CONNECT FEATURES

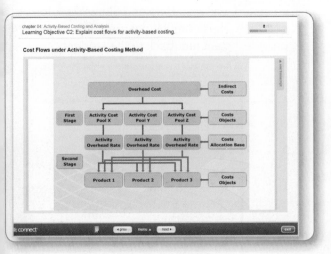

Interactive Presentations

Interactive Presentations cover each chapter's core learning objectives with narrated, animated presentations that pause frequently to check for comprehension. Interactive Presentations harness the full power of technology to appeal to all learning styles. Interactive Presentations are a great way to improve online or hybrid sections, but also extend the learning opportunity for traditional classes, such as in facilitating a "flipped classroom."

Guided Examples

Guided Examples provide narrated and animated step-by-step walkthroughs of algorithmic versions of assigned exercises. This allows students to identify, review, or reinforce the concepts and activities covered in class. Guided Examples provide immediate feedback and focus on the areas where students need the most guidance.

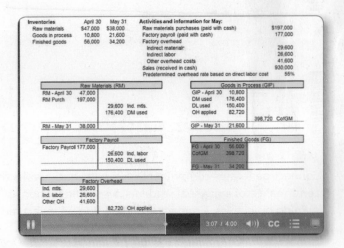

End-of-Chapter Material

McGraw-Hill Education redesigned the student interface for our end-of-chapter assessment content. The new interface provides improved answer acceptance to reduce students' frustration with formatting issues (such as rounding) and, for select questions, provides an expanded table that guides students through the process of solving the problem. Many questions have been redesigned to more fully test students' mastery of the content.

2. value: 10.00 points

	Marsh Concert Promotions	Ellis Home Builders
Actual indirect materials costs	$ 22,000	$ 12,500
Actual indirect labor costs	46,000	46,500
Other overhead costs	17,000	47,000
Overhead applied	88,200	105,200

Marsh Concert Promotions

Determine whether overhead is overapplied or underapplied.

Factory Overhead			
Indirect materials	22,000	88,200	Applied overhead
Indirect labor	46,000		
Other overhead costs	17,000		
			Overapplied overhead
		3,200	

General Ledger

New to 5e are General Ledger problems that offer students the ability to see how transactions post from the general journal all the way through the financial statements. General Ledger (GL) questions provide auto-grading in the same intelligent design as our end-of-chapter content. Critical thinking and analysis components are added to each GL problem to ensure understanding of the entire process.

Excel Simulations

Assignable within Connect Accounting, Excel Simulations allow students to practice their Excel skills—such as basic formulas and formatting—with the context of accounting. These questions feature animated, narrated Help and Show Me tutorials (w enabled). These simulations are auto-graded and provide instant feedback to the student.

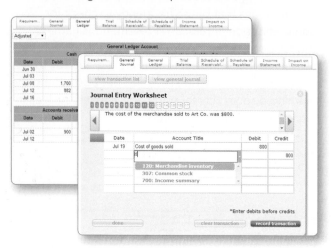

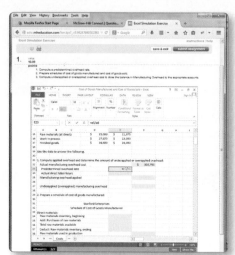

POWERFUL PERFORMANCE REPORTING

Connect generates comprehensive reports and graphs that provide instructors with an instant view of the performance of individual students, a specific section, or multiple sections. Since all content is mapped to learning objectives, Connect reporting is ideal for accreditation or other administrative documentation.

At a Glance Insights | Assignment Results & Statistics Reports | Student Performance Reports | Item Analysis Reports | Category Analysis Reports | At-Risk Student Reports | LearnSmart Reports

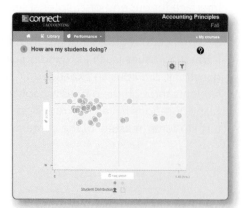

Connect Insight

The first and only analytics tool of its kind, Connect Insight is a series of visual data displays that are each framed by an intuitive question and provide at-a-glance information regarding how an instructor's class is performing. Connect Insight is available through Connect titles.

Managerial Accounting

5th edition

John J. Wild

University of Wisconsin at Madison

Ken W. Shaw

University of Missouri at Columbia

Mc Graw Hill Education

To my students and family, especially **Kimberly, Jonathan, Stephanie** and **Trevor.**
To my wife **Linda** and children **Erin, Emily** and **Jacob.**

MANAGERIAL ACCOUNTING, FIFTH EDITION

Published by McGraw-Hill Education, 2 Penn Plaza, New York, NY 10121. Copyright © 2016 by McGraw-Hill Education. All rights reserved. Printed in the United States of America. Previous editions © 2013, 2011, and 2009. No part of this publication may be reproduced or distributed in any form or by any means, or stored in a database or retrieval system, without the prior written consent of McGraw-Hill Education, including, but not limited to, in any network or other electronic storage or transmission, or broadcast for distance learning.

Some ancillaries, including electronic and print components, may not be available to customers outside the United States.

This book is printed on acid-free paper.

1 2 3 4 5 6 7 8 9 0 DOW/DOW 1 0 9 8 7 6 5

ISBN 978-1-259-17649-4
MHID 1-259-17649-5

Senior Vice President, Products & Markets: *Kurt L. Strand*
Vice President, General Manager, Products & Markets: *Marty Lange*
Vice President, Content Design & Delivery: *Kimberly Meriwether David*
Managing Director: *Tim Vertovec*
Marketing Director: *Brad Parkins*
Brand Manager: *Steve Schuetz*
Director, Product Development: *Rose Koos*
Director of Digital Content: *Patricia Plumb*
Lead Product Developer: *Ann Torbert*
Product Developer: *Lindsey Schauer*
Marketing Manager: *Michelle Nolte*
Digital Product Analyst: *Xin Lin*
Director, Content Design & Delivery: *Linda Avenarius*
Program Manager: *Daryl Horrocks*
Content Project Managers: *Lori Koetters, Brian Nacik*
Buyer: *Carol A. Bielski*
Design: *Debra Kubiak*
Content Licensing Specialists: *DeAnna Dausener, Keri Johnson*
Cover Image: *Yuri_Arcurs/Getty Images*
Compositor: *Aptara®, Inc.*
Printer: *R.R. Donnelley*

All credits appearing on page or at the end of the book are considered to be an extension of the copyright page.

Library of Congress Control Number: 2014957125

The Internet addresses listed in the text were accurate at the time of publication. The inclusion of a website does not indicate an endorsement by the authors or McGraw-Hill Education, and McGraw-Hill Education does not guarantee the accuracy of the information presented at these sites.

www.mhhe.com

Adapting to the Needs of Today's Students

Managerial Accounting, 5e

Enhancements in technology have changed how we live and learn. Working with learning resources across devices, whether smartphones, tablets, or laptop computers, empowers students to drive their own learning by putting increasingly intelligent technology into their hands.

Whether the goal is to become an accountant, a business-person, or simply an informed consumer of accounting information, *Managerial Accounting (MA)* has helped generations of students succeed. Its leading-edge accounting content, paired with state-of-the-art technology, supports student learning and elevates understanding of key accounting principles.

MA excels at **engaging students** with content that will help them see the relevance of accounting. Its chapter-opening vignettes showcase dynamic, successful entrepreneurial individuals and companies and **highlight the usefulness of accounting to business owners**. This edition's featured companies—**Apple, Google,** and **Samsung**—capture student interest with their products, and their annual reports serve as a pathway for learning financial statements. New in this edition, Need-to-Know illustrations in each chapter demonstrate how to apply key accounting procedures. They are supported by guided video presentations.

MA also delivers innovative technology to help student performance. ***Connect Accounting*** provides students with a media-rich eBook version of the textbook and offers instant grading and feedback for assignments that are completed online. Our system for completing exercise and problem material takes accounting content to the next level, delivering assessment material in a **more intuitive, less restrictive** format that adapts to the needs of today's students.

This technology features:

- **an auto-calculation** feature that allows students to focus on concepts rather than rote tasks.
- **a smart (auto-fill) drop-down design**.
- **a general journal interface** that looks and feels more like that found in practice.

The end result is content that better prepares students for the real world.

Connect Accounting also includes digitally based, interactive, adaptive learning tools that provide an opportunity to engage students more effectively by offering varied instructional methods and more personalized learning paths that build on different learning styles, interests, and abilities.

The revolutionary technology of the LearnSmart Advantage Series—consisting of **LearnSmart®** and **SmartBook®**—is available only from McGraw-Hill Education. These products are based on an intelligent learning system that uses a series of adaptive questions to pinpoint each student's knowledge gaps and then provides an optimal learning path. Students spend less time in areas they already know and more time in areas they don't. The result: Students study more efficiently, learn faster, and retain more knowledge. Valuable reports provide insights into how students are progressing through textbook content and information useful for shaping in-class time or assessment.

Interactive Presentations teach each chapter's core learning objectives in a rich, multimedia format, bringing the content to life. Your students will come to class prepared when you assign Interactive Presentations. Students can also review the Interactive Presentations as they study. Further, **Guided Examples** provide students with narrated, animated, step-by-step walk-throughs of algorithmic versions of assigned exercises. Students appreciate the Guided Examples, which help them learn accounting and complete assignments outside of class.

A **General Ledger (GL) application,** new to 5e, offers students the ability to see how transactions post from the general journal all the way through the financial statements. It uses the intuitive, less restrictive format used for other homework, and it adds critical thinking components to each GL question, to ensure understanding of the entire process.

The first and only analytics tool of its kind, **Connect Insight®** is a series of visual data displays—each framed by an intuitive question—to provide at-a-glance information about how your class is doing. Connect Insight provides a quick analysis on five key dimensions, available at a moment's notice from a tablet device: *How are my students doing? How is my section doing? How is this student doing? How are my assignments going?* and *How is this assignment going?*

"This is an excellent book that is well-written and contains excellent illustrations. It has the best online supplements of any of the texts that I have reviewed. . . . This is an excellent book that I would recommend to all of my colleagues."

—**KAREN CRISONINO, County College of Morris**

About the Authors

JOHN J. WILD is a distinguished professor of accounting at the University of Wisconsin at Madison. He previously held appointments at Michigan State University and the University of Manchester in England. He received his BBA, MS, and PhD from the University of Wisconsin.

Professor Wild teaches accounting courses at both the undergraduate and graduate levels. He has received numerous teaching honors, including the Mabel W. Chipman Excellence-in-Teaching Award, the departmental Excellence-in-Teaching Award, and the Teaching Excellence Award from the 2003 and 2005 business graduates at the University of Wisconsin. He also received the Beta Alpha Psi and Roland F. Salmonson Excellence-in-Teaching Award from Michigan State University. Professor Wild has received several research honors and is a past KPMG Peat Marwick National Fellow and is a recipient of fellowships from the American Accounting Association and the Ernst and Young Foundation.

Professor Wild is an active member of the American Accounting Association and its sections. He has served on several committees of these organizations, including the Outstanding Accounting Educator Award, Wildman Award, National Program Advisory, Publications, and Research Committees. Professor Wild is author of *Fundamental Accounting Principles, Financial Accounting, Financial and Managerial Accounting,* and *College Accounting,* each published by McGraw-Hill Education. His research articles on accounting and analysis appear in *The Accounting Review; Journal of Accounting Research; Journal of Accounting and Economics; Contemporary Accounting Research; Journal of Accounting, Auditing and Finance; Journal of Accounting and Public Policy;* and other journals. He is past associate editor of *Contemporary Accounting Research* and has served on several editorial boards including *The Accounting Review.* Professor Wild is a recognized expert in accounting and financial analysis, and is known for his teaching innovations within an active learning classroom environment.

In his leisure time, Professor Wild enjoys hiking, sports, travel, people, and spending time with family and friends.

KEN W. SHAW is an associate professor of accounting and the Deloitte Professor of Accounting at the University of Missouri. He previously was on the faculty at the University of Maryland at College Park. He has also taught in international programs at the University of Bergamo (Italy) and the University of Alicante (Spain). He received an accounting degree from Bradley University and an MBA and PhD from the University of Wisconsin. He is a Certified Public Accountant with work experience in public accounting.

Professor Shaw teaches accounting at the undergraduate and graduate levels. He has received numerous School of Accountancy, College of Business and university-level teaching awards. He was voted the "Most Influential Professor" by three School of Accountancy graduating classes, and is a two-time recipient of the O'Brien Excellence in Teaching Award. He is the advisor to his school's chapter of the Association of Certified Fraud Examiners.

Professor Shaw is an active member of the American Accounting Association and its sections. He has served on many committees of these organizations and presented his research papers at national and regional meetings. Professor Shaw's research appears in the *Journal of Accounting Research; The Accounting Review; Contemporary Accounting Research; Journal of Financial and Quantitative Analysis; Journal of the American Taxation Association; Strategic Management Journal; Journal of Accounting, Auditing, and Finance; Journal of Financial Research;* and other journals. He has served on the editorial boards of *Issues in Accounting Education; Journal of Business Research;* and *Research in Accounting Regulation.* Professor Shaw is co-author of *Fundamental Accounting Principles, Financial and Managerial Accounting,* and *College Accounting,* all published by McGraw-Hill Education.

In his leisure time, Professor Shaw enjoys tennis, cycling, music, and coaching his children's sports teams.

Dear Colleagues and Friends,

As we roll out the new edition of *Managerial Accounting,* we thank each of you who provided suggestions to improve the textbook and its teaching resources. This new edition reflects the advice and wisdom of many dedicated reviewers, symposium and workshop participants, students, and instructors. Throughout the revision process, we steered this textbook and its teaching tools in the manner you directed. As you'll find, the new edition offers a rich set of features—especially digital features—to improve student learning and assist instructor teaching and grading. We believe you and your students will like what you find in this new edition.

Many talented educators and professionals have worked hard to create the materials for this product, and for their efforts, we're grateful. **We extend a special thank-you to our contributing and technology supplement authors,** who have worked so diligently to support this product:

Contributing Author: Kathleen O'Donnell, *Onondaga Community College*

Accuracy Checkers: Dave Krug, *Johnson County Community College;* Mark McCarthy, *East Carolina University;* Helen Roybark, *Radford University;* Barbara Schnathorst; and Beth Woods

LearnSmart Author: April Mohr, *Jefferson Community and Technical College, SW*

Interactive Presentations: Jeannie Folk, *College of DuPage*

PowerPoint Presentations: Beth Kane, *Northwestern University*

Instructor Resource Manual: Patricia Walczak, *Lansing Community College*

Test Bank Contributors: Anna Boulware, *St. Charles Community College,* and Brenda J. McVey, *University of Mississippi*

Digital Contributor, Connect Content, General Ledger Problems, and Exercise PowerPoints: Kathleen O'Donnell, *Onondaga Community College*

In addition to the invaluable help from the colleagues listed above, we thank the entire *MA,* 5e, team at McGraw-Hill Education: Tim Vertovec, Steve Schuetz, Michelle Nolte, Lindsey Schauer, Lori Koetters, Ann Torbert, Brad Parkins, Patricia Plumb, Xin Lin, Kevin Moran, Debra Kubiak, Carol Bielski, Keri Johnson, DeAnna Dausener, Sarah Evertson, Ben Pearsall, Brian Nacik, Ron Nelms, and Daryl Horrocks. We could not have completed this new edition without your efforts.

John J. Wild   Ken W. Shaw

| ACCOUNTING Easy to Use. Proven Effective

McGraw-Hill *CONNECT ACCOUNTING*

McGraw-Hill *Connect Accounting* is a digital teaching and learning environment that gives students the means to better connect with their coursework, with their instructors, and with the important concepts they will need to know for success now and in the future. With *Connect Accounting,* instructors can easily deliver assignments, quizzes, and tests online. Students can review course material and practice important skills.

McGraw-Hill *Connect Accounting* provides all of the following learning and teaching resources:

- SmartBook, powered by LearnSmart
- Auto-graded online homework
- General ledger problems
- Auto-graded Excel simulations
- Interactive Presentations
- Guided Examples

In short, *Connect Accounting* offers students powerful tools and features that optimize their time and energy, enabling them to focus on learning.

SmartBook, Powered by LearnSmart

SMARTBOOK McGraw-Hill LearnSmart® is the market-leading adaptive study resource that is proven to strengthen memory recall, increase class retention, and boost grades. LearnSmart allows students to study more efficiently because they are made aware of what they know and don't know.

SmartBook®, which is powered by LearnSmart, is the first and only adaptive reading experience designed to change the way students read and learn. It creates a personalized reading experience by highlighting the most impactful concepts a student needs to learn at that moment in time. As a student engages with SmartBook, the reading experience continuously adapts by highlighting content based on what the student knows and doesn't know. This ensures that the focus is on the content he or she needs to learn, while simultaneously promoting long-term retention of material.

Use SmartBook's real-time reports to quickly identify the concepts that require more attention from individual students—or the entire class. The end result? Students are more engaged with course content, can better prioritize their time, and come to class ready to participate.

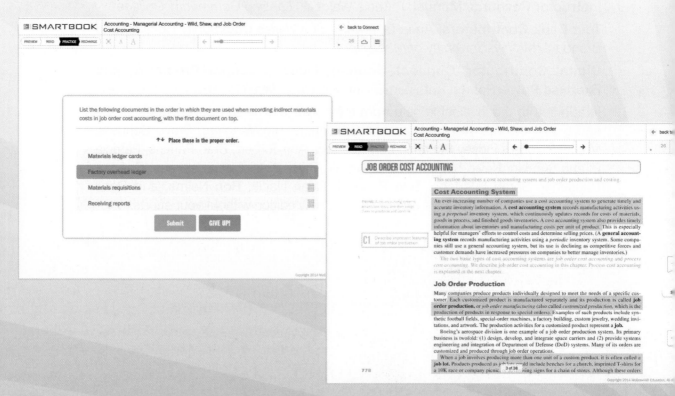

Tailored to You.

Online Assignments

Connect Accounting helps students learn more efficiently by providing feedback and practice material when they need it, where they need it. *Connect* grades homework automatically and gives immediate feedback on any questions students may have missed. Our assignable, gradable end-of-chapter content includes a general journal application that looks and feels more like what you would find in a general ledger software package. Also, select questions have been redesigned to test students' knowledge more fully. They now include tables for students to work through rather than requiring that all calculations be done off-line. McGraw-Hill's redesigned student interface provides a real-world feel to interactive assignments and end-of-chapter assessment content. This robust accounting software allows for flexibility in learning styles and provides opportunities for courses to be delivered in traditional, online, and blended settings.

General Ledger Problems

New General Ledger problems for select questions enable students to see how transactions post from the general journal all the way through the financial statements. It provides a much-improved experience for students working with accounting cycle questions. Students' work in the general journal is automatically posted to the ledger, navigation is much simpler, scrolling is no longer an issue, and students can easily link back to their original entries simply by clicking the ledger if edits are needed. Many questions now have critical thinking components added, to maximize students' foundational knowledge of accounting concepts and principles.

Interactive Presentations

Interactive Presentations provide engaging narratives of all chapter learning objectives in an assignable interactive online format. They follow the structure of the text and are organized to match the specific learning objectives within each chapter. While the Interactive Presentations are not meant to replace the textbook, they provide additional explanation and enhancement of material from the text chapter, allowing students to learn, study, and practice at their own pace, with instant feedback.

Guided Examples

The Guided Examples in *Connect Accounting* provide a narrated, animated, step-by-step walkthrough of select exercises similar to those assigned. These short presentations, which can be turned on or off by instructors, provide reinforcement when students need it most.

Excel Simulations

Simulated Excel questions, assignable within *Connect Accounting,* allow students to practice their Excel skills—such as basic formulas and formatting—within the context of accounting. These questions feature animated, narrated Help and Show Me tutorials (when enabled), as well as automatic feedback and grading for both students and professors.

 **connect** |ACCOUNTING **Easy to Use. Proven Effectiv**

McGraw-Hill *CONNECT ACCOUNTING* Features

Simple Assignment Management and Smart Grading

With *Connect Accounting,* creating assignments is easier than ever, enabling instructors to spend more time teaching and less time managing. Simple assignment management and smart grading allow you to:

- Create and deliver assignments easily with selectable end-of-chapter questions and Test Bank items.
- Have assignments scored automatically, giving students immediate feedback on their work and side-by-side comparisons with correct answers.
- Access and review each response, manually change grades, or leave comments for students to review.
- Reinforce classroom concepts with practice assignments and instant quizzes and exams.

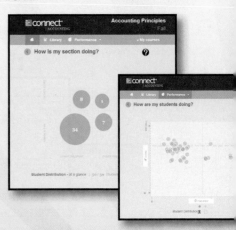

Powerful Instructor and Student Reports

Connect Accounting keeps instructors informed about how each student, section, and class is performing, allowing for more productive use of lecture and office hours. The progress-tracking function enables you to:

- View scored work immediately and track individual or group performance with assignment and grade reports.
- Access an instant view of student or class performance relative to learning objectives.
- Collect data and generate reports required by many accreditation organizations, such as AACSB and AICPA.

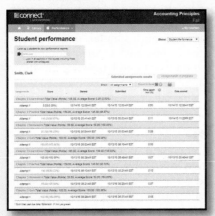

Connect Insight

The first and only analytics tool of its kind, McGraw-Hill Connect® Insight is a series of visual data displays—each framed by an intuitive question—to provide at-a-glance information about how your class is doing.

Connect Insight provides a quick analysis on five key insights, available at a moment's notice from your tablet device:

- How are my students doing?
- How is my section doing?
- How is this student doing?
- How are my assignments going?
- How is this assignment going?

Instructor Library

The *Connect Accounting* Instructor Library is a repository for additional resources to improve student engagement in and out of class. You can select and use any asset that enhances your lecture. The *Connect Accounting* Instructor Library includes:

- Presentation slides.
- Animated PowerPoint exhibits and exercises.
- Solutions Manual.
- Test Bank.
- Instructor's Resource Manual.

The *Connect Accounting* Instructor Library also allows you to upload your own files.

For more information about *Connect Accounting,* go to **http://connect.mheducation.com,** or contact your local McGraw-Hill Higher Education representative.

Tailored to You.

Other Technology Offered by McGraw-Hill

Tegrity Campus: Lectures 24/7

 Tegrity Campus is a service that makes class time available 24/7 by automatically capturing every lecture. With a simple one-click start-and-stop process, you capture all computer screens and corresponding audio in a format that is easily searchable, frame by frame. Students can replay any part of any recorded class with easy-to-use browser-based viewing on a PC, Mac, or mobile device.

Help turn your students' study time into learning moments immediately supported by your lecture. With Tegrity Campus, you also increase intent listening and class participation by easing students' concerns about note-taking.

To learn more about Tegrity, watch a two-minute Flash demo at **http://tegritycampus.mhhe.com.**

McGraw-Hill Campus

 McGraw-Hill Campus® is a new one-stop teaching and learning experience available to users of any learning management system. This institutional service allows faculty and students to enjoy single sign-on (SSO) access to all McGraw-Hill Higher Education materials, including the award-winning McGraw-Hill *Connect* platform, from directly within the institution's website. To learn more about McGraw-Hill Campus, visit **http://mhcampus.mhhe.com.**

Custom Publishing through Create

McGraw-Hill Create™ is a self-service website that allows instructors to create custom course materials by drawing upon McGraw-Hill's comprehensive, cross-disciplinary content. Instructors can add their own content quickly and easily and tap into other rights-secured, third-party sources as well, then arrange the content in a way that makes the most sense for their course.

Through Create, you can:

- Combine material from different sources and even upload your own content.
- Personalize your product with the course name and information.
- Choose the best format for your students—color print, black-and-white print, or eBook.
- Edit and update your course materials as often as you'd like.

Begin creating now at **www.mcgrawhillcreate.com.**

ALEKS: A Superior, Student-Friendly Accounting Experience

ALEKS®

Artificial intelligence: Fills knowledge gaps.

Cycle of learning and assessment: Increases learning momentum and engages students.

Customizable curriculum: Aligns with your course syllabi and textbooks.

Dynamic, automated reports: Monitors detailed student and class progress.

To learn more, visit **www.aleks.com/highered/business.**

CourseSmart

 CourseSmart is a way for faculty to find and review eTextbooks. It's also a great option for students who are interested in accessing their course materials digitally and saving money.

CourseSmart offers thousands of the most commonly adopted textbooks across hundreds of courses from a wide variety of higher education publishers. With the CourseSmart eTextbook, students can save up to 45 percent off the cost of a print book, reduce their impact on the environment, and access powerful web tools for learning. CourseSmart is an online eTextbook, which means users access and view their textbook online when connected to the Internet. Students can also print sections of the book for maximum portability. CourseSmart eTextbooks are available in one standard online reader with full text search, notes and highlighting, and e-mail tools for sharing notes between classmates. For more information on CourseSmart, go to **www.coursesmart.com.**

McGraw-Hill Customer Experience Group Contact Information
At McGraw-Hill, we understand that getting the most from new technology can be challenging. That's why our services don't stop after you purchase our products. You can contact our Product Specialists 24 hours a day to get product training online. Or you can search the knowledge bank of Frequently Asked Questions on our support website. For customer support, call **800-331-5094** or visit **www.mhhe.com/support.**

Innovative Textbook Features . . .

Using Accounting for Decisions

Whether we prepare, analyze, or apply accounting information, one skill remains essential: decision making. To help develop good decision-making habits and to illustrate the relevance of accounting, we use a pedagogical framework we call the Decision Center. This framework encompasses a variety of approaches and subject areas, giving students insight into every aspect of business decision making; see the four nearby examples for the different types of decision boxes, including those that relate to ethics. Answers to Decision Maker and Ethics boxes are at the end of each chapter.

Decision Insight

Make or Buy IT Companies apply make or buy decisions to their services. Many now outsource their information technology activities. Information technology companies provide infrastructure and services to enable businesses to focus on their key activities. It is argued that outsourcing saves money and streamlines operations, and without the headaches. ■

Decision Ethics

Production Manager You invite three friends to a restaurant. When the dinner check arrives, David, a self-employed entrepreneur, picks it up saying, "Here, let me pay. I'll deduct it as a business expense on my tax return." Denise, a salesperson, takes the check from David's hand and says, "I'll put this on my company's credit card. It won't cost us anything." Derek, a factory manager for a company, laughs and says, "Neither of you understands. I'll put this on my company's credit card and call it overhead on a cost-plus contract my company has with a client." (*A cost-plus contract means the company receives its costs plus a percent of those costs.*) Adds Derek, "That way, my company pays for dinner *and* makes a profit." Who should pay the bill? Why? ■ [Answers follow the chapter's Summary.]

Decision Analysis ▢▢▢ Setting Product Price

A2 Determine product selling price based on total costs.

Relevant costs are useful to management in determining prices for special short-term decisions. But longer run pricing decisions of management need to cover both variable and fixed costs, and yield a profit.

There are several methods to help management in setting prices. The *cost-plus* methods are probably the most common, where management adds a **markup** to cost to reach a target price. We will describe the **total cost method**, where management sets price equal to the product's total costs plus a desired profit on the product. This is a four-step process:

1. Determine total costs.

$$\text{Total costs} = \frac{\text{Production (direct materials,}}{\text{direct labor, and overhead) costs}} + \frac{\text{Nonproduction (selling and}}{\text{administrative) costs}}$$

Decision Maker

Partner You are a partner in a small accounting firm that specializes in keeping the books and preparing taxes for clients. A local restaurant is interested in obtaining these services from your firm. Identify factors that are relevant in deciding whether to accept the engagement. ■ [Answers follow the chapter's Summary.]

"Authors do a good job of relating material to real-life situations and putting students in the decision-maker role."

—**MORGAN ROCKETT, Moberly Area Community College**

Chapter Preview

Each chapter opens with a visual chapter preview. Students can begin their reading with a clear understanding of what they will learn and when, allowing them to stay more focused and organized along the way. Learning objective numbers highlight the location of related content.

Chapter Preview

DECENTRALIZATION	RESPONSIBILITY ACCOUNTING	PROFIT CENTERS	INVESTMENT CENTERS
Advantages	Controllable versus uncontrollable costs	C1 Direct and indirect expenses	A1 ROI and residual income
Disadvantages	Responsibility accounting system	P2 Allocation of indirect expenses	A2 Margin and turnover
Performance evaluation	P1 Responsibility accounting report	P3 Departmental income statements	A3 Nonfinancial performance measures
		Departmental contribution to overhead	A4 Cycle time
			C2 Transfer pricing
			C3 Joint costs allocation

CAP Model

The Conceptual/Analytical/Procedural (CAP) Model allows courses to be specially designed to meet the teaching needs of a diverse faculty. This model identifies learning objectives, textual materials, assignments, and test items by C, A, or P, allowing different instructors to teach from the same materials, yet easily customize their courses toward a conceptual, analytical, or procedural approach (or a combination thereof) based on personal preferences.

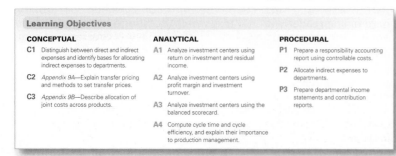

Learning Objectives

CONCEPTUAL

C1 Distinguish between direct and indirect expenses and identify bases for allocating indirect expenses to departments.

C2 *Appendix 9A*—Explain transfer pricing and methods to set transfer prices.

C3 *Appendix 9B*—Describe allocation of joint costs across products.

ANALYTICAL

A1 Analyze investment centers using return on investment and residual income.

A2 Analyze investment centers using profit margin and investment turnover.

A3 Analyze investment centers using the balanced scorecard.

A4 Compute cycle time and cycle efficiency, and explain their importance to production management.

PROCEDURAL

P1 Prepare a responsibility accounting report using controllable costs.

P2 Allocate indirect expenses to departments.

P3 Prepare departmental income statements and contribution reports.

Bring Accounting to Life

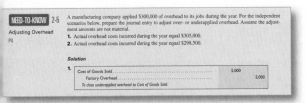

Need-to-Know Illustrations

New in this edition are several Need-to-Know illustrations located at key junctures in each chapter. These illustrations pose questions about the material just presented—content that students "need to know" to successfully learn accounting. Accompanying solutions walk students through key procedures and analysis necessary to be successful with homework and test materials. Need-to-Know illustrations are supplemented with narrated, animated, step-by-step walk-through videos led by an instructor and available via *Connect*.

Global View

The Global View section explains international accounting practices relating to the material covered in that chapter. The aim of this section is to describe accounting practices and to identify the similarities and differences in international accounting practices versus those in the United States. As we move toward global convergence in accounting practices, and as we witness the likely convergence of U.S. GAAP to IFRS, the importance of student familiarity with international accounting grows. This innovative section helps us begin down that path. This section is purposefully located at the end of each chapter so that each instructor can decide what emphasis, if at all, is to be assigned to it.

GLOBAL VIEW

Porsche AG manufactures high-performance cars. Each car is built according to individual customer specifications. Customers can use the Internet to place orders for their dream cars. Porsche employs just-in-time inventory techniques to ensure a flexible production process that can respond rapidly to customer orders. For a recent year, Porsche reported €33,781 million in costs of materials and €9,038 million in personnel costs, which helped generate €57,081 million in revenue.

Sustainability and Accounting   Porsche's sustainability efforts extend beyond its manufacturing operations to event management. Each year when the company sponsors a professional tennis tournament, it uses a Porsche Cayenne Hybrid to shuttle players to and from the venue. In addition, the company sells event tickets that include public transportation, thus reducing the number of distinct journeys to the venue by about 30%. In addition, **Middleton Made Knives** applies sustainablity through Quintin Middleton's choice of materials. The steel used for his knife blades can be recycled, and new trees can be planted to supply the wood for his knife blades.

Sean Gallup/Getty Images

Sustainability and Accounting

New in this edition are brief sections that highlight the importance of sustainability within the broader context of global accounting (and accountability). Companies increasingly address sustainability in their public reporting and consider the sustainability accounting standards (from the Sustainability Accounting Standards Board) and the expectations of our global society. These boxes, located near the end of the Global View section, cover different aspects of sustainability, often within the context of the chapter's featured entrepreneurial company.

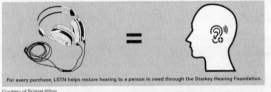

Sustainability and Accounting   LSTN, as introduced in this chapter's opening feature, places an emphasis on being a socially conscious and environmentally friendly alternative within the luxury headphone market. LSTN partners with The Starkey Hearing Foundation "to provide hearing for children in deaf schools," explains Bridget Hilton, its founder. "Ninety-five percent of children in deaf schools worldwide can be helped . . . [and] eighty percent of those people live in developing countries." LSTN also recognizes the need to work within the local markets so that its successes are sustainable. Our hearing products and services "will not undercut the local economies—these are basic senses that everyone on earth should be able to experience," explains Bridget. "To me, success in business is doing something you love while being financially secure." That is something we all hope is sustainable.

For every purchase, LSTN helps restore hearing to a person in need through the Starkey Hearing Foundation.

Courtesy of Bridget Hilton

> "I like the layout of the text and the readability. The illustrations and comics in the book make the text seem less intimidating and boring for students. The PowerPoint slides are easy to understand and use, the pictorials are great, and the text has great coverage of accounting material. The addition of IFRS information and the updates to the opening stories are great. I like that the decision insights are about businesses the students can relate to (i.e., Facebook, women start-up businesses, etc.)."
>
> **—JEANNIE LIU, Chaffey College**

Outstanding Assignment Material . . .

Once a student has finished reading the chapter, how well he or she retains the material can depend greatly on the questions, exercises, and problems that reinforce it. This book leads the way in comprehensive, accurate assignments.

Comprehensive Need-to-Know Problems present both a problem and a complete solution, allowing students to review the entire problem-solving process and achieve success.

Chapter Summaries provide students with a review organized by learning objectives. Chapter Summaries are a component of the CAP model (see page xii), which recaps each conceptual, analytical, and procedural objective.

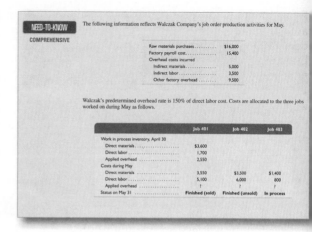

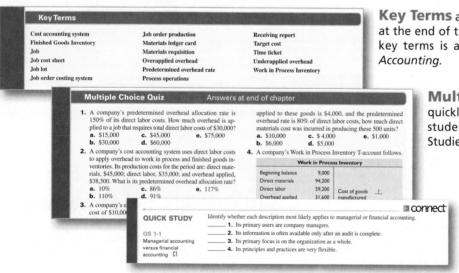

Key Terms are bolded in the text and repeated at the end of the chapter. A complete glossary of key terms is available online through *Connect Accounting.*

Multiple Choice Quiz questions quickly test chapter knowledge before a student moves on to complete Quick Studies, Exercises, and Problems.

Quick Study assignments are short exercises that often focus on one learning objective. Most are included in *Connect Accounting.* There are at least 10–15 Quick Study assignments per chapter.

Exercises are one of this book's many strengths and a competitive advantage. There are at least 10–15 per chapter, and most are included in *Connect Accounting.*

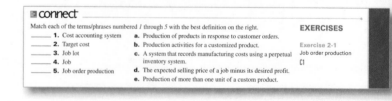

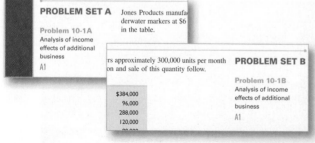

Problem Sets A & B are proven problems that can be assigned as homework or for in-class projects. All problems are coded according to the CAP model (see page xii), and Set A is included in *Connect Accounting.*

Helps Students Master Key Concepts

Beyond the Numbers exercises ask students to use accounting figures and understand their meaning. Students also learn how accounting applies to a variety of business situations. These creative and fun exercises are all new or updated and are divided into sections:

- Reporting in Action
- Comparative Analysis
- Ethics Challenge
- Communicating in Practice
- Taking It to the Net
- Teamwork in Action
- Hitting the Road
- Entrepreneurial Decision
- Global Decision

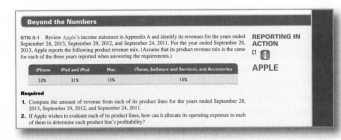

Serial Problems use a continuous running case study to illustrate chapter concepts in a familiar context. The Serial Problem can be followed continuously from the first chapter or picked up at any later point in the book; enough information is provided to ensure students can get right to work.

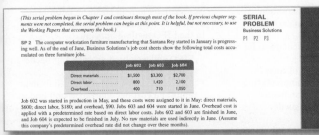

"The serial problems are excellent.... I like the continuation of the same problem to the next chapters if applicable. I use the Quick Studies as practice problems. . . . Students have commented that this really works for them if they work (these questions) before attempting the assigned exercises and problems. I also like the discussion (questions) and make this an assignment. You have done an outstanding job presenting accounting to our students."

—**JERRI TITTLE, Rose State College**

General Ledger Problems New General Ledger problems enable students to see how transactions post. Students can track an amount in any financial statement all the way back to the original journal entry. Critical thinking components then challenge students to analyze the business activities in the problem.

The **General Ledger** tool in *Connect* automates several of the procedural steps in accounting so that the financial professional can focus on the impacts of each transaction on various reports and performance measures.

GL 2-1   General Ledger assignment GL 2-1, based on Problem 2-1A, focuses on transactions related to job-order costing. Prepare summary journal entries to record the cost of jobs and their flow through the manufacturing environment. Then prepare a schedule of cost of goods manufactured and a partial income statement.

GENERAL LEDGER PROBLEM

Available in Connect

The End of the Chapter Is Only the Beginning Our valuable and proven assignments aren't just confined to the book. From problems that require technological solutions to materials found exclusively online, this book's end-of-chapter material is fully integrated with its technology package.

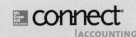

- Quick Studies, Exercises, and Problems available in *Connect* are marked with an icon.
- Assignments that focus on global accounting practices and companies are identified with an icon.
- Assignments that involve decision analysis are identified with an icon.

Content Revisions Enhance Learning

This edition's revisions are driven by feedback from instructors and students.

- Many new, revised, and updated assignments throughout, including serial problem and entrepreneurial assignments.
- New Need-to-Know illustrations added to each chapter at key junctures to reinforce key topics.
- New Sustainability section for each chapter, with examples linked to the company featured in the chapter opener.
- New annual reports and comparison assignments: Apple, Google, and Samsung.
- New streamlined opening layout for each chapter.
- Revised art program, visual infographics, and text layout.

- Updated ratio/tool analysis, using data from well-known firms.
- New General Ledger questions added to most chapters.
- New and revised entrepreneurial examples and elements.
- New technology content integrated and referenced in the book.
- Revised terminology from *goods in process* to *work in process.*
- Changed the title of *Manufacturing Statement* to *Schedule of Cost of Goods Manufactured* due to its use in practice.

Chapter 1

SunSaluter **NEW opener.**
Revised discussions of the purpose of managerial accounting and cost classifications and their uses.
Reduced number of cost classifications from five to three.
Revised exhibit and example of direct vs. indirect costs.
Added new exhibit comparing the balance sheet and income statement for different types of companies.
Reduced level of detail in exhibit on income statement reporting.
Revised discussion of the flow of manufacturing costs.
New four-step process to illustrate the schedule of cost of goods manufactured (COGM).
Added T-accounts to show the flow of costs for the COGM.
Added a third column to the schedule of COGM, for enhanced presentation.
Simplified exhibit on cost flows across the financial statements.
New discussion of corporate social responsibility.
Added 6 Quick Studies and 4 Exercises.

Chapter 2

Middleton Made Knives **NEW opener.**
New discussion of differences between job order and process operations.
Moved discussion of job order costing for services to later in chapter.
Revised/simplified discussions of cost flows and job cost sheets.
Simplified journal entries for labor costs.
New exhibits to show postings of product cost journal entries to general ledger accounts and to job cost sheets.
Revised exhibits on materials and labor cost flows.
Revised text and new exhibit on four-step process to record overhead.
Revised discussion of applying overhead and recording actual overhead.

Added new discussion and presentation of journal entries for indirect materials and indirect labor.
Added new exhibit showing calculations for overhead applied to individual jobs.
Added new exhibit on the flow of costs to general ledger accounts, the manufacturing statement, and the financial statements.
Added new schedule of cost of goods manufactured exhibit.
Added 2 Quick Studies and 2 Exercises.

Chapter 3

Kar's Nuts **NEW opener.**
Major change: Revised the overview exhibit of process operations and expanded the illustration to show *two departments.*
Major change: Combined coverage of direct labor and overhead into *conversion costs.*
Revised exhibits/examples to show fewer processes and simpler, more engaging products (tennis balls and trail mix).
Added discussion, with journal entries, of transfers of costs across departments.
Added discussion of multiple work in process (WIP) inventory accounts.
Revised discussion of job order vs. process costing.
Revised discussion, with new exhibit, on computation of equivalent units.
Added conversion costs per unit to equivalent units discussion.
Added a section differentiating the weighted-average and FIFO methods.
New exhibit showing units transferred out and units remaining in ending work in process inventory.
Added formula for computing equivalent units under the weighted-average method.
Moved discussion of journal entries to later in the chapter.
Revised the process costing summary report to focus on direct materials and conversion costs.
Revised journal entries to show two WIP Inventory accounts and to eliminate the Factory Payroll account.
Added discussion of Volkswagen's use of robotics in process operations.
Revised and added Comprehensive Need-to-Knows to reflect changes in chapter (including *two processes*).

New exhibits showing transfer of units and costs across departments, using T-accounts.
In the FIFO method appendix:
- Added discussion of differences between FIFO and weighted-average approaches to computing equivalent units.
- Added exhibits on computing equivalent units and cost per equivalent unit under FIFO.
- Revised discussion of applying four-step process using FIFO.
Added 16 Quick Studies and 7 Exercises.

Chapter 4

Suja Juice Company **NEW opener.**
Clarified departmental overhead rate method and ABC methods as four-step processes.
Re-graded heading levels to highlight plantwide and departmental overhead rate method topics.
Expanded discussion of examples used in the ABC application, to enhance clarity.
Revised Exhibit 4.16, separating Costs of Good Quality from Costs of Poor Quality, thus highlighting the Cost of Quality Report.
4 new Quick Studies, and some old Quick Studies repurposed to Exercises.

Chapter 5

Fast Yeti Custom Tees **NEW opener.**
Revised discussion of fixed and variable costs.
Revised discussion of *relevant range.*
Reorganized discussion of the high-low method as a three-step process.
Enhanced exhibit on high-low method.
Revised discussion of how changes in estimates affect break-even points.
Revised *target income* discussion to focus on pretax income.
Simplified exhibit on using the contribution margin income statement to compute sales needed for target income.
Revised discussion of sensitivity analyses, with examples of buying a new machine or increasing advertising.
Added exhibit on using the contribution margin income statement in sensitivity analysis.

Eliminated the *weighted-average contribution margin* method of computing multiproduct break-even.
Added two exhibits on calculations of *operating leverage.*
Added appendix on variable costing.
Added 5 Quick Studies and 6 Exercises.

Chapter 6

Happy Family Brands **UPDATED opener.**
Added new discussion of the three-step process to determine product selling price in the "Setting Prices" section.
Added short section on sources of data for CVP Analysis when preparing income statement under variable costing versus absorption costing.
Replaced previous break-even Decision Analysis example with special-order using IceAge Company.
3 new Quick Studies and 4 new Exercises.

Chapter 7

Solben **NEW opener.**
Major change: Uses a *manufacturing company* as the example within the chapter.
Budgeting for a *merchandising company* now appears in the chapter-end appendix.
Shortened/tightened section on budget process and administration.
Added section on the benefits of budgeting.
New section on the master budget differences between manufacturers and merchandisers.
Revised exhibit on the sequence of preparing the master budget for a *manufacturer.*
Reformatted sales budget exhibit.
Streamlined and reformatted several exhibits in Excel format.
Rewrote sections on preparing the direct materials, direct labor, and factory overhead budgets.
Clarified explanation of capital expenditures budget.
Slightly expanded section on preparation of the cash budget.
Added section on using the master budget.
In appendix, added new exhibit on the master budget sequence for a merchandiser.
Added 5 Quick Studies and 6 Exercises.

Chapter 8

Niner Bikes **NEW opener.**
Revised discussions of fixed and flexible budget performance reports.
Revised several flexible budget exhibits.
Revised discussion of setting standard costs.

Revised discussion of computing and analyzing cost variances.
Revised exhibits on computing direct materials and direct labor variances.
Revised sections on analyzing materials, labor, and overhead variances.
Simplified discussion of setting overhead standards.
Revised discussion of computing the predetermined overhead rate.
Revised exhibits on overhead variances and overhead variance report.
Revised discussion of sales variances in Decision Analysis.
Added learning objective for overhead spending and efficiency variances (in appendix).
In the appendix, added discussion, with an exhibit, on the standard costing income statement.
Added 7 Exercises.

Chapter 9

United by Blue **UPDATED opener.**
Added discussion of advantages and disadvantages of decentralization.
Reorganized discussion of cost, profit, and investment centers into a bulleted list, with examples using Kraft Foods Group.
Revised discussion and exhibit of responsibility accounting for cost centers.
Streamlined and clarified discussion and exhibits in the allocation of indirect expenses example.
Added discussion of the usefulness of departmental income statements in decision making.
Revised discussion of the use of return on investment and residual income in decision making.
Revised example of profit margin and investment turnover calculations, using Walt Disney Company
Added 3 Quick Studies, 5 Exercises, and 1 Problem.

Chapter 10

Charlie's Brownies **UPDATED opener.**
Expanded discussion and exhibits for short-term decisions, including additional business, make or buy, scrap or rework, sell or process further, sales mix, and segment elimination.
Added a Need-to-Know illustration for each short-term decision.
New Global View on segment elimination.
Added 3 Quick Studies.

Chapter 11

Adafruit Industries **NEW opener.**
Revised separate discussions of the accounting rate of return, net present value, and internal rate of return.
Updated graphic showing cost of capital estimates by industry.
Revised discussion of profitability index, with new exhibit.
Added 7 Quick Studies and 6 Exercises.

Chapter 12

LSTN **NEW opener.**
New infographics for operating, investing, and financing activities.
New linkage of cash flow classifications to balance sheet.
Simplified discussion of noncash investing and financing.
New, simplified preparation steps for statement of cash flows.
New, overall summary T-account for preparing statement of cash flows.
New reconstruction entries to help determine cash.
Updated cash flow analysis using Nike.
Several new Quick Studies and revised Exercises and Problems.

Chapter 13

Motley Fool **REVISED opener.**
New companies—Apple, Google, and Samsung—throughout the text and exhibits.
New boxed discussion of the role of financial statement analysis to fight and prevent fraud.
Enhanced horizontal and vertical ratio analysis using new companies and industry data.
New analysis for segment data.

Appendix C

New layout showing financial statements drawn from trial balance.
New preliminary coverage of classified and unclassified balance sheets.
Changed selected numbers for FastForward.
Revised Piaggio's (IFRS) balance sheet.
Updated debt ratio section using Skechers.

Appendix D

New LLC example using STARZ.
New T-accounts to enhance learning of partnership capital.

Instructor Resources

Connect is your all-in-one location for a variety of instructor resources. You can create custom presentations from your own materials and access all of the following. Here's what you'll find there:

- **Instructor's Resource Manual**

  Written by April Mohr, Jefferson Community and Technical College, SW.

  This manual contains (for each chapter) a Lecture Outline, a chart linking all assignment materials to learning objectives, and additional visuals with transparency masters.

- **Solutions Manual**

  Written by John J. Wild, University of Wisconsin–Madison, and Ken W. Shaw, University of Missouri–Columbia.

- **Test Bank, Computerized Test Bank**

  Revised by James Racic, Lakeland Community College

- **PowerPoint® Presentations**

  Prepared by Anna Boulware, St. Charles Community College.

  Presentations allow for revision of lecture slide, and include a viewer, allowing screens to be shown with or without the software.

- **Exercise PowerPoints**

  Prepared by Kathleen O'Donnell, Onondaga Community College.

  Exercise PowerPoints are animated walk-throughs of end-of-chapter exercises that you can edit and customize for your classroom use. These presentations are a powerful tool for the smart classroom, allowing you to spend more time teaching and less time writing on the board.

Student Supplements

Working Papers

Available on demand through Create.

Written by John J. Wild.

Connect Accounting with LearnSmart Access Code Card

ISBN: 9781259296284
MHID: 1259296288

"This textbook does address many learning styles and at the same time allows for many teaching styles ... our faculty have been very pleased with the continued revisions and supplements. From paper working papers ... to continually improved homework sites and ebooks. I'm a 'Wild' fan!"

—RITA HAYS, Southwestern Oklahoma State University

Meeting Accreditation Needs

Assurance of Learning Ready

Many educational institutions today are focused on the notion of assurance of learning, an important element of some accreditation standards. *Managerial Accounting* is designed specifically to support your assurance of learning initiatives with a simple, yet powerful solution. Each test bank question for *Managerial Accounting* maps to a specific chapter learning objective listed in the text. You can use our test bank software, EZ Test Online, or *Connect Accounting* to easily query for learning objectives that directly relate to the learning objectives for your course. You can then use the EZ Test reporting features to aggregate student results in similar fashion, making the collection and presentation of assurance of learning data simple and easy.

> "*Connect* certainly offers so much for the students and at the same time helps the professors. The professors can offer more learning opportunities to the students without intensive time investment."
>
> —CONSTANCE HYLTON, George Mason University

AACSB Statement

The McGraw-Hill Companies is a proud corporate member of AACSB International. Understanding the importance and value of AACSB accreditation, *Managerial Accounting* recognizes the curricula guidelines detailed in the AACSB standards for business accreditation by connecting selected questions in the test bank to the general knowledge and skill guidelines in the AACSB standards. The statements contained in *Managerial Accounting* are provided only as a guide for the users of this textbook. The AACSB leaves content coverage and assessment within the purview of individual schools, the mission of the school, and the faculty. While *Managerial Accounting* and the teaching package make no claim of any specific AACSB qualification or evaluation, we have within *Managerial Accounting* labeled select questions according to the general knowledge and skills areas.

Acknowledgments

John J. Wild, Ken W. Shaw, and McGraw-Hill Education recognize the following instructors for their valuable feedback and involvement in the development of *Managerial Accounting,* 5e. We are thankful for their suggestions, counsel, and encouragement.

Khaled Abdou, Penn State University–Berks
Anne Marie Anderson, Raritan Valley Community College
Elaine Anes, Heald College–Fresno
Jerome Apple, University of Akron
Jack Aschkenazi, American Intercontinental University
Sidney Askew, Borough of Manhattan Community College
Lawrence Awopetu, University of Arkansas–Pine Bluff
Jon Backman, Spartanburg Community College
Charles Baird, University of Wisconsin–Stout
Michael Barendse, Grossmont College
Richard Barnhart, Grand Rapids Community College
Beverly R. Beatty, Anne Arundel Community College
Anna Beavers, Laney College
Judy Benish, Fox Valley Technical College
Patricia Bentley, Keiser University
Teri Bernstein, Santa Monica College
Jaswinder Bhangal, Chabot College
Sandra Bitenc, University of Texas at Arlington
Susan Blizzard, San Antonio College
Marvin Blye, Wor-Wic Community College
Patrick Borja, Citrus College
Anna Boulware, St. Charles Community College
Gary Bower, Community College of Rhode Island–Flanagan
Leslee Brock, Southwest Mississippi Community College
Gregory Brookins, Santa Monica College
Regina Brown, Eastfield College
Tracy L. Bundy, University of Louisiana at Lafayette
Roy Carson, Anne Arundel Community College
Deborah Carter, Coahoma Community College
Roberto Castaneda, DeVry University Online
Martha Cavalaris, Miami Dade College
Amy Chataginer, Mississippi Gulf Coast Community College
Gerald Childs, Waukesha County Technical College
Colleen Chung, Miami Dade College–Kendall
Shifei Chung, Rowan University
Robert Churchman, Harding University
Marilyn Ciolino, Delgado Community College
Thomas Clement, University of North Dakota
Oyinka Coakley, Broward College
Susan Cockrell, Birmingham-Southern College
Lisa Cole, Johnson County Community College
Robbie R. Coleman, Northeast Mississippi Community College
Christie Comunale, Long Island University–C.W. Post Campus
Jackie Conrecode, Florida Gulf Coast University
Debora Constable, Georgia Perimeter College
Susan Cordes, Johnson County Community College
Anne Cordozo, Broward College
Cheryl Corke, Genesee Community College
James Cosby, John Tyler Community College
Ken Couvillion, Delta College
Loretta Darche, Southwest Florida College
Judy Daulton, Piedmont Technical College
Annette Davis, Glendale Community College

Dorothy Davis, University of Louisiana–Monroe
Walter DeAguero, Saddleback College
Mike Deschamps, MiraCosta College
Pamela Donahue, Northern Essex Community College
Steve Doster, Shawnee State University
Larry Dragosavac, Edison Community College
Samuel Duah, Bowie State University
Robert Dunlevy, Montgomery County Community College
Jerrilyn Eisenhauer, Tulsa Community College–Southeast
Ronald Elders, Virginia College
Terry Elliott, Morehead State University
Patricia Feller, Nashville State Community College
Albert Fisher, College of Southern Nevada
Annette Fisher, Glendale Community College
Ron Fitzgerald, Santa Monica College
David Flannery, Bryant and Stratton College
Hollie Floberg, Tennessee Wesleyan College
Linda Flowers, Houston Community College
Jeannie Folk, College of DuPage
Rebecca Foote, Middle Tennessee State University
Paul Franklin, Kaplan University
Tim Garvey, Westwood College
Barbara Gershman, Northern Virginia Community College–Woodbridge
Barbara Gershowitz, Nashville State Technical Community College
Mike Glasscock, Amarillo College
Diane Glowacki, Tarrant County College
Ernesto Gonzalez, Florida National College
Lori Grady, Bucks County Community College
Gloria Grayless, Sam Houston State University
Ann Gregory, South Plains College
Rameshwar Gupta, Jackson State University
Amy Haas, Kingsborough Community College
Pat Halliday, Santa Monica College
Keith Hallmark, Calhoun Community College
Rebecca Hancock, El Paso Community College–Valley Verde
Mechelle Harris, Bossier Parish Community College
Tracey Hawkins, University of Cincinnati–Clermont College
Thomas Hayes, University of Arkansas–Ft. Smith
Laurie Hays, Western Michigan University
Roger Hehman, University of Cincinnati–Clermont College
Cheri Hernandez, Des Moines Area Community College
Margaret Hicks, Howard University
Melanie Hicks, Liberty University
James Higgins, Holy Family University
Patricia Holmes, Des Moines Area Community College
Barbara Hopkins, Northern Virginia Community College–Manassas
Wade Hopkins, Heald College
Aileen Huang, Santa Monica College
Les Hubbard, Solano College
Deborah Hudson, Gaston College
James Hurst, National College

Constance Hylton, George Mason University
Christine Irujo, Westfield State University
Tamela Jarvais, Prince George's Community College
Fred Jex, Macomb Community College
Gina M. Jones, Aims Community College
Jeff Jones, College of Southern Nevada
Rita Jones, Columbus State University
Odessa Jordan, Calhoun Community College
Dmitriy Kalyagin, Chabot College
Thomas Kam, Hawaii Pacific University
Naomi Karolinski, Monroe Community College
Shirly A. Kleiner, Johnson County Community College
Kenneth A. Koerber, Bucks County Community College
Jill Kolody, Anne Arundel Community College
Tamara Kowalczyk, Appalachian State University
Anita Kroll, University of Wisconsin–Madison
David Krug, Johnson County Community College
Christopher Kwak, DeAnza College
Tara Laken, Joliet Junior College
Jeanette Landin, Empire College
Beth Lasky, Delgado Community College
Neal Leviton, Santa Monica College
Danny Litt, University of California Los Angeles
James L. Lock, Northern Virginia Community College
Steve Ludwig, Northwest Missouri State University
Debra Luna, El Paso Community College
Amado Mabul, Heald College
Lori Major, Luzerne County Community College
Jennifer Malfitano, Delaware County Community College
Maria Mari, Miami Dade College–Kendall
Thomas S. Marsh, Northern Virginia Community College–Annandale
Karen Martinson, University of Wisconsin–Stout
Brenda Mattison, Tri-County Technical College
Stacie Mayes, Rose State College
Clarice McCoy, Brookhaven College
Tammy Metzke, Milwaukee Area Technical College
Jeanine Metzler, Northampton Community College
Theresa Michalow, Moraine Valley Community College
Julie Miller, Chippewa Valley Tech College
Tim Miller, El Camino College
John Minchin, California Southern University
Edna C. Mitchell, Polk State College
Jill Mitchell, Northern Virginia Community College
Lynn Moore, Aiken Technical College
Angela Mott, Northeast Mississippi Community College
Andrea Murowski, Brookdale Community College
Timothy Murphy, Diablo Valley College
Kenneth F. O'Brien, Farmingdale State College
Kathleen O'Donnell, Onondaga Community College
Ahmed Omar, Burlington County College
Robert A. Pacheco, Massasoit Community College
Margaret Parilo, Cosumnes River College
Paige Paulsen, Salt Lake Community College
Yvonne Phang, Borough of Manhattan Community College
Gary Pieroni, Diablo Valley College
Debbie Porter, Tidewater Community College, Virginia Beach
Kristen Quinn, Northern Essex Community College
James Racic, Lakeland Community College
David Ravetch, University of California Los Angeles
Ruthie Reynolds, Howard University
Cecile Roberti, Community College of Rhode Island

Morgan Rockett, Moberly Area Community College
Patrick Rogan, Cosumnes River College
Paul Rogers, Community College of Beaver County
Brian Routh, Washington State University–Vancouver
Helen Roybark, Radford University
Alphonse Ruggiero, Suffolk County Community College
Joan Ryan, Clackamas Community College
Martin Sabo, Community College of Denver
Arjan Sadhwani, South University
Gary K. Sanborn, Northwestern Michigan College
Kin Kin Sandhu, Heald College
Marcia Sandvold, Des Moines Area Community College
Gary Schader, Kean University
Barbara Schnathorst, The Write Solution, Inc.
Darlene Schnuck, Waukesha County Technical College
Elizabeth Serapin, Columbia Southern University
Geeta Shankhar, University of Dayton
Regina Shea, Community College of Baltimore County–Essex
James Shelton, Liberty University
Jay Siegel, Union County College
Gerald Singh, New York City College of Technology
Lois Slutsky, Broward College–South
Gerald Smith, University of Northern Iowa
Kathleen Sobieralski, University of Maryland University College
Charles Spector, State University of New York at Oswego
Diane Stark, Phoenix College
Thomas Starks, Heald College
Carolyn L. Strauch, Crowder College
Latazia Stuart, Fortis University Online
Gene Sullivan, Liberty University
David Sulzen, Ferrum College
Dominique Svarc, William Rainey Harper College
Linda Sweeney, Sam Houston State University
Carl Swoboda, Southwest Tennessee Community College, Macon
Margaret Tanner, University of Arkansas–Ft. Smith
Ulysses Taylor, Fayetteville State University
Anthony Teng, Saddleback College
Paula Thomas, Middle Tennessee State University
Teresa Thompson, Chaffey Community College
Leslie Thysell, John Tyler Community College
Melanie Torborg, Globe University
Shafi Ullah, Broward College
Bob Urell, Irvine Valley College
Adam Vitalis, Georgia Tech
Patricia Walczak, Lansing Community College
Terri Walsh, Seminole State College–Oviedo
Shunda Ware, Atlanta Technical College
Janis Weber, University of Louisiana–Monroe
Dave Welch, Franklin University
Jean Wells-Jessup, Howard University
Christopher Widmer, Tidewater Community College
Andrew Williams, Edmonds Community College
Jonathan M. Wild, University of Wisconsin–Madison
Wanda Wong, Chabot College
John Woodward, Polk State College
Patricia Worsham, Norco College, Riverside Community College
Gail E. Wright, Stevenson University
Lynnette Yerbury, Salt Lake Community College
Judy Zander, Grossmont College
Mary Zenner, College of Lake County
Jane Zlojutro, Northwestern Michigan College

Brief Contents

*Appendixes C & D are available in McGraw-Hill *Connect* and as print copies from a McGraw-Hill representative.

Contents

4 Activity-Based Costing and Analysis 130

5 Cost Behavior and Cost-Volume-Profit Analysis 172

6 Variable Costing and Analysis 212

**13 Analysis of Financial
Statements 508**

Managerial Accounting

Managerial Accounting Concepts and Principles

MANAGERIAL ACCOUNTING BASICS

C1 Purpose of managerial accounting

Nature of managerial accounting

Managerial decisions

Fraud and ethics in managerial accounting

MANAGERIAL COST CONCEPTS

C2 Types of cost classifications

C3 Identification of cost classifications

Cost concepts for service companies

REPORTING

C4 Manufacturer costs

Balance sheet

P1 Income statement

C5 Flow of activities

P2 Schedule of cost of goods manufactured

C6 Managerial accounting trends

A1 Inventory analysis

Learning Objectives

CONCEPTUAL

C1 Explain the purpose and nature of, and the role of ethics in, managerial accounting.

C2 Describe accounting concepts useful in classifying costs.

C3 Define product and period costs and explain how they impact financial statements.

C4 Explain how balance sheets and income statements for manufacturing, merchandising, and service companies differ.

C5 Explain manufacturing activities and the flow of manufacturing costs.

C6 Describe trends in managerial accounting.

ANALYTICAL

A1 Assess raw materials inventory management using raw materials inventory turnover and days' sales in raw materials inventory.

PROCEDURAL

P1 Compute cost of goods sold for a manufacturer and for a merchandiser.

P2 Prepare a schedule of cost of goods manufactured and explain its purpose and links to financial statements.

Follow the Sun

CALGARY, CANADA—As a child, Eden Full experimented with solar electricity, starting with a desktop solar car she built from a kit as a 10-year-old. In high school, Eden tinkered with how to arrange solar panels to generate the most electricity. "I found that to get the most electricity, you have to face your solar panels toward the sun," says Eden. Thus was born the SunSaluter, Eden's invention that uses a water filtration system to automatically rotate solar panels to follow the sun's path each day.

> *"If it's beneficial and sustainable, you have to keep pushing"*
> **—Eden Full**

Like most successful entrepreneurs, Eden is finding success by creating a niche. While solar tracking is not a novel idea, Eden notes that "solar trackers can be expensive, many require electricity, and they often involve complex mechanisms prone to failure. A lot of technologies fail simply because they are too complicated." Because Eden's product does not use electricity, and it creates clean filtered water while it also produces solar electricity, its use has great potential benefit in developing countries. "When I realized I could invent a technology for social good, I fell in love with tinkering with something that mattered," she says.

With her product and a desire to change the world, Eden started her company, **SunSaluter.** Though still small, her company generates enough revenue to cover its costs. Eden stresses it is good to start a business when one is young. Risk is low, and "if the owners are passionate about their idea, someone will provide financing." In addition to passion and seed money, aspiring entrepreneurs need to understand basic managerial principles, cost classifications, and cost flows. Managerial accounting information enables Eden to plan and control costs and make good decisions. But, as Eden notes, "innovators must execute what they plan to do," and information on costs can help owners see if their plans are working.

Eden notes that it took her a while to "understand how to develop a realistic product with market potential." While financial success ultimately rests on monitoring and controlling operations, Eden measures success by more than just profits. "Anything that provides economic value should have a positive social impact," claims Eden. "You have to think about long-term returns." Eden offers sound advice for aspiring entrepreneurs: "Find your passion. But, no matter what your dream is, there will be tough days. Don't give up." And, of course, follow the sun.

Sources: *SunSaluter website,* January 2015; *Conscious Magazine; Entrepreneur.com,* April 18, 2013; *Carbon Talks,* www.carbontalks.ca/innovator-profile/eden-full; *EnergyMatters.com,* June 10, 2011; *NPR,* December 2012

MANAGERIAL ACCOUNTING BASICS

Managerial accounting is an activity that provides financial and nonfinancial information to an organization's managers. Managers include, for example, employees in charge of a company's divisions; the heads of marketing, information technology, and human resources; and top-level managers such as the chief executive officer (CEO) and chief financial officer (CFO). To do their jobs, such managers need more than just the general-purpose financial statements provided by the financial accounting system. This section explains the purpose of managerial accounting (also called *management accounting*) and compares it with financial accounting.

Purpose of Managerial Accounting

C1

Explain the purpose and nature of, and the role of ethics in, managerial accounting.

The purpose of managerial accounting is to provide useful information to managers of an organization. Managerial accounting helps managers with three key tasks: (1) determining the costs of an organization's products and services, (2) planning future activities, and (3) comparing actual results to planned results. For example, managerial accounting information can help the marketing manager decide whether to advertise on social media such as **Twitter**; it also can help the information technology manager decide whether to buy new computers. Managerial accounting information also helps the CEO decide which divisions to expand and which to eliminate.

Point: Costs are important to managers because they impact both the financial position and profitability of a business. Managerial accounting assists in analysis, planning, and control of costs.

The remainder of this book looks carefully at how managerial accounting information is gathered and how managers use it. We begin by showing how the managerial accounting system collects cost information and assigns it to an organization's products and services. Information about such costs is important for many decisions that managers make, such as predicting the future costs of a product or service. Predicted costs are used in product pricing, profitability analysis, and in deciding whether to make or buy a product or component. More generally, much of managerial accounting involves gathering information about costs for planning and control decisions.

Planning is the process of setting goals and making plans to achieve them. Companies make long-term strategic plans that usually span a 5- to 10-year horizon. Strategic plans usually set a firm's long-term direction based on opportunities such as new products, new markets, and capital investments. A strategic plan's goals and objectives are broadly defined given its long-term orientation. With long-term plans in place, companies then set short-term plans, which are more operational in nature. Short-term plans translate the strategic plan into actions, and they are more concrete and consist of better-defined objectives and goals. A short-term plan often covers a one-year period that, when translated in monetary terms, is known as a budget.

Control is the process of monitoring planning decisions and evaluating an organization's activities and employees. It includes the measurement and evaluation of actions, processes, and outcomes. Feedback provided by the control function allows managers to revise their plans. Measurement of actions and processes also allows managers to take corrective actions to obtain better outcomes. For example, managers periodically compare actual results with planned results. Exhibit 1.1 portrays the important management functions of planning and control. In later chapters, we explain how managers also use this information to direct and improve business operations.

EXHIBIT 1.1

Planning and Control (including monitoring and feedback)

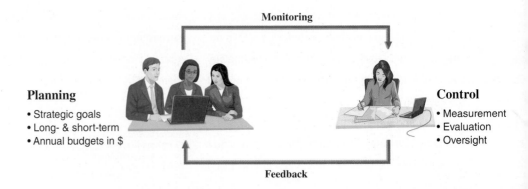

Monitoring

Planning
- Strategic goals
- Long- & short-term
- Annual budgets in $

Control
- Measurement
- Evaluation
- Oversight

Feedback

Nature of Managerial Accounting

Managerial accounting differs from financial accounting. We discuss seven key differences in this section, as summarized in Exhibit 1.2.

EXHIBIT 1.2

Key Differences between Managerial Accounting and Financial Accounting

	Financial Accounting	Managerial Accounting
1. Users	External: Investors, creditors, and others outside of the managers of the organization	Internal: Managers, employees, and decision makers inside the organization
2. Purpose of information	Help external users make investment, credit, and other decisions	Help managers make planning and control decisions
3. Flexibility of reporting	Structured and often controlled by GAAP	Relatively flexible (no GAAP constraints)
4. Timeliness of information	Often available only after an audit is complete	Available quickly without the need to wait for an audit
5. Time dimension	The past; historical information with some predictions	The future; many projections and estimates, with some historical information
6. Focus of information	The whole organization	An organization's projects, processes, and divisions
7. Nature of information	Monetary information	Mostly monetary; but also nonmonetary information

Users and Decision Makers   Companies accumulate, process, and report financial accounting and managerial accounting information for different groups of decision makers. Financial accounting information is provided primarily to external users including investors, creditors, analysts, and regulators. External users rarely have a major role in managing a company's daily activities. Managerial accounting information, in contrast, is provided primarily to internal users who are responsible for making and implementing decisions about a company's business activities.

Purpose of Information   Investors, creditors, and other external users of financial accounting information must often decide whether to invest in or lend to a company. If they have already done so, they must decide whether to continue owning the company or carrying the loan. Internal decision makers must plan a company's future. They seek to take advantage of opportunities or to overcome obstacles. They also try to control activities. Managerial accounting information helps internal users make both planning and control decisions.

Flexibility of Practice   External users compare companies by using financial reports, and they need protection against false or misleading information. Thus, financial accounting relies on accepted principles that are enforced through an extensive set of rules and guidelines, or GAAP. Internal users need managerial accounting information for planning and controlling their company's activities rather than for external comparisons. Internal users require different types of information, depending on the activity and the type of organization. Thus, managerial accounting systems are flexible and differ across companies. The design of a company's managerial accounting system depends largely on the nature of the business and the arrangement of its internal operations. Managers can decide for themselves what information they want and how they want it reported. Even within a single company, different managers often design their own systems to meet their special needs. The important question a manager must ask is whether the information being collected and reported is useful for planning, decision making, and control purposes.

Point: It is desirable to accumulate certain information for management reports in a database separate from financial accounting records.

Point: The *Institute of Management Accountants* issues statements that govern the practice of managerial accounting. Accountants who pass a qualifying exam are awarded the CMA.

Timeliness of Information   Formal financial statements reporting past transactions and events are not immediately available to outside parties. Independent certified public accountants often must *audit* a company's financial statements before providing them to external users. Thus, because audits often take several weeks to complete, financial reports to outsiders usually are not available until well after the period-end. However, managers can quickly obtain managerial accounting information. External auditors need not review it. Estimates and projections are acceptable. To get information quickly, managers often accept less precision in reports. As an example, an early internal report to management prepared right after the year-end could report net income for the year between $4.2 and $4.8 million. An audited income statement could later show net income for the year at $4.6 million. The internal report is not precise, but its information can be more useful because it is available earlier.

Point: Financial statements are usually issued several weeks after the period-end. GAAP requires the reporting of important events that occur while the statements are being prepared. These events are called *subsequent events*.

Internal auditing plays an important role in managerial accounting. Internal auditors evaluate the flow of information not only inside but also outside the company. Managers are responsible for preventing and detecting fraudulent activities in their companies.

Time Dimension   To protect external users from false expectations, financial reports deal primarily with results of both past activities and current conditions. While some predictions such as service lives and salvage values of plant assets are necessary, financial accounting avoids predictions whenever possible. In contrast, managerial accounting regularly includes predictions of conditions and events. As an example, one important managerial accounting report is a budget, which predicts revenues, expenses, and other items. If managerial accounting reports were restricted to the past and present, managers would be less able to plan activities and less effective in managing and evaluating current activities.

EXHIBIT 1.3

Focus of External Reports

Reports to external users focus on company as a whole

Focus of Information   Companies often organize into divisions and departments, but investors rarely can buy shares in one division or department. Nor do creditors lend money to a company's single division or department. Instead, they own shares in or make loans to the entire company. Financial accounting focuses primarily on a company as a whole as depicted in Exhibit 1.3.

The focus of managerial accounting is different. While top-level managers are responsible for managing the whole company, most other managers are responsible for much smaller sets of activities. These middle-level and lower-level managers need managerial accounting reports dealing with specific activities, projects, and subdivisions for which they are responsible. For instance, division sales managers are directly responsible only for the results achieved in their divisions. Accordingly, to improve performance, they need only information about results achieved in their own divisions. This information includes the level of success achieved by each individual, product, or department in each division of the whole company as depicted in Exhibit 1.4.

EXHIBIT 1.4

Focus of Internal Reports

Reports to internal users focus on company units and divisions

Nature of Information   Both financial and managerial accounting systems report monetary information. Managerial accounting systems also report considerable nonmonetary information. Monetary information is an important part of managerial decisions, and nonmonetary information also plays a crucial role, especially when monetary effects are difficult to measure. Common examples of nonmonetary information include customer and employee satisfaction data, the percentage of on-time deliveries, and product defect rates.

Managerial Decision Making

Although there are differences between financial and managerial accounting, the two are not entirely separate. Some similar information is useful to both external and internal users. For instance, information about costs of manufacturing products is useful to all users in making decisions. Also, both financial and managerial accounting affect people's actions. For example, Trek's sales compensation plan affects the behavior of its salesforce when selling it

manufactured bikes. Trek also must estimate the effects of promotions on buying patterns of customers. These estimates impact the equipment purchase decisions for manufacturing and can affect the supplier selection criteria established by purchasing. Thus, financial and managerial accounting systems do more than measure; they also affect people's decisions and actions.

Fraud and Ethics in Managerial Accounting

Fraud, and the role of ethics in reducing fraud, are important factors in running business operations. Fraud involves the use of one's job for personal gain through the deliberate misuse of the employer's assets. Examples include theft of the employer's cash or other assets, overstating reimbursable expenses, payroll schemes, and financial statement fraud. Three factors must exist for a person to commit fraud: opportunity, financial pressure, and rationalization. This is known as the *fraud triangle*. Fraud affects all business and it is costly: A 2014 *Report to the Nation* from the Association of Certified Fraud Examiners (ACFE) estimates the average U.S. business loses 5% of its annual revenues to fraud.

The most common type of fraud, where employees steal or misuse the employer's resources, results in an average loss of $130,000 per occurrence. For example, in a billing fraud, an employee sets up a bogus supplier. The employee then prepares bills from the supplier and pays these bills from the employer's checking account. The employee cashes the checks sent to the bogus supplier and uses them for his or her own personal benefit. An organization's best chance to minimize fraud is through reducing opportunities for employees to commit fraud.

Implications for Managerial Accounting Fraud increases a business's costs, and an important goal of managerial accounting is accurate cost information. Left undetected, inflated costs can result in poor pricing decisions, an improper product mix, and faulty performance evaluations. All of these can lead to poor financial results for the company. Management can develop accounting systems to closely track costs and identify deviations from expected amounts. In addition, managers rely on an **internal control system** to monitor and control business activities. An internal control system is the policies and procedures managers use to:

- Ensure reliable accounting.
- Protect assets.
- Urge adherence to company policies.
- Promote efficient operations.

Combating fraud and other dilemmas requires ethics in accounting. **Ethics** are beliefs that distinguish right from wrong. They are accepted standards of good and bad behavior. Identifying the ethical path can be difficult. The **Institute of Management Accountants (IMA),** the professional association for management accountants, has issued a code of ethics to help accountants involved in solving ethical dilemmas. The IMA's Statement of Ethical Professional Practice requires that management accountants be competent, maintain confidentiality, act with integrity, and communicate information in a fair and credible manner.

The IMA provides a "road map" for resolving ethical conflicts. It suggests that an employee follow the company's policies on how to resolve such conflicts. If the conflict remains unresolved, an employee should contact the next level of management (such as the immediate supervisor) who is not involved in the ethical conflict.

Point: The IMA also issues the Certified Management Accountant (CMA) and the Certified Financial Manager (CFM) certifications. Employees with the CMA or CFM certifications typically earn higher salaries than those without.

Point: The **Sarbanes-Oxley Act** requires each issuer of securities to disclose whether it has adopted a code of ethics for its senior officers and the content of that code.

■ Decision Ethics

Production Manager You invite three friends to a restaurant. When the dinner check arrives, David, a self-employed entrepreneur, picks it up saying, "Here, let me pay. I'll deduct it as a business expense on my tax return." Denise, a salesperson, takes the check from David's hand and says, "I'll put this on my company's credit card. It won't cost us anything." Derek, a factory manager for a company, laughs and says, "Neither of you understands. I'll put this on my company's credit card and call it overhead on a cost-plus contract my company has with a client." (*A cost-plus contract means the company receives its costs plus a percent of those costs.*) Adds Derek, "That way, my company pays for dinner *and* makes a profit." Who should pay the bill? Why? ■ [Answers follow the chapter's Summary.]

QC1

MANAGERIAL COST CONCEPTS

C2

Describe accounting concepts useful in classifying costs.

Because managers use costs for many different purposes, organizations classify costs in different ways (that is, different costs for different purposes). This section explains common ways to classify costs and links them to managerial decisions. We illustrate these cost classifications with Rocky Mountain Bikes, a manufacturer of bicycles.

Types of Cost Classifications

Fixed versus Variable   At a basic level, a cost can be classified by how it behaves with changes in the volume of activity. Thus, a cost can be classified as fixed or variable. A **fixed cost** does not change with changes in the volume of activity (within a range of activity known as an activity's *relevant range*). For example, straight-line depreciation on equipment is a fixed cost. A **variable cost** changes in proportion to changes in the volume of activity. Sales commissions computed as a percent of sales revenue are variable costs. Additional examples of fixed and variable costs for a bike manufacturer are provided in Exhibit 1.5. Classification of costs as fixed or variable is helpful in cost-volume-profit analyses and short-term decision making. We discuss these in Chapters 5 and 11.

EXHIBIT 1.5

Fixed and Variable Costs

Fixed Cost: Rent for Rocky Mountain Bikes' building is $22,000, and it doesn't change with the number of bikes produced.

Variable Cost: Cost of bicycle tires is variable with the number of bikes produced—this cost is $15 per pair.

Direct versus Indirect   A cost is often traced to a **cost object,** which is a product, process, department, or customer to which costs are assigned. **Direct costs** are traceable to a single cost object. **Indirect costs** cannot be easily and cost-beneficially traced to a single cost object. Assuming the cost object is a bicycle, Rocky Mountain Bikes will first identify the costs that can be directly traced to bicycles. The direct costs traceable to a bicycle as a cost object would include direct material and direct labor costs used in its production. Such direct costs include wheels, brakes, chains, and seat, plus the wages and benefits of the employees who work directly on making the bike.

What are indirect costs associated with bicycles? One example is the salary of the supervisor. She monitors the production process and other factory activities, but she does not actually work on producing any bikes. Thus, her salary cannot be directly traced to bikes. Likewise, depreciation (other than the units-of-production method) on manufacturing warehouses cannot be traced to individual bikes. Another example is a maintenance department that provides services to two or more departments of a company making bicycles and strollers. If the cost object is the bicycle, the wages of the maintenance department employees who clean the factory area every night would be indirect costs. Exhibit 1.6 identifies more examples of direct and indirect costs when the cost object is a bicycle.

 **Decision Maker**

Entrepreneur   You wish to trace as many of your assembly department's direct costs as possible. You can trace 90% of them in an economical manner. To trace the other 10%, you need sophisticated and costly accounting software. Do you purchase this software? ■   [Answers follow the chapter's Summary.]

EXHIBIT 1.6

Direct and Indirect Costs
for a Bicycle

Direct Costs (for bicycle)		**Indirect Costs (for bicycle)**	
• Tires	• Frames	• Factory accounting	• Factory light and heat
• Seats	• Chains	• Factory administration	• Factory intranet
• Handlebars	• Brakes	• Factory rent	• Insurance on factory
• Bike maker wages	• Bike maker benefits	• Factory manager's salary	• Factory equipment depreciation*

* For all depreciation methods other than units-of-production.

Product versus Period Costs   All production (or factory) costs are product costs. **Product costs** are those production costs necessary to create a product and consist of: direct materials, direct labor, and factory overhead. Overhead refers to production costs other than direct materials and direct labor. Product costs are capitalized as inventory during and after completion of the products; they are recorded as cost of goods sold when those products are sold.

Period costs are non-production costs and are usually more associated with activities linked to a time period than with completed products. Common examples of period costs include salaries of the sales staff, wages of maintenance workers, advertising expenses, and depreciation on office furniture and equipment. Period costs are expensed in the period when incurred either as selling expenses or as general and administrative expenses.

A distinction between product and period costs is important because period costs are expensed when incurred and reported on the income statement whereas product costs are capitalized as inventory on the balance sheet until that inventory is sold. An ability to understand and identify product costs and period costs is crucial to using and interpreting a *schedule of cost of goods manufactured,* described later in this chapter.

Exhibit 1.7 shows the different effects of product and period costs. Period costs flow directly to the current income statement as expenses. They are not reported as assets. Product costs are

C3

Define product and period costs and explain how they impact financial statements.

Point: Product costs are either in the income statement as part of cost of goods sold or in the balance sheet as inventory. Period costs appear only on the income statement under operating expenses.

EXHIBIT 1.7

Period and Product Costs in Financial Statements

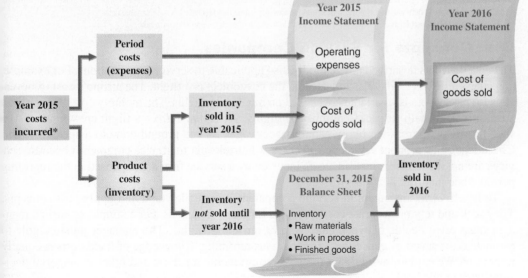

Point: For a team approach to identifying period and product costs, see *Teamwork in Action* in the *Beyond the Numbers* section.

* This diagram excludes costs to acquire assets other than inventory.

first assigned to inventory. Their final treatment depends on when inventory is sold or disposed of. Product costs assigned to finished goods that are sold in year 2015 are reported on the 2015 income statement as cost of goods sold. Product costs assigned to unsold inventory are carried forward on the balance sheet at the end of year 2015. If this inventory is sold in year 2016, product costs assigned to it are reported as cost of goods sold in that year's income statement.

Exhibit 1.8 summarizes typical managerial decisions for common cost classifications.

EXHIBIT 1.8

Summary of Cost Classifications and Example Managerial Decisions

Point: In subsequent chapters, we discuss some other ways to classify costs. The three cost classifications presented here are the foundation.

Costs Classified As	Example Managerial Decision
Variable or Fixed	How many units must we sell to break even?
	What will profit be if we raise the selling price?
	Should we add a new line of business?
Direct or Indirect	How well did our departments perform?
Product or Period	What is the cost of our inventory?
	Are selling expenses too high?

Identification of Cost Classifications

It is important to understand that a cost can be classified using any one (or combination) of the three different means described here. Understanding how to classify costs in several different ways enables managers to use cost information for a variety of decisions. Factory rent, for instance, is classified as a *product* cost; it is *fixed* with respect to the number of units produced, and it is *indirect* with respect to the product. Potential multiple classifications are shown in Exhibit 1.9 using different cost items incurred in manufacturing mountain bikes. The finished bike is the cost object. Proper allocation of these costs and the managerial decisions based on cost data depend on a correct cost classification.

EXHIBIT 1.9

Examples of Multiple Cost Classifications

Cost Item	Fixed or Variable	Direct or Indirect	Product or Period
Bicycle tires and wheels.	Variable	Direct	Product
Wages of assembly worker*	Variable	Direct	Product
Advertising	Fixed	Indirect	Period
Production manager's salary	Fixed	Indirect	Product
Office depreciation	Fixed	Indirect	Period
Factory depreciation (straight-line)	Fixed	Indirect	Product
Oil and grease applied to gears/chains**	Variable	Indirect	Product
Sales commissions	Variable	Indirect	Period

*In some cases wages can be classified as fixed costs. For example, union contracts might limit an employer's ability to adjust its labor force in response to changes in demand. In this book, unless told otherwise, assume that factory wages are variable costs.
**Oil and grease are indirect costs as it is not practical to track how much of each is applied to each bike.

Cost Concepts for Service Companies

The cost concepts described are generally also applicable to service organizations. For example, consider **Southwest Airlines**, and assume the cost object is a flight. The airline's cost of beverages for passengers is a variable cost based on number of flights. The monthly cost of leasing an aircraft is fixed with respect to number of flights. We can also trace a flight crew's salary to a specific flight whereas we likely cannot trace wages for the ground crew to a specific flight. Classification as product versus period costs is not relevant to service companies because services are not inventoried. Instead, costs incurred by a service firm are expensed in the reporting period when incurred.

To be effective, managers in service companies must understand and apply cost concepts. They seek and rely on accurate cost estimates for many decisions. For example, an airline manager must often decide between canceling or rerouting flights. The manager must be able to estimate costs saved by canceling a flight versus rerouting. Knowledge of fixed costs is equally important. We explain more about the cost requirements for these and other managerial decisions later in this book.

Justin Sullivan/Getty Images

Service Costs

• Beverages and snacks
• Cleaning fees
• Pilot and copilot salaries
• Attendant salaries
• Fuel and oil costs
• Travel agent fees
• Ground crew salaries

Following are selected costs of a company that manufactures computer chips. Classify each as either a product cost or a period cost. Then classify each of the product costs as direct material, direct labor, or overhead.

1. Plastic boards used to mount chips
2. Advertising costs
3. Factory maintenance workers' salaries
4. Real estate taxes paid on the sales office
5. Real estate taxes paid on the factory
6. Factory supervisor salary
7. Depreciation on factory equipment
8. Assembly worker hourly pay to make chips

Cost Classification

C2   C3

QC2

Do More: QS 1-4, QS 1-5, E 1-5

Solution

	Product Costs			Period Cost
	Direct Material	Direct Labor	Overhead	
1. Plastic boards used to mount chips	X			
2. Advertising costs.				X
3. Factory maintenance workers' salaries.			X	
4. Real estate taxes paid on the sales office.				X
5. Real estate taxes paid on the factory.			X	
6. Factory supervisor salary			X	
7. Depreciation on factory equipment.			X	
8. Assembly worker hourly pay to make chips.		X		

REPORTING

Companies with manufacturing activities differ from both merchandising and service companies. The main difference between merchandising and manufacturing companies is that merchandisers buy goods ready for sale while manufacturers produce goods from materials and labor. **Amazon.com** is an example of a merchandising company. It buys and sells goods without physically changing them. **Adidas** is primarily a manufacturer of shoes, apparel, and accessories. It purchases materials such as leather, cloth, dye, plastic, rubber, glue, and laces and then uses employees' labor to convert these materials to products. Southwest Airlines is a service company that transports people and items. Some companies have several types of activities. For example, **Best Buy** is a merchandiser that also provides services via its Geek Squad.

The next section discusses costs for manufacturing companies. We then discuss the reporting of activities for manufacturing, merchandising, and service companies. Importantly, as these types of organizations have different kinds of costs and they classify costs in different ways, their accounting reports will also differ in some respects.

Manufacturers' Costs

Direct Materials   Direct materials are tangible components of a finished product. **Direct material costs** are the expenditures for direct materials that are separately and readily traced through the manufacturing process to finished goods. Examples of direct materials in manufacturing a mountain bike include its tires, seat, frame, pedals, brakes, cables, gears, and handlebars. The chart in the margin shows that direct materials generally make up about 45% of manufacturing costs in today's products, but this amount varies across industries and companies.

Typical Manufacturing Costs in Today's Products

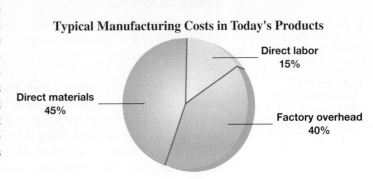

Direct materials 45%

Direct labor 15%

Factory overhead 40%

Direct Labor   **Direct labor** refers to the efforts of employees who physically convert materials to finished product. **Direct labor costs** are the wages and salaries for direct labor that are separately and readily traced through the manufacturing process to finished goods. Examples of direct labor in manufacturing a mountain bike include operators directly involved in converting raw materials into finished products (welding, painting, forming) and assembly workers who attach materials such as tires, seats, pedals, and brakes to the bike frames.

Factory Overhead   **Factory overhead,** also called *manufacturing overhead,* consists of all manufacturing costs that are not direct materials or direct labor. **Factory overhead costs** cannot be separately or readily traced to finished goods. Thus, all factory overhead costs are considered indirect costs. These costs include indirect materials, **indirect labor,** and other costs not directly traceable to the product. **Indirect materials** are materials used in manufacturing and become part of the final product, but they are *not* clearly identified with specific product units. Often, direct materials are classified as indirect materials when their costs are low. Examples include screws and nuts used in assembling mountain bikes, and staples and glue used in manufacturing shoes. Applying the *materiality principle,* companies may decide it does not make economic sense to individually trace costs of each of these materials to individual products. For example, keeping detailed records of the amount of glue used to manufacture one shoe is not cost-beneficial.

   Indirect labor costs refer to the costs of workers who assist in or supervise the manufacturing process. Examples include costs for employees who maintain the manufacturing equipment and salaries of production supervisors. Those workers do not assemble products. These costs are not linked to specific units of product, though they are indirectly related to production. Overtime premiums paid to direct laborers are also included in overhead because overtime is due to delays, interruptions, or constraints not necessarily identifiable to a specific product or batches of product.

   Factory overhead costs also include maintenance of the mountain bike factory, supervision of its employees, repairing manufacturing equipment, factory utilities (water, gas, electricity), factory manager's salary, factory rent, depreciation on factory buildings and equipment, factory insurance, property taxes on factory buildings and equipment, and factory accounting and legal services. Factory overhead does *not* include selling and administrative expenses because they are not incurred in manufacturing products. These expenses are *period costs,* and they are recorded as expenses on the income statement when incurred.

EXHIBIT 1.10

Prime and Conversion Costs and Their Makeup

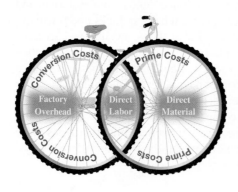

Prime costs = Direct materials + Direct labor.
Conversion costs = Direct labor + Factory overhead.

Prime and Conversion Costs   Direct material costs and direct labor costs are also called **prime costs**—expenditures directly associated with the manufacture of finished goods. Direct labor costs and overhead costs are called **conversion costs**—expenditures incurred in the process of converting raw materials to finished goods. Direct labor costs are considered both prime costs and conversion costs. Exhibit 1.10 conveys the relation between prime and conversion costs and their components of direct material, direct labor, and factory overhead.

Balance Sheet

Manufacturers carry several unique assets and usually have three inventories instead of the single inventory that merchandisers carry. The three inventories are raw materials, work in process, and finished goods.

Raw Materials Inventory   **Raw materials inventory** refers to the goods a company acquires to use in making products. Companies use raw materials in two ways: directly and indirectly. Raw materials that are possible and practical to trace to an end-product are called *direct materials;* they are included in raw materials inventory. Raw materials that are either impossible or impractical to trace to an end-product are classified as indirect materials (such as solder used for welding); they often come from factory supplies or raw materials inventory.

Work in Process Inventory   Another inventory held by manufacturers is **work in process inventory,** also called *goods in process inventory.* It consists of products in the process of being manufactured but not yet complete. The amount of work in process inventory depends on the type of production process. If the time required to produce a unit of product is short, the work in process inventory is likely small; but if weeks or months are needed to produce a unit, the work in process inventory is usually larger.

Finished Goods Inventory   A third inventory owned by a manufacturer is **finished goods inventory,** which consists of completed products ready for sale. This inventory is similar to merchandise inventory owned by a merchandising company.

Marco Prosch/Getty Images

Balance Sheets for Merchandising and Service Companies   The current assets section of the balance sheet will look different for merchandising and service companies as compared to manufacturing companies. A merchandiser will report only merchandise inventory rather than the three types of inventory reported by a manufacturer. A service company's balance sheet does not have any inventory held for sale. Exhibit 1.11 shows the current assets section of the balance sheet for a manufacturer, a merchandiser, and a service company. Note that the manufacturer, Rocky Mountain Bikes, shows three different inventories. The merchandiser, Tele-Mart, shows one inventory, and the service provider, Northeast Air, shows no inventory of goods for sale.

Manufacturers also often own unique plant assets such as small tools, factory buildings, factory equipment, and patents to manufacture products. Merchandisers and service providers also typically own fixed assets.

EXHIBIT 1.11

Balance Sheets for Manufacturer, Merchandiser, and Service Provider

ROCKY MOUNTAIN BIKES Balance Sheet (partial) December 31, 2015	
Assets	
Current assets	
Cash	$11,000
Accounts receivable, net . . .	30,150
Raw materials inventory	9,000
Work in process inventory . .	7,500
Finished goods inventory	10,300
Factory supplies	350
Prepaid insurance	300
Total current assets	$68,600

TELE-MART (Merchandiser) Balance Sheet (partial) December 31, 2015	
Assets	
Current assets	
Cash	$11,000
Accounts receivable, net . . .	30,150
Merchandise inventory	21,000
Supplies	350
Prepaid insurance	300
Total current assets	$62,800

NORTHEAST AIR (Service Provider) Balance Sheet (partial) December 31, 2015	
Assets	
Current assets	
Cash	$11,000
Accounts receivable, net	30,150
Supplies	350
Prepaid insurance	300
Total current assets	$41,800

Income Statement

The main difference between the income statement of a manufacturer and that of a merchandiser involves the items making up cost of goods sold. In this section, we look at how manufacturers determine and report cost of goods sold.

P1

Compute cost of goods sold for a manufacturer, and for a merchandiser.

Cost of Goods Sold   Exhibit 1.12 compares the components of cost of goods sold for a merchandiser with those for a manufacturer. To determine its cost of goods sold, a *merchandiser* adds cost of goods purchased to beginning merchandise inventory and then subtracts ending merchandise inventory. To determine its cost of goods sold, a *manufacturer* adds cost of goods manufactured to beginning finished goods inventory and then subtracts ending finished goods inventory.

In computing cost of goods sold, a merchandiser uses *merchandise* inventory while a manufacturer uses *finished goods* inventory. A manufacturer's inventories of raw materials and work in process are not included in finished goods because they are not available for

EXHIBIT 1.12

Cost of Goods Sold
Computation

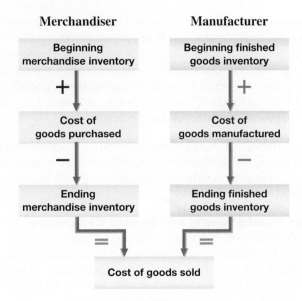

sale. A manufacturer also shows cost of goods *manufactured* instead of cost of goods *purchased*. This difference occurs because a manufacturer produces its goods instead of purchasing them ready for sale. The Cost of Goods Sold sections for both a merchandiser (Tele-Mart) and a manufacturer (Rocky Mountain Bikes) are shown in Exhibit 1.13 to highlight these differences. The remaining income statement sections are similar for merchandisers and manufacturers.

EXHIBIT 1.13

Cost of Goods Sold for
a Merchandiser and
Manufacturer

Merchandising Company (Tele-Mart)	
Cost of goods sold	
Beginning *merchandise* inventory	$ 14,200
Cost of merchandise *purchased*	234,150
Goods available for sale	248,350
Less ending *merchandise* inventory	12,100
Cost of goods sold	$236,250

Manufacturing Company (Rocky Mtn. Bikes)	
Cost of goods sold	
Beginning *finished goods* inventory	$ 11,200
Cost of goods *manufactured**	170,500
Goods available for sale	181,700
Less ending *finished goods* inventory	10,300
Cost of goods sold	$171,400

* Cost of goods manufactured is reported in the income statement of Exhibit 1.14.

Although the cost of goods sold computations are similar, the numbers in these computations reflect different activities. A merchandiser's cost of goods purchased is the cost of buying products to be sold. A manufacturer's cost of goods manufactured is the sum of direct materials, direct labor, and factory overhead costs incurred in producing products.

Income Statement for Service Company   Since a service provider does not make or buy inventory to be sold, it does not report cost of goods manufactured or cost of goods sold. Instead, its operating expenses include all of the costs it incurred in providing its service. Southwest Airlines, for example, reports large operating expenses for employee pay and benefits, fuel and oil, and depreciation.

Point: Manufacturers treat costs such as depreciation and rent as product costs if they are related to manufacturing.

Reporting Performance   Exhibit 1.14 shows the income statement for Rocky Mountain Bikes. Its operating expenses include selling expenses and general and administrative expenses, which include salaries for those business functions as well as depreciation for related equipment. Operating expenses do not include manufacturing costs such as factory workers' wages and depreciation of production equipment and the factory buildings. These manufacturing costs are reported as part of cost of goods manufactured and included in cost of goods sold. This exhibit also shows the income statement for Tele-Mart (merchandiser) and Northeast Air (service provider). Note that Tele-Mart reports *cost of merchandise purchased* instead of cost of goods manufactured. Tele-Mart reports its operating expenses like those of the manufacturing company. Finally, the income statement for Northeast Air shows only operating expenses.

EXHIBIT 1.14

Income Statements for Manufacturer, Merchandiser, and Service Provider

ROCKY MOUNTAIN BIKES (Manufacturer)
Income Statement
For Year Ended December 31, 2015

Sales		$310,000
Cost of goods sold		
Finished goods inventory, Dec. 31, 2014	$ 11,200	
Cost of goods manufactured (from Exhibit 1.16)	170,500	
Goods available for sale	181,700	
Less finished goods inventory, Dec. 31, 2015	10,300	
Cost of goods sold		171,400
Gross profit		138,600
Operating expenses		
Selling expenses	38,150	
General and administrative expenses	21,750	
Total operating expenses		59,900
Income before income taxes		78,700
Income tax expense		32,600
Net income		$ 46,100

TELE-MART (Merchandiser)
Income Statement
For Year Ended December 31, 2015

Sales		$345,000
Cost of goods sold		
Merchandise inventory, Dec. 31, 2014	$ 14,200	
Cost of merchandise purchased	234,150	
Goods available for sale	248,350	
Merchandise inventory, Dec. 31, 2015	12,100	
Cost of goods sold		236,250
Gross profit		108,750
Operating expenses		
Selling expenses	38,150	
General and administrative expenses	21,750	
Total operating expenses		59,900
Income before income taxes		48,850
Income tax expense		20,235
Net income		$ 28,615

NORTHEAST AIR (Service Provider)
Income Statement
For Year Ended December 31, 2015

Service revenue		$425,000
Operating expenses		
Salaries and wages	$127,750	
Fuel and oil	159,375	
Maintenance and repairs	29,750	
Rent	42,500	
Depreciation	14,000	
General and admin. expenses	20,000	
Total operating expenses		393,375
Income before income taxes		31,625
Income tax expense		13,100
Net income		$ 18,525

Indicate whether the following financial statement items apply to a manufacturer, a merchandiser, or a service provider. Some items apply to more than one type of organization.

NEED-TO-KNOW 1-2

Organization Costs and Types

C4

_____ **1.** Merchandise inventory   _____ **4.** Operating expenses
_____ **2.** Finished goods inventory   _____ **5.** Cost of goods manufactured
_____ **3.** Cost of goods sold   _____ **6.** Supplies inventory

Solution

	Manufacturer	Merchandiser	Service Provider
1. Merchandise inventory		✓	
2. Finished goods inventory	✓		
3. Cost of goods sold	✓	✓	
4. Operating expenses	✓	✓	✓
5. Cost of goods manufactured	✓		
6. Supplies inventory	✓	✓	✓

Do More: E 1-7

QC3

Flow of Manufacturing Activities

C5

Explain manufacturing
activities and the flow of
manufacturing costs.

In addition to income statements and balance sheets, manufacturing companies typically prepare additional reports to help managers plan and control the manufacturing process. In order to understand these reports, we must first understand the flow of manufacturing activities and costs. Exhibit 1.15 shows the flow of manufacturing activities and the cost flows of those activities. As you can see (across the top row), the activities flow consists of *materials activity* followed by *production activity* followed by *sales activity*. The boxes below those activities show the costs for each activity and how costs flow across the three manufacturing activities. We explain further in this section.

EXHIBIT 1.15

Activities and Cost Flows
in Manufacturing

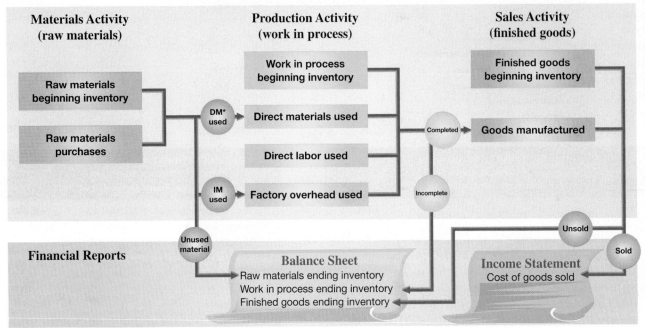

* DM = direct materials, IM = indirect materials.

Point: Knowledge of
managerial accounting provides
us a means of measuring
manufacturing costs and is a
sound foundation for studying
advanced business topics.

Materials Activity   The far left side of Exhibit 1.15 shows the flow of raw materials. Manufacturers usually start a period with some beginning raw materials inventory left over from the previous period. The company then acquires additional raw materials in the current period. Adding these purchases to beginning inventory gives *total raw materials available for use* in production. These raw materials are then either used in production in the current period or remain in inventory at the end of the period for use in future periods.

Production Activity   The middle section of Exhibit 1.15 describes production activity. Four factors come together in production: beginning work in process inventory, raw materials, direct labor, and overhead. *Beginning work in process inventory* consists of partially complete products from the previous period. To the beginning work in process inventory are added direct materials, direct labor, and manufacturing overhead.

  The production activity that takes place in the period from those inputs results in products that are either finished or remain unfinished. The cost of finished products makes up the **cost of goods manufactured** for the current period. The cost of goods manufactured is the total cost of making and finishing products in the period. That amount is included on the income statement in the computation of cost of goods sold, as we showed in Exhibit 1.14. Unfinished products are identified as *ending work in process inventory*. The cost of unfinished products consists of raw materials, direct labor, and factory overhead, and is reported on the current period's balance sheet. The costs of both finished goods manufactured and work in process are *product costs*.

Sales Activity   The far right side of Exhibit 1.15 shows what happens to the finished goods. The company combines the beginning inventory of finished goods with the newly completed units (goods manufactured). Together, they make up *total finished goods available for sale* in the current period. These goods now are ready for sales activity. As they are sold, the cost of finished products sold is reported on the income statement as cost of goods sold. The cost of any finished products not sold in the period is reported as a current asset, *finished goods inventory,* on the current period's balance sheet.

Schedule of Cost of Goods Manufactured

Managers of manufacturing firms typically analyze product costs in detail. Such analysis can help managers make better decisions about materials, labor, and overhead in order to reduce the cost of goods manufactured and maximize the company's profits. A company's manufacturing activities are described in a separate report, called a **schedule of cost of goods manufactured.** (It is also called a *manufacturing statement,* a *statement of cost of goods manufactured,* or a similar term.) By whatever name, the schedule of cost of goods manufactured summarizes the types and amounts of costs incurred in a company's manufacturing process. Exhibit 1.16 shows the schedule of cost of goods manufactured for Rocky Mountain Bikes. The schedule is divided into four parts: *direct materials, direct labor, overhead,* and *computation of cost of goods manufactured.* The schedule of cost of goods manufactured is completed in the following steps.

P2

Prepare a schedule of cost of goods manufactured and explain its purpose and links to financial statements.

① Compute direct materials used. Add the beginning raw materials inventory of $8,000 to the current period's purchases of $86,500. This yields $94,500 of total raw materials available for use. A physical count of inventory shows $9,000 of ending raw materials inventory. If $94,500 of materials were available for use, and $9,000 of materials remains in inventory, then $85,500 of materials were used in the period. (*Note:* All raw materials are direct materials for Rocky Mountain Bikes.)

Raw Materials Inventory			
Beg. bal.	8,000		
Purch.	86,500		
		Mtls. used	85,500
End. bal.	9,000		

② Compute direct labor costs used. Rocky Mountain Bikes had total direct labor costs of $60,000 for the period. This amount includes payroll taxes and fringe benefits.

ROCKY MOUNTAIN BIKES Schedule of Cost of Goods Manufactured For Year Ended December 31, 2015			
Direct materials			
① Raw materials inventory, Dec. 31, 2014	$ 8,000		
Raw materials purchases	86,500		
Raw materials available for use	94,500		
Less raw materials inventory, Dec. 31, 2015	9,000		
Direct materials used		$ 85,500	
② Direct labor		60,000	
Factory overhead			
Indirect labor	9,000		
Factory supervision	6,000		
Factory utilities	2,600		
Repairs—Factory equipment	2,500		
Property taxes—Factory building	1,900		
③ Factory supplies used	600		
Factory insurance expired	1,100		
Depreciation expense—Small tools	200		
Depreciation expense—Factory equipment	3,500		
Depreciation expense—Factory building	1,800		
Amortization expense—Patents (on factory equipment)	800		
Total factory overhead		30,000	
Total manufacturing costs		$175,500	
Add work in process inventory, Dec. 31, 2014		2,500	
④ Total cost of work in process		178,000	
Less work in process inventory, Dec. 31, 2015		7,500	
Cost of goods manufactured		$170,500	

EXHIBIT 1.16

Schedule of Cost of Goods Manufactured

Point: Manufacturers sometimes report variable and fixed overhead separately in the schedule of cost of goods manufactured to provide more information to managers about cost behavior.

③ Compute total factory overhead costs used. The statement lists each important factory overhead item and its cost. All of these costs are indirectly related to manufacturing activities. In addition, period expenses, such as selling expenses and other costs not related to manufacturing activities, are *not* reported on this statement. Total factory overhead cost for the period is $30,000. Some companies report only *total* factory overhead on the schedule of cost of goods manufactured and attach a separate schedule listing individual overhead costs.

④ Compute the *cost of goods manufactured.* Total manufacturing costs for the period are $175,500 ($85,500 + $60,000 + $30,000), the sum of direct materials used and direct labor and overhead costs incurred. This amount is added to beginning work in process inventory. This gives the total work in process during the period of $178,000 ($175,500 + $2,500). A physical count shows $7,500 of work in process inventory remains at the end of the period. We then compute the current period's cost of goods manufactured of $170,500 by taking the $178,000 total work in process and subtracting the $7,500 cost of ending work in process inventory. The cost of goods manufactured amount is also called *net cost of goods manufactured* or *cost of goods completed.*

Work in Process Inventory

Beg. bal. 2,500	
Mfg. costs 175,500	
	COG Mfg. 170,500
End. bal. 7,500	

Using the Schedule of Cost of Goods Manufactured   Management uses information in the schedule of cost of goods manufactured to plan and control the company's manufacturing activities. To provide timely information for decision making, the statement is often prepared monthly, weekly, or even daily. In anticipation of release of its much-hyped iPad, **Apple** grew its inventory of critical components, and its finished goods inventory. The schedule of cost of goods manufactured contains information useful to external users, but it is not a general-purpose financial statement. Companies rarely publish this schedule because managers view this information as proprietary and potentially harmful to the company if released to competitors.

Jin Lee/Bloomberg/Getty Images

Manufacturing Cost Flows across Accounting Reports   The previous section showed manufacturing activities and cost flows and their reporting in the schedule of cost of goods manufactured. This cost information is also used to complete the financial statements at the end of an accounting period. Exhibit 1.17 summarizes how product costs flow through the accounting system: Direct materials, direct labor, and overhead costs are summarized in the schedule of cost of goods manufactured; then the amount of the cost of goods manufactured from that statement is used to compute cost of goods sold on the income statement. Physical counts determine the dollar amounts of ending raw materials inventory and work in process inventory, and those amounts are included on the end-of-period balance sheet. (*Note:* This exhibit shows only partial reports.)

EXHIBIT 1.17

Manufacturing Cost Flows across Accounting Reports

ROCKY MOUNTAIN BIKES Schedule of Cost of Goods Manufactured For Year Ended December 31, 2015	
Direct materials used*	$ 85,500
Direct labor used	60,000
Factory overhead**	30,000
Total manuf. costs	175,500
Beg. work in process	2,500
Total work in process	178,000
End. work in process	(7,500)
Cost of goods manuf.	$170,500

*Direct materials used is computed in Exhibit 1.16.
** Overhead items are listed in Exhibit 1.16.

ROCKY MOUNTAIN BIKES Income Statement For Year Ended December 31, 2015	
Sales	$310,000
Cost of goods sold	
Beg. finished goods	11,200
Cost of goods manuf.	170,500
End. finished goods	(10,300)
Cost of goods sold	171,400
Gross profit	138,600
Operating expenses	59,900
Income before tax	$ 78,700

ROCKY MOUNTAIN BIKES Balance Sheet–PARTIAL December 31, 2015	
Cash	$11,000
Accounts receivable, net	30,150
Raw materials inventory	9,000
Work in process inventory	7,500
Finished goods inventory	10,300
Factory supplies	350
Prepaid insurance	300
Total current assets	$68,600

Compute the following three measures using the information below.

_____ **1.** Cost of materials used

_____ **2.** Cost of goods manufactured

_____ **3.** Cost of goods sold

NEED-TO-KNOW 1-3

Key Cost Measures

P1   P2

Beginning raw materials inventory	$15,500	Ending raw materials inventory..............	$10,600
Beginning work in process inventory	29,000	Ending work in process inventory............	44,000
Beginning finished goods inventory...........	24,000	Ending finished goods inventory	37,400
Raw materials purchased....................	66,000	Direct labor used........................	38,000
Total factory overhead used	80,000		

Do More: QS 1-8, QS 1-9, QS 1-10, E 1-8, E 1-11

Solution

QC4

1. $70,900   **2.** $173,900   **3.** $160,500

Raw Materials Inventory			Work in Process Inventory			Finished Goods Inventory		
Begin. Inv.	15,500		Begin. Inv.	29,000		Begin. Inv.	24,000	
			➤Materials	70,900				
			Labor	38,000				
			Overhead	80,000				
Purchases	66,000		Overhead	80,000		➤Cost of goods mfg	173,900	
Avail for use	81,500		Avail for mfg.	217,900		Avail for sale	197,900	
		Matls used 70,900—			Cost of goods mfg 173,900—			Cost of goods sold 160,500
End. Inv.	10,600		End. Inv.	44,000		End. Inv.	37,400	

Trends in Managerial Accounting

The analytical tools and techniques of managerial accounting have always been useful, and their relevance and importance continue to increase. This is so because of changes in the business environment. This section describes some of these changes and their impact on managerial accounting.

C6

Describe trends in managerial accounting.

Customer Orientation   There is an increased emphasis on *customers* as the most important constituent of a business. Customers expect to derive a certain value for the money they spend to buy products and services. Specifically, they expect that their suppliers will offer them the right service (or product) at the right time and the right price. This implies that companies accept the notion of **customer orientation,** which means that employees understand the changing needs and wants of their customers and align their management and operating practices accordingly.

Global Economy   Our *global economy* expands competitive boundaries and provides customers more choices. The global economy also produces changes in business activities. One notable case that reflects these changes in customer demand and global competition is auto manufacturing. The top three Japanese auto manufacturers (Honda, Nissan, and Toyota) once controlled more than 40% of the U.S. auto market. Customers perceived that Japanese auto manufacturers provided value not available from other manufacturers. Many European and North American auto manufacturers responded to this challenge and regained much of the lost market share.

E-Commerce   People have become increasingly interconnected via smartphones, text messaging, and other electronic applications. Consumers thus expect and demand to be able to buy items electronically, whenever and wherever they want. Many businesses have enhanced their websites to allow for online transactions. Online sales now make up about 6% of total retail sales.

Point: Goals of a TQM process include reduced waste, better inventory control, fewer defects, and continuous improvement. Just-in-time concepts have similar goals.

Service Economy   Businesses that provide services, such as telecommunications and health care, constitute an ever-growing part of our economy. In developed economies like the United States, service businesses typically account for over 60% to 70% of total economic activity.

Companies must be alert to these and other factors. Many companies have responded by adopting the **lean business model,** whose goal is to *eliminate waste* while "satisfying the customer" and "providing a positive return" to the company.

"My boss wants us to appeal to a younger and hipper crowd. So, I'd like to get a tattoo that says-- 'Accounting rules!'"

Copyright © Jerry King, www.artizans.com

Lean Practices   **Continuous improvement** rejects the notions of "good enough" or "acceptable" and challenges employees and managers to continuously experiment with new and improved business practices. This has led companies to adopt practices such as total quality management (TQM) and just-in-time (JIT) manufacturing. The philosophy underlying both practices is continuous improvement; the difference is in the focus.

Total quality management focuses on quality improvement and applies this standard to all aspects of business activities. In doing so, managers and employees seek to uncover waste in business activities including accounting activities such as payroll and disbursements. To encourage an emphasis on quality, the U.S. Congress established the Malcolm Baldrige National Quality Award (MBNQA). Entrants must conduct a thorough analysis and evaluation of their business using guidelines from the Baldrige committee. Ritz Carlton Hotel is a recipient of the Baldrige award in the service category. The company applies a core set of values, collectively called *The Gold Standards,* to improve customer service.

Just-in-time manufacturing is a system that acquires inventory and produces only when needed. An important aspect of JIT is that companies manufacture products only after they receive an order (a *demand-pull* system) and then deliver the customer's requirements on time. This means that processes must be aligned to eliminate any delays and inefficiencies including inferior inputs and outputs. Companies must also establish good relations and communications with their suppliers. On the downside, JIT is more susceptible to disruption than traditional systems. As one example, several General Motors plants were temporarily shut down due to a strike at an assembly division; the plants supplied components *just in time* to the assembly division.

Point: The time between buying raw materials and selling finished goods is called *throughput time.*

Value Chain   The **value chain** refers to the series of activities that add value to a company's products or services. Exhibit 1.18 illustrates a possible value chain for a retail cookie company. Companies can use lean practices across the value chain to increase efficiency and profits.

EXHIBIT 1.18

Typical Value Chain (Cookie Retailer)

Acquire raw materials   Baking   Sales   Service

Implications for Managerial Accounting   Adopting the lean business model can be challenging because to foster its implementation, all systems and procedures that a company follows must be realigned. Managerial accounting has an important role to play by providing accurate cost and performance information. Companies must understand the nature and sources of cost and must develop systems that capture costs accurately. Developing such a system is important to measuring the "value" provided to customers. The price that customers pay for acquiring goods and services is an important determinant of value. In turn, the costs a company incurs are key determinants of price. All else being equal, the better a company is at controlling its costs, the better its performance.

Corporate Social Responsibility   In addition to maximizing shareholder value, when making decisions corporations often must consider the demands of other stakeholders, including employees, suppliers, and society in general. **Corporate social responsibility (CSR)** is a concept that goes beyond just following the law. For example, to reduce its impact on the environment, **Three Twins Ice Cream** uses only cups and spoons made from organic ingredients. **United By Blue**, an apparel and jewelry company, removes one pound of trash from waterways for every product sold. Companies like **Microsoft**, **Google**, and **Walt Disney**, ranked at the top of large multinational companies in terms of CSR, report progress on their CSR goals on their company websites.

Decision Insight

Balanced Scorecard   The *balanced scorecard* aids continuous improvement by augmenting financial measures with information on the "drivers" (indicators) of future financial performance along four dimensions: (1) *financial*—profitability and risk, (2) *customer*—value creation and product and service differentiation, (3) *internal business processes*—business activities that create customer and owner satisfaction, and (4) *learning and growth*—organizational change, innovation, and growth. ■

GLOBAL VIEW

Managerial accounting is more flexible than financial accounting and does not follow a set of strict rules. However, many international businesses use the managerial accounting concepts and principles described in this chapter.

Customer Focus   **Nestlé**, one of the world's leading nutrition and wellness companies, adopts a customer focus and strives to understand its customers' tastes. For example, Nestlé employees spent three days living with people in Lima, Peru, to understand their motivations, routines, buying habits, and everyday lives. This allowed Nestlé to adjust its products to suit local tastes.

Reporting Manufacturing Activities   Nestlé must classify and report costs. In reporting inventory, Nestlé includes direct production costs, production overhead, and factory depreciation. A recent Nestlé annual report shows the following:

(in millions of Swiss francs)	Ending Inventory	Beginning Inventory
Raw materials, work in progress, and sundry supplies	3,499	3,815
Finished goods	5,138	5,302

Nestlé managers use this information, along with the more detailed information found in a schedule of cost of goods manufactured, to plan and control manufacturing activities.

Sustainability and Accounting   Nestlé's version of corporate social responsibility focuses on sustainability. The company seeks to increase shareholder value by reducing water usage, improving farmers' operations, and enhancing children's nutrition in developing countries. Eden Full, founder of this chapter's opening company **SunSaluter**, designed her company around the development of sustainable energy and water conservation.

Courtesy of SunSaluter

Raw Materials Inventory Turnover and Days' Sales in Raw Materials Inventory   □□□   **Decision Analysis**

Managerial accounting information helps business managers perform detailed analyses that are not readily available to external users of accounting information. Inventory management is one example. Using publicly available financial statements, an external user can compute the *inventory turnover* ratio. However, a managerial accountant can go much further.

A1

Assess raw materials inventory management using raw materials inventory turnover and days' sales in raw materials inventory.

Raw Materials Inventory Turnover

A business manager can assess how effectively a company manages its *raw materials* inventory by computing the **raw materials inventory turnover** ratio as shown in Exhibit 1.19.

EXHIBIT 1.19

Raw Materials Inventory Turnover

> **Raw materials inventory turnover = Raw materials used/Average raw materials inventory**

This ratio reveals how many times a company turns over (uses in production) its raw materials inventory during a period. Generally, a high ratio of raw materials inventory turnover is preferred, as long as raw materials inventory levels are adequate to meet demand. To illustrate, Rocky Mountain Bikes reports direct (raw) materials used of $85,500 for a year, with a beginning raw materials inventory of $8,000 and an ending raw materials inventory of $9,000 (see Exhibit 1.16). Raw materials inventory turnover for Rocky Mountain Bikes for that year is computed as in Exhibit 1.20.

EXHIBIT 1.20

Raw Materials Inventory Turnover Computed

Raw materials inventory turnover = $85,500/[($8,000 + $9,000)/2] = 10.06 (rounded).

Days' Sales in Raw Materials Inventory

To further assess raw materials inventory management, a manager can measure the adequacy of raw materials inventory to meet production demand. **Days' sales in raw materials inventory** reveals how much raw materials inventory is available in terms of the number of days' sales. It is a measure of how long it takes raw materials to be used in production. It is defined and computed for Rocky Mountain Bikes in Exhibit 1.21.

EXHIBIT 1.21

Days' Sales in Raw Materials Inventory Turnover

Days' sales in raw materials inventory = Ending raw materials inventory/Raw materials used × 365

$$= \$9,000/\$85,500 \times 365 = 38.4 \text{ days (rounded)}$$

This computation suggests that it will take 38 days for Rocky Mountain Bikes' raw materials inventory to be used in production. Assuming production needs can be met, companies usually prefer a *lower* number of days' sales in raw materials inventory. Just-in-time manufacturing techniques can be useful in lowering days' sales in raw materials inventory; for example, Dell keeps less than seven days of production needs in raw materials inventory for most of its computer components.

NEED-TO-KNOW

COMPREHENSIVE

The following account balances and other information are from SUNN Corporation's accounting records for year-end December 31, 2015. Use this information to prepare (1) a table listing factory overhead costs, (2) a schedule of cost of goods manufactured (show only the total factory overhead cost), and (3) an income statement.

Advertising expense	$ 85,000	Work in process inventory, Dec. 31, 2014	$ 8,000
Amortization expense—Factory patents	16,000	Work in process inventory, Dec. 31, 2015	9,000
Bad debts expense	28,000	Income taxes	53,400
Depreciation expense—Office equipment	37,000	Indirect labor	26,000
Depreciation expense—Factory building	133,000	Interest expense	25,000
Depreciation expense—Factory equipment	78,000	Miscellaneous expense	55,000
Direct labor	250,000	Property taxes on factory equipment	14,000
Factory insurance used up	62,000	Raw materials inventory, Dec. 31, 2014	60,000
Factory supervisor salary	74,000	Raw materials inventory, Dec. 31, 2015	78,000
Factory supplies used	21,000	Raw materials purchases	313,000
Factory utilities	115,000	Repairs expense—Factory equipment	31,000
Finished goods inventory, Dec. 31, 2014	15,000	Salaries expense	150,000
Finished goods inventory, Dec. 31, 2015	12,500	Sales	1,630,000

PLANNING THE SOLUTION

● Analyze the account balances and select those that are part of factory overhead costs.

● Arrange these costs in a table that lists factory overhead costs for the year.

- Analyze the remaining costs and select those related to production activity for the year; selected costs should include the materials and work in process inventories and direct labor.
- Prepare a schedule of cost of goods manufactured for the year showing the calculation of the cost of materials used in production, the cost of direct labor, and the total factory overhead cost. When presenting overhead cost on this statement, report only total overhead cost from the table of overhead costs for the year. Show the costs of beginning and ending work in process inventory to determine cost of goods manufactured.
- Organize the remaining revenue and expense items into the income statement for the year. Combine cost of goods manufactured from the schedule of cost of goods manufactured with the finished goods inventory amounts to compute cost of goods sold for the year.

SOLUTION

SUNN CORPORATION
Factory Overhead Costs
For Year Ended December 31, 2015

Amortization expense—Factory patents	$ 16,000
Depreciation expense—Factory building	133,000
Depreciation expense—Factory equipment	78,000
Factory insurance used up	62,000
Factory supervisor salary	74,000
Factory supplies used	21,000
Factory utilities	115,000
Indirect labor	26,000
Property taxes on factory equipment	14,000
Repairs expense—Factory equipment	31,000
Total factory overhead	$570,000

SUNN CORPORATION
Schedule of Cost of Goods Manufactured
For Year Ended December 31, 2015

Direct materials		
Raw materials inventory, Dec. 31, 2014	$ 60,000	
Raw materials purchase	313,000	
Raw materials available for use	373,000	
Less raw materials inventory, Dec. 31, 2015	78,000	
Direct materials used		295,000
Direct labor		250,000
Factory overhead		570,000
Total manufacturing costs		1,115,000
Add work in process inventory, Dec. 31, 2014		8,000
Total cost of work in process.................		1,123,000
Less work in process inventory, Dec. 31, 2015 ...		9,000
Cost of goods manufactured		$1,114,000

SUNN CORPORATION
Income Statement
For Year Ended December 31, 2015

Sales		$1,630,000
Cost of goods sold		
Finished goods inventory, Dec. 31, 2014	$ 15,000	
Cost of goods manufactured	1,114,000	
Goods available for sale	1,129,000	
Less finished goods inventory, Dec. 31, 2015...	12,500	
Cost of goods sold		1,116,500
Gross profit		513,500
Operating expenses		
Advertising expense	85,000	
Bad debts expense	28,000	
Depreciation expense—Office equipment.....	37,000	
Interest expense	25,000	
Miscellaneous expense	55,000	
Salaries expense	150,000	
Total operating expenses..................		380,000
Income before income taxes		133,500
Income taxes		53,400
Net income		$ 80,100

Raw Materials Inventory

12/31/2014	60,000	
Purch.	313,000	
Avail.	373,000	
		Dir. Mtls. Used 295,000
12/31/2015	78,000	

Work in Process Inventory

12/31/2014	8,000	
Dir. Mtls. Used	295,000	
Dir. Labor	250,000	
FOH	570,000	
Avail.	1,123,000	
		COGM 1,114,000
12/31/2015	9,000	

Finished Goods Inventory

12/31/2014	15,000	
COGM	1,114,000	
Avail.	1,129,000	
		COGS 1,116,500
12/31/2015	12,500	

Summary

C1   **Explain the purpose and nature of, and the role of ethics in, managerial accounting.** The purpose of managerial accounting is to provide useful information to management and other internal decision makers. It does this by collecting, managing, and reporting both monetary and nonmonetary information in a manner useful to internal users. Major characteristics of managerial accounting include (1) focus on internal decision makers, (2) emphasis on planning and control, (3) flexibility, (4) timeliness, (5) reliance on forecasts and estimates, (6) focus on segments and projects, and (7) reporting both monetary and nonmonetary information. Ethics are beliefs that distinguish right from wrong. Ethics can be important in reducing fraud in business operations.

C2   **Describe accounting concepts useful in classifying costs.** We can classify costs as (1) fixed vs. variable, (2) direct vs. indirect, and (3) product vs. period. A cost can be classified in more than one way, depending on the purpose for which the cost is being determined. These classifications help us understand cost patterns, analyze performance, and plan operations.

C3   **Define product and period costs and explain how they impact financial statements.** Costs that are capitalized because they are expected to have future value are called *product costs;* costs that are expensed are called *period costs.* This classification is important because it affects the amount of costs expensed in the income statement and the amount of costs assigned to inventory on the balance sheet. Product costs are commonly made up of direct materials, direct labor, and overhead. Period costs include selling and administrative expenses.

C4   **Explain how balance sheets and income statements for manufacturing, merchandising, and service companies differ.** The main difference is that manufacturers usually carry three inventories on their balance sheets—raw materials, work in process, and finished goods—instead of one inventory that merchandisers carry. Service company balance sheets do not include inventories of items for sale. The main difference between income statements of manufacturers and merchandisers is the items making up cost of goods sold. A merchandiser uses merchandise inventory and the cost of goods purchased to compute cost of goods sold; a manufacturer uses finished goods inventory and the cost of goods manufactured to compute cost of goods sold. A service company's income statement does not include cost of goods sold.

C5   **Explain manufacturing activities and the flow of manufacturing costs.** Manufacturing activities consist of materials, production, and sales activities. The materials activity consists of the purchase and issuance of materials to production. The production activity consists of converting materials into finished goods. At this stage in the process, the materials, labor, and overhead costs have been incurred and the schedule of cost of goods manufactured is prepared. The sales activity consists of selling some or all of finished goods available for sale. At this stage, the cost of goods sold is determined.

C6   **Describe trends in managerial accounting.** Important trends in managerial accounting include an increased focus on satisfying customers, the impact of a global economy, and the growing presence of e-commerce and service-based businesses. The lean business model, designed to eliminate waste and satisfy customers, can be useful in responding to recent trends. Concepts such as total quality management, just-in-time production, and the value chain often aid in application of the lean business model.

A1   **Assess raw materials inventory management using raw materials inventory turnover and days' sales in raw materials inventory.** A high raw materials inventory turnover suggests a business is more effective in managing its raw materials inventory. We use days' sales in raw materials inventory to assess the likelihood of production being delayed due to inadequate levels of raw materials. We prefer a high raw materials inventory turnover ratio and a small number of days' sales in raw materials inventory, provided that raw materials inventory levels are adequate to keep production steady.

P1   **Compute cost of goods sold for a manufacturer and for a merchandiser.** A manufacturer adds beginning finished goods inventory to cost of goods manufactured and then subtracts ending finished goods inventory to get cost of goods sold. A merchandiser adds beginning merchandise inventory to cost of goods purchased and then subtracts ending merchandise inventory to get cost of goods sold.

P2   **Prepare a schedule of cost of goods manufactured and explain its purpose and links to financial statements.** This schedule reports the computation of cost of goods manufactured for the period. It begins by showing the period's costs for direct materials, direct labor, and overhead and then adjusts these numbers for the beginning and ending inventories of the work in process to yield cost of goods manufactured.

Guidance Answers to Decision Maker and Decision Ethics

Production Manager   It appears that all three friends want to pay the bill with someone else's money. David is using money belonging to the tax authorities, Denise is taking money from her company, and Derek is defrauding the client. To prevent such practices, companies have internal audit mechanisms. Many companies also adopt ethical codes of conduct to help guide employees. We must recognize that some entertainment expenses are justifiable and even encouraged. For example, the tax law allows certain deductions for entertainment that have a business purpose. Corporate policies also sometimes allow and encourage reimbursable spending for social activities, and contracts can include entertainment as allowable costs. Nevertheless, without further details, payment for this bill should be made from personal accounts.

Entrepreneur   Tracing all costs directly to cost objects is always desirable, but you need to be able to do so in an economically feasible manner. In this case, you are able to trace 90% of the assembly department's direct costs. It may not be economical to spend more money on a new software to trace the final 10% of costs. You need to make a cost-benefit trade-off. If the software offers benefits beyond tracing the remaining 10% of the assembly department's costs, your decision should consider this.

Key Terms

Continuous improvement	Ethics	Lean business model
Control	Factory overhead	Managerial accounting
Conversion costs	Factory overhead costs	Period costs
Corporate social responsibility (CSR)	Finished goods inventory	Planning
Cost object	Fixed cost	Prime costs
Cost of goods manufactured	Indirect costs	Product costs
Customer orientation	Indirect labor	Raw materials inventory
Days' sales in raw materials inventory	Indirect labor costs	Raw materials inventory turnover
Direct costs	Indirect materials	Schedule of cost of goods manufactured
Direct labor	Institute of Management Accountants (IMA)	Total quality management (TQM)
Direct labor costs		Value chain
Direct materials	Internal control system	Variable cost
Direct material costs	Just-in-time (JIT) manufacturing	Work in process inventory

Multiple Choice Quiz   Answers at end of chapter

1. Continuous improvement
   a. Is used to reduce inventory levels.
   b. Is applicable only in service businesses.
   c. Rejects the notion of "good enough."
   d. Is used to reduce ordering costs.
   e. Is applicable only in manufacturing businesses.

2. A direct cost is one that is
   a. Variable with respect to the cost object.
   b. Traceable to the cost object.
   c. Fixed with respect to the cost object.
   d. Allocated to the cost object.
   e. A period cost.

3. Costs that are incurred as part of the manufacturing process, but are not clearly traceable to the specific unit of product or batches of product, are called
   a. Period costs.   d. Operating expenses.
   b. Factory overhead.   e. Fixed costs.
   c. Variable costs.

4. The three major cost components of manufacturing a product are
   a. Direct materials, direct labor, and factory overhead.
   b. Period costs, product costs, and conversion costs.
   c. Indirect labor, indirect materials, and fixed expenses.
   d. Variable costs, fixed costs, and period costs.
   e. Overhead costs, fixed costs, and direct costs.

5. A company reports the following for the current year.

Finished goods inventory, beginning year	$6,000
Finished goods inventory, ending year	3,200
Cost of goods sold	7,500

   Its cost of goods manufactured for the current year is
   a. $1,500.   d. $2,800.
   b. $1,700.   e. $4,700.
   c. $7,500.

🚪 Icon denotes assignments that involve decision making.

Discussion Questions

1. Describe the managerial accountant's role in business planning, control, and decision making.

2. Distinguish between managerial and financial accounting on
   a. Users and decision makers.   b. Purpose of information.
   c. Flexibility of practice.   d. Time dimension.
   e. Focus of information.   f. Nature of information.

3. 🚪 Identify the usual changes that a company must make when it adopts a customer orientation.

4. Distinguish between direct labor and indirect labor.

5. Distinguish between (a) factory overhead and (b) selling and administrative overhead.

6. Distinguish between direct material and indirect material.

7. What product cost is listed as both a prime cost and a conversion cost?

8. 🔹 Assume that we tour **Samsung**'s factory where it makes its products. **Samsung** List three direct costs and three indirect costs that we are likely to see.

9. 🔹 Should we evaluate a production manager's performance on the basis of operating expenses? Why?

10. 🔹 Explain why knowledge of cost behavior is useful in product performance evaluation.

11. Explain why product costs are capitalized but period costs are expensed in the current accounting period.

12. 🔹 Explain how business activities and inventories for a manufacturing company, a merchandising company, and a service company differ.

13. 🔹 Why does managerial accounting often involve working with numerous predictions and estimates?

14. How do an income statement and a balance sheet for a manufacturing company and a merchandising company differ?

15. Besides inventories, what other assets often appear on manufacturers' balance sheets but not on merchandisers' balance sheets?

16. Why does a manufacturing company require three different inventory categories?

17. Manufacturing activities of a company are described in the _____. This schedule summarizes the types and amounts of costs incurred in its manufacturing _____.

18. What are the three categories of manufacturing costs?

19. List several examples of factory overhead.

20. 🔹 List the four components of a schedule of cost of goods manufactured and provide specific examples of each for **Apple**. **APPLE**

21. 🔹 Prepare a proper title for the annual schedule of cost of goods manufactured of **Google**. Does the date match the balance sheet or income statement? Why? **GOOGLE**

22. 🔹 Describe the relations among the income statement, the schedule of cost of goods manufactured, and a detailed listing of factory overhead costs.

23. 🔹 Define and describe two measures to assess raw materials inventory management.

24. 🔹 Can management of a company such as **Apple** use cycle time and cycle efficiency as useful measures of performance? Explain. **APPLE**

25. Access **Dell**'s annual report (10-K) for the fiscal year ended February 1, 2013, at the SEC's EDGAR database (**SEC.gov**) or its website (**Dell.com**). From its financial statement notes, identify the titles and amounts of its inventory components.

---

connect

QUICK STUDY

QS 1-1

Managerial accounting versus financial accounting   C1

Identify whether each description most likely applies to managerial or financial accounting.

_____ **1.** Its primary users are company managers.

_____ **2.** Its information is often available only after an audit is complete.

_____ **3.** Its primary focus is on the organization as a whole.

_____ **4.** Its principles and practices are very flexible.

QS 1-2

Fixed and variable costs

C2

A cell phone company offers two different plans. Plan A costs $80 per month for unlimited talk and text. Plan B costs $0.20 per minute plus $0.10 per text message sent. You need to purchase a plan for your 14-year-old sister. Your sister currently uses 1,700 minutes and sends 1,600 texts each month.

1. What is your sister's total cost under each of the two plans?

2. Suppose your sister doubles her monthly usage to 3,400 minutes and sends 3,200 texts. What is your sister's total cost under each of the two plans?

QS 1-3

Direct and indirect costs

C2

Diez Company produces sporting equipment, including leather footballs. Identify each of the following costs as direct or indirect. The cost object is a football produced by Diez.

_____ **1.** Electricity used in the production plant.

_____ **2.** Labor used on the football production line.

_____ **3.** Salary of manager who supervises the entire plant.

_____ **4.** Depreciation on equipment used to produce footballs.

_____ **5.** Leather used to produce footballs.

QS1-4

Classifying product costs

C2

Identify each of the following costs as either direct materials, direct labor, or factory overhead. The company manufactures tennis balls.

_____ **1.** Rubber used to form the cores

_____ **2.** Factory maintenance

_____ **3.** Wages paid to assembly workers

_____ **4.** Glue used in binding rubber cores to felt covers

_____ **5.** Depreciation—Factory equipment

_____ **6.** Cans to package the balls

Identify each of the following costs as either a product cost or a period cost.

_____ **1.** Factory maintenance   _____ **5.** Rent on factory building

_____ **2.** Sales commissions   _____ **6.** Interest expense

_____ **3.** Depreciation—Factory equipment   _____ **7.** Office manager salary

_____ **4.** Depreciation—Office equipment   _____ **8.** Indirect materials used in making goods

QS 1-5
Product and period costs
C3

Compute ending work in process inventory for a manufacturer with the following information.

Raw materials purchased	$124,800
Raw materials used in production	74,300
Direct labor used	55,000
Total factory overhead	95,700
Work in process inventory, beginning of year	26,500
Cost of goods manufactured	221,800

QS 1-6
Inventory reporting for manufacturers
C4

Compute cost of goods sold for 2015 using the following information.

Finished goods inventory, Dec. 31, 2014	$345,000
Work in process inventory, Dec. 31, 2014	83,500
Work in process inventory, Dec. 31, 2015	72,300
Cost of goods manufactured, 2015	918,700
Finished goods inventory, Dec. 31, 2015	283,600

QS 1-7
Cost of goods sold
P1

Compute cost of goods sold using the following information:

Finished goods inventory, beginning	$ 500
Cost of goods manufactured	4,000
Finished goods inventory, ending	750

QS 1-8
Cost of goods sold
P1

Compute the total manufacturing cost for a manufacturer with the following information for the month.

Raw materials purchased	$32,400
Raw materials used in production	53,750
Direct labor used	12,000
Factory supervisor salary	8,000
Salesperson commissions	6,200
Depreciation expense—Factory building	3,500
Depreciation expense—Delivery equipment	2,200
Indirect materials	1,250

QS 1-9
Manufacturing cost flows
C5

Prepare the 2015 schedule of cost of goods manufactured for Barton Company using the following information.

Direct materials	$190,500
Direct labor	63,150
Factory overhead costs	24,000
Work in process, Dec. 31, 2014	157,600
Work in process, Dec. 31, 2015	142,750

QS 1-10
Cost of goods manufactured
P2

QS 1-11
Direct materials used
P2

Use the following information to compute the cost of direct materials used for the current year.

	January 1	December 31
Inventories		
Raw materials inventory	$ 6,000	$7,500
Work in process inventory	12,000	9,000
Finished goods inventory.	8,500	5,500
Activity during current year		
Materials purchased.		$123,500
Direct labor		94,000
Factory overhead.		39,000

QS 1-12
Trends in managerial
accounting
C6

Match each concept with its best description by entering its letter in the blank.

_____ **1.** Just-in-time manufacturing

_____ **2.** Continuous improvement

_____ **3.** Customer orientation

_____ **4.** Total quality management

A. Focuses on quality throughout the production process.

B. Flexible product designs can be modified to accommodate customer choices.

C. Every manager and employee constantly looks for ways to improve company operations.

D. Inventory is acquired or produced only as needed.

QS 1-13
Direct materials used
C5

Nestlé reports beginning raw materials inventory of 3,815 and ending raw materials inventory of 3,499 (both numbers in millions of Swiss francs). If Nestlé purchased 13,860 (in millions of Swiss francs) of raw materials during the year, what is the amount of raw materials it used during the year?

QS 1-14
Raw materials inventory
management   **A1**

Nestlé reports beginning raw materials inventory of 3,815 and ending raw materials inventory of 3,499 (both numbers in millions of Swiss francs). Assume Nestlé purchased 13,860 and used 14,176 (both amounts in millions of Swiss francs) in raw materials during the year. Compute raw materials inventory turnover and the number of days' sales in raw materials inventory.

connect

EXERCISES

Exercise 1-1
Sources of accounting
information
C1

Both managerial accounting and financial accounting provide useful information to decision makers. Indicate in the following chart the most likely source of information for each business decision.

	Primary Information Source	
Business Decision	**Managerial**	**Financial**
1. Determine whether to lend to a company	_____	_____
2. Evaluate a purchasing department's performance	_____	_____
3. Report financial performance to board of directors	_____	_____
4. Estimate product cost for a new line of shoes	_____	_____
5. Plan the budget for next quarter	_____	_____
6. Measure profitability of an individual store	_____	_____
7. Prepare financial reports according to GAAP	_____	_____
8. Determine location and size for a new plant	_____	_____

Exercise 1-2
Cost classification
C2

Listed here are product costs for the production of soccer balls. Classify each cost (a) as either variable or fixed and (b) as either direct or indirect. What patterns do you see regarding the relation between costs classified in these two ways?

Product Cost	Variable or Fixed		Direct or Indirect	
	Variable	**Fixed**	**Direct**	**Indirect**
1. Leather covers for soccer balls	___	___	___	___
2. Annual flat fee paid for office security	___	___	___	___
3. Coolants for machinery	___	___	___	___
4. Wages of assembly workers	___	___	___	___
5. Lace to hold leather together	___	___	___	___
6. Taxes on factory	___	___	___	___
7. Machinery depreciation (straight-line)	___	___	___	___

TechPro offers instructional courses in e-commerce website design. The company holds classes in a building that it owns. Classify each of TechPro's costs below as (a) variable or fixed and (b) direct or indirect. Assume the cost object is an individual class.

_____ **1.** Depreciation on classroom building

_____ **2.** Monthly Internet connection cost

_____ **3.** Instructional manuals for students

_____ **4.** Travel expenses for salesperson

_____ **5.** Depreciation on computers used for classes

_____ **6.** Instructor wage (per class)

Exercise 1-3
Cost classifications for a service provider
C2

Listed below are costs of providing an airline service. Classify each cost as (a) either variable or fixed, and (b) either direct or indirect. Consider the cost object to be a flight.

Exercise 1-4
Cost classifications for a service company
C2

Cost	Variable or Fixed		Direct or Indirect	
	Variable	**Fixed**	**Direct**	**Indirect**
1. Advertising	___	___	___	___
2. Beverages and snacks.....................	___	___	___	___
3. Regional vice-president salary	___	___	___	___
4. Depreciation on ground equipment	___	___	___	___
5. Fuel and oil used in planes	___	___	___	___
6. Flight attendant salaries	___	___	___	___
7. Pilot salaries	___	___	___	___
8. Maintenance worker wages..................	___	___	___	___
9. Customer service salaries	___	___	___	___

Some costs related to **Apple**'s iPad are listed below. Classify each cost as either direct materials, direct labor, factory overhead, selling expenses, or general and administrative expenses.

_____ **1.** Display screen

_____ **2.** Assembly-line supervisor salary

_____ **3.** Wages for assembly workers

_____ **4.** Salary of the chief executive officer

_____ **5.** Glue to hold iPad cases together

_____ **6.** Uniforms provided for each factory worker

_____ **7.** Wages for retail store worker

_____ **8.** Depreciation (straight-line) on robotic equipment used in assembly

Exercise 1-5
Classifying manufacturing costs
C3

Georgia Pacific, a manufacturer, incurs the following costs. (1) Classify each cost as either a product or a period cost. If a product cost, identify it as direct materials, direct labor, or factory overhead, and then as a prime and/or conversion cost. (2) Classify each product cost as either a direct cost or an indirect cost using the product as the cost object.

Exercise 1-6
Cost classification
C3

| | Product Cost | | | | | | |
| | Prime | | Conversion | | | | |
Cost	Direct Materials	Direct Labor	Direct Labor	Overhead	Period Cost	Direct Cost	Indirect Cost
1. Factory utilities	___	___	___	___	___	___	___
2. Advertising	___	___	___	___	___	___	___
3. Amortization of patents on factory machine...........	___	___	___	___	___	___	___
4. State and federal income taxes	___	___	___	___	___	___	___
5. Office supplies used	___	___	___	___	___	___	___
6. Insurance on factory building	___	___	___	___	___	___	___
7. Wages to assembly workers	___	___	___	___	___	___	___

Exercise 1-7
Balance sheet identification and preparation

C4

Current assets for two different companies at fiscal year-end 2015 are listed here. One is a manufacturer, Rayzer Skis Mfg., and the other, Sunrise Foods, is a grocery distribution company. (1) Identify which set of numbers relates to the manufacturer and which to the merchandiser. (2) Prepare the current asset section for each company from this information. Discuss why the current asset section for these two companies is different.

Account	Company 1	Company 2
Cash	$ 7,000	$ 5,000
Raw materials inventory	—	42,000
Merchandise inventory	45,000	—
Work in process inventory	—	30,000
Finished goods inventory	—	50,000
Accounts receivable, net	62,000	75,000
Prepaid expenses	1,500	900

Exercise 1-8
Cost of goods manufactured and cost of goods sold computation

P1   P2

Using the following data, compute (1) the cost of goods manufactured and (2) the cost of goods sold for both Garcon Company and Pepper Company for the year ended December 31, 2015.

	Garcon Company	Pepper Company
Beginning finished goods inventory...........	$12,000	$16,450
Beginning work in process inventory	14,500	19,950
Beginning raw materials inventory	7,250	9,000
Rental cost on factory equipment	27,000	22,750
Direct labor	19,000	35,000
Ending finished goods inventory	17,650	13,300
Ending work in process inventory	22,000	16,000
Ending raw materials inventory..............	5,300	7,200
Factory utilities	9,000	12,000
Factory supplies used.......................	8,200	3,200
General and administrative expenses	21,000	43,000
Indirect labor	1,250	7,660
Repairs—Factory equipment	4,780	1,500
Raw materials purchases....................	33,000	52,000
Selling expenses	50,000	46,000
Sales	195,030	290,010
Cash....................................	20,000	15,700
Factory equipment, net.....................	212,500	115,825
Accounts receivable, net...................	13,200	19,450

Check Garcon COGS, $91,030

Use the data in Exercise 1-8 to prepare an income statement and the current assets section of the balance sheet for each company. Ignore income taxes.

Exercise 1-9
Prepare financial statements for a manufacturer C4 P2

Refer to the data in Exercise 1-8. Compute the total (1) prime costs and (2) conversion costs for each company.

Exercise 1-10
Cost classification C2

Compute cost of goods sold for each of these two companies for the year ended December 31, 2015.

Exercise 1-11
Cost of goods sold computation

P1

	A	B	C
1 2		**Unimart**	**Precision Manufacturing**
3	Beginning inventory		
4	Merchandise	$275,000	
5	Finished goods		$450,000
6	Cost of purchases	500,000	
7	Cost of goods manufactured		900,000
8	Ending inventory		
9	Merchandise	115,000	
10	Finished goods		375,000
11			

Check Unimart COGS, $660,000

For each of the following accounts for a manufacturing company, place a ✓ in the appropriate column indicating that it appears on the balance sheet, the income statement, the schedule of cost of goods manufactured, and/or a detailed listing of factory overhead costs. *Assume that the income statement shows the calculation of cost of goods sold and the schedule of cost of goods manufactured shows only the total amount of factory overhead.* (An account can appear on more than one report.)

Exercise 1-12
Components of accounting reports

P2

	A	B	C	D	E
1 2	**Account**	**Balance Sheet**	**Income Statement**	**Sched. of Cost of Goods Manuf'd.**	**Overhead Report**
3	Accounts receivable				
4	Computer supplies used (office)				
5	Beginning finished goods inventory				
6	Beginning work in process inventory				
7	Cash				
8	Depreciation expense—Factory building				
9	Depreciation expense—Office building				
10	Direct labor				
11	Ending work in process inventory				
12	Ending raw materials inventory				
13	Factory maintenance wages				
14	Income taxes				
15	Insurance on factory building				
16	Property taxes on factory building				
17	Raw materials purchases				
18	Sales				
19					

Given the following selected account balances of Delray Mfg. prepare its schedule of cost of goods manufactured for the year ended December 31, 2015. Include a listing of the individual overhead account balances in this schedule.

Exercise 1-13
Preparation of schedule of cost of goods manufactured P2

Sales	$1,250,000	Repairs—Factory equipment	$ 5,250
Raw materials inventory, Dec. 31, 2014	37,000	Rent cost of factory building	57,000
Work in process inventory, Dec. 31, 2014 ...	53,900	Advertising expense	94,000
Finished goods inventory, Dec. 31, 2014	62,750	General and administrative expenses	129,300
Raw materials purchases	175,600	Raw materials inventory, Dec. 31, 2015	42,700
Direct labor	225,000	Work in process inventory, Dec. 31, 2015 ...	41,500
Factory computer supplies used	17,840	Finished goods inventory, Dec. 31, 2015	67,300
Indirect labor	47,000		

Check Cost of goods manufactured, $534,390

Exercise 1-14
Income statement
preparation **P2**

Use the information in Exercise 1-13 to prepare an income statement for Delray Mfg. (a manufacturer). Assume that its cost of goods manufactured is $534,390.

Exercise 1-15
Schedule of cost of goods
manufactured and cost of
goods sold **P1   P2**

Beck Manufacturing reports the information below for 2015. Using this information:
1. Prepare the schedule of cost of goods manufactured for the year.
2. Compute cost of goods sold for the year.

Raw Materials Inventory			Work in Process Inventory			Finished Goods Inventory		
Begin. Inv.	10,000		Begin. Inv.	14,000		Begin. Inv.	16,000	
			Materials	46,500				
			Direct labor	27,500				
Purchases	45,000		Overhead	55,000		Cost of goods mfg	131,000	
Avail for Use	55,000		Avail for mfg.	143,000		Avail for sale	147,000	
		Matls used 46,500			Cost of goods mfg 131,000			Cost of goods sold 129,000
End. Inv.	8,500		End. Inv.	12,000		End. Inv.	18,000	

Exercise 1-16
Cost flows in
manufacturing
C5

The following chart shows how costs flow through a business as a product is manufactured. Some boxes in the flowchart show cost amounts. Compute the cost amounts for the boxes that contain question marks.

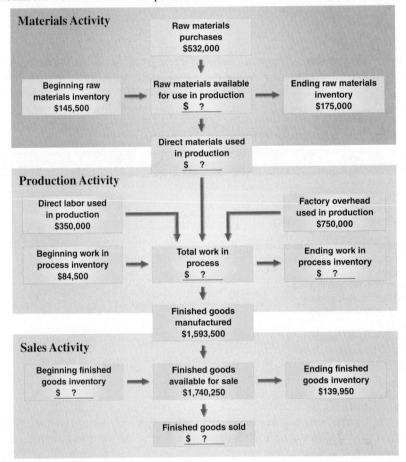

Exercise 1-17
Lean business concepts
C6

Many fast-food restaurants compete on lean business concepts. Match each of the following activities at a fast-food restaurant with the lean business concept it strives to achieve. Some activities might relate to more than one lean business concept.

_____ **1.** Courteous employees
_____ **2.** Food produced to order
_____ **3.** Clean tables and floors
_____ **4.** Orders filled within three minutes
_____ **5.** Standardized food making processes
_____ **6.** New product development

a. Just-in-time (JIT)
b. Continuous improvement (CI)
c. Total quality management (TQM)

≡connect

Listed here are the total costs associated with the 2015 production of 1,000 drum sets manufactured by TrueBeat. The drum sets sell for $500 each.

Costs	Variable or Fixed		Product or Period	
	Variable	**Fixed**	**Product**	**Period**
1. Plastic for casing—$17,000	$17,000	———	$17,000	———
2. Wages of assembly workers—$82,000	———	———	———	———
3. Property taxes on factory—$5,000	———	———	———	———
4. Accounting staff salaries—$35,000	———	———	———	———
5. Drum stands (1,000 stands purchased)—$26,000	———	———	———	———
6. Rent cost of equipment for sales staff—$10,000	———	———	———	———
7. Upper management salaries—$125,000	———	———	———	———
8. Annual flat fee for factory maintenance service—$10,000	———	———	———	———
9. Sales commissions—$15 per unit	———	———	———	———
10. Machinery depreciation, straight-line—$40,000	———	———	———	———

Required

1. Classify each cost and its amount as (a) either variable or fixed and (b) either product or period. (The first cost is completed as an example.)

2. Compute the manufacturing cost per drum set.

Analysis Component

3. Assume that 1,200 drum sets are produced in the next year. What do you predict will be the total cost of plastic for the casings and the per unit cost of the plastic for the casings? Explain.

4. Assume that 1,200 drum sets are produced in the next year. What do you predict will be the total cost of property taxes and the per unit cost of the property taxes? Explain.

The following calendar year-end information is taken from the December 31, 2015, adjusted trial balance and other records of Leone Company.

Advertising expense	$ 28,750	Miscellaneous production costs	$ 8,425
Depreciation expense—Office equipment	7,250	Office salaries expense	63,000
Depreciation expense—Selling equipment	8,600	Raw materials purchases	925,000
Depreciation expense—Factory equipment ...	33,550	Rent expense—Office space	22,000
Factory supervision	102,600	Rent expense—Selling space	26,100
Factory supplies used	7,350	Rent expense—Factory building	76,800
Factory utilities	33,000	Maintenance expense—Factory equipment ...	35,400
Direct labor	675,480	Sales	4,462,500
Indirect labor	56,875	Sales salaries expense	392,560

Required

1. Identify and classify each of the costs above as either a product or period cost.

2. Classify each of the product costs as either direct materials, direct labor, or factory overhead.

3. Classify each of the period costs as either selling or general and administrative expenses.

Using the data from Problem 1-2A and the inventory information for Leone Company below, complete the requirements below. Assume income tax expense is $233,725 for the year.

Inventories	
Raw materials, December 31, 2014	$166,850
Raw materials, December 31, 2015	182,000
Work in process, December 31, 2014	15,700
Work in process, December 31, 2015	19,380
Finished goods, December 31, 2014..........	167,350
Finished goods, December 31, 2015..........	136,490

PROBLEM SET A

Problem 1-1A
Cost computation, classification, and analysis

C2   C3   ♟

Check (1) Total variable production cost, $125,000

Problem 1-2A
Classifying costs

C2   C3

Problem 1-3A
Schedule of cost of goods manufactured and income statement; inventory analysis

P2   A1

Required

1. Prepare the company's 2015 schedule of cost of goods manufactured.
2. Prepare the company's 2015 income statement that reports separate categories for (*a*) selling expenses and (*b*) general and administrative expenses.

Analysis Component

3. Compute the (*a*) inventory turnover, defined as cost of goods sold divided by average inventory, and (*b*) days' sales in inventory, defined as 365 times ending inventory divided by cost of goods sold, for both its raw materials inventory and its finished goods inventory. (To compute turnover and days' sales in inventory for raw materials, use raw materials used rather than cost of goods sold.) Discuss some possible reasons for differences between these ratios for the two types of inventories. Round answers to one decimal place.

Problem 1-4A
Ending inventory
computation and
evaluation

C4

Nazaro's Boot Company makes specialty boots for the rodeo circuit. On December 31, 2014, the company had (*a*) 300 pairs of boots in finished goods inventory and (*b*) 1,200 heels at a cost of $8 each in raw materials inventory. During 2015, the company purchased 35,000 additional heels at $8 each and manufactured 16,600 pairs of boots.

Required

1. Determine the unit and dollar amounts of raw materials inventory in heels at December 31, 2015.

Analysis Component

2. Write a one-half page memorandum to the production manager explaining why a just-in-time inventory system for heels should be considered. Include the amount of working capital that can be reduced at December 31, 2015, if the ending heel raw material inventory is cut by half.

Problem 1-5A
Inventory computation
and reporting

C4   P1

Shown here are annual financial data at December 31, 2015, taken from two different companies.

	Music World Retail	Wave-Board Manufacturing
Beginning inventory		
Merchandise	$200,000	
Finished goods		$500,000
Cost of purchases	300,000	
Cost of goods manufactured		875,000
Ending inventory		
Merchandise	175,000	
Finished goods		225,000

Required

1. Compute the cost of goods sold section of the income statement at December 31, 2015, for each company. Include the proper title and format in the solution.
2. Write a half-page memorandum to your instructor (*a*) identifying the inventory accounts and (*b*) describing where each is reported on the income statement and balance sheet for both companies.

PROBLEM SET B

Listed here are the total costs associated with the 2015 production of 15,000 Blu-ray Discs (BDs) manufactured by Maxwell. The BDs sell for $18 each.

Problem 1-1B
Cost computation,
classification, and
analysis

C2   C3

Costs	Variable or Fixed		Product or Period	
	Variable	Fixed	Product	Period
1. Plastic for BDs—$1,500	$1,500		$1,500	
2. Wages of assembly workers—$30,000				
3. Cost of factory rent—$6,750				
4. Systems staff salaries—$15,000				
5. Labeling—$0.25 per BD				
6. Cost of office equipment rent—$1,050				
7. Upper management salaries—$120,000				
8. Annual fixed fee for cleaning service—$4,520				
9. Sales commissions—$0.50 per BD				
10. Machinery depreciation, straight-line—$18,000				

Required

1. Classify each cost and its amount as (*a*) either variable or fixed and (*b*) either product or period. (The first cost is completed as an example.)
2. Compute the manufacturing cost per BD.

Check   (2) Total variable production cost, $35,250

Analysis Component

3. Assume that 10,000 BDs are produced in the next year. What do you predict will be the total cost of plastic for the BDs and the per unit cost of the plastic for the BDs? Explain.
4. Assume that 10,000 BDs are produced in the next year. What do you predict will be the total cost of factory rent and the per unit cost of the factory rent? Explain.

The following calendar year-end information is taken from the December 31, 2015, adjusted trial balance and other records of Best Bikes.

Problem 1-2B
Classifying costs

C2   C3

Advertising expense	$ 20,250	Miscellaneous production costs	$ 8,440
Depreciation expense—Office equipment....	8,440	Office salaries expense	70,875
Depreciation expense—Selling equipment ...	10,125	Raw materials purchases	894,375
Depreciation expense—Factory equipment ...	35,400	Rent expense—Office space	23,625
Factory supervision	121,500	Rent expense—Selling space	27,000
Factory supplies used	6,060	Rent expense—Factory building	93,500
Factory utilities	37,500	Maintenance expense—Factory equipment ...	30,375
Direct labor	562,500	Sales	4,942,625
Indirect labor	59,000	Sales salaries expense	295,300

Required

1. Identify and classify each of the costs above as either a product or period cost.
2. Classify each of the product costs as either direct materials, direct labor, or factory overhead.
3. Classify each of the period costs as either selling or general and administrative expenses.

Using the information from Problem 1-2B and the inventory information for Best Bikes below, complete the requirements below. Assume income tax expense is $136,700 for the year.

Problem 1-3B
Schedule of cost of goods manufactured and income statement; analysis of inventories

P2   A1

Inventories	
Raw materials, December 31, 2014	$ 40,375
Raw materials, December 31, 2015	70,430
Work in process, December 31, 2014	12,500
Work in process, December 31, 2015	14,100
Finished goods, December 31, 2014	177,200
Finished goods, December 31, 2015	141,750

Required

1. Prepare the company's 2015 schedule of cost of goods manufactured.
2. Prepare the company's 2015 income statement that reports separate categories for (*a*) selling expenses and (*b*) general and administrative expenses.

Check   (1) Cost of goods manufactured, $1,816,995

Analysis Component

3. Compute the (*a*) inventory turnover, defined as cost of goods sold divided by average inventory, and (*b*) days' sales in inventory, defined as 365 times ending inventory divided by cost of goods sold, for both its raw materials inventory and its finished goods inventory. (To compute turnover and days' sales in inventory for raw materials, use raw materials used rather than cost of goods sold.) Discuss some possible reasons for differences between these ratios for the two types of inventories. Round answers to one decimal place.

Problem 1-4B
Ending inventory
computation and
evaluation   C4

Racer's Edge makes specialty skates for the ice skating circuit. On December 31, 2014, the company had (a) 1,500 skates in finished goods inventory and (b) 2,500 blades at a cost of $20 each in raw materials inventory. During 2015, Racer's Edge purchased 45,000 additional blades at $20 each and manufactured 20,750 pairs of skates.

Required

1. Determine the unit and dollar amounts of raw materials inventory in blades at December 31, 2015.

Analysis Component

2. Write a one-half page memorandum to the production manager explaining why a just-in-time inventory system for blades should be considered. Include the amount of working capital that can be reduced at December 31, 2015, if the ending blade raw materials inventory is cut in half.

Problem 1-5B
Inventory computation
and reporting

C4   P1

Shown here are annual financial data at December 31, 2015, taken from two different companies.

	TeeMart (Retail)	Aim Labs (Manufacturing)
Beginning inventory		
Merchandise	$100,000	
Finished goods		$300,000
Cost of purchases	250,000	
Cost of goods manufactured		586,000
Ending inventory		
Merchandise	150,000	
Finished goods		200,000

Required

1. Compute the cost of goods sold section of the income statement at December 31, 2015, for each company. Include the proper title and format in the solution.

2. Write a half-page memorandum to your instructor (a) identifying the inventory accounts and (b) identifying where each is reported on the income statement and balance sheet for both companies.

**SERIAL
PROBLEM**

Business Solutions

C2   C4   P2

(This serial problem begins in this chapter and continues through most of the book. It is helpful, but not necessary, to use the Working Papers that accompany the book.)

SP 1   Santana Rey, owner of Business Solutions, decides to diversify her business by also manufacturing computer workstation furniture.

Required

1. Classify the following manufacturing costs of Business Solutions as either (a) variable or fixed and (b) direct or indirect.

	Variable or Fixed		Direct or Indirect	
Product Costs	**Variable**	**Fixed**	**Direct**	**Indirect**
1. Monthly flat fee to clean workshop........................	___	___	___	___
2. Laminate coverings for desktops...........................	___	___	___	___
3. Taxes on assembly workshop	___	___	___	___
4. Glue to assemble workstation component parts..............	___	___	___	___
5. Wages of desk assembler	___	___	___	___
6. Electricity for workshop	___	___	___	___
7. Depreciation on tools	___	___	___	___

2. Prepare a schedule of cost of goods manufactured for Business Solutions for the month ended January 31, 2016. Assume the following manufacturing costs:

Direct materials: $2,200

Factory overhead: $490

Direct labor: $900

Beginning work in process: none (December 31, 2015)

Ending work in process: $540 (January 31, 2016)

Beginning finished goods inventory: none (December 31, 2015)

Ending finished goods inventory: $350 (January 31, 2016)

3. Prepare the cost of goods sold section of a partial income statement for Business Solutions for the month ended January 31, 2016.

Check   (3) COGS, $2,700

Beyond the Numbers

BTN 1-1   Managerial accounting is more than recording, maintaining, and reporting financial results. Managerial accountants must provide managers with both financial and nonfinancial information including estimates, projections, and forecasts. An important estimate for **Apple** is its reserve for warranty claims, and the company must provide shareholders information on these estimates.

REPORTING IN ACTION
C1

APPLE

Required

1. Access and read Apple's "Warranty costs" section of the "Critical Accounting Policies and Estimates" footnote to its financial statements, from Appendix A. How does management establish and adjust the warranty reserve? What are some of the effects if the company's actual results differ from its estimates?

2. What is the management accountant's role in determining those estimates?

3. What are some factors that could impact the warranty accrual in a given year?

Fast Forward

4. Access **Apple's** annual report for a fiscal year ending after September 28, 2013, from either its website [Apple.com] or the SEC's EDGAR database [SEC.gov]. Answer the questions in parts 1, 2, and 3 after reading the current "Critical Accounting Policies and Estimates." Identify any major changes.

BTN 1-2   Both **Apple** and **Google** have audit committees as part of their boards of directors. Access each company's website (investor.apple.com or investor.google.com) and read about the purpose of the audit committee.

COMPARATIVE ANALYSIS
C2

APPLE
GOOGLE

Required

1. From Apple's website, select Leadership & Governance, Committee Charters, and Audit and Finance. What is the purpose of Apple's audit committee?

2. From Google's website, select Corporate Governance, Board Committees, and Audit. What is the purpose of Google's audit committee?

3. Based on your answers to parts 1 and 2, how would management accountants be involved in assisting the audit committee in carrying out its responsibilities?

BTN 1-3   Assume that you are the managerial accountant at Infostore, a manufacturer of hard drives, CDs, and DVDs. Its reporting year-end is December 31. The chief financial officer is concerned about having enough cash to pay the expected income tax bill because of poor cash flow management. On November 15, the purchasing department purchased excess inventory of CD raw materials in anticipation of rapid growth of this product beginning in January. To decrease the company's tax liability, the chief financial officer tells you to record the purchase of this inventory as part of supplies and expense it in the current year; this would decrease the company's tax liability by increasing expenses.

ETHICS CHALLENGE
C1   C3

Required

1. In which account should the purchase of CD raw materials be recorded?

2. How should you respond to this request by the chief financial officer?

COMMUNICATING IN PRACTICE

C6

BTN 1-4   Write a one-page memorandum to a prospective college student about salary expectations fo graduates in business. Compare and contrast the expected salaries for accounting (including differen subfields such as public, corporate, tax, audit, and so forth), marketing, management, and finance majors Prepare a graph showing average starting salaries (and those for experienced professionals in those field if available). To get this information, stop by your school's career services office; libraries also have thi information. The website **JobStar.org** (click on "Salary Info") also can get you started.

TAKING IT TO THE NET

C1

BTN 1-5   Managerial accounting professionals follow a code of ethics. As a member of the Institute o Management Accountants, the managerial accountant must comply with Standards of Ethical Conduct.

Required

1. Identify, print, and read the *Statement of Ethical Professional Practice* posted at **www.IMAnet.org** (Under "Resources and Publications" select "Ethics Center," and then select "IMA Statement o Ethical Professional Practice.")
2. What four overarching ethical principles underlie the IMA's statement?
3. Describe the courses of action the IMA recommends in resolving ethical conflicts.

TEAMWORK IN ACTION

C5   P2

BTN 1-6   The following calendar-year information is taken from the December 31, 2015, adjusted tria balance and other records of Dahlia Company.

Advertising expense	$ 19,125	Direct labor	$ 650,750
Depreciation expense—Office equipment	8,750	Indirect labor	60,000
Depreciation expense—Selling equipment	10,000	Miscellaneous production costs	8,500
Depreciation expense—Factory equipment	32,500	Office salaries expense	100,875
Factory supervision	122,500	Raw materials purchases	872,500
Factory supplies used	15,750	Rent expense—Office space	21,125
Factory utilities	36,250	Rent expense—Selling space	25,750
Inventories		Rent expense—Factory building	79,750
Raw materials, December 31, 2014	177,500	Maintenance expense—Factory equipment	27,875
Raw materials, December 31, 2015	168,125	Sales	3,275,000
Work in process, December 31, 2014	15,875	Sales discounts	57,500
Work in process, December 31, 2015	14,000	Sales salaries expense	286,250
Finished goods, December 31, 2014	164,375		
Finished goods, December 31, 2015	129,000		

Required

1. *Each* team member is to be responsible for computing **one** of the following amounts. You are not t duplicate your teammates' work. Get any necessary amounts from teammates. Each member is to ex plain the computation to the team in preparation for reporting to class.

    a. Materials used.   **d.** Total cost of work in process.

    b. Factory overhead.   **e.** Cost of goods manufactured.

    c. Total manufacturing costs.

2. Check your cost of goods manufactured with the instructor. If it is correct, proceed to part 3.

3. *Each* team member is to be responsible for computing **one** of the following amounts. You are not t duplicate your teammates' work. Get any necessary amounts from teammates. Each member is to ex plain the computation to the team in preparation for reporting to class.

    a. Net sales.   **d.** Total operating expenses.

    b. Cost of goods sold.   **e.** Net income or loss before taxes.

    c. Gross profit.

Point: Provide teams with transparencies and markers for presentation purposes.

BTN 1-7   Eden Full of SunSaluter must understand manufacturing costs to effectively operate and suc-ceed as a profitable and efficient business.

Required

1. What are the three main categories of manufacturing costs Eden must monitor and control? Provide examples of each.

2. What are four goals of a total quality management process? How can SunSaluter use TQM to improve its business activities?

BTN 1-8   Visit your favorite fast-food restaurant. Observe its business operations.

Required

1. Describe all business activities from the time a customer arrives to the time that customer departs.

2. List all costs you can identify with the separate activities described in part 1.

3. Classify each cost from part 2 as fixed or variable, and explain your classification.

BTN 1-9   Access Samsung's 2013 annual report from its website (www.samsung.com). Like Apple, Samsung offers warranties on its products.

Required

1. Access and read footnote 18, "Provisions," included in Samsung's 2013 annual report. What amount of warranty expense did Samsung record during 2013? What amount of warranty claims did Samsung pay in 2013?

2. Access and read information on Apple's accrued warranty in footnote 10 of its 2013 annual report. What amount of warranty expense did Apple record during 2013? What amount of warranty claims did Apple pay in 2013?

3. Using your answer from parts 1 and 2, which company was more accurate in estimating warranty claims for 2013?

ANSWERS TO MULTIPLE CHOICE QUIZ

1. c

2. b

3. b

4. a

5. e; Beginning finished goods + Cost of goods manufactured
(COGM) − Ending finished goods = Cost of goods sold
$6,000 + COGM − $3,200 = $7,500
COGM = $4,700

chapter 2

Job Order Costing and Analysis

Chapter Preview

JOB ORDER COSTING

Cost accounting system

C1 Job order production

Comparing job order and process operations

Production activities in job order costing

Cost flows

C2 Job cost sheet

JOB ORDER COST FLOWS AND REPORTS

P1 Materials cost flows and documents

P2 Labor cost flows and documents

P3 Overhead cost flows and recording applied overhead

Recording actual overhead

Summary of cost flows

Schedule of cost of goods manufactured

ADJUSTING FACTORY OVERHEAD AND PRICING

Overhead T-account and actual vs applied overhead

P4 Underapplied or overapplied overhead

A1 Pricing services

Learning Objectives

CONCEPTUAL

C1 Describe important features of job order production.

C2 Explain job cost sheets and how they are used in job order costing.

ANALYTICAL

A1 Apply job order costing in pricing services.

PROCEDURAL

P1 Describe and record the flow of materials costs in job order costing.

P2 Describe and record the flow of labor costs in job order costing.

P3 Describe and record the flow of overhead costs in job order costing.

P4 Determine adjustments for overapplied and underapplied factory overhead.

ST. STEPHEN, SC—Growing up, Quintin Middleton was fascinated by swords. "It all started with the movies . . . *Star Wars* and *He-Man*," laughs Quintin. Working part-time at a knife shop to help pay for his study of aircraft mechanics at a local technical school, Quintin decided he wanted to make knives. But not just any knives. Quintin makes handmade culinary knives of the very highest quality. Although his business, **Middleton Made Knives (Middletonmadeknives.com)**, is young and small, Quintin has sold his knives to chefs of both local and national renown. One top chef, Craig Deihl, says buying one of Quintin's knives "is like buying a tailored suit. Everything is made to order, and Quintin gives personalized attention."

Quintin uses direct labor (his own!) in making knives. He begins with only the highest-quality raw materials, including high-carbon steel, stainless steel, and exotic woods for the handles. His production process is labor-intensive; every step, from knife design to grinding the edges, is done by hand. Quintin keeps his overhead costs low by working out of a 12-by-16-foot storage shed in his backyard. "I also keep fixed costs low by not stocking inventory," explains Quintin, who makes his knives to order. Quintin uses a job order costing system—the topic of this chapter—to track his costs and to make quick business decisions regarding costs and selling prices. In Quintin's case, he separately tracks the costs of making each special-order knife and the costs of making each group ("job lot") of standard knives. Job order costing enables entrepreneurs like Quintin to better isolate costs and avoid the runaway costs often experienced by start-ups that fail to use such costing techniques.

Like many entrepreneurs who build their own businesses, Quintin started with little more than a dream. He used his own money to buy his equipment. Although not a chef, he wanted to make knives for chefs, and after many rejections he "finally made a knife that [a top chef] liked." Quintin's dream continues to grow with his business. Someday he hopes to have a small knife "factory," with about 10 employees. Expanding his business will increase Quintin's materials, labor, and overhead costs, and he will need to rely even more on accurate cost information to succeed.

Courtesy of Quintin Middleton

Sharpest Knife in the Shed

"Passion creates quality"
—**Quintin Middleton**

Quintin notes that "to succeed in any business you need a great product." In Quintin's case that means constantly striving to make better knives. In addition to a passion for quality, persistence is critical, believes Quintin, and he encourages young entrepreneurs to believe in themselves. "Follow your great ideas, and always have a plan," says Quintin.

Sources: *Middleton Made Knives website,* January 2015; *The Local Palate,* July 8, 2013; *The Post and Courier,* September 29, 2012; *Entrepreneur.com,* September 28, 2011

JOB ORDER COSTING

This section describes a cost accounting system, job order production and costing, and contrasts job order production with process operations.

Cost Accounting System

Point: Cost accounting systems accumulate costs and then assign them to products and services.

Companies use cost accounting systems to generate timely and accurate cost information. A **cost accounting system** records manufacturing activities using a *perpetual* inventory system, which continuously updates records for costs of materials, work in process, and finished goods inventories. A cost accounting system also provides timely information about inventories and manufacturing costs per unit of product. This is especially helpful for managers' efforts to control costs and determine selling prices.

The two basic types of cost accounting systems are *job order costing* and *process costing.* In the next section we differentiate between job order operations and process operations. We then describe job order costing in this chapter and process costing in the next chapter.

C1

Describe important features of job order production.

Job Order Production

Many companies produce products individually designed to meet the needs of a specific customer. Each customized product is manufactured separately and its production is called **job order production,** or *job order manufacturing* (also called *customized production,* which is the production of products in response to special orders). Examples of such products or services include special-order machines, a factory building, custom jewelry, wedding invitations, tattoos, and audits by an accounting firm. The production activities for a customized product represent a **job.**

A key feature of job order production is the diversity, often called *heterogeneity,* of the products produced. That is, each customer order differs from another customer order in some important respect. These differences can be large or small. For example, Nike allows custom orders over the Internet, enabling customers to select materials and colors and to personalize their shoes with letters and numbers.

Maddie Meyer/Getty Images

When a job involves producing more than one unit of a custom product, it is often called a **job lot.** Products produced as job lots could include benches for a church, imprinted T-shirts for a 10K race or company picnic, or advertising signs for a chain of stores. Although these orders involve more than one unit, the volume of production is typically low, such as 50 benches, 200 T-shirts, or 100 signs.

Comparing Job Order and Process Operations

Point: Many professional examinations, including the CPA and CMA exams, require knowledge of job order and process costing.

Process operations, also called *process manufacturing* or *process production,* is the mass production of products in a continuous flow of steps. Unlike job order production, where every product differs depending on customer needs, process operations are designed to mass-produce large quantities of identical products. For example, each year Penn makes millions of tennis balls, and The Hershey Company produces over a billion pounds of chocolate.

Exhibit 2.1 lists important features of job order and process operations. Both types of operations are used by manufacturers and also by service companies. Movies made by Walt Disney and financial audits done by KPMG are examples of job order service operations. Order processing in large mail-order firms like L.L. Bean is an example of a process service operation.

EXHIBIT 2.1

Comparing Job Order and Process Operations

Job Order Operations	Process Operations
• Custom orders	• Repetitive procedures
• Heterogeneous products and services	• Homogeneous products and services
• Low production volume	• High production volume
• High product flexibility	• Low product flexibility
• Low to medium standardization	• High standardization

Production Activities in Job Order Costing

An overview of job order production activity and cost flows is shown in Exhibit 2.2. This exhibit shows the March production activity of Road Warriors, which installs entertainment systems and security devices in cars and trucks. The company customizes any vehicle by adding speakers, amplifiers, video systems, alarms, and reinforced exteriors.

EXHIBIT 2.2

Job Order Production
Activities and Cost Flows

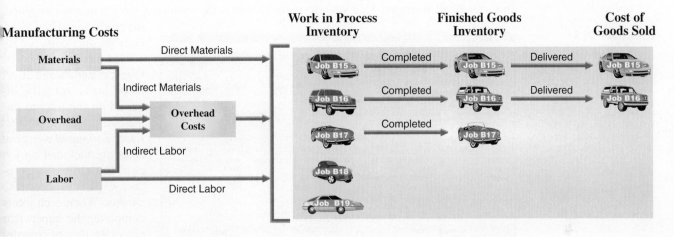

Job order production for Road Warriors requires materials, labor, and overhead costs. Recall that direct materials are used in manufacturing and can be clearly identified with a particular job. Similarly, direct labor is effort devoted to a particular job. Overhead costs support production of more than one job. Common overhead items are depreciation on factory buildings and equipment, factory supplies (indirect materials), supervision and maintenance (indirect labor), cleaning, and utilities.

Point: Factory insurance and property taxes are included in overhead.

Exhibit 2.2 shows that materials, labor, and overhead are added to Jobs B15, B16, B17, B18, and B19, which were started during the month (March). Alarm systems are added to Jobs B15 and B16; Job B17 receives a high-end audio and video entertainment system. Road Warriors completed Jobs B15, B16, and B17 in March and delivered Jobs B15 and B16 to customers. At the end of March, Jobs B18 and B19 remain in work in process inventory and Job B17 is in finished goods inventory.

Decision Insight

Target Costing   Many producers determine a target cost for their jobs. Target cost is determined as follows: Expected selling price − Desired profit = Target cost. If the projected target cost of the job as determined by job costing is too high, the producer can apply *value engineering*, which is a method of determining ways to reduce job cost until the target cost is met. ■

Cost Flows

Because they are product costs, manufacturing costs flow through inventory accounts (Raw Materials Inventory, Work in Process Inventory, and Finished Goods Inventory) until the related goods are sold. While a job is being produced, its accumulated costs are kept in **Work in Process Inventory.** When a job is finished, its accumulated costs are transferred from Work in Process Inventory to **Finished Goods Inventory.** When a finished job is delivered to a customer, its accumulated costs are transferred from Finished Goods Inventory to Cost of Goods Sold.

These general ledger inventory accounts, however, do not provide enough detail for managers of job order operations to plan and control production activities. Managers need to know the costs of each individual job (or job lot). Subsidiary records store this information about the manufacturing costs for each individual job. The next section describes the use of these subsidiary records.

Job Cost Sheet

C2
Explain job cost sheets and how they are used in job order costing.

A major aim of a **job order costing system** is to determine the cost of producing each job or job lot. In the case of a job lot, the system also aims to compute the cost per unit. The accounting system must include separate records for each job to accomplish this, and it must capture information about costs incurred and charge these costs to each job.

A **job cost sheet** is a separate record maintained for each job. Exhibit 2.3 shows a job cost sheet for Road Warriors. This job cost sheet identifies the customer, the job number assigned, the product, and key dates. Only product costs are recorded on job cost sheets. Direct materials and direct labor costs actually incurred on the job are immediately recorded on this sheet. *Estimated* overhead costs are included on job cost sheets, through a process we discuss later in the chapter. When each job is complete, the supervisor enters the date of completion, records any remarks, and signs the sheet. The balance in the Work in Process Inventory account at any point in time is the

EXHIBIT 2.3

Job Cost Sheet

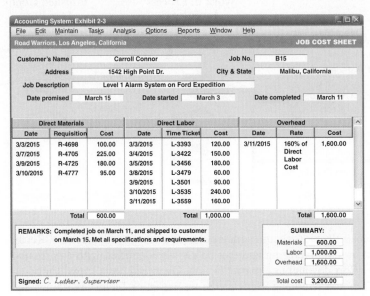

sum of the costs on job cost sheets for all jobs that are not yet complete. The balance in the Finished Goods Inventory account at any point in time is the sum of the costs on job cost sheets for all jobs that *are* complete and awaiting sale. The balance in Cost of Goods Sold is the sum of all job sheets for jobs that have been sold and delivered to the customer. Managers use job cost sheets to monitor costs incurred to date and to predict and control costs for each job. In the next section we use Road Warriors' production and sales activity for March to illustrate job order costing and the use of job cost sheets.

Point: Documents (electronic and paper) are crucial in a job order system. The job cost sheet is the cornerstone. Understanding it aids in grasping concepts of capitalizing product costs and product cost flow.

QC1

JOB ORDER COST FLOWS AND REPORTS

The previous section provided an overview of job order costing. Next we look at job order costing in more detail, including the source documents for each cost flow. In this example, Road Warriors begins the month (March) with $1,000 in Raw Materials Inventory and nothing in the Work in Process Inventory or Finished Goods Inventory accounts.

P1
Describe and record the flow of materials costs in job order costing.

Materials

Materials Cost Flows and Documents

This section focuses on the flow of materials costs and the related documents in a job order costing system. We begin analysis of the flow of materials costs by examining Exhibit 2.4. When materials are first received from suppliers, the employees count and inspect them and record the items' quantity and cost on a receiving report. The **receiving report** serves as the *source document* for recording materials received in both a materials ledger card and in the general ledger. In nearly all job order cost systems, **materials ledger cards** (or electronic files) are perpetual records that are updated each time materials are purchased and each time materials are issued for use in production.

Point: Some companies certify certain suppliers based on the quality of their materials. Goods received from these suppliers are not always inspected by the purchaser to save costs.

To illustrate the purchase of materials, Road Warriors acquired $2,750 of materials on credit on March 4, 2015. These include both direct and indirect materials. This purchase is recorded as shown below. After this entry is recorded, each individual materials ledger card is updated to

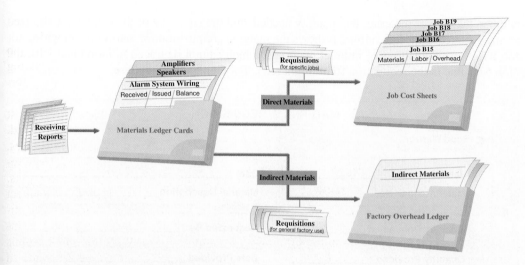

EXHIBIT 2.4

Materials Cost Flows

reflect the added materials. In addition, the entry is posted to the Raw Materials Inventory and Accounts Payable general ledger accounts.

Mar. 4	Raw Materials Inventory............................	2,750	
	Accounts Payable............................		2,750
	To record purchase of materials for production.		

Assets = Liabilities + Equity
+2,750   +2,750

Exhibit 2.4 shows that materials can be requisitioned for use either on a specific job (direct materials) or as overhead (indirect materials). Direct materials include costs, such as alarm system wiring, that are easily traced to individual jobs. Indirect materials include costs, such as those for screws, that are not easily traced to jobs. Cost of direct materials flows from the materials ledger card to the job cost sheets. The cost of indirect materials flows from the materials ledger card to the Indirect Materials account in the factory overhead ledger, which is a subsidiary ledger controlled by the Factory Overhead account in the general ledger. The factory overhead ledger includes all of the individual overhead costs.

Exhibit 2.5 shows a materials ledger card for one type of material received and issued by Road Warriors. The card identifies the item as alarm system wiring and shows the item's stock number, its location in the storeroom, information about the maximum and minimum quantities that should be available, and the reorder quantity. For example, two units of alarm system wiring were purchased on March 4, 2015, as evidenced by receiving report C-7117. After this purchase the company has three units of alarm system wiring on hand. Materials ledger cards would also be updated for each of the other materials purchased.

When materials are needed in production, a production manager prepares a **materials requisition** and sends it to the materials manager. For direct materials, the requisition shows the job

EXHIBIT 2.5

Materials Ledger Card

MATERIALS LEDGER CARD

Road Warriors
Los Angeles, California

| Item | Alarm system wiring | Stock No. | M–347 | Location in Storeroom | Bin 137 |
| Maximum quantity | 5 units | Minimum quantity | 1 unit | Quantity to reorder | 2 units |

	Received				Issued				Balance		
Date	Receiving Report Number	Units	Unit Price	Total Price	Requi- sition Number	Units	Unit Price	Total Price	Units	Unit Price	Total Price
									1	225.00	225.00
3/4/2015	C-7117	2	225.00	450.00					3	225.00	675.00
3/7/2015					R–4705	1	225.00	225.00	2	225.00	450.00

number, the type of material, the quantity needed, and the signature of the manager authorized to make the requisition. Exhibit 2.6 shows the materials requisition for alarm system wiring for Job B15. For requisitions of indirect materials, which cannot be traced to individual jobs, the "Job No." line in the requisition form might read "For General Factory Use."

EXHIBIT 2.6

Materials Requisition

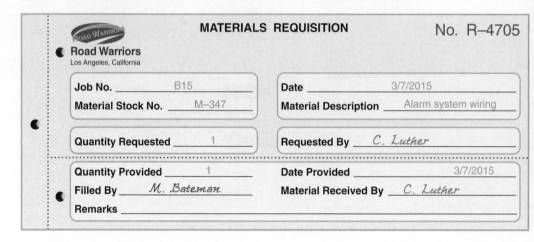

Requisitions are often accumulated and recorded in one journal entry. The frequency of entries depends on the job, the industry, and management procedures. In this example, Road Warriors records materials requisitions at the end of each week. These materials requisitions are shown below.

Direct materials—requisitioned for specific jobs	
Job B15.........................	$ 600
Job B16.........................	300
Job B17.........................	500
Job B18.........................	150
Job B19.........................	250
Total direct materials	**$1,800**
Indirect materials—requisitioned for general factory use............	550
Total...........................	$ 2,350

The use of direct materials for the week (including alarm system wiring for Job B15) yields the following entry.

Assets = Liabilities + Equity
+1,800
−1,800

Mar. 7	Work in Process Inventory	1,800	
	Raw Materials Inventory		1,800
	To record use of direct materials.		

This entry is posted both to general ledger accounts and to subsidiary records. Posting to subsidiary records includes debits to job cost sheets and credits to materials ledger cards. Exhibit 2.7 shows the postings to general ledger accounts (Work in Process Inventory and Raw Materials Inventory) and to the job cost sheets (subsidiary records). The Raw Materials Inventory account began the month with $1,000 of beginning inventory; it was increased for the March 7 purchase of $2,750. The $1,800 cost of materials used reduces Raw Materials Inventory and increases Work in Process Inventory. Note that the total amount of direct materials used so far ($1,800) is reflected in Work in Process Inventory and in the job cost sheets. Later we show the accounting for indirect materials. At this point, it is important only to know that requisitions of indirect materials do not directly impact Work in Process Inventory.

EXHIBIT 2.7

Posting Direct Materials
Used to the General
Ledger and Job Cost
Sheets

General Ledger Accounts	Raw Materials Inventory		
	Beg. bal.	1,000	
	Purch.	2,750	
			Mtls. used 1,800
	End. bal.	1,950*	

	Work in Process Inventory		
	Beg. bal.	0	
	Mtls. used	1,800	
	End. bal.	1,800	

Subsidiary Job Cost Sheets

Job B15	**Job B16**	**Job B17**	**Job B18**	**Job B19**
Dir. Mtls. $600	Dir. Mtls. $300	Dir. Mtls. $500	Dir. Mtls. $150	Dir. Mtls. $250

Total direct materials on job cost sheets = $600 + $300 + $500 + $150 + $250 = $1,800.

* Equals total amount from all materials ledger cards (not shown in this exhibit).

A manufacturing company purchased $1,200 of materials (on account) for use in production. The company used $200 of direct materials on Job 1 and $350 of direct materials on Job 2. Prepare journal entries to record these two transactions.

Solution

Raw Materials Inventory...	1,200	
Accounts Payable		1,200
To record purchase of materials on account.		
Work in Process Inventory...	550	
Raw Materials Inventory.......................................		550
To record use of direct materials in production.		

NEED-TO-KNOW 2-1

Recording Direct
Materials

P1

Do More: QS 2-4, E 2-8

Labor Cost Flows and Documents

Labor is the next manufacturing cost to account for. Exhibit 2.8 shows that factory labor costs are classified as either direct or indirect. Direct labor costs flow to individual job cost sheets. To assign direct labor costs to individual jobs, companies use **time tickets** to track how each employee's time is used. Employees fill out time tickets to record how much time they spent on each job. For many companies, this process is automated: Employees swipe electronic identification badges, and a computer system assigns employees' hours worked to individual jobs. An employee who works on several jobs during a day completes separate time tickets for each job. In all cases, supervisors check and approve the accuracy of time tickets.

Indirect labor includes factory costs like supervisor salaries and maintenance worker wages. These costs cannot be assigned directly to individual jobs. Instead, the company determines the amounts of supervisor salaries from their salary contracts and the amounts of maintenance worker wages from time tickets, and classifies those costs as overhead. These costs flow to the factory overhead ledger. Later in the chapter we show how these overhead costs are allocated to specific jobs.

Labor

P2

Describe and record the
flow of labor costs in job
order costing.

Point: Many employee
fraud schemes involve payroll,
including overstated hours on
time tickets.

EXHIBIT 2.8

Labor Cost Flows

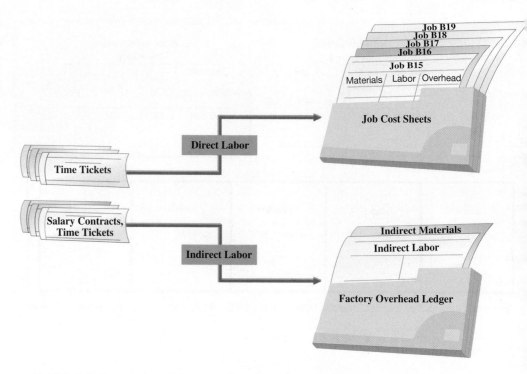

Exhibit 2.9 shows a time ticket reporting the time a Road Warrior employee spent working o▌
Job B15. The employee's supervisor signed the ticket to confirm its accuracy. The hourly rat▌
and total labor cost are computed after the time ticket is turned in.

EXHIBIT 2.9

Time Ticket

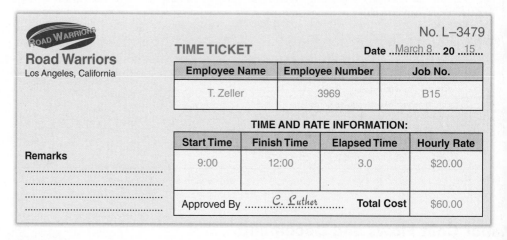

Time tickets are often accumulated and recorded in one journal entry. The frequency of thes▌
entries varies across companies. In this example, Road Warriors journalizes direct labor monthly▌
During March, Road Warriors' factory payroll costs total $5,300. Of this amount, $4,200 can b▌
traced directly to jobs, and the remaining $1,100 is classified as indirect labor, as shown below▌

Direct labor—traceable to specific jobs	
Job B15	$ 1,000
Job B16	800
Job B17	1,100
Job B18	700
Job B19	600
Total direct labor	$4,200
Indirect labor	1,100
Total	$ 5,300

The following entry records direct labor for the month, based on all the direct labor time tickets for the month.

Mar. 31	Work in Process Inventory	4,200	
	Factory Wages Payable.		4,200
	To record direct labor used for the month.		

Assets = Liabilities + Equity
+4,200   +4,200

This entry is posted to the general ledger accounts, Work in Process Inventory and Factory Wages Payable (or Cash, if paid), and to individual job cost sheets. Exhibit 2.10 shows these postings. Time tickets are used to determine how much of the monthly total direct labor cost ($4,200) to assign to specific jobs. This total matches the amount of direct labor posted to the Work in Process Inventory general ledger account. After this entry is posted, the balance in Work in Process Inventory is $6,000, consisting of $1,800 of direct materials and $4,200 of direct labor. Later we show the accounting for indirect labor. At this point it is important only to know that the use of indirect labor does not impact Work in Process Inventory.

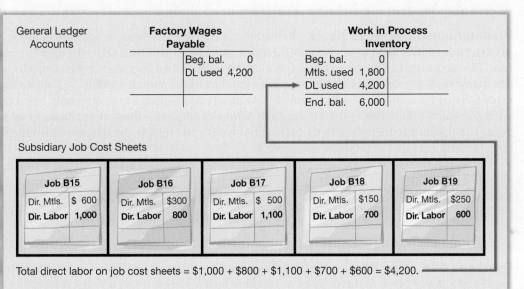

EXHIBIT 2.10

Posting Direct Labor to General Ledger and Job Cost Sheets

A manufacturing company used $5,400 of direct labor in production activities in May. Of this amount, $3,100 of direct labor was used on Job A1 and $2,300 of direct labor was used on Job A2. Prepare the journal entry to record direct labor used.

Solution

Work in Process Inventory.	5,400	
Factory Wages Payable.		5,400
To record direct labor used in production.		

NEED-TO-KNOW 2-2

Recording Direct Labor

P2

Do More: QS 2-5, E 2-9

Overhead Cost Flows and Recording Applied Overhead

We turn now to overhead costs. Unlike direct materials and direct labor, overhead costs cannot be traced directly to individual jobs. Instead, the accounting for overhead costs follows the four-step process shown in Exhibit 2.11. Overhead accounting requires managers to first estimate what total overhead costs will be for the coming period. We cannot wait until the end of a period to allocate overhead to jobs, because a job order costing system uses perpetual inventory records that require

Overhead

P3

Describe and record the flow of overhead costs in job order costing.

EXHIBIT 2.11

Four-Step Process for
Overhead

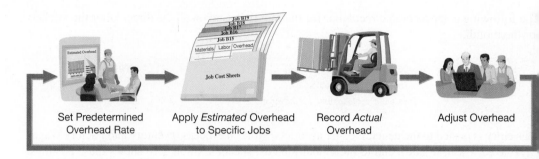

| Set Predetermined Overhead Rate | Apply *Estimated* Overhead to Specific Jobs | Record *Actual* Overhead | Adjust Overhead |

up-to-date costs. This estimated overhead cost, even if it is not exactly precise, is needed to estimate a job's total costs before its completion. Such estimated costs are useful for managers in
many decisions, including setting prices and identifying costs that are out of control. At the end
of the year, the company adjusts its estimated overhead to the actual amount of overhead incurred for that year, and then considers whether to change its predetermined overhead rate for
the next year. We discuss each of these steps below.

Predetermined Overhead Rates   Being able to estimate overhead in advance requires a
predetermined overhead rate, also called *predetermined overhead allocation* (or *application*
rate. The predetermined overhead rate requires an estimate of total overhead cost and an allocation factor such as total direct labor cost *before* the start of the period. Exhibit 2.12 shows the
usual formula for computing a predetermined overhead rate (estimates are commonly based on
annual amounts). This rate is used during the period to allocate estimated overhead to jobs.
Some companies use multiple activity (allocation) bases and multiple predetermined overhead
rates for different types of products and services.

EXHIBIT 2.12

Predetermined Overhead
Rate Formula

$$\text{Predetermined overhead rate} = \frac{\text{Estimated}}{\text{overhead costs}} \div \frac{\text{Estimated}}{\text{activity base}}$$

Overhead Allocation Bases   We generally allocate overhead by linking it to another factor
used in production, such as direct labor or machine hours. The factor to which overhead costs
are linked is known as the *activity (or allocation) base.* The allocation should reflect a "cause
and effect" relation between the base and overhead costs. A manager must think carefully about
how many and which activity bases to use. This managerial decision influences the accuracy
with which overhead costs are allocated to individual jobs. In turn, the cost of individual jobs
might impact a manager's decisions for pricing or performance evaluation.

© Royalty-Free/Corbis

Recording Applied Overhead   To illustrate, Road Warriors applies (also termed *allocates,*
assigns, or *charges*) overhead by linking it to direct labor. At the start of the current year, management estimates total direct labor costs of $125,000 and total overhead costs of $200,000.
Using these estimates, management computes its predetermined overhead rate as 160% of direct
labor cost ($200,000 ÷ $125,000). Earlier we showed that Road Warriors used $4,200 of direct
labor in March. We then use the predetermined overhead rate of 160% to allocate $6,720 (equal
to $4,200 × 1.60) of overhead. The entry to record this allocation is:

Mar. 31	Work in Process Inventory	6,720	
	Factory Overhead		6,720
	To apply overhead at 160% of direct labor.		

Then, overhead is allocated to each individual job based on the amount of the activity base
that job used (in this example, direct labor). Exhibit 2.13 shows these calculations for Road
Warriors' March production activity.

EXHIBIT 2.13

Allocating Overhead to
Specific Jobs

Job	Direct Labor Cost	Predetermined Overhead Rate*	Allocated Overhead
B15	$1,000	1.6	$1,600
B16	800	1.6	1,280
B17	1,100	1.6	1,760
B18	700	1.6	1,120
B19	600	1.6	960
Total	$4,200		$6,720

*160% of direct labor cost

After overhead is journalized in the general journal and the amounts of overhead to allocate to each job are determined (Exhibit 2.13), postings to general ledger accounts and to individual job cost sheets follow, as in Exhibit 2.14.

EXHIBIT 2.14

Posting Overhead to
General Ledger and Job
Cost Sheets

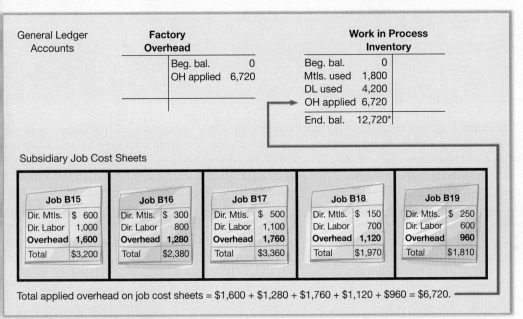

Total applied overhead on job cost sheets = $1,600 + $1,280 + $1,760 + $1,120 + $960 = $6,720.

* Total product costs assigned to jobs = $3,200 + $2,380 + $3,360 + $1,970 + $1,810 = $12,720, equal to the ending balance in Work in Process Inventory in the general ledger.

At this point, estimated (allocated) overhead has been posted to general ledger accounts and to individual job cost sheets. In addition, we verified that the balance in the Work in Process Inventory account equals the sum of the accumulated balances in the job cost sheets. In the next section we discuss how to record *actual* overhead.

A manufacturing company estimates it will incur $240,000 of overhead costs in the next year. The company allocates overhead using machine hours, and estimates it will use 1,600 machine hours in the next year. During the month of June, the company used 80 machine hours on Job 1 and 70 machine hours on Job 2.

1. Compute the predetermined overhead rate to be used to apply overhead during the year.
2. Determine how much overhead should be applied to Job 1 and to Job 2 for June.
3. Prepare the journal entry to record overhead applied for June.

Solution

1. $240,000/1,600 = $150 per machine hour.
2. 80 × $150 = $12,000 applied to Job 1; 70 × $150 = $10,500 applied to Job 2.
3.

Work in Process Inventory..	22,500	
Factory Overhead...		22,500
To record applied overhead.		

NEED-TO-KNOW 2-3

Recording Applied
Overhead

P3

QC2

Do More: QS 2-6, QS 2-8,
QS 2-11, E 2-10

Recording Actual Overhead

Point: Companies also incur *nonmanufacturing* costs, such as advertising, salesperson's salaries, and depreciation on assets not used in production. These types of costs are not considered overhead, but instead are treated as period costs and charged directly to the income statement. These period costs can be relevant to managers' pricing decisions.

Factory overhead includes all factory costs other than direct materials and direct labor. Two sources of overhead costs are *indirect* materials and *indirect* labor. These costs are recorded from materials requisition forms for indirect materials and from salary contracts or time tickets for indirect labor. Two other sources of overhead are (1) vouchers authorizing payment for factory items such as supplies or utilities and (2) adjusting journal entries for costs such as depreciation on factory assets.

Factory overhead usually contains many different costs. These costs are recorded with debits to the Factory Overhead general ledger account, and with credits to various accounts. Next we show how to record journal entries for actual overhead costs. While journal entries for different types of overhead costs might be recorded with varying frequency, in our example we assume these entries are each made at the end of the month.

Recording Indirect Materials Used   During March, Road Warriors incurred $550 of actual indirect materials costs, as supported by materials requisitions. The use of these indirect materials yields the following entry.

Mar. 31	Factory Overhead	550	
	Raw Materials Inventory		550
	To record indirect materials used during the month.		

This entry is posted to the general ledger accounts, Factory Overhead and Raw Materials Inventory, and is posted to Indirect Materials in the subsidiary factory overhead ledger. Note that unlike the recording of *direct* materials, actual *indirect* materials costs incurred are not immediately recorded in Work in Process Inventory and are not posted to job cost sheets.

Recording Indirect Labor Used   During March, Road Warriors incurred $1,100 of actual indirect labor costs. These costs might be supported by time tickets for maintenance workers or by salary contracts for production supervisors. The use of this indirect labor yields the following entry.

Mar. 31	Factory Overhead	1,100	
	Factory Wages Payable.		1,100
	To record indirect labor used during the month.		

This entry is posted to the general ledger accounts, Factory Overhead and Factory Wages Payable, and is posted to Indirect Labor in the subsidiary factory overhead ledger. Note that unlike the recording of *direct* labor, actual *indirect* labor costs incurred are not recorded immediately in Work in Process Inventory and are not posted to job cost sheets.

Recording Other Overhead Costs   During March, Road Warriors incurred $5,270 of actual other overhead costs. These costs could include items such as factory building rent, depreciation on the factory building, factory utilities, and other such costs indirectly related to production activities. These costs are recorded with debits to Factory Overhead and credits to other accounts such as Cash, Accounts Payable, Utilities Payable, and Accumulated Depreciation—Factory Equipment. The entry to record these other overhead costs for March is as follows.

Mar. 31	Factory Overhead	5,270	
	Accumulated Depreciation—Factory Equipment . . .		2,400
	Rent Payable.		1,620
	Utilities Payable		250
	Prepaid Insurance.		1,000
	To record actual overhead costs for the month.		

This entry is posted to the general ledger account, Factory Overhead, and is posted to separate accounts for each of the overhead items in the subsidiary factory overhead ledger. Note that actual overhead costs incurred are not recorded in Work in Process Inventory and are not posted to job cost sheets. Only applied overhead is recorded in Work in Process Inventory and posted to job cost sheets.

A manufacturing company used $400 of indirect materials and $2,000 of indirect labor during the month. The company also incurred $1,200 of depreciation on factory equipment, $500 of depreciation on office equipment, and $300 of factory utilities. Prepare the journal entry to record actual factory overhead costs incurred during the month.

NEED-TO-KNOW 2-4

Recording Actual
Overhead

P3

Solution

Factory Overhead...	3,900	
Raw Materials Inventory..		400
Factory Wages Payable..		2,000
Accumulated Depreciation—Factory Equipment*.................		1,200
Utilities Payable...		300
To record actual overhead costs used in production.		

QC3

Do More: QS 2-7, E 2-10

*Depreciation on office equipment is a period cost and is excluded from factory overhead.

Summary of Cost Flows

In this section we summarize the flow of costs. Exhibit 2.15 shows how costs for a manufacturing company flow to its financial statements.

EXHIBIT 2.15

Cost Flows and Reports

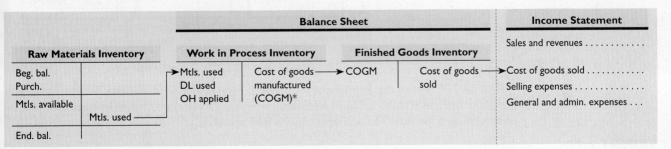

*Reported on the schedule of cost of goods manufactured.

Exhibit 2.15 shows that direct materials used, direct labor used, and factory overhead applied flow through the Work in Process Inventory and Finished Goods balance sheet accounts. The cost of goods manufactured (COGM) is computed and shown on the schedule of cost of goods manufactured. When goods are sold, their costs are transferred from Finished Goods Inventory to the income statement as cost of goods sold.

Period costs do not impact inventory accounts. As a result, they do not impact cost of goods sold, and they are not reported on the schedule of cost of goods manufactured. They are reported on the income statement as operating expenses.

We next show the flow of costs and their reporting for our Road Warriors example. The upper part of Exhibit 2.16 shows the flow of Road Warriors' product costs through general ledger accounts. Arrow lines are numbered to show the flows of costs for March. Each numbered cost flow reflects journal entries made in March. The lower part of Exhibit 2.16 shows summarized job cost sheets and their status at the end of March. The sum of costs assigned to the two jobs in process ($1,970 + $1,810) equals the $3,780 balance in Work in Process Inventory. Also, costs assigned to Job B17 equal the $3,360 balance in Finished Goods Inventory. These balances in Work in Process Inventory and Finished Goods Inventory are reported on the end-of-period balance sheet. The sum of costs assigned to Jobs B15 and B16 ($3,200 + $2,380) equals the $5,580 balance in Cost of Goods Sold. This amount is reported on the income statement for the period.

EXHIBIT 2.16

Job Order Cost Flows and Ending Job Cost Sheets

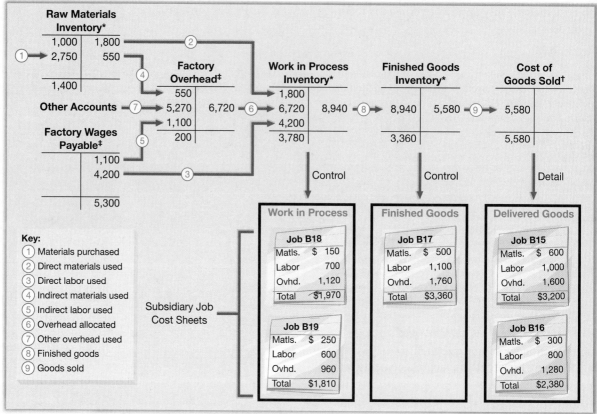

* The ending balances in the inventory accounts are carried to the balance sheet.

† The Cost of Goods Sold balance is carried to the income statement.

‡ Factory Overhead is considered a temporary account; when these costs are allocated to jobs, its balance is reduced.

Exhibit 2.17 shows the journal entries made in March. Each entry is numbered to link with the arrow lines in Exhibit 2.16. In addition, Exhibit 2.17 concludes with the summary journal entry to record the sales (on account) of Jobs B15 and B16.

EXHIBIT 2.17

Entries for Job Order Production Costs*

①	Raw Materials Inventory..................	2,750	
	Accounts Payable		2,750
	Acquired raw materials.		
②	Work in Process Inventory..............	1,800	
	Raw Materials Inventory.............		1,800
	To assign costs of direct materials used.		
③	Work in Process Inventory..............	4,200	
	Factory Wages Payable..............		4,200
	To assign costs of direct labor used.		
④	Factory Overhead......................	550	
	Raw Materials Inventory.............		550
	To record use of indirect materials.		
⑤	Factory Overhead......................	1,100	
	Factory Wages Payable..............		1,100
	To record indirect labor costs.		

⑥	Work in Process Inventory..............	6,720	
	Factory Overhead..................		6,720
	To apply overhead at 160% of direct labor.		
⑦	Factory Overhead......................	5,270	
	Cash (and other accounts)..........		5,270
	To record factory overhead costs such as insurance, utilities, rent, and depreciation.		
⑧	Finished Goods Inventory	8,940	
	Work in Process Inventory..........		8,940
	To record completion of Jobs B15, B16, and B17.		
⑨	Cost of Goods Sold	5,580	
	Finished Goods Inventory		5,580
	To record cost of goods sold for Jobs B15 and B16.		
⑩	Accounts Receivable...................	7,780	
	Sales		7,780
	To record sale of Jobs B15 and B16.		

* Exhibit 2.17 provides summary journal entries. *Actual* overhead is debited to Factory Overhead. *Applied* overhead is credited to Factory Overhead.

Schedule of Cost of Goods Manufactured

We end the Road Warriors example with the schedule of cost of goods manufactured in Exhibit 2.18. This schedule is similar to the one reported in the previous chapter, with one key difference: *Total manufacturing costs includes overhead applied rather than actual overhead costs.* In this example, actual overhead costs were $6,920, while applied overhead was $6,720. We discuss how to account for this difference in the next section.

Work in Process Inventory			
Beg. bal.	0		
Mtls. used	1,800		
DL used	4,200		
OH applied	6,720		
Ttl mfg. costs	12,720		
		COGM 8,940	
End. bal.	3,780		

ROAD WARRIORS	
Schedule of Cost of Goods Manufactured	
For the Month of March 2015	
Direct materials used	$ 1,800
Direct labor used..........................	4,200
Factory overhead applied*....................	6,720
Total manufacturing costs...................	$12,720
Add: Work in process, March 1, 2015	0
Total cost of work in process.................	12,720
Less: Work in process, March 31, 2015	3,780
Cost of goods manufactured.................	$ 8,940

* Actual overhead = $6,920. Overhead is $200 underapplied.

EXHIBIT 2.18

Schedule of Cost of Goods Manufactured

ADJUSTING FACTORY OVERHEAD

Refer to the debits in the Factory Overhead account in Exhibit 2.16 (or Exhibit 2.17). The total cost of factory overhead incurred during March is $6,920 ($550 + $5,270 + $1,100). The $6,920 of actual overhead costs does not equal the $6,720 of overhead applied to work in process inventory (see ⑥). This leaves a debit balance of $200 in the Factory Overhead account. Companies usually wait until the end of the year to adjust the Factory Overhead account for differences between actual and applied overhead. We show how this is done in the next section.

Factory Overhead T-Account

Exhibit 2.19 shows a Factory Overhead T-account. The company applies overhead (credits the Factory Overhead account) using a predetermined rate estimated at the beginning of the

Factory Overhead	
Actual amounts	Applied amounts

EXHIBIT 2.19

Factory Overhead T-account

year. During the year, the company records actual overhead costs with debits to the Factory Overhead account. Exhibit 2.20 shows what to do when, at year-end, actual overhead does not equal applied overhead. First, we determine whether the applied overhead is more or less than the actual overhead:

- When *less* overhead is applied than is actually incurred, the remaining debit balance in the Factory Overhead account is called **underapplied overhead.**
- When *more* overhead is applied than is actually incurred, the resulting credit balance in the Factory Overhead account is called **overapplied overhead.**

When overhead is underapplied, it means that individual jobs have not been charged enough overhead during the year, and cost of goods sold for the year is too low. When overhead is overapplied, it means that jobs have been charged too much overhead during the year, and cost of goods sold is too high. In either case, a journal entry is needed to adjust Factory Overhead and Cost of Goods Sold. Exhibit 2.20 summarizes this entry.

EXHIBIT 2.20

Adjusting Factory
Overhead

Overhead Costs	Factory Overhead Balance Is	Overhead Is	Journal Entry Required		
Actual > Applied	Debit	Underapplied	Cost of Goods Sold	#	
			Factory Overhead		#
Actual < Applied	Credit	Overapplied	Factory Overhead	#	
			Cost of Goods Sold		#

P4

Determine adjustments
for overapplied and
underapplied factory
overhead.

Example: If we do not adjust
for underapplied overhead,
will net income be overstated
or understated? *Answer:*
Overstated.

Underapplied or Overapplied Overhead

To illustrate, assume that Road Warriors applied $200,000 of overhead to jobs during 2015.
This equals the amount of overhead that management estimated in advance for the year. We
further assume that Road Warriors incurred a total of $200,480 of actual overhead cost
during 2015. Thus, at the end of the year, the Factory Overhead account has a debit balance
of $480.

The $480 debit balance reflects manufacturing costs not assigned to jobs. This means that
the balances in Work in Process Inventory, Finished Goods Inventory, and Cost of Goods
Sold do not include all production costs incurred. The required journal entry depends on
whether the difference (under- or overapplied) is material. When the underapplied overhead
amount is immaterial, it is closed to the Cost of Goods Sold account with the following adjusting entry.

Dec. 31	Cost of Goods Sold	480	
	Factory Overhead		480
	To adjust for underapplied overhead costs.		

The $480 debit (increase) to Cost of Goods Sold reduces income by $480. After this entry,
the Factory Overhead account has a zero balance. (When the underapplied or overapplied
overhead is material, the amount is normally allocated to the Cost of Goods Sold, Finished
Goods Inventory, and Work in Process Inventory accounts. This process is covered in advanced courses.) We treat overapplied overhead at the end of the period in the same way we
treat underapplied overhead, except that we debit Factory Overhead and credit Cost of Goods
Sold for the amount.

NEED-TO-KNOW 2-5

Adjusting Overhead
P4

A manufacturing company applied $300,000 of overhead to its jobs during the year. For the independent
scenarios below, prepare the journal entry to adjust over- or underapplied overhead. Assume the adjustment amounts are not material.
1. Actual overhead costs incurred during the year equal $305,000.
2. Actual overhead costs incurred during the year equal $298,500.

Solution

1.

Cost of Goods Sold	5,000	
Factory Overhead..		5,000
To close underapplied overhead to Cost of Goods Sold.		

2.

Factory Overhead..	1,500	
Cost of Goods Sold		1,500
To close overapplied overhead to Cost of Goods Sold.		

Do More: QS 2-9, QS 2-10,
E 2-11, E 2-12

Job Order Costing of Services

The principle of customization also applies to service companies. Most service companies meet customers' needs by performing a custom service for a specific customer. Examples of such services include an accountant auditing a client's financial statements, an interior designer remodeling an office, a wedding consultant planning and supervising a reception, and a lawyer defending a client. Whether the setting is manufacturing or services, job order operations involve meeting the needs of customers by producing or performing custom jobs. We show an example of job order costing for an advertising service in the Decision Analysis section of this chapter.

 Decision Maker

Management Consultant One of your tasks is to control and manage costs for a consulting company. At the end of a recent month, you find that three consulting jobs were completed and two are 60% complete. Each unfinished job is estimated to cost $10,000 and to earn a revenue of $12,000. You are unsure how to recognize work in process inventory and record costs and revenues. Do you recognize any inventory? If so, how much? How much revenue is recorded for unfinished jobs this month? ■ [Answers follow the chapter's Summary.]

GLOBAL VIEW

Porsche AG manufactures high-performance cars. Each car is built according to individual customer specifications. Customers can use the Internet to place orders for their dream cars. Porsche employs just-in-time inventory techniques to ensure a flexible production process that can respond rapidly to customer orders. For a recent year, Porsche reported €33,781 million in costs of materials and €9,038 million in personnel costs, which helped generate €57,081 million in revenue.

Sean Gallup/Getty Images

Sustainability and Accounting Porsche's sustainability efforts extend beyond its manufacturing operations to event management. Each year when the company sponsors a professional tennis tournament, it uses a Porsche Cayenne Hybrid to shuttle players to and from the venue. In addition, the company sells event tickets that include public transportation, thus reducing the number of distinct journeys to the venue by about 30%. In addition, **Middleton Made Knives** applies sustainablity through Quintin Middleton's choice of materials. The steel used for his knife blades can be recycled, and new trees can be planted to supply the wood for his knife blades.

Pricing for Services **Decision Analysis**

The chapter described job order costing mainly using a manufacturing setting. However, these concepts and procedures are applicable to a service setting. Consider AdWorld, an advertising agency that develops Web-based ads for small firms. Each of its customers has unique requirements, so costs for each individual job must be tracked separately.

A1

Apply job order costing in pricing services.

AdWorld uses two types of labor: Web designers ($65 per hour) and computer staff ($50 per hour). It also incurs overhead costs that it assigns using two different predetermined overhead allocation rates: $125 per designer hour and $96 per staff hour. For each job, AdWorld must estimate the number of designer and staff hours needed. Then total costs pertaining to each job are determined using the procedures in the chapter. [*Note:* Most service firms have neither the raw materials inventory nor finished goods inventory. Such firms do typically have inventories of supplies, and they can have work in process inventory (services in process inventory).]

To illustrate, a manufacturer of golf balls requested a quote from AdWorld for an advertising engagement. AdWorld estimates that the job will require 43 designer hours and 61 staff hours, with the following total estimated cost for this job.

Direct Labor

Designers (43 hours × $65)...............	$ 2,795	
Staff (61 hours × $50)	3,050	
Total direct labor........................		$ 5,845

Overhead

Designer related (43 hours × $125)	5,375	
Staff related (61 hours × $96).............	5,856	
Total overhead...........................		11,231
Total estimated job cost..................		$17,076

AdWorld can use this cost information to help determine the price quote for the job (see *Decision Maker, Sales Manager,* below).

Another source of information that AdWorld must consider is the market, that is, how much competitors will quote for this job. Competitor information is often unavailable; therefore, AdWorld's managers must use estimates based on their assessment of the competitive environment.

■ Decision Maker

Sales Manager   As AdWorld's sales manager, assume that you estimate costs pertaining to a proposed job as $17,076. Your normal pricing policy is to apply a markup of 18% from total costs. However, you learn that three other agencies are likely to bid for the same job, and that their quotes will range from $16,500 to $22,000. What price should you quote? What factors other than cost must you consider? ■   [Answers follow the chapter's Summary.]

NEED-TO-KNOW

COMPREHENSIVE

The following information reflects Walczak Company's job order production activities for May.

Raw materials purchases..........	$16,000
Factory payroll cost..............	15,400
Overhead costs incurred	
Indirect materials.............	5,000
Indirect labor................	3,500
Other factory overhead	9,500

Walczak's predetermined overhead rate is 150% of direct labor cost. Costs are allocated to the three jobs worked on during May as follows.

	Job 401	Job 402	Job 403
Work in process inventory, April 30			
Direct materials	$3,600		
Direct labor	1,700		
Applied overhead	2,550		
Costs during May			
Direct materials	3,550	$3,500	$1,400
Direct labor	5,100	6,000	800
Applied overhead	?	?	?
Status on May 31	**Finished (sold)**	**Finished (unsold)**	**In process**

Required

1. Determine the total cost of:

   a. The April 30 inventory of jobs in process.

   b. Materials (direct and indirect) used during May.

   c. Labor (direct and indirect) used during May.

   d. Factory overhead incurred and applied during May and the amount of any over- or underapplied overhead on May 31.

   e. The total cost of each job as of May 31, the May 31 inventories of both work in process and finished goods, and the cost of goods sold during May.

2. Prepare summarized journal entries for the month to record:

   a. Materials purchases (on credit), direct materials used in production, direct labor used in production, and overhead applied.

   b. Actual overhead costs, including indirect materials, indirect labor, and other overhead costs.

   c. Transfer of each completed job to the Finished Goods Inventory account.

   d. Cost of goods sold.

   e. The sale (on account) of Job 401 for $35,000.

   f. Removal of any underapplied or overapplied overhead from the Factory Overhead account. (Assume the amount is not material.)

3. Prepare a schedule of cost of goods manufactured for May.

PLANNING THE SOLUTION

- Determine the cost of the April 30 work in process inventory by totaling the materials, labor, and applied overhead costs for Job 401.
- Compute the cost of materials used and labor by totaling the amounts assigned to jobs and to overhead.
- Compute the total overhead incurred by summing the amounts for the three components. Compute the amount of applied overhead by multiplying the total direct labor cost by the predetermined overhead rate. Compute the underapplied or overapplied amount as the difference between the actual cost and the applied cost.
- Determine the total cost charged to each job by adding the costs incurred in April (if any) to the cost of materials, labor, and overhead applied during May.
- Group the costs of the jobs according to their completion status.
- Record the direct materials costs assigned to the three jobs.
- Transfer costs of Jobs 401 and 402 from Work in Process Inventory to Finished Goods.
- Record the costs of Job 401 as cost of goods sold.
- Record the sale (on account) of Job 401 for $35,000.
- On the schedule of cost of goods manufactured, remember to include the beginning and ending work in process inventories and to use applied rather than actual overhead.

SOLUTION

1. Total cost of

   a. April 30 inventory of jobs in process (Job 401).

Direct materials..........	$3,600
Direct labor.............	1,700
Applied overhead	2,550
Total cost..............	$7,850

   b. Materials used during May.

Direct materials	
Job 401.................	$ 3,550
Job 402.................	3,500
Job 403.................	1,400
Total direct materials	8,450
Indirect materials	5,000
Total materials used	$13,450

c. Labor used during May.

Direct labor

Job 401..............	$ 5,100
Job 402..............	6,000
Job 403..............	800
Total direct labor........	11,900
Indirect labor...........	3,500
Total labor used.........	$15,400

d. Factory overhead incurred in May.

Actual overhead

Indirect materials......................	$ 5,000
Indirect labor.........................	3,500
Other factory overhead	9,500
Total actual overhead	18,000
Overhead applied (150% × $11,900)........	17,850
Underapplied overhead...................	$ 150

e. Total cost of each job.

	401	402	403
Work in process, April 30			
Direct materials................	$ 3,600		
Direct labor...................	1,700		
Applied overhead*.............	2,550		
Cost incurred in May			
Direct materials (from part b)	3,550	$ 3,500	$1,400
Direct labor...................	5,100	6,000	800
Applied overhead*.............	7,650	9,000	1,200
Total costs.....................	$24,150	$18,500	$3,400

* Equals 150% of the direct labor cost.

Total cost of the May 31 inventory of work in process (Job 403) = $3,400

Total cost of the May 31 inventory of finished goods (Job 402) = $18,500

Total cost of goods sold during May (Job 401) = $24,150

2. Journal entries.

a. Record raw materials purchases, direct materials used, direct labor used, and overhead applied.

Raw Materials Inventory...........................	16,000	
Accounts Payable		16,000
To record materials purchases.		
Work in Process Inventory	8,450	
Raw Materials Inventory		8,450
To assign direct materials to jobs.		
Work in Process Inventory	11,900	
Factory Payroll Payable.......................		11,900
To assign direct labor to jobs.		
Work in Process Inventory	17,850	
Factory Overhead		17,850
To apply overhead to jobs.		

b. Record actual overhead costs.

Factory Overhead	5,000	
Raw Materials Inventory		5,000
To record indirect materials.		
Factory Overhead	3,500	
Factory Payroll Payable.......................		3,500
To record indirect labor.		
Factory Overhead	9,500	
Cash		9,500
To record other actual factory overhead.		

c. Transfer of completed jobs to Finished Goods Inventory.

Finished Goods Inventory	42,650	
Work in Process Inventory		42,650
To record completion of jobs		
($24,150 for Job 401 + $18,500 for Job 402).		

d. Record cost of job sold.

Cost of Goods Sold............................	24,150	
Finished Goods Inventory		24,150
To record costs for sale of Job 401.		

e. Record sales for job sold.

Accounts Receivable	35,000	
Sales		35,000
To record sale of Job 401.		

f. Close overhead to cost of goods sold.

Cost of Goods Sold	150	
Factory Overhead		150
To assign underapplied overhead to Cost of Goods Sold.		

3.

WALCZAK COMPANY	
Schedule of Cost of Goods Manufactured	
For Month Ended May 31	
Direct materials.........................	$ 8,450
Direct labor	11,900
Factory overhead applied*..................	17,850
Total manufacturing costs	38,200
Add: Work in process, April 30	7,850
Total cost of work in process	46,050
Less: Work in process, May 31	3,400
Cost of goods manufactured................	$42,650

* Actual overhead = $18,000. Overhead is $150 underapplied.

Summary

C1 **Describe important features of job order production.**
Certain companies called *job order manufacturers* produce custom-made products for customers. These customized products are produced in response to a customer's orders. A job order manufacturer produces products that usually are different and, typically, produced in low volumes. The production systems of job order companies are flexible and are not highly standardized.

C2 **Explain job cost sheets and how they are used in job order costing.** In a job order costing system, the costs of producing each job are accumulated on a separate job cost sheet. Costs of direct materials, direct labor, and overhead applied are accumulated separately on the job cost sheet and then added to determine the total cost of a job. Job cost sheets for jobs in process, finished jobs, and jobs sold make up subsidiary records controlled by general ledger accounts.

A1 **Apply job order costing in pricing services.** Job order costing can usefully be applied to a service setting. The resulting job cost estimate can then be used to help determine a price for services.

P1 **Describe and record the flow of materials costs in job order costing.** Costs of direct materials flow to the Work in Process Inventory account and to job cost sheets. Costs of indirect materials flow to the Factory Overhead account and to the factory overhead subsidiary ledger. Receiving reports evidence the purchase of raw materials, and requisition forms evidence the use of materials in production.

P2 **Describe and record the flow of labor costs in job order costing.** Costs of direct labor flow to the Work in Process Inventory account and to job cost sheets. Costs of

indirect labor flow to the Factory Overhead account and to the factory overhead subsidiary ledger. Time tickets document the use of labor.

P3 **Describe and record the flow of overhead costs in job order costing.** Overhead costs are charged to jobs using a predetermined overhead rate. Actual overhead costs incurred are accumulated in the Factory Overhead account that controls the subsidiary factory overhead ledger.

P4 **Determine adjustments for overapplied and underapplied factory overhead.** At the end of each year, the Factory Overhead account usually has a residual debit (underapplied overhead) or credit (overapplied overhead) balance. Assuming the balance is not material, it is transferred to Cost of Goods Sold, and the Factory Overhead account is closed.

Guidance Answers to Decision Maker

Management Consultant Service companies (such as this consulting firm) do not recognize work in process inventory or finished goods inventory—an important difference between service and manufacturing companies. For the two jobs that are 60% complete, you could recognize revenues and costs at 60% of the total expected amounts. This means you could recognize revenue of $7,200 (0.60 × $12,000) and costs of $6,000 (0.60 × $10,000), yielding net income of $1,200 from each job.

Sales Manager The price based on AdWorld's normal pricing policy is $20,150 ($17,076 × 1.18), which is within the price range offered by competitors. One option is to apply normal pricing policy and quote a price of $20,150. On the other hand, assessing the competition, particularly in terms of their service quality and other benefits they might offer, would be useful. Although price is an input customers use to select suppliers, factors such as quality and timeliness (responsiveness) of suppliers are important. Accordingly, your price can reflect such factors.

Key Terms

Cost accounting system	Job order production	Receiving report
Finished Goods Inventory	Materials ledger card	Target cost
Job	Materials requisition	Time ticket
Job cost sheet	Overapplied overhead	Underapplied overhead
Job lot	Predetermined overhead rate	Work in Process Inventory
Job order costing system	Process operations	

Multiple Choice Quiz   Answers at end of chapter

1. A company's predetermined overhead allocation rate is 150% of its direct labor costs. How much overhead is applied to a job that requires total direct labor costs of $30,000?
a. $15,000   **c.** $45,000   **e.** $75,000
b. $30,000   **d.** $60,000

2. A company's cost accounting system uses direct labor costs to apply overhead to work in process and finished goods inventories. Its production costs for the period are: direct materials, $45,000; direct labor, $35,000; and overhead applied, $38,500. What is its predetermined overhead allocation rate?
a. 10%   **c.** 86%   **e.** 117%
b. 110%   **d.** 91%

3. A company's ending inventory of finished goods has a total cost of $10,000 and consists of 500 units. If the overhead

applied to these goods is $4,000, and the predetermined overhead rate is 80% of direct labor costs, how much direct materials cost was incurred in producing these 500 units?
a. $10,000   **c.** $ 4,000   **e.** $1,000
b. $6,000   **d.** $5,000

4. A company's Work in Process Inventory T-account follows.

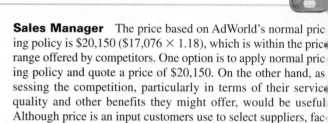

Work in Process Inventory			
Beginning balance	9,000		
Direct materials	94,200		
Direct labor	59,200	Cost of goods	?
Overhead applied	31,600	manufactured	
Ending balance	17,800		

The Cost of Goods Manufactured is
a. $193,000   **c.** $185,000   **e.** $176,200
b. $211,800   **d.** $144,600

5. At the end of its current year, a company learned that its overhead was underapplied by $1,500 and that this amount is not considered material. Based on this information, the company should
 a. Close the $1,500 to Finished Goods Inventory.
 b. Close the $1,500 to Cost of Goods Sold.
 c. Carry the $1,500 to the next period.
 d. Do nothing about the $1,500 because it is not material and it is likely that overhead will be overapplied by the same amount next year.
 e. Carry the $1,500 to the income statement as "Other Expense."

Icon denotes assignments that involve decision making.

Discussion Questions

1. Why must a company estimate the amount of factory overhead assigned to individual jobs or job lots?

2. The chapter used a percent of labor cost to assign factory overhead to jobs. Identify another factor (or base) a company might reasonably use to assign overhead costs.

3. What information is recorded on a job cost sheet? How do management and employees use job cost sheets?

4. In a job order costing system, what records serve as a subsidiary ledger for Work in Process Inventory? For Finished Goods Inventory?

5. What journal entry is recorded when a materials manager receives a materials requisition and then issues materials (both direct and indirect) for use in the factory?

6. How does the materials requisition help safeguard a company's assets?

7. **Samsung** uses a "time ticket" for some employees. How are time tickets used in job order costing? **Samsung**

8. What events cause debits to be recorded in the Factory Overhead account? What events cause credits to be recorded in the Factory Overhead account?

9. **Google** applies overhead to product costs. What account(s) is(are) used to eliminate overapplied or underapplied overhead from the Factory Overhead account, assuming the amount is not material? **GOOGLE**

10. Assume that **Apple** produces a batch of 1,000 iPhones. Does it account for this as 1,000 individual jobs or as a job lot? Explain (consider costs and benefits). **APPLE**

11. Why must a company use predetermined overhead rates when using job order costing?

12. How would a hospital apply job order costing? Explain.

13. **Harley-Davidson** manufactures 30 custom-made, luxury-model motorcycles. Does it account for these motorcycles as 30 individual jobs or as a job lot? Explain.

14. Assume **Sprint** will install and service a server to link all of a customer's employees' smartphones to a centralized company server, for an up-front flat price. How can Sprint use a job order costing system?

connect

Determine which of the following are most likely to be considered as a job and which as a job lot.

_____ 1. Hats imprinted with company logo.

_____ 2. Little League trophies.

_____ 3. A hand-crafted table.

_____ 4. A 90-foot motor yacht.

_____ 5. Wedding dresses for a chain of stores.

_____ 6. A custom-designed home.

QUICK STUDY

QS 2-1
Jobs and job lots

C1

The left column lists the titles of documents and accounts used in job order costing. The right column presents short descriptions of the purposes of the documents. Match each document in the left column to its numbered description in the right column.

A. Time ticket

B. Materials ledger card

C. Voucher

D. Factory Overhead account

E. Materials requisition

_____ 1. Shows amount of time an employee works on a job.

_____ 2. Accumulates the cost of incurred overhead and the overhead cost assigned to specific jobs.

_____ 3. Perpetual inventory record of raw materials received, used, and available for use.

_____ 4. Shows amount approved for payment of an overhead or other cost.

_____ 5. Communicates the need for materials to complete a job.

QS 2-2
Documents in job order costing

P1 P2 P3

QS 2-3
Job cost sheets **C2**

Clemens Cars' job cost sheet for Job A40 shows that the cost to add security features to a car was $10,500. The car was delivered to the customer, who paid $14,900 in cash for the added features. What journal entries should Clemens record for the completion and delivery of Job A40?

QS 2-4
Direct materials journal entries **P1**

During the current month, a company that uses job order costing purchases $50,000 in raw materials for cash. It then uses $12,000 of raw materials indirectly as factory supplies and uses $32,000 of raw materials as direct materials. Prepare journal entries to record these three transactions.

QS 2-5
Direct labor journal entries **P2**

During the current month, a company that uses job order costing incurred a monthly factory payroll of $180,000. Of this amount, $40,000 is classified as indirect labor and the remainder as direct. Prepare journal entries to record these transactions.

QS 2-6
Factory overhead rates
P3

A company incurred the following manufacturing costs this period: direct labor, $468,000; direct materials, $390,000; and factory overhead, $117,000. Compute its overhead cost as a percent of (1) direct labor and (2) direct materials. Express your answers as percents, rounded to the nearest whole number.

QS 2-7
Factory overhead journal entries **P3**

During the current month, a company that uses job order costing incurred a monthly factory payroll of $175,000. Of this amount, $44,000 is classified as indirect labor and the remainder as direct labor for the production of Job 65A. Factory overhead is applied at 90% of direct labor. Prepare the journal entry to apply factory overhead to this job.

QS 2-8
Predetermined overhead rate **P3**

At the beginning of a year, a company predicts total direct materials costs of $900,000 and total overhead costs of $1,170,000. If the company uses direct materials costs as its activity base to allocate overhead, what is the predetermined overhead rate it should use during the year?

QS 2-9
Entry for over- or underapplied overhead
P4

A company's Factory Overhead T-account shows total debits of $624,000 and total credits of $646,000 at the end of the year. Prepare the journal entry to close the balance in the Factory Overhead account to Cost of Goods Sold.

QS 2-10
Entry for over- or underapplied overhead
P4

A company allocates overhead at a rate of 150% of direct labor cost. Actual overhead cost for the current period is $950,000, and direct labor cost is $600,000. Prepare the journal entry to close over- or underapplied overhead to Cost of Goods Sold.

QS 2-11
Applied overhead
P3

On March 1 a dressmaker starts work on three custom-designed wedding dresses. The company uses job order costing and applies overhead to each job (dress) at the rate of 40% of direct materials costs. During the month, the jobs used direct materials as shown below. Compute the amount of overhead applied to each of the three jobs.

	Job 1	Job 2	Job 3
Direct materials used.........	$5,000	$7,000	$1,500

QS 2-12
Manufacturing cost flows
P1 P2 P3

Refer to the information in QS 2-11. During the month, the jobs used direct labor as shown below. Jobs 1 and 3 are not finished by the end of March, and Job 2 is finished but not sold by the end of March. (1) Determine the amounts of direct materials, direct labor, and factory overhead applied that would be reported on job cost sheets for each of the three jobs for March. (2) Determine the total dollar amount of Work in Process Inventory at the end of March. (3) Determine the total dollar amount of Finished Goods Inventory at the end of March. Assume the company has no beginning Work in Process or Finished Goods inventories.

	Job 1	Job 2	Job 3
Direct labor used...........	$9,000	$4,000	$3,000

An advertising agency is estimating costs for advertising a music festival. The job will require 200 direct labor hours at a cost of $50 per hour. Overhead costs are applied at a rate of $65 per direct labor hour. What is the total estimated cost for this job?

QS 2-13
Job order costing
of services   A1

Refer to this chapter's Global View. **Porsche AG** is the manufacturer of the Porsche automobile line. Does Porsche produce in jobs or in job lots? Explain.

QS 2-14
Job order production

C1

connect

Match each of the terms/phrases numbered *1* through *5* with the best definition on the right.

_____ **1.** Cost accounting system
_____ **2.** Target cost
_____ **3.** Job lot
_____ **4.** Job
_____ **5.** Job order production

a. Production of products in response to customer orders.
b. Production activities for a customized product.
c. A system that records manufacturing costs using a perpetual inventory system.
d. The expected selling price of a job minus its desired profit.
e. Production of more than one unit of a custom product.

EXERCISES

Exercise 2-1
Job order production

C1

The following information is from the materials requisitions and time tickets for Job 9-1005 completed by Great Bay Boats. The requisitions are identified by code numbers starting with the letter Q and the time tickets start with W. At the start of the year, management estimated that overhead cost would equal 110% of direct labor cost for each job. Determine the total cost on the job cost sheet for Job 9-1005.

Exercise 2-2
Job cost computation

C2

Date	Document	Amount
7/1/2015.................	Q-4698	$1,250
7/1/2015.................	W-3393	600
7/5/2015.................	Q-4725	1,000
7/5/2015.................	W-3479	450
7/10/2015.................	W-3559	300

As of the end of June, the job cost sheets at Racing Wheels, Inc., show the following total costs accumulated on three custom jobs.

Exercise 2-3
Analysis of cost flows

C2 P1 P2 P3

	Job 102	Job 103	Job 104
Direct materials.........	$15,000	$33,000	$27,000
Direct labor	8,000	14,200	21,000
Overhead applied........	4,000	7,100	10,500

Job 102 was started in production in May and the following costs were assigned to it in May: direct materials, $6,000; direct labor, $1,800; and overhead, $900. Jobs 103 and 104 are started in June. Overhead cost is applied with a predetermined rate based on direct labor cost. Jobs 102 and 103 are finished in June, and Job 104 is expected to be finished in July. No raw materials are used indirectly in June. Using this information, answer the following questions. (Assume this company's predetermined overhead rate did not change across these months.)

1. What is the cost of the raw materials requisitioned in June for each of the three jobs?
2. How much direct labor cost is incurred during June for each of the three jobs?
3. What predetermined overhead rate is used during June?
4. How much total cost is transferred to finished goods during June?

Check   (4) $81,300

Exercise 2-4

Overhead rate; costs assigned to jobs

P3

Check   (2) $22,710

In December 2014, Shire Computer's management establishes the 2015 predetermined overhead rate based on direct labor cost. The information used in setting this rate includes estimates that the company will incur $747,500 of overhead costs and $575,000 of direct labor cost in year 2015. During March 2015, Shire began and completed Job No. 13-56.

1. What is the predetermined overhead rate for 2015?

2. Use the information on the following job cost sheet to determine the total cost of the job.

JOB COST SHEET

| Customer's Name | Keiser Co. | | | | | Job No. | 13-56 |

Job Description   5 plasma monitors—61 inch

	Direct Materials			Direct Labor		Overhead Costs Applied	
Date	Requisition No.	Amount		Time-Ticket No.	Amount	Rate	Amount
Mar. 8	4-129	$5,000		T-306	$ 700		
Mar. 11	4-142	7,020		T-432	1,250		
Mar. 18	4-167	3,330		T-456	1,250		
Totals							

Exercise 2-5

Analysis of costs assigned to work in process

P3

Lorenzo Company uses a job order costing system that charges overhead to jobs on the basis of direct material cost. At year-end, the Work in Process Inventory account shows the following.

	A	B	C	D	E
1		Work in Process Inventory			
2		Acct. No. 121			
3	Date	Explanation	Debit	Credit	Balance
4	2015				
5	Dec. 31	Direct materials cost	1,500,000		1,500,000
6	31	Direct labor cost	300,000		1,800,000
7	31	Overhead applied	600,000		2,400,000
8	31	To finished goods		2,350,000	50,000
9					

Check   (2) Direct labor cost, $8,000

1. Determine the predetermined overhead rate used (based on direct material cost).

2. Only one job remained in work in process inventory at December 31, 2015. Its direct materials cost is $30,000. How much direct labor cost and overhead cost are assigned to this job?

Exercise 2-6

Recording product costs

P1   P2   P3

Starr Company reports the following information for August.

Raw materials purchased on account	$76,200
Direct materials used in production	$48,000
Factory wages earned (direct labor)	$15,350
Overhead rate	120% of direct labor cost

Prepare journal entries to record the following events.

1. Raw materials purchased.

2. Direct materials used in production.

3. Direct labor used in production.

4. Applied overhead.

The following information is available for Lock-Tite Company, which produces special-order security products and uses a job order costing system.

Exercise 2-7
Cost flows in a job order
costing system
P1   P2   P3   P4

	April 30	May 31
Inventories		
Raw materials	$43,000	$ 52,000
Work in process	10,200	21,300
Finished goods	63,000	35,600
Activities and information for May		
Raw materials purchases (paid with cash)		210,000
Factory payroll (paid with cash)		345,000
Factory overhead		
Indirect materials......................................		15,000
Indirect labor		80,000
Other overhead costs		120,000
Sales (received in cash)		1,400,000
Predetermined overhead rate based on direct labor cost		70%

Compute the following amounts for the month of May.
1. Cost of direct materials used.
2. Cost of direct labor used.
3. Cost of goods manufactured.
4. Cost of goods sold.*
5. Gross profit.
6. Overapplied or underapplied overhead.

*Do not consider any underapplied or overapplied overhead.

Check   (3) $625,400

Use information in Exercise 2-7 to prepare journal entries for the following events for the month of May.
1. Raw materials purchases for cash.
2. Direct materials usage.
3. Indirect materials usage.

Exercise 2-8
Journal entries for
materials   P1

Use information in Exercise 2-7 to prepare journal entries for the following events for the month of May.
1. Direct labor usage.
2. Indirect labor usage.
3. Total payroll paid in cash.

Exercise 2-9
Journal entries for labor

P2

Use information in Exercise 2-7 to prepare journal entries for the following events for the month of May.
1. Incurred other overhead costs (record credit to Other Accounts).
2. Application of overhead to work in process.

Exercise 2-10
Journal entries for
overhead   P3

Refer to information in Exercise 2-7. Prepare the journal entry to allocate (close) overapplied or underapplied overhead to Cost of Goods Sold.

Exercise 2-11
Adjusting factory
overhead   P4

Record the journal entry to close over- or underapplied factory overhead to Cost of Goods Sold for each of the two companies below.

Exercise 2-12
Adjusting factory
overhead   P4

	Storm Concert Promotions	Valle Home Builders
Actual indirect materials costs	$22,000	$ 12,500
Actual indirect labor costs	46,000	46,500
Other overhead costs	17,000	47,000
Overhead applied	88,200	105,200

Exercise 2-13
Recording events in job order costing

P1   P2   P3   P4

Using Exhibit 2.17 as a guide, prepare summary journal entries to record the following transactions and events *a* through *g* for a company in its first month of operations.

a. Raw materials purchased on account, $90,000.

b. Direct materials used in production, $36,500. Indirect materials used in production, $19,200.

c. Paid cash for factory payroll, $50,000. Of this total, $38,000 is for direct labor and $12,000 is for indirect labor.

d. Paid cash for other actual overhead costs, $11,475.

e. Applied overhead at the rate of 125% of direct labor cost.

f. Transferred cost of jobs completed to finished goods, $56,800.

g. Sold jobs on account for $82,000. The jobs had a cost of $56,800.

Exercise 2-14
Factory overhead computed, applied, and adjusted

P3   P4

In December 2014, Custom Mfg. established its predetermined overhead rate for jobs produced during 2015 by using the following cost predictions: overhead costs, $750,000, and direct labor costs, $625,000. At year-end 2015, the company's records show that actual overhead costs for the year are $830,000. Actual direct labor cost had been assigned to jobs as follows.

Jobs completed and sold	$513,750
Jobs in finished goods inventory	102,750
Jobs in work in process inventory	68,500
Total actual direct labor cost	$685,000

1. Determine the predetermined overhead rate for 2015.

2. Set up a T-account for Factory Overhead and enter the overhead costs incurred and the amounts applied to jobs during the year using the predetermined overhead rate.

Check   (3) $8,000 underapplied

3. Determine whether overhead is overapplied or underapplied (and the amount) during the year.

4. Prepare the adjusting entry to allocate any over- or underapplied overhead to Cost of Goods Sold.

Exercise 2-15
Factory overhead computed, applied, and adjusted

P3   P4

In December 2014, Infodeo established its predetermined overhead rate for movies produced during 2015 by using the following cost predictions: overhead costs, $1,680,000, and direct labor costs, $480,000. At year-end 2015, the company's records show that actual overhead costs for the year are $1,652,000. Actual direct labor cost had been assigned to jobs as follows.

Movies completed and released	$425,000
Movies still in production	50,000
Total actual direct labor cost	$475,000

1. Determine the predetermined overhead rate for 2015.

2. Set up a T-account for overhead and enter the overhead costs incurred and the amounts applied to movies during the year using the predetermined overhead rate.

Check   (3) $10,500 overapplied

3. Determine whether overhead is overapplied or underapplied (and the amount) during the year.

4. Prepare the adjusting entry to allocate any over- or underapplied overhead to Cost of Goods Sold.

Exercise 2-16
Overhead rate calculation, allocation, and analysis

P3

Moonrise Bakery applies factory overhead based on direct labor costs. The company incurred the following costs during 2015: direct materials costs, $650,000; direct labor costs, $3,000,000; and factory overhead costs applied, $1,800,000.

1. Determine the company's predetermined overhead rate for 2015.

2. Assuming that the company's $71,000 ending Work in Process Inventory account for 2015 had $20,000 of direct labor costs, determine the inventory's direct materials costs.

Check   (3) $90,000 overhead costs

3. Assuming that the company's $490,000 ending Finished Goods Inventory account for 2015 had $250,000 of direct materials costs, determine the inventory's direct labor costs and its overhead costs.

Custom Cabinetry has one job in process (Job 120) as of June 30; at that time, its job cost sheet reports direct materials of $6,000, direct labor of $2,800, and applied overhead of $2,240. Custom Cabinetry applies overhead at the rate of 80% of direct labor cost. During July, Job 120 is sold (on account) for $22,000, Job 121 is started and completed, and Job 122 is started and still in process at the end of the month. Custom Cabinetry incurs the following costs during July.

Exercise 2-17
Manufacturing cost flows
P1   P2   P3

July Product Costs	Job 120	Job 121	Job 122	Total
Direct materials...........	$1,000	$6,000	$2,500	$9,500
Direct labor	2,200	3,700	2,100	8,000
Overhead applied.........	?	?	?	?

1. Prepare journal entries for the following in July.
   a. Direct materials used in production.   **d.** The sale of Job 120.
   b. Direct labor used in production.   **e.** Cost of goods sold for Job 120.
   c. Overhead applied.
2. Compute the July 31 balances of the Work in Process Inventory and the Finished Goods Inventory general ledger accounts.

Hansel Corporation has requested bids from several architects to design its new corporate headquarters. Frey Architects is one of the firms bidding on the job. Frey estimates that the job will require the following direct labor.

Exercise 2-18
Job order costing
for services
A1

	A	B	C
1	**Labor**	**Estimated Hours**	**Hourly Rate**
2	Architects	150	$300
3	Staff	300	75
4	Clerical	500	20
5			

Frey applies overhead to jobs at 175% of direct labor cost. Frey would like to earn at least $80,000 profit on the architectural job. Based on past experience and market research, it estimates that the competition will bid between $285,000 and $350,000 for the job.

1. What is Frey's estimated cost of the architectural job?
2. What bid would you suggest that Frey submit?

Check   (1) $213,125

A recent balance sheet for Porsche AG shows beginning raw materials inventory of €83 million and ending raw materials inventory of €85 million. Assume the company purchased raw materials (on account) for €3,108 million during the year. (1) Prepare journal entries to record (a) the purchase of raw materials and (b) the use of raw materials in production. (2) What do you notice about the € amounts in your journal entries?

Exercise 2-19
Direct materials journal
entries   P1

connect

Marcelino Co.'s March 31 inventory of raw materials is $80,000. Raw materials purchases in April are $500,000, and factory payroll cost in April is $363,000. Overhead costs incurred in April are: indirect materials, $50,000; indirect labor, $23,000; factory rent, $32,000; factory utilities, $19,000; and factory equipment depreciation, $51,000. The predetermined overhead rate is 50% of direct labor cost. Job 306 is sold for $635,000 cash in April. Costs of the three jobs worked on in April follow.

PROBLEM SET A

Problem 2-1A
Production costs
computed and recorded;
reports prepared
C2   P1   P2   P3   P4

	Job 306	Job 307	Job 308
Balances on March 31			
Direct materials............	$ 29,000	$ 35,000	
Direct labor	20,000	18,000	
Applied overhead..........	10,000	9,000	
Costs during April			
Direct materials...........	135,000	220,000	$100,000
Direct labor	85,000	150,000	105,000
Applied overhead..........	?	?	?
Status on April 30	Finished (sold)	Finished (unsold)	In process

Required

1. Determine the total of each production cost incurred for April (direct labor, direct materials, and applied overhead), and the total cost assigned to each job (including the balances from March 31).
2. Prepare journal entries for the month of April to record the following.
   a. Materials purchases (on credit).
   b. Direct materials used in production.
   c. Direct labor paid and assigned to Work in Process Inventory.
   d. Indirect labor paid and assigned to Factory Overhead.
   e. Overhead costs applied to Work in Process Inventory.
   f. Actual overhead costs incurred, including indirect materials. (Factory rent and utilities are paid in cash.)
   g. Transfer of Jobs 306 and 307 to Finished Goods Inventory.
   h. Cost of goods sold for Job 306.
   i. Revenue from the sale of Job 306.
   j. Assignment of any underapplied or overapplied overhead to the Cost of Goods Sold account. (The amount is not material.)
3. Prepare a schedule of cost of goods manufactured.
4. Compute gross profit for April. Show how to present the inventories on the April 30 balance sheet.

Check   (2*j*) $5,000 underapplied

(3) Cost of goods manufactured, $828,500

Analysis Component

5. The over- or underapplied overhead is closed to Cost of Goods Sold. Discuss how this adjustment impacts business decision making regarding individual jobs or batches of jobs.

Problem 2-2A
Source documents, journal entries, overhead, and financial reports

P1   P2   P3   P4

Bergamo Bay's computer system generated the following trial balance on December 31, 2015. The company's manager knows something is wrong with the trial balance because it does not show any balance for Work in Process Inventory but does show a balance for the Factory Overhead account. In addition, the accrued factory payroll (Factory Payroll Payable) has not been recorded.

	Debit	Credit
Cash	$170,000	
Accounts receivable	75,000	
Raw materials inventory	80,000	
Work in process inventory	0	
Finished goods inventory	15,000	
Prepaid rent	3,000	
Accounts payable		$ 17,000
Notes payable		25,000
Common stock		50,000
Retained earnings		271,000
Sales		373,000
Cost of goods sold	218,000	
Factory overhead	115,000	
Operating expenses	60,000	
Totals	$736,000	$736,000

After examining various files, the manager identifies the following six source documents that need to be processed to bring the accounting records up to date.

Materials requisition 21-3010:	$10,200 direct materials to Job 402
Materials requisition 21-3011:	$18,600 direct materials to Job 404
Materials requisition 21-3012:	$5,600 indirect materials
Labor time ticket 6052:	$36,000 direct labor to Job 402
Labor time ticket 6053:	$23,800 direct labor to Job 404
Labor time ticket 6054:	$8,200 indirect labor

obs 402 and 404 are the only units in process at year-end. The predetermined overhead rate is 200% of direct labor cost.

Required

1. Use information on the six source documents to prepare journal entries to assign the following costs.
   a. Direct materials costs to Work in Process Inventory.
   b. Direct labor costs to Work in Process Inventory.
   c. Overhead costs to Work in Process Inventory.
   d. Indirect materials costs to the Factory Overhead account.
   e. Indirect labor costs to the Factory Overhead account.
2. Determine the revised balance of the Factory Overhead account after making the entries in part 1. Determine whether there is any under- or overapplied overhead for the year. Prepare the adjusting entry to allocate any over- or underapplied overhead to Cost of Goods Sold, assuming the amount is not material.
3. Prepare a revised trial balance.
4. Prepare an income statement for 2015 and a balance sheet as of December 31, 2015.

Analysis Component

5. Assume that the $5,600 on materials requisition 21-3012 should have been direct materials charged to Job 404. Without providing specific calculations, describe the impact of this error on the income statement for 2015 and the balance sheet at December 31, 2015.

Check (2) $9,200 underapplied overhead

(3) T. B. totals, $804,000

(4) Net income, $85,800

Vidmer Watercraft's predetermined overhead rate for 2015 is 200% of direct labor. Information on the company's production activities during May 2015 follows.
a. Purchased raw materials on credit, $200,000.
b. Materials requisitions record use of the following materials for the month.

Problem 2-3A
Source documents, journal entries, and accounts in job order costing

P1   P2   P3

Job 136.	$ 48,000
Job 137.	32,000
Job 138.	19,200
Job 139.	22,400
Job 140.	6,400
Total direct materials.	128,000
Indirect materials.	19,500
Total materials used.	$147,500

c. Paid $15,000 cash to a computer consultant to reprogram factory equipment.
d. Time tickets record use of the following labor for the month. These wages were paid in cash.

Job 136	$ 12,000
Job 137	10,500
Job 138	37,500
Job 139	39,000
Job 140	3,000
Total direct labor	102,000
Indirect labor	24,000
Total	$126,000

e. Applied overhead to Jobs 136, 138, and 139.
f. Transferred Jobs 136, 138, and 139 to Finished Goods.
g. Sold Jobs 136 and 138 on credit at a total price of $525,000.

h. The company incurred the following overhead costs during the month (credit Prepaid Insurance for expired factory insurance).

Depreciation of factory building	$68,000
Depreciation of factory equipment	36,500
Expired factory insurance	10,000
Accrued property taxes payable	35,000

i. Applied overhead at month-end to the Work in Process Inventory account (Jobs 137 and 140) using the predetermined overhead rate of 200% of direct labor cost.

Required

1. Prepare a job cost sheet for each job worked on during the month. Use the following simplified form.

Job No. _____	
Materials	$ _____
Labor.	_____
Overhead.	_____
Total cost	$ _____

Check   (2e) Cr. Factory
Overhead, $177,000

2. Prepare journal entries to record the events and transactions *a* through *i*.

3. Set up T-accounts for each of the following general ledger accounts, each of which started the month with a zero balance: Raw Materials Inventory; Work in Process Inventory; Finished Goods Inventory; Factory Overhead; Cost of Goods Sold. Then post the journal entries to these T-accounts and determine the balance of each account.

Check   (4) Finished Goods
Inventory, $139,400

4. Prepare a report showing the total cost of each job in process and prove that the sum of their costs equals the Work in Process Inventory account balance. Prepare similar reports for Finished Goods Inventory and Cost of Goods Sold.

Problem 2-4A
Overhead allocation and adjustment using a predetermined overhead rate

P3   P4

In December 2014, Learer Company's manager estimated next year's total direct labor cost assuming 50 persons working an average of 2,000 hours each at an average wage rate of $25 per hour. The manager also estimated the following manufacturing overhead costs for 2015.

Indirect labor	$ 319,200
Factory supervision	240,000
Rent on factory building	140,000
Factory utilities	88,000
Factory insurance expired.	68,000
Depreciation—Factory equipment	480,000
Repairs expense—Factory equipment	60,000
Factory supplies used	68,800
Miscellaneous production costs	36,000
Total estimated overhead costs	$1,500,000

At the end of 2015, records show the company incurred $1,520,000 of actual overhead costs. It completed and sold five jobs with the following direct labor costs: Job 201, $604,000; Job 202, $563,000; Job 203, $298,000; and Job 204, $716,000; and Job 205, $314,000. In addition, Job 206 is in process at the end of 2015 and had been charged $17,000 for direct labor. No jobs were in process at the end of 2014. The company's predetermined overhead rate is based on direct labor cost.

Required

1. Determine the following.

   a. Predetermined overhead rate for 2015.

   b. Total overhead cost applied to each of the six jobs during 2015.

   c. Over- or underapplied overhead at year-end 2015.

2. Assuming that any over- or underapplied overhead is not material, prepare the adjusting entry to allocate any over- or underapplied overhead to Cost of Goods Sold at the end of 2015.

Check   (1c) 12,800 underapplied

            (2) Cr. Factory Overhead $12,800

Sager Company manufactures variations of its product, a technopress, in response to custom orders from its customers. On May 1, the company had no inventories of work in process or finished goods but held the following raw materials.

Problem 2-5A
Production transactions, subsidiary records, and source documents

P1   P2   P3   P4

Material M	200 units @ $250 =	$50,000
Material R	95 units @ 180 =	17,100
Paint	55 units @ 75 =	4,125
Total cost		$71,225

On May 4, the company began working on two technopresses: Job 102 for Worldwide Company and Job 103 for Reuben Company.

Required

Using Exhibit 2.3 as a guide, prepare Job cost sheets for Jobs 102 and 103. Using Exhibit 2.5 as a guide, prepare materials ledger cards for Material M, Material R, and paint. Enter the beginning raw materials inventory dollar amounts for each of these materials on their respective ledger cards. Then, follow the instructions in this list of activities.

a. Purchased raw materials on credit and recorded the following information from receiving reports and invoices.

> Receiving Report No. 426, Material M, 250 units at $250 each.
> Receiving Report No. 427, Material R, 90 units at $180 each.

Instructions: Record these purchases with a single journal entry. Enter the receiving report information on the materials ledger cards.

b. Requisitioned the following raw materials for production.

> Requisition No. 35, for Job 102, 135 units of Material M.
> Requisition No. 36, for Job 102, 72 units of Material R.
> Requisition No. 37, for Job 103, 70 units of Material M.
> Requisition No. 38, for Job 103, 38 units of Material R.
> Requisition No. 39, for 15 units of paint.

Instructions: Enter amounts for direct materials requisitions on the materials ledger cards and the job cost sheets. Enter the indirect material amount on the materials ledger card. Do not record a journal entry at this time.

c. Received the following employee time tickets for work in May.

> Time tickets Nos. 1 to 10 for direct labor on Job 102, $90,000.
> Time tickets Nos. 11 to 30 for direct labor on Job 103, $65,000.
> Time tickets Nos. 31 to 36 for equipment repairs, $19,250.

Instructions: Record direct labor from the time tickets on the job cost sheets. Do not record a journal entry at this time.

d. Paid cash for the following items during the month: factory payroll, $174,250, and miscellaneou overhead items, $102,000. Use the time tickets to record the total direct and indirect labor costs.

Instructions: Record these payments with journal entries.

e. Finished Job 102 and transferred it to the warehouse. The company assigns overhead to each job wit a predetermined overhead rate equal to 80% of direct labor cost.

Instructions: Enter the allocated overhead on the cost sheet for Job 102, fill in the cost summary sec tion of the cost sheet, and then mark the cost sheet "Finished." Prepare a journal entry to record th job's completion and its transfer to Finished Goods.

f. Delivered Job 102 and accepted the customer's promise to pay $400,000 within 30 days.

Instructions: Prepare journal entries to record the sale of Job 102 and the cost of goods sold.

g. Applied overhead to Job 103 based on the job's direct labor to date.

Instructions: Enter overhead on the job cost sheet but do not make a journal entry at this time.

Check (*h*) Dr. Work in Process Inventory, $71,050

h. Recorded the total direct and indirect materials costs as reported on all the requisitions for the month

Instructions: Prepare a journal entry to record these costs.

Check   Balance in Factory Overhead, $1,625 Cr., overapplied

i. Recorded the total overhead costs applied to jobs.

Instructions: Prepare a journal entry to record the allocation of these overhead costs.

j. Compute the balance in the Factory Overhead account as of the end of May.

PROBLEM SET B

Problem 2-1B
Production costs computed and recorded; reports prepared

C2   P1   P2   P3   P4

Perez Mfg.'s August 31 inventory of raw materials is $150,000. Raw materials purchases in September ar $400,000, and factory payroll cost in September is $232,000. Overhead costs incurred in September are indirect materials, $30,000; indirect labor, $14,000; factory rent, $20,000; factory utilities, $12,000; an factory equipment depreciation, $30,000. The predetermined overhead rate is 50% of direct labor cos Job 114 is sold for $380,000 cash in September. Costs for the three jobs worked on in September follow

	Job 114	Job 115	Job 116
Balances on August 31			
Direct materials.	$ 14,000	$ 18,000	
Direct labor	18,000	16,000	
Applied overhead.	9,000	8,000	
Costs during September			
Direct materials	100,000	170,000	$ 80,000
Direct labor	30,000	68,000	120,000
Applied overhead.	?	?	?
Status on September 30	Finished (sold)	Finished (unsold)	In process

Required

1. Determine the total of each production cost incurred for September (direct labor, direct materials, an applied overhead), and the total cost assigned to each job (including the balances from August 31).

2. Prepare journal entries for the month of September to record the following.

    a. Materials purchases (on credit).

    b. Direct materials used in production.

    c. Direct labor paid and assigned to Work in Process Inventory.

    d. Indirect labor paid and assigned to Factory Overhead.

    e. Overhead costs applied to Work in Process Inventory.

    f. Actual overhead costs incurred, including indirect materials. (Factory rent and utilities are pai in cash.)

    g. Transfer of Jobs 114 and 115 to the Finished Goods Inventory.

    h. Cost of Job 114 in the Cost of Goods Sold account.

    i. Revenue from the sale of Job 114.

Check (*2j*) $3,000 overapplied

    j. Assignment of any underapplied or overapplied overhead to the Cost of Goods Sold account. (Th amount is not material.)

3. Prepare a schedule of cost of goods manufactured.

4. Compute gross profit for September. Show how to present the inventories on the September 30 balance sheet.

(3) Cost of goods manufactured, $500,000

Analysis Component

5. The over- or underapplied overhead adjustment is closed to Cost of Goods Sold. Discuss how this adjustment impacts business decision making regarding individual jobs or batches of jobs.

Cavallo Mfg.'s computer system generated the following trial balance on December 31, 2015. The company's manager knows that the trial balance is wrong because it does not show any balance for Work in Process Inventory but does show a balance for the Factory Overhead account. In addition, the accrued factory payroll (Factory Payroll Payable) has not been recorded.

Problem 2-2B
Source documents, journal entries, overhead, and financial reports

P1   P2   P3   P4

	Debit	Credit
Cash	$ 64,000	
Accounts receivable	42,000	
Raw materials inventory	26,000	
Work in process inventory	0	
Finished goods inventory	9,000	
Prepaid rent	3,000	
Accounts payable		$ 10,500
Notes payable		13,500
Common stock		30,000
Retained earnings		87,000
Sales		180,000
Cost of goods sold	105,000	
Factory overhead	27,000	
Operating expenses	45,000	
Totals	$321,000	$321,000

After examining various files, the manager identifies the following six source documents that need to be processed to bring the accounting records up to date.

Materials requisition 94-231:	$4,600 direct materials to Job 603
Materials requisition 94-232:	$7,600 direct materials to Job 604
Materials requisition 94-233:	$2,100 indirect materials
Labor time ticket 765:	$5,000 direct labor to Job 603
Labor time ticket 766:	$8,000 direct labor to Job 604
Labor time ticket 777:	$3,000 indirect labor

Jobs 603 and 604 are the only units in process at year-end. The predetermined overhead rate is 200% of direct labor cost.

Required

1. Use information on the six source documents to prepare journal entries to assign the following costs.

   a. Direct materials costs to Work in Process Inventory.

   b. Direct labor costs to Work in Process Inventory.

   c. Overhead costs to Work in Process Inventory.

   d. Indirect materials costs to the Factory Overhead account.

   e. Indirect labor costs to the Factory Overhead account.

2. Determine the revised balance of the Factory Overhead account after making the entries in part 1. Determine whether there is under- or overapplied overhead for the year. Prepare the adjusting entry to allocate any over- or underapplied overhead to Cost of Goods Sold, assuming the amount is not material.

3. Prepare a revised trial balance.

4. Prepare an income statement for 2015 and a balance sheet as of December 31, 2015.

Analysis Component

5. Assume that the $2,100 indirect materials on materials requisition 94-233 should have been direct materials charged to Job 604. Without providing specific calculations, describe the impact of this error on the income statement for 2015 and the balance sheet at December 31, 2015.

Problem 2-3B
Source documents,
journal entries, and
accounts in job order
costing

P1   P2   P3

Starr Mfg.'s predetermined overhead rate is 200% of direct labor. Information on the company's production activities during September 2015 follows.

a. Purchased raw materials on credit, $125,000.

b. Materials requisitions record use of the following materials for the month.

Job 487	$30,000
Job 488	20,000
Job 489	12,000
Job 490	14,000
Job 491	4,000
Total direct materials	80,000
Indirect materials	12,000
Total materials used	$92,000

c. Paid $11,000 cash for miscellaneous factory overhead costs.

d. Time tickets record use of the following labor for the month. These wages are paid in cash.

Job 487	$ 8,000
Job 488	7,000
Job 489	25,000
Job 490	26,000
Job 491	2,000
Total direct labor	68,000
Indirect labor	16,000
Total	$84,000

e. Allocated overhead to Jobs 487, 489, and 490.

f. Transferred Jobs 487, 489, and 490 to Finished Goods.

g. Sold Jobs 487 and 489 on credit for a total price of $340,000.

h. The company incurred the following overhead costs during the month (credit Prepaid Insurance for expired factory insurance).

Depreciation of factory building	$37,000
Depreciation of factory equipment	21,000
Expired factory insurance	7,000
Accrued property taxes payable	31,000

i. Applied overhead at month-end to the Work in Process Inventory account (Jobs 488 and 491) using the predetermined overhead rate of 200% of direct labor cost.

Required

1. Prepare a job cost sheet for each job worked on in the month. Use the following simplified form.

| Job No. _____ |
| Materials .... $ _____ |
| Labor........... _____ |
| Overhead .... _____ |
| Total cost .... $ _____ |

Check   (2e) Cr. Factory Overhead, $118,000
(3) Finished Goods Inventory, $92,000 bal.

2. Prepare journal entries to record the events and transactions *a* through *i*.

3. Set up T-accounts for each of the following general ledger accounts, each of which started the month with a zero balance: Raw Materials Inventory, Work in Process Inventory, Finished Goods Inventory, Factory Overhead, Cost of Goods Sold. Then post the journal entries to these T-accounts and determine the balance of each account.

4. Prepare a report showing the total cost of each job in process and prove that the sum of their costs equals the Work in Process Inventory account balance. Prepare similar reports for Finished Goods Inventory and Cost of Goods Sold.

In December 2014, Pavelka Company's manager estimated next year's total direct labor cost assuming 50 persons working an average of 2,000 hours each at an average wage rate of $15 per hour. The manager also estimated the following manufacturing overhead costs for 2015.

Problem 2-4B
Overhead allocation and adjustment using a predetermined overhead rate

P3   P4

Indirect labor	$159,600
Factory supervision	120,000
Rent on factory building..................	70,000
Factory utilities	44,000
Factory insurance expired	34,000
Depreciation—Factory equipment	240,000
Repairs expense—Factory equipment	30,000
Factory supplies used	34,400
Miscellaneous production costs	18,000
Total estimated overhead costs	$750,000

At the end of 2015, records show the company incurred $725,000 of actual overhead costs. It completed and sold five jobs with the following direct labor costs: Job 625, $354,000; Job 626, $330,000; Job 627, $175,000; Job 628, $420,000; and Job 629, $184,000. In addition, Job 630 is in process at the end of 2015 and had been charged $10,000 for direct labor. No jobs were in process at the end of 2014. The company's predetermined overhead rate is based on direct labor cost.

Required

1. Determine the following.

  a. Predetermined overhead rate for 2015.

  b. Total overhead cost applied to each of the six jobs during 2015.

  c. Over- or underapplied overhead at year-end 2015.

2. Assuming that any over- or underapplied overhead is not material, prepare the adjusting entry to allocate any over- or underapplied overhead to Cost of Goods Sold at the end of year 2015.

Check   (1c) $11,500 overapplied
(2) Dr. Factory Overhead, $11,500

King Company produces variations of its product, a megatron, in response to custom orders from its customers. On June 1, the company had no inventories of work in process or finished goods but held the following raw materials.

Problem 2-5B
Production transactions, subsidiary records, and source documents

P1   P2   P3   P4

Material M	120 units @ $200 =	$24,000
Material R	80 units @ 160 =	12,800
Paint	44 units @ 72 =	3,168
Total cost		$39,968

On June 3, the company began working on two megatrons: Job 450 for Encinita Company and Job 451 for Fargo, Inc.

Required

Using Exhibit 2.3 as a guide, prepare job cost sheets for Jobs 450 and 451. Using Exhibit 2.5 as a guide, prepare materials ledger cards for Material M, Material R, and paint. Enter the beginning raw materials inventory dollar amounts for each of these materials on their respective ledger cards. Then, follow instructions in this list of activities.

a. Purchased raw materials on credit and recorded the following information from receiving reports and invoices.

> Receiving Report No. 20, Material M, 150 units at $200 each.
> Receiving Report No. 21, Material R, 70 units at $160 each.

Instructions: Record these purchases with a single journal entry. Enter the receiving report information on the materials ledger cards.

b. Requisitioned the following raw materials for production.

> Requisition No. 223, for Job 450, 80 units of Material M.
> Requisition No. 224, for Job 450, 60 units of Material R.
> Requisition No. 225, for Job 451, 40 units of Material M.
> Requisition No. 226, for Job 451, 30 units of Material R.
> Requisition No. 227, for 12 units of paint.

Instructions: Enter amounts for direct materials requisitions on the materials ledger cards and the job cost sheets. Enter the indirect material amount on the materials ledger card. Do not record a journal entry at this time.

c. Received the following employee time tickets for work in June.

> Time tickets Nos. 1 to 10 for direct labor on Job 450, $40,000.
> Time tickets Nos. 11 to 20 for direct labor on Job 451, $32,000.
> Time tickets Nos. 21 to 24 for equipment repairs, $12,000.

Instructions: Record direct labor from the time tickets on the job cost sheets. Do not record a journal entry at this time.

d. Paid cash for the following items during the month: factory payroll, $84,000, and miscellaneous overhead items, $36,800. Use the time tickets to record the total direct and indirect labor costs.

Instructions: Record these payments with journal entries.

e. Finished Job 450 and transferred it to the warehouse. The company assigns overhead to each job with a predetermined overhead rate equal to 70% of direct labor cost.

Instructions: Enter the allocated overhead on the cost sheet for Job 450, fill in the cost summary section of the cost sheet, and then mark the cost sheet "Finished." Prepare a journal entry to record the job's completion and its transfer to Finished Goods.

f. Delivered Job 450 and accepted the customer's promise to pay $290,000 within 30 days.

Instructions: Prepare journal entries to record the sale of Job 450 and the cost of goods sold.

g. Applied overhead cost to Job 451 based on the job's direct labor used to date.

Instructions: Enter overhead on the job cost sheet but do not make a journal entry at this time.

Check (*h*) Dr. Work in Process Inventory, $38,400

h. Recorded the total direct and indirect materials costs as reported on all the requisitions for the month.

Instructions: Prepare a journal entry to record these.

i. Recorded the total overhead costs applied to jobs.

   Instructions: Prepare a journal entry to record the allocation of these overhead costs.

j. Compute the balance in the Factory Overhead account as of the end of June.

Check   Balance in
Factory Overhead, $736 Cr.,
overapplied

This serial problem began in Chapter 1 and continues through most of the book. If previous chapter seg-ments were not completed, the serial problem can begin at this point. It is helpful, but not necessary, to use the Working Papers that accompany the book.)

**SERIAL
PROBLEM**
Business Solutions

P1   P2   P3

SP 2   The computer workstation furniture manufacturing that Santana Rey started in January is progress-ing well. As of the end of June, Business Solutions's job cost sheets show the following total costs accu-mulated on three furniture jobs.

	Job 602	Job 603	Job 604
Direct materials	$1,500	$3,300	$2,700
Direct labor	800	1,420	2,100
Overhead	400	710	1,050

Job 602 was started in production in May, and these costs were assigned to it in May: direct materials, $600; direct labor, $180; and overhead, $90. Jobs 603 and 604 were started in June. Overhead cost is applied with a predetermined rate based on direct labor costs. Jobs 602 and 603 are finished in June, and Job 604 is expected to be finished in July. No raw materials are used indirectly in June. (Assume this company's predetermined overhead rate did not change over these months).

Required

1. What is the cost of the raw materials used in June for each of the three jobs and in total?

2. How much total direct labor cost is incurred in June?

3. What predetermined overhead rate is used in June?

4. How much cost is transferred to Finished Goods Inventory in June?

Check   (1) Total materials,
$6,900

(3) 50%

The **General Ledger** tool in *Connect* automates several of the procedural steps in accounting so that the financial professional can focus on the impacts of each transaction on various reports and performance measures.

GL 2-1   General Ledger assignment GL 2-1, based on Problem 2-1A, focuses on transactions related to job-order costing. Prepare summary journal entries to record the cost of jobs and their flow through the manufacturing environment. Then prepare a schedule of cost of goods manufactured and a partial income statement.

**GL GENERAL
LEDGER
PROBLEM**

Available in Connect

|ACCOUNTING

Beyond the Numbers

BTN 2-1   Apple's financial statements and notes in Appendix A provide evidence of growth potential in its sales.

**REPORTING IN
ACTION**

C1

APPLE

Required

1. Identify at least two types of costs that will predictably increase as a percent of sales with growth in sales.

2. Explain why you believe the types of costs identified for part 1 will increase, and describe how you might assess Apple's success with these costs. (*Hint:* You might consider the gross margin ratio.)

Fast Forward

3. Access Apple's annual report for a fiscal year ending after September 28, 2013, from its website [Apple.com] or the SEC's EDGAR database [www.SEC.gov]. Review and report its growth in sales along with its cost and income levels (including its gross margin ratio).

COMPARATIVE ANALYSIS

C1

APPLE
GOOGLE

BTN 2-2 Manufacturers and merchandisers can apply just-in-time (JIT) to their inventory management Both **Apple** and **Google** want to know the impact of a JIT inventory system for their operating cash flows Review each company's statement of cash flows in Appendix A to answer the following.

Required

1. Identify the impact on operating cash flows (increase or decrease) for changes in inventory levels (increase or decrease) for both companies for each of the three most recent years.
2. What impact would a JIT inventory system have on both Apple's and Google's operating income? Link the answer to your response for part 1.
3. Would the move to a JIT system have a one-time or recurring impact on operating cash flow?

ETHICS CHALLENGE

P3

Point: Students could compare responses and discuss differences in concerns with allocating overhead.

BTN 2-3 An accounting professional requires at least two skill sets. The first is to be technically competent. Knowing how to capture, manage, and report information is a necessary skill. Second, the ability to assess manager and employee actions and biases for accounting analysis is another skill. For instance knowing how a person is compensated helps anticipate information biases. Draw on these skills and write a half-page memo to the financial officer on the following practice of allocating overhead.

Background: Assume that your company sells portable housing to both general contractors and the government. It sells jobs to contractors on a bid basis. A contractor asks for three bids from different manufacturers. The combination of low bid and high quality wins the job. However, jobs sold to the government are bid on a cost-plus basis. This means price is determined by adding all costs plus a profit based on cost at a specified percent, such as 10%. You observe that the amount of overhead allocated to government jobs is higher than that allocated to contract jobs. These allocations concern you and motivate your memo.

COMMUNICATING IN PRACTICE

C1 C2

Point: Have students present a mock interview, one assuming the role of the president of the company and the other the applicant.

BTN 2-4 Assume that you are preparing for a second interview with a manufacturing company. The company is impressed with your credentials but has indicated that it has several qualified applicants. You anticipate that in this second interview, you must show what you offer over other candidates. You learn the company currently uses a periodic inventory system and is not satisfied with the timeliness of its information and its inventory management. The company manufactures custom-order holiday decorations and display items. To show your abilities, you plan to recommend that it use a cost accounting system.

Required

In preparation for the interview, prepare notes outlining the following:
1. Your cost accounting system recommendation and why it is suitable for this company.
2. A general description of the documents that the proposed cost accounting system requires.
3. How the documents in part 2 facilitate the operation of the cost accounting system.

TAKING IT TO THE NET

C1

BTN 2-5 Many contractors work on custom jobs that require a job order costing system.

Required

Access the website **AMSI.com**; click on "Construction Management Software," and then on "STARBUILDER." Prepare a one-page memorandum for the CEO of a construction company providing information about the job order costing software this company offers. Would you recommend that the company purchase this software?

TEAMWORK IN ACTION

C1

BTN 2-6 Consider the activities undertaken by a medical clinic in your area.

Required

1. Do you consider a job order costing system appropriate for the clinic?
2. Identify as many factors as possible to lead you to conclude that it uses a job order system.

BTN 2-7   Refer to the chapter opener regarding Quintin Middleton and his company, Middleton Made Knives. All successful businesses track their costs, and it is especially important for start-up businesses to monitor and control costs.

ENTREPRENEURIAL DECISION

C1   C2

Required

1. Assume that Middleton Made Knives uses a job order costing system. For the basic cost category of direct materials, explain how a job cost sheet for Middleton Made Knives would differ from a job cost sheet for a service company.

2. For the basic cost categories of direct labor and overhead, provide examples of the types of costs that would fall into each category for Middleton Made Knives.

BTN 2-8   Job order costing is frequently used by home builders.

HITTING THE ROAD

C2   P1   P2   P3

Required

1. You (or your team) are to prepare a job cost sheet for a single-family home under construction. List four items of both direct materials and direct labor. Explain how you think overhead should be applied.

2. Contact a builder and compare your job cost sheet to this builder's job cost sheet. If possible, speak to that company's accountant. Write your findings in a short report.

BTN 2-9   Apple and Samsung are competitors in the global marketplace. Apple's and Samsung's financial statements are in Appendix A.

GLOBAL DECISION

C1

APPLE

Samsung

Required

1. Determine the change in Apple's and Samsung's inventories for the most recent year reported. Then identify the impact on net resources generated by operating activities (increase or decrease) for the change in inventory level (increase or decrease) for Apple and Samsung for that same year.

2. How would the move to a just-in-time (JIT) system likely impact future operating cash flows and operating income?

3. Would a move to a JIT system likely impact Apple more than it would Samsung? Explain.

ANSWERS TO MULTIPLE CHOICE QUIZ

1. c; $30,000 \times 150\% = \underline{\$45,000}$

2. b; $38,500/$35,000 = \underline{110\%}$

3. e; Direct materials + Direct labor + Overhead = Total cost;
   Direct materials + ($4,000/.80) + $4,000 = $10,000
   Direct materials = $\underline{\$1,000}$

4. e; $9,000 + $94,200 + $59,200 + $31,600 − Finished goods
   = $17,800
   Thus, finished goods = $\underline{\$176,200}$

5. b

chapter 3

Process Costing and Analysis

Chapter Preview

PROCESS OPERATIONS

C1 Organization of process operations

A1 Process cost vs. job order systems

C2 Equivalent units (EUP)

PROCESS COSTING ILLUSTRATION

C3 Overview of GenX Company

Physical flow of units

Computing EUP

Cost per EUP

Cost reconciliation

Process cost summary

ACCOUNTING AND REPORTING

P1 Accounting for materials

P2 Accounting for labor

P3 Accounting for overhead

P4 Accounting for transfers

A2 Hybrid costing system

C4 *Appendix:* FIFO method

Learning Objectives

CONCEPTUAL

C1 Explain process operations and the way they differ from job order operations.

C2 Define and compute equivalent units and explain their use in process costing.

C3 Describe accounting for production activity and preparation of a process cost summary using weighted average.

C4 *Appendix 3A*—Describe accounting for production activity and preparation of a process cost summary using FIFO.

ANALYTICAL

A1 Compare process costing and job order costing.

A2 Explain and illustrate a hybrid costing system.

PROCEDURAL

P1 Record the flow of materials costs in process costing.

P2 Record the flow of labor costs in process costing.

P3 Record the flow of factory overhead costs in process costing.

P4 Record the transfer of goods across departments, to Finished Goods Inventory, and to Cost of Goods Sold.

Mixing It Up

MADISON HEIGHTS, MI—Like many small businesses, **Kar's Nuts (karsnuts.com)** started at home, where Sue Kar roasted peanuts to sell at nearby Tiger Stadium. From humble beginnings, the company now has the country's best-selling branded trail mix, Sweet 'n Salty Mix. Kar's CEO and family-owner Nick Nicolay notes that "Sweet 'n Salty is our flagship item, and we sell over 15 million pounds of it each year."

Unlike products made in job order operations, Kar's operates a continuous production line that runs around the clock, processing over 26 million pounds of different trail mixes during the year. High production volumes are characteristic of products made in process operations. This operation requires production managers to track costs differently than in job order systems, and Kar's relies on a process costing system to monitor and control its costs. These systems track the costs of each process, which in Kar's case include roasting, blending, and packaging.

Each of Kar's processes adds direct materials costs. In the roasting department, thousand-pound supersacks of peanuts and sunflower kernels are roasted and then transferred to the blending department. "We're choosy with ingredients, and use only jumbo peanuts because they taste better," says Nick. In the blending department, direct materials like dark chocolate chunks, raisins, and various berries are blended with the roasted nuts.

Like many process operations, Kar's relies heavily on automation. Much of the work is done by machines, including roasters, conveyors, bucket elevators, and robots. The overhead costs of running the machines must be carefully monitored and (as in job order costing) allocated. In process costing,

> *"We roast around the clock . . . the demand is there"*
> — **Nick Nicolay**

overhead costs are allocated to individual processes, such as roasting, blending, and packaging, rather than to individual jobs. With costly raw materials and overhead costs, Nick and his production managers must be adept at interpreting process cost summary reports to monitor and control costs.

While Kar's has been in business for many years, Nick stresses the need for the company to remain entrepreneurial and creative: "Coming up with innovative, new products can be challenging. No one's creating new fruits or nuts, so our charge is to take what's out there and continue to come up with unique, tasty, healthy combinations to meet new demand." A 30-minute internal meeting was the genesis of the idea for Sweet 'n Salty. According to Nicolay, "We thought a sweet and salty trail mix would be a good alternative to candy bars in vending machines in the summertime. . . . But it quickly became more than a seasonal item." Likewise, Kar's developed Second Nature, a line focused on meeting trends toward even healthier snacks. "We saw that consumers wanted a more premium, upscale, healthy eating option, and we responded with this line of mixes that includes all-natural ingredients," says Nick.

Nick encourages young entrepreneurs to "enjoy what you do and work hard." Though he started as a banker, Nick realized that "snack food is in my family's blood," and he made the move to Kar's. Now, the company boasts yearly sales of over $90 million, and Nick has plans for his products to be sold in nearly all the top grocery stores in the United States within the next few years. "There is a lot of geography left," notes Nick.

Source: *Kar's Nuts website,* January 2015; *mibiz.com,* October 9, 2013; *plantemoran.com,* October 16, 2013; *Crain's Detroit Business,* May 5, 2013

PROCESS OPERATIONS

C1

Explain process operations and the way they differ from job order operations.

In the previous chapter we described differences in job order and process operations and illustrated job order costing. Recall that job order operations involve individual, customized jobs, with little standardization of work activities. **Process operations** involve the mass production of similar products in a continuous flow of sequential processes. A key feature of process operations is the high level of standardization needed if the system is to produce large volumes of products. Thus, process operations use a standardized process to make similar products; job order operations use a customized process to make unique products.

Penn, a maker of tennis balls, reflects a process operation. Tennis players want every tennis ball to be the same in terms of bounce, playability, and durability. This uniformity requires Penn to use a production process that can repeatedly make large volumes of tennis balls to the same specifications. Such a process is unlike job order operations, where customers want products or services customized to their individual needs. Process operations also extend to services, such as mail sorting in large post offices and order processing in retailers like **Amazon.com**. Other companies using process operations include:

Company*	Product	Company	Product
Kellogg	Cereals	Heinz	Ketchup
Pfizer	Pharmaceuticals	Mars	M&Ms
Procter & Gamble	Household products	Hershey	Chocolate
Coca-Cola	Soft drinks	Suja	Organic juice

*For virtual tours of process operations visit PennRacquet.com/video.html (tennis balls) and Hersheys.com/ads-and-videos/how-we-make-chocolate.aspx (chocolate).

Organization of Process Operations

Each of these products involves operations having a series of repetitive *processes,* or steps, resulting in a noncustomized product or service. A production operation that makes tennis balls, for instance, might include the three steps shown in Exhibit 3.1. Understanding such processes for companies with process operations is crucial for measuring their costs. Increasingly, process operations use machines and automation to control product quality and reduce manufacturing costs.

EXHIBIT 3.1

Process Operations: Making of Tennis Balls

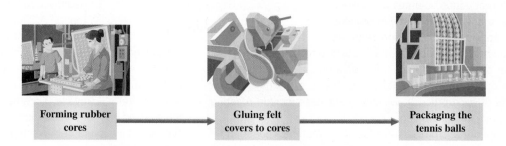

Forming rubber cores → Gluing felt covers to cores → Packaging the tennis balls

In a process operation, each process is identified as a separate *production department, workstation,* or *work center.* With the exception of the first process or department, each receives the output from the prior department as a partially processed product. Depending on the nature of the process, each process applies direct labor, overhead, and, perhaps, additional direct materials to move the product toward completion. Only the final process or department in the series produces finished goods ready for sale to customers. In Exhibit 3.1, the first step in tennis ball production involves cutting rubber into pellets and forming the core of each ball. These rubber cores are passed to the second department, where felt is cut into covers and glued to the rubber cores. The completed tennis balls are then passed to the final department for quality checks and packaging.

Tracking costs for several related departments can seem complex. Yet because process cost-ing procedures are applied to *the activity of each department or process separately,* we need to consider only one process at a time. This simplifies the procedures. In addition, as we will show in this chapter, many of the journal entries in a process costing system are like those in a job order costing system.

Comparing Process and Job Order Costing Systems

Both **job order costing systems** and **process costing systems** track direct materials, direct la-bor, and overhead costs. The measurement focus in a job order costing system is on the indi-vidual job or batch, whereas in a process costing system, it is on the individual process. Regardless of the measurement focus, we are ultimately interested in determining the cost per unit of product (or service) resulting from either system.

While both measure costs per unit, these two accounting systems differ in terms of how they do so. A job order system measures cost per unit upon completion of a job, by dividing the total cost for that job by the number of units in that job. As we showed in the previous chapter, job cost sheets accumulate the costs for each job. In a job order system, the cost object is a job. A process costing system measures unit costs at the end of a period (for example, a month) by combining the costs per equivalent unit (explained in the next section) from each separate de-partment. In process costing, the cost object is the process. Differences in the way these two systems apply materials, labor, and overhead costs are highlighted in Exhibit 3.2.

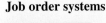

A1

Compare process costing and job order costing.

Point: The cost object in a job order system is the specific job; the cost object in a process costing system is the process.

QC1

EXHIBIT 3.2

Cost Flows: Comparing Job Order and Process Costing Systems

Job order systems

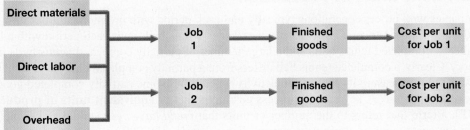

Process systems

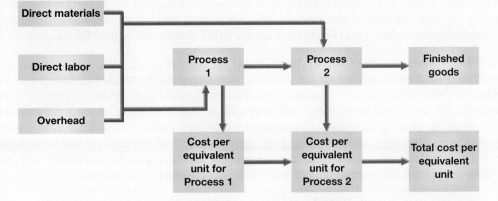

Transferring Costs across Departments   A key difference between job order and pro-cess costing arises with respect to work in process inventory: Job order costing often uses *only one* Work in Process Inventory account; the balance in this account agrees with the accumulated balances across all the job cost sheets for the jobs still in process. Process costing, however, uses *separate* Work in Process Inventory accounts for each department. When the production process is complete in process costing, the completed goods and the accumulated costs are transferred from the Work in Process Inventory account for the final department in the series of processes to the Finished Goods Inventory account. Exhibit 3.3 summarizes the journal entries to capture this flow of costs for a tennis ball manufacturer.

EXHIBIT 3.3

Flow of Costs through
Separate Work in Process
Accounts

Work in Process Inventory—Felt department . . . .   ##

    Work in Process Inventory—Core department . . . .   ##

    To transfer costs of partially completed goods to the next department.

Finished Goods Inventory . . . .   ##

    Work in Process Inventory—Felt department . . . .   ##

    To transfer costs of completed products to finished goods.

NEED-TO-KNOW 3-1

Job Order vs. Process
Costing Systems

C1   A1

Do More: QS 3-1, QS 3-2,
E 3-1, E 3-2

QC2

Complete the following table with either a yes or no regarding the attributes of job order and process costing systems.

	Job Order	Process
Uses direct materials, direct labor, and overhead costs	a.	e.
Uses job cost sheets to accumulate costs	b.	f.
Typically uses several Work in Process Inventory accounts	c.	g.
Yields a cost per unit of product	d.	h.

Solution

a. yes   **b.** yes   **c.** no   **d.** yes   **e.** yes   **f.** no   **g.** yes   **h.** yes

Equivalent Units of Production

C2

Define and compute
equivalent units and
explain their use in
process costing.

Companies with process operations typically end each period with inventories of both finished goods and work in process. For example, a maker of tennis balls ends each period with a large number of completed tennis balls and a large number of partially completed tennis balls in inventory. Clearly, a completed tennis ball differs from a partially completed one. How, then, does a manufacturer measure its production activity when it has some partially completed goods at the end of a period? A key idea in process costing is that of **equivalent units of production (EUP),** a term that refers to the number of units that *could have been* started and completed given the costs incurred during the period. For example, 100,000 tennis balls that are 60% through the production process is equivalent to 60,000 (100,000 units × 60%) tennis balls that have completed the entire production process. This means that the cost to put 100,000 units 60% of the way through the production process is *equivalent to* the cost to put 60,000 units completely through the production process. Having information about the costs of partially completed goods makes it possible to measure the firm's production activity for the period.

EUP for Materials and Conversion Costs   In many processes, the equivalent units of production for direct materials are not the same with respect to direct labor and overhead. For example, direct materials, like rubber for tennis ball cores, might enter production entirely at the beginning of a process; direct labor and overhead, in contrast, might be used continuously throughout the process. How does a manufacturer account for these timing differences? Again, by measuring equivalent units of production. For example, if all of the direct materials to produce 10,000 units have entered the production process, but those units have received only 20% of their direct labor and overhead costs, equivalent units would be computed as:

$$
\begin{aligned}
\text{EUP for direct materials} &= 10,000 \times 100\% = 10,000 \\
\text{EUP for direct labor} &= 10,000 \times 20\% = 2,000 \\
\text{EUP for overhead} &= 10,000 \times 20\% = 2,000
\end{aligned}
$$

As discussed in a previous chapter, direct labor and factory overhead can be classified as *conversion costs*—that is, as costs of converting direct materials into finished products. Many businesses with process operations compute **conversion cost per equivalent unit,** which is the combined costs of direct labor and factory overhead per equivalent unit. If, as shown in the example above, direct labor and overhead enter the production process at the same rate, it is convenient to combine them and focus on them, together, as conversion costs. In addition, advances in technology

Point: When overhead is applied based on direct labor cost, the percentage of completion for direct labor and overhead will be the same.

enable companies to automate their production processes and reduce direct labor costs. For these reasons, many companies with process operations use the categories of direct materials and conversion costs both for accounting and decision-making purposes. We illustrate this in the next section.

Weighted Average versus FIFO   As we will show later, there are different ways to compute the number of equivalent units. These methods make different assumptions about how costs flow. The **weighted-average method** combines units and costs *across two periods* in computing equivalent units. The **FIFO method** computes equivalent units based only on production activity in the *current period*. The objectives, concepts, and journal entries (but not amounts) are the same under the weighted-average and FIFO methods; the computations of equivalent units differ. While the FIFO method is generally considered to be more precise than the weighted-average method, it requires more calculations. Often, the differences between the two methods are not large. When using a just-in-time inventory system, these different methods will yield very similar results because inventories are immaterial. **In this chapter we assume the weighted-average method for inventory costs and illustrate the FIFO method in the appendix.**

PROCESS COSTING ILLUSTRATION

In this section we provide a step-by-step illustration of process costing. Each process (or department) in a process operation follows these steps:

1. Determine the physical flow of units.
2. Compute the equivalent units of production.
3. Compute the cost per equivalent unit of production.
4. Assign and reconcile costs.

The next section shows these steps for the first of two sequential processes used by a company to produce one of its products.

C3

Describe accounting for production activity and preparation of a process cost summary using weighted average.

Overview of GenX Company's Process Operation

The GenX Company produces an organic trail mix called FitMix. Its target customers are active people who are interested in fitness and the environment. GenX sells FitMix to wholesale distributors, who in turn sell it to retailers. FitMix is manufactured in a continuous, two-process operation (roasting and blending), shown in Exhibit 3.4.

EXHIBIT 3.4

GenX's Process Operation

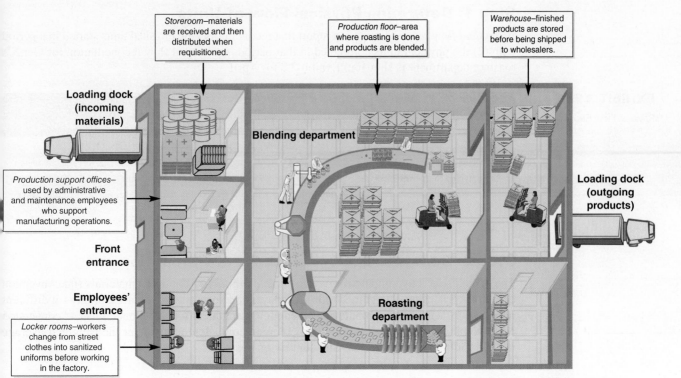

Storeroom—materials are received and then distributed when requisitioned.

Production floor—area where roasting is done and products are blended.

Warehouse—finished products are stored before being shipped to wholesalers.

Loading dock (incoming materials)

Blending department

Loading dock (outgoing products)

Production support offices—used by administrative and maintenance employees who support manufacturing operations.

Front entrance

Employees' entrance

Locker rooms—workers change from street clothes into sanitized uniforms before working in the factory.

Roasting department

In the first process (roasting department), GenX roasts, oils, and salts organically grown peanuts. These peanuts are then passed to the blending department, the second process. In the blending department, machines blend organic chocolate pieces and organic dried fruits with the peanuts from the first process. The blended mix is then inspected and packaged for delivery. In both departments, direct materials enter production at the beginning of the process, while conversion costs occur continuously throughout each department's processing. Exhibit 3.5 presents production data (in units) for GenX's roasting department. This exhibit includes the percentage of completion for both materials and conversion; for example, beginning work in process inventory is 100% complete with respect to materials but only 65% complete with respect to conversion.

EXHIBIT 3.5

Production Data (in units) for Roasting Department

Roasting Department	Units	Percentage of Completion	
		Direct Materials	Conversion
Beginning work in process inventory (March 31)	30,000	100%	65%
Units started this period	+90,000	—	—
Units completed and transferred out	−100,000	100%	100%
Ending work in process inventory (April 30)	20,000	100%	25%

Exhibit 3.6 presents production cost data for GenX's roasting department. We will use the data in Exhibits 3.5 and 3.6 to illustrate the four-step approach to process costing.

EXHIBIT 3.6

Roasting Department Production Cost Data

GenX—Roasting Department		
Beginning work in process inventory (March 31)		
Direct materials costs	$ 81,000	
Conversion costs	108,900	$189,900
Costs during the current period (April)		
Direct materials costs	279,000	
Direct labor costs*	171,000	
Factory overhead costs applied (120% of direct labor)*	205,200	655,200
Total production costs		$845,100

*Total conversion costs for the month equal $376,200 ($171,000 + $205,200).

Step 1: Determine Physical Flow of Units

A *physical flow reconciliation* is a report that reconciles (1) the physical units started in a period with (2) the physical units completed in that period. A physical flow reconciliation for GenX's roasting department is shown in Exhibit 3.7 for April.

EXHIBIT 3.7

Physical Flow Reconciliation

GenX—Roasting Department				
Units to Account For		Units Accounted For		
Beginning work in process inventory	30,000 units	Units completed and transferred out		100,000 units
Units started this period	90,000 units	Ending work in process inventory		20,000 units
Total units to account for	**120,000 units**	Total units accounted for		**120,000 units**

reconciled

Step 2: Compute Equivalent Units of Production

The second step is to compute *equivalent units of production* for direct materials and conversion costs for April. Since direct materials and conversion costs typically enter a process at different rates, departments must compute equivalent units separately for direct materials and conversion costs. Exhibit 3.8 shows the formula to compute equivalent units under the weighted-average method for both direct materials and conversion costs.

$$\text{Equivalent units of production (EUP)} = \frac{\text{Number of whole units completed}}{\text{and transferred to next department*}} + \frac{\text{Number of equivalent units in}}{\text{ending work in process inventory}}$$

*Or transferred to finished goods inventory.

EXHIBIT 3.8

Computing EUP—
Weighted-Average Method

For GenX's roasting department, we must convert the 120,000 physical units measure to *equivalent units* based on how each input has been used. The roasting department fully completed its work on 100,000 units, and partially completed its work on 20,000 units (from Exhibit 3.5). Equivalent units are computed by multiplying the number of units accounted for (from step 1) by the percentage of completion for each input—see Exhibit 3.9.

EXHIBIT 3.9

Equivalent Units of
Production—Weighted
Average

GenX—Roasting Department		
Equivalent Units of Production	**Direct Materials**	**Conversion**
Equivalent units completed and transferred out (100,000 × 100%)	100,000 EUP	100,000 EUP
Equivalent units for ending work in process		
Direct materials (20,000 × 100%).........................	20,000 EUP	
Conversion (20,000 × 25%)		5,000 EUP
Equivalent units of production	120,000 EUP	105,000 EUP

The first row of Exhibit 3.9 reflects units transferred out in April. The roasting department entirely completed its work on the 100,000 units transferred out. These units have 100% of the materials and conversion required, or 100,000 equivalent units of each input (100,000 × 100%).

GenX ended the month with 20,000 partially completed units. For direct materials, the units in ending work in process inventory include all materials required, so there are 20,000 equivalent units (20,000 × 100%) of materials in the unfinished physical units. Regarding conversion, the units in ending work in process inventory include 25% of the conversion required, which implies 5,000 equivalent units of conversion (20,000 × 25%).

The final row reflects the total equivalent units of production, which is whole units of product that could have been manufactured with the amount of inputs used to create some complete and some incomplete units. For GenX, the amount of inputs used to produce 100,000 complete units and to start 20,000 additional units is equivalent to the amount of direct materials in 120,000 whole units and the amount of conversion in 105,000 whole units.

Ken Whitmore/Stone/Getty Images

A department began the month with 8,000 units in work in process inventory. These units were 100% complete with respect to direct materials and 40% complete with respect to conversion. During the current month, the department started 56,000 units and completed 58,000 units. Ending work in process inventory includes 6,000 units, 100% complete with respect to direct materials and 70% complete with respect to conversion. Use the weighted-average method of process costing to:

1. Compute the department's equivalent units of production for the month for direct materials.
2. Compute the department's equivalent units of production for the month for conversion.

Solution

1. EUP for materials = 58,000 + (6,000 × 100%) = 64,000 EUP
2. EUP for conversion = 58,000 + (6,000 × 70%) = 62,200 EUP

NEED-TO-KNOW 3-2

EUP—Direct Materials
and Conversion
(Weighted Average)
C2

Do More: QS 3-5, QS 3-6,
QS 3-10, E 3-4, E 3-8

QC3

Step 3: Compute Cost per Equivalent Unit

Under the weighted-average method, the computation of EUP does not separate the units in beginning inventory from those started this period, as shown above. Similarly, the weighted-average method combines the costs of beginning work in process inventory with the costs incurred in the current period. This total cost is then divided by the equivalent units of production (from step 2), to compute the average cost per equivalent unit. This process is illustrated in

Point: The weighted-average method mixes production activity and costs across two periods.

Point: Managers can examine changes in monthly costs per equivalent unit to help control the production process.

Exhibit 3.10. For direct materials, the cost averages $3.00 per EUP. For conversion, the cost per equivalent unit averages $4.62 per unit.

EXHIBIT 3.10

Cost per Equivalent Unit of Production—Weighted Average

GenX—Roasting Department		
Cost per Equivalent Unit of Production	**Direct Materials**	**Conversion**
Costs of beginning work in process inventory***........	$ 81,000	$108,900
Costs incurred this period***	279,000	376,200**
Total costs......................................	$360,000	$485,100
÷ Equivalent units of production (from step 2)...........	120,000 EUP	105,000 EUP
= Cost per equivalent unit of production...............	$3.00 per EUP*	$4.62 per EUP†

*$360,000 ÷ 120,000 EUP   **$171,000 + $205,200   †$485,100 ÷ 105,000 EUP   *** From Exhibit 3.6

Step 4: Assign and Reconcile Costs

The EUP from step 2 and the cost per EUP from step 3 are used in step 4 to assign costs to (a) units that the roasting department completed and transferred to the blending department (100,000 units), and (b) units that remain in process in the roasting department (20,000 units). This is illustrated in Exhibit 3.11.

EXHIBIT 3.11

Report of Costs Accounted For—Weighted Average

GenX—Roasting Department		
Cost of units completed and transferred to blending dept.		
Direct materials (100,000 EUP × $3.00 per EUP)............	$300,000	
Conversion (100,000 EUP × $4.62 per EUP)	462,000	
Cost of units completed this period......................		$762,000
Cost of ending work in process inventory		
Direct materials (20,000 EUP × $3.00 per EUP)	60,000	
Conversion (5,000 EUP × $4.62 per EUP)	23,100	
Cost of ending work in process inventory..................		83,100
Total costs accounted for		$845,100

Cost of Units Completed and Transferred   The 100,000 units completed and transferred to the blending department required 100,000 EUP of direct materials and 100,000 EUP of conversion. Thus, we assign $300,000 (100,000 EUP × $3.00 per EUP) of direct materials cost to those units. Similarly, we assign $462,000 (100,000 EUP × $4.62 per EUP) of conversion to those units. The total cost of the 100,000 completed and transferred units is $762,000 ($300,000 + $462,000) and their average cost per unit is $7.62 ($762,000 ÷ 100,000 units).

Cost of Units for Ending Work in Process   There are 20,000 incomplete units in work in process inventory at period-end. For direct materials, those units have 20,000 EUP of material (from step 2) at a cost of $3.00 per EUP (from step 3), which yields the materials cost of work in process inventory of $60,000 (20,000 EUP × $3.00 per EUP). For conversion, the in-process units reflect 5,000 EUP (from step 2). Using the $4.62 conversion cost per EUP (from step 3) we obtain conversion costs for in-process inventory of $23,100 (5,000 EUP × $4.62 per EUP). Total cost of work in process inventory at period-end is $83,100 ($60,000 + $23,100).

As a check, management verifies that total costs assigned to units completed and transferred plus the costs of units in process (from Exhibit 3.11) equal the costs incurred by production. Exhibit 3.12 shows the costs incurred by production this period. We then reconcile the *costs accounted for* in Exhibit 3.11 with the *costs to account for* in Exhibit 3.12.

GenX—Roasting Department

Cost of beginning work in process inventory		
Direct materials.	$ 81,000	
Conversion	108,900	$ 189,900
Cost incurred this period		
Direct materials.	279,000	
Conversion	376,200	655,200
Total costs to account for		**$845,100**

EXHIBIT 3.12

Report of Costs to Account For—Weighted Average

The roasting department manager is responsible for $845,100 in costs: $189,000 from beginning work in process plus $655,200 of materials and conversion incurred in the period. At period-end, that manager must show where these costs are assigned. The roasting department manager reports that $83,100 are assigned to units in process and $762,000 are assigned to units transferred out to the blending department (per Exhibit 3.11). The sum of these amounts equals $845,100. Thus, the total *costs to account for* equal the total *costs accounted for* (minor differences can sometimes occur from rounding).

A department began the month with conversion costs of $65,000 in its beginning work in process inventory. During the current month, the department incurred $55,000 of conversion costs. Equivalent units of production for conversion for the month was 15,000 units. The department completed and transferred 12,000 units to the next department. The department uses the weighted-average method of process costing.

1. Compute the department's cost per equivalent unit for conversion for the month.
2. Compute the department's conversion cost of units transferred to the next department for the month.

Solution

1. ($65,000 + $55,000)/15,000 units = $8.00 per EUP for conversion

2. 12,000 units × $8.00 = $96,000 conversion cost transferred to next department

NEED-TO-KNOW 3-3

Cost per EUP— Conversion, with Transfer

C3

Do More: QS 3-11, QS 3-13, E 3-6

QC4

Process Cost Summary

An important managerial accounting report for a process costing system is the **process cost summary** (also called *production report*), which is prepared separately for each process or production department. Three reasons for the summary are to (1) help department managers control and monitor their departments, (2) help factory managers evaluate department managers' performances, and (3) provide cost information for financial statements. A process cost summary achieves these purposes by describing the costs charged to each department, reporting the equivalent units of production achieved by each department, and determining the costs assigned to each department's output. For our purposes, it is prepared using a combination of Exhibits 3.7, 3.9, 3.10, 3.11, and 3.12.

The process cost summary for the roasting department is shown in Exhibit 3.13. The report is divided into three sections. Section ① lists the total costs charged to the department, including direct materials and conversion costs incurred, as well as the cost of the beginning work in process inventory. Section ② describes the equivalent units of production for the department. Equivalent units for materials and conversion are in separate columns. It also reports direct materials and conversion costs per equivalent unit. Section ③ allocates total costs among units worked on in the period. The $762,000 is the total cost of the 100,000 units transferred out of the roasting department to the blending department. The $83,100 is the cost of the 20,000 partially completed units in ending inventory in the roasting department. The assigned costs are then added to show that the total $845,100 cost charged to the roasting department in section ① is now assigned to the units in section ③.

Point: The key report in a job order costing system is a job cost sheet, which reports manufacturing costs per job. A process cost summary reports manufacturing costs per equivalent unit of a process or department.

EXHIBIT 3.13

Process Cost Summary
(Weighted-Average)

GenX COMPANY—ROASTING DEPARTMENT
Process Cost Summary (Weighted-Average Method)
For Month Ended April 30, 2015

① Costs Charged to Production

Costs of beginning work in process

Direct materials	$ 81,000	
Conversion	108,900	$ 189,900

Costs incurred this period

Direct materials	279,000	
Conversion	376,200	655,200
Total costs to account for		**$845,100** ◄

Unit Information

Units to account for:		Units accounted for:	
Beginning work in process	30,000	Completed and transferred out	100,000
Units started this period	90,000	Ending work in process	20,000
Total units to account for	120,000	Total units accounted for	120,000

② Equivalent Units of Production (EUP)

	Direct Materials	Conversion
Units completed and transferred out (100,000 × 100%)	100,000 EUP	100,000 EUP
Units of ending work in process		
Direct materials (20,000 × 100%)	20,000 EUP	
Conversion (20,000 × 25%)		5,000 EUP
Equivalent units of production	120,000 EUP	105,000 EUP

Cost per EUP

	Direct Materials	Conversion
Costs of beginning work in process	$ 81,000	$108,900
Costs incurred this period	279,000	376,200
Total costs	$360,000	$485,100
÷ EUP	120,000 EUP	105,000 EUP
Cost per EUP	$3.00 per EUP	$4.62 per EUP

③ Cost Assignment and Reconciliation

Costs transferred out (cost of goods manufactured)

Direct materials (100,000 EUP × $3.00 per EUP)	$300,000	
Conversion (100,000 EUP × $4.62 per EUP)	462,000	$ 762,000

Costs of ending work in process

Direct materials (20,000 EUP × $3.00 per EUP)	60,000	
Conversion (5,000 EUP × $4.62 per EUP)	23,100	83,100
Total costs accounted for		**$845,100** ◄

ACCOUNTING AND REPORTING FOR PROCESS COSTING

In this section we illustrate the journal entries to account for the operations of a process manufacturer. We continue to focus on GenX Company's roasting department. Exhibit 3.14 illustrates the flow of costs for GenX. Materials, labor, and overhead costs flow into the manufacturing processes. GenX keeps separate Work in Process Inventory accounts for the roasting and blending departments; when goods are packaged and ready for sale, their costs are transferred to the Finished Goods Inventory account.

Like a job order costing system, a process costing system relies on source documents. For example, *materials requisitions* are used to signal the use of direct and indirect materials. *Time tickets* are used to record the use of direct and indirect labor. While some companies might combine direct labor and overhead into conversion costs when computing costs per equivalent unit (as we showed previously), labor and overhead costs are accounted for separately within the company's accounts. In addition, since overhead costs typically cannot be tied to individual processes, but rather benefit all processes or departments, most companies use a single Factory Overhead account to accumulate actual and applied overhead costs.

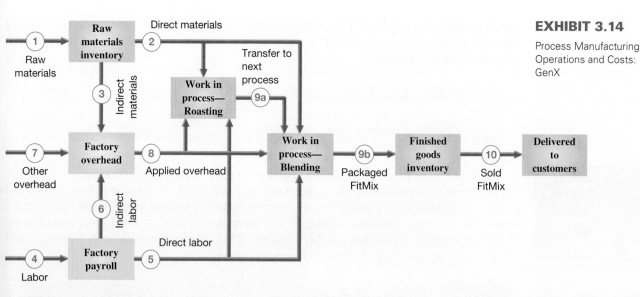

EXHIBIT 3.14

Process Manufacturing Operations and Costs: GenX

As with job order costing, process manufacturers must allocate, or apply, overhead to processes. This requires such companies to find good *allocation bases,* such as direct labor hours or machine hours used. With increasing automation, companies with process operations use fewer direct labor hours and thus are more likely to use machine hours to allocate overhead.

For some companies, a single allocation base will not provide good overhead allocations. For example, direct labor cost might be a good allocation base for GenX's roasting department, but not for its blending department, depending on the amounts of direct labor used in each of those departments. As a result, a process manufacturer can use different overhead allocation rates for different production departments. However, all applied overhead is credited to a single Factory Overhead account.

Exhibit 3.15 presents cost data for GenX. Roasting department costs are from Exhibit 3.6. We use these data next to show the journal entries in a process costing system.

EXHIBIT 3.15

Cost Data—GenX

Raw materials inventory (March 31).................	$100,000
Beginning work in process inventories (March 31)	
Work in process—Roasting	$189,900
Work in process—Blending	151,688
Materials purchased (on account)...................	$400,000
Materials requisitions during April	
Direct materials—Roasting......................	$279,000
Direct materials—Blending.....................	102,000
Indirect materials................................	71,250
Factory payroll for April	
Direct labor—Roasting..........................	$171,000
Direct labor—Blending..........................	183,160
Indirect labor...................................	78,350
Other actual overhead costs during April	
Insurance expense—Factory......................	$ 11,930
Utilities payable—Factory.......................	7,945
Depreciation expense—Factory equipment	220,650
Other (paid in cash)	21,875

Accounting for Materials Costs

In Exhibit 3.14, arrow line ① reflects the arrival of materials at GenX's factory. These materials include organic peanuts, chocolate pieces, dried fruits, oil, salt, and packaging. They also include supplies for the production support office. GenX uses a perpetual inventory system and

P1

Record the flow of materials costs in process costing.

makes all purchases on credit. The summary entry for receipts of raw materials in April follows (dates in journal entries are omitted because they are summary entries, often reflecting two or more transactions or events).

Assets = Liabilities + Equity
+400,000   +400,000

①	Raw Materials Inventory..........................	400,000	
	Accounts Payable...........................		400,000
	Acquired materials on credit for factory use.		

Natalia Kolesnikova/AFP/Getty Images

Arrow line ② in Exhibit 3.14 reflects the flow of direct materials to production in the roasting and blending departments. These direct materials are physically combined into the finished product. The manager of a process usually obtains materials by submitting a *materials requisition* to the materials storeroom manager. The entry to record the use of direct materials by GenX's production departments in April follows. These direct materials costs flow into each department's separate Work in Process Inventory account.

Assets = Liabilities + Equity
+279,000
+102,000
−381,000

②	Work in Process—Roasting......................	279,000	
	Work in Process—Blending.....................	102,000	
	Raw Materials Inventory		381,000
	To assign costs of direct materials used in production.		

In Exhibit 3.14, arrow line ③ reflects the flow of indirect materials from the storeroom to factory overhead. These materials are not clearly linked with any specific production process or department but are used to support overall production activity. As these costs cannot be linked directly to either the roasting or blending departments, they are recorded in GenX's single Factory Overhead account. The following entry records the cost of indirect materials used by GenX in April.

③	Factory Overhead	71,250	
	Raw Materials Inventory		71,250
	To record indirect materials used in April.		

Accounting for Labor Costs

P2

Record the flow of labor costs in process costing.

Exhibit 3.14 shows GenX's factory payroll costs as reflected in arrow line ④. Exhibit 3.15 shows costs of $171,000 for roasting department direct labor, $183,160 for blending department direct labor, and $78,350 for indirect labor. This total payroll of $432,510 is a product cost, and it is allocated to either Work in Process Inventory or Factory Overhead, as we show next.

Time reports from the production departments and the production support office trigger payroll entries. (For simplicity, we do not separately identify withholdings and additional payroll taxes for employees.) In a process operation, the direct labor of a production department includes all labor used exclusively by that department. This is the case even if the labor is not applied to the product itself. If a production department in a process operation, for instance, has a full-time manager and a full-time maintenance worker, their salaries are direct labor costs of that process and are not factory overhead.

Arrow line ⑤ in Exhibit 3.14 shows GenX's use of direct labor. The following entry then records direct labor used. These direct labor costs flow into each department's separate Work in Process Inventory account.

Assets = Liabilities + Equity
+171,000   +354,160
+183,160

⑤	Work in Process Inventory—Roasting	171,000	
	Work in Process Inventory—Blending	183,160	
	Factory Payroll Payable......................		354,160
	To record direct labor used in production.		

Arrow line ⑥ in Exhibit 3.14 reflects GenX's indirect labor costs. These employees provide clerical, maintenance, and other services that help production in both the roasting and blending departments. For example, they order materials, deliver them to the factory floor, repair equipment, operate and program computers used in production, keep payroll and other production records, clean up, and move goods across departments. The following entry records these indirect labor costs.

Point: A department's indirect labor cost might include an allocated portion of the salary of a manager who supervises two or more departments. Allocation of costs between departments is discussed in a later chapter.

⑥	Factory Overhead	78,350	
	Factory Payroll Payable		78,350
	To record indirect labor as overhead.		

After GenX posts these entries for direct and indirect labor, the Factory Payroll Payable account has a balance of $432,510 ($354,160 + $78,350). The entry below shows the payment of this total payroll. After this entry, the Factory Payroll Payable account has a zero balance.

④	Factory Payroll Payable	432,510	
	Cash		432,510
	To record factory wages for April.		

Assets = Liabilities + Equity
−432,510   −432,510

Accounting for Factory Overhead

Overhead costs other than indirect materials and indirect labor are reflected by arrow line ⑦ in Exhibit 3.14. These overhead items include the costs of insuring production assets, renting the factory building, using factory utilities, and depreciating factory equipment not directly related to a specific process. The following entry records these other overhead costs for April.

P3

Record the flow of factory overhead costs in process costing.

⑦	Factory Overhead	262,400	
	Prepaid Insurance		11,930
	Utilities Payable		7,945
	Cash		21,875
	Accumulated Depreciation—Factory Equipment		220,650
	To record other overhead costs incurred in April.		

Applying Overhead to Work in Process   Recall that companies use *predetermined overhead rates* to apply overhead. These rates are estimated at the beginning of a period and used to apply overhead during the period. The application of overhead allows managers to obtain up-to-date estimates of the costs of their processes during the period. This is important for process costing, where goods are transferred across departments before the entire production process is complete.

Arrow line ⑧ in Exhibit 3.14 reflects the application of factory overhead to the two production departments. Factory overhead is applied to processes by relating overhead cost to another variable such as direct labor hours or machine hours used. In many situations, a single allocation basis such as direct labor hours (or a single rate for the entire plant) fails to provide useful allocations. As a result, management may use different rates for different production departments. In our example, GenX applies overhead on the basis of direct labor cost as shown in Exhibit 3.16.

Point: The time it takes to process (cycle) products through a process is sometimes used to allocate costs.

EXHIBIT 3.16

Applying Factory Overhead

Production Department	Direct Labor Cost	Predetermined Rate	Overhead Applied
Roasting	$171,000	120%	$205,200
Blending	183,160	120	219,792
Total			$424,992

GenX records its applied overhead with the following entry.

⑧	Work in Process Inventory—Roasting	205,200	
	Work in Process Inventory—Blending	219,792	
	Factory Overhead		424,992
	Applied overhead costs to production departments at 120% of direct labor cost.		

■ Decision Ethics

Budget Officer   You are working to identify the direct and indirect costs of a new processing department that has several machines. This department's manager instructs you to classify a majority of the costs as indirect to take advantage of the direct labor-based overhead allocation method so it will be charged a lower amount of overhead (because of its small direct labor cost). This would penalize other departments with higher allocations. It also will cause the performance ratings of managers in these other departments to suffer. What action do you take? ■

[Answers follow the chapter's Summary.]

NEED-TO-KNOW 3-4

Overhead Rate and Costs

P1   P2   P3

Tower Mfg. estimates it will incur $200,000 of total overhead costs during 2015. Tower allocates overhead based on machine hours; it estimates it will use a total of 10,000 machine hours during 2015. During February 2015, the assembly department of Tower Mfg. uses 375 machine hours. In addition, Tower incurred actual overhead costs as follows during February: indirect materials, $1,800; indirect labor, $5,700; depreciation on factory equipment, $8,000; factory utilities, $500.

1. Compute the company's predetermined overhead rate for 2015.
2. Prepare journal entries to record (a) overhead applied for the assembly department for the month and (b) actual overhead costs used during the month.

Solution

1. Predetermined overhead rate = Estimated overhead costs ÷ Estimated activity base
   = $200,000/10,000 = $20 per machine hour.

2a.

	Work in Process Inventory—Assembly..........................	7,500	
	Factory Overhead.......................................		7,500
	To record applied overhead (375 hours × $20 per hour).		

2b.

	Factory Overhead	16,000	
	Raw Materials Inventory.....................................		1,800
	Factory Payroll Payable......................................		5,700
	Accumulated Depreciation—Factory Equipment		8,000
	Utilities Payable		500
	To record actual overhead.		

Do More: QS 3-25, E 3-23, E 3-25

QC5

Accounting for Transfers

P4

Record the transfer of goods across departments, to Finished Goods Inventory, and to Cost of Goods Sold.

Assets = Liabilities + Equity
+762,000
−762,000

Transfers across Departments   Arrow line ⑨a in Exhibit 3.14 reflects the transfer of units from the roasting department to the blending department. The process cost summary for the roasting department (Exhibit 3.13) shows that the 100,000 units transferred to the blending department are assigned a cost of $762,000. The entry to record this transfer follows.

⑨a	Work in Process Inventory—Blending	762,000	
	Work in Process Inventory—Roasting		762,000
	To record the transfer of 100,000 units from the roasting department to the blending department.		

Units and costs *transferred out* of the roasting department are *transferred into* the blending department. Exhibit 3.17 shows this transfer using T-accounts for the separate Work in Process Inventory accounts (first in units and then in dollars).

EXHIBIT 3.17

Production and Cost Activity—Transfer to Blending Department

Roasting Department—Units			
Beg. inv.	30,000 units		
Started	90,000 units		
Total	120,000 units		
		100,000 units transferred out	
End. inv.	20,000 units		

Blending Department—Units			
Beg. inv.	12,000 units		
Transferred in	100,000 units		
Total	112,000 units		
		97,000 units transferred to Finished Goods	
End. inv.	15,000 units		

WIP—Roasting Dept.			
Beg. inv.*	189,900		
DM	279,000		
Conv.	376,200		
Total	845,100		
		762,000 Transferred out	
End. Inv.	83,100		

WIP—Blending Dept.			
Beg. inv.†	151,688		
Transferred in	762,000		
DM	102,000		
Conv.	402,952		
Total	1,418,640		

*$81,000 direct materials + $108,900 conversion

†$91,440 transferred-in + $10,000 DM + $50,248 conversion

As Exhibit 3.17 shows, the blending department began the month with 12,000 units in beginning inventory, with a related cost of $151,688. In computing its production activity and costs, the blending department must also consider the units and costs transferred in from the roasting department, as shown in Exhibit 3.17. The 100,000 units transferred in from the roasting department, and their related costs of $762,000, are added to the blending department's number of units and separate Work in Process (WIP) Inventory account.

The blending department then adds additional direct materials and conversion costs. The blending department incurred direct materials costs of $102,000 and conversion costs of $402,952 during the month. (Although not illustrated here, the concepts and methods used in this second department would be similar to those we showed in detail for the first department.)

Accounting for Transfer to Finished Goods   Arrow line ⑨ᵇ in Exhibit 3.14 reflects the transfer of units and their related costs from the blending department to finished goods inventory. At the end of the month, the blending department transferred 97,000 completed units, with a related cost of $1,262,940, to finished goods. The entry to record this transfer follows.

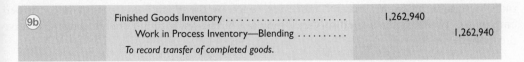

⑨ᵇ	Finished Goods Inventory	1,262,940	
	Work in Process Inventory—Blending		1,262,940
	To record transfer of completed goods.		

Assets = Liabilities + Equity
+1,262,940
−1,262,940

Accounting for Transfer to Cost of Goods Sold   Arrow line ⑩ reflects the sale of finished goods. Assume that GenX sold 106,000 units of FitMix this period, and that its beginning finished goods inventory was 26,000 units with a cost of $338,520. Also assume that its ending finished goods inventory consists of 20,000 units at a cost of $260,400. Using this information, cost of goods sold is computed as in Exhibit 3.18.

Finished Goods Inventory		
Beg. bal. 338,520		
COGM 1,262,940		
Avail. 1,601,460		
	COGS 1,341,060	
End. bal. 260,400		

Beginning finished goods inventory	$ 338,520	
+ Cost of goods manufactured this period.........	1,262,940	
= Cost of goods available for sale	1,601,460	
− Ending finished goods inventory................	260,400	
= Cost of goods sold	$1,341,060	

EXHIBIT 3.18

Cost of Goods Sold

The summary entry to record cost of goods sold for this period follows:

Assets = Liabilities + Equity
−1,341,060   −1,341,060

⑩	Cost of Goods Sold........................	1,341,060	
	Finished Goods Inventory		1,341,060
	To record cost of goods sold for April.		

Trends in Process Operations

Some recent trends in process operations are discussed in the following paragraphs.

Process Design Management concerns with production efficiency can lead companies to entirely reorganize production processes. For example, instead of producing different types of computers in a series of departments, a separate work center for each computer can be established in one department. The process cost system is then changed to account for each work center's costs.

Just-in-Time Production Companies are increasingly adopting just-in-time techniques. With a just-in-time inventory system, inventory levels can be minimal. If raw materials are not ordered or received until needed, a Raw Materials Inventory account might be unnecessary. Instead, materials cost is immediately debited to the Work in Process Inventory account. Similarly, a Finished Goods Inventory account may not be needed. Instead, cost of finished goods may be immediately debited to the Cost of Goods Sold account.

Automation Companies are increasingly automating their production processes and using robots. For example, **Volkswagen** recently began using robots on tasks that are hard for humans to perform. This automation resulted in reduced direct labor costs and a healthier workforce.

Continuous Processing In some companies, materials move continuously through the manufacturing process. **Pepsi Bottling** uses a process in which inventory moves continuously through the system. In these cases, a **materials consumption report** summarizes the materials used and replaces materials requisitions.

Services Service-based businesses are increasingly prevalent. For routine, standardized services like oil changes and simple tax returns, computing costs based on the process is simpler and more useful than a cost per individual job. More complex service companies use process departments to perform specific tasks for consumers. Hospitals, for example, have radiology and physical therapy facilities, each with special equipment and trained employees. When patients need services, they are processed through departments to receive prescribed care.

Customer Orientation Focus on customer orientation also leads to improved processes. A manufacturer of control devices improved quality and reduced production time by forming teams to study processes and suggest improvements. An ice cream maker studied customer tastes to develop a more pleasing ice cream texture.

GLOBAL VIEW

As part of a series of global environmental goals, **Anheuser-Busch InBev** set targets to reduce its water usage. The company uses massive amounts of water in beer production and in its cleaning and cooling processes. To meet these goals, the company followed recent trends in process operations. These included extensive redesign of production processes and the use of advanced technology to increase efficiency at wastewater treatment plants. As a result water usage decreased by almost 37 percent in its global operations.

Sustainability and Accounting   As society becomes more attuned to health issues, businesses must respond. As described in the opener to this chapter, **Kar's Nuts** met demand for healthier snacks by offering trail mixes based on all-natural ingredients. The company also takes precautions to ensure its production process is allergen-free. For example, when transitioning its production line from products with allergens, such as wheat, workers perform a detailed cleaning of all conveyors and packaging equipment. These cleaning efforts add costs but help Kar's fulfill its obligations to its customers and ensure a sustainable product and business.

Hybrid Costing System   ⬛⬛⬜   Decision Analysis

This chapter explained the process costing system and contrasted it with the job order costing system. Many organizations use a *hybrid system* that contains features of both process and job order operations. A recent survey of manufacturers revealed that a majority use hybrid systems (also called *operation cost systems*).

A2

Explain and illustrate a hybrid costing system.

To illustrate, consider a car manufacturer's assembly line. On one hand, the line resembles a process operation in that the assembly steps for each car are nearly identical. On the other hand, the specifications of most cars have several important differences. At the **Ford** Mustang plant, each car assembled on a given day can be different from the previous car and the next car. This means that the costs of materials (subassemblies or components) for each car can differ. Accordingly, while the conversion costs (direct labor and overhead) can be accounted for using a process costing system, the component costs (direct materials) are accounted for using a job order system (separately for each car or type of car).

A hybrid system of processes requires a *hybrid costing system* to properly cost products or services. In the Ford plant, the assembly costs per car are readily determined using process costing. The costs of additional components can then be added to the assembly costs to determine each car's total cost (as in job order costing). To illustrate, consider the following information for a daily assembly process at Ford.

Assembly process costs	
Direct materials	$10.6 million
Conversion costs	$12.0 million
Number of cars assembled	1,000
Costs of three different types of steering wheels	$240, $330, $480
Costs of three different types of seats	$620, $840, $1,360

The assembly process costs $22,600 per car. Depending on the type of steering wheel and seats the customer requests, the cost of a car can range from $23,460 to $24,440 (a $980 difference).

Today companies are increasingly trying to standardize processes while attempting to meet individual customer needs. To the extent that differences among individual customers' requests are large, understanding the costs to satisfy those requests is important. Thus, monitoring and controlling both process and job order costs are important.

◼ Decision **Ethics**

Entrepreneur   You operate a process production company making similar products for three different customers. One customer demands 100% quality inspection of products at your location before shipping. The added costs of that inspection are spread across all customers, not just the one demanding it. If you charge the added costs to that customer, you could lose that customer and experience a loss. Moreover, your other two customers have agreed to pay 110% of full costs. What actions (if any) do you take? ◼ [Answers follow the chapter's Summary.]

Pennsylvania Company produces a product that passes through two processes: grinding and mixing
Information related to its grinding department manufacturing activities for July follows. The company
uses the weighted-average method of process costing.

Grinding Department
Raw Materials

Beginning inventory	$100,000
Raw materials purchased on credit	211,400
Direct materials used	(190,000)
Indirect materials used	(51,400)
Ending inventory	$ 70,000

Factory Payroll

Direct labor incurred	$ 55,500
Indirect labor incurred	50,625
Total payroll	$106,125

Factory Overhead

Indirect materials used	$ 51,400
Indirect labor used	50,625
Other overhead costs	71,725
Total factory overhead incurred	$173,750

Factory Overhead Applied

Overhead applied (200% of direct labor)	$111,000

Grinding Department

Beginning work in process inventory (units)	5,000
Percentage completed—Materials	100%
Percentage completed—Conversion	70%
Beginning work in process inventory (costs)	
Direct materials used	$ 20,000
Direct labor incurred	9,600
Overhead applied (200% of direct labor)	19,200
Total costs of beginning work in process	$ 48,800
Units started this period	20,000
Units transferred to mixing this period	17,000
Ending work in process inventory (units)	8,000
Percentage completed—Materials	100%
Percentage completed—Conversion	20%

Required

Complete the requirements below for the grinding department.
1. Prepare a physical flow reconciliation for July.
2. Compute the equivalent units of production in July for direct materials and conversion.
3. Compute the costs per equivalent units of production in July for direct materials and conversion.
4. Prepare a report of costs accounted for and a report of costs to account for.

PLANNING THE SOLUTION

- Track the physical flow to determine the number of units completed in July.
- Compute the equivalent units of production for direct materials and conversion.
- Compute the costs per equivalent unit of production with respect to direct materials and conversion and determine the cost per unit for each.
- Compute the total cost of the goods transferred to mixing by using the equivalent units and unit costs. Determine (a) the cost of the beginning work in process inventory, (b) the materials and conversion costs added to the beginning work in process inventory, and (c) the materials and conversion costs added to the units started and completed in the month.

SOLUTION

1. Physical flow reconciliation.

Units to Account For		Units Accounted For	
Beginning work in process inventory	5,000 units	Units completed and transferred out	17,000 units
Units started this period	20,000 units	Ending work in process inventory	8,000 units
Total units to account for	**25,000 units**	Total units accounted for	**25,000 units**

reconciled

. Equivalent units of production (weighted-average).

Equivalent Units of Production	Direct Materials	Conversion
Equivalent units completed and transferred out ...	17,000 EUP	17,000 EUP
Equivalent units in ending work in process		
Direct materials (8,000 × 100%).............	8,000 EUP	
Conversion (8,000 × 20%).................		1,600 EUP
Equivalent units of production	25,000 EUP	18,600 EUP

. Costs per equivalent unit of production (weighted-average).

Costs per Equivalent Unit of Production	Direct Materials	Conversion
Costs of beginning work in process	$ 20,000	$ 28,800
Costs incurred this period	190,000	166,500*
Total costs..................................	$210,000	$195,300
÷ Equivalent units of production (from part 2)	25,000 EUP	18,600 EUP
= Costs per equivalent unit of production	$8.40 per EUP	$10.50 per EUP

*Direct labor of $55,500 + overhead applied of $111,000

. Reports of costs accounted for and of costs to account for (weighted-average).

Report of Costs Accounted For

Cost of units transferred out (cost of goods manufactured)
Direct materials ($8.40 per EUP × 17,000 EUP) $142,800
Conversion ($10.50 per EUP × 17,000 EUP) 178,500
Cost of units completed this period .... $ 321,300

Cost of ending work in process inventory
Direct materials ($8.40 per EUP × 8,000 EUP) 67,200
Conversion ($10.50 per EUP × 1,600 EUP) 16,800
Cost of ending work in process inventory 84,000
Total costs accounted for .... **$405,300** ◄

Report of Costs to Account For

Cost of beginning work in process inventory
Direct materials .... $ 20,000
Conversion .... 28,800 $ 48,800

Cost incurred this period
Direct materials 190,000
Conversion 166,500   356,500
Total costs to account for .... **$405,300** ◄

reconciled

NEED-TO-KNOW

COMPREHENSIVE 2

FIFO Method

Refer to the information given for the weighted-average method version of this Comprehensive Need-To-Know. For the grinding department, complete requirements 1 through 4 using the FIFO method. (Round the cost per equivalent unit of conversion to two decimal places.)

SOLUTION

1. Physical flow reconciliation (FIFO).

Units to Account For		Units Accounted For	
Beginning work in process inventory..........	5,000 units	Units completed and transferred out...................	17,000 units
Units started this period......	20,000 units	Ending work in process inventory......	8,000 units
Total units to account for.....	**25,000 units**	Total units accounted for.............	**25,000 units**

reconciled

2. Equivalent units of production (FIFO).

Equivalent Units of Production	Direct Materials	Conversion
(a) Equivalent units complete beginning work in process		
Direct materials (5,000 × 0%).........................	0 EUP	
Conversion (5,000 × 30%).............................		1,500 EUP
(b) Equivalent units started and completed...................	12,000 EUP	12,000 EUP
(c) Equivalent units in ending work in process		
Direct materials (8,000 × 100%).......................	8,000 EUP	
Conversion (8,000 × 20%)............................		1,600 EUP
Equivalent units of production............................	20,000 EUP	15,100 EUP

3. Costs per equivalent unit of production (FIFO).

Costs per Equivalent Unit of Production	Direct Materials	Conversion
Costs incurred this period..........................	$190,000	$166,500
÷ Equivalent units of production (from part 2).........	20,000 EUP	15,100 EUP
= Costs per equivalent unit of production	$9.50 per EUP	$11.03 per EUP**

*Direct labor of $55,500 plus overhead applied of $111,000   **Rounded

4. Reports of costs accounted for and of costs to account for (FIFO).

Report of Costs Accounted For
Cost of units transferred out (cost of goods manufactured)

Cost of beginning work in process inventory............................		$ 48,800
Cost to complete beginning work in process		
Direct materials ($9.50 per EUP × 0 EUP)	$ 0	
Conversion ($11.03 per EUP × 1,500 EUP).........................	16,545	16,545
Cost of units started and completed this period		
Direct materials ($9.50 per EUP × 12,000 EUP)	114,000	
Conversion ($11.03 per EUP × 12,000 EUP).........................	132,360	246,360
Total cost of units finished this period		311,705
Cost of ending work in process inventory		
Direct materials ($9.50 per EUP × 8,000 EUP)	76,000	
Conversion ($11.03 per EUP × 1,600 EUP).........................	17,648	
Total cost of ending work in process inventory.........................		93,648
Total costs accounted for		**$405,353** ◄
Report of Costs to Account For		
Cost of beginning work in process inventory		
Direct materials	$ 20,000	
Conversion	28,800	$ 48,800
Costs incurred this period		
Direct materials	190,000	
Conversion	166,500	356,500
Total costs to account for		**$405,300** ◄

reconciled (with $53 rounding difference)

Garcia Manufacturing produces a product that passes through a molding process and then through an assembly process. Partial information related to its manufacturing activities for July follows.

COMPREHENSIVE 3

Journal Entries for
Process Costing

Direct materials

Raw materials purchased on credit	$400,000
Direct materials used—Molding	190,000
Direct materials used—Assembly	88,600

Direct Labor

Direct labor—Molding	$ 42,000
Direct labor—Assembly.............	55,375

Factory Overhead (Actual costs)

Indirect materials used	$ 51,400
Indirect labor used	50,625
Other overhead costs	71,725
Total factory overhead incurred	$173,750

Factory Overhead Applied

Molding (150% of direct labor)..........	$ 63,000
Assembly (200% of direct labor)	110,750
Total factory overhead applied..........	$173,750

Cost Transfers

From molding to assembly	$277,200
From assembly to finished goods........	578,400
From finished goods to cost of goods sold.....................	506,100

Required

Prepare summary journal entries to record the transactions and events of July for: (a) raw materials purchases, (b) direct materials usage, (c) indirect materials usage, (d) direct labor usage, (e) indirect labor usage, (f) other overhead costs (credit Other Accounts), (g) application of overhead to the two departments, (h) transfer of partially completed goods from molding to assembly, (i) transfer of finished goods out of assembly, and (j) the cost of goods sold.

SOLUTION

Summary journal entries for the transactions and events in July.

a.	Raw Materials Inventory..................	400,000	
	Accounts Payable		400,000
	To record raw materials purchases.		
b.	Work in Process Inventory—Molding	190,000	
	Work in Process Inventory—Assembly	88,600	
	Raw Materials Inventory..............		278,600
	To record direct materials usage.		
c.	Factory Overhead	51,400	
	Raw Materials Inventory		51,400
	To record indirect materials usage.		
d.	Work in Process Inventory—Molding	42,000	
	Work in Process Inventory—Assembly	55,375	
	Factory Payroll Payable..............		97,375
	To record direct labor usage.		
e.	Factory Overhead......................	50,625	
	Factory Payroll Payable..............		50,625
	To record indirect labor usage.		

f.	Factory Overhead......................	71,725	
	Other Accounts		71,725
	To record other overhead costs.		
g.	Work in Process Inventory—Molding	63,000	
	Work in Process Inventory—Assembly......	110,750	
	Factory Overhead		173,750
	To record application of overhead.		
h.	Work in Process Inventory—Assembly......	277,200	
	Work in Process Inventory—Molding ...		277,200
	To record transfer of partially completed goods from molding to assembly.		
i.	Finished Goods Inventory	578,400	
	Work in Process Inventory—Assembly..		578,400
	To record transfer of finished goods out of assembly.		
j.	Cost of Goods Sold	506,100	
	Finished Goods Inventory		506,100
	To record cost of goods sold.		

APPENDIX

FIFO Method of Process Costing

3A

The FIFO method of process costing assigns costs to units assuming a first-in, first-out flow of product. The key difference between the FIFO and weighted-average methods lies in the treatment of beginning work in process inventory. Under the weighted-average method, the number of units and the costs in beginning work in process inventory are combined with production activity in the current period to compute

C4____

Appendix—Describe accounting for production activity and preparation of a process cost summary using FIFO.

costs per equivalent unit. Thus, the weighted-average method combines production activity across two periods.

The FIFO method, in contrast, focuses on production activity *in the current period only*. The FIFO method assumes that the units that were in process at the beginning of the period are completed during the current period. Thus, under the FIFO method equivalent units of production are computed as shown in Exhibit 3A.1.

EXHIBIT 3A.1

Computing EUP—FIFO Method

$$
\begin{array}{rcl}
\text{Equivalent units of} & = & \text{Number of equivalent} \\
\text{production (EUP)} & & \text{units needed to complete} \\
& & \text{beginning work in} \\
& & \text{process inventory}
\end{array}
+
\begin{array}{c}
\text{Number of whole units} \\
\text{started, completed, and} \\
\text{transferred to the next} \\
\text{department*}
\end{array}
+
\begin{array}{c}
\text{Number of equivalent} \\
\text{units in ending work} \\
\text{in process inventory}
\end{array}
$$

*Or to Finished Goods Inventory

In computing cost per equivalent unit, the FIFO method ignores the cost of beginning work in process inventory. Instead, FIFO uses *only the costs incurred in the current period*, as shown in Exhibit 3A.2.

EXHIBIT 3A.2

Cost per EUP—FIFO Method

$$
\text{Cost per EUP (FIFO)} = \frac{\text{Manufacturing costs added during the current period}}{\text{Equivalent units of production during current period}}
$$

We use the data in Exhibit 3A.3 to illustrate the FIFO method for GenX's roasting department.

EXHIBIT 3A.3

Production Data—Roasting Department

GenX—Roasting Department	
Beginning work in process inventory (March 31)	
Units of product	30,000 units
Percentage of completion—Direct materials	100%
Percentage of completion—Conversion costs	65%
Direct materials costs	$ 81,000
Conversion costs	$108,900
Activities during the current period (April)	
Units started this period	90,000 units
Units transferred out (completed)	100,000 units
Direct materials costs	$279,000
Direct labor costs	$171,000
Factory overhead costs applied (120% of direct labor)	$205,200
Ending work in process inventory (April 30)	
Units of product	20,000 units
Percentage of completion—Direct materials	100%
Percentage of completion—Conversion	25%

Exhibit 3A.3 shows selected information from GenX's roasting department for the month of April. Accounting for a department's activity for a period includes four steps: (1) determine physical flow, (2) compute equivalent units, (3) compute cost per equivalent unit, and (4) determine cost assignment and reconciliation. This appendix describes each of these steps using the FIFO method for process costing.

Step 1: Determine Physical Flow of Units   A *physical flow reconciliation* is a report that reconciles (1) the physical units started in a period with (2) the physical units completed in that period. The physical flow reconciliation for GenX's roasting department is shown in Exhibit 3A.4 for April.

EXHIBIT 3A.4

Physical Flow Reconciliation

GenX—Roasting Department			
Units to Account For		**Units Accounted For**	
Beginning work in process inventory	30,000 units	Units completed and transferred out	100,000 units
Units started this period	90,000 units	Ending work in process inventory	20,000 units
Total units to account for	**120,000 units**	Total units accounted for	**120,000 units**

reconciled

Step 2: Compute Equivalent Units of Production—FIFO   Exhibit 3A.4 shows that the roasting department completed 100,000 units during the month. The FIFO method assumes that the units in beginning inventory were the first units completed during the month. Thus, FIFO assumes that of the 100,000 completed units, 30,000 consist of units in beginning work in process inventory that were completed during the month. This means that 70,000 (100,000 − 30,000) units were both started and completed during the month. This also means that 20,000 units were started but not completed during the month (90,000 units started − 70,000 units started and completed). Exhibit 3A.5 shows how units flowed through the roasting department, assuming FIFO.

EXHIBIT 3A.5

FIFO—Flow of Units

Roasting Department—Units		
Beg. inv.	30,000	→30,000 Completed and transferred out
Started	90,000	70,000 Started and completed
Total	120,000	
		100,000 Transferred out
End. inv.	20,000	

In computing the equivalent units of production, the roasting department must consider these three distinct groups of units:

Units in beginning work in process inventory (30,000).
Units started and completed during the month (70,000).
Units in ending work in process inventory (20,000).

GenX's roasting department then computes equivalent units of production under FIFO as shown in Exhibit 3A.6. We compute EUP for each of the three distinct groups of units, and sum them to find total EUP.

EXHIBIT 3A.6

Equivalent Units of Production—FIFO

GenX—Roasting Department		
Equivalent Units of Production	Direct Materials	Conversion
(a) Equivalent units to complete beginning work in process		
Direct materials (30,000 × 0%)	0 EUP	
Conversion (30,000 × 35%)		10,500 EUP
(b) Equivalent units started and completed*	70,000 EUP	70,000 EUP
(c) Equivalent units in ending work in process		
Direct materials (20,000 × 100%)	20,000 EUP	
Conversion (20,000 × 25%)		5,000 EUP
Equivalent units of production	90,000 EUP	85,500 EUP

*Units completed this period .... 100,000 units
Less units in beginning work in process .... 30,000 units
Units started and completed this period .... 70,000 units

Direct Materials   To calculate the equivalent units of production for direct materials, we start with the equivalent units in beginning work in process inventory. We see that beginning work in process inventory was 100% complete with respect to materials; no materials were needed to complete these units. Thus, this group of units required 0 EUP during the month. Next, we consider the units started and completed during the month. In terms of direct materials, the 70,000 units started and completed during the month received 100% of their materials during the month. Thus, EUP for this group is 70,000 units (70,000 × 100%). Finally, we consider the units in ending work in process inventory. The roasting department started but *did not* complete 20,000 units during the month. This group received all of its materials during the month. Thus, EUP for this group is 20,000 units (20,000 × 100%). The sum of the EUP for these three distinct groups of units is 90,000 (computed as 0 + 70,000 + 20,000), which is the total number of equivalent units of production for direct materials during the month.

Conversion   To calculate the equivalent units of production for conversion, we start by determining the percentage of conversion costs needed to complete the beginning work in process inventory. As Exhibit 3A.3 shows, the beginning work in process inventory of 30,000 units was 65% complete with respect to conversion. Thus, this group of units required an additional 35% of conversion costs during the period t̶ complete those units (100% − 65%), or 10,500 EUP (30,000 × 35%). Next, we consider the units starte̶ and completed during the month. The units started and completed during the month incurred 100% o̶ their conversion costs during the month. Thus, EUP for this group is 70,000 units (70,000 × 100%̶ Finally, we consider the units in ending work in process inventor̶ incurred 25% of its conversion costs (see Exhibit 3A.3) during the month. Thus, EUP for this group i̶ 5,000 units (20,000 × 25%). The sum of the EUP for these three distinct groups of units is 85,500 (con̶ puted as 10,500 + 70,000 + 5,000). Thus, the roasting department's equivalent units of production fo̶ conversion for the month is 85,500 units.

NEED-TO-KNOW 3-5

EUP—Direct Materials and Conversion (FIFO)

C4

A department began the month with 50,000 units in work in process inventory. These units were 60̶ complete with respect to direct materials and 40% complete with respect to conversion. During the mon̶ the department started 286,000 units; 220,000 of these units were completed during the month. The re̶ maining 66,000 units are in ending work in process inventory, 80% complete with respect to direct mater̶ als and 30% complete with respect to conversion. Use the FIFO method of process costing to:

1. Compute the department's equivalent units of production for the month for direct materials.
2. Compute the department's equivalent units of production for the month for conversion.

Solution

Do More: QS 3-14, QS 3-15,
E 3-5, E 3-10

1. EUP for materials = (50,000 × 40%) + (220,000 × 100%) + (66,000 × 80%) = 292,800 EUP
2. EUP for conversion = (50,000 × 60%) + (220,000 × 100%) + (66,000 × 30%) = 269,800 EUP

Step 3: Compute Cost per Equivalent Unit—FIFO   To compute cost per equivalent uni̶ we take the direct materials and conversion costs added in April and divide by the equivalent units of pr̶ duction from step 2. Exhibit 3A.7 illustrates these computations.

EXHIBIT 3A.7

Cost per Equivalent Unit of Production—FIFO

GenX—Roasting Department		
Cost per Equivalent Unit of Production	**Direct Materials**	**Conversion**
Costs incurred this period (from Exhibit 3A.3)	$279,000	$376,200
÷ Equivalent units of production (from step 2)	90,000 EUP	85,500 EUP
Cost per equivalent unit of production	$3.10 per EUP	$4.40 per EUP

It is essential to compute costs per equivalent unit for *each* input because production inputs are added a̶ different times in the process. The FIFO method computes the cost per equivalent unit based solely on thi̶ period's EUP and costs (unlike the weighted-average method, which adds in the costs of the beginnin̶ work in process inventory).

NEED-TO-KNOW 3-6

Cost per EUP—Direct Materials and Conversion (FIFO)

C4

A department started the month with beginning work in process inventory of $130,000 ($90,000 for direc̶ materials and $40,000 for conversion). During the month, the department incurred additional direct mate̶ rials costs of $700,000 and conversion costs of $500,000. Assume that equivalent units for the month wer̶ computed as 250,000 for materials and 200,000 for conversion.

1. Compute the department's cost per equivalent unit of production for the month for direct materials.
2. Compute the department's cost per equivalent unit of production for the month for conversion.

Solution

Do More: QS 3-15, QS 3-17,
E 3-7

1. Cost per EUP of materials = $700,000/250,000 = $2.80
2. Cost per EUP of conversion = $500,000/200,000 = $2.50

Step 4: Assign and Reconcile Costs   The equivalent units determined in step 2 and the cost per equivalent unit computed in step 3 are both used to assign costs (1) to units that the production department completed and transferred to the blending department and (2) to units that remain in process at period-end.

In Exhibit 3A.8, under the section for cost of units transferred out, we see that the cost of units completed in April includes the $189,900 cost carried over from March for work already applied to the 30,000 units that make up beginning work in process inventory, plus the $46,200 incurred in April to complete those units. This section also includes the $525,000 of cost assigned to the 70,000 units started and completed this period. Thus, the total cost of goods manufactured in April is $761,100. The average cost per unit for goods completed in April is $7.611 ($761,100 ÷ 100,000 completed units).

EXHIBIT 3A.8

Report of Costs Accounted For—FIFO

Cost of units transferred out (cost of goods manufactured)		
Cost of beginning work in process inventory..........................		$ 189,900
Cost to complete beginning work in process		
Direct materials ($3.10 per EUP × 0 EUP)..........................	$ 0	
Conversion ($4.40 per EUP × 10,500 EUP)..........................	46,200	46,200
Cost of units started and completed this period		
Direct materials ($3.10 per EUP × 70,000 EUP).....................	217,000	
Conversion ($4.40 per EUP × 70,000 EUP).........................	308,000	525,000
Total cost of units finished this period..............................		761,100
Cost of ending work in process inventory		
Direct materials ($3.10 per EUP × 20,000 EUP).....................	62,000	
Conversion ($4.40 per EUP × 5,000 EUP)...........................	22,000	
Total cost of ending work in process inventory......................		84,000
Total costs accounted for...		**$845,100**

The computation for cost of ending work in process inventory is in the lower part of Exhibit 3A.8. That cost of $84,000 ($62,000 + $22,000) also is the ending balance for the Work in Process Inventory—Roasting account.

The roasting department manager verifies that the total costs assigned to units transferred out and units still in process equal the total costs incurred by production. We reconcile the costs accounted for (in Exhibit 3A.8.) to the costs that production was charged for as shown in Exhibit 3A.9.

EXHIBIT 3A.9

Report of Costs to Account For—FIFO

Cost of beginning work in process inventory		
Direct materials	$ 81,000	
Conversion	108,900	$ 189,900
Costs incurred this period		
Direct materials	279,000	
Conversion	376,200	655,200
Total costs to account for		**$845,100**

The roasting department production manager is responsible for $845,100 in costs: $189,900 that had been assigned to the department's work in process inventory as of April 1 plus $655,200 of costs the department incurred in April. At period-end, the manager must identify where those costs were assigned. The production manager can report that $761,100 of cost was assigned to units completed in April and $84,000 was assigned to units still in process at period-end.

Process Cost Summary   The final report is the process cost summary, which summarizes key information from previous exhibits. Reasons for the summary are to (1) help managers control and monitor costs, (2) help upper management assess department manager performance, and (3) provide cost information for financial reporting. The process cost summary, using FIFO, for GenX's roasting department is in Exhibit 3A.10. Section ① lists the total costs charged to the department, including direct materials and conversion costs incurred, as well as the cost of the beginning work in process inventory. Section ② describes the equivalent units of production for the department. Equivalent units for conversion are in separate columns. It also reports direct materials and conversion costs per equivalent unit. Section ③ allocates total costs among units worked on in the period.

EXHIBIT 3A.10

Process Cost Summary
(FIFO)

GenX COMPANY— ROASTING DEPARTMENT
Process Cost Summary (FIFO Method)
For Month Ended April 30, 2015

Costs charged to production

Costs of beginning work in process inventory

Direct materials		$ 81,000	
Conversion		108,900	$ 189,900

Costs incurred this period

Direct materials		279,000	
Conversion		376,200	655,200
Total costs to account for			$845,100 ◄

Unit information

Units to account for		Units accounted for	
Beginning work in process	30,000	Transferred out	100,000
Units started this period	90,000	Ending work in process	20,000
Total units to account for	120,000	Total units accounted for	120,000

Equivalent units of production	**Direct Materials**	**Conversion**
Equivalent units to complete beginning work in process		
Direct materials (30,000 × 0%)	0 EUP	
Conversion (30,000 × 35%)		10,500 EUP
Equivalent units started and completed	70,000 EUP	70,000 EUP
Equivalent units in ending work in process		
Direct materials (20,000 × 100%)	20,000 EUP	
Conversion (20,000 × 25%)		5,000 EUP
Equivalent units of production	90,000 EUP	85,500 EUP

Cost per equivalent unit of production	**Direct Materials**	**Conversion**
Costs incurred this period	$279,000	$376,200
÷ Equivalent units of production	90,000 EUP	85,500 EUP
Cost per equivalent unit of production	$3.10 per EUP	$4.40 per EUP

Cost assignment and reconciliation

(cost of units completed and transferred out)

Cost of beginning work in process			$ 189,900
Cost to complete beginning work in process			
Direct materials ($3.10 per EUP × 0 EUP)		$ 0	
Conversion ($4.40 per EUP × 10,500 EUP)		46,200	46,200
Cost of units started and completed this period			
Direct materials ($3.10 per EUP × 70,000 EUP)		217,000	
Conversion ($4.40 per EUP × 70,000 EUP)		308,000	525,000
Total cost of units finished this period			761,100
Cost of ending work in process			
Direct materials ($3.10 per EUP × 20,000 EUP)		62,000	
Conversion ($4.40 per EUP × 5,000 EUP)		22,000	
Total cost of ending work in process			84,000
Total costs accounted for			$845,100 ◄

■ **Decision Maker** ▬▬▬▬▬▬▬▬▬▬▬▬▬▬▬▬▬▬▬▬▬▬▬▬▬▬

Cost Manager As cost manager for an electronics manufacturer, you apply a process costing system using FIFO. Your company plans to adopt a just-in-time system and eliminate inventories. What is the impact of the use of FIFO (versus the weighted-average method) given these plans? ■ [Answers follow the chapter's Summary.]

Summary

C1 **Explain process operations and the way they differ from job order operations.** Process operations produce large quantities of similar products or services by passing them through a series of processes, or steps, in production. Like job order operations, they combine direct materials, direct labor, and overhead in the operations. Unlike job order operations that assign the responsibility for each job to a manager, process operations assign the responsibility for each *process* to a manager.

C2 **Define and compute equivalent units and explain their use in process costing.** Equivalent units of production measure the activity of a process as the number of units that would be completed in a period if all effort had been applied to units that were started and finished. This measure of production activity is used to compute the cost per equivalent unit and to assign costs to finished goods and work in process inventory. To compute equivalent units, determine the number of units that would have been finished if all materials (or conversion) had been used to produce units that were started and completed during the period. The costs incurred by a process are divided by its equivalent units to yield cost per equivalent unit.

C3 **Describe accounting for production activity and preparation of a process cost summary using weighted average.** A process cost summary reports on the activities of a production process or department for a period. It describes the costs charged to the department, the equivalent units of production for the department, and the costs assigned to the output. The report aims to (1) help managers control their departments, (2) help factory managers evaluate department managers' performances, and (3) provide cost information for financial statements. A process cost summary includes the physical flow of units, equivalent units of production, costs per equivalent unit, and a cost reconciliation. It reports the units and costs to account for during the period and how they were accounted for during the period. In terms of units, the summary includes the beginning work in process inventory and the units started during the month. These units are accounted for in terms of the goods completed and transferred out, and the ending work in process inventory. With respect to costs, the summary includes materials and conversion costs assigned to the process during the period. It shows how these costs are assigned to goods completed and transferred out, and to ending work in process inventory.

C4 *Appendix—Describe accounting for production activity and preparation of a process cost summary using FIFO.* The FIFO method for process costing is applied and illustrated to (1) report the physical flow of units, (2) compute the equivalent units of production, (3) compute the cost per equivalent unit of production, and (4) assign and reconcile costs.

A1 **Compare process costing and job order costing.** Process and job order manufacturing operations are similar in that both combine materials, and conversion to produce products or services. They differ in the way they are organized and managed. In job order operations, the job order costing system assigns product costs to specific jobs. In process operations, the process costing system assigns product costs to specific processes. The total costs associated with each process are then divided by the number of units passing through that process to get cost per equivalent unit. The costs per equivalent unit for all processes are added to determine the total cost per unit of a product or service.

A2 **Explain and illustrate a hybrid costing system.** A hybrid costing system contains features of both job order and process costing systems. Generally, certain direct materials are accounted for by individual products as in job order costing, but direct labor and overhead costs are accounted for similar to process costing.

P1 **Record the flow of materials costs in process costing.** Materials purchased are debited to a Raw Materials Inventory account. As direct materials are issued to processes, they are separately accumulated in a Work in Process Inventory account for that process. As indirect materials are used their costs are debited to Factory Overhead.

P2 **Record the flow of labor costs in process costing.** Direct labor costs are assigned to the Work in Process Inventory account pertaining to each process. As indirect labor is used its cost is debited to Factory Overhead.

P3 **Record the flow of factory overhead costs in process costing.** Actual overhead costs are recorded as debits to the Factory Overhead account. Estimated overhead costs are allocated, using a predetermined overhead rate, to the different processes. This allocated amount is credited to the Factory Overhead account and debited to the Work in Process Inventory account for each separate process.

P4 **Record the transfer of goods across departments, to Finished Goods Inventory, and to Cost of Goods Sold.** As units are passed through processes, their accumulated costs are transferred across separate Work in Process Inventory accounts for each process. As units complete the final process and are eventually sold, their accumulated cost is transferred to Finished Goods Inventory and finally to Cost of Goods Sold.

Guidance Answers to Decision Maker and Decision Ethics

Budget Officer By instructing you to classify a majority of costs as indirect, the manager is passing some of his department's costs to a common overhead pool that other departments will partially absorb. Since overhead costs are allocated on the basis of direct labor for this company and the new department has a relatively low direct labor cost, the new department will be assigned less overhead. Such action suggests unethical behavior

by this manager. You must object to such reclassification. If this manager refuses to comply, you must inform someone in a more senior position.

Entrepreneur By spreading the added quality-related costs across three customers, the entrepreneur is probably trying to remain competitive with respect to the customer that demands the

100% quality inspection. Moreover, the entrepreneur is partly covering the added costs by recovering two-thirds of them from the other two customers who are paying 110% of total costs. This act likely breaches the trust placed by the two customers in this entrepreneur's application of its costing system. The costing system should be changed, and the entrepreneur should consider renegotiating the pricing and/or quality test agreement with this one customer (at the risk of losing this currently loss-producing customer).

Cost Manager   Differences between the FIFO and weighted average methods are greatest when large work in process inventories exist and when costs fluctuate. The method used if inventories are eliminated does not matter; both produce identical costs.

Key Terms

Conversion cost per equivalent unit

Equivalent units of production (EUP)

FIFO method

Job order costing system

Materials consumption report

Process costing system

Process cost summary

Process operations

Weighted-average method

Multiple Choice Quiz   Answers at end of chapter

1. Equivalent units of production are equal to
   a. Physical units that were completed this period from all effort being applied to them.
   b. The number of units introduced into the process this period.
   c. The number of finished units actually completed this period.
   d. The number of units that could have been started and completed given the cost incurred.
   e. The number of units in the process at the end of the period.

2. Recording the cost of raw materials purchased for use in a process costing system includes a
   a. Credit to Raw Materials Inventory.
   b. Debit to Work in Process Inventory.
   c. Debit to Factory Overhead.
   d. Credit to Factory Overhead.
   e. Debit to Raw Materials Inventory.

3. The production department started the month with a beginning work in process inventory of $20,000. During the month, it was assigned the following costs: direct materials, $152,000; direct labor, $45,000; overhead applied at the rate of 40% of direct labor cost. Inventory with a cost of $218,000 was transferred to finished goods. The ending balance of work in process inventory is

   a. $330,000.
   b. $ 17,000.
   c. $220,000.
   d. $112,000.
   e. $118,000.

4. A company's beginning work in process inventory consists of 10,000 units that are 20% complete with respect to conversion costs. A total of 40,000 units are completed this period. There are 15,000 units in work in process, one-third complete for conversion, at period-end. The equivalent units of production (EUP) with respect to conversion at period-end, assuming the weighted-average method, are
   a. 45,000 EUP.
   b. 40,000 EUP.
   c.   5,000 EUP.
   d. 37,000 EUP.
   e. 43,000 EUP.

5. Assume the same information as in question 4. Also assume that beginning work in process had $6,000 in conversion cost and that $84,000 in conversion is added during this period. What is the cost per EUP for conversion?
   a. $0.50 per EUP
   b. $1.87 per EUP
   c. $2.00 per EUP
   d. $2.10 per EUP
   e. $2.25 per EUP

A
  Superscript letter A denotes assignments based on Appendix 3A.

🔲 Icon denotes assignments that involve decision making.

Discussion Questions

1. 🔲 What is the main factor for a company in choosing between the job order costing and process costing systems? Give two likely applications of each system.

2. The focus in a job order costing system is the job or batch. Identify the main focus in process costing.

3. 🔲 Can services be delivered by means of process operations? Support your answer with an example.

4. Are the journal entries that match cost flows to product flows in process costing primarily the same or much different than those in job order costing? Explain.

5. Identify the control document for materials flow when a materials requisition slip is not used.

6. 🔋 Explain in simple terms the notion of equivalent units of production (EUP). Why is it necessary to use EUP in process costing?

7. 🔋 What are the two main inventory methods used in process costing? What are the differences between these methods?

8. 🔋 Why is it possible for direct labor in process operations to include the labor of employees who do not work directly on products or services?

9. Assume that a company produces a single product by processing it first through a single production department. Direct labor costs flow through what accounts in this company's process cost system?

10. At the end of a period, what balance should remain in the Factory Overhead account?

11. 🔋 Is it possible to have under- or overapplied overhead costs in a process costing system? Explain.

12. Explain why equivalent units of production for both direct labor and overhead can be the same as, and why they can be different from, equivalent units for direct materials.

13. Companies such as **Samsung** apply process operations. List the four steps in accounting for production activity in a reporting period (for process operations). **Samsung**

14. Companies such as **Apple** commonly prepare a process cost summary. What purposes does a process cost summary serve? **APPLE**

15. 🔋 Are there situations where Google can use process costing? Identify at least one and explain it. **GOOGLE**

16. 🔋 **Samsung** produces digital televisions with a multiple process production line. Identify and list some of its production processing steps and departments. **Samsung**

⬛ **connect**

For each of the following products and services, indicate whether it is more likely produced in a process operation or in a job order operation.

_____ **1.** Tennis courts

_____ **2.** Organic juice

_____ **3.** Audit of financial statements

_____ **4.** Luxury yachts

_____ **5.** Vanilla ice cream

_____ **6.** Tennis balls

QUICK STUDY

QS 3-1
Process vs. job order
operations **C1**

Label each statement below as either true ("T") or false ("F").

_____ **1.** The cost per equivalent unit is computed as the total costs of a process divided by the number of equivalent units passing through that process.

_____ **2.** Service companies are not able to use process costing.

_____ **3.** Costs per job are computed in both job order and process costing systems.

_____ **4.** Job order and process operations both combine materials, labor, and overhead in producing products or services.

QS 3-2
Process vs. job order
costing

A1

For each of the following products and services, indicate whether it is more likely produced in a process operation or a job order operation.

_____ **1.** Beach toys

_____ **2.** Concrete swimming pool

_____ **3.** iPhones

_____ **4.** Wedding reception

_____ **5.** Custom suits

_____ **6.** Juice

_____ **7.** Tattoos

_____ **8.** Guitar picks

QS 3-3
Process vs. job order
operations

C1

The following refers to units processed in Sunflower Printing's binding department in March. Prepare a physical flow reconciliation.

QS 3-4
Physical flow
reconciliation

C2

	Units of Product	Percent of Conversion Added
Beginning work in process..........	150,000	80%
Goods started	310,000	100
Goods completed	340,000	100
Ending work in process	120,000	25

QS 3-5
Weighted average:
Computing equivalent
units of production   C2

Refer to QS 3-4. Compute the total equivalent units of production with respect to conversion for March using the weighted-average inventory method.

QS 3-6[A]
FIFO: Computing
equivalent units   C4

Refer to QS 3-4. Compute the total equivalent units of production with respect to conversion for March using the FIFO inventory method.

QS 3-7
Weighted average:
Cost per EUP

C3

A production department's beginning inventory cost includes $394,900 of conversion costs. This department incurs an additional $907,500 in conversion costs in the month of March. Equivalent units of production for conversion total 740,000 for March. Calculate the cost per equivalent unit of conversion using the weighted-average method.

QS 3-8
Weighted average:
Computing equivalent
units of production

C2

The following refers to units processed by an ice cream maker in July. Compute the total equivalent units of production with respect to conversion for July using the weighted-average inventory method.

	Gallons of Product	Percent of Conversion Added
Beginning work in process	320,000	25%
Goods started	620,000	100
Goods completed	680,000	100
Ending work in process	260,000	75

QS 3-9[A]
FIFO: Computing
equivalent units   C4

Refer to QS 3-8 and compute the total equivalent units of production with respect to conversion for July using the FIFO inventory method.

QS 3-10
Weighted average:
Equivalent units of
production   C2

The following information applies to QS 3-10 through QS 3-17.

The Carlberg Company has two manufacturing departments, assembly and painting. The assembly department started 10,000 units during November. The following production activity unit and cost information refers to the assembly department's November production activities.

Assembly Department	Units	Percent of Direct Materials Added	Percent of Conversion Added
Beginning work in process.........	2,000	60%	40%
Units transferred out.............	9,000	100%	100%
Ending work in process	3,000	80%	30%

Beginning work in process inventory—Assembly dept.....................	$1,581 (includes $996 for direct materials and $585 for conversion)
Costs added during the month:	
Direct materials............................	$10,404
Conversion................................	$12,285

Required

Calculate the assembly department's equivalent units of production for materials and for conversion for November. Use the weighted-average method.

QS 3-11
Weighted average:
Cost per EUP   C2

Refer to the information in QS 3-10. Calculate the assembly department's cost per equivalent unit of production for materials and for conversion for November. Use the weighted-average method.

Refer to the information in QS 3-10. Assign costs to the assembly department's output—specifically, the units transferred out to the painting department and the units that remain in process in the assembly department at month-end. Use the weighted-average method.

QS 3-12
Weighted average:
Assign costs to output C3

Refer to the information in QS 3-10. Prepare the November 30 journal entry to record the transfer of units (and costs) from the assembly department to the painting department. Use the weighted-average method.

QS 3-13
Weighted average:
Journal entry to transfer costs P4

Refer to the information in QS 3-10. Calculate the assembly department's equivalent units of production for materials and for conversion for November. Use the FIFO method.

QS 3-14[A]
FIFO: Equivalent units of production C4

Refer to the information in QS 3-10. Calculate the assembly department's cost per equivalent unit of production for materials and for conversion for November. Use the FIFO method.

QS 3-15[A]
FIFO: Cost per EUP C4

Refer to the information in QS 3-10. Assign costs to the assembly department's output—specifically, the units transferred out to the painting department and the units that remain in process in the assembly department at month-end. Use the FIFO method.

QS 3-16[A]
FIFO: Assign costs to output C4

Refer to the information in QS 3-10. Prepare the November 30 journal entry to record the transfer of units (and costs) from the assembly department to the painting department. Use the FIFO method.

QS 3-17[A]
FIFO: Journal entry to transfer costs C4 P4

The Plastic Flowerpots Company has two manufacturing departments, molding and packaging. At the beginning of the month, the molding department has 2,000 units in inventory, 70% complete as to materials. During the month, the molding department started 18,000 units. At the end of the month, the molding department had 3,000 units in ending inventory, 80% complete as to materials. Units completed in the molding department are transferred into the packaging department.

Cost information for the molding department for the month follows:

QS 3-18
Weighted average:
Computing equivalent units and cost per EUP (direct materials)
C2 C3

Beginning work in process inventory (direct materials)....	$ 1,200
Direct materials added during the month.............	27,900

Using the weighted-average method, compute the molding department's (a) equivalent units of production for materials and (b) cost per equivalent unit of production for materials for the month. (Round to two decimal places.)

Refer to information in QS 3-18. Using the weighted-average method, assign direct materials costs to the molding department's output—specifically, the units transferred out to the packaging department and the units that remain in process in the molding department at month-end.

QS 3-19
Weighted average:
Assigning costs to output
C3

Azule Co. manufactures in two sequential processes, cutting and binding. The two departments report the information below for a recent month. Determine the ending balances in the Work in Process Inventory accounts of each department.

QS 3-20
Transfer of costs; ending WIP balances
C3

	Cutting	Binding
Beginning work in process		
Transferred in from cutting dept.		$ 1,200
Direct materials....................	$ 845	1,926
Conversion......................	2,600	3,300
Costs added during March		
Direct materials....................	$ 8,240	$ 6,356
Conversion......................	11,100	18,575
Transferred in from cutting dept.		15,685
Transferred to finished goods		30,000

QS 3-21[A]
FIFO: Computing equivalent units and cost per EUP (direct materials)
C4

BOGO Inc. has two sequential processing departments, roasting and mixing. At the beginning of the month, the roasting department has 2,000 units in inventory, 70% complete as to materials. During the month, the roasting department started 18,000 units. At the end of the month, the roasting department had 3,000 units in ending inventory, 80% complete as to materials.

Cost information for the roasting department for the month is as follows:

Beginning work in process inventory (direct materials)	$ 2,170
Direct materials added during the month.	27,900

Using the FIFO method, compute the roasting department's (a) equivalent units of production for materials and (b) cost per equivalent unit of production for materials for the month.

QS 3-22[A]
FIFO: Assigning costs to output   C4

Refer to QS 3-21. Using the FIFO method, assign direct materials costs to the roasting department's output—specifically, the units transferred out to the mixing department and the units that remain in process in the roasting department at month-end.

QS 3-23
Recording costs of materials   P1

Hotwax makes surfboard wax in a single operation. This period, Hotwax purchased $62,000 in raw materials. Its production department requisitioned $50,000 of those materials for use in production. Prepare journal entries to record its (1) purchase of raw materials and (2) requisition of direct materials.

QS 3-24
Recording costs of labor
P2

Prepare journal entries to record the following production activities for Hotwax.
1. Incurred direct labor of $125,000 (credit Factory Payroll Payable).
2. Incurred indirect labor of $10,000 (credit Factory Payroll Payable).
3. Total factory payroll of $135,000 was paid in cash.

QS 3-25
Recording costs of factory overhead
P1   P3

Prepare journal entries to record the following production activities for Hotwax.
1. Requisitioned $9,000 of indirect materials for use in production of surfboard wax.
2. Incurred $156,000 overhead costs (credit "Other accounts").
3. Applied overhead at the rate of 140% of direct labor costs. Direct labor costs were $125,000.

QS 3-26
Recording transfer of costs to finished goods
P4

Hotwax completed products costing $275,000 and transferred them to finished goods. Prepare its journal entry to record the transfer of units from production to finished goods inventory.

QS 3-27
Process cost summary
C3

Anheuser-Busch InBev is attempting to reduce its water usage. How could a company manager use a process cost summary to determine if the program to reduce water usage is successful?

■ connect

EXERCISES

Exercise 3-1
Matching of product to cost accounting system
C1

For each of the following products and services, indicate whether it is more likely produced in a process operation or in a job order operation.

_____ **1.** Beach towels   _____ **5.** Designed patio   _____ **9.** Concrete swimming pools
_____ **2.** Bolts and nuts   _____ **6.** Door hardware   _____ **10.** Custom tailored dresses
_____ **3.** Lawn chairs   _____ **7.** Cut flower arrangements   _____ **11.** Grand pianos
_____ **4.** Headphones   _____ **8.** House paints   _____ **12.** Table lamps

Label each item *a* through *h* below as a feature of either a job order or process operation.

_____ **a.** Heterogeneous products and services

_____ **b.** Custom orders

_____ **c.** Low production volume

_____ **d.** Routine, repetitive procedures

_____ **e.** Focus on individual batch

_____ **f.** Low product standardization

_____ **g.** Low product flexibility

_____ **h.** Focus on standardized units

Exercise 3-2

Compare process and job order operations

C1

Match each of the following items A through G with the best numbered description of its purpose.

A. Factory Overhead account

B. Process cost summary

C. Equivalent units of production

D. Work in Process Inventory account

E. Raw Materials Inventory account

F. Materials requisition

G. Finished Goods Inventory account

_____ **1.** Notifies the materials manager to send materials to a production department.

_____ **2.** Holds costs of indirect materials, indirect labor, and similar costs until assigned to production.

_____ **3.** Holds costs of direct materials, direct labor, and applied overhead until products are transferred from production to finished goods (or another department).

_____ **4.** Standardizes partially completed units into equivalent completed units.

_____ **5.** Holds costs of finished products until sold to customers.

_____ **6.** Describes the activity and output of a production department for a period.

_____ **7.** Holds costs of materials until they are used in production or as factory overhead.

Exercise 3-3

Terminology in process costing

C1 A1 P1 P2 P3

The production department in a process manufacturing system completed 80,000 units of product and transferred them to finished goods during a recent period. Of these units, 24,000 were in process at the beginning of the period. The other 56,000 units were started and completed during the period. At period-end, 16,000 units were in process. Compute the department's equivalent units of production with respect to direct materials under each of three separate assumptions, using the weighted average method:

1. All direct materials are added to products when processing begins.

2. Beginning inventory is 40% complete as to materials and conversion costs. Ending inventory is 75% complete as to materials and conversion costs.

3. Beginning inventory is 60% complete as to materials and 40% complete as to conversion costs. Ending inventory is 30% complete as to materials and 60% complete as to conversion costs.

Exercise 3-4

Weighted average: Equivalent units computed

C2

Check (3) EUP for materials, 84,800

Refer to the information in Exercise 3-4 and complete the requirements for each of the three separate assumptions using the FIFO method for process costing.

Exercise 3-5[A]

FIFO: Equivalent units computed C4

Check (3) EUP for materials, 70,400

The Fields Company has two manufacturing departments, forming and painting. The company uses the weighted-average method of process costing. At the beginning of the month, the forming department has 25,000 units in inventory, 60% complete as to materials and 40% complete as to conversion costs. The beginning inventory cost of $60,100 consisted of $44,800 of direct material costs and $15,300 of conversion cost.

During the month, the forming department started 300,000 units. At the end of the month, the forming department had 30,000 units in ending inventory, 80% complete as to materials and 30% complete as to conversion. Units completed in the forming department are transferred to the painting department.

Cost information for the forming department is as follows:

Exercise 3-6

Weighted average: Cost per EUP and costs assigned to output

C2

Beginning work in process inventory	$ 60,100
Direct materials added during the month	1,231,200
Conversion added during the month	896,700

1. Calculate the equivalent units of production for the forming department.

2. Calculate the costs per equivalent unit of production for the forming department.

3. Using the weighted-average method, assign costs to the forming department's output—specifically, its units transferred to painting and its ending work in process inventory.

Exercise 3-7[A]
FIFO: Costs per EUP
C4

Refer to the information in Exercise 3-6. Assume that Fields uses the FIFO method of process costing.
1. Calculate the equivalent units of production for the forming department.
2. Calculate the costs per equivalent unit of production for the forming department.

Exercise 3-8
Weighted average:
Computing equivalent
units of production
C2

During April, the production department of a process manufacturing system completed a number of unit
of a product and transferred them to finished goods. Of these transferred units, 60,000 were in process i
the production department at the beginning of April and 240,000 were started and completed in April
April's beginning inventory units were 60% complete with respect to materials and 40% complete wit
respect to conversion. At the end of April, 82,000 additional units were in process in the production de
partment and were 80% complete with respect to materials and 30% complete with respect to conversion
1. Compute the number of units transferred to finished goods.
2. Compute the number of equivalent units with respect to both materials used and conversion used in the
production department for April using the weighted-average method.

Check (2) EUP for
materials, 365,600

Exercise 3-9
Weighted average:
Costs assigned to output
and inventories **C2**

The production department described in Exercise 3-8 had $850,368 of direct materials and $649,296 o
conversion costs charged to it during April. Also, its beginning inventory of $167,066 consists of $118,47:
of direct materials cost and $48,594 of conversion costs.
1. Compute the direct materials cost and the conversion cost per equivalent unit for the department.
2. Using the weighted-average method, assign April's costs to the department's output—specifically, it
units transferred to finished goods and its ending work in process inventory.

Check (1) $2.65 per EUP
of direct materials

Exercise 3-10[A]
FIFO: Computing
equivalent units of
production   **C4**

Refer to the information in Exercise 3-8 to compute the number of equivalent units with respect to bot
materials used and conversion costs in the production department for April using the FIFO method.

Exercise 3-11[A]
FIFO: Costs assigned to
output   **C4**   **P4**

Refer to the information in Exercise 3-9 and complete its parts 1 and 2 using the FIFO method.

Exercise 3-12
Weighted average:
Completing a process
cost summary
C3

The following partially completed process cost summary describes the July production activities of Ashad
Company. Its production output is sent to its warehouse for shipping. All direct materials are added to
products when processing begins. Beginning work in process inventory is 20% complete with respect to
conversion. Prepare its process cost summary using the weighted-average method.

Equivalent Units of Production	Direct Materials	Conversion
Units transferred out.................................	32,000 EUP	32,000 EUP
Units of ending work in process	2,500 EUP	1,500 EUP
Equivalent units of production	34,500 EUP	33,500 EUP
Costs per EUP	**Direct Materials**	**Conversion**
Costs of beginning work in process	$ 18,550	$ 2,280
Costs incurred this period	357,500	188,670
Total costs	$376,050	$190,950
Units in beginning work in process (all completed during July)		2,000
Units started this period..		32,500
Units completed and transferred out		32,000
Units in ending work in process		2,500

Refer to the information in Exercise 3-12. Prepare a process cost summary using the FIFO method. (Round cost per equivalent unit calculations to two decimal places.)

Exercise 3-13[A]
FIFO: Completing a
process cost summary

C3   C4

Pro-Weave manufactures stadium blankets by passing the products through a weaving department and a sewing department. The following information is available regarding its June inventories:

Exercise 3-14
Production cost flow and
measurement; journal
entries

P1   P2   P3   P4

	Beginning Inventory	Ending Inventory
Raw materials inventory	$ 120,000	$ 185,000
Work in process inventory—Weaving	300,000	330,000
Work in process inventory—Sewing	570,000	700,000
Finished goods inventory.	1,266,000	1,206,000

The following additional information describes the company's manufacturing activities for June:

Raw materials purchases (on credit).	$ 500,000
Factory payroll cost (paid in cash).	3,060,000
Other factory overhead cost (Other Accounts credited) . . .	156,000
Materials used	
Direct—Weaving	$ 240,000
Direct—Sewing	75,000
Indirect.	120,000
Labor used	
Direct—Weaving	$1,200,000
Direct—Sewing	360,000
Indirect.	1,500,000
Overhead rates as a percent of direct labor	
Weaving	80%
Sewing	150%
Sales (on credit).	$4,000,000

Required

1. Compute the (a) cost of products transferred from weaving to sewing, (b) cost of products transferred from sewing to finished goods, and (c) cost of goods sold.
2. Prepare journal entries dated June 30 to record (a) goods transferred from weaving to sewing, (b) goods transferred from sewing to finished goods, and (c) sale of finished goods.

Check   (1c) Cost of goods
sold $3,275,000

Refer to the information in Exercise 3-14. Prepare journal entries dated June 30 to record: (a) raw materials purchases, (b) direct materials usage, (c) indirect materials usage, (d) direct labor usage, (e) indirect labor usage, (f) other overhead costs, (g) overhead applied, and (h) payment of total payroll costs.

Exercise 3-15
Recording product costs

P1   P2   P3

Elliott Company produces large quantities of a standardized product. The following information is available for its production activities for March.

Exercise 3-16
Weighted average:
Process cost summary
units and costs   C3

Units		Costs		
Beginning work in process inventory..........	2,000	Beginning work in process inventory		
Started.....................................	20,000	Direct materials	$2,500	
Ending work in process inventory	5,000	Conversion.........................	6,360	$ 8,860
		Direct materials added..................		168,000
Status of ending work in process inventory		Direct labor added		199,850
Materials—Percent complete..............	100%	Overhead applied (140% of direct labor) ...		279,790
Conversion—Percent complete............	35%	Total costs to account for		$656,500
		Ending work in process inventory		$ 84,110

Prepare a process cost summary report for this company, showing costs charged to production, unit cost information, equivalent units of production, cost per EUP, and its cost assignment and reconciliation. Use the weighted-average method.

Exercise 3-17
Weighted average:
Process cost summary

C3

Oslo Company produces large quantities of a standardized product. The following information is available for its production activities for May.

Units		Costs		
Beginning work in process inventory	4,000	Beginning work in process inventory		
Started	12,000	Direct materials	$2,880	
Ending work in process inventory.............	3,000	Conversion	5,358	$ 8,238
		Direct materials added		197,120
Status of ending work in process inventory		Direct labor added		123,680
Materials—Percent complete	100%	Overhead applied (90% of direct labor)...		111,312
Conversion—Percent complete............	25%	Total costs to account for		$440,350
		Ending work in process inventory		$ 50,610

Prepare a process cost summary report for this company, showing costs charged to production, unit cost information, equivalent units of production, cost per EUP, and its cost assignment and reconciliation. Use the weighted-average method.

Exercise 3-18[A]
FIFO: Equivalent units

C4   P4

RSTN Co. produces its product through two sequential processing departments. Direct materials and conversion are added to the product evenly throughout the process. The company uses monthly reporting periods for its process costing system. During October, the company finished and transferred 150,000 units of its product to Department 2. Of these units, 30,000 were in process at the beginning of the month and 120,000 were started and completed during the month. The beginning work in process inventory was 30% complete. At the end of the month, the work in process inventory consisted of 20,000 units that were 80% complete. Compute the number of equivalent units of production for October. Use the FIFO method.

Exercise 3-19
Production cost flows

P1   P2   P3   P4

The flowchart below shows the August production activity of the punching and bending departments of Wire Box Company. Use the amounts shown on the flowchart to compute the missing numbers identified by question marks.

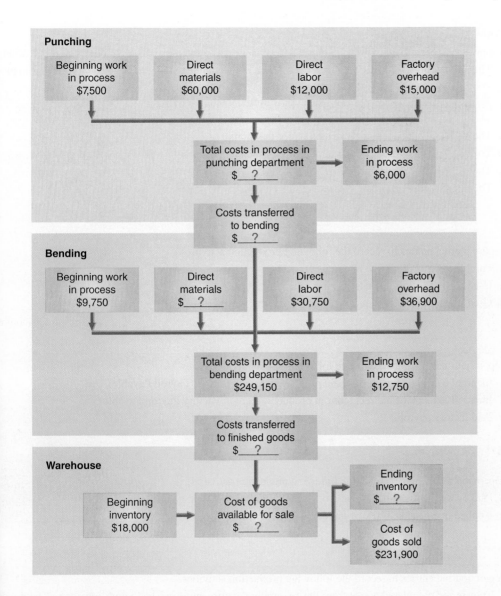

Punching

| Beginning work in process $7,500 | Direct materials $60,000 | Direct labor $12,000 | Factory overhead $15,000 |

Total costs in process in punching department $___?___ → Ending work in process $6,000

Costs transferred to bending $___?___

Bending

| Beginning work in process $9,750 | Direct materials $___?___ | Direct labor $30,750 | Factory overhead $36,900 |

Total costs in process in bending department $249,150 → Ending work in process $12,750

Costs transferred to finished goods $___?___

Warehouse

Beginning inventory $18,000 → Cost of goods available for sale $___?___

Ending inventory $___?___

Cost of goods sold $231,900

Hi-Test Company uses the weighted-average method of process costing to assign production costs to its products. Information for September follows. Assume that all materials are added at the beginning of its production process, and that conversion costs are added uniformly throughout the process.

Exercise 3-20
Weighted average:
Process cost summary
C3

Work in process inventory, September 1 (2,000 units, 100% complete with respect to direct materials, 80% complete with respect to direct labor and overhead; includes $45,000 of direct material cost, $25,600 in direct labor cost, $30,720 overhead cost)	$101,320
Units started in April	28,000
Units completed and transferred to finished goods inventory	23,000
Work in process inventory, September 30 (? units, 100% complete with respect to direct materials, 40% complete with respect to direct labor and overhead)	$?
Costs incurred in September	
Direct materials	$375,000
Conversion.	$341.000

Required

Compute each of the following, assuming Hi-Test uses the weighted-average method of process costing.

1. The number of physical units that were transferred out and the number that are in ending work in process inventory.
2. The number of equivalent units for materials for the month.
3. The number of equivalent units for conversion for the month.
4. The cost per equivalent unit of materials for the month.
5. The cost per equivalent unit for conversion for the month.
6. The total cost of goods transferred out.
7. The total cost of ending work in process inventory.

Exercise 3-21
Recording costs of materials
P1

Prepare journal entries to record the following production activities.

1. Purchased $80,000 of raw materials on credit.
2. Used $42,000 of direct materials in production.
3. Used $22,500 of indirect materials in production.

Exercise 3-22
Recording costs of labor
P2

Prepare journal entries to record the following production activities.

1. Incurred $75,000 of direct labor in production (credit Factory Payroll Payable).
2. Incurred $20,000 of indirect labor in production (credit Factory Payroll Payable).
3. Paid factory payroll.

Exercise 3-23
Recording overhead costs   P3

Prepare journal entries to record the following production activities.

1. Paid overhead costs (other than indirect materials and indirect labor) of $38,750.
2. Applied overhead at 110% of direct labor costs. Direct labor costs were $75,000.

Exercise 3-24
Recording cost of completed goods   P4

Prepare journal entries to record the following production activities.

1. Transferred completed goods from the Assembly department to finished goods inventory. The goods cost $135,600.
2. Sold $315,000 of goods on credit. Their cost is $175,000.

Exercise 3-25
Recording cost flows in a process cost system
P1 P2 P3 P4

Laffer Lumber produces bagged bark for use in landscaping. Production involves packaging bark chips in plastic bags in a bagging department. The following information describes production operations for October.

	A	B
1		**Bagging**
2		**Department**
3	Direct materials used	$ 522,000
4	Direct labor used	$ 130,000
5	Predetermined overhead rate (based on direct labor)	175%
6	Goods transferred from bagging to finished goods	$(595,000)
7		

The company's revenue for the month totaled $950,000 from credit sales, and its cost of goods sold for the month is $540,000. Prepare summary journal entries dated October 31 to record its October production activities for (1) direct material usage, (2) direct labor incurred (3) overhead allocation, (4) goods transfer from production to finished goods, and (5) credit sales.

Check (3) Cr. Factory Overhead, $227,500

The following journal entries are recorded in Kiesha Co.'s process costing system. Kiesha produces apparel and accessories. Overhead is applied to production based on direct labor cost for the period. Prepare a brief explanation (including any overhead rates applied) for each journal entry *a* through *j*.

Exercise 3-26
Interpretation of journal entries in process costing

P1   P2   P3   P4

a.	Raw Materials Inventory.............	52,000		g.	Factory Payroll Payable.............	38,000	
	Accounts Payable		52,000		Cash		38,000
b.	Work in Process Inventory...........	42,000		h.	Work in Process Inventory...........	33,600	
	Raw Materials Inventory.........		42,000		Factory Overhead..............		33,600
c.	Work in Process Inventory...........	32,000		i.	Finished Goods Inventory	88,000	
	Factory Payroll Payable...........		32,000		Work in Process Inventory........		88,000
d.	Factory Overhead..................	6,000		j.	Accounts Receivable.................	250,000	
	Factory Payroll Payable...........		6,000		Sales		250,000
e.	Factory Overhead..................	12,000			Cost of Goods Sold	100,000	
	Cash		12,000		Finished Goods Inventory		100,000
f.	Factory Overhead..................	10,000					
	Raw Materials Inventory..........		10,000				

Explain a hybrid costing system. Identify a product or service operation that might well fit a hybrid costing system.

Exercise 3-27
Hybrid costing system

A2

☰ connect

Sierra Company manufactures woven blankets and accounts for product costs using process costing. The company uses a single processing department. The following information is available regarding its May inventories.

PROBLEM SET A

Problem 3-1A
Production cost flow and measurement; journal entries

P1   P2   P3   P4

	Beginning Inventory	Ending Inventory
Raw materials inventory	$ 60,000	$ 92,500
Work in process inventory	435,000	515,000
Finished goods inventory	633,000	605,000

The following additional information describes the company's production activities for May.

Raw materials purchases (on credit)	$ 250,000
Factory payroll cost (paid in cash)	1,530,000
Other overhead cost (Other Accounts credited)	87,000
Materials used	
Direct	$ 157,500
Indirect	60,000
Labor used	
Direct	$ 780,000
Indirect	750,000
Overhead rate as a percent of direct labor...............	115%
Sales (on credit)	$2,500,000

Required

1. Compute the cost of (a) products transferred from production to finished goods, and (b) goods sold.
2. Prepare summary journal entries dated May 31 to record the following production activities during May: (a) raw materials purchases, (b) direct materials usage, (c) indirect materials usage, (d) direct labor costs incurred, (e) indirect labor costs incurred, (f) payment of factory payroll, (g) other overhead costs, (h) overhead applied, (i) goods transferred from production to finished goods, and (j) sale of finished goods.

Check (1b) Cost of goods sold, $1,782,500

Problem 3-2A
Weighted average: Cost per equivalent unit; costs assigned to products

C2   C3

Victory Company uses weighted-average process costing to account for its production costs. Conversion cost is added evenly throughout the process. Direct materials are added at the beginning of the process. During November, the company transferred 700,000 units of product to finished goods. At the end of November, the work in process inventory consists of 180,000 units that are 30% complete with respect to conversion. Beginning inventory had $420,000 of direct materials and $139,000 of conversion cost. The direct material cost added in November is $2,220,000, and the conversion cost added is $3,254,000. Beginning work in process consisted of 60,000 units that were 100% complete with respect to direct materials and 80% complete with respect to conversion. Of the units completed, 60,000 were from beginning work in process and 640,000 units were started and completed during the period.

Required

Check   (2) Conversion cost per equivalent unit, $4.50
(3b) $783,000

1. Determine the equivalent units of production with respect to (a) direct materials and (b) conversion.
2. Compute both the direct material cost and the conversion cost per equivalent unit.
3. Compute the direct material cost and the conversion cost assigned to (a) units completed and transferred out, and (b) ending work in process inventory.

Analysis Component

4. The company sells and ships all units to customers as soon as they are completed. Assume that an error is made in determining the percentage of completion for units in ending inventory. Instead of being 30% complete with respect to labor, they are actually 60% complete. Write a one-page memo to the plant manager describing how this error affects its November financial statements.

Problem 3-3A
Weighted average: Process cost summary; equivalent units

C2   C3   P4

Fast Co. produces its product through a single processing department. Direct materials are added at the start of production, and conversion costs are added evenly throughout the process. The company uses monthly reporting periods for its weighted-average process costing system. The Work in Process Inventory account has a balance of $84,300 as of October 1, which consisted of $17,100 of direct materials and $67,200 of conversion costs. During the month the company incurred the following costs:

Direct materials.........	$144,400
Conversion............	862,400

During October, the company started 140,000 units and transferred 150,000 units to finished goods. At the end of the month, the work in process inventory consisted of 20,000 units that were 80% complete with respect to conversion costs.

Required

Check   (1) Costs transferred out to finished goods, $982,500

1. Prepare the company's process cost summary for October using the weighted-average method.
2. Prepare the journal entry dated October 31 to transfer the cost of the completed units to finished goods inventory.

Problem 3-4A
Weighted average: Process cost summary, equivalent units, cost estimates

C2   C3   P4

Tamar Co. manufactures a single product in one department. All direct materials are added at the beginning of the manufacturing process. Conversion costs are added evenly throughout the process. During May, the company completed and transferred 22,200 units of product to finished goods inventory. Its 3,000 units of beginning work in process consisted of $19,800 of direct materials and $221,940 of conversion costs. It has 2,400 units (100% complete with respect to direct materials and 80% complete with respect to conversion) in process at month-end. During the month, $496,800 of direct material costs and $2,165,940 of conversion costs were charged to production.

Required

Check   (1) EUP for conversion, 24,120
(2) Cost transferred out to finished goods, $2,664,000

1. Prepare the company's process cost summary for May using the weighted-average method.
2. Prepare the journal entry dated May 31 to transfer the cost of completed units to finished goods inventory.

Analysis Components

3. The costing process depends on numerous estimates.
   a. Identify two major estimates that determine the cost per equivalent unit.
   b. In what direction might you anticipate a bias from management for each estimate in part 3a (assume that management compensation is based on maintaining low inventory amounts)? Explain your answer.

Refer to the data in Problem 3-4A. Assume that Tamar uses the FIFO method to account for its process costing system. The following additional information is available:

- Beginning work in process consisted of 3,000 units that were 100% complete with respect to direct materials and 40% complete with respect to conversion.
- Of the 22,200 units completed, 3,000 were from beginning work in process. The remaining 19,200 were units started and completed during May.

Required

1. Prepare the company's process cost summary for May using FIFO.
2. Prepare the journal entry dated May 31 to transfer the cost of completed units to finished goods inventory.

Problem 3-5A[A]
FIFO: Process cost summary; equivalent units; cost estimates
C3 C4 P4

Check (1) EUP for conversion, 22,920
(2) Cost transferred out to finished goods, $2,667,840

During May, the production department of a process manufacturing system completed a number of units of a product and transferred them to finished goods. Of these transferred units, 37,500 were in process in the production department at the beginning of May and 150,000 were started and completed in May. May's beginning inventory units were 60% complete with respect to materials and 40% complete with respect to conversion. At the end of May, 51,250 additional units were in process in the production department and were 60% complete with respect to materials and 20% complete with respect to conversion. The production department had $505,035 of direct materials and $396,568 of conversion cost charged to it during May. Its beginning inventory included $74,075 of direct materials cost and $28,493 of conversion cost.

1. Compute the number of units transferred to finished goods.
2. Compute the number of equivalent units with respect to both materials used and conversion used in the production department for May using the FIFO method.
3. Compute the direct materials cost and the conversion cost per equivalent unit for the department.
4. Using the FIFO method, assign May's costs to the units transferred to finished goods and assign costs to its ending work in process inventory.

Problem 3-6A[A]
FIFO: Costs per equivalent unit; costs assigned to products
C2 C4

Check (2) EUP for materials, 195,750

Dengo Co. makes a trail mix in two departments: roasting and blending. Direct materials are added at the beginning of each process, and conversion costs are added evenly throughout each process. The company uses the FIFO method of process costing. During October, the roasting department completed and transferred 22,200 units to the blending department. Of the units completed, 3,000 were from beginning inventory and the remaining 19,200 were started and completed during the month. Beginning work in process was 100% complete with respect to direct materials and 40% complete with respect to conversion. The company has 2,400 units (100% complete with respect to direct materials and 80% complete with respect to conversion) in process at month-end. Information on the roasting department's costs of beginning work in process inventory and costs added during the month follows.

Problem 3-7A[A]
FIFO: Process cost summary, equivalent units, cost estimates
C2 C3 C4 P4

Cost	Direct Materials	Conversion
Of beginning work in process inventory.........	$ 9,900	$ 110,970
Added during the month....................	248,400	1,082,970

Required

1. Prepare the roasting department's process cost summary for October using the FIFO method.
2. Prepare the journal entry dated October 31 to transfer the cost of completed units to the blending department.

Analysis Component

3. The company provides incentives to department managers by paying monthly bonuses based on their success in controlling costs per equivalent unit of production. Assume that a production department underestimates the percentage of completion for units in ending inventory with the result that its equivalent units of production for October are understated. What impact does this error have on the October bonuses paid to that department's managers? What impact, if any, does this error have on November bonuses?

Check (1) EUP for conversion, 22,920
(2) Cost transferred out to blending, $1,333,920

PROBLEM SET B

Problem 3-1B
Production cost flow and measurement; journal entries

P1 P2 P3 P4

Dream Toys Company manufactures video game consoles and accounts for product costs using process costing. The company uses a single processing department. The following information is available regarding its June inventories.

	Beginning Inventory	Ending Inventory
Raw materials inventory	$ 72,000	$110,000
Work in process inventory	156,000	250,000
Finished goods inventory	160,000	198,000

The following additional information describes the company's production activities for June.

Raw materials purchases (on credit)	$200,000
Factory payroll cost (paid in cash)	400,000
Other overhead cost (Other Accounts credited)	170,500
Materials used	
Direct	$120,000
Indirect	42,000
Labor used	
Direct	$350,000
Indirect	50,000
Overhead rate as a percent of direct labor	75%
Sales (on credit)	$1,000,000

Required

Check (1b) Cost of goods sold, $600,500

1. Compute the cost of (a) products transferred from production to finished goods, and (b) goods sold.
2. Prepare journal entries dated June 30 to record the following production activities during June: (a) raw materials purchases, (b) direct materials usage, (c) indirect materials usage, (d) direct labor costs, (e) indirect labor costs, (f) payment of factory payroll (g) other overhead costs, (h) overhead applied, (i) goods transferred from production to finished goods, and (j) sale of finished goods.

Problem 3-2B
Weighted average:
Cost per equivalent unit; costs assigned to products

C2 C3

Abraham Company uses process costing to account for its production costs. Conversion is added evenly throughout the process. Direct materials are added at the beginning of the process. During September, the production department transferred 80,000 units of product to finished goods. Beginning work in process consisted of 2,000 units that were 100% complete with respect to direct materials and 85% complete with respect to conversion. Of the units completed, 2,000 were from beginning work in process and 78,000 units were started and completed during the period. Beginning work in process had $58,000 of direct materials and $86,400 of conversion cost. At the end of September, the work in process inventory consists of 8,000 units that are 25% complete with respect to conversion. The direct materials cost added in September is $712,000, and conversion cost added is $1,980,000. The company uses the weighted-average method.

Required

1. Determine the equivalent units of production with respect to (a) conversion and (b) direct materials.

Check (2) Conversion cost per equivalent unit, $25.20

(3b) $120,400

2. Compute both the conversion cost and the direct materials cost per equivalent unit.
3. Compute both conversion cost and direct materials cost assigned to (a) units completed and transferred out and (b) ending work in process inventory.

Analysis Component

4. The company sells and ships all units to customers as soon as they are completed. Assume that an error is made in determining the percentage of completion for units in ending inventory. Instead of being 25% complete with respect to conversion, they are actually 75% complete. Write a one-page memo to the plant manager describing how this error affects its September financial statements.

Braun Company produces its product through a single processing department. Direct materials are added at the beginning of the process. Conversion costs are added to the product evenly throughout the process. The company uses monthly reporting periods for its weighted-average process costing. The Work in Process Inventory account had a balance of $21,300 on November 1, which consisted of $6,800 of direct materials and $14,500 of conversion costs.

During the month the company incurred the following costs:

Direct materials.........	$ 116,400
Conversion............	1,067,000

During November, the company finished and transferred 100,000 units of its product to finished goods. At the end of the month, the work in process inventory consisted of 12,000 units that were 100% complete with respect to direct materials and 25% complete with respect to conversion.

Required

1. Prepare the company's process cost summary for November using the weighted-average method.
2. Prepare the journal entry dated November 30 to transfer the cost of the completed units to finished goods inventory.

Problem 3-3B
Weighted average:
Process cost summary;
equivalent units

C2   C3   P4

Check   (1) Cost transferred out to finished goods, $1,160,000

Switch Co. manufactures a single product in one department. Direct labor and overhead are added evenly throughout the process. Direct materials are added as needed. The company uses monthly reporting periods for its weighted-average process costing. During January, Switch completed and transferred 220,000 units of product to finished goods inventory. Its 10,000 units of beginning work in process consisted of $7,500 of direct materials and $49,850 of conversion. In process at month-end are 40,000 units (50% complete with respect to direct materials and 30% complete with respect to conversion). During the month, the company used direct materials of $112,500 in production, and incurred conversion costs of $616,000.

Required

1. Prepare the company's process cost summary for January using the weighted-average method.
2. Prepare the journal entry dated January 31 to transfer the cost of completed units to finished goods inventory.

Analysis Components

3. The cost accounting process depends on several estimates.
   a. Identify two major estimates that affect the cost per equivalent unit.
   b. In what direction might you anticipate a bias from management for each estimate in part 3a (assume that management compensation is based on maintaining low inventory amounts)? Explain your answer.

Problem 3-4B
Weighted average:
Process cost summary;
equivalent units; cost
estimates

C2   C3   P4

Check   (1) EUP for conversion, 232,000
(2) Cost transferred out to finished goods, $741,400

Refer to the information in Problem 3-4B. Assume that Switch uses the FIFO method to account for its process costing system. The following additional information is available.

• Beginning work in process consists of 10,000 units that were 75% complete with respect to direct materials and 60% complete with respect to conversion.
• Of the 220,000 units completed, 10,000 were from beginning work in process; the remaining 210,000 were units started and completed during January.

Required

1. Prepare the company's process cost summary for January using FIFO. Round cost per EUP to three decimal places.
2. Prepare the journal entry dated January 31 to transfer the cost of completed units to finished goods inventory.

Problem 3-5B[A]
FIFO: Process cost
summary; equivalent
units; cost estimates

C3   C4   P4

Check   (1) Conversion EUP, 226,000
(2) Cost transferred out, $743,554

Problem 3-6B[A]
FIFO: Costs per equivalent unit; costs assigned to products

C2   C4

During May, the production department of a process manufacturing system completed a number of units of a product and transferred them to finished goods. Of these transferred units, 62,500 were in process in the production department at the beginning of May and 175,000 were started and completed in May. May's beginning inventory units were 40% complete with respect to materials and 80% complete with respect to conversion. At the end of May, 76,250 additional units were in process in the production department and were 80% complete with respect to materials and 20% complete with respect to conversion. The production department had $683,750 of direct materials and $446,050 of conversion cost charged to it during May. Its beginning inventory included $99,075 of direct materials cost and $53,493 of conversion cost.

1. Compute the number of units transferred to finished goods.

Check   (2) EUP for materials, 273,500

2. Compute the number of equivalent units with respect to both materials used and conversion used in the production department for May using the FIFO method.

3. Compute the direct materials cost and the conversion cost per equivalent unit for the department.

4. Using the FIFO method, assign May's costs to the units transferred to finished goods and assign costs to its ending work in process inventory.

Problem 3-7B[A]
FIFO: Process cost summary, equivalent units, cost estimates

C2   C3   C4   P4

Belda Co. makes organic juice in two departments: cutting and blending. Direct materials are added at the beginning of each process, and conversion costs are added evenly throughout each process. The company uses the FIFO method of process costing. During March, the cutting department completed and transferred 220,000 units to the blending department. Of the units completed, 10,000 were from beginning inventory and the remaining 210,000 were started and completed during the month. Beginning work in process was 75% complete with respect to direct materials and 60% complete with respect to conversion. The company has 40,000 units (50% complete with respect to direct materials and 30% complete with respect to conversion) in process at month-end. Information on the cutting department's costs of beginning work in process inventory and costs added during the month follows.

Cost	Direct Materials	Conversion
Of beginning work in process inventory.........	$ 16,800	$ 97,720
Added during the month....................	223,200	1,233,960

Required

Check   (1) EUP for conversion, 226,000

(2) Cost transferred out, $1,486,960

1. Prepare the cutting department's process cost summary for March using the FIFO method.

2. Prepare the journal entry dated March 31 to transfer the cost of completed units to the blending department.

Analysis Component

3. The company provides incentives to department managers by paying monthly bonuses based on their success in controlling costs per equivalent unit of production. Assume that the production department overestimates the percentage of completion for units in ending inventory with the result that its equivalent units of production for March are overstated. What impact does this error have on bonuses paid to the managers of the production department? What impact, if any, does this error have on these managers' April bonuses?

SERIAL PROBLEM
Business Solutions

C1   A1

(This serial problem began in Chapter 1 and continues through most of the book. If previous chapter segments were not completed, the serial problem can begin at this point.)

SP 3   The computer workstation furniture manufacturing that Santana Rey started is progressing well. At this point, Santana is using a job order costing system to account for the production costs of this product line. Santana has heard about process costing and is wondering whether process costing might be a better method for her to keep track of and monitor her production costs.

Required

1. What are the features that distinguish job order costing from process costing?

2. Do you believe that Santana should continue to use job order costing or switch to process costing for her workstation furniture manufacturing? Explain.

CP 3   Major League Bat Company manufactures baseball bats. In addition to its work in process inventories, the company maintains inventories of raw materials and finished goods. It uses raw materials as direct materials in production and as indirect materials. Its factory payroll costs include direct labor for production and indirect labor. All materials are added at the beginning of the process, and conversion costs are applied uniformly throughout the production process.

COMPREHENSIVE PROBLEM

Major League Bat Company

Weighted average:
Review of
Chapter 1

Required

You are to maintain records and produce measures of inventories to reflect the July events of this company. Set up the following general ledger accounts and enter the June 30 balances: Raw Materials Inventory, $25,000; Work in Process Inventory, $8,135 ($2,660 of direct materials and $5,475 of conversion); Finished Goods Inventory, $110,000; Sales, $0; Cost of Goods Sold, $0; Factory Payroll Payable, $0; and Factory Overhead, $0.

1. Prepare journal entries to record the following July transactions and events.

   a. Purchased raw materials for $125,000 cash (the company uses a perpetual inventory system).

   b. Used raw materials as follows: direct materials, $52,440; and indirect materials, $10,000.

   c. Recorded factory payroll payable costs as follows: direct labor, $202,250; and indirect labor, $25,000.

   d. Paid factory payroll cost of $227,250 with cash (ignore taxes).

   e. Incurred additional factory overhead costs of $80,000 paid in cash.

   f. Allocated factory overhead to production at 50% of direct labor costs.

2. Information about the July inventories follows. Use this information with that from part 1 to prepare a process cost summary, assuming the weighted-average method is used.

Check (1f) Cr. Factory Overhead, $101,125

Check (2) EUP for conversion, 14,200

Units	
Beginning inventory	5,000 units
Started	14,000 units
Ending inventory	8,000 units
Beginning inventory	
Materials—Percent complete	100%
Conversion—Percent complete	75%
Ending inventory	
Materials—Percent complete	100%
Conversion—Percent complete	40%

3. Using the results from part 2 and the available information, make computations and prepare journal entries to record the following:

   g. Total costs transferred to finished goods for July (label this entry g).

   h. Sale of finished goods costing $265,700 for $625,000 in cash (label this entry h).

(3g) $271,150

4. Post entries from parts 1 and 3 to the ledger accounts set up at the beginning of the problem.

5. Compute the amount of gross profit from the sales in July. (*Note:* Add any underapplied overhead to, or deduct any overapplied overhead from, the cost of goods sold. Ignore the corresponding journal entry.)

The **General Ledger** tool in *Connect* automates several of the procedural steps in accounting so that the financial professional can focus on the impacts of each transaction on various reports and performance measures.

GL 3-1   General Ledger assignment GL 3-1, based on Problem 3-1A, focuses on transactions related to process costing. Prepare summary journal entries to record the cost of units manufactured and their flow through the manufacturing environment. Then prepare a schedule of cost of goods manufactured and a partial income statement.

GENERAL LEDGER PROBLEM

Available in Connect

Beyond the Numbers

REPORTING IN ACTION

C2

APPLE

BTN 3-1 **Apple** reports in notes to its financial statements that, in addition to its products sold, it includes the following costs (among others) in cost of sales: customer shipping and handling expenses and warranty expenses.

Required

1. Why do you believe Apple includes these costs in its cost of sales?
2. What effect does this cost accounting policy for its cost of sales have on Apple's financial statements and any analysis of those statements? Explain.

Fast Forward

3. Access Apple's financial statements for the years after September 28, 2013, from its website (**Apple.com**) or the SEC's EDGAR website (**SEC.gov**). Review its footnote relating to Summary of Significant Accounting Policies. Has Apple changed its policy with respect to what costs are included in the cost of sales? Explain.

COMPARATIVE ANALYSIS

C1

APPLE
GOOGLE

BTN 3-2 Manufacturers such as **Apple** and **Google** usually work to maintain a high-quality and low-cost operation. One ratio routinely computed for this assessment is the cost of goods sold divided by total expenses. A decline in this ratio can mean that the company is spending too much on selling and administrative activities. An increase in this ratio beyond a reasonable level can mean that the company is not spending enough on selling activities. (Assume for this analysis that total expenses equal the cost of goods sold plus total operating expenses.)

Required

1. For Apple and Google refer to Appendix A and compute the ratios of cost of goods sold to total expenses for their two most recent fiscal years. (Record answers as percents, rounded to one decimal.)
2. Comment on the similarities or differences in the ratio results across both years between the companies.

ETHICS CHALLENGE

C1

BTN 3-3 Many accounting and accounting-related professionals are skilled in financial analysis, but most are not skilled in manufacturing. This is especially the case for process manufacturing environments (for example, a bottling plant or chemical factory). To provide professional accounting and financial services, one must understand the industry, product, and processes. We have an ethical responsibility to develop this understanding before offering services to clients in these areas.

Required

Write a one-page action plan, in memorandum format, discussing how you would obtain an understanding of key business processes of a company that hires you to provide financial services. The memorandum should specify an industry, a product, and one selected process and should draw on at least one reference, such as a professional journal or industry magazine.

COMMUNICATING IN PRACTICE

A1 C1 P1 P2

BTN 3-4 You hire a new assistant production manager whose prior experience is with a company that produced goods to order. Your company engages in continuous production of homogeneous products that go through various production processes. Your new assistant e-mails you questioning some cost classifications on an internal report—specifically why the costs of some materials that do not actually become part of the finished product, including some labor costs not directly associated with producing the product, are classified as direct costs. Respond to this concern via memorandum.

TAKING IT TO THE NET

C1

BTN 3-5 Many companies acquire software to help them monitor and control their costs and as an aid to their accounting systems. One company that supplies such software is **proDacapo** (**prodacapo.com**). There are many other such vendors. Access proDacapo's website, click on "Products," then click on "Prodacapo Process Management," and review the information displayed.

Required

How is process management software helpful to businesses? Explain with reference to costs, efficiency, and examples, if possible.

BTN 3-6   The purpose of this team activity is to ensure that each team member understands process operations and the related accounting entries. Find the activities and flows identified in Exhibit 3.14 with numbers ①–⑩. Pick a member of the team to start by describing activity number ① in this exhibit, then verbalizing the related journal entry, and describing how the amounts in the entry are computed. The other members of the team are to agree or disagree; discussion is to continue until all members express understanding. Rotate to the next numbered activity and next team member until all activities and entries have been discussed. If at any point a team member is uncertain about an answer, the team member may pass and get back in the rotation when he or she can contribute to the team's discussion.

BTN 3-7   This chapter's opener featured Nick Nicolay and his company **Kar's Nuts.**

Required

1. Kar's Nuts uses three processes: roasting, blending, and packaging. What are some benefits of using separate process cost summary reports for each process?
2. Nick tries to order raw materials just-in-time for their use in production. How does holding raw materials inventories increase costs? If the items are not used in production, how can they impact profits? Explain.
3. Suppose Kar's Nuts decides to allow customers to make their own unique trail mix flavors. Why might the company then use a hybrid costing system?

BTN 3-8   In process costing, the process is analyzed first and then a unit measure is computed in the form of equivalent units for direct materials, conversion (direct labor and overhead), and both types of costs combined. The same analysis applies to both manufacturing and service processes.

Required

Visit your local **U.S. Mail** center. Look into the back room, and you will see several ongoing processes. Select one process, such as sorting, and list the costs associated with this process. Your list should include materials, labor, and overhead; be specific. Classify each cost as fixed or variable. At the bottom of your list, outline how overhead should be assigned to your identified process. The following format (with an example) is suggested.

Point: The class can compare and discuss the different processes studied and the answers provided.

Cost Description	Direct Material	Conversion Direct Labor	Conversion Overhead	Variable Cost	Fixed Cost
Manual sorting		X		X	
. .					
Overhead allocation suggestions:					

BTN 3-9   **Samsung, Apple,** and **Google** are competitors in the global marketplace. Selected data for Samsung follow.

(billions of Korean won)	Current Year	Prior Year
Cost of goods sold	₩137,696.3	₩126,651.9
Operating expenses	54,211.3	45,402.3
Total expenses	₩191,907.6	₩172,054.2

Samsung

APPLE

GOOGLE

Required

1. Review the discussion of the importance of the cost of goods sold divided by total expenses ratio in BTN 3-2. Compute the cost of goods sold to total expenses ratio for Samsung for the two years of data provided. (Record answers as percents, rounded to one decimal.)
2. Comment on the similarities or differences in the ratio results calculated in part 1 and in BTN 3-2 across years and companies. (Record answers as percents, rounded to one decimal.)

ANSWERS TO MULTIPLE CHOICE QUIZ

1. d

2. e

3. b; $20,000 + $152,000 + $45,000 + $18,000 − $218,000 = $17,000

4. a; 40,000 + (15,000 × 1/3) = 45,000 EUP

5. c; ($6,000 + $84,000) ÷ 45,000 EUP = $2 per EUP

4 | chapter

Activity-Based Costing and Analysis

Chapter Preview

ASSIGNING OVERHEAD COSTS

C1 Alternative methods

P1 Single plantwide overhead rate method

P2 Multiple departmental overhead rate method

A1 Assessing plantwide and departmental rate methods

C2 Activity-based costing rates and methods

APPLYING ACTIVITY-BASED COSTING

P3 Step 1 Identify activities and their costs

Step 2 Trace overhead costs to cost pools

Step 3 Determine activity rates

Step 4 Assign overhead costs to cost objects

ASSESSING ACTIVITY-BASED COSTING

A2 Advantages of activity-based costing

Disadvantages of activity-based costing

Activity-based costing for service providers

C3 Types of activities

Learning Objectives

CONCEPTUAL

C1 Distinguish between the plantwide overhead rate method, the departmental overhead rate method, and the activity-based costing method.

C2 Explain cost flows for activity-based costing.

C3 Describe the four types of activities that cause overhead costs.

ANALYTICAL

A1 Identify and assess advantages and disadvantages of the plantwide overhead and departmental overhead rate methods.

A2 Identify and assess advantages and disadvantages of activity-based costing.

PROCEDURAL

P1 Allocate overhead costs to products using the plantwide overhead rate method.

P2 Allocate overhead costs to products using the departmental overhead rate method.

P3 Allocate overhead costs to products using activity-based costing.

Juicin' Profits

SAN DIEGO—Chance encounters sometimes lead to great opportunities. "I was just into eating healthy food, surfing, and doing a lot of yoga," says Eric Ethans. Stressed out from law school, Annie Lawless devoted herself to teaching yoga and making fresh juices. "I would bring juice to yoga classes, and people started to buy it," says Annie. One day, Eric strode into Annie's yoga class carrying his own homemade juice. "We became instant best friends, talking about all things juice and health-related," says Annie. Together, these best friends started **Suja Juice Co. (Sujajuice.com)**, a maker of cold-pressed juices made from organic fruits and vegetables.

"Do what you love and learn all you can about it"

—Annie Lawless

The duo started small, making juices in Ethans's beach bungalow and selling mainly to Annie's yoga class. Then they started a home-delivery service for their juices, and demand skyrocketed. Ethans found himself delivering juice via his skateboard, sometimes at night. Former customer (and company co-founder) James Brennan recalls, "One day Eric rode up on his skateboard and dropped the juice, shattering glass everywhere. I said, 'Eric, what's your plan here? If you ever really want to do something with this, let me know.'" Eric and Annie, exhausted after working so much and making little profit, asked Brennan to join their venture. In turn, Brennan introduced them to Jeff Church, a serial entrepreneur and now company CEO.

Making cold-pressed juice begins with organic fruits and vegetables, grown on the company's own farms, and cut and inspected by trained chefs. To extend the shelf life of its juices, the company relies on expensive high-pressure processing instead of pasteurization or the use of chemical preservatives. "People don't want the additives and concentrates we grew up with," notes Brennan, "they want things that are organic and natural and raw." Making Suja's juices is expensive, and

the use of costly raw materials and overhead costs require company managers to understand product costs.

While Eric and Annie focus mainly on developing new juices, they understand that overhead cost allocation is vital for managerial decisions such as product pricing and product mix. Overhead costs, such as plant maintenance, supervision, and clean-up costs, must be allocated to products. In smaller businesses with few product lines, a single plantwide overhead allocation rate is often sufficient. But, as businesses grow and offer more diverse product lines, more sophisticated costing techniques are often needed. The departmental overhead rate method improves upon the plantwide rate method by using more than one overhead allocation rate. Activity-based costing (ABC), which focuses on the activities that cause costs, can help managers monitor and control overhead costs and ensure product quality. ABC can be especially useful in companies like Suja, where different product lines require different processes and varying levels of overhead.

So far, Suja's recipe is clearly working. Founded in 2012, the company generated sales of $17 million in 2013 and about $50 million in 2014. "I don't think anyone here thought this was going to be as big as it is," says Eric. "I would have been happy even if it was much smaller." Still, the owners are planning for even more rapid growth. "Natural cold-pressed organic juices—this is the hottest beverage market on the planet right now," says Brennan. In addition to stressing the importance of partnering with experienced and talented mentors, Annie encourages young entrepreneurs to "constantly push forward and never settle. Put in the extra work to make things extraordinary."

Sources: *Suja Juice Co. website,* January 2015; *Forbes,* February 10, 2014; *San Diego Business Journal,* May 20, 2013; *Livetheprocess.com; Wellandgoodnyc.com,* December 31, 2013

ASSIGNING OVERHEAD COSTS

C1

Distinguish between the plantwide overhead rate method, the departmental overhead rate method, and the activity-based costing method.

Managerial activities such as product pricing, product mix decisions, and cost control depend on accurate product cost information. Distorted product cost information can result in poor decisions. Knowing accurate costs for producing, delivering, and servicing products helps managers set a price to cover product costs and yield a profit.

In competitive markets, price is established through the forces of supply and demand. In these situations, managers must understand product costs to assess whether the market price is high enough to justify the cost of entering the market. Disparities between market prices and producer costs give managers insight into their efficiency relative to competitors.

Product costs consist of direct materials, direct labor, and overhead (indirect costs). Since the physical components of a product (direct materials) and the work of making a product (direct labor) can be traced to units of output, the assignment of costs of these factors is usually straightforward. Overhead costs, however, are not directly related to production volume and therefore cannot be traced to units of product in the same way that direct materials and direct labor can.

Point: Evidence suggests overhead costs have steadily increased while direct labor costs have steadily decreased as a percentage of total manufacturing costs over recent decades. This puts greater importance on accurate cost allocations.

For example, we can trace the cost of putting tires on a car because we know there is a logical relation between the number of cars produced and the number of tires needed for each car. The cost to heat an automobile manufacturing factory, however, is not readily linked to the number of cars made. Consequently, we must use an allocation system to assign overhead costs such as utilities and factory maintenance. This chapter introduces three methods of overhead allocation: (1) the single plantwide overhead rate method, (2) the departmental overhead rate method, and (3) the activity-based costing method.

Alternative Methods of Overhead Allocation

Exhibit 4.1 summarizes some key features of these three alternative methods. Both the *plantwide overhead rate method* and the *departmental overhead rate method* use volume-based measures such as direct labor hours, direct labor dollars, or machine hours to allocate overhead costs to products. These methods differ in that the plantwide method uses a single rate for allocating overhead costs, and the departmental rate method uses at least two rates. The departmental method arguably provides more accurate cost allocations than the single rate allocations of the plantwide method. In contrast, *activity-based costing* focuses on activities and the costs of carrying out activities. Rates based on these activities are then used to assign overhead to products in proportion to the amount of activity required to produce them. Activity-based costing typically uses more overhead allocation rates than the plantwide and departmental methods.

EXHIBIT 4.1

Overhead Cost Allocation Methods

Allocation Method	Overhead Allocations Based on	Overhead Allocation Rates Based on
Plantwide rate	One rate	Volume-based measures such as direct labor hours or machine hours
Departmental rate	Two or more rates	Volume-based measures such as direct labor hours or machine hours
Activity-based costing	At least two (but often many) rates	Activities that drive costs, such as number of batches of product produced

Plantwide Overhead Rate Method

P1

Allocate overhead costs to products using the plantwide overhead rate method.

The first method of allocating overhead costs to products is known as the *single plantwide overhead rate method,* or simply the *plantwide overhead rate method.*

Cost Flows under Plantwide Overhead Rate Method   For the plantwide overhead rate method, the target of the cost assignment, or **cost object,** is the unit of product—see Exhibit 4.2. The overhead rate is determined using volume-related measures such as direct labor hours, direct labor cost dollars, or machine hours, which are readily available in most manufacturing settings. In some industries, overhead costs are closely related to these volume-related measures. In such cases it is logical to use this method to assign overhead costs to products.

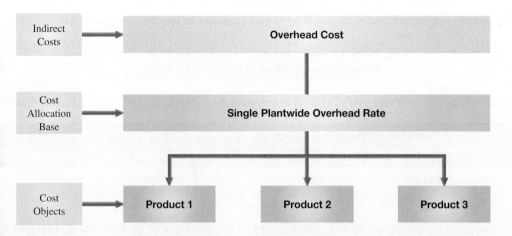

EXHIBIT 4.2

Plantwide Overhead Rate
Method

Applying the Plantwide Overhead Rate Method   Under the single plantwide overhead rate method, total budgeted overhead costs are combined into one overhead cost pool. This cost pool is then divided by the chosen allocation base, such as total direct labor hours, to arrive at a single plantwide overhead rate. This rate then is applied to assign costs to all products based on their usage of the allocation base.

To illustrate, consider data from KartCo, a go-kart manufacturer that produces both standard and custom go-karts for amusement parks. The standard go-kart is a basic model sold primarily to amusement parks that service county and state fairs. Custom go-karts are produced for theme parks who want unique go-karts that coordinate with their respective themes.

Assume that KartCo applies the plantwide overhead rate method and uses direct labor hours (DLH) as its overhead allocation base. KartCo's budgeted DLH information is in Exhibit 4.3.

	Number of Units	Direct Labor Hours per Unit	Total Direct Labor Hours
Standard go-kart ...	5,000	15	75,000
Custom go-kart	1,000	25	25,000
Total.............			100,000

EXHIBIT 4.3

KartCo's Budgeted Direct
Labor Hours

KartCo's budgeted overhead cost information is in Exhibit 4.4. Its overhead cost consists of indirect labor and factory utilities.

	Budgeted Cost
Indirect labor cost	$4,000,000
Factory utilities	800,000
Total budgeted overhead cost	$4,800,000

EXHIBIT 4.4

KartCo's Budgeted
Overhead Cost

The single plantwide overhead rate for KartCo is computed as follows.

$$\begin{aligned}\text{Plantwide} \atop \text{overhead rate} &= {\text{Total budgeted} \atop \text{overhead cost}} \div {\text{Total budgeted direct} \atop \text{labor hours}} \\ &= \$4{,}800{,}000 \div 100{,}000 \text{ DLH} \\ &= \$48 \text{ per DLH}\end{aligned}$$

This plantwide overhead rate is then used to allocate overhead cost to products based on the number of direct labor hours required to produce each unit as follows.

Overhead allocated to each product unit = Plantwide overhead rate × DLH per unit

For KartCo, overhead cost is allocated to its two products as follows (on a per unit basis).

Standard go-kart:	$48 per DLH × 15 DLH = $ 720
Custom go-kart:	$48 per DLH × 25 DLH = $1,200

KartCo uses these per unit overhead costs to compute the total unit cost of each product as follows.

	Product Cost per Unit Using the Plantwide Rate Method			
	Direct Materials	Direct Labor	Overhead	Total Cost per Unit
Standard go-kart	$400	$350	$ 720	$1,470
Custom go-kart	600	500	1,200	2,300

© Getty Images

During the most recent period, KartCo sold its standard model go-karts for $2,000 and its custom go-karts for $3,500. A recent report from its marketing staff indicates that competitors are selling go-karts similar to KartCo's standard model for as low as $1,200. KartCo management knows the company must be competitive, but management is concerned that meeting this lower price would result in a loss of $270 ($1,200 − $1,470) on each standard go-kart sold.

In the case of its custom go-kart, KartCo has been swamped with orders and cannot meet demand. Accordingly, management is considering dropping the standard model and concentrating on the custom model. Yet management recognizes that its pricing and cost decisions are influenced by its cost allocations. Thus, before making any strategic decisions, management has directed its cost analysts to further review production costs for both the standard and custom go-kart models. To pursue this analysis, the cost analysts first turned to the departmental overhead rate method.

Departmental Overhead Rate Method

P2

Allocate overhead costs to products using the departmental overhead rate method.

Many companies have several departments that produce various products and consume overhead resources in substantially different ways. Under such circumstances, use of a single plantwide overhead rate can produce cost assignments that fail to accurately reflect the cost to manufacture a specific product. In these cases, use of multiple overhead rates can result in better overhead cost allocations and improve management decisions.

Cost Flows under Departmental Overhead Rate Method   The *departmental overhead rate method* uses a different overhead rate for each production department. This is usually done through a four-step process (see Exhibit 4.5):

1. Assign overhead costs to departmental *cost pools.*
2. Select an allocation base for each department.
3. Compute overhead allocation rates for each department.
4. Use departmental overhead rates to assign overhead costs to cost objects (products).

EXHIBIT 4.5

Departmental Overhead Rate Method

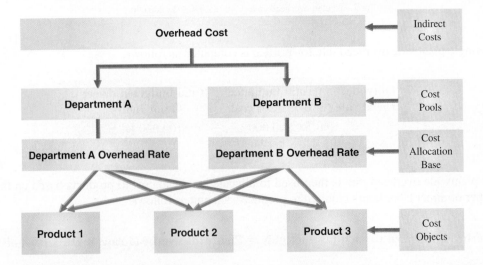

Exhibit 4.5 shows that under the departmental overhead rate method, overhead costs are first determined separately for each production department. Next, an overhead rate is computed for each production department to allocate the overhead costs of each department to products passing through that department. The departmental overhead rate method allows each department to have its own overhead rate and its own allocation base. For example, an assembly department can use direct labor hours to allocate its overhead cost while a machining department can use machine hours as its base.

Applying the Departmental Overhead Rate Method   To illustrate the departmental overhead rate method, let's return to KartCo. KartCo has two production departments, the machining department and the assembly department. The first step requires that KartCo assign its $4,800,000 overhead cost to its two production departments. KartCo determines from an analysis of its indirect labor and factory utilities that $4,200,000 of overhead costs are traceable to its machining department and the remaining $600,000 are traceable to its assembly department.

The second step requires each department to determine an allocation base. For KartCo, the machining department uses machine hours (MH) as a base for allocating its overhead; the assembly department uses direct labor hours (DLH) as the base for allocating its overhead. The relevant information for KartCo's machining and assembly departments is in Exhibit 4.6.

Point: In some cases it is difficult for companies to trace overhead costs to distinct departments as some overhead costs can be common to several departments. In these cases, companies must allocate overhead to departments applying reasonable allocation bases.

	Number of Units	Machining Department		Assembly Department	
		Hours per Unit	Total Hours	Hours per Unit	Total Hours
Standard go-kart	5,000	10 MH per unit	50,000 MH	5 DLH per unit	25,000 DLH
Custom go-kart	1,000	20 MH per unit	20,000 MH	5 DLH per unit	5,000 DLH
Totals			70,000 MH		30,000 DLH

EXHIBIT 4.6

Allocation Information for Machining and Assembly Departments

In step three, each department computes its own overhead rate using the following formula.

$$\text{Departmental overhead rate} = \frac{\text{Total budgeted departmental overhead cost}}{\text{Total amount of departmental allocation base}}$$

KartCo's departmental overhead rates are computed as follows.

$$\text{Machining department overhead rate} = \frac{\$4,200,000}{70,000 \text{ MH}} = \$60 \text{ per MH}$$

$$\text{Assembly department overhead rate} = \frac{\$600,000}{30,000 \text{ DLH}} = \$20 \text{ per DLH}$$

Step four is to apply overhead costs to each product based on departmental overhead rates. For KartCo, since each standard go-kart requires 10 MH from the machining department and five DLH from the assembly department, the overhead cost allocated to each standard go-kart is $600 from the machining department (10 MH × $60 per MH) and $100 from the assembly department (5 DLH × $20 per DLH). The same procedure is applied for its custom go-kart. The allocation of overhead costs to KartCo's standard and custom go-karts is summarized in Exhibit 4.7.

	Departmental Overhead Rate	Standard Go-Kart		Custom Go-Kart	
		Hours per Unit	Overhead Allocated	Hours per Unit	Overhead Allocated
Machining department	$60 per MH	10 MH per unit	$600	20 MH per unit	$1,200
Assembly department	$20 per DLH	5 DLH per unit	100	5 DLH per unit	100
Totals			$700		$1,300

EXHIBIT 4.7

Overhead Allocation Using Departmental Overhead Rates

Point: Total budgeted overhead costs are the same under both the plantwide and departmental rate methods.

Allocated overhead costs vary depending upon the allocation methods used. Exhibit 4.8 summarizes and compares the allocated overhead costs for standard and custom go-karts under the single plantwide overhead rate and the departmental overhead rate methods. The overhead cost allocated to each standard go-kart decreased from $720 under the plantwide overhead rate method to $700 under the departmental overhead rate method, whereas overhead cost allocated to each custom go-kart increased from $1,200 to $1,300. These differences occur because the custom go-kart requires more hours in the machining department (20 MH) than the standard go-kart requires (10 MH).

EXHIBIT 4.8

Comparison of Plantwide Overhead Rate and Departmental Overhead Rate Methods

Overhead per Unit Using:	Standard Go-Kart	Custom Go-Kart
Plantwide overhead rate method	$720	$1,200
Departmental overhead rate method.	$700	$1,300

Compared to the plantwide overhead rate method, the departmental overhead rate method usually results in more accurate overhead allocations. When cost analysts are able to logically trace overhead costs to different cost allocation bases, costing accuracy is improved. For KartCo, using the multiple departmental overhead rate method yields the following total costs per unit.

	Product Cost per Unit Using Departmental Rate Method			
	Direct Materials	Direct Labor	Overhead	Total Cost per Unit
Standard go-kart.	$400	$350	$ 700	$1,450
Custom go-kart	600	500	1,300	2,400

These costs per unit under the departmental overhead rate method are different from those under the plantwide overhead rate method. Further, this information suggests that KartCo management seriously review future production for its standard go-kart product. Specifically, these cost data imply that KartCo cannot make a profit on its standard go-kart if it meets competitors' $1,200 price.

NEED-TO-KNOW 4-1

Plantwide and Departmental Rate Methods

P1   P2

A manufacturer reports the following budgeted data for its two production departments.

	Machining	Assembly
Manufacturing overhead costs.	$600,000	$300,000
Machine hours to be used (MH)	20,000	0
Direct labor hours to be used (DLH).	20,000	5,000

1. What is the company's single plantwide overhead rate based on direct labor hours?
2. What are the company's departmental overhead rates if the machining department assigns overhead based on machine hours and the assembly department assigns overhead based on direct labor hours?
3. Using the departmental overhead rates from part 2, how much overhead should be assigned to a job that uses 16 machine hours in the machining department and 5 direct labor hours in the assembly department?

Solution

1. Plantwide overhead rate $= \dfrac{\$600,000 + \$300,000}{20,000 \text{ DLH} + 5,000 \text{ DLH}} = \dfrac{\$900,000}{25,000 \text{ DLH}} = \$36$ per direct labor hour

2. Machining department rate $= \dfrac{\$600,000}{20,000 \text{ MH}} = \$30$ per machine hour

   Assembly department rate $= \dfrac{\$300,000}{5,000 \text{ DLH}} = \$60$ per direct labor hour

Do More: QS 4-3, QS 4-4, QS 4-5, E 4-1

3. Overhead assigned to job = (16 MH × $30 per MH) + (5 DLH × $60 per DLH) = $780

Assessing the Plantwide and Departmental Overhead Rate Methods

A1

Identify and assess advantages and disadvantages of the plantwide overhead and departmental overhead rate methods.

The plantwide and departmental overhead rate methods have three key advantages: (1) They are based on readily available information, like direct labor hours. (2) They are easy to implement. (3) They are consistent with GAAP and can be used for external reporting needs. Both suffer from an important disadvantage, in that overhead costs are frequently too complex to be explained by one factor like direct labor hours or machine hours. Further, technological advances often lower direct labor costs as a percentage of total manufacturing costs, meaning direct labor hours might not be a good allocation base.

Plantwide Overhead Rate Method   The usefulness of overhead allocations based on the single plantwide overhead rate for managerial decisions depends on two critical assumptions: (1) overhead costs change with the allocation base (such as direct labor hours); and (2) all products use overhead costs in the same proportions.

The reasonableness of these assumptions varies. For companies that manufacture few products or whose operations are labor-intensive, the single plantwide method can yield reasonably useful information for managerial decisions. However, for companies with many different products or those with products that use overhead costs in very different ways, the assumptions of the single plantwide rate are not reasonable. When overhead costs, like machinery depreciation, bear little if any relation to direct labor hours used, allocating overhead cost using a single plantwide overhead rate based on direct labor hours can distort product cost and lead to poor managerial decisions. Despite such shortcomings, some companies continue to use the plantwide method for its simplicity.

Departmental Overhead Rate Method   The departmental overhead rate method is more refined than the plantwide overhead rate method, but it too can distort product costs. The departmental overhead rate method assumes that different products are similar in volume, complexity, and batch size, and that departmental overhead costs are directly proportional to the department allocation base (such as direct labor hours and machine hours for KartCo). When products differ in batch size and complexity, they usually consume different amounts of overhead costs. This is likely the case for KartCo with its high-volume standard model and its low-volume custom model built to customer specifications. In addition, since the departmental overhead rate method still allocates overhead costs based on measures closely related to production volume, it also fails to accurately assign many overhead costs, like machine depreciation or utility costs, that are not driven by production volume.

The next section describes the activity-based costing method, which is designed to overcome some of the limitations of the plantwide and departmental overhead rate methods.

Decision Ethics

Department Manager   Three department managers jointly decide to hire a consulting firm for advice on increasing departmental effectiveness and efficiency. The consulting firm spends 50% of its efforts on department "A" and 25% on each of the other two departments. The manager for department "A" suggests that the three departments equally share the consulting fee. As a manager of one of the other two departments, do you believe equal sharing is fair? ■ [Answers follow the chapter's Summary.]

Activity-Based Costing Rates and Method

Activity-based costing (ABC) attempts to more accurately assign overhead costs to the users of overhead by focusing on *activities*. Unlike the plantwide rate method, ABC uses more than a single rate. Unlike the departmental rate method, ABC focuses on activities rather than departments. In the next section we illustrate the activity-based costing method of assigning overhead costs.

C2

Explain cost flows for activity-based costing.

Cost Flows under Activity-Based Costing Method   The basic principle underlying activity-based costing is that an **activity,** which is a task, operation, or procedure, is what causes costs to be incurred. For example, cutting raw materials consumes labor and machine hours.

Likewise, warehousing products consumes resources (costs) such as employee time for driving a forklift, the electricity to power the forklift, and the wear and tear on a forklift. Also, training employees drives costs such as fees or salaries paid to trainers and the training supplies required. Generally, all activities of an organization can be linked to use of resources. An **activity cost pool** is a collection of costs that are related to the same or similar activity. Pooling costs to determine an **activity overhead (pool) rate** for all costs incurred by the same activity reduces the number of cost assignments required.

There are four basic steps to the ABC method (see Exhibit 4.9):

1. Identify activities and the overhead costs they cause.
2. Trace overhead costs to activity cost pools.
3. Compute overhead allocation rates for each activity.
4. Use the activity overhead rates to assign overhead costs to cost objects (products).

EXHIBIT 4.9

Activity-Based Costing
Method

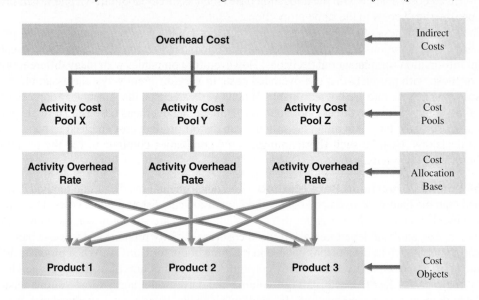

To reduce the total number of activities that must be assigned costs, similar activities (those caused by the same factor) are grouped into activity cost *pools*. For example, handling raw materials requires several activities, including wages of receiving department employees, wages of forklift employees who move materials, and depreciation on forklifts. These activities can be grouped into a single cost pool since they are all caused by the amount of materials moved. Next we apply the ABC method to KartCo.

QC1

APPLYING ACTIVITY-BASED COSTING

Activity-based costing accumulates overhead costs into activity cost pools and then uses activity rates to allocate those costs to products. This involves four steps: (1) identify activities and the costs they cause; (2) trace overhead costs to activity cost pools; (3) determine an activity rate for each activity cost pool; and (4) allocate overhead costs to products using those activity rates. To illustrate, let's return to KartCo and apply steps 1 through 4.

Step 1: Identify Activities and the Costs They Cause

Step 1 in applying ABC is to identify activities and the costs they cause. This is commonly done through discussions with employees in production departments and through reviews of production activities. The more activities that ABC tracks, the more accurately overhead costs are assigned. However, tracking too many activities makes the system cumbersome and costly to maintain. It is often necessary to reduce the number of activities tracked by combining similar activities. An activity can also involve several related tasks. The aim of this first step is to understand actions performed in the organization that drive costs.

KartCo has total overhead costs of $4,800,000 consisting of $4,000,000 indirect labor costs and $800,000 factory utilities costs. Details gathered by KartCo about its overhead costs are shown in Exhibit 4.10. Column totals for indirect labor and factory utilities correspond to amounts in Exhibit 4.4. Activity-based costing provides more detail about the activities and the costs they cause than is provided from traditional costing methods.

P3

Allocate overhead costs to products using activity-based costing.

EXHIBIT 4.10

KartCo Overhead Cost Details

Activity	Indirect Labor	Factory Utilities	Total Overhead
Machine setup	$ 700,000	—	$ 700,000
Machine repair	1,300,000	—	1,300,000
Factory maintenance	800,000	—	800,000
Engineer salaries	1,200,000	—	1,200,000
Assembly line power	—	$600,000	600,000
Heating and lighting	—	200,000	200,000
Totals	$4,000,000	$800,000	$4,800,000

Step 2: Trace Overhead Costs to Activity Cost Pools

Step 2 in applying ABC is to assign activities and their overhead costs to activity cost pools. Overhead costs are commonly accumulated by each department in a traditional accounting system. Instead of combining costs from different activities into one plantwide pool or multiple departmental pools, ABC focuses on activities as the cost object in the first step of cost assignment. We are then able to *trace* costs to a cost object and then combine activities that are used by products in similar ways to reduce the number of cost allocations.

After a review and analysis of its activities, KartCo management assigns its overhead costs into its four activity cost pools: craftsmanship, setup, design modification, and plant services (see Exhibit 4.11). To assign costs to pools, management looks for costs that are caused by similar activities.

EXHIBIT 4.11

Assigning Overhead to Activity Cost Pools

Activity Pools	Activity Cost	Pool Cost
Craftsmanship		
Assembly line power	$ 600,000	$ 600,000
Setup		
Machine setup	700,000	
Machine repair	1,300,000	2,000,000
Design modification		
Engineer salaries	1,200,000	1,200,000
Plant services		
Factory maintenance	800,000	
Heating and lighting	200,000	1,000,000
Total overhead cost		$4,800,000

Exhibit 4.11 shows that $600,000 of overhead costs are assigned to the craftsmanship cost pool; $2,000,000 to the setup cost pool; $1,200,000 to the design-modification cost pool; and $1,000,000 to the plant services cost pool. This reduces the potential number of overhead rates from six (one for each of its six activities) to four (one for each activity pool).

Step 3: Determine Activity Rates

Step 3 is to compute activity rates used to assign overhead costs to final cost objects such as products. Proper determination of activity rates depends on (1) proper identification of the factor that drives the cost in each activity cost pool and (2) proper measures of activities.

The factor that drives cost, or **activity cost driver,** is that activity causing costs in the pool to be incurred. For KartCo's overhead, craftsmanship costs are mainly driven by the direct labor

© AP Images/Christof Stache

hours used to assemble products; setup costs are driven by the number of batches produced; design-modification costs are driven by the number of new designs; and plant service costs are driven by the square feet of building space occupied. These activity cost drivers serve as the allocation base for each activity cost pool. KartCo then determines an expected activity level for each activity pool, as shown below.

Activity Cost Pool	Activity Driver (# of)	Expected Activity Level
Craftsmanship	Direct labor hours	30,000 DLH
Setup	Batches	200 batches
Design modification	Designs	10 design modifications
Plant services	Square feet	20,000 square feet

In general, cost pool activity rates are computed as:

Cost pool activity rate = Overhead costs assigned to pool ÷ Expected activity level

For KartCo, the activity rate for the craftsmanship cost pool is computed as:

Craftsmanship cost pool activity rate = $600,000 ÷ 30,000 DLH = $20 per DLH

The activity rate computations for KartCo are summarized in Exhibit 4.12.

EXHIBIT 4.12

Activity Rates for KartCo

Activity Cost Pools	Activity Driver	Overhead Costs Assigned to Pool	÷ Expected Activity Level	= Activity Rate
Craftsmanship	DLH	$ 600,000	30,000 DLH	$20 per DLH
Setup	Batches	2,000,000	200 batches	$10,000 per batch
Design modification	Number of designs	1,200,000	10 designs	$120,000 per design
Plant services	Square feet	1,000,000	20,000 sq. ft.	$50 per sq. ft.

Step 4: Assign Overhead Costs to Cost Objects

Step 4 is to assign overhead costs in each activity cost pool to final cost objects using activity rates. To do this, overhead costs are allocated to products based on the *actual* levels of activities used.

For KartCo, overhead costs in each pool are allocated to the standard go-karts and the custom go-karts using the activity rates from Exhibit 4.12. The actual activities used by each product line and the overhead costs allocated to standard and custom go-karts under ABC for KartCo are summarized in Exhibit 4.13. To illustrate, of the $600,000 of overhead costs in the craftsmanship cost pool, $500,000 is allocated to standard go-karts as follows.

Overhead from craftsmanship pool	=	**Activities consumed**	×	**Activity rate**
allocated to standard go-kart	=	25,000 DLH	×	$20 per DLH
	=	$500,000		

Point: In ABC, overhead is allocated based on the actual level of activities used, multiplied by a predetermined activity rate for each cost pool.

We know that standard go-karts require 25,000 direct labor hours and the activity rate for craftsmanship is $20 per direct labor hour. Multiplying the number of direct labor hours by the activity rate yields the craftsmanship costs assigned to standard go-karts ($500,000). Custom go-karts consumed 5,000 direct labor hours, so we assign $100,000 (5,000 DLH × $20 per DLH) of craftsmanship costs to that product line. We similarly allocate overhead of setup, design modification, and plant services pools to each type of go-kart.

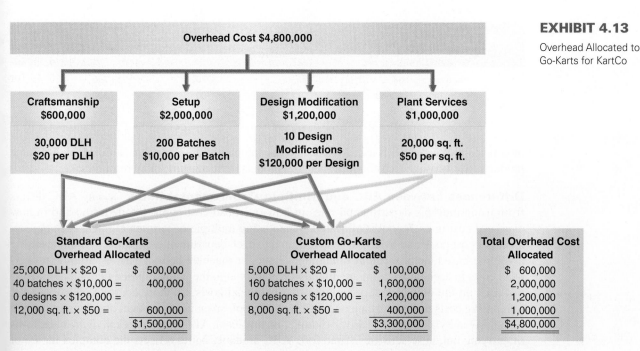

EXHIBIT 4.13

Overhead Allocated to
Go-Karts for KartCo

In assigning overhead costs to products, KartCo assigned no design-modification costs to standard go-karts because standard go-karts are sold as "off-the-shelf" items. Using ABC, a total of $1,500,000 of overhead costs is allocated to standard go-karts and a total of $3,300,000 is allocated to custom go-karts. While the total overhead cost allocated ($4,800,000) is the same as under the plantwide and departmental rate methods, the amounts allocated to the two product lines differ.

Overhead cost per unit is computed by dividing total overhead cost allocated to each product line by the number of product units. KartCo's overhead cost per unit for its standard and custom go-karts is computed and shown in Exhibit 4.14.

	(A) Total Overhead Cost Allocated	(B) Units Produced	(A ÷ B) Overhead Cost per Unit
Standard go-kart	$1,500,000	5,000 units	$ 300 per unit
Custom go-kart	3,300,000	1,000 units	$3,300 per unit

EXHIBIT 4.14

Overhead Cost per Unit for
Go-Karts Using ABC

Total cost per unit for KartCo using ABC for its two products follows.

	Direct Materials	Direct Labor	Overhead	Total Cost per Unit
Standard go-kart ...	$400	$350	$ 300	$1,050
Custom go-kart	600	500	3,300	4,400

Assuming that ABC more accurately assigns costs, we now are able to help KartCo's management understand how its competitors can sell their standard models at $1,200 and why KartCo is flooded with orders for custom go-karts. Specifically, if the cost to produce a standard go-kart is $1,050, as shown above (and not $1,470 as computed using the plantwide rate or $1,450 computed using departmental rates), a profit of $150 ($1,200 − $1,050) occurs on each standard unit sold at the competitive $1,200 market price. Further, selling its custom go-kart at $3,500 is a mistake by KartCo management because it is losing $900 ($3,500 − $4,400) on each custom go-kart sold. That is, KartCo has underpriced its custom go-kart relative to its production costs and competitors' prices, which explains why the company has more custom orders than it can supply.

Exhibit 4.15 summarizes overhead allocation per go-kart under the single plantwide rate method, multiple departmental rate method, and ABC. Overhead cost allocated to standard go-karts is much less under ABC than under either of the volume-based costing methods. One reason for this difference is the large design-modification costs that were spread over all go-karts under both the plantwide rate and the departmental rate methods even though standard go-karts require no engineering

Point: Accurately assigning costs to products is key to setting many product prices. If product costs are inaccurate and result in prices that are too low, the company loses money on each item sold. Likewise, if product prices are improperly set too high, the company loses business to competitors. ABC can be used to more accurately set prices.

EXHIBIT 4.15

Comparison of Overhead
Allocations by Method

Overhead Cost Allocation Method	Overhead Cost per Go-Kart	
	Standard Go-Kart	Custom Go-Kart
Plantwide method	$720	$1,200
Departmental method....................	700	1,300
Activity-based costing	300	3,300

modification. When ABC is used, overhead costs commonly shift from standardized, high-volume products to low-volume, customized specialty products that consume more resources.

Differences between ABC and Multiple Departmental Rates   Using ABC differs from using multiple departmental rates in how overhead cost pools are identified and in how overhead cost in each pool is allocated. When using multiple departmental rates, each *department* is a cost pool, and overhead cost allocated to each department is assigned to products using a volume-based factor (such as direct labor hours or machine hours). This assumes that overhead costs in each department are directly proportional to the volume-based factor.

ABC, on the other hand, recognizes that overhead costs are more complex. For example, purchasing costs might make up one activity cost pool, spanning more than one department and being driven by a single cost driver (number of invoices). ABC emphasizes *activities* and costs of carrying out these activities. Therefore, ABC arguably better reflects the complex nature of overhead costs and how these costs are used in making products.

■ Decision Maker

Entrepreneur   You are the entrepreneur of a start-up pharmaceutical company. You are assigning overhead to product units based on machine hours in the packaging area. Profits are slim due to increased competition. One of your larger overhead costs is $10,000 for cleaning and sterilization that occurs each time the packaging system is converted from one product to another. These overhead costs average $0.10 per product unit. Can you reduce cleaning and sterilizing costs by reducing the number of units produced? If not, what should you do to control these overhead costs? ■   [Answers follow the chapter's Summary.]

Activity-Based Costing

P3

A manufacturer makes two types of snowmobiles, Basic and Deluxe, and reports the following data to be used in applying activity-based costing. The company budgets production of 6,000 Basic snowmobiles and 2,000 Deluxe snowmobiles.

Activity Cost Pool	Activity Cost Driver	Cost Assigned to Pool	Basic	Deluxe
Machine setup	Number of setups	$ 150,000	200 setups	300 setups
Materials handling ...	Number of parts	250,000	10 parts per unit	20 parts per unit
Machine depreciation	Machine hours (MH)	720,000	1 MH per unit	1.5 MH per unit
Total		$1,120,000		

1. Compute overhead activity rates for each cost pool using ABC.
2. Compute the total amount of overhead cost to be allocated to each of the company's product lines using ABC.
3. Compute the overhead cost per unit for each product line using ABC.

Solution

1. Machine setup activity rate $= \dfrac{\$150,000}{200 + 300} = \$300$ per machine setup

   Materials handling activity rate $= \dfrac{\$250,000}{60,000 + 40,000^*} = \$2.50$ per part

   *(6,000 units $\times$ 10 parts per unit for Basic, 2,000 units $\times$ 20 parts per unit for Deluxe)

   Machine depreciation activity rate $= \dfrac{\$720,000}{6,000 + 3,000^{**}} = \$80$ per machine hour

   **(6,000 units $\times$ 1 MH per unit for Basic, 2,000 units $\times$ 1.5 MH per unit for Deluxe)

2.

Activity Cost Pool	Activity Pool Rate	Basic		Deluxe	
Machine setup	$300 per setup	$300 × 200 =	$ 60,000	$300 × 300 =	$ 90,000
Materials handling. . .	$2.50 per part	$2.50 × 6,000 × 10 =	150,000	$2.50 × 2,000 × 20 =	100,000
Machine depreciation	$80 per MH	$80 × 6,000 × 1 =	480,000	$80 × 2,000 × 1.5 =	240,000
Totals			$690,000		$430,000

3. Basic snowmobile overhead cost per unit $= \dfrac{\$690,000}{6,000} = \$115$ per unit

Deluxe snowmobile overhead cost per unit $= \dfrac{\$430,000}{2,000} = \$215$ per unit

QC2

Do More: QS 4-8, QS 4-9, QS 4-10, E 4-2, E 4-11, E 4-12

ASSESSING ACTIVITY-BASED COSTING

While activity-based costing can improve the accuracy of overhead cost allocations to products, it too has limitations. This section describes the major advantages and disadvantages of activity-based costing.

A2
Identify and assess advantages and disadvantages of activity-based costing.

Advantages of Activity-Based Costing

More Accurate Overhead Cost Allocation   Companies have typically used either a plantwide overhead rate or multiple departmental overhead rates because these methods are more straightforward than ABC and are acceptable under GAAP for external reporting. Under these traditional systems, overhead costs are pooled in a few large pools and are spread uniformly across high- and low-volume products. With ABC, overhead costs are grouped into activity pools. There are usually more activity pools under ABC than cost pools under traditional costing, which usually increases costing accuracy. More important is that overhead costs in each ABC pool are caused by a single activity. This means that overhead costs in each activity pool are allocated to products based on the cost of resources consumed by a product (input) rather than on how many units are produced (output). In sum, overhead cost allocation under ABC is more accurate because (1) there are more cost pools, (2) costs in each pool are more similar, and (3) allocation is based on activities that cause overhead costs.

Point: ABC is not acceptable under GAAP for external financial reporting.

Point: ABC can allocate the selling and administrative costs expensed by GAAP to activities; such costs can include marketing costs, costs to process orders, and costs to process customer returns.

More Effective Overhead Cost Control   Using the plantwide or departmental rate methods, companies usually allocate overhead costs to products based on either direct labor hours or machine hours. Such allocation typically leads management to focus attention on direct labor cost or machine hours. Yet, direct labor or machine hours are often not the cause of overhead costs and often not even linked with these volume-related measures. As we saw with KartCo, design modifications markedly affect its overhead costs. Consequently, a plantwide overhead rate or departmental overhead rate based on direct labor or machine hours can mislead managers, preventing effective control of overhead costs and leading to product mispricing. ABC, on the other hand, can be used to identify activities that can benefit from process improvement. ABC can also help managers effectively control overhead costs by focusing on processes or activities such as setups, order processing, and design modifications instead of focusing only on direct labor or machine hours. For KartCo, identification of large design-modification costs would allow managers to work on ways to improve this process. Besides controlling overhead costs, KartCo's better assignment of overhead costs (particularly design-modification costs) for its go-karts helps its managers make better production and pricing decisions.

Focus on Relevant Factors   Basing cost assignment on activities is not limited to determining product costs. ABC can be used to assign costs to any cost object that is of management interest. For instance, a marketing manager often wants to determine the profitability of various market segments. Activity-based costing can be used to accurately assign costs of shipping, advertising, order-taking, and customer service that are unrelated to sales and costs of products sold. Such an activity-based analysis can reveal to the marketing department some customers that are better left to the competition if they consume a larger amount of marketing resources than the gross profit generated by sales to

Point: Many companies use ABC techniques for these types of special projects even if they don't use ABC in determining overall product costs.

© Getty Images

those customers. Generally, ABC provides better customer profitability information by including all resources consumed to serve a customer. This allows managers to make better pricing decisions on custom orders and to better manage customers by focusing on those that are most profitable.

Better Management of Activities   Being competitive requires that managers be able to use resources efficiently. Understanding how costs are incurred is a first step toward controlling costs. One important contribution of ABC is helping managers identify the causes of costs, that is, the activities driving them. **Activity-based management (ABM)** is an outgrowth of ABC that draws on the link between activities and cost incurrence for better management. Activity-based management can be useful in distinguishing **value-added activities,** which add value to a product, from *non-value-added activities,* which do not. For KartCo, its value-added activities include machining, assembly, and the costs of engineering design changes. Its non-value-added activity is machine repair. The way to control a cost requires changing how much of an activity is performed.

▢ Decision Insight

The ABCs of Decisions   Business managers must make long-term strategic decisions, day-to-day operating decisions, and decisions on the type of financing the business needs. Survey evidence suggests that managers find ABC more useful in making strategic, operating, and financing decisions than non-ABC methods. ▪

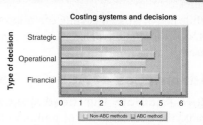

Average response, 0=Not useful, 6=Extremely useful
Source: Stratton et al., Management Accounting Quarterly, 2009

Costs of Quality   A focus on the costs of activities, via ABC and ABM, lends itself to assessments of the **costs of quality.** These costs refer to costs resulting from manufacturing defective products or providing services that do not meet customer expectations. Exhibit 4.16 summarizes the typical costs of quality. These costs can be summarized in a **cost of quality report,** which lists the costs of quality activities by category. A focus on activities and quality costs can lead to higher quality and lower costs.

EXHIBIT 4.16

Types of Quality Costs

Costs of Good Quality

Prevention costs

Appraisal costs

Costs of Poor Quality

Internal failure costs

External failure costs

Cost of Quality Report	
	Cost
Prevention	
Training	$ 22,000
Appraisal	
Inspecting materials	37,500
Testing finished goods	14,200
Internal failure	
Rework	8,250
Scrap	11,750
External failure	
Warranty claims	45,700
Total cost of quality	$139,400

Point: Prevention and appraisal costs are usually considered value-added costs, while internal and external costs are considered non-value-added costs.

Prevention and *appraisal costs* are incurred before a good or service is provided to a customer. The purpose of these costs is to reduce the chance the customer is provided a defective good or service. These are the costs of trying to ensure that only good-quality items are produced. Prevention activities focus on quality training and improvement programs to ensure quality is built into the product or service. Common appraisal costs include the costs of inspections to ensure that materials and supplies meet specifications and inspections of finished goods.

Internal and external failure costs are the costs of making poor-quality items. *Internal failure costs* are incurred after a company has manufactured a defective product but before that product has been delivered to a customer. Internal failure costs include the costs of reworking products, reinspecting reworked products, and scrap.

Finally, *external failure costs* are incurred after a customer has been provided a defective product or service. Examples of this type of cost include costs of warranty repairs and costs of recalling products. This category also includes lost profits due to dissatisfied customers buying from other companies.

Disadvantages of Activity-Based Costing

Costs to Implement and Maintain ABC   Designing and implementing an activity-based costing system requires management commitment and financial resources. For ABC to be effective, a thorough analysis of cost activities must be performed and appropriate cost pools must be determined. Collecting and analyzing cost data is expensive and so is maintaining an ABC system. While technology, such as bar coding, has made it possible for many companies to use ABC, it is still too costly for some. Managers must weigh the cost of implementing and maintaining an ABC system against the potential benefits of ABC in light of company circumstances.

Uncertainty with Decisions Remains   As with all cost information, managers must interpret ABC data with caution in making decisions. In the KartCo case, given the huge design-modification costs for custom go-karts determined under the ABC system, a manager might be tempted to decline some custom go-kart orders to save overhead costs. However, in the short run, some or all of the design-modification costs cannot be saved even if some custom go-kart orders are rejected. Managers must examine carefully the controllability of costs before making decisions.

ABC for Service Providers

Although we've shown how to use ABC in a manufacturing setting, ABC also applies to service providers. The only requirements for ABC are the existence of costs and demand for reliable cost information. **First Tennessee National Corporation**, a bank, applied ABC and found that 30% of its certificate of deposit (CD) customers provided nearly 90% of its profits from CDs. Further, 30% of the bank's CD customers were actually losing money for the bank. The bank's management used ABC to correct the problem and increase profits. Laboratories performing medical tests, accounting and law offices, and advertising agencies are other examples of service firms that can benefit from ABC. (Refer to this chapter's Decision Analysis for an example of applying ABC to assess customer profitability and this chapter's Comprehensive Need-To-Know for an example of applying ABC to a law firm.)

Types of Activities

Activities causing overhead costs can be separated into four levels of types of activities: (1) **unit-level activities**, (2) **batch-level activities**, (3) **product-level activities**, and (4) **facility-level activities**. These four activities are described as follows.

C3

Describe the four types of activities that cause overhead costs.

Activity Levels

Unit-level activities are performed on each product unit. For example, the machining department needs electricity to power the machinery to produce each unit of product. Unit-level costs tend to change with the number of units produced.

Batch-level activities are performed only on each batch or group of units. For example, machine setup is needed only for each batch regardless of the units in that batch, and customer order processing must be performed for each order regardless of the number of units ordered. Batch-level costs do not vary with the number of units, but instead vary with the number of batches.

Product-level activities are performed on each product line and are not affected by either the numbers of units or batches. For example, product design is needed only for each product line. Product-level costs do not vary with the number of units or batches produced.

Facility-level activities are performed to sustain facility capacity as a whole and are not caused by any specific product. For example, rent and factory maintenance costs are incurred no matter what is being produced. Facility-level costs do not vary with what is manufactured, how many batches are produced, or the output quantity.

In the KartCo example, the craftsmanship pool reflects unit-level costs, the setup pool reflects batch-level costs, the design-modification pool reflects product-level costs, and plant services reflect facility-level costs.

Exhibit 4.17 shows additional examples of activities commonly found within each of the four activity levels. This is not a complete list, but reviewing it can help in understanding this hierarchy of production activities. This list also includes common measures used to reflect the specific activity identified. Knowing this hierarchy can help us simplify and understand activity-based costing.

EXHIBIT 4.17

Examples of Activities by Activity Level

Activity Level	Examples of Activity	Activity Driver (Measure)
Unit level	Cutting parts	Machine hours
	Assembling components	Direct labor hours
	Printing checks	Number of checks
Batch level	Calibrating machines	Number of batches
	Receiving shipments	Number of orders
	Sampling product quality	Number of lots produced
Product level	Designing modifications	Change requests
	Organizing production	Engineering hours
	Controlling inventory	Parts per product
Facility level	Cleaning workplace	Square feet of floors*
	Providing electricity	Kilowatt hours*
	Providing personnel support	Number of employees*

* Facility-level costs are not traceable to individual product lines, batches, or units. They are normally assigned to units using a unit-level driver such as direct labor hours or machine hours even though they are caused by another activity.

GLOBAL VIEW

© Robert Gallagher/Forbes Magazine/
Forbes Collection/Corbis Outline

Toyota Motor Corporation pioneered *lean manufacturing,* which focuses on eliminating waste while satisfying customers. Many lean manufacturers embrace **lean accounting,** which has two key components. First, the company applies lean thinking to eliminate waste in its accounting process. Second, instead of focusing on cost allocation methods such as activity-based costing, the company develops alternative performance measures that better reflect the benefits of manufacturing process changes. Examples include the percentage of products produced without defects, the percentage of ontime deliveries, and the level of sales per employee.

Sustainability and Accounting   Suja Juice Co. also relies on lean techniques. The company must use extremely fresh raw materials, thus it employs just-in-time inventory management. Likewise, its finished product has a limited shelf life, so managers must carefully monitor sales demand to ensure that no juice is wasted.

 Decision Analysis **Customer Profitability**

Are all customers equal? To help answer this, let's return to the KartCo case and assume that costs of providing customer support (such as delivery, installation, and warranty work) are related to the distance a technician must travel to provide services. Also assume that, as a result of applying activity-based costing, KartCo plans to sell its standard go-kart for $1,200 per unit. If the annual cost of customer services is expected to be $250,000 and the distance traveled by technicians is 100,000 miles annually, KartCo would want to link the cost of customer services with individual customers to make efficient marketing decisions.

Using these data, an activity rate of $2.50 per mile ($250,000/100,000 miles) is computed for assigning customer service costs to individual customers. For KartCo, it would compute a typical customer profitability report for one of its customers, Six Flags, as follows.

Customer Profitability Report—Six Flags		
Sales (10 standard go-karts × $1,200).............................		$12,000
Less: Product costs		
Direct materials (10 go-karts × $400 per go-kart)	$4,000	
Direct labor (10 go-karts × $350 per go-kart)...................	3,500	
Overhead (10 go-karts × $300 per go-kart, Exhibit 4.14)	3,000	10,500
Product profit margin		1,500
Less: Customer service costs (200 miles × $2.50 per mile)		500
Customer profit margin.......................................		$ 1,000

Analysis indicates that a total profit margin of $1,000 is generated from this customer. The management of KartCo can see that if this customer requires service technicians to travel more than 600 miles ($1,500 ÷ $2.50 per mile), the sale of 10 standard go-karts to this customer would be unprofitable. ABC encourages management to consider all resources consumed to serve a customer, not just manufacturing costs that are the focus of traditional costing methods.

Silver Law Firm provides litigation and mediation services to a variety of clients. Attorneys keep track of the time they spend on each case, which is used to charge fees to clients at a rate of $300 per hour. A management advisor commented that activity-based costing might prove useful in evaluating the costs of its legal services, and the firm has decided to evaluate its fee structure by comparing ABC to its alternative cost allocations. The following data relate to a typical month at the firm. During a typical month the firm handles seven mediation cases and three litigation cases.

	Activity Driver	Total Amount	Consumption by Service Type		Activity Cost
			Litigation	Mediation	
Providing legal advice.................	Billable hours	200	75	125	$30,000
Overhead costs					
Internal support departments					
Preparing documents	Documents	30	16	14	$ 4,000
Occupying office space	Billable hours	200	75	125	1,200
Heating and lighting of office	Billable hours	200	75	125	350
External support departments					
Registering court documents	Documents	30	16	14	1,250
Retaining consultants (investigators, psychiatrists)	Court dates	6	5	1	10,000
Using contract services (couriers, security guards)	Court dates	6	5	1	5,000
Total overhead costs					$21,800

Required

1. Determine the cost of providing legal services to each type of case using activity-based costing (ABC).
2. Determine the cost of each type of case using a single plantwide rate for nonattorney costs based on billable hours.
3. Determine the cost of each type of case using multiple departmental overhead rates for the internal support department (based on number of documents) and external support department (based on billable hours).
4. Compare and discuss the costs assigned under each method for management decisions.

PLANNING THE SOLUTION

- Compute pool rates and assign costs to cases using ABC.
- Compute costs for the cases using the volume-based methods and discuss differences between these costs and the costs computed using ABC.

SOLUTION

1. We need to set up activity pools and compute pool rates for ABC. All activities except "occupying office space" and "heating and lighting" are unit-level activities (meaning they are traceable to the individual cases handled by the law firm). "Preparing documents" and "registering documents" are both driven by the number of documents associated with each case. We can therefore combine these activities and their costs into a single pool, which we call "clerical support." Similarly, "retaining consultants" and "using services" are related to the number of times the attorneys must go to court (court dates). We combine these activities and their costs into another activity cost pool labeled "litigation support." The costs associated with occupying office space and the heating and lighting are facility level activities and are not traceable to individual cases. Yet they are costs that must be covered by fees charged to clients. We assign these costs using a convenient base—in this example we use the number of billable hours, which attorneys record for each client. Providing legal advice is the direct labor for law firm.

Activity Pool	Activity Cost	Pool Cost	Activity Driver	Pool Rate (Pool Cost ÷ Activity Driver)
Providing legal advice	$30,000	$30,000	200 billable hours	$150 per billable hour
Clerical support				
Preparing documents	4,000			
Registering documents	1,250	5,250	30 documents	$175 per document
Litigation support				
Retaining consultants	10,000			
Using services	5,000	15,000	6 court dates	$2,500 per court date
Facility costs				
Occupying office space	1,200			
Heating and lighting	350	1,550	200 billable hours	$7.75 per billable hour

We next determine the cost of providing each type of legal service as shown in the following table. Specifically, the pool rates from above are used to assign costs to each type of service provided by the law firm. Since litigation consumed 75 billable hours of attorney time, we assign $11,250 (75 billable hours × $150 per billable hour) of the cost of providing legal advice to this type of case. Mediation required 125 hours of attorney time, so $18,750 (125 billable hours × $150 per billable hour) of the cost to provide legal advice is assigned to mediation cases. Clerical support costs $175 per document, so the cost associated with activities in this cost pool are assigned to litigation cases (16 documents × $175 per document = $2,800) and mediation cases (14 documents × $175 per document = $2,450). The costs of activities in the litigation support and the facility cost pools are similarly assigned to the two case types.

We compute the total cost of litigation ($27,131.25) and mediation ($24,668.75) and divide these totals by the number of cases of each type to determine the average cost of each case type: $9,044 for litigation and $3,524 for mediation. This analysis shows that charging clients $300 per billable hour without regard to the type of case results in litigation clients being charged less than the cost to provide that service ($7,500 versus $9,044).

	Pool Rate	Litigation		Mediation	
Providing legal advice.	$150 per billable hour	75 hours	$11,250.00	125 hours	$18,750.00
Clerical support.	$175 per document	16 docs	2,800.00	14 docs	2,450.00
Litigation support	$2,500 per court date	5 court dates	12,500.00	1 court date	2,500.00
Facility costs	$7.75 per billable hour	75 hours	581.25	125 hours	968.75
Total cost.			$27,131.25		$24,668.75
÷ Number of cases.			3 cases		7 cases
Average cost per case.			**$9,044**		**$3,524**
Average fee per case.			**$7,500***		**$5,357**†

* (75 billable hours × $300 per hour) ÷ 3 cases   † (125 billable hours × $300 per hour) ÷ 7 cases

2. The cost of each type of case using a single plantwide rate for nonattorney costs (that is, all costs except for those related to providing legal advice) based on billable hours is as follows.

Total overhead cost/Total billable hours = $21,800/200 billable hours = $109 per hour

We then determine the cost of providing each type of legal service as follows.

		Litigation		Mediation	
Providing legal advice...........	$150 per billable hour	75 hours	$11,250	125 hours	$18,750
Overhead (from part 2)	$109 per billable hour	75 hours	8,175	125 hours	13,625
Total cost....................			$19,425		$32,375
÷ Number of cases...........			3 cases		7 cases
Average cost per case.........			$6,475		$4,625
Average fee per case........... (from part 1)			$7,500		$5,357

3. The cost of each type of case using multiple departmental overhead rates for the internal support department (based on number of documents) and external support department (based on billable hours) is determined as follows.

	Departmental Cost	Base	Departmental Rate (Departmental Cost ÷ Base)
Internal support departments			
Preparing documents.........	$ 4,000		
Occupying office space	1,200		
Heating and lighting of office ...	350	$ 5,550	30 documents	$185 per document
External support departments			
Registering documents	1,250		
Retaining consultants	10,000		
Using contract services.......	5,000	16,250	200 billable hours	$81.25 per hour

The departmental overhead rates computed above are used to assign overhead costs to the two types of legal services. For the internal support department we use the overhead rate of $185 per document to assign $2,960 ($185 × 16 documents) to litigation and $2,590 ($185 × 14 documents) to mediation. For the external support department we use the overhead rate of $81.25 per hour to assign $6,093.75 ($81.25 × 75 hours) to litigation and $10,156.25 ($81.25 × 125 hours) to mediation. As shown below, the resulting average costs of litigation cases and mediation cases are $6,768 and $4,499, respectively. Using this method of cost assignment, it *appears* that the fee of $300 per billable hour is adequate to cover costs associated with each case.

		Litigation		Mediation	
Attorney fees..........	$150 per billable hour	75 hours	$11,250.00	125 hours	$18,750.00
Internal support........	$185 per document	16 documents	2,960.00	14 documents	2,590.00
External support	$81.25 per hour	75 hours	6,093.75	125 hours	10,156.25
Total cost.............			$20,303.75		$31,496.25
÷ Number of cases.....			3 cases		7 cases
Average cost per case...			$6,768		$4,499
Average fee per case.... (from part 1)			$7,500		$5,357

4. A comparison and discussion of the costs assigned under each method follows.

Average Cost per Case	Method of Assigning Overhead Costs		
	Activity-Based Costing	Plantwide Overhead Rate	Departmental Overhead Rates
Litigation cases...................	$9,044	$6,475	$6,768
Mediation cases	3,524	4,625	4,499

The departmental and plantwide overhead rate methods assign overhead on the basis of volume-related measures (billable hours and document filings). Litigation costs *appear* profitable under these methods, because the average costs are below the average revenue of $7,500. ABC, however, focuses attention on activities that drive costs. A large part of overhead costs was for consultants and contract services, which were unrelated to the number of cases, but related to the type of cases consuming those resources. Using ABC, the costs shift from the high-volume cases (mediation) to the low-volume cases (litigation). When the firm considers the consumption of resources for these cases using ABC, it finds that the fees charged to litigate cases is insufficient (average revenue of $7,500 versus average cost of $9,044). The law firm is charging too little for the complex cases that require litigation.

Summary

C1 **Distinguish between the plantwide overhead rate method, the departmental overhead rate method, and the activity-based costing method.** Overhead costs can be assigned to cost objects using a plantwide rate that combines all overhead costs into a single rate, usually based on direct labor hours, machine hours, or direct labor cost. Multiple departmental overhead rates that include overhead costs traceable to departments are used to allocate overhead based on departmental functions. ABC links overhead costs to activities and assigns overhead based on how much of each activity is required for a product.

C2 **Explain cost flows for activity-based costing.** With ABC, overhead costs are first traced to the activities that cause them, and then cost pools are formed combining costs caused by the same activity. Overhead rates based on these activities are then used to assign overhead to products in proportion to the amount of activity required to produce them.

C3 **Describe the four types of activities that cause overhead costs.** The four types of activities that cause overhead costs are: (1) unit-level activities, (2) batch-level activities, (3) product-level activities, and (4) facility-level activities. Unit-level activities are performed on each unit, batch-level activities are performed only on each group of units, and product-level activities are performed only on each product line. Facility-level activities are performed to sustain facility capacity and are not caused by any specific product. Understanding these types of activities can help in applying activity-based costing.

A1 **Identify and assess advantages and disadvantages of the plantwide overhead and departmental overhead rate methods.** A single plantwide overhead rate is a simple way to assign overhead cost. A disadvantage is that it can inaccurately assign costs when costs are caused by multiple factors and when different products consume different amounts of

inputs. Overhead costing accuracy is improved by use of multiple departmental rates because differences across departmental functions can be linked to costs incurred in departments. Yet, accuracy of cost assignment with departmental rates suffers from the same problems associated with plantwide rates because activities required for each product are not identified with costs of providing those activities.

A2 **Identify and assess advantages and disadvantages of activity-based costing.** ABC improves product costing accuracy and draws management attention to relevant factors to control. The cost of constructing and maintaining an ABC system can sometimes outweigh its value.

P1 **Allocate overhead costs to products using the plantwide overhead rate method.** The plantwide overhead rate equals total budgeted overhead divided by budgeted plant volume, the latter often measured in direct labor hours or machine hours. This rate multiplied by the number of direct labor hours (or machine hours) required for each product provides the overhead assigned to each product.

P2 **Allocate overhead costs to products using the departmental overhead rate method.** When using multiple departmental rates, overhead costs must first be traced to each department and then divided by the measure of output for that department to yield the departmental overhead rate. Overhead is applied to products using this rate as products pass through each department.

P3 **Allocate overhead costs to products using activity-based costing.** With ABC, overhead costs are matched to activities that cause them. If there is more than one cost with the same activity, these costs are combined into pools. An overhead rate for each pool is determined by dividing total cost for that pool by its activity measure. Overhead costs are assigned to products by multiplying the ABC pool rate by the amount of the activity required for each product.

Guidance Answers to Decision Maker and Decision Ethics

Department Manager When dividing a bill, common sense suggests fairness. That is, if one department consumes more services than another, we attempt to share the bill in proportion to consumption. Equally dividing the bill among the number of departments is fair if each consumed equal services. This same notion applies in assigning costs to products and services. For

example, dividing overhead costs by the number of units is fair if all products consumed overhead in equal proportion.

Entrepreneur Cleaning and sterilizing costs are not directly related to the volume of product manufactured. Thus, changing the number of units produced does not necessarily reduce these costs. Further, expressing costs of cleaning and sterilizing on a per unit basis is often misleading for the person responsible for controlling costs. Costs of cleaning and sterilizing are related to changing from one product line to another. Consequently, the

way to control those costs is to control the number of times the packaging system has to be changed for a different product line. Thus, efficient product scheduling would help reduce those overhead costs and improve profitability.

Key Terms

Activity

Activity-based costing (ABC)

Activity-based management (ABM)

Activity cost driver

Activity cost pool

Activity overhead (pool) rate

Batch-level activities

Cost object

Cost of quality report

Costs of quality

Facility-level activities

Lean accounting

Product-level activities

Unit-level activities

Value-added activities

Multiple Choice Quiz   Answers at end of chapter

1. In comparison to a traditional cost system, and when there are batch-level or product-level costs, an activity-based costing system usually:
   a. Shifts costs from low-volume to high-volume products.
   b. Shifts costs from high-volume to low-volume products.
   c. Shifts costs from standardized to specialized products.
   d. Shifts costs from specialized to standardized products.

2. Which of the following statements is (are) true?
   a. An activity-based costing system is generally easier to implement and maintain than a traditional costing system.
   b. One of the goals of activity-based management is the elimination of waste by allocating costs to products that waste resources.
   c. Activity-based costing uses a number of activity cost pools, each of which is allocated to products on the basis of direct labor hours.
   d. Activity rates in activity-based costing are computed by dividing costs from the first-stage allocations by the activity measure for each activity cost pool.

3. All of the following are examples of batch-level activities except:
   a. Purchase order processing.
   b. Setting up equipment.
   c. Clerical activity associated with processing purchase orders to produce an order for a standard product.
   d. Employee recreational facilities.

4. A company has two products: A and B. It uses activity-based costing and prepares the following analysis showing budgeted cost and activity for each of its three activity cost pools.

Activity Cost Pool	Budgeted Overhead Cost	Budgeted Activity		
		Product A	Product B	Total
Activity 1	$ 80,000	200	800	1,000
Activity 2	58,400	1,000	500	1,500
Activity 3	360,000	600	5,400	6,000

Annual production and sales level of Product A is 18,188 units, and the annual production and sales level of Product B is 31,652 units. The approximate overhead cost per unit of Product B under activity-based costing is:
   a. $2.02   c. $12.87
   b. $5.00   d. $22.40

5. A company uses activity-based costing to determine the costs of its two products: A and B. The budgeted cost and activity for each of the company's three activity cost pools follow.

Activity Cost Pool	Budgeted Cost	Budgeted Activity		
		Product A	Product B	Total
Activity 1	$19,800	800	300	1,100
Activity 2	16,000	2,200	1,800	4,000
Activity 3	14,000	400	300	700

The activity rate under the activity-based costing method for Activity 3 is.
   a. $4.00   c. $18.00
   b. $8.59   d. $20.00

Icon denotes assignments that involve decision making.

Discussion Questions

1. Why are overhead costs allocated to products and not traced to products as direct materials and direct labor are?

2. What are three common methods of assigning overhead costs to a product?

3. Why are direct labor hours and machine hours commonly used as the bases for overhead allocation?

4. What are the advantages of using a single plantwide overhead rate?

5. The usefulness of a single plantwide overhead rate is based on two assumptions. What are those assumptions?

6. What is a cost object?

7. 🔘 Explain why a single plantwide overhead rate can distort the cost of a particular product.

8. 🔘 Why are multiple departmental overhead rates more accurate for product costing than a single plantwide overhead rate?

9. In what way are departmental overhead rates similar to a single plantwide overhead rate? How are they different?

10. Why is overhead allocation under ABC usually more accurate than either the plantwide overhead allocation method or the departmental overhead allocation method?

11. 🔘 **Google** reports costs in financial **GOOGLE** statements. If plantwide overhead rates are allowed for reporting costs to external users, why might a company choose to use a more complicated and more expensive method for assigning overhead costs to products?

12. What is the first step in applying activity-based costing?

13. What is an activity cost driver?

14. **Apple**'s production requires activities. What are value-added activities? **APPLE**

15. What are the four activity levels associated with activity-based costing? Define each.

16. 🔘 **Samsung** is a manufacturer. "Activity-based costing is only useful for manufacturing companies." Is this a true statement? Explain. **Samsung**

17. 🔘 **Apple** must assign overhead costs to its products. Activity-based costing is generally **APPLE** considered more accurate than other methods of assigning overhead. If this is so, why don't all manufacturing companies use it?

🖥 **connect**

QUICK STUDY

In the blank next to each of the following terms, place the letter *A* through *D* that corresponds to the description of that term. Some letters are used more than once.

QS 4-1

Overhead cost allocation methods

C1

_____ **1.** Activity-based costing
_____ **2.** Plantwide overhead rate method
_____ **3.** Departmental overhead rate method

A. Uses more than one rate to allocate overhead costs to products.

B. Uses only volume-based measures such as direct labor hours to allocate overhead costs to products.

C. Typically uses the most overhead allocation rates.

D. Focuses on the costs of carrying out activities.

QS 4-2

Cost allocation methods

C1

1. Which costing method assumes all products use overhead costs in the same proportions?
   a. Activity-based costing
   b. Plantwide overhead rate method
   c. Departmental overhead rate method
   d. All cost allocation methods

2. Which of the following would usually *not* be used in computing plantwide overhead rates?
   a. Direct labor hours
   b. Number of quality inspections
   c. Direct labor dollars
   d. Machine hours

3. With ABC, overhead costs should be traced to which cost object first?
   a. Units of product
   b. Departments
   c. Activities
   d. Product batches

QS 4-3

Plantwide rate method

P1

A manufacturer uses machine hours to assign overhead costs to products. Budgeted information for the next year follows. Compute the plantwide overhead rate for the next year based on machine hours.

Budgeted factory overhead costs	$544,000
Budgeted machine hours	6,400

QS 4-4

Compute plantwide overhead rates

P1

Rafner Manufacturing identified the following budgeted data in its two production departments.

	Assembly	Finishing
Manufacturing overhead costs.........	$1,200,000	$600,000
Direct labor hours..................	12,000 DLH	20,000 DLH
Machine hours	6,000 MH	16,000 MH

1. What is the company's single plantwide overhead rate based on direct labor hours?
2. What is the company's single plantwide overhead rate based on machine hours? (Round your answer to two decimal places.)

Refer to the information in QS 4-4. What are the company's departmental overhead rates if the assembly department assigns overhead based on direct labor hours and the finishing department assigns overhead based on machine hours?

QS 4-5
Compute departmental
overhead rates   P2

List the three main advantages of the plantwide and departmental overhead rate methods.

QS 4-6
Advantages of plantwide
and departmental rate
methods   A1

In the blank next to the following terms, place the letter A through D corresponding to the best description of that term.

_____ **1.** Activity
_____ **2.** Activity driver
_____ **3.** Cost object
_____ **4.** Cost pool

A. Measurement associated with an activity.
B. A group of costs that have the same activity drivers.
C. Anything to which costs will be assigned.
D. A task that causes a cost to be incurred.

QS 4-7
Costing terminology
C2

A manufacturer uses activity-based costing to assign overhead costs to products. Budgeted information for selected activities for next year follows. Form two cost pools and compute activity rates for each of the cost pools.

QS 4-8
Computing activity rates
P3

Activity	Expected Cost	Cost Driver	Expected Usage of Cost Driver
Purchasing	$135,000	Purchase orders	4,500 purchase orders
Cleaning factory..........	32,000	Square feet	5,000 square feet
Providing utilities	65,000	Square feet	5,000 square feet

---

Aziz Company sells two types of products, Basic and Deluxe. The company provides technical support for users of its products, at an expected cost of $250,000 per year. The company expects to process 10,000 customer service calls per year.
1. Determine the company's cost of technical support per customer service call.
2. During the month of January, Aziz received 550 calls for customer service on its Deluxe model and 250 calls for customer service on its Basic model. Assign technical support costs to each model using activity-based costing (ABC).

QS 4-9
Assigning costs using
ABC
P3

A company uses activity-based costing to determine the costs of its three products: A, B, and C. The budgeted cost and cost driver activity for each of the company's three activity cost pools follow. Compute the activity rates for each of the company's three activities.

QS 4-10
Computing activity rates
P3

Activity Cost Pool	Budgeted Cost	Budgeted Activity of Cost Driver		
		Product A	Product B	Product C
Activity 1	$140,000	20,000	9,000	6,000
Activity 2	$ 90,000	8,000	15,000	7,000
Activity 3	$ 82,000	1,625	1,000	2,500

QS 4-11
Multiple choice overhead
questions   A2

1. If management wants the most accurate product cost, which of the following costing methods should be used?
   - **a.** Volume-based costing using departmental overhead rates
   - **b.** Volume-based costing using a plantwide overhead rate
   - **c.** Normal costing using a plantwide overhead rate
   - **d.** Activity-based costing
2. Which costing method tends to overstate the cost of high-volume products?
   - **a.** Traditional volume-based costing
   - **b.** Activity-based costing
   - **c.** Job order costing
   - **d.** Differential costing
3. Disadvantages of activity-based costing include
   - **a.** It is not acceptable under GAAP for external reporting.
   - **b.** It can be costly to implement.
   - **c.** It can be used in an activity-based management.
   - **d.** Both a. and b.

QS 4-12
Costs of quality

A2

A list of activities that generate quality costs is provided below. For each activity, indicate whether it relates to a prevention activity (P), appraisal activity (A), internal failure activity (I), or external failure activity (E).
- **a.** Inspecting raw materials
- **b.** Training workers in quality techniques
- **c.** Collecting data on a manufacturing process
- **d.** Overtime labor to rework products
- **e.** Cost of additional materials to rework a product
- **f.** Inspecting finished goods inventory
- **g.** Scrapping defective goods
- **h.** Lost sales due to customer dissatisfaction

QS 4-13
Identify activity levels

C3

Classify each of the following activities as unit level (U), batch level (B), product level (P), or facility level (F) for a manufacturer of organic juices.
- _____ **1.** Cutting fruit
- _____ **2.** Developing new types of juice
- _____ **3.** Blending fruit into juice
- _____ **4.** Receiving fruit shipments
- _____ **5.** Cleaning blending machines

QS 4-14
Identify activity levels

C3

Classify each of the following activities as unit level (U), batch level (B), product level (P), or facility level (F) for a manufacturer of trail mix.
- _____ **1.** Roasting peanuts
- _____ **2.** Cleaning roasting machines
- _____ **3.** Sampling product quality
- _____ **4.** Providing utilities for factory
- _____ **5.** Calibrating mixing machines

QS 4-15
Lean accounting and ABC

A2

Toyota embraces lean techniques, including lean accounting. What are the two key components of lean accounting?

EXERCISES

Exercise 4-1
Compute plantwide
overhead rates

P1

Xie Company identified the following activities, costs, and activity drivers for 2015. The company manufactures two types of go-karts: Deluxe and Basic.

Activity	Expected Costs	Expected Activity
Handling materials	$625,000	100,000 parts
Inspecting product	900,000	1,500 batches
Processing purchase orders	105,000	700 orders
Paying suppliers	175,000	500 invoices
Insuring the factory	300,000	40,000 square feet
Designing packaging	75,000	2 models

Required

1. Compute a single plantwide overhead rate assuming that the company assigns overhead based on 125,000 budgeted direct labor hours.
2. In January 2015 the Deluxe model required 2,500 direct labor hours, and the Standard model required 6,000 direct labor hours. Assign overhead costs to each model using the single plantwide overhead rate.

Refer to the information in Exercise 4-1. Compute the activity rate for each activity, assuming the company uses activity-based costing.

Exercise 4-2
Compute overhead rates
under ABC   P3

Refer to the information in Exercise 4-1. Assume that the following information is available for the company's two products for the first quarter of 2015.

Exercise 4-3
Assigning costs using
ABC

P3

	Deluxe Model	Basic Model
Production volume.........	10,000 units	30,000 units
Parts required	20,000 parts	30,000 parts
Batches made.............	250 batches	100 batches
Purchase orders	50 orders	20 orders
Invoices	50 invoices	10 invoices
Space occupied	10,000 square feet	7,000 square feet
Models	1 model	1 model

Required

Compute activity rates for each activity and assign overhead costs to each product model using activity-based costing (ABC). What is the overhead cost per unit of each model?

Textra Plastics produces parts for a variety of small machine manufacturers. Most products go through two operations, molding and trimming, before they are ready for packaging. Expected costs and activities for the molding department and for the trimming department for 2015 follow.

Exercise 4-4
Plantwide overhead rate

P1

	Molding	Trimming
Direct labor hours...............	52,000 DLH	48,000 DLH
Machine hours	30,500 MH	3,600 MH
Overhead costs	$730,000	$590,000

Data for two special order parts to be manufactured by the company in 2015 follow:

	Part A27C	Part X82B
Number of units	9,800 units	54,500 units
Machine hours		
Molding	5,100 MH	1,020 MH
Trimming	2,600 MH	650 MH
Direct labor hours		
Molding	5,500 DLH	2,150 DLH
Trimming	700 DLH	3,500 DLH

Required

1. Compute the plantwide overhead rate using direct labor hours as the base.
2. Determine the overhead cost assigned to each product line using the plantwide rate computed in requirement 1.

Refer to the information in Exercise 4-4.

Exercise 4-5
Departmental overhead
rates

P2

Required

1. Compute a departmental overhead rate for the molding department based on machine hours and a department overhead rate for the trimming department based on direct labor hours.
2. Determine the total overhead cost assigned to each product line using the departmental overhead rates from requirement 2.
3. Determine the overhead cost per unit for each product line using the departmental rate.

Exercise 4-6
Assigning overhead costs using the plantwide rate and departmental rate methods

P1   P2

Laval produces lamps and home lighting fixtures. Its most popular product is a brushed aluminum desk lamp. This lamp is made from components shaped in the fabricating department and assembled in its assembly department. Information related to the 35,000 desk lamps produced annually follow.

Direct materials	$280,000
Direct labor	
Fabricating department (7,000 DLH × $20 per DLH)	$140,000
Assembly department (16,000 DLH × $29 per DLH)	$464,000
Machine hours	
Fabricating department	15,040 MH
Assembly department	21,000 MH

Expected overhead cost and related data for the two production departments follow.

	Fabricating	Assembly
Direct labor hours	75,000 DLH	125,000 DLH
Machine hours	80,000 MH	62,500 MH
Overhead cost	$300,000	$200,000

Required

1. Determine the plantwide overhead rate for Laval using direct labor hours as a base.

Check (2) $26.90 per unit

2. Determine the total manufacturing cost per unit for the aluminum desk lamp using the plantwide overhead rate.

3. Compute departmental overhead rates based on machine hours in the fabricating department and direct labor hours in the assembly department.

Check (4) $27.60 per unit

4. Use departmental overhead rates from requirement 3 to determine the total manufacturing cost per unit for the aluminum desk lamps.

Exercise 4-7
Using the plantwide overhead rate to assess prices

P1

Way Cool produces two different models of air conditioners. The company produces the mechanical systems in their components department. The mechanical systems are combined with the housing assembly in its finishing department. The activities, costs, and drivers associated with these two manufacturing processes and the production support process follow.

Process	Activity	Overhead Cost	Driver	Quantity
Components	Changeover	$ 500,000	Number of batches	800
	Machining	279,000	Machine hours	6,000
	Setups	225,000	Number of setups	120
		$1,004,000		
Finishing	Welding	$ 180,300	Welding hours	3,000
	Inspecting	210,000	Number of inspections	700
	Rework	75,000	Rework orders	300
		$ 465,300		
Support	Purchasing	$ 135,000	Purchase orders	450
	Providing space	32,000	Number of units	5,000
	Providing utilities	65,000	Number of units	5,000
		$ 232,000		

Additional production information concerning its two product lines follows.

	Model 145	Model 212
Units produced	1,500	3,500
Welding hours	800	2,200
Batches	400	400
Number of inspections	400	300
Machine hours	1,800	4,200
Setups	60	60
Rework orders	160	140
Purchase orders	300	150

Required

1. Using a plantwide overhead rate based on machine hours, compute the overhead cost per unit for each product line.
2. Determine the total cost per unit for each product line if the direct labor and direct materials costs per unit are $250 for Model 145 and $180 for Model 212.
3. If the market price for Model 145 is $820 and the market price for Model 212 is $480, determine the profit or loss per unit for each model. Comment on the results.

Check   (3) Model 212,
$(40.26) per unit loss

Refer to the information in Exercise 4-7 to answer the following requirements.

Exercise 4-8
Using departmental overhead rates to assess prices
P2

Required

1. Determine departmental overhead rates and compute the overhead cost per unit for each product line. Base your overhead assignment for the components department on machine hours. Use welding hours to assign overhead costs to the finishing department. Assign costs to the support department based on number of purchase orders.
2. Determine the total cost per unit for each product line if the direct labor and direct materials costs per unit are $250 for Model 145 and $180 for Model 212.
3. If the market price for Model 145 is $820 and the market price for Model 212 is $480, determine the profit or loss per unit for each model. Comment on the results.

Check   (3) Model 212,
$(20.38) per unit loss

Refer to the information in Exercise 4-7 to answer the following requirements.

Exercise 4-9
Using ABC to assess prices
P3

Required

1. Using ABC, compute the overhead cost per unit for each product line.
2. Determine the total cost per unit for each product line if the direct labor and direct materials costs per unit are $250 for Model 145 and $180 for Model 212.
3. If the market price for Model 145 is $820 and the market price for Model 212 is $480, determine the profit or loss per unit for each model. Comment on the results.

Check   (3) Model 212,
$34.88 per unit profit

Consider the following data for two products of Gitano Manufacturing.

Exercise 4-10
Using ABC for strategic decisions
P1   P3

	Overhead Cost	Product A	Product B
Number of units produced		10,000 units	2,000 units
Direct labor cost (@$24 per DLH)		0.20 DLH per unit	0.25 DLH per unit
Direct materials cost.....................		$2 per unit	$3 per unit
Activity			
Machine setup	$121,000		
Materials handling	48,000		
Quality control inspections.............	80,000		
	$249,000		

Required

1. Using direct labor hours as the basis for assigning overhead costs, determine the total production cost per unit for each product line.

2. If the market price for Product A is $20 and the market price for Product B is $60, determine the profit or loss per unit for each product. Comment on the results.

3. Consider the following additional information about these two product lines. If ABC is used for assigning overhead costs to products, what is the cost per unit for Product A and for Product B?

	Product A	Product B
Number of setups required for production	10 setups	12 setups
Number of parts required	1 part/unit	3 parts/unit
Inspection hours required	40 hours	210 hours

4. Determine the profit or loss per unit for each product. Should this information influence company strategy? Explain.

Exercise 4-11
Activity-based costing and overhead cost allocation
P3

The following is taken from Ronda Co.'s internal records of its factory with two production departments. The cost driver for indirect labor and supplies is direct labor costs, and the cost driver for the remaining overhead items is number of hours of machine use. Compute the total amount of overhead cost allocated to Department 1 using activity-based costing.

	Direct Labor	Machine Use Hours
Department 1	$18,800	2,000
Department 2	13,200	1,200
Totals	$32,000	3,200
Factory overhead costs		
Rent and utilities	$12,200	
Indirect labor	5,400	
General office expense	4,000	
Depreciation—Equipment	3,000	
Supplies	2,600	
Total factory overhead.	$27,200	

Exercise 4-12
Activity-based costing rates and allocations
P3

A company has two products: standard and deluxe. The company expects to produce 36,375 standard units and 62,240 deluxe units. It uses activity-based costing and has prepared the following analysis showing budgeted cost and cost driver activity for each of its three activity cost pools.

Activity Cost Pool	Budgeted Cost	Budgeted Activity of Cost Driver	
		Standard	Deluxe
Activity 1	$93,000	2,500	5,250
Activity 2	$92,000	4,500	5,500
Activity 3	$87,000	3,000	2,800

Required

1. Compute overhead rates for each of the three activities.

2. What is the expected overhead cost per unit for the standard units?

3. What is the expected overhead cost per unit for the deluxe units?

Cardiff and Delp is an architectural firm that provides services for residential construction projects. The following data pertain to a recent reporting period.

Exercise 4-13
Using ABC in a service
company
P3

	Activities	Costs
Design department		
Client consultation	1,500 contact hours	$270,000
Drawings	2,000 design hours	115,000
Modeling	40,000 square feet	30,000
Project management department		
Supervision	600 days	$120,000
Billings	8 jobs	10,000
Collections	8 jobs	12,000

Required

1. Using ABC, compute the firm's activity overhead rates. Form activity cost pools where appropriate.
2. Assign costs to a 9,200-square-foot job that requires 450 contact hours, 340 design hours, and 200 days to complete.

Check   (2) $150,200

Glassworks Inc. produces two types of glass shelving, rounded edge and squared edge, on the same production line. For the current period, the company reports the following data.

Exercise 4-14
Activity-based costing
P3   A2

	Rounded Edge	Squared Edge	Total
Direct materials	$19,000	$ 43,200	$ 62,200
Direct labor	12,200	23,800	36,000
Overhead (300% of direct labor cost)	36,600	71,400	108,000
Total cost............................	$67,800	$138,400	$206,200
Quantity produced	10,500 ft.	14,100 ft.	
Average cost per ft. (rounded)	$ 6.46	$ 9.82	

Glassworks's controller wishes to apply activity-based costing (ABC) to allocate the $108,000 of overhead costs incurred by the two product lines to see whether cost per foot would change markedly from that reported above. She has collected the following information.

Overhead Cost Category (Activity Cost Pool)	Cost
Supervision	$ 5,400
Depreciation of machinery	56,600
Assembly line preparation...	46,000
Total overhead..	$108,000

She has also collected the following information about the cost drivers for each category (cost pool) and the amount of each driver used by the two product lines.

Overhead Cost Category (Activity Cost Pool)	Driver	Usage		
		Rounded Edge	Squared Edge	Total
Supervision	Direct labor cost ($)	$12,200	$23,800	$36,000
Depreciation of machinery	Machine hours	500 hours	1,500 hours	2,000 hours
Assembly line preparation	Setups (number)	40 times	210 times	250 times

Required

1. Assign these three overhead cost pools to each of the two products using ABC.
2. Determine average cost per foot for each of the two products using ABC.
3. Compare the average cost per foot under ABC with the average cost per foot under the current method for each product. Explain why a difference between the two cost allocation methods exists.

Check   (2) Rounded edge,
$5.19; Squared edge, $10.76

Exercise 4-15

Activity-based costing

P3

Surgery Center is an outpatient surgical clinic that was profitable for many years, but Medicare has cut its reimbursements by as much as 40%. As a result, the clinic wants to better understand its costs. It decides to prepare an activity-based cost analysis, including an estimate of the average cost of both general surgery and orthopedic surgery. The clinic's three activity cost pools and their cost drivers follow.

Activity Cost Pool	Cost	Cost Driver	Driver Quantity
Professional salaries...............	$1,600,000	Professional hours	10,000
Patient services and supplies	27,000	Number of patients	600
Building cost	150,000	Square feet	1,500

The two main surgical units and their related data follow.

Service	Hours	Square Feet*	Patients
General surgery.....................	2,500	600	400
Orthopedic surgery..................	7,500	900	200

* Orthopedic surgery requires more space for patients, supplies, and equipment.

Required

Check   (2) Average cost of general (orthopedic) surgery, $1,195 ($6,495) per patient

1. Compute the cost per cost driver for each of the three activity cost pools.
2. Use the results from part 1 to allocate costs to both the general surgery and the orthopedic surgery units. Compute total cost and average cost per patient for both the general surgery and the orthopedic surgery units.

Exercise 4-16

Comparing costs under ABC to traditional plantwide overhead rate

P1 P3 A1 A2

Smythe Crystal makes fine tableware in its Ireland factory. The following data are taken from its production plans for the year.

Direct labor costs	€5,870,000
Setup costs..	630,000

	Wineglasses	Commemorative Vases
Expected production.......................	211,000 units	17,000 units
Direct labor hours required	254,000 DLH	16,400 DLH
Machine setups required	200 setups	800 setups

Required

1. Determine the setup cost per unit for the wineglasses and for the commemorative vases if setup costs are assigned using a single plantwide overhead rate based on direct labor hours.

Check   (2) Vases, €29.65 per unit

2. Determine setup costs per unit for the wineglasses and for the commemorative vases if the setup costs are assigned based on the number of setups.
3. Which method is better for assigning costs to each product? Explain.

Exercise 4-17

Identify activity levels

C3

Identify each of the following activities as unit level (U), batch level (B), product level (P), or facility level (F) to indicate the way each is incurred with respect to production.

_____ **1.** Paying real estate taxes on the factory building

_____ **2.** Attaching labels to collars of shirts

_____ **3.** Redesigning a bicycle seat in response to customer feedback

_____ **4.** Cleaning the assembly department

_____ **5.** Polishing of gold wedding rings

_____ **6.** Mixing of bread dough in a commercial bakery

_____ **7.** Sampling cookies to determine quality

Following are activities in providing medical services at Healthsmart Clinic.

Exercise 4-18
Activity classification
C3

A. Registering patients
B. Cleaning beds
C. Stocking examination rooms
D. Washing linens
E. Ordering medical equipment
F. Heating the clinic
G. Providing security services
H. Filling prescriptions

Required

1. Classify each activity as unit level (U), batch level (B), product level (P), or facility level (F).
2. Identify an activity driver that might be used to measure these activities at the clinic.

connect

The following data are for the two products produced by Tadros Company.

PROBLEM SET A

Problem 4-1A
Comparing costs using
ABC with the plantwide
overhead rate

P1   P3   A1   A2

	Product A	Product B
Direct materials	$15 per unit	$24 per unit
Direct labor hours	0.3 DLH per unit	1.6 DLH per unit
Machine hours	0.1 MH per unit	1.2 MH per unit
Batches	125 batches	225 batches
Volume	10,000 units	2,000 units
Engineering modifications	12 modifications	58 modifications
Number of customers	500 customers	400 customers
Market price	$30 per unit	$120 per unit

The company's direct labor rate is $20 per direct labor hour (DLH). Additional information follows.

	Costs	Driver
Indirect manufacturing		
Engineering support	$24,500	Engineering modifications
Electricity	34,000	Machine hours
Setup costs	52,500	Batches
Nonmanufacturing		
Customer service	81,000	Number of customers

Required

1. Compute the manufacturing cost per unit using the plantwide overhead rate based on direct labor hours. What is the gross profit per unit?

Check   (1) Product A,
$26.37 per unit cost

2. How much gross profit is generated by each customer of Product A using the plantwide overhead rate? How much gross profit is generated by each customer of Product B using the plantwide overhead rate? What is the cost of providing customer service to each customer? What information is provided by this comparison?

3. Determine the manufacturing cost per unit of each product line using ABC. What is the gross profit per unit?

(3) Product A,
$24.30 per unit cost

4. How much gross profit is generated by each customer of Product A using ABC? How much gross profit is generated by each customer of Product B using ABC? Is the gross profit per customer adequate?
5. Which method of product costing gives better information to managers of this company? Explain why.

Xylon Company manufactures custom-made furniture for its local market and produces a line of home furnishings sold in retail stores across the country. The company uses traditional volume-based methods of assigning direct materials and direct labor to its product lines. Overhead has always been assigned by using a plantwide overhead rate based on direct labor hours. In the past few years, management has seen its line of retail products continue to sell at high volumes, but competition has forced it to lower prices on these items. The prices are declining to a level close to its cost of production.

Problem 4-2A
Assessing impacts of
using a plantwide
overhead rate
versus ABC

A1   A2

Meanwhile, its custom-made furniture is in high demand and customers have commented on its favorable (lower) prices compared to its competitors. Management is considering dropping its line of retail products and devoting all of its resources to custom-made furniture.

Required

1. What reasons could explain why competitors are forcing the company to lower prices on its high-volume retail products?
2. Why do you believe the company charges less for custom-order products than its competitors?
3. Does a company's costing method have any effect on its pricing decisions? Explain.
4. Aside from the differences in volume of output, what production differences do you believe exist between making custom-order furniture and mass-market furnishings?
5. What information might the company obtain from using ABC that it might not obtain using volume-based costing methods?

Problem 4-3A
Applying activity-based costing
P1 P3 A1 A2 C3

Craft Pro Machining produces machine tools for the construction industry. The following details about overhead costs were taken from its company records.

Production Activity	Indirect Labor	Indirect Materials	Other Overhead
Grinding	$320,000		
Polishing		$135,000	
Product modification	600,000		
Providing power			$255,000
System calibration	500,000		

Additional information on the drivers for its production activities follows.

Grinding	13,000 machine hours
Polishing	13,000 machine hours
Product modification	1,500 engineering hours
Providing power	17,000 direct labor hours
System calibration	400 batches

Required

1. Classify each activity as unit level, batch level, product level, or facility level.
2. Compute the activity overhead rates using ABC. Form cost pools as appropriate.
3. Determine overhead costs to assign to the following jobs using ABC.

	Job 3175	Job 4286
Number of units	200 units	2,500 units
Machine hours	550 MH	5,500 MH
Engineering hours	26 eng. hours	32 eng. hours
Batches	30 batches	90 batches
Direct labor hours	500 DLH	4,375 DLH

Check (4) Job 3175, $373.25 per unit

4. What is the overhead cost per unit for Job 3175? What is the overhead cost per unit for Job 4286?
5. If the company used a plantwide overhead rate based on direct labor hours, what is the overhead cost for each unit of Job 3175? Of Job 4286?
6. Compare the overhead costs per unit computed in requirements 4 and 5 for each job. Which method more accurately assigns overhead costs?

Bright Day Company produces two beverages, Hi-Voltage and EasySlim. Data about these products follow.

Problem 4-4A
Evaluating product
line costs and prices
using ABC

P3

	Hi-Voltage	EasySlim
Production volume	12,500 bottles	180,000 bottles
Liquid materials	1,400 gallons	37,000 gallons
Dry materials	620 pounds	12,000 pounds
Bottles	12,500 bottles	180,000 bottles
Labels..	3 labels per bottle	1 label per bottle
Machine setups	500 setups	300 setups
Machine hours	200 MH	3,750 MH

Additional data from its two production departments follow.

Department	Driver	Cost
Mixing department		
Liquid materials	Gallons	$ 2,304
Dry materials............................	Pounds	6,941
Utilities.....................................	Machine hours	1,422
Bottling department		
Bottles	Units	$77,000
Labeling	Labels per bottle	6,525
Machine setup	Setups	20,000

Required

1. Determine the cost of each product line using ABC.
2. What is the cost per bottle for Hi-Voltage? What is the cost per bottle of EasySlim? (*Hint:* Your answer should draw on the total cost for each product line computed in requirement 1.)
3. If Hi-Voltage sells for $3.75 per bottle, how much profit does the company earn per bottle of Hi-Voltage that it sells?
4. What is the minimum price that the company should set per bottle of EasySlim? Explain.

Check (3) $2.22 profit per
bottle

Sara's Salsa Company produces its condiments in two types: Extra Fine for restaurant customers and Family Style for home use. Salsa is prepared in department 1 and packaged in department 2. The activities, overhead costs, and drivers associated with these two manufacturing processes and the company's production support activities follow.

Problem 4-5A
Pricing analysis with
ABC and a plantwide
overhead rate

A1 A2 P1 P3

Process	Activity	Overhead Cost	Driver	Quantity
Department 1	Mixing	$ 4,500	Machine hours	1,500
	Cooking	11,250	Machine hours	1,500
	Product testing	112,500	Batches	600
		$128,250		
Department 2	Machine calibration	$250,000	Production runs	400
	Labeling	12,000	Cases of output	120,000
	Defects	6,000	Cases of output	120,000
		$268,000		
Support	Recipe formulation	$ 90,000	Focus groups	45
	Heat, lights, and water	27,000	Machine hours	1,500
	Materials handling	65,000	Container types	8
		$182,000		

Additional production information about its two product lines follows.

	Extra Fine	Family Style
Units produced	20,000 cases	100,000 cases
Batches...........................	200 batches	400 batches
Machine hours	500 MH	1,000 MH
Focus groups	30 groups	15 groups
Container types.....................	5 containers	3 containers
Production runs.....................	200 runs	200 runs

Required

1. Using a plantwide overhead rate based on cases, compute the overhead cost that is assigned to each case of Extra Fine Salsa and each case of Family Style Salsa.

Check (2) Cost per case: Extra Fine, $10.82; Family Style, $9.82

2. Using the plantwide overhead rate, determine the total cost per unit for the two products if the direct materials and direct labor cost is $6 per case of Extra Fine and $5 per case of Family Style.

3. If the market price of Extra Fine Salsa is $18 per case and the market price of Family Style Salsa is $9 per case, determine the gross profit per case for each product. What might management conclude about each product line?

(4) Cost per case: Extra Fine, $20.02; Family Style, $7.98

4. Using ABC, compute the total cost per case for each product type if the direct labor and direct materials cost is $6 per case of Extra Fine and $5 per case of Family Style.

5. If the market price is $18 per case of Extra Fine and $9 per case of Family Style, determine the gross profit per case for each product. How should management interpret the market prices given your computations?

6. Would your pricing analysis be improved if the company used departmental rates based on machine hours in department 1 and number of cases in department 2, instead of ABC? Explain.

PROBLEM SET B

Wade Company makes two distinct products with the following information available for each.

Problem 4-1B
Comparing costs using ABC with the plantwide overhead rate

A1   A2   P1   P3

	Standard	Deluxe
Direct materials	$4 per unit	$8 per unit
Direct labor hours	4 DLH per unit	5 DLH per unit
Machine hours	3 MH per unit	3 MH per unit
Batches	175 batches	75 batches
Volume......................	40,000 units	10,000 units
Engineering modifications	50 modifications	25 modifications
Number of customers...........	1,000 customers	1,000 customers
Market price	$92 per unit	$125 per unit

The company's direct labor rate is $20 per direct labor hour (DLH). Additional information follows.

	Costs	Driver
Indirect manufacturing		
Engineering support	$ 56,250	Engineering modifications
Electricity..................	112,500	Machine hours
Setup costs.................	41,250	Batches
Nonmanufacturing		
Customer service............	250,000	Number of customers

Required

1. Compute the manufacturing cost per unit using the plantwide overhead rate based on machine hours. What is the gross profit per unit?

2. How much gross profit is generated by each customer of the standard product using the plantwide overhead rate? How much gross profit is generated by each customer of the deluxe product using the plantwide overhead rate? What is the cost of providing customer service to each customer? What information is provided by this comparison?

3. Determine the manufacturing cost per unit of each product line using ABC. What is the gross profit per unit?

4. How much gross profit is generated by each customer of the standard product using ABC? How much gross profit is generated by each customer of the deluxe product using ABC? Is the gross profit per customer adequate?

5. Which method of product costing gives better information to managers of this company? Explain.

Check (1) Gross profit per unit: Standard, $3.80; Deluxe, $12.80

(3) Gross profit per unit: Standard, $4.09; Deluxe, $11.64

Midwest Paper produces cardboard boxes. The boxes require designing, cutting, and printing. (The boxes are shipped flat and customers fold them as necessary.) Midwest has a reputation for providing high-quality products and excellent service to customers, who are major U.S. manufacturers. Costs are assigned to products based on the number of machine hours required to produce them.

Three years ago, a new marketing executive was hired. She suggested the company offer custom design and manufacturing services to small specialty manufacturers. These customers required boxes for their products and were eager to have Midwest as a supplier. Within one year Midwest found that it was so busy with orders from small customers, it had trouble supplying boxes to all its customers on a timely basis. Large, long-time customers began to complain about slow service, and several took their business elsewhere. Within another 18 months, Midwest was in financial distress with a backlog of orders to be filled.

Problem 4-2B
Assessing impacts of using a plantwide overhead rate versus ABC
A1 A2

Required

1. What do you believe are the major costs of making its boxes? How are those costs related to the volume of boxes produced?

2. How did Midwest's new customers differ from its previous customers?

3. Would the unit cost to produce a box for new customers be different from the unit cost to produce a box for its previous customers? Explain.

4. Could Midwest's fate have been different if it had used ABC for determining the cost of its boxes?

5. What information would have been available with ABC that might have been overlooked using a traditional volume-based costing method?

Ryan Foods produces gourmet gift baskets that it distributes online as well as from its small retail store. The following details about overhead costs are taken from its records.

Problem 4-3B
Applying activity-based costing
P1 P3 A1 A2 C3

Production Activity	Indirect Labor	Indirect Materials	Other Overhead
Wrapping	$300,000	$200,000	
Assembling	400,000		
Product design	180,000		
Obtaining business licenses			$100,000
Cooking	150,000	120,000	

Additional information on the drivers for its production activities follows.

Wrapping	100,000 units
Assembling.	20,000 direct labor hours
Product design	3,000 design hours
Obtaining business licenses	20,000 direct labor hours
Cooking	1,000 batches

Required

1. Classify each activity as unit level, batch level, product level, or facility level.
2. Compute the activity overhead rates using ABC. Form cost pools as appropriate.
3. Determine the overhead cost to assign to the following jobs using ABC.

	Holiday Basket	Executive Basket
Number of units	8,000 units	1,000 units
Direct labor hours................................	2,000 DLH	500 DLH
Design hours	40 design hours	40 design hours
Batches...	80 batches	200 batches

Check (4) Holiday Basket, $14.25 per unit

4. What is the overhead cost per unit for the Holiday Basket? What is the overhead cost per unit for the Executive Basket?

(5) Holiday Basket, $18.13 per unit

5. If the company used a plantwide overhead rate based on direct labor hours, what is the overhead cost for each Holiday Basket unit? What would be the overhead cost for each Executive Basket unit if a single plantwide overhead rate is used?

6. Compare the costs per unit computed in requirements 4 and 5 for each job. Which cost assignment method provides the most accurate cost? Explain.

Problem 4-4B
Evaluating product line costs and prices using ABC

P3

Mathwerks produces two electronic, handheld educational games: *Fun with Fractions* and *Count Calculus*. Data on these products follow.

	Fun with Fractions	*Count Calculus*
Production volume	150,000 units	10,000 units
Components	450,000 parts	100,000 parts
Direct labor hours	15,000 DLH	2,000 DLH
Packaging materials	150,000 boxes	10,000 boxes
Shipping cartons	100 units per carton	25 units per carton
Machine setups	52 setups	52 setups
Machine hours	5,000 MH	2,000 MH

Additional data from its two production departments follow.

Department	Driver	Cost
Assembly department		
Component cost	Parts	$495,000
Assembly labor................................	Direct labor hours	244,800
Maintenance	Machine hours	100,800
Wrapping department		
Packaging materials	Boxes	$460,800
Shipping	Cartons	27,360
Machine setup	Setups	187,200

Required

1. Using ABC, determine the cost of each product line.
2. What is the cost per unit for *Fun with Fractions*? What is the cost per unit of *Count Calculus*?

Check (3) $32.37 profit per unit

3. If *Count Calculus* sells for $59.95 per unit, how much profit does the company earn per unit of *Count Calculus* sold?
4. What is the minimum price that the company should set per unit of *Fun with Fractions*? Explain.

ent Pro produces two lines of tents sold to outdoor enthusiasts. The tents are cut to specifications in epartment A. In department B the tents are sewn and folded. The activities, costs, and drivers associ- ed with these two manufacturing processes and the company's production support activities follow.

Problem 4-5B
Pricing analysis with ABC and a plantwide overhead rate

A1 A2 P1 P3

Process	Activity	Overhead Cost	Driver	Quantity
Department A	Pattern alignment	$ 64,400	Batches	560
	Cutting	50,430	Machine hours	12,300
	Moving product	100,800	Moves	2,400
		$215,630		
Department B	Sewing	$327,600	Direct labor hours	4,200
	Inspecting	24,000	Inspections	600
	Folding	47,880	Units	22,800
		$399,480		
Support	Design	$280,000	Modification orders	280
	Providing space	51,600	Square feet	8,600
	Materials handling	184,000	Square yards	920,000
		$515,600		

Additional production information on the two lines of tents follows.

	Pup Tent	Pop-Up Tent
Units produced	15,200 units	7,600 units
Moves.	800 moves	1,600 moves
Batches.	140 batches	420 batches
Number of inspections	240 inspections	360 inspections
Machine hours	7,000 MH	5,300 MH
Direct labor hours.	2,600 DLH	1,600 DLH
Modification orders	70 modification orders	210 modification orders
Space occupied	4,300 square feet	4,300 square feet
Material required	450,000 square yards	470,000 square yards

Required

1. Using a plantwide overhead rate based on direct labor hours, compute the overhead cost that is as- signed to each pup tent and each pop-up tent.
2. Using the plantwide overhead rate, determine the total cost per unit for the two products if the direct materials and direct labor cost is $25 per pup tent and $32 per pop-up tent.
3. If the market price of the pup tent is $65 and the market price of the pop-up tent is $200, determine the gross profit per unit for each tent. What might management conclude about the pup tent?
4. Using ABC, compute the total cost per unit for each tent if the direct labor and direct materials cost is $25 per pup tent and $32 per pop-up tent.
5. If the market price is $65 per pup tent and $200 per pop-up tent, determine the gross profit per unit for each tent. Comment on the results.
6. Would your pricing analysis be improved if the company used, instead of ABC, departmental rates determined using machine hours in department A and direct labor hours in department B? Explain.

Check (4) Pup tent, $58.46 per unit cost

This serial problem began in Chapter 1 and continues through most of the book. If previous chapter seg- ments were not completed, the serial problem can begin at this point. It is helpful, but not necessary, to use he Working Papers that accompany the book.)

SERIAL PROBLEM
Business Solutions

P3

SP 4 After reading an article about activity-based costing in a trade journal for the furniture industry, Santana Rey wondered if it was time to critically analyze overhead costs at Business Solutions. In a recent month, Santana found that setup costs, inspection costs, and utility costs made up most of its overhead. Additional information about overhead follows.

Activity	Cost	Driver
Setting up machines	$20,000	25 batches
Inspecting components	$ 7,500	5,000 parts
Providing utilities	$10,000	5,000 machine hours

Overhead has been applied to output at a rate of 50% of direct labor costs. The following data pertain to Job 615.

Direct materials	$2,500
Direct labor	$3,500
Batches.	2 batches
Number of parts	400 parts
Machine hours	600 machine hours

Required

1. Classify each of its three overhead activities as unit level, batch level, product level, or facility level.
2. What is the total cost of Job 615 if Business Solutions applies overhead at 50% of direct labor cost?
3. What is the total cost of Job 615 if Business Solutions uses activity-based costing?
4. Which approach to assigning overhead gives a better representation of the costs incurred to produce Job 615? Explain.

Beyond the Numbers

REPORTING IN ACTION

C3   A2

APPLE

GOOGLE

BTN 4-1   Refer to financial statements of Apple (Apple.com) and Google (Google.com) to answer the following.

Required

1. Identify at least two activities at Apple and at Google that cause costs to be incurred. Do you believe these companies should be concerned about controlling costs of the activities you identified? Explain.
2. Would you classify Apple and Google as service, merchandising, or manufacturing companies? Explain.
3. Is activity-based costing useful for companies such as Apple and Google? Explain.

COMPARATIVE ANALYSIS

C2   A2

APPLE

GOOGLE

BTN 4-2   Apple and Google are competitors in the sales of electronic devices. Compare these companies' income statements and answer the following.

Required

1. Which company has a higher ratio of costs, defined as cost of goods sold plus total operating expenses, to revenues? Use the two most recent years' income statements from Appendix A. Show your analysis.
2. How might the use of activity-based costing help the less competitive company become *more* competitive?
3. Assume Apple is considering opening a new retail store. What are the activities associated with opening a new retail store?

TN 4-3   In conducting interviews and observing factory operations to implement an activity-based costing system, you determine that several activities are unnecessary or redundant. For example, warehouse personnel were inspecting purchased components as they were received at the loading dock. Later that day, the components were inspected again on the shop floor before being installed in the final product. Both of these activities caused costs to be incurred but were not adding value to the product. If you include this observation in your report, one or more employees who perform inspections will likely lose their jobs.

ETHICS CHALLENGE
A2   C3

Required

1. As a plant employee, what is your responsibility to report your findings to superiors?
2. Should you attempt to determine if the redundancy is justified? Explain.
3. What is your responsibility to the employees whose jobs will likely be lost because of your report?
4. What facts should you consider before making your decision to report or not?

TN 4-4   The chief executive officer (CEO) of your company recently returned from a luncheon meeting where activity-based costing was presented and discussed. Though her background is not in accounting, she has worked for the company for 15 years and is thoroughly familiar with its operations. Her impression of the presentation about ABC was that it was just another way of dividing up total overhead cost and that the total would still be the same "no matter how you sliced it."

COMMUNICATING IN PRACTICE
A2

Required

Write a memorandum to the CEO, no more than one page, explaining how ABC is different from traditional volume-based costing methods. Also, identify its advantages and disadvantages vis-à-vis traditional methods. Be sure it is written to be understandable to someone who is not an accountant.

TN 4-5   Accounting professionals who work for private companies often obtain the Certified Management Accountant (CMA) designation to indicate their proficiency in several business areas in addition to managerial accounting. The CMA examination is administered by the Institute of Management Accountants (IMA).

TAKING IT TO THE NET
A2

Required

Go to the IMA website (**IMAnet.org**) and determine which parts of the CMA exam likely cover activity-based costing. A person planning to become a CMA should take what college course work?

TN 4-6   Observe the operations at your favorite fast-food restaurant.

TEAMWORK IN ACTION
C2   C3

Required

1. How many people does it take to fill a typical order of sandwich, beverage, and one side order?
2. Describe the activities involved in its food service process.
3. What costs are related to each activity identified in requirement 2?

TN 4-7   Suja Juice Co. has expanded its product offerings to include many varieties of cold-pressed organic juices. Company founders know that financial success depends on cost control as well as revenue generation.

ENTREPRENEURIAL DECISION
C3

Required

1. If Suja Juice Co. wanted to expand its product line to include organic energy bars, what activitie[s] would it need to perform that are not required for its current product lines?
2. Related to part 1, should the additional overhead costs related to new product lines be shared by exist[t]-ing product lines? Explain your reasoning.

HITTING THE ROAD
C2   C3

BTN 4-8   Visit and observe the processes of three different fast-food restaurants—these visits can b[e] done as individuals or as teams. The objective of activity-based costing is to accurately assign costs t[o] products and to improve operational efficiency.

Required

1. Individuals (or teams) can be assigned to each of three different fast-food establishments. Make a lis[t] of the activities required to process an order of a sandwich, beverage, and one side order at each res[t]aurant. Record the time required for each process, from placing the order to receiving the complete[] order.
2. What activities do the three establishments have in common? What activities are different across th[e] establishments?
3. Is the number of activities related to the time required to process an order? Is the number of activitie[s] related to the price charged to customers? Explain both.
4. Make recommendations for improving the processes you observe. Would your recommendations in[]-crease or decrease the cost of operations?

GLOBAL DECISION
C3

Samsung
APPLE

BTN 4-9   Visit the websites and review the financial statements for Apple (Apple.com) an[d] Samsung (Samsung.com). Each of these companies sells electronic devices like smartphones i[n] global markets.

Required

1. For Apple in 2013, what are the largest three geographic markets in which it sells products? What i[s] the amount (in millions of dollars) of sales in each market?
2. For Samsung in 2013, what are the largest three geographic markets in which it sells products[?] What is the amount (in millions of Korean won) of sales in each market? (Use "revenue from exter[]-nal customers.")
3. How would customer service activities differ across different geographic markets?

ANSWERS TO MULTIPLE CHOICE QUIZ

1. b; Under traditional costing methods, overhead costs are allocated to products on the basis of some measure of volume such as direct labor hours or machine hours. This results in much of the overhead cost being allocated to high-volume products. In contrast, under activity-based costing, some overhead costs are allocated on the basis of batch-level or product-level activities. This change in allocation bases results in shifting overhead costs from high-volume products to low-volume products.

2. d; Generally, an activity-based costing system is more difficult to implement and maintain than a traditional costing system (thus answer **a** is false). Instead of eliminating waste by allocating costs to products that waste resources, activity-based management is a management approach that focuses on managing activities as a means of eliminating waste and reducing delays and defects (thus

answer **b** is false). Instead of using a single allocation base (suc[h] as direct labor hours), activity-based costing uses a number of a[l]location bases for assigning costs to products (thus answer **c** [is] false). Answer **d** is true.

3. d; Batch-level activities are activities that are performed each time [a] batch of goods is handled or processed, regardless of how man[y] units are in a batch. Further, the amount of resources consumed de[]-pends on the number of batches rather than on the number of units i[n] the batch. Worker recreational facilities relate to the organization a[s] a whole rather than to specific batches and, as such, are not consid[]-ered to be batch level. On the other hand, purchase order processing[,] setting up equipment, and the clerical activities described are activi[]-ties that are performed each time a batch of goods is handled o[r] processed, and, as such, are batch-level activities.

4. c;

	(A) Activity Rate (Budgeted overhead cost ÷ Budgeted activity)	(B) Actual Activity	(A × B) Overhead Cost Applied to Production
Activity 1....	($80,000 ÷ 1,000) = $80.00	800	$ 64,000
Activity 2....	($58,400 ÷ 1,500) = $38.93*	500	19,465
Activity 3....	($360,000 ÷ 6,000) = $60.00	5,400	324,000
Total overhead cost per unit for Product B			$407,465
Divided by number of units produced			÷ 31,652
Overhead cost per unit of Product B			$ 12.87

*rounded

5. d; The activity rate for Activity 3 is determined as follows:

Budgeted cost ÷ Budgeted activity = Activity rate
$14,000 ÷ 700 = $20

5 chapter

Cost Behavior and Cost-Volume-Profit Analysis

Chapter Preview

IDENTIFYING COST BEHAVIOR

C1 Fixed costs

Variable costs

Mixed costs

Step-wise costs and relevant range

Curvilinear costs

MEASURING COST BEHAVIOR

P1 Scatter diagrams

High-low method

Least-squares regression

Comparison of cost estimation methods

CONTRIBUTION MARGIN AND BREAK-EVEN ANALYSIS

A1 Computing contribution margin

P2 Computing break-even

Computing margin of safety

P3 Preparing a cost-volume-profit chart

Impact of estimates on break-even analysis

APPLYING COST-VOLUME-PROFIT ANALYSIS

C2 Computing income from sales and costs

Computing sales for target income

Sensitivity analysis

P4 Computing multi-product break-even

A2 Analyzing sales with operating leverage

Learning Objectives

CONCEPTUAL

C1 Describe different types of cost behavior in relation to production and sales volume.

C2 Describe several applications of cost-volume-profit analysis.

ANALYTICAL

A1 Compute the contribution margin and describe what it reveals about a company's cost structure.

A2 Analyze changes in sales using the degree of operating leverage.

PROCEDURAL

P1 Determine cost estimates using the scatter diagram, high-low, and regression methods of estimating costs.

P2 Compute the break-even point for a single product company.

P3 Graph costs and sales for a single product company.

P4 Compute the break-even point for a multiproduct company.

Find the Yeti

COLUMBIA, MO—After finishing his marketing degree and obtaining over 13 years of professional marketing and design experience, Reid Lyle needed a change. "I wanted to produce creative quality products with talented, genuine people in a business that I could actually influence for the better" says Reid. Reid, along with partners Ryan Montgomery and Jordan Roudenis, opened a custom T-shirt shop, **Fast Yeti Custom Tees (fastyetitees.com)**.

"We all contributed to every aspect of starting this business" says Reid. That includes brainstorming to find a name for their company. The trio came up with a mythical character, Freddie the Yeti, who allegedly trekked from the Ozark Mountains to convince the group to start a business. "Fast Yeti is memorable and fun," says Reid. "It's interesting. It raises questions." During the week, Freddie roams the streets of Columbia, and customers who capture a photo of him receive a discount on merchandise. "A common misconception is that he's a human wearing a costume," jokes Ryan. "It's a real yeti."

While humor is a large part of their business, the owners have a serious focus on providing high-quality products to meet customer demands. "Everyone has a favorite T-shirt," says Reid. "We want to be the shop that designs and sells it." Jordan, the company's production manager, says he "is very particular about how I do things. If I mess up, I fix it and try not to let it happen again. I try to perfect what I do."

"The T-shirt is the epitome of creativity"
—**Reid Lyle**

Operating at a small scale, in a highly competitive industry, requires the owners to understand and control their costs. Successful entrepreneurs must understand cost behavior to succeed. Identifying fixed and variable costs is key to understanding break-even points determining the amount of sales required to make a target income, key topics in this chapter. In addition to selling custom T-shirts, Fast Yeti also sells custom hats and polo shirts. Understanding multiproduct break-even points and sales mix is important in companies with diverse product lines. Contribution margin income statements, which separate fixed and variable costs, enable entrepreneurs to quickly see how changes in selling prices, variable costs, or fixed costs impact profit. Understanding contribution margins and cost-volume-profit analyses enables small businesses to profit and grow.

Reid, Ryan, and Jordan agree that young entrepreneurs should follow their passion and "make it happen." "We all are interested in apparel, humor, and design," says Reid. "Still, we all had to strip out old carpet and make our own shelves to get this store opened." While still a young company, the trio is seeing their hard work rewarded with increasing sales. "We work hard," says Ryan, "but it's really fun." And, if you see a yeti roaming around . . . take a photo.

Sources: *Fast Yeti Custom Tees website,* January 2015; *Columbia Missourian,* May 14, 2014; *Columbia Daily Tribune,* June 16, 2014

IDENTIFYING COST BEHAVIOR

Planning a company's future activities and events is crucial to successful management. One of the first steps in planning is to predict the volume of activity, the costs to be incurred, sales to be made, and profit to be earned. An important tool in such planning is **cost-volume-profit (CVP) analysis,** which helps managers predict how changes in costs and sales levels affect profit. In its basic form, CVP analysis involves computing the sales level at which a company neither earns an income nor incurs a loss, called the *break-even point.* For this reason, this basic form of cost-volume-profit analysis is often called *break-even analysis.*

Managers use variations of CVP analysis to answer questions like:

- How much does income increase if we install a new machine to reduce labor costs?
- What is the change in income if selling prices decline and sales volume increases?
- How will income change if we change the sales mix of our products or services?
- What sales volume is needed to earn a target income?

Consequently, cost-volume-profit analysis is useful in a wide range of business decisions.

The concept of *relevant range* is important to classifying costs for CVP analysis. The **relevant range of operations** is the normal operating range for a business. Except for unusually good or bad times, management typically plans for operations within a range of volume neither close to zero nor at maximum capacity. The relevant range excludes extremely high or low operating levels that are unlikely to recur. CVP analysis requires management to classify costs as either *fixed* or *variable* with respect to production or sales volume, within the relevant range of operations. The remainder of this section discusses concepts of cost behavior as they relate to CVP analysis.

Fixed Costs

C1
Describe different types of cost behavior in relation to production and sales volume.

Fixed costs remain unchanged despite variations in the volume of activity within a relevant range. For example, $32,000 in monthly rent paid for a factory building remains the same whether the factory operates with a single eight-hour shift or around the clock with three shifts. This means that rent cost is the same each month at any level of output from zero to the plant's full productive capacity. Common examples of fixed costs include depreciation, property taxes, office salaries, and many service department costs.

Be sure to realize that the idea of fixed cost not changing as the level of production changes applies to the *total* dollar amount. It does not apply to the per unit amount. Rather, the fixed cost *per unit* of output decreases as volume increases. For instance, if 200 units are produced when monthly rent is $32,000, the average rent cost per unit is $160 (computed as $32,000/200 units). When production increases to 1,000 units per month, the average rent cost per unit decreases to $32 (computed as $32,000/1,000 units).

When production volume and costs are graphed, units of product are usually plotted on the *horizontal axis* and dollars of cost are plotted on the *vertical axis.* Fixed costs then are

gerenme/Vetta/Getty Images

represented as a horizontal line because they remain constant at all levels of production. To illustrate, the top graph in Exhibit 5.1 shows that fixed costs remain at $32,000 at all production levels up to the company's monthly capacity of 2,000 units of output. The bottom graph in Exhibit 5.1 shows that fixed costs per unit fall as production levels increase. This drop in costs per unit as production levels increase is known as *economies of scale.* The *relevant range* for fixed costs in Exhibit 5.1 is 0 to 2,000 units. If the relevant range changes (that is, production capacity extends beyond this range), the amount of fixed costs will likely change.

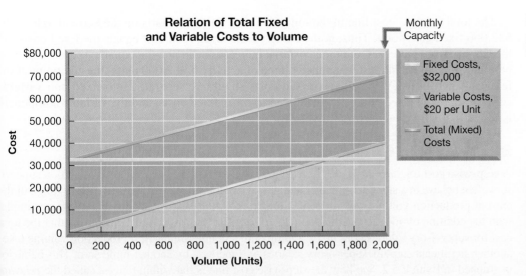

Relation of Total Fixed
and Variable Costs to Volume

Monthly
Capacity

EXHIBIT 5.1

Relations of Total and Per
Unit Costs to Volume

Example: If the fixed cost
line in Exhibit 5.1 is shifted
upward, does the total cost line
shift up, down, or remain in the
same place? *Answer:* It shifts up
by the same amount.

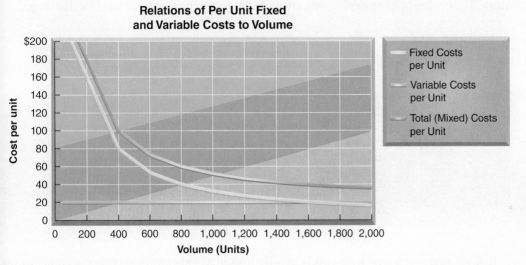

Relations of Per Unit Fixed
and Variable Costs to Volume

Example: If the level of fixed
costs in Exhibit 5.1 changes,
does the slope of the total cost
line change? *Answer:* No, the
slope doesn't change. The total
cost line is simply shifted
upward or downward.

Variable Costs

Variable costs change in proportion to changes in volume of activity. The direct materials cost of a product is one example of a variable cost. If one unit of product requires materials costing $20, total materials costs are $200 when 10 units of product are manufactured, $400 for 20 units, $600 for 30 units, and so on. In addition to direct materials, common variable costs include direct labor (if employees are paid per unit), sales commissions, shipping costs, and some overhead costs.

Point: Fixed costs are constant in total but vary (decline) per unit as more units are produced. Variable costs vary in total but are fixed per unit.

Notice that variable cost *per unit* remains constant but the *total* amount of variable cost changes with the level of production. When variable costs are plotted on a graph of cost and volume, they appear as a straight line starting at the zero cost level. This straight line is upward (positive) sloping. The line rises as volume of activity increases. A variable cost line using a $20 per unit cost is graphed in Exhibit 5.1. The bottom graph in Exhibit 5.1 shows that variable cost per unit is constant as production levels change.

Mixed Costs

Are costs either fixed or variable? No—another category, **mixed costs,** includes both fixed and variable cost components. For example, compensation for sales representatives often includes a fixed monthly salary and a variable commission based on sales. Utilities can also be considered a mixed cost; even if no units are produced, it is not likely a manufacturing plant will use no electricity or water. Like a fixed cost, a mixed cost is greater than zero when volume is zero; but unlike a fixed cost, it increases steadily in proportion to increases in volume.

The total (mixed) cost line in the top graph in Exhibit 5.1 starts on the vertical axis at the $32,000 fixed cost point. Thus, at the zero volume level, total cost equals the fixed costs. As the activity level increases, the total cost line increases at an amount equal to the variable cost per unit. This line is highest when the volume of activity is at 2,000 units (the end point of the relevant range). In CVP analysis, mixed costs should be separated into fixed and variable components. The fixed component is added to other fixed costs, and the variable component is added to other variable costs.

Step-wise Costs and the Relevant Range

A **step-wise cost** (or *stair-step cost*) reflects a step pattern in costs. Salaries of production supervisors often behave in a step-wise manner in that their salaries are fixed within a *relevant range* of the current production volume. However, if production volume expands significantly (for example, with the addition of another shift), additional supervisors must be hired. This means that the total cost for supervisory salaries goes up by a lump-sum amount. Similarly, if production volume takes another significant step up, supervisory salaries will increase by another lump sum. This behavior is graphed in Exhibit 5.2. See how the step-wise cost line is flat within ranges, called the *relevant range*. Then, when volume significantly changes, the cost shifts to another level for that range.

EXHIBIT 5.2

Step-wise and Curvilinear Costs

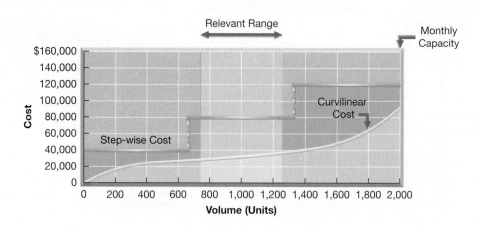

In CVP analysis, a step-wise cost is usually treated as either a fixed cost or a variable cost. This treatment involves manager judgment and depends on the width of the relevant range and the expected volume. To illustrate, suppose after the production of every 25 snowboards, an operator lubricates the finishing machine. The cost of this lubricant reflects a step-wise pattern. Also, suppose that after the production of every 1,000 units, the snowboard cutting tool is replaced. Again, this is a step-wise cost. Note that the relevant range of 25 snowboards is much narrower than the relevant range of 1,000 snowboards. Some managers might treat the lubricant cost as a variable cost and the cutting tool cost as a fixed cost.

Point: Computer spreadsheets are important and effective tools for CVP analysis and for analyzing alternative "what-if" strategies.

Curvilinear Costs

As shown earlier, variable costs increase at a constant rate as the volume of activity increases. For example, a salesperson's commission of 7% of sales volume would increase at a constant rate as sales volume increases. **Curvilinear costs** also increase as volume increases, but at a nonconstant rate. The curved line in Exhibit 5.2 shows a curvilinear cost beginning at zero (when production is zero) and increasing at different rates as volume increases.

An example of a curvilinear cost is total direct labor cost when workers are paid by the hour. For example, a company might add new employees assigned to specialize in certain tasks. When production levels are relatively low, adding those specialized employees often yields more output. This is reflected in a flatter slope in the curvilinear cost graph in Exhibit 5.2. At some point, however, adding still more employees creates inefficiencies (they get in each other's way); this inefficiency is reflected in a steeper slope for the curvilinear cost graph. In CVP analysis, curvilinear costs are often treated as variable costs, within a relevant range. This is reasonable for most types of curvilinear costs.

Determine whether each of the following is best described as a fixed, variable, mixed, step-wise, or curvilinear cost with respect to product units.

NEED-TO-KNOW 5-1

Classifying Costs

C1

	Type of Cost
Rubber used to manufacture tennis balls	a. _____
Depreciation (straight-line method)	b. _____
Electricity usage.	c. _____
Supervisory salaries	d. _____
A salesperson's commission is 7% for sales of up to $100,000, and 10% of sales for sales above $100,000	e. _____

Solution

a. variable   **b.** fixed   **c.** mixed   **d.** fixed*   **e.** curvilinear

*If more shifts are added, then supervisory salaries behave like a step-wise cost with respect to the number of shifts.

Do More: QS 5-1, QS 5-2, E 5-1, E 5-2, E 5-3

QC1

MEASURING COST BEHAVIOR

Identifying and measuring cost behavior requires careful analysis and judgment. An important part of this process is to identify costs that can be classified as either fixed or variable, which often requires analysis of past cost behavior. A goal of classifying costs is to develop a *cost equation*. The cost equation expresses total costs as a function of fixed costs plus variable cost per unit. Three methods are commonly used to analyze past costs: scatter diagrams, the high-low method, and least-squares regression. Each method is discussed in this section using the unit and cost data shown in Exhibit 5.3, which are taken from a start-up company that uses units produced as the activity base in estimating cost behavior.

P1

Determine cost estimates using the scatter diagram, high-low, and regression methods of estimating costs.

EXHIBIT 5.3

Data for Estimating Cost Behavior

Month	Units Produced	Total Cost
January	27,500	$21,500
February	17,500	20,500
March	25,000	25,000
April	35,000	21,500
May	47,500	25,500
June	22,500	18,500
July	30,000	23,500
August	52,500	28,500
September	37,500	26,000
October	67,500	29,000
November	62,500	31,000
December	57,500	26,000

Scatter Diagrams

Scatter diagrams display past cost and unit data in graphical form. In preparing a scatter diagram, units are plotted on the horizontal axis, and costs are plotted on the vertical axis. Each individual point on a scatter diagram reflects the cost and number of units for a prior period. In Exhibit 5.4, the prior 12 months' costs and numbers of units are graphed. Each point reflects total costs incurred and units produced for one of those months. For instance, the point labeled March had units produced of 25,000 and costs of $25,000.

The **estimated line of cost behavior** is drawn on a scatter diagram to reflect the relation between cost and unit volume. This line best visually "fits" the points in a scatter diagram. Fitting this line demands judgment, or can be done with spreadsheet software, as we illustrate

EXHIBIT 5.4

Scatter Diagram

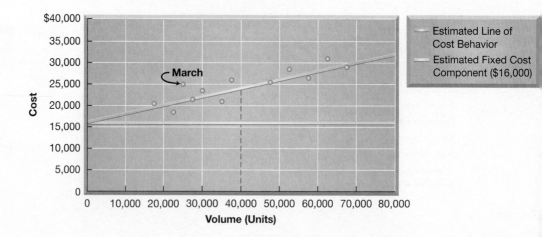

in Appendix 5A. The line drawn in Exhibit 5.4 intersects the vertical axis at approximately $16,000, which reflects fixed cost. To compute variable cost per unit, or the slope, we perform three steps. First, we select any two points on the horizontal axis (units), say 0 and 40,000. Second, we draw a vertical line from each of these points to intersect the estimated line of cost behavior. The point on the vertical axis (cost) corresponding to the 40,000 units point that intersects the estimated line is roughly $24,000. Similarly, the cost corresponding to zero units is $16,000 (the fixed cost point). Third, we compute the slope of the line, or variable cost, as the change in cost divided by the change in units. Exhibit 5.5 shows this computation.

EXHIBIT 5.5

Variable Cost per Unit
(Scatter Diagram)

$$\frac{\text{Change in cost}}{\text{Change in units}} = \frac{\$24,000 - \$16,000}{40,000 - 0} = \frac{\$8,000}{40,000} = \$0.20 \text{ per unit}$$

Example: In Exhibits 5.4 and 5.5, if units are projected at 30,000, what is the predicted cost? *Answer:* Approximately $22,000.

Variable cost is $0.20 per unit. Thus, the cost equation that management will use to estimate costs for different unit levels is **$16,000 plus $0.20 per unit produced**.

High-Low Method

The **high-low method** is a way to estimate the cost equation using just two points: the highest and lowest volume levels. The high-low method follows these steps:

Step 1: Identify the highest and lowest volume levels. It is important to note that these might not be the highest or lowest levels of *costs*.

Step 2: Compute the slope (variable cost per unit) using the high and low activity levels.

Step 3: Compute the total fixed costs by computing the total variable cost at either the high or low activity level, and then subtracting that amount from the total cost at that activity level.

We illustrate the high-low method next.

Step 1: In our case, the lowest number of units is 17,500, and the highest is 67,500. The costs corresponding to these unit volumes are $20,500 and $29,000, respectively (see the data in Exhibit 5.3).

Step 2: The variable cost per unit is calculated using a simple formula: change in cost divided by the change in units. Using the data from the high and low unit volumes, this results in a slope, or variable cost per unit, of $0.17 as computed in Exhibit 5.6.

EXHIBIT 5.6

Variable Cost per Unit
(High-Low Method)

$$\frac{\text{Change in cost}}{\text{Change in units}} = \frac{\$29,000 - \$20,500}{67,500 - 17,500} = \frac{\$8,500}{50,000} = \$0.17 \text{ per unit}$$

Step 3: To estimate the fixed cost for the high-low method, we use the knowledge that total cost equals fixed cost plus variable cost per unit times the number of units. Then we pick either the high or low point to determine the fixed cost. This computation is shown in Exhibit 5.7—where we use the high point (67,500 units) in determining the fixed cost of $17,525. (Use of the low point yields the same fixed cost estimate.)

Total cost = Fixed cost + (Variable cost per unit × Units)

$29,000 = Fixed cost + ($0.17 per unit × 67,500 units)

$29,000 = Fixed cost + $11,475

Fixed cost = $17,525

EXHIBIT 5.7

Determining Fixed Costs (High-Low Method)

Thus, the cost equation from the high-low method is **$17,525 plus $0.17 per unit produced.** This cost equation differs slightly from that determined from the scatter diagram method. A weakness of the high-low method is that it ignores all cost points except the highest and lowest volume levels.

Example: Using information from Exhibit 5.6, what is the amount of fixed cost at the low level of volume? *Answer:* $17,525, computed as $29,000 − ($0.17 × 17,500 units).

Least-Squares Regression

Least-squares regression is a statistical method for identifying cost behavior. For our purposes, we use the cost equation estimated from this method but leave the computational details for more advanced courses. Such computations for least-squares regression are readily done using most spreadsheet programs or calculators. We illustrate this using Excel in Appendix 5A. Using least-squares regression, the cost equation for the data presented in Exhibit 5.3 is **$16,947 plus $0.19 per unit produced;** that is, the fixed cost is estimated as $16,947 and the variable cost at $0.19 per unit.

Comparison of Cost Estimation Methods

The three cost estimation methods result in slightly different estimates of fixed and variable costs as summarized in Exhibit 5.8. Estimates from the scatter diagram, unless done with spreadsheet software, are based on a visual fit of the cost line and are subject to interpretation. Estimates from the high-low method use only two sets of values corresponding to the lowest and highest unit volumes. Sometimes these two extreme activity levels do not reflect the more usual conditions likely to recur. Estimates from least-squares regression use a statistical technique and all available data points.

Estimation Method	Fixed Cost	Variable Cost
Scatter diagram	$16,000	$0.20 per unit
High-low method	17,525	0.17 per unit
Least-squares regression	16,947	0.19 per unit

EXHIBIT 5.8

Comparison of Cost Estimation Methods

We must remember that all three methods use *past data.* Thus, cost estimates resulting from these methods are only as good as the data used for estimation. Managers must establish that the data are reliable in deriving cost estimates for the future. If the data are reliable, the use of more data points, as in the regression or scatter diagram methods, should yield more accurate estimates than the high-low method. However, the high-low method is easier to apply and thus might be useful for obtaining a quick cost equation estimate.

Using the information below, apply the high-low method to determine the *cost equation* (total fixed costs plus variable costs per unit).

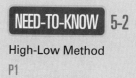

NEED-TO-KNOW 5-2

High-Low Method

P1

Activity Level	Units Produced	Total Cost
Lowest	1,600	$ 9,800
Highest	4,000	17,000

Solution

The variable cost per unit is computed as: [$17,000 − $9,800]/[4,000 units − 1,600 units] = $3 per unit. Total fixed costs using the lowest activity level is computed from the following equation: $9,800 = Fixed costs − ($3 × 1,600 units); thus, fixed costs = $5,000. This implies the cost equation is **$5,000 plus $3 per unit produced.** We can prove the accuracy of this cost equation at either the highest or lowest point shown here.

<table>
<tr><td>Highest point:</td><td>Lowest point:</td></tr>
<tr><td>Total cost = $5,000 + ($3 per unit × 4,000 units)</td><td>Total cost = $5,000 + ($3 per unit × 1,600 units)</td></tr>
<tr><td>= $5,000 + $12,000</td><td>= $5,000 + $4,800</td></tr>
<tr><td>= $17,000</td><td>= $9,800</td></tr>
</table>

Do More: QS 5-3, E 5-6

QC2

CONTRIBUTION MARGIN AND BREAK-EVEN ANALYSIS

In this section we introduce the concept of *contribution margin,* the key measure in cost-volume-profit analysis. We also discuss break-even analysis, an important special case of cost-volume-profit analysis.

Contribution Margin and Its Measures

A1

Compute the contribution margin and describe what it reveals about a company's cost structure.

CVP analysis requires managers to classify costs as being fixed or variable with respect to volume of activity. In manufacturing companies, volume of activity usually refers to the number of units produced. We then classify a cost as either fixed or variable, depending on whether total cost changes as the number of units produced changes. Once we classify costs by behavior, we can then compute a product's contribution margin. **Contribution margin per unit,** or *unit contribution margin,* is the amount by which a product's unit selling price exceeds its total variable cost per unit. This amount contributes to covering fixed costs and generating profits. Exhibit 5.9 shows the formula used to calculate contribution margin per unit.

EXHIBIT 5.9

Contribution Margin per Unit

$$\text{Contribution margin per unit} = \text{Selling price per unit} - \text{Total variable cost per unit}$$

Another way to calculate contribution margin is as a ratio. The **contribution margin ratio,** which is the percent of a unit's selling price that exceeds total unit variable cost, is also useful for business decisions. It can be interpreted as the percent of each sales dollar that remains after deducting the total unit variable cost. Exhibit 5.10 shows the formula for the contribution margin ratio.

EXHIBIT 5.10

Contribution Margin Ratio

$$\text{Contribution margin ratio} = \frac{\text{Contribution margin per unit}}{\text{Selling price per unit}}$$

AP Images/Skip Peterson

To illustrate the use of contribution margin, let's consider Rydell, which sells footballs for $100 each and incurs variable costs of $70 per football sold. Its fixed costs are $24,000 per month with monthly capacity of 1,800 units (footballs). Rydell's contribution margin per unit is $30, which is computed as follows.

Selling price per unit	$100
Variable cost per unit	70
Contribution margin per unit	$ 30

Thus, at a selling price of $100 per unit, Rydell covers its variable costs and makes $30 per football to contribute to fixed costs and profit. Rydell's contribution margin ratio is 30%, computed as $30/$100. A contribution margin ratio of 30% implies that for each $1 in sales, Rydell has $0.30 that contributes to fixed cost and profit. Next we show how to use these contribution margin measures in break-even analysis.

■ Decision Maker

Sales Manager   You are evaluating orders from two customers but can accept only one of the orders because of your company's limited capacity. The first order is for 100 units of a product with a contribution margin ratio of 60% and a selling price of $1,000 per unit. The second order is for 500 units of a product with a contribution margin ratio of 20% and a selling price of $800 per unit. The incremental fixed costs are the same for both orders. Which order do you accept? ■   [Answers follow the chapter's Summary.]

Computing the Break-Even Point

The **break-even point** is the sales level at which a company neither earns a profit nor incurs a loss. The concept of break-even applies to nearly all organizations, activities, and events. A key concern when launching a project is whether it will break even—that is, whether sales will at least cover total costs. The break-even point can be expressed in either units or dollars of sales.

To illustrate break-even analysis, let's again look at Rydell, which sells footballs for $100 per unit and incurs $70 of variable costs per unit sold. Its fixed costs are $24,000 per month. We compute the break-even point using the formula in Exhibit 5.11. This formula uses the contribution margin per unit (calculated above), which for Rydell is $30 ($100 − $70). From this we can compute the break-even sales volume in units as follows:

$$\text{Break-even point in units} = \frac{\text{Fixed costs}}{\text{Contribution margin per unit}}$$
$$= \$24,000/\$30$$
$$= 800 \text{ units per month}$$

P2
Compute the break-even point for a single product company.

Point: Selling prices and variable costs are usually expressed in per unit amounts. Fixed costs are usually expressed in total amounts.

EXHIBIT 5.11

Formula for Computing Break-Even Sales (in Units)

If Rydell sells 800 units, its profit will be zero. Profit increases or decreases by $30 for every unit sold above or below that break-even point; if Rydell sells 801 units, profit will equal $30. We also can calculate the break-even point in dollars. Also called *break-even sales dollars,* it uses the contribution margin ratio to determine the required sales dollars needed for the company to break even. Exhibit 5.12 shows the formula and Rydell's break-even point in dollars:

$$\text{Break-even point in dollars} = \frac{\text{Fixed costs}}{\text{Contribution margin ratio}}$$
$$= \$24,000/30\%$$
$$= \$24,000/0.30$$
$$= \$80,000 \text{ of monthly sales}$$

EXHIBIT 5.12

Formula for Computing Break-Even Sales (in Dollars)

Point: Even if a company operates at a level above its break-even point, management may decide to stop operating because it is not earning a reasonable return on investment.

To verify that Rydell's monthly break-even point equals $80,000 (or 800 units), we prepare a simplified income statement in Exhibit 5.13. It shows that the $80,000 revenue from sales of 800 units exactly equals the sum of variable and fixed costs.

EXHIBIT 5.13

Contribution Margin Income Statement for Break-Even Sales

RYDELL COMPANY Contribution Margin Income Statement (at Break-Even) For Month Ended January 31, 2015	
Sales (800 units at $100 each)	$80,000
Variable costs (800 units at $70 each)	56,000
Contribution margin	24,000
Fixed costs	24,000
Net income	$ 0

Point: A contribution margin income statement is also referred to as a *variable costing income statement.* This differs from the traditional *absorption costing* approach where all product costs are assigned to units sold and to units in ending inventory. Recall that variable costing expenses all fixed product costs. Thus, income for the two approaches differs depending on the level of finished goods inventory; the lower inventory is, the more similar the two approaches are. GAAP requires financial statements for external users be prepared using absorption costing.

The statement in Exhibit 5.13 is called a *contribution margin income statement.* It differs in format from a conventional income statement in two ways. First, it separately classifies costs and expenses as variable or fixed. Second, it reports contribution margin (Sales − Variable costs). We will use the contribution margin income statement format in this chapter's assignment materials because of its usefulness in CVP analysis.

Computing the Margin of Safety

All companies wish to sell more than the break-even number of units. The excess of expected sales over the break-even sales level is called a company's **margin of safety,** the amount that sales can drop before the company incurs a loss. It is often expressed in dollars or as a percent of the expected sales level.

To illustrate, recall that Rydell's break-even point in dollars is $80,000. If its expected sales are $100,000, the margin of safety is $20,000 (= $100,000 − $80,000). As a percent, the margin of safety is 20% of expected sales as shown in Exhibit 5.14.

EXHIBIT 5.14

Computing Margin of Safety (in Percent)

$$\text{Margin of safety (in percent)} = \frac{\text{Expected sales} - \text{Break-even sales}}{\text{Expected sales}}$$

$$= \frac{\$100,000 - \$80,000}{\$100,000}$$

$$= \$20,000/\$100,000$$

$$= 20\%$$

Management must assess whether the margin of safety is adequate in light of factors such as sales variability, competition, consumer tastes, and economic conditions.

NEED-TO-KNOW   5-3

Contribution Margin, Break-Even Point, Margin of Safety

A1   P2

Do More: QS 5-5, QS 5-6, QS 5-10, E 5-8, E 5-9, E 5-16

A manufacturer predicts fixed costs of $400,000 for the next year. Its one product sells for $170 per unit, and it incurs variable costs of $150 per unit. The company predicts total sales of 25,000 units for the next year.

1. Compute the contribution margin per unit.
2. Compute the break-even point (in units).
3. Compute the margin of safety (in dollars).

Solution

1. Contribution margin per unit = $170 − $150 = $20
2. Break-even point = $400,000/$20 = 20,000 units
3. Margin of safety = [25,000 × $170] − [20,000 × $170] = $850,000

Preparing a Cost-Volume-Profit Chart

P3

Graph costs and sales for a single product company.

Point: CVP charts can also be drawn with computer programs.

Exhibit 5.15 is a graph of Rydell's cost-volume-profit relations. This graph is called a **cost-volume-profit (CVP) chart,** or a *break-even chart* or *break-even graph.* The horizontal axis is the number of units produced and sold, and the vertical axis is dollars of sales and costs. The lines in the chart depict both sales and costs at different output levels.

We follow three steps to prepare a CVP chart:

1. Plot fixed costs on the vertical axis ($24,000 for Rydell). Draw a horizontal line at this level to show that fixed costs remain unchanged regardless of output volume (drawing this fixed cost line is not essential to the chart).

2. Draw the total (variable plus fixed) cost line for a relevant range of volume levels. This line starts at the fixed costs level on the vertical axis because total costs equal fixed costs

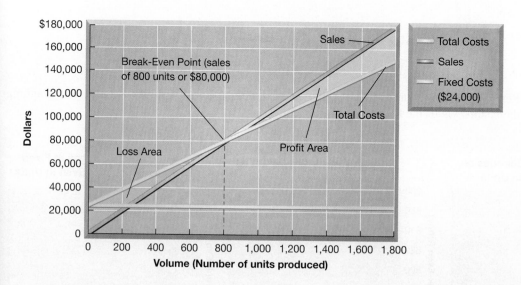

EXHIBIT 5.15

Cost-Volume-Profit Chart

at zero volume. The slope of the total cost line equals the variable cost per unit ($70). To draw the line, compute the total costs for any volume level, and connect this point with the vertical axis intercept ($24,000). Do not draw this line beyond the productive capacity for the planning period (1,800 units for Rydell).

3. Draw the sales line. Start at the origin (zero units and zero dollars of sales) and make the slope of this line equal to the selling price per unit ($100). To draw the line, compute dollar sales for any volume level and connect this point with the origin. Do not extend this line beyond the productive capacity. Total sales will be highest at maximum capacity.

The total cost line and the sales line intersect at 800 units in Exhibit 5.15, which is the break-even point—the point where total dollar sales of $80,000 equals the sum of both fixed and variable costs ($80,000). (Note that 800 units is the same result we calculated earlier using the formula in Exhibit 5.11.)

On either side of the break-even point, the vertical distance between the sales line and the total cost line at any specific volume reflects the profit or loss expected at that point. At volume levels to the left of the break-even point, this vertical distance is the amount of the expected loss because the total costs line is above the total sales line. At volume levels to the right of the break-even point, the vertical distance represents the expected profit because the total sales line is above the total cost line.

Working with Changes in Estimates

Because CVP analysis uses estimates, knowing how changes in those estimates impact break-even is useful. For example, a manager might form three estimates for each of the components of break-even: optimistic, most likely, and pessimistic. Then ranges of break-even points in units can be computed, using the formula from Exhibit 5.11. To illustrate, assume Rydell's managers provide the set of estimates in Exhibit 5.16.

Point: CVP analysis is often based on *sales volume*, using either units sold or dollar sales. Other output measures, such as the number of units produced, can also be used.

Example: In Exhibit 5.15, the sales line intersects the total cost line at 800 units. At what point would the two lines intersect if selling price is increased by 20% to $120 per unit? *Answer:* $24,000/($120 − $70) = 480 units

QC3

EXHIBIT 5.16

Alternative Estimates for Break-Even Analysis

	Selling Price per Unit	Variable Cost per Unit	Total Fixed Costs
Optimistic	$105	$68	$21,000
Most likely	100	70	24,000
Pessimistic	95	72	27,000

If, for example, Rydell's managers believe they can raise the selling price of a football to $105, without any change in unit variable or total fixed costs, then the revised contribution margin per football is $35 ($105 − $70), and the revised break-even in units follows in Exhibit 5.17.

EXHIBIT 5.17

Revised Break-Even
in Units

$$\text{Revised break-even point in units} = \frac{\$24,000}{\$35} = 686 \text{ units (rounded)}$$

EXHIBIT 5.18

Break-Even Points for
Alternative Estimates

Repeating this calculation using each of the other eight separate estimates above, and graphing the results, yields the three graphs in Exhibit 5.18.

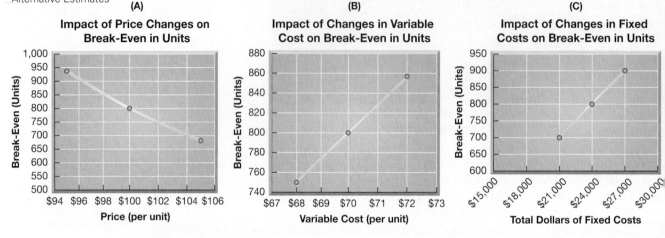

(A) Impact of Price Changes on Break-Even in Units

(B) Impact of Changes in Variable Cost on Break-Even in Units

(C) Impact of Changes in Fixed Costs on Break-Even in Units

These graphs show how changes in selling prices, variable costs, and fixed costs impact break-even. When selling prices can be increased without impacting unit variable costs or total fixed costs, break-even decreases (graph A). When competition reduces selling prices, and the company cannot reduce costs, break-even increases (graph A). Increases in either variable (graph B) or fixed costs (graph C), if they cannot be passed on to customers via higher selling prices, will increase break-even. If costs can be reduced and selling prices held constant, the break-even point decreases.

Point: This analysis changed only one estimate at a time; managers can examine how combinations of changes in estimates will impact break-even.

 Decision Ethics

Supervisor   Your team is conducting a cost-volume-profit analysis for a new product. Different sales projections have different incomes. One member suggests picking numbers yielding favorable income because any estimate is "as good as any other." Another member points to a diagram of 20 months' production on a comparable product and suggests dropping unfavorable data points for cost estimation. What do you do? ■   [Answers follow the chapter's Summary.]

APPLYING COST-VOLUME-PROFIT ANALYSIS

Managers consider a variety of strategies in planning business operations. Cost-volume-profit analysis is useful in helping managers evaluate the likely effects of these strategies.

Computing Income from Sales and Costs

C2

Describe several applications of cost-volume-profit analysis.

An important question managers often ask is "What is the predicted income from a predicted level of sales?" To answer this, we look at four variables in CVP analysis—sales, variable costs, contribution margin, and fixed costs. Exhibit 5.19 shows these variables and their relations to income (pretax). We use these relations to compute expected income from predicted sales and cost levels.

EXHIBIT 5.19

Income Relations in
CVP Analysis

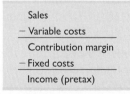

Sales
− Variable costs
Contribution margin
− Fixed costs
Income (pretax)

To illustrate, let's assume that Rydell's management expects to sell 1,500 units in January 2015. What is the amount of income if this sales level is achieved? Using the calculation format in Exhibit 5.19, we compute Rydell's expected income in Exhibit 5.20.

RYDELL COMPANY Contribution Margin Income Statement For Month Ended January 31, 2015	
Sales (1,500 units at $100 each)	$150,000
Variable costs (1,500 units at $70 each)	105,000
Contribution margin	45,000
Fixed costs	24,000
Income (pretax)	$ 21,000

EXHIBIT 5.20

Computing Expected Pretax Income from Expected Sales

This income amount can also be computed as (units sold × contribution margin per unit) − fixed costs, or (1,500 × $30) − $24,000. The $21,000 income is pretax. To find the amount of *after-tax* income from selling 1,500 units, management must apply the proper tax rate. Assume that the tax rate is 25%. Then we can prepare a projected after-tax income statement, shown in Exhibit 5.21. We can also compute pretax income as after-tax income divided by (1 − tax rate); for Rydell, this is $15,750/(1 − 0.25), or $21,000.

Point: 1,500 units of sales is 700 units above Rydell's break-even point. Income can also be computed as 700 units × $30 contribution margin per unit.

RYDELL COMPANY Contribution Margin Income Statement For Month Ended January 31, 2015	
Sales (1,500 units at $100 each)	$150,000
Variable costs (1,500 units at $70 each)	105,000
Contribution margin	45,000
Fixed costs	24,000
Pretax income	21,000
Income taxes (25%)	5,250
Net income (after tax)	$ 15,750

EXHIBIT 5.21

Computing Expected After-Tax Income from Expected Sales

Management then assesses whether this income is an adequate return on assets invested. Management should also consider whether sales and income can be increased by raising or lowering prices. CVP analysis is a good tool for addressing these kinds of "what-if" questions.

"How many units must we sell to earn $50,000?"

Computing Sales for a Target Income

Many companies' annual plans are based on certain income targets (sometimes called *budgets*). Rydell's income target for this year is to increase income by 10% over the prior year. When prior year income is known, Rydell easily computes its target income. CVP analysis helps to determine the sales level needed to achieve the target income. Planning for the year is then based on this level.

We use the formula shown in Exhibit 5.22 to compute sales for a target income (pretax). To illustrate, Rydell has monthly fixed costs of $24,000 and a 30% contribution margin ratio. Assume that it sets a target monthly income of $12,000. Using the formula in Exhibit 5.22, we find that Rydell needs $120,000 of sales to produce a $12,000 pretax target income.

EXHIBIT 5.22

Computing Sales (Dollars) for a Target Income

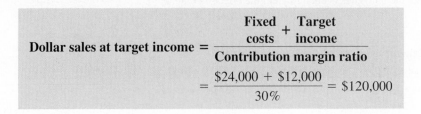

$$\text{Dollar sales at target income} = \frac{\text{Fixed costs} + \text{Target income}}{\text{Contribution margin ratio}}$$

$$= \frac{\$24,000 + \$12,000}{30\%} = \$120,000$$

Point: Break-even is a special case of the formulas in Exhibits 5.22 and 5.23; simply set target income to $0 and the formulas reduce to those in Exhibits 5.11 and 5.12.

Alternatively, we can compute *unit sales* instead of dollar sales. To do this, we substitute *contribution margin per unit* for the contribution margin ratio in the denominator. This gives the number of units to sell to reach the target income. Exhibit 5.23 illustrates this for Rydell. The two computations in Exhibits 5.22 and 5.23 are equivalent because sales of 1,200 units at $100 per unit equal $120,000 of sales.

EXHIBIT 5.23

Computing Sales (Units) for a Target Income

$$\text{Unit sales at target income} = \frac{\text{Fixed costs} + \text{Target income}}{\text{Contribution margin per unit}}$$

$$= \frac{\$24,000 + \$12,000}{\$30} = 1,200 \text{ units}$$

We can also use the contribution margin income statement approach to compute sales for a target income, in two steps.

Step 1: Insert the fixed costs ($24,000) and the target profit level ($12,000) into a contribution margin income statement, as shown in Exhibit 5.24. To cover its fixed costs of $24,000 and yield target income of $12,000, Rydell must generate a contribution margin of $36,000 (computed as $24,000 plus $12,000).

Step 2: Enter $36,000 in the contribution margin row as step 2. With a contribution margin ratio of 30%, sales must be $120,000, computed as $36,000/0.30, to yield a contribution margin of $36,000. We enter $120,000 in the sales row of the contribution margin income statement and solve for variable costs of $84,000 (computed as $120,000 − $36,000). At a selling price of $100 per unit, Rydell must sell 1,200 units ($120,000/$100) to earn a target income of $12,000.

EXHIBIT 5.24

Using the Contribution Margin Income Statement to Find Target Sales

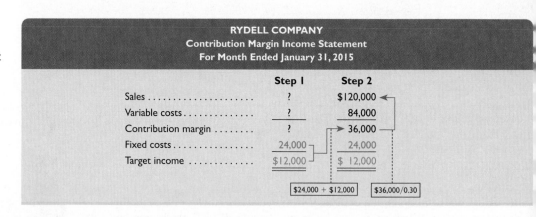

RYDELL COMPANY		
Contribution Margin Income Statement		
For Month Ended January 31, 2015		
	Step 1	Step 2
Sales	?	$120,000
Variable costs	?	84,000
Contribution margin	?	36,000
Fixed costs	24,000	24,000
Target income	$12,000	$ 12,000
	$24,000 + $12,000	$36,000/0.30

NEED-TO-KNOW 5-4

Contribution Margin and Target Income

A1 C2

A manufacturer predicts fixed costs of $502,000 for the next year. Its one product sells for $180 per unit, and it incurs variable costs of $126 per unit. Its target (pretax) income is $200,000.

1. Compute the contribution margin ratio.

2. Compute the dollar sales needed to yield the target income.

3. Compute the unit sales needed to yield the target income.

Solution

1. Contribution margin ratio = [$180 − $126]/$180 = 30%

2. Dollar sales at target income = [$502,000 + $200,000]/0.30 = $2,340,000

3. Unit sales at target income = [$502,000 + $200,000]/[$180 − $126] = 13,000 units

Do More: QS 5-9, QS 5-13, E 5-12, E 5-17

Using Sensitivity Analysis

Earlier we showed how changing one of the estimates in a CVP analysis impacts break-even. We can also examine strategies that impact several estimates in the CVP analysis. For instance, we might want to know what happens to income if we automate a currently manual process. We can use *sensitivity analysis* to predict income if we can describe how these changes affect a company's fixed costs, variable costs, selling price, and volume. CVP analyses based on different estimates can be useful to management in planning business strategy. We provide examples next.

Buy a New Machine   Assume Rydell is considering buying a new machine that would increase monthly fixed costs from $24,000 to $30,000 and would decrease variable costs by $10 per unit (from $70 per unit to $60 per unit). Recall from Exhibit 5.12 that Rydell's break-even point in dollars is currently $80,000. Management needs to know how the new machine would affect Rydell's break-even point in dollars. If Rydell maintains its selling price of $100 per unit, its contribution margin per unit will increase to $40—computed as the sales price of $100 per unit minus the (new) variable costs of $60 per unit. With this new machine, the revised contribution margin ratio per unit is 40% (computed as $40/$100). Rydell's revised break-even point in dollars would be $75,000, as computed in Exhibit 5.25. The new machine would lower Rydell's break-even point by $5,000, or 50 units, per month. The revised margin of safety increases to 25%, computed as ($100,000 − $75,000)/$100,000.

EXHIBIT 5.25

Revised Break-Even

$$\text{Revised break-even point in dollars} = \frac{\text{Revised fixed costs}}{\text{Revised contribution margin ratio}} = \frac{\$30,000}{40\%} = \$75,000$$

Increase Advertising   Instead of buying a new machine, Rydell's advertising manager suggests increasing advertising instead. She believes that an increase of $3,000 in the monthly advertising budget will increase sales by $25,000 per month (at a selling price of $100 per unit). The contribution margin will continue to be $30 per unit. Recall from Exhibit 5.14 that the company's margin of safety was 20% when Rydell's expected sales level was $100,000. Management wants to know how a new advertising campaign would affect Rydell's break-even point and margin of safety. With the advertising campaign, Rydell's revised break-even point in dollars is $90,000, as computed in Exhibit 5.26.

EXHIBIT 5.26

Revised Break-Even (in dollars)

$$\text{Revised break-even point in dollars} = \frac{\text{Revised fixed costs}}{\text{Revised contribution margin ratio}} = \frac{\$27,000}{30\%} = \$90,000$$

The revised margin of safety is then computed as shown in Exhibit 5.27. Without considering other factors, the advertising campaign would increase Rydell's margin of safety from 20% (see Exhibit 5.14) to 28%.

QC4

EXHIBIT 5.27

Revised Margin of Safety (in percent)

$$\text{Revised margin of safety (in percent)} = \frac{\text{Expected sales} - \text{Break-even sales}}{\text{Expected sales}}$$
$$= \frac{\$125,000 - \$90,000}{\$125,000} = 28\%$$

Computing a Multiproduct Break-Even Point

P4

Compute the break-even point for a multiproduct company.

E+/Getty Images

So far we have looked only at cases where the company sells a single product or service. However, many companies sell multiple products or services, and we can modify the CVP analysis for use in these cases. An important assumption in a multiproduct setting is that the sales mix of different products is known and remains constant during the planning period. **Sales mix** is the ratio (proportion) of the sales volumes for the various products. For instance, if a company normally sells 10,000 footballs, 5,000 softballs, and 4,000 basketballs per month, its sales mix can be expressed as 10:5:4 for footballs, softballs, and basketballs.

In multiproduct CVP analysis, we estimate the break-even point by using a **composite unit**, which summarizes the sales mix and contribution margins of each product. Multiproduct CVP analysis treats this composite unit as a single product. To illustrate, let's look at Hair-Today, a styling salon that offers three cuts: basic, ultra, and budget in the ratio of 4 basic units to 2 ultra units to 1 budget unit (expressed as 4:2:1). Management wants to estimate its break-even point for next year. Unit selling prices for these three cuts are basic, $20; ultra, $32; and budget, $16. Using the 4:2:1 sales mix, the selling price of a composite unit of the three products is computed as follows.

Selling price per composite unit	
4 units of basic @ $20 per unit.	$ 80
2 units of ultra @ $32 per unit	64
1 unit of budget @ $16 per unit	16
Selling price of a composite unit	**$160**

Hair-Today's fixed costs are $192,000 per year, and its unit variable costs of the three products are basic, $13; ultra, $18; and budget, $8. Variable costs for a composite unit of these products follow.

Variable costs per composite unit	
4 units of basic @ $13 per unit.	$52
2 units of ultra @ $18 per unit	36
1 unit of budget @ $8 per unit	8
Variable costs of a composite unit	**$96**

We calculate the contribution margin for a *composite unit* using essentially the same formula used earlier (see Exhibit 5.9), as shown in Exhibit 5.28:

EXHIBIT 5.28

Contribution Margin per Composite Unit

$$\begin{array}{ccc} \textbf{Contribution margin} & \textbf{Selling price} & \textbf{Variable cost} \\ \textbf{per composite unit} = & \textbf{per composite unit} - & \textbf{per composite unit} \\ \$64 \quad = & \$160 \quad - & \$96 \end{array}$$

We then use the contribution margin per composite unit to determine Hair-Today's break-even point in composite units in Exhibit 5.29.

EXHIBIT 5.29

Break-Even Point in Composite Units

$$\text{Break-even point in composite units} = \frac{\text{Fixed costs}}{\text{Contribution margin per composite unit}}$$
$$= \frac{\$192,000}{\$64} = 3,000 \text{ composite units}$$

This computation implies that Hair-Today breaks even when it sells 3,000 composite units. To determine how many units of each product it must sell to break even, we use the expected sales mix of 4:2:1 and multiply the number of units of each product in the composite by 3,000 as follows.

Point: The break-even point in dollars for Exhibit 5.29 is $192,000/($64/$160) = $480,000.

Basic:	4 × 3,000	12,000 units
Ultra:	2 × 3,000	6,000 units
Budget:	1 × 3,000	3,000 units
		21,000 units

Point: Each composite unit represents 7 haircuts. Total haircuts at the break-even point equal 21,000 (3,000 composite units × 7 haircuts per composite unit).

Exhibit 5.30 verifies the results for composite units by showing Hair-Today's sales and costs at this break-even point using a forecasted contribution margin income statement.

EXHIBIT 5.30

Multiproduct Break-Even Income Statement

HAIR-TODAY Forecasted Contribution Margin Income Statement (at Break-Even)				
	Basic	**Ultra**	**Budget**	**Total**
Sales				
Basic (12,000 @ $20)..........	$240,000			
Ultra (6,000 @ $32)...........		$192,000		
Budget (3,000 @ $16)			$48,000	
Total sales..................				$480,000
Variable costs				
Basic (12,000 @ $13)..........	156,000			
Ultra (6,000 @ $18)...........		108,000		
Budget (3,000 @ $8)			24,000	
Total variable costs...........				288,000
Contribution margin	$ 84,000	$ 84,000	$24,000	192,000
Fixed costs				192,000
Net income				$ 0

A CVP analysis using composite units can be used to answer a variety of planning questions. Once a product mix is set, all answers are based on the assumption that the mix remains constant at all relevant sales levels as other factors in the analysis do. If the sales mix changes, it is likely that the break-even point will change also. For example, if Hair-Today sells more ultra cuts and fewer basic cuts, its break-even point will decrease. We can vary the sales mix to see what happens under alternative strategies.

Point: Enterprise resource planning (ERP) systems can quickly generate multiproduct break-even analyses.

Decision Maker

Entrepreneur   A CVP analysis indicates that your start-up, which markets electronic products, will break even with the current sales mix and price levels. You have a target income in mind. What analysis might you perform to assess the likelihood of achieving this income? ■   [Answers follow the chapter's Summary.]

The sales mix of a company's two products, X and Y, is 2:1. Unit variable costs for both products are $2, and unit selling prices are $5 for X and $4 for Y. The company has $640,000 of fixed costs.
1. What is the contribution margin per composite unit?
2. What is the break-even point in composite units?
3. How many units of X and how many units of Y will be sold at the break-even point?

NEED-TO-KNOW 5-5

Contribution Margin and Break-Even Point, Composite Units

P4

Solution

1.

Selling price of a composite unit		Variable costs of a composite unit	
2 units of X @ $5 per unit	$10	2 units of X @ $2 per unit	$4
1 unit of Y @ $4 per unit	4	1 unit of Y @ $2 per unit	2
Selling price of a composite unit	$14	Variable costs of a composite unit	$6

Do More: QS 5-14, E 5-21,
E 5-23

QC5

Therefore, the contribution margin per composite unit is $8.

2. The break-even point in composite units = $640,000/$8 = 80,000 units.

3. At break-even, the company will sell 160,000 units (80,000 × 2) of X and 80,000 units of Y (80,000 × 1

Making Assumptions in Cost-Volume-Profit Analysis

CVP analysis assumes that costs can be classified as variable or fixed. CVP analysis also as
sumes that selling prices per unit, variable costs per unit, and total fixed costs are all held con
stant. Further, multiproduct CVP analysis assumes a constant sales mix. If the expected cost
and sales behavior differ from the assumptions, the results of CVP analysis can be limited
While the behavior of individual costs and sales may not be perfectly consistent with CVP as
sumptions, we can still perform useful analyses in spite of these assumptions' limitations, fo
reasons we describe next.

Summing Costs Offsets Individual Deviations   Deviations from assumptions wit
individual costs are often minor when these costs are summed. That is, individual variabl
cost items may not be perfectly variable, but when we sum these variable costs, their in
dividual deviations can offset each other. This means the assumption of variable cost be
havior can be proper for total variable costs. Similarly, an assumption that total fixe
costs are constant can be proper even when individual fixed cost items are not exactl
constant.

CVP Applies to a Relevant Range of Operations   Sales, variable costs, and fixe
costs often are reasonably reflected in straight lines on a graph when the assumptions are ap
plied over a relevant range. The validity of assuming that a specific cost is fixed or variable i
more acceptable when operations are within the relevant range. As shown in Exhibit 5.2,
curvilinear cost can be treated as variable and linear if the relevant range covers volume
where it has a nearly constant slope. If the normal range of activity changes, some costs migh
need reclassification.

CVP Analysis Yields Estimates   CVP analysis yields approximate answers to question
about costs, volumes, and profits. These answers do not have to be precise because the analy
sis makes rough estimates about the future. As long as managers understand that CVP analysi
gives estimates, it can be a useful tool for starting the planning process. Other qualitative fac
tors also must be considered.

GLOBAL VIEW

Survey evidence shows that many German companies have elaborate and detailed cost accounting sys
tems. Over 90 percent of companies surveyed report their systems focus on *contribution margin*. Thi
focus helps German companies like **Volkswagen** control costs and plan their production levels. Recently
Volkswagen announced it expects its Spanish brand *SEAT* to break even within five years. For 2012, th
SEAT brand lost €156 million on revenue of €6.485 billion.

Sustainability and Accounting   Volkswagen (VW) is regarded as the most sustainable automotive group in the Dow Jones Sustainability Index—in part because of its efforts to embrace opportunities and manage risks deriving from economic, environmental, and social developments. The company recently entered a long-term contract to buy wind-generated power for several of its Mexican manufacturing facilities. VW expects the use of wind power not only to reduce its carbon emissions but also to save $3.5 million per year in electric utility costs. Smaller companies can also make a difference. Fast Yeti Custom Tees, this chapter's feature company, buys its T-shirts from suppliers with good environmental practices. All of the company's shirts are made from 100% cotton, a natural and renewable fiber.

Degree of Operating Leverage **Decision Analysis**

CVP analysis is especially useful when management begins the planning process and wishes to predict outcomes of alternative strategies. These strategies can involve changes in selling prices, fixed costs, variable costs, sales volume, and product mix. Managers are interested in seeing the effects of changes in some or all of these factors.

A2

Analyze changes in sales using the degree of operating leverage.

One goal of all managers is to get maximum benefits from their fixed costs. Managers would like to use 100% of their output capacity so that fixed costs are spread over the largest number of units. This would decrease fixed cost per unit and increase income. The extent, or relative size, of fixed costs in the total cost structure is known as **operating leverage.** Companies having a higher proportion of fixed costs in their total cost structure are said to have higher operating leverage. An example of this is a company that chooses to automate its processes instead of using direct labor, increasing its fixed costs and lowering its variable costs.

A useful managerial measure to help assess the effect of changes in the level of sales on income is the **degree of operating leverage (DOL),** calculated as shown in Exhibit 5.31.

DOL = Total contribution margin (in dollars)/Pretax income

EXHIBIT 5.31

Degree of Operating Leverage

To illustrate, let's return to Rydell Company and assume it sells 1,200 footballs. At this sales level, its contribution margin (in dollars) and pretax income are computed as:

Sales (1,200 × $100)................	$120,000
Variable costs (1,200 × $70).........	84,000
Contribution margin.............	36,000
Fixed costs.......................	24,000
Income (pretax).................	$ 12,000

Rydell's degree of operating leverage (DOL) is then computed as shown in Exhibit 5.32.

DOL = Total contribution margin (in dollars)/Pretax income
DOL = $36,000/$12,000 = 3.0

EXHIBIT 5.32

Rydell's Degree of Operating Leverage

We then can use DOL to measure the effect of changes in the level of sales on pretax income. For example, if Rydell expects sales can either increase or decrease by 10%, and these changes would be within Rydell's relevant range, we can compute the change in pretax income using DOL as shown in Exhibit 5.33.

Change in income (%) = DOL × Change in sales (%)
= 3.0 × 10%
= 30%

EXHIBIT 5.33

Impact of Change in Sales on Income

Thus, if Rydell's sales *increase* by 10%, its income will increase by $3,600 (computed as $12,000 × 30%), to $15,600. If, instead, Rydell's sales decrease by 10%, its net income will decrease by $3,600, to $8,400. We can prove these results with contribution margin income statements, as shown below.

	Current	Sales Increase by 10%	Sales Decrease by 10%
Sales	$120,000	$132,000	$108,000
Variable costs.	84,000	92,400	75,600
Contribution margin	$ 36,000	$ 39,600	$ 32,400
Fixed costs.	24,000	24,000	24,000
Target (pretax) income	$ 12,000	$ 15,600	$ 8,400

NEED-TO-KNOW

COMPREHENSIVE

Sport Caps Co. manufactures and sells caps for different sporting events. The fixed costs of operating the company are $150,000 per month, and the variable costs are $5 per cap. The caps are sold for $8 per unit. The fixed costs provide a production capacity of up to 100,000 caps per month.

Required

1. Use the formulas in the chapter to compute the following:
   a. Contribution margin per cap.
   b. Break-even point in terms of the number of caps produced and sold.
   c. Amount of income at 30,000 caps sold per month (ignore taxes).
   d. Amount of income at 85,000 caps sold per month (ignore taxes).
   e. Number of caps to be produced and sold to provide $60,000 of income (pretax).
2. Draw a CVP chart for the company, showing cap output on the horizontal axis. Identify (a) the break-even point and (b) the amount of pretax income when the level of cap production is 70,000. (Omit the fixed cost line.)
3. Use the formulas in the chapter to compute the
   a. Contribution margin ratio.
   b. Break-even point in terms of sales dollars.
   c. Amount of income at $250,000 of sales per month (ignore taxes).
   d. Amount of income at $600,000 of sales per month (ignore taxes).
   e. Dollars of sales needed to provide $60,000 of pretax income.

PLANNING THE SOLUTION

● Identify the formulas in the chapter for the required items expressed in units and solve them using the data given in the problem.
● Draw a CVP chart that reflects the facts in the problem. The horizontal axis should plot the volume in units up to 100,000, and the vertical axis should plot the total dollars up to $800,000. Plot the total cost line as upward sloping, starting at the fixed cost level ($150,000) on the vertical axis and increasing until it reaches $650,000 at the maximum volume of 100,000 units. Verify that the break-even point (where the two lines cross) equals the amount you computed in part 1.
● Identify the formulas in the chapter for the required items expressed in dollars and solve them using the data given in the problem.

SOLUTION

1. a. Contribution margin per cap $= $ Selling price per unit $-$ Variable cost per unit

$= \$8 - \$5 = \underline{\underline{\$3}}$

b. Break-even point in caps $= \dfrac{\text{Fixed costs}}{\text{Contribution margin per cap}} = \dfrac{\$150,000}{\$3} = \underline{\underline{50,000 \text{ caps}}}$

c. Income at 30,000 caps sold

$= $ (Units $\times$ Contribution margin per unit) $-$ Fixed costs
$= (30,000 \times \$3) - \$150,000 = \underline{\$(60,000)\ \text{loss}}$

d. Income at 85,000 caps sold

$= $ (Units $\times$ Contribution margin per unit) $-$ Fixed costs
$= (85,000 \times \$3) - \$150,000 = \underline{\$105,000\ \text{profit}}$

e. Units needed for $60,000 income $= \dfrac{\text{Fixed costs} + \text{Target income}}{\text{Contribution margin per cap}}$

$= \dfrac{\$150,000 + \$60,000}{\$3} = \underline{70,000\ \text{caps}}$

2. CVP chart.

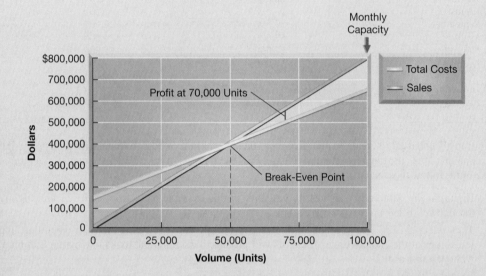

3. a. Contribution margin ratio

$= \dfrac{\text{Contribution margin per unit}}{\text{Selling price per unit}} = \dfrac{\$3}{\$8} = \underline{\underline{0.375, \text{ or } 37.5\%}}$

b. Break-even point in dollars

$= \dfrac{\text{Fixed costs}}{\text{Contribution margin ratio}} = \dfrac{\$150,000}{37.5\%} = \underline{\underline{\$400,000}}$

c. Income at sales of $250,000

$= $ (Sales $\times$ Contribution margin ratio) $-$ Fixed costs
$= (\$250,000 \times 37.5\%) - \$150,000 = \underline{\$(56,250)\ \text{loss}}$

d. Income at sales of $600,000

$= $ (Sales $\times$ Contribution margin ratio) $-$ Fixed costs
$= (\$600,000 \times 37.5\%) - \$150,000 = \underline{\$75,000\ \text{income}}$

e. Dollars of sales to yield
$60,000 pretax income

$= \dfrac{\text{Fixed costs} + \text{Target pretax income}}{\text{Contribution margin ratio}}$

$= \dfrac{\$150,000 + \$60,000}{37.5\%} = \underline{\$560,000}$

Using Excel to Estimate Least-Squares Regression

5A

Microsoft Excel® and other spreadsheet software can be used to perform least-squares regressions to identify cost behavior. In Excel, the INTERCEPT and SLOPE functions are used. The following screen shot
reports the data from Exhibit 5.3 in cells Al through C13 and shows the cell contents to find the intercept
(cell B15) and slope (cell B16). Cell B15 uses Excel to find the intercept from a least-squares regression
of total cost (shown as C2:C13 in cell B15) on units produced (shown as B2:B13 in cell B15). Spreadsheet

software is useful in understanding cost behavior when many data points (such as monthly total costs and units produced) are available.

	A	B	C	
1	**Month**	**Units Produced**	**Total Cost**	
2	January	27,500	$21,500	
3	February	17,500	20,500	
4	March	25,000	25,000	
5	April	35,000	21,500	
6	May	47,500	25,500	
7	June	22,500	18,500	
8	July	30,000	23,500	
9	August	52,500	28,500	
10	September	37,500	26,000	
11	October	67,500	29,000	
12	November	62,500	31,000	
13	December	57,500	26,000	
14			**Result**	
15	**Intercept**	=INTERCEPT(C2:C13, B2:B13)	$16,947.17	
16	**Slope**	=SLOPE(C2:C13, B2:B13)	$ 0.1930	
17				

Excel can also be used to create scatter diagrams such as that in Exhibit 5.4. In contrast to visually drawing a line that "fits" the data, Excel more precisely fits the regression line. To draw a scatter diagram with a line of fit, follow these steps:

1. Highlight the data cells you wish to diagram; in this example, start from cell C13 and highlight through cell B2.
2. Then select "Insert" and "Scatter" from the drop-down menus. Selecting the chart type in the upper left corner of the choices under "Scatter" will produce a diagram that looks like that in Exhibit 5.4 without a line of fit.
3. To add a line of fit (also called a trend line), select "Layout" and "Trendline" from the drop-down menus. Selecting "Linear Trendline" will produce a diagram that looks like that in Exhibit 5.4, including the line of fit.

APPENDIX

5B   Variable Costing and Performance Reporting

This chapter showed the usefulness of *contribution margin,* or selling price minus variable costs, in CVP analysis. The contribution margin income statement introduced in this chapter is also known as a **variable costing income statement.** In **variable costing,** only costs that change in total with changes in production levels are included in product costs. These costs include direct materials, direct labor, and *variable* overhead costs. Thus, under variable costing, *fixed* overhead costs are excluded from product costs. As we showed in this chapter, a variable costing approach can be useful in many managerial analyses and decisions.

The variable costing method is not allowed, however, for external financial reporting. Instead, GAAP requires **absorption costing.** Under absorption costing, product costs include direct materials, direct labor, *and all overhead,* both variable and fixed. Managers can use variable costing information for internal decision making, but they must use absorption costing for external reporting purposes.

Exhibit 5B.1 shows product cost per unit computations for both absorption and variable costing.

EXHIBIT 5B.1

Unit Cost Computation

	Absorption Costing	Variable Costing
Direct materials cost per unit..............	$ 4	$ 4
Direct labor cost per unit.................	8	8
Overhead cost		
Variable overhead cost per unit	3	3
Fixed overhead cost per unit	10	—
Total product cost per unit...............	$25	$15

Summary

C1 **Describe different types of cost behavior in relation to production and sales volume.** Cost behavior is described in terms of how its amount changes in relation to changes in volume of activity within a relevant range. Fixed costs remain constant to changes in volume. Total variable costs change in direct proportion to volume changes. Mixed costs display the effects of both fixed and variable components. Step-wise costs remain constant over a small volume range, then change by a lump sum and remain constant over another volume range, and so on. Curvilinear costs change in a nonlinear relation to volume changes.

C2 **Describe several applications of cost-volume-profit analysis.** Cost-volume-profit analysis can be used to predict what can happen under alternative strategies concerning sales volume, selling prices, variable costs, or fixed costs. Applications include "what-if" analysis, computing sales for a target income, and break-even analysis.

A1 **Compute the contribution margin and describe what it reveals about a company's cost structure.** Contribution margin per unit is a product's selling price less its total variable costs. Contribution margin ratio is a product's contribution margin per unit divided by its selling price. Unit contribution margin is the amount received from each sale that contributes to fixed costs and income. The contribution margin ratio reveals what portion of each sales dollar is available as contribution to fixed costs and income.

A2 **Analyze changes in sales using the degree of operating leverage.** The extent, or relative size, of fixed costs in a company's total cost structure is known as *operating leverage.* One tool useful in assessing the effect of changes in sales on income is the degree of operating leverage, or DOL. DOL is the ratio of the contribution margin divided by pretax income. This ratio can be used to determine the expected percent change in income given a percent change in sales.

P1 **Determine cost estimates using the scatter diagram, high-low, and regression methods of estimating costs.** Three different methods used to estimate costs are the scatter diagram, the high-low method, and least-squares regression. All three methods use past data to estimate costs. Cost estimates from a scatter diagram are based on a visual fit of the cost line. Estimates from the high-low method are based only on costs corresponding to the lowest and highest sales. The least-squares regression method is a statistical technique and uses all data points.

P2 **Compute the break-even point for a single product company.** A company's break-even point for a period is the sales volume at which total revenues equal total costs. To compute a break-even point in terms of sales units, we divide total fixed costs by the contribution margin per unit. To compute a break-even point in terms of sales dollars, divide total fixed costs by the contribution margin ratio.

P3 **Graph costs and sales for a single product company.** The costs and sales for a company can be graphically illustrated using a CVP chart. In this chart, the horizontal axis represents the number of units sold and the vertical axis represents dollars of sales or costs. Straight lines are used to depict both costs and sales on the CVP chart.

P4 **Compute the break-even point for a multiproduct company.** CVP analysis can be applied to a multiproduct company by expressing sales volume in terms of composite units. A composite unit consists of a specific number of units of each product in proportion to their expected sales mix. Multiproduct CVP analysis treats this composite unit as a single product.

Guidance Answers to Decision Maker and Decision Ethics

Sales Manager   The contribution margin per unit for the first order is $600 (60% of $1,000); the contribution margin per unit for the second order is $160 (20% of $800). You are likely tempted to accept the first order based on its high contribution margin per unit, but you must compute the total contribution margin based on the number of units sold for each order. Total contribution margin is $60,000 ($600 per unit × 100 units) and $80,000 ($160 per unit × 500 units) for the two orders, respectively. The second order provides the largest return in absolute dollars and is the order you would accept. Another factor to consider in your selection is the potential for a long-term relationship with these customers including repeat sales and growth.

Supervisor   Your dilemma is whether to go along with the suggestions to "manage" the numbers to make the project look like it will achieve sufficient profits. You should not succumb to these suggestions. Many people will likely be affected negatively if you manage the predicted numbers and the project eventually is unprofitable. Moreover, if it does fail, an investigation would likely reveal that data in the proposal were "fixed" to make it look good. Probably the only benefit from managing the numbers is the short-term payoff of pleasing those who proposed the product. One way to deal with this dilemma is to prepare several analyses showing results under different assumptions and then let senior management make the decision.

Entrepreneur   You must first compute the level of sales required to achieve the desired net income. Then you must conduct sensitivity analysis by varying the price, sales mix, and cost estimates. Results from the sensitivity analysis provide information you can use to assess the possibility of reaching the target sales level. For instance, you might have to pursue aggressive marketing strategies to push the high-margin products, or you might have to cut prices to increase sales and profits, or another strategy might emerge.

Key Terms

Absorption costing	Curvilinear cost	Operating leverage
Break-even point	Degree of operating leverage (DOL)	Relevant range of operations
Composite unit	Estimated line of cost behavior	Sales mix
Contribution margin per unit	High-low method	Scatter diagram
Contribution margin ratio	Least-squares regression	Step-wise cost
Cost-volume-profit (CVP) analysis	Margin of safety	Variable costing
Cost-volume-profit (CVP) chart	Mixed cost	Variable costing income statement

Multiple Choice Quiz   Answers at end of chapter

1. A company's only product sells for $150 per unit. Its variable costs per unit are $100, and its fixed costs total $75,000. What is its contribution margin per unit?
   - **a.** $50
   - **b.** $250
   - **c.** $100
   - **d.** $150
   - **e.** $25

2. Using information from question 1, what is the company's contribution margin ratio?
   - **a.** 66⅔%
   - **b.** 100%
   - **c.** 50%
   - **d.** 0%
   - **e.** 33⅓%

3. Using information from question 1, what is the company's break-even point in units?
   - **a.** 500 units
   - **b.** 750 units
   - **c.** 1,500 units
   - **d.** 3,000 units
   - **e.** 1,000 units

4. A company's forecasted sales are $300,000 and its sales at break-even are $180,000. Its margin of safety in dollars is
   - **a.** $180,000.
   - **b.** $120,000.
   - **c.** $480,000.
   - **d.** $60,000.
   - **e.** $300,000.

5. A product sells for $400 per unit and its variable costs per unit are $260. The company's fixed costs are $840,000. If the company desires $70,000 pretax income, what is the required dollar sales?
   - **a.** $2,400,000
   - **b.** $200,000
   - **c.** $2,600,000
   - **d.** $2,275,000
   - **e.** $1,400,000

^A *Superscript letter A denotes assignments based on Appendix 5A.*

🔲 Icon denotes assignments that involve decision making.

Discussion Questions

1. What is a variable cost? Identify two variable costs.
2. 🔲 When output volume increases, do variable costs per unit increase, decrease, or stay the same within the relevant range of activity? Explain.
3. 🔲 When output volume increases, do fixed costs per unit increase, decrease, or stay the same within the relevant range of activity? Explain.
4. 🔲 How is cost-volume-profit analysis useful?
5. How do step-wise costs and curvilinear costs differ?
6. Describe the contribution margin ratio in layperson's terms.
7. Define and explain the *contribution margin ratio.*
8. Define and describe *contribution margin per unit.*
9. In performing CVP analysis for a manufacturing company, what simplifying assumption is usually made about the volume of production and the volume of sales?
10. What two arguments tend to justify classifying all costs as either fixed or variable even though individual costs might not behave exactly as classified?
11. 🔲 How does assuming that operating activity occurs within a relevant range affect cost-volume-profit analysis?
12. List three methods to measure cost behavior.
13. How is a scatter diagram used to identify and measure the behavior of a company's costs?
14. In cost-volume-profit analysis, what is the estimated profit at the break-even point?
15. 🔲 Assume that a straight line on a CVP chart intersects the vertical axis at the level of fixed costs and has a positive slope that rises with each additional unit of volume by the amount of the variable costs per unit. What does this line represent?
16. **Apple** has both fixed and variable costs. Why are fixed costs depicted as a horizontal line on a CVP chart? **APPLE**
17. 🔲 Each of two similar companies has sales of $20,000 and total costs of $15,000 for a month. Company A's total costs include $10,000 of variable costs and $5,000 of fixed costs. If Company B's total costs include $4,000 of variable costs and $11,000 of fixed costs, which company will enjoy more profit if sales double?
18. _____ of _____ reflects expected sales in excess of the level of break-even sales.

19. Google produces tablet computers for sale. Identify some of the variable and fixed product costs associated with that production. [*Hint:* Limit costs to product costs.]

GOOGLE

20. Should Apple use single product or multiproduct break-even analysis? Explain.

APPLE

21. Samsung is thinking of expanding sales of its most popular smartphone model by 65%. Should we expect its variable and fixed costs for this model to stay within the relevant range? Explain.

Samsung

connect

Listed here are four series of separate costs measured at various volume levels. Examine each series and identify whether it is best described as a fixed, variable, step-wise, or curvilinear cost. (It can help to graph the cost series.)

QUICK STUDY

QS 5-1
Cost behavior
identification   C1

Volume (Units)	Series 1	Series 2	Series 3	Series 4
0	$ 0	$450	$ 800	$100
100	800	450	800	105
200	1,600	450	800	120
300	2,400	450	1,600	145
400	3,200	450	1,600	190
500	4,000	450	2,400	250
600	4,800	450	2,400	320

Determine whether each of the following is best described as a fixed, variable, or mixed cost with respect to product units.

_____ **1.** Rubber used to manufacture athletic shoes.

_____ **2.** Maintenance of factory machinery.

_____ **3.** Packaging expense.

_____ **4.** Wages of an assembly-line worker paid on the basis of acceptable units produced.

_____ **5.** Factory supervisor's salary.

_____ **6.** Taxes on factory building.

_____ **7.** Depreciation expense of warehouse.

QS 5-2
Cost behavior
identification

C1

The following information is available for a company's maintenance cost over the last seven months. Using the high-low method, estimate both the fixed and variable components of its maintenance cost.

QS 5-3
Cost behavior
estimation—high-low
method

P1

Month	Maintenance Hours	Maintenance Cost
June..............	9	$5,450
July	18	6,900
August	12	5,100
September	15	6,000
October...........	21	6,900
November	24	8,100
December	6	3,600

This scatter diagram reflects past maintenance hours and their corresponding maintenance costs.

QS 5-4
Cost behavior
estimation—scatter
diagram

P1

1. Draw an estimated line of cost behavior.

2. Estimate the fixed and variable components of maintenance costs.

QS 5-5 Contribution margin ratio A1	Compute and interpret the contribution margin ratio using the following data: sales, $5,000; total variable cost, $3,000.

QS 5-6 Contribution margin per unit and break-even units P2	SBD Phone Company sells its waterproof phone case for $90 per unit. Fixed costs total $162,000, and variable costs are $36 per unit. Determine the (1) contribution margin per unit and (2) break-even point in units.

QS 5-7 Assumptions in CVP analysis C2	SBD Phone Company sells its waterproof phone case for $90 per unit. Fixed costs total $162,000, and variable costs are $36 per unit. How will the break-even point in units change in response to each of the following independent changes in selling price per unit, variable cost per unit, or total fixed costs? Use I for increase and D for decrease. (It is not necessary to compute new break-even points.)

Change	Break-Even in Units Will
1. Total fixed costs to $190,000	_____
2. Variable costs to $34 per unit	_____
3. Selling price per unit to $80	_____
4. Variable costs to $67 per unit	_____
5. Total fixed costs to $150,000	_____
6. Selling price per unit to $120	_____

QS 5-8 Contribution margin ratio and break-even dollars P2	SBD Phone Company sells its waterproof phone case for $90 per unit. Fixed costs total $162,000, and variable costs are $36 per unit. Determine the (1) contribution margin ratio and (2) break-even point in dollars.

QS 5-9 CVP analysis and target income P2	SBD Phone Company sells its waterproof phone case for $90 per unit. Fixed costs total $162,000, and variable costs are $36 per unit. Compute the units of product that must be sold to earn pretax income of $200,000. (Round to the nearest whole unit.)

QS 5-10 Computing break- even P2	Zhao Co. has fixed costs of $354,000. Its single product sells for $175 per unit, and variable costs are $116 per unit. Determine the break-even point in units.

QS 5-11 Margin of safety P2	Zhao Co. has fixed costs of $354,000. Its single product sells for $175 per unit, and variable costs are $116 per unit. If the company expects sales of 10,000 units, compute its margin of safety (a) in dollars and (b) as a percent of expected sales.

QS 5-12 Contribution margin income statement P2	Zhao Co. has fixed costs of $354,000. Its single product sells for $175 per unit, and variable costs are $116 per unit. The company expects sales of 10,000 units. Prepare a contribution margin income statement for the year ended December 31, 2015.

QS 5-13 Target income C2	Zhao Co. has fixed costs of $354,000. Its single product sells for $175 per unit, and variable costs are $116 per unit. Compute the level of sales in units needed to produce a target (pretax) income of $118,000.

QS 5-14 Multiproduct break- even P4	US-Mobile manufactures and sells two products, tablet computers and smartphones, in the ratio of 5:3. Fixed costs are $105,000, and the contribution margin per composite unit is $125. What number of each type of product is sold at the break-even point?

QS 5-15 CVP graph P3	Corme Company expects sales of $34 million (400,000 units). The company's total fixed costs are $17.5 million and its variable costs are $35 per unit. Prepare a CVP chart from this information.

QS 5-16 Operating leverage analysis A2	Singh Co. reports a contribution margin of $960,000 and fixed costs of $720,000. (1) Compute the company's degree of operating leverage. (2) If sales increase by 15%, what amount of income will Singh Co. report?

A recent income statement for **Volkswagen** reports the following (in € millions). Assume 75 percent of the cost of sales and 75 percent of the selling and administrative costs are variable costs, and the remaining 25 percent of each is fixed. Compute the contribution margin (in € millions). (Round computations using percentages to the nearest whole euro.)

Sales	€126,875
Cost of sales	105,431
Selling and administrative expenses	15,500

connect

Following are five graphs representing various cost behaviors. (1) Identify whether the cost behavior in each graph is mixed, step-wise, fixed, variable, or curvilinear. (2) Identify the graph (by number) that best illustrates each cost behavior: (a) Factory policy requires one supervisor for every 30 factory workers; (b) real estate taxes on factory; (c) electricity charge that includes the standard monthly charge plus a charge for each kilowatt hour; (d) commissions to salespersons; and (e) costs of hourly paid workers that provide substantial gains in efficiency when a few workers are added but gradually smaller gains in efficiency when more workers are added.

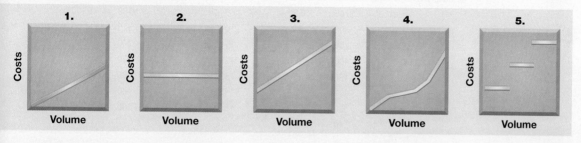

The left column lists several cost classifications. The right column presents short definitions of those costs. In the blank space beside each of the numbers in the right column, write the letter of the cost best described by the definition.

A. Total cost

B. Mixed cost

C. Variable cost

D. Curvilinear cost

E. Step-wise cost

F. Fixed cost

_____ **1.** This cost is the combined amount of all the other costs.

_____ **2.** This cost remains constant over a limited range of volume; when it reaches the end of its limited range, it changes by a lump sum and remains at that level until it exceeds another limited range.

_____ **3.** This cost has a component that remains the same over all volume levels and another component that increases in direct proportion to increases in volume.

_____ **4.** This cost increases when volume increases, but the increase is not constant for each unit produced.

_____ **5.** This cost remains constant over all volume levels within the productive capacity for the planning period.

_____ **6.** This cost increases in direct proportion to increases in volume; its amount is constant for each unit produced.

Following are five series of costs A through E measured at various volume levels. Examine each series and identify which is fixed, variable, mixed, step-wise, or curvilinear.

	A	B	C	D	E	F
	Volume (Units)	**Series A**	**Series B**	**Series C**	**Series D**	**Series E**
1	0	$ 0	$2,500	$ 0	$1,000	$5,000
2	400	3,600	3,100	6,000	1,000	5,000
3	800	7,200	3,700	6,600	2,000	5,000
4	1,200	10,800	4,300	7,200	2,000	5,000
5	1,600	14,400	4,900	8,200	3,000	5,000
6	2,000	18,000	5,500	9,600	3,000	5,000
7	2,400	21,600	6,100	13,500	4,000	5,000

Exercise 5-4
Measurement of cost
behavior using a scatter
diagram

P1

A company reports the following information about its sales and its cost of sales. Each unit of its produc
sells for $500. Use these data to prepare a scatter diagram. Draw an estimated line of cost behavior an
determine whether the cost appears to be variable, fixed, or mixed.

Period	Sales	Cost of Sales	Period	Sales	Cost of Sales
1.............	$22,500	$15,150	4.............	$11,250	$ 8,250
2.............	17,250	11,250	5.............	13,500	9,000
3.............	15,750	10,500	6.............	18,750	14,250

Exercise 5-5
Scatter diagram and
measurement of cost
behavior

P1

Use the following information about sales and costs to prepare a scatter diagram. Draw a cost line tha
reflects the behavior displayed by this cost. Determine whether the cost is variable, step-wise, fixed
mixed, or curvilinear.

Period	Sales	Costs	Period	Sales	Costs
1.............	$760	$590	9.............	$580	$390
2.............	800	560	10.............	320	240
3.............	200	230	11.............	240	230
4.............	400	400	12.............	720	550
5.............	480	390	13.............	280	260
6.............	620	550	14.............	440	410
7.............	680	590	15.............	380	260
8.............	540	430			

Exercise 5-6
Cost behavior
estimation—scatter
diagram and high-low

P1

Felix & Co. reports the following information about its sales and cost of sales. Draw an estimated line o
cost behavior using a scatter diagram, and compute fixed costs and variable costs per unit sold. Then us
the high-low method to estimate the fixed and variable components of the cost of sales.

Period	Units Sold	Cost of Sales	Period	Units Sold	Cost of Sales
1.............	0	$2,500	6.............	2,000	$5,500
2.............	400	3,100	7.............	2,400	6,100
3.............	800	3,700	8.............	2,800	6,700
4.............	1,200	4,300	9.............	3,200	7,300
5.............	1,600	4,900	10.............	3,600	7,900

Exercise 5-7[A]
Measurement of
cost behavior using
regression   P1

Refer to the information from Exercise 5-6. Use spreadsheet software to use ordinary least-squares regres
sion to estimate the cost equation, including fixed and variable cost amounts.

Exercise 5-8
Contribution margin

A1

A jeans maker is designing a new line of jeans called Slims. The jeans will sell for $205 per pair an
cost $164 per pair in variable costs to make.
1. Compute the contribution margin per pair.
2. Compute the contribution margin ratio.
3 Describe what the contribution margin ratio reveals about this new jeans line.

Blanchard Company manufactures a single product that sells for $180 per unit and whose total variable costs are $135 per unit. The company's annual fixed costs are $562,500. Use this information to compute the company's (a) contribution margin, (b) contribution margin ratio, (c) break-even point in units, and (d) break-even point in dollars of sales.

Exercise 5-9
Contribution margin and break-even P2

Blanchard Company manufactures a single product that sells for $180 per unit and whose total variable costs are $135 per unit. The company's annual fixed costs are $562,500. Prepare a CVP chart for the company.

Exercise 5-10
CVP chart P3

Blanchard Company manufactures a single product that sells for $180 per unit and whose total variable costs are $135 per unit. The company's annual fixed costs are $562,500.

1. Prepare a contribution margin income statement for Blanchard Company showing sales, variable costs, and fixed costs at the break-even point.
2. If the company's fixed costs increase by $135,000, what amount of sales (in dollars) is needed to break even? Explain.

Exercise 5-11
Income reporting and break-even analysis C2

Blanchard Company manufactures a single product that sells for $180 per unit and whose total variable costs are $135 per unit. The company's annual fixed costs are $562,500. Management targets an annual pretax income of $1,012,500. Assume that fixed costs remain at $562,500. Compute the (1) unit sales to earn the target income and (2) dollar sales to earn the target income.

Exercise 5-12
Computing sales to achieve target income C2

Blanchard Company manufactures a single product that sells for $180 per unit and whose total variable costs are $135 per unit. The company's annual fixed costs are $562,500. The sales manager predicts that annual sales of the company's product will soon reach 40,000 units and its price will increase to $200 per unit. According to the production manager, the variable costs are expected to increase to $140 per unit but fixed costs will remain at $562,500. The income tax rate is 20%. What amounts of pretax and after-tax income can the company expect to earn from these predicted changes? (*Hint:* Prepare a forecasted contribution margin income statement as in Exhibit 5.21.)

Exercise 5-13
Forecasted income statement C2

Check Forecasted after-tax income, $1,470,000

Bloom Company management predicts that it will incur fixed costs of $160,000 and earn pretax income of $164,000 in the next period. Its expected contribution margin ratio is 25%. Use this information to compute the amounts of (1) total dollar sales and (2) total variable costs.

Exercise 5-14
Predicting sales and variable costs using contribution margin C2

Cooper Company expects to sell 200,000 units of its product next year, which would generate total sales of $17 million. Management predicts that pretax net income for next year will be $1,250,000 and that the contribution margin per unit will be $25. Use this information to compute next year's total expected (a) variable costs and (b) fixed costs.

Exercise 5-15
Computation of variable and fixed costs C2

Hudson Co. reports the contribution margin income statement for 2015 below. Using this information, compute Hudson Co.'s (1) break-even point in units and (2) break-even point in sales dollars.

Exercise 5-16
Break-even P2

HUDSON CO.	
Contribution Margin Income Statement	
For Year Ended December 31, 2015	
Sales (9,600 units at $225 each)	$2,160,000
Variable costs (9,600 units at $180 each)	1,728,000
Contribution margin	$ 432,000
Fixed costs	324,000
Pretax income	$ 108,000

Exercise 5-17
Target income and
margin of safety
(in dollars) **C2**

Refer to the information in Exercise 5-16.

1. Assume Hudson Co. has a target pretax income of $162,000 for 2016. What amount of sales (in dollars) is needed to produce this target income?

2. If Hudson achieves its target pretax income for 2016, what is its margin of safety (in percent)? (Round to one decimal place.)

Exercise 5-18
Sensitivity analysis **C2**

Refer to the information in Exercise 5-16. Assume the company is considering investing in a new machine that will increase its fixed costs by $40,500 per year and decrease its variable costs by $9 per unit. Prepare a forecasted contribution margin income statement for 2016 assuming the company purchases this machine.

Exercise 5-19
Sensitivity analysis **C2**

Refer to the information in Exercise 5-16. If the company raises its selling price to $240 per unit, compute its (1) contribution margin per unit, (2) contribution margin ratio, (3) break-even point in units, and (4) break-even point in sales dollars.

Exercise 5-20
Sensitivity analysis **C2**

Refer to the information in Exercise 5-16. The marketing manager believes that increasing advertising costs by $81,000 in 2016 will increase the company's sales volume to 11,000 units. Prepare a forecasted contribution margin income statement for 2016 assuming the company incurs the additional advertising costs.

Exercise 5-21
Predicting unit and dollar
sales **C2**

Nombre Company management predicts $390,000 of variable costs, $430,000 of fixed costs, and a pretax income of $155,000 in the next period. Management also predicts that the contribution margin per unit will be $9. Use this information to compute the (1) total expected dollar sales for next period and (2) number of units expected to be sold next period.

Exercise 5-22
CVP analysis using
composite units **P4**

Check   (3) 1,000
composite units

Handy Home sells windows and doors in the ratio of 8:2 (windows:doors). The selling price of each window is $200 and of each door is $500. The variable cost of a window is $125 and of a door is $350. Fixed costs are $900,000. Use this information to determine the (1) selling price per composite unit, (2) variable costs per composite unit, (3) break-even point in composite units, and (4) number of units of each product that will be sold at the break-even point.

Exercise 5-23
CVP analysis using
composite units
P4

R&R Tax Service offers tax and consulting services to individuals and small businesses. Data for fees and costs of three types of tax returns follow. R&R provides services in the ratio of 5:3:2 (easy, moderate, business). Fixed costs total $18,000 for the tax season. Use this information to determine the (1) selling price per composite unit, (2) variable costs per composite unit, (3) break-even point in composite units, and (4) number of units of each product that will be sold at the break-even point.

Type of Return	Fee Charged	Variable Cost per Return
Easy (Form 1040EZ)	$ 50	$ 30
Moderate (Form 1040)	125	75
Business	275	100

Exercise 5-24
Operating leverage
computed and applied

A2

Company A is a manufacturer with current sales of $6,000,000 and a 60% contribution margin. Its fixed costs equal $2,600,000. Company B is a consulting firm with current service revenues of $4,500,000 and a 25% contribution margin. Its fixed costs equal $375,000. Compute the degree of operating leverage (DOL) for each company. Identify which company benefits more from a 20% increase in sales and explain why.

Refer to the information in Exercise 5-16.

1. Compute the company's degree of operating leverage for 2015.

2. If sales decrease by 5% in 2016, what will be the company's pretax income?

3. Assume sales for 2016 decrease by 5%. Prepare a contribution margin income statement for 2016.

Exercise 5-25
Degree of operating
leverage   A2

connect

The following costs result from the production and sale of 1,000 drum sets manufactured by Tight Drums Company for the year ended December 31, 2015. The drum sets sell for $500 each. The company has a 25% income tax rate.

PROBLEM SET A

Problem 5-1A
Contribution margin
income statement and
contribution margin ratio
A1

Variable production costs	
Plastic for casing	$ 17,000
Wages of assembly workers	82,000
Drum stands	26,000
Variable selling costs	
Sales commissions	15,000
Fixed manufacturing costs	
Taxes on factory	5,000
Factory maintenance	10,000
Factory machinery depreciation	40,000
Fixed selling and administrative costs	
Lease of equipment for sales staff.........	10,000
Accounting staff salaries	35,000
Administrative management salaries	125,000

Required

1. Prepare a contribution margin income statement for the company.

2. Compute its contribution margin per unit and its contribution margin ratio.

Check (1) Net income, $101,250

Analysis Component

3. Interpret the contribution margin and contribution margin ratio from part 2.

Alden Co.'s monthly sales and cost data for its operating activities of the past year follow. Management wants to use these data to predict future fixed and variable costs.

Problem 5-2A
Scatter diagram and cost
behavior estimation
P1

Month	Sales	Total Cost	Month	Sales	Total Cost
1.............	$320,000	$160,000	7	$340,000	$220,000
2.............	160,000	100,000	8	280,000	160,000
3.............	280,000	220,000	9	80,000	64,000
4.............	200,000	100,000	10	160,000	140,000
5.............	300,000	230,000	11	100,000	100,000
6.............	200,000	120,000	12	110,000	80,000

Required

1. Prepare a scatter diagram for these data with sales volume (in $) plotted on the horizontal axis and total cost plotted on the vertical axis.

2. Estimate both the variable costs per sales dollar and the total monthly fixed costs using the high-low method. Draw the total costs line on the scatter diagram in part 1.

3. Use the estimated line of cost behavior and results from part 2 to predict future total costs when sales volume is (a) $200,000 and (b) $300,000.

Check (2) Variable costs, $0.60 per sales dollar; fixed costs, $16,000

Problem 5-3A
CVP analysis and
charting   P2   P3

Praveen Co. manufactures and markets a number of rope products. Management is considering the future of Product XT, a special rope for hang gliding, that has not been as profitable as planned. Since Product XT is manufactured and marketed independently of the other products, its total costs can be precisely measured. Next year's plans call for a $200 selling price per 100 yards of XT rope. Its fixed costs for the year are expected to be $270,000, up to a maximum capacity of 700,000 yards of rope. Forecasted variable costs are $140 per 100 yards of XT rope.

Required

Check (1a) Break-even
sales, 4,500 units

1. Estimate Product XT's break-even point in terms of (a) sales units and (b) sales dollars.
2. Prepare a CVP chart for Product XT like that in Exhibit 5.15. Use 7,000 units (700,000 yards/100 yards) as the maximum number of sales units on the horizontal axis of the graph, and $1,400,000 as the maximum dollar amount on the vertical axis.
3. Prepare a contribution margin income statement showing sales, variable costs, and fixed costs for Product XT at the break-even point.

Problem 5-4A
Break-even analysis;
income targeting and
forecasting

C2   P2   A1

Astro Co. sold 20,000 units of its only product and incurred a $50,000 loss (ignoring taxes) for the current year as shown here. During a planning session for year 2016's activities, the production manager notes that variable costs can be reduced 50% by installing a machine that automates several operations. To obtain these savings, the company must increase its annual fixed costs by $200,000. The maximum output capacity of the company is 40,000 units per year.

ASTRO COMPANY	
Contribution Margin Income Statement	
For Year Ended December 31, 2015	
Sales	$1,000,000
Variable costs.	800,000
Contribution margin	200,000
Fixed costs	250,000
Net loss	$ (50,000)

Required

1. Compute the break-even point in dollar sales for year 2015.
2. Compute the predicted break-even point in dollar sales for year 2016 assuming the machine is installed and there is no change in the unit selling price.

Check (3) Net income,
$150,000

3. Prepare a forecasted contribution margin income statement for 2016 that shows the expected results with the machine installed. Assume that the unit selling price and the number of units sold will not change, and no income taxes will be due.

   (4) Required sales,
$1,083,333 or 21,667 units
(both rounded)

4. Compute the sales level required in both dollars and units to earn $200,000 of target pretax income in 2016 with the machine installed and no change in unit sales price. Round answers to whole dollars and whole units.
5. Prepare a forecasted contribution margin income statement that shows the results at the sales level computed in part 4. Assume no income taxes will be due.

Problem 5-5A
Break-even analysis,
different cost structures,
and income calculations

C2   A1   P4

Henna Co. produces and sells two products, T and O. It manufactures these products in separate factories and markets them through different channels. They have no shared costs. This year, the company sold 50,000 units of each product. Sales and costs for each product follow.

	Product T	Product O
Sales	$2,000,000	$2,000,000
Variable costs.	1,600,000	250,000
Contribution margin	400,000	1,750,000
Fixed costs.	125,000	1,475,000
Income before taxes	275,000	275,000
Income taxes (32% rate)	88,000	88,000
Net income	$ 187,000	$ 187,000

Required

1. Compute the break-even point in dollar sales for each product. (Round the answer to whole dollars.)

2. Assume that the company expects sales of each product to decline to 30,000 units next year with no change in unit selling price. Prepare forecasted financial results for next year following the format of the contribution margin income statement as just shown with columns for each of the two products (assume a 32% tax rate). Also, assume that any loss before taxes yields a 32% tax benefit.

3. Assume that the company expects sales of each product to increase to 60,000 units next year with no change in unit selling price. Prepare forecasted financial results for next year following the format of the contribution margin income statement shown with columns for each of the two products (assume a 32% tax rate).

Analysis Component

4. If sales greatly decrease, which product would experience a greater loss? Explain.

5. Describe some factors that might have created the different cost structures for these two products.

Check (2) After-tax income: T, $78,200; O, $(289,000)

(3) After-tax income: T, $241,400; O, $425,000

This year Burchard Company sold 40,000 units of its only product for $25 per unit. Manufacturing and selling the product required $200,000 of fixed manufacturing costs and $325,000 of fixed selling and administrative costs. Its per unit variable costs follow.

Problem 5-6A
Analysis of price, cost, and volume changes for contribution margin and net income

P2   A1

Material	$8.00
Direct labor (paid on the basis of completed units).	5.00
Variable overhead costs	1.00
Variable selling and administrative costs	0.50

Next year the company will use new material, which will reduce material costs by 50% and direct labor costs by 60% and will not affect product quality or marketability. Management is considering an increase in the unit selling price to reduce the number of units sold because the factory's output is nearing its annual output capacity of 45,000 units. Two plans are being considered. Under plan 1, the company will keep the selling price at the current level and sell the same volume as last year. This plan will increase income because of the reduced costs from using the new material. Under plan 2, the company will increase the selling price by 20%. This plan will decrease unit sales volume by 10%. Under both plans 1 and 2, the total fixed costs and the variable costs per unit for overhead and for selling and administrative costs will remain the same.

Required

1. Compute the break-even point in dollar sales for both (a) plan 1 and (b) plan 2.

2. Prepare a forecasted contribution margin income statement with two columns showing the expected results of plan 1 and plan 2. The statements should report sales, total variable costs, contribution margin, total fixed costs, income before taxes, income taxes (30% rate), and net income.

Check (1) Break-even: Plan 1, $750,000; Plan 2, $700,000

(2) Net income: Plan 1, $122,500; Plan 2, $199,500

Patriot Co. manufactures and sells three products: red, white, and blue. Their unit selling prices are red, $20; white, $35; and blue, $65. The per unit variable costs to manufacture and sell these products are red, $12; white, $22; and blue, $50. Their sales mix is reflected in a ratio of 5:4:2 (red:white:blue). Annual fixed costs shared by all three products are $250,000. One type of raw material has been used to manufacture all three products. The company has developed a new material of equal quality for less cost. The new material would reduce variable costs per unit as follows: red, by $6; white, by $12; and blue, by $10. However, the new material requires new equipment, which will increase annual fixed costs by $50,000. (Round answers to whole composite units.)

Problem 5-7A
Break-even analysis with composite units

P4

Required

1. If the company continues to use the old material, determine its break-even point in both sales units and sales dollars of each individual product.

2. If the company uses the new material, determine its new break-even point in both sales units and sales dollars of each individual product.

Analysis Component

3. What insight does this analysis offer management for long-term planning?

Check (1) Old plan break-even, 2,050 composite units (rounded)

(2) New plan break-even, 1,364 composite units (rounded)

PROBLEM SET B

Problem 5-1B
Contribution margin
income statement and
contribution margin ratio

A1

The following costs result from the production and sale of 12,000 CD sets manufactured by Gilmore Company for the year ended December 31, 2015. The CD sets sell for $18 each. The company has a 25% income tax rate.

Variable manufacturing costs	
Plastic for CD sets	$ 1,500
Wages of assembly workers	30,000
Labeling	3,000
Variable selling costs	
Sales commissions	6,000
Fixed manufacturing costs	
Rent on factory	6,750
Factory cleaning service	4,520
Factory machinery depreciation	20,000
Fixed selling and administrative costs	
Lease of office equipment	1,050
Systems staff salaries	15,000
Administrative management salaries........	120,000

Required

Check   (1) Net income,
$6,135

1. Prepare a contribution margin income statement for the company.
2. Compute its contribution margin per unit and its contribution margin ratio.

Analysis Component

3. Interpret the contribution margin and contribution margin ratio from part 2.

Problem 5-2B
Scatter diagram and cost
behavior estimation

P1

Sun Co.'s monthly sales and cost data for its operating activities of the past year follow. Management wants to use these data to predict future fixed and variable costs. (Dollar amounts are in thousands.)

Month	Sales	Total Cost	Month	Sales	Total Cost
1.............	$195	$ 97	7	$145	$ 93
2.............	125	87	8	185	105
3.............	105	73	9	135	85
4.............	155	89	10	85	58
5.............	95	81	11	175	95
6.............	215	110	12	115	79

Required

Check   (2) Variable costs,
$0.40 per sales dollar; fixed
costs, $24,000

1. Prepare a scatter diagram for these data with sales volume (in $) plotted on the horizontal axis and total costs plotted on the vertical axis.
2. Estimate both the variable costs per sales dollar and the total monthly fixed costs using the high-low method. Draw the total costs line on the scatter diagram in part 1.
3. Use the estimated line of cost behavior and results from part 2 to predict future total costs when sales volume is (a) $100 and (b) $170.

Problem 5-3B
CVP analysis and
charting

P2   P3

Hip-Hop Co. manufactures and markets several products. Management is considering the future of one product, electronic keyboards, that has not been as profitable as planned. Since this product is manufactured and marketed independently of the other products, its total costs can be precisely measured. Next year's plans call for a $350 selling price per unit. The fixed costs for the year are expected to be $42,000 up to a maximum capacity of 700 units. Forecasted variable costs are $210 per unit.

Required

1. Estimate the keyboards' break-even point in terms of (a) sales units and (b) sales dollars.

2. Prepare a CVP chart for keyboards like that in Exhibit 5.15. Use 700 keyboards as the maximum number of sales units on the horizontal axis of the graph, and $250,000 as the maximum dollar amount on the vertical axis.

3. Prepare a contribution margin income statement showing sales, variable costs, and fixed costs for keyboards at the break-even point.

Check   (1) Break-even sales, 300 units

Rivera Co. sold 20,000 units of its only product and incurred a $50,000 loss (ignoring taxes) for the current year as shown here. During a planning session for year 2016's activities, the production manager notes that variable costs can be reduced 50% by installing a machine that automates several operations. To obtain these savings, the company must increase its annual fixed costs by $150,000. The maximum output capacity of the company is 40,000 units per year.

Problem 5-4B
Break-even analysis; income targeting and forecasting
C2 P2 A1

RIVERA COMPANY	
Contribution Margin Income Statement	
For Year Ended December 31, 2015	
Sales	$750,000
Variable costs	600,000
Contribution margin	150,000
Fixed costs	200,000
Net loss	$ (50,000)

Required

1. Compute the break-even point in dollar sales for year 2015.

2. Compute the predicted break-even point in dollar sales for year 2016 assuming the machine is installed and no change occurs in the unit selling price. (Round the change in variable costs to a whole number.)

3. Prepare a forecasted contribution margin income statement for 2016 that shows the expected results with the machine installed. Assume that the unit selling price and the number of units sold will not change, and no income taxes will be due.

4. Compute the sales level required in both dollars and units to earn $200,000 of target pretax income in 2016 with the machine installed and no change in unit sales price. (Round answers to whole dollars and whole units.)

5. Prepare a forecasted contribution margin income statement that shows the results at the sales level computed in part 4. Assume no income taxes will be due.

Check   (3) Net income, $100,000

(4) Required sales, $916,667 or 24,445 units (both rounded)

Stam Co. produces and sells two products, BB and TT. It manufactures these products in separate factories and markets them through different channels. They have no shared costs. This year, the company sold 50,000 units of each product. Sales and costs for each product follow.

Problem 5-5B
Break-even analysis, different cost structures, and income calculations
C2 P4 A1

	Product BB	Product TT
Sales	$800,000	$800,000
Variable costs	560,000	100,000
Contribution margin	240,000	700,000
Fixed costs	100,000	560,000
Income before taxes	140,000	140,000
Income taxes (32% rate)	44,800	44,800
Net income	$ 95,200	$ 95,200

Required

1. Compute the break-even point in dollar sales for each product. (Round the answer to the next whole dollar.)

2. Assume that the company expects sales of each product to decline to 33,000 units next year with no change in the unit selling price. Prepare forecasted financial results for next year following the format

Check   (2) After-tax income: BB, $39,712; TT, $(66,640)

of the contribution margin income statement as shown here with columns for each of the two products (assume a 32% tax rate, and that any loss before taxes yields a 32% tax benefit).

(3) After-tax income: BB, $140,896; TT, $228,480

3. Assume that the company expects sales of each product to increase to 64,000 units next year with no change in the unit selling prices. Prepare forecasted financial results for next year following the format of the contribution margin income statement as shown here with columns for each of the two products (assume a 32% tax rate).

Analysis Component

4. If sales greatly increase, which product would experience a greater increase in profit? Explain.

5. Describe some factors that might have created the different cost structures for these two products.

Problem 5-6B
Analysis of price, cost, and volume changes for contribution margin and net income

A1   P2

This year Best Company earned a disappointing 5.6% after-tax return on sales (net income/sales) from marketing 100,000 units of its only product. The company buys its product in bulk and repackages it for resale at the price of $20 per unit. Best incurred the following costs this year.

Total variable unit costs..............	$800,000
Total variable packaging costs	$100,000
Fixed costs.......................	$950,000
Income tax rate	25%

The marketing manager claims that next year's results will be the same as this year's unless some changes are made. The manager predicts the company can increase the number of units sold by 80% if it reduces the selling price by 20% and upgrades the packaging. This change would increase variable packaging costs by 20%. Increased sales would allow the company to take advantage of a 25% quantity purchase discount on the cost of the bulk product. Neither the packaging change nor the volume discount would affect fixed costs, which provide an annual output capacity of 200,000 units.

Required

Check (1*b*) Break-even sales for new strategy, $1,727,273 (rounded)

(2) Net income: Existing strategy, $112,500; new strategy, $475,500

1. Compute the break-even point in dollar sales under the (a) existing business strategy and (b) new strategy that alters both unit selling price and variable costs. (Round answers to the next whole dollar.)

2. Prepare a forecasted contribution margin income statement with two columns showing the expected results of (a) the existing strategy and (b) changing to the new strategy. The statements should report sales, total variable costs (unit and packaging), contribution margin, fixed costs, income before taxes, income taxes, and net income. Also determine the after-tax return on sales for these two strategies.

Problem 5-7B
Break-even analysis with composite units

P4

Milano Co. manufactures and sells three products: product 1, product 2, and product 3. Their unit selling prices are product 1, $40; product 2, $30; and product 3, $20. The per unit variable costs to manufacture and sell these products are product 1, $30; product 2, $15; and product 3, $8. Their sales mix is reflected in a ratio of 6:4:2. Annual fixed costs shared by all three products are $270,000. One type of raw material has been used to manufacture products 1 and 2. The company has developed a new material of equal quality for less cost. The new material would reduce variable costs per unit as follows: product 1 by $10 and product 2 by $5. However, the new material requires new equipment, which will increase annual fixed costs by $50,000.

Required

Check (1) Old plan break-even, 1,875 composite units

1. If the company continues to use the old material, determine its break-even point in both sales units and sales dollars of each individual product.

(2) New plan break-even, 1,429 composite units (rounded)

2. If the company uses the new material, determine its new break-even point in both sales units and sales dollars of each individual product. (Round to the next whole unit.)

Analysis Component

3. What insight does this analysis offer management for long-term planning?

(This serial problem began in Chapter 1 and continues through most of the book. If previous chapter segments were not completed, the serial problem can begin at this point. It is helpful, but not necessary, to use the working papers that accompany the book.)

SP 5   Business Solutions sells upscale modular desk units and office chairs in the ratio of 3:2 (desk unit:chair). The selling prices are $1,250 per desk unit and $500 per chair. The variable costs are $750 per desk unit and $250 per chair. Fixed costs are $120,000.

SERIAL PROBLEM

Business Solutions

P4

Required

1. Compute the selling price per composite unit.
2. Compute the variable costs per composite unit.
3. Compute the break-even point in composite units.
4. Compute the number of units of each product that would be sold at the break-even point.

Check   (3) 60 composite units

Beyond the Numbers

BTN 5-1   Apple offers extended service contracts that provide repair coverage for its products. As you complete the following requirements, assume that Apple's repair services department uses many of the company's existing resources such as its facilities, repair machinery, and computer systems.

REPORTING IN ACTION

C1

APPLE

Required

1. Identify several of the variable, mixed, and fixed costs that Apple's repair services department is likely to incur in carrying out its services.
2. Assume that Apple's repair service revenues are expected to grow by 25% in the next year. How would we expect the costs identified in part 1 to change, if at all?
3. Based on the answer to part 2, can Apple use the contribution margin ratio to predict how income will change in response to increases in Apple's repair service revenues?

BTN 5-2   Both Apple and Google sell electronic devices like phones and computers, and each of these companies has a different product mix.

COMPARATIVE ANALYSIS

P2 A2

APPLE
GOOGLE

Required

1. Assume the following data are available for both companies. Compute each company's break-even point in unit sales. (Each company sells many devices at many different selling prices, and each has its own variable costs. This assignment assumes an *average* selling price per unit and an *average* cost per item.)

	Apple	Google
Average selling price per unit sold.	$550 per unit	$470 per unit
Average variable cost per unit sold.	$250 per unit	$270 per unit
Total fixed costs ($ in millions)	$36,000	$10,000

2. If unit sales were to decline, which company would experience the larger decline in operating profit? Explain.

BTN 5-3   Labor costs of an auto repair mechanic are seldom based on actual hours worked. Instead, the amount paid a mechanic is based on an industry average of time estimated to complete a repair job. The repair shop bills the customer for the industry average amount of time at the repair center's billable cost per hour. This means a customer can pay, for example, $120 for two hours of work on a car when the actual time worked was only one hour. Many experienced mechanics can complete repair jobs faster than the industry average. The average data are compiled by engineering studies and surveys conducted in the auto

ETHICS CHALLENGE

C1

repair business. Assume that you are asked to complete such a survey for a repair center. The survey calls for objective input, and many questions require detailed cost data and analysis. The mechanics and owners know you have the survey and encourage you to complete it in a way that increases the average billable hours for repair work.

Required

Write a one-page memorandum to the mechanics and owners that describes the direct labor analysis you will undertake in completing this survey.

COMMUNICATING IN PRACTICE

C2

BTN 5-4 Several important assumptions underlie CVP analysis. Assumptions often help simplify and focus our analysis of sales and costs. A common application of CVP analysis is as a tool to forecast sales, costs, and income.

Required

Assume that you are actively searching for a job. Prepare a half-page report identifying (1) three assumptions relating to your expected revenue (salary) and (2) three assumptions relating to your expected costs for the first year of your new job. Be prepared to discuss your assumptions in class.

TAKING IT TO THE NET

C1

BTN 5-5 Access and review the entrepreneurial information at **Business Owner's Toolkit** [Toolkit.com]. Access and review its *New Business Cash Needs Checklist* (or similar worksheets related to controls of cash and costs) under the "Start Up" link. (Look under the heading "Free Startup Downloads.")

Required

Write a half-page report that describes the information and resources available at the Business Owner's Toolkit to help the owner of a start-up business to control and monitor its cash flows and costs.

TEAMWORK IN ACTION

C2

BTN 5-6 A local movie theater owner explains to you that ticket sales on weekends and evenings are strong, but attendance during the weekdays, Monday through Thursday, is poor. The owner proposes to offer a contract to the local grade school to show educational materials at the theater for a set charge per student during school hours. The owner asks your help to prepare a CVP analysis listing the cost and sales projections for the proposal. The owner must propose to the school's administration a charge per child. At a minimum, the charge per child needs to be sufficient for the theater to break even.

Required

Your team is to prepare two separate lists of questions that enable you to complete a reliable CVP analysis of this situation. One list is to be answered by the school's administration, the other by the owner of the movie theater.

ENTREPRENEURIAL DECISION

C1   A1

BTN 5-7 **Fast Yeti Custom Tees**, launched by entrepreneurs Reid Lyle, Jordan Roudenis, and Ryan Montgomery, produces apparel products. The company has a diverse product line of T-shirts, hats, and polo shirts.

Required

1. Identify at least two fixed costs that will not change regardless of how many T-shirts Fast Yeti produces.
2. How could overly optimistic sales estimates potentially hurt Fast Yeti's business?
3. Explain how cost-volume-profit analysis can help Reid, Jordan, and Ryan manage Fast Yeti.

HITTING THE ROAD

P4

BTN 5-8 Multiproduct break-even analysis is often viewed differently when actually applied in practice. You are to visit a local fast-food restaurant and count the number of items on the menu. To apply multiproduct break-even analysis to the restaurant, similar menu items must often be fit into groups. A reasonable approach is to classify menu items into approximately five groups. We then estimate average selling price and average variable cost to compute average contribution margin. (*Hint:* For fast-food restaurants, the highest contribution margin is with its beverages, at about 90%.)

Required

1. Prepare a one-year multiproduct break-even analysis for the restaurant you visit. Begin by establishing groups. Next, estimate each group's volume and contribution margin. These estimates are necessary to compute each group's contribution margin. Assume that annual fixed costs in total are $500,000 per year. (*Hint:* You must develop your own estimates on volume and contribution margin for each group to obtain the break-even point and sales.)

2. Prepare a one-page report on the results of your analysis. Comment on the volume of sales necessary to break even at a fast-food restaurant.

BTN 5-9   Access and review **Samsung**'s website (www.samsung.com) to answer the following questions.

GLOBAL DECISION

P4

Required

1. Do you believe that Samsung's managers use single product CVP analysis or multiproduct break-even analysis? Explain.

2. How does the addition of a new product line affect Samsung's CVP analysis?

Samsung

ANSWERS TO MULTIPLE CHOICE QUIZ

1. a; $150 − $100 = $50
2. e; ($150 − $100)/$150 = 33⅓%
3. c; $75,000/$50 CM per unit = 1,500 units
4. b; $300,000 − $180,000 = $120,000
5. c; Contribution margin ratio = ($400 − $260)/$400 = 0.35
   Targeted sales = ($840,000 + $70,000)/0.35 = $2,600,000

6

Variable Costing and Analysis

Chapter Preview

VARIABLE COSTING AND ABSORPTION COSTING

Absorption costing

Variable costing

P1 Computing unit costs

INCOME REPORTING IMPLICATIONS

P2 When production equals sales

When production exceeds sales

When production is less than sales

Income reporting

P3 Converting income under variable costing to absorption costing

COMPARING VARIABLE COSTING AND ABSORPTION COSTING

C1 Planning production

P4 Setting prices

Controlling costs

CVP analysis

Limitations of variable costing

Variable costing for services

A1 Pricing special orders with variable costing

Learning Objectives

CONCEPTUAL

C1 Describe how absorption costing can result in overproduction.

ANALYTICAL

A1 Use variable costing in pricing special orders.

PROCEDURAL

P1 Compute unit cost under both absorption and variable costing.

P2 Prepare and analyze an income statement using absorption costing and using variable costing.

P3 Convert income under variable costing to the absorption cost basis.

P4 Determine product selling price based on absorption costing.

NEW YORK—Shazi Visram grew up in Alabama, and she felt entrepreneurship was her calling. "I always knew that I wanted to be my own boss," recalls Shazi. "I had this idea to make baby food the way moms would." However, entrepreneurship had its challenges. "There was an evening when I got to the subway with nothing in my wallet but maxed out credit cards and no way to pay for my ride home," admits Shazi. "The path of entrepreneurship isn't smooth . . . it's a rollercoaster!" From these modest beginnings, Shazi created **Happy Family Brands (HappyBabyFood.com),** which is committed to quality foods for the entire family.

"We are an authentic mom-run company; we are real people behind this business who care about the quality of our products," explains Shazi. "I made the first recipes in my kitchen, using the best organic ingredients. Then, I subjected these recipes to the critics; hundreds of babies, including my own!" Along the way, Shazi set up an accounting system to measure, track, summarize, and report on operations. An important part of this accounting system is a focus on variable costs and product contribution margins. "We are a small business with a big vision and a big heart," says Shazi. "Quality is of the utmost concern," explains Shazi.

"We've grown exponentially . . . now we're in over 17,000 stores," says Shazi. "What's important [in both business and accounting] is . . . being adaptable!" A variable costing approach allows Shazi to adapt to changing market conditions and unique opportunities.

Shazi's company is riding high, and she recently sold a large portion of her company to Danone, a multinational corporation based in France. "Our mission is to remove toxins from children's lives. With a mission that big, we need our company to be as big as possible," says Shazi. "What an incredible opportunity to build a meaningful brand," says Shazi. "[We] make a difference in a child's life." Shazi adds, "We have been really blessed!"

Courtesy of Happy Family Brands

Happy Times

"We let our investors see, and share, our passion"

—**Shazi Visram**

Sources: *Happy Family Brands website,* January 2015; *Inc.,* August 2011, March 2012, and September 2013; *New Hope 360,* March 2011; *FOXBusiness,* November 2011

INTRODUCING VARIABLE COSTING AND ABSORPTION COSTING

Product costs consist of direct materials, direct labor, and overhead. Direct materials and direct labor costs are those that can be identified and traced to the product(s). Overhead, which consists of costs such as electricity, equipment depreciation, and supervisor salaries, is not traceable to the product. Overhead costs must be allocated to products.

There are a variety of costing methods for identifying and allocating overhead costs to products. A prior chapter focused on *how* to allocate overhead costs to products. This chapter focuses on *what* overhead costs are included in product costs.

Under the traditional costing approach, *all* manufacturing costs are assigned to products. Those costs consist of direct materials, direct labor, and manufacturing overhead, both variable and fixed. This traditional approach is referred to as **absorption costing** (also called *full costing*), which assumes that products *absorb* all costs incurred to produce them. While widely used for external financial reporting (GAAP), this costing method can result in misleading product cost information for managers' business decisions.

Under **variable costing,** only costs that change in total with changes in production level are included in product costs. Those consist of direct materials, direct labor, and variable manufacturing overhead. Fixed manufacturing overhead does not change with changes in production and, thus, it is excluded from product costs under variable costing. Instead, fixed overhead is treated as a *period cost,* meaning it is expensed in the period when it is incurred.

Point: Under variable costing, fixed overhead is expensed at the time the units are produced. Under absorption costing, fixed overhead is expensed at the time the units are sold (as a component of cost of goods sold).

Exhibit 6.1 compares the absorption and variable costing methods. Under both methods, direct materials, direct labor, and variable overhead are included in product costs. The key difference between the methods lies in their treatment of *fixed* overhead costs—such costs are included in product costs under absorption costing but included in period expenses under variable costing. Recall that product costs are included in inventory until the goods are sold, at which time they are included in cost of goods sold. Period expenses are reported as expenses immediately in the period in which they are incurred.

EXHIBIT 6.1

Absorption versus Variable Costing

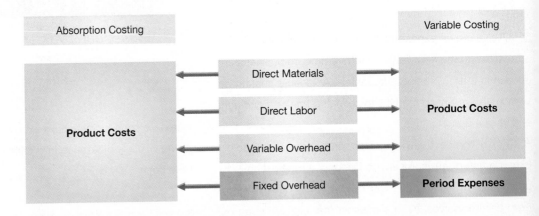

Exhibit 6.1 helps us understand when the absorption and variable costing methods will yield different income amounts over a period. In particular, differences in income resulting from the alternative costing methods will be *small* when:

● Fixed overhead is small as a percentage of total manufacturing costs.

● Inventory levels are low. As more companies adopt lean techniques, including just-in-time manufacturing, inventory levels fall. Lower inventory levels reduce income differences between absorption and variable costing.

● Inventory turnover is rapid. The more quickly inventory turns over, the more product costs are included in cost of goods sold, relative to the product costs that remain in inventory.

● The period of analysis is long. For example, different costing methods might yield very different income numbers over a quarter or year, but these differences will decrease as income is compared over longer periods.

Computing Unit Cost

To illustrate the difference between absorption costing and variable costing, let's consider the product cost data in Exhibit 6.2 from IceAge, a skate manufacturer.

Direct materials cost	$4 per unit
Direct labor cost	$8 per unit
Overhead cost	
Variable overhead cost	$ 180,000
Fixed overhead cost	600,000
Total overhead cost.	$ 780,000
Expected units produced	60,000 units

P1

Compute unit cost under both absorption and variable costing.

EXHIBIT 6.2

Summary Product Cost Data

Drawing on the product cost data, Exhibit 6.3 shows the product cost per unit computations for both absorption and variable costing. These computations are shown both in a tabular format (left side of exhibit) and a visual format (right side of exhibit). For absorption costing, the product cost per unit is $25, which consists of $4 in direct materials, $8 in direct labor, $3 in variable overhead ($180,000/60,000 units), and $10 in fixed overhead ($600,000/60,000 units).

For variable costing, the product cost per unit is $15, which consists of $4 in direct materials, $8 in direct labor, and $3 in variable overhead. Fixed overhead costs of $600,000 are treated as a period cost and are recorded as expense in the period incurred. *The difference between the two costing methods is the exclusion of fixed overhead from product costs for variable costing.*

©TOSHIFUMI KITAMURA/AFP/ Getty Images

EXHIBIT 6.3

Unit Cost Computation

	Product Cost per Unit	
	Absorption Costing	**Variable Costing**
Direct materials.	$ 4	$ 4
Direct labor	8	8
Overhead costs		
Variable overhead.	3	3
Fixed overhead.	10	—
Total product cost per unit.	$25	$15

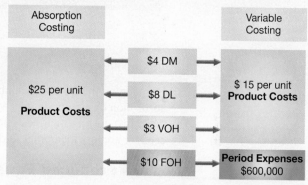

A manufacturer reports the following data.

Direct materials cost.	$6 per unit	Variable overhead	$220,000 per year
Direct labor cost	$14 per unit	Fixed overhead	$680,000 per year
Expected units produced	20,000 units		

1. Compute the total product cost per unit under absorption costing.
2. Compute the total product cost per unit under variable costing.

NEED-TO-KNOW 6-1

Computing Product Cost per Unit

P1

Solution

Per Unit Costs	(1) Absorption Costing	(2) Variable Costing
Direct materials	$ 6	$ 6
Direct labor	14	14
Variable overhead ($220,000/20,000)	11	11
Fixed overhead ($680,000/20,000)*	34	—
Total product cost per unit	$65	$31

Do More: QS 6-1, QS 6-2, E 6-1, E 6-2

*Not included in product costs under variable costing.

QC1

INCOME REPORTING IMPLICATIONS

The prior section showed how the different treatment of fixed overhead costs leads to different product costs per unit under absorption and variable costing. This section shows the implications of this difference for income reporting.

To illustrate the income reporting implications, we return to IceAge Company. Below are the manufacturing cost data for IceAge as well as additional data on selling and administrative expenses. Assume that IceAge's variable costs per unit are constant and that its annual fixed costs remain unchanged during the three-year period 2013 through 2015.

Manufacturing Costs		Selling and Administrative Expenses	
Direct materials cost..........	$4 per unit	Variable...................	$2 per unit
Direct labor cost.............	$8 per unit	Fixed.....................	$200,000 per year
Variable overhead cost........	$3 per unit		
Fixed overhead cost..........	$600,000 per year		

The reported sales and production information for IceAge follows. Its sales price was a constant $40 per unit over this time period. We see that the units produced equal those sold for 2013, exceed those sold for 2014, and are less than those sold for 2015. IceAge began 2013 with no units in beginning inventory.

	Units Produced	Units Sold	Units in Ending Inventory
2013	60,000	60,000	0
2014	60,000	40,000	20,000
2015	60,000	80,000	0

Drawing on the information above, we next prepare income statements for IceAge both under absorption costing and under variable costing. Our purpose is to highlight differences between these two costing methods under three different cases: when units produced are equal to, exceed, or are less than units sold.

P2

Prepare and analyze an income statement using absorption costing and using variable costing.

Units Produced Equal Units Sold

Exhibit 6.4 presents the 2013 income statement for both costing methods (2014 and 2015 statements will follow). The income statement under variable costing (on the right) is referred to as the **contribution margin income statement.** Contribution margin is the excess of sales over variable costs. This margin contributes to covering all fixed costs and earning income. Under

EXHIBIT 6.4

Income for 2013—Quantity Produced Equals Quantity Sold*

Point: Contribution margin (Sales − Variable expenses) is different from gross margin (Sales − Cost of sales).

A performance report that excludes fixed expenses and net income is a *contribution margin report.* Its bottom line is contribution margin.

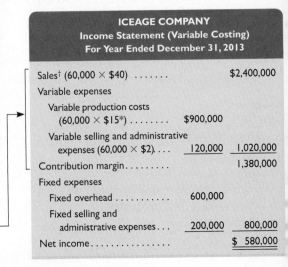

ICEAGE COMPANY		
Income Statement (Absorption Costing)		
For Year Ended December 31, 2013		
Sales† (60,000 × $40)		$2,400,000
Cost of goods sold (60,000 × $25**) ..		1,500,000
Gross margin		900,000
Selling and administrative expenses		
[$200,000 + (60,000 × $2)]......		320,000
Net income		$ 580,000

* ($4 DM + $8 DL + $3 VOH)
** ($4 DM + $8 DL + $3 VOH + $10 FOH)
† Units produced equal 60,000; units sold equal 60,000.

ICEAGE COMPANY		
Income Statement (Variable Costing)		
For Year Ended December 31, 2013		
Sales† (60,000 × $40)		$2,400,000
Variable expenses		
Variable production costs		
(60,000 × $15*)	$900,000	
Variable selling and administrative		
expenses (60,000 × $2). ...	120,000	1,020,000
Contribution margin.........		1,380,000
Fixed expenses		
Fixed overhead	600,000	
Fixed selling and		
administrative expenses...	200,000	800,000
Net income................		$ 580,000

variable costing, expenses are grouped according to cost behavior—variable or fixed, and production or nonproduction. Under the traditional format of absorption costing, expenses are grouped according to function but not separated into variable and fixed components.

Exhibit 6.4 reveals that *reported income is identical under absorption costing and variable costing when the number of units produced equals the number of units sold.* Because variable costing results in expensing of fixed manufacturing overhead based on the number of units produced (60,000 × $10), and absorption costing results in expensing of fixed manufacturing overhead based on the number of units sold (also 60,000 × $10), the net income is the same under either method when units produced equals units sold.

Exhibit 6.5 reorganizes the information from Exhibit 6.4 to show the assignment of costs to different expenses and assets under both absorption costing and variable costing. In this year, there are no units in ending inventory, so the finished goods inventory is $0 under both methods. When quantity produced equals quantity sold, there is no difference in total expenses reported on the income statement. Yet, there is a difference in what categories receive those costs. Absorption costing assigns $1,500,000 to cost of goods sold compared to $900,000 for variable costing. The $600,000 difference is a period cost for variable costing.

Point: Contribution margin income statements prepared under variable costing are useful in performing cost-volume-profit analyses.

EXHIBIT 6.5

Production Cost Assignment for 2013

Absorption Costing		For Year 2013
Beginning finished goods inventory		$ 0
Cost of goods manufactured		
Direct materials.	$240,000	
Direct labor	480,000	
Variable manufacturing overhead	180,000	
Fixed manufacturing overhead	600,000	1,500,000
Cost of goods available for sale		1,500,000
Less: Ending finished goods inventory . . .		0
Cost of goods sold		$1,500,000

Variable Costing		For Year 2013
Beginning finished goods inventory		$ 0
Cost of goods manufactured		
Direct materials.	$240,000	
Direct labor	480,000	
Variable manufacturing overhead	180,000	
Fixed manufacturing overhead	0	900,000
Cost of goods available for sale		900,000
Less: Ending finished goods inventory . . .		0
Cost of goods sold		900,000
Period costs		
Fixed manufacturing overhead		600,000
Total costs		$1,500,000

Decision Insight

Manufacturing Margin Some managers compute **manufacturing margin** (also called *production margin*), which is sales less variable production costs. Some managers also require that internal income statements show this amount to highlight the impact of variable product costs on income. The contribution margin section of IceAge's variable costing income statement would appear as follows (compare this to Exhibit 6.4).

Sales.	$2,400,000
Variable production costs	900,000
Manufacturing margin	1,500,000
Variable selling & admin. exp.	120,000
Contribution margin	$1,380,000

©Steve Mason/Getty Images

Units Produced Exceed Units Sold

Exhibit 6.6 shows absorption costing and variable costing income statements for 2014. In 2014, 60,000 units were produced, which is the same as in 2013. However, only 40,000 units were sold, which means 20,000 units remain in ending inventory.

The income statements reveal that for 2014, income is $320,000 under absorption costing. Under variable costing, income is $120,000, which is $200,000 less than under absorption costing. The cause of this $200,000 difference is due to the different treatment of fixed overhead under the two costing methods. Because variable costing expenses fixed manufacturing overhead (FOH) based on the number of units produced (60,000 × $10), and absorption costing

EXHIBIT 6.6

Income for 2014—Quantity Produced Exceeds Quantity Sold

ICEAGE COMPANY Income Statement (Absorption Costing) For Year Ended December 31, 2014		
Sales† (40,000 × $40)		$1,600,000
Cost of goods sold (40,000 × $25**)...		1,000,000
Gross margin		600,000
Selling and administrative expenses [$200,000 + (40,000 × $2)]		280,000
Net income......................		$ 320,000

* ($4 DM + $8 DL + $3 VOH)
** ($4 DM + $8 DL + $3 VOH + $10 FOH)
† Units produced equal 60,000; units sold equal 40,000.

ICEAGE COMPANY Income Statement (Variable Costing) For Year Ended December 31, 2014		
Sales† (40,000 × $40)		$1,600,000
Variable expenses		
Variable production costs (40,000 × $15*)	$600,000	
Variable selling and administrative expenses (40,000 × $2)....	80,000	680,000
Contribution margin.........		920,000
Fixed expenses		
Fixed overhead	600,000	
Fixed selling and administrative expense	200,000	800,000
Net income................		$ 120,000

expenses FOH based on the number of units sold (40,000 × $10), net income is lower under variable costing by $200,000 (20,000 units × $10).

Under variable costing, the entire $600,000 fixed overhead cost is treated as an expense in computing 2014 income. Under absorption costing, the fixed overhead cost is allocated to each unit of product at the rate of $10 per unit (from Exhibit 6.3). When production exceeds sales by 20,000 units (60,000 versus 40,000), the $200,000 ($10 × 20,000 units) of fixed overhead cost allocated to these 20,000 units is included in the cost of ending inventory (see Exhibit 6.7). This means that $200,000 of fixed overhead cost incurred in 2014 is not expensed until future years, when it is reported in cost of goods sold as those products are sold. Consequently, income for 2014 under absorption costing is $200,000 higher than income under variable costing. Even though sales (of 40,000 units) and the number of units produced (totaling 60,000) are the same under both costing methods, net income differs greatly due to the treatment of fixed overhead.

EXHIBIT 6.7

Production Cost Assignment for 2014

Absorption Costing		For Year 2014
Beginning finished goods inventory		$ 0
Cost of goods manufactured		
Direct materials.................... $240,000		
Direct labor...................... 480,000		
Variable manufacturing overhead 180,000		
Fixed manufacturing overhead 600,000	1,500,000	
Cost of goods available for sale.......	1,500,000	
Less: Ending finished goods inventory ...	500,000*	
Cost of goods sold	$1,000,000	

* 20,000 units × $25 per unit
** 20,000 units × $15 per unit

Variable Costing		For Year 2014
Beginning finished goods inventory		$ 0
Cost of goods manufactured		
Direct materials.................... $240,000		
Direct labor...................... 480,000		
Variable manufacturing overhead 180,000		
Fixed manufacturing overhead 0	900,000	
Cost of goods available for sale......	900,000	
Less: Ending finished goods inventory ..	300,000**	
Cost of goods sold	600,000	
Period costs		
Fixed manufacturing overhead	600,000	
Total costs	$1,200,000	

Exhibit 6.7 reorganizes the information from Exhibit 6.6 to show the assignment of costs to different expenses and assets under both absorption costing and variable costing. When quantity produced exceeds quantity sold, there is a difference in total expenses. Under absorption costing, cost of goods sold is $200,000 lower than the total costs ($1,200,000) under variable costing. As a result, income (and ending finished goods inventory) under absorption costing is $200,000 greater than under variable costing because of the fixed overhead cost allocated to ending inventory (asset) under absorption costing.

Units Produced Are Less Than Units Sold

Exhibit 6.8 shows absorption costing and variable costing income statements for 2015. In 2015, IceAge produced 60,000 units and sold 80,000 units. Thus, IceAge produced 20,000 units fewer than it sold. This means IceAge sold all that it produced during the period, and it sold all of its beginning finished goods inventory. IceAge's income is $840,000 under absorption costing, but it is $1,040,000 under variable costing.

Point: IceAge can sell more units than it produced in 2015 because of inventory carried over from 2014.

EXHIBIT 6.8

Income for 2015—Quantity Produced Is Less Than Quantity Sold

ICEAGE COMPANY
Income Statement (Absorption Costing)
For Year Ended December 31, 2015

Sales† (80,000 × $40)	$3,200,000
Cost of goods sold (80,000 × $25*) . . .	2,000,000
Gross margin	1,200,000
Selling and administrative expenses	
[$200,000 + (80,000 × $2)]	360,000
Net income.	$ 840,000

* ($4 DM + $8 DL + $3 VOH)
** ($4 DM + $8 DL + $3 VOH + $10 FOH)
† Units produced equal 60,000; units sold equal 80,000.

ICEAGE COMPANY
Income Statement (Variable Costing)
For Year Ended December 31, 2015

Sales† (80,000 × $40)		$3,200,000
Variable expenses		
Variable production costs		
(80,000 × $15**)	$1,200,000	
Variable selling and		
administrative expenses		
(80,000 × $2)	160,000	1,360,000
Contribution margin.		1,840,000
Fixed expenses		
Fixed overhead	600,000	
Fixed selling and administrative		
expense.	200,000	800,000
Net income.		$1,040,000

The cause of this $200,000 income difference lies with the treatment of fixed overhead. Beginning inventory in 2015 under absorption costing included $200,000 of fixed overhead cost incurred in 2014, which is assigned to cost of goods sold in 2015 under absorption costing. Because variable costing expenses fixed manufacturing overhead (FOH) based on the number of units produced (60,000 × $10), and absorption costing expenses FOH based on the number of units sold (80,000 × $10), net income is higher under variable costing by $200,000 (20,000 units × $10).

Exhibit 6.9 reorganizes the information from Exhibit 6.8 to show the assignment of costs to different expenses and assets under both absorption costing and variable costing. When quantity produced is less than quantity sold, there is a difference in total costs assigned.

EXHIBIT 6.9

Production Cost Assignment for 2015

Absorption Costing		For Year 2015
Beginning finished goods inventory		$ 500,000*
Cost of goods manufactured		
Direct materials.	$240,000	
Direct labor	480,000	
Variable manufacturing overhead	180,000	
Fixed manufacturing overhead	600,000	1,500,000
Cost of goods available for sale		2,000,000
Less: Ending finished goods inventory . . .		0
Cost of goods sold		$2,000,000

* 20,000 units × $25 per unit
** 20,000 units × $15 per unit

Variable Costing		For Year 2015
Beginning finished goods inventory		$ 300,000**
Cost of goods manufactured		
Direct materials.	$240,000	
Direct labor	480,000	
Variable manufacturing overhead	180,000	
Fixed manufacturing overhead	0	900,000
Cost of goods available for sale		1,200,000
Less: Ending finished goods inventory . . .		0
Cost of goods sold		1,200,000
Period costs		
Fixed manufacturing overhead		600,000
Total costs		$1,800,000

Specifically, ending inventory in 2014 under absorption costing was $500,000 (20,000 units × $25) whereas it was only $300,000 (20,000 units × $15) under variable costing—see Exhibit 6.7. Consequently, when that inventory is sold in 2015, that $200,000 difference in ending inventory is included in cost of goods sold under absorption costing. Thus, the 2015 income under absorption costing is $200,000 less than the income under variable costing. That inventory cost difference flows through cost of goods sold and then to income.

Summarizing Income Reporting

Income reported under both variable costing and absorption costing for the years 2013 through 2015 for IceAge is summarized in Exhibit 6.10. We see that total income is $1,740,000 for this time period for *both* methods. Further, income under absorption costing and that under variable costing differ whenever the quantity produced and the quantity sold differ. These differences in income are due to the different timing with which fixed overhead costs are reported in income under the two methods. Specifically, *income under absorption costing is higher when more units are produced relative to units sold and is lower when fewer units are produced than are sold.*

EXHIBIT 6.10

Summary of Income Reporting

	Units Produced	Units Sold	Income under Absorption Costing	Income under Variable Costing	Income Differences
2013	60,000	60,000	$ 580,000	$ 580,000	$ 0
2014	60,000	40,000	320,000	120,000	200,000
2015	60,000	80,000	840,000	1,040,000	(200,000)
Totals	180,000	180,000	$1,740,000	$1,740,000	$ 0

Point: In our illustration the company produces the same number of units (60,000) each year. We provide an example with varying yearly production levels in the Comprehensive Need-To-Know at the end of the chapter.

In our illustration using IceAge, the total number of units produced over 2013–2015 was exactly equal to the number of units sold over that period. This meant that the difference between absorption costing income and variable costing income for the *total* three-year period is zero. In reality, it is unusual for production and sales quantities to exactly equal each other over such a short period of time. This means that we normally continue to see differences in income for these two methods extending over several years.

NEED-TO-KNOW 6-2

Computing Income under Absorption and Variable Costing

P2

ZBest Mfg. reports the following data for 2015.

Direct materials cost.....	$6 per unit	Units produced	20,000 units
Direct labor cost........	$11 per unit	Units sold	14,000 units
Variable overhead cost ...	$3 per unit	Variable selling and administrative expenses ..	$2 per unit
Fixed overhead	$680,000 per year	Fixed selling and administrative expenses....	$112,000 per year
Sales price	$80 per unit		

1. Prepare an income statement for 2015 under absorption costing.
2. Prepare an income statement for 2015 under variable costing.

Solution

ZBEST MFG.
Income Statement (Absorption Costing)
For Year Ended December 31, 2015

Sales (14,000 × $80)	$1,120,000
Cost of goods sold (14,000 × $54)* ...	756,000
Gross margin	364,000
Selling and admin. expenses [$112,000 + (14,000 × $2)]	140,000
Net income.......................	$ 224,000

ZBEST MFG.
Income Statement (Variable Costing)
For Year Ended December 31, 2015

Sales (14,000 × $80)		$1,120,000
Variable expenses		
Variable production costs (14,000 × $20)†	$280,000	
Variable selling and admin. expenses**	28,000	308,000
Contribution margin..........		812,000
Fixed expenses		
Fixed overhead	680,000	
Fixed selling and admin. expenses	112,000	792,000
Net income.................		$ 20,000

Do More: QS 6-3, QS 6-4, E 6-3, E 6-4, E 6-5.

* $6 DM + $11 DL + $3 VOH + $20 FOH ($680,000/20,000) = $54 per unit
** 14,000 × $2 per unit.
† $6 DM + $11 DL + $3 VOH = $20 per unit

The difference in income between the two methods ($204,000) can be computed as the 6,000 units added to ending inventory × $34 FOH per unit.

QC2

Converting Income under Variable Costing to Absorption Costing

P3

Convert income under variable costing to the absorption cost basis.

Companies commonly use variable costing for internal reporting and business decisions, and they use absorption costing for external reporting and tax reporting. For companies concerned about the cost of maintaining two costing systems, it is comforting to know that we can readily convert reports under variable costing to those using absorption costing.

Income under variable costing is restated to that under absorption costing by adding the fixed overhead cost in ending inventory and subtracting the fixed overhead cost in beginning inventory. Exhibit 6.11 shows the formula for this calculation.

Income under absorption costing	=	Income under variable costing	+	Fixed overhead cost in ending inventory	−	Fixed overhead cost in beginning inventory

EXHIBIT 6.11

Formula to Convert Variable Costing Income to Absorption Costing

Using IceAge's data, in 2014, absorption costing income was $200,000 higher than variable costing income. The $200,000 difference was because the fixed overhead cost incurred in 2014 was allocated to the 20,000 units of ending inventory under absorption costing (and not expensed in 2014 under absorption costing). On the other hand, the $200,000 fixed overhead costs (along with all other fixed costs) were expensed in 2014 under variable costing.

Exhibit 6.12 shows the computations for restating income under the two costing methods. To restate variable costing income to absorption costing income for 2014, we must add back the **fixed overhead cost deferred in** (ending) **inventory.** Similarly, to restate variable costing income to absorption costing income for 2015, we must deduct the **fixed overhead cost recognized from** (beginning) **inventory,** which was incurred in 2014, but expensed in the 2015 cost of goods sold when the inventory was sold.

	2013	2014	2015
Variable costing income (Exhibit 6.10)	$580,000	$120,000	$1,040,000
Add: Fixed overhead cost deferred in ending inventory			
(20,000 × $10)	0	200,000	0
Less: Fixed overhead cost recognized from beginning inventory			
(20,000 × $10)	0	0	(200,000)
Absorption costing income	$580,000	$320,000	$ 840,000

EXHIBIT 6.12

Converting Variable Costing Income to Absorption Costing Income

COMPARING VARIABLE COSTING AND ABSORPTION COSTING

This section compares the roles of absorption and variable costing in managers' business decisions.

Planning Production

C1

Describe how absorption costing can result in overproduction.

Production planning is an important managerial function. Producing too much leads to excess inventory, which in turn leads to higher storage and financing costs, and to greater risk of product obsolescence. On the other hand, producing too little can lead to lost sales and customer dissatisfaction.

Production levels should be based on reliable sales forecasts. However, overproduction and inventory buildup can occur because of how managers are evaluated and rewarded. For instance, many companies link manager bonuses to income computed under absorption costing because this is how income is reported to shareholders (per GAAP).

To illustrate how a reward system can lead to overproduction under absorption costing, let's use IceAge's 2013 data with one change: assume that its manager decides to produce 100,000 units instead of 60,000. Since only 60,000 units are sold, the 40,000 units of excess production will be stored in ending finished goods inventory.

The left side of Exhibit 6.13 shows the unit cost when 60,000 units are produced (same as Exhibit 6.3). The right side shows unit cost when 100,000 units are produced. The exhibit is prepared under absorption costing for 2013.

EXHIBIT 6.13

Unit Cost under Absorption Costing for Different Production Levels

Absorption Costing When 60,000 Units Are Produced		Absorption Costing When 100,000 Units Are Produced	
Direct materials cost	$ 4 per unit	Direct materials cost	$ 4 per unit
Direct labor cost	8 per unit	Direct labor cost	8 per unit
Variable overhead cost	3 per unit	Variable overhead cost	3 per unit
Total variable cost	15 per unit	Total variable cost	15 per unit
Fixed overhead ($600,000/60,000 units)	10 per unit	Fixed overhead ($600,000/100,000 units)	6 per unit
Total product cost	$25 per unit	Total product cost	$21 per unit

Total production cost *per unit* is $4 less when 100,000 units are produced. Specifically, cost per unit is $21 when 100,000 units are produced versus $25 per unit at 60,000 units. The reason for this difference is because the company is spreading the $600,000 fixed overhead cost over more units when 100,000 units are produced than when 60,000 units are produced.

The difference in cost per unit impacts income reporting. Exhibit 6.14 presents the 2013 income statement under absorption costing for the two alternative production levels.

EXHIBIT 6.14

Income under Absorption Costing for Different Production Levels

ICEAGE COMPANY Income Statement (Absorption Costing) For Year Ended December 31, 2013 [60,000 Units Produced; 60,000 Units Sold]			ICEAGE COMPANY Income Statement (Absorption Costing) For Year Ended December 31, 2013 [100,000 Units Produced; 60,000 Units Sold]		
Sales (60,000 × $40)		$2,400,000	Sales (60,000 × $40)		$2,400,000
Cost of goods sold (60,000 × $25)		1,500,000	Cost of goods sold (60,000 × $21).....		1,260,000
Gross margin		900,000	Gross margin		1,140,000
Selling and administrative expenses			Selling and administrative expenses		
Variable (60,000 × $2) ...	$120,000		Variable (60,000 × $2) ..	$120,000	
Fixed	200,000	320,000	Fixed	200,000	320,000
Net income		$ 580,000	Net income		$ 820,000

Common sense suggests that because the company's variable cost per unit, total fixed costs, and sales are identical in both cases, merely producing more units and creating excess ending inventory should not increase income. Yet, as we see in Exhibit 6.14, income under absorption costing is $240,000 greater if management produces 40,000 more units than necessary and builds up ending inventory. The reason is that $240,000 of fixed overhead (40,000 units × $6) is assigned to ending inventory instead of being expensed as cost of goods sold in 2013. This shows that under absorption costing, a manager can report increased income merely by producing more and disregarding whether the excess units can be sold or not.

Manager bonuses are tied to income computed under absorption costing for many companies. Accordingly, these managers may be enticed to increase production that increases income and their bonuses. This incentive problem encourages inventory buildup, which leads to increased costs in storage, financing, and obsolescence. If the excess inventory is never sold, it will be disposed of at a loss.

The manager incentive problem can be avoided when income is measured using variable costing. To illustrate, Exhibit 6.15 reports income under variable costing for the same production levels used in Exhibit 6.14. This demonstrates that managers cannot increase income under variable costing by merely increasing production without increasing sales.

Why is income under absorption costing affected by the production level when that for variable costing is not? The answer lies in the different treatment of fixed overhead costs for the two methods. Under absorption costing, fixed overhead *per unit* is lower when 100,000 units are produced than when 60,000 units are produced, and then fixed overhead cost is allocated to more units—recall Exhibit 6.13. If those excess units produced are not sold, the fixed overhead cost allocated to those units is not expensed until a future period when those units are sold.

ICEAGE COMPANY Income Statement (Variable Costing) For Year Ended December 31, 2013 [60,000 Units Produced; 60,000 Units Sold]		
Sales (60,000 × $40)		$2,400,000
Variable expenses		
Variable production costs (60,000 × $15)	$900,000	
Variable selling and administrative expenses (60,000 × $2)	120,000	1,020,000
Contribution margin		1,380,000
Fixed expenses		
Fixed overhead	600,000	
Fixed selling and administrative expense	200,000	800,000
Net income		$ 580,000

ICEAGE COMPANY Income Statement (Variable Costing) For Year Ended December 31, 2013 [100,000 Units Produced; 60,000 Units Sold]		
Sales (60,000 × $40) . . .		$2,400,000
Variable expenses		
Variable production costs (60,000 × $15) . . .	$900,000	
Variable selling and administrative expenses (60,000 × $2)	120,000	1,020,000
Contribution margin . . .		1,380,000
Fixed expenses		
Fixed overhead	600,000	
Fixed selling and administrative expenses	200,000	800,000
Net income		$ 580,000

EXHIBIT 6.15

Income under Variable Costing for Different Production Levels

   Reported income under variable costing, on the other hand, is not affected by production level changes because *all* fixed production costs are expensed in the year when incurred. Under variable costing, companies increase reported income by selling more units—it is not possible to increase income just by producing more units and creating excess inventory.

Decision Ethics

Production Manager   Your company produces and sells MP3 players. Due to competition, your company projects sales to be 35% less than last year. In a recent meeting, the CEO expressed concern that top executives may not receive bonuses because of the expected sales decrease. The controller suggests that if the company continues to produce as many units as last year, reported income might achieve the level for bonuses to be paid. Should your company produce excess inventory to maintain income? What ethical issues arise? ■   [Answers follow the chapter's Summary.]

Setting Prices

Setting prices for products and services is one of the more complex and important managerial decisions. Although many factors impact pricing, cost is a crucial factor. Cost information from both absorption costing and variable costing can aid managers in pricing.

   Over the long run, prices must be high enough to cover all costs, including variable costs and fixed costs, and still provide an acceptable return to owners. For this purpose, absorption cost information is useful because it reflects the full costs that sales must exceed for the company to be profitable. We can use a three-step process to determine product selling prices:

P4_____

Determine product selling price based on absorption costing.

Step 1: Determine the product cost per unit using absorption costing.

Step 2: Determine the target *markup* on product cost per unit.

Step 3: Add the target markup to the product cost to find the target selling price.

   To illustrate, consider IceAge. Under absorption costing, its product cost is $25 per unit (from Exhibit 6.3). IceAge's management must then determine a target markup on this product cost. This target markup could be based on industry averages, prices that have been charged in the past, or other information. In addition, this markup must be set high enough to cover selling and administrative expenses (both variable and fixed) that are excluded from product costs. In this example, IceAge targets a markup of 60% of absorption cost. With that information, the company computes a target selling price as in Exhibit 6.16.

EXHIBIT 6.16

Determining Selling Price
with Absorption Costing

Step 1	Absorption cost per unit (from Exhibit 6.3)	$25
Step 2	Target markup per unit ($25 × 60%)	15
Step 3	Target selling price per unit	$40

IceAge can use this target selling price as a starting point in setting prices. Management must also consider the level of competition in its industry and customer preferences. If customers are not willing to pay $40 per unit, IceAge must either lower its target markup or find ways to reduce its costs.

While absorption cost information is useful in setting long-run prices, it can lead to misleading decisions in analyzing special orders. We show how variable cost information can be used to analyze special order decisions in the Decision Analysis at the end of the chapter.

Controlling Costs

Every company strives to control costs to be competitive. An effective cost control practice is to hold managers responsible only for their **controllable costs.** A cost is controllable if a manager has the power to determine or at least markedly affect the amount incurred. **Uncontrollable costs** are not within the manager's control or influence. For example, direct materials cost is controllable by a production supervisor. On the other hand, costs related to production capacity are not controllable by that supervisor as that supervisor does not have authority to change factory size or add new machinery. Generally, variable production costs and fixed production costs are controlled at different levels of management. Similarly, variable selling and administrative costs are usually controlled at a level of management different from that which controls fixed selling and administrative costs.

Under absorption costing, both variable production costs and fixed production costs are included in product cost. This makes it difficult to evaluate the effectiveness of cost control by different levels of managers. Variable costing separates the variable costs from fixed costs and, therefore, makes it easier to identify and assign control over costs.

Decisions to change a company's fixed costs are usually assigned to higher-level managers. This is different from most variable costs that are assigned to lower-level managers and supervisors. When we separately report variable and fixed cost elements, as is done with an income statement in the **contribution format,** it highlights the impact of each cost element for income. This makes it easier for us to identify problem areas and to take cost control measures by appropriate levels of management. This approach is also useful in evaluating the performance of managers of different segments within a company.

■ Decision Maker

Internal Auditor Your company uses absorption costing for preparing its GAAP-based income statement and balance sheet. Management is disappointed because its external auditors are requiring it to write off an inventory amount because it exceeds what the company could reasonably sell in the foreseeable future. Why would management produce more than it sells? Why would management be disappointed about the write-off? ■ [Answers follow the chapter's Summary.]

CVP Analysis

The previous chapter discussed cost-volume-profit (CVP) analysis for making managerial decisions. If the income statement is prepared under variable costing and presented in the contribution format, the data needed for CVP analysis are readily available. However, if the income statement is prepared under absorption costing, the data needed for CVP analysis are not readily available. Thus, if absorption costing is used, substantial effort is needed to reclassify cost data in order to conduct CVP analysis.

Limitations of Reports Using Variable Costing

An important generally accepted accounting principle is that of matching. Most managers interpret the matching principle as expensing all manufacturing costs, both variable and fixed, in the period when the related product is sold rather than when costs are incurred. Thus, and despite the many useful applications and insights provided by variable cost reports, *absorption costing is the only acceptable basis for external reporting under both U.S. GAAP and IFRS*. Also, as we discussed, top executives are often awarded bonuses based on income computed using absorption costing. For income tax purposes, absorption costing is the only acceptable basis for filings with the Internal Revenue Service (IRS) under the Tax Reform Act of 1986. These realities contribute to the widespread use of absorption costing by companies.

QC3

Variable Costing for Service Firms

Although this chapter's examples used data for a manufacturer, variable costing also applies to service companies. Since service companies do not produce inventory, the differences in income from absorption and variable costing shown for a manufacturer do not apply. Still, a focus on variable costs can be useful in managerial decisions for service firms. One example is "special order" pricing for airlines when they sell tickets a day or so before a flight at deeply discounted prices. Provided the discounted price exceeds variable costs, such sales increase contribution margin and net income.

GLOBAL VIEW

U.S. multinational companies must change their business processes when moving their operations to international locations. These changes can impact the company's cost structure. For example, both **McDonald's** and **Yum Brands** offer delivery services in major international cities like Beijing (China) and Seoul (South Korea). Cities like these are heavily populated and real estate costs are high. These factors discourage the building of drive-through facilities, which would increase fixed overhead costs. Fixed overhead costs also fall as these companies process more orders over the Internet and thus build fewer call centers. As fixed overhead costs decrease, the difference in net income that would result from applying variable costing versus absorption costing also decreases.

Sustainability and Accounting **Happy Family Brands**'s focus on sustainability extends beyond organic raw materials to the packaging of its products. Many of the company's packaging materials are made from recyclable materials. Such materials increase variable costs but are consistent with the company's philosophy.

©Krzysztof Dydynski/Getty Images/Lonely Planet Images

 Pricing Special Orders **Decision Analysis**

Over the long run, prices must cover all fixed and variable costs. Over the short run, however, fixed production costs such as the cost to maintain plant capacity do not change with changes in production levels. With excess capacity, increases in production levels would increase variable production costs, but not fixed costs. This implies that while managers try to maintain the long-run price on existing orders, which covers all production costs, managers should accept special orders *provided the special order price exceeds variable cost*.

To illustrate, let's return to the data of IceAge Company. Recall that its variable production cost per unit is $15 and its total production cost per unit is $25 (at production level of 60,000 units). Assume that it receives a special order for 1,000 pairs of skates at an offer price of $22 per pair from a foreign skating school. This special order will not affect IceAge's regular sales and its plant has excess capacity to fill the order.

A1
Use variable costing in pricing special orders.

Drawing on absorption costing information, we observe that cost is $25 per unit and that the special order price is $22 per unit. These data would suggest that management reject the order as it would lose $3,000, computed as 1,000 units at $3 loss per pair ($22 − $25).

However, closer analysis suggests that this order should be accepted. This is because the $22 order price exceeds the $15 variable cost of the product. Specifically, Exhibit 6.17 reveals that the incremental revenue from accepting the order is $22,000 (1,000 units at $22 per unit), whereas the incremental production cost of the order is $15,000 (1,000 units at $15 per unit) and the incremental variable selling and administrative cost is $2,000 (1,000 units at $2 per unit). Thus, both its contribution margin and net income would increase by $5,000 from accepting the order. Variable costing reveals this profitable opportunity while absorption costing hides it.

Point: Use of relevant costs in special order and other managerial decisions is covered more extensively in a later chapter.

EXHIBIT 6.17

Computing Incremental Income for a Special Order

Rejecting Special Order		Accepting Special Order	
Incremental sales	$ 0	Incremental sales (1,000 × $22)	$22,000
Incremental costs	0	Incremental costs	
		Variable production cost (1,000 × $15)	15,000
		Variable selling and admin. expense (1,000 × $2)	2,000
Incremental income	$ 0	Incremental income.................................	$ 5,000

Point: Fixed overhead costs won't increase when these additional units are sold because the company already has the capacity.

The reason for increased income from accepting the special order lies in the different behavior of variable and fixed production costs. We see that if the order is rejected, only variable costs are saved. Fixed costs, on the other hand, do not change in the short run regardless of rejecting or accepting this order. Since incremental revenue from the order exceeds incremental costs (only variable cost in this case), accepting the special order increases company income.

NEED-TO-KNOW

COMPREHENSIVE

Navaroli Company began operations on January 5, 2014. Cost and sales information for its first two calendar years of operations are summarized below.

Manufacturing costs		Production and sales data	
Direct materials..................	$80 per unit	Units produced, 2014	200,000 units
Direct labor.....................	$120 per unit	Units sold, 2014................	140,000 units
Factory overhead costs for the year		Units in ending inventory, 2014 ...	60,000 units
Variable overhead	$30 per unit	Units produced, 2015	80,000 units
Fixed overhead.................	$14,000,000	Units sold, 2015................	140,000 units
Nonmanufacturing costs		Units in ending inventory, 2015 ...	0 units
Variable selling and administrative ...	$10 per unit	Sales price per unit	$600 per unit
Fixed selling and administrative	$ 8,000,000		

Required

1. Prepare an income statement for the company for 2014 under absorption costing.
2. Prepare an income statement for the company for 2014 under variable costing.
3. Explain the source(s) of the difference in reported income for 2014 under the two costing methods.
4. Prepare an income statement for the company for 2015 under absorption costing.
5. Prepare an income statement for the company for 2015 under variable costing.
6. Prepare a schedule to convert variable costing income to absorption costing income for each of the years 2014 and 2015. Use the format in Exhibit 6.12.

PLANNING THE SOLUTION

- Set up a table to compute the unit cost under the two costing methods (refer to Exhibit 6.3).
- Prepare an income statement under both of the two costing methods (refer to Exhibit 6.6).
- Consider differences in the treatment of fixed production costs for the income statement to answer requirements 3 and 6.

SOLUTION

Before the income statement for 2014 is prepared, unit costs for 2014 are computed under the two costing methods as follows.

	Production Cost Per Unit	
	Absorption Costing	Variable Costing
Direct materials	$ 80	$ 80
Direct labor.	120	120
Overhead		
Variable overhead	30	30
Fixed overhead*	70	—
Total production cost per unit	$300	$230

*Fixed overhead per unit = $14,000,000 ÷ 200,000 units = $70 per unit.

1. Absorption costing income statement for 2014.

NAVAROLI COMPANY
Income Statement (Absorption Costing)
For Year Ended December 31, 2014

Sales (140,000 × $600)	$84,000,000
Cost of goods sold (140,000 × $300)	42,000,000
Gross margin	42,000,000
Selling and administrative expenses ($1,400,000 + $8,000,000)	9,400,000
Net income	$32,600,000

2. Variable costing income statement for 2014.

NAVAROLI COMPANY
Income Statement (Variable Costing)
For Year Ended December 31, 2014

Sales (140,000 × $600)		$84,000,000
Variable expenses		
Variable production costs (140,000 × $230).	$32,200,000	
Variable selling and administrative costs.	1,400,000	33,600,000
Contribution margin.		50,400,000
Fixed expenses		
Fixed overhead	14,000,000	
Fixed selling and administrative	8,000,000	22,000,000
Net income.		$28,400,000

3. Income under absorption costing is $4,200,000 more than that under variable costing even though sales are identical for each. This difference is due to the different treatment of fixed overhead cost. Under variable costing, the entire $14,000,000 of fixed overhead is expensed on the 2014 income statement. However, under absorption costing, $70 of fixed overhead cost is allocated to each of the 200,000 units produced. Since there were 60,000 units unsold at year-end, $4,200,000 (60,000 units × $70 per unit) of fixed overhead cost allocated to these units will be carried on its balance sheet in ending inventory. Consequently, reported income under absorption costing is $4,200,000 higher than variable costing income for the current period.

Before the income statement for 2015 is prepared, unit costs for production in 2015 are computed under the two costing methods as follows.

	Production Cost Per Unit	
	Absorption Costing	Variable Costing
Direct materials	$ 80	$ 80
Direct labor.........................	120	120
Overhead		
Variable overhead	30	30
Fixed overhead*	175	
Total production cost...............	$405	$230

*Fixed overhead per unit = $14,000,000/80,000 units = $175 per unit.

4. Absorption costing income statement for 2015.

NAVAROLI COMPANY
Income Statement (Absorption Costing)
For Year Ended December 31, 2015

Sales (140,000 × $600)		$84,000,000
Cost of goods sold		
From beginning inventory (60,000 × $300)	$18,000,000	
Produced during the year (80,000 × $405)	32,400,000	50,400,000
Gross margin...		33,600,000
Selling and administrative expenses ($1,400,000 + $8,000,000)		9,400,000
Net income		$24,200,000

5. Variable costing income statement for 2015.

NAVAROLI COMPANY
Income Statement (Variable Costing)
For Year Ended December 31, 2015

Sales (140,000 × $600)		$84,000,000
Variable expenses		
Variable production costs (140,000 × $230).........	$32,200,000	
Variable selling and administrative costs.............	1,400,000	33,600,000
Contribution margin.............................		50,400,000
Fixed expenses		
Fixed overhead	14,000,000	
Fixed selling and administrative	8,000,000	22,000,000
Net income		$28,400,000

6. Conversion of variable costing income to absorption costing income.

	2014	2015
Variable costing income............................	$28,400,000	$28,400,000
Add: Fixed overhead cost deferred in ending inventory (60,000 × $70)	4,200,000	0
Less: Fixed overhead cost recognized from beginning inventory (60,000 × $70)	0	(4,200,000)
Absorption costing income.........................	$32,600,000	$24,200,000

Point: Total income across the two years equals $56,800,000 under both costing methods. This is because the total number of units produced over these two years equals the total number of units sold over these two years.

Summary

C1 **Describe how absorption costing can result in overproduction.** Under absorption costing, fixed overhead costs are allocated to all units including both units sold and units in ending inventory. Consequently, expenses associated with the fixed overhead allocated to ending inventory are deferred to a future period. As a result, the larger ending inventory is, the more overhead cost is deferred to the future, and the greater current period income is.

A1 **Use variable costing in pricing special orders.** Over the short run, fixed production costs such as cost of maintaining plant capacity do not change with changes in production levels. When there is excess capacity, increases in production levels would only increase variable costs. Thus, managers should accept special orders as long as the order price is greater than the variable cost. This is because accepting the special order would increase only variable costs.

P1 **Compute unit cost under both absorption and variable costing.** Absorption cost per unit includes direct materials, direct labor, and *all* overhead, whereas variable cost per unit includes direct materials, direct labor, and only *variable* overhead.

P2 **Prepare and analyze an income statement using absorption costing and using variable costing.** The variable costing income statement differs from the absorption

costing income statement in that it classifies expenses based on cost behavior rather than function. Instead of gross margin, the variable costing income statement shows contribution margin. This contribution margin format focuses attention on the relation between costs and sales that is not evident from the absorption costing format. Under absorption costing, some fixed overhead cost is allocated to ending inventory and is carried on the balance sheet to the next period. However, all fixed costs are expensed in the period incurred under variable costing. Consequently, absorption costing income is generally greater than variable costing income if units produced exceed units sold, and conversely.

P3 **Convert income under variable costing to the absorption cost basis.** Variable costing income can be adjusted to absorption costing income by adding the fixed cost allocated to ending inventory and subtracting the fixed cost previously allocated to beginning inventory.

P4 **Determine product selling price based on absorption costing.** Target selling prices can be determined by adding a markup to the total product cost under absorption costing. The markup should be enough to cover selling and administrative expenses, provide for a target profit, and yield a competitive price.

Guidance Answers to Decision Maker and Decision Ethics

Production Manager   Under absorption costing, fixed production costs are spread over all units produced. Thus, fixed cost for each unit will be lower if more units are produced because the fixed cost is spread over more units. This means the company can increase income by producing excess units even if sales remain constant. With sales lagging, producing excess inventory leads to increased financing cost and inventory obsolescence. Also, producing excess inventory to meet income levels for bonuses harms company owners and is unethical. You must discuss this with the appropriate managers.

Internal Auditor   If manager bonuses are tied to income, they would have incentives to increase income for personal gain. If absorption costing is used to determine income, management can reduce current period expenses (and raise income) with overproduction, which shifts fixed production costs to future periods. This decision fails to consider whether there is a viable market for all units that are produced. If there is not, an auditor can conclude that the inventory does not have "future economic value" and pressure management to write it off. Such a write-off reduces income by the cost of the excess inventory.

Key Terms

Absorption costing (also called **full** costing)

Contribution format

Contribution margin income statement

Controllable costs

Fixed overhead cost deferred in inventory

Fixed overhead cost recognized from inventory

Manufacturing margin

Uncontrollable costs

Variable costing (also called **direct** or marginal costing)

Multiple Choice Quiz   Answers at end of chapter

Answer questions 1 and 2 using the following company data.

Units produced	1,000
Variable costs	
Direct materials	$3 per unit
Direct labor	$5 per unit
Variable overhead.	$3 per unit
Variable selling and administrative	$1 per unit
Fixed overhead.	$3,000 total
Fixed selling and administrative	$1,000 total

1. Product cost per unit under absorption costing is:
   a. $11   d. $15
   b. $12   e. $16
   c. $14

2. Product cost per unit under variable costing is:
   a. $11   d. $15
   b. $12   e. $16
   c. $14

3. Under variable costing, which costs are included in product cost?
   a. All variable product costs, including direct materials, direct labor, and variable overhead.

b. All variable and fixed allocations of product costs, including direct materials, direct labor, and both variable and fixed overhead.
   c. All variable product costs except for variable overhead.
   d. All variable and fixed allocations of product costs, except for both variable and fixed overhead.

4. The difference between product cost per unit under absorption costing as compared to that under variable costing is:
   a. Direct materials and direct labor.
   b. Fixed and variable portions of overhead.
   c. Fixed overhead only.
   d. Variable overhead only.

5. When production exceeds sales, which of the following is true?
   a. No change occurs to inventories for either absorption costing or variable costing methods.
   b. Use of absorption costing produces a higher net income than the use of variable costing.
   c. Use of absorption costing produces a lower net income than the use of variable costing.
   d. Use of absorption costing causes inventory value to decrease more than it would through the use of variable costing.

🔲 Icon denotes assignments that involve decision making.

Discussion Questions

1. What costs are normally included in product costs under variable costing?

2. What costs are normally included in product costs under absorption costing?

3. 🔲 When units produced exceed units sold for a reporting period, would income under variable costing be greater than, equal to, or less than income under absorption costing? Explain.

4. Describe how the following items are computed: *a.* Gross margin, and *b.* Contribution margin.

5. 🔲 How can absorption costing lead to incorrect short-run pricing decisions?

6. What conditions must exist to achieve accurate short-run pricing decisions using variable costing?

7. 🔲 Describe the usefulness of variable costing for controlling company costs.

8. 🔲 Describe how use of absorption costing in determining income can lead to overproduction and a buildup of inventory. Explain how variable costing can avoid this same problem.

9. What are the major limitations of variable costing?

10. **Google** uses variable costing for **GOOGLE** several business decisions. How can variable costing income statements be converted to absorption costing?

11. 🔲 Explain how contribution margin analysis is useful for managerial decisions and performance evaluations.

12. 🔲 **Samsung**'s managers rely on reports of variable costs. How can **Samsung** variable costing reports prepared using the contribution margin format help managers in computing break-even volume in units?

13. 🔲 Assume that **Apple** has received a special order from a retailer for 1,000 specially outfitted iPads. This is a one-time order, which will not require any additional capacity or fixed costs. What should Apple consider when determining a selling price for these iPads?

14. 🔲 How can **Samsung** use variable costing to help better understand its **Samsung** operations and to make better pricing decisions?

■ connect

Vijay Company reports the following information regarding its production costs. Compute its production cost per unit under absorption costing.

Direct materials...........................	$10 per unit
Direct labor...............................	$20 per unit
Overhead costs for the year	
Variable overhead	$10 per unit
Fixed overhead	$160,000
Units produced	20,000 units

QUICK STUDY

QS 6-1
Computing unit cost
under absorption costing
P1

Refer to Vijay Company's data in QS 6-1. Compute its production cost per unit under variable costing.

QS 6-2
Computing unit cost
under variable costing   P1

Aces Inc., a manufacturer of tennis rackets, began operations this year. The company produced 6,000 rackets and sold 4,900. Each racket was sold at a price of $90. Fixed overhead costs are $78,000 and fixed selling and administrative costs are $65,200. The company also reports the following per unit costs for the year. Prepare an income statement under variable costing.

Variable production costs	$25.00
Variable selling and administrative expenses.........	2.00

QS 6-3
Variable costing income
statement   P2

Aces Inc., a manufacturer of tennis rackets, began operations this year. The company produced 6,000 rackets and sold 4,900. Each racket was sold at a price of $90. Fixed overhead costs are $78,000 and fixed selling and administrative costs are $65,200. The company also reports the following per unit costs for the year. Prepare an income statement under absorption costing.

Variable production costs	$25.00
Variable selling and administrative expenses.........	2.00

QS 6-4
Absorption costing
income statement   P2

Ramort Company reports the following cost data for its single product. The company regularly sells 20,000 units of its product at a price of $60 per unit. Compute gross margin under absorption costing.

Direct materials...........................	$10 per unit
Direct labor	$12 per unit
Overhead costs for the year	
Variable overhead.......................	$3 per unit
Fixed overhead per year	$40,000
Selling and adminstrative costs for the year	
Variable...............................	$2 per unit
Fixed...................................	$65,200
Normal production level (in units)	20,000 units

QS 6-5
Absorption costing and
gross margin
P2

Refer to the information about Ramort Company in QS 6-5. If Ramort doubles its production to 40,000 units while sales remain at the current 20,000-unit level, by how much would the company's gross margin increase or decrease under absorption costing?

QS 6-6
Absorption costing and
gross margin   P2

Refer to the information about Ramort Company in QS 6-5. Compute contribution margin under variable costing.

QS 6-7
Variable costing and
contribution margin   P2

Refer to the information about Ramort Company in QS 6-5. If Ramort doubles its production to 40,000 units while sales remain at the current 20,000-unit level, by how much would the company's contribution margin increase or decrease under variable costing?

QS 6-8
Variable costing and
contribution margin   P2

QS 6-9
Computing manufacturing margin   P2

D'Souza Company sold 10,000 units of its product at a price of $80 per unit. Total variable cost is $50 per unit, consisting of $40 in variable production cost and $10 in variable selling and administrative cost. Compute the manufacturing (production) margin for the company under variable costing.

QS 6-10
Computing contribution margin   P2

D'Souza Company sold 10,000 units of its product at a price of $80 per unit. Total variable cost is $50 per unit, consisting of $40 in variable production cost and $10 in variable selling and administrative cost. Compute the contribution margin.

QS 6-11
Converting variable costing income to absorption costing

P3

Diaz Company reports the following variable costing income statement for its single product. This company's sales totaled 50,000 units, but its production was 80,000 units. It had no beginning finished goods inventory for the current period.

DIAZ COMPANY	
Income Statement (Variable Costing)	
Sales (50,000 units × $60 per unit)......................................	$3,000,000
Variable expenses	
Variable manufacturing expense (50,000 units × $28 per unit)............	1,400,000
Variable selling and admin. expense (50,000 units × $5 per unit)..........	250,000
Total variable expenses.....................................	1,650,000
Contribution margin..	1,350,000
Fixed expenses	
Fixed overhead	320,000
Fixed selling and administrative expense	160,000
Total fixed expenses.......................................	480,000
Net income..	$ 870,000

1. Convert this company's variable costing income statement to an absorption costing income statement.
2. Explain the difference in income between the variable costing and absorption costing income statement.

QS 6-12
Converting variable costing income to absorption costing income
P3

Ming Company had net income of $772,200 based on variable costing. Beginning and ending inventories were 7,800 units and 5,200 units, respectively. Assume the fixed overhead per unit was $3.00 for both the beginning and ending inventory. What is net income under absorption costing?

QS 6-13
Converting variable costing income to absorption costing income
P3

Mortech had net income of $250,000 based on variable costing. Beginning and ending inventories were 50,000 units and 48,000 units, respectively. Assume the fixed overhead per unit was $0.75 for both the beginning and ending inventory. What is net income under absorption costing?

QS 6-14
Converting variable costing income to absorption costing income   P3

Hong Co. had net income of $386,100 under variable costing. Beginning and ending inventories were 2,600 units and 3,900 units, respectively. Fixed overhead cost was $4.00 per unit for both the beginning and ending inventory. What is net income under absorption costing?

QS 6-15
Converting variable costing income to absorption costing income   P3

E-Com had net income of $130,000 under variable costing. Beginning and ending inventories were 1,200 units and 4,900 units, respectively. Fixed overhead cost was $2.50 per unit for both the beginning and ending inventory. What is net income under absorption costing?

Under absorption costing a company had the following per unit costs when 10,000 units were produced.

Direct labor	$ 2
Direct material	3
Variable overhead.	4
Total variable cost	9
Fixed overhead ($50,000/10,000 units)	5
Total production cost per unit	$14

1. Compute the company's total production cost per unit if 12,500 units had been produced.
2. Why might a manager of a company using absorption costing produce more units than can currently be sold?

A manufacturer reports the following information on its product. Compute the target selling price per unit under absorption costing.

Direct materials cost	$50 per unit
Direct labor cost	$12 per unit
Variable overhead cost	$6 per unit
Fixed overhead cost.	$2 per unit
Target markup	40%

Li Company produces a product that sells for $84 per unit. A customer contacts Li and offers to purchase 2,000 units of its product at a price of $68 per unit. Variable production costs with this order would be $30 per unit, and variable selling expenses would be $18 per unit. Assuming that this special order would not require any additional fixed costs, and that Li has sufficient capacity to produce the product without affecting regular sales, explain to Li's management why it might be a good decision to accept this special order.

connect
_____

Trio Company reports the following information for the current year, which is its first year of operations.

EXERCISES

Exercise 6-1
Computing unit and
inventory costs under
absorption costing
P1

Direct materials	$15 per unit
Direct labor	$16 per unit
Overhead costs for the year	
Variable overhead.	$ 80,000 per year
Fixed overhead	$160,000 per year
Units produced this year	20,000 units
Units sold this year	14,000 units
Ending finished goods inventory in units	6,000 units

1. Compute the cost per unit using absorption costing.
2. Determine the cost of ending finished goods inventory using absorption costing.
3. Determine the cost of goods sold using absorption costing.

Refer to the information in Exercise 6-1. Assume instead that Trio Company uses variable costing.
1. Compute the cost per unit using variable costing.
2. Determine the cost of ending finished goods inventory using variable costing.
3. Determine the cost of goods sold using variable costing.

Exercise 6-2
Computing unit and
inventory costs under
variable costing   P2

Check (1) Variable cost per
unit, $35

Exercise 6-3

Income reporting under absorption costing and variable costing

P2

Sims Company, a manufacturer of tablet computers, began operations on January 1, 2015. Its cost and sales information for this year follows.

Manufacturing costs	
Direct materials	$40 per unit
Direct labor	$60 per unit
Overhead costs for the year	
Variable overhead	$3,000,000
Fixed overhead	$7,000,000
Selling and administrative costs for the year	
Variable	$ 770,000
Fixed	$4,250,000
Production and sales for the year	
Units produced	100,000 units
Units sold	70,000 units
Sales price per unit	$350 per unit

Check   (1) Variable costing income, $3,380,000

1. Prepare an income statement for the year using variable costing.
2. Prepare an income statement for the year using absorption costing.
3. Under what circumstance(s) is reported income identical under both absorption costing and variable costing?

Exercise 6-4

Variable costing income statement

P2

Kenzi Kayaking, a manufacturer of kayaks, began operations this year. During this first year, the company produced 1,050 kayaks and sold 800 at a price of $1,050 each. At this first year-end, the company reported the following income statement information using absorption costing.

Sales (800 × $1,050)	$840,000
Cost of goods sold (800 × $500)	400,000
Gross margin	440,000
Selling and administrative expenses	230,000
Net income	$210,000

Additional Information

a. Production cost per kayak totals $500, which consists of $400 in variable production cost and $100 in fixed production cost—the latter amount is based on $105,000 of fixed production costs allocated to the 1,050 kayaks produced.

b. The $230,000 in selling and administrative expense consists of $75,000 that is variable and $155,000 that is fixed.

1. Prepare an income statement for the current year under variable costing.
2. Explain the difference in income between the variable costing and absorption costing income statement.

Exercise 6-5

Absorption costing and variable costing income statements

P2

Rey Company's single product sells at a price of $216 per unit. Data for its single product for its first year of operations follow. Prepare an income statement for the year assuming (a) absorption costing and (b) variable costing.

Direct materials	$20 per unit
Direct labor	$28 per unit
Overhead costs	
Variable overhead	$ 6 per unit
Fixed overhead per year	$160,000 per year
Selling and administrative expenses	
Variable	$ 18 per unit
Fixed	$200,000 per year
Units produced (and sold)	20,000 units

Hayek Bikes prepares the income statement under variable costing for its managerial reports, and it prepares the income statement under absorption costing for external reporting. For its first month of operations, 375 bikes were produced and 225 were sold; this left 150 bikes in ending inventory. The income statement information under variable costing follows.

Exercise 6-6
Absorption costing
income statement
P2

Sales (225 × $1,600)	$360,000
Variable production cost (225 × $625)	140,625
Variable selling and administrative expenses (225 × $65)	14,625
Contribution margin	204,750
Fixed overhead cost	56,250
Fixed selling and administrative expense	75,000
Net income	$ 73,500

1. Prepare this company's income statement for its first month of operations under absorption costing.
2. Explain the difference in income between the variable costing and absorption costing income statement.

Oak Mart, a producer of solid oak tables, reports the following data from its second year of business.

Exercise 6-7
Income reporting under
absorption costing and
variable costing
P2

Sales price per unit	$320 per unit	Manufacturing costs this year		
Units produced this year	115,000 units	Direct materials		$40 per unit
Units sold this year	118,000 units	Direct labor		$62 per unit
Units in beginning-year inventory	3,000 units	Overhead costs this year		
Beginning inventory costs		Variable overhead		$3,220,000
Variable (3,000 units × $135)	$405,000	Fixed overhead		$7,400,000
Fixed (3,000 units × $80)	240,000	Selling and adminstrative costs this year		
Total	$645,000	Variable		$1,416,000
		Fixed		4,600,000

1. Prepare the current year income statement for the company using variable costing.
2. Prepare the current year income statement for the company using absorption costing.
3. Explain any difference between the two income numbers under the two costing methods in parts 1 and 2.

Check (2) Absorption
costing income, $8,749,000

Polarix is a retailer of ATVs (all-terrain vehicles) and accessories. An income statement for its Consumer ATV Department for the current year follows. ATVs sell for $3,800 each. Variable selling expenses are $270 per ATV. The remaining selling expenses are fixed. Administrative expenses are 40% variable and 60% fixed. The company does not manufacture its own ATVs; it purchases them from a supplier for $1,830 each.

Exercise 6-8
Contribution margin
format income statement
P2

POLARIX
Income Statement—Consumer ATV Department
For Year Ended December 31, 2015

Sales		$646,000
Cost of goods sold		311,100
Gross margin		334,900
Operating expenses		
Selling expenses	$135,000	
Administrative expenses	59,500	194,500
Net income		$140,400

1. Prepare an income statement for this current year using the contribution margin format.
2. For each ATV sold during this year, what is the contribution toward covering fixed expenses and earning income?

Check (2) $1,560

Exercise 6-9
Income statement under absorption costing and variable costing
P1   P2

Cool Sky reports the following costing data on its product for its first year of operations. During this first year, the company produced 44,000 units and sold 36,000 units at a price of $140 per unit.

Manufacturing costs	
Direct materials per unit	$60
Direct labor per unit.......................................	$22
Variable overhead per unit	$8
Fixed overhead for the year.....................................	$528,000
Selling and administrative costs	
Variable selling and administrative cost per unit	$11
Fixed selling and administrative cost per year	$105,000

Check (1a) Absorption cost per unit, $102

(2a) Variable cost per unit, $90

1. Assume the company uses absorption costing.
   a. Determine its product cost per unit.
   b. Prepare its income statement for the year under absorption costing.
2. Assume the company uses variable costing.
   a. Determine its product cost per unit.
   b. Prepare its income statement for the year under variable costing.

Exercise 6-10
Computing absorption costing income
P3

A manufacturer reports the information below for three recent years. Compute income for each of the three years using absorption costing.

	Year 1	Year 2	Year 3
Variable costing income.....................	$110,000	$114,400	$118,950
Beginning finished goods inventory (units)	0	1,200	700
Ending finished goods inventory (units)	1,200	700	800
Fixed manufacturing overhead per unit.........	$ 2.50	$ 2.50	$ 2.50

Exercise 6-11
Absorption costing and product pricing
P4

Sirhuds Inc., a maker of smartwatches, reports the information below on its product. The company uses absorption costing and has a target markup of 40% of absorption cost per unit. Compute the target selling price per unit under absorption costing.

Direct materials cost	$100 per unit
Direct labor cost...	$30 per unit
Variable overhead cost	$8 per unit
Fixed overhead cost.......................................	$600,000 per year
Variable selling and administrative expenses..................	$3 per unit
Fixed selling and administrative expenses	$120,000 per year
Expected production (and sales)...........................	50,000 units per year

Exercise 6-12
Absorption costing and overproduction
C1

Jacquie Inc. reports the following annual cost data for its single product.

Normal production and sales level	60,000 units
Sales price	$56.00 per unit
Direct materials...	$9.00 per unit
Direct labor..	$6.50 per unit
Variable overhead.......................................	$11.00 per unit
Fixed overhead	$720,000 in total

If Jacquie increases its production to 80,000 units, while sales remain at the current 60,000-unit level, by how much would the company's gross margin increase or decrease under absorption costing? Assume the company has idle capacity to double current production.

Grand Garden is a luxury hotel with 150 suites. Its regular suite rate is $250 per night per suite. The hotel's cost per night is $140 per suite and consists of the following.

Variable direct labor and materials cost	$ 30
Fixed cost	110
Total cost per night per suite	$140

The hotel manager received an offer to hold the local Bikers' Club annual meeting at the hotel in March, which is the hotel's low season with an occupancy rate of under 50%. The Bikers' Club would reserve 50 suites for three nights if the hotel could offer a 50% discount, or a rate of $125 per night. The hotel manager is inclined to reject the offer because the cost per suite per night is $140. Prepare an analysis of this offer for the hotel manager. Explain (with supporting computations) whether the offer from the Bikers' Club should be accepted or rejected.

Exercise 6-13
Variable cost analysis for a services company
A1

Empire Plaza Hotel is a luxury hotel with 400 rooms. Its regular room rate is $300 per night per room. The hotel's cost is $165 per night per room and consists of the following.

Variable direct labor and materials cost	$ 40
Fixed cost	125
Total cost per night per room...........	$165

The hotel manager received an offer to hold the Junior States of America (JSA) convention at the hotel in February, which is the hotel's low season with an occupancy rate of under 45%. JSA would reserve 100 rooms for four nights if the hotel could offer a 50% discount, or a rate of $150 per night. The hotel manager is inclined to reject the offer because the cost per room per night is $165. Prepare an analysis of this offer for the hotel manager. Explain (with supporting computations) whether the offer from JSA should be accepted or rejected.

Exercise 6-14
Variable cost analysis for a services company
A1

MidCoast Airlines provides charter airplane services. In October of this year, the company was operating at 60% of its capacity when it received a bid from the local community college. The college was organizing a Washington, D.C., trip for its international student group. The college budgeted only $30,000 for round-trip airfare. MidCoast Airlines normally charges between $50,000 and $60,000 for such service. MidCoast determined its cost for the round-trip flight to Washington to be $44,000, which consists of the following:

Variable cost......................	$15,000
Fixed cost (allocated)...............	29,000
Total cost.......................	$44,000

Although the manager at MidCoast supports the college's educational efforts, she could not justify accepting the $30,000 bid for the trip given the projected $14,000 loss. Still, she decides to consult with you, an independent financial consultant. Do you believe the airline should accept the bid from the college? Prepare a memorandum, with supporting computations, explaining why or why not.

Exercise 6-15
Variable costing for services
A1

A recent annual report for **McDonald's** reports the following operating income for its United States and Europe geographic segments:

In $ millions	2013	2012
United States	$3,779	$3,750
Europe	3,371	3,196

Exercise 6-16
Analyzing income growth
P2

Required

1. Is operating income growing faster in the United States or in the Europe segment? Explain.

. Is the difference in operating income growth due to the use of different costing methods (absorption or variable costing) in the two geographic segments? Explain.

PROBLEM SET A

Problem 6-1A
Variable costing income
statement and
conversion to absorption
costing income (two
consecutive years)
P2   P3

Dowell Company produces a single product. Its income statements under absorption costing for its first two years of operation follow.

	2014	2015
Sales ($46 per unit)	$920,000	$1,840,000
Cost of goods sold ($31 per unit)	620,000	1,240,000
Gross margin	300,000	600,000
Selling and administrative expenses	290,000	340,000
Net income	$ 10,000	$ 260,000

Additional Information

a. Sales and production data for these first two years follow.

	2014	2015
Units produced	30,000	30,000
Units sold	20,000	40,000

b. Variable cost per unit and total fixed costs are unchanged during 2014 and 2015. The company's $31 per unit product cost consists of the following.

Direct materials	$ 5
Direct labor	9
Variable overhead	7
Fixed overhead ($300,000/30,000 units)	10
Total product cost per unit	$31

c. Selling and administrative expenses consist of the following.

	2014	2015
Variable selling and administrative expenses ($2.50 per unit)	$ 50,000	$100,000
Fixed selling and administrative expenses	240,000	240,000
Total selling and administrative expenses	$290,000	$340,000

Required

Check   (1) 2014 net loss,
$(90,000)

1. Prepare income statements for the company for each of its first two years under variable costing.

2. Explain any difference between the absorption costing income and the variable costing income for these two years.

Problem 6-2A
Variable costing income
statement and
conversion to absorption
costing income
P2   P3

Trez Company began operations this year. During this first year, the company produced 100,000 units and sold 80,000 units. The absorption costing income statement for this year follows.

Sales (80,000 units × $50 per unit)		$4,000,000
Cost of goods sold		
Beginning inventory	$ 0	
Cost of goods manufactured (100,000 units × $30 per unit)	3,000,000	
Cost of goods available for sale	3,000,000	
Ending inventory (20,000 × $30)	600,000	
Cost of goods sold		2,400,000
Gross margin		1,600,000
Selling and administrative expenses		530,000
Net income		$1,070,000

Additional Information

a. Selling and administrative expenses consist of $350,000 in annual fixed expenses and $2.25 per unit in variable selling and administrative expenses.

b. The company's product cost of $30 per unit is computed as follows.

Direct materials	$5 per unit
Direct labor	$14 per unit
Variable overhead.	$2 per unit
Fixed overhead ($900,000/100,000 units)	$9 per unit

Required

1. Prepare an income statement for the company under variable costing.

2. Explain any difference between the income under variable costing (from part 1) and the income reported above.

Check (1) Variable costing income, $890,000

Blazer Chemical produces and sells an ice-melting granular used on roadways and sidewalks in winter. It annually produces and sells about 100 tons of its granular. In its nine-year history, the company has never reported a net loss. However, because of this year's unusually mild winter, projected demand for its product is only 60 tons. Based on its predicted production and sales of 60 tons, the company projects the following income statement (under absorption costing).

Problem 6-3A
Income reporting, absorption costing, and managerial ethics

P2   C1

Sales (60 tons at $21,000 per ton)	$1,260,000
Cost of goods sold (60 tons at $16,000 per ton)	960,000
Gross margin	300,000
Selling and administrative expenses	318,600
Net loss	$ (18,600)

Its product cost information follows and consists mainly of fixed cost because of its automated production process requiring expensive equipment.

Variable direct labor and material costs per ton	$ 3,500
Fixed cost per ton ($750,000 ÷ 60 tons)	12,500
Total product cost per ton	$16,000

Selling and administrative expenses consist of variable selling and administrative expenses of $310 per ton and fixed selling and administrative expenses of $300,000 per year. The company's president is concerned about the adverse reaction from its creditors and shareholders if the projected net loss is reported. The operations manager mentions that since the company has large storage capacity, it can report a net income by keeping its production at the usual 100-ton level even though it expects to sell only 60 tons. The president was puzzled by the suggestion that the company can report income by producing more without increasing sales.

Required

1. Can the company report a net income by increasing production to 100 tons and storing the excess production in inventory? Your explanation should include an income statement (using absorption costing) based on production of 100 tons and sales of 60 tons.

2. Should the company produce 100 tons given that projected demand is 60 tons? Explain, and also refer to any ethical implications of such a managerial decision.

Azule Company produces a single product. Its income statements under absorption costing for its first two years of operation follow.

PROBLEM SET B

Problem 6-1B
Variable costing income statement and conversion to absorption costing income (two consecutive years)

P2   P3

	2014	2015
Sales ($35 per unit)	$1,925,000	$2,275,000
Cost of goods sold ($26 per unit)	1,430,000	1,690,000
Gross margin	495,000	585,000
Selling and administrative expenses	465,000	495,000
Net income	$ 30,000	$ 90,000

Additional Information

a. Sales and production data for these first two years follow:

	2014	2015
Units produced	60,000	60,000
Units sold	55,000	65,000

b. Its variable cost per unit and total fixed costs are unchanged during 2014 and 2015. Its $26 per unit product cost consists of the following.

Direct materials	$ 4
Direct labor	6
Variable overhead	8
Fixed overhead ($480,000/60,000 units)	8
Total product cost per unit	$26

c. Its selling and administrative expenses consist of the following.

	2014	2015
Variable selling and administrative expenses ($3 per unit)	$165,000	$195,000
Fixed selling and administrative expenses	300,000	300,000
Total selling and administrative expenses	$465,000	$495,000

Required

Check (1) 2014 net loss, $(10,000)

1. Prepare this company's income statements under variable costing for each of its first two years.

2. Explain any difference between the absorption costing income and the variable costing income for these two years.

Problem 6-2B

Variable costing income statement and conversion to absorption costing income

P2   P3

E'Lonte Company began operations this year. During this first year, the company produced 300,000 units and sold 250,000 units. Its income statement under absorption costing for this year follows.

Sales (250,000 units × $18 per unit)		$4,500,000
Cost of goods sold		
Beginning inventory	$ 0	
Cost of goods manufactured (300,000 units × $7.50 per unit)	2,250,000	
Cost of goods available for sale	2,250,000	
Ending inventory (50,000 × $7.50)	375,000	
Cost of goods sold		1,875,000
Gross margin		2,625,000
Selling and administrative expenses		2,200,000
Net income		$ 425,000

Additional Information

a. Selling and administrative expenses consist of $1,200,000 in annual fixed expenses and $4 per unit in variable selling and administrative expenses.

b. The company's product cost of $7.50 per unit is computed as follows.

Direct materials	$2.00 per unit
Direct labor	$2.40 per unit
Variable overhead	$1.60 per unit
Fixed overhead ($450,000/300,000 units)	$1.50 per unit

Required

Check (1) Variable costing income, $350,000

1. Prepare the company's income statement under variable costing.

2. Explain any difference between the company's income under variable costing (from part 1) and the income reported above.

Chem-Melt produces and sells an ice-melting granular used on roadways and sidewalks in winter. The company annually produces and sells about 300,000 pounds of its granular. In its ten-year history, the company has never reported a net loss. Because of this year's unusually mild winter, projected demand for its product is only 250,000 pounds. Based on its predicted production and sales of 250,000 pounds, the company projects the following income statement under absorption costing.

Problem 6-3B
Income reporting,
absorption costing, and
managerial ethics

P2   C1

Sales (250,000 lbs. at $8 per lb.)	$2,000,000
Cost of goods sold (250,000 lbs. at $6.80 per lb.)	1,700,000
Gross margin	300,000
Selling and administrative expenses	450,000
Net loss	$ (150,000)

Its product cost information follows and consists mainly of fixed production cost because of its automated production process requiring expensive equipment.

Variable direct labor and materials costs per pound	$2.00
Fixed production cost per pound ($1,200,000/250,000 lbs.)	4.80
Total product cost per pound	$6.80

The company's selling and administrative expenses are all fixed. The president is concerned about the adverse reaction from its creditors and shareholders if the projected net loss is reported. The controller suggests that since the company has large storage capacity, it can report a net income by keeping its production at the usual 300,000-pound level even though it expects to sell only 250,000 pounds. The president was puzzled by the suggestion that the company can report a profit by producing more without increasing sales.

Required

1. Can the company report a net income by increasing production to 300,000 pounds and storing the excess production in inventory? Your explanation should include an income statement (using absorption costing) based on production of 300,000 pounds and sales of 250,000 pounds.

2. Should the company produce 300,000 pounds given that projected demand is 250,000 pounds? Explain, and also refer to any ethical implications of such a managerial decision.

(This serial problem began in Chapter 1 and continues through most of the book. If previous chapter segments were not completed, the serial problem can begin at this point. It is helpful, but not necessary, to use the Working Papers that accompany the book.)

**SERIAL
PROBLEM**
Business Solutions

P2   P3

SP 6   Santana Rey expects sales of her line of computer workstation furniture to equal 300 workstations (at a sales price of $3,000) for 2016. The workstations' manufacturing costs include the following.

Direct materials	$800 per unit
Direct labor	$400 per unit
Variable overhead	$100 per unit
Fixed overhead	$24,000 per year

The selling expenses related to these workstations follow.

Variable selling expenses	$50 per unit
Fixed selling expenses	$4,000 per year

Santana is considering how many workstations to produce in 2016. She is confident that she will be able to sell any workstations in her 2016 ending inventory during 2017. However, Santana does not want to overproduce as she does not have sufficient storage space for many more workstations.

Required

1. Compute Business Solutions's absorption costing income assuming
   a. 300 workstations are produced.
   b. 320 workstations are produced.

[continued on next page]

2. Compute Business Solutions's variable costing income assuming
   a. 300 workstations are produced.
   b. 320 workstations are produced.
3. Explain to Santana any differences in the income figures determined in parts 1 and 2. How should Santana use the information from parts 1 and 2 to help make production decisions?

Beyond the Numbers

REPORTING IN ACTION

P2

APPLE

BTN 6-1   Apple's ending inventory amounts (in $ millions) are shown below:

	2013	2012	2011
Ending inventory	$1,764	$791	$776

Required

1. Assume Apple uses variable costing for some of its internal reports. For each of the years 2013 and 2012, would net income based on variable costing be higher, lower, or no different from net income based on absorption costing? Explain.
2. Assume Apple is considering implementing a just-in-time (JIT) inventory system. Would a JIT system increase, decrease, or have no effect on differences in net income between absorption costing and variable costing? Explain.

COMPARATIVE ANALYSIS

P2

APPLE
GOOGLE

BTN 6-2   Apple offers repair service on its products. Assume that Google wants to offer in-home and online services for computer repair and support.

Required

1. What are some of the costs that Google must consider when deciding to offer these additional computer services? Are these costs different from what Apple must consider when offering additional new types of repair and support services?
2. Would variable or absorption costing be more useful to Google in analyzing whether repair and support services are profitable?

ETHICS CHALLENGE

C1

BTN 6-3   FDP Company produces a variety of home security products. Gary Price, the company's president, is concerned with the fourth quarter market demand for the company's products. Unless something is done in the last two months of the year, the company is likely to miss its earnings expectation of Wall Street analysts. Price still remembers when FDP's earnings were below analysts' expectation by two cents a share three years ago, and the company's share price fell 19% the day earnings were announced. In a recent meeting, Price told his top management that something must be done quickly. One proposal by the marketing vice president was to give a deep discount to the company's major customers to increase the company's sales in the fourth quarter. The company controller pointed out that while the discount could increase sales, it may not help the bottom line; to the contrary, it could lower income. The controller said, "Since we have enough storage capacity, we might simply increase our production in the fourth quarter to increase our reported profit."

Required

1. Gary Price is not sure how the increase in production without a corresponding increase in sales could help boost the company's income. Explain to Price how reported income varies with respect to production level.
2. Is there an ethical concern in this situation? If so, which parties are affected? Explain.

COMMUNICATING IN PRACTICE

P3

BTN 6-4   Mertz Chemical has three divisions. Its consumer product division faces strong competition from companies overseas. During its recent teleconference, Ryan Peterson, the consumer product division manager, reported that his division's sales for the current year were below its break-even point. However, when the division's annual reports were received, Billie Mertz, the company president, was surprised that the consumer product division actually reported a profit of $264,000. How could this be possible?

Required

Assume that you work in the corporate controller's office. Write a half-page memorandum to the president explaining how the division can report income even if its sales are below the break-even point.

BTN 6-5   This chapter discussed the variable costing method and how to use variable costing information to make various business decisions. We also can find several websites on variable costing and its business applications.

TAKING IT TO THE NET
P2

Required

1. Review the website of **Value Based Management** at <u>ValueBasedManagement.net</u>. Identify and print the site page on the topic of variable costing (<u>valuebasedmanagement.net/methods_variable_costing.html</u>).
2. What other phrases are used in practice for *variable costing*?
3. According to this website, what are the consequences of variable costing for profit calculation?

BTN 6-6   This chapter identified several decision contexts in which managers use product cost information.

TEAMWORK IN ACTION
P4

Required

Break into teams and identify at least one specific decision context in which absorption costing information is more relevant than variable costing information and at least one decision context in which variable costing information is more relevant than absorption costing. Be prepared to discuss your answers in class.

BTN 6-7   **Happy Family Brands**, which was launched by entrepreneur Shazi Visram, produces high-quality organic foods for babies, young children, and adults.

ENTREPRENEURIAL DECISION
P3

Required

1. The founder of Happy Family Brands uses variable costing in her business decisions. If Happy Family Brands used absorption costing, would you expect the company's income to be more, less than, or about the same as its income measured under variable costing? Explain.

BTN 6-8   Visit a local hotel and observe its daily operating activities. The costs associated with some of its activities are variable while others are fixed with respect to occupancy levels.

HITTING THE ROAD
A1

Required

1. List cost items that are likely variable for the hotel.
2. List cost items that are likely fixed for the hotel.
3. Compare the fixed cost items with variable cost items. Rank costs within each category based on your perception of which ones you believe are the larger.
4. Based on your observations and the answers to parts 1 through 3, explain why many hotels offer discounts as high as 50% or more during their low occupancy season.

BTN 6-9   Assume that **Samsung** (<u>Samsung.com</u>) is considering offering a service similar to **Apple**'s iTunes music download store. However, instead of developing the division internally, Samsung is considering buying a company that already offers such services.

GLOBAL DECISION
P2

Samsung
APPLE

Required

Would absorption or variable costing be most useful to Samsung in evaluating whether to acquire an existing business that provides services similar to iTunes? Explain.

ANSWERS TO MULTIPLE CHOICE QUIZ

1. c; $14, computed as $3 + $5 + $3 + ($3,000/1,000 units).
2. a; $11, computed as $3 + $5 + $3 (consisting of all variable product costs).
3. a
4. c
5. b

7

Master Budgets and Performance Planning

Chapter Preview

BUDGET PROCESS AND ADMINISTRATION

C1 Budgeting as a management tool

    Benefits of budgeting

    Budgeting and human behavior

    Budget reporting and timing

    Budget committee

THE MASTER BUDGET

C2 Budget components

P1 Operating budgets—including sales; production; selling; administrative

    Direct materials budget

    Direct labor budget

    Factory overhead budget

    Capital expenditures budget

P2 Cash budget

BUDGETED FINANCIAL STATEMENTS

P3 Budgeted income statement

    Budgeted balance sheet

    Using the master budget

A1 Activity-based budgeting

P4 *Appendix:* Master budget—merchandiser

Learning Objectives

CONCEPTUAL

C1 Describe the benefits of budgeting and the process of budget administration.

C2 Describe a master budget and the process of preparing it.

ANALYTICAL

A1 Analyze expense planning using activity-based budgeting.

PROCEDURAL

P1 Prepare the operating budget components of a master budget—for a manufacturing company.

P2 Prepare a cash budget.

P3 Prepare budgeted financial statements.

P4 *Appendix 7A*—Prepare each component of a master budget and link each to the budgeting process—for a merchandising company.

MONTERREY, MEXICO—To fulfill requirements for his high school degree, Daniel Gómez Iñiguez completed a project on how to make biodiesel fuel from vegetable oil and animal fats. "Searching the Internet, I realized it is real easy to make biodiesel at your home," explains Daniel. As Daniel's interest in making biodiesel grew, he expanded his knowledge by taking college courses on biodiesel production and joining an informal biodiesel club. His efforts led to connections with three partners—Guillermo Colunga, Antonio Lopez, and Maurico Pareja—and the group started **Solben**, a company that sells technology for biodiesel production.

Like most entrepreneurs, the partners faced challenges in getting their business going. "We regularly entered entrepreneurship competitions, knowing we had no chance to win," admits Daniel. "The competitions wanted business plans and budgets, and we didn't have those. But we learned something every time." This continual learning enabled the company to find a niche by developing technology that can be effective in a developing economy. "Large plants are costly to build and expensive to operate," says Daniel, "but most homegrown systems produce low-quality fuel. Our system makes high-quality fuel, even at small volumes, and it is modular, so the plant can grow as demand grows."

As Solben grew, budgeting and the budgeting process became increasingly important. Daniel explains that budgets help formalize business plans and goals and help direct and monitor employees. Budgeted income statements enable managers to assess how changes in materials, labor, and overhead impact the bottom line. As Solben expanded its sales and its work force grew, the partners began developing more formal plans and budgets. "Budgeting gives us a plan of where we want to go," asserts Daniel. "Still, we must never stop learning and adapting our plans." Although budgets are expressed in monetary terms, Daniel says that "money is not the only way to measure success. Success is based on the number of people you can impact in a positive way."

Daniel offers advice for budding entrepreneuers. "Do something you are really passionate about. And don't be afraid of failure. Failure is positive if you learn from it. Always keep learning." In Solben's case, this emphasis on learning has led to sales of over $3 million in a recent year, and an over 85 percent share of Mexico's market for biodiesel technology production.

Courtesy of Daniel E. Gómez Iñiguez and Solben

Full of Energy

"Success is a path . . . you determine how long it is"
—**Daniel Gómez Iñiguez**

And, the company continues to plan for more growth—into the United States and ultimately a listing on the Mexican stock exchange.

Sources: *Solben website,* January 2015; *billionsuccess.com* interview, July 21, 2012; *Mother Nature Network,* April 27, 2012; *news.niagara.edu,* November 15, 2012

BUDGET PROCESS AND ADMINISTRATION

Budgeting as a Management Tool

An important management objective in large companies is to ensure that activities of all departments contribute to meeting the company's overall goals. This requires coordination. Budgeting helps to achieve this coordination. The budgeting process coordinates the activities of various departments to meet the company's overall goals.

Most companies prepare long-term strategic plans spanning 5 to 10 years. They then fine-tune them in medium-term and short-term plans. Long-term strategic plans provide a road map for the future about potential opportunities such as new products, markets, and investments. Medium- and short-term plans are more operational and translate strategic plans into actions. These action plans are fairly concrete and consist of defined objectives and goals.

Short-term financial plans are called *budgets* and typically cover a one-year period. A **budget** is a formal statement of a company's future plans. It is usually expressed in monetary terms because the economic or financial aspects of the business are the primary factors driving management's decisions. All managers should be involved in **budgeting,** the process of planning future business actions and expressing them as formal plans. Managers who participate in a budgeting process increase the likelihood of both personal and company success.

Benefits of Budgeting

Budgets help fulfill the key managerial functions of planning and controlling. There are several benefits to having a written budget:

- A budget focuses on the future opportunities and threats to the organization. This focus on the future is important, because the daily pressures of operating an organization can divert management's attention to planning. The budgeting system counteracts this tendency by formalizing the planning process and demanding input. Budgeting makes planning an explicit management responsibility.

- The control function requires management to evaluate (benchmark) operations against some norm. Since budgeted performance takes into account important company, industry, and economic factors, a comparison of actual to budgeted performance provides an effective monitoring and control system. This evaluation assists management in identifying problems and taking corrective actions if necessary.

- An important management objective in large companies is to ensure that the activities of all departments contribute to meeting the company's overall goals. This requires coordination. Budgeting helps to achieve this coordination across departments.

- A written budget is an effective way to communicate management's specific action plans to all employees. When plans are not written down, conversations can lead to uncertainty and confusion among employees.

- Budgets can be used to motivate employees. Budgeted performance levels can provide goals for employees to attain or even exceed. Many companies provide incentives, like cash bonuses, for employee performance that meets or exceeds budget goals.

Decision Insight

Incentive Pay Budgets are important in determining managers' pay. A recent survey shows that 82% of large companies tie managers' bonus payments to beating budget goals. For these companies, bonus payments are frequently more than 20% of total manager pay. ■

Budgeting and Human Behavior

Budgets provide standards for evaluating performance and can affect the attitudes of employees evaluated by them. Budgeting can be used to create a positive effect on employees' attitudes, but it can also create negative effects if not properly applied. Budgeted levels of performance, for instance, must be realistic to avoid discouraging employees. Personnel who will be evaluated should be consulted and involved in preparing the budget to increase their commitment to meeting it. Performance evaluations must allow the affected employees to explain the reasons for apparent performance deficiencies.

The budgeting process has three important guidelines:

1. Employees affected by a budget should be consulted when it is prepared (*participatory budgeting*).
2. Goals reflected in a budget should be attainable.
3. Evaluations should be made carefully with opportunities to explain differences between actual and budgeted amounts.

Budgeting can be a positive motivating force when these guidelines are followed.

Managers must also be aware of potential negative outcomes of budgeting. Under participatory budgeting, some employees might understate sales budgets and overstate expense budgets to allow themselves a cushion, or *budgetary slack,* to aid in meeting targets. For some businesses, pressure to meet budgeted results might lead employees to engage in unethical behavior or commit fraud. Finally, some employees might always spend their budgeted amounts, even on unnecessary items, to ensure their budgets aren't reduced for the next period.

Example: Assume a company's sales force receives a bonus when sales exceed the budgeted amount. How would this arrangement affect the participatory sales forecasts? *Answer:* Sales reps may understate their budgeted sales.

Budget Reporting and Timing

The budget period usually coincides with the accounting period. Most companies prepare at least an annual budget, which reflects the objectives for the next year. To provide specific guidance, the annual budget usually is separated into quarterly or monthly budgets. These short-term budgets allow management to periodically evaluate performance and take corrective action.

The time period required for the annual budgeting process can vary considerably. Large, complex organizations usually require a longer time to prepare their budgets than do smaller organizations. This is so because considerable effort is required to coordinate the different units (departments) within large organizations.

Many companies apply **continuous budgeting** by preparing **rolling budgets.** As each monthly or quarterly budget period goes by, these companies revise their entire set of budgets for the months or quarters remaining and add new monthly or quarterly budgets to replace the ones that have lapsed. Thus, at any point in time, monthly or quarterly budgets are available for the next 12 months or four quarters. Exhibit 7.1 shows rolling budgets prepared at the end of five consecutive periods. The first set (at top) is prepared in December 2014 and covers the four calendar quarters of 2015. In March 2015, the company prepares another rolling budget for the next four quarters through March 2016. This same process is repeated every three months. As a result, management is continuously planning ahead.

Exhibit 7.1 reflects an annual budget composed of four quarters, prepared four times per year using the most recent information available. When continuous budgeting is not used, the fourth-quarter budget is nine months old and perhaps out of date when applied.

Companies Using Rolling Budgets

No 55% Yes 45%

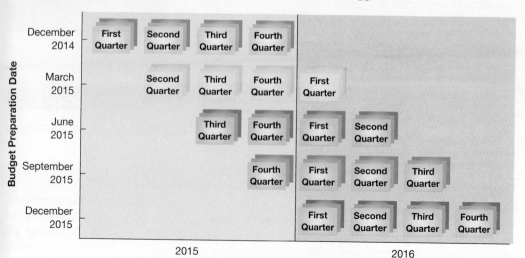

EXHIBIT 7.1

Rolling Budgets

Decision Insight

Budget Calendar Many companies use long-range operating budgets. For large companies, three groups usually determine or influence the budgets: creditors, directors, and management. All three are interested in the companies' future cash flows and earnings. The annual budget process often begins six months or more before the budget is due to the board of directors. When rolling budgets are used, directors must be aware that management's updated budgets might be used to mask poor performance. ■

Budget Committee

The task of preparing a budget should not be the sole responsibility of any one department. Similarly, the budget should not be simply handed down as top management's final word. Instead, budget figures and budget estimates developed through a *bottom-up* process usually

are more useful. This includes, for instance, involving the sales department in preparing sales estimates. Likewise, the production department should have initial responsibility for preparing its own expense budget. Without active employee involvement in preparing budget figures, there is a risk these employees will feel that the numbers fail to reflect their special problems and needs.

Although most budgets should be developed using a bottom-up process, the budgeting system requires central guidance. This guidance is supplied by a budget committee of department heads and other executives responsible for seeing that budgeted amounts are realistic and coordinated. If a department submits initial budget figures that do not reflect efficient performance, the budget committee should return them with explanatory comments on how to improve them. Then the originating department must either adjust its proposals or explain why they are acceptable. Communication between the originating department and the budget committee should continue as needed to ensure that both parties accept the budget as reasonable, attainable, and desirable.

Point: In a large company, developing a budget through a bottom-up process can involve hundreds of employees and take several weeks to finalize.

Decision Insight

Strategic Planning Most companies allocate dollars based on budgets submitted by department managers. These managers verify the numbers and monitor the budget. Managers must remember, however, that a budget is judged by its success in helping achieve the company's mission. One analogy is that a hiker must know the route to properly plan a hike and monitor hiking progress. ■

Pixland/AGE fotostock

THE MASTER BUDGET

C2

Describe a master budget and the process of preparing it.

A **master budget** is a formal, comprehensive plan for a company's future. It contains several individual budgets that are linked with each other to form a coordinated plan.

Master Budget Components

Exhibit 7.2 summarizes the master budgeting process. The master budgeting process typically begins with the sales budget and ends with a cash budget and budgeted financial statements. The master budget includes individual budgets for sales, production (or purchases), various expenses, capital expenditures, and cash.

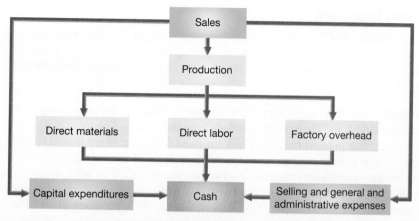

Budgeted financial statements

EXHIBIT 7.2

Master Budget Process
for a Manufacturer

The usual number and types of budgets included in a master budget depend on the company's size and complexity. A manufacturer's master budget should include, at a minimum, several operating budgets (shown in yellow in Exhibit 7.2), a capital expenditures budget, and a cash budget. Managers also often express the expected financial results of these planned activities with a budgeted balance sheet and a budgeted income statement. Some budgets require the input of other budgets. For example, direct materials and direct labor budgets cannot be prepared until a production budget is prepared. A company cannot plan its production until it prepares a sales budget.

Point: Merchandisers prepare *merchandise purchase* budgets instead of the operating budgets in Exhibit 7.2.

The rest of this chapter explains how Toronto Sticks Company (TSC), a manufacturer of youth hockey sticks, prepares its master budget. Its master budget includes operating, capital expenditures, and cash budgets for each month in each quarter. It also includes a budgeted income statement for each quarter and a budgeted balance sheet as of the last day of each quarter. We show how TSC prepares budgets for October, November, and December 2015. Exhibit 7.3 presents TSC's balance sheet at the start of this budgeting period, which we often refer to as we prepare the component budgets.

Courtesy of JJW Images

EXHIBIT 7.3

Balance Sheet Prior to the
Budgeting Periods

TORONTO STICKS COMPANY
Balance Sheet
September 30, 2015

Assets

Cash		$ 20,000
Accounts receivable		25,200
Raw materials inventory (178 pounds @ $20)		3,560
Finished goods inventory (1,010 units @ $17)		17,170
Equipment*	$200,000	
Less: Accumulated depreciation	36,000	164,000
Total assets		$229,930

Liabilities and Equity

Liabilities		
Accounts payable	$ 7,060	
Income taxes payable (due 10/31/2015)	20,000	
Note payable	10,000	$ 37,060
Stockholders' equity		
Common stock	150,000	
Retained earnings	42,870	192,870
Total liabilities and equity		$229,930

* Equipment is depreciated on a straight-line basis over 10 years (salvage value is $20,000).

P1

Prepare the operating
budget components of a
master budget—for a
manufacturing company.

Operating Budgets

This section explains TSC's preparation of operating budgets. Its operating budgets consist of the sales budget, production and manufacturing budgets, selling expense budget, and general and administrative expense budget. (The preparation of merchandising budgets is described in Appendix 7A.)

Sales Budget   The first step in preparing the master budget is the **sales budget,** which shows the planned sales units and the expected dollars from these sales. The sales budget is the starting point in the budgeting process because plans for most departments are linked to sales.

The sales budget should emerge from a careful analysis of forecasted economic and market conditions, business capacity, proposed selling expenses (such as advertising), and predictions of unit sales. A company's sales personnel are usually asked to develop predictions of sales for each territory and department. To illustrate, in September 2015, TSC sold 700 hockey sticks at $60 per unit. After considering sales predictions and market conditions, TSC prepares its sales budget for the next three months (see Exhibit 7.4). Note that the sales budget in Exhibit 7.4 includes forecasts of both unit sales and unit prices. Some sales budgets are expressed only in total sales dollars, but most are more detailed. Management finds it useful to know budgeted units and unit prices for many different products, regions, departments, and sales representatives.

EXHIBIT 7.4

Sales Budget

	A	B	C	D	E
1		TORONTO STICKS COMPANY			
2		Sales Budget			
3		October 2015–December 2015			
4		October	November	December	Totals
5	Budgeted sales (units)	1,000	800	1,400	3,200
6	Selling price per unit	× $ 60	× $ 60	× $ 60	× $ 60
7	Total budgeted sales (dollars)	$60,000	$48,000	$84,000	$192,000
8					

■ Decision Maker

Entrepreneur   You run a start-up that manufactures designer clothes. Business is seasonal, and fashions and designs quickly change. How do you prepare reliable annual sales budgets? ■   [Answers follow the chapter's Summary.]

Production Budget   A manufacturer prepares a **production budget,** which shows the number of units to be produced in a period. The production budget is based on the unit sales projected in the sales budget, along with inventory considerations. Manufacturers often determine a certain amount of **safety stock,** a quantity of inventory that provides protection against lost sales caused by unfulfilled demands from customers or delays in shipments from suppliers. Exhibit 7.5 shows the general computation of the production required for a period. *A production budget does not show costs; it is always expressed in units of product.*

EXHIBIT 7.5

Computing Production
Requirements

$$\text{Budgeted ending inventory (units of safety stock)} + \text{Budgeted sales units for the period (from the sales budget)} = \text{Required units needed for the period} - \text{Number of units in beginning inventory} = \text{Total units to be produced in the period}$$

In a *safety stock inventory system,* companies maintain sufficient inventory to reduce the risk and cost of running short. This practice requires enough production or purchases to satisfy the budgeted sales amounts. To illustrate, after assessing the cost of keeping inventory along with the risk and cost of inventory shortages, TSC decided that the number of units in its finished goods inventory at each month-end should equal 90% of next month's predicted sales. For example, inventory at the end of October should equal 90% of budgeted November sales, and so on. This information along with knowledge of 1,010 units in inventory at September 30 (see Exhibit 7.3) allows the company to prepare the production budget shown in Exhibit 7.6. The

Example: Under a JIT system, how will a sales budget differ from a merchandise purchases or production budget? *Answer:* The two budgets will be similar because future inventory should be near zero.

	A	B	C	D
1	**TORONTO STICKS COMPANY**			
2	**Production Budget**			
3	**October 2015–December 2015**			
4		**October**	**November**	**December**
5	Next month's budgeted sales (units) from Sales Budget*	800	1,400	900
6	Ratio of inventory to future sales	× 90%	× 90%	× 90%
7	Budgeted ending inventory (units)	720	1,260	810
8	Add: Budgeted sales (units)	1,000	800	1,400
9	Required units of available production	1,720	2,060	2,210
10	Deduct: Beginning inventory (units)	1,010**	720	1,260
11	Units to be produced	710	1,340	950
12				

*From Sales Budget (Exhibit 7.4); January budgeted sales of 900 units from next quarter's sales budget.
**October's beginning inventory (1,010 units) is inconsistent with company policy.

EXHIBIT 7.6

Production Budget

actual number of units of ending inventory at September 30 is not consistent with TSC's policy. This is not uncommon, as sales forecasts are uncertain and production can sometimes be disrupted.

The first three lines of TSC's production budget determine the budgeted ending inventories (in units). Budgeted unit sales are then added to the budgeted ending inventory to give the required units of production. We then subtract beginning inventory to determine the budgeted number of units to be produced. The information about units to be produced provides the basis for *manufacturing budgets* for the production costs of those units—direct materials, direct labor, and overhead.

Courtesy of JJW Images

Decision Insight

Just-in-Time Inventory Systems   Managers of *just-in-time* (JIT) inventory systems use sales budgets for short periods (often as few as one or two days) to order just enough merchandise or materials to satisfy the immediate sales demand. This keeps the amount of inventory to a minimum (or zero in an ideal situation). A JIT system minimizes the costs of maintaining inventory, but it is practical only if customers are content to order in advance or if managers can accurately determine short-term sales demand. Suppliers also must be able and willing to ship small quantities regularly and promptly. ■

Point: Accurate estimates of future sales are crucial in a JIT system.

A manufacturing company predicts sales of 220 units for May and 250 units for June. The company wants each month's ending inventory to equal 30% of next month's predicted unit sales. Beginning inventory for May is 66 units. Compute the company's budgeted production in units for May.

Solution

Production Budget	Units
Budgeted ending inventory for May (250 × 30%)	75
Plus: Budgeted sales for May	220
Required units of available production	295
Less: Beginning inventory	(66)
Total units to be produced	229

NEED-TO-KNOW 7-1

Production Budget

P1

QC1

Do More: QS 7-12, QS 7-16, QS 7-17, E 7-3, E 7-10, E 7-11

Direct Materials Budget   The **direct materials budget** shows the budgeted costs for the direct materials that will need to be purchased to satisfy the estimated production for the period. Whereas the production budget shows *units* to be produced, the direct materials budget translates the units to be produced into budgeted *costs*. (The same is true for the other two manufacturing budgets that we will discuss below—the direct labor budget and the factory overhead budget).

To develop a direct materials budget, companies need the following inputs:

- Number of units to produce (from the production budget).
- Materials requirements per unit—How many units (pounds, gallons, etc.) of direct materials go into each unit of finished product?
- Budgeted ending inventory (in units) of direct materials—As with finished goods, most companies maintain a safety stock of materials to ensure that production can continue.
- Beginning inventory (in units) of direct materials.
- Cost per unit of direct materials.

Using these inputs the company can then prepare a direct materials budget. As an example, Exhibit 7.7 shows the direct materials budget for TSC. This budget begins with the budgeted production, taken directly from the production budget. Next, TSC needs to know the amount of direct materials needed for each of the units to be produced—in this case, half a pound (.5) of wood. With these two inputs we can now compute the amount of direct materials needed for production. For example, to produce 710 hockey sticks in October, TSC will need 355 pounds of wood (710 units × 0.5 lbs. = 355 lbs.).

EXHIBIT 7.7

Direct Materials Budget

	A	B	C	D
1	TORONTO STICKS COMPANY			
2	Direct Materials Budget			
3	October 2015–December 2015			
4		October	November	December
5	Budgeted production units*	710	1,340	950
6	Materials requirements per unit	× 0.5	× 0.5	× 0.5
7	Materials needed for production (pounds)	355	670	475
8	Add: Budgeted ending inventory (pounds)	335	237.5	247.5**
9	Total materials requirements (pounds)	690	907.5	722.5
10	Deduct: Beginning inventory (pounds)	(178)	(335)	(237.5)
11	Materials to be purchased (pounds)	512	572.5	485.0
12				
13	Material price per pound	$ 20	$ 20	$ 20
14	Total cost of direct materials purchases	$10,240	$11,450	$9,700
15				

*From Production Budget (Exhibit 7.6)
**Computed from January 2016 production requirements, assumed to be 990 units.

The company then needs to consider its safety stock of direct materials. TSC has determined that it wants to have a safety stock of direct materials on hand at the end of each month to complete 50% of the budgeted units to be produced in the next month. Since TSC expects to produce 1,340 units in November, requiring 670 pounds of materials, it needs ending inventory of direct materials of 335 pounds (50% × 670) at the end of October. TSC's total direct materials requirement for October is therefore 690 pounds (355 + 335).

TSC already has 178 pounds of direct materials in its beginning inventory (refer to Exhibit 7.3). TSC deducts the amount of direct materials that were in beginning inventory from the total materials requirements for the month. For October, the calculation is 690 pounds − 178 pounds, resulting in the need for 512 pounds of direct materials to be purchased in October.

The direct materials budget next translates the *pounds* of direct materials to be purchased into budgeted *costs*. TSC estimates that the cost of direct materials will be $20 per pound over the quarter. At $20 per pound, purchasing 512 pounds of direct materials for October production will cost $10,240 (computed as $20 × 512). Similar calculations are done to compute the cost of direct materials purchases for November ($11,450) and December ($9,700). (For December, assume the budgeted ending inventory of direct materials, based on January's production requirements, is 247.5 pounds). (*Note*: If the company expects direct materials costs to change in the future, it can easily work those changes into the direct materials budget. For example, if it expected the price of wood to jump to $25 per pound in December—say, because a long-term contract with the supplier was about to expire—it could simply change that number in the direct materials budget.)

Direct Labor Budget   The **direct labor budget** shows the budgeted costs for the direct labor that will be needed to satisfy the estimated production for the period. Because there is no
"inventory" of labor, the direct labor budget is easier to prepare than the direct materials budget.
TSC's direct labor budget is shown in Exhibit 7.8. Fifteen minutes of labor time (a quarter of an
hour) is required to produce one unit. Labor is paid at the rate of $12 per hour. Budgeted labor
hours are computed by multiplying the budgeted production level for each month by one-quarter
(0.25) of an hour. Direct labor cost is then computed by multiplying budgeted labor hours by the
labor rate of $12 per hour.

Point: A quarter of an hour
can be expressed as 0.25 hours.

	A	B	C	D
1		TORONTO STICKS COMPANY		
2		Direct Labor Budget		
3		October 2015–December 2015		
4		October	November	December
5	Budgeted production (units)*	710	1,340	950
6	Labor requirements per unit (hours)	× 0.25	× 0.25	× 0.25
7	Total labor hours needed	177.5	335	237.5
8				
9	Labor rate (per hour)	$ 12	$ 12	$ 12
10	Labor dollars	$2,130	$4,020	$2,850
11				

*From Production Budget (Exhibit 7.6)

EXHIBIT 7.8

Direct Labor Budget

As before, estimated changes in direct labor costs can be easily shown in the budgeting process.
Companies thus can ensure the right amount of labor for periods in which production is expected to change or to take into account expected changes in hourly labor rates.

A manufacturing company budgets production of 800 units during June and 900 units during July. Each
unit of finished goods requires 2 pounds of direct materials, at a cost of $8 per pound. The company main-
tains an inventory of direct materials equal to 10% of next month's budgeted production. Beginning direct
materials inventory for June is 160 pounds. Each finished unit requires 1 hour of direct labor at the rate of
$14 per hour. Compute the budgeted (a) cost of direct materials purchases for June and (b) direct labor
cost for June.

NEED-TO-KNOW 7-2

Direct Materials and
Direct Labor Budgets

P1

Solution

a.

Direct Materials Budget

Budgeted production (units)	800
Materials requirements per unit (lbs.)	× 2
Materials needed for production (lbs.)	1,600
Add: Budgeted ending inventory (lbs.)	180*
Total materials requirements (lbs.)	1,780
Less: Beginning inventory (lbs.)	(160)
Materials to be purchased (lbs.)	1,620
Material price per pound	$ 8
Total cost of direct materials purchases	$12,960

*900 units × 2 lbs. per unit × 10% = 180 lbs.

b.

Direct Labor Budget

Budgeted production (units)	800
Labor requirements per unit (hours)	× 1
Total direct labor hours needed	800
Labor rate (per hour)	$ 14
Direct labor cost (June)	$11,200

Do More: QS 7-7, QS 7-8,
QS 7-13, QS 7-14, E 7-4,
E 7-5, E 7-8

Factory Overhead Budget   The **factory overhead budget** shows the budgeted costs for
factory overhead that will be needed to complete the estimated production for the period. TSC's
factory overhead budget is shown in Exhibit 7.9. TSC separates variable and fixed overhead
costs in its overhead budget, as do many companies.

EXHIBIT 7.9

Factory Overhead Budget

	A	B	C	D
1		**TORONTO STICKS COMPANY**		
2		**Factory Overhead Budget**		
3		**October 2015–December 2015**		
4		**October**	**November**	**December**
5	Budgeted production (units)*	710	1,340	950
6	Variable factory overhead rate	× $ 2.50	× $ 2.50	× $ 2.50
7	Budgeted variable overhead	1,775	3,350	2,375
8	Budgeted fixed overhead	1,500	1,500	1,500
9	Budgeted total overhead	$3,275	$4,850	$3,875
10				

*From Production Budget (Exhibit 7.6)

Point: Companies can use scatter diagrams, the high-low method, or regression analysis to classify overhead costs as fixed or variable.

Separating variable and fixed overhead costs enables companies to more closely estimate changes in overhead costs as production volume varies. The variable portion of overhead is assigned at the rate of $2.50 per unit of production. This predetermined overhead rate might be based on inputs such as direct materials costs, machine hours, direct labor hours, or other activity measures. TSC's fixed overhead consists entirely of depreciation on manufacturing equipment. From Exhibit 7.3, this is computed as $18,000 per year [($200,000 − $20,000)/10 years], or $1,500 per month ($18,000/12 months). This fixed portion stays constant at $1,500 per month.

The budget in Exhibit 7.9 is in condensed form; most overhead budgets are more detailed, listing each overhead cost item. Other costs included on overhead budgets commonly include supervisor salaries, indirect materials, indirect labor, utilities, and maintenance of manufacturing equipment. We explain these more detailed overhead budgets in the next chapter.

Product Cost Per Unit   With the information from the three manufacturing budgets (direct materials, direct labor, and factory overhead), we can compute TSC's product cost per unit. This is useful in computing cost of goods sold and preparing a budgeted income statement, as we show later. For budgeting purposes, TSC assumes it will normally produce 3,000 units of product each quarter, yielding fixed overhead of $1.50 per unit. TSC's other product costs are all variable. Exhibit 7.10 summarizes the product cost per unit calculation.

EXHIBIT 7.10

Product Cost Per Unit

Product Cost	Per Unit
Direct materials: ½ pound of materials × $20 per pound of materials....................	$10.00
Direct labor: 0.25 hours of direct labor × $12 per hour of direct labor	3.00
Variable overhead (given)..	2.50
Fixed overhead ($4,500 total fixed overhead per quarter/3,000 units of expected production per quarter......................	1.50
Total product cost per unit*..	$17.00

*At the normal production level of 3,000 units per quarter.

Selling Expense Budget   The **selling expense budget** is an estimate of the types and amounts of selling expenses expected during the budget period. It is usually prepared by the vice president of marketing or an equivalent sales manager. Budgeted selling expenses are based on the sales budget, plus a fixed amount of sales manager salaries.

To illustrate, TSC's selling expense budget is in Exhibit 7.11. The firm's selling expenses consist of commissions paid to sales personnel and a $2,000 monthly salary paid to the sales manager. Sales commissions equal 10% of total sales and are paid in the month sales occur. Sales commissions are variable with respect to sales volume, but the sales manager's salary is fixed. No advertising expenses are budgeted for this particular quarter.

Point: Other common selling expenses include advertising, delivery expenses, and marketing expenses.

	A	B	C	D	E
1		TORONTO STICKS COMPANY			
2		Selling Expense Budget			
3		October 2015–December 2015			
4		October	November	December	Totals
5	Budgeted sales*	$60,000	$48,000	$ 84,000	$192,000
6	Sales commission percent	× 10%	× 10%	× 10%	× 10%
7	Sales commissions	6,000	4,800	8,400	19,200
8	Salary for sales manager	2,000	2,000	2,000	6,000
9	Total selling expenses	$ 8,000	$ 6,800	$ 10,400	$ 25,200
10					

*From Sales Budget (Exhibit 7.4)

EXHIBIT 7.11

Selling Expense Budget

Example: If TSC expects a 12% sales commission will result in budgeted sales of $220,000 for the quarter, what is the total amount of selling expenses for the quarter? Answer: $32,400.

General and Administrative Expense Budget   The **general and administrative expense budget** plans the predicted operating expenses not included in the selling expenses or manufacturing budgets. The office manager responsible for general administration often is responsible for preparing the general and administrative expense budget.

Exhibit 7.12 shows TSC's general and administrative expense budget. It includes salaries of $54,000 per year, or $4,500 per month (paid each month when they are earned). Insurance, taxes, and depreciation on nonmanufacturing assets are other common examples of general and administrative expenses.

Point: Some companies combine selling and general administrative expenses into a single budget.

	A	B	C	D	E
1		TORONTO STICKS COMPANY			
2		General and Administrative Expense Budget			
3		October 2015–December 2015			
4		October	November	December	Totals
5	Administrative salaries	$4,500	$4,500	$4,500	$13,500
6	Total general and administrative expenses	$4,500	$4,500	$4,500	$13,500
7					

EXHIBIT 7.12

General and Administrative Expense Budget

Decision Insight

No Biz Like Snow Biz   Ski resorts' costs of making snow are in the millions of dollars for equipment alone. Snowmaking involves spraying droplets of water into the air, causing them to freeze and come down as snow. Making snow can cost more than $2,000 an hour. Snowmaking accounts for 40 to 50 percent of the budgeted costs for many ski resorts. ■

Gail Shotlander/Getty Images

Example: In Exhibit 7.12, how would a rental agreement of $5,000 per month plus 1% of sales affect the general and administrative expense budget? (Budgeted sales are in Exhibit 7.4.) Answer: Rent expense: Oct. = $5,600; Nov. = $5,480; Dec. = $5,840; Total = $16,920; Revised total general and administrative expenses: Oct. = $10,100; Nov. = $9,980; Dec. = $10,340; Total = $30,420.

A manufacturing company budgets sales of $70,000 during July. It pays sales commissions of 5% of sales and also pays a sales manager a salary of $3,000 per month. Other monthly costs include depreciation on office equipment ($500), insurance expense ($200), advertising ($1,000), and office manager salary of $2,500 per month. For the month of July, compute the total (a) budgeted selling expense and (b) budgeted general and administrative expense.

NEED-TO-KNOW 7-3

Selling and General and Administrative Expense Budgets

P1

Solution

a. Total budgeted selling expense = ($70,000 × 5%) + $3,000 + $1,000 = $7,500
b. Total budgeted general and administrative expense = $500 + $200 + $2,500 = $3,200

Do More: QS 7-5, QS 7-11

QC2

At this point we have illustrated how a manufacturing company prepares its operating budgets. Information from these operating budgets is useful in preparing the capital expenditures budget, the cash budget, and budgeted financial statements, as we show next.

Capital Expenditures Budget   The **capital expenditures budget** shows dollar amounts estimated to be spent to purchase additional plant assets the company will use to carry out its budgeted business activities. It also shows any amounts expected to be received from plant asset disposals, as companies replace old assets with new ones. Thus, the capital expenditures budget shows the company's expected investing activities in plant assets. It is usually prepared after the operating budgets. Since a company's plant assets determine its productive capacity, this budget is usually affected by long-range plans for the business. Yet the process of preparing other budgets can reveal that the company requires more (or less) capacity, which implies more (or less) plant assets.

Capital budgeting is the process of evaluating and planning for capital (plant asset) expenditures. This is an important management task because these expenditures often involve long-run commitments of large amounts, affect predicted cash flows, and impact future debt and equity financing. This means that the capital expenditures budget is often linked with management's evaluation of the company's ability to take on more debt. We describe capital budgeting in a later chapter.

TSC does not anticipate disposal of any plant assets through December 2015, but it does plan to acquire additional equipment for $25,000 cash near the end of December 2015. This is the only budgeted capital expenditure from October 2015 through December 2015. Thus, no separate budget is shown. TSC's cash budget will reflect this $25,000 planned expenditure.

Cash Budget

P2
_____
Prepare a cash budget.

After developing budgets for sales, manufacturing costs, expenses, and capital expenditures, the next step is to prepare the **cash budget,** which shows expected cash inflows and outflows during the budget period. The cash budget is especially important because it helps the company maintain a cash balance necessary to meet ongoing obligations. Most companies set an amount of cash they want to have on hand. By preparing a cash budget, management can prearrange loans to cover anticipated cash shortages before they are needed. A cash budget also helps management avoid a cash balance that is too large. Too much cash is undesirable because it earns a relatively low (if any) return. Exhibit 7.13 shows the general formula for the cash budget.

EXHIBIT 7.13

General Formula for Cash Budget

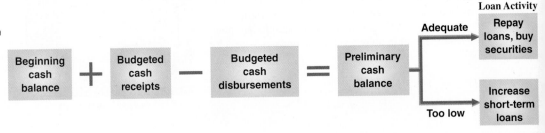

When preparing a cash budget, we add expected cash receipts to the beginning cash balance and deduct expected cash disbursements. If the expected (preliminary) cash balance is too low, additional cash requirements appear in the budget as planned increases from short-term loans. If the preliminary cash balance exceeds the balance the company wants to maintain, the excess is used to repay loans (if any) or to acquire short-term investments. Information for preparing the cash budget is mainly taken from the operating and capital expenditures budgets. Preparing the cash budget typically requires the preparation of other supporting schedules; we show the first of these, a schedule of cash receipts from sales, next.

Cash Receipts from Sales   Managers use the sales budget, combined with knowledge about how frequently customers pay on credit sales, to budget monthly cash receipts. To illustrate, Exhibit 7.14 presents TSC's schedule of budgeted cash receipts.

EXHIBIT 7.14

Computing Budgeted Cash
Receipts from Sales

	A	B	C	D	E
1		TORONTO STICKS COMPANY			
2		Schedule of Cash Receipts from Sales			
3		October 2015–December 2015			
4		September	October	November	December
5	Sales*	$42,000	$60,000	$48,000	$84,000
6	Less: Ending accounts receivable (60%)	25,200**	36,000	28,800	50,400
7	Cash receipts from				
8	Cash sales (40% of sales)		24,000	19,200	33,600
9	Collections of prior month's receivables		25,200	36,000	28,800
10	Total cash receipts		$49,200	$55,200	$62,400
11					

*From Sales Budget (Exhibit 7.4)
**Accounts receivable balance from September 30 balance sheet (Exhibit 7.3)

We begin with reference to TSC's budgeted sales (Exhibit 7.4). Analysis of past sales indicates that 40% of the firm's sales are for cash. The remaining 60% are credit sales; these customers are expected to pay in full in the month following the sales. We now can compute the budgeted cash receipts from customers, as shown in Exhibit 7.14. October's budgeted cash receipts consist of $24,000 from expected cash sales ($60,000 × 40%) plus the anticipated collection of $25,200 of accounts receivable from the end of September.

Cash Payments for Materials   Managers use the beginning balance sheet (Exhibit 7.3) and the direct materials budget (Exhibit 7.7) to help prepare a schedule of cash disbursements for materials. Managers must also know *how* TSC purchases direct materials (pay cash or on account), and for credit purchases, how quickly TSC pays. TSC's materials purchases are entirely on account. It makes full payment during the month following its purchases. Using this information, the schedule of cash payments for materials is shown in Exhibit 7.15.

EXHIBIT 7.15

Computing Cash Payments
for Materials Purchases

	A	B	C	D
1		TORONTO STICKS COMPANY		
2		Schedule of Cash Payments for Direct Materials		
3		October 2015–December 2015		
4		October	November	December
5	Materials purchases*	$10,240	$11,450	$ 9,700
6	Cash disbursements for			
7	Current month purchases (0%)	0	0	0
8	Prior month purchases (100%)	7,060**	10,240	11,450
9	Total cash disbursements for direct materials	$ 7,060	$10,240	$11,450
10				

*From Direct Materials Budget (Exhibit 7.7)
**Accounts payable balance from September 30 balance sheet (Exhibit 7.3)

The schedule above can be modified for alternative payment timing. For example, if Toronto Sticks Company paid for 20% of its purchases in the month of purchase, and paid the remaining 80% of a month's purchases in the following month, its cash disbursements in December would equal $11,100, computed as (20% × $9,700) plus (80% × $11,450).

Preparing the Cash Budget   Managing cash flows is vital for a company's success. The cash budget is useful in this regard because it summarizes many other budgets in terms of their effects on cash. To prepare the cash budget, TSC's managers use the budgets and other schedules listed below.

1. Cash receipts from sales (Exhibit 7.14).
2. Cash payments for direct materials (Exhibit 7.15).
3. Cash payments for direct labor (Exhibit 7.8).
4. Cash payments for variable overhead (Exhibit 7.9).
5. Cash payments for selling expenses (Exhibit 7.11).
6. Cash payments for general and administrative expenses (Exhibit 7.12).

Note that the *fixed overhead* assigned to depreciation in the factory overhead budget (Exhibit 7.9) does not require a cash payment. Therefore, it is not included in the cash budget. Other types of fixed overhead—such as payments for property taxes and insurance—*are* included if they require cash payments.

Additional information is typically needed to prepare the cash budget. For TSC, this additional information includes:

1. Income taxes payable (from the beginning balance sheet, Exhibit 7.3).
2. Expected dividend payments: TSC plans to pay $3,000 of cash dividends in the second month of each quarter.
3. Loan activity: TSC's managers want to maintain a minimum cash balance of $20,000 at each month-end. This is important, as it helps ensure TSC maintains enough liquidity to pay its bills as they come due.

Exhibit 7.16 shows the full cash budget for TSC. The company begins October with $20,000 in cash. To this is added $49,200 in expected cash receipts from sales (from Exhibit 7.14). We next subtract expected cash payments for direct materials, direct labor, overhead, selling expenses, and general and administrative expenses. Income taxes of $20,000 were due as of the end of September 30, 2015, and payable in October. We next discuss TSC's loan activity, including any interest payments.

Courtesy of JJW Images

EXHIBIT 7.16

Cash Budget

	A	B	C	D
1		TORONTO STICKS COMPANY		
2		Cash Budget		
3		October 2015–December 2015		
4		October	November	December
5	Beginning cash balance	$20,000	$20,000	$38,881
6	Add: Cash receipts from customers (Exhibit 7.14)	49,200	55,200	62,400
7	Total cash available	69,200	75,200	101,281
8	Less: Cash payments for			
9	Direct materials (Exhibit 7.15)	7,060	10,240	11,450
10	Direct labor (Exhibit 7.8)	2,130	4,020	2,850
11	Variable overhead (Exhibit 7.9)	1,775	3,350	2,375
12	Sales commissions (Exhibit 7.11)	6,000	4,800	8,400
13	Sales salaries (Exhibit 7.11)	2,000	2,000	2,000
14	General and administrative expenses (Exhibit 7.12)	4,500	4,500	4,500
15	Income taxes payable (Exhibit 7.3)	20,000		
16	Dividends		3,000	
17	Interest on bank loan			
18	October ($10,000 × 1%)*	100		
19	November ($4,365 × 1%)**		44	
20	Purchase of equipment			25,000
21	Total cash disbursements	43,565	31,954	56,575
22	Preliminary cash balance	$25,635	$43,246	$44,706
23	Loan activity			
24	Additional loan from bank			
25	Repayment of loan to bank	5,635	4,365	
26	Ending cash balance	$20,000	$38,881	$44,706
27	Loan balance, end of month	$ 4,365	$ 0	$ 0
28				

* Beginning loan balance (note payable) from Exhibit 7.3   ** Rounded to the nearest dollar.

Loan Activity   TSC has an agreement with its bank that promises additional loans at each month-end, if necessary, so that the company keeps a minimum cash balance of $20,000. If the cash balance exceeds $20,000 at a month-end, TSC uses the excess to repay loans. If the cash balance is less than $20,000 at month-end, the bank loans TSC the difference.

At the end of each month, TSC pays the bank interest on any outstanding loan amount, at the monthly rate of 1% of the beginning balance of these loans. For October, this payment is 1% of the $10,000 note payable amount reported in the balance sheet of Exhibit 7.3. For November, TSC expects to pay interest of $44, computed as 1% of the $4,365 expected loan balance at October 31. No interest is budgeted for December because the company expects to repay the loans in full at the end of November. Exhibit 7.16 shows that the October 31 cash balance increases to $25,635 (before any loan-related activity). This amount is more than the $20,000 minimum. Thus, TSC will pay off a portion of its outstanding loan. At the end of November, TSC's cash balance is sufficient to pay off its remaining loan balance. Had TSC's preliminary cash balance been below the $20,000 minimum in any month, TSC would have increased its loan from the bank so that the ending cash balance was $20,000. We show an example of this situation in Need-To-Know Comprehensive 2 at the end of this chapter.

▮ Decision Insight

Cash Cushion   Why do some companies maintain a minimum cash balance even when the budget shows extra cash is not needed? For example, Apple's cash and short-term investments balance is over $40 billion. According to Apple's CEO, Tim Cook, the cushion provides "flexibility and security," important in navigating uncertain economic times. A cash cushion also enables companies to jump on new ventures or acquisitions that may present themselves. ▮

Kevork Djansezian/Getty Images

BUDGETED FINANCIAL STATEMENTS

One of the final steps in the budgeting process is summarizing the financial statement effects. We next illustrate TSC's budgeted income statement and budgeted balance sheet.

P3

Prepare budgeted financial statements.

Budgeted Income Statement

The **budgeted income statement** is a managerial accounting report showing predicted amounts of sales and expenses for the budget period. It summarizes the income effects of the budgeted activities. Information needed to prepare a budgeted income statement is primarily taken from already-prepared budgets. The volume of information summarized in the budgeted income statement is so large for some companies that they often use spreadsheets to accumulate the budgeted transactions and classify them by their effects on income.

We condense TSC's budgeted income statement and show it in Exhibit 7.17. All information in this exhibit is taken from the component budgets we've examined in this chapter. Also, we now can predict the amount of income tax expense for the quarter, computed as 40% of the budgeted pretax income. For TSC, these taxes are not payable until January 31, 2016. Thus, these taxes are not shown on the October–December 2015 cash budget in Exhibit 7.16, but they are included on the December 31, 2015, balance sheet (shown next).

Point: Lenders often require potential borrowers to provide cash budgets, budgeted income statements, and budgeted balance sheets, as well as data on past performance.

EXHIBIT 7.17

Budgeted Income Statement

TORONTO STICKS COMPANY		
Budgeted Income Statement		
For Three Months Ended December 31, 2015		
Sales (Exhibit 7.4, 3,200 units @ $60)		$192,000
Cost of goods sold (3,200 units @ $17)*		54,400
Gross profit		137,600
Operating expenses		
Sales commissions (Exhibit 7.11)	$19,200	
Sales salaries (Exhibit 7.11)	6,000	
Administrative salaries (Exhibit 7.12)	13,500	
Interest expense (Exhibit 7.16)	144	38,844
Income before income taxes		98,756
Income tax expense ($98,756 × 40%)**		39,502
Net income		$ 59,254

*$17 product cost per unit from Exhibit 7.10   **Rounded to the nearest dollar

Budgeted Balance Sheet

The final step in preparing the master budget is summarizing the company's financial position. The **budgeted balance sheet** shows predicted amounts for the company's assets, liabilities, and equity as of the end of the budget period. TSC's budgeted balance sheet in Exhibit 7.18 is prepared using information from the other budgets. The sources of amounts are reported in the notes to the budgeted balance sheet.

EXHIBIT 7.18

Budgeted Balance Sheet

TORONTO STICKS COMPANY Budgeted Balance Sheet December 31, 2015		
Assets		
Cash[a]		$ 44,706
Accounts receivable[b]		50,400
Raw materials inventory[c]		4,950
Finished goods inventory[d]		13,770
Equipment[e]	$225,000	
Less: Accumulated depreciation[f]	40,500	184,500
Total assets		$298,326
Liabilities and Equity		
Liabilities		
Accounts payable[g]	$ 9,700	
Income taxes payable[h]	39,502	$ 49,202
Stockholders' equity		
Common stock[i]	150,000	
Retained earnings[j]	99,124	249,124
Total liabilities and equity		$298,326

[a] Ending balance for December from the cash budget (in Exhibit 7.16).
[b] 60% of $84,000 sales budgeted for December from the sales budget (in Exhibit 7.4).
[c] 247.5 pounds of raw materials in budgeted ending inventory at the budgeted cost of $20 per unit (direct materials budget, Exhibit 7.7).
[d] 810 units in budgeted finished goods inventory (Exhibit 7.6) at the budgeted cost of $17 per unit (Exhibit 7.10).
[e] September 30 balance of $200,000 from the beginning balance sheet in Exhibit 7.3 plus $25,000 cost of new equipment from the cash budget in Exhibit 7.16.
[f] September 30 balance of $36,000 from the beginning balance sheet in Exhibit 7.3 plus $4,500 depreciation expense from the factory overhead budget in Exhibit 7.9.
[g] Budgeted cost of materials purchases for December from Exhibit 7.7, to be paid in January.
[h] Income tax expense from the budgeted income statement for the fourth quarter in Exhibit 7.17, to be paid in January.
[i] Unchanged from the beginning balance sheet in Exhibit 7.3.
[j] September 30 balance of $42,870 from the beginning balance sheet in Exhibit 7.3 plus budgeted net income of $59,254 from the budgeted income statement in Exhibit 7.17 minus budgeted cash dividends of $3,000 from the cash budget in Exhibit 7.16.

Using the Master Budget

For a master budget to be useful, managers must employ it in their planning and controlling activities. With respect to *planning,* the master budget is clearly a plan for future activities. In addition, any stage in the master budgeting process might reveal undesirable outcomes. The new information can cause management to change its decisions. For example, an early version of the cash budget could show an insufficient amount of cash unless cash outlays are reduced. This information could yield a reduction in planned equipment purchases. Likewise, a budgeted balance sheet might reveal too much debt from too many planned equipment purchases; the company could reduce its planned equipment purchases and thus reduce its need for borrowing.

In *controlling* operations, managers typically compare actual results to budgeted results. Differences between actual and budgeted results are called *variances.* Management examines variances, particularly large ones, to identify areas for improvement and take corrective action. We discuss variances in more detail in the next chapter.

QC3

GLOBAL VIEW

Royal Philips Electronics of the Netherlands is a diversified company. Preparing budgets and evaluating progress helps the company achieve its goals. In a recent annual report the company reports that it budgets sales to grow at a faster pace than overall economic growth. Based on this sales target, company managers prepare detailed operating, capital expenditure, and financial budgets.

Budgeted and actual results of companies that do global business are impacted by changes in foreign currency exchange rates. While most of Royal Philips's cash disbursements are in euros, the company's sales are in euros, U.S. dollars, Chinese yuan, Brazilian real, and other currencies. Forecasting future exchange rates and their impact on sales budgets is difficult. In addition, global economic and political uncertainties add to budgeting challenges.

Sustainability and Accounting   Solben, this chapter's opener company, is focused on alternative fuels. According to the U.S. Department of Energy, burning biodiesel instead of petroleum diesel reduces tailpipe emissions and is better for the environment. Daniel Gómez Iñiguez, one of Solben's founders, notes that "the benefits of biodiesel technology extend beyond earth-friendly fuel. Our plants can be built in remote locations, and thus create local jobs. Companies like ours can have a global impact, and be an example of how socially responsible businesses can also be profitable." The sustainability of Solben's operations, and operations like it, is arguably one path to making business accountable.

Steve McAlister/The Image Bank/Getty Images

Activity-Based Budgeting  **Decision Analysis**

Activity-based budgeting (ABB) is a budget system based on expected activities. Knowledge of expected activities and their levels for the budget period enables management to plan for resources required to perform the activities. Exhibit 7.19 contrasts a traditional budget with an activity-based budget for a company's accounting department. Traditional budgeting systems list items such as salaries, supplies, equipment, and utilities. With a traditional budget, management often makes across-the-board budget cuts or increases. For example, management might decide that each of the line items in the traditional budget must be cut by 5%. This might not be a good strategic decision. In contrast, ABB requires management to list activities performed by, say, the accounting department such as auditing, tax reporting, financial reporting, and cost accounting. An understanding of the resources required to perform the activities, the costs associated with these resources, and the way resource use changes with changes in activity levels allows management to better assess how expenses will change to accommodate changes in activity levels. Moreover, by knowing the relation between activities and costs, management can attempt to reduce costs by eliminating nonvalue-added activities.

A1

Analyze expense planning using activity-based budgeting.

EXHIBIT 7.19

Activity-Based Budgeting versus Traditional Budgeting (for an accounting department)

Traditional Budget		Activity-Based Budget	
Salaries	$152,000	Auditing	$ 58,000
Supplies.	22,000	Tax reporting	71,000
Depreciation	36,000	Financial reporting	63,000
Utilities	14,000	Cost accounting	32,000
Total.	$224,000	Total.	$224,000

Decision Maker

Environmental Manager   You hold the new position of environmental control manager for a chemical company. You are asked to develop a budget for your job and identify job responsibilities. How do you proceed? ■   [Answers follow the chapter's Summary.]

NEED-TO-KNOW

COMPREHENSIVE 1

Master Budget—
Manufacturer

Payne Company's management asks you to prepare its master budget using the following information. The budget is to cover the months of April, May, and June of 2015.

PAYNE COMPANY
Balance Sheet
March 31, 2015

Assets			Liabilities and Equity		
Cash	$ 50,000		Accounts payable	$ 63,818	
Accounts receivable	175,000		Short-term notes payable	12,000	
Raw materials inventory	30,798*		Total current liabilities		$ 75,818
Finished goods inventory	96,600**		Long-term note payable		200,000
Total current assets		$352,398	Total liabilities		275,818
Equipment	480,000		Common stock	435,000	
Less: Accumulated depreciation . . .	(90,000)		Retained earnings	31,580	
Equipment, net		390,000	Total stockholders' equity		466,580
Total assets		$742,398	Total liabilities and equity		$742,398

*2,425 pounds @$12.70, rounded to nearest whole dollar   **8,400 units @ $11.50 per unit

Additional Information

a. Sales for March total 10,000 units. Expected sales (in units) are: 10,500 (April), 9,500 (May), 10,000 (June), and 10,500 (July). The product's selling price is $25 per unit.

b. Company policy calls for a given month's ending finished goods inventory to equal 80% of the next month's expected unit sales. The March 31 finished goods inventory is 8,400 units, which complies with the policy. The product's manufacturing cost is $11.50 per unit, including per unit costs of $6.35 for materials (.5 lbs. at $12.70 per lb.), $3.75 for direct labor (1/4 hour × $15 direct labor rate per hour), $0.90 for variable overhead, and $0.50 for fixed overhead. Fixed overhead consists entirely of $5,000 of monthly depreciation expense. Company policy also calls for a given month's ending raw materials inventory to equal 50% of next month's expected materials needed for production. The March 31 inventory is 2,425 units of materials, which complies with the policy. The company expects to have 2,100 units of materials inventory on June 30.

c. Sales representatives' commissions are 12% of sales and are paid in the month of the sales. The sales manager's monthly salary will be $3,500 in April and $4,000 per month thereafter.

d. Monthly general and administrative expenses include $8,000 administrative salaries and 0.9% monthly interest on the long-term note payable.

e. The company expects 30% of sales to be for cash and the remaining 70% on credit. Receivables are collected in full in the month following the sale (none is collected in the month of the sale).

f. All direct materials purchases are on credit, and no payables arise from any other transactions. One month's purchases are fully paid in the next month. Materials cost $12.70 per pound.

g. The minimum ending cash balance for all months is $50,000. If necessary, the company borrows enough cash using a short-term note to reach the minimum. Short-term notes require an interest payment of 1% at each month-end (before any repayment). If the ending cash balance exceeds the minimum, the excess will be applied to repaying the short-term notes payable balance.

h. Dividends of $100,000 are to be declared and paid in May.

i. No cash payments for income taxes are to be made during the second calendar quarter. Income taxes will be assessed at 35% in the quarter.

j. Equipment purchases of $55,000 are scheduled for June.

Required

Prepare the following budgets and other financial information as required:

1. Sales budget, including budgeted sales for July.
2. Production budget.
3. Direct materials budget. Round costs of materials purchases to the nearest dollar.
4. Direct labor budget.

5. Factory overhead budget.

6. Selling expense budget.

7. General and administrative expense budget.

8. Expected cash receipts from customers and the expected June 30 balance of accounts receivable.

9. Expected cash payments for purchases and the expected June 30 balance of accounts payable.

0. Cash budget.

11. Budgeted income statement, budgeted statement of retained earnings, and budgeted balance sheet.

SOLUTION

	A	B	C	D	E
1	**Sales Budget**	**April**	**May**	**June**	**Quarter**
2	Projected unit sales	10,500	9,500	10,000	
3	Selling price per unit	× $ 25	× $ 25	× $ 25	
4	Projected sales	$262,500	$237,500	$250,000	$750,000
5					

	A	B	C	D	E
1	**Production Budget**	**April**	**May**	**June**	**Quarter**
2	Next period's unit sales (part I)	9,500	10,000	10,500	
3	Ending inventory percent	× 80%	× 80%	× 80%	
4	Desired ending inventory	7,600	8,000	8,400	
5	Current period's unit sales (part I)	10,500	9,500	10,000	
6	Required units of available production	18,100	17,500	18,400	
7	Less: Beginning inventory	8,400	7,600	8,000	
8	Total units to be produced	9,700	9,900	10,400	
9					

	A	B	C	D
1	**Direct Materials Budget**	**April**	**May**	**June**
2	Budgeted production (units) (part 2)	9,700	9,900	10,400
3	Materials requirements per unit (pounds)	× 0.5	× 0.5	× 0.5
4	Materials needed for production (pounds)	4,850	4,950	5,200
5	Add: Budgeted ending inventory (pounds)	2,475	2,600	2,100
6	Total material requirements (pounds)	7,325	7,550	7,300
7	Deduct: Beginning inventory (pounds)	2,425	2,475	2,600
8	Materials to be purchased (pounds)	4,900	5,075	4,700
9				
10	Materials price per pound	$ 12.70	$ 12.70	$ 12.70
11	Total cost of direct materials purchases	$62,230	$64,453*	$59,690
12				

*Rounded to nearest dollar

	A	B	C	D
1	**Direct Labor Budget**	**April**	**May**	**June**
2	Budgeted production (units) (part 2)	9,700	9,900	10,400
3	Labor requirements per unit (hours)	× 0.25	× 0.25	× 0.25
4	Total labor hours needed	2,425	2,475	2,600
5				
6	Labor rate (per hour)	$ 15	$ 15	$ 15
7				
8	Total direct labor cost	$36,375	$37,125	$39,000
9				

	A	B	C	D
1	**Factory Overhead Budget**	**April**	**May**	**June**
2	Budgeted production (units) (part 2)	9,700	9,900	10,400
3	Variable factory overhead rate	× $ 0.90	× $ 0.90	× $ 0.90
4	Budgeted variable overhead	8,730	8,910	9,360
5	Budgeted fixed overhead	5,000	5,000	5,000
6	Budgeted total overhead	$13,730	$13,910	$14,360
7				

6.

	A	B	C	D	E
1	**Selling Expense Budget**	**April**	**May**	**June**	**Quarter**
2	Budgeted sales (part 1)	$262,500	$237,500	$250,000	$750,000
3	Commission percent	× 12%	× 12%	× 12%	× 12%
4	Sales commissions	31,500	28,500	30,000	90,000
5	Manager's salary	3,500	4,000	4,000	11,500
6	Budgeted selling expenses	$ 35,000	$ 32,500	$ 34,000	$101,500
7					

7.

	A	B	C	D	E
1	**General and Administrative Expense Budget**	**April**	**May**	**June**	**Quarter**
2	Administrative salaries	$8,000	$8,000	$8,000	$24,000
3	Interest on long-term note				
4	payable (0.9% × $200,000)	1,800	1,800	1,800	5,400
5	Budgeted general and administrative expenses	$9,800	$9,800	$9,800	$29,400
6					

8.

	A	B	C	D	E
1	**Schedule of Cash Receipts**	**April**	**May**	**June**	**Quarter**
2	Budgeted sales (part 1)	$262,500	$237,500	$250,000	
3	Ending accounts receivable (70%)	$183,750	$166,250	$175,000	
4	Cash receipts				
5	Cash sales (30% of budgeted sales)	$ 78,750	$ 71,250	$ 75,000	$225,000
6	Collections of prior month's receivables	175,000*	183,750	166,250	525,000
7	Total cash to be collected	$253,750	$255,000	$241,250	$750,000
8					

*Accounts receivable balance from March 31 balance sheet

9.

	A	B	C	D	E
1	**Schedule of Cash Payments for Materials**	**April**	**May**	**June**	**Quarter**
2	Cash payments (equal to prior month's				
3	materials purchases)	$63,818*	$62,230	$64,453	$190,501
4	Expected June 30 balance of accounts				
5	payable (June purchases)			$59,690	
6					

*Accounts payable balance from March 31 balance sheet

10.

	A	B	C	D
1	**Cash Budget**	**April**	**May**	**June**
2	Beginning cash balance	$ 50,000	$137,907	$142,342
3	Cash receipts from customers (part 8)	253,750	255,000	241,250
4	Total cash available	303,750	392,907	383,592
5	Cash disbursements			
6	Payments for materials (part 9)	63,818	62,230	64,453
7	Payments for direct labor (part 4)	36,375	37,125	39,000
8	Payments for variable overhead (part 5)	8,730	8,910	9,360
9	Sales commissions (part 6)	31,500	28,500	30,000
10	Salaries			
11	Sales (part 6)	3,500	4,000	4,000
12	Administrative (part 7)	8,000	8,000	8,000
13	Dividends		100,000	
14	Interest on long-term note (part 7)	1,800	1,800	1,800
15	Interest on bank loan			
16	October ($12,000 × 1%)	120		
17	Purchase of equipment			55,000
18	Total cash disbursements	153,843	250,565	211,613
19	Preliminary cash balance	$149,907	$142,342	$171,979
20	Additional loan from bank			
21	Repayment of loan to bank	12,000	0	0
22	Ending cash balance	$137,907	$142,342	$171,979
23	Loan balance, end of month	$ 0	$ 0	$ 0
24				

1.

PAYNE COMPANY
Budgeted Income Statement
For Quarter Ended June 30, 2015

Sales (part 1)		$750,000
Cost of goods sold (30,000 @ $11.50)		345,000
Gross profit		405,000
Operating expenses		
Sales commissions (part 6)	$90,000	
Sales salaries (part 6)	11,500	
Administrative salaries (part 7)	24,000	
Interest on long-term note (part 7)	5,400	
Interest on short-term notes (part 10)	120	
Total operating expenses		131,020
Income before income taxes		273,980
Income taxes (35%)		95,893
Net income		$178,087

PAYNE COMPANY
Budgeted Statement of Retained Earnings
For Quarter Ended June 30, 2015

Beginning retained earnings (given)	$ 31,580
Net income	178,087
	209,667
Less: Cash dividends (part 10)	100,000
Ending retained earnings	$109,667

PAYNE COMPANY
Budgeted Balance Sheet
June 30, 2015

Assets			Liabilities and Equity		
Cash (part 10)		$171,979	Accounts payable (part 9)	$ 59,690	
Accounts receivable (part 8)		175,000	Income taxes payable	95,893	
Raw materials inventory (2,100 pounds @$12.70)*		26,671	Total current liabilities		$155,583
Finished goods inventory (8,400 units @$11.50)		96,600	Long-term note payable (Mar. 31 bal.)		200,000
Total current assets		$470,250	Total liabilities		355,583
Equipment (Mar. 31 bal. plus purchase)		535,000	Common stock (Mar. 31 bal.)	435,000	
Less: Accumulated depreciation			Retained earnings	109,667	
(Mar. 31 bal. plus depreciation expense)	105,000	430,000	Total stockholders' equity		544,667
Total assets		$900,250	Total liabilities and equity		$900,250

*Plus $1 rounding difference

Wild Wood Company's management asks you to prepare its master budget using the following information. The budget is to cover the months of April, May, and June of 2015.

WILD WOOD COMPANY
Balance Sheet
March 31, 2015

Assets		Liabilities and Equity	
Cash	$ 50,000	Accounts payable	$156,000
Accounts receivable	175,000	Short-term notes payable	12,000
Inventory	126,000	Total current liabilities	168,000
Total current assets	351,000	Long-term note payable	200,000
Equipment, gross	480,000	Total liabilities	368,000
Accumulated depreciation	(90,000)	Common stock	235,000
Equipment, net	390,000	Retained earnings	138,000
		Total stockholders' equity	373,000
Total assets	$741,000	Total liabilities and equity	$741,000

NEED-TO-KNOW

COMPREHENSIVE 2

Master Budget—
Merchandiser

Additional Information

a. Sales for March total 10,000 units. Each month's sales are expected to exceed the prior month's result by 5%. The product's selling price is $25 per unit.

b. Company policy calls for a given month's ending inventory to equal 80% of the next month's expected unit sales. The March 31 inventory is 8,400 units, which complies with the policy. The purchase price is $15 per unit.

c. Sales representatives' commissions are 12.5% of sales and are paid in the month of the sales. The sales manager's monthly salary will be $3,500 in April and $4,000 per month thereafter.

d. Monthly general and administrative expenses include $8,000 administrative salaries, $5,000 depreciation, and 0.9% monthly interest on the long-term note payable.

e. The company expects 30% of sales to be for cash and the remaining 70% on credit. Receivables are collected in full in the month following the sale (none is collected in the month of the sale).

f. All merchandise purchases are on credit, and no payables arise from any other transactions. One month's purchases are fully paid in the next month.

g. The minimum ending cash balance for all months is $50,000. If necessary, the company borrows enough cash using a short-term note to reach the minimum. Short-term notes require an interest payment of 1% at each month-end (before any repayment). If the ending cash balance exceeds the minimum, the excess will be applied to repaying the short-term notes payable balance.

h. Dividends of $100,000 are to be declared and paid in May.

i. No cash payments for income taxes are to be made during the second calendar quarter. Income taxes will be assessed at 35% in the quarter.

j. Equipment purchases of $55,000 are scheduled for June.

Required

Prepare the following budgets and other financial information as required:

1. Sales budget, including budgeted sales for July.

2. Purchases budget.

3. Selling expense budget.

4. General and administrative expense budget.

5. Expected cash receipts from customers and the expected June 30 balance of accounts receivable.

6. Expected cash payments for purchases and the expected June 30 balance of accounts payable.

7. Cash budget.

8. Budgeted income statement, budgeted statement of retained earnings, and budgeted balance sheet.

PLANNING THE SOLUTION

● The sales budget shows expected sales for each month in the quarter. Start by multiplying March sales by 105% and then do the same for the remaining months. July's sales are needed for the purchases budget. To complete the budget, multiply the expected unit sales by the selling price of $25 per unit.

● Use these results and the 80% inventory policy to budget the size of ending inventory for April, May, and June. Add the budgeted sales to these numbers and subtract the actual or expected beginning inventory for each month. The result is the number of units to be purchased each month. Multiply these numbers by the per unit cost of $15. Find the budgeted cost of goods sold by multiplying the unit sales in each month by the $15 cost per unit. Compute the cost of the June 30 ending inventory by multiplying the expected units available at that date by the $15 cost per unit.

● The selling expense budget has only two items. Find the amount of the sales representatives' commissions by multiplying the expected dollar sales in each month by the 12.5% commission rate. Then include the sales manager's salary of $3,500 in April and $4,000 in May and June.

● The general and administrative expense budget should show three items. Administrative salaries are fixed at $8,000 per month, and depreciation is $5,000 per month. Budget the monthly interest expense on the long-term note by multiplying its $200,000 balance by the 0.9% monthly interest rate.

● Determine the amounts of cash sales in each month by multiplying the budgeted sales by 30%. Add to this amount the credit sales of the prior month (computed as 70% of prior month's sales). April's cash receipts from collecting receivables equals the March 31 balance of $175,000. The expected June 30 accounts receivable balance equals 70% of June's total budgeted sales.

● Determine expected cash payments on accounts payable for each month by making them equal to the merchandise purchases in the prior month. The payments for April equal the March 31 balance of accounts payable shown on the beginning balance sheet. The June 30 balance of accounts payable equals merchandise purchases for June.

- Prepare the cash budget by combining the given information and the amounts of cash receipts and cash payments on account that you computed. Complete the cash budget for each month by either borrowing enough to raise the preliminary balance to the minimum or paying off short-term debt as much as the balance allows without falling below the minimum. Show the ending balance of the short-term note in the budget.

- Prepare the budgeted income statement by combining the budgeted items for all three months. Determine the income before income taxes and multiply it by the 35% rate to find the quarter's income tax expense.

- The budgeted statement of retained earnings should show the March 31 balance plus the quarter's net income minus the quarter's dividends.

- The budgeted balance sheet includes updated balances for all items that appear in the beginning balance sheet and an additional liability for unpaid income taxes. Amounts for all asset, liability, and equity accounts can be found either in the budgets, other calculations, or by adding amounts found there to the beginning balances.

SOLUTION

1.

	A	B	C	D	E
1	**Calculation of Unit Sales**	**April**	**May**	**June**	**July**
2	Prior period's unit sales	10,000	10,500	11,025	11,576
3	Plus 5% growth*	500	525	551	579
4	Projected unit sales	10,500	11,025	11,576	12,155
5					

*Rounded to nearest whole unit

	A	B	C	D	E
1	**Sales Budget**	**April**	**May**	**June**	**Quarter**
2	Projected unit sales	10,500	11,025	11,576	
3	Selling price per unit	× $ 25	× $ 25	× $ 25	
4	Projected sales	$262,500	$275,625	$289,400	$827,525
5					

2.

	A	B	C	D	E
1	**Purchases Budget**	**April**	**May**	**June**	**Quarter**
2	Next period's unit sales (part 1)	11,025	11,576	12,155	
3	Ending inventory percent	× 80%	× 80%	× 80%	
4	Desired ending inventory (units)	8,820	9,261	9,724	
5	Current period's unit sales (part 1)	10,500	11,025	11,576	
6	Units to be available	19,320	20,286	21,300	
7	Less: Beginning inventory (units)	8,400	8,820	9,261	
8	Units to be purchased	10,920	11,466	12,039	
9	Budgeted cost per unit	× $ 15	× $ 15	× $ 15	
10	Budgeted purchases	$163,800	$171,990	$180,585	$516,375
11					

3.

	A	B	C	D	E
1	**Selling Expense Budget**	**April**	**May**	**June**	**Quarter**
2	Budgeted sales (part 1)	$262,500	$275,625	$289,400	$827,525
3	Commission percent	× 12.5%	× 12.5%	× 12.5%	× 12.5%
4	Sales commissions*	32,813	34,453	36,175	103,441
5	Manager's salary	3,500	4,000	4,000	11,500
6	Budgeted selling expenses*	$ 36,313	$ 38,453	$ 40,175	$114,941
7					

*Rounded to the nearest dollar

4.

	A	B	C	D	E
1	**General and Administrative Expense Budget**	**April**	**May**	**June**	**Quarter**
2	Administrative salaries	$ 8,000	$ 8,000	$ 8,000	$24,000
3	Depreciation	5,000	5,000	5,000	15,000
4	Interest on long-term note payable (0.9% × $200,000)	1,800	1,800	1,800	5,400
5	Budgeted expenses	$14,800	$14,800	$14,800	$44,400
6					

5.

	A	B	C	D	E
1	**Schedule of Cash Receipts from Sales**	**April**	**May**	**June**	**Quarter**
2	Budgeted sales (part 1)	$262,500	$275,625	$289,400	
3	Ending accounts receivable (70%)	$183,750	$192,938	$202,580	
4	Cash receipts				
5	Cash sales (30% of budgeted sales)	$ 78,750	$ 82,687	$ 86,820	$248,257
6	Collections of prior month's receivables	175,000*	183,750	192,938	551,688
7	Total cash to be collected	$253,750	$266,437	$279,758	$799,945
8					

*March 31 Accounts Receivable balance (from Balance Sheet)

6.

	A	B	C	D	E
1	**Schedule of Cash Payments to Suppliers**	**April**	**May**	**June**	**Quarter**
2	Cash payments (equal to prior month's				
3	purchases)	$156,000*	$163,800	$171,990	$491,790
4	Expected June 30 balance of accounts				
5	payable (June purchases)			$180,585	
6					

*March 31 Accounts Payable balance (from Balance Sheet)

7.

	A	B	C	D
1	**Cash Budget**	**April**	**May**	**June**
2	Beginning cash balance	$ 50,000	$ 89,517	$ 50,000
3	Cash receipts (part 5)	253,750	266,437	279,758
4	Total cash available	303,750	355,954	329,758
5	Cash payments			
6	Payments for merchandise (part 6)	156,000	163,800	171,990
7	Sales commissions (part 3)	32,813	34,453	36,175
8	Salaries			
9	Sales (part 3)	3,500	4,000	4,000
10	Administrative (part 4)	8,000	8,000	8,000
11	Interest on long-term note (part 4)	1,800	1,800	1,800
12	Dividends		100,000	
13	Equipment purchase			55,000
14	Interest on short-term notes			
15	April ($12,000 × 1%)	120		
16	June ($6,099 × 1%)			61
17	Total cash payments	202,233	312,053	277,026
18	Preliminary balance	101,517	43,901	52,732
19	Loan activity			
20	Additional loan		6,099	
21	Loan repayment	(12,000)		(2,732)
22	Ending cash balance	$ 89,517	$ 50,000	$ 50,000
23	Ending short-term notes	$ 0	$ 6,099	$ 3,367
24				

8.

WILD WOOD COMPANY
Budgeted Income Statement
For Quarter Ended June 30, 2015

Sales (part 1)		$827,525
Cost of goods sold*		496,515
Gross profit		331,010
Operating expenses		
Sales commissions (part 3)	$103,441	
Sales salaries (part 3)	11,500	
Administrative salaries (part 4)	24,000	
Depreciation (part 4)	15,000	
Interest on long-term note (part 4)	5,400	
Interest on short-term notes (part 7)	181	
Total operating expenses		159,522
Income before income taxes		171,488
Income taxes (35%)		60,021
Net income		$111,467

WILD WOOD COMPANY
Budgeted Statement of Retained Earnings
For Quarter Ended June 30, 2015

Beginning retained earnings (Mar. 31 bal.)	$138,000
Net income	111,467
	249,467
Less: Cash dividends (Mar. 31 bal.)	100,000
Ending retained earnings	$149,467

*33,101 units sold @ $15 per unit

WILD WOOD COMPANY
Budgeted Balance Sheet
June 30, 2015

Assets			Liabilities and Equity		
Cash (part 7)	$ 50,000		Accounts payable (part 6)	$180,585	
Accounts receivable (part 5)	202,580		Short-term notes payable (part 7)	3,367	
Inventory (9,724 units @ $15 each)	145,860		Income taxes payable	60,021	
Total current assets		$398,440	Total current liabilities		$243,973
			Long-term note payable (Mar. 31 bal.) ...		200,000
			Total liabilities		443,973
Equipment (Mar. 31 bal. plus purchase)	535,000		Common stock (Mar. 31 bal.)	235,000	
Less: Accumulated depreciation			Retained earnings	149,467	
(Mar. 31 bal. plus depreciation expense)	105,000	430,000	Total stockholders' equity		384,467
Total assets		$828,440	Total liabilities and equity		$828,440

Merchandise Purchases Budget

Exhibit 7A.1 shows the master budget sequence for a merchandiser. Unlike a manufacturing company, a merchandiser must prepare a merchandise purchases budget rather than a production budget. In addition, a merchandiser does not prepare direct materials, direct labor, or factory overhead budgets. In this appendix we show the merchandise purchases budget for Hockey Den (HD), a retailer of hockey sticks.

P4

Prepare each component of a master budget and link each to the budgeting process—for a merchandising company.

EXHIBIT 7A.1

Master Budget Sequence—Merchandiser

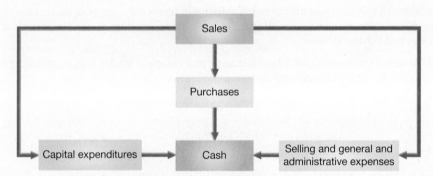

Budgeted financial statements

Merchandise purchases budget preparation.   Toronto Sticks Company is an exclusive supplier of hockey sticks to Hockey Den, meaning that the companies rely on the same budgeted sales figures (Exhibit 7.4) in preparing budgets. A merchandiser usually expresses a **merchandise purchases budget** in both units and dollars. Exhibit 7A.2 shows the general layout for this budget in equation form. If this formula is expressed in units and only one product is involved, we can compute the number of dollars of inventory to be purchased for the budget by multiplying the units to be purchased by the cost per unit.

EXHIBIT 7A.2

General Formula for Merchandise Purchases Budget

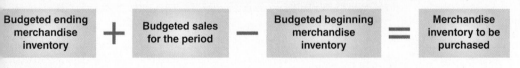

To illustrate, after assessing the cost of keeping inventory along with the risk and cost of inventory shortages, HD decided that the number of units in its inventory at each month-end should equal 90% of next month's predicted sales. For example, inventory at the end of October should equal 90% of budgeted November sales, and the November ending inventory should equal 90% of budgeted December sales, and so on. Also, HD expects the September 2015 per unit purchase cost of $60 to remain unchanged through January 2016. This information along with knowledge of 1,010 units in inventory at September 30 (given) allows the company to prepare the merchandise purchases budget shown in Exhibit 7A.3.

EXHIBIT 7A.3

Merchandise Purchases
Budget

	A	B	C	D
1		**HOCKEY DEN**		
2		**Merchandise Purchases Budget**		
3		**October 2015–December 2015**		
4		**October**	**November**	**December**
5	Next month's budgeted sales (units)	800	1,400	900
6	Ratio of inventory to future sales	× 90%	× 90%	× 90%
7	Budgeted ending inventory (units)	720	1,260	810
8	Add: Budgeted sales (units)	1,000	800	1,400
9	Required units of available merchandise	1,720	2,060	2,210
10	Deduct: Beginning inventory (units)	1,010*	720	1,260
11	Total units to be purchased	710	1,340	950
12				
13	Budgeted cost per unit	$ 60	$ 60	$ 60
14	Budgeted cost of merchandise purchases	$42,600	$80,400	$57,000
15				

*Does not comply with company policy.

The first three lines of HD's merchandise purchases budget determine the required ending inventories (in units). Budgeted unit sales are then added to the desired ending inventory to give the required units of available merchandise. We then subtract beginning inventory to determine the budgeted number of units to be purchased. The last line is the budgeted cost of the purchases, computed by multiplying the number of units to be purchased by the predicted cost per unit.

Other Master Budget Differences—Merchandiser vs. Manufacturer   In addition to preparing a purchases budget instead of production, direct materials, direct labor, and overhead budgets, other key differences in master budgets for merchandisers include:

1. Depreciation expense is included in the general and administrative expense budget of the merchandiser. For the manufacturer, depreciation on manufacturing assets is included in the factory overhead budget and treated as a product cost.

2. The budgeted balance sheet for the merchandiser will report only one asset for inventory. The balance sheet for the manufacturer will typically report three inventory assets: raw materials, work in process, and finished goods.

See Need-To-Know Comprehensive 2 for illustration of a complete master budget, including budgeted financial statements, for a merchandising company.

NEED-TO-KNOW 7-4

Merchandise
Purchases Budget

P4

In preparing monthly budgets for the third quarter, a company budgeted sales of 120 units for July and 140 units for August. Management wants each month's ending inventory to be 60% of next month's sales. The June 30 inventory consists of 72 units. How many units should be purchased in July?

Solution

Purchases Budget	July
Next month's budgeted sales (units)............	140
Ratio of inventory to future sales	× 60%
Budgeted ending inventory (units)	84
Add: Budgeted sales (units)...................	+120
Required units of available merchandise	204
Deduct: Beginning inventory (units)	− 72
Units to be purchased.......................	132

Do More: QS 7-28, QS 7-29,
QS 7-30, E 7-23

Summary

C1 **Describe the benefits of budgeting and the process of budget administration.** Planning is a management responsibility of critical importance to business success. Budgeting is the process management uses to formalize its plans. Budgeting promotes management analysis and focuses its attention on the future. Budgeting also provides a basis for evaluating performance, serves as a source of motivation, is a means of coordinating activities, and communicates management's plans and instructions to employees. Budgeting is a detailed activity that requires administration. At least three aspects are important: budget committee, budget reporting, and budget timing. A budget committee oversees the budget preparation. The budget period pertains to the time period for which the budget is prepared such as a year or month.

C2 Describe a master budget and the process of preparing it. A master budget is a formal overall plan for a company. It consists of plans for business operations and capital expenditures, plus the financial results of those activities. The budgeting process begins with a sales budget. Based on expected sales volume, companies can budget production and manufacturing costs, selling expenses, and administrative expenses. Next, the capital expenditures budget is prepared, followed by the cash budget and budgeted financial statements. Merchandisers must budget merchandise purchases instead of manufacturing costs.

A1 Analyze expense planning using activity-based budgeting. Activity-based budgeting requires management to identify activities performed by departments, plan necessary activity levels, identify resources required to perform these activities, and budget the resources.

P1 Prepare the operating budget components of a master budget—for a manufacturing company. From budgeted sales a manufacturer prepares a *production budget*. A *manufacturing budget* shows the budgeted production costs for direct materials, direct labor, and overhead. *Selling* and *general and administrative expense* budgets complete the operating budgets of the master budget.

P2 Prepare a cash budget. The cash budget shows expected cash inflows and outflows during a budgeting period. This budget helps management maintain the company's desired cash balance.

P3 Prepare budgeted financial statements. The operating budgets, capital expenditures budget, and cash budget contain much of the information to prepare a budgeted income statement for the budget period and a budgeted balance sheet at the end of the budget period. Budgeted financial statements show the expected financial consequences of the planned activities described in the budgets.

P4A Prepare each component of a master budget and link each to the budgeting process—for a merchandising company. The term *master budget* refers to a collection of individual component budgets. Each component budget is designed to guide persons responsible for activities covered by that component. A master budget must reflect the components of a company and their interaction in pursuit of company goals.

Guidance Answers to Decision Maker

Entrepreneur   You must deal with two issues. First, because fashions and designs frequently change, you cannot heavily rely on previous budgets. As a result, you must carefully analyze the market to understand what designs are in vogue. This will help you plan the product mix and estimate demand. The second issue is the budgeting period. An annual sales budget may be unreliable because tastes can quickly change. Your best bet might be to prepare monthly and quarterly sales budgets that you continuously monitor and revise.

Environmental Manager   You are unlikely to have data on this new position to use in preparing your budget. In this situation, you can use activity-based budgeting. This requires developing a list of activities to conduct, the resources required to perform these activities, and the expenses associated with these resources. You should challenge yourself to be absolutely certain that the listed activities are necessary and that the listed resources are required.

Key Terms

Activity-based budgeting (ABB)	Continuous budgeting	Merchandise purchases budget
Budget	Direct labor budget	Production budget
Budgeted balance sheet	Direct materials budget	Rolling budgets
Budgeted income statement	Factory overhead budget	Safety stock
Budgeting	General and administrative expense budget	Sales budget
Capital expenditures budget		Selling expense budget
Cash budget	Master budget	

Multiple Choice Quiz   Answers at end of chapter

1. A plan that reports the units of merchandise to be produced by a manufacturing company during the budget period is called a
   a. Capital expenditures budget.
   b. Cash budget.
   c. Production budget.
   d. Manufacturing budget.
   e. Sales budget.

2.A A hardware store has budgeted sales of $36,000 for its power tool department in July. Management wants to have $7,000 in power tool inventory at the end of July. Its beginning inventory of power tools is expected to be $6,000. What is the budgeted dollar amount of merchandise purchases?
   a. $36,000   c. $42,000   e. $37,000
   b. $43,000   d. $35,000

3. A store has the following budgeted sales for the next five months.

May	$210,000
June	186,000
July	180,000
August	220,000
September	240,000

Cash sales are 25% of total sales and all credit sales are expected to be collected in the month following the sale. The total amount of cash expected to be received from customers in September is

a. $240,000   **c.** $60,000   **e.** $220,000
b. $225,000   **d.** $165,000

4. A plan that shows the expected cash inflows and cash outflows during the budget period, including receipts from loans needed to maintain a minimum cash balance and repayments of such loans, is called

a. A rolling budget.   **d.** A cash budget.
b. An income statement.   **e.** An operating budget.
c. A balance sheet.

5. The following sales are predicted for a company's next four months.

	September	October	November	December
Unit sales ...	480	560	600	480

Each month's ending inventory of finished goods should be 30% of the next month's sales. At September 1, the finished goods inventory is 140 units. The budgeted production of units for October is

a. 572 units.   **c.** 548 units.   **e.** 180 units.
b. 560 units.   **d.** 600 units.

A   *Superscript letter A denotes assignments based on Appendix 7A, which relates to budgets for merchandising companies.*

🛈 Icon denotes assignments that involve decision making.

Discussion Questions

1. 🛈 Identify at least three roles that budgeting plays in helping managers control and monitor a business.

2. What two common benchmarks can be used to evaluate actual performance? Which of the two is generally more useful?

3. 🛈 What is the benefit of continuous budgeting?

4. Identify three usual time horizons for short-term planning and budgets.

5. 🛈 Why should each department participate in preparing its own budget?

6. 🛈 How does budgeting help management coordinate and plan business activities?

7. 🛈 Why is the sales budget so important to the budgeting process?

8. What is a selling expense budget? What is a capital expenditures budget?

9. Budgeting promotes good decision making by requiring managers to conduct _____ and by focusing their attention on the _____.

10. Google prepares a cash budget. What is a cash budget? Why must operating budgets and the capital expenditures budget be prepared before the cash budget?   **GOOGLE**

11. Apple regularly uses budgets. What is the difference between a production budget and a manufacturing budget?   **APPLE**

12. 🛈 Would a manager of an Apple retail store participate more in budgeting than a manager at the corporate offices? Explain.   **APPLE**

13. 🛈 Does the manager of a Samsung distribution center participate in long-term budgeting? Explain.   **Samsung**

14. 🛈 Assume that Samsung's consumer electronics division is charged with preparing a master budget. Identify the participants—for example, the sales manager for the sales budget—and describe the information each person provides in preparing the master budget.   **Samsung**

🔲 connect

QUICK STUDY

QS 7-1
Budget motivation   C1

The motivation of employees is one goal of budgeting. Identify three guidelines that organizations should follow if budgeting is to serve effectively as a source of motivation for employees.

QS 7-2
Budgeting process   C1

🛈

Good management includes good budgeting. (1) Explain why the bottom-up approach to budgeting is considered a more successful management technique than a top-down approach. (2) Provide an example of implementation of the bottom-up approach to budgeting.

Identify which of the following sets of items are necessary components of the master budget.

_____ **1.** Operating budgets, historical income statement, and budgeted balance sheet.

_____ **2.** Prior sales reports, capital expenditures budget, and financial budgets.

_____ **3.** Sales budget, operating budgets, and historical financial budgets.

_____ **4.** Operating budgets, financial budgets, and capital expenditures budget.

QS 7-3
Components of a master budget
C2

Grace manufactures and sells miniature digital cameras for $250 each. 1,000 units were sold in May, and management forecasts 4% growth in unit sales each month. Determine (a) the number of units of camera sales and (b) the dollar amount of camera sales for the month of June.

QS 7-4
Sales budget P1

Zilly Co. predicts sales of $400,000 for June. Zilly pays a sales manager a monthly salary of $6,000 and a commission of 8% of sales dollars. Prepare a selling expense budget for the month of June.

QS 7-5
Selling expense budget
P1

Liza's predicts sales of $40,000 for May and $52,000 for June. Assume 60% of Liza's sales are for cash. The remaining 40% are credit sales; these customers pay in the month following the sale. Compute the budgeted cash receipts for June.

QS 7-6
Cash budget P2

Zortek Corp. budgets production of 400 units in January and 200 units in February. Each finished unit requires five pounds of raw material Z, which costs $2 per pound. Each month's ending inventory of raw materials should be 40% of the following month's budgeted production. The January 1 raw materials inventory has 130 pounds of Z. Prepare a direct materials budget for January.

QS 7-7
Manufacturing: Direct materials budget P1

Tora Co. plans to produce 1,020 units in July. Each unit requires two hours of direct labor. The direct labor rate is $20 per hour. Prepare a direct labor budget for July.

QS 7-8
Manufacturing: Direct labor budget P1

Scora, Inc., is preparing its master budget for the quarter ending March 31. It sells a single product for $50 per unit. Budgeted sales for the next four months follow. Prepare a sales budget for the months of January, February, and March.

QS 7-9
Sales budget
P1

	January	February	March	April
Sales in units	1,200	2,000	1,600	1,400

X-Tel budgets sales of $60,000 for April, $100,000 for May, and $80,000 for June. In addition, sales are 40% cash and 60% on credit. All credit sales are collected in the month following the sale. The April 1 balance in accounts receivable is $15,000. Prepare a schedule of budgeted cash receipts for April, May, and June.

QS 7-10
Cash receipts budget P2

X-Tel budgets sales of $60,000 for April, $100,000 for May, and $80,000 for June. In addition, sales commissions are 10% of sales dollars and the company pays a sales manager a salary of $6,000 per month. Sales commissions and salaries are paid in the month incurred. Prepare a selling expense budget for April, May, and June.

QS 7-11
Selling expense budget
P1

Champ, Inc., predicts the following sales in units for the coming three months:

QS 7-12
Manufacturing:
Production budget
P1

	May	June	July
Sales in units	180	200	240

Each month's ending inventory of finished units should be 60% of the next month's sales. The April 30 finished goods inventory is 108 units. Compute Champ's budgeted production (in units) for May.

QS 7-13
Manufacturing: Direct materials budget
P1

Miami Solar manufactures solar panels for industrial use. The company budgets production of 5,000 units (solar panels) in July and 5,300 units in August. Each unit requires 3 pounds of direct materials, which cost $6 per pound. The company's policy is to maintain direct materials inventory equal to 30% of the next month's direct materials requirement. As of June 30, the company has 4,500 pounds of direct materials in inventory, which complies with the policy. Prepare a direct materials budget for July.

QS 7-14
Manufacturing: Direct labor budget   P1

Miami Solar budgets production of 5,000 solar panels in July. Each unit requires 4 hours of direct labor at a rate of $16 per hour. Prepare a direct labor budget for July.

QS 7-15
Manufacturing: Factory overhead budget   P1

Miami Solar budgets production of 5,300 solar panels for August. Each unit requires 4 hours of direct labor at a rate of $16 per hour. Variable factory overhead is budgeted to be 70% of direct labor cost, and fixed factory overhead is $180,000 per month. Prepare a factory overhead budget for August.

QS 7-16
Manufacturing:
Production budget
P1

Atlantic Surf manufactures surfboards. The company's sales budget for the next three months is shown below. In addition, company policy is to maintain finished goods inventory equal (in units) to 40% of the next month's unit sales. As of June 30, the company has 1,600 finished surfboards in inventory, which complies with the policy. Prepare a production budget for the months of July and August.

	July	August	September
Sales (in units)	4,000	6,500	3,500

QS 7-17
Manufacturing:
Production budget
P1

Forrest Company manufactures phone chargers and has a JIT policy that ending inventory must equal 10% of the next month's sales. It estimates that October's actual ending inventory will consist of 40,000 units. November and December sales are estimated to be 400,000 and 350,000 units, respectively. Compute the number of units to be produced that would appear on the company's production budget for the month of November.

QS 7-18
Manufacturing: Factory overhead budget   P1

Hockey Pro budgets production of 3,900 hockey pucks during May. The company assigns variable overhead at the rate of $1.50 per unit. Fixed overhead equals $46,000 per month. Prepare a factory overhead budget for May.

QS 7-19
Cash receipts   P2

Music World reports the following sales forecast: August, $150,000; September, $170,000. Cash sales are normally 40% of total sales and all credit sales are expected to be collected in the month following the date of sale. Prepare a schedule of cash receipts for September.

QS 7-20
Cash receipts, with uncollectible accounts
P2

The Guitar Shoppe reports the following sales forecast: August, $150,000; September, $170,000. Cash sales are normally 40% of total sales, 55% of credit sales are collected in the month following sale, and the remaining 5% of credit sales are written off as uncollectible. Prepare a schedule of cash receipts for September.

QS 7-21
Cash receipts, with uncollectible accounts   P2

Wells Company reports the following sales forecast: September, $55,000; October, $66,000; and November, $80,000. All sales are on account. Collections of credit sales are received as follows: 25% in the month of sale, 60% in the first month after sale, and 10% in the second month after sale. 5% of all credit sales are written off as uncollectible. Prepare a schedule of cash receipts for November.

QS 7-22
Computing budgeted accounts receivable
P2

Lighthouse Company anticipates total sales for June and July of $420,000 and $398,000, respectively. Cash sales are normally 60% of total sales. Of the credit sales, 20% are collected in the same month as the sale, 70% are collected during the first month after the sale, and the remaining 10% are collected in the second month. Determine the amount of accounts receivable reported on the company's budgeted balance sheet as of July 31.

QS 7-23
Budgeted loan activity
P2

Messers Company is preparing a cash budget for February. The company has $20,000 cash at the beginning of February and anticipates $75,000 in cash receipts and $100,250 in cash disbursements during February. What amount, if any, must the company borrow during February to maintain a $5,000 cash balance? The company has no loans outstanding on February 1.

Use the following information to prepare a cash budget for the month ended on March 31 for Gado Company. The budget should show expected cash receipts and cash disbursements for the month of March and the balance expected on March 31.

a. Beginning cash balance on March 1, $72,000.
b. Cash receipts from sales, $300,000.
c. Budgeted cash disbursements for purchases, $140,000.
d. Budgeted cash disbursements for salaries, $80,000.
e. Other budgeted cash expenses, $45,000.
f. Cash repayment of bank loan, $20,000.

QS 7-24
Cash budget
P2

Following are selected accounts for a company. For each account, indicate whether it will appear on a budgeted income statement (BIS) or a budgeted balance sheet (BBS). If an item will not appear on either budgeted financial statement, label it NA.

QS 7-25
Budgeted financial statements
P3

Sales	_____	Interest expense on note payable . . .	_____
Office salaries expense	_____	Cash dividends paid	_____
Accumulated depreciation	_____	Bank loan owed	_____
Amortization expense	_____	Cost of goods sold	_____

Gordands purchased $600,000 of merchandise in August and expects to purchase $720,000 in September. Merchandise purchases are paid as follows: 25% in the month of purchase and 75% in the following month. Compute cash disbursements for merchandise for September.

QS 7-26[A]
Merchandising: Cash disbursements for merchandise P4

Meyer Co. forecasts merchandise purchases of $15,800 in January, $18,600 in February, and $20,200 in March; 40% of purchases are paid in the month of purchase and 60% are paid in the following month. At December 31 of the prior year, the balance of accounts payable (for December purchases) is $22,000. Prepare a schedule of cash disbursements for merchandise for each of the months of January, February, and March.

QS 7-27[A]
Merchandising: Cash disbursements for merchandise P4

Raider-X Company forecasts sales of 18,000 units for April. Beginning inventory is 3,000 units. The desired ending inventory is 30% higher than the beginning inventory. How many units should Raider-X purchase in April?

QS 7-28[A]
Merchandising: Computing purchases
P4

Lexi Company forecasts unit sales of 1,040,000 in April, 1,220,000 in May, 980,000 in June, and 1,020,000 in July. Beginning inventory on April 1 is 280,000 units, and the company wants to have 30% of next month's sales in inventory at the end of each month. Prepare a merchandise purchases budget for the months of April, May, and June.

QS 7-29[A]
Merchandising: Computing purchases
P4

Montel Company's July sales budget calls for sales of $600,000. The store expects to begin July with $50,000 of inventory and to end the month with $40,000 of inventory. Gross margin is typically 40% of sales. Determine the budgeted cost of merchandise purchases for July.

QS 7-30[A]
Merchandising: Purchases budget P4

Activity-based budgeting is a budget system based on *expected activities*. (1) Describe activity-based budgeting, and explain its preparation of budgets. (2) How does activity-based budgeting differ from traditional budgeting?

QS 7-31
Activity-based budgeting
A1

Royal Philips Electronics of the Netherlands reports sales of €25,400 million for a recent year. Assume that the company expects sales growth of 3 percent for the next year. Also assume that selling expenses are typically 20 percent of sales, while general and administrative expenses are 4 percent of sales.

1. Compute budgeted sales for the next year.
2. Assume budgeted sales for next year is €26,000 million, and then compute budgeted selling expenses and budgeted general and administrative expenses for the next year.

QS 7-32
Operating budgets
P1

EXERCISES

Exercise 7-1

Budget consequences

C1

Participatory budgeting can sometimes lead to negative consequences. From the following list of outcomes that can arise from participatory budgeting, identify those with potentially *negative* consequences.

_____ **a.** Budgetary slack will not be available to meet budgeted results.

_____ **b.** Employees might understate expense budgets.

_____ **c.** Employees might commit unethical or fraudulent acts to meet budgeted results.

_____ **d.** Employees set sales targets too high.

_____ **e.** Employees always spend budgeted amounts, even if on unnecessary items.

_____ **f.** Employees might understate sales budgets and overstate expense budgets.

Exercise 7-2

Master budget definitions

C2

Match the definitions 1 through 9 with the term or phrase *a* through *i*.

A. Budget

B. Merchandise purchases budget

C. Cash budget

D. Safety stock

E. Budgeted income statement

F. General and administrative expense budget

G. Sales budget

H. Master budget

I. Budgeted balance sheet

_____ **1.** A comprehensive business plan that includes specific plans for expected sales, the units of product to be produced, the merchandise or materials to be purchased, the expenses to be incurred, the long-term assets to be purchased, and the amounts of cash to be borrowed or loans to be repaid, as well as a budgeted income statement and balance sheet.

_____ **2.** A quantity of inventory or materials over the minimum to reduce the risk of running short.

_____ **3.** A plan showing the units of goods to be sold and the sales to be derived; the usual starting point in the budgeting process.

_____ **4.** An accounting report that presents predicted amounts of the company's revenues and expenses for the budgeting period.

_____ **5.** An accounting report that presents predicted amounts of the company's assets, liabilities, and equity balances at the end of the budget period.

_____ **6.** A plan that shows the units or costs of merchandise to be purchased by a merchandising company during the budget period.

_____ **7.** A formal statement of a company's future plans, usually expressed in monetary terms.

_____ **8.** A plan that shows predicted operating expenses not included in the selling expenses budget.

_____ **9.** A plan that shows the expected cash inflows and cash outflows during the budget period, including receipts from any loans needed to maintain a minimum cash balance and repayments of such loans.

Exercise 7-3

Manufacturing:
Production budget

P1

Hospitable Co. provides the following sales forecast for the next four months:

	April	May	June	July
Sales (units)	500	580	540	620

The company wants to end each month with ending finished goods inventory equal to 25% of next month's sales. Finished goods inventory on April 1 is 190 units. Assume July's budgeted production is 540 units. Prepare a production budget for the months of April, May, and June.

Exercise 7-4

Manufacturing: Direct materials budget P1

Refer to the information in Exercise 7-3. In addition, each finished unit requires five pounds of raw materials and the company wants to end each month with raw materials inventory equal to 30% of next month's production needs. Beginning raw materials inventory for April was 663 pounds. Assume direct materials cost $4 per pound. Prepare a direct materials budget for April, May, and June.

The production budget for Manner Company shows units to be produced as follows: July, 620; August, 680; September, 540. Each unit produced requires two hours of direct labor. The direct labor rate is currently $20 per hour but is predicted to be $21 per hour in September. Prepare a direct labor budget for the months July, August, and September.

Exercise 7-5
Manufacturing: Direct labor budget P1

Rida, Inc., a manufacturer in a seasonal industry, is preparing its direct materials budget for the second quarter. It plans production of 240,000 units in the second quarter and 52,500 units in the third quarter. Raw material inventory is 43,200 pounds at the beginning of the second quarter. Other information follows. Prepare a direct materials budget for the second quarter.

Exercise 7-6
Manufacturing: Direct materials budget
P1

Direct materials	Each unit requires 0.60 pounds of a key raw material, priced at $175 per pound. The company plans to end each quarter with an ending inventory of materials equal to 30% of next quarter's budgeted materials requirements.

Addison Co. budgets production of 2,400 units during the second quarter. In addition, information on its direct labor and its variable and fixed overhead is shown below. For the second quarter, prepare (1) a direct labor budget and (2) a factory overhead budget.

Exercise 7-7
Manufacturing: Direct labor and factory overhead budgets P1

Direct labor	Each finished unit requires 4 direct labor hours, at a cost of $9 per hour.
Variable overhead.	Applied at the rate of $11 per direct labor hour
Fixed overhead	Budgeted at $450,000 per quarter

---

Rad Co. provides the following sales forecast and production budget for the next four months:

Exercise 7-8
Manufacturing: Direct materials budget
P1

	April	May	June	July
Sales (units)	500	580	530	600
Budgeted production (units)	442	570	544	540

The company plans for finished goods inventory of 120 units at the end of June. In addition, each finished unit requires 5 pounds of raw materials and the company wants to end each month with raw materials inventory equal to 30% of next month's production needs. Beginning raw materials inventory for April was 663 pounds. Each finished unit requires 0.50 hours of direct labor at the rate of $16 per hour. The company budgets variable overhead at the rate of $20 per direct labor hour and budgets fixed overhead of $8,000 per month. Prepare a raw materials budget for April, May, and June.

Refer to Exercise 7-8. For April, May, and June, prepare (1) a direct labor budget and (2) a factory overhead budget.

Exercise 7-9
Manufacturing: Direct labor and factory overhead budgets P1

Blue Wave Co. predicts the following unit sales for the coming four months: September, 4,000 units; October, 5,000 units; November, 7,000 units; and December, 7,600 units. The company's policy is to maintain finished goods inventory equal to 60% of the next month's sales. At the end of August, the company had 2,400 finished units on hand. Prepare a production budget for each of the months of September, October, and November.

Exercise 7-10
Manufacturing: Production budget P1

Tyler Co. predicts the following unit sales for the next four months: April, 3,000 units; May, 4,000 units; June, 6,000 units; and July, 2,000 units. The company's policy is to maintain finished goods inventory equal to 30% of the next month's sales. At the end of March, the company had 900 finished units on hand. Prepare a production budget for each of the months of April, May, and June.

Exercise 7-11
Manufacturing: Production budget
P1

Exercise 7-12
Manufacturing:
Preparing production
budgets (for two periods)
P1

Check   Second quarter
production, 480,000 units

Electro Company manufactures an innovative automobile transmission for electric cars. Management predicts that ending finished goods inventory for the first quarter will be 75,000 units. The following unit sales of the transmissions are expected during the rest of the year: second quarter, 450,000 units; third quarter, 525,000 units; and fourth quarter, 475,000 units. Company policy calls for the ending finished goods inventory of a quarter to equal 20% of the next quarter's budgeted sales. Prepare a production budget for both the second and third quarters that shows the number of transmissions to manufacture. Ending inventory for the first quarter does not comply with company policy.

Exercise 7-13
Manufacturing: Direct
materials budget   P1

Electro Company budgets production of 450,000 transmissions in the second quarter and 520,000 transmissions in the third quarter. Each transmission requires 0.80 pounds of a key raw material. Electro Company aims to end each quarter with an ending inventory of direct materials equal to 20% of next quarter's budgeted materials requirements. Beginning inventory of this raw material is 72,000 pounds. Direct materials cost $1.70 per pound. Prepare a direct materials budget for the second quarter.

Exercise 7-14
Manufacturing: Direct
labor budget   P1

Branson Belts makes hand-crafted belts. The company budgets production of 4,500 belts during the second quarter. Each belt requires 4 direct labor hours, at a cost of $12 per hour. Prepare a direct labor budget for the second quarter.

Exercise 7-15
Manufacturing: Direct
materials, direct labor,
and overhead budgets
P1

MCO Leather Goods manufactures leather purses. Each purse requires 2 pounds of direct materials at a cost of $4 per pound and 0.8 direct labor hours at a rate of $16 per hour. Variable manufacturing overhead is charged at a rate of $2 per direct labor hour. Fixed manufacturing overhead is $10,000 per month. The company's policy is to end each month with direct materials inventory equal to 40% of the next month's materials requirement. At the end of August the company had 3,680 pounds of direct materials in inventory. The company's production budget reports the following. Prepare budgets for September *and* October for (1) direct materials, (2) direct labor, and (3) factory overhead.

Production Budget	September	October	November
Units to be produced	4,600	6,200	5,800

Exercise 7-16
Manufacturing: Direct
materials, direct labor,
and overhead budgets
P1

Ornamental Sculptures Mfg. manufactures garden sculptures. Each sculpture requires 8 pounds of direct materials at a cost of $3 per pound and 0.5 direct labor hours at a rate of $18 per hour. Variable manufacturing overhead is charged at a rate of $3 per direct labor hour. Fixed manufacturing overhead is $4,000 per month. The company's policy is to maintain direct materials inventory equal to 20% of the next month's materials requirement. At the end of March the company had 5,280 pounds of direct materials in inventory. The company's production budget reports the following. Prepare budgets for March *and* April for (1) direct materials, (2) direct labor, and (3) factory overhead.

Production Budget	March	April	May
Units to be produced	3,300	4,600	4,800

Exercise 7-17
Preparation of cash
budgets (for three
periods)

P2

Kayak Co. budgeted the following cash receipts (excluding cash receipts from loans received) and cash disbursements (excluding cash disbursements for loan principal and interest payments) for the first three months of next year.

	Cash Receipts	Cash Disbursements
January	$525,000	$475,000
February	400,000	350,000
March	450,000	525,000

According to a credit agreement with the company's bank, Kayak promises to have a minimum cash balance of $30,000 at each month-end. In return, the bank has agreed that the company can borrow up to $150,000 at an annual interest rate of 12%, paid on the last day of each month. The interest is computed based on the beginning balance of the loan for the month. The company repays loan principal with available cash on the last day of each month. The company has a cash balance of $30,000 and a loan balance of $60,000 at January 1. Prepare monthly cash budgets for each of the first three months of next year.

Check January ending cash balance, $30,000

Jasper Company has sales on account and for cash. Specifically, 70% of its sales are on account and 30% are for cash. Credit sales are collected in full in the month following the sale. The company forecasts sales of $525,000 for April, $535,000 for May, and $560,000 for June. The beginning balance of accounts receivable is $400,000 on April 1. Prepare a schedule of budgeted cash receipts for April, May, and June.

Exercise 7-18
Budgeted cash receipts
P2

Karim Corp. requires a minimum $8,000 cash balance. If necessary, loans are taken to meet this requirement at a cost of 1% interest per month (paid monthly). Any excess cash is used to repay loans at month-end. The cash balance on July 1 is $8,400 and the company has no outstanding loans. Forecasted cash receipts (other than for loans received) and forecasted cash payments (other than for loan or interest payments) follow. Prepare a cash budget for July, August, and September. Round interest payments to the nearest whole dollar.

Exercise 7-19
Cash budget
P2

	July	August	September
Cash receipts	$20,000	$26,000	$40,000
Cash disbursements	28,000	30,000	22,000

Foyert Corp. requires a minimum $30,000 cash balance. If necessary, loans are taken to meet this requirement at a cost of 1% interest per month (paid monthly). Any excess cash is used to repay loans at month-end. The cash balance on October 1 is $30,000 and the company has an outstanding loan of $10,000. Forecasted cash receipts (other than for loans received) and forecasted cash payments (other than for loan or interest payments) follow. Prepare a cash budget for October, November, and December. Round interest payments to the nearest whole dollar.

Exercise 7-20
Cash budget
P2

	October	November	December
Cash receipts.............	$110,000	$80,000	$100,000
Cash disbursements	120,000	75,000	80,000

Use the following information to prepare the September cash budget for PTO Manufacturing Co. The following information relates to expected cash receipts and cash disbursements for the month ended September 30.

a. Beginning cash balance, September 1, $40,000.

b. Budgeted cash receipts from sales in September, $255,000.

c. Raw materials are purchased on account. Purchase amounts are: August (actual), $80,000, and September (budgeted), $110,000. Payments for direct materials are made as follows: 65% in the month of purchase and 35% in the month following purchase.

d. Budgeted cash disbursements for direct labor in September, $40,000.

e. Budgeted depreciation expense for September, $4,000.

f. Other cash expenses budgeted for September, $60,000.

g. Accrued income taxes payable in September, $10,000.

h. Bank loan interest payable in September, $1,000.

Exercise 7-21
Manufacturing: Cash budget
P2

Mike's Motors Corp. manufactures motors for dirt bikes. The company requires a minimum $30,000 cash balance at each month-end. If necessary, the company takes a loan to meet this requirement, at a cost of 2% interest per month (paid at the end of each month). Any cash balance above $30,000 at month-end is used to repay loans. The cash balance on July 1 is $34,000, and the company has no outstanding loans at that time. Forecasted cash receipts and forecasted cash payments (other than for loan activity) are as follows. Prepare a cash budget for July, August, and September.

Exercise 7-22
Manufacturing: Cash budget
P2

	Cash Receipts	Cash Disbursements
July	$ 85,000	$113,000
August	111,000	99,900
September	150,000	127,400

Exercise 7-23[A]
Merchandising:
Preparation of purchases budgets (for three periods)
P4

Walker Company prepares monthly budgets. The current budget plans for a September ending inventory of 30,000 units. Company policy is to end each month with merchandise inventory equal to a specified percent of budgeted sales for the following month. Budgeted sales and merchandise purchases for the next three months follow.

1. Prepare the merchandise purchases budget for the months of July, August, and September.
2. Compute the ratio of ending inventory to the next month's sales for each budget prepared in part 1.
3. How many units are budgeted for sale in October?

	Sales (Units)	Purchases (Units)
July	180,000	200,250
August	315,000	308,250
September	270,000	259,500

Exercise 7-24[A]
Merchandising:
Preparation of a cash budget
P4

Use the following information to prepare the July cash budget for Acco Co. It should show expected cash receipts and cash disbursements for the month and the cash balance expected on July 31.

a. Beginning cash balance on July 1: $50,000.
b. Cash receipts from sales: 30% is collected in the month of sale, 50% in the next month, and 20% in the second month after sale (uncollectible accounts are negligible and can be ignored). Sales amounts are: May (actual), $1,720,000; June (actual), $1,200,000; and July (budgeted), $1,400,000.
c. Payments on merchandise purchases: 60% in the month of purchase and 40% in the month following purchase. Purchases amounts are: June (actual), $700,000; and July (budgeted), $750,000.
d. Budgeted cash disbursements for salaries in July: $275,000.
e. Budgeted depreciation expense for July: $36,000.
f. Other cash expenses budgeted for July: $200,000.
g. Accrued income taxes due in July: $80,000.
h. Bank loan interest paid in July: $6,600.

Check Ending cash balance, $122,400

Exercise 7-25[A]
Merchandising:
Preparing a budgeted income statement and balance sheet
P4

Use the information in Exercise 7-24 and the following additional information to prepare a budgeted income statement for the month of July and a budgeted balance sheet for July 31.

a. Cost of goods sold is 55% of sales.
b. Inventory at the end of June is $80,000 and at the end of July is $60,000.
c. Salaries payable on June 30 are $50,000 and are expected to be $60,000 on July 31.
d. The equipment account balance is $1,600,000 on July 31. On June 30, the accumulated depreciation on equipment is $280,000.
e. The $6,600 cash payment of interest represents the 1% monthly expense on a bank loan of $660,000.
f. Income taxes payable on July 31 are $30,720, and the income tax rate applicable to the company is 30%.
g. The only other balance sheet accounts are: Common Stock, with a balance of $600,000 on June 30; and Retained Earnings, with a balance of $964,000 on June 30.

Check Net income, $71,680; Total assets, $2,686,400

Exercise 7-26[A]
Merchandising:
Computing budgeted cash payments for purchases   **P4**

Hardy Company's cost of goods sold is consistently 60% of sales. The company plans to carry ending merchandise inventory for each month equal to 20% of the next month's budgeted cost of goods sold. All merchandise is purchased on credit, and 50% of the purchases made during a month is paid for in that month. Another 35% is paid for during the first month after purchase, and the remaining 15% is paid for during the second month after purchase. Expected sales are: August (actual), $325,000; September (actual), $320,000; October (estimated), $250,000; and November (estimated), $310,000. Use this information to determine October's expected cash payments for purchases.

Check Budgeted purchases: August, $194,400; October, $157,200

Exercise 7-27[A]
Merchandising:
Computing budgeted purchases and cost of goods sold   **P4**

Quick Dollar Company purchases all merchandise on credit. It recently budgeted the following month-end accounts payable balances and merchandise inventory balances. Cash payments on accounts payable during each month are expected to be: May, $1,600,000; June, $1,490,000; July, $1,425,000; and August, $1,495,000. Use the available information to compute the budgeted amounts of (1) merchandise purchases for June, July, and August and (2) cost of goods sold for June, July, and August.

[continued on next page]

	Accounts Payable	Merchandise Inventory
May 31	$150,000	$250,000
June 30	200,000	400,000
July 31	235,000	300,000
August 31	195,000	330,000

Check June purchases, $1,540,000; June cost of goods sold, $1,390,000

Big Sound, a merchandising company specializing in home computer speakers, budgets its monthly cost of goods sold to equal 70% of sales. Its inventory policy calls for ending inventory in each month to equal 20% of the next month's budgeted cost of goods sold. All purchases are on credit, and 25% of the purchases in a month is paid for in the same month. Another 60% is paid for during the first month after purchase, and the remaining 15% is paid for in the second month after purchase. The following sales budgets are set: July, $350,000; August, $290,000; September, $320,000; October, $275,000; and November, $265,000.

Compute the following: (1) budgeted merchandise purchases for July, August, September, and October; (2) budgeted payments on accounts payable for September and October; and (3) budgeted ending balances of accounts payable for September and October. (*Hint:* For part *1,* refer to Exhibits 7A.2 and 7A.3 for guidance, but note that budgeted sales are in dollars for this assignment.)

Exercise 7-28^A

Exercise 7-28A
Merchandising:
Computing budgeted accounts payable and purchases—sales forecast in dollars P4

Check July purchases, $236,600; Sept. payments on accts. pay., $214,235

Hector Company reports the following sales and purchases data. Payments for purchases are made in the month after purchase. Selling expenses are 10% of sales, administrative expenses are 8% of sales, and both are paid in the month of sale. Rent expense of $7,400 is paid monthly. Depreciation expense is $2,300 per month. Prepare a schedule of budgeted cash disbursements for August and September.

Exercise 7-29A
Merchandising:
Budgeted cash disbursements
P4

	July	August	September
Sales	$50,000	$72,000	$66,000
Purchases	14,400	19,200	21,600

Castor, Inc., is preparing its master budget for the quarter ended June 30. Budgeted sales and cash payments for merchandise for the next three months follow:

Exercise 7-30A
Merchandising: Cash budget
P4

Budgeted	April	May	June
Sales	$32,000	$40,000	$24,000
Cash payments for merchandise	20,200	16,800	17,200

Sales are 50% cash and 50% on credit. All credit sales are collected in the month following the sale. The March 30 balance sheet includes balances of $12,000 in cash, $12,000 in accounts receivable, $11,000 in accounts payable, and a $2,000 balance in loans payable. A minimum cash balance of $12,000 is required. Loans are obtained at the end of any month when a cash shortage occurs. Interest is 1% per month based on the beginning of the month loan balance and is paid at each month-end. If an excess balance of cash exists, loans are repaid at the end of the month. Operating expenses are paid in the month incurred and consist of sales commissions (10% of sales), shipping (2% of sales), office salaries ($5,000 per month), and rent ($3,000 per month). Prepare a cash budget for each of the months of April, May, and June (round all dollar amounts to the nearest whole dollar).

Kelsey is preparing its master budget for the quarter ended September 30. Budgeted sales and cash payments for merchandise for the next three months follow:

Exercise 7-31A
Merchandising: Cash budget
P4

Budgeted	July	August	September
Sales	$64,000	$80,000	$48,000
Cash payments for merchandise	40,400	33,600	34,400

Sales are 20% cash and 80% on credit. All credit sales are collected in the month following the sale. The June 30 balance sheet includes balances of $15,000 in cash; $45,000 in accounts receivable; $4,500 in accounts payable; and a $5,000 balance in loans payable. A minimum cash balance of $15,000 is required. Loans are obtained at the end of any month when a cash shortage occurs. Interest is 1% per month based on the beginning of the month loan balance and is paid at each month-end. If an excess balance of cash exists, loans are repaid at the end of the month. Operating expenses are paid in the month incurred and consist of sales commissions (10% of sales), office salaries ($4,000 per month), and rent ($6,500 per month). (1) Prepare a cash receipts budget for July, August, and September. (2) Prepare a cash budget for each of the months of July, August, and September. (Round all dollar amounts to the nearest whole dollar.)

Exercise 7-32ᴬ
Merchandising:
Budgeted balance sheet
P4

The following information is available for Zetrov Company:

a. The cash budget for March shows an ending bank loan of $10,000 and an ending cash balance of $50,000.

b. The sales budget for March indicates sales of $140,000. Accounts receivable are expected to be 70% of the current-month sales.

c. The merchandise purchases budget indicates that $89,000 in merchandise will be purchased on account in March. Purchases on account are paid 100% in the month following the purchase. Ending inventory for March is predicted to be 600 units at a cost of $35 each.

d. The budgeted income statement for March shows net income of $48,000. Depreciation expense of $1,000 and $26,000 in income tax expense were used in computing net income for March. Accrued taxes will be paid in April.

e. The balance sheet for February shows equipment of $84,000 with accumulated depreciation of $46,000, common stock of $25,000, and ending retained earnings of $8,000. There are no changes budgeted in the Equipment or Common Stock accounts.

Prepare a budgeted balance sheet for March.

Exercise 7-33ᴬ
Merchandising:
Budgeted income
statement
P4

Fortune, Inc., is preparing its master budget for the first quarter. The company sells a single product at a price of $25 per unit. Sales (in units) are forecasted at 45,000 for January, 55,000 for February, and 50,000 for March. Cost of goods sold is $14 per unit. Other expense information for the first quarter follows. Prepare a budgeted income statement for this first quarter.

Commissions	8% of sales dollars
Rent	$14,000 per month
Advertising	15% of sales dollars
Office salaries	$75,000 per month
Depreciation	$40,000 per month
Interest	15% annually on a $250,000 note payable
Tax rate	30%

Exercise 7-34
Activity-based budgeting
A1

Render Co. CPA is preparing activity-based budgets for 2015. The partners expect the firm to generate billable hours for the year as follows:

Data entry	2,200 hours
Auditing	4,800 hours
Tax	4,300 hours
Consulting	750 hours

The company pays $10 per hour to data-entry clerks, $40 per hour to audit personnel, $50 per hour to tax personnel, and $50 per hour to consulting personnel. Prepare a schedule of budgeted labor costs for 2015 using activity-based budgeting.

≣ connect

Black Diamond Company produces snow skis. Each ski requires 2 pounds of carbon fiber. The company's management predicts that 5,000 skis and 6,000 pounds of carbon fiber will be in inventory on June 30 of the current year and that 150,000 skis will be sold during the next (third) quarter. A set of two skis sells for $300. Management wants to end the third quarter with 3,500 skis and 4,000 pounds of carbon fiber in inventory. Carbon fiber can be purchased for $15 per pound. Each ski requires 0.5 hours of direct labor at $20 per hour. Variable overhead is applied at the rate of $8 per direct labor hour. The company budgets fixed overhead of $1,782,000 for the quarter.

Required

1. Prepare the third-quarter production budget for skis.
2. Prepare the third-quarter direct materials (carbon fiber) budget; include the dollar cost of purchases.
3. Prepare the direct labor budget for the third quarter.
4. Prepare the factory overhead budget for the third quarter.

PROBLEM SET A

Problem 7-1A
Manufacturing:
Preparing production and manufacturing budgets

C2   P1

Check   (1) Units manuf.,
148,500;
         (2) Cost of carbon
fiber purchases, $4,425,000

Built-Tight is preparing its master budget for the quarter ended September 30, 2015. Budgeted sales and cash payments for product costs for the quarter follow:

Problem 7-2A
Manufacturing: Cash budget

P2

	A	B	C	D
1		**July**	**August**	**September**
2	Budgeted sales	$64,000	$80,000	$48,000
3	Budgeted cash payments for			
4	Direct materials	16,160	13,440	13,760
5	Direct labor	4,040	3,360	3,440
6	Factory overhead	20,200	16,800	17,200
7				

Sales are 20% cash and 80% on credit. All credit sales are collected in the month following the sale. The June 30 balance sheet includes balances of $15,000 in cash; $45,000 in accounts receivable; $4,500 in accounts payable; and a $5,000 balance in loans payable. A minimum cash balance of $15,000 is required. Loans are obtained at the end of any month when a cash shortage occurs. Interest is 1% per month based on the beginning of the month loan balance and is paid at each month-end. If an excess balance of cash exists, loans are repaid at the end of the month. Operating expenses are paid in the month incurred and consist of sales commissions (10% of sales), office salaries ($4,000 per month), and rent ($6,500 per month).

1. Prepare a cash receipts budget for July, August, and September.
2. Prepare a cash budget for each of the months of July, August, and September. (Round amounts to the dollar.)

Merline Manufacturing makes its product for $75 per unit and sells it for $150 per unit. The sales staff receives a 10% commission on the sale of each unit. Its December income statement follows.

Problem 7-3A
Manufacturing:
Preparation and analysis of budgeted income statements

P3

MERLINE MANUFACTURING
Income Statement
For Month Ended December 31, 2015

Sales	$2,250,000
Cost of goods sold	1,125,000
Gross profit	1,125,000
Operating expenses	
Sales commissions (10%)	225,000
Advertising	250,000
Store rent	30,000
Administrative salaries	45,000
Depreciation—Office equipment	50,000
Other expenses	10,000
Total expenses	610,000
Net income	$ 515,000

Management expects December's results to be repeated in January, February, and March of 2016 without any changes in strategy. Management, however, has an alternative plan. It believes that unit sales will increase at a rate of 10% *each* month for the next three months (beginning with January) if the item's selling price is reduced to $125 per unit and advertising expenses are increased by 15% and remain at that level for all three months. The cost of its product will remain at $75 per unit, the sales staff will continue to earn a 10% commission, and the remaining expenses will stay the same.

Required

Check (1) Budgeted net income: January, $196,250; February, $258,125; March, $326,187

1. Prepare budgeted income statements for each of the months of January, February, and March that show the expected results from implementing the proposed changes. Use a three-column format, with one column for each month.

Analysis Component

2. Use the budgeted income statements from part 1 to recommend whether management should implement the proposed changes. Explain.

Problem 7-4A
Manufacturing:
Preparation of a complete master budget

P1   P2   P3

The management of Zigby Manufacturing prepared the following estimated balance sheet for March, 2015:

ZIGBY MANUFACTURING Estimated Balance Sheet March 31, 2015			
Assets		**Liabilities and Equity**	
Cash	$ 40,000	Accounts payable	$ 200,500
Accounts receivable	342,248	Short-term notes payable	12,000
Raw materials inventory...........	98,500	Total current liabilities	212,500
Finished goods inventory	325,540	Long-term note payable	500,000
Total current assets	806,288	Total liabilities	712,500
Equipment, gross.................	600,000	Common stock	335,000
Accumulated depreciation	(150,000)	Retained earnings	208,788
Equipment, net	450,000	Total stockholders' equity	543,788
Total assets	$1,256,288	Total liabilities and equity	$1,256,288

To prepare a master budget for April, May, and June of 2015, management gathers the following information:

   a. Sales for March total 20,500 units. Forecasted sales in units are as follows: April, 20,500; May, 19,500; June, 20,000; and July, 20,500. Sales of 240,000 units are forecasted for the entire year. The product's selling price is $23.85 per unit and its total product cost is $19.85 per unit.

   b. Company policy calls for a given month's ending raw materials inventory to equal 50% of the next month's materials requirements. The March 31 raw materials inventory is 4,925 units, which complies with the policy. The expected June 30 ending raw materials inventory is 4,000 units. Raw materials cost $20 per unit. Each finished unit requires 0.50 units of raw materials.

   c. Company policy calls for a given month's ending finished goods inventory to equal 80% of the next month's expected unit sales. The March 31 finished goods inventory is 16,400 units, which complies with the policy.

   d. Each finished unit requires 0.50 hours of direct labor at a rate of $15 per hour.

   e. Overhead is allocated based on direct labor hours. The predetermined variable overhead rate is $2.70 per direct labor hour. Depreciation of $20,000 per month is treated as fixed factory overhead.

   f. Sales representatives' commissions are 8% of sales and are paid in the month of the sales. The sales manager's monthly salary is $3,000.

   g. Monthly general and administrative expenses include $12,000 administrative salaries and 0.9% monthly interest on the long-term note payable.

   h. The company expects 30% of sales to be for cash and the remaining 70% on credit. Receivables are collected in full in the month following the sale (none is collected in the month of the sale).

i. All raw materials purchases are on credit, and no payables arise from any other transactions. One month's raw materials purchases are fully paid in the next month.

j. The minimum ending cash balance for all months is $40,000. If necessary, the company borrows enough cash using a short-term note to reach the minimum. Short-term notes require an interest payment of 1% at each month-end (before any repayment). If the ending cash balance exceeds the minimum, the excess will be applied to repaying the short-term notes payable balance.

k. Dividends of $10,000 are to be declared and paid in May.

l. No cash payments for income taxes are to be made during the second calendar quarter. Income tax will be assessed at 35% in the quarter and paid in the third calendar quarter.

m. Equipment purchases of $130,000 are budgeted for the last day of June.

Required

Prepare the following budgets and other financial information as required. All budgets and other financial information should be prepared for the second calendar quarter, except as otherwise noted below. Round calculations up to the nearest whole dollar, except for the amount of cash sales, which should be rounded down to the nearest whole dollar.

1. Sales budget.
2. Production budget.
3. Raw materials budget.
4. Direct labor budget.
5. Factory overhead budget.
6. Selling expense budget.
7. General and administrative expense budget.
8. Cash budget.
9. Budgeted income statement for the entire second quarter (not for each month separately).
10. Budgeted balance sheet as of the end of the second calendar quarter.

Check (2) Units to produce: April, 19,700; May, 19,900
(3) Cost of raw materials purchases, April, $198,000
(5) Total overhead cost, May, $46,865
(8) Ending cash balance: April, $83,346; May, $124,295
(10) Budgeted total assets, June 30: $1,299,440

Keggler's Supply is a merchandiser of three different products. The company's February 28 inventories are footwear, 20,000 units; sports equipment, 80,000 units; and apparel, 50,000 units. Management believes that excessive inventories have accumulated for all three products. As a result, a new policy dictates that ending inventory in any month should equal 30% of the expected unit sales for the following month. Expected sales in units for March, April, May, and June follow.

Problem 7-5A[A]
Merchandising:
Preparation and analysis of purchases budgets
P4

	Budgeted Sales in Units			
	March	April	May	June
Footwear	15,000	25,000	32,000	35,000
Sports equipment	70,000	90,000	95,000	90,000
Apparel	40,000	38,000	37,000	25,000

Required

1. Prepare a merchandise purchases budget (in units) for each product for each of the months of March, April, and May.

Analysis Component

2. The purchases budgets in part 1 should reflect fewer purchases of all three products in March compared to those in April and May. What factor caused fewer purchases to be planned? Suggest business conditions that would cause this factor to both occur and impact the company in this way.

Check (l) March budgeted purchases: Footwear, 2,500; Sports equip., 17,000; Apparel, 1,400

During the last week of August, Oneida Company's owner approaches the bank for a $100,000 loan to be made on September 2 and repaid on November 30 with annual interest of 12%, for an interest cost of $3,000. The owner plans to increase the store's inventory by $80,000 during September and needs the loan to pay for inventory acquisitions. The bank's loan officer needs more information about Oneida's ability to repay the loan and asks the owner to forecast the store's November 30 cash position. On September 1, Oneida is expected to have a $5,000 cash balance, $159,100 of net accounts receivable, and $125,000

Problem 7-6A[A]
Merchandising:
Preparation of cash budgets (for three periods)
P4

of accounts payable. Its budgeted sales, merchandise purchases, and various cash disbursements for the next three months follow.

	A	B	C	D
1	**Budgeted Figures***	**September**	**October**	**November**
2	Sales	$250,000	$375,000	$400,000
3	Merchandise purchases	240,000	225,000	200,000
4	Cash disbursements			
5	Payroll	20,000	22,000	24,000
6	Rent	10,000	10,000	10,000
7	Other cash expenses	35,000	30,000	20,000
8	Repayment of bank loan			100,000
9	Interest on the bank loan			3,000
10				

*Operations began in August; August sales were $215,000 and purchases were $125,000.

The budgeted September merchandise purchases include the inventory increase. All sales are on account. The company predicts that 25% of credit sales is collected in the month of the sale, 45% in the month following the sale, 20% in the second month, 9% in the third, and the remainder is uncollectible. Applying these percents to the August credit sales, for example, shows that $96,750 of the $215,000 will be collected in September, $43,000 in October, and $19,350 in November. All merchandise is purchased on credit; 80% of the balance is paid in the month following a purchase, and the remaining 20% is paid in the second month. For example, of the $125,000 August purchases, $100,000 will be paid in September and $25,000 in October.

Required

Prepare a cash budget for September, October, and November for Oneida Company. Show supporting calculations as needed.

Problem 7-7A[A]

Merchandising:
Preparation and analysis of cash budgets with supporting inventory and purchases budgets

P4

Aztec Company sells its product for $180 per unit. Its actual and budgeted sales follow.

	Units	Dollars
April (actual)	4,000	$ 720,000
May (actual)	2,000	360,000
June (budgeted)	6,000	1,080,000
July (budgeted)	5,000	900,000
August (budgeted)	3,800	684,000

All sales are on credit. Recent experience shows that 20% of credit sales is collected in the month of the sale, 50% in the month after the sale, 28% in the second month after the sale, and 2% proves to be uncollectible. The product's purchase price is $110 per unit. All purchases are payable within 12 days. Thus, 60% of purchases made in a month is paid in that month and the other 40% is paid in the next month. The company has a policy to maintain an ending monthly inventory of 20% of the next month's unit sales plus a safety stock of 100 units. The April 30 and May 31 actual inventory levels are consistent with this policy. Selling and administrative expenses for the year are $1,320,000 and are paid evenly throughout the year in cash. The company's minimum cash balance at month-end is $100,000. This minimum is maintained, if necessary, by borrowing cash from the bank. If the balance exceeds $100,000, the company repays as much of the loan as it can without going below the minimum. This type of loan carries an annual 12% interest rate. On May 31, the loan balance is $25,000, and the company's cash balance is $100,000. (Round amounts to the nearest dollar.)

Required

1. Prepare a table that shows the computation of cash collections of its credit sales (accounts receivable) in each of the months of June and July.

2. Prepare a table that shows the computation of budgeted ending inventories (in units) for April, May, June, and July.

3. Prepare the merchandise purchases budget for May, June, and July. Report calculations in units and then show the dollar amount of purchases for each month.

4. Prepare a table showing the computation of cash payments on product purchases for June and July.

5. Prepare a cash budget for June and July, including any loan activity and interest expense. Compute the loan balance at the end of each month.

(5) Budgeted ending loan balance: June, $43,650; July, $0

Analysis Component

6. Refer to your answer to part 5. Aztec's cash budget indicates the company will need to borrow more than $18,000 in June. Suggest some reasons that knowing this information in May would be helpful to management.

Near the end of 2015, the management of Dimsdale Sports Co., a merchandising company, prepared the following estimated balance sheet for December 31, 2015.

Problem 7-8A[A]

Merchandising:
Preparation of a complete master budget P4

DIMSDALE SPORTS COMPANY Estimated Balance Sheet December 31, 2015				
Assets			**Liabilities and Equity**	
Cash	$ 36,000		Accounts payable	$360,000
Accounts receivable	525,000		Bank loan payable	15,000
Inventory	150,000		Taxes payable (due 3/15/2016)	90,000
Total current assets		$ 711,000	Total liabilities	$ 465,000
Equipment	540,000		Common stock	472,500
Less: Accumulated depreciation ...	67,500		Retained earnings	246,000
Equipment, net..............		472,500	Total stockholders' equity	718,500
Total assets		$1,183,500	Total liabilities and equity	$1,183,500

To prepare a master budget for January, February, and March of 2016, management gathers the following information.

a. Dimsdale Sports's single product is purchased for $30 per unit and resold for $55 per unit. The expected inventory level of 5,000 units on December 31, 2015, is more than management's desired level for 2016, which is 20% of the next month's expected sales (in units). Expected sales are: January, 7,000 units; February, 9,000 units; March, 11,000 units; and April, 10,000 units.

b. Cash sales and credit sales represent 25% and 75%, respectively, of total sales. Of the credit sales, 60% is collected in the first month after the month of sale and 40% in the second month after the month of sale. For the December 31, 2015, accounts receivable balance, $125,000 is collected in January and the remaining $400,000 is collected in February.

c. Merchandise purchases are paid for as follows: 20% in the first month after the month of purchase and 80% in the second month after the month of purchase. For the December 31, 2015, accounts payable balance, $80,000 is paid in January and the remaining $280,000 is paid in February.

d. Sales commissions equal to 20% of sales are paid each month. Sales salaries (excluding commissions) are $60,000 per year.

e. General and administrative salaries are $144,000 per year. Maintenance expense equals $2,000 per month and is paid in cash.

f. Equipment reported in the December 31, 2015, balance sheet was purchased in January 2015. It is being depreciated over eight years under the straight-line method with no salvage value. The following amounts for new equipment purchases are planned in the coming quarter: January, $36,000; February, $96,000; and March, $28,800. This equipment will be depreciated under the straight-line method over eight years with no salvage value. A full month's depreciation is taken for the month in which equipment is purchased.

g. The company plans to acquire land at the end of March at a cost of $150,000, which will be paid with cash on the last day of the month.

h. Dimsdale Sports has a working arrangement with its bank to obtain additional loans as needed. The interest rate is 12% per year, and interest is paid at each month-end based on the beginning balance. Partial or full payments on these loans can be made on the last day of the month. The company has agreed to maintain a minimum ending cash balance of $25,000 in each month.

i. The income tax rate for the company is 40%. Income taxes on the first quarter's income will not be paid until April 15.

Required

Prepare a master budget for each of the first three months of 2016; include the following component budgets (show supporting calculations as needed, and round amounts to the nearest dollar):

Check   (2) Budgeted
purchases: January, $114,000;
February, $282,000
         (3) Budgeted
selling expenses: January,
$82,000; February, $104,000
         (6) Ending cash bal.:
January, $30,100; February,
$210,300
         (8) Budgeted total
assets at March 31,
$1,568,650

1. Monthly sales budgets (showing both budgeted unit sales and dollar sales).
2. Monthly merchandise purchases budgets.
3. Monthly selling expense budgets.
4. Monthly general and administrative expense budgets.
5. Monthly capital expenditures budgets.
6. Monthly cash budgets.
7. Budgeted income statement for the entire first quarter (not for each month).
8. Budgeted balance sheet as of March 31, 2016.

PROBLEM SET B

Problem 7-1B
Manufacturing:
Preparing production and
manufacturing budgets

C2   P1

NSA Company produces baseball bats. Each bat requires 3 pounds of aluminum alloy. Management predicts that 8,000 bats and 15,000 pounds of aluminum alloy will be in inventory on March 31 of the current year and that 250,000 bats will be sold during this year's second quarter. Bats sell for $80 each. Management wants to end the second quarter with 6,000 finished bats and 12,000 pounds of aluminum alloy in inventory. Aluminum alloy can be purchased for $4 per pound. Each bat requires 0.5 hours of direct labor at $18 per hour. Variable overhead is applied at the rate of $12 per direct labor hour. The company budgets fixed overhead of $1,776,000 for the quarter.

Required

Check   (1) Units manuf.,
248,000
         (2) Cost of
materials purchases,
$2,964,000

1. Prepare the second-quarter production budget for bats.
2. Prepare the second-quarter direct materials (aluminum alloy) budget; include the dollar cost of purchases.
3. Prepare the direct labor budget for the second quarter.
4. Prepare the factory overhead budget for the second quarter.

Problem 7-2B
Manufacturing: Cash
budget

P2   A1

A1 Manufacturing is preparing its master budget for the quarter ended September 30, 2015. Budgeted sales and cash payments for product costs for the quarter follow.

	A	B	C	D
1		**July**	**August**	**September**
2	Budgeted sales	$63,400	$80,600	$48,600
3	Budgeted cash payments for			
4	Direct materials	12,480	9,900	10,140
5	Direct labor	10,400	8,250	8,450
6	Factory overhead	18,720	14,850	15,210
7				

Sales are 20% cash and 80% on credit. All credit sales are collected in the month following the sale. The June 30 balance sheet includes balances of $12,900 in cash; $47,000 in accounts receivable; $5,100 in accounts payable; and a $2,600 balance in loans payable. A minimum cash balance of $12,600 is required. Loans are obtained at the end of any month when a cash shortage occurs. Interest is 1% per month based on the beginning of the month loan balance and is paid at each month-end. If an excess balance of cash exists, loans are repaid at the end of the month. Operating expenses are paid in the month incurred and consist of sales commissions (10% of sales), office salaries ($4,600 per month), and rent ($7,100 per month).

1. Prepare a cash receipts budget for July, August, and September.
2. Prepare a cash budget for each of the months of July, August, and September. (Round amounts to the dollar.)

HCS Mfg. makes its product for $60 and sells it for $130 per unit. The sales staff receives a 10% commission on the sale of each unit. Its June income statement follows.

Problem 7-3B
Manufacturing:
Preparation and analysis
of budgeted income
statements   P3

HCS MFG.	
Income Statement	
For Month Ended June 30, 2015	
Sales	$1,300,000
Cost of goods sold	600,000
Gross profit	700,000
Operating expenses	
Sales commissions (10%)	130,000
Advertising	200,000
Store rent	24,000
Administrative salaries	40,000
Depreciation—Office equipment	50,000
Other expenses	12,000
Total expenses	456,000
Net income	$ 244,000

Management expects June's results to be repeated in July, August, and September without any changes in strategy. Management, however, has another plan. It believes that unit sales will increase at a rate of 10% *each* month for the next three months (beginning with July) if the item's selling price is reduced to $115 per unit and advertising expenses are increased by 25% and remain at that level for all three months. The cost of its product will remain at $60 per unit, the sales staff will continue to earn a 10% commission, and the remaining expenses will stay the same.

Required

1. Prepare budgeted income statements for each of the months of July, August, and September that show the expected results from implementing the proposed changes. Use a three-column format, with one column for each month.

Check Budgeted net
income: July, $102,500;
August, $150,350;
September, $202,985

Analysis Component

2. Use the budgeted income statements from part 1 to recommend whether management should implement the proposed plan. Explain.

The management of Nabar Manufacturing prepared the following estimated balance sheet for June, 2015:

Problem 7-4B
Manufacturing:
Preparation of a
complete master budget

P1   P2   P3

NABAR MANUFACTURING				
Estimated Balance Sheet				
June 30, 2015				
Assets		**Liabilities and Equity**		
Cash	$ 40,000	Accounts payable	$ 51,400
Accounts receivable	249,900	Income taxes payable.	10,000
Raw materials inventory	35,000	Short-term notes payable	24,000
Finished goods inventory	241,080	Total current liabilities	85,400
Total current assets	565,980	Long-term note payable	300,000
Equipment, gross.	720,000	Total liabilities	385,400
Accumulated depreciation	(240,000)	Common stock	600,000
Equipment, net	480,000	Retained earnings	60,580
		Total stockholders' equity	660,580
Total assets	$1,045,980	Total liabilities and equity	$1,045,980

To prepare a master budget for July, August, and September of 2015, management gathers the following information:

a. Sales were 20,000 units in June. Forecasted sales in units are as follows: July, 21,000; August, 19,000; September, 20,000; October, 24,000. The product's selling price is $17 per unit and its total product cost is $14.35 per unit.

b. Company policy calls for a given month's ending finished goods inventory to equal 70% of the next month's expected unit sales. The June 30 finished goods inventory is 16,800 units, which does not comply with the policy.

c. Company policy calls for a given month's ending raw materials inventory to equal 20% of the next month's materials requirements. The June 30 raw materials inventory is 4,375 units (which also fails to meet the policy). The budgeted September 30 raw materials inventory is 1,980 units. Raw materials cost $8 per unit. Each finished unit requires 0.50 units of raw materials.

d. Each finished unit requires 0.50 hours of direct labor at a rate of $16 per hour.

e. Overhead is allocated based on direct labor hours. The predetermined variable overhead rate is $2.70 per direct labor hour. Depreciation of $20,000 per month is treated as fixed factory overhead.

f. Monthly general and administrative expenses include $9,000 administrative salaries and 0.9% monthly interest on the long-term note payable.

g. Sales representatives' commissions are 10% of sales and are paid in the month of the sales. The sales manager's monthly salary is $3,500 per month.

h. The company expects 30% of sales to be for cash and the remaining 70% on credit. Receivables are collected in full in the month following the sale (none are collected in the month of the sale).

i. All raw materials purchases are on credit, and no payables arise from any other transactions. One month's raw materials purchases are fully paid in the next month.

j. Dividends of $20,000 are to be declared and paid in August.

k. Income taxes payable at June 30 will be paid in July. Income tax expense will be assessed at 35% in the quarter and paid in October.

l. Equipment purchases of $100,000 are budgeted for the last day of September.

m. The minimum ending cash balance for all months is $40,000. If necessary, the company borrows enough cash using a short-term note to reach the minimum. Short-term notes require an interest payment of 1% at each month-end (before any repayment). If the ending cash balance exceeds the minimum, the excess will be applied to repaying the short-term notes payable balance.

Required

Prepare the following budgets and other financial information as required. All budgets and other financial information should be prepared for the third calendar quarter, except as otherwise noted below. Round calculations to the nearest whole dollar.

Check   (2) Units to produce: July, 17,500; August, 19,700

(3) Cost of raw materials purchases, July, $50,760

(5) Total overhead cost, August, $46,595

(8) Ending cash balance: July, $96,835; August, $141,180

(10) Budgeted total assets, Sept. 30: $1,054,920

1. Sales budget.
2. Production budget.
3. Raw materials budget.
4. Direct labor budget.
5. Factory overhead budget.
6. Selling expense budget.
7. General and administrative expense budget.
8. Cash budget.
9. Budgeted income statement for the entire quarter (not for each month separately).
10. Budgeted balance sheet as of September 30, 2015.

Problem 7-5B[A]

Merchandising:

Preparation and analysis of purchases budgets

P4 🔧

H2O Sports Company is a merchandiser of three different products. The company's March 31 inventories are water skis, 40,000 units; tow ropes, 90,000 units; and life jackets, 150,000 units. Management believes that excessive inventories have accumulated for all three products. As a result, a new policy dictates that ending inventory in any month should equal 10% of the expected unit sales for the following month. Expected sales in units for April, May, June, and July follow.

	Budgeted Sales in Units			
	April	**May**	**June**	**July**
Water skis	70,000	90,000	130,000	100,000
Tow ropes	100,000	90,000	110,000	100,000
Life jackets	160,000	190,000	200,000	120,000

Required

1. Prepare a merchandise purchases budget (in units) for each product for each of the months of April, May, and June.

Analysis Component

2. The purchases budgets in part 1 should reflect fewer purchases of all three products in April compared to those in May and June. What factor caused fewer purchases to be planned? Suggest business conditions that would cause this factor to both occur and affect the company as it has.

Check   (1) April budgeted purchases: Water skis, 39,000; Tow ropes, 19,000; Life jackets, 29,000

During the last week of March, Sony Stereo's owner approaches the bank for an $80,000 loan to be made on April 1 and repaid on June 30 with annual interest of 12%, for an interest cost of $2,400. The owner plans to increase the store's inventory by $60,000 in April and needs the loan to pay for inventory acquisitions. The bank's loan officer needs more information about Sony Stereo's ability to repay the loan and asks the owner to forecast the store's June 30 cash position. On April 1, Sony Stereo is expected to have a $3,000 cash balance, $135,000 of accounts receivable, and $100,000 of accounts payable. Its budgeted sales, merchandise purchases, and various cash disbursements for the next three months follow.

Problem 7-6B[A]

Merchandising: Preparation of cash budgets (for three periods)

P4

	A	B	C	D
1	**Budgeted Figures***	**April**	**May**	**June**
2	Sales	$220,000	$300,000	$380,000
3	Merchandise purchases	210,000	180,000	220,000
4	Cash disbursements			
5	Payroll	16,000	17,000	18,000
6	Rent	6,000	6,000	6,000
7	Other cash expenses	64,000	8,000	7,000
8	Repayment of bank loan			80,000
9	Interest on the bank loan			2,400
10				

*Operations began in March; March sales were $180,000 and purchases were $100,000.

The budgeted April merchandise purchases include the inventory increase. All sales are on account. The company predicts that 25% of credit sales is collected in the month of the sale, 45% in the month following the sale, 20% in the second month, 9% in the third, and the remainder is uncollectible. Applying these percents to the March credit sales, for example, shows that $81,000 of the $180,000 will be collected in April, $36,000 in May, and $16,200 in June. All merchandise is purchased on credit; 80% of the balance is paid in the month following a purchase and the remaining 20% is paid in the second month. For example, of the $100,000 March purchases, $80,000 will be paid in April and $20,000 in May.

Required

Prepare a cash budget for April, May, and June for Sony Stereo. Show supporting calculations as needed.

Check   Budgeted cash balance: April, $53,000; May, $44,000; June, $34,800

Connick Company sells its product for $22 per unit. Its actual and budgeted sales follow.

Problem 7-7B[A]

Merchandising: Preparation and analysis of cash budgets with supporting inventory and purchases budgets

P4

	Units	Dollars
January (actual)	18,000	$396,000
February (actual)	22,500	495,000
March (budgeted)	19,000	418,000
April (budgeted)	18,750	412,500
May (budgeted)	21,000	462,000

All sales are on credit. Recent experience shows that 40% of credit sales is collected in the month of the sale, 35% in the month after the sale, 23% in the second month after the sale, and 2% proves to be uncollectible. The product's purchase price is $12 per unit. All purchases are payable within 21 days. Thus, 30% of purchases made in a month is paid in that month and the other 70% is paid in the next month. The company has a policy to maintain an ending monthly inventory of 20% of the next month's unit sales plus a safety stock of 100 units. The January 31 and February 28 actual inventory levels are consistent with this policy. Selling and administrative expenses for the year are $1,920,000 and are paid evenly throughout the year in cash. The company's minimum cash balance for month-end is $50,000. This minimum is maintained, if necessary, by borrowing cash from the bank. If the balance exceeds $50,000, the company repays as much of the loan as it can without going below the minimum. This type of loan carries an annual 12% interest rate. At February 28, the loan balance is $12,000, and the company's cash balance is $50,000.

Required

Check (1) Cash collections: March, $431,530; April, $425,150

(3) Budgeted purchases: February, $261,600; March, $227,400

(5) Ending cash balance: March, $58,070; April, $94,920

1. Prepare a table that shows the computation of cash collections of its credit sales (accounts receivable) in each of the months of March and April.

2. Prepare a table showing the computations of budgeted ending inventories (units) for January, February, March, and April.

3. Prepare the merchandise purchases budget for February, March, and April. Report calculations in units and then show the dollar amount of purchases for each month.

4. Prepare a table showing the computation of cash payments on product purchases for March and April.

5. Prepare a cash budget for March and April, including any loan activity and interest expense. Compute the loan balance at the end of each month.

Analysis Component

6. Refer to your answer to part 5. Connick's cash budget indicates whether the company must borrow additional funds at the end of March. Suggest some reasons that knowing the loan needs in advance would be helpful to management.

Problem 7-8B[A]
Merchandising:
Preparation of a complete master budget

P4

Near the end of 2015, the management of Isle Corp., a merchandising company, prepared the following estimated balance sheet for December 31, 2015.

ISLE CORPORATION Estimated Balance Sheet December 31, 2015				
Assets			**Liabilities and Equity**	
Cash	$ 36,000		Accounts payable	$360,000
Accounts receivable	525,000		Bank loan payable	15,000
Inventory	150,000		Taxes payable (due 3/15/2016)	90,000
Total current assets		$ 711,000	Total liabilities	$ 465,000
Equipment	540,000		Common stock	472,500
Less: Accumulated depreciation	67,500		Retained earnings	246,000
Equipment, net...............		472,500	Total stockholders' equity	718,500
Total assets		$1,183,500	Total liabilities and equity	$1,183,500

To prepare a master budget for January, February, and March of 2016, management gathers the following information.

a. Isle Corp.'s single product is purchased for $30 per unit and resold for $45 per unit. The expected inventory level of 5,000 units on December 31, 2015, is more than management's desired level for 2016, which is 25% of the next month's expected sales (in units). Expected sales are: January, 6,000 units; February, 8,000 units; March, 10,000 units; and April, 9,000 units.

b. Cash sales and credit sales represent 25% and 75%, respectively, of total sales. Of the credit sales, 60% is collected in the first month after the month of sale and 40% in the second month after the month of sale. For the $525,000 accounts receivable balance at December 31, 2015, $315,000 is collected in January 2014 and the remaining $210,000 is collected in February 2016.

c. Merchandise purchases are paid for as follows: 20% in the first month after the month of purchase and 80% in the second month after the month of purchase. For the $360,000 accounts payable balance at December 31, 2015, $72,000 is paid in January 2016 and the remaining $288,000 is paid in February 2016.

d. Sales commissions equal to 20% of sales are paid each month. Sales salaries (excluding commissions) are $90,000 per year.

e. General and administrative salaries are $144,000 per year. Maintenance expense equals $3,000 per month and is paid in cash.

f. Equipment reported in the December 31, 2015, balance sheet was purchased in January 2015. It is being depreciated over eight years under the straight-line method with no salvage value. The following amounts for new equipment purchases are planned in the coming quarter: January, $72,000; February, $96,000; and March, $28,800. This equipment will be depreciated using the straight-line method over eight years with no salvage value. A full month's depreciation is taken for the month in which equipment is purchased.

g. The company plans to acquire land at the end of March at a cost of $150,000, which will be paid with cash on the last day of the month.

h. Isle Corp. has a working arrangement with its bank to obtain additional loans as needed. The interest rate is 12% per year, and interest is paid at each month-end based on the beginning balance. Partial or full payments on these loans can be made on the last day of the month. Isle has agreed to maintain a minimum ending cash balance of $36,000 in each month.

i. The income tax rate for the company is 40%. Income taxes on the first quarter's income will not be paid until April 15.

Required

Prepare a master budget for each of the first three months of 2016; include the following component budgets (show supporting calculations as needed, and round amounts to the nearest dollar):

1. Monthly sales budgets (showing both budgeted unit sales and dollar sales).
2. Monthly merchandise purchases budgets.
3. Monthly selling expense budgets.
4. Monthly general and administrative expense budgets.
5. Monthly capital expenditures budgets.
6. Monthly cash budgets.
7. Budgeted income statement for the entire first quarter (not for each month).
8. Budgeted balance sheet as of March 31, 2016.

Check (2) Budgeted purchases: January, $90,000; February, $255,000
(3) Budgeted selling expenses: January, $61,500; February, $79,500
(6) Ending cash bal.: January, $182,850; February, $107,850
(8) Budgeted total assets at March 31, $1,346,875

This serial problem began in Chapter 1 and continues through most of the book. If previous chapter segments were not completed, the serial problem can begin at this point. It is helpful, but not necessary, to use the Working Papers that accompany the book.)

SERIAL PROBLEM
Business Solutions
P3

SP 7 Santana Rey expects second-quarter 2016 sales of her new line of computer furniture to be the same as the first quarter's sales (reported below) without any changes in strategy. Monthly sales averaged 40 desk units (sales price of $1,250) and 20 chairs (sales price of $500).

BUSINESS SOLUTIONS	
Segment Income Statement*	
For Quarter Ended March 31, 2016	
Sales†	$180,000
Cost of goods sold‡	115,000
Gross profit	65,000
Expenses	
Sales commissions (10%)	18,000
Advertising expenses	9,000
Other fixed expenses	18,000
Total expenses	45,000
Net income	$ 20,000

* Reflects revenue and expense activity only related to the computer furniture segment.
† Revenue: (120 desks × $1,250) + (60 chairs × $500) = $150,000 + $30,000 = $180,000
‡ Cost of goods sold: (120 desks × $750) + (60 chairs × $250) + $10,000 = $115,000

Santana Rey believes that sales will increase each month for the next three months (April, 48 desks, 32 chairs; May, 52 desks, 35 chairs; June, 56 desks, 38 chairs) *if* selling prices are reduced to $1,150 for desks and $450 for chairs, and advertising expenses are increased by 10% and remain at that level for all three months. The products' variable cost will remain at $750 for desks and $250 for chairs. The sales staff will continue to earn a 10% commission, the fixed manufacturing costs per month will remain at $10,000, and other fixed expenses will remain at $6,000 per month.

Required

Check (1) Budgeted
income (loss): April, $(660);
May, $945

1. Prepare budgeted income statements for each of the months of April, May, and June that show the expected results from implementing the proposed changes. Use a three-column format, with one column for each month.

2. Use the budgeted income statements from part 1 to recommend whether Santana Rey should implement the proposed changes. Explain.

Beyond the Numbers

REPORTING IN ACTION

P2

APPLE

BTN 7-1   Financial statements often serve as a starting point in formulating budgets. Review Apple's financial statements in Appendix A to determine its cash paid for acquisitions of property, plant, and equipment in the current year and the budgeted cash needed for such acquisitions in the next year.

Required

1. Which financial statement reports the amount of cash paid for acquisitions of property, plant, and equipment? Explain where on the statement this information is reported.

2. Indicate the amount of cash (a) paid for acquisitions of property and equipment in the year ended September 28, 2013, and (b) to be paid (budgeted for) next year under the assumption that annual acquisitions of property and equipment equal 20% of the prior year's net income.

Fast Forward

3. Access Apple's financial statements for a year ending after September 28, 2013, from either its web site [Apple.com] or the SEC's EDGAR database [www.SEC.gov]. Compare your answer for part 2 with actual cash paid for acquisitions of property and equipment for that fiscal year. Compute the error, if any, in your estimate. Speculate as to why cash paid for acquisitions of property and equipment was higher or lower than your estimate.

COMPARATIVE ANALYSIS

P2

APPLE
GOOGLE

BTN 7-2   One source of cash savings for a company is improved management of inventory. To illustrate, assume that Apple and Google both have $1 billion per month in sales of one model of smartphone in Canada, and both forecast this level of sales per month for the next 24 months. Also assume that both Apple and Google have a 20% contribution margin, their fixed costs are equal, and that cost of goods sold is the only variable cost. Assume that the main difference between Apple and Google is the distribution system. Apple uses a just-in-time system and requires ending inventory of only 10% of next month's sales in inventory at each month-end. However, Google is building an improved distribution system and currently requires 30% of next month's sales in inventory at each month-end.

Required

1. Compute the amount by which Google can reduce its inventory level if it can match Apple's system of maintaining an inventory equal to 10% of next month's sales. (*Hint:* Focus on the facts given and only on the Canadian market.)

2. Explain how the analysis in part 1 that shows ending inventory levels for both the 30% and 10% required inventory policies can help justify a just-in-time inventory system. Assume a 15% interest cost for resources that are tied up in ending inventory.

ETHICS CHALLENGE

C1

BTN 7-3   Both the budget process and budgets themselves can impact management actions, both positively and negatively. For instance, a common practice among not-for-profit organizations and government agencies is for management to spend any amounts remaining in a budget at the end of the budget period, a practice often called "use it or lose it." The view is that if a department manager does not spend the budgeted amount, top management will reduce next year's budget by the amount not spent. To avoid losing budget dollars, department managers often spend all budgeted amounts regardless of the value added to products or services. All of us pay for the costs associated with this budget system.

Required

Write a half-page report to a local not-for-profit organization or government agency offering a solution to the "use it or lose it" budgeting problem.

BTN 7-4   The sales budget is usually the first and most crucial of the component budgets in a master budget because all other budgets usually rely on it for planning purposes.

COMMUNICATING IN PRACTICE

C2

Required

Assume that your company's sales staff provides information on expected sales and selling prices for items making up the sales budget. Prepare a one-page memorandum to your supervisor outlining concerns with the sales staff's input in the sales budget when its compensation is at least partly tied to these budgets. More generally, explain the importance of assessing any potential bias in information provided to the budget process.

BTN 7-5   Access information on e-budgets through The Manage Mentor website (themanagementor.com/kuniverse/kmailers_universe/finance_kmailers/cfa/budgeting2.htm). Read the information provided.

TAKING IT TO THE NET

C1

Required

1. Assume the role of a senior manager in a large, multidivision company. What are the benefits of using e-budgets?

2. As a senior manager, what concerns do you have with the concept and application of e-budgets?

BTN 7-6   Your team is to prepare a budget report outlining the costs of attending college (full-time) for the next two semesters (30 hours) or three quarters (45 hours). This budget's focus is solely on attending college; do not include personal items in the team's budget. Your budget must include tuition, books, supplies, club fees, food, housing, and all costs associated with travel to and from college. This budgeting exercise is similar to the initial phase in activity-based budgeting. Include a list of any assumptions you use in completing the budget. Be prepared to present your budget in class.

TEAMWORK IN ACTION

A1

BTN 7-7   Solben sells technology to use in the production of biodiesel. Company founder Daniel Gómez Iñiguez stresses the importance of planning and budgeting for business success.

ENTREPRENEURIAL DECISION

C1

Required

1. How can budgeting help Daniel efficiently develop and operate his business?

2. Daniel plans to expand his business. How can a budget be useful in expanding a business's operations?

BTN 7-8   To help understand the factors impacting a sales budget, you are to visit three businesses with the same ownership or franchise membership. Record the selling prices of two identical products at each location, such as regular and premium gas sold at Chevron stations. You are likely to find a difference in prices for at least one of the three locations you visit.

HITTING THE ROAD

C2   P1

Required

1. Identify at least three external factors that must be considered when setting the sales budget. (*Note:* There is a difference between internal and external factors that impact the sales budget.)

2. What factors might explain any differences identified in the prices of the businesses you visited?

BTN 7-9   Access Samsung's income statement (in Appendix A) for the business year 2013.

GLOBAL DECISION

P1

Required

1. Is Samsung's selling and administrative expenses budget likely to be an important budget in its master budgeting process? Explain.

2. Identify three types of expenses that would be reported as selling and administrative expenses on Samsung's income statement.

Samsung

3. Who likely has the initial responsibility for Samsung's selling and administrative expense budget? Explain.

ANSWERS TO MULTIPLE CHOICE QUIZ

1. c

2. e; Budgeted purchases = $36,000 + $7,000 − $6,000 = $37,000

3. b; Cash collected = 25% of September sales + 75% of August sales =
    (0.25 × $240,000) + (0.75 × $220,000) = $225,000

4. d

5. a; 560 units + (0.30 × 600 units) − (0.30 × 560 units) = 572 units

chapter

8

Flexible Budgets and Standard Costs

Chapter Preview

FIXED BUDGET REPORTS	FLEXIBLE BUDGET REPORTS	MATERIALS AND LABOR STANDARDS	OVERHEAD STANDARDS AND VARIANCES
Fixed budget performance report	Purpose	**C1** Identifying standard costs	Flexible overhead budget
Fixed budget reports for evaluation	**P1** Preparation	Setting standard costs	Setting overhead standards
	Flexible budget performance report	**C2** Cost variance analysis	**P3** Computing overhead variances
		Cost variance computation	**A1** Sales variances
		P2 Materials and labor variances	**P4** Overhead variances
			P5 Standard cost entries

Learning Objectives

CONCEPTUAL

C1 Define *standard costs* and explain how standard cost information is useful for management by exception.

C2 Describe cost variances and what they reveal about performance.

ANALYTICAL

A1 Analyze changes in sales from expected amounts.

PROCEDURAL

P1 Prepare a flexible budget and interpret a flexible budget performance report.

P2 Compute materials and labor variances.

P3 Compute overhead controllable and volume variances.

P4 *Appendix 8A*—Compute overhead spending and efficiency variances.

P5 *Appendix 8A*—Prepare journal entries for standard costs and account for price and quantity variances.

Roll On

FORT COLLINS, CO—Avid mountain biker Chris Sugai was looking for a better bike. "I wanted a higher-end bike, one that was better at climbing, braking, and descending. I noticed that no one was making it, so I decided to do it." Chris and his company, **Niner Bikes (www.ninerbikes.com)**, staked their future on 29-inch-wheel bikes, a radical departure from the more standard 26-inch wheel. "Everyone thought we were crazy," laughs Chris, "but we're convinced the 29-inch wheel gives the best ride quality." Apparently, many customers agree, as evidenced by the company's over 400% increase in sales over the past few years.

"Great products come from great people"
—Chris Sugai

Chris considers Niner Bikes to be a "virtual company." The company does much of its work online via Google Docs. The company collects new product ideas from customer chat rooms, and an engineering and design team uses software to perform virtual testing and simulation. The resulting information is shared electronically with a marketing team to develop graphics. "I need to get the best people possible, and I can't force them to move to a certain location. With Skype, iPads, and cell phones, I don't need to. I'm very much for freedom and allowing people to work how they work best."

Manufacturers like Niner Bikes must control materials, labor, and overhead costs. Determining standard costs helps. Since Niner Bikes makes only bikes with 29-inch wheels, it is able to better understand how design elements and bike components work together, enabling the company to develop very precise manufacturing specifications and standards. "We are able to focus on the minutest details. We just spent four hours talking about a cable routing system for braking." This attention to detail, and analysis of any variances in the actual manufacturing process from standards, helps Chris keep the manufacturing process on track.

Materials price and quantity variances are important in controlling the costs of expensive raw materials like carbon steel. Chris stresses the need for "precise specifications and controls; we don't use any material that does not meet our requirements." Unfavorable materials price variances could result from rising raw materials prices, which might cause the company to consider alternative suppliers or to raise its selling prices.

From sales of $2.7 million in 2009 to over $14 million currently, Niner Bikes has seen rapid growth. When production activity changes so rapidly, budgets can quickly become outdated. The use of flexible budgets, which reflect budgeted costs at several different production levels, can be useful in analyzing performance and making business decisions. While attention to budgeting, standard costs, and variances is important, Chris encourages potential entrepreneurs to build a business they are passionate about and to give back. "Part of our company's mission statement is to give back to the community that makes what we do possible. Helping organizations that support the development and maintenance of bike trails is important for our company and the right thing to do."

Sources: *Niner Bikes website,* January 2015; *Wired.com,* September 10, 2012; Interbike interview, http://vimeo.com/ninerbikes/; *Northern Colorado Business Report,* August 20, 2013

Section 1—Flexible Budgets

To monitor and control operations, companies exercise budgetary control and require budget reports. **Budgetary control** refers to management's use of budgets to see that planned objectives are met. **Budget reports** contain relevant information that compares actual results to planned activities. Budget reports are sometimes viewed as progress reports, or *report cards,* on management's performance in achieving planned objectives. These reports can be prepared at any time and for any period. Three common periods for a budget report are a month, quarter, and year.

Point: Budget reports are often used to determine bonuses of managers.

The budgetary control process involves at least four steps: (1) develop the budget from planned objectives, (2) compare actual results to budgeted amounts and analyze any differences, (3) take corrective and strategic actions, and (4) establish new planned objectives and prepare a new budget. Exhibit 8.1 shows this continual process of budgetary control. Budget reports and related documents are effective tools for managers to obtain the greatest benefits from this budgetary process.

EXHIBIT 8.1

Process of Budgetary Control

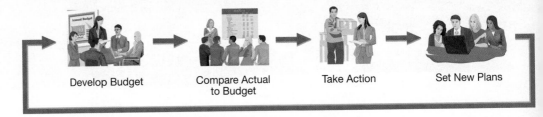

| Develop Budget | Compare Actual to Budget | Take Action | Set New Plans |

Because budgets are the main vehicle by which companies monitor and control operations, we need to look at them in some detail. As we showed in the previous chapter, a *master budget* is based on a predicted level of activity, such as sales volume, for the budget period. In preparing a master budget, two alternative approaches can be used: *fixed budgeting* or *flexible budgeting*. A **fixed budget,** also called a *static budget,* is based on a single predicted amount of sales or other activity measure. A **flexible budget,** also called a *variable budget,* is based on several different amounts of sales. As we will show in this section, a flexible budget is more useful than a fixed budget when the actual level of sales activity differs from the level of sales activity predicted at the beginning of the period. We look first at fixed budgets; understanding the limitations of fixed budgets better enables us to appreciate the benefits of flexible budgets later.

FIXED BUDGET REPORTS

Fixed Budget Performance Report

One use of a budget is to compare actual results with planned activities. Information useful for this analysis is often presented in a *performance report* that shows budgeted amounts, actual amounts, and *variances* (differences between budgeted and actual amounts). In a fixed budget control system, the master budget is based on a *single prediction* for sales volume, and the budgeted amount for each cost essentially assumes that a specific (or *fixed*) amount of sales will occur.

We illustrate fixed budget performance reports with Optel, which manufactures eyeglasses, frames, contact lenses, and related supplies. For 2015, Optel based its fixed budget on a prediction of 10,000 (composite) units of sales; costs also were budgeted based on 10,000 composite units of sales. Exhibit 8.2 shows a **fixed budget performance report,** a report that compares actual results with the results expected under a fixed budget. As the report shows, Optel's actual sales for the year were 12,000 composite units. In addition, Optel produced 12,000 composite units during the year (its inventory level did not change). The final column in the performance report shows the differences (variances) between the budgeted and actual amounts for each budget item.

OPTEL Fixed Budget Performance Report For Month Ended January 31, 2015	Fixed Budget	Actual Results	Variances*
Sales (in units)	10,000	12,000	
Sales (in dollars).......................	$100,000	$125,000	$25,000 F
Cost of goods sold			
Direct materials	10,000	13,000	3,000 U
Direct labor	15,000	20,000	5,000 U
Overhead			
Factory supplies	2,000	2,100	100 U
Utilities..........................	3,000	4,000	1,000 U
Depreciation—machinery.............	8,000	8,000	0
Supervisory salaries	11,000	11,000	0
Selling expenses			
Sales commissions	9,000	10,800	1,800 U
Shipping expenses	4,000	4,300	300 U
General and administrative expenses			
Office supplies	5,000	5,200	200 U
Insurance expenses	1,000	1,200	200 U
Depreciation—office equipment..........	7,000	7,000	0
Administrative salaries..................	13,000	13,000	0
Total expenses	88,000	99,600	11,600 U
Income from operations	$ 12,000	$ 25,400	$13,400 F

* F = Favorable variance; U = Unfavorable variance.

EXHIBIT 8.2

Fixed Budget Performance Report

This type of performance report designates differences between budgeted and actual results as *variances*. We use the letters *F* and *U* to describe the variances, with meanings as follows:

F = **Favorable variance** When compared to budget, the actual cost or revenue contributes to a *higher* income. That is, actual revenue is higher than budgeted revenue, or actual cost is lower than budgeted cost.

U = **Unfavorable variance** When compared to budget, the actual cost or revenue contributes to a *lower* income; actual revenue is lower than budgeted revenue, or actual cost is higher than budgeted cost.

This convention is common in practice and is used throughout this chapter.

Example: How is it that the favorable sales variance in Exhibit 8.2 is linked with so many unfavorable cost and expense variances? *Answer:* Costs have increased with the increase in sales.

Budget Reports for Evaluation

A primary use of budget reports is as a tool for management to monitor and control operations. From the fixed budget performance report in Exhibit 8.2, Optel's management might raise questions such as:

- Why is actual income from operations $13,400 higher than budgeted?
- Is manufacturing using too much direct material?
- Is manufacturing using too much direct labor?
- Why are sales commissions higher than budgeted?
- Why are so many of the variances unfavorable?

The performance report in Exhibit 8.2 will not be very useful in answering these types of questions. This is because it is not based on an "apples to apples" comparison. That is, the budgeted dollar amounts are based on 10,000 units of sales, but the actual dollar amounts are based on

12,000 units of sales. Clearly, the costs to make 12,000 units will be greater than the costs to make 10,000 units, so it is no surprise that Optel's total expense variance is unfavorable. In addition, the costs in Exhibit 8.2 with the highest unfavorable variances (direct materials, direct labor, and sales commissions) are typically considered *variable* costs, which increase directly with sales activity. In general, the fixed budget performance report is not very useful in analyzing performance when actual sales differ from predicted sales. In the next section we show how a flexible budget can be useful in analyzing performance.

■ Decision Insight

Cruise Control   Budget reporting and evaluation are used at service providers such as **Royal Caribbean Cruises Ltd**. It regularly prepares performance plans and budget requests for its fleet of cruise ships, which describe performance goals, measure outcomes, and analyze variances. ■

Melanie Stetson Freeman/The Christian Science Monitor/Getty Images

FLEXIBLE BUDGET REPORTS

Purpose of Flexible Budgets

To help address limitations with the fixed budget performance report, particularly from the effects of changes in sales volume, management can use a flexible budget. Since flexible budgets vary by level of activity, they are useful both before and after the period's activities are complete.

A flexible budget prepared before the period is often based on several levels of activity. Budgets for those different levels can provide a "what-if" look at operations. The different levels often include both a best-case and worst-case scenario. This allows management to make adjustments to avoid or lessen the effects of the worst-case scenario.

A flexible budget prepared after the period helps management evaluate past performance. It is especially useful for such an evaluation because it reflects budgeted revenues and costs based on the actual level of activity. Thus, the flexible budget gives an "apples to apples" comparison because the budgeted activity level is the same as the actual activity level. With a flexible budget, comparisons of actual results with budgeted performance are likely to be able to identify the causes of any differences. Such information can help managers focus attention on real problem areas and implement corrective actions.

Preparation of Flexible Budgets

P1
_____

Prepare a flexible budget and interpret a flexible budget performance report.

A flexible budget is designed to reveal the effects of different activity levels on revenues and costs. To prepare a flexible budget, management must classify costs as variable or fixed, within a relevant range. Recall that the total amount of a variable cost changes in direct proportion to a change in activity level. The total amount of fixed cost remains unchanged regardless of changes in the level of activity within a relevant (normal) operating range.

When we create the numbers in a flexible budget, we express each variable cost in one of two ways: either as (1) a constant amount per unit of sales or as (2) a percentage of a sales dollar. In the case of a fixed cost, we express its budgeted amount as the total amount expected to occur at any sales volume within the relevant range.

Point: The usefulness of a flexible budget depends on valid classification of variable and fixed costs. Some costs are mixed and must be analyzed to determine their variable and fixed portions.

Exhibit 8.3 shows a set of flexible budgets for Optel for January 2015. Seven of its expenses are classified as variable costs. Optel expects these costs to change in total as sales change. Its remaining five expenses are fixed costs. These classifications result from management's investigation of each expense. Variable and fixed expense categories are *not* the same for every company, and we must avoid drawing conclusions from specific cases. For example, depending on the nature of a company's operations, office supplies expense can be either fixed or variable with respect to sales.

EXHIBIT 8.3

Flexible Budgets

OPTEL
Flexible Budgets
For Month Ended January 31, 2015

	Flexible Budget		Flexible Budget for Unit Sales of		
	Variable Amount per Unit	Total Fixed Cost	10,000	12,000	14,000
Sales	$10.00		$100,000	$120,000	$140,000
Variable costs					
Direct materials	1.00		10,000	12,000	14,000
Direct labor	1.50		15,000	18,000	21,000
Factory supplies	0.20		2,000	2,400	2,800
Utilities	0.30		3,000	3,600	4,200
Sales commissions	0.90		9,000	10,800	12,600
Shipping expenses	0.40		4,000	4,800	5,600
Office supplies	0.50		5,000	6,000	7,000
Total variable costs	4.80		48,000	57,600	67,200
Contribution margin	$ 5.20		$ 52,000	$ 62,400	$ 72,800
Fixed costs					
Depreciation—machinery		$ 8,000	8,000	8,000	8,000
Supervisory salaries		11,000	11,000	11,000	11,000
Insurance expense		1,000	1,000	1,000	1,000
Depreciation—office equipment		7,000	7,000	7,000	7,000
Administrative salaries		13,000	13,000	13,000	13,000
Total fixed costs		$40,000	40,000	40,000	40,000
Income from operations			$ 12,000	$ 22,400	$ 32,800

The layout for the flexible budgets in Exhibit 8.3 follows a *contribution margin format*—beginning with sales followed by variable costs and then fixed costs. Both the expected individual and total variable costs are reported and then subtracted from sales. Sales minus variable costs equals contribution margin. The expected amounts of fixed costs are listed next, followed by the expected income from operations before taxes.

The first column of numbers in Exhibit 8.3 shows the variable costs per unit for each of Optel's variable costs. The second column of numbers shows Optel's fixed costs, which won't change as sales volume changes. The third, fourth, and fifth number columns show the flexible budget amounts computed for three different sales volumes. For instance, the third number column's flexible budget is based on 10,000 units. In this column, total variable costs for each of Optel's seven variable costs are computed as the variable cost per unit (from column 1) multiplied by 10,000 units. Also, the total fixed costs in this column are the same as those in the second number column.

Overall, the numbers in the third number column of Exhibit 8.3 are the same as those in the fixed budget of Exhibit 8.2 because the expected sales volume (10,000 units) is the same for both budgets. In addition, the flexible budget in Exhibit 8.3 reports budgeted costs for activity levels of 12,000 and 14,000 units. Note that the total variable costs increase as the activity levels increase, but the total fixed costs stay unchanged as activity increases. A flexible budget like that in Exhibit 8.3 can be useful to management in planning operations. In addition, as we will show in the next section, a flexible budget is particularly useful in analyzing performance when actual sales volume differs from that predicted by a fixed budget.

Flexible Budget Performance Report

Recall that Optel's actual sales volume for January was 12,000 units. This sales volume is 2,000 units more than the 10,000 units originally predicted in the fixed budget. So, when management evaluates Optel's performance, it needs a flexible budget showing actual and budgeted dollar amounts at 12,000 units.

Example: Using Exhibit 8.3, what is the budgeted income from operations for unit sales of (a) 11,000 and (b) 13,000? *Answers:* $17,200 for unit sales of 11,000; $27,600 for unit sales of 13,000.

Point: Flexible budgeting allows a budget to be prepared at the *actual* output level. Performance reports are then prepared comparing the flexible budget to actual revenues and costs.

A **flexible budget performance report** compares actual performance and budgeted performance based on actual sales volume (or other activity level). This report directs management's attention to those costs or revenues that differ substantially from budgeted amounts. In Optel's case, we prepare this report after January's sales volume is known to be 12,000 units. Exhibit 8.4 shows Optel's flexible budget performance report for January. The flexible budget report shows a favorable net income variance of $3,000. Management then uses this report to investigate variances and evaluate Optel's performance. Quite often management will focus on large variances. This report shows a $5,000 favorable variance in total dollar sales. Because actual and budgeted volumes are both 12,000 units, the $5,000 sales variance must have resulted from a higher than expected selling price. Management would like to determine if the conditions that resulted in higher selling prices are likely to continue.

EXHIBIT 8.4

Flexible Budget
Performance Report

OPTEL Flexible Budget Performance Report For Month Ended January 31, 2015	Flexible Budget (12,000 units)	Actual Results (12,000 units)	Variances*
Sales	$120,000	$125,000	$5,000 F
Variable costs			
Direct materials	12,000	13,000	1,000 U
Direct labor	18,000	20,000	2,000 U
Factory supplies	2,400	2,100	300 F
Utilities	3,600	4,000	400 U
Sales commissions	10,800	10,800	0
Shipping expenses	4,800	4,300	500 F
Office supplies	6,000	5,200	800 F
Total variable costs	57,600	59,400	1,800 U
Contribution margin	62,400	65,600	3,200 F
Fixed costs			
Depreciation—machinery	8,000	8,000	0
Supervisory salaries	11,000	11,000	0
Insurance expense	1,000	1,200	200 U
Depreciation—office equipment	7,000	7,000	0
Administrative salaries	13,000	13,000	0
Total fixed costs	40,000	40,200	200 U
Income from operations	$ 22,400	$ 25,400	$3,000 F

* F = Favorable variance; U = Unfavorable variance.

The other variances in Exhibit 8.4 also direct management's attention to areas where corrective actions can help control Optel's operations. For example, both the direct materials and direct labor variances are relatively large and unfavorable. On the other hand, relatively large favorable variances are observed for shipping expenses and office supplies. Management will try to determine the causes for these variances, both favorable and unfavorable, and make changes to Optel's operations if needed.

In addition to analyzing variances using a flexible budget performance report, management can also take a more detailed approach based on a *standard cost* system. We illustrate this form of variance analysis next in the Standard Costs section of this chapter.

■ **Decision Maker**

Entrepreneur   The heads of both the strategic consulting and tax consulting divisions of your financial services firm complain to you about the unfavorable variances on their performance reports. "We worked on more consulting assignments than planned. It's not surprising our costs are higher than expected. To top it off, this report characterizes our work as *poor*!" How do you respond? ■   [Answers follow the chapter's Summary.]

A manufacturing company reports the fixed budget and actual results for the past year as shown below. The company's fixed budget assumes a selling price of $40 per unit. The fixed budget is based on 20,000 units of sales, and the actual results are based on 24,000 units of sales. Prepare a flexible budget performance report for the past year.

NEED-TO-KNOW 8-1

Flexible Budget

P1

	Fixed Budget (20,000 units)	Actual Results (24,000 units)
Sales	$800,000	$972,000
Variable costs*	160,000	240,000
Fixed costs	500,000	490,000

*Budgeted variable cost per unit = $160,000/20,000 = $8.00

Solution

Flexible Budget Performance Report			
	Flexible Budget (24,000 units)	Actual Results (24,000 units)	Variances
Sales	$960,000*	$972,000	$12,000 F
Variable costs	192,000**	240,000	48,000 U
Contribution margin	768,000	732,000	36,000 U
Fixed costs	500,000	490,000	10,000 F
Income from operations	$268,000	$242,000	$26,000 U

*24,000 × $40   **24,000 × $8

Do More: QS 8-1, QS 8-2, QS 8-3, QS 8-4, E 8-3, E 8-4

QC1

Section 2—Standard Costs

In this section we show how *standard costs* can be used in a flexible budgeting system to enable management to better understand the reasons for variances. **Standard costs** are preset costs for delivering a product or service under normal conditions. These costs are established by personnel, engineering, and accounting studies using past experiences and data. Standard costs vary across companies. Management can use standard costs to assess the reasonableness of actual costs incurred for producing the product or providing the service. When actual costs vary from standard costs, management follows up to identify potential problems and take corrective actions. **Management by exception** means that managers focus attention on the most significant differences between actual costs and standard costs and give less attention to areas where performance is reasonably close to standard. Management by exception is especially useful when directed at controllable items, enabling top management to affect the actions of lower-level managers responsible for the company's revenues and costs.

Standard costs are often used in preparing budgets because they are the anticipated costs incurred under normal conditions. Terms such as *standard materials cost, standard labor cost,* and *standard overhead cost* are often used to refer to amounts budgeted for direct materials, direct labor, and overhead.

While many managers use standard costs to investigate manufacturing costs, standard costs can also help control *nonmanufacturing* costs. Companies providing services instead of products can also benefit from the use of standard costs. For example, while quality medical service is paramount, efficiency in providing that service is also important to medical professionals. The use of budgeting and standard costing is touted as an effective means to control and monitor medical costs, especially overhead.

C1

Define *standard costs* and explain how standard cost information is useful for management by exception.

Point: Business practice often uses the word *budget* when speaking of total amounts and *standard* when discussing per unit amounts.

MATERIALS AND LABOR STANDARDS

This section explains how to set direct materials and direct labor standards and how to prepare a standard cost card.

Identifying Standard Costs

Managerial accountants, engineers, personnel administrators, and other managers combine their efforts to set standard costs. To identify standards for direct labor costs, we can conduct time and motion studies for each labor operation in the process of providing a product or service. From these studies, management can learn the best way to perform the operation and then set the standard labor time required for the operation under normal conditions. Similarly, standards for direct materials are set by studying the quantity, grade, and cost of each material used. (Standards for overhead costs are explained later in the chapter.)

Regardless of the care used in setting standard costs and in revising them as conditions change, actual costs frequently differ from standard costs. For instance, the actual quantity of material used can differ from the standard, or the price paid per unit of material can differ from the standard. Quantity and price differences from standard amounts can also occur for labor. That is, the actual labor time and actual labor rate can vary from what was expected.

Example: What factors might be considered when deciding whether to revise standard costs? *Answer:* Changes in the processes and/or resources needed to carry out the processes.

 Decision Insight

Cruis'n Standards   The **Corvette** consists of hundreds of parts for which engineers set standards. Various types of labor are also involved in its production, including machining, assembly, painting, and welding, and standards are set for each. Actual results are periodically compared with standards to assess performance. ∎

Car Culture/Getty Images

Setting Standard Costs

To illustrate the setting of standard costs, we consider baseball bats manufactured by ProBat. Its engineers have determined that manufacturing one bat requires 0.90 kilograms (kg) of high-grade wood. They also expect some loss of material as part of the process because of inefficiencies and waste. This results in adding an *allowance* of 0.10 kg, making the standard requirement 1.0 kg of wood for each bat.

The 0.90 kg portion is called an *ideal standard;* it is the quantity of material required if the process is 100% efficient without any loss or waste. Reality suggests that some loss of material usually occurs with any process. The standard of 1.0 kg is known as the *practical standard,* the quantity of material required under normal application of the process. Most companies use practical rather than ideal standards.

Point: Companies promoting continuous improvement strive to achieve ideal standards by eliminating inefficiencies and waste.

ProBat needs to develop standard costs for direct materials, direct labor, and overhead. For direct materials and direct labor, ProBat must develop standard quantities and standard prices. For overhead, ProBat must consider the activities that drive overhead costs.

- High-grade wood can be purchased at a standard price of $25 per kg. The purchasing department sets this price as the expected price for the budget period. To determine this price, the purchasing department considers factors such as the quality of materials, future economic conditions, supply factors (shortages and excesses), and any available discounts.
- The engineers also decide that two hours of labor time (after including allowances) are required to manufacture a bat. The wage rate is $20 per hour (better-than-average skilled labor is required).
- ProBat assigns all overhead at the rate of $10 per labor hour.

The standard costs of direct materials, direct labor, and overhead for one bat are shown in Exhibit 8.5 in what is called a *standard cost card.* These standard cost amounts are then used to prepare manufacturing budgets for a budgeted level of production.

STANDARD COST CARD			
Production factor	**Standard Quantity**	**Standard Cost per Unit**	**Total Standard Cost**
Direct materials (wood)	1 kg	$25 per kg	$25
Direct labor	2 hours	$20 per hour	40
Overhead	2 labor hours	$10 per hour	20
		Total	**$85**

COST VARIANCE ANALYSIS

Knowing the standard costs they expect, companies have a way to monitor and analyze differences from the standards. A **cost variance,** also simply called a *variance,* is the difference between actual and standard costs. Cost variances can be favorable (F) or unfavorable (U). If actual cost is less than standard cost, the variance is considered favorable. If actual costs are greater than standard costs, the variance is unfavorable.[1] This section discusses cost variance analysis.

Exhibit 8.6 shows the flow of events in **variance analysis:** (1) preparing a standard cost performance report, (2) computing and analyzing variances, (3) identifying questions and their explanations, and (4) taking corrective and strategic actions. These variance analysis steps are interrelated and are frequently applied in good organizations.

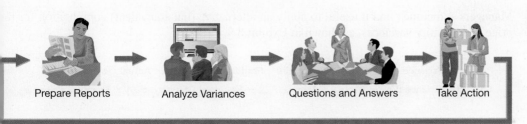

Prepare Reports   Analyze Variances   Questions and Answers   Take Action

Cost Variance Computation

Management needs information about the factors causing a cost variance, but first it must properly compute the variance. In its most simple form, a cost variance (CV) is computed as shown in Exhibit 8.7.

Cost Variance (CV) = Actual Cost (AC) − Standard Cost (SC)

where:

Actual Cost (AC) = Actual Quantity (AQ) × Actual Price (AP)
Standard Cost (SC) = Standard Quantity (SQ) × Standard Price (SP)

A cost variance is further defined by its components. Actual quantity (AQ) is the input (material or labor) used to manufacture the quantity of output. Standard quantity (SQ) is the standard input for the quantity of output. For example, if ProBat's actual output is 500 bats, its standard quantity of direct labor is 1,000 hours (500 bats × 2 hours per bat). Actual price (AP) is the actual amount paid to acquire the input (material or labor), and standard price (SP) is the standard price.

---

[1] Short-term favorable variances can sometimes lead to long-term unfavorable variances. For instance, if management spends less than the budgeted amount on maintenance or insurance, the performance report would show a favorable variance. Cutting these expenses can lead to major losses in the long run if machinery wears out prematurely or insurance coverage proves inadequate.

Two main factors cause a cost variance:

1. The difference between actual price per unit of input and standard price per unit of input results in a **price** (or rate) **variance**
2. The difference between actual quantity of input used and standard quantity of input used results in a **quantity** (or usage or efficiency) **variance.**

To assess the impacts of these two factors in a cost variance, we use the formulas in Exhibit 8.8.

EXHIBIT 8.8

Price Variance and Quantity
Variance Formulas

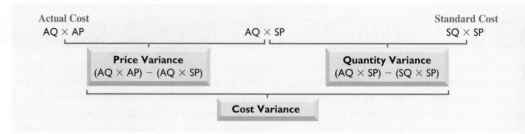

Exhibit 8.8 illustrates three important general rules in computing cost variances:

1. In computing a price variance, the quantity (actual) is held constant.
2. In computing a quantity variance, the price (standard) is held constant.
3. The cost variance, or total variance, is the sum of the price and quantity variances.

Managers sometimes find it useful to apply an alternative (but equivalent) computation for the price and quantity variances, as shown in Exhibit 8.9.

EXHIBIT 8.9

Alternative Price Variance
and Quantity Variance
Formulas

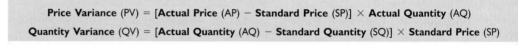

Price Variance (PV) = [**Actual Price (AP)** − **Standard Price (SP)**] × **Actual Quantity (AQ)**

Quantity Variance (QV) = [**Actual Quantity (AQ)** − **Standard Quantity (SQ)**] × **Standard Price (SP)**

The results from applying the formulas in Exhibits 8.8 and 8.9 are identical.

Computing Materials and Labor Variances

P2

Compute materials and
labor variances.

We illustrate the computation of the materials and labor cost variances using data from G-Max, a company that makes specialty golf equipment and accessories for individual customers. This company has set the following standard quantities and costs for direct materials and direct labor per unit for one of its handcrafted golf clubheads:

Direct materials (0.5 lb. per unit at $20 per lb.)	$10.00
Direct labor (1 hr. per unit at $8 per hr.)	8.00
Total standard direct cost per unit	$18.00

Materials Cost Variances   During May 2015, G-Max budgeted to produce 4,000 clubheads (units). It actually produced only 3,500 units. It used 1,800 pounds of direct materials (titanium) costing $21 per pound, meaning its total direct materials cost was $37,800. To produce 3,500 units, G-Max should have used 1,750 pounds of direct materials (3,500 × 0.5 lb. per unit). This information allows us to compute both actual and standard direct materials costs for G-Max's 3,500 units and its total direct materials cost variance as follows:

Direct Materials	Quantity	Price per Unit	Cost
Actual cost	1,800 lbs.	@ $21.00 per lb. =	$37,800
Standard cost	1,750 lbs.*	@ $20.00 per lb. =	35,000
Direct materials cost variance (unfavorable)		=	$ 2,800

*Standard quantity = 3,500 units × 0.5 lb. per unit

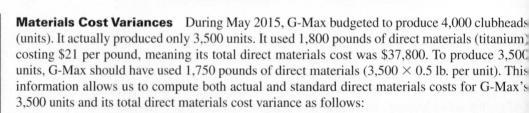

Kristjan Maack/Getty Images/
Nordic Photos

Management would like to determine if this unfavorable cost variance is due to unfavorable quantity or price variances, or both. To better isolate the causes of this $2,800 unfavorable total direct materials cost variance, the materials price and quantity variances for these G-Max clubheads are computed and shown in Exhibit 8.10.

EXHIBIT 8.10

Materials Price and Quantity Variances*

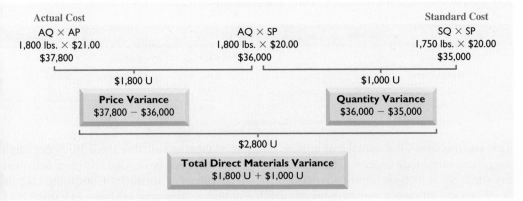

*AQ is actual quantity; AP is actual price; SP is standard price; SQ is standard quantity allowed for actual output.

We now can see the two components of the $2,800 unfavorable variance: The $1,800 unfavorable price variance results from paying $1 more per pound than the standard price, computed as 1,800 lbs. × $1. G-Max also used 50 pounds more materials than the standard quantity (1,800 actual pounds − 1,750 standard pounds). The $1,000 unfavorable quantity variance is computed as [(1,800 actual lbs. − 1,750 standard lbs.) × $20 standard price per lb.]. Detailed price and quantity variances allow management to ask the responsible individuals for explanations and corrective actions.

Example: Identify at least two factors that might have caused the unfavorable quantity variance and the unfavorable price variance in Exhibit 8.10. *Answer:* Poor-quality materials or untrained workers for the former; poor price negotiation or higher-quality materials for the latter.

Evaluating Materials Variances   The purchasing department is usually responsible for the price paid for materials. Responsibility for explaining the price variance in this case rests with the purchasing manager if a price higher than standard caused the variance. The production department is usually responsible for the amount of material used. In this case the production manager is responsible for explaining why the process used more than the standard amount of materials.

Variance analysis presents challenges. For instance, the production department could have used more than the standard amount of material because the materials' quality did not meet specifications and led to excessive waste. In this case, the purchasing manager is responsible for explaining why inferior materials were acquired. However, if analysis shows that waste was due to inefficiencies, not poor-quality material, the production manager is responsible for explaining what happened.

In evaluating price variances, managers must recognize that a favorable price variance can indicate a problem with poor product quality. **Redhook Ale**, a microbrewery in the Pacific Northwest, can probably save 10% to 15% in material prices by buying six-row barley malt instead of the better two-row from Washington's Yakima valley. Attention to quality, however, has helped Redhook Ale increase its sales. Purchasing activities are judged on both the quality of the materials and the purchase price variance.

© ColorBlind Images/Corbis

A manufacturing company reports the following for one of its products. Compute the direct materials *(a)* price variance and *(b)* quantity variance and indicate whether they are favorable or unfavorable.

NEED-TO-KNOW 8-2

Direct Materials Variances

P2

Direct materials standard	8 pounds at $6 per pound
Actual direct materials used	83,000 pounds @ $5.80 per pound
Actual finished units produced	10,000

Solution

a. Price variance   = (Actual quantity × Actual price) − (Actual quantity × Standard price)

= (83,000 × $5.80) − (83,000 × $6) = $16,600 favorable

b. Quantity variance = (Actual quantity × Standard price) − (Standard quantity* × Standard price)

= (83,000 × $6) − (80,000 × $6) = $18,000 unfavorable

*Standard quantity = 10,000 units × 8 standard pounds per unit = 80,000 pounds

Do More: QS 8-8, E 8-9, E 8-11, E 8-12, E 8-13

Labor Cost Variances   Labor cost for a specific product or service depends on the number of hours worked (quantity) and the wage rate paid to employees (price). To illustrate, G-Max's direct labor standard for 3,500 units of its handcrafted clubheads is one direct labor hour per unit, or 3,500 hours at $8 per hour. But because only 3,400 hours at $8.30 per hour were actually used to complete the units, the actual and standard direct labor costs are

Direct Labor	Quantity	Rate per Hour	Cost
Actual cost....................................	3,400 hrs.	@ $8.30 per hr. =	$28,220
Standard cost................................	3,500 hrs.*	@ $8.00 per hr. =	28,000
Direct labor cost variance (unfavorable)		=	$ 220

*Standard quantity = 3,500 units × 1 standard DLH per unit

This analysis shows that actual cost is merely $220 over the standard; that small difference might suggest no immediate concern. The direct labor cost variance can be divided into price and quantity variances, which are almost always called *rate* and *efficiency* variances. Computing both the labor rate and efficiency variances reveals a different picture, however, as shown in Exhibit 8.11.

EXHIBIT 8.11

Labor Rate and Efficiency
Variances*

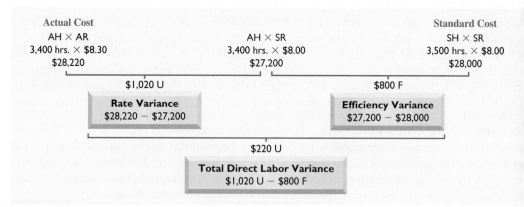

* Here, we employ hours (H) for quantity (Q), and the wage rate (R) for price (P). Thus: AH is actual direct labor hours: AR is actual wage rate; SH is standard direct labor hours allowed for actual output; SR is standard wage rate.

Evaluating Labor Variances   Exhibit 8.11 shows that the total unfavorable labor cost variance results from an $800 favorable efficiency variance and a $1,020 unfavorable rate variance. The favorable efficiency variance results from using 100 fewer direct labor (3,400 actual DLH − 3,500 standard DLH) hours than standard for the units produced. The unfavorable rate variance results from paying a wage rate that is $0.30 per hour higher ($8.30 actual rate − $8.00 standard rate) than standard. The personnel administrator or the production manager needs to explain why the wage rate is higher than expected. The production manager should also explain how the labor hours were reduced. If this experience can be repeated and transferred to other departments, more savings are possible.

One possible explanation of these labor rate and efficiency variances is the use of workers with different skill levels. If this is the reason, senior management must discuss the implications with the production manager who has the responsibility to assign workers to tasks with the appropriate skill level. In this case, an investigation might show that higher-skilled workers were used to produce 3,500 units of hand-crafted clubheads. As a result, fewer labor hours might be required for the work, but the wage rate paid these workers is higher than standard because of their greater skills. The effect of this strategy is a higher than standard total cost, which would require actions to remedy the situation or adjust the standard.

■ **Decision** Maker

Production Manager   You receive the manufacturing variance report for June and discover a large unfavorable labor efficiency (quantity) variance. What factors do you investigate to identify its possible causes? ■   [Answers follow the chapter's Summary.]

The following information is available for York Company. Compute the direct labor rate and efficiency variances.

Actual direct labor cost (6,250 hours @ $13.10 per hour).........	$81,875
Standard direct labor hours per unit.........................	2.0 hours
Standard rate per hour	$13.00
Actual production (units)	2,500 units
Budgeted production (units)	3,000 units

Solution

Total standard hours = 2,500 × 2.0 = 5,000
Rate variance   = ($13.10 − $13.00) × 6,250 = $625 unfavorable
Efficiency variance = (6,250 − 5,000) × $13.00 = $16,250 unfavorable

OVERHEAD STANDARDS AND VARIANCES

In previous chapters we showed how companies can use *predetermined overhead rates* to allocate overhead costs to products or services. In a standard costing system this allocation is done using the *standard* amount of the overhead allocation base, such as standard labor hours or standard machine hours. Next we show how to use standard costs to develop flexible overhead budgets.

Flexible Overhead Budgets

Standard overhead costs are the overhead amounts expected to occur at a certain activity level. Unlike direct materials and direct labor, overhead includes fixed costs and variable costs. This requires management to classify overhead costs as fixed or variable (within a relevant range), and to develop a flexible budget for overhead costs.

To illustrate, the first two number columns of Exhibit 8.12 show the overhead cost structure to develop G-Max's flexible overhead budgets for May 2015. At the beginning of the year, G-Max predicted variable overhead costs of $1.00 per unit (clubhead), comprised of $0.40 per unit for indirect labor, $0.30 per unit for indirect materials, $0.20 per unit for power and lights, and $0.10 per unit for factory maintenance. In addition, G-Max predicts monthly fixed overhead of $4,000.

With these variable and fixed overhead cost amounts, G-Max can prepare flexible overhead budgets at various capacity levels (four right-most number columns in Exhibit 8.12). At its maximum capacity (100% column), G-Max could produce 5,000 clubheads. At 70% of maximum capacity, G-Max could produce 3,500 (computed as 5,000 × 70%) clubheads. Recall that total variable costs will increase as production activity increases, but total fixed costs will not change as production activity changes. At 70% capacity, variable overhead costs are budgeted at $3,500 (3,500 × $1.00), while at 100% capacity variable costs are budgeted at $5,000 (5,000 × $1.00). At all capacity levels, fixed overhead costs are budgeted at $4,000 per month.

Point: With increased automation, machine hours are frequently used in applying overhead instead of labor hours.

Setting Overhead Standards

To allocate overhead costs to products or services, management needs to establish the standard overhead cost rate. To do that, management must determine (1) an allocation base and (2) a predicted activity level.

Allocation Base   The allocation base is some measure of input that management believes is related to overhead costs. Examples include direct labor hours or machine hours. In this section

EXHIBIT 8.12

Flexible Overhead Budgets

G-MAX Flexible Overhead Budgets For Month Ended May 31, 2015	Flexible Budget		Flexible Budget at Capacity Level of			
	Variable Amount per Unit	Total Fixed Cost	70%	80%	90%	100%
Production (in units)	I unit		3,500	4,000	4,500	5,000
Factory overhead						
Variable costs						
Indirect labor	$0.40/unit		$1,400	$1,600	$1,800	$2,000
Indirect materials	0.30/unit		1,050	1,200	1,350	1,500
Power and lights	0.20/unit		700	800	900	1,000
Maintenance	0.10/unit		350	400	450	500
Total variable overhead costs	$1.00/unit		3,500	4,000	4,500	5,000
Fixed costs (per month)						
Building rent		$1,000	1,000	1,000	1,000	1,000
Depreciation—machinery		1,200	1,200	1,200	1,200	1,200
Supervisory salaries		1,800	1,800	1,800	1,800	1,800
Total fixed overhead costs.		$4,000	4,000	4,000	4,000	4,000
Total factory overhead			$7,500	$8,000	$8,500	$9,000
Standard direct labor hours I hr./unit . .			3,500 hrs.	4,000 hrs.	4,500 hrs.	5,000 hrs.
Predetermined overhead rate per standard direct labor hour				$ 2.00		

we assume that G-Max uses direct labor hours as an allocation base, and it has a standard of one direct labor hour per finished unit.

Predicted Activity Level When choosing the predicted activity level, management considers many factors. The level could be set at 100% of capacity, but this is rare. Difficulties in scheduling work, equipment breakdowns, and insufficient product demand typically cause the activity level to be less than full capacity. Also, good long-run management practices usually call for some excess plant capacity, to allow for special opportunities and demand changes. G-Max managers predicted an 80% activity level for May, or a production volume of 4,000 clubheads.

Standard Overhead Rate At the predicted activity level of 4,000 units, the flexible budget in Exhibit 8.12 predicts total overhead of $8,000. At this activity level of 4,000 units, G-Max's standard direct labor hours is 4,000 hours (4,000 units × 1 direct labor hour per unit). G-Max's standard overhead rate is then computed as:

$$\text{Standard overhead rate} = \frac{\text{Total overhead cost at predicted activity level}}{\text{Total direct labor hours at predicted activity level}}$$

$$= \frac{\$8,000}{4,000} = \$2 \text{ per direct labor hour}$$

This standard overhead rate will be used in computing overhead cost variances, as we show next, and in recording journal entries in a standard cost system, which we show in the appendix to this chapter.

Decision Insight

Measuring Up In the spirit of continuous improvement, competitors compare their processes and performance standards against benchmarks established by industry leaders. Those that use **benchmarking** include Jiffy Lube, All Tune and Lube, and SpeeDee Oil Change and Tune-Up. ■

Computing Overhead Cost Variances

When standard costs are used, the cost accounting system applies overhead to the units produced using the predetermined standard overhead rate. The standard overhead applied is based on the predetermined overhead rate (at the predicted activity level) and the standard number of hours that *should have been used,* based on the actual production. Actual overhead incurred might be different from the overhead cost applied for a period, and management will again use *variance analysis*. The difference between the total overhead cost applied to products and the total overhead cost actually incurred is called an **overhead cost variance** (total overhead variance), which is defined in Exhibit 8.13.

P3
Compute overhead controllable and volume variances.

EXHIBIT 8.13
Overhead Cost Variance

Overhead cost variance (OCV) = Actual overhead incurred (AOI) − Standard overhead applied (SOA)

To illustrate, G-Max produced 3,500 units during the month, which should have used 3,500 direct labor hours. Recall that management expected to produce 4,000 units during the month; thus G-Max operated below its expected level. From Exhibit 8.12, G-Max's predetermined overhead rate at the predicted capacity level of 4,000 units was $2.00 per direct labor hour, so the standard overhead applied is $7,000 (computed as 3,500 direct labor hours × $2.00). Additional data from cost reports show that the actual overhead cost incurred in the month is $7,650. Using the formula in Exhibit 8.13, we find that G-Max's total overhead variance is $650, computed as:

Actual total overhead (given)	$7,650
Standard overhead applied (3,500 DLH × $2.00 per DLH).........	7,000
Total overhead variance (unfavorable)........................	$ 650

This variance is unfavorable: G-Max's actual overhead was higher than it should have been based on budgeted amounts.

Overhead Controllable and Volume Variances To help identify factors causing the overhead cost variance, managers separate out the *overhead controllable* and *overhead volume variances,* as illustrated in Exhibit 8.14. The results provide information useful for taking strategic actions to improve company performance.

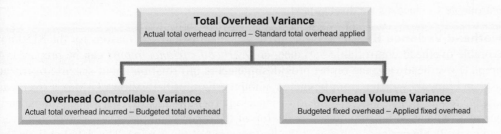

EXHIBIT 8.14

Framework for Understanding Total Overhead Variance

The **controllable variance** is the difference between actual overhead costs incurred and the budgeted overhead costs based on a flexible budget. The controllable variance is so named because it refers to activities usually under management control. Since G-Max only produced 3,500 units during the month, we need to compare the *actual* overhead costs to make 3,500 units to the *budgeted* cost to make 3,500 units.

Point: The budgeted overhead cost is from a flexible budget.

A **volume variance** occurs when there is a difference between the actual volume of production and the standard volume of production. The volume variance is based solely on *fixed* overhead. The budgeted fixed overhead amount is the same regardless of the volume of production (within the relevant range). The applied fixed overhead is based, however, on the standard direct labor hours allowed for the actual volume of production. When a company operates at a capacity level different from what it expected, a volume variance will exist. We next compute the controllable and volume variances for G-Max.

The flexible budget in Exhibit 8.12 shows budgeted factory overhead of $7,500 at the production volume of 3,500 units. The controllable variance is computed as:

Overhead Controllable Variance	
Actual total overhead (given)	$7,650
Budgeted total overhead (from flexible budget)	7,500
Controllable variance (unfavorable)	$ 150

Next, we compute the volume variance. G-Max's budgeted fixed overhead at the predicted capacity level for the month (4,000 units) was $4,000. Recall from Exhibit 8.12 that G-Max's predetermined fixed overhead rate at the predicted capacity level of 4,000 units was $1 per direct labor hour. Thus, G-Max's applied fixed overhead was $3,500, computed as 3,500 direct labor hours × $1.00 per unit. G-Max's volume variance is computed as:

Overhead Volume Variance	
Budgeted fixed overhead (at predicted capacity)	$4,000
Applied fixed overhead (3,500 DLH × $1.00 per DLH)	3,500
Volume variance (unfavorable)	$ 500

Analyzing Overhead Controllable and Volume Variances   How should the top management of G-Max interpret the unfavorable overhead controllable and volume variances? An unfavorable volume variance means that the company did not reach its predicted operating level. In this case, 80% of manufacturing capacity was budgeted but only 70% was used. Management needs to know why the actual level of production differs from the expected level. The main purpose of the volume variance is to identify what portion of the total overhead variance is caused by failing to meet the expected production level. Often the reasons for failing to meet this expected production level are due to factors, for example customer demand, that are beyond employees' control. This information permits management to focus on explanations for the controllable variance, as we discuss next.

Overhead Variance Reports   To help management isolate the reasons for the $150 unfavorable overhead controllable variance, an *overhead variance report* can be prepared. A complete overhead variance report provides managers information about specific overhead costs and how they differ from budgeted amounts. Exhibit 8.15 shows G-Max's overhead variance report for May. The overhead variance report shows the total overhead volume variance of $500 unfavorable (shown near the top of the report) and the $150 unfavorable overhead controllable variance (shown at the bottom right of the report). The detailed listing of individual overhead costs reveals the following: (1) Fixed overhead costs and variable factory maintenance costs were incurred as expected. (2) Costs for indirect labor and power and lights were higher than expected. (3) Indirect materials cost was less than expected. Management can use the variance overhead report to identify the individual overhead costs it wants to investigate.

Appendix 8A describes an expanded analysis of overhead variances.

EXHIBIT 8.15

Overhead Variance Report

G-MAX
Overhead Variance Report
For Month Ended May 31, 2015

Overhead Volume Variance

Expected production level	80% of capacity (4,000 units)	
Production level achieved	70% of capacity (3,500 units)	
Budgeted fixed overhead (4,000 DLH × $1.00)	$4,000	
Fixed overhead applied (3,500 DLH × $1.00)	$3,500	
Volume variance	$ 500 (unfavorable)	

Overhead Controllable Variance	**Flexible Budget**	**Actual Results**	**Variances***
Variable overhead costs			
Indirect labor	$1,400	$1,525	$125 U
Indirect materials.	1,050	1,025	25 F
Power and lights	700	750	50 U
Maintenance.	350	350	0
Total variable overhead costs	3,500	3,650	150 U
Fixed overhead costs			
Building rent	1,000	1,000	0
Depreciation—machinery.	1,200	1,200	0
Supervisory salaries.	1,800	1,800	0
Total fixed overhead costs	4,000	4,000	0
Total overhead costs	$7,500	$7,650	$150 U

Total overhead variance = $650 unfavorable

* F = Favorable variance; U = Unfavorable variance.

A manufacturing company uses standard costs and reports the information below for January. The company uses machine hours to allocate overhead, and the standard is two machine hours per finished unit. Compute the total overhead cost variance, overhead controllable variance, and overhead volume variance for January. Indicate whether each variance is favorable or unfavorable.

Predicted activity level.	1,500 units
Variable overhead rate budgeted.	$2.50 per machine hour
Fixed overhead budgeted.	$6,000 per month ($2.00 per machine hour at predicted activity level)
Actual activity level	1,800 units
Actual overhead costs	$15,800

Solution

Total overhead cost variance

Actual total overhead cost (given)	$15,800
Standard overhead applied (1,800 × 2 × $4.50)	16,200
Total overhead variance (favorable).	$ 400

Overhead controllable variance

Actual total overhead cost (given)	$15,800
Flexible budget total overhead (1,800 × 2 × $2.50) + $6,000	15,000
Overhead controllable variance (unfavorable)	$ 800

Overhead volume variance

Budgeted fixed overhead	$ 6,000
Applied fixed overhead (1,800 × 2 × $2)	7,200
Overhead volume variance (favorable)	$ 1,200

GLOBAL VIEW

BMW, a German automobile manufacturer, uses concepts of standard costing and variance analysis. Production begins with huge rolls of steel and aluminum, which are then cut and pressed by large machines. Material must meet high quality standards, and the company sets standards for each of its machine operations. In the assembly department, highly trained employees complete the assembly of the painted car chassis, often to customer specifications. Again, BMW sets standards for how much labor should be used and monitors its employee performance. The company then computes and analyzes materials price and quantity variances and labor rate and efficiency variances and takes action as needed. Like most manufacturers, BMW uses *practical standards* and thus must address waste of raw materials in its production process. In a recent year, BMW used over 3 million tons of steel, plastic, and aluminum to make over 1.8 million cars. Of the 665,000 tons of these raw materials wasted in production, over 98% are recyclable.

Sustainability and Accounting   Niner Bikes employs standard cost principles in making bikes. But, founder and CEO Chris Sugai offers flexible work schedules for his employees and insists that employees stay home after they or their spouses give birth. These benefits are costly, but they allow Chris to sustain a loyal workforce.

Decision Analysis ▢▢▢   Sales Variances

A1

Analyze changes in sales
from expected amounts.

This chapter explained the computation and analysis of cost variances. A similar variance analysis can be applied to sales. For this analysis, the budgeted amount of unit sales is the predicted activity level, and the budgeted selling price can be treated as a "standard" price. To illustrate, consider the following sales data from G-Max for two of its golf products, Excel golf balls and Big Bert drivers.

	Budgeted	Actual
Sales of Excel golf balls (units)...........	1,000 units	1,100 units
Sales price per Excel golf ball.............	$10	$10.50
Sales of Big Bert drivers (units)...........	150 units	140 units
Sales price per Big Bert driver............	$200	$190

Using this information, we compute both the *sales price variance* and the *sales volume variance* as shown in Exhibit 8.16. The total sales price variance is $850 unfavorable, and the total sales volume variance is $1,000 unfavorable. However, further analysis of these total sales variances reveals that both the sales price and sales volume variances for Excel golf balls are favorable, while both variances are unfavorable for the Big Bert driver.

EXHIBIT 8.16

Computing Sales
Variances*

Excel Golf Balls	Actual Results AS × AP	Flexible Budget AS × BP	Fixed Budget BS × BP
Sales dollars (balls)	(1,100 × $10.50) **$11,550**	(1,100 × $10) **$11,000**	(1,000 × $10) **$10,000**
		$550 F	$1,000 F
		Sales Price Variance (AS × AP) − (AS × BP)	**Sales Volume Variance** (AS × BP) − (BS × BP)
Big Bert Drivers			
Sales dollars (drivers)	(140 × $190) **$26,600**	(140 × $200) **$28,000**	(150 × $200) **$30,000**
		$1,400 U	$2,000 U
		Sales Price Variance (AS × AP) − (AS × BP)	**Sales Volume Variance** (AS × BP) − (BS × BP)
Total		<u>$850 U</u>	<u>$1,000 U</u>

* AS = actual sales units; AP = actual sales price; BP = budgeted sales price; BS = budgeted sales units (fixed budget).

Managers use sales variances for planning and control purposes. G-Max sold 90 combined total units (both balls and drivers) more than budgeted, yet its total sales price and sales volume variances are unfavorable. The unfavorable sales price variance is due mainly to a decrease in the selling price of Big

Bert drivers by $10 per unit. Management must assess whether this price decrease will continue. Likewise, the unfavorable sales volume variance is due to G-Max selling fewer Big Bert drivers (140) than was budgeted (150). Management must assess whether this decreased demand for Big Bert drivers will persist.

Overall, management can use the detailed sales variances to examine what caused the company to sell more golf balls and fewer drivers. Managers can also use this information to evaluate and even reward salespeople. Extra compensation is paid to salespeople who contribute to a higher profit margin.

Decision Maker

Sales Manager   The current performance report reveals a large favorable sales volume variance but an unfavorable sales price variance. You did not expect to see a large increase in sales volume. What steps do you take to analyze this situation? ■   [Answers follow the chapter's Summary.]

Pacific Company provides the following information about its budgeted and actual results for June 2015. Although the expected June volume was 25,000 units produced and sold, the company actually produced and sold 27,000 units as detailed here:

NEED-TO-KNOW

COMPREHENSIVE

	Budget (25,000 units)	Actual (27,000 units)
Selling price	$5.00 per unit	$141,210
Variable costs (per unit)		
Direct materials.	1.24 per unit	$30,800
Direct labor	1.50 per unit	37,800
Factory supplies*	0.25 per unit	9,990
Utilities*	0.50 per unit	16,200
Selling costs	0.40 per unit	9,180
Fixed costs (per month)		
Depreciation—machinery*	$3,750	$3,710
Depreciation—factory building*	2,500	2,500
General liability insurance.	1,200	1,250
Property taxes on office equipment.	500	485
Other administrative expense.	750	900

* Indicates factory overhead item; $0.75 per unit or $3 per direct labor hour for variable overhead, and $0.25 per unit or $1 per direct labor hour for fixed overhead.

Standard costs based on expected output of 25,000 units:

	Standard Quantity	Total Cost
Direct materials, 4 oz. per unit @ $0.31/oz.	100,000 oz.	$31,000
Direct labor, 0.25 hrs. per unit @ $6.00/hr.	6,250 hrs.	37,500
Overhead, 6,250 standard hours × $4.00 per DLH		25,000

Actual costs incurred to produce 27,000 units:

	Actual Quantity	Total Cost
Direct materials, 110,000 oz. @ $0.28/oz.	110,000 oz.	$30,800
Direct labor, 5,400 hrs. @ $7.00/hr.	5,400 hrs.	37,800
Overhead ($9,990 + $16,200 + $3,710 + $2,500).		32,400

Required

1. Prepare June flexible budgets showing expected sales, costs, and net income assuming 20,000, 25,000, and 30,000 units of output produced and sold.

2. Prepare a flexible budget performance report that compares actual results with the amounts budgeted if the actual volume of 27,000 units had been expected.

3. Apply variance analysis for direct materials and direct labor.

4. Compute the total overhead variance, and the overhead controllable and overhead volume variances.

5. Compute spending and efficiency variances for overhead. (Refer to Appendix 8A.)

6. Prepare journal entries to record standard costs, and price and quantity variances, for direct materials, direct labor, and factory overhead. (Refer to Appendix 8A.)

PLANNING THE SOLUTION

- Prepare a table showing the expected results at the three specified levels of output. Compute the variable costs by multiplying the per unit variable costs by the expected volumes. Include fixed costs at the given amounts. Combine the amounts in the table to show total variable costs, contribution margin, total fixed costs, and income from operations.

- Prepare a table showing the actual results and the amounts that should be incurred at 27,000 units. Show any differences in the third column and label them with an *F* for favorable if they increase income or a *U* for unfavorable if they decrease income.

- Using the chapter's format, compute these total variances and the individual variances requested:
  - Total materials variance (including the direct materials quantity variance and the direct materials price variance).
  - Total direct labor variance (including the direct labor efficiency variance and rate variance).
  - Total overhead variance (including both controllable and volume overhead variances and their component variances). Variable overhead is applied at the rate of $3.00 per direct labor hour. Fixed overhead is applied at the rate of $1.00 per direct labor hour.

SOLUTION

1.

PACIFIC COMPANY Flexible Budgets For Month Ended June 30, 2015					
	Flexible Budget				
	Variable Amount per Unit	**Total Fixed Cost**	**Flexible Budget for Unit Sales of**		
			20,000	**25,000**	**30,000**
Sales	$5.00		$100,000	$125,000	$150,000
Variable costs					
Direct materials.	1.24		24,800	31,000	37,200
Direct labor	1.50		30,000	37,500	45,000
Factory supplies	0.25		5,000	6,250	7,500
Utilities	0.50		10,000	12,500	15,000
Selling costs	0.40		8,000	10,000	12,000
Total variable costs	3.89		77,800	97,250	116,700
Contribution margin	$1.11		22,200	27,750	33,300
Fixed costs					
Depreciation—machinery		$3,750	3,750	3,750	3,750
Depreciation—factory building.		2,500	2,500	2,500	2,500
General liability insurance		1,200	1,200	1,200	1,200
Property taxes on office equipment		500	500	500	500
Other administrative expense		750	750	750	750
Total fixed costs.		$8,700	8,700	8,700	8,700
Income from operations			$ 13,500	$ 19,050	$ 24,600

2.

PACIFIC COMPANY
Flexible Budget Performance Report
For Month Ended June 30, 2015

	Flexible Budget	Actual Results	Variance**
Sales (27,000 units)	$135,000	$141,210	$6,210 F
Variable costs			
Direct materials	33,480	30,800	2,680 F
Direct labor	40,500	37,800	2,700 F
Factory supplies*	6,750	9,990	3,240 U
Utilities*	13,500	16,200	2,700 U
Selling costs	10,800	9,180	1,620 F
Total variable costs	105,030	103,970	1,060 F
Contribution margin	29,970	37,240	7,270 F
Fixed costs			
Depreciation—machinery*	3,750	3,710	40 F
Depreciation—factory building*	2,500	2,500	0
General liability insurance	1,200	1,250	50 U
Property taxes on office equipment	500	485	15 F
Other administrative expense	750	900	150 U
Total fixed costs	8,700	8,845	145 U
Income from operations	$ 21,270	$ 28,395	$7,125 F

* Indicates factory overhead item   ** Abbreviations: F = Favorable variance; U = Unfavorable variance.

3. Variance analysis of materials and labor costs.

Direct materials cost variances

Actual cost	110,000 oz. @ $0.28	$30,800
Standard cost	108,000 oz. @ $0.31	33,480
Direct materials cost variance (favorable)		$ 2,680

Price and quantity variances (based on formulas in Exhibit 8.10):

Actual Cost		**Standard Cost**
AQ × AP	AQ × SP	SQ* × SP
110,000 oz. × $0.28	110,000 oz. × $0.31	108,000 oz. × $0.31
$30,800	$34,100	$33,480

$3,300 F — **Price Variance**

$620 U — **Quantity Variance**

$2,680 F — **Total Direct Materials Variance**

*SQ = 27,000 actual units of output × 4 oz. standard quantity rate per unit

Direct labor cost variances

Actual cost	5,400 hrs. @ $7.00	$37,800
Standard cost	6,750 hrs. @ $6.00	40,500
Direct labor cost variance (favorable)		$ 2,700

Rate and efficiency variances (based on formulas in Exhibit 8.11):

Actual Cost		**Standard Cost**
AH × AR	AH × SR	SH** × SR
5,400 hrs. × $7	5,400 hrs. × $6	6,750 hrs. × $6
$37,800	$32,400	$40,500

$5,400 U — **Rate Variance**

$8,100 F — **Efficiency Variance**

$2,700 F — **Total Direct Labor Variance**

**SH = 27,000 actual units of output × 0.25 standard DLH per unit.

4. Total, controllable, and volume variances for overhead.

Total overhead cost variance

Total overhead cost incurred . . . . (given)	$32,400
Total overhead applied . . . . (27,000 units × .25 DLH per unit × $4 per DLH)	27,000
Overhead cost variance (unfavorable)	$ 5,400

Controllable variance

Total overhead cost incurred (given)	$32,400
Budgeted overhead (from flexible budget for 27,000 units)	26,500
Controllable variance (unfavorable)	$ 5,900

Volume variance

Budgeted fixed overhead (at predicted capacity)	$ 6,250
Applied fixed overhead (6,750 standard DLH × $1.00 fixed overhead rate per DLH)	6,750
Volume variance (favorable)	$ 500

5. Variable overhead spending variance, variable overhead efficiency variance, fixed overhead spending variance, and fixed overhead volume variance. (See Appendix 8A.)

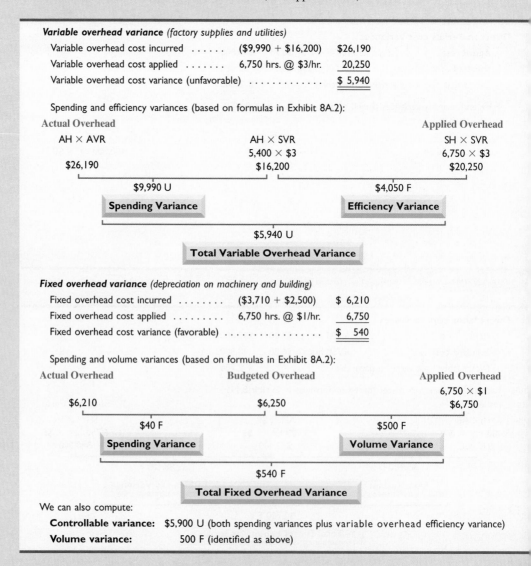

Variable overhead variance (factory supplies and utilities)

Variable overhead cost incurred	($9,990 + $16,200)	$26,190
Variable overhead cost applied	6,750 hrs. @ $3/hr.	20,250
Variable overhead cost variance (unfavorable)		$ 5,940

Spending and efficiency variances (based on formulas in Exhibit 8A.2):

Actual Overhead		Applied Overhead
AH × AVR	AH × SVR	SH × SVR
	5,400 × $3	6,750 × $3
$26,190	$16,200	$20,250

$9,990 U — **Spending Variance**

$4,050 F — **Efficiency Variance**

$5,940 U — **Total Variable Overhead Variance**

Fixed overhead variance (depreciation on machinery and building)

Fixed overhead cost incurred	($3,710 + $2,500)	$ 6,210
Fixed overhead cost applied	6,750 hrs. @ $1/hr.	6,750
Fixed overhead cost variance (favorable)		$ 540

Spending and volume variances (based on formulas in Exhibit 8A.2):

Actual Overhead	Budgeted Overhead	Applied Overhead
		6,750 × $1
$6,210	$6,250	$6,750

$40 F — **Spending Variance**

$500 F — **Volume Variance**

$540 F — **Total Fixed Overhead Variance**

We can also compute:

Controllable variance: $5,900 U (both spending variances plus variable overhead efficiency variance)

Volume variance: 500 F (identified as above)

6. Journal entries under a standard cost system. (Refer to Appendix 8A.)

Work in Process Inventory	33,480	
Direct Materials Quantity Variance	620	
Direct Materials Price Variance		3,300
Raw Materials Inventory		30,800
Work in Process Inventory	40,500	
Direct Labor Rate Variance	5,400	
Direct Labor Efficiency Variance		8,100
Factory Payroll Payable		37,800
Work in Process Inventory*	27,000	
Variable Overhead Spending Variance	9,990	
Variable Overhead Efficiency Variance		4,050
Fixed Overhead Spending Variance		40
Fixed Overhead Volume Variance		500
Factory Overhead**		32,400

* Overhead applied = 6,750 standard DLH × \$4 per DLH
** Overhead incurred = \$9,990 + \$16,200 + \$3,710 + \$2,500

Expanded Overhead Variances and Standard Cost Accounting System

8A

Expanded Overhead Variances Similar to analysis of direct materials and direct labor, overhead variances can be more completely analyzed. Exhibit 8A.1 shows an expanded framework for understanding these component overhead variances.

This framework uses classifications of overhead costs as either variable or fixed. Within those two classifications are further types of variances—spending, efficiency, and volume variances. We looked at the latter in the body of the chapter.

A **spending variance** occurs when management pays an amount different from the standard price to acquire an item. For instance, the actual wage rate paid to indirect labor might be higher than the standard rate. Similarly, actual supervisory salaries might be different than expected. Spending variances such as these cause management to investigate the reasons that the amount paid differs from the standard. Both variable and fixed overhead costs can yield their own spending variances.

Analyzing variable overhead also includes computing an **efficiency variance,** which occurs when standard direct labor hours (the allocation base) expected for actual production differ from the actual direct labor hours used. This efficiency variance reflects on the cost-effectiveness in using the overhead allocation base (such as direct labor).

Exhibit 8A.1 shows that we can combine the variable overhead spending variance, the fixed overhead spending variance, and the variable overhead efficiency variance to get the controllable variance.

P4

Compute overhead spending and efficiency variances.

EXHIBIT 8A.1

Expanded Framework for Total Overhead Variance

Computing Variable and Fixed Overhead Cost Variances To illustrate the computation of more detailed overhead cost variances, we return to the G-Max data. We know that G-Max produced 3,500 units when

4,000 units were budgeted. Additional data from cost reports (from Exhibit 8.15) show that the actual over-head cost incurred is $7,650 (the variable portion of $3,650 and the fixed portion of $4,000). Recall from Exhibit 8.12 that each unit requires one hour of direct labor, that variable overhead is applied at a rate of $1.00 per direct labor hour, and that the predetermined fixed overhead rate is $1.00 per direct labor hour. Using this information, we can compute overhead variances for both variable and fixed overhead as follows:

Variable Overhead Variance	
Actual variable overhead (given)	$3,650
Applied variable overhead (3,500 units × 1 standard DLH × $1.00 VOH rate per DLH)	3,500
Variable overhead variance (unfavorable)	$ 150

Fixed Overhead Variance	
Actual fixed overhead (given)	$4,000
Applied fixed overhead (3,500 units × 1 standard DLH × $1.00 FOH rate per DLH)	3,500
Fixed overhead variance (unfavorable)	$ 500

Management should seek to determine the causes of these unfavorable variances and take corrective action. To help better isolate the causes of these variances, more detailed overhead variances can be used, as shown in the next section.

Expanded Overhead Variance Formulas   Exhibit 8A.2 shows formulas to use in computing detailed overhead variances that can better identify reasons for variable and fixed overhead variances.

EXHIBIT 8A.2

Variable and Fixed Overhead Variances

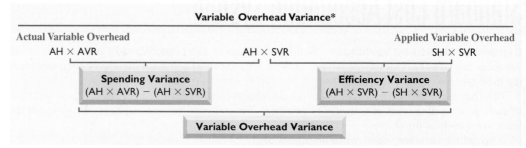

* AH = actual direct labor hours; AVR = actual variable overhead rate; SH = standard direct labor hours; SVR = standard variable overhead rate.

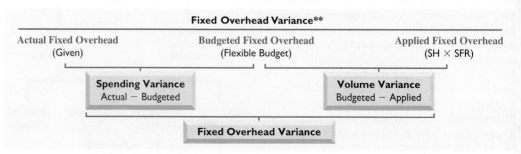

**SH = standard direct labor hours; SFR = standard fixed overhead rate.

Variable Overhead Cost Variances   Using these formulas, Exhibit 8A.3 offers insight into the causes of G-Max's $150 unfavorable variable overhead cost variance. Recall that G-Max applies overhead based on direct labor hours as the allocation base. We know that it used 3,400 direct labor hours to produce 3,500 units. This compares favorably to the standard requirement of 3,500 direct labor hours at one labor hour per unit. At a standard variable overhead rate of $1.00 per direct labor hour, this should have resulted in variable overhead costs of $3,400 (middle column of Exhibit 8A.3).

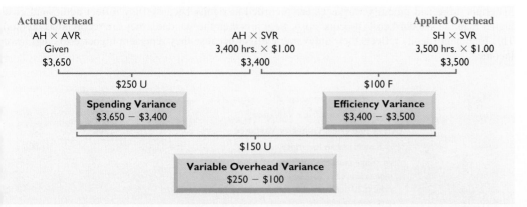

EXHIBIT 8A.3

Computing Variable
Overhead Cost Variances

G-Max's cost records, however, report actual variable overhead of $3,650, or $250 higher than expected. This means G-Max has an unfavorable variable overhead spending variance of $250 ($3,650 − $3,400). On the other hand, G-Max used 100 fewer labor hours than expected to make 3,500 units, and its actual variable overhead is lower than its applied variable overhead. Thus, G-Max has a favorable variable overhead efficiency variance of $100 ($3,400 − $3,500).

Fixed Overhead Cost Variances   Exhibit 8A.4 provides insight into the causes of G-Max's $500 unfavorable fixed overhead variance. G-Max reports that it incurred $4,000 in actual fixed overhead; this amount equals the budgeted fixed overhead for May at the expected production level of 4,000 units (see Exhibit 8.12). Thus, the fixed overhead spending variance is zero, suggesting good control of fixed overhead costs. G-Max's budgeted fixed overhead application rate is $1 per hour ($4,000/4,000 direct labor hours), but the actual production level is only 3,500 units.

Using this information, we can compute the fixed overhead volume variance shown in Exhibit 8A.4. The applied fixed overhead is computed by multiplying 3,500 standard hours allowed for the actual production by the $1 fixed overhead allocation rate. The volume variance of $500 occurs because 500 fewer units are produced than budgeted; namely, 80% of the manufacturing capacity is budgeted but only 70% is used. Management needs to know why the actual level of production differs from the expected level.

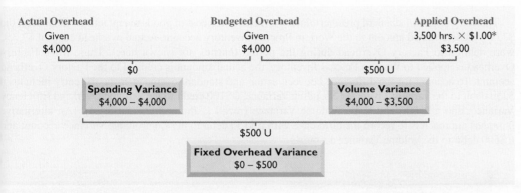

EXHIBIT 8A.4

Computing Fixed Overhead
Cost Variances

*3,500 units × 1 DLH per unit × $1.00 FOH rate per DLH

Standard Cost Accounting System   We have shown how companies use standard costs in management reports. Most standard cost systems also record these costs and variances in accounts. This practice simplifies recordkeeping and helps in preparing reports. Although we do not need knowledge of standard cost accounting practices to understand standard costs and their use, we must know how to interpret the accounts in which standard costs and variances are recorded. The entries in this section briefly illustrate the important aspects of this process for G-Max's standard costs and variances for May.

The first of these entries records standard materials cost incurred in May in the Work in Process Inventory account. This part of the entry is similar to the usual accounting entry, but the amount of the debit equals the standard cost ($35,000) instead of the actual cost ($37,800). This entry credits Raw Materials Inventory for actual cost. The difference between standard and actual direct materials costs is recorded with debits to two separate materials variance accounts (recall Exhibit 8.10). Both the

P5

Prepare journal entries
for standard costs and
account for price and
quantity variances.

materials price and quantity variances are recorded as debits because they reflect additional costs higher than the standard cost (if actual costs were less than the standard, they are recorded as credits). This treatment (debit) reflects their unfavorable effect because they represent higher costs and lower income.

May 31	Work in Process Inventory	35,000	
	Direct Materials Price Variance*	**1,800**	
	Direct Materials Quantity Variance	**1,000**	
	Raw Materials Inventory		37,800
	To charge production for standard quantity of materials used (1,750 lbs.) at the standard price ($20 per lb.), and to record material price and material quantity variances.		

* Many companies record the materials price variance when materials are purchased. For simplicity, we record both the materials price and quantity variances when materials are issued to production.

The second entry debits Work in Process Inventory for the standard labor cost of the goods manufactured during May ($28,000). Actual labor cost ($28,220) is recorded with a credit to the Factory Payroll Payable account. The difference between standard and actual labor costs is explained by two variances (see Exhibit 8.11). The direct labor rate variance is unfavorable and is debited to that account. The direct labor efficiency variance is favorable and that account is credited. The direct labor efficiency variance is favorable because it represents a lower cost and a higher net income.

May 31	Work in Process Inventory	28,000	
	Direct Labor Rate Variance	**1,020**	
	Direct Labor Efficiency Variance		**800**
	Factory Payroll Payable............................		28,220
	To charge production with 3,500 standard hours of direct labor at the standard $8 per hour rate, and to record the labor rate and efficiency variances.		

The entry to assign standard predetermined overhead to the cost of goods manufactured must debit the $7,000 predetermined amount to the Work in Process Inventory account. Actual overhead costs of $7,650 were debited to Factory Overhead during the period (entries not shown here). Thus, when Factory Overhead is applied to Work in Process Inventory, the actual amount is credited to the Factory Overhead account. To account for the difference between actual and standard overhead costs, the entry includes a $250 debit to the Variable Overhead Spending Variance, a $100 credit to the Variable Overhead Efficiency Variance, and a $500 debit to the Volume Variance (recall Exhibits 8A.3 and 8A.4). (An alternative [simpler] approach is to record the difference with a $150 debit to the Controllable Variance account and a $500 debit to the Volume Variance account.)

May 31	Work in Process Inventory	7,000	
	Volume Variance	**500**	
	Variable Overhead Spending Variance.............	**250**	
	Variable Overhead Efficiency Variance		**100**
	Factory Overhead		7,650
	To apply overhead at the standard rate of $2 per standard direct labor hour (3,500 hours), and to record overhead variances.		

Point: If variances are material they can be allocated between Work in Process Inventory, Finished Goods Inventory, and Cost of Goods Sold. This closing process is explained in advanced courses.

The balances of these different variance accounts accumulate until the end of the accounting period. As a result, the unfavorable variances of some months can offset the favorable variances of other months.

These ending variance account balances, which reflect results of the period's various transactions and events, are closed at period-end. If the amounts are *immaterial,* they are added to or subtracted from the balance of the Cost of Goods Sold account. This process is similar to that shown in the job order costing chapter for eliminating an underapplied or overapplied balance in the Factory Overhead account. (*Note:* These variance balances, which represent differences between actual and standard costs, must be added to or subtracted from the materials, labor, and overhead costs recorded. In this way, the recorded costs equal the actual costs incurred in the period; a company must use actual costs in external financial statements prepared in accordance with generally accepted accounting principles.)

Standard Costing Income Statement   In addition to the reports discussed in this chapter, management can use a **standard costing income statement** to summarize company performance for a period. This income statement reports sales and cost of goods sold at their standard amounts, and then lists the individual sales and cost variances to compute gross profit at actual cost. Exhibit 8A.5 provides an example. Unfavorable variances are added to cost of goods sold at standard cost; favorable variances are subtracted from cost of goods sold at standard cost.

EXHIBIT 8A.5

Standard Costing Income Statement

G-MAX Standard Costing Income Statement For Year Ended December 31, 2015		
Sales revenue (at standard)...............	•••••	
Sales price variance.....................	•••	
Sales volume variance...................	•••	•••
Sales revenue (actual)....................	•••••	
Cost of goods sold (at standard)............	•••••	
Manufacturing cost variances		
Direct materials price variance	•••	
Direct materials quantity variance..........	•••	
Direct labor rate variance	•••	
Direct labor efficiency variance	•••	
Variable overhead spending variance........	•••	
Variable overhead efficiency variance........	•••	
Fixed overhead spending variance	•••	
Fixed overhead volume variance	•••	
Total manufacturing cost variances	•••	
Cost of goods sold (actual)	•••••	
Gross profit............................	••••	
Selling expenses	•••	
General and administrative expenses..........	•••	
Income from operations....................	•••••	

Add unfavorable variances; subtract favorable variances.

A company uses a standard cost accounting system. Prepare the journal entry to record these direct materials variances:

Direct materials cost actually incurred	$73,200
Direct materials quantity variance (favorable)	3,800
Direct materials price variance (unfavorable)..........	1,300

NEED-TO-KNOW 8-5

Recording Variances

P4

Solution

Work in Process Inventory.......................	75,700	
Direct Materials Price Variance	1,300	
Direct Materials Quantity Variance		3,800
Raw Materials Inventory........................		73,200

Do More: QS 8-17, E 8-14

Summary

C1 **Define *standard costs* and explain how standard cost information is useful for management by exception.** Standard costs are the normal costs that should be incurred to produce a product or perform a service. They should be based on a careful examination of the processes used to produce a product or perform a service as well as the quantities and prices that should be incurred in carrying out those processes. On a performance report, standard costs (which are flexible budget amounts) are compared to actual costs, and the differences are presented as variances. Standard cost accounting provides management information about costs that differ from budgeted (expected) amounts. Performance reports disclose the costs or areas of operations that have significant variances from budgeted amounts. This allows managers to focus more attention on the exceptions and less attention on areas proceeding normally.

C2 **Describe cost variances and what they reveal about performance.** Management can use variances to monitor and control activities. Total cost variances can be broken into price and quantity variances to direct management's attention to those responsible for quantities used and prices paid.

A1 **Analyze changes in sales from expected amounts.** Actual sales can differ from budgeted sales, and managers can investigate this difference by computing both the sales price and sales volume variances. The *sales price variance* refers to that portion of total variance resulting from a difference between actual and budgeted selling prices. The *sales volume variance* refers to that portion of total variance resulting from a difference between actual and budgeted sales quantities.

P1 **Prepare a flexible budget and interpret a flexible budget performance report.** A flexible budget expresses variable costs in per unit terms so that it can be used to develop budgeted amounts for any volume level within the relevant range. Thus, managers compute budgeted amounts for evaluation after a period for the volume that actually occurred. To prepare a flexible budget, we express each variable cost as a constant amount per unit of sales (or as a percent of sales dollars). In contrast, the budgeted amount of each fixed cost is expressed as a total amount expected to occur at any sales

volume within the relevant range. The flexible budget is then determined using these computations and amounts for fixed and variable costs at the expected sales volume.

P2 **Compute materials and labor variances.** Materials and labor variances are due to differences between the actual costs incurred and the budgeted costs. The price (or rate) variance is computed by comparing the actual cost with the flexible budget amount that should have been incurred to acquire the actual quantity of resources. The quantity (or efficiency) variance is computed by comparing the flexible budget amount that should have been incurred to acquire the actual quantity of resources with the flexible budget amount that should have been incurred to acquire the standard quantity of resources.

P3 **Compute overhead controllable and volume variances.** Overhead variances are due to differences between the actual overhead costs incurred and the overhead applied to production. The overhead controllable variance equals the actual overhead minus the budgeted overhead, based on a flexible budget. The volume variance equals the budgeted fixed overhead minus the applied fixed overhead.

P4ᴬ **Compute overhead spending and efficiency variances.** An overhead spending variance occurs when management pays an amount different from the standard price to acquire an item. An overhead efficiency variance occurs when the standard amount of the allocation base to assign overhead differs from the actual amount of the allocation base used.

P5ᴬ **Prepare journal entries for standard costs and account for price and quantity variances.** When a company records standard costs in its accounts, the standard costs of direct materials, direct labor, and overhead are debited to the Work in Process Inventory account. Based on an analysis of the material, labor, and overhead costs, each quantity variance, price variance, volume variance, and controllable variance is recorded in a separate account. At period-end, if the variances are not material, they are debited (if unfavorable) or credited (if favorable) to the Cost of Goods Sold account.

Guidance Answers to Decision Maker

Entrepreneur   From the complaints, this performance report appears to compare actual results with a fixed budget. This comparison is useful in determining whether the amount of work actually performed was more or less than planned, but it is not useful in determining whether the divisions were more or less efficient than planned. If the two consulting divisions worked on more assignments than expected, some costs will certainly increase. Therefore, you should prepare a flexible budget using the actual number of consulting assignments and then compare actual performance to the flexible budget.

Production Manager   As production manager, you should investigate the causes for any labor-related variances although you may not be responsible for them. An unfavorable labor efficiency variance occurs because more labor hours than standard were used during the period. There are at least three possible reasons for this: (1) materials quality could be poor, resulting in more labor consumption due to rework; (2) unplanned interruptions (strike, breakdowns, accidents) could have occurred during the period; and (3) a different labor mix might have occurred for a strategic reason such as to expedite orders. This new labor mix could have consisted of a larger proportion of untrained labor, which resulted in more labor hours.

Sales Manager The unfavorable sales price variance suggests that actual prices were lower than budgeted prices. As the sales manager, you want to know the reasons for a lower than expected price. Perhaps your salespeople lowered the price of certain prod-

ucts by offering quantity discounts. You then might want to know what prompted them to offer the quantity discounts (perhaps competitors were offering discounts). You want to break the sales volume variance into both the sales mix and sales quantity variances. You could find that although the sales quantity variance is favorable, the sales mix variance is not. Then you need to investigate why the actual sales mix differs from the budgeted sales mix.

Key Terms

Benchmarking	Fixed budget	Quantity variance
Budget report	Fixed budget performance report	Spending variance
Budgetary control	Flexible budget	Standard costing income statement
Controllable variance	Flexible budget performance report	Standard costs
Cost variance	Management by exception	Unfavorable variance
Efficiency variance	Overhead cost variance	Variance analysis
Favorable variance	Price variance	Volume variance

Multiple Choice Quiz   Answers at end of chapter

1. A company predicts its production and sales will be 24,000 units. At that level of activity, its fixed costs are budgeted at $300,000, and its variable costs are budgeted at $246,000. If its activity level declines to 20,000 units, what will be its fixed costs and its variable costs?
  a. Fixed, $300,000; variable, $246,000
  b. Fixed, $250,000; variable, $205,000
  c. Fixed, $300,000; variable, $205,000
  d. Fixed, $250,000; variable, $246,000
  e. Fixed, $300,000; variable, $300,000

2. Using the following information about a single product company, compute its total actual cost of direct materials used.
  • Direct materials standard cost: 5 lbs. × $2 per lb. = $10.
  • Total direct materials cost variance: $15,000 unfavorable.
  • Actual direct materials used: 300,000 lbs.
  • Actual units produced: 60,000 units.
  a. $585,000   **c.** $300,000   **e.** $615,000
  b. $600,000   **d.** $315,000

3. A company uses four hours of direct labor to produce a product unit. The standard direct labor cost is $20 per hour.

This period the company produced 20,000 units and used 84,160 hours of direct labor at a total cost of $1,599,040. What is its labor rate variance for the period?
  a. $83,200 F   **c.** $84,160 F   **e.** $960 F
  b. $84,160 U   **d.** $83,200 U

4. A company's standard for a unit of its single product is $6 per unit in variable overhead (4 hours × $1.50 per hour). Actual data for the period show variable overhead costs of $150,000 and production of 24,000 units. Its total variable overhead cost variance is
  a. $6,000 F   **c.** $114,000 U   **e.** $0
  b. $6,000 U   **d.** $114,000 F

5. A company's standard for a unit of its single product is $4 per unit in fixed overhead ($24,000 total/6,000 units budgeted). Actual data for the period show total actual fixed overhead of $24,100 and production of 4,800 units. Its volume variance is
  a. $4,800 U   **c.** $100 U   **e.** $4,900 U
  b. $4,800 F   **d.** $100 F

[A] *Superscript letter A denotes assignments based on Appendix 8A.*
[I] Icon denotes assignments that involve decision making.

Discussion Questions

1. [I] What limits the usefulness to managers of fixed budget performance reports?

2. [I] Identify the main purpose of a flexible budget for managers.

3. Prepare a flexible budget performance report title (in proper form) for Spalding Company for the calendar year 2015. Why is a proper title important for this or any report?

4. [I] What type of analysis does a flexible budget performance report help management perform?

5. In what sense can a variable cost be considered constant?

6. [I] What department is usually responsible for a direct labor rate variance? What department is usually responsible for a direct labor efficiency variance? Explain.

7. What is a price variance? What is a quantity variance?

8. 🔟 What is the purpose of using standard costs?

9. Google monitors its fixed overhead. In an analysis of fixed overhead cost variances, what is the volume variance? **GOOGLE**

10. What is the predetermined standard overhead rate? How is it computed?

11. In general, variance analysis is said to provide information about _____ and _____ variances.

12. 🔟 Samsung monitors its overhead. In an analysis of overhead cost variances, what is the controllable variance and what causes it? **Samsung**

13. What are the relations among standard costs, flexible budgets, variance analysis, and management by exception?

14. 🔟 How can the manager of advertising sales at Google use flexible budgets to enhance performance? **GOOGLE**

15. 🔟 Is it possible for a retail store such as Apple to use variances in analyzing its operating performance? Explain. **APPLE**

16. 🔟 Assume that Samsung is budgeted to operate at 80% of capacity but actually operates at 75% of capacity. What effect will the 5% deviation have on its controllable variance? Its volume variance? **Samsung**

≡ connect

QUICK STUDY

QS 8-1
Flexible budget performance report
P1

Beech Company produced and sold 105,000 units of its product in May. For the level of production achieved in May, the budgeted amounts were: sales, $1,300,000; variable costs, $750,000; and fixed costs, $300,000. The following actual financial results are available for May. Prepare a flexible budget performance report for May.

	Actual
Sales (105,000 units)	$1,275,000
Variable costs	712,500
Fixed costs	300,000

QS 8-2
Flexible budget P1

Based on predicted production of 24,000 units, a company anticipates $300,000 of fixed costs and $246,000 of variable costs. If the company actually produces 20,000 units, what are the flexible budget amounts of fixed and variable costs?

QS 8-3
Flexible budget
P1

Brodrick Company expects to produce 20,000 units for the year ending December 31. A flexible budget for 20,000 units of production reflects sales of $400,000; variable costs of $80,000; and fixed costs of $150,000. If the company instead expects to produce and sell 26,000 units for the year, calculate the expected level of income from operations.

QS 8-4
Flexible budget performance report P1

Refer to information in QS 8-3. Assume that actual sales for the year are $480,000, actual variable costs for the year are $112,000, and actual fixed costs for the year are $145,000. Prepare a flexible budget performance report for the year.

QS 8-5
Standard cost card C1

BatCo makes metal baseball bats. Each bat requires 1 kg of aluminum at $18 per kg and 0.25 direct labor hours at $20 per hour. Overhead is assigned at the rate of $40 per direct labor hour. What amounts would appear on a standard cost card for BatCo?

QS 8-6
Cost variances C2

Refer to information in QS 8-5. Assume the actual cost to manufacture one metal bat was $40. Compute the cost variance and classify it as favorable or unfavorable.

QS 8-7
Management by exception C1 🔟

Managers use *management by exception* for control purposes.
1. Describe the concept of management by exception.
2. Explain how standard costs help managers apply this concept to monitor and control costs.

QS 8-8
Materials variances
P2

Tercer reports the following on one of its products. Compute the direct materials price and quantity variances.

Direct materials standard (4 lbs. @ $2/lb.)	$8 per finished unit
Actual direct materials used	300,000 lbs.
Actual finished units produced	60,000 units
Actual cost of direct materials used	$535,000

For the current period, Kayenta Company's manufacturing operations yield a $4,000 unfavorable price variance on its direct materials usage. The actual price per pound of material is $78; the standard price is $77.50 per pound. How many pounds of material were used in the current period?

QS 8-9
Materials cost variances
P2

Juan Company's output for the current period was assigned a $150,000 standard direct materials cost. The direct materials variances included a $12,000 favorable price variance and a $2,000 favorable quantity variance. What is the actual total direct materials cost for the current period?

QS 8-10
Materials cost variances
P2

The following information describes a company's usage of direct labor in a recent period. Compute the direct labor rate and efficiency variances for the period.

Actual direct labor hours used	65,000
Actual direct labor rate per hour	$15
Standard direct labor rate per hour	$14
Standard direct labor hours for units produced	67,000

QS 8-11
Direct labor variances
P2

Frontera Company's output for the current period results in a $20,000 unfavorable direct labor rate variance and a $10,000 unfavorable direct labor efficiency variance. Production for the current period was assigned a $400,000 standard direct labor cost. What is the actual total direct labor cost for the current period?

QS 8-12
Labor cost variances
P2

Fogel Co. expects to produce 116,000 units for the year. The company's flexible budget for 116,000 units of production shows variable overhead costs of $162,400 and fixed overhead costs of $124,000. For the year, the company incurred actual overhead costs of $262,800 while producing 110,000 units. Compute the controllable overhead variance.

QS 8-13
Controllable overhead variance   P3

AirPro Corp. reports the following for November. Compute the controllable overhead variance for November.

Actual total factory overhead incurred	$28,175
Standard factory overhead:	
Variable overhead	$3.10 per unit produced
Fixed overhead	
($12,000/12,000 predicted units to be produced)	$1 per unit
Predicted units to produce	12,000 units
Actual units produced	9,800 units

QS 8-14
Controllable overhead variance
P3

Refer to information in QS 8-14. Compute the overhead volume variance for November.

QS 8-15
Volume variance   P3

Alvarez Company's output for the current period yields a $20,000 favorable overhead volume variance and a $60,400 unfavorable overhead controllable variance. Standard overhead applied to production for the period is $225,000. What is the actual total overhead cost incurred for the period?

QS 8-16
Overhead cost variances
P3

Refer to the information in QS 8-16. Alvarez records standard costs in its accounts. Prepare the journal entry to charge overhead costs to the Work in Process Inventory account and to record any variances.

QS 8-17ᴬ
Preparing overhead entries   P5

Mosaic Company applies overhead using machine hours and reports the following information. Compute the total variable overhead cost variance.

Actual machine hours used	4,700 hours
Standard machine hours (for actual production)	5,000 hours
Actual variable overhead rate per hour	$4.15
Standard variable overhead rate per hour	$4.00

QS 8-18
Total variable overhead cost variance
P3

QS 8-19ᴬ
Overhead spending and
efficiency variances   **P4**

Refer to the information from QS 8-18. Compute the variable overhead spending variance and the variable overhead efficiency variance.

QS 8-20
Computing sales price and
volume variances   **A1**

Farad, Inc., specializes in selling used SUVs. During the month, the dealership sold 50 trucks at an average price of $9,000 each. The budget for the month was to sell 45 trucks at an average price of $9,500 each. Compute the dealership's sales price variance and sales volume variance for the month.

QS 8-21
Sales variances   **A1**

In a recent year, **BMW** sold 216,944 of its 1 Series cars. Assume the company expected to sell 225,944 of these cars during the year. Also assume the budgeted sales price for each car was $30,000, and the actual sales price for each car was $30,200. Compute the sales price variance and the sales volume variance.

🔲 **connect**

EXERCISES

Exercise 8-1
Classification of costs as
fixed or variable

P1

JPAK Company manufactures and sells mountain bikes. It normally operates eight hours a day, five days a week. Using this information, classify each of the following costs as fixed or variable. If additional information would affect your decision, describe the information.

____ **a.** Bike frames	____ **e.** Bike tires
____ **b.** Screws for assembly	____ **f.** Gas used for heating
____ **c.** Repair expense for tools	____ **g.** Incoming shipping expenses
____ **d.** Direct labor	____ **h.** Taxes on property

____ **i.** Office supplies
____ **j.** Depreciation on tools
____ **k.** Management salaries

Exercise 8-2
Preparation of flexible
budgets

P1

Tempo Company's fixed budget (based on sales of 7,000 units) for the first quarter of calendar year 2015 reveals the following. Prepare flexible budgets following the format of Exhibit 8.3 that show variable costs per unit, fixed costs, and three different flexible budgets for sales volumes of 6,000, 7,000, and 8,000 units.

		Fixed Budget
Sales (7,000 units)		$2,800,000
Cost of goods sold		
Direct materials	$280,000	
Direct labor	490,000	
Production supplies	175,000	
Plant manager salary	65,000	1,010,000
Gross profit		1,790,000
Selling expenses		
Sales commissions	140,000	
Packaging	154,000	
Advertising	125,000	419,000
Administrative expenses		
Administrative salaries	85,000	
Depreciation—office equip.	35,000	
Insurance	20,000	
Office rent	36,000	176,000
Income from operations		$1,195,000

Check   Income (at 6,000
units), $972,000

Exercise 8-3
Preparation of a flexible
budget performance
report

P1

Solitaire Company's fixed budget performance report for June follows. The $315,000 budgeted expenses include $294,000 variable expenses and $21,000 fixed expenses. Actual expenses include $27,000 fixed expenses. Prepare a flexible budget performance report showing any variances between budgeted and actual results. List fixed and variable expenses separately.

	Fixed Budget	**Actual Results**	**Variances**
Sales (in units)	8,400	10,800	
Sales (in dollars)	$420,000	$540,000	$120,000 F
Total expenses	315,000	378,000	63,000 U
Income from operations	$105,000	$162,000	$ 57,000 F

Check   Income variance,
$21,000 F

Bay City Company's fixed budget performance report for July follows. The $647,500 budgeted total expenses include $487,500 variable expenses and $160,000 fixed expenses. Actual expenses include $158,000 fixed expenses. Prepare a flexible budget performance report that shows any variances between budgeted results and actual results. List fixed and variable expenses separately.

Exercise 8-4
Preparation of a flexible budget performance report
P1

	Fixed Budget	Actual Results	Variances
Sales (in units)	7,500	7,200	
Sales (in dollars)	$750,000	$737,000	$13,000 U
Total expenses	647,500	641,000	6,500 F
Income from operations	$102,500	$ 96,000	$ 6,500 U

Check Income variance, $4,000 F

Match the terms *a–e* with their correct definition 1–5.

a. Standard cost card
b. Management by exception
c. Standard cost
d. Ideal standard
e. Practical standard

____ **1.** Quantity of input required under normal conditions.
____ **2.** Quantity of input required if a production process is 100% efficient.
____ **3.** Managing by focusing on large differences from standard costs.
____ **4.** Record that accumulates standard cost information.
____ **5.** Preset cost for delivering a product or service under normal conditions.

Exercise 8-5
Standard costs
C1

Resset Co. provides the following results of April's operations: F indicates favorable and U indicates unfavorable. Applying the management by exception approach, which of the variances are of greatest concern? Why?

Exercise 8-6
Analyzing variances
C1

Direct materials price variance	$ 300 F
Direct materials quantity variance	3,000 U
Direct labor rate variance	100 U
Direct labor efficiency variance	2,200 F
Controllable overhead variance	400 U
Fixed overhead volume variance	500 F

Presented below are terms preceded by letters *a* through *j* and a list of definitions 1 through 10. Enter the letter of the term with the definition, using the space preceding the definition.

Exercise 8-7
Cost variances
C2

a. Fixed budget
b. Standard costs
c. Price variance
d. Quantity variance
e. Volume variance
f. Controllable variance
g. Cost variance
h. Flexible budget
i. Variance analysis
j. Management by exception

____ **1.** The difference between actual and budgeted sales or cost caused by the difference between the actual price per unit and the budgeted price per unit.
____ **2.** A planning budget based on a single predicted amount of sales or production volume; unsuitable for evaluations if the actual volume differs from the predicted volume.
____ **3.** Preset costs for delivering a product, component, or service under normal conditions.
____ **4.** A process of examining the differences between actual and budgeted sales or costs and describing them in terms of the amounts that resulted from price and quantity differences.
____ **5.** The difference between the total budgeted overhead cost and the overhead cost that was allocated to products using the predetermined fixed overhead rate.
____ **6.** A budget prepared based on predicted amounts of revenues and expenses corresponding to the actual level of output.
____ **7.** The difference between actual and budgeted cost caused by the difference between the actual quantity and the budgeted quantity.
____ **8.** The combination of both overhead spending variances (variable and fixed) and the variable overhead efficiency variance.
____ **9.** A management process to focus on significant variances and give less attention to areas where performance is close to the standard.
____ **10.** The difference between actual cost and standard cost, made up of a price variance and a quantity variance.

Exercise 8-8
Standard unit cost; total cost variance
C2

A manufactured product has the following information for June.

	Standard	Actual
Direct materials.	(6 lbs. @ $8 per lb.)	48,500 lbs. @ $8.10 per lb.
Direct labor.	(2 hrs. @ $16 per hr.)	15,700 hrs. @ $16.50 per hr.
Overhead.	(2 hrs. @ $12 per hr.)	$198,000
Units manufactured.		8,000

Compute the (1) standard cost per unit and (2) total cost variance for June. Indicate whether the cost variance is favorable or unfavorable.

Exercise 8-9
Direct materials variances P2

Refer to the information in Exercise 8-8 and compute the (1) direct materials price and (2) direct materials quantity variances. Indicate whether each variance is favorable or unfavorable.

Exercise 8-10
Direct labor variances
P2

Refer to the information in Exercise 8-8 and compute the (1) direct labor rate and (2) direct labor efficiency variances. Indicate whether each variance is favorable or unfavorable.

Exercise 8-11
Direct materials and direct labor variances
P2

Hutto Corp. has set the following standard direct materials and direct labor costs per unit for the product it manufactures.

Direct materials (15 lbs. @ $4 per lb.).	$60
Direct labor (3 hrs. @ $15 per hr.).	45

During May the company incurred the following actual costs to produce 9,000 units.

Direct materials (138,000 lbs. @ $3.75 per lb.).	$517,500
Direct labor (31,000 hrs. @ $15.10 per hr.).	468,100

Compute the (1) direct materials price and quantity variances and (2) direct labor rate and efficiency variances. Indicate whether each variance is favorable or unfavorable.

Exercise 8-12
Direct materials and direct labor variances
P2

Reed Corp. has set the following standard direct materials and direct labor costs per unit for the product it manufactures.

Direct materials (10 lbs. @ $3 per lb.).	$30
Direct labor (4 hrs. @ $6 per hr.).	24

During June the company incurred the following actual costs to produce 9,000 units.

Direct materials (92,000 lbs. @ $2.95 per lb.).	$271,400
Direct labor (37,600 hrs. @ $6.05 per hr.).	227,480

Compute the (1) direct materials price and quantity variances and (2) direct labor rate and efficiency variances. Indicate whether each variance is favorable or unfavorable.

Exercise 8-13
Computation and interpretation of materials variances P2

Check Price variance, $2,200 U

Hart Company made 3,000 bookshelves using 22,000 board feet of wood costing $266,200. The company's direct materials standards for one bookshelf are 8 board feet of wood at $12 per board foot.

1. Compute the direct materials price and quantity variances incurred in manufacturing these bookshelves.
2. Interpret the direct materials variances.

Refer to Exercise 8-13. Hart Company records standard costs in its accounts and its materials variances in separate accounts when it assigns materials costs to the Work in Process Inventory account.

1. Show the journal entry that both charges the direct materials costs to the Work in Process Inventory account and records the materials variances in their proper accounts.
2. Assume that Hart's materials variances are the only variances accumulated in the accounting period and that they are immaterial. Prepare the adjusting journal entry to close the variance accounts at period-end.
3. Identify the variance that should be investigated according to the management by exception concept. Explain.

Exercise 8-14^A
Materials variances
recorded and closed

P5 ♟

Check (2) Cr. to Cost of
Goods Sold, $21,800

The following information describes production activities of Mercer Manufacturing for the year:

Actual direct materials used	16,000 lbs. at $4.05 per lb.
Actual direct labor used	5,545 hours for a total of $105,355
Actual units produced	30,000

Budgeted standards for each unit produced are 0.50 pounds of direct material at $4.00 per pound and 10 minutes of direct labor at $20 per hour.

1. Compute the direct materials price and quantity variances.
2. Compute the direct labor rate and efficiency variances. Indicate whether each variance is favorable or unfavorable.

Exercise 8-15
Direct materials and
direct labor variances

P2

After evaluating Null Company's manufacturing process, management decides to establish standards of 3 hours of direct labor per unit of product and $15 per hour for the labor rate. During October, the company uses 16,250 hours of direct labor at a $247,000 total cost to produce 5,600 units of product. In November, the company uses 22,000 hours of direct labor at a $335,500 total cost to produce 6,000 units of product.

1. Compute the direct labor rate variance, the direct labor efficiency variance, and the total direct labor cost variance for each of these two months.
2. Interpret the October direct labor variances.

Exercise 8-16
Computation and
interpretation of labor
variances **P2** ♟

Check (1) October rate
variance, $3,250 U

Sedona Company set the following standard costs for one unit of its product for 2015.

Direct material (20 lbs. @ $2.50 per lb.)	$ 50
Direct labor (10 hrs. @ $8.00 per hr.)	80
Factory variable overhead (10 hrs. @ $4.00 per hr.)	40
Factory fixed overhead (10 hrs. @ $1.60 per hr.)	16
Standard cost	$186

Exercise 8-17
Computation of total
variable and fixed
overhead variances

P3 ♟

The $5.60 ($4.00 + $1.60) total overhead rate per direct labor hour is based on an expected operating level equal to 75% of the factory's capacity of 50,000 units per month. The following monthly flexible budget information is also available.

	A	B	C	D
1		**Operating Levels (% of capacity)**		
2	**Flexible Budget**	**70%**	**75%**	**80%**
3	Budgeted output (units)	35,000	37,500	40,000
4	Budgeted labor (standard hours)	350,000	375,000	400,000
5	Budgeted overhead (dollars)			
6	Variable overhead	$1,400,000	$1,500,000	$1,600,000
7	Fixed overhead	600,000	600,000	600,000
8	Total overhead	$2,000,000	$2,100,000	$2,200,000
9				

During the current month, the company operated at 70% of capacity, employees worked 340,000 hours and the following actual overhead costs were incurred.

Variable overhead costs	$1,375,000
Fixed overhead costs	628,600
Total overhead costs	$2,003,600

Check (2) Variable overhead cost variance, $25,000 F

1. Show how the company computed its predetermined overhead application rate per hour for total overhead, variable overhead, and fixed overhead.
2. Compute the total variable and total fixed overhead variances.

Exercise 8-18[A]
Computation and interpretation of overhead spending, efficiency, and volume variances   P4

Check (1) Variable overhead: Spending, $15,000 U; Efficiency, $40,000 F

Refer to the information from Exercise 8-17. Compute and interpret the following.
1. Variable overhead spending and efficiency variances.
2. Fixed overhead spending and volume variances.
3. Controllable variance.

Exercise 8-19
Computation of total overhead rate and total overhead variance

P3

Check (1) Variable overhead rate, $11.00 per hour

World Company expects to operate at 80% of its productive capacity of 50,000 units per month. At this planned level, the company expects to use 25,000 standard hours of direct labor. Overhead is allocated to products using a predetermined standard rate based on direct labor hours. At the 80% capacity level, the total budgeted cost includes $50,000 fixed overhead cost and $275,000 variable overhead cost. In the current month, the company incurred $305,000 actual overhead and 22,000 actual labor hours while producing 35,000 units.

1. Compute the overhead application rate for total overhead.
2. Compute the total overhead variance.

Exercise 8-20
Computation of volume and controllable overhead variances   P3

Check (2) $14,375 U

Refer to the information from Exercise 8-19. Compute the (1) overhead volume variance and (2) overhead controllable variance.

Exercise 8-21
Overhead controllable and volume variances; overhead variance report

P3

James Corp. applies overhead on the basis of direct labor hours. For the month of May, the company planned production of 8,000 units (80% of its production capacity of 10,000 units) and prepared the following overhead budget:

	Operating Level
Overhead Budget	**80%**
Production in units	8,000
Standard direct labor hours	24,000
Budgeted overhead	
Variable overhead costs	
Indirect materials...............	$15,000
Indirect labor	24,000
Power........................	6,000
Maintenance....................	3,000
Total variable costs	48,000
Fixed overhead costs	
Rent of factory building	15,000
Depreciation—machinery	10,000
Supervisory salaries	19,400
Total fixed costs	44,400
Total overhead costs	$92,400

During May, the company operated at 90% capacity (9,000 units) and incurred the following actual overhead costs:

Overhead costs	
Indirect materials	$15,000
Indirect labor	26,500
Power	6,750
Maintenance	4,000
Rent of factory building	15,000
Depreciation—machinery	10,000
Supervisory salaries	22,000
Total actual overhead costs	$99,250

1. Compute the overhead controllable variance.
2. Compute the overhead volume variance.
3. Prepare an overhead variance report at the actual activity level of 9,000 units.

Blaze Corp. applies overhead on the basis of direct labor hours. For the month of March, the company planned production of 8,000 units (80% of its production capacity of 10,000 units) and prepared the following budget:

Exercise 8-22
Overhead controllable and volume variances; overhead variance report

P3

Overhead Budget	Operating Level 80%
Production in units	8,000
Standard direct labor hours	32,000
Budgeted overhead	
Variable overhead costs	
Indirect materials	$10,000
Indirect labor	16,000
Power	4,000
Maintenance	2,000
Total variable costs	32,000
Fixed overhead costs	
Rent of factory building	12,000
Depreciation—machinery	20,000
Taxes and insurance	2,400
Supervisory salaries	13,600
Total fixed costs	48,000
Total overhead costs	$80,000

During March, the company operated at 90% capacity (9,000 units), and it incurred the following actual overhead costs:

Overhead costs	
Indirect materials	$10,000
Indirect labor	16,000
Power	4,500
Maintenance	3,000
Rent of factory building	12,000
Depreciation—machinery	19,200
Taxes and insurance	3,000
Supervisory salaries	14,000
Total actual overhead costs	$81,700

1. Compute the overhead controllable variance.
2. Compute the overhead volume variance.
3. Prepare an overhead variance report at the actual activity level of 9,000 units.

Comp Wiz sells computers. During May 2015, it sold 350 computers at a $1,200 average price each. The May 2015 fixed budget included sales of 365 computers at an average price of $1,100 each.
1. Compute the sales price variance and the sales volume variance for May 2015.
2. Interpret the findings.

Exercise 8-23
Computing and interpreting sales variances   A1

PROBLEM SET A

Problem 8-1A
Preparation and analysis
of a flexible budget

P1

Phoenix Company's 2015 master budget included the following fixed budget report. It is based on an expected production and sales volume of 15,000 units.

PHOENIX COMPANY Fixed Budget Report For Year Ended December 31, 2015		
Sales		$3,000,000
Cost of goods sold		
Direct materials..................................	$975,000	
Direct labor	225,000	
Machinery repairs (variable cost)	60,000	
Depreciation—plant equipment (straight-line)........	300,000	
Utilities ($45,000 is variable)	195,000	
Plant management salaries	200,000	1,955,000
Gross profit		1,045,000
Selling expenses		
Packaging	75,000	
Shipping	105,000	
Sales salary (fixed annual amount)	250,000	430,000
General and administrative expenses		
Advertising expense	125,000	
Salaries..	241,000	
Entertainment expense	90,000	456,000
Income from operations		$ 159,000

Required

1. Classify all items listed in the fixed budget as variable or fixed. Also determine their amounts per unit or their amounts for the year, as appropriate.

2. Prepare flexible budgets (see Exhibit 8.3) for the company at sales volumes of 14,000 and 16,000 units.

3. The company's business conditions are improving. One possible result is a sales volume of 18,000 units. The company president is confident that this volume is within the relevant range of existing capacity. How much would operating income increase over the 2015 budgeted amount of $159,000 if this level is reached without increasing capacity?

4. An unfavorable change in business is remotely possible; in this case, production and sales volume for 2015 could fall to 12,000 units. How much income (or loss) from operations would occur if sales volume falls to this level?

Check (2) Budgeted
income at 16,000 units,
$260,000

(4) Potential
operating loss, $(144,000)

Problem 8-2A
Preparation and analysis
of a flexible budget
performance report

P1 P2 A1

Refer to the information in Problem 8-1A. Phoenix Company's actual income statement for 2015 follows

PHOENIX COMPANY Statement of Income from Operations For Year Ended December 31, 2015		
Sales (18,000 units)		$3,648,000
Cost of goods sold		
Direct materials..................................	$1,185,000	
Direct labor	278,000	
Machinery repairs (variable cost)	63,000	
Depreciation—plant equipment	300,000	
Utilities (fixed cost is $147,500)	200,500	
Plant management salaries........................	210,000	2,236,500
Gross profit		1,411,500
Selling expenses		
Packaging	87,500	
Shipping	118,500	
Sales salary (annual).............................	268,000	474,000
General and administrative expenses		
Advertising expense	132,000	
Salaries..	241,000	
Entertainment expense	93,500	466,500
Income from operations		$ 471,000

Required

1. Prepare a flexible budget performance report for 2015.

Analysis Component

2. Analyze and interpret both the (a) sales variance and (b) direct materials cost variance.

Antuan Company set the following standard costs for one unit of its product.

Direct materials (6 lbs. @ $5 per lb.)	$ 30
Direct labor (2 hrs. @ $17 per hr.).................................	34
Overhead (2 hrs. @ $18.50 per hr.)	37
Total standard cost	$101

The predetermined overhead rate ($18.50 per direct labor hour) is based on an expected volume of 75% of the factory's capacity of 20,000 units per month. Following are the company's budgeted overhead costs per month at the 75% capacity level.

Overhead Budget (75% Capacity)		
Variable overhead costs		
Indirect materials	$ 45,000	
Indirect labor	180,000	
Power	45,000	
Repairs and maintenance	90,000	
Total variable overhead costs		$360,000
Fixed overhead costs		
Depreciation—building	24,000	
Depreciation—machinery	80,000	
Taxes and insurance...........................	12,000	
Supervision	79,000	
Total fixed overhead costs.....................		195,000
Total overhead costs		$555,000

The company incurred the following actual costs when it operated at 75% of capacity in October.

Direct materials (91,000 lbs. @ $5.10 per lb.)		$ 464,100
Direct labor (30,500 hrs. @ $17.25 per hr.)		526,125
Overhead costs		
Indirect materials	$ 44,250	
Indirect labor	177,750	
Power	43,000	
Repairs and maintenance	96,000	
Depreciation—building	24,000	
Depreciation—machinery	75,000	
Taxes and insurance...........................	11,500	
Supervision	89,000	560,500
Total costs		$1,550,725

Required

1. Examine the monthly overhead budget to (a) determine the costs per unit for each variable overhead item and its total per unit costs, and (b) identify the total fixed costs per month.

2. Prepare flexible overhead budgets (as in Exhibit 8.12) for October showing the amounts of each variable and fixed cost at the 65%, 75%, and 85% capacity levels.

3. Compute the direct materials cost variance, including its price and quantity variances.

(4) Labor variances:
Rate, $7,625 U; Efficiency,
$8,500 U

4. Compute the direct labor cost variance, including its rate and efficiency variances.

5. Prepare a detailed overhead variance report (as in Exhibit 8.15) that shows the variances for individual items of overhead.

Problem 8-4A
Computation of
materials, labor, and
overhead variances

P2   P3

Trico Company set the following standard unit costs for its single product.

Direct materials (30 lbs. @ $4 per lb.)	$120
Direct labor (5 hrs. @ $14 per hr.)	70
Factory overhead—variable (5 hrs. @ $8 per hr.)	40
Factory overhead—fixed (5 hrs. @ $10 per hr.)	50
Total standard cost	$280

The predetermined overhead rate is based on a planned operating volume of 80% of the productive capacity of 60,000 units per quarter. The following flexible budget information is available.

	Operating Levels		
	70%	80%	90%
Production in units	42,000	48,000	54,000
Standard direct labor hours	210,000	240,000	270,000
Budgeted overhead			
Fixed factory overhead	$2,400,000	$2,400,000	$2,400,000
Variable factory overhead	$1,680,000	$1,920,000	$2,160,000

During the current quarter, the company operated at 90% of capacity and produced 54,000 units of product; actual direct labor totaled 265,000 hours. Units produced were assigned the following standard costs:

Direct materials (1,620,000 lbs. @ $4 per lb.)	$ 6,480,000
Direct labor (270,000 hrs. @ $14 per hr.)	3,780,000
Factory overhead (270,000 hrs. @ $18 per hr.)	4,860,000
Total standard cost	$15,120,000

Actual costs incurred during the current quarter follow:

Direct materials (1,615,000 lbs. @ $4.10 per lb.)	$ 6,621,500
Direct labor (265,000 hrs. @ $13.75 per hr.)	3,643,750
Fixed factory overhead costs	2,350,000
Variable factory overhead costs	2,200,000
Total actual costs..	$14,815,250

Check   (1) Materials
variances: Price, $161,500 U;
Quantity, $20,000 F
          (2) Labor variances:
Rate, $66,250 F; Efficiency,
$70,000 F

Required

1. Compute the direct materials cost variance, including its price and quantity variances.

2. Compute the direct labor cost variance, including its rate and efficiency variances.

3. Compute the overhead controllable and volume variances.

Problem 8-5A[A]
Expanded overhead
variances

P4

Refer to information in Problem 8-4A.

Required

Compute these variances: (a) variable overhead spending and efficiency, (b) fixed overhead spending and volume, and (c) total overhead controllable.

Boss Company's standard cost accounting system recorded this information from its December operations.

Standard direct materials cost...........................	$100,000
Direct materials quantity variance (unfavorable)	3,000
Direct materials price variance (favorable).......................	500
Actual direct labor cost...............................	90,000
Direct labor efficiency variance (favorable).....................	7,000
Direct labor rate variance (unfavorable)......................	1,200
Actual overhead cost................................	375,000
Volume variance (unfavorable)........................	12,000
Controllable variance (unfavorable)	9,000

Problem 8-6A[A]
Materials, labor, and overhead variances recorded and analyzed

C1   P5

Required

1. Prepare December 31 journal entries to record the company's costs and variances for the month. (Do not prepare the journal entry to close the variances.)

Analysis Component

2. Identify the variances that would attract the attention of a manager who uses management by exception. Explain what action(s) the manager should consider.

Check (1) Dr. Work in Process Inventory (for overhead), $354,000

Tohono Company's 2015 master budget included the following fixed budget report. It is based on an expected production and sales volume of 20,000 units.

PROBLEM SET B

Problem 8-1B
Preparation and analysis of a flexible budget

P1   A1

TOHONO COMPANY Fixed Budget Report For Year Ended December 31, 2015		
Sales		$3,000,000
Cost of goods sold		
Direct materials.............................	$1,200,000	
Direct labor	260,000	
Machinery repairs (variable cost)	57,000	
Depreciation—machinery (straight-line)..............	250,000	
Utilities (25% is variable cost)......................	200,000	
Plant manager salaries	140,000	2,107,000
Gross profit		893,000
Selling expenses		
Packaging	80,000	
Shipping	116,000	
Sales salary (fixed annual amount)...................	160,000	356,000
General and administrative expenses		
Advertising......................................	81,000	
Salaries..	241,000	
Entertainment expense..........................	90,000	412,000
Income from operations		$ 125,000

Required

1. Classify all items listed in the fixed budget as variable or fixed. Also determine their amounts per unit or their amounts for the year, as appropriate.
2. Prepare flexible budgets (see Exhibit 8.3) for the company at sales volumes of 18,000 and 24,000 units.
3. The company's business conditions are improving. One possible result is a sales volume of 28,000 units. The company president is confident that this volume is within the relevant range of existing capacity. How much would operating income increase over the 2015 budgeted amount of $125,000 if this level is reached without increasing capacity?
4. An unfavorable change in business is remotely possible; in this case, production and sales volume for 2015 could fall to 14,000 units. How much income (or loss) from operations would occur if sales volume falls to this level?

Check (2) Budgeted income at 24,000 units, $372,400

(4) Potential operating loss, $(246,100)

Problem 8-2B

Preparation and analysis of a flexible budget performance report

P1   A1

Refer to the information in Problem 8-1B. Tohono Company's actual income statement for 2015 follows.

TOHONO COMPANY Statement of Income from Operations For Year Ended December 31, 2015		
Sales (24,000 units)		$3,648,000
Cost of goods sold		
Direct materials	$1,400,000	
Direct labor	360,000	
Machinery repairs (variable cost)	60,000	
Depreciation—machinery	250,000	
Utilities (variable cost, $64,000)	218,000	
Plant manager salaries	155,000	2,443,000
Gross profit		1,205,000
Selling expenses		
Packaging	90,000	
Shipping	124,000	
Sales salary (annual)	162,000	376,000
General and administrative expenses		
Advertising expense	104,000	
Salaries	232,000	
Entertainment expense	100,000	436,000
Income from operations		$ 393,000

Required

1. Prepare a flexible budget performance report for 2015.

Analysis Component

2. Analyze and interpret both the (a) sales variance and (b) direct materials cost variance.

Problem 8-3B

Flexible budget preparation; computation of materials, labor, and overhead variances; and overhead variance report

P1   P2   P3   C2

Suncoast Company set the following standard costs for one unit of its product.

Direct materials (4.5 lbs. @ $6 per lb.).	$27
Direct labor (1.5 hrs. @ $12 per hr.)	18
Overhead (1.5 hrs. @ $16 per hr.)	24
Total standard cost	$69

The predetermined overhead rate ($16.00 per direct labor hour) is based on an expected volume of 75% of the factory's capacity of 20,000 units per month. Following are the company's budgeted overhead costs per month at the 75% capacity level.

Overhead Budget (75% Capacity)		
Variable overhead costs		
Indirect materials	$22,500	
Indirect labor	90,000	
Power	22,500	
Repairs and maintenance	45,000	
Total variable overhead costs		$180,000
Fixed overhead costs		
Depreciation—building	24,000	
Depreciation—machinery	72,000	
Taxes and insurance	18,000	
Supervision	66,000	
Total fixed overhead costs.		180,000
Total overhead costs		$360,000

The company incurred the following actual costs when it operated at 75% of capacity in December.

Direct materials (69,000 lbs. @ $6.10 per lb.)		$ 420,900
Direct labor (22,800 hrs. @ $12.30 per hr.)		280,440
Overhead costs		
Indirect materials	$21,600	
Indirect labor	82,260	
Power	23,100	
Repairs and maintenance	46,800	
Depreciation—building	24,000	
Depreciation—machinery	75,000	
Taxes and insurance	16,500	
Supervision	66,000	355,260
Total costs		$1,056,600

Required

1. Examine the monthly overhead budget to (a) determine the costs per unit for each variable overhead item and its total per unit costs, and (b) identify the total fixed costs per month.
2. Prepare flexible overhead budgets (as in Exhibit 8.12) for December showing the amounts of each variable and fixed cost at the 65%, 75%, and 85% capacity levels.
3. Compute the direct materials cost variance, including its price and quantity variances.
4. Compute the direct labor cost variance, including its rate and efficiency variances.
5. Prepare a detailed overhead variance report (as in Exhibit 8.15) that shows the variances for individual items of overhead.

Check (2) Budgeted total overhead at 17,000 units, $384,000
(3) Materials variances: Price, $6,900 U; Quantity, $9,000 U
(4) Labor variances: Rate, $6,840 U; Efficiency, $3,600 U

Kryll Company set the following standard unit costs for its single product.

Problem 8-4B
Computation of materials, labor, and overhead variances

P2 P3

Direct materials (25 lbs. @ $4 per lb.).............................	$100
Direct labor (6 hrs. @ $8 per hr.)...................................	48
Factory overhead—variable (6 hrs. @ $5 per hr.)	30
Factory overhead—fixed (6 hrs. @ $7 per hr.)	42
Total standard cost	$220

The predetermined overhead rate is based on a planned operating volume of 80% of the productive capacity of 60,000 units per quarter. The following flexible budget information is available.

	Operating Levels		
	70%	80%	90%
Production in units	42,000	48,000	54,000
Standard direct labor hours	252,000	288,000	324,000
Budgeted overhead			
Fixed factory overhead	$2,016,000	$2,016,000	$2,016,000
Variable factory overhead	1,260,000	1,440,000	1,620,000

During the current quarter, the company operated at 70% of capacity and produced 42,000 units of product; direct labor hours worked were 250,000. Units produced were assigned the following standard costs:

Direct materials (1,050,000 lbs. @ $4 per lb.)	$4,200,000
Direct labor (252,000 hrs. @ $8 per hr.)	2,016,000
Factory overhead (252,000 hrs. @ $12 per hr.)	3,024,000
Total standard cost	$9,240,000

Actual costs incurred during the current quarter follow:

Direct materials (1,000,000 lbs. @ $4.25 per lb.)	$4,250,000
Direct labor (250,000 hrs. @ $7.75 per hr.).......................	1,937,500
Fixed factory overhead costs.......................................	1,960,000
Variable factory overhead costs....................................	1,200,000
Total actual costs..	$9,347,500

Check (1) Materials variances: Price, $250,000 U; Quantity, $200,000 F (2) Labor variances: Rate, $62,500 F; Efficiency, $16,000 F

Required

1. Compute the direct materials cost variance, including its price and quantity variances.
2. Compute the direct labor cost variance, including its rate and efficiency variances.
3. Compute the total overhead controllable and volume variances.

Problem 8-5B[A]
Expanded overhead variances
P4

Refer to information in Problem 8-4B.

Required

Compute these variances: (a) variable overhead spending and efficiency, (b) fixed overhead spending and volume, and (c) total overhead controllable.

Problem 8-6B[A]
Materials, labor, and overhead variances recorded and analyzed

C1   P5

Kenya Company's standard cost accounting system recorded this information from its June operations.

Standard direct materials cost.......................................	$130,000
Direct materials quantity variance (favorable)......................	5,000
Direct materials price variance (favorable).........................	1,500
Actual direct labor cost..	65,000
Direct labor efficiency variance (favorable).........................	3,000
Direct labor rate variance (unfavorable)............................	500
Actual overhead cost..	250,000
Volume variance (unfavorable).....................................	12,000
Controllable variance (unfavorable)	8,000

Check (1) Dr. Work in Process Inventory (for overhead), $230,000

Required

1. Prepare journal entries dated June 30 to record the company's costs and variances for the month. (Do not prepare the journal entry to close the variances.)

Analysis Component

2. Identify the variances that would attract the attention of a manager who uses management by exception. Describe what action(s) the manager should consider.

SERIAL PROBLEM
Business Solutions
P1

(This serial problem began in Chapter 1 and continues through most of the book. If previous chapter segments were not completed, the serial problem can begin at this point. It is helpful, but not necessary, to use the working papers that accompany the book.)

SP 8 Business Solutions's second quarter 2016 fixed budget performance report for its computer furniture operations follows. The $156,000 budgeted expenses include $108,000 in variable expenses for desks and $18,000 in variable expenses for chairs, as well as $30,000 fixed expenses. The actual expenses include $31,000 fixed expenses. Prepare a flexible budget performance report that shows any variances between budgeted results and actual results. List fixed and variable expenses separately.

	Fixed Budget	Actual Results	Variances
Desk sales (in units).............	144	150	
Chair sales (in units)	72	80	
Desk sales	$180,000	$186,000	$6,000 F
Chair sales	36,000	41,200	5,200 F
Total expenses................	156,000	163,880	7,880 U
Income from operations	$ 60,000	$ 63,320	$3,320 F

Check Variances: Fixed expenses, $1,000 U

Beyond the Numbers

BTN 8-1   Analysis of flexible budgets and standard costs emphasizes the importance of a similar unit of measure for meaningful comparisons and evaluations. When **Apple** compiles its financial reports in compliance with GAAP, it applies the same unit of measurement, U.S. dollars, for most measures of business operations. One issue for Apple is how best to adjust account values for its subsidiaries that compile financial reports in currencies other than the U.S. dollar.

REPORTING IN ACTION
C1
APPLE

Required

1. Read Apple's Note 1 in Appendix A and identify the financial statement where it reports the annual adjustment for foreign currency translation for subsidiaries that do not use the U.S. dollar as their functional currency.
2. Translating financial statements requires the use of a currency exchange rate. For each of the following financial statement items, explain the exchange rate the company would apply to translate into U.S. dollars.
   a. Cash
   b. Sales revenue
   c. Property, plant and equipment

BTN 8-2   The usefulness of budgets, variances, and related analyses often depends on the accuracy of management's estimates of future sales activity.

COMPARATIVE ANALYSIS
A1
APPLE
GOOGLE

Required

1. Identify and record the prior three years' sales (in dollars) for **Apple** and **Google** using their financial statements in Appendix A.
2. Using the data in part *1*, predict both companies' sales activity for the next two to three years. (If possible, compare your predictions to actual sales figures for those years.)

BTN 8-3   Setting materials, labor, and overhead standards is challenging. If standards are set too low, companies might purchase inferior products and employees might not work to their full potential. If standards are set too high, companies could be unable to offer a quality product at a profitable rate and employees could be overworked. The ethical challenge is to set a high but reasonable standard. Assume that as a manager you are asked to set the standard materials price and quantity for the new 1,000 CKB Mega-Max chip, a technically advanced product. To properly set the price and quantity standards, you assemble a team of specialists to provide input.

ETHICS CHALLENGE
C1

Required

Identify four types of specialists that you would assemble to provide information to help set the materials price and quantity standards. Briefly explain why you chose each individual.

BTN 8-4   The reason we use the words *favorable* and *unfavorable* when evaluating variances is made clear when we look at the closing of accounts. To see this, consider that (1) all variance accounts are closed at the end of each period (temporary accounts), (2) a favorable variance is always a credit balance, and (3) an unfavorable variance is always a debit balance. Write a half-page memorandum to your instructor with three parts that answer the three following requirements. (Assume that variance accounts are closed to Cost of Goods Sold.)

COMMUNICATING IN PRACTICE
P5 C2

Required

1. Does Cost of Goods Sold increase or decrease when closing a favorable variance? Does gross margin increase or decrease when a favorable variance is closed to Cost of Goods Sold? Explain.

2. Does Cost of Goods Sold increase or decrease when closing an unfavorable variance? Does gross margin increase or decrease when an unfavorable variance is closed to Cost of Goods Sold? Explain.

3. Explain the meaning of a favorable variance and an unfavorable variance.

TAKING IT TO THE NET

C1

BTN 8-5   Access iSixSigma's website (<u>iSixSigma.com</u>) to search for and read information about *benchmarking* to complete the following requirements. (*Hint:* Look in the "dictionary" link.)

Required

1. Write a one-paragraph explanation (in layperson's terms) of benchmarking.

2. How does standard costing relate to benchmarking?

TEAMWORK IN ACTION

C2

BTN 8-6   Many service industries link labor rate and time (quantity) standards with their processes. One example is the standard time to board an aircraft. The reason time plays such an important role in the service industry is that it is viewed as a competitive advantage: best service in the shortest amount of time. Although the labor rate component is difficult to observe, the time component of a service delivery standard is often readily apparent—for example, "Lunch will be served in less than five minutes, or it is free."

Required

Break into teams and select two service industries for your analysis. Identify and describe all the time elements each industry uses to create a competitive advantage.

ENTREPRENEURIAL DECISION

C1 C2

BTN 8-7   **Niner Bikes**, as discussed in the chapter opener, uses a costing system with standard costs for direct materials, direct labor, and overhead costs. Two comments frequently are mentioned in relation to standard costing and variance analysis: "Variances are not explanations" and "Management's goal is not to minimize variances."

Required

Write a short memo to Chris Sugai, Niner Bikes' president, (no more than one page) interpreting these two comments in the context of his business.

HITTING THE ROAD

C1

BTN 8-8   Training employees to use standard amounts of materials in production is common. Typically, large companies invest in this training but small organizations do not. One can observe these different practices in a trip to two different pizza businesses. Visit both a local pizza business and a national pizza chain business and then complete the following.

Required

1. Observe and record the number of raw material items used to make a typical cheese pizza. Also observe how the person making the pizza applies each item when preparing the pizza.

2. Record any differences in how items are applied between the two businesses.

3. Estimate which business is more profitable from your observations. Explain.

BTN 8-9   Access the annual report of Samsung (at <u>samsung.com</u>) for the year ended December 31, 2013. The usefulness of its budgets, variances, and related analyses depends on the accuracy of management's estimates of future sales activity.

GLOBAL DECISION

A1

Samsung

Required

1. Identify and record the prior two years' sales (in ₩ millions) for Samsung from its income statement.
2. Using the data in part *1*, predict sales activity for Samsung for the next two years. Explain your prediction process.

ANSWERS TO MULTIPLE CHOICE QUIZ

1. c; Fixed costs remain at $300,000; Variable costs = ($246,000/24,000 units) × 20,000 units = $205,000
2. e; Budgeted direct materials + Unfavorable variance = Actual cost of direct materials used; or, 60,000 units × $10 per unit = $600,000 + $15,000 U = $615,000
3. c; (AH × AR) − (AH × SR) = $1,599,040 − (84,160 hours × $20 per hour) = $84,160 F

4. b; Actual variable overhead − Variable overhead applied to production = Variable overhead cost variance; or $150,000 − (96,000 hours × $1.50 per hour) = $6,000 U
5. a; Budgeted fixed overhead − Fixed overhead applied to production = Volume variance; or $24,000 − (4,800 units × $4 per unit) = $4,800 U

chapter 9

Performance Measurement and Responsibility Accounting

Chapter Preview

DECENTRALIZATION

Advantages

Disadvantages

Performance evaluation

RESPONSIBILITY ACCOUNTING

Controllable versus uncontrollable costs

Responsibility accounting system

P1 Responsibility accounting report

PROFIT CENTERS

C1 Direct and indirect expenses

P2 Allocation of indirect expenses

P3 Departmental income statements

Departmental contribution to overhead

INVESTMENT CENTERS

A1 ROI and residual income

A2 Margin and turnover

A3 Nonfinancial performance measures

A4 Cycle time

C2 Transfer pricing

C3 Joint costs allocation

Learning Objectives

CONCEPTUAL

C1 Distinguish between direct and indirect expenses and identify bases for allocating indirect expenses to departments.

C2 *Appendix 9A*—Explain transfer pricing and methods to set transfer prices.

C3 *Appendix 9B*—Describe allocation of joint costs across products.

ANALYTICAL

A1 Analyze investment centers using return on investment and residual income.

A2 Analyze investment centers using profit margin and investment turnover.

A3 Analyze investment centers using the balanced scorecard.

A4 Compute cycle time and cycle efficiency, and explain their importance to production management.

PROCEDURAL

P1 Prepare a responsibility accounting report using controllable costs.

P2 Allocate indirect expenses to departments.

P3 Prepare departmental income statements and contribution reports.

Saving Troubled Waters

PHILADELPHIA—Brian Linton has a passion for oceans. Growing up in Singapore, Brian spent time scuba diving and tending to his 30 fish tanks. Traveling the world enabled Brian to see the "good, the bad, and the ugly of oceans and waterways." Combining his love of the water with an entrepreneurial spirit, Brian started his company **United By Blue (UnitedByBlue.com),** an apparel and jewelry company that removes one pound of trash in oceans and waterways for every product sold. As Brian notes, the company's unique business model was driven by "a quest for concrete ways to contribute to real and significant conservation efforts."

Building off Brian's college experiences selling jewelry he imported from Thailand, United By Blue sells men's and women's clothing, bags, and jewelry. The company uses organic cotton and creative designs to make products that elicit a fun vibe associated with oceans and harbor villages. Offering a diverse product line requires Brian to pay attention to cost management and departmental profits. The Sand Shack, a product in the company's jewelry department, "is a line of jewelry with chunky turquoise stones that generates much of the profits the company runs on," says Brian. His managers monitor direct, indirect, and controllable costs; allocate indirect costs to departments; and "measure return on investment (ROI)," explains Brian.

While focusing on controlling costs, United By Blue also strives to remove plastic from its packaging. "The number one material we collect during cleanups is plastic debris. We try to eliminate as much plastic as we can from our supply chain," says Brian. Apparel tags are made from biodegradable substances, infused with flower seeds. T-shirts are packaged in banana fiber paper. "We use things that go back to the earth in a very natural way and actually grow life." While these materials are more costly than plastic, they better fit the company's philosophy and, Brian believes, help generate new business. "We have customers that double their orders the next season because of the cleanups," Brian notes.

As United By Blue continues to grow, Brian focuses on financial *and* nonfinancial performance measures. From $330,000 in 2010, revenues have grown to over $2 million in 2013. A focus on departmental contribution margins enables the company to operate efficiently to finance future growth. Likewise, more revenues mean the company collects more trash, over 170,000 pounds through early 2014 and a goal of over a million pounds. As company founder and chief trash collector, this nonfinancial indicator measures progress toward Brian's vision of "doing the most good possible."

Brian encourages young entrepreneurs to "leave a positive impact on this world" by focusing on what you love. "My heart is in the ocean, so whatever I am doing is going to be in that realm. Whatever your passion is, leave that positive impact."

"Do the dirty work yourself"
—**Brian Linton**

Sources: *United By Blue website,* January 2015; *Philly.com,* September 5, 2013; *Bloomberg Businessweek,* January 9, 2012; *businessinterviews.com,* interview, September 2014; *Philadelphia Magazine,* July 2011; *PRweb.com,* January 2012

DECENTRALIZATION

Companies are divided into smaller units, called *divisions, segments, departments,* or *subunits,* when they become too large to be managed effectively as a single unit. In these **decentralized organizations,** decisions are made by managers throughout the company rather than by a few top executives. Common ways to decentralize organizations are by geography or product line (also called *brand*). For example, **LinkedIn** organizes its operations into three geographic segments: North America, Europe, and Asia-Pacific. **Callaway Golf** organizes its operations around two product lines, golf balls and golf clubs, and **Kraft Foods Group (Kraft)** organizes its operations around six product lines.

In this section we discuss the motivation for and the advantages and disadvantages of decentralization. In later sections of this chapter we discuss performance measurement in decentralized organizations.

Advantages of Decentralization

Many companies are so large and complex that they are broken into separate divisions for efficiency and/or effectiveness purposes. Divisions then are usually organized into separate departments. Each department is often placed under the direction of a manager. Providing lower-level managers with decision-making authority offers several advantages:

- Lower-level managers have timely access to detailed information about their departments. This enables these managers to better oversee and control their departments' operations.
- Providing lower-level managers with authority to make day-to-day decisions for their departments enables top-level managers to focus more on long-term strategy for the entire organization.
- Managing a division can be good training for employees who later might be promoted to top-level management.
- Having decision-making authority often boosts employee morale and retention.

Disadvantages of Decentralization

Decentralization has potential disadvantages which organizations should consider:

- Because they are so focused on their own departments, department managers might make decisions that do not reflect the organization's overall strategy.
- When an organization has several departments, the decisions of individual departments might conflict with one another.
- Departments might duplicate certain activities (for example, payroll accounting or purchasing); such duplication increases costs. In many decentralized organizations, activities like payroll, purchasing, and other administrative functions are *centralized* to reduce costs.

Performance Evaluation

When a company is decentralized, managers need to know how each department is performing. The accounting system must supply information about resources used and outputs achieved by each department. This requires a system to measure and accumulate revenue and expense information for each department.

Departmental information is prepared for internal managers to help control operations, appraise performance, allocate resources, and plan strategy. If a department is highly profitable, management may decide to expand its operations; if a department is performing poorly, information about revenues or expenses can suggest useful changes. Departmental information is rarely distributed publicly, because of its potential usefulness to competitors.

Financial information used to evaluate a department depends on whether it is evaluated as a cost center, profit center, or investment center.

- A **cost center** incurs costs without directly generating revenues. The manufacturing departments of a manufacturer and its service departments, such as accounting, advertising, and purchasing, are all cost centers. **Kraft**'s Delaware manufacturing plant is a cost center.

- A **profit center** generates revenues and incurs costs. Product lines and selling departments are often evaluated as profit centers. Kraft's Kool-Aid and Capri Sun drinks are examples of profit centers. A profit center manager would not have the authority to make significant investing decisions, such as the decision to build a new manufacturing plant.

- An **investment center** generates revenues and incurs costs, and its manager is also responsible for the investments made in operating assets. For example, the manager of Kraft's beverage division has the authority to make decisions such as building a new manufacturing plant.

Evaluation of managers' performance depends on whether they are responsible for cost centers, profit centers, or investment centers. Cost center managers are evaluated on their ability to control costs. Profit center managers are judged on their ability to generate revenues in excess of the profit center's costs. Investment center managers are evaluated on their use of investment-center assets to generate income. In the remainder of this chapter we discuss alternative ways to measure performance for these different types of departments.

RESPONSIBILITY ACCOUNTING

A **responsibility accounting system** can be set up to control costs and evaluate managers' performance by assigning costs to the managers responsible for controlling them. We discuss responsibility accounting and cost control in this section.

P1

Prepare a responsibility accounting report using controllable costs.

Controllable versus Uncontrollable Costs

We often evaluate a manager's performance using responsibility accounting reports that describe a department's activities in terms of whether a cost is controllable. **Controllable costs** are those for which a manager has the power to determine or at least significantly affect the amount incurred. **Uncontrollable costs** are not within the manager's control or influence. For example, department managers often have little or no control over depreciation expense because they cannot affect the amount of equipment assigned to their departments. Also, department managers rarely control their own salaries. However, they can control or influence items such as the cost of supplies used in their department. When evaluating managers' performances, we should use data reflecting their departments' outputs along with their controllable costs and expenses.

Point: *Cost* refers to a monetary outlay to acquire some resource that has a future benefit. *Expense* usually refers to an expired cost.

Distinguishing between controllable and uncontrollable costs depends on the particular manager and time period under analysis. For example, the cost of property insurance is usually not controllable at the department manager's level, but it is controllable by the executive responsible for obtaining the company's insurance coverage. Likewise, this executive does not control expenses resulting from insurance policies already in force. However, when a policy expires, this executive can renegotiate a replacement policy and then controls these costs. Therefore, all costs are controllable at some management level if the time period is sufficiently long. We must use good judgment in identifying controllable costs.

QC1

Responsibility Accounting System

A responsibility accounting system uses the concept of controllable costs to assign managers the responsibility for costs and expenses under their control. Prior to each reporting period, a company prepares plans that identify costs and expenses under each manager's control. These **responsibility accounting budgets** are typically based on the flexible budgeting approach we showed in the previous chapter. However, a responsibility accounting budget includes only controllable costs.

A responsibility accounting system also involves performance reports. A **responsibility accounting performance report** reports actual expenses that a manager is responsible for and their budgeted amounts. Management's analysis of differences between budgeted and actual amounts often results in corrective or strategic managerial actions. Upper-level management uses performance reports to evaluate the effectiveness of lower-level managers in keeping costs within budgeted amounts.

Point: Responsibility accounting does not place blame. Instead, responsibility accounting is used to identify opportunities for improving performance.

EXHIBIT 9.1

Organizational
Responsibility Chart

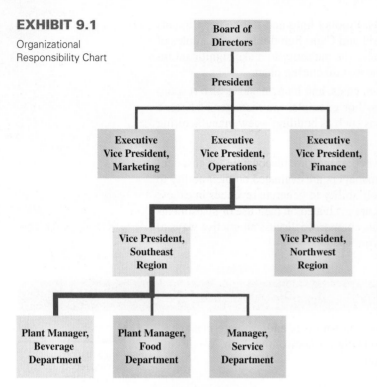

A responsibility accounting system recognizes that control over costs and expenses belongs to several levels of management. We illustrate this in the organization chart in Exhibit 9.1. The lines in this chart connecting the managerial positions reflect channels of authority. For example, the three department managers (beverage, food, and service) in this company are responsible for controllable costs incurred in their departments. These department managers report to the vice president (VP) of the Southeast region, and thus these same costs are subject to the overall control of this VP. Similarly, the costs of the Southeast region are reported to and subject to the control of the executive vice president (EVP) of operations, the president, and, ultimately, the board of directors.

Responsibility Accounting Report

Exhibit 9.2 shows summarized performance reports for the three management levels identified in Exhibit 9.1. The beverage department is a cost center, and its manager is responsible for controlling costs. Exhibit 9.2 shows that costs under the control of the beverage department plant manager are totaled and included among the controllable costs of the VP of the Southeast region. Costs under the control of this VP are totaled and included among

EXHIBIT 9.2

Responsibility Accounting
Performance Reports

Executive Vice President, Operations	For July		
Controllable Costs	**Budgeted Amount**	**Actual Amount**	**Over (Under) Budget**
Salaries, VPs	$ 80,000	$ 80,000	$ 0
Quality control costs	21,000	22,400	1,400
Office costs	29,500	28,800	(700)
Southeast region	276,700	279,500	2,800 ←
Northwest region	390,000	380,600	(9,400)
Totals	$ 797,200	$ 791,300	$ (5,900)

Vice President, Southeast Region	For July		
Controllable Costs	**Budgeted Amount**	**Actual Amount**	**Over (Under) Budget**
Salaries, department managers	$ 75,000	$ 76,500	$ 1,500
Depreciation	10,600	10,600	0
Insurance	6,800	6,300	(500)
Beverage department	79,600	79,900	300
Food department	61,500	64,200	2,700
Service department	43,200	42,000	(1,200)
Totals	$276,700	$279,500	$2,800

Plant Manager, Beverage Department	For July		
Controllable Costs	**Budgeted Amount**	**Actual Amount**	**Over (Under) Budget**
Direct materials	$ 51,600	$ 52,500	$ 900
Direct labor	20,000	19,600	(400)
Overhead	8,000	7,800	(200)
Totals	$ 79,600	$ 79,900	$ 300

the controllable costs of the EVP of operations. In this way, responsibility accounting reports provide relevant information for each management level. (If the VP and EVP are responsible for more than just costs, the responsibility accounting system will be expanded, as we show later in this chapter.)

The number of controllable costs reported varies across management levels. At lower levels, managers have limited responsibility and thus few controllable costs. Responsibility and control broaden for higher-level managers; therefore, their reports span a wider range of costs. However, reports to higher-level managers usually are summarized because: (1) lower-level managers are often responsible for these detailed costs, and (2) detailed reports can obscure the broader issues facing the top managers of an organization.

Point: Responsibility accounting usually divides a company into subunits, or *responsibility centers.* A center manager is evaluated on how well the center performs, as reported in responsibility accounting reports.

PROFIT CENTERS

When departments are organized as profit centers, responsibility accounting focuses on how well each department controlled costs *and* generated revenues. This information leads to **departmental income statements** as a common way to report profit center performance. When a company computes departmental profits, it confronts some accounting challenges that involve allocating expenses across departments. We next illustrate these allocations and departmental income reporting.

Direct and Indirect Expenses

Direct expenses are costs readily traced to a department because they are incurred for that department's sole benefit. They require no allocation across departments. For example, the salary of an employee who works in only one department is a direct expense of that one department. Direct expenses are often, but not always, controllable costs.

Indirect expenses are costs that are incurred for the joint benefit of more than one department; they cannot be readily traced to only one department. For example, if two or more departments share a single building, all enjoy the benefits of the expenses for rent, heat, and light. Likewise, the *operating departments* that perform an organization's main functions, for example manufacturing and selling, benefit from the work of *service departments.* Service departments, like payroll and human resource management, do not generate revenues, but their support is crucial for the operating departments' success.

When we need information about departmental profits, indirect expenses are allocated across departments benefiting from them. Ideally, we allocate indirect expenses by using a cause-effect relation. When we cannot identify cause-effect relations, we allocate each indirect expense on a basis approximating the relative benefit each department receives.

C1

Distinguish between direct and indirect expenses and identify bases for allocating indirect expenses to departments.

Illustration of Indirect Expense Allocation To illustrate how to allocate an indirect expense, we consider a retail store that hires an outside company to provide cleaning services. Management allocates this cost across the store's three departments according to the floor space each occupies. Costs of cleaning services for a recent month are $800. Exhibit 9.3 shows the square feet of floor space each department occupies. The store computes the percent of total square feet allotted to each department and uses the percentages to allocate the $800 cost.

Specifically, because the jewelry department occupies 60% of the floor space, 60% of the total $800 cost is assigned to it. The same procedure is applied to the other departments. When

Department	Department Square Feet	Percent of Total Square Feet	Cost Allocated to Department
Jewelry..............	2,400	60%	$480
Watch repair..........	600	15	120
China and silver........	1,000	25	200
Totals...............	4,000	100%	$800

EXHIBIT 9.3

Indirect Expense Allocation

the allocation process is complete, these and other allocated costs are deducted from the gross profit for each department to determine net income for each.

Allocation of Indirect Expenses

Allocate indirect expenses to departments.

Purestock/SuperStock

Point: Some companies ask supervisors to estimate time spent supervising specific departments for purposes of expense allocation.

We've just seen one example of how to allocate indirect expenses across departments—by percentage of floor space for cleaning services. Many other bases exist for allocating indirect expenses. This section describes how to identify appropriate allocation bases.

No standard rule identifies the best basis because expense allocation involves several factors, and the relative importance of these factors varies across departments and organizations. Judgment is required, and people do not always agree. Employee morale suffers when allocations are perceived as unfair. Thus, it is important to carefully design and explain the allocation of service department costs.

Wages and Salaries   Employee wages and salaries can be either direct or indirect expenses. If their time is spent entirely in one department, their wages are direct expenses of that department. However, if employees work for the benefit of more than one department, their wages are indirect expenses and must be allocated across the departments benefited. An employee's contribution to a department usually depends on the number of hours worked in contributing to that department. Thus, a reasonable basis for allocating employee wages and salaries is the *relative amount of time spent in each department.* In the case of a supervisor who manages more than one department, recording the time spent in each department may not always be practical. Instead, a company can allocate the supervisor's salary to departments on the basis of the number of employees or the amount of sales in each department.

Rent and Related Expenses   Rent expense for a building is reasonably allocated to a department on the basis of floor space it occupies. Location can often make some floor space more valuable than other space. Ground floor retail space, for instance, is often more valuable than basement or upper-floor space because all customers pass departments near the entrance but fewer go beyond the first floor. Thus, the allocation method can charge departments that occupy more valuable space a higher expense per square foot.

When no precise measures of floor space values exist, basing allocations on data such as customer traffic and real estate assessments is helpful. When a company owns its building, its expenses for depreciation, taxes, insurance, and other related building expenses are allocated like rent expense.

Advertising Expenses   Effective advertising of a department's products increases its sales and customer traffic. Moreover, advertising products for some departments usually helps other departments' sales because customers also often buy unadvertised products. Thus, many stores treat advertising as an indirect expense allocated on the basis of each department's proportion of total sales. For example, a department with 10% of a store's total sales is assigned 10% of advertising expense. Another method is to analyze each advertisement to compute the web/newspaper space or TV/radio time devoted to the products of a department and charge that department for the proportional costs of advertisements. Management must consider whether this more detailed and costly method is justified.

Equipment and Machinery Depreciation   Depreciation on equipment and machinery used in only one department is a direct expense of that department. Depreciation on equipment and machinery used by more than one department is an indirect expense to be allocated across departments. Accounting for each department's depreciation expense requires a company to keep records showing which departments use specific assets. The number of hours that a department uses equipment and machinery is a reasonable basis for allocating depreciation.

Utilities Expenses   Utilities expenses such as heating and lighting are usually allocated on the basis of floor space occupied by departments. This practice assumes their use is uniform across departments. When this is not so, a more involved allocation can be necessary, although there is often a trade-off between the usefulness of more precise allocations and the effort to compute them. Manufacturers often allocate electricity cost to departments on the basis of the machine hours used or the horsepower of equipment located in each department.

Service Department Expenses   To generate revenues, operating departments require support services provided by departments such as personnel, payroll, and purchasing. Such service departments are typically evaluated as *cost centers* because they do not produce revenues. A departmental accounting system can accumulate and report costs incurred by each service department for this purpose. The system then allocates a service department's expenses to operating departments benefiting from them. Exhibit 9.4 shows some commonly used bases for allocating service department expenses to operating departments. In the next section we illustrate how to allocate costs to operating departments.

Service Department	Common Allocation Bases
Office expenses	Number of employees or sales in each department
Personnel expenses	Number of employees in each department
Payroll expenses	Number of employees in each department
Purchasing costs	Dollar amounts of purchases or number of purchase orders processed
Maintenance expenses	Square feet of floor space occupied

EXHIBIT 9.4

Bases for Allocating Service Department Expenses

Departmental Income Statements

An income statement can be prepared for each operating department once expenses have been assigned to it. Its expenses include both direct expenses and its share of indirect expenses. For this purpose, it is useful to compile all expenses incurred in service departments before assigning those expenses to operating departments. We illustrate the steps to prepare departmental income statements using **A-1 Hardware** and its five departments. Two of them (office and purchasing) are service departments; the other three (hardware, housewares, and appliances) are operating (selling) departments. Allocating costs to operating departments and preparing departmental income statements involves four steps.

P3

Prepare departmental income statements and contribution reports.

Step 1: Accumulating revenues and direct expenses by department.

Step 2: Allocating indirect expenses across departments.

Step 3: Allocating service department expenses to operating departments.

Step 4: Preparing departmental income statements.

Exhibit 9.5 summarizes these steps in preparing departmental performance reports for cost centers and profit centers (links to the steps are coded with circled numbers *1* through *4*). A-1 Hardware's service departments (general office and purchasing) are cost centers, so their performance will be based on how well they controlled total service department expenses. The company's operating departments (hardware, housewares, and appliances) are profit centers, and their performance will be based on how well they generated departmental net income.

Point: Operating departments generate revenues. Service departments do not generate revenues.

Step 1:   Step 1 accumulates revenues and direct expenses in departmental accounts for each department. As cost centers, the service departments do not generate revenues. Direct expenses

EXHIBIT 9.5

Departmental Performance Reporting

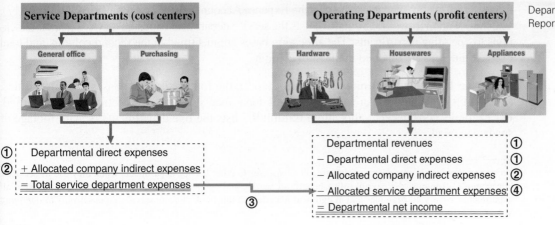

for all five departments include salaries, wages, and other expenses that each department incurs but does not share with any other department.

Step 2: Step 2 allocates indirect company expenses across all service and operating departments. Indirect expenses can include items such as depreciation, rent, advertising, and any other expenses that cannot be directly assigned to a department. Indirect expenses are first recorded in *company* accounts. Then, an allocation base is identified for each expense, and costs are allocated using a *departmental expense allocation spreadsheet,* described next.

Step 3: Step 3 allocates service department expenses to operating departments. Service department expenses typically are not allocated to other service departments.[1] Exhibit 9.6 shows the use of a departmental allocation spreadsheet. It uses various allocation bases to allocate all of the direct and indirect expenses of service departments to operating departments. After this allocation, no expenses remain in the service departments, as shown in row 21 of Exhibit 9.6.

EXHIBIT 9.6

Departmental Expense Allocation Spreadsheet

			A	B	C	D	E	F	G
1				**A-1 HARDWARE**					
2				**Departmental Expense Allocations**					
3				**For Year Ended December 31, 2015**					
4						**Allocation of Expenses to Departments**				
5					Expense	General	Purchas-	Hard-	House-	Appli-
6					Account	Office	ing	ware	wares	ances
7		**Allocation Base**			Balance	Dept.	Dept.	Dept.	Dept.	Dept.
8	**Direct expenses**									
9	Salaries expense.................	Payroll records.....................			$51,900	$13,300	$8,200	$15,600	$ 7,000	$ 7,800
10	Depreciation—Equipment......	Depreciation records.............			1,500	500	300	400	100	200
11	Supplies expense..................	Requisitions...........................			900	200	100	300	200	100
12	**Indirect expenses**									
13	Rent expense	Amount and value of space..			12,000	600	600	4,860	3,240	2,700
14	Utilities expense.....................	Floor space............................			2,400	300	300	810	540	450
15	Advertising expense..............	Sales......................................			1,000			500	300	200
16	Insurance expense.................	Value of insured assets			2,500	400	200	900	600	400
17	Total department expenses				72,200	15,300	9,700	23,370	11,980	11,850
18	**Service department expenses**									
19	General office department.....	Sales......................................				(15,300)		↳7,650	↳4,590	↳3,060
20	Purchasing department	Purchase orders...................					(9,700)	↳3,880	↳2,630	↳3,190
21	**Total expenses allocated to operating departments**..				$72,200	$ 0	$ 0	$34,900	$19,200	$18,100
22										

Computations for steps 2 and 3 are commonly made using a departmental expense allocation spreadsheet.

Accumulate Revenues and Direct Expenses First, direct and indirect expenses are accumulated by department and reported in the Expense Account Balance column (rows 8 through 17). The third section (rows 18 through 20) lists the service department expenses and shows their allocations to operating departments. The allocation bases are identified in the second column, and total expense amounts are reported in the third column.

Allocate Indirect Expenses Second (step 2), the four indirect expenses of rent, utilities, advertising, and insurance are allocated to all departments using the allocation bases identified. For example, consider rent allocation. Exhibit 9.7 lists the five departments' square footage of space occupied.

---

[1]In some cases we allocate a service department's expenses to other service departments when they use its services. For example, expenses of a payroll office benefit all service and operating departments and can be assigned to all departments. Nearly all examples and assignment materials in this book allocate service expenses *only to operating departments* for simplicity.

EXHIBIT 9.7

Departments' Allocation Bases

Department	Floor Space (Square Feet)	Value of Insured Assets ($)	Sales ($)	Number of Purchase Orders*
General office	1,500	$ 38,000		—
Purchasing	1,500	19,000		—
Hardware	4,050	85,500	$119,500	394
Housewares	2,700	57,000	71,700	267
Appliances	2,250	38,000	47,800	324
Total	12,000	$237,500	$239,000	985

*Purchasing department tracks purchase orders by department.

The two service departments (office and purchasing) occupy 25% of the total space (3,000 sq. feet/12,000 sq. feet). However, they are located near the back of the building, which is of lower value than space near the front that is occupied by operating departments. Management estimates that space near the back accounts for $1,200 (10%) of the total rent expense of $12,000. Exhibit 9.8 shows how we allocate the $1,200 rent expense between these two service

EXHIBIT 9.8

Allocating Indirect (Rent) Expense to Service Departments

Department	Square Feet	Percent of Total	Allocated Cost*
General office	1,500	50.0%	$ 600
Purchasing	1,500	50.0	600
Totals	3,000	100.0%	$1,200

*See row 13 of departmental expense allocation spreadsheet (Exhibit 9.6).

departments in proportion to their square footage. The calculations in Exhibit 9.8 show a simple rule for cost allocations:

> Allocated cost = Percentage of allocation base × Total cost to allocate

We then have the remaining amount of $10,800 ($12,000 − $1,200) of rent expense to allocate to the three operating departments, as shown in Exhibit 9.9.

EXHIBIT 9.9

Allocating Indirect (Rent) Expense to Operating Departments

Department	Square Feet	Percent of Total	Allocated Cost*
Hardware	4,050	45.0%	$ 4,860
Housewares	2,700	30.0	3,240
Appliances	2,250	25.0	2,700
Totals	9,000	100.0%	$10,800

*See row 13 of departmental expense allocation spreadsheet (Exhibit 9.6).

We continue step 2 by allocating the $2,400 of utilities expense to all departments based on the square footage occupied, as shown in Exhibit 9.10.

EXHIBIT 9.10

Allocating Indirect (Utilities) Expense to All Departments

Department	Square Feet	Percent of Total	Allocated Cost*
General office	1,500	12.50%	$ 300
Purchasing	1,500	12.50	300
Hardware	4,050	33.75	810
Housewares	2,700	22.50	540
Appliances	2,250	18.75	450
Totals	12,000	100.00%	$2,400

*See row 14 of departmental expense allocation spreadsheet (Exhibit 9.6).

Exhibit 9.11 shows the allocation of $1,000 of advertising expense to the three operating departments on the basis of sales dollars. We exclude the service departments from this allocation because they do not generate sales.

EXHIBIT 9.11

Allocating Indirect (Advertising) Expense to Operating Departments

Department	Sales	Percent of Total	Allocated Cost*
Hardware	$119,500	50.0%	$ 500
Housewares	71,700	30.0	300
Appliances	47,800	20.0	200
Totals	$239,000	100.0%	$1,000

*See row 15 of departmental expense allocation spreadsheet (Exhibit 9.6).

Finally, to complete step 2 we allocate insurance expense to each service and operating department, as shown in Exhibit 9.12.

EXHIBIT 9.12

Allocating Indirect (Insurance) Expense to All Departments

Department	Value of Insured Assets	Percent of Total	Allocated Cost*
General office	$ 38,000	16.0%	$ 400
Purchasing	19,000	8.0	200
Hardware	85,500	36.0	900
Housewares	57,000	24.0	600
Appliances	38,000	16.0	400
Total	$237,500	100.0%	$2,500

*See row 16 of departmental expense allocation spreadsheet (Exhibit 9.6).

Allocate Service Department Expenses   Third (step 3), total expenses of the two service departments are allocated to the three operating departments. Exhibit 9.13 shows the allocation of total general office expenses ($15,300) to operating departments.

EXHIBIT 9.13

Allocating Service Department (General Office) Expenses to Operating Departments

Department	Sales	Percent of Total	Allocated Cost*
Hardware	$119,500	50.0%	$ 7,650
Housewares	71,700	30.0	4,590
Appliances	47,800	20.0	3,060
Total	$239,000	100.0%	$15,300

*See row 19 of departmental expense allocation spreadsheet (Exhibit 9.6).

Exhibit 9.14 shows the allocation of total purchasing department expenses ($9,700) to operating departments.

EXHIBIT 9.14

Allocating Service Department (Purchasing) Expenses to Operating Departments

Department	Number of Purchase Orders	Percent of Total	Allocated Cost*
Hardware	394	40.00%	$3,880
Housewares	267	27.11	2,630
Appliances	324	32.89	3,190
Total	985	100.00%	$9,700

*See row 20 of departmental expense allocation spreadsheet (Exhibit 9.6).

Step 4:   The departmental expense allocation spreadsheet can now be used to prepare departmental performance reports. The general office and purchasing departments are cost centers, and their managers will be evaluated on their control of costs, as we showed in Exhibit 9.2.

Exhibit 9.15 shows income statements for A-1 Hardware's three operating departments. This exhibit uses the spreadsheet (in Exhibit 9.6) for its operating expenses; information on sales and cost of goods sold comes from departmental records.

EXHIBIT 9.15

Departmental Income Statements (Operating Departments)

A-1 HARDWARE Departmental Income Statements For Year Ended December 31, 2015	Hardware Department	Housewares Department	Appliances Department	Combined	
Sales	$119,500	$71,700	$47,800	$239,000	
Cost of goods sold	73,800	43,800	30,200	147,800	
Gross profit	45,700	27,900	17,600	91,200	
Operating expenses					
Salaries expense	15,600	7,000	7,800	30,400	⎤
Depreciation expense—Equipment	400	100	200	700	Direct expenses
Supplies expense	300	200	100	600	⎦
Rent expense	4,860	3,240	2,700	10,800	⎤
Utilities expense	810	540	450	1,800	Allocated indirect expenses
Advertising expense	500	300	200	1,000	
Insurance expense	900	600	400	1,900	⎦
Share of general office expenses	7,650	4,590	3,060	15,300	⎤ Allocated service
Share of purchasing expenses	3,880	2,630	3,190	9,700	⎦ department expenses
Total operating expenses	34,900	19,200	18,100	72,200	
Operating income (loss)	$10,800	$8,700	$(500)	$19,000	

Higher-level managers can use departmental income statements to determine which of a company's departments are most profitable. After considering all costs, A-1 Hardware's hardware department is its most profitable. As such, the company might attempt to expand its hardware department.

Departmental Contribution to Overhead

Exhibit 9.15 shows that the appliances department reported an operating loss of $(500). Should this department be eliminated? We must be careful when indirect expenses are a large portion of total expenses and when weaknesses in assumptions and decisions in allocating indirect expenses can markedly affect income. Also, operating department managers might have no control over the level of service department services they use. In these and other cases, we might better evaluate profit center performance using the **departmental contribution to overhead,** a measure of the amount of sales less *direct* expenses. A department's contribution is said to be "to overhead" because of the practice of considering all indirect expenses as overhead. Thus, the excess of a department's sales over direct expenses is a contribution toward at least a portion of its total overhead.

The upper half of Exhibit 9.16 shows a departmental contribution to overhead, as part of an expanded income statement. This format is common when reporting departmental contributions to overhead.

Using the information in Exhibits 9.15 and 9.16, we can evaluate the profitability of the three profit centers. For instance, let's compare the performance of the appliances department as described in these two exhibits. Exhibit 9.15 shows a $500 loss resulting from this department's operations. Yet Exhibit 9.16 shows a $9,500 positive contribution to overhead. The difference arises because the loss includes allocated indirect expenses while the contribution to overhead does not. The contribution of the appliances department is not as large as those of the other selling departments, but a $9,500 contribution to overhead is better than a $500 loss. This tells us that the appliances department is not a money loser. On the contrary, it is contributing $9,500 toward defraying total indirect expenses of $40,500.

Example: If the $15,300 general office expenses in Exhibit 9.6 are allocated equally across departments, what is income for the hardware department and for the combined company? *Answer:* Hardware income, $13,350; combined income, $19,000.

EXHIBIT 9.16

Departmental Contribution
to Overhead

A-I HARDWARE				
Income Statement Showing Departmental Contribution to Overhead				
For Year Ended December 31, 2015				
	Hardware Department	**Housewares Department**	**Appliances Department**	**Combined**
Sales	$119,500	$ 71,700	$47,800	$239,000
Cost of goods sold	73,800	43,800	30,200	147,800
Gross profit	45,700	27,900	17,600	91,200
Direct expenses				
Salaries expense	15,600	7,000	7,800	30,400
Depreciation expense—Equipment	400	100	200	700
Supplies expense	300	200	100	600
Total direct expenses.................	16,300	7,300	8,100	31,700
Departmental contributions				
to overhead........................	**$29,400**	**$20,600**	**$ 9,500**	**$59,500**
Indirect expenses				
Rent expense				10,800
Utilities expense				1,800
Advertising expense...................				1,000
Insurance expense				1,900
General office department expense				15,300
Purchasing department expense				9,700
Total indirect expenses				40,500
Operating income				$19,000

Point: Operating income is
the same in Exhibits 9.15 and
9.16. The method of reporting
indirect expenses in Exhibit 9.16
does not change total income
but does identify each operating
department's contribution to
overhead.

Behavioral Aspects of Departmental Performance Reports An organization must consider potential effects on employee behavior from departmental income statements and contribution to overhead reports. These include:

● Indirect expenses are typically uncontrollable costs for a department manager. Thus departmental contribution to overhead might be a better way to evaluate department manager performance. Including uncontrollable costs in performance evaluation is inconsistent with responsibility accounting and can reduce department manager morale.

● On the other hand, including indirect expenses in the department manager's performance evaluation can lead the manager to be more careful in using service departments, which can reduce the organization's costs.

● Some companies allocate *budgeted* service department costs rather than actual service department costs. In this way, operating departments are not held responsible for excessive costs from service departments, and service departments are more likely to try to control their costs.

QC2

EVALUATING INVESTMENT CENTER PERFORMANCE

We now come to the third type of responsibility center, the investment center. This section introduces both financial and nonfinancial measures of investment center performance.

Financial Performance Evaluation Measures

A1

Analyze investment
centers using return on
investment and residual
income.

Investment center managers are typically evaluated using performance measures that combine income and assets. These measures include return on investment, residual income, profit margin, and investment turnover. Consider the following data for ZTel, a company that operates two divisions: LCD and S-Phone. The LCD division manufactures liquid crystal display (LCD) touch-screen monitors and sells them for use in computers, cellular phones, and other products. The S-Phone division sells smartphones. Exhibit 9.17 shows current-year income and assets for those divisions.

	LCD Division	S-Phone Division
Investment center income.....................	$ 526,500	$ 417,600
Investment center average invested assets.........	2,500,000	1,850,000

EXHIBIT 9.17

Investment Center Income and Assets

Investment Center Return on Investment   One measure to evaluate division performance is the investment center **return on investment (ROI),** commonly called *return on assets* (ROA). This measure is computed as follows:

$$\text{Return on investment} = \frac{\text{Investment center income}}{\text{Investment center average invested assets}}$$

The return on investment for the LCD division is 21% (rounded), computed as $526,500/$2,500,000. The S-Phone division's return on investment is 23% (rounded), computed as $417,600/$1,850,000. ZTel's management can use ROI as part of its performance evaluation for its investment center managers. For example, the actual ROI can be compared to a targeted ROI or to the ROI for similar departments at competing businesses.

Investment Center Residual Income   Another way to evaluate division performance is to compute investment center **residual income,** which is computed as follows:

$$\text{Residual income} = \frac{\text{Investment center}}{\text{income}} - \frac{\text{Target investment center}}{\text{income}}$$

princigalli/iStock/360/Getty Images

Assume ZTel's top management sets target income at 8% of investment center assets. For an investment center, this target is typically the cost of obtaining financing. Applying this target rate using the data from Exhibit 9.17 yields the residual income for ZTel's divisions shown in Exhibit 9.18.

	LCD Division	S-Phone Division
Investment center income.....................	$526,500	$417,600
Less: Target investment center income		
$2,500,000 × 8%.........................	200,000	
$1,850,000 × 8%.........................		148,000
Investment center residual income..............	$326,500	$269,600

EXHIBIT 9.18

Investment Center Residual Income

Notice that residual income is expressed in dollars, not as a percentage. The LCD division produced more dollars of residual income than the S-Phone division. Ztel's management can use residual income, along with ROI, to evaluate investment center manager performance.

Using residual income to evaluate division performance encourages division managers to accept all opportunities that return more than the target income, thus increasing company value. For example, the S-Phone division might (mistakenly) not want to accept a new customer that will provide a 15% return on investment, since that will reduce the S-Phone division's overall return on investment (23% as shown above). However, the S-Phone division should accept this opportunity because the new customer would increase residual income by providing income above the target income of 8% of invested assets.

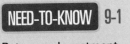

NEED-TO-KNOW 9-1

Return on Investment
A1

Do More: QS 9-9, QS 9-10,
E 9-8, E 9-9, E 9-10

The media division of a company reports income of $600,000, average invested assets of $7,500,000, and a target income of 6% of invested assets. Compute the division's (a) return on investment and (b) residual income.

Solution

a. $600,000/$7,500,000 = 8%
b. $600,000 − ($7,500,000 × 6%) = $150,000

Issues in Computing Return on Investment and Residual Income   Evaluations of investment center performance using return on investment and residual income can be affected by how a company answers the questions below:

1. How do you compute *average* invested assets? It is common to compute the average by adding the year's beginning amount of invested assets to the year's ending amount of invested assets, and dividing that sum by 2. Averages based on monthly or quarterly asset amounts are also acceptable.

2. How do you measure invested assets? It is common to measure invested assets using their *net* book values. For example, depreciable assets would be measured at their cost minus accumulated depreciation. As net book value declines over a depreciable asset's useful life, the result is that return on investment and residual income would increase over that asset's life. This might cause managers not to invest in new assets. In addition, in measuring invested assets, companies commonly exclude assets that are not used in generating investment center income, such as land held for resale.

Point: *Economic Value Added* (EVA®), developed and trademarked by Stern, Stewart, and Co., is an approach to address issues in computing residual income. This method uses a variety of adjustments to compute income, assets, and the target rate.

3. How do you measure investment center income? It is common to exclude both interest expense and tax expense from investment center income. Interest expense reflects a company's financing decisions, and tax expense is typically considered outside the control of an investment center manager. Excluding interest and taxes in these calculations enables more meaningful comparisons of return on investment and residual income across investment centers and companies.

■ **Decision** Insight ━━━━━━━━━━━━━━━━━━━━━━━━━━━━

In-the-Money   Executive pay is often linked to performance measures. Bonus payments are often based on exceeding a target return on investment or certain balanced scorecard indicators. Stock awards, such as stock options and restricted stock, reward executives when their company's stock price rises. The goal of bonus plans and stock awards is to encourage executives to make decisions that increase company performance and value. ■

A2

Analyze investment centers using profit margin and investment turnover.

Investment Center Profit Margin and Investment Turnover   We can further examine investment center (division) performance by splitting return on investment into two measures— profit margin and investment turnover, as follows.

Return on investment	=	Profit margin	×	Investment turnover

$$\frac{\text{Investment center income}}{\text{Investment center average assets}} = \frac{\text{Investment center income}}{\text{Investment center sales}} \times \frac{\text{Investment center sales}}{\text{Investment center average assets}}$$

Point: This partitioning of return on investment is sometimes referred to as DuPont analysis.

Profit margin measures the income earned per dollar of sales. Profit margin for the entire organization is calculated as net income divided by sales. In analyzing investment center performance, we typically use a measure of income *before* tax. Thus, for an investment center, profit margin is computed as investment center income divided by investment center sales. Likewise, **investment turnover** measures how efficiently an investment center generates sales from its invested assets. It is calculated as investment center sales divided by investment center average assets. Profit margin is expressed as a percent, while investment turnover is interpreted as the number of times assets were converted into sales. Higher profit margin and higher investment turnover indicate better performance.

To illustrate, consider **Walt Disney Co.**, which reports in Exhibit 9.19 results for two of its operating divisions: Media Networks and Parks and Resorts.

($ millions)	Media Networks	Parks and Resorts
Sales......................	$20,356	$14,089
Income....................	6,818	2,220
Average invested assets........	28,644	21,504

EXHIBIT 9.19

Walt Disney Division Sales, Income, and Assets

Profit margin and investment turnover for these two divisions are computed and shown in Exhibit 9.20:

($ millions)	Media Networks	Parks and Resorts
Profit margin		
$6,818/$20,356............	33.49%	
$2,220/$14,089............		15.76%
Investment turnover		
$20,356/$28,644..........	0.71	
$14,089/$21,504..........		0.66
Return on investment		
33.49% × 0.71.............	23.78%	
15.76% × 0.66.............		10.40%

EXHIBIT 9.20

Walt Disney Division Profit Margin and Investment Turnover

Disney's Media Networks division generates 33.49 cents of profit for every dollar of sales, while its Parks and Resorts division generates 15.76 cents of profit per dollar of sales. The Media Networks division (0.71 investment turnover) is slightly more efficient than the Parks and Resorts division (0.66 investment turnover) in using assets. Top management can use profit margin and investment turnover to evaluate the performance of division managers. The measures can also aid management when considering further investment in its divisions. As a result of both a much higher profit margin and more rapid investment turnover, the Media Networks division's return on investment (23.78%) is much greater than that of the Parks and Resorts division (10.40%).

■ **Decision** Maker ●━━━━━━━━━━━━━━━━━━━━━━━━━━━━

Division Manager   You manage a division in a highly competitive industry. You will receive a cash bonus if your division achieves an ROI above 12%. Your division's profit margin is 7%, equal to the industry average, and your division's investment turnover is 1.5. What actions can you take to increase your chance of receiving the bonus? ■   [Answers follow the chapter's Summary.]

A division reports sales of $50,000, income of $2,000, and average invested assets of $10,000. Compute the division's (a) profit margin, (b) investment turnover, and (c) return on investment.

Solution

a. $2,000/$50,000 = 4%
b. $50,000/$10,000 = 5
c. $2,000/$10,000 = 20%

NEED-TO-KNOW 9-2

Margin, Turnover, and Return

A2

Do More: QS 9-12, E 9-10, E 9-11, E 9-13

Nonfinancial Performance Evaluation Measures

Evaluating performance solely on financial measures such as return on investment or residual income has limitations. For example, some investment center managers might forgo profitable opportunities to keep their return on investment high. Also, residual income is less useful when comparing investment centers of different size. And, both return on investment and residual income can encourage managers to focus too heavily on short-term financial goals.

A3

Analyze investment centers using the balanced scorecard.

In response to these limitations, companies consider nonfinancial measures. For example, a delivery company such as **FedEx** might track the percentage of on-time deliveries. The percentage of defective tennis balls manufactured can be used to assess performance of **Penn**'s production managers. **Walmart**'s credit card screens commonly ask customers at checkout whether the cashier was friendly or the store was clean. This kind of information can help division managers run their divisions and help top management evaluate division manager performance. A popular measure that uses some nonfinancial indicators is the balanced scorecard.

Balanced Scorecard   The **balanced scorecard** is a system of performance measures, including nonfinancial measures, used to assess company and division manager performance. The balanced scorecard requires managers to think of their company from four perspectives:

1. **Customer:** What do customers think of us?
2. **Internal processes:** Which of our operations are critical to meeting customer needs?
3. **Innovation and learning:** How can we improve?
4. **Financial:** What do our owners think of us?

Point: One survey indicates that nearly 60% of global companies use some form of a balanced scorecard.

The balanced scorecard collects information on several key performance indicators within each of the four perspectives. These key indicators vary across companies. Exhibit 9.21 lists some common performance indicators used in the balanced scorecard.

EXHIBIT 9.21

Balanced Scorecard Performance Indicators

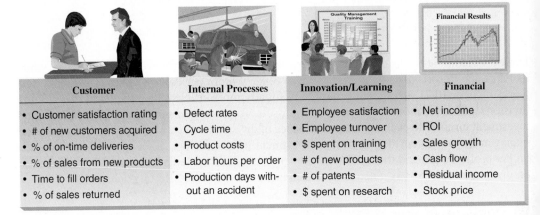

Customer	Internal Processes	Innovation/Learning	Financial
• Customer satisfaction rating	• Defect rates	• Employee satisfaction	• Net income
• # of new customers acquired	• Cycle time	• Employee turnover	• ROI
• % of on-time deliveries	• Product costs	• $ spent on training	• Sales growth
• % of sales from new products	• Labor hours per order	• # of new products	• Cash flow
• Time to fill orders	• Production days without an accident	• # of patents	• Residual income
• % of sales returned		• $ spent on research	• Stock price

After selecting key performance indicators, companies collect data on each indicator and compare actual amounts to expected amounts to assess performance. For example, a company might have a goal of filling 98% of customer orders within two hours. Balanced scorecard reports are often presented in graphs or tables that can be updated frequently. Such timely information aids division managers in their decisions and can be used by top management to evaluate division manager performance.

Exhibit 9.22 is an example of balanced scorecard reporting on the customer perspective for an Internet retailer. This scorecard reports that the retailer is getting 62% of its potential customers successfully through the checkout process, and that 2.2% of all orders are returned. The *color* of the arrows in the right-most column reveals whether the company is exceeding its goal (green), barely meeting the goal (yellow), or not meeting the goal (red). The *direction* of the arrows

EXHIBIT 9.22

Balanced Scorecard Reporting: Internet Retailer

Customer Perspective	Actual	Goal
Checkout success	62%	↑
Orders returned	2.2%	↔
Customer satisfaction rating	9.5	↑
Number of customer complaints	142	↓

reveals any trend in performance: an upward arrow indicates improvement, a downward arrow indicates declining performance, and an arrow pointing sideways indicates no change. A review of these arrows' color and direction suggests the retailer is meeting or exceeding its goals on checkout success, orders returned, and customer satisfaction. Further, checkout success and customer satisfaction are improving. The red arrow shows the company has received more customer complaints than was hoped for; however, the number of customer complaints is declining. A manager would combine this information with similar information on the internal process, innovation and learning, and financial perspectives to get an overall view of division performance.

▉ Decision Maker

Center Manager   Your center's usual return on total assets is 19%. You are considering two new investments for your center. The first requires a $250,000 average investment and is expected to yield annual net income of $50,000. The second requires a $1 million average investment with an expected annual net income of $175,000. Do you pursue either? ▉   [Answers follow the chapter's Summary.]

GLOBAL VIEW

L'Oréal is an international cosmetics company incorporated in France. With multiple brands and operations in over 100 countries, the company uses concepts of departmental accounting and controllable costs to evaluate performance. For example, for 2012 the company reports the following for the major divisions in its cosmetics branch:

Division	Operating Profit (€ millions)	
Consumer products...........	€2,051	
Professional products.........	615	
Luxury products.............	1,077	
Active cosmetics	311	€4,054 ◄
Nonallocated costs		(577)
Cosmetics branch total........		€3,477 ◄

Similar to "Departmental contributions to overhead" in Exhibit 9.16

Similar to "Operating income" in Exhibit 9.16

For L'Oréal, nonallocated costs include costs that are not controllable by division managers, including fundamental research and development and costs of service operations like insurance and banking. Excluding noncontrollable costs enables L'Oréal to prepare more meaningful division performance evaluations.

Sustainability and Accounting   Kraft's cream cheese-making process generates a lot of a by-product called whey. Kraft recently retrofitted a manufacturing plant to convert whey into energy. Here, a "digestion" system converts whey into a biogas, which is then used to create steam to power manufacturing machines. In this way, the company has converted a by-product into a source of sustainable energy and yielded cost savings. United By Blue, this chapter's feature company, uses recyclable packaging and eliminates as much plastic as possible from its supply chain. Although they add costs, company founder Brian Linton believes these sustainability efforts increase customer loyalty and sales.

Cycle Time and Cycle Efficiency ▉▉▉ **Decision Analysis**

Manufacturing companies commonly use nonfinancial measures to evaluate the performance of their production processes. For example, as lean manufacturing practices help companies move toward just-in-time manufacturing, it is important for these companies to reduce the time to manufacture their products and to improve manufacturing efficiency. One metric that measures that time element is **cycle time (CT)**, which describes the time it takes to produce a product or service. It is defined in Exhibit 9.23.

$$\text{Cycle time} = \text{Process time} + \text{Inspection time} + \text{Move time} + \text{Wait time}$$

Process time is the time spent producing the product. *Inspection time* is the time spent inspecting (1) raw materials when received, (2) work in process while in production, and (3) finished goods prior to shipment. *Move time* is the time spent moving (1) raw materials from storage to production and (2) work in process

A4 _____

Compute cycle time and cycle efficiency, and explain their importance to production management.

EXHIBIT 9.23

Cycle Time

from one factory location to another factory location. *Wait time* is the time that an order or job sits with no production applied to it. Wait time can be due to order delays, bottlenecks in production, or poor scheduling.

Process time is considered **value-added time:** it is the only activity in cycle time that adds value to the product from the customer's perspective. The other three time activities are considered **non-value-added time:** they add no value to the customer.

Companies strive to reduce non-value-added time to improve **cycle efficiency (CE),** which is a measure of production efficiency. Cycle efficiency is the ratio of value-added time to total cycle time, as shown in Exhibit 9.24.

EXHIBIT 9.24

Cycle Efficiency

$$\text{Cycle efficiency} = \frac{\text{Value-added time}}{\text{Cycle time}}$$

To illustrate, assume that Rocky Mountain Bikes receives and produces an order for 500 Tracker mountain bikes. Assume that it took the following times to produce this order.

Process time... 1.8 days   **Inspection time... 0.5 days**   **Move time... 0.7 days**   **Wait time... 3.0 days**

In this case, cycle time is 6.0 days (1.8 + 0.5 + 0.7 + 3.0 days). Also, cycle efficiency is 0.3, or 30%, computed as 1.8 days divided by 6.0 days. This means that Rocky Mountain Bikes' value-added time (its process time, or time spent working on the product) is 30%. The other 70% is spent on non-value-added activities.

If a company has a CE of 1, it means that its time is spent entirely on value-added activities. If the CE is low, the company should evaluate its production process to see if it can identify ways to reduce non-value-added activities. The 30% CE for Rocky Mountain Bikes is low, and its management should look for ways to reduce non-value-added activities.

NEED-TO-KNOW

COMPREHENSIVE

Management requests departmental income statements for Gamer's Haven, a computer store that has five departments. Three are operating departments (hardware, software, and repairs) and two are service departments (general office and purchasing).

	General Office	Purchasing	Hardware	Software	Repairs
Sales	—	—	$960,000	$600,000	$840,000
Cost of goods sold	—	—	500,000	300,000	200,000
Direct expenses					
Payroll	$60,000	$45,000	80,000	25,000	325,000
Depreciation	6,000	7,200	33,000	4,200	9,600
Supplies	15,000	10,000	10,000	2,000	25,000

The departments incur several indirect expenses. To prepare departmental income statements, the indirect expenses must be allocated across the five departments. Then the expenses of the two service departments must be allocated to the three operating departments. Total cost amounts and the allocation bases for each indirect expense follow.

Indirect Expense	Total Cost	Allocation Basis
Rent	$150,000	Square footage occupied
Utilities	50,000	Square footage occupied
Advertising	125,000	Dollars of sales
Insurance	30,000	Value of assets insured
Service departments		
General office	?	Number of employees
Purchasing	?	Dollars of cost of goods sold

The following additional information is needed for indirect expense allocations.

Department	Square Feet	Sales	Insured Assets	Employees	Cost of Goods Sold
General office	500		$ 60,000		
Purchasing	500		72,000		
Hardware	4,000	$ 960,000	330,000	5	$ 500,000
Software	3,000	600,000	42,000	5	300,000
Repairs	2,000	840,000	96,000	10	200,000
Totals	10,000	$2,400,000	$600,000	20	$1,000,000

Required

1. Prepare a departmental expense allocation spreadsheet for Gamer's Haven.
2. Prepare a departmental income statement reporting net income for each operating department and for all operating departments combined.

PLANNING THE SOLUTION

- Set up and complete four tables to allocate the indirect expenses—one each for rent, utilities, advertising, and insurance.
- Allocate the departments' indirect expenses using a spreadsheet like the one in Exhibit 9.6. Enter the given amounts of the direct expenses for each department. Then enter the allocated amounts of the indirect expenses that you computed.
- Complete two tables for allocating the general office and purchasing department costs to the three operating departments. Enter these amounts on the spreadsheet and determine the total expenses allocated to the three operating departments.
- Prepare departmental income statements like the one in Exhibit 9.15. Show sales, cost of goods sold, gross profit, individual expenses, and net income for each of the three operating departments and for the combined company.

SOLUTION

Allocations of the four indirect expenses across the five departments.

Rent	Square Feet	Percent of Total	Allocated Cost
General office	500	5.0%	$ 7,500
Purchasing	500	5.0	7,500
Hardware	4,000	40.0	60,000
Software	3,000	30.0	45,000
Repairs	2,000	20.0	30,000
Totals	10,000	100.0%	$150,000

Utilities	Square Feet	Percent of Total	Allocated Cost
General office	500	5.0%	$ 2,500
Purchasing	500	5.0	2,500
Hardware	4,000	40.0	20,000
Software	3,000	30.0	15,000
Repairs	2,000	20.0	10,000
Totals	10,000	100.0%	$50,000

Advertising	Sales Dollars	Percent of Total	Allocated Cost
Hardware	$ 960,000	40.0%	$ 50,000
Software	600,000	25.0	31,250
Repairs	840,000	35.0	43,750
Totals	$2,400,000	100.0%	$125,000

Insurance	Assets Insured	Percent of Total	Allocated Cost
General office	$ 60,000	10.0%	$ 3,000
Purchasing	72,000	12.0	3,600
Hardware	330,000	55.0	16,500
Software	42,000	7.0	2,100
Repairs	96,000	16.0	4,800
Totals	$600,000	100.0%	$30,000

1. Allocations of service department expenses to the three operating departments.

General Office Allocations to	Employees	Percent of Total	Allocated Cost
Hardware............	5	25.0%	$23,500
Software............	5	25.0	23,500
Repairs	10	50.0	47,000
Totals	20	100.0%	$94,000

Purchasing Allocations to	Cost of Goods Sold	Percent of Total	Allocated Cost
Hardware............	$ 500,000	50.0%	$37,900
Software............	300,000	30.0	22,740
Repairs	200,000	20.0	15,160
Totals	$1,000,000	100.0%	$75,800

GAMER'S HAVEN
Departmental Expense Allocations
For Year Ended December 31, 2015

	Allocation Base	Expense Account Balance	General Office Dept.	Purchasing Dept.	Hardware Dept.	Software Dept.	Repairs Dept.
Direct Expenses							
Payroll................................		$ 535,000	$ 60,000	$ 45,000	$ 80,000	$ 25,000	$ 325,000
Depreciation		60,000	6,000	7,200	33,000	4,200	9,600
Supplies		62,000	15,000	10,000	10,000	2,000	25,000
Indirect Expenses							
Rent	Square ft.	150,000	7,500	7,500	60,000	45,000	30,000
Utilities.............................	Square ft.	50,000	2,500	2,500	20,000	15,000	10,000
Advertising..........................	Sales	125,000	—	—	50,000	31,250	43,750
Insurance	Assets	30,000	3,000	3,600	16,500	2,100	4,800
Total expenses.......................		1,012,000	94,000	75,800	269,500	124,550	448,150
Service Department Expenses							
General office	Employees		(94,000)		23,500	23,500	47,000
Purchasing	Goods sold			(75,800)	37,900	22,740	15,160
Total expenses allocated to operating departments		$1,012,000	$ 0	$ 0	$330,900	$170,790	$510,310

2. Departmental income statements.

GAMER'S HAVEN
Departmental Income Statements
For Year Ended December 31, 2015

	Hardware	Software	Repairs	Combined
Sales	$ 960,000	$ 600,000	$ 840,000	$2,400,000
Cost of goods sold	500,000	300,000	200,000	1,000,000
Gross profit	460,000	300,000	640,000	1,400,000
Expenses				
Payroll	80,000	25,000	325,000	430,000
Depreciation	33,000	4,200	9,600	46,800
Supplies	10,000	2,000	25,000	37,000
Rent	60,000	45,000	30,000	135,000
Utilities	20,000	15,000	10,000	45,000
Advertising..................	50,000	31,250	43,750	125,000
Insurance	16,500	2,100	4,800	23,400
Share of general office	23,500	23,500	47,000	94,000
Share of purchasing	37,900	22,740	15,160	75,800
Total expenses...............	330,900	170,790	510,310	1,012,000
Operating income	$129,100	$129,210	$129,690	$ 388,000

Transfer Pricing

C2

Explain transfer pricing and methods to set transfer prices.

Divisions in decentralized companies sometimes do business with one another. For example, a separate division of **Harley-Davidson** manufactures its plastic and fiberglass parts used in the company's motorcycles. **Anheuser-Busch**'s metal container division makes cans and lids used in its brewing operations, and also sells cans and lids to soft-drink companies. A division of **Prince** produces strings used in tennis rackets made by Prince and other manufacturers. The price used to record transfers of goods across divisions of the same company is called the **transfer price.** Transfer prices can be used in cost, profit, and investment centers. Determining how to set transfer prices is the focus of this appendix.

In decentralized organizations, division managers have input on or decide transfer prices. Since these transfers are not with customers outside the company, the transfer price has no direct impact on the company's overall profits. However, transfer prices can impact performance evaluations and, if set incorrectly, lead to bad decisions.

Point: Transfer pricing can impact company profits when divisions are located in countries with different tax rates; this is covered in advanced courses.

Alternative Transfer Prices   The top portion of Exhibit 9A.1 reports data on the LCD division of ZTel. That division manufactures liquid crystal display (LCD) touch-screen monitors for use in ZTel's S-Phone division's smartphones. The monitors can also be used in other products. The LCD division can sell its monitors to the S-Phone division as well as to buyers other than S-Phone. Likewise, the S-Phone division can purchase monitors from suppliers other than LCD.

EXHIBIT 9A.1

LCD Division Manufacturing Information—Monitors

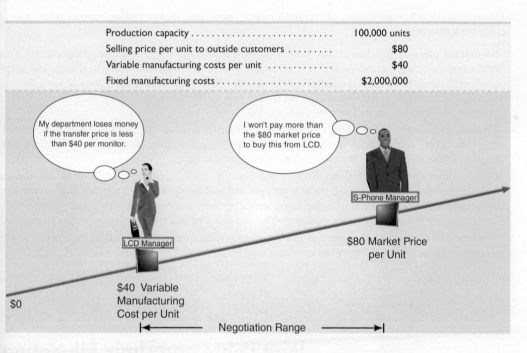

Production capacity	100,000 units
Selling price per unit to outside customers	$80
Variable manufacturing costs per unit	$40
Fixed manufacturing costs	$2,000,000

The bottom portion of Exhibit 9A.1 reveals the range of transfer prices for transfers of monitors from LCD to S-Phone. As you can see, the transfer price can reasonably range from $40 (the variable manufacturing cost per unit) to $80 (the cost of buying the monitor from an outside supplier). The manager of LCD wants to report a divisional profit. Thus, this manager will not accept a transfer price less than $40; a price less than $40 would cause the division to lose money on each monitor transferred. The LCD manager will consider transfer prices of only $40 or more. On the other hand, the S-Phone division manager also wants to report a divisional profit. Thus, this manager will not pay more than $80 per monitor because similar monitors can be bought from outside suppliers at that price. The S-Phone manager will consider transfer prices of only $80 or less.

As any transfer price between $40 and $80 per monitor is possible, how does ZTel determine the transfer price? The answer depends in part on whether the LCD division has excess capacity to manufacture monitors.

No Excess Capacity   If the LCD division can sell every monitor it produces (100,000 units) at a market price of $80 per monitor, LCD managers would not accept any transfer price less than $80 per monitor. This is a **market-based transfer price**—one based on the market price of the good or service being transferred. Any transfer price less than $80 would cause the LCD division managers to incur an unnecessary *opportunity cost* that would lower the division's income and hurt its managers' performance evaluation.

Typically, a division operating at full capacity will sell to external customers rather than sell internally. Still, the market-based transfer price of $80 can be considered the maximum possible transfer price when there is excess capacity, which is the case we consider next.

Excess Capacity   Now assume that the LCD division has excess capacity. For example, the LCD division might currently be producing only 80,000 units. Because LCD has $2,000,000 of fixed manufacturing costs, both the LCD division and the top management of ZTel prefer that the S-Phone division purchases its monitors from LCD. For example, if S-Phone purchases its monitors from an outside supplier at the market price of $80 each, LCD manufactures no units. Then, LCD reports a division loss equal to its fixed costs, and ZTel overall reports a lower net income as its costs are higher. Consequently, with excess capacity, LCD should accept any transfer price of $40 per unit or greater, and S-Phone should purchase monitors from LCD. This will allow LCD to recover some (or all) of its fixed costs and increase ZTel's overall profits.

For example, if a transfer price of $50 per monitor is used, the S-Phone manager is pleased to buy from LCD, since that price is below the market price of $80. For each monitor transferred from LCD to S-Phone at $50, the LCD division receives a *contribution margin* of $10 (computed as $50 transfer price less $40 variable cost) to contribute toward recovering its fixed costs. This form of transfer pricing is called **cost-based transfer pricing.** Under this approach the transfer price might be based on variable costs, total costs, or variable costs plus a markup. Determining the transfer price under excess capacity is complex and is covered in advanced courses.

Additional Issues in Transfer Pricing   Several additional issues arise in determining transfer prices which include the following:

Transfer Pricing Approaches Used by Companies

Cost 46%

Market 37%

Negotiated 17%

- **No market price exists.** Sometimes there is no market price for the product being transferred. The product might be a key component that requires additional conversion costs at the next stage and is not easily replicated by an outside company. For example, there is no market for a console for a Nissan Maxima and there is no substitute console Nissan can use in assembling a Maxima. In this case a market-based transfer price cannot be used.

- **Cost control.** To provide incentives for cost control, transfer prices might be based on standard, rather than actual costs. For example, if a transfer price of actual variable costs plus a markup of $20 per unit is used in the case above, LCD has no incentive to control its costs.

- **Division managers' negotiation.** With excess capacity, division managers will often negotiate a transfer price that lies between the variable cost per unit and the market price per unit. In this case, the **negotiated transfer price** and resulting departmental performance reports reflect, in part, the negotiating skills of the respective division managers. This might not be best for overall company performance.

- **Nonfinancial factors.** Factors such as quality control, reduced lead times, and impact on employee morale can be important factors in determining transfer prices.

APPENDIX

9B   Joint Costs and Their Allocation

C3

Describe allocation of joint costs across products.

Most manufacturing processes involve **joint costs,** which refer to costs incurred to produce or purchase two or more products at the same time. For example, a sawmill company incurs joint costs when it buys logs that it cuts into lumber as shown in Exhibit 9B.1. The joint costs include the logs (raw material) and their being cut (conversion) into boards classified as Clear, Select, No. 1 Common, No. 2 Common, No. 3 Common, and other types of lumber and by-products. After the logs are cut into boards, any further processing costs on the boards are not joint costs.

When a joint cost is incurred, a question arises as to whether to allocate it to different products resulting from it. The answer is that when management wishes to estimate the costs of individual products, joint costs are included and must be allocated to these joint products. However, when management needs information to help decide whether to sell a product at a certain point in the production process or to process it further, the joint costs are ignored. (We study this sell-or-process-further decision in a later chapter.)

Financial statements prepared according to GAAP must assign joint costs to products. To do this, management must decide how to allocate joint costs across products benefiting from these costs. If some products are sold and others remain in inventory, allocating joint costs involves assigning costs to both cost of goods sold and ending inventory.

The two usual methods to allocate joint costs are the (1) *physical basis* and (2) *value basis.* The physical basis typically involves allocating a joint cost using physical characteristics such as the ratio of pounds, cubic feet, or gallons of each joint product to the total pounds, cubic feet, or gallons of all joint products flowing from the cost. This method is not preferred because the resulting cost allocations do not reflect the relative market values the joint cost generates. The preferred approach is the value basis, which allocates a joint cost in proportion to the sales value of the output produced by the process at the "split-off point"; see Exhibit 9B.1. The split-off point is the point at which separate products can be identified.

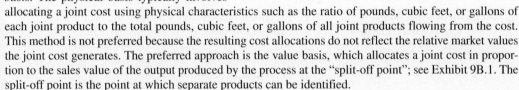

EXHIBIT 9B.1

Joint Products from Logs

Physical Basis Allocation of Joint Costs   To illustrate the physical basis of allocating a joint cost, we consider a sawmill that bought logs for $30,000. When cut, these logs produce 100,000 board feet of lumber in the grades and amounts shown in Exhibit 9B.2. The logs produce 20,000 board feet of No. 3 Common lumber, which is 20% of the total. With physical allocation, the No. 3 Common lumber is assigned 20% of the $30,000 cost of the logs, or $6,000 ($30,000 × 20%). Because this low-grade lumber sells for $4,000, this allocation gives a $2,000 loss from its production and sale. The physical basis for allocating joint costs does not reflect the extra value flowing into some products or the inferior value flowing into others. That is, the portion of a log that produces Clear and Select grade lumber is worth more than the portion used to produce the three grades of common lumber, but the physical basis fails to reflect this.

EXHIBIT 9B.2

Allocating Joint Costs on a Physical Basis

Grade of Lumber	Board Feet Produced	Percent of Total	Allocated Cost	Sales Value	Gross Profit
Clear and Select............	10,000	10.0%	$ 3,000	$12,000	$ 9,000
No. 1 Common	30,000	30.0	9,000	18,000	9,000
No. 2 Common	40,000	40.0	12,000	16,000	4,000
No. 3 Common	20,000	20.0	6,000	4,000	(2,000)
Totals	100,000	100.0%	$30,000	$50,000	$20,000

Value Basis Allocation of Joint Costs   Exhibit 9B.3 illustrates the value basis method of allocation. It determines the percents of the total costs allocated to each grade by the ratio of each grade's sales value at the split-off point to the total sales value of $50,000 (sales value is the unit selling price multiplied by the number of units produced). The Clear and Select lumber grades receive 24% of the total cost ($12,000/$50,000) instead of the 10% portion using a physical basis. The No. 3 Common lumber receives only 8% of the total cost, or $2,400, which is much less than the $6,000 assigned to it using the physical basis.

EXHIBIT 9B.3

Allocating Joint Costs on a Value Basis

Grade of Lumber	Sales Value	Percent of Total	Allocated Cost	Gross Profit
Clear and Select	$12,000	24.0%	$ 7,200	$ 4,800
No. 1 Common.	18,000	36.0	10,800	7,200
No. 2 Common.	16,000	32.0	9,600	6,400
No. 3 Common.	4,000	8.0	2,400	1,600
Totals.	$50,000	100.0%	$30,000	$20,000

Example: Refer to Exhibit 9B.3. If the sales value of Clear and Select lumber is changed to $10,000, what is the revised ratio of the market value of No. 1 Common to the total? *Answer:* $18,000/$48,000 = 37.5%

An outcome of value basis allocation is that *each* grade produces exactly the same 40% gross profit at the split-off point. This 40% rate equals the gross profit rate from selling all the lumber made from the $30,000 logs for a combined price of $50,000. It is this closer matching of cost and revenues that makes the value basis allocation of joint costs the preferred method.

Summary

C1 **Distinguish between direct and indirect expenses and identify bases for allocating indirect expenses to departments.** Direct expenses are traced to a specific department and are incurred for the sole benefit of that department. Indirect expenses benefit more than one department. Indirect expenses are allocated to departments when computing departmental net income. Ideally, we allocate indirect expenses by using a cause-effect relation for the allocation base. When a cause-effect relation is not identifiable, each indirect expense is allocated on a basis reflecting the relative benefit received by each department.

C2 **Explain transfer pricing and methods to set transfer prices.** Transfer prices are used to record transfers of items between divisions of the same company. Transfer prices can be based on costs or market prices, or can be negotiated by division managers.

C3 **Describe allocation of joint costs across products.** A joint cost refers to costs incurred to produce or purchase two or more products at the same time. When income statements are prepared, joint costs are usually allocated to the resulting joint products using either a physical or value basis.

A1 **Analyze investment centers using return on investment and residual income.** A financial measure often used to evaluate an investment center manager is the *return on investment,* also called *return on assets.* This measure is computed as the center's income divided by the center's average total assets. Residual income, computed as investment center income minus a target income is an alternative financial measure of investment center performance.

A2 **Analyze investment centers using profit margin and investment turnover.** Return on investment can also be computed as profit margin times investment turnover. Profit margin (equal to income/sales) measures the income earned per dollar of sales, and investment turnover (equal to sales/assets) measures how efficiently a division uses its assets.

A3 **Analyze investment centers using the balanced scorecard.** A balanced scorecard uses a combination of financial and nonfinancial measures to evaluate performance. Customer, internal process, and innovation and learning are the three primary perspectives of nonfinancial measures used in balanced scorecards.

A4 **Compute cycle time and cycle efficiency, and explain their importance to production management.** It is important for companies to reduce the time to produce their products and to improve manufacturing efficiency. One measure of that time is cycle time (CT), defined as Process time + Inspection time + Move time + Wait time. Process time is value-added time; the others are non-value-added time. Cycle efficiency (CE) is the ratio of value-added time to total cycle time. If CE is low, management should evaluate its production process to see if it can reduce non-value-added activities.

P1 **Prepare a responsibility accounting report using controllable costs.** Responsibility accounting systems provide information for evaluating the performance of department managers. A responsibility accounting system's performance reports for evaluating department managers should include only the expenses (and revenues) that each manager controls.

P2 **Allocate indirect expenses to departments.** Indirect expenses include items like depreciation, rent, advertising, and other expenses that cannot be assigned directly to departments. Indirect expenses are recorded in company accounts, an allocation base is identified for each expense, and costs are allocated to departments. Departmental expense allocation spreadsheets are often used in allocating indirect expenses to departments.

P3 **Prepare departmental income statements and contribution reports.** Each profit center (department) is assigned its expenses to yield its own income statement. These costs include its direct expenses and its share of indirect expenses. The departmental income statement lists its revenues and costs of goods sold to determine gross profit. Its operating expenses (direct expenses and its indirect expenses allocated to the department) are deducted from gross profit to yield departmental net income. The departmental contribution report is similar to the departmental income statement in terms of computing the gross profit for each department. Then the direct operating expenses for each department are deducted from gross profit to determine the contribution generated by each department. Indirect operating expenses are deducted *in total* from the company's combined contribution.

Guidance Answers to Decision Maker

Division Manager Your division's ROI without further action is 10.5% (equal to 7% × 1.5). In a highly competitive industry, it is difficult to increase profit margins by raising prices. Your division might be better able to control its costs to increase its profit margin. In addition, you might engage in a marketing program to increase sales without increasing your division's invested assets. Investment turnover and thus ROI will increase if the marketing campaign attracts customers.

Center Manager We must first realize that the two investment opportunities are not comparable on the basis of absolute dollars of income or on assets. For instance, the second investment provides a higher income in absolute dollars but requires a higher investment. Accordingly, we need to compute return on investment for each alternative: (1) $50,000 ÷ $250,000 = 20%, and (2) $175,000 ÷ $1 million = 17.5%. Alternative 1 has the higher return and is preferred over alternative 2. Do you pursue one, both, or neither? Because alternative 1's return is higher than the center's usual return of 19%, it should be pursued, assuming its risks are acceptable. Also, since alternative 1 requires a small investment, top management is likely to be more agreeable to pursuing it. Alternative 2's return is lower than the usual 19% and is not likely to be acceptable.

Key Terms

Balanced scorecard	Indirect expenses	Responsibility accounting budget
Controllable costs	Investment center	Responsibility accounting performance
Cost-based transfer pricing	Investment turnover	report
Cost center	Joint cost	Responsibility accounting system
Cycle efficiency (CE)	Market-based transfer price	Return on investment
Cycle time (CT)	Negotiated transfer price	Transfer price
Decentralized organization	Non-value-added time	Uncontrollable costs
Departmental contribution to overhead	Profit center	Value-added time
Departmental income statements	Profit margin	
Direct expenses	Residual income	

Multiple Choice Quiz   Answers at end of chapter

1. A retailer has three departments—housewares, appliances, and clothing—and buys advertising that benefits all departments. Advertising expense is $150,000 for the year, and departmental sales for the year follow: housewares, $356,250; appliances, $641,250; and clothing, $427,500. How much advertising expense is allocated to appliances if allocation is based on departmental sales?
   a. $37,500   d. $150,000
   b. $67,500   e. $641,250
   c. $45,000

2. Indirect expenses
   a. Cannot be readily traced to one department.
   b. Are allocated to departments based on the relative benefit each department receives.
   c. Are the same as uncontrollable expenses.
   d. *a, b,* and *c* above are all true.
   e. *a* and *b* above are true.

3. A division reports the information below. What is the division's investment (asset) turnover?

Sales	$500,000
Income	75,000
Average assets	200,000

   a. 37.5%   d. 2.67
   b. 15   e. 4
   c. 2.5

4. A company operates three retail departments as profit centers, and the following information is available for each. Which department has the largest dollar amount of departmental contribution to overhead, and what is the dollar amount contributed?

Department	Sales	Cost of Goods Sold	Direct Expenses	Allocated Indirect Expenses
X.	$500,000	$350,000	$50,000	$40,000
Y	200,000	75,000	20,000	50,000
Z.	350,000	150,000	75,000	10,000

   a. Department Y, $55,000
   b. Department Z, $125,000
   c. Department X, $500,000
   d. Department Z, $200,000
   e. Department X, $60,000

5. Using the data in question 4, Department X's contribution to overhead as a percentage of sales is
   a. 20%   d. 48%
   b. 30%   e. 32%
   c. 12%

A(B) *Superscript letter A (B) denotes assignments based on Appendix 9A (9B).*
🏿 Icon denotes assignments that involve decision making.

Discussion Questions

1. Why are many companies divided into departments?
2. What is the difference between operating departments and service departments?
3. 🏿 What are controllable costs?
4. Controllable and uncontrollable costs must be identified with a particular _____ and a definite _____ period.

5. 🏿 Why should managers be closely involved in preparing their responsibility accounting budgets?
6. 🏿 What are two main goals in managerial accounting for reporting on and analyzing departments?
7. 🏿 Is it possible to evaluate a cost center's profitability? Explain.

8. What is the difference between direct and indirect expenses?

9. 🔋 Suggest a reasonable basis for allocating each of the following indirect expenses to departments: (a) salary of a supervisor who manages several departments, (b) rent, (c) heat, (d) electricity for lighting, (e) janitorial services, (f) advertising, (g) expired insurance on equipment, and (h) property taxes on equipment.

10. Samsung has many departments. How is a department's contribution to overhead measured? **Samsung**

11. 🔋 Google aims to give its managers timely cost reports. In responsibility accounting, who receives timely cost reports and specific cost information? Explain. **GOOGLE**

12.ᴬ What is a transfer price? Under what conditions is a market-based transfer price most likely to be used?

13.ᴮ What is a joint cost? How are joint costs usually allocated among the products produced from them?

14.ᴮ 🔋 Give two examples of products with joint costs.

15. 🔋 Each **Apple** retail store has several departments. Why is it useful for its management to (a) collect accounting information about each department and (b) treat each department as a profit center? **APPLE**

16. 🔋 **Apple** delivers its products to locations around the world. List three controllable and three uncontrollable costs for its delivery department. **APPLE**

17. 🔋 Define and describe *cycle time* and identify the components of cycle time.

18. 🔋 Explain the difference between value-added time and non-value-added time.

19. Define and describe *cycle efficiency*.

20. 🔋 Can management of a company such as Samsung use cycle time and cycle efficiency as useful measures of performance? Explain. **Samsung**

---

connect

QUICK STUDY

QS 9-1
Allocating costs to departments
P1

Macee Department Store has three departments, and it conducts advertising campaigns that benefit all departments. Advertising costs are $100,000 this year, and departmental sales for this year follow. How much advertising cost is allocated to each department if the allocation is based on departmental sales?

Department	Sales
Department 1	$220,000
Department 2	400,000
Department 3	180,000

QS 9-2
Allocating costs to departments
P1

Mervon Company has two operating departments: mixing and bottling. Mixing has 300 employees and occupies 22,000 square feet. Bottling has 200 employees and occupies 18,000 square feet. Indirect factory costs for the current period follow: administrative, $160,000; and maintenance, $200,000. Administrative costs are allocated to operating departments based on the number of workers. Determine the administrative costs allocated to each operating department.

QS 9-3
Allocating costs to departments   P1

Mervon Company has two operating departments: mixing and bottling. Mixing has 300 employees and occupies 22,000 square feet. Bottling has 200 employees and occupies 18,000 square feet. Indirect factory costs for the current period follow: administrative, $160,000; and maintenance, $200,000. If the maintenance costs are allocated to operating departments based on square footage, determine the amount of maintenance costs allocated to each operating department.

QS 9-4
Allocation and measurement terms
C1

In each blank next to the following terms, place the identifying letter of its best description.

1. _____ Cost center
2. _____ Investment center
3. _____ Departmental accounting system
4. _____ Operating department
5. _____ Profit center
6. _____ Responsibility accounting system
7. _____ Service department

A. Incurs costs without directly yielding revenues.

B. Provides information used to evaluate the performance of a department.

C. Holds manager responsible for revenues, costs, and investments.

D. Engages directly in manufacturing or in making sales directly to customers.

E. Does not directly manufacture products but contributes to profitability of the entire company.

F. Incurs costs and also generates revenues.

G. Provides information used to evaluate the performance of a department manager.

For each of the following types of indirect expenses and service department expenses, identify one allocation basis that could be used to distribute it to the departments indicated.

_____ **1.** Computer service expenses of production scheduling for operating departments.

_____ **2.** General office department expenses of the operating departments.

_____ **3.** Maintenance department expenses of the operating departments.

_____ **4.** Electric utility expenses of all departments.

QS 9-5
Basis for cost allocation
C1

In each blank next to the following terms, place the identifying letter of its best description.

_____ **1.** Indirect expenses

_____ **2.** Controllable costs

_____ **3.** Direct expenses

_____ **4.** Uncontrollable costs

A. Costs not within a manager's control or influence

B. Costs that can be readily traced to a department

C. Cost that a manager has the ability to affect

D. Costs incurred for the joint benefit of more than one department

QS 9-6
Responsibility accounting terms

C1

Car Mart pays $130,000 rent each year for its two-story building. The space in this building is occupied by five departments as specified here.

QS 9-7
Rent expense allocated to departments

P2

Paint department	1,440 square feet of first-floor space
Engine department	3,360 square feet of first-floor space
Window department	2,016 square feet of second-floor space
Electrical department	960 square feet of second-floor space
Accessory department	1,824 square feet of second-floor space

The company allocates 65% of total rent expense to the first floor and 35% to the second floor, and then allocates rent expense for each floor to the departments occupying that floor on the basis of space occupied. Determine the rent expense to be allocated to each department. (Round percents to the nearest one-tenth and dollar amounts to the nearest whole dollar.)

Check   Allocated to paint dept., $25,350

Use the information in the following table to compute each department's contribution to overhead (both in dollars and as a percent). Which department contributes the largest dollar amount to total overhead? Which contributes the highest percent (as a percent of sales)? Round percents to one decimal.

QS 9-8
Departmental contribution to overhead

P3

	Dept. A	Dept. B	Dept. C
Sales	$53,000	$180,000	$84,000
Cost of goods sold	34,185	103,700	49,560
Gross profit	18,815	76,300	34,440
Total direct expenses	3,660	37,060	7,386
Contribution to overhead	$_____	$_____	$_____
Contribution percent (of sales).	_____ %	_____ %	_____ %

Compute return on investment for each of the divisions below (each is an investment center). Comment on the relative performance of each investment center.

QS 9-9
Computing return on investment

A1

Investment Center	Net Income	Average Assets	Return on Investment
Cameras and camcorders	$4,500,000	$20,000,000	_____
Phones and communications.	1,500,000	12,500,000	_____
Computers and accessories	800,000	10,000,000	_____

Refer to information in QS 9-9. Assume a target income of 12% of average invested assets. Compute residual income for each division.

QS 9-10
Computing residual income   A1

QS 9-11

Performance measures

A1   A2

Fill in the blanks in the schedule below for two separate investment centers A and B. Round answers to the nearest whole percent.

	Investment Center	
	A	**B**
Sales	$_____	$10,400,000
Net income	$ 352,000	$_____
Average invested assets	$1,400,000	_____
Profit margin.	8%	_____%
Investment turnover	_____	1.5
Return on investment	_____%	12%

QS 9-12

Computing profit margin and investment turnover

A2

A company's shipping division (an investment center) has sales of $2,420,000, net income of $516,000, and average invested assets of $2,250,000. Compute the division's profit margin and investment turnover.

QS 9-13

Performance measures— balanced scorecard

A3

Classify each of the performance measures below into the most likely balanced scorecard perspective it relates to. Label your answers using C (customer), P (internal process), I (innovation and growth), or F (financial).

_____ **1.** Customer wait time

_____ **2.** Number of days of employee absences

_____ **3.** Profit margin

_____ **4.** Number of new products introduced

_____ **5.** Change in market share

_____ **6.** Employee training sessions attended

_____ **7.** Length of time raw materials are in inventory

_____ **8.** Customer satisfaction index

QS 9-14

Performance measures— balanced scorecard

A3

Walt Disney reports the following information for its two Parks and Resorts divisions.

	U.S.		International	
	Current year	**Prior year**	**Current year**	**Prior year**
Hotel occupancy rates.	81%	82%	85%	88%

Assume Walt Disney uses a balanced scorecard and sets a target of 85% occupancy in its resorts. Using Exhibit 9.22 as a guide, show how the company's performance on hotel occupancy would appear on a balanced scorecard report.

QS 9-15

Manufacturing cycle time and efficiency

A4

Compute and interpret (*a*) manufacturing cycle time and (*b*) manufacturing cycle efficiency using the following information from a manufacturing company.

Process time	15 minutes
Inspection time	2 minutes
Move time	6.4 minutes
Wait time	36.6 minutes

QS 9-16[A]

Determining transfer prices without excess capacity   C2

The windshield division of Fast Car Co. makes windshields for use in Fast Car's assembly division. The windshield division incurs variable costs of $200 per windshield and has capacity to make 500,000 windshields per year. The market price is $450 per windshield. The windshield division incurs total fixed costs of $3,000,000 per year. If the windshield division is operating at full capacity, what transfer price should be used on transfers between the windshield and assembly divisions? Explain.

The windshield division of Fast Car Co. makes windshields for use in Fast Car's assembly division. The windshield division incurs variable costs of $200 per windshield and has capacity to make 500,000 windshields per year. The market price is $450 per windshield. The windshield division incurs total fixed costs of $3,000,000 per year. If the windshield division has excess capacity, what is the range of possible transfer prices that could be used on transfers between the windshield and assembly divisions? Explain.

QS 9-17^A
Determining transfer prices with excess capacity   C2

A company purchases a 10,020 square-foot commercial building for $325,000 and spends an additional $50,000 to divide the space into two separate rental units and prepare it for rent. Unit A, which has the desirable location on the corner and contains 3,340 square feet, will be rented for $1.00 per square foot. Unit B contains 6,680 square feet and will be rented for $0.75 per square foot. How much of the joint cost should be assigned to Unit B using the value basis of allocation?

QS 9-18^B
Joint cost allocation
C3

For a recent year **L'Oréal** reported operating profit of €3,385 (in millions) for its cosmetics division. Total assets were €12,888 (in millions) at the beginning of the year and €13,099 (in millions) at the end of the year. Compute return on investment for the year. State your answer as a percent, rounded to one decimal.

QS 9-19
Return on investment

A1

connect

Marvin Dinardo manages an auto dealership's service department. Costs and expenses for a recent quarter for his department follows. List the controllable costs that would appear on a responsibility accounting report for the service department.

EXERCISES

Exercise 9-1
Responsibility accounting report

P1

Costs and expenses	
Cost of parts sold	$30,000
Building depreciation (allocated)	9,300
Manager's salary	12,000
Supplies	15,900
Utilities (allocated)...................	4,400
Wages	16,000

Marathon Running Shop has two service departments (advertising and administrative) and two operating departments (shoes and clothing). During 2015, the departments had the following direct expenses and occupied the following amount of floor space.

Exercise 9-2
Departmental expense allocation-spreadsheet

P2

Department	Direct Expenses	Square Feet
Advertising	$ 18,000	1,120
Administrative	25,000	1,400
Shoes	103,000	7,140
Clothing	15,000	4,340

The advertising department developed and distributed 120 advertisements during the year. Of these, 90 promoted shoes and 30 promoted clothing. The store sold $350,000 of merchandise during the year. Of this amount, $273,000 is from the shoes department, and $77,000 is from the clothing department. The utilities expense of $64,000 is an indirect expense to all departments. Prepare a departmental expense allocation spreadsheet for Marathon Running Shop. The spreadsheet should assign (1) direct expenses to each of the four departments, (2) the $64,000 of utilities expense to the four departments on the basis of floor space occupied, (3) the advertising department's expenses to the two operating departments on the basis of the number of ads placed that promoted a department's products, and (4) the administrative department's expenses to the two operating departments based on the amount of sales. Provide supporting computations for the expense allocations.

Check   Total expenses allocated to shoes dept., $177,472

The following is a partially completed lower section of a departmental expense allocation spreadsheet for Cozy Bookstore. It reports the total amounts of direct and indirect expenses allocated to its five departments. Complete the spreadsheet by allocating the expenses of the two service departments (advertising and purchasing) to the three operating departments.

Exercise 9-3
Service department expenses allocated to operating departments   P2

	A	B	C	D	E	F	G
1				**Allocation of Expenses to Departments**			
2 3 4	**Allocation Base**	**Expense Account Balance**	**Advertising Dept.**	**Purchasing Dept.**	**Books Dept.**	**Magazines Dept.**	**Newspapers Dept.**
5	Total department expenses..........	$698,000	$24,000	$34,000	$425,000	$90,000	$125,000
6	**Service department expenses**						
7	Advertising department............. Sales		?		?	?	?
8	Purchasing department............ Purch. orders			?	?	?	?
9	Total expenses allocated to						
10	operating departments.............	?	$ 0	$ 0	?	?	?

Advertising and purchasing department expenses are allocated to operating departments on the basis of dollar sales and purchase orders, respectively. Information about the allocation bases for the three operating departments follows.

Department	Sales	Purchase Orders
Books	$495,000	516
Magazines	198,000	360
Newspapers	207,000	324
Total	$900,000	1,200

Check Total expenses allocated to books dept., $452,820

Exercise 9-4
Indirect payroll expense allocated to departments

P2

Jessica Porter works in both the jewelry department and the hosiery department of a retail store. Porter assists customers in both departments and arranges and stocks merchandise in both departments. The store allocates Porter's $30,000 annual wages between the two departments based on a sample of the time worked in the two departments. The sample is obtained from a diary of hours worked that Porter kept in a randomly chosen two-week period. The diary showed the following hours and activities spent in the two departments. Allocate Porter's annual wages between the two departments.

Selling in jewelry department	51 hours
Arranging and stocking merchandise in jewelry department	6 hours
Selling in hosiery department	12 hours
Arranging and stocking merchandise in hosiery department	7 hours
Idle time spent waiting for a customer to enter one of the selling departments	4 hours

Check Assign $7,500 to hosiery

Exercise 9-5
Departmental expense allocations

P2

Woh Che Co. has four departments: materials, personnel, manufacturing, and packaging. In a recent month, the four departments incurred three shared indirect expenses. The amounts of these indirect expenses and the bases used to allocate them follow.

Indirect Expense	Cost	Allocation Base
Supervision	$ 82,500	Number of employees
Utilities	50,000	Square feet occupied
Insurance	22,500	Value of assets in use
Total	$155,000	

Departmental data for the company's recent reporting period follow.

Department	Employees	Square Feet	Asset Values
Materials	27	25,000	$ 6,000
Personnel	9	5,000	1,200
Manufacturing	63	55,000	37,800
Packaging	51	15,000	15,000
Total	150	100,000	$60,000

1. Use this information to allocate each of the three indirect expenses across the four departments.
2. Prepare a summary table that reports the indirect expenses assigned to each of the four departments.

Check   (2) Total of $29,600 assigned to materials dept.

Below are departmental income statements for a guitar manufacturer. The manufacturer is considering dropping its electric guitar department since it has a net loss. The company classifies advertising, rent, and utilities expenses as indirect.

Exercise 9-6
Departmental contribution report
P3

WHOLESALE GUITARS Departmental Income Statements For Year Ended December 31, 2015		
	Acoustic	**Electric**
Sales	$112,500	$105,500
Cost of goods sold	55,675	66,750
Gross profit	56,825	38,750
Operating expenses		
Advertising expense	8,075	6,250
Depreciation expense—equipment	10,150	9,000
Salaries expense	17,300	13,500
Supplies expense	2,030	1,700
Rent expense	6,105	5,950
Utilities expense............	3,045	2,550
Total operating expenses	46,705	38,950
Net income (loss)	$ 10,120	($200)

1. Prepare a departmental contribution report that shows each department's contribution to overhead.
2. Based on contribution to overhead, should the electric guitar department be eliminated?

Jansen Company reports the following for its ski department for the year 2015. All of its costs are direct, except as noted.

Exercise 9-7
Departmental income statement and contribution to overhead
P3

Sales	$605,000
Cost of goods sold..........	425,000
Salaries	112,000 ($15,000 is indirect)
Utilities...................	14,000 ($3,000 is indirect)
Depreciation	42,000 ($10,000 is indirect)
Office expenses	20,000 (all indirect)

Prepare a (1) departmental income statement for 2015 and (2) departmental contribution to overhead report for 2015. (3) Based on these two performance reports, should Jansen eliminate the ski department?

You must prepare a return on investment analysis for the regional manager of Fast & Great Burgers. This growing chain is trying to decide which outlet of two alternatives to open. The first location (A) requires a $1,000,000 average investment and is expected to yield annual net income of $160,000. The second location (B) requires a $600,000 average investment and is expected to yield annual net income of $108,000. Compute the return on investment for each Fast & Great Burgers alternative and then make your recommendation in a half-page memorandum to the regional manager. (The chain currently generates an 18% return on total assets.)

Exercise 9-8
Investment center analysis   A1

Megamart, a retailer of consumer goods, provides the following information on two of its departments (each considered an investment center).

Exercise 9-9
Computing return on investment and residual income; investing decision
A1

Investment Center	Sales	Income	Average Invested Assets
Electronics	$40,000,000	$2,880,000	$16,000,000
Sporting goods..............	20,000,000	2,040,000	12,000,000

1. Compute return on investment for each department. Using return on investment, which department is most efficient at using assets to generate returns for the company?
2. Assume a target income level of 12% of average invested assets. Compute residual income for each department. Which department generated the most residual income for the company?
3. Assume the electronics department is presented with a new investment opportunity that will yield a 15% return on investment. Should the new investment opportunity be accepted? Explain.

Exercise 9-10
Computing margin and turnover; department efficiency   A2

Refer to information in Exercise 9-9. Compute profit margin and investment turnover for each department. Which department generates the most net income per dollar of sales? Which department is most efficient at generating sales from average invested assets?

Exercise 9-11
Return on investment
A1   A2

Kraft Foods Group reports the following for two of its divisions for a recent year. All numbers are in millions of dollars.

($ millions)	Beverage Division	Cheese Division
Invested assets, beginning	$2,662	$4,455
Invested assets, ending............	2,593	4,400
Sales	2,681	3,925
Operating income	349	634

For each division, compute (1) return on investment, (2) profit margin, and (3) investment turnover for the year. Round answers to two decimal places.

Exercise 9-12
Residual income   A1

Refer to the information in Exercise 9-11. Assume that each of the company's divisions has a required rate of return of 7%. Compute residual income for each division.

Exercise 9-13
Profit margin   A2

Apple Inc. reports the following for three of its geographic segments for a recent year. All numbers are in millions of dollars.

($ millions)	Americas	Europe	China
Operating income	$22,817	$13,025	$ 8,541
Sales	62,739	37,883	25,417

Compute profit margin for each division. Express answers as percentages, rounded to one decimal place.

Exercise 9-14
Return on investment
A1   A2

ZNet Co. is a web-based retail company. The company reports the following for 2015.

Sales	$ 5,000,000
Operating income	1,000,000
Average invested assets	12,500,000

The company's CEO believes that sales for 2016 will increase by 20%, and both profit margin (%) and the level of average invested assets will be the same as for 2015.

1. Compute return on investment for 2015.
2. Compute profit margin for 2015.
3. If the CEO's forecast is correct, what will return on investment equal for 2016?
4. If the CEO's forecast is correct, what will investment turnover equal for 2016?

USA Airlines uses the following performance measures. Classify each of the performance measures below into the most likely balanced scorecard perspective it relates to. Label your answers using *C* (customer), *P* (internal process), *I* (innovation and growth), or *F* (financial).

———— **1.** Cash flow from operations
———— **2.** Number of reports of mishandled or lost baggage
———— **3.** Percentage of on-time departures
———— **4.** On-time flight percentage
———— **5.** Percentage of ground crew trained
———— **6.** Return on investment
———— **7.** Market value
———— **8.** Accidents or safety incidents per mile flown
———— **9.** Customer complaints
———— **10.** Flight attendant training sessions attended
———— **11.** Time airplane is on ground between flights
———— **12.** Airplane miles per gallon of fuel
———— **13.** Revenue per seat
———— **14.** Cost of leasing airplanes

Exercise 9-15
Performance measures—
balanced scorecard
A3

Oakwood Company produces maple bookcases to customer order. It received an order from a customer to produce 5,000 bookcases. The following information is available for the production of the bookcases.

Process time..........	6.0 days	Move time	3.2 days
Inspection time	0.8 days	Wait time	5.0 days

1. Compute the company's manufacturing cycle time.
2. Compute the company's manufacturing cycle efficiency. Interpret your answer.
3. Oakwood believes it can reduce move time by 1.2 days and wait time by 2.8 days by adopting lean manufacturing techniques. Compute the company's manufacturing cycle efficiency assuming the company's predictions are correct.

Exercise 9-16
Manufacturing cycle time
and efficiency
A4

Check (2) Manufacturing cycle efficiency, 0.40

Best Ink produces ink-jet printers for personal computers. It received an order for 500 printers from a customer. The following information is available for this order.

Process time..........	16.0 hours	Move time	9.0 hours
Inspection time	3.5 hours	Wait time	21.5 hours

1. Compute the company's manufacturing cycle time.
2. Compute the company's manufacturing cycle efficiency. Interpret your answer.
3. Assume that Best Ink wishes to increase its manufacturing cycle efficiency to 0.80. What are some ways that it can accomplish this?

Exercise 9-17
Manufacturing cycle time
and efficiency
A4

The trailer division of Baxter Bicycles makes bike trailers that attach to bicycles and can carry children or cargo. The trailers have a retail price of $200 each. Each trailer incurs $80 of variable manufacturing costs. The trailer division has capacity for 40,000 trailers per year and incurs fixed costs of $1,000,000 per year.

1. Assume the assembly division of Baxter Bicycles wants to buy 15,000 trailers per year from the trailer division. If the trailer division can sell all of the trailers it manufactures to outside customers, what price should be used on transfers between Baxter Bicycles' divisions? Explain.
2. Assume the trailer division currently only sells 20,000 trailers to outside customers, and the assembly division wants to buy 15,000 trailers per year from the trailer division. What is the range of acceptable prices that could be used on transfers between Baxter Bicycles' divisions? Explain.
3. Assume transfer prices of either $80 per trailer or $140 per trailer are being considered. Comment on the preferred transfer prices from the perspectives of the trailer division manager, the assembly division manager, and the top management of Baxter Bicycles.

Exercise 9-18ᴬ
Determining transfer
prices
C2

Exercise 9-19B
Joint real estate costs assigned **C3**

Check Total Hilltop cost, $3,000,000

Heart & Home Properties is developing a subdivision that includes 600 home lots. The 450 lots in the Canyon section are below a ridge and do not have views of the neighboring canyons and hills; the 150 lots in the Hilltop section offer unobstructed views. The expected selling price for each Canyon lot is $55,000 and for each Hilltop lot is $110,000. The developer acquired the land for $4,000,000 and spent another $3,500,000 on street and utilities improvements. Assign the joint land and improvement costs to the lots using the value basis of allocation and determine the average cost per lot.

Exercise 9-20B
Joint product costs assigned

C3

Check (2) Inventory cost, $2,268

Pirate Seafood Company purchases lobsters and processes them into tails and flakes. It sells the lobster tails for $21 per pound and the flakes for $14 per pound. On average, 100 pounds of lobster are processed into 52 pounds of tails and 22 pounds of flakes, with 26 pounds of waste. Assume that the company purchased 2,400 pounds of lobster for $4.50 per pound and processed the lobsters with an additional labor cost of $1,800. No materials or labor costs are assigned to the waste. If 1,096 pounds of tails and 324 pounds of flakes are sold, what is (1) the allocated cost of the sold items and (2) the allocated cost of the ending inventory? The company allocates joint costs on a value basis. (Round the dollar cost per pound to the nearest thousandth.)

Exercise 9-21
Profit margin and investment turnover

A2

L'Oréal reports the following for a recent year for the major divisions in its cosmetics branch.

(€ millions)	Sales	Income	Total Assets End of Year	Total Assets Beginning of Year
Professional products	€ 2,717	€ 552	€ 2,624	€ 2,516
Consumer products	9,530	1,765	5,994	5,496
Luxury products	4,507	791	3,651	4,059
Active cosmetics	1,386	278	830	817
Total	€18,140	€3,386	€13,099	€12,888

1. Compute profit margin for each division. State your answers as percents, rounded to two decimal places. Which L'Oréal division has the highest profit margin?
2. Compute investment turnover for each division. Round your answers to two decimal places. Which L'Oréal division has the best investment turnover?

connect

PROBLEM SET A

Problem 9-1A
Responsibility accounting performance reports; controllable and budgeted costs

P1

Billie Whitehorse, the plant manager of Travel Free's Indiana plant, is responsible for all of that plant's costs other than her own salary. The plant has two operating departments and one service department. The camper and trailer operating departments manufacture different products and have their own managers. The office department, which Whitehorse also manages, provides services equally to the two operating departments. A budget is prepared for each operating department and the office department. The company's responsibility accounting system must assemble information to present budgeted and actual costs in performance reports for each operating department manager and the plant manager. Each performance report includes only those costs that a particular operating department manager can control: raw materials, wages, supplies used, and equipment depreciation. The plant manager is responsible for the department managers' salaries, utilities, building rent, office salaries other than her own, and other office costs plus all costs controlled by the two operating department managers. The annual departmental budgets and actual costs for the two operating departments follow.

	Budget			Actual		
	Campers	Trailers	Combined	Campers	Trailers	Combined
Raw materials	$195,000	$275,000	$ 470,000	$194,200	$273,200	$ 467,400
Employee wages	104,000	205,000	309,000	106,600	206,400	313,000
Dept. manager salary	43,000	52,000	95,000	44,000	53,500	97,500
Supplies used	33,000	90,000	123,000	31,700	91,600	123,300
Depreciation—Equip.	60,000	125,000	185,000	60,000	125,000	185,000
Utilities.................	3,600	5,400	9,000	3,300	5,000	8,300
Building rent	5,700	9,300	15,000	5,300	8,700	14,000
Office department costs	68,750	68,750	137,500	67,550	67,550	135,100
Totals	$513,050	$830,450	$1,343,500	$512,650	$830,950	$1,343,600

The office department's annual budget and its actual costs follow.

	Budget	Actual
Plant manager salary	$ 80,000	$ 82,000
Other office salaries	32,500	30,100
Other office costs	25,000	23,000
Totals	$137,500	$135,100

Required

1. Prepare responsibility accounting performance reports like those in Exhibit 9.2 that list costs controlled by the following:

   a. Manager of the camper department.

   b. Manager of the trailer department.

   c. Manager of the Indiana plant.

In each report, include the budgeted and actual costs and show the amount that each actual cost is over or under the budgeted amount.

Check (1*a*) $500 total over budget

(1*c*) Indiana plant controllable costs, $1,900 total under budget

Analysis Component

2. Did the plant manager or the operating department managers better manage costs? Explain.

National Bank has several departments that occupy both floors of a two-story building. The departmental accounting system has a single account, Building Occupancy Cost, in its ledger. The types and amounts of occupancy costs recorded in this account for the current period follow.

Problem 9-2A
Allocation of building occupancy costs to departments

P2

Depreciation—Building	$18,000
Interest—Building mortgage	27,000
Taxes—Building and land	9,000
Gas (heating) expense.............	3,000
Lighting expense	3,000
Maintenance expense	6,000
Total occupancy cost	$66,000

The building has 4,000 square feet on each floor. In prior periods, the accounting manager merely divided the $66,000 occupancy cost by 8,000 square feet to find an average cost of $8.25 per square foot and then charged each department a building occupancy cost equal to this rate times the number of square feet that it occupied.

Diane Linder manages a first-floor department that occupies 1,000 square feet, and Juan Chiro manages a second-floor department that occupies 1,800 square feet of floor space. In discussing the departmental reports, the second-floor manager questions whether using the same rate per square foot for all departments makes sense because the first-floor space is more valuable. This manager also references a recent real estate study of average local rental costs for similar space that shows first-floor space worth $30 per square foot and second-floor space worth $20 per square foot (excluding costs for heating, lighting, and maintenance).

Required

1. Allocate occupancy costs to the Linder and Chiro departments using the current allocation method.

2. Allocate the depreciation, interest, and taxes occupancy costs to the Linder and Chiro departments in proportion to the relative market values of the floor space. Allocate the heating, lighting, and maintenance costs to the Linder and Chiro departments in proportion to the square feet occupied (ignoring floor space market values).

Check (1) Total allocated to Linder and Chiro, $23,100; (2) total occupancy cost to Linder, $9,600

Analysis Component

3. Which allocation method would you prefer if you were a manager of a second-floor department? Explain.

Problem 9-3A
Departmental income statements; forecasts

P3

Williams Company began operations in January 2015 with two operating (selling) departments and one service (office) department. Its departmental income statements follow.

WILLIAMS COMPANY Departmental Income Statements For Year Ended December 31, 2015			
	Clock	**Mirror**	**Combined**
Sales	$130,000	$55,000	$185,000
Cost of goods sold	63,700	34,100	97,800
Gross profit	66,300	20,900	87,200
Direct expenses			
Sales salaries	20,000	7,000	27,000
Advertising	1,200	500	1,700
Store supplies used	900	400	1,300
Depreciation—Equipment	1,500	300	1,800
Total direct expenses.................	23,600	8,200	31,800
Allocated expenses			
Rent expense	7,020	3,780	10,800
Utilities expense	2,600	1,400	4,000
Share of office department expenses	10,500	4,500	15,000
Total allocated expenses	20,120	9,680	29,800
Total expenses..........................	43,720	17,880	61,600
Net income	$ 22,580	$ 3,020	$ 25,600

Williams plans to open a third department in January 2016 that will sell paintings. Management predicts that the new department will generate $50,000 in sales with a 55% gross profit margin and will require the following direct expenses: sales salaries, $8,000; advertising, $800; store supplies, $500; and equipment depreciation, $200. It will fit the new department into the current rented space by taking some square footage from the other two departments. When opened the new painting department will fill one-fifth of the space presently used by the clock department and one-fourth used by the mirror department. Management does not predict any increase in utilities costs, which are allocated to the departments in proportion to occupied space (or rent expense). The company allocates office department expenses to the operating departments in proportion to their sales. It expects the painting department to increase total office department expenses by $7,000. Since the painting department will bring new customers into the store, management expects sales in both the clock and mirror departments to increase by 8%. No changes for those departments' gross profit percents or their direct expenses are expected except for store supplies used, which will increase in proportion to sales.

Required

Check   2016 forecasted combined net income (sales), $43,472 ($249,800)

Prepare departmental income statements that show the company's predicted results of operations for calendar year 2016 for the three operating (selling) departments and their combined totals. (Round percents to the nearest one-tenth and dollar amounts to the nearest whole dollar.)

Problem 9-4A
Departmental contribution to income

P3

Vortex Company operates a retail store with two departments. Information about those departments follows.

	Department A	**Department B**
Sales	$800,000	$450,000
Cost of goods sold	497,000	291,000
Direct expenses		
Salaries	125,000	88,000
Insurance	20,000	10,000
Utilities................	24,000	14,000
Depreciation	21,000	12,000
Maintenance............	7,000	5,000

The company also incurred the following indirect costs.

Salaries	$36,000
Insurance	6,000
Depreciation	15,000
Office expenses	50,000

Indirect costs are allocated as follows: salaries on the basis of sales; insurance and depreciation on the basis of square footage; and office expenses on the basis of number of employees. Additional information about the departments follows.

Department	Square footage	Number of employees
A	28,000	75
B	12,000	50

Required

1. For each department, determine the departmental contribution to overhead and the departmental net income.
2. Should Department B be eliminated? Explain.

Check   (1) Dept. A net income, $38,260

Georgia Orchards produced a good crop of peaches this year. After preparing the following income statement, the company believes it should have given its No. 3 peaches to charity and saved its efforts.

Problem 9-5A[B]
Allocation of joint costs

C3

GEORGIA ORCHARDS				
Income Statement				
For Year Ended December 31, 2015				
	No. 1	No. 2	No. 3	Combined
Sales (by grade)				
No. 1: 300,000 lbs. @ $1.50/lb	$450,000			
No. 2: 300,000 lbs. @ $1.00/lb		$300,000		
No. 3: 750,000 lbs. @ $0.25/lb			$ 187,500	
Total sales				$937,500
Costs				
Tree pruning and care @ $0.30/lb	90,000	90,000	225,000	405,000
Picking, sorting, and grading @ $0.15/lb	45,000	45,000	112,500	202,500
Delivery costs	15,000	15,000	37,500	67,500
Total costs	150,000	150,000	375,000	675,000
Net income (loss)	$300,000	$150,000	$(187,500)	$262,500

In preparing this statement, the company allocated joint costs among the grades on a physical basis as an equal amount per pound. The company's delivery cost records show that $30,000 of the $67,500 relates to crating the No. 1 and No. 2 peaches and hauling them to the buyer. The remaining $37,500 of delivery costs is for crating the No. 3 peaches and hauling them to the cannery.

Required

1. Prepare reports showing cost allocations on a sales value basis to the three grades of peaches. Separate the delivery costs into the amounts directly identifiable with each grade. Then allocate any shared delivery costs on the basis of the relative sales value of each grade.
2. Using your answers to part 1, prepare an income statement using the joint costs allocated on a sales value basis.

Check   (1) $129,600 tree pruning and care costs allocated to No. 2

(2) Net income from No. 1 & No. 2 peaches, $140,400 & $93,600

Analysis Component

3. Do you think delivery costs fit the definition of a joint cost? Explain.

PROBLEM SET B

Problem 9-1B
Responsibility accounting
performance reports;
controllable and
budgeted costs

P1

Britney Brown, the plant manager of LMN Co.'s Chicago plant, is responsible for all of that plant's costs other than her own salary. The plant has two operating departments and one service department. The refrigerator and dishwasher operating departments manufacture different products and have their own managers. The office department, which Brown also manages, provides services equally to the two operating departments. A monthly budget is prepared for each operating department and the office department. The company's responsibility accounting system must assemble information to present budgeted and actual costs in performance reports for each operating department manager and the plant manager. Each performance report includes only those costs that a particular operating department manager can control: raw materials, wages, supplies used, and equipment depreciation. The plant manager is responsible for the department managers' salaries, utilities, building rent, office salaries other than her own, and other office costs plus all costs controlled by the two operating department managers. The April departmental budgets and actual costs for the two operating departments follow.

	Budget			Actual		
	Refrigerators	**Dishwashers**	**Combined**	**Refrigerators**	**Dishwashers**	**Combined**
Raw materials	$400,000	$200,000	$ 600,000	$385,000	$202,000	$ 587,000
Employee wages	170,000	80,000	250,000	174,700	81,500	256,200
Dept. manager salary	55,000	49,000	104,000	55,000	46,500	101,500
Supplies used	15,000	9,000	24,000	14,000	9,700	23,700
Depreciation—Equip.	53,000	37,000	90,000	53,000	37,000	90,000
Utilities	30,000	18,000	48,000	34,500	20,700	55,200
Building rent	63,000	17,000	80,000	65,800	16,500	82,300
Office department costs . . .	70,500	70,500	141,000	75,000	75,000	150,000
Totals	$856,500	$480,500	$1,337,000	$857,000	$488,900	$1,345,900

The office department's budget and its actual costs for April follow.

	Budget	Actual
Plant manager salary	$ 80,000	$ 85,000
Other office salaries	40,000	35,200
Other office costs	21,000	29,800
Totals	$141,000	$150,000

Required

Check   (1a) $11,300 total
under budget

       (1c) Chicago plant
controllable costs, $3,900
total over budget

1. Prepare responsibility accounting performance reports like those in Exhibit 9.2 that list costs controlled by the following:

   a. Manager of the refrigerator department.

   b. Manager of the dishwasher department.

   c. Manager of the Chicago plant.

   In each report, include the budgeted and actual costs for the month and show the amount by which each actual cost is over or under the budgeted amount.

Analysis Component

2. Did the plant manager or the operating department managers better manage costs? Explain.

Problem 9-2B
Allocation of building
occupancy costs to
departments

P2

Harmon's has several departments that occupy all floors of a two-story building that includes a basement floor. Harmon rented this building under a long-term lease negotiated when rental rates were low. The departmental accounting system has a single account, Building Occupancy Cost, in its ledger. The types and amounts of occupancy costs recorded in this account for the current period follow.

Building rent	$400,000
Lighting expense	25,000
Cleaning expense	40,000
Total occupancy cost	$465,000

The building has 7,500 square feet on each of the upper two floors but only 5,000 square feet in the basement. In prior periods, the accounting manager merely divided the $465,000 occupancy cost by 20,000 square feet to find an average cost of $23.25 per square foot and then charged each department a building occupancy cost equal to this rate times the number of square feet that it occupies.

Jordan Style manages a department that occupies 2,000 square feet of basement floor space. In discussing the departmental reports with other managers, she questions whether using the same rate per square foot for all departments makes sense because different floor space has different values. Style checked a recent real estate report of average local rental costs for similar space that shows first-floor space worth $40 per square foot, second-floor space worth $20 per square foot, and basement space worth $10 per square foot (excluding costs for lighting and cleaning).

Required

1. Allocate occupancy costs to Style's department using the current allocation method.

2. Allocate the building rent cost to Style's department in proportion to the relative market value of the floor space. Allocate to Style's department the lighting and cleaning costs in proportion to the square feet occupied (ignoring floor space market values). Then, compute the total occupancy cost allocated to Style's department.

Check Total costs allocated to Style's dept., (1) $46,500; (2) Total occupancy cost to Style $22,500

Analysis Component

3. Which allocation method would you prefer if you were a manager of a basement department?

Bonanza Entertainment began operations in January 2015 with two operating (selling) departments and one service (office) department. Its departmental income statements follow.

Problem 9-3B
Departmental income statements; forecasts

P3

BONANZA ENTERTAINMENT Departmental Income Statements For Year Ended December 31, 2015			
	Movies	**Video Games**	**Combined**
Sales	$600,000	$200,000	$800,000
Cost of goods sold	420,000	154,000	574,000
Gross profit	180,000	46,000	226,000
Direct expenses			
Sales salaries	37,000	15,000	52,000
Advertising	12,500	6,000	18,500
Store supplies used	4,000	1,000	5,000
Depreciation—Equipment	4,500	3,000	7,500
Total direct expenses.	58,000	25,000	83,000
Allocated expenses			
Rent expense	41,000	9,000	50,000
Utilities expense	7,380	1,620	9,000
Share of office department expenses	56,250	18,750	75,000
Total allocated expenses	104,630	29,370	134,000
Total expenses	162,630	54,370	217,000
Net income (loss)	$ 17,370	$ (8,370)	$ 9,000

The company plans to open a third department in January 2016 that will sell compact discs. Management predicts that the new department will generate $300,000 in sales with a 35% gross profit margin and will require the following direct expenses: sales salaries, $18,000; advertising, $10,000; store supplies, $2,000; and equipment depreciation, $1,200. The company will fit the new department into the current rented space by taking some square footage from the other two departments. When opened, the new compact disc department will fill one-fourth of the space presently used by the movie department and one-third of the space used by the video game department. Management does not predict any increase in utilities costs, which are allocated to the departments in proportion to occupied space (or rent expense). The company allocates office department expenses to the operating departments in proportion to their sales. It expects the compact disc department to increase total office department expenses by $10,000. Since the compact disc department will bring new customers into the store, management expects sales in both the movie and video game departments to increase by 8%. No changes for those departments' gross profit percents or for their direct expenses are expected, except for store supplies used, which will increase in proportion to sales.

Required

Prepare departmental income statements that show the company's predicted results of operations for calendar year 2016 for the three operating (selling) departments and their combined totals. (Round percents to the nearest one-tenth and dollar amounts to the nearest whole dollar.)

Problem 9-4B
Departmental
contribution to income

P3

Sadar Company operates a store with two departments: videos and music. Information about those departments follows.

	Videos Department	Music Department
Sales	$370,500	$279,500
Cost of goods sold	320,000	175,000
Direct expenses		
Salaries	35,000	25,000
Maintenance	12,000	10,000
Utilities	5,000	4,500
Insurance	4,200	3,700

The company also incurred the following indirect costs.

Advertising	$15,000
Salaries	27,000
Office expenses	3,200

Indirect costs are allocated as follows: advertising on the basis of sales; salaries on the basis of number of employees; and office expenses on the basis of square footage. Additional information about the departments follows.

Department	Square footage	Number of employees
Videos	5,000	3
Music	3,000	2

Required

1. For each department, determine the departmental contribution to overhead and the departmental net income.

2. Should the video department be eliminated? Explain.

Problem 9-5B[B]
Allocation of joint costs

C3

Rita and Rick Redding own and operate a tomato grove. After preparing the following income statement, Rita believes they should have offered the No. 3 tomatoes to the public for free and saved themselves time and money.

RITA AND RICK REDDING Income Statement For Year Ended December 31, 2015				
	No. 1	No. 2	No. 3	Combined
Sales (by grade)				
No. 1: 500,000 lbs. @ $1.80/lb	$900,000			
No. 2: 400,000 lbs. @ $1.25/lb		$500,000		
No. 3: 100,000 lbs. @ $0.40/lb			$ 40,000	
Total sales.				$1,440,000
Costs				
Land preparation, seeding, and cultivating @ $0.70/lb	350,000	280,000	70,000	700,000
Harvesting, sorting, and grading @ $0.04/lb..................	20,000	16,000	4,000	40,000
Delivery costs	10,000	7,000	3,000	20,000
Total costs	380,000	303,000	77,000	760,000
Net income (loss)	$520,000	$197,000	$(37,000)	$ 680,000

In preparing this statement, Rita and Rick allocated joint costs among the grades on a physical basis as an equal amount per pound. Also, their delivery cost records show that $17,000 of the $20,000 relates to crating the No. 1 and No. 2 tomatoes and hauling them to the buyer. The remaining $3,000 of delivery costs is for crating the No. 3 tomatoes and hauling them to the cannery.

Required

1. Prepare reports showing cost allocations on a sales value basis to the three grades of tomatoes. Separate the delivery costs into the amounts directly identifiable with each grade. Then allocate any shared delivery costs on the basis of the relative sales value of each grade. (Round percents to the nearest one-tenth and dollar amounts to the nearest whole dollar.)

2. Using your answers to part 1, prepare an income statement using the joint costs allocated on a sales value basis.

Analysis Component

3. Do you think delivery costs fit the definition of a joint cost? Explain.

Check (1) $1,120 harvesting, sorting and grading costs allocated to No. 3

(2) Net income from No. 1 & No. 2 tomatoes, $426,569 & $237,151

(This serial problem began in Chapter 1 and continues through most of the book. If previous chapter segments were not completed, the serial problem can begin at this point. It is helpful, but not necessary, to use the Working Papers that accompany the book.)

SP 9   Santana Rey's two departments, computer consulting services and computer workstation furniture manufacturing, have each been profitable. Santana has heard of the balanced scorecard and wants you to provide details on how it could be used to measure performance of her departments.

SERIAL PROBLEM
Business Solutions
A3

Required

1. Explain the four performance perspectives included in a balanced scorecard.
2. For each of the four performance perspectives included in a balanced scorecard, provide examples of measures Santana could use to measure performance of her departments.

Beyond the Numbers

BTN 9-1   Review Apple's income statement in Appendix A and identify its revenues for the years ended September 28, 2013, September 29, 2012, and September 24, 2011. For the year ended September 28, 2013, Apple reports the following product revenue mix. (Assume that its product revenue mix is the same for each of the three years reported when answering the requirements.)

REPORTING IN ACTION
C1

APPLE

iPhone	iPad and iPod	Mac	iTunes, Software and Services, and Accessories
53%	21%	13%	13%

Required

1. Compute the amount of revenue from each of its product lines for the years ended September 28, 2013, September 29, 2012, and September 24, 2011.
2. If Apple wishes to evaluate each of its product lines, how can it allocate its operating expenses to each of them to determine each product line's profitability?

Fast Forward

3. Access Apple's annual report for a fiscal year ending after September 28, 2013, from its website (Apple.com) or the SEC's EDGAR database (www.SEC.gov). Locate its table of "Net Sales by Product" in the footnotes. How has its product mix changed from 2013?

BTN 9-2   Apple and Google compete in several product categories. Sales, income, and asset information is provided for fiscal year 2013 for each company below.

COMPARATIVE ANALYSIS
A2

APPLE
GOOGLE

(in millions)	Apple	Google
Sales	$170,910	$ 59,825
Net income	37,037	12,920
Invested assets, beginning of year	176,064	93,798
Invested assets, end of year.	207,000	110,920

Required

1. Compute profit margin for each company.

2. Compute investment turnover for each company.

Analysis Component

3. Using your answers to the questions above, compare the companies' performance for the year.

ETHICS CHALLENGE

P3

BTN 9-3   Super Security Co. offers a range of security services for athletes and entertainers. Each type of service is considered within a separate department. Marc Pincus, the overall manager, is compensated partly on the basis of departmental performance by staying within the quarterly cost budget. He often revises operations to make sure departments stay within budget. Says Pincus, "I will not go over budget even if it means slightly compromising the level and quality of service. These are minor compromises that don't significantly affect my clients, at least in the short term."

Required

1. Is there an ethical concern in this situation? If so, which parties are affected? Explain.

2. Can Marc Pincus take action to eliminate or reduce any ethical concerns? Explain.

3. What is Super Security's ethical responsibility in offering professional services?

COMMUNICATING IN PRACTICE

P2

BTN 9-4   Improvement Station is a national home improvement chain with more than 100 stores throughout the country. The manager of each store receives a salary plus a bonus equal to a percent of the store's net income for the reporting period. The following net income calculation is on the Denver store manager's performance report for the recent monthly period.

Sales	$2,500,000
Cost of goods sold	800,000
Wages expense	500,000
Utilities expense	200,000
Home office expense	75,000
Net income	$ 925,000
Manager's bonus (0.5%)	$ 4,625

In previous periods, the bonus had also been 0.5%, but the performance report had not included any charges for the home office expense, which is now assigned to each store as a percent of its sales.

Required

Assume that you are the national office manager. Write a half-page memorandum to your store managers explaining why home office expense is in the new performance report.

TAKING IT TO THE NET

P2

BTN 9-5   This chapter described and used spreadsheets to prepare various managerial reports (see Exhibit 9-6). You can download from websites various tutorials showing how spreadsheets are used in managerial accounting and other business applications.

Required

1. Link to the website Lacher.com. Select "Table of Contents" under "Microsoft Excel Examples." Identify and list three tutorials for review.

2. Describe in a half-page memorandum to your instructor how the applications described in each tutorial are helpful in business and managerial decision making.

TEAMWORK IN ACTION

P1

APPLE

Samsung

BTN 9-6   Apple and Samsung compete across the world in several markets.

Required

1. Design a three-tier responsibility accounting organizational chart assuming that you have available internal information for both companies. Use Exhibit 9.1 as an example. The goal of this assignment is to design a reporting framework for the companies; numbers are not required. Limit your reporting framework to sales activity only.

2. Explain why it is important to have similar performance reports when comparing performance within a company (and across different companies). Be specific in your response.

BTN 9-7   Brian Linton's company, **United By Blue**, sells jewelry and apparel. His company plans for continued expansion into other types of products.

ENTREPRENEURIAL DECISION

P3

Required

1. How can United By Blue use departmental income statements to assist in understanding and controlling operations?
2. Are departmental income statements always the best measure of a department's performance? Explain.
3. Provide examples of nonfinancial performance indicators United By Blue might use as part of a balanced scorecard system of performance evaluation.

BTN 9-8   Visit a local movie theater and check out both its concession area and its showing areas. The manager of a theater must confront questions such as:

HITTING THE ROAD

C1   P1

- How much return do we earn on concessions?
- What types of movies generate the greatest sales?
- What types of movies generate the greatest net income?

Required

Assume that you are the new accounting manager for a 16-screen movie theater. You are to set up a responsibility accounting reporting framework for the theater.

1. Recommend how to segment the different departments of a movie theater for responsibility reporting.
2. Propose an expense allocation system for heat, rent, insurance, and maintenance costs of the theater.

BTN 9-9   Selected product data from **Samsung** (www.samsung.com) follow.

GLOBAL DECISION

P3

Samsung

Product Segment for Year Ended (billions of Korean won)	Net Sales		Operating Income	
	Dec. 31, 2013	Dec. 31, 2012	Dec. 31, 2013	Dec. 31, 2012
Consumer electronics	₩ 50,332	₩ 51,105	₩ 1,673	₩ 2,324
IT and mobile communications	138,817	105,845	24,958	19,418

Required

1. Compute the percentage growth in net sales for each product line from fiscal year 2012 to 2013. Round percents to one decimal.
2. Which product line's net sales grew the fastest?
3. Which segment was the most profitable?
4. How can Samsung's managers use this information?

ANSWERS TO MULTIPLE CHOICE QUIZ

1. b; [$641,250/($356,250 + $641,250 + $427,500)] × $150,000 = $67,500
2. d;
3. c; $500,000/200,000 = 2.5
4. b;

	Department X	Department Y	Department Z
Sales	$500,000	$200,000	$350,000
Cost of goods sold	350,000	75,000	150,000
Gross profit	150,000	125,000	200,000
Direct expenses.	50,000	20,000	75,000
Departmental contribution to overhead . . .	$100,000	$105,000	$125,000

5. a; $100,000/$500,000 = 20%

10

Relevant Costing for Managerial Decisions

Chapter Preview

DECISIONS AND INFORMATION

Decision making

C1 Relevant costs and benefits

P1 Identify relevant costs

DECISION SCENARIOS

A1 Additional business

Make or buy

Scrap or rework

Sell or process further

Sales mix selection

Segment elimination

Keep or replace

A2 Determine selling price

Learning Objectives

CONCEPTUAL

C1 Describe the importance of relevant costs for short-term decisions.

ANALYTICAL

A1 Evaluate short-term managerial decisions using relevant costs.

A2 Determine product selling price based on total costs.

PROCEDURAL

P1 Identify relevant costs and apply them to managerial decisions.

LOS ANGELES—Noticing long lines and an inadequate supply of sweets to satisfy his high school friends' cravings, Charlie Fyffe began making brownies and selling them at school. His brownies were an instant hit, and as his clientele and passion for baking grew, so did his desire to start his own business. "I started **Charlie's Brownies** (**CharliesBrownies.com**) because sweets make people happy and baking is a fun industry," explains Charlie. "I developed a quality original recipe and started selling brownies in simple cake boxes. Staying simple and consistent opened the door to a viable business."

After six months of professional baking classes to sharpen his skills, Charlie turned to the business side. "I had a lot to learn," admits Charlie. "I read entrepreneurial books and did internships to learn how to run a business. Becoming an entrepreneur was hard work, but it allows me a life of freedom outside the cubicle and the opportunity to pursue my dreams and visions." Charlie had to learn how to use accounting information to make important business decisions. For example, attention to contribution margins enables Charlie to decide if adding new product lines, like vegan and gluten-free brownies, would increase profits. Focusing on contribution margins, his own and his competition's, also helps Charlie decide whether to eliminate certain products because they are not profitable.

Charlie applies high standards to his production process. Unlike some companies that can rework substandard materials into a viable product, Charlie explains that "raw materials that don't meet our standards never enter the baking process." Further, although expensive, exotic ingredients like "pink Himalayan salt and organic coconut palm sugar create a pop and that undeniable urge to eat another brownie. You can't help but to want another one!" Charlie has also managed to control overhead costs by doing much of the baking, marketing, and delivery himself. "I do whatever it takes to get the job done" he says. "There is never a dull moment!"

Much of Charlie's Brownies business is done online. To meet Charlie's goal of developing the company into a "nationwide and global Brownie Experience," he must focus on relevant costs to help him make good decisions. Determining the optimal sales mix requires Charlie to understand product contribution margins. Charlie sees farmers' markets and retail distribution as central to his vision and explains that "we need to upgrade our space and add to our capacity." The decision to

Courtesy of Charlie's Brownies

Sweet Success

"Put all of your love into your product"
—**Charlie Fyffe**

keep or replace equipment is common in growing businesses and assessing relevant costs helps Charlie with this and other key managerial decisions.

Charlie advises young entrepreneurs to follow their passion. "Hang out with other overachievers and young entrepreneurs to stay one step ahead," he says. "Stay focused, work hard, and seek guidance from other successful businesspeople." Sounds like a recipe for success.

Sources: *Charlie's Brownies website*, January 2015; *JaredSurnamer.com*, August 2011; *PopularFinesse.tumblr.com*, October 2011; *Twentity.com*, February 2011

This chapter focuses on methods that use accounting information to make several important managerial decisions. Most of these involve short-term decisions. This differs from methods used for longer-term managerial decisions that are described in the first section of this chapter and in several other chapters of this book.

DECISIONS AND INFORMATION

This section explains how managers make decisions and the information relevant to those decisions.

Decision Making

Managerial decision making involves five steps: (1) define the decision task, (2) identify alternative courses of action, (3) collect relevant information and evaluate each alternative, (4) select the preferred course of action, and (5) analyze and assess decisions made. These five steps are illustrated in Exhibit 10.1.

EXHIBIT 10.1

Managerial Decision Making

| Define Task and Goal | Identify Alternative Actions | Collect Relevant Information | Select Course of Action | Analyze and Assess Decision |

Both managerial and financial accounting information play an important role in most management decisions. The accounting system is expected to provide primarily *financial* information such as performance reports and budget analyses for decision making. *Nonfinancial* information is also relevant, however; it includes information on environmental effects, political sensitivities, and social responsibility.

Relevant Costs and Benefits

C1

Describe the importance of relevant costs for short-term decisions.

Most financial measures of revenues and costs from accounting systems are based on historical costs. Although historical costs are important and useful for many tasks such as product pricing and the control and monitoring of business activities, their use can lead to incorrect decisions in some instances. Instead, an analysis of *relevant costs,* or *avoidable costs,* is especially useful in managers' short-term decisions. Three types of costs are pertinent to our discussion of relevant costs: sunk costs, out-of-pocket costs, and opportunity costs.

A *sunk cost* arises from a past decision and cannot be avoided or changed; it is irrelevant to future decisions. An example is the cost of computer equipment previously purchased by a company. This cost is not relevant to the decision of whether to replace the computer equipment. Likewise, depreciation of the original cost of plant (and intangible) assets are sunk costs. Most of a company's allocated costs, including fixed overhead items such as depreciation and administrative expenses, are sunk costs.

An *out-of-pocket cost* requires a future outlay of cash and is relevant for current and future decision making. These costs are usually the direct result of management's decisions. For instance, future purchases of computer equipment involve out-of-pocket costs. The cost of future computer purchases is relevant to the decision of whether to replace the computer equipment.

"Sunk costs are not relevant to my decision."

"I must consider out-of-pocket and opportunity costs."

An *opportunity cost* is the potential benefit lost by taking a specific action when two or more alternative choices are available. An example is a student giving up wages from a job to attend summer school. The forgone wages should be considered as part of the total cost of attending summer school. Companies continually must choose from alternative courses of action. For instance, a company making standardized products might be approached by a customer to supply a special (nonstandard) product. A decision to accept or reject the special order must consider not only the profit to be made from the special order but also the profit given up by devoting time and resources to this order instead of pursuing an alternative project. The profit given up is an opportunity cost. Consideration of opportunity costs is important. Although opportunity costs are not entered in accounting records, they are relevant to many managerial decisions.

In sum, the relevant costs in making decisions are the **incremental costs,** also called *differential costs,* which are the additional costs incurred if a company pursues a certain course of action.

Besides relevant costs, management must also consider the relevant benefits associated with a decision. **Relevant benefits** refer to the additional or *incremental* revenue generated by selecting a particular course of action over another. In making decisions, managers should focus on those for which the relevant benefits exceed the relevant costs. As we will show, however, managers must also consider qualitative factors that are not easily expressed in terms of costs and benefits.

MANAGERIAL DECISION SCENARIOS

Managers experience many different scenarios that require analyzing alternative actions and making a decision. We describe several different types of decision scenarios in this section. We set these tasks in the context of FasTrac, a manufacturer of exercise equipment and supplies. *We treat each of these decision tasks as separate from each other.*

A1_____

Evaluate short-term managerial decisions using relevant costs.

Additional Business

FasTrac is operating at its normal level of 80% of full capacity. At this level, it produces and sells approximately 100,000 units of product annually. Its per unit and annual total sales and costs are shown in the contribution margin income statement in Exhibit 10.2. Its normal selling price is $10.00 per unit, and each unit sold generates $1.00 per unit of operating income.

FASTRAC Contribution Margin Income Statement For Year Ended December 31, 2015		
	Per Unit	**Annual Total**
Sales (100,000 units)..............	$10.00	$1,000,000
Variable costs		
Direct materials	(3.50)	(350,000)
Direct labor	(2.20)	(220,000)
Variable overhead.............	(0.50)	(50,000)
Selling expenses	(1.40)	(140,000)
Contribution margin.............	2.40	240,000
Fixed costs		
Fixed overhead	0.60	60,000
Administrative expenses........	0.80	80,000
Operating income...............	$ 1.00	$ 100,000

EXHIBIT 10.2

Selected Operating Income Data

A current buyer of FasTrac's products wants to purchase additional units of its product and export them to another country. This buyer offers to buy 10,000 units of the product at $8.50 per unit, or $1.50 less than the current price. The offer price is low, but FasTrac is considering the proposal because this sale would be several times larger than any single previous sale and it would use idle capacity. Also, the units will be exported, so this new business will not affect current sales.

To determine whether to accept or reject this order, management needs to know whether accepting the offer will increase net income. The analysis in Exhibit 10.3 shows that if management relies incorrectly on per unit historical costs, it would reject the sale because the selling price ($8.50) per unit is less than the total historical costs per unit ($9.00), and it thus yields a loss.

EXHIBIT 10.3

Analysis of Additional
Business Using Historical
Costs

Additional Business	Per Unit	Total
Sales (10,000 additional units)...............	$ 8.50	$ 85,000
Total costs and expenses (historical)	(9.00)	(90,000)
Operating loss	$(0.50)	$(5,000)

P1_____

Identify relevant costs and
apply them to managerial
decisions.

To correctly make its decision, FasTrac must analyze the costs of this potential new business differently. The $9.00 historical cost per unit is not necessarily the incremental cost of this order. The following information regarding the order is available:

● The variable manufacturing costs to produce this order will be the same as for FasTrac's normal business—$3.50 per unit for direct materials, $2.20 per unit for direct labor, and $0.50 per unit for variable overhead.

● Selling expenses for this order will be $0.20 per unit, which is less than the selling expenses of FasTrac's normal business.

● Fixed overhead expenses will not change regardless of whether this order is accepted.

● This order will incur *incremental* administrative expenses of $1,000 for clerical work. These are additional fixed costs due to this order.

We use this information to determine whether FasTrac should accept this new business. The analysis of relevant benefits and costs in Exhibit 10.4 suggests that the additional business should be accepted. It would yield $20,000 of additional pretax income. More generally, FasTrac would increase its income with any price that exceeded $6.50 per unit ($65,000 incremental cost/10,000 additional units). The key point is that *management must not blindly use historical costs, especially allocated overhead costs.* Instead, management must focus on the incremental costs to be incurred if the additional business is accepted.

EXHIBIT 10.4

Analysis of Additional
Business Using Relevant
Costs

FASTRAC Contribution Margin Income Statement (for special order) For Year Ended December 31, 2015		
	Per Unit	Annual Total
Sales (10,000 units).................	$8.50	$85,000
Variable costs		
Direct materials	(3.50)	(35,000)
Direct labor	(2.20)	(22,000)
Variable overhead................	(0.50)	(5,000)
Selling expenses	(0.20)	(2,000)
Contribution margin................	2.10	21,000
Fixed costs		
Fixed overhead	—	—
Administrative expenses...........	(0.10)	(1,000)
Operating income (incremental)	$2.00	$20,000

Point: The income statement
in Exhibit 10.4 is based on the
incremental revenues and costs
of the special order.

Other Factors An analysis of the incremental costs pertaining to the additional volume is always relevant for this type of decision. We must proceed cautiously, however, when the additional volume approaches or exceeds the factory's existing available capacity. If the additional volume requires the company to expand its capacity by obtaining more equipment, more space, or more personnel, the incremental costs could quickly exceed the incremental revenue. Another cautionary note is the effect on existing sales. All new units of the extra business will be sold outside FasTrac's normal domestic sales channels. If accepting additional business would cause existing sales to decline, this information must be included in our analysis. The contribution margin lost from a decline in sales is an opportunity cost. The company must also consider whether this customer is really a one-time customer. If not, can the company continue to offer this low price in the long run?

Example: Exhibit 10.4
uses quantitative information.
Suggest some qualitative factors
to be considered when deciding
whether to accept this project.
Answer: (1) Impact on relationships with other customers and
(2) improved relationship with
customer buying additional
units.

A company receives a special order for 200 units that requires stamping the buyer's name on each unit, yielding an additional fixed cost of $400 to its normal costs. Without the order, the company is operating at 75% of capacity and produces 7,500 units of product at the costs below. The company's normal selling price is $22 per unit.

Direct materials	$37,500
Direct labor	60,000
Overhead (30% variable)	20,000
Selling expenses (60% variable)	25,000

The sales price for the special order is $18 per unit. The special order will not affect normal unit sales and will not increase fixed overhead or fixed selling expenses. Variable selling expenses on the special order are reduced to one-half the normal amount. Should the company accept the special order?

Solution

Incremental variable costs per unit for this order of 200 units are computed as follows:

Direct materials ($37,500/7,500)	$ 5.00
Direct labor ($60,000/7,500)	8.00
Variable overhead [(0.30 × $20,000)/7,500]	0.80
Variable selling expenses [(0.60 × $25,000 × 0.5)/7,500]	1.00
Total incremental variable costs per unit	$14.80

The contribution margin from the special order is $640, computed as [($18.00 − $14.80) × 200]. This will cover the incremental fixed costs of $400 and yield incremental income of $240. The offer should be accepted.

■ **Decision** Maker

Partner You are a partner in a small accounting firm that specializes in keeping the books and preparing taxes for clients. A local restaurant is interested in obtaining these services from your firm. Identify factors that are relevant in deciding whether to accept the engagement. ■ [Answers follow the chapter's Summary.]

Make or Buy

The managerial decision to make or buy a component is common. For example, **Apple** buys the component parts for its electronic products, but it could consider making these components in its own manufacturing facilities. This decision depends on incremental costs. We return to Fas-Trac to illustrate. FasTrac currently buys part 417, a component of the main product it sells, for $1.20 per unit. FasTrac has excess productive capacity, and management is wondering whether the company should make part 417 instead of buy it. FasTrac estimates that making part 417 would incur variable costs of $0.45 for direct materials and $0.50 for direct labor. FasTrac's normal predetermined overhead application rate is 100% of direct labor cost. If management *incorrectly* relies on this historical overhead rate, it will prepare the analysis in Exhibit 10.5.

(per unit)	Make	Buy
Direct materials	$0.45	—
Direct labor	0.50	—
Overhead costs (using historical rate)	**0.50**	—
Purchase price	—	$1.20
Total costs	$1.45	$1.20

EXHIBIT 10.5

Make or Buy Analysis Using Historical Costs

Using the data in Exhibit 10.5, management would mistakenly believe that the cost to make the component part is $1.45 per unit and conclude that the company is better off buying the part at $1.20 per unit. This analysis is flawed, however, because it uses the historical predetermined overhead rate.

As we explained earlier, only *incremental* overhead costs are relevant to this make or buy decision. Incremental overhead costs might include, for example, additional power for operating machines, extra supplies, added cleanup costs, materials handling, and quality control. Assume that management computes an *incremental overhead rate* of $0.20 per unit if it makes the part. We can then prepare a per unit analysis, using relevant costs, as shown in Exhibit 10.6.

EXHIBIT 10.6

Make or Buy Analysis Using Relevant Costs

(per unit)	Make	Buy
Direct materials	$0.45	—
Direct labor	0.50	—
Overhead costs (using incremental rate)	0.20	—
Purchase price..................................	—	$1.20
Total costs.....................................	$1.15	$1.20

Exhibit 10.6 shows that the relevant cost to make part 417 is $1.15. Based on this analysis, it is cheaper to make the part than to buy it. We can see that if incremental overhead costs are less than $0.25 per unit, the total cost of making the part will be less than the purchase price of $1.20 per unit.

Other Factors While our analysis suggests it is cheaper to make part 417, FasTrac must also consider several nonfinancial factors in the make or buy decision. These factors might include product quality, timeliness of delivery (especially in a just-in-time setting), reactions of customers and suppliers, and other intangibles like employee morale and workload. It must also consider whether making the part requires incremental fixed costs to expand plant capacity. When these additional factors are considered, small cost differences might not matter.

Make or Buy

A1

A company currently pays $5 per unit to buy a key part for a product it manufactures. The company believes it can make the part for $1.50 per unit for direct materials and $2.50 per unit for direct labor. The company allocates overhead costs at the rate of 50% of direct labor. Incremental overhead costs to make this part are $0.75 per unit. Should the company make or buy the part?

Solution

(per unit)	Make	Buy
Direct materials	$1.50	—
Direct labor	2.50	—
Overhead	0.75	—
Cost to buy the part	—	$5.00
Total	$4.75	$5.00

Do More: QS 10-7, QS 10-8, E 10-4, E 10-5

The company should make the part because the cost to make it is less than the cost to buy it.

█ Decision Insight ━━━━━━━━━━━━━━━━━━━━━━━━━━━━━━━━━━━

Make or Buy IT Companies apply make or buy decisions to their services. Many now outsource their information technology activities. Information technology companies provide infrastructure and services to enable businesses to focus on their key activities. It is argued that outsourcing saves money and streamlines operations, and without the headaches. ■

Scrap or Rework

Manufacturing processes sometimes yield defective products. In such cases, managers must make a decision on whether to scrap or rework products in process. Two points are important here. First, costs already incurred in manufacturing the defective units are sunk and not relevant. Second, we must consider opportunity costs—reworking the defective products uses productive capacity that could be devoted to normal operations.

To illustrate, assume that FasTrac has 10,000 defective units of a product that have already cost $1 per unit to manufacture. These units can be sold as is (as scrap) for $0.40 each, or they can be reworked for $0.80 per unit and then sold for their full price of $1.50 each. Should FasTrac sell the units as scrap or rework them?

The $1 per unit manufacturing cost already incurred is irrelevant. Further, if FasTrac is operating near its maximum capacity, reworking the defects means that FasTrac is unable to manufacture 10,000 *new* units with an incremental cost of $1 per unit and a selling price of $1.50 per unit, meaning it incurs an *opportunity cost* of $0.50 per unit ($1.50 selling price − $1.00 incremental cost). Our analysis is then reflected in Exhibit 10.7.

	Scrap	Rework
Sale of scrapped/reworked units (10,000 units).................	$ 4,000	$15,000*
Less out-of-pocket costs to rework defects ($0.80 per unit).............		(8,000)
Less opportunity cost of not making new units ($0.50 per unit).....		**(5,000)**
Incremental net income.......................	$4,000	$ 2,000

*10,000 × $1.50

EXHIBIT 10.7

Scrap or Rework Analysis

Scrapping the units would yield incremental income of $4,000; reworking the units would yield only $2,000 of income. Based on this analysis, the defective units should be scrapped and sold as is for $0.40 each. If we had failed to include the opportunity costs of $5,000, the rework option would have shown an income of $7,000 instead of $2,000, mistakenly making reworking appear more favorable than scrapping.

Sell or Process Further

Some companies must decide whether to sell partially completed products as is or to process them further for sale as other products. For example, a peanut grower could sell its peanut harvest as is, or it could process peanuts into other products such as peanut butter, trail mix, and candy. The decision depends on the incremental costs and benefits of further processing, as we show next.

To illustrate, suppose that FasTrac has 40,000 units of partially finished Product Q. It has already spent $30,000 to manufacture these 40,000 units. FasTrac can sell the 40,000 units to another manufacturer as raw material for $50,000. Alternatively, it can process them further and produce finished Products X, Y, and Z. Processing the units further will cost an additional $80,000 and will yield total revenues of $150,000. FasTrac must decide whether the added revenues from selling finished Products X, Y, and Z exceed the costs of finishing them.

Exhibit 10.8 presents the analysis.

	Sell as Product Q	Process Further into Products X, Y, and Z
Incremental revenue	$50,000	$150,000
Incremental cost	—	(80,000)
Incremental income.	$50,000	$ 70,000

EXHIBIT 10.8

Sell or Process Further Analysis

The analysis shows that the incremental income from processing further ($70,000) is greater than the incremental income ($50,000) from selling Product Q as is. Therefore, FasTrac should process further; by doing so, it will earn an additional $20,000 of income ($70,000 − $50,000).

Notice that the $30,000 of previously incurred manufacturing costs are *excluded* from the analysis. These costs are sunk, and they are not relevant to the decision. The incremental revenue from selling Product Q as is ($50,000) is properly included. It is the opportunity cost associated with processing further.

For each of the two independent scenarios below, determine whether the company should sell the partially completed product as is or process it further into other saleable products.

1. $10,000 of manufacturing costs have been incurred to produce Product Alpha. Alpha can be sold as is for $30,000 or processed further into two separate products. The further processing will cost $15,000, and the resulting products can be sold for total revenues of $60,000.

2. $5,000 of manufacturing costs have been incurred to produce Product Delta. Delta can be sold as is for $150,000 or processed further into two separate products. The further processing will cost $75,000, and the resulting products can be sold for total revenues of $200,000.

Solution

1.

Alpha	Sell As Is	Process Further
Incremental revenue	$30,000	$60,000
Incremental cost	—	(15,000)
Incremental income	$30,000	$45,000

Alpha should be processed further; doing so will yield an extra $15,000 ($45,000 − $30,000) of income.

2.

Delta	Sell As Is	Process Further
Incremental revenue	$150,000	$200,000
Incremental cost	—	(75,000)
Incremental income	$150,000	$125,000

Delta should be sold as is; doing so will yield an extra $25,000 ($150,000 − $125,000) of income.

Sales Mix Selection When Resources Are Constrained

When a company sells a mix of products, some are likely to be more profitable than others. Management concentrates sales efforts on more profitable products. If production facilities or other factors are limited, producing more of one product usually requires producing less of others. In this case, management must identify the most profitable combination, or *sales mix*, of products. To identify the best sales mix, management focuses on the *contribution margin per unit of scarce resource.*

Point: A method called *linear programming* is useful for finding the optimal sales mix for several products subject to many market and production constraints. This method is described in advanced courses.

To illustrate, assume that FasTrac makes and sells two products, A and B. The same machines are used to produce both products. A and B have the following selling prices and variable costs per unit:

(per unit)	Product A	Product B
Selling price	$5.00	$7.50
Variable costs.........	3.50	5.50

FasTrac has an existing capacity of 100,000 machine hours per year. In addition, Product A uses 1 machine hour per unit while Product B uses 2 machine hours per unit. With limited resources, FasTrac should focus its productive capacity on the product that yields the highest contribution margin per machine hour, until market demand for that product is satisfied. Exhibit 10.9 shows the relevant analysis.

	Product A	Product B
Selling price per unit	$5.00	$7.50
Variable costs per unit	3.50	5.50
Contribution margin per unit (a)...........................	$1.50	$2.00
Machine hours per unit (b)	1.0	2.0
Contribution margin per machine hour (a) ÷ (b).........	$1.50	$1.00

EXHIBIT 10.9

Sales Mix Analysis

Exhibit 10.9 shows that although Product B has a higher contribution margin per *unit,* Product A has a higher contribution margin per *machine hour*. In this case, FasTrac should produce as much of Product A as possible, up to the market demand. For example, if the demand for Product A is unlimited, FasTrac should produce 100,000 units of Product A and none of Product B. This sales mix would yield a contribution margin of $150,000 per year, the maximum the company could make subject to its resource constraint.

If demand for Product A is limited—say, to 80,000 units—FasTrac will begin by producing those 80,000 units. This production level would leave 20,000 machine hours to devote to production of Product B. FasTrac would use these remaining machine hours to produce 10,000 units (20,000 machine hours/2 machine hours per unit) of Product B. This sales mix would yield the contribution margin shown in Exhibit 10.10.

	Contribution Margin	Machine Hours Used
Product A (80,000 × $1.50 per unit)	$120,000	80,000
Product B (10,000 × $2.00 per unit)	20,000	20,000
Total......................................	$140,000	100,000

EXHIBIT 10.10

Contribution Margin from Sales Mix, with Resource Constraint

With limited demand for Product A, the optimal sales mix yields a contribution margin of $140,000, the best the company can do subject to its resource constraint and market demand. In general, if demand for products is limited, management should produce its most profitable product (per unit of scarce resource) up to the point of total demand (or its capacity constraint). It then uses remaining capacity to produce its next most profitable product.

Point: FasTrac might consider buying more machines to reduce the constraint on production. A strategy designed to reduce the impact of constraints or bottlenecks on production is called the *theory of constraints*.

A company produces two products, Gamma and Omega. Gamma sells for $10 per unit and Omega sells for $12.50 per unit. Variable costs are $7 per unit of Gamma and $8 per unit of Omega. The company has a capacity of 5,000 machine hours per month. Gamma uses 1 machine hour per unit, and Omega uses 3 machine hours per unit.

1. Compute the contribution margin per machine hour for each product.
2. Assume demand for Gamma is limited to 3,800 units per month. How many units of Gamma and Omega should the company produce, and what will be the total contribution margin from this sales mix?

NEED-TO-KNOW 10-4

Sales Mix with Constrained Resources

A1

Solution

1.

	Gamma	Omega
Selling price per unit	$10.00	$12.50
Variable costs per unit	7.00	8.00
Contribution margin per unit	$ 3.00	$ 4.50
Machine hours per unit	1	3
Contribution margin per machine hour	$ 3.00	$ 1.50

2. The company will begin by producing Gamma to meet the market demand of 3,800 units. This production level will consume 3,800 machine hours, leaving 1,200 machine hours to produce Omega. With 1,200 machine hours, the company can produce 400 units (1,200 machine hours/3 machine hours per unit) of Omega. The total contribution margin from this sales mix is:

Gamma......................	3,800 units × $3.00 per unit =	$11,400
Omega	400 units × $4.50 per unit =	1,800
Total.......................		$13,200

Do More: QS 10-12, E 10-9

Decision Insight

Companies such as **Gap, Abercrombie & Fitch**, and **American Eagle** must continuously monitor and manage the sales mix of their product lists. Selling their products worldwide further complicates their decision process. The contribution margin of each product is crucial to their product mix strategies. ▪

BananaStock/Punchstock

Segment Elimination

When a segment, division, or store is performing poorly, management must consider eliminating it. As we showed in a previous chapter, determining a segment's *contribution to overhead* is an important first step in this analysis. Segments with revenues less than direct costs are candidates for elimination. However, contribution to overhead is not sufficient for this decision. Instead, we must further classify the segment's expenses as avoidable or unavoidable. **Avoidable expenses** are amounts the company would not incur if it eliminated the segment. **Unavoidable expenses** are amounts that would continue even if the segment was eliminated.

Example: How can insurance be classified as either avoidable or unavoidable? *Answer:* It depends on whether the assets insured can be removed and the premiums canceled.

To illustrate, FasTrac is considering eliminating its treadmill division, which reported a $500 operating loss for the recent year, as shown in Exhibit 10.11. From Exhibit 10.11, we see that the treadmill division contributes $9,700 to recovery of overhead costs. The next step is to classify the division's costs as either avoidable or unavoidable. Variable costs, such as cost of goods sold and

EXHIBIT 10.11

Classification of Segment Operating Expenses for Analysis

Treadmill Division	Total	Avoidable Expenses	Unavoidable Expenses
Sales	$47,800		
Cost of goods sold............................	30,000	$30,000	
Gross profit	17,800		
Direct expenses			
Wages expense	7,900	7,900	
Depreciation expense—Equipment	200		$ 200
Total direct expenses........................	8,100		
Departmental contribution to overhead............	$ 9,700		
Indirect expenses			
Rent and utilities expense	3,150		3,150
Advertising expense..........................	400	400	
Insurance expense	400	300	100
Share of office department expenses	3,060	2,200	860
Share of purchasing department expenses	3,190	1,000	2,190
Total indirect expenses	10,200		
Operating income (loss)	$ (500)		
Total avoidable expenses..........................		$41,800	
Total unavoidable expenses.......................			$6,500

Point: The analysis is summarized as:

Sales	$47,800
Avoidable expenses	(41,800)
Reduction in income	$ 6,000

Because sales > avoidable expenses, do *not* eliminate division.

wages expense, are avoidable. In addition, some of the division's indirect expenses are avoidable; for example, if the treadmill division were eliminated, FasTrac could reduce its overall advertising expense by $400 and its overall insurance expense by $300. In addition, FasTrac could avoid office department expenses of $2,200 and purchasing expenses of $1,000 if the treadmill division were eliminated. It is important to realize that these *avoidable* expenses would not be allocated to other divisions of the company; rather, these expenses would be eliminated. Unavoidable expenses, however, will be reallocated to other divisions if the treadmill division is eliminated.

FasTrac's analysis shows that it can avoid a total of $41,800 of expenses if it eliminates the treadmill division. However, because this division's sales are $47,800, eliminating the division would reduce FasTrac's income by $6,000 ($47,800 − $41,800). Based on this analysis, FasTrac should not eliminate its treadmill division. *Our decision rule is that a segment is a candidate for elimination if its revenues are less than its avoidable expenses.* Avoidable expenses can be viewed as the costs to generate this segment's revenues.

Other Factors When considering elimination of a segment, we must assess its impact on other segments. A segment could be unprofitable on its own, but it might still contribute to other segments' revenues and profits. It is possible then to continue a segment even when its revenues are less than its avoidable expenses. Similarly, a profitable segment might be discontinued if its space, assets, or staff can be more profitably used by expanding existing segments or by creating new ones. Our decision to keep or eliminate a segment requires a more complex analysis than simply looking at a segment's performance report.

Example: Give an example of a segment that a company might profitably use to attract customers even though it might incur a loss. *Answer:* Warranty and post-sales services.

A bike maker is considering eliminating its tandem bike division because it operates at a loss of $6,000 per year. Sales for the year total $40,000, and the company reports the costs for this division as shown below. Should the tandem bike division be eliminated?

NEED-TO-KNOW 10-5

Segment Elimination

A1

	Avoidable Expenses	Unavoidable Expenses
Cost of goods sold..............	$30,000	$ —
Direct expenses	8,000	—
Indirect expenses................	2,500	3,000
Service department costs	250	2,250
Total........................	$40,750	$5,250

Solution

Total avoidable costs of $40,750 are greater than the division's sales of $40,000, suggesting the division should be eliminated. Other factors might be relevant, since the shortfall in sales ($750) is low. For example, are sales expected to increase in the future? Does the sale of tandem bikes help sales of other types of products?

Do More: QS 10-13, QS 10-14, E 10-10

Keep or Replace Equipment

Businesses periodically must decide whether to keep using equipment or replace it. Advances in technology typically mean newer equipment can operate more efficiently and at lower cost than older equipment. If the reduction in *variable* manufacturing costs with the new equipment is greater than its net purchase price, the equipment should be replaced. In this setting, the net purchase price of the equipment is its total cost minus any trade-in allowance or cash receipt for the old equipment.

For example, FasTrac has a piece of manufacturing equipment with a book value (cost minus accumulated depreciation) of $20,000 and a remaining useful life of four years. At the end of four years the equipment will have a salvage value of zero. The market value of the equipment is currently $25,000.

FasTrac can purchase a new machine for $100,000 and receive $25,000 in return for trading in its old machine. The new machine will reduce FasTrac's variable manufacturing costs by $18,000 per year over the four-year life of the new machine. FasTrac's incremental analysis is shown in Exhibit 10.12.

EXHIBIT 10.12

Keep or Replace Analysis

	Increase or (Decrease) in Net Income
Cost to buy new machine	$(100,000)
Cash received to trade in old machine	25,000
Reduction in variable manufacturing costs	72,000*
Total increase (decrease) in net income	$ (3,000)

*18,000 × 4 years

The analysis in Exhibit 10.12 shows that FasTrac should not replace the old equipment with this newer version as it will decrease income by $3,000. Note, the book value of the old equipment ($20,000) is not relevant to this analysis. Book value is a sunk cost, and it cannot be changed regardless of whether FasTrac keeps or replaces this equipment.

GLOBAL VIEW

Courtesy of Charlie's Brownies

Heinz India Private Limited, headquartered in India, is a maker of ketchup, energy drinks, and other products. The company recently decided to eliminate several unprofitable segments, including those that made biscuits and ready-to-eat packaged foods, in order to focus on more profitable segments. Analyses of avoidable and unavoidable expenses, along with consideration of these segments' potential impact on other segments, support such decisions.

Sustainability and Accounting   Charlie Fyffe of **Charlie's Brownies** strives to reduce the impact his company has on the environment while also growing sales. Unlike companies that make brownies with animal fats, Charlie makes his brownies entirely from plant-based, organic raw materials. The use of such materials enables Charlie to expand his sales to customers who follow vegan diets.

Decipher Analysis Setting Product Price

A2

Determine product selling price based on total costs.

Relevant costs are useful to management in determining prices for special short-term decisions. But longer run pricing decisions of management need to cover both variable and fixed costs, and yield a profit.

There are several methods to help management in setting prices. The *cost-plus* methods are probably the most common, where management adds a **markup** to cost to reach a target price. We will describe the **total cost method,** where management sets price equal to the product's total costs plus a desired profit on the product. This is a four-step process:

1. Determine total costs.

$$\text{Total costs} = \begin{array}{c}\textbf{Production (direct materials,}\\ \textbf{direct labor, and overhead) costs}\end{array} + \begin{array}{c}\textbf{Nonproduction (selling and}\\ \textbf{administrative) costs}\end{array}$$

2. Determine total cost per unit.

$$\textbf{Total cost per unit = Total costs} \div \textbf{Total units expected to be produced and sold}$$

3. Determine the dollar markup per unit.

$$\textbf{Markup per unit = Total cost per unit} \times \textbf{Markup percentage}$$

where Markup percentage = Desired profit/Total costs

4. Determine selling price per unit.

$$\textbf{Selling price per unit = Total cost per unit + Markup per unit}$$

To illustrate, consider a company that produces MP3 players. The company desires a 20% return on its assets of $1,000,000, and it expects to produce and sell 10,000 players. The following additional company information is available:

Variable costs (per unit)	
Production costs.............	$44
Nonproduction costs	6
Fixed costs (in dollars)	
Overhead..................	$140,000
Nonproduction	60,000

We apply our four-step process to determine price.

1. Total costs = Production costs + Nonproduction costs
   = [($44 × 10,000 units) + $140,000] + [($6 × 10,000 units) + $60,000]
   = $700,000

2. Total cost per unit = Total costs/Total units expected to be produced and sold
   = $700,000/10,000
   = $70

3. Markup per unit = Total cost per unit × (Desired profit/Total costs)
   = $70 × [(20% × $1,000,000)/$700,000]
   = $20

4. Selling price per unit = Total cost per unit + Markup per unit
   = $70 + $20
   = $90

To verify that our price yields the $200,000 desired profit (20% × $1,000,000), we compute the following simplified income statement using the information above.

Sales ($90 × 10,000)	$900,000
Expenses	
Variable ($50 × 10,000).............	500,000
Fixed ($140,000 + $60,000)	200,000
Income	$200,000

Companies use cost-plus pricing as a starting point for determining selling prices. Many factors determine price, including consumer preferences and competition.

Determine the appropriate action in each of the following managerial decision situations.

NEED-TO-KNOW

COMPREHENSIVE

1. Packer Company is operating at 80% of its manufacturing capacity of 100,000 product units per year. A chain store has offered to buy an additional 10,000 units at $22 each and sell them to customers so as not to compete with Packer Company. The following data are available.

Costs at 80% Capacity	Per Unit	Total
Direct materials	$ 8.00	$ 640,000
Direct labor	7.00	560,000
Overhead (fixed and variable)	12.50	1,000,000
Totals	$27.50	$2,200,000

In producing 10,000 additional units, fixed overhead costs would remain at their current level but incremental variable overhead costs of $3 per unit would be incurred. Should the company accept or reject this order?

2. Green Company uses Part JR3 in manufacturing its products. It has always purchased this part from a supplier for $40 each. It recently upgraded its own manufacturing capabilities and has enough excess

capacity (including trained workers) to begin manufacturing Part JR3 instead of buying it. The company prepares the following cost projections of making the part, assuming that overhead is allocated to the part at the normal predetermined rate of 200% of direct labor cost.

Direct materials	$11
Direct labor	15
Overhead (fixed and variable) (200% of direct labor)	30
Total	$56

The required volume of output to produce the part will not require any incremental fixed overhead. Incremental variable overhead cost will be $17 per unit. Should the company make or buy this part?

3. Gold Company's manufacturing process causes a relatively large number of defective parts to be produced. The defective parts can be (a) sold for scrap, (b) melted to recover the recycled metal for reuse, or (c) reworked to be good units. Reworking defective parts reduces the output of other good units because no excess capacity exists. Each unit reworked means that one new unit cannot be produced. The following information reflects 500 defective parts currently available.

Proceeds of selling as scrap	$2,500
Additional cost of melting down defective parts	400
Cost of purchases avoided by using recycled metal from defects	4,800
Cost to rework 500 defective parts	
Direct materials	0
Direct labor	1,500
Incremental overhead	1,750
Cost to produce 500 new parts	
Direct materials	6,000
Direct labor	5,000
Incremental overhead	3,200
Selling price per good unit	40

Should the company melt the parts, sell them as scrap, or rework them?

PLANNING THE SOLUTION

● Determine whether Packer Company should accept the additional business by finding the incremental costs of materials, labor, and overhead that will be incurred if the order is accepted. Omit fixed costs that the order will not increase. If the incremental revenue exceeds the incremental cost, accept the order.

● Determine whether Green Company should make or buy the component by finding the incremental cost of making each unit. If the incremental cost exceeds the purchase price, the component should be purchased. If the incremental cost is less than the purchase price, make the component.

● Determine whether Gold Company should sell the defective parts, melt them down and recycle the metal, or rework them. To compare the three choices, examine all costs incurred and benefits received from the alternatives in working with the 500 defective units versus the production of 500 new units. For the scrapping alternative, include the costs of producing 500 new units and subtract the $2,500 proceeds from selling the old ones. For the melting alternative, include the costs of melting the defective units, add the net cost of new materials in excess over those obtained from recycling, and add the direct labor and overhead costs. For the reworking alternative, add the costs of direct labor and incremental overhead. Select the alternative that has the lowest cost. The cost assigned to the 500 defective units is sunk and not relevant in choosing among the three alternatives.

SOLUTION

1. This decision involves accepting additional business. Since current unit costs are $27.50, it appears initially as if the offer to sell for $22 should be rejected, but the $27.50 cost includes fixed costs. When the analysis includes only *incremental* costs, the per unit cost is as shown in the following table. The

offer should be accepted because it will produce $4 of additional profit per unit (computed as $22 price less $18 incremental cost), which yields a total profit of $40,000 for the 10,000 additional units.

Direct materials	$ 8.00
Direct labor	7.00
Variable overhead (given)	3.00
Total incremental cost	$18.00

2. For this make or buy decision, the analysis must not include the $13 nonincremental overhead per unit ($30 − $17). When only the $17 incremental overhead is included, the relevant unit cost of manufacturing the part is shown in the following table. It would be better to continue buying the part for $40 instead of making it for $43.

Direct materials	$11.00
Direct labor	15.00
Variable overhead	17.00
Total incremental cost	$43.00

3. The goal of this scrap or rework decision is to identify the alternative that produces the greatest net benefit to the company. To compare the alternatives, we determine the net cost of obtaining 500 marketable units as follows:

Incremental Cost to Produce 500 Marketable Units	Sell As Is	Melt and Recycle	Rework Units
Direct materials			
New materials	$ 6,000	$6,000	
Recycled metal materials...............................		(4,800)	
Net materials cost....................................		1,200	
Melting costs		400	
Total direct materials cost	6,000	1,600	
Direct labor	5,000	5,000	$1,500
Incremental overhead	3,200	3,200	1,750
Cost to produce 500 marketable units	14,200	9,800	3,250
Less proceeds of selling defects as scrap	(2,500)		
Opportunity costs*			5,800
Net cost	$11,700	$9,800	$9,050

* The $5,800 opportunity cost is the lost contribution margin from not being able to produce and sell 500 units because of reworking, computed as ($40 − [$14,200/500 units]) × 500 units.

The incremental cost of 500 marketable parts is smallest if the defects are reworked.

Summary

C1   **Describe the importance of relevant costs for short-term decisions.** A company must rely on relevant costs pertaining to alternative courses of action rather than historical costs. Out-of-pocket expenses and opportunity costs are relevant because these are avoidable; sunk costs are irrelevant because they result from past decisions and are therefore unavoidable. Managers must also consider the relevant benefits associated with alternative decisions.

A1   **Evaluate short-term managerial decisions using relevant costs.** Relevant costs are useful in making decisions such as to accept additional business, make or buy, and sell as is or process further. For example, the relevant factors in deciding whether to produce and sell additional units of product are

incremental costs and incremental revenues from the additional volume.

A2   **Determine product selling price based on total costs.** Product selling price is estimated using total production and nonproduction costs plus a markup. Price is set to yield management's desired profit for the company.

P1   **Identify relevant costs and apply them to managerial decisions.** Several illustrations apply relevant costs to managerial decisions, such as whether to accept additional business; make or buy; scrap or rework products; sell products or process them further; or eliminate a segment and how to select the best sales mix.

Guidance Answer to Decision Maker

Partner   You should identify the differences between existing clients and this potential client. A key difference is that the restaurant business has additional inventory components (groceries, vegetables, meats, etc.) and is likely to have a higher proportion of depreciable assets. These differences imply that the partner must spend more hours auditing the records and understanding the business, regulations, and standards that pertain to the restaurant business. Such differences suggest that the partner must use a different "formula" for quoting a price to this potential client vis-à-vis current clients.

Key Terms

Avoidable expense	Markup	Total cost method
Incremental cost	Relevant benefits	Unavoidable expense

Multiple Choice Quiz   Answers at end of chapter

1. A company inadvertently produced 3,000 defective MP3 players. The players cost $12 each to produce. A recycler offers to purchase the defective players as they are for $8 each. The production manager reports that the defects can be corrected for $10 each, enabling them to be sold at their regular market price of $19 each. The company should:
   a. Correct the defect and sell them at the regular price.
   b. Sell the players to the recycler for $8 each.
   c. Sell 2,000 to the recycler and repair the rest.
   d. Sell 1,000 to the recycler and repair the rest.
   e. Throw the players away.

2. A company's productive capacity is limited to 480,000 machine hours. Product X requires 10 machine hours to produce; Product Y requires 2 machine hours to produce. Product X sells for $32 per unit and has variable costs of $12 per unit; Product Y sells for $24 per unit and has variable costs of $10 per unit. Assuming that the company can sell as many of either product as it produces, it should:
   a. Produce X and Y in the ratio of 57% and 43%.
   b. Produce X and Y in the ratio of 83% X and 17% Y.
   c. Produce equal amounts of Product X and Product Y.
   d. Produce only Product X.
   e. Produce only Product Y.

3. A company receives a special one-time order for 3,000 units of its product at $15 per unit. The company has excess capacity and it currently produces and sells the units at $20 each to its regular customers. Production costs are $13.50 per unit, which includes $9 of variable costs. To produce the special order, the company must incur additional fixed costs of $5,000. Should the company accept the special order?
   a. Yes, because incremental revenue exceeds incremental costs.
   b. No, because incremental costs exceed incremental revenue.
   c. No, because the units are being sold for $5 less than the regular price.
   d. Yes, because incremental costs exceed incremental revenue.
   e. No, because incremental costs exceed $15 per unit when total costs are considered.

4. A cost that cannot be changed because it arises from a past decision and is irrelevant to future decisions is
   a. An uncontrollable cost.   d. An opportunity cost.
   b. An out-of-pocket cost.   e. An incremental cost.
   c. A sunk cost.

5. The potential benefit of one alternative that is lost by choosing another is known as
   a. An alternative cost.   d. An opportunity cost.
   b. A sunk cost.   e. An out-of-pocket cost.
   c. A differential cost.

[I] Icon denotes assignments that involve decision making.

Discussion Questions

1. [I] Identify the five steps involved in the managerial decision-making process.

2. Is nonfinancial information ever useful in managerial decision making?

3. What is a relevant cost? Identify the two types of relevant costs.

4. [I] Why are sunk costs irrelevant in deciding whether to sell a product in its present condition or to make it into a new product through additional processing?

5. [I] Identify some qualitative factors that should be considered when making managerial decisions.

6. **Google** has many types of costs. What is an out-of-pocket cost? What is an opportunity cost? Are opportunity costs recorded in the accounting records?   **GOOGLE**

7. [I] **Samsung** must confront sunk costs. Why are sunk costs irrelevant in deciding whether to sell a product in its present   **Samsung**

condition or to make it into a new product through additional processing?

8. 📖 Identify the incremental costs incurred by Apple for shipping one additional iPod **APPLE** from a warehouse to a retail store along with the store's normal order of 75 iPods.

9. 📖 Apple is considering eliminating one of its stores in a large U.S. city. What are some **APPLE** factors that it should consider in making this decision?

10. 📖 Assume that Samsung manufactures and sells 60,000 units of a **Samsung** product at $11,000 per unit in domestic markets. It costs $6,000 per unit to manufacture ($4,000 variable cost per unit, $2,000 fixed cost per unit). Can you describe a situation under which the company is willing to sell an additional 8,000 units of the product in an international market at $5,000 per unit?

📖 connect

Helix Company has been approached by a new customer to provide 2,000 units of its regular product at a special price of $6 per unit. The regular selling price of the product is $8 per unit. Helix is operating at 75% of its capacity of 10,000 units. Identify whether the following costs are relevant to Helix's decision as to whether to accept the order at the special selling price. No additional fixed manufacturing overhead will be incurred because of this order. The only additional selling expense on this order will be a $0.50 per unit shipping cost. There will be no additional administrative expenses because of this order. Place an X in the appropriate column to identify whether the cost is relevant or irrelevant to accepting this order.

QUICK STUDY

QS 10-1
Identification of relevant costs
P1

Item	Relevant	Not relevant
a. Selling price of $6.00 per unit	____	____
b. Direct materials cost of $1.00 per unit	____	____
c. Direct labor of $2.00 per unit	____	____
d. Variable manufacturing overhead of $1.50 per unit	____	____
e. Fixed manufacturing overhead of $0.75 per unit	____	____
f. Regular selling expenses of $1.25 per unit	____	____
g. Additional selling expenses of $0.50 per unit	____	____
h. Administrative expenses of $0.60 per unit	____	____

Refer to the data in QS 10-1. Based on financial considerations alone, should Helix accept this order at the special price? Explain.

QS 10-2
Analysis of relevant costs   A1

Refer to QS 10-1 and QS 10-2. What nonfinancial factors should Helix consider before accepting this order? Explain.

QS 10-3
Identification of relevant nonfinancial factors   P1

Garcia Company has 10,000 units of its product that were produced last year at a total cost of $150,000. The units were damaged in a rainstorm because the warehouse where they were stored developed a leak in the roof. Garcia can sell the units as is for $2 each or it can repair the units at a total cost of $18,000 and then sell them for $5 each. Should Garcia sell the units as is or repair them and then sell them? Explain.

QS 10-4
Sell or process
P1 A1

Label each of the following statements as either true ("T") or false ("F").
1. Relevant costs are also known as unavoidable costs.
2. Incremental costs are also known as differential costs.
3. An out-of-pocket cost requires a current and/or future outlay of cash.
4. An opportunity cost is the potential benefit that is lost by taking a specific action when two or more alternative choices are available.
5. A sunk cost will change with a future course of action.

QS 10-5
Relevant costs
C1

Radar Company sells bikes for $300 each. The company currently sells 3,750 bikes per year and could make as many as 5,000 bikes per year. The bikes cost $225 each to make; $150 in variable costs per bike and $75 of fixed costs per bike. Radar received an offer from a potential customer who wants to buy 750 bikes for $250 each. Incremental fixed costs to make this order are $50,000. No other costs will change if this order is accepted. Compute Radar's additional income (ignore taxes) if it accepts this order.

QS 10-6
Decision to accept additional business   A1

QS 10-7
Make or buy
A1

Kando Company incurs a $9 per unit cost for Product A, which it currently manufactures and sells for $13.50 per unit. Instead of manufacturing and selling this product, the company can purchase Product B for $5 per unit and sell it for $12 per unit. If it does so, unit sales would remain unchanged and $5 of the $9 per unit costs assigned to Product A would be eliminated. Should the company continue to manufacture Product A or purchase Product B for resale?

QS 10-8
Make or buy
A1

Xia Co. currently buys a component part for $5 per unit. Xia believes that making the part would require $2.25 per unit of direct materials and $1.00 per unit of direct labor. Xia allocates overhead using a predetermined overhead rate of 200% of direct labor cost. Xia estimates an incremental overhead rate of $0.75 per unit to make the part. Should Xia make or buy the part?

QS 10-9
Scrap or rework
A1

Signal mistakenly produced 1,000 defective cell phones. The phones cost $60 each to produce. A salvage company will buy the defective phones as they are for $30 each. It would cost Signal $80 per phone to rework the phones. If the phones are reworked, Signal could sell them for $120 each. Assume there is no opportunity cost associated with reworking the phones. Compute the incremental net income from reworking the phones.

QS 10-10
Sell or process further
A1

Holmes Company produces a product that can either be sold as is or processed further. Holmes has already spent $50,000 to produce 1,250 units that can be sold now for $67,500 to another manufacturer. Alternatively, Holmes can process the units further at an incremental cost of $250 per unit. If Holmes processes further, the units can be sold for $375 each. Compute the incremental income if Holmes processes further.

QS 10-11
Sell or process further A1

A company has already incurred $5,000 of costs in producing 6,000 units of Product XY. Product XY can be sold as is for $15 per unit. Instead, the company could incur further processing costs of $8 per unit and sell the resulting product for $21 per unit. Should the company sell Product XY as is or process it further?

QS 10-12
Selection of sales mix
A1

Excel Memory Company can sell all units of computer memory X and Y that it can produce, but it has limited production capacity. It can produce two units of X per hour *or* three units of Y per hour, and it has 4,000 production hours available. Contribution margin is $5 for Product X and $4 for Product Y. What is the most profitable sales mix for this company?

QS 10-13
Segment elimination
A1

A guitar manufacturer is considering eliminating its electric guitar division because its $76,000 expenses are higher than its $72,000 sales. The company reports the following expenses for this division. Should the division be eliminated?

	Avoidable Expenses	Unavoidable Expenses
Cost of goods sold	$56,000	
Direct expenses	9,250	$1,250
Indirect expenses	470	1,600
Service department costs	6,000	1,430

QS 10-14
Segment elimination
A1

A division of a large company reports the information shown below for a recent year. Variable costs and direct fixed costs are avoidable, and 40% of the indirect fixed costs are avoidable. Based on this information, should the division be eliminated?

	Total
Sales	$200,000
Variable costs	145,000
Fixed costs	
Direct	30,000
Indirect	50,000
Operating loss	$ (25,000)

Rory Company has a machine with a book value of $75,000 and a remaining five-year useful life. A new machine is available at a cost of $112,500, and Rory can also receive $60,000 for trading in its old machine. The new machine will reduce variable manufacturing costs by $13,000 per year over its five-year useful life. Should the machine be replaced?

QS 10-15
Keep or replace decision
A1

connect

Fill in each of the blanks below with the correct term.

1. A _____ arises from a past decision and cannot be avoided or changed; it is irrelevant to future decisions.
2. _____ refer to the incremental revenue generated from taking one particular action over another.
3. Relevant costs are also known as _____.
4. An _____ requires a future outlay of cash and is relevant for current and future decision making.
5. An _____ is the potential benefit lost by taking a specific action when two or more alternative choices are available.

EXERCISES

Exercise 10-1
Relevant costs
C1

Farrow Co. expects to sell 150,000 units of its product in the next period with the following results.

Sales (150,000 units)	$2,250,000
Costs and expenses	
Direct materials	300,000
Direct labor	600,000
Overhead	150,000
Selling expenses	225,000
Administrative expenses	385,500
Total costs and expenses	1,660,500
Net income	$ 589,500

Exercise 10-2
Accept new business or not
A1

The company has an opportunity to sell 15,000 additional units at $12 per unit. The additional sales would not affect its current expected sales. Direct materials and labor costs per unit would be the same for the additional units as they are for the regular units. However, the additional volume would create the following incremental costs: (1) total overhead would increase by 15% and (2) administrative expenses would increase by $64,500. Prepare an analysis to determine whether the company should accept or reject the offer to sell additional units at the reduced price of $12 per unit.

Check Income increase, $3,000

Goshford Company produces a single product and has capacity to produce 100,000 units per month. Costs to produce its current sales of 80,000 units follow. The regular selling price of the product is $100 per unit. Management is approached by a new customer who wants to purchase 20,000 units of the product for $75 per unit. If the order is accepted, there will be no additional fixed manufacturing overhead, and no additional fixed selling and administrative expenses. The customer is not in the company's regular selling territory, so there will be a $5 per unit shipping expense in addition to the regular variable selling and administrative expenses.

Exercise 10-3
Accept new business or not
A1

	Per Unit	Costs at 80,000 Units
Direct materials	$12.50	$1,000,000
Direct labor	15.00	1,200,000
Variable manufacturing overhead	10.00	800,000
Fixed manufacturing overhead	17.50	1,400,000
Variable selling and administrative expenses	14.00	1,120,000
Fixed selling and administrative expenses	13.00	1,040,000
Totals	$82.00	$6,560,000

1. Determine whether management should accept or reject the new business.
2. What nonfinancial factors should management consider when deciding whether to take this order?

Check (1) Additional volume effect on net income, $370,000

Exercise 10-4

Make or buy decision

A1

Check $9,500 increased costs to buy

Gilberto Company currently manufactures 65,000 units per year of one of its crucial parts. Variable costs are $1.95 per unit, fixed costs related to making this part are $75,000 per year, and allocated fixed costs are $62,000 per year. Allocated fixed costs are unavoidable whether the company makes or buys the part. Gilberto is considering buying the part from a supplier for a quoted price of $3.25 per unit guaranteed for a three-year period. Should the company continue to manufacture the part, or should it buy the part from the outside supplier? Support your answer with analyses.

Exercise 10-5

Make or buy

A1

Check   Increased cost to make, $3,000

Gelb Company currently manufactures 40,000 units per year of a key component for its manufacturing process. Variable costs are $1.95 per unit, fixed costs related to making this component are $65,000 per year, and allocated fixed costs are $58,500 per year. The allocated fixed costs are unavoidable whether the company makes or buys this component. The company is considering buying this component from a supplier for $3.50 per unit. Should it continue to manufacture the component, or should it buy this component from the outside supplier? Support your decision with analysis of the data provided.

Exercise 10-6

Scrap or rework

A1

A company must decide between scrapping or reworking units that do not pass inspection. The company has 22,000 defective units that cost $6 per unit to manufacture. The units can be sold as is for $2.50 each, or they can be reworked for $4.50 each and then sold for the full price of $8.50 each. If the units are sold as is, the company will be able to build 22,000 replacement units at a cost of $6 each, and sell them at the full price of $8.50 each. (1) What is the incremental income from selling the units as scrap? (2) What is the incremental income from reworking and selling the units? (3) Should the company sell the units as scrap or rework them?

Exercise 10-7

Scrap or rework   A1

Check   Incremental net income of reworking, $(6,000)

Varto Company has 7,000 units of its sole product in inventory that it produced last year at a cost of $22 each. This year's model is superior to last year's and the 7,000 units cannot be sold at last year's regular selling price of $35 each. Varto has two alternatives for these items: (1) they can be sold to a wholesaler for $8 each, or (2) they can be reworked at a cost of $125,000 and then sold for $25 each. Prepare an analysis to determine whether Varto should sell the products as is or rework them and then sell them.

Exercise 10-8

Sell or process further

A1

Cobe Company has already manufactured 28,000 units of Product A at a cost of $28 per unit. The 28,000 units can be sold at this stage for $700,000. Alternatively, the units can be further processed at a $420,000 total additional cost and be converted into 5,600 units of Product B and 11,200 units of Product C. Per unit selling price for Product B is $105 and for Product C is $70. Prepare an analysis that shows whether the 28,000 units of Product A should be processed further or not.

Exercise 10-9

Sales mix determination and analysis

A1

Check   (2) $55,940

Colt Company owns a machine that can produce two specialized products. Production time for Product TLX is two units per hour and for Product MTV is five units per hour. The machine's capacity is 2,750 hours per year. Both products are sold to a single customer who has agreed to buy all of the company's output up to a maximum of 4,700 units of Product TLX and 2,500 units of Product MTV. Selling prices and variable costs per unit to produce the products follow. Determine (1) the company's most profitable sales mix and (2) the contribution margin that results from that sales mix.

	Product TLX	Product MTV
Selling price per unit	$15.00	$9.50
Variable costs per unit	4.80	5.50

Exercise 10-10

Analysis of income effects from eliminating departments

A1

Suresh Co. expects its five departments to yield the following income for next year.

	A	B	C	D	E	F	G
1		Dept. M	Dept. N	Dept. O	Dept. P	Dept. T	Total
2	Sales	$63,000	$35,000	$56,000	$42,000	$ 28,000	$224,000
3	Expenses						
4	Avoidable	9,800	36,400	22,400	14,000	37,800	120,400
5	Unavoidable	51,800	12,600	4,200	29,400	9,800	107,800
6	Total expenses	61,600	49,000	26,600	43,400	47,600	228,200
7	Net income (loss)	$ 1,400	$(14,000)	$29,400	$(1,400)	$ (19,600)	$ (4,200)
8							

Recompute and prepare the departmental income statements (including a combined total column) for the company under each of the following separate scenarios: Management (1) eliminates departments with expected net losses, and (2) eliminates departments with sales dollars that are less than avoidable expenses. Explain your answers to parts 1 and 2.

Check   Total income (loss)
(1) $(21,000), (2) $7,000

Childress Company produces three products, K1, S5, and G9. Each product uses the same type of direct material. K1 uses 4 pounds of the material, S5 uses 3 pounds of the material, and G9 uses 6 pounds of the material. Demand for all products is strong, but only 50,000 pounds of material are available. Information about the selling price per unit and variable cost per unit of each product follows. Orders for which product should be produced and filled first, then second, and then third? Support your answer.

Exercise 10-11
Sales mix
A1

	K1	S5	G9
Selling price	$160	$112	$210
Variable costs	96	85	144

Check   K1 contribution
margin per pound, $16

Xinhong Company is considering replacing one of its manufacturing machines. The machine has a book value of $45,000 and a remaining useful life of 5 years, at which time its salvage value will be zero. It has a current market value of $52,000. Variable manufacturing costs are $36,000 per year for this machine. Information on two alternative replacement machines follows. Should Xinhong keep or replace its manufacturing machine? If the machine should be replaced, which alternative new machine should Xinhong purchase?

Exercise 10-12
Keep or replace
A1

	Alternative A	Alternative B
Cost	$115,000	$125,000
Variable manufacturing costs per year.........	19,000	15,000

Marinette Company makes several products, including canoes. The company has been experiencing losses from its canoe segment and is considering dropping that product line. The following information is available regarding its canoe segment. Should management discontinue the manufacturing of canoes? Support your decision.

Exercise 10-13
Income analysis of eliminating departments
A1

MARINETTE COMPANY
Income Statement—Canoe Segment

Sales		$2,000,000
Variable costs		
Direct materials......................	$450,000	
Direct labor	500,000	
Variable overhead....................	300,000	
Variable selling and administrative.........	200,000	
Total variable costs		1,450,000
Contribution margin		550,000
Fixed costs		
Direct...........................	375,000	
Indirect........................	300,000	
Total fixed costs......................		675,000
Net income		$ (125,000)

Check   Income impact if
canoe segment dropped,
$(175,000)

PROBLEM SET A

Problem 10-1A
Analysis of income
effects of additional
business

A1

Jones Products manufactures and sells to wholesalers approximately 400,000 packages per year of underwater markers at $6 per package. Annual costs for the production and sale of this quantity are shown in the table.

Direct materials...............	$ 576,000
Direct labor...................	144,000
Overhead.....................	320,000
Selling expenses...............	150,000
Administrative expenses.........	100,000
Total costs and expenses........	$1,290,000

A new wholesaler has offered to buy 50,000 packages for $5.20 each. These markers would be marketed under the wholesaler's name and would not affect Jones Products's sales through its normal channels. A study of the costs of this additional business reveals the following:

● Direct materials costs are 100% variable.
● Per unit direct labor costs for the additional units would be 50% higher than normal because their production would require overtime pay at 1½ times the usual labor rate.
● Twenty-five percent of the normal annual overhead costs are fixed at any production level from 350,000 to 500,000 units. The remaining 75% of the annual overhead cost is variable with volume.
● Accepting the new business would involve no additional selling expenses.
● Accepting the new business would increase administrative expenses by a $5,000 fixed amount.

Required

Check Operating income:
(1) $1,110,000
(2) $126,000

Prepare a three-column comparative income statement that shows the following:
1. Annual operating income without the special order (column 1).
2. Annual operating income received from the new business only (column 2).
3. Combined annual operating income from normal business and the new business (column 3).

Problem 10-2A
Analysis of income
effects of additional
business

P1   A1

Calla Company produces skateboards that sell for $50 per unit. The company currently has the capacity to produce 90,000 skateboards per year, but is selling 80,000 skateboards per year. Annual costs for 80,000 skateboards follow.

Direct materials...............	$ 800,000
Direct labor...................	640,000
Overhead.....................	960,000
Selling expenses...............	560,000
Administrative expenses.........	480,000
Total costs and expenses........	$3,440,000

A new retail store has offered to buy 10,000 of its skateboards for $45 per unit. The store is in a different market from Calla's regular customers and would not affect regular sales. A study of its costs in anticipation of this additional business reveals the following:

● Direct materials and direct labor are 100% variable.
● Thirty percent of overhead is fixed at any production level from 80,000 units to 90,000 units; the remaining 70% of annual overhead costs are variable with respect to volume.
● Selling expenses are 60% variable with respect to number of units sold, and the other 40% of selling expenses are fixed.
● There will be an additional $2 per unit selling expense for this order.
● Administrative expenses would increase by a $1,000 fixed amount.

Required

1. Prepare a three-column comparative income statement that reports the following:

   a. Annual income without the special order.

   b. Annual income from the special order.

   c. Combined annual income from normal business and the new business.

Check   (1b) Added income from order, $123,000

2. Should Calla accept this order? What nonfinancial factors should Calla consider? Explain.

Analysis Component

3. Assume that the new customer wants to buy 15,000 units instead of 10,000 units—it will only buy 15,000 units or none and will not take a partial order. Without any computations, how does this change your answer for part 2?

Haver Company currently produces component RX5 for its sole product. The current cost per unit to manufacture the required 50,000 units of RX5 follows.

Problem 10-3A
Make or buy

P1   A1

Direct materials	$ 5.00
Direct labor	8.00
Overhead	9.00
Total cost per unit	$22.00

Direct materials and direct labor are 100% variable. Overhead is 80% fixed. An outside supplier has offered to supply the 50,000 units of RX5 for $18.00 per unit.

Required

1. Determine whether the company should make or buy the RX5.

2. What factors besides cost must management consider when deciding whether to make or buy RX5?

Check   (1) Incremental cost to make RX5, $740,000

Harold Manufacturing produces denim clothing. This year, it produced 5,000 denim jackets at a manufacturing cost of $45 each. These jackets were damaged in the warehouse during storage. Management investigated the matter and identified three alternatives for these jackets.

Problem 10-4A
Sell or process

P1   A1

1. Jackets can be sold to a secondhand clothing shop for $6 each.

2. Jackets can be disassembled at a cost of $32,000 and sold to a recycler for $12 each.

3. Jackets can be reworked and turned into good jackets. However, with the damage, management estimates it will be able to assemble the good parts of the 5,000 jackets into only 3,000 jackets. The remaining pieces of fabric will be discarded. The cost of reworking the jackets will be $102,000, but the jackets can then be sold for their regular price of $45 each.

Required

Which alternative should Harold choose? Show analysis for each alternative.

Check   Incremental income for alternative 2, $28,000

Edgerron Company is able to produce two products, G and B, with the same machine in its factory. The following information is available.

Problem 10-5A
Analysis of sales mix strategies

A1

	Product G	Product B
Selling price per unit	$120	$160
Variable costs per unit	40	90
Contribution margin per unit	$ 80	$ 70
Machine hours to produce 1 unit	0.4 hours	1.0 hours
Maximum unit sales per month	600 units	200 units

The company presently operates the machine for a single eight-hour shift for 22 working days each month. Management is thinking about operating the machine for two shifts, which will increase its productivity by another eight hours per day for 22 days per month. This change would require $15,000 additional fixed costs per month.

Required

1. Determine the contribution margin per machine hour that each product generates.

2. How many units of Product G and Product B should the company produce if it continues to operate with only one shift? How much total contribution margin does this mix produce each month?

3. If the company adds another shift, how many units of Product G and Product B should it produce? How much total contribution margin would this mix produce each month? Should the company add the new shift? Explain.

4. Suppose that the company determines that it can increase Product G's maximum sales to 700 units per month by spending $12,000 per month in marketing efforts. Should the company pursue this strategy and the double shift? Explain.

Problem 10-6A

Analysis of possible elimination of a department

A1

Elegant Decor Company's management is trying to decide whether to eliminate Department 200, which has produced losses or low profits for several years. The company's 2015 departmental income statements show the following.

ELEGANT DECOR COMPANY Departmental Income Statements For Year Ended December 31, 2015			
	Dept. 100	Dept. 200	Combined
Sales	$436,000	$290,000	$726,000
Cost of goods sold	262,000	207,000	469,000
Gross profit	174,000	83,000	257,000
Operating expenses			
Direct expenses			
Advertising.........................	17,000	12,000	29,000
Store supplies used	4,000	3,800	7,800
Depreciation—Store equipment	5,000	3,300	8,300
Total direct expenses	26,000	19,100	45,100
Allocated expenses			
Sales salaries	65,000	39,000	104,000
Rent expense.......................	9,440	4,720	14,160
Bad debts expense	9,900	8,100	18,000
Office salary	18,720	12,480	31,200
Insurance expense	2,000	1,100	3,100
Miscellaneous office expenses	2,400	1,600	4,000
Total allocated expenses	107,460	67,000	174,460
Total expenses........................	133,460	86,100	219,560
Net income (loss)	$ 40,540	$ (3,100)	$ 37,440

In analyzing whether to eliminate Department 200, management considers the following:

a. The company has one office worker who earns $600 per week, or $31,200 per year, and four sales-clerks who each earn $500 per week, or $26,000 per year for each salesclerk.

b. The full salaries of two salesclerks are charged to Department 100. The full salary of one salesclerk is charged to Department 200. The salary of the fourth clerk, who works half-time in both departments, is divided evenly between the two departments.

c. Eliminating Department 200 would avoid the sales salaries and the office salary currently allocated to it. However, management prefers another plan. Two salesclerks have indicated that they will be quit-ting soon. Management believes that their work can be done by the other two clerks if the one office worker works in sales half-time. Eliminating Department 200 will allow this shift of duties. If this change is implemented, half the office worker's salary would be reported as sales salaries and half would be reported as office salary.

d. The store building is rented under a long-term lease that cannot be changed. Therefore, Department 100 will use the space and equipment currently used by Department 200.

e. Closing Department 200 will eliminate its expenses for advertising, bad debts, and store supplies; 70% of the insurance expense allocated to it to cover its merchandise inventory; and 25% of the miscella-neous office expenses presently allocated to it.

Required

1. Prepare a three-column report that lists items and amounts for (a) the company's total expenses (including cost of goods sold)—in column 1, (b) the expenses that would be eliminated by closing Department 200—in column 2, and (c) the expenses that will continue—in column 3.

2. Prepare a forecasted annual income statement for the company reflecting the elimination of Department 200 assuming that it will not affect Department 100's sales and gross profit. The statement should reflect the reassignment of the office worker to one-half time as a salesclerk.

Analysis Component

3. Reconcile the company's combined net income with the forecasted net income assuming that Department 200 is eliminated (list both items and amounts). Analyze the reconciliation and explain why you think the department should or should not be eliminated.

Check   (1) Total expenses:
(a) $688,560, (b) $284,070

(2) Forecasted net income without Department 200, $31,510

Windmire Company manufactures and sells to local wholesalers approximately 300,000 units per month at a sales price of $4 per unit. Monthly costs for the production and sale of this quantity follow.

Direct materials	$384,000
Direct labor	96,000
Overhead	288,000
Selling expenses	120,000
Administrative expenses	80,000
Total costs and expenses.	$968,000

A new out-of-state distributor has offered to buy 50,000 units next month for $3.44 each. These units would be marketed in other states and would not affect Windmire's sales through its normal channels. A study of the costs of this new business reveals the following:

● Direct materials costs are 100% variable.

● Per unit direct labor costs for the additional units would be 50% higher than normal because their production would require overtime pay at 1½ times their normal rate to meet the distributor's deadline.

● Twenty-five percent of the normal annual overhead costs are fixed at any production level from 250,000 to 400,000 units. The remaining 75% is variable with volume.

● Accepting the new business would involve no additional selling expenses.

● Accepting the new business would increase administrative expenses by a $4,000 fixed amount.

Required

Prepare a three-column comparative income statement that shows the following:

1. Monthly operating income without the special order (column 1).
2. Monthly operating income received from the new business only (column 2).
3. Combined monthly operating income from normal business and the new business (column 3).

Check   Operating income:
(1) $232,000, (2) $44,000

PROBLEM SET B

Problem 10-1B
Analysis of income effects of additional business

A1

Mervin Company produces circuit boards that sell for $8 per unit. It currently has capacity to produce 600,000 circuit boards per year, but is selling 550,000 boards per year. Annual costs for the 550,000 circuit boards follow.

Direct materials	$ 825,000
Direct labor	1,100,000
Overhead	1,375,000
Selling expenses	275,000
Administrative expenses	550,000
Total costs and expenses.	$4,125,000

Problem 10-2B
Analysis of income effects of additional business

P1   A1

An overseas customer has offered to buy 50,000 circuit boards for $6 per unit. The customer is in a different market from Mervin's regular customers and would not affect regular sales. A study of its costs in anticipation of this additional business reveals the following:

- Direct materials and direct labor are 100% variable.
- Twenty percent of overhead is fixed at any production level from 550,000 units to 600,000 units; the remaining 80% of annual overhead costs are variable with respect to volume.
- Selling expenses are 40% variable with respect to number of units sold, and the other 60% of selling expenses are fixed.
- There will be an additional $0.20 per unit selling expense for this order.
- Administrative expenses would increase by a $700 fixed amount.

Required

1. Prepare a three-column comparative income statement that reports the following:
   a. Annual income without the special order.

Check (1b) Additional income from order, $4,300

   b. Annual income from the special order.
   c. Combined annual income from normal business and the new business.
2. Should management accept the order? What nonfinancial factors should Mervin consider? Explain.

Analysis Component

3. Assume that the new customer wants to buy 100,000 units instead of 50,000 units—it will only buy 100,000 units or none and will not take a partial order. Without any computations, how does this change your answer in part 2?

Problem 10-3B
Make or buy
P1 A1

Alto Company currently produces component TH1 for its sole product. The current cost per unit to manufacture its required 400,000 units of TH1 follows.

Direct materials	$1.20
Direct labor	1.50
Overhead.	6.00
Total cost per unit	$8.70

Direct materials and direct labor are 100% variable. Overhead is 75% fixed. An outside supplier has offered to supply the 400,000 units of TH1 for $4 per unit.

Required

Check (1) Incremental cost to make TH1, $1,680,000

1. Determine whether management should make or buy the TH1.
2. What factors besides cost must management consider when deciding whether to make or buy TH1?

Problem 10-4B
Sell or process
P1 A1

Micron Manufacturing produces electronic equipment. This year, it produced 7,500 oscilloscopes at a manufacturing cost of $300 each. These oscilloscopes were damaged in the warehouse during storage and, while usable, cannot be sold at their regular selling price of $500 each. Management has investigated the matter and has identified three alternatives for these oscilloscopes.

1. They can be sold to a wholesaler for $75 each.
2. They can be disassembled at a cost of $400,000 and the parts sold to a recycler for $130 each.
3. They can be reworked and turned into good units. The cost of reworking the units will be $3,200,000, after which the units can be sold at their regular price of $500 each.

Required

Check Incremental income for alternative 2, $575,000

Which alternative should management pursue? Show analysis for each alternative.

Sung Company is able to produce two products, R and T, with the same machine in its factory. The following information is available.

Problem 10-5B
Analysis of sales mix strategies

A1

	Product R	Product T
Selling price per unit	$60	$80
Variable costs per unit.	20	45
Contribution margin per unit	$40	$35
Machine hours to produce 1 unit	0.4 hours	1.0 hours
Maximum unit sales per month.	550 units	175 units

The company presently operates the machine for a single eight-hour shift for 22 working days each month. Management is thinking about operating the machine for two shifts, which will increase its productivity by another eight hours per day for 22 days per month. This change would require $3,250 additional fixed costs per month.

Required

1. Determine the contribution margin per machine hour that each product generates.

2. How many units of Product R and Product T should the company produce if it continues to operate with only one shift? How much total contribution margin does this mix produce each month?

3. If the company adds another shift, how many units of Product R and Product T should it produce? How much total contribution margin would this mix produce each month? Should the company add the new shift? Explain.

4. Suppose that the company determines that it can increase Product R's maximum sales to 675 units per month by spending $4,500 per month in marketing efforts. Should the company pursue this strategy and the double shift? Explain.

Check Units of Product R:
(2) 440

(3) 550

Esme Company's management is trying to decide whether to eliminate Department Z, which has produced low profits or losses for several years. The company's 2015 departmental income statements show the following.

Problem 10-6B
Analysis of possible elimination of a department

A1

ESME COMPANY
Departmental Income Statements
For Year Ended December 31, 2015

	Dept. A	Dept. Z	Combined
Sales	$700,000	$175,000	$875,000
Cost of goods sold	461,300	125,100	586,400
Gross profit	238,700	49,900	288,600
Operating expenses			
Direct expenses			
Advertising.	27,000	3,000	30,000
Store supplies used	5,600	1,400	7,000
Depreciation—Store equipment	14,000	7,000	21,000
Total direct expenses	46,600	11,400	58,000
Allocated expenses			
Sales salaries	70,200	23,400	93,600
Rent expense.	22,080	5,520	27,600
Bad debts expense	21,000	4,000	25,000
Office salary	20,800	5,200	26,000
Insurance expense.	4,200	1,400	5,600
Miscellaneous office expenses	1,700	2,500	4,200
Total allocated expenses	139,980	42,020	182,000
Total expenses.	186,580	53,420	240,000
Net income (loss)	$ 52,120	$ (3,520)	$ 48,600

In analyzing whether to eliminate Department Z, management considers the following items:

a. The company has one office worker who earns $500 per week or $26,000 per year and four salesclerks who each earn $450 per week or $23,400 per year for each salesclerk.

b. The full salaries of three salesclerks are charged to Department A. The full salary of one salesclerk is charged to Department Z.

c. Eliminating Department Z would avoid the sales salaries and the office salary currently allocated to it. However, management prefers another plan. Two salesclerks have indicated that they will be quitting soon. Management believes that their work can be done by the two remaining clerks if the one office worker works in sales half-time. Eliminating Department Z will allow this shift of duties. If this change is implemented, half the office worker's salary would be reported as sales salaries and half would be reported as office salary.

d. The store building is rented under a long-term lease that cannot be changed. Therefore, Department A will use the space and equipment currently used by Department Z.

e. Closing Department Z will eliminate its expenses for advertising, bad debts, and store supplies; 65% of the insurance expense allocated to it to cover its merchandise inventory; and 30% of the miscellaneous office expenses presently allocated to it.

Required

Check   (1) Total expenses: (a) $826,400, (b) $181,960

(2) Forecasted net income without Department Z, $55,560

1. Prepare a three-column report that lists items and amounts for (a) the company's total expenses (including cost of goods sold)—in column 1, (b) the expenses that would be eliminated by closing Department Z—in column 2, and (c) the expenses that will continue—in column 3.

2. Prepare a forecasted annual income statement for the company reflecting the elimination of Department Z assuming that it will not affect Department A's sales and gross profit. The statement should reflect the reassignment of the office worker to one-half time as a salesclerk.

Analysis Component

3. Reconcile the company's combined net income with the forecasted net income assuming that Department Z is eliminated (list both items and amounts). Analyze the reconciliation and explain why you think the department should or should not be eliminated.

SERIAL PROBLEM
Business Solutions

A1

(This serial problem began in Chapter 1 and continues through most of the book. If previous chapter segments were not completed, the serial problem can begin at this point. It is helpful, but not necessary, to use the Working Papers that accompany the book.)

SP 10   Santana Rey has found that her line of computer desks and chairs has become very popular and she is finding it hard to keep up with demand. She knows that she cannot fill all of her orders for both items, so she decides she must determine the optimal sales mix given the resources she has available. Information about the desks and chairs follows.

	Desks	Chairs
Selling price per unit	$1,125	$375
Variable costs per unit	500	200
Contribution margin per unit	$ 625	$175
Direct labor hours per unit	5 hours	4 hours
Expected demand for next quarter	175 desks	50 chairs

Santana has determined that she only has 1,015 direct labor hours available for the next quarter and wants to optimize her contribution margin given the limited number of direct labor hours available.

Required

Determine the optimal sales mix and the contribution margin the business will earn at that sales mix.

Beyond the Numbers

BTN 10-1 Apple currently chooses to buy (mainly from suppliers located in Asia)—rather than make—nearly all of its manufactured products. Assume you have been asked to analyze whether Apple should instead make its products.

REPORTING IN ACTION
P1 C1
APPLE

Required

1. Provide examples of relevant costs that Apple should consider in this make or buy decision.
2. Provide examples of qualitative (nonfinancial) factors Apple should consider in this decision.

BTN 10-2 Apple and Google sell a variety of products, including smartphones and tablet computers. Some products are more profitable than others. Teams of employees in each company make advertising, investment, and product mix decisions. A certain portion of advertising for both companies is on a local basis to a target audience.

COMPARATIVE ANALYSIS
A1
APPLE
GOOGLE

Required

1. Contact the local newspaper and ask the approximate cost of ad space (for example, cost of one page or one-half page of advertising) for a company's product or group of products (such as Apple iPads).
2. Estimate how many products this advertisement must sell to justify its cost. Begin by taking the product's sales price advertised for each company and assume a 20% contribution margin.
3. Prepare a half-page memorandum explaining the importance of effective advertising when making a product mix decision. Be prepared to present your ideas in class.

BTN 10-3 Bert Asiago, a salesperson for Convertco, received an order from a potential new customer for 50,000 units of Convertco's single product at a price $25 below its regular selling price of $65. Asiago knows that Convertco has the capacity to produce this order without affecting regular sales. He has spoken to Convertco's controller, Bia Morgan, who has informed Asiago that at the $40 selling price, Convertco will not be covering its variable costs of $42 for the product, and she recommends the order not be accepted. Asiago knows that variable costs include his sales commission of $4 per unit. If he accepts a $2 per unit commission, the sale will produce a contribution margin of zero. Asiago is eager to get the new customer because he believes that this could lead to the new customer becoming a regular customer.

ETHICS CHALLENGE
A1

Required

1. Determine the contribution margin per unit on the order as determined by the controller.
2. Determine the contribution margin per unit on the order as determined by Asiago if he takes the lower commission.
3. Do you recommend Convertco accept the special order? What factors must management consider?

BTN 10-4 Assume that you work for Greeble's Department Store, and your manager requests that you outline the pros and cons of discontinuing its hardware department. That department appears to be generating losses, and your manager believes that discontinuing it will increase overall store profits.

COMMUNICATING IN PRACTICE
P1

Required

Prepare a memorandum to your manager outlining what Greeble's management should consider when trying to decide whether to discontinue its hardware department.

TAKING IT TO THE NET

A1

BTN 10-5 Many companies must determine whether to internally produce their component parts or to outsource them. Further, some companies now outsource key components or business processes to international providers. Access the website sourcingmag.com and review the available information on business process outsourcing (click on "What is BPO?").

Required

1. According to this website, what is business process outsourcing?
2. What types of processes are commonly outsourced, according to this website?
3. What are some of the benefits of business process outsourcing?

TEAMWORK IN ACTION

P1

BTN 10-6 Break into teams and identify costs that an airline such as Delta Airlines would incur on a flight from Green Bay to Minneapolis. (1) Identify the individual costs as variable or fixed. (2) Assume that Delta is trying to decide whether to drop this flight because it seems to be unprofitable. Determine which costs are likely to be saved if the flight is dropped. Set up your answer in the following format.

Cost	Variable or Fixed	Cost Saved if Flight Is Dropped	Rationale

ENTREPRENEURIAL DECISION

A1

BTN 10-7 Charlie Fyffe of Charlie's Brownies makes brownies and other sweets. Charlie must decide on the best sales mix for his products. Assume that his company has a capacity of 400 hours of processing time available each month and it makes two types of brownies, Deluxe and Premium. Information on these foods follows.

	Deluxe	Premium
Selling price per carton	$70	$90
Variable costs per carton	$40	$50
Processing minutes per carton	60 minutes	120 minutes

Required

1. Assume the markets for both cartons of brownies are unlimited. How many Deluxe cartons and how many Premium cartons should the company make each month? Explain. How much total contribution margin does this mix produce each month?
2. Assume the market for the Deluxe carton is limited to 60 cartons per month, with no market limit for the Premium cartons. How many Deluxe cartons and how many Premium cartons should the company make each month? Explain. How much total contribution margin does this mix produce each month?

HITTING THE ROAD

P1

BTN 10-8 Restaurants often add and remove menu items. Visit a restaurant and identify a new food item. Make a list of costs that the restaurant must consider when deciding whether to add that new item. Also, make a list of nonfinancial factors that the restaurant must consider when adding that item.

GLOBAL DECISION

C1

Samsung

BTN 10-9 Access Samsung's 2013 Corporate Sustainability Report, from its website www.samsung.com. Identify and read the section "Social Responsibility: Making Contributions Around the Globe."

Required

Samsung's 2013 Corporate Sustainability Report notes that the company spent 245 billion Korean won in 2012 for programs devoted to better health and education for children. Why would a company like Samsung pursue such a costly program?

ANSWERS TO MULTIPLE CHOICE QUIZ

1. a; Reworking provides incremental revenue of $11 per unit ($19 − $8); it costs $10 to rework them. The company is better off by $1 per unit when it reworks these products and sells them at the regular price.

2. e; Product X has a $2 contribution margin per machine hour [($32 − $12)/10 MH]; Product Y has a $7 contribution margin per machine hour [($24 − $10)/2 MH]. It should produce as much of Product Y as possible.

3. a; Total revenue from the special order = 3,000 units × $15 per unit = $45,000; total costs for the special order = (3,000 units × $9 per unit) + $5,000 = $32,000. Net income from the special order = $45,000 − $32,000 = $13,000. Thus, yes, it should accept the order.

4. c

5. d

11

Capital Budgeting and Investment Analysis

Chapter Preview

NONPRESENT VALUE METHODS	PRESENT VALUE METHODS	COMPARISON AND ANALYSIS
P1 Payback period	**P3** Net present value	Comparison of methods
P2 Accounting rate of return	**P4** Internal rate of return	**A1** Break-even time

Learning Objectives

ANALYTICAL

A1 Analyze a capital investment project using break-even time.

PROCEDURAL

P1 Compute payback period and describe its use.

P2 Compute accounting rate of return and explain its use.

P3 Compute net present value and describe its use.

P4 Compute internal rate of return and explain its use.

NEW YORK—Studying computer science and electrical engineering, Limor Fried used the skills she learned in class to make electrical devices like MP3 players, synthesizers, and toys. Thinking others might like her designs, she posted instructions for her projects on her website. Inundated with requests to sell her designs as project kits, Limor invested her tuition money in a large quantity of parts and began designing. The result is her company **Adafruit Industries**, which now boasts sales of over $22 million per year.

Adafruit started small, with one employee (Limor) operating out of her dorm room. "The company took off," says Limor, "because we sold learning projects that you would actually use or want to keep." Projects like MintyBoost (a mobile-device charger assembled from an Altoids tin and electronic components), a set of bicycle lights that spell out words and draw symbols as you ride, and a mini-electric guitar are both fun to make and fun to use. "The idea is that people will learn a little about electronics by assembling the kits, and, in the end have a handmade good that is also useful."

Limor uses accounting information to make business decisions. She priced her kits to yield about a $10 contribution margin per kit. These profits enabled her to hire more employees and expand her business. Focusing on contribution margins enables Adafruit to add more-profitable products and eliminate less-profitable products. In addition to profits, Limor must consider qualitative factors in her decisions, and she focuses on customer satisfaction. "Everything is designed to be painless," says Ada. "I spend a lot of time thinking about how customers will interact with products, and we always give good documentation."

In addition to short-term decisions involving sales mix, Limor had to confront decisions regarding capital investments. Recently, the company moved from a small loft into a 12,000-square-foot industrial space. The industrial-grade power supply in this new space enabled investments in large equipment, enabling faster production. Net present value calculations, based on the cost of this new equipment and the future cash flows from additional sales, support such decisions. "It's a new chapter in our business," exclaims Limor. "I think we can quadruple our current size."

Courtesy of Adafruit Industries

High Energy

"We put our heart and soul into it . . . every day"
—Limor Fried

For Limor, though, business is not just about making more profit. She is passionate about education, and in particular about encouraging young women to pursue engineering and related technical fields. "It is possible to help people all while running a business," she says. Limor encourages young entrepreneurs to "go for it." "Entrepreneurship is cool," says Limor. "It's about freedom, the ability to do great work with great people for great customers. It's hard to do this if you are working for someone else."

Sources: *Adafruit Industries website,* January 2015; *Entrepreneur.com,* December 18, 2012; *New York Times,* November 15, 2007

Capital budgeting is the process of analyzing alternative long-term investments and deciding which assets to acquire or sell. Common examples of capital budgeting decisions include buying a machine or a building or acquiring an entire company. An objective for these decisions is to earn a satisfactory return on investment.

Capital budgeting decisions require careful analysis because they are usually the most difficult and risky decisions that managers make. These decisions are difficult because they require predicting events that will not occur until well into the future. Many of these predictions are tentative and potentially unreliable. Specifically, a capital budgeting decision is risky because (1) the outcome is uncertain, (2) large amounts of money are usually involved, (3) the investment involves a long-term commitment, and (4) the decision could be difficult or impossible to reverse, no matter how poor it turns out to be. Risk is especially high for investments in technology due to innovations and uncertainty.

Managers use several methods to evaluate capital budgeting decisions. Nearly all of these methods involve predicting future cash inflows and cash outflows of proposed investments, assessing the risk of and returns on those cash flows, and then choosing the investments to make. Management often restates future cash flows in terms of their present value. This approach applies the time value of money: A dollar today is worth more than a dollar tomorrow. Similarly, a dollar tomorrow is worth less than a dollar today. The process of restating future cash flows in terms of their present value is called *discounting*. The time value of money is important when evaluating capital investments, but managers sometimes apply evaluation methods that ignore present value. This chapter describes four methods for comparing alternative investments.

Point: The nature of capital spending has changed with the business environment. Budgets for information technology have increased from about 25% of corporate capital spending 20 years ago to an estimated 35% today.

METHODS NOT USING TIME VALUE OF MONEY

All investments, whether they involve the purchase of a machine or another long-term asset, are expected to produce net cash flows. *Net cash flow* is cash inflows minus cash outflows. Sometimes managers perform simple analyses of the financial feasibility of an investment's net cash flow without using the time value of money. This section explains two of the most common methods in this category: (1) payback period and (2) accounting rate of return.

Payback Period

P1
_____

Compute payback period and describe its use.

An investment's **payback period (PBP)** is the expected amount of time to recover the initial investment amount. Managers prefer investing in assets with shorter payback periods to reduce the risk of an unprofitable investment over the long run. Acquiring assets with short payback periods reduces a company's risk from potentially inaccurate long-term predictions of future cash flows.

Computing Payback Period with Even Cash Flows   To illustrate use of the payback period for an investment with even cash flows, we look at data from FasTrac, a manufacturer of exercise equipment and supplies. (*Even cash flows* are cash flows that are the same each and every year; *uneven cash flows* are cash flows that are not all equal in amount.) FasTrac is considering several different capital investments, one of which is to purchase a machine to use in manufacturing a new product. This machine costs $16,000 and is expected to have an eight-year life with no salvage value. Management predicts this machine will produce 1,000 units of product each year and that the new product will be sold for $30 per unit. Exhibit 11.1 shows the expected net income and expected annual net cash flows for this asset over its life.

The amount of net cash flow from the machinery is computed by subtracting expected cash outflows from expected cash inflows. The Expected Net Cash Flow column of Exhibit 11.1 excludes all noncash revenues and expenses. Depreciation is FasTrac's only noncash item. Alternatively, managers can adjust the projected net income for revenue and expense items that do not affect cash flows. For FasTrac, this means taking the $2,100 net income and adding back the $2,000 depreciation, to yield $4,100 of net cash flow.

Point: Annual net cash flow in Exhibit 11.1 equals net income plus depreciation (a noncash expense).

EXHIBIT 11.1

Cash Flow Analysis

FASTRAC Cash Flow Analysis—Machinery Investment January 15, 2015	Expected Net Income	Expected Net Cash Flow
Annual sales of new product	$30,000	$30,000
Deduct annual expenses		
Cost of materials, labor, and overhead (except depreciation)	15,500	15,500
Depreciation—Machinery	2,000	
Additional selling and administrative expenses....................	9,500	9,500
Annual pretax income	3,000	
Income taxes (30%)	900	900
Annual net income	$ 2,100	
Annual net cash flow...		$ 4,100

The formula for computing the payback period of an investment that yields even net cash flows is in Exhibit 11.2.

$$\text{Payback period} = \frac{\text{Cost of investment}}{\text{Annual net cash flow}}$$

EXHIBIT 11.2

Payback Period Formula with Even Cash Flows

The payback period reflects the amount of time for the investment to generate enough net cash flow to return (or pay back) the cash initially invested to purchase it. FasTrac's payback period for this machine is just under four years:

$$\text{Payback period} = \frac{\$16,000}{\$4,100} = 3.9 \text{ years}$$

The initial investment is fully recovered in 3.9 years, or just before reaching the halfway point of this machine's useful life of eight years.

Example: If an alternative machine (with different technology) yields a payback period of 3.5 years, which one does a manager choose? *Answer:* The alternative (3.5 is less than 3.9).

■ Decision Insight

e-Payback Health care providers are increasingly using electronic systems to improve their operations. With *e-charting*, doctors' orders and notes are saved electronically. Such systems allow for more personalized care plans, more efficient staffing, and reduced costs. Investments in such systems must be evaluated on the basis of payback periods and other financial measures. ■

Tetra Images/Getty Images

Computing Payback Period with Uneven Cash Flows Computing the payback period in the prior section assumed even net cash flows. What happens if the net cash flows are uneven? In this case, the payback period is computed using the *cumulative total of net cash flows*. The word *cumulative* refers to the addition of each period's net cash flows as we progress through time. To illustrate, consider data for another investment that FasTrac is considering. This machine is predicted to generate uneven net cash flows over the next eight years. The relevant data and payback period computation are shown in Exhibit 11.3.

Year 0 refers to the period of initial investment in which the $16,000 cash outflow occurs at the end of year 0 to acquire the machinery. By the end of year 1, the cumulative net cash flow is reduced to $(13,000), computed as the $(16,000) initial cash outflow plus year 1's $3,000 cash inflow. This process continues throughout the asset's life. The cumulative net cash flow amount changes from negative to positive in year 5. Specifically, at the end of year 4, the cumulative net cash flow is $(1,000). As soon as FasTrac receives net cash inflow of $1,000 during the fifth year,

Example: Find the payback period in Exhibit 11.3 if net cash flows for the first 4 years are:
Year 1 = $6,000; Year 2 = $5,000;
Year 3 = $4,000; Year 4 = $3,000.
Answer: 3.33 years

EXHIBIT 11.3

Payback Period Calculation with Uneven Cash Flows

Period*	Expected Net Cash Flows	Cumulative Net Cash Flows	
Year 0	$(16,000)	$(16,000)	
Year 1	3,000	(13,000)	
Year 2	4,000	(9,000)	
Year 3	4,000	(5,000)	
Year 4	4,000	**(1,000)**	} Payback occurs between years 4 and 5.
Year 5	**5,000**	**4,000**	
Year 6	3,000	7,000	
Year 7	2,000	9,000	
Year 8	2,000	11,000	
Payback period = 4 years + $1,000/$5,000 of year 5 = 4.2 years			

* All cash inflows and outflows occur uniformly during years 1 through 8.

it has fully recovered the $16,000 initial investment. If we assume that cash flows are received uniformly *within* each year, receipt of the $1,000 occurs about one-fifth (0.20) of the way through the fifth year. This is computed as $1,000 divided by year 5's total net cash flow of $5,000, or 0.20. This yields a payback period of 4.2 years, computed as 4 years plus 0.20 of year 5.

Using the Payback Period   Companies like short payback periods to increase return and reduce risk. The more quickly a company receives cash, the sooner it is available for other uses and the less time it is at risk of loss. A shorter payback period also improves the company's ability to respond to unanticipated changes and lowers its risk of having to keep an unprofitable investment.

Payback period should never be the only consideration in evaluating investments because it ignores at least three important factors. First, it fails to reflect differences in the timing of net cash flows within the payback period. In Exhibit 11.3, FasTrac's net cash flows in the first five years were $3,000, $4,000, $4,000, $4,000, and $5,000. If another investment had predicted cash flows of $9,000, $3,000, $2,000, $1,800, and $1,000 in these five years, its payback period would also be 4.2 years, but this second alternative could be more desirable because it returns cash more quickly. Second, payback period ignores *all* cash flows after the point where an investment's costs are fully recovered. For example, one investment might pay back its cost in 3 years but stop producing cash after 4 years. A second investment might require 5 years to pay back its cost yet continue to produce net cash flows for another 15 years. A focus on only the payback period would mistakenly lead management to choose the first investment over the second. Third, payback period ignores the time value of money.

Payback Period

P1

QC1

Do More: QS 11-1, QS 11-5, E 11-1, E 11-3, E 11-5

A company is considering purchasing equipment costing $75,000. Future annual net cash flows from this equipment are $30,000, $25,000, $15,000, $10,000, and $5,000. Cash flows occur uniformly during the year. What is this investment's payback period?

Solution

Period	Expected Net Cash Flows	Cumulative Net Cash Flows
Year 0..........	$(75,000)	$(75,000)
Year 1..........	30,000	(45,000)
Year 2..........	25,000	(20,000)
Year 3..........	15,000	(5,000)
Year 4..........	10,000	5,000
Year 5..........	5,000	10,000
Payback period = 3.5 years, computed as 3 + $5,000/$10,000		

Accounting Rate of Return

P2

Compute accounting rate of return and explain its use.

The **accounting rate of return** is the percentage accounting return on annual average investment. It is called an "accounting" return because it is based on net income, rather than on cash flows. It is computed by dividing a project's after-tax net income by the average amount invested in it. To illustrate, we return to FasTrac's $16,000 machinery investment described in

Exhibit 11.1. We first compute (1) the after-tax net income and (2) the average amount invested. The $2,100 after-tax net income is already available from Exhibit 11.1.

If a company uses straight-line depreciation, we can find the average amount invested by using the formula in Exhibit 11.4. Because FasTrac uses straight-line depreciation, its average amount invested for the eight years equals the sum of the book value at the beginning of the asset's investment period and the book value at the end of its investment period, divided by 2, as shown in Exhibit 11.4.

Point: Amount invested includes all costs that must be incurred to get the asset in its location and ready for use.

$$\text{Annual average investment} = \frac{\text{Beginning book value} + \text{Ending book value}}{2}$$
(straight-line case only)
$$= \frac{\$16,000 + \$0}{2} = \$8,000$$

EXHIBIT 11.4

Computing Average Amount Invested under Straight-Line Depreciation

If an investment has a salvage value, the average amount invested when using straight-line depreciation is computed as (Beginning book value + Salvage value)/2.

If a company uses a depreciation method other than straight-line, for example MACRS for tax purposes, the calculation of average book value is more complicated. In this case, the book value of the asset is computed for *each year* of its life. The general formula for the annual average investment is shown in Exhibit 11.5.

$$\text{Annual average investment} = \frac{\text{Sum of individual years' average book values}}{\text{Number of years of the planned investment}}$$
(general case)

EXHIBIT 11.5

General Formula for Average Amount Invested

Once we determine the annual after-tax net income and the annual average amount invested, the accounting rate of return is computed as shown in Exhibit 11.6.

$$\text{Accounting rate of return} = \frac{\text{Annual after-tax net income}}{\text{Annual average investment}}$$
$$= \frac{\$2,100}{\$8,000} = 26.25\%$$

EXHIBIT 11.6

Accounting Rate of Return Formula

FasTrac management must decide whether a 26.25% accounting rate of return is satisfactory. To make this decision, we must factor in the investment's risk. For instance, we cannot say an investment with a 26.25% return is preferred over one with a lower return unless we consider any differences in risk. When comparing investments with similar lives and risk, a company will prefer the investment with the higher accounting rate of return.

Using the Accounting Rate of Return   The accounting rate of return should never be the only consideration in evaluating investments because it has at least two important limitations: First, an asset's net income may vary from year to year. In this case, the accounting rate of return will also vary across years, and the project might appear desirable in some years and not in others. Second, the accounting rate of return ignores the time value of money.

The following data relate to a company's decision on whether to purchase a machine:

Cost.	$180,000
Salvage value	15,000
Annual after-tax net income.	40,000

Assume net cash flows occur uniformly over each year and the company uses straight-line depreciation. What is the machine's accounting rate of return?

NEED-TO-KNOW 11-2

Accounting Rate of Return

P2

QC2

Solution

Annual average investment = ($180,000 + $15,000)/2 = $97,500
Accounting rate of return   = $40,000/$97,500 = 41% (rounded)

Do More: QS 11-6, QS 11-7, E 11-7, E 11-8

METHODS USING TIME VALUE OF MONEY

Methods Using Time Value of Money

P3

Compute net present value and describe its use.

This section describes two methods that help managers with capital budgeting decisions and that use the time value of money: (1) net present value and (2) internal rate of return. *(To apply these methods, you need a basic understanding of the concept of present value. An expanded explanation of present value concepts is in Appendix B near the end of the book. You can use the present value tables at the end of Appendix B to solve many of this chapter's assignments that use the time value of money.)*

Net Present Value

Net present value analysis applies the time value of money to future cash inflows and cash outflows so management can evaluate a project's benefits and costs at one point in time. Specifically, **net present value (NPV)** is computed by discounting the future net cash flows from the investment at the project's required rate of return and then subtracting the initial amount invested. A company's required return, often called its *hurdle rate,* is typically its **cost of capital,** which is an average of the rate the company must pay to its long-term creditors and shareholders. (Computation of the cost of capital is covered in advanced courses.)

Point: The assumption of end-of-year cash flows simplifies computations and is common in practice.

To illustrate, let's return to FasTrac's proposed machinery purchase described in Exhibit 11.1. Does this machine provide a satisfactory return while recovering the amount invested? Recall that the machine requires a $16,000 investment and is expected to provide $4,100 annual net cash inflows for the next eight years. If we assume that net cash inflows from this machine are received at each year-end and that FasTrac requires a 12% annual return, net present value can be computed as in Exhibit 11.7.

EXHIBIT 11.7

Net Present Value Calculation with Equal Cash Flows

	Net Cash Flows*	Present Value of 1 at 12%**	Present Value of Net Cash Flows
Year 1	$ 4,100	0.8929	$ 3,661
Year 2	4,100	0.7972	3,269
Year 3	4,100	0.7118	2,918
Year 4	4,100	0.6355	2,606
Year 5	4,100	0.5674	2,326
Year 6	4,100	0.5066	2,077
Year 7	4,100	0.4523	1,854
Year 8	4,100	0.4039	1,656
Totals	$32,800		20,367
Amount invested (at year 0).			(16,000)
Net present value			$ 4,367

* Cash flows occur at the end of each year.
** Present value of 1 factors are taken from Table B.1 in Appendix B.

Example: What is the net present value in Exhibit 11.7 if a 10% return is applied? *Answer:* $5,873

Cost of Capital by Industry

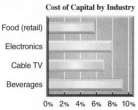

Source: www.stern.nyu.edu/adamordoran, data as of January 2014.

The first number column of Exhibit 11.7 shows the annual net cash flows. Present value of 1 factors, also called *discount factors,* are shown in the second column. Taken from Table B.1 in Appendix B, they assume that net cash flows are received at each year-end. *(To simplify present value computations and for assignment material at the end of this chapter, we assume that net cash flows are received at each year-end.)* Annual net cash flows from the first column of Exhibit 11.7 are multiplied by the discount factors in the second column to give present values of annual net cash flows shown in the third column. These annual amounts are summed to yield the total present value of net cash flows ($20,367). The last three lines of this exhibit show the final NPV computations. The asset's $16,000 initial cost is deducted from the $20,367 total present value of all future net cash flows to give this asset's NPV of $4,367. Thus, the present value of this machine's future net cash flows exceeds the initial $16,000 investment by $4,367. FasTrac should invest in this machine.

Net Present Value Decision Rule   The decision rule in applying NPV is as follows: When an asset's expected future cash flows yield a *positive* net present value when discounted at the required rate of return, the asset should be acquired. This decision rule is reflected in the graphic below. When comparing several investment opportunities of similar cost and risk, we prefer the one with the highest positive net present value.

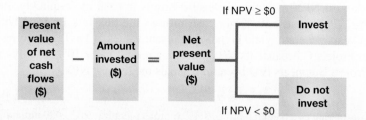

Simplifying Computations   The computations in Exhibit 11.7 use separate present value of 1 factors for each of the eight years. Each year's net cash flow is multiplied by its present value of 1 factor to determine its present value. The individual present values for each of the eight net cash flows are added to give the asset's total present value. This computation can be simplified if annual net cash flows are equal in amount. A series of cash flows of equal dollar amount is called an **annuity.** One way is to use Table B.3, which gives the present value of 1 to be received periodically for a number of periods. To determine the present value of these eight annual receipts discounted at 12%, go down the 12% column of Table B.3 to the factor on the eighth line. This cumulative discount factor, also known as an *annuity* factor, is 4.9676. We then compute the $20,367 present value for these eight annual $4,100 receipts, computed as 4.9676 × $4,100.

Example: Why does the net present value of an investment increase when a lower discount rate is used? *Answer:* The present value of net cash flows increases.

Another way to simplify present value calculations, whether net cash flows are equal in amount or not, is to use a calculator with compound interest functions or a spreadsheet program. We show how to use Excel functions to compute net present value in this chapter's appendix. Whatever procedure you use, it is important to understand the concepts behind these computations.

▉ Decision Ethics ━━━━━━━━━━━━━━━

Systems Manager   Top management adopts a policy requiring purchases in excess of $5,000 to be submitted with cash flow projections to the cost analyst for capital budget approval. As systems manager, you want to upgrade your computers at a $25,000 cost. You consider submitting several orders all under $5,000 to avoid the approval process. You believe the computers will increase profits and wish to avoid a delay. What do you do? ▉ [Answers follow the chapter's Summary.]

Uneven Cash Flows   Net present value analysis can also be applied when net cash flows are uneven (unequal). To illustrate, assume that FasTrac can choose only one capital investment from among Projects A, B, and C. Each project requires the same $12,000 initial investment. Future net cash flows for each project are shown in the first three number columns of Exhibit 11.8.

	Net Cash Flows			Present Value of 1 at 10%	Present Value of Net Cash Flows		
	A	**B**	**C**		**A**	**B**	**C**
Year 1	$ 5,000	$ 8,000	$ 1,000	0.9091	$ 4,546	$ 7,273	$ 909
Year 2	5,000	5,000	5,000	0.8264	4,132	4,132	4,132
Year 3	5,000	2,000	9,000	0.7513	3,757	1,503	6,762
Totals	$15,000	$15,000	$15,000		12,435	12,908	11,803
Amount invested					(12,000)	(12,000)	(12,000)
Net present value					$ 435	$ 908	$ (197)

EXHIBIT 11.8

Net Present Value Calculation with Uneven Cash Flows

The three projects in Exhibit 11.8 have the same expected total net cash flows of $15,000. Project A is expected to produce equal amounts of $5,000 each year. Project B is expected to produce a larger amount in the first year. Project C is expected to produce a larger amount in the third year. The fourth column of Exhibit 11.8 shows the present value of 1 factors from Table B.1 assuming 10% required return.

Computations in the right-most columns show that Project A has a $435 positive NPV. Project B has the largest NPV of $908, because it brings in cash more quickly. Project C has a $(197) *negative* NPV because its larger cash inflows are delayed. Projects with higher cash flows in earlier years generally yield higher net present values. If FasTrac requires a 10% return, it should reject Project C because its NPV implies a return *under* 10%. If only one project can be accepted, Project B appears best because it yields the highest NPV.

NEED-TO-KNOW 11-3

Net Present Value

P3

A company is considering two potential projects. Each project requires a $20,000 initial investment and is expected to generate end-of-period annual cash flows as shown below. Assuming a discount rate of 10%, compute the net present value of each project.

| | **Net Cash Inflows** | | | |
	Year 1	Year 2	Year 3	Total
Project A.........	$12,000	$8,500	$ 4,000	$24,500
Project B.........	4,500	8,500	13,000	26,000

Solution

Net present values are computed as follows:

| | | **Project A** | | **Project B** | |
Year	Present Value of 1 at 10%	Net Cash Flows	Present Value of Net Cash Flows	Net Cash Flows	Present Value of Net Cash Flows
1	0.9091	$12,000	$10,909	$ 4,500	$ 4,091
2	0.8264	8,500	7,024	8,500	7,024
3	0.7513	4,000	3,005	13,000	9,767
Totals		$24,500	$20,938	$26,000	$20,882
Amount invested			(20,000)		(20,000)
Net present value			**$ 938**		**$ 882**

QC3

Salvage Value   FasTrac predicted the $16,000 machine to have zero salvage value at the end of its useful life (recall Exhibit 11.1). In many cases, assets are expected to have salvage values. If so, this amount is an additional net cash inflow expected to be received at the end of the final year of the asset's life. All other computations remain the same. For example, the net present value of the $16,000 investment that yields $4,100 of net cash flows for eight years is $4,367, as shown in Exhibit 11.7. If that machine is expected to have a $1,500 salvage value at the end of its eight-year life, the present value of this salvage amount is $606 (computed as $1,500 × 0.4039). The net present value of the machine, including the present value of its expected salvage amount, is $4,973 (computed as $4,367 + $606).

Accelerated Depreciation   Depreciation computations also affect net present value analysis. FasTrac computes depreciation using the straight-line method. Accelerated depreciation is also commonly used, especially for income tax purposes. Accelerated depreciation produces larger depreciation deductions in the early years of an asset's life and smaller deductions in later years. This pattern results in smaller income tax payments in early years and larger payments in later years. Accelerated depreciation does not change the basics of a present value analysis, but it can change the result. Using accelerated depreciation for tax reporting affects the NPV of an asset's cash flows because it produces larger net cash inflows in the early years of the asset's life and smaller ones in later years. Being able to use accelerated depreciation for tax reporting always makes an investment more desirable because early cash flows are more valuable than later ones.

Point: Tax savings from depreciation is called *depreciation tax shield.*

Comparing Positive NPV Projects   In deciding whether to make a capital investment, we invest if the NPV is positive; we do not invest if the NPV is negative. When considering several projects of similar investment amounts and risk levels, we can compare the different projects' NPVs and rank them on the basis of their NPVs. However, if the amount invested differs substantially across projects, the NPV is of limited value for comparison purposes. One way to compare projects, especially when a company cannot fund all positive net present value projects, is to use the **profitability index,** which is computed as:

Example: When is it appropriate to use different discount rates for different projects? *Answer:* When risk levels are different.

$$\text{Profitability index} = \frac{\text{Present value of net cash flows}}{\text{Investment}}$$

Exhibit 11.9 illustrates the computation of the profitability index for three potential investments.

	Investment		
	1	2	3
Present value of net cash flows (a)	$900,000	$375,000	$270,000
Amount invested (b)	750,000	250,000	300,000
Profitability index (a)/(b)	1.2	1.5	0.90

EXHIBIT 11.9

Profitability Index

A profitability index less than 1 indicates an investment with a *negative* net present value. These potential investments, like Investment 3 in Exhibit 11.9, are eliminated from further consideration. Both Investments 1 and 2 have profitability indexes greater than 1, thus they have positive net present values. For example, Investment 1's NPV equals $150,000 (computed as $900,000 − $750,000); Investment 2's NPV equals $125,000 (computed as $375,000 − $250,000). Ideally, the company would accept all positive NPV projects, but if forced to choose, it should select the project with the higher profitability index. Thus, Investment 2 would be ranked ahead of Investment 1, based on its higher profitability index.

Inflation   Large price-level increases should be considered in NPV analyses. Discount rates should already include inflation forecasts. Net cash flows can be adjusted for inflation by using *future value* computations. For example, if the expected net cash inflow in year 1 is $4,100 and 5% inflation is expected, then the expected net cash inflow in year 2 is $4,305, computed as $4,100 × 1.05 (1.05 is the future value of $1 [Table B.2] for one period with a 5% rate).

Internal Rate of Return

Another means to evaluate capital investments is to use the **internal rate of return (IRR),** which equals the discount rate that yields an NPV of zero for an investment. This means that if we compute the total present value of a project's net cash flows using the IRR as the discount rate and then subtract the initial investment from this total present value, we get a zero NPV.

P4

Compute internal rate of return and explain its use.

To illustrate, we use the data for FasTrac's Project A from Exhibit 11.8 to compute its IRR. Below is the two-step process for computing IRR with even cash flows.

Step 1: **Compute the present value factor for the investment project.**

$$\text{Present value factor} = \frac{\text{Amount invested}}{\text{Net cash flows}} = \frac{\$12,000}{\$5,000} = 2.4000$$

Step 2: **Identify the discount rate (IRR) yielding the present value factor.**
Search Table B.3 for a present value factor of 2.4000 in the three-year row (equaling the 3-year project duration). The 12% discount rate yields a present value factor of 2.4018. This implies that the IRR is approximately 12%.

When cash flows are equal, as with Project A, we compute the present value factor by dividing the initial investment by its annual net cash flows. We then use an annuity table to determine the discount rate equal to this present value factor. For FasTrac's Project A, we look across the three-period row of Table B.3 and find that the discount rate corresponding to the present value factor of 2.4000 roughly equals the 2.4018 value for the 12% rate.* This row of Table B.3 is reproduced here:

Present Value of an Annuity of 1 for Three Periods					
	Discount Rate				
Periods	1%	5%	10%	12%	15%
3	2.9410	2.7232	2.4869	**2.4018**	2.2832

The 12% rate is the project's IRR. A more precise IRR estimate can be computed using an Excel function, as we show in this chapter's appendix.

Uneven Cash Flows   If net cash flows are uneven, it is best to use either a calculator or spreadsheet software to compute the IRR. However, we can also use trial and error to compute the IRR. We do this by selecting any reasonable discount rate and computing the NPV. If the amount is positive (negative), we recompute the NPV using a higher (lower) discount rate. We continue these steps until we reach a point where two consecutive computations result in NPVs having different signs (positive and negative). Because the NPV is zero using IRR, we know that the IRR lies between these two discount rates. We can then estimate its value.

■ **Decision** Insight ◀━━━◗

CEO-IRR   A survey reported that 41% of top managers would reject a project with an internal rate of return *above* the cost of capital *if* the project would cause the firm to miss its earnings forecast. The roles of benchmarks and manager compensation plans must be considered in capital budgeting decisions. ■

REJECTED

Robert Kirk/Stockbyte/Getty Images

Use of Internal Rate of Return   When we use the IRR to evaluate a project, we compare it to a predetermined **hurdle rate,** which is a minimum acceptable rate of return. The decision rule using IRR is applied as follows.

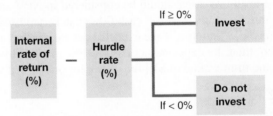

Example: How can management evaluate the risk of an investment? *Answer:* It must assess the uncertainty of future cash flows.

Top management selects the hurdle rate to use in evaluating capital investments. If the IRR is higher than the hurdle rate, the investment is made.

Comparing Projects Using IRR   Multiple projects are often ranked by the extent to which their IRR exceeds the hurdle rate. The hurdle rate for individual projects is often different,

---

* Since the present value factor of 2.4000 is not exactly equal to the 12% factor of 2.4018, we can more precisely estimate the IRR as follows:

Discount Rate	Present Value Factor from Table B.3
12%	2.4018
15%	2.2832
	0.1186 = difference

Then, IRR $= 12\% + \left[(15\% - 12\%) \times \dfrac{2.4018 - 2.4000}{0.1186} \right] = \underline{\underline{12.05\%}}$

depending on the risk involved. IRR is not subject to the limitations of NPV when comparing projects with different amounts invested because the IRR is expressed as a percent rather than as a dollar value in NPV.

◾ **Decision** Maker

Entrepreneur   You are developing a new product and you use a 12% discount rate to compute its NPV. Your banker, from whom you hope to obtain a loan, expresses concern that your discount rate is too low. How do you respond? ◾ [Answers follow the chapter's Summary.]

A machine costing $58,880 is expected to generate net cash flows of $8,000 per year for each of the next 10 years.

1. Compute the machine's internal rate of return (IRR).

2. If a company's hurdle rate is 6.5%, use IRR to determine whether the company should purchase this machine.

> **NEED-TO-KNOW** 11-4
>
> Internal Rate of Return
>
> P4

Solution

1. Amount invested/net cash flows = $58,880/$8,000 = 7.36. Scanning the "Periods equal 10" row in Table B.3 for a present value factor near 7.36 indicates the IRR is 6%.

2. The machine should not be purchased because its IRR (6%) is less than the company's hurdle rate (6.5%).

> Do More: QS 11-3, QS 11-13,
> E 11-13, E 11-14

Comparison of Capital Budgeting Methods

We explained four methods that managers use to evaluate capital investment projects. How do these methods compare with each other? Exhibit 11.10 addresses that question. Neither the payback period nor the accounting rate of return considers the time value of money. On the other hand, both the net present value and the internal rate of return do.

EXHIBIT 11.10

Comparing Capital
Budgeting Methods

	Payback Period	Accounting Rate of Return	Net Present Value	Internal Rate of Return
Measurement basis	• Cash flows	• Accrual income	• Cash flows	• Cash flows
Measurement unit	• Years	• Percent	• Dollars	• Percent
Strengths	• Easy to understand • Allows comparison of projects	• Easy to understand • Allows comparison of projects	• Reflects time value of money • Reflects varying risks over project's life	• Reflects time value of money • Allows comparisons of dissimilar projects
Limitations	• Ignores time value of money • Ignores cash flows after payback period	• Ignores time value of money • Ignores annual rates over life of project	• Difficult to compare dissimilar projects	• Ignores varying risks over life of project

The payback period is probably the simplest method. It gives managers an estimate of how soon they will recover their initial investment. Managers sometimes use this method when they have limited cash to invest and a number of projects to choose from. The accounting rate of return yields a percent measure computed using accrual income instead of cash flows. The accounting rate of return is an average rate for the entire investment period. Net present value considers all estimated net cash flows for the project's expected life. It can be applied to even and uneven cash flows and can reflect changes in the level of risk over a project's life. Since NPV yields a dollar measure, comparing projects of unequal sizes is more difficult. The profitability index, based on each project's net present value, can be used in this case. The internal rate of return considers all cash flows from a project. It is readily computed when the cash flows are even but requires some trial and error or use of a computer estimation when cash flows are uneven. Because the IRR is a percent measure, it is readily used to compare projects with different investment amounts. However, IRR does not reflect changes in risk over a project's life.

Decision Insight

And the Winner Is . . .   How do we choose among the methods for evaluating capital investments? Management surveys consistently show the internal rate of return (IRR) as the most popular method followed by the payback period and net present value (NPV). Few companies use the accounting rate of return (ARR), but nearly all use more than one method. ■

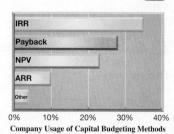

Company Usage of Capital Budgeting Methods

GLOBAL VIEW

Siemens AG is a global electrical engineering and electronics company headquartered in Germany. Recently, the company announced plans to invest £160 million to build a wind turbine plant in the United Kingdom. Net present value analyses support such decisions. In this case, Siemens foresees strong future cash flows based on increased demand for clean sources of energy, like wind power.

Sustainability and Accounting   Net present value calculations extend to investments in sustainable energy sources like solar power. Predicting the future benefits of solar panel installations, in terms of reduced energy costs, is challenging for several reasons. First, the amount of solar energy that can be produced depends on geographic location, with locations nearer the equator typically better. Second, south-facing roofs are better able to capture solar energy than other orientations. Third, cost savings from solar energy require predictions of the future costs of other sources of power, which can be volatile. While challenging, these factors must be considered when performing a net present value calculation on a potential investment in solar power.

Sustainability extends beyond natural resources. **Adafruit**'s founder Limor Fried invests in programs to educate future engineers and entrepreneurs. In this way Limor is helping to develop and sustain the human capital that will benefit society in the future.

Decision Analysis   ▢▢▢   Break-Even Time

A1
_____
Analyze a capital investment project using break-even time.

The first section of this chapter explained several methods to evaluate capital investments. Break-even time of an investment project is a variation of the payback period method that overcomes the limitation of not using the time value of money. **Break-even time (BET)** is a time-based measure used to evaluate a capital investment's acceptability. Its computation yields a measure of expected time, reflecting the time period until the *present value* of the net cash flows from an investment equals the initial cost of the investment. In basic terms, break-even time is computed by restating future cash flows in terms of present values and then determining the payback period using these present values.

To illustrate, we return to the FasTrac case described in Exhibit 11.1 involving a $16,000 investment in machinery. The annual net cash flows from this investment are projected at $4,100 for eight years. Exhibit 11.11 shows the computation of break-even time for this investment decision.

EXHIBIT 11.11

Break-Even Time Analysis*

Year	Cash Flows	Present Value of 1 at 10%	Present Value of Cash Flows	Cumulative Present Value of Cash Flows
0	$(16,000)	1.0000	$(16,000)	$(16,000)
1	4,100	0.9091	3,727	(12,273)
2	4,100	0.8264	3,388	(8,885)
3	4,100	0.7513	3,080	(5,805)
4	4,100	0.6830	2,800	(3,005)
5	4,100	0.6209	2,546	(459)
6	4,100	0.5645	2,314	1,855
7	4,100	0.5132	2,104	3,959
8	4,100	0.4665	1,913	5,872

* The time of analysis is the start of year 1 (same as end of year 0). All cash flows occur at the end of each year.

The right-most column of this exhibit shows that break-even time is between 5 and 6 years, or about 5.2 years—also see margin graph (where the line crosses the zero point). This is the time the project takes to break even after considering the time value of money (recall that the payback period computed without considering the time value of money was 3.9 years). We interpret this as cash flows earned after 5.2 years contribute to a positive net present value that, in this case, eventually amounts to $5,872.

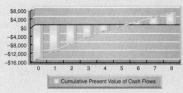

Cumulative Present Value of Cash Flows

Break-even time is a useful measure for managers because it identifies the point in time when they can expect the cash flows to begin to yield net positive returns. Managers expect a positive net present value from an investment if break-even time is less than the investment's estimated life. The method allows managers to compare and rank alternative investments, giving the project with the shortest break-even time the highest rank.

Decision Maker

Investment Manager Management asks you, the investment manager, to evaluate three alternative investments. Investment recovery time is crucial because cash is scarce. The time value of money is also important. Which capital budgeting method(s) do you use to assess the investments? ■ [Answers follow the chapter's Summary.]

White Company can invest in one of two projects, TD1 or TD2. Each project requires an initial investment of $101,250 and produces the year-end cash inflows shown in the following table.

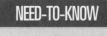

NEED-TO-KNOW

COMPREHENSIVE

	Net Cash Flows	
	TDI	**TD2**
Year 1.........	$ 20,000	$ 40,000
Year 2.........	30,000	40,000
Year 3.........	70,000	40,000
Totals	$120,000	$120,000

Required

1. Compute the payback period for both projects. Which project has the shortest payback period?
2. Assume that the company requires a 10% return from its investments. Compute the net present value of each project.
3. Drawing on your answers to parts 1 and 2, determine which project, if any, should be chosen.
4. Compute the internal rate of return for project TD2. Based on its internal rate of return, should project TD2 be chosen?

PLANNING THE SOLUTION

- Compute the payback period for the series of unequal cash flows (Project TD1) and for the series of equal cash flows (Project TD2).
- Compute White Company's net present value of each investment using a 10% discount rate.
- Use the payback and net present value rules to determine which project, if any, should be selected.
- Compute the internal rate of return for the series of equal cash flows (Project TD2) and determine whether that internal rate of return is greater than the company's 10% discount rate.

SOLUTION

1. The payback period for a project with a series of equal cash flows is computed as follows:

$$\text{Payback period} = \frac{\text{Cost of investment}}{\text{Annual net cash flow}}$$

For project TD2, the payback period equals 2.53 (rounded), computed as $101,250/$40,000. This means that the company expects to recover its investment in Project TD2 after approximately two and one-half years of its three-year life.

Next, determining the payback period for a series of unequal cash flows (as in Project TD1) requires us to compute the cumulative net cash flows from the project at the end of each year. Assuming the cash outflow for Project TD1 occurs at the end of year 0, and cash inflows occur continuously over years 1, 2, and 3, the payback period calculation follows.

TD1:

Period	Expected Net Cash Flows	Cumulative Net Cash Flows
0	$(101,250)	$(101,250)
1	20,000	(81,250)
2	30,000	(51,250)
3	70,000	18,750

The cumulative net cash flow for Project TD1 changes from negative to positive in year 3. As cash flows are received continuously, the point at which the company has recovered its investment into year 3 is 0.73 (rounded), computed as $51,250/$70,000. This means that the payback period for TD1 is 2.73 years, computed as 2 years plus 0.73 of year 3.

2. TD1:

	Net Cash Flows	Present Value of 1 at 10%	Present Value of Net Cash Flows
Year 1.....................	$ 20,000	0.9091	$ 18,182
Year 2.....................	30,000	0.8264	24,792
Year 3.....................	70,000	0.7513	52,591
Totals	$120,000		95,565
Amount invested			(101,250)
Net present value.........			$ (5,685)

TD2:

	Net Cash Flows	Present Value of 1 at 10%	Present Value of Net Cash Flows
Year 1.....................	$ 40,000	0.9091	$ 36,364
Year 2.....................	40,000	0.8264	33,056
Year 3.....................	40,000	0.7513	30,052
Totals	$120,000		99,472
Amount invested			(101,250)
Net present value.........			$ (1,778)

3. White Company should not invest in either project. Both are expected to yield a negative net present value, and it should invest only in positive net present value projects. Although the company expects to recover its investment from both projects before the end of these projects' useful lives, the projects are not acceptable after considering the time value of money.

4. To compute Project TD2's internal rate of return, we first compute a present value factor as follows:

$$\text{Present value factor} = \frac{\text{Amount invested}}{\text{Net cash flow}} = \$101,250/\$40,000 = 2.5313 \text{ (rounded)}$$

Then, we search Table B.3 for the discount rate that corresponds to the present value factor of 2.5313 for three periods. From Table B.3, this discount rate is 9%. Project TD2's internal rate of return of 9% is below this company's hurdle rate of 10%. Thus, Project TD2 should *not* be chosen.

Using Excel to Compute Net Present Value and Internal Rate of Return

11A

Computing present values and internal rates of return for projects with uneven cash flows is tedious and error prone. These calculations can be performed simply and accurately by using functions built into Excel. Many calculators and other types of spreadsheet software can perform them too. To illustrate, consider FasTrac, a company that is considering investing in a new machine with the expected cash flows shown in the following spreadsheet. Cash outflows are entered as negative numbers, and cash inflows are entered as positive numbers. Assume FasTrac requires a 12% annual return, entered as 0.12 in cell C1.

	A	B	C	D
1	Annual discount rate		0.12	
2	Initial investment, made at beginning of period 1		-16000	
3	Annual cash flows received at end of period:			
4		1	3000	
5		2	4000	
6		3	4000	
7		4	4000	
8		5	5000	
9		6	3000	
10		7	2000	
11		8	2000	
12				
13			=NPV(C1,C4:C11)+C2	
14				
15			=IRR(C2:C11)	
16				

To compute the net present value of this project, the following is entered into cell C13:

$$=NPV(C1,C4:C11)+C2$$

This instructs Excel to use its NPV function to compute the present value of the cash flows in cells C4 through C11, using the discount rate in cell C1, and then add the amount of the (negative) initial investment. For this stream of cash flows and a discount rate of 12%, the net present value is $1,326.03.

To compute the internal rate of return for this project, the following is entered into cell C15:

$$=IRR(C2:C11)$$

This instructs Excel to use its IRR function to compute the internal rate of return of the cash flows in cells C2 through C11. By default, Excel starts with a guess of 10%, and then uses trial and error to find the IRR. The IRR equals 14% for this project.

Summary

A1 **Analyze a capital investment project using break-even time.** Break-even time (BET) is a method for evaluating capital investments by restating future cash flows in terms of their present values (discounting the cash flows) and then calculating the payback period using these present values of cash flows.

P1 **Compute payback period and describe its use.** One way to compare potential investments is to compute and compare their payback periods. The payback period is an estimate of the expected time before the cumulative net cash inflow from the investment equals its initial cost. A payback period analysis

fails to reflect risk of the cash flows, differences in the timing of cash flows within the payback period, and cash flows that occur after the payback period.

P2 **Compute accounting rate of return and explain its use.** A project's accounting rate of return is computed by dividing the expected annual after-tax net income by the average amount of investment in the project. When the net cash flows are received evenly throughout each period and straight-line depreciation is used, the average investment is computed as the average of the investment's initial book value and its salvage value.

P3 **Compute net present value and describe its use.** An investment's net present value is determined by predicting the future cash flows it is expected to generate, discounting them at a rate that represents an acceptable return, and then by subtracting the investment's initial cost from the sum of the present values. This technique can deal with any pattern of expected cash flows and applies a superior concept of return on investment.

P4 **Compute internal rate of return and explain its use.** The internal rate of return (IRR) is the discount rate that results in a zero net present value. When the cash flows are equal, we can compute the present value factor corresponding to the IRR by dividing the initial investment by the annual cash flows. We then use the annuity tables to determine the discount rate corresponding to this present value factor.

Guidance Answers to Decision Maker and Decision Ethics

Systems Manager Your dilemma is whether to abide by rules designed to prevent abuse or to bend them to acquire an investment that you believe will benefit the firm. You should not pursue the latter action because breaking up the order into small components is dishonest and there are consequences of being caught at a later stage. Develop a proposal for the entire package and then do all you can to expedite its processing, particularly by pointing out its benefits. When faced with controls that are not working, there is rarely a reason to overcome its shortcomings by dishonesty. A direct assault on those limitations is more sensible and ethical.

Entrepreneur The banker is probably concerned because new products are risky and should therefore be evaluated using a higher

rate of return. You should conduct a thorough technical analysis and obtain detailed market data and information about any similar products available in the market. These factors might provide sufficient information to support the use of a lower return. You must convince yourself that the risk level is consistent with the discount rate used. You should also be confident that your company has the capacity and the resources to handle the new product.

Investment Manager You should probably focus on either the payback period or break-even time because both the time value of money and recovery time are important. Break-even time method is superior because it accounts for the time value of money, which is an important consideration in this decision.

Key Terms

Accounting rate of return

Annuity

Break-even time (BET)

Capital budgeting

Cost of capital

Hurdle rate

Internal rate of return (IRR)

Net present value (NPV)

Payback period (PBP)

Profitability index

Multiple Choice Quiz   Answers at end of chapter

1. The minimum acceptable rate of return for an investment decision is called the
   a. Hurdle rate of return.
   b. Payback rate of return.
   c. Internal rate of return.
   d. Average rate of return.
   e. Maximum rate of return.

2. A corporation is considering the purchase of new equipment costing $90,000. The projected after-tax annual net income from the equipment is $3,600, after deducting $30,000 depreciation. Assume that revenue is to be received at each year-end, and the machine has a useful life of three years with zero salvage value. Management requires a 12% return on its investments. What is the net present value of this machine?
   a. $ 60,444   c. $(88,560)   e. $ (9,300)
   b. $ 80,700   d. $ 90,000

3. A disadvantage of using the payback period to compare investment alternatives is that it
   a. Ignores cash flows beyond the payback period.
   b. Cannot be used to compare alternatives with different initial investments.

   c. Cannot be used when cash flows are not uniform.
   d. Involves the time value of money.
   e. Cannot be used if a company records depreciation.

4. A company is considering the purchase of equipment for $270,000. Projected annual cash inflow from this equipment is $61,200 per year. The payback period is:
   a. 0.2 years   c. 4.4 years   e. 3.9 years
   b. 5.0 years   d. 2.3 years

5. A company buys a machine for $180,000 that has an expected life of nine years and no salvage value. The company expects an annual net income (after taxes of 30%) of $8,550. What is the accounting rate of return?
   a. 4.75%   c. 2.85%   e. 6.65%
   b. 42.75%   d. 9.50%

🚹 Icon denotes assignments that involve decision making.

Discussion Questions

1. Capital budgeting decisions require careful analysis because they are generally the _____ _____ and _____ decisions that management faces.
2. What is capital budgeting?
3. 🚹 Identify four reasons that capital budgeting decisions by managers are risky.
4. Identify two disadvantages of using the payback period for comparing investments.
5. 🚹 Why is an investment more attractive to management if it has a shorter payback period?
6. What is the average amount invested in a machine during its predicted five-year life if it costs $200,000 and has a $20,000 salvage value? Assume that net income is received evenly throughout each year and straight-line depreciation is used.
7. If the present value of the expected net cash flows from a machine, discounted at 10%, exceeds the amount to be invested, what can you say about the investment's expected rate of return? What can you say about the expected rate of return if the present value of the net cash flows, discounted at 10%, is less than the investment amount?
8. Why is the present value of $100 that you expect to receive one year from today worth less than $100 received today?

What is the present value of $100 that you expect to receive one year from today, discounted at 12%?

9. 🚹 If a potential investment's internal rate of return is above the company's hurdle rate, should the investment be made?
10. 🚹 Google managers must select depreciation methods. Why does the use **GOOGLE** of the accelerated depreciation method (instead of straight-line) for income tax reporting increase an investment's value?
11. The management of Samsung is planning to invest in a new compa- **Samsung** nywide computerized inventory tracking system. What makes this potential investment risky?
12. The management of Google is planning to acquire new equipment to manufac- **GOOGLE** ture tablet computers. What are some of the costs and benefits that would be included in Google's analysis?
13. 🚹 Apple is considering expanding a store. Identify three methods management can use **APPLE** to evaluate whether to expand.

ⓜ connect

Park Co. is considering an investment that requires immediate payment of $27,000 and provides expected cash inflows of $9,000 annually for four years. What is the investment's payback period?

QUICK STUDY

QS 11-1
Payback period P1

Park Co. is considering an investment that requires immediate payment of $27,000 and provides expected cash inflows of $9,000 annually for four years. If Park Co. requires a 10% return on its investments, what is the net present value of this investment? (Round your calculations to the nearest dollar.)

QS 11-2
Net present value P3

Park Co. is considering an investment that requires immediate payment of $27,000 and provides expected cash inflows of $9,000 annually for four years. Assume Park Co. requires a 10% return on its investments. Based on its internal rate of return, should Park Co. make the investment?

QS 11-3
Internal rate of return P4

Howard Co. is considering two alternative investments. The payback period is 3.5 years for Investment A and 4 years for Investment B. (1) If management relies on the payback period, which investment is preferred? (2) Why might Howard's analysis of these two alternatives lead to the selection of B over A?

QS 11-4
Analyzing payback periods P1

Project A requires a $280,000 initial investment for new machinery with a five-year life and a salvage value of $30,000. The company uses straight-line depreciation. Project A is expected to yield annual net income of $20,000 per year for the next five years. Compute Project A's payback period.

QS 11-5
Payback period P1

QS 11-6
Accounting rate of return
P2

Project A requires a $280,000 initial investment for new machinery with a five-year life and a salvage value of $30,000. The company uses straight-line depreciation. Project A is expected to yield annual net income of $20,000 per year for the next five years. Compute Project A's accounting rate of return. Express your answer as a percentage, rounded to two decimal places.

QS 11-7
Computation of
accounting rate of return
P2

Peng Company is considering an investment expected to generate an average net income after taxes of $1,950 for three years. The investment costs $45,000 and has an estimated $6,000 salvage value. Compute the accounting rate of return for this investment; assume the company uses straight-line depreciation. Express your answer as a percentage, rounded to two decimal places.

QS 11-8
Net present value   P3

Peng Company is considering an investment expected to generate an average net income after taxes of $1,950 for three years. The investment costs $45,000 and has an estimated $6,000 salvage value. Assume Peng requires a 15% return on its investments. Compute the net present value of this investment. (Round each present value calculation to the nearest dollar.)

QS 11-9
Computation of net
present value   P3

If Quail Company invests $50,000 today, it can expect to receive $10,000 at the end of each year for the next seven years, plus an extra $6,000 at the end of the seventh year. What is the net present value of this investment assuming a required 10% return on investments? (Round present value calculations to the nearest dollar.)

QS 11-10
Profitability index
P3

Yokam Company is considering two alternative projects. Project 1 requires an initial investment of $400,000 and has a present value of cash flows of $1,100,000. Project 2 requires an initial investment of $4 million and has a present value of cash flows of $6 million. Compute the profitability index for each project. Based on the profitability index, which project should the company prefer? Explain.

QS 11-11
Net present value
P3

Following is information on an investment considered by Hudson Co. The investment has zero salvage value. The company requires a 12% return from its investments. Compute this investment's net present value.

	Investment A1
Initial investment	($200,000)
Expected net cash flows in year:	
1	100,000
2	90,000
3	75,000

QS 11-12
Net present value, with
salvage value   P3

Refer to the information in QS 11-11 and instead assume the investment has a salvage value of $20,000. Compute the investment's net present value.

QS 11-13
Internal rate of return   P4

A company is considering investing in a new machine that requires a cash payment of $47,947 today. The machine will generate annual cash flows of $21,000 for the next three years. What is the internal rate of return if the company buys this machine?

QS 11-14
Net present value   P3

A company is considering investing in a new machine that requires a cash payment of $47,947 today. The machine will generate annual cash flows of $21,000 for the next three years. Assume the company uses an 8% discount rate. Compute the net present value of this investment. (Round your answer to the nearest dollar.)

QS 11-15
Computation of break-
even time
A1

Heels, a shoe manufacturer, is evaluating the costs and benefits of new equipment that would custom fit each pair of athletic shoes. The customer would have his or her foot scanned by digital computer equipment; this information would be used to cut the raw materials to provide the customer a perfect fit. The new equipment costs $90,000 and is expected to generate an additional $35,000 in cash flows for five years. A bank will make a $90,000 loan to the company at a 10% interest rate for this equipment's purchase. Use the following table to determine the break-even time for this equipment. (Round the present value of cash flows to the nearest dollar.)

Year	Cash Flows*	Present Value of 1 at 10%	Present Value of Cash Flows	Cumulative Present Value of Cash Flows
0	$(90,000)	1.0000	_____	_____
1	35,000	0.9091	_____	_____
2	35,000	0.8264	_____	_____
3	35,000	0.7513	_____	_____
4	35,000	0.6830	_____	_____
5	35,000	0.6209	_____	_____

* All cash flows occur at year-end.

Siemens AG invests €80 million to build a manufacturing plant to build wind turbines. The company predicts net cash flows of €16 million per year for the next eight years. Assume the company requires an 8% rate of return from its investments.

1. What is the payback period of this investment?
2. What is the net present value of this investment?

QS 11-16
Capital budgeting
methods   P1   P3

≡connect

Beyer Company is considering the purchase of an asset for $180,000. It is expected to produce the following net cash flows. The cash flows occur evenly throughout each year. Compute the payback period for this investment (round years to two decimals).

	Year 1	Year 2	Year 3	Year 4	Year 5	Total
Net cash flows	$60,000	$40,000	$70,000	$125,000	$35,000	$330,000

EXERCISES

Exercise 11-1
Payback period
computation; uneven
cash flows   P1
Check   3.08 years

Refer to the information in Exercise 11-1 and assume that Beyer requires a 10% return on its investments. Compute the net present value of this investment. (Round to the nearest dollar.) Should Beyer accept the investment?

Exercise 11-2
Net present value   P3

A machine can be purchased for $150,000 and used for five years, yielding the following net incomes. In projecting net incomes, straight-line depreciation is applied, using a five-year life and a zero salvage value. Compute the machine's payback period (ignore taxes). (Round the payback period to three decimals.)

	Year 1	Year 2	Year 3	Year 4	Year 5
Net income	$10,000	$25,000	$50,000	$37,500	$100,000

Exercise 11-3
Payback period
computation; straight-
line depreciation
P1

Refer to the information in Exercise 11-3 and assume instead that double-declining depreciation is applied. Compute the machine's payback period (ignore taxes). (Round the payback period to three decimals.)

Exercise 11-4
Payback period;
accelerated depreciation

P1
Check   2.265 years

Compute the payback period for each of these two separate investments (round the payback period to two decimals):

a. A new operating system for an existing machine is expected to cost $520,000 and have a useful life of six years. The system yields an incremental after-tax income of $150,000 each year after deducting its straight-line depreciation. The predicted salvage value of the system is $10,000.

b. A machine costs $380,000, has a $20,000 salvage value, is expected to last eight years, and will generate an after-tax income of $60,000 per year after straight-line depreciation.

Exercise 11-5
Payback period
computation; even
cash flows
P1

Exercise 11-6
Net present value   P3

Refer to the information in Exercise 11-5. Assume the company requires a 10% rate of return on its invest-ments. Compute the net present value of each potential investment. (Round to the nearest dollar.)

Exercise 11-7
Accounting rate of return
P2

A machine costs $700,000 and is expected to yield an after-tax net income of $52,000 each year. Management predicts this machine has a 10-year service life and a $100,000 salvage value, and it uses straight-line depreciation. Compute this machine's accounting rate of return.

Exercise 11-8
Payback period and accounting rate of return on investment
P1   P2

B2B Co. is considering the purchase of equipment that would allow the company to add a new product to its line. The equipment is expected to cost $360,000 with a 12-year life and no salvage value. It will be depreciated on a straight-line basis. The company expects to sell 144,000 units of the equipment's product each year. The expected annual income related to this equipment follows. Compute the (1) payback period and (2) accounting rate of return for this equipment.

Sales	$225,000
Costs	
Materials, labor, and overhead (except depreciation on new equipment)	120,000
Depreciation on new equipment	30,000
Selling and administrative expenses	22,500
Total costs and expenses...	172,500
Pretax income	52,500
Income taxes (30%)..	15,750
Net income	$ 36,750

Check   (1) 5.39 years
(2) 20.42%

Exercise 11-9
Computing net present value   P3

After evaluating the risk of the investment described in Exercise 11-8, B2B Co. concludes that it must earn at least an 8% return on this investment. Compute the net present value of this investment. (Round the net present value to the nearest dollar.)

Exercise 11-10
NPV and profitability index
P3

Following is information on two alternative investments being considered by Jolee Company. The com-pany requires a 10% return from its investments.

	Project A	Project B
Initial investment	$(160,000)	$(105,000)
Expected net cash flows in year:		
1	40,000	32,000
2	56,000	50,000
3	80,295	66,000
4	90,400	72,000
5	65,000	24,000

For each alternative project compute the (a) net present value, and (b) profitability index. (Round your answers in part *b* to two decimal places.) If the company can only select one project, which should it choose? Explain.

Exercise 11-11
Net present value, profitability index
P3

Following is information on two alternative investments being considered by Tiger Co. The company re-quires a 4% return from its investments.

	Project X1	Project X2
Initial investment	($80,000)	($120,000)
Expected net cash flows in year:		
1	25,000	60,000
2	35,500	50,000
3	60,500	40,000

Compute each project's (a) net present value and (b) profitability index. (Round present value calculations to the nearest dollar and round the profitability index to two decimal places.) If the company can choose only one project, which should it choose? Explain.

Refer to the information in Exercise 11-11 and instead assume the company requires a 12% return on its investments. Compute each project's (a) net present value and (b) profitability index. (Round present value calculations to the nearest dollar.) Express the profitability index as a percentage (rounded to two decimal places). If the company can choose only one project, which should it choose? Explain.

Exercise 11-12
Net present value, profitability index   P3

Refer to the information in Exercise 11-11. Create an Excel spreadsheet to compute the internal rate of return for each of the projects. Based on internal rate of return, determine whether the company should accept either of the two projects.

Exercise 11-13^A
Internal rate of return   P4

Phoenix Company can invest in each of three cheese-making projects: C1, C2, and C3. Each project requires an initial investment of $228,000 and would yield the following annual cash flows.

Exercise 11-14
Computation and interpretation of net present value and internal rate of return

P3   P4

	C1	C2	C3
Year 1........	$ 12,000	$ 96,000	$180,000
Year 2	108,000	96,000	60,000
Year 3	168,000	96,000	48,000
Totals	$288,000	$288,000	$288,000

(1) Assuming that the company requires a 12% return from its investments, use net present value to determine which projects, if any, should be acquired. (2) Using the answer from part 1, explain whether the internal rate of return is higher or lower than 12% for Project C2.

Refer to the information in Exercise 11-10. Create an Excel spreadsheet to compute the internal rate of return for each of the projects. Round the percentage return to two decimals.

Exercise 11-15^A
Using Excel to compute IRR   P4

This chapter explained two methods to evaluate investments using recovery time, the payback period and break-even time (BET). Refer to QS 11-15 and (1) compute the recovery time for both the payback period and break-even time, (2) discuss the advantage(s) of break-even time over the payback period, and (3) list two conditions under which payback period and break-even time are similar.

Exercise 11-16
Comparison of payback and BET

P1   A1

■connect

Factor Company is planning to add a new product to its line. To manufacture this product, the company needs to buy a new machine at a $480,000 cost with an expected four-year life and a $20,000 salvage value. All sales are for cash, and all costs are out-of-pocket, except for depreciation on the new machine. Additional information includes the following.

PROBLEM SET A

Problem 11-1A
Computation of payback period, accounting rate of return, and net present value

P1   P2   P3

Expected annual sales of new product	$1,840,000
Expected annual costs of new product	
Direct materials	480,000
Direct labor	672,000
Overhead (excluding straight-line depreciation on new machine)	336,000
Selling and administrative expenses	160,000
Income taxes	30%

Required

1. Compute straight-line depreciation for each year of this new machine's life. (Round depreciation amounts to the nearest dollar.)
2. Determine expected net income and net cash flow for each year of this machine's life. (Round answers to the nearest dollar.)
3. Compute this machine's payback period, assuming that cash flows occur evenly throughout each year. (Round the payback period to two decimals.)

4. Compute this machine's accounting rate of return, assuming that income is earned evenly throughout each year. (Round the percentage return to two decimals.)

5. Compute the net present value for this machine using a discount rate of 7% and assuming that cash flows occur at each year-end. (*Hint:* Salvage value is a cash inflow at the end of the asset's life. Round the net present value to the nearest dollar.)

Problem 11-2A
Analysis and computation of payback period, accounting rate of return, and net present value   P1 P2 P3

Most Company has an opportunity to invest in one of two new projects. Project Y requires a $350,000 investment for new machinery with a four-year life and no salvage value. Project Z requires a $350,000 investment for new machinery with a three-year life and no salvage value. The two projects yield the following predicted annual results. The company uses straight-line depreciation, and cash flows occur evenly throughout each year.

	Project Y	Project Z
Sales	$350,000	$280,000
Expenses		
Direct materials	49,000	35,000
Direct labor.........................	70,000	42,000
Overhead including depreciation	126,000	126,000
Selling and administrative expenses	25,000	25,000
Total expenses	270,000	228,000
Pretax income	80,000	52,000
Income taxes (30%)	24,000	15,600
Net income	$ 56,000	$ 36,400

Required

1. Compute each project's annual expected net cash flows. (Round the net cash flows to the nearest dollar.)

2. Determine each project's payback period. (Round the payback period to two decimals.)

3. Compute each project's accounting rate of return. (Round the percentage return to one decimal.)

4. Determine each project's net present value using 8% as the discount rate. For part 4 only, assume that cash flows occur at each year-end. (Round the net present value to the nearest dollar.)

Analysis Component

5. Identify the project you would recommend to management and explain your choice.

Problem 11-3A
Computation of cash flows and net present values with alternative depreciation methods

P3

Manning Corporation is considering a new project requiring a $90,000 investment in test equipment with no salvage value. The project would produce $66,000 of pretax income before depreciation at the end of each of the next six years. The company's income tax rate is 40%. In compiling its tax return and computing its income tax payments, the company can choose between the two alternative depreciation schedules shown in the table.

	Straight-Line Depreciation	MACRS Depreciation*
Year 1.........	$ 9,000	$18,000
Year 2.........	18,000	28,800
Year 3.........	18,000	17,280
Year 4.........	18,000	10,368
Year 5.........	18,000	10,368
Year 6.........	9,000	5,184
Totals	$90,000	$90,000

* The modified accelerated cost recovery system (MACRS) for depreciation is discussed in financial accounting courses.

Required

1. Prepare a five-column table that reports amounts (assuming use of straight-line depreciation) for each of the following for each of the six years: (a) pretax income before depreciation, (b) straight-line depreciation expense, (c) taxable income, (d) income taxes, and (e) net cash flow. Net cash flow equals the amount of income before depreciation minus the income taxes. (Round answers to the nearest dollar.)

2. Prepare a five-column table that reports amounts (assuming use of MACRS depreciation) for each of the following for each of the six years: (a) pretax income before depreciation, (b) MACRS depreciation expense, (c) taxable income, (d) income taxes, and (e) net cash flow. Net cash flow equals the income amount before depreciation minus the income taxes. (Round answers to the nearest dollar.)

3. Compute the net present value of the investment if straight-line depreciation is used. Use 10% as the discount rate. (Round the net present value to the nearest dollar.)

4. Compute the net present value of the investment if MACRS depreciation is used. Use 10% as the discount rate. (Round the net present value to the nearest dollar.)

Check Net present value:
(3) $108,518
(4) $110,303

Analysis Component

5. Explain why the MACRS depreciation method increases this project's net present value.

Interstate Manufacturing is considering either replacing one of its old machines with a new machine or having the old machine overhauled. Information about the two alternatives follows. Management requires a 10% rate of return on its investments.

Problem 11-4A
Computing net present value of alternate investments

P3

Alternative 1: Keep the old machine and have it overhauled. If the old machine is overhauled, it will be kept for another five years and then sold for its salvage value.

Cost of old machine	$112,000
Cost of overhaul	150,000
Annual expected revenues generated	95,000
Annual cash operating costs after overhaul	42,000
Salvage value of old machine in 5 years	15,000

Alternative 2: Sell the old machine and buy a new one. The new machine is more efficient and will yield substantial operating cost savings with more product being produced and sold.

Cost of new machine	$300,000
Salvage value of old machine now	29,000
Annual expected revenues generated	100,000
Annual cash operating costs	32,000
Salvage value of new machine in 5 years	20,000

Required

1. Determine the net present value of alternative 1.

2. Determine the net present value of alternative 2.

3. Which alternative do you recommend that management select? Explain.

Check (1) Net present value of alternative 1, $60,226

Sentinel Company is considering an investment in technology to improve its operations. The investment will require an initial outlay of $250,000 and will yield the following expected cash flows. Management requires investments to have a payback period of three years, and it requires a 10% return on investments.

Problem 11-5A
Payback period, break-even time, and net present value

P1 A1

Period	Cash Flow
1	$ 47,000
2	52,000
3	75,000
4	94,000
5	125,000

Required

1. Determine the payback period for this investment. (Round the answer to one decimal.)
2. Determine the break-even time for this investment. (Round the answer to one decimal.)
3. Determine the net present value for this investment.

Analysis Component
4. Should management invest in this project? Explain.

Problem 11-6A
Payback period, break-even time, and net present value

P1 A1

Lenitnes Company is considering an investment in technology to improve its operations. The investment will require an initial outlay of $250,000 and will yield the following expected cash flows. Management requires investments to have a payback period of three years, and it requires a 10% return on its investments.

Period	Cash Flow
1	$125,000
2	94,000
3	75,000
4	52,000
5	47,000

Required

1. Determine the payback period for this investment. (Round the answer to one decimal.)
2. Determine the break-even time for this investment. (Round the answer to one decimal.)
3. Determine the net present value for this investment.

Analysis Component
4. Should management invest in this project? Explain.
5. Compare your answers for parts 1 through 4 with those for Problem 11-5A. What are the causes of the differences in results and your conclusions?

PROBLEM SET B

Problem 11-1B
Computation of payback period, accounting rate of return, and net present value

P1   P2   P3

Cortino Company is planning to add a new product to its line. To manufacture this product, the company needs to buy a new machine at a $300,000 cost with an expected four-year life and a $20,000 salvage value. All sales are for cash and all costs are out-of-pocket, except for depreciation on the new machine. Additional information includes the following.

Expected annual sales of new product	$1,150,000
Expected annual costs of new product	
Direct materials.......................................	300,000
Direct labor	420,000
Overhead (excluding straight-line depreciation on new machine).........	210,000
Selling and administrative expenses	100,000
Income taxes	30%

Required

1. Compute straight-line depreciation for each year of this new machine's life. (Round depreciation amounts to the nearest dollar.)
2. Determine expected net income and net cash flow for each year of this machine's life. (Round answers to the nearest dollar.)
3. Compute this machine's payback period, assuming that cash flows occur evenly throughout each year. (Round the payback period to two decimals.)

4. Compute this machine's accounting rate of return, assuming that income is earned evenly throughout each year. (Round the percentage return to two decimals.)

5. Compute the net present value for this machine using a discount rate of 7% and assuming that cash flows occur at each year-end. (*Hint:* Salvage value is a cash inflow at the end of the asset's life.)

Aikman Company has an opportunity to invest in one of two projects. Project A requires a $240,000 investment for new machinery with a four-year life and no salvage value. Project B also requires a $240,000 investment for new machinery with a three-year life and no salvage value. The two projects yield the following predicted annual results. The company uses straight-line depreciation, and cash flows occur evenly throughout each year.

Problem 11-2B
Analysis and computation of payback period, accounting rate of return, and net present value

P1 P2 P3

	Project A	Project B
Sales	$250,000	$200,000
Expenses		
Direct materials	35,000	25,000
Direct labor	50,000	30,000
Overhead including depreciation	90,000	90,000
Selling and administrative expenses	18,000	18,000
Total expenses	193,000	163,000
Pretax income	57,000	37,000
Income taxes (30%)	17,100	11,100
Net income	$ 39,900	$ 25,900

Required

1. Compute each project's annual expected net cash flows. (Round net cash flows to the nearest dollar.)
2. Determine each project's payback period. (Round the payback period to two decimals.)
3. Compute each project's accounting rate of return. (Round the percentage return to one decimal.)
4. Determine each project's net present value using 8% as the discount rate. For part 4 only, assume that cash flows occur at each year-end. (Round net present values to the nearest dollar.)

Check For Project A:
(2) 2.4 years
(3) 33.3%
(4) $90,879

Analysis Component

5. Identify the project you would recommend to management and explain your choice.

Grossman Corporation is considering a new project requiring a $30,000 investment in an asset having no salvage value. The project would produce $12,000 of pretax income before depreciation at the end of each of the next six years. The company's income tax rate is 40%. In compiling its tax return and computing its income tax payments, the company can choose between two alternative depreciation schedules as shown in the table.

Problem 11-3B
Computation of cash flows and net present values with alternative depreciation methods

P3

	Straight-Line Depreciation	MACRS Depreciation*
Year 1	$ 3,000	$ 6,000
Year 2	6,000	9,600
Year 3	6,000	5,760
Year 4	6,000	3,456
Year 5	6,000	3,456
Year 6	3,000	1,728
Totals	$30,000	$30,000

* The modified accelerated cost recovery system (MACRS) for depreciation is discussed in financial accounting courses.

Required

1. Prepare a five-column table that reports amounts (assuming use of straight-line depreciation) for each of the following items for each of the six years: (a) pretax income before depreciation, (b) straight-line depreciation expense, (c) taxable income, (d) income taxes, and (e) net cash flow. Net cash flow equals the amount of income before depreciation minus the income taxes. (Round answers to the nearest dollar.)
2. Prepare a five-column table that reports amounts (assuming use of MACRS depreciation) for each of the following items for each of the six years: (a) pretax income before depreciation, (b) MACRS depreciation expense, (c) taxable income, (d) income taxes, and (e) net cash flow. Net cash flow equals the amount of income before depreciation minus the income taxes. (Round answers to the nearest dollar.)

3. Compute the net present value of the investment if straight-line depreciation is used. Use 10% as the discount rate. (Round the net present value to the nearest dollar.)

4. Compute the net present value of the investment if MACRS depreciation is used. Use 10% as the discount rate. (Round the net present value to the nearest dollar.)

Analysis Component

5. Explain why the MACRS depreciation method increases the net present value of this project.

Problem 11-4B
Computing net present
value of alternate
investments

P3

Archer Foods has a freezer that is in need of repair and is considering whether to replace the old freezer with a new freezer or have the old freezer extensively repaired. Information about the two alternatives follows. Management requires a 10% rate of return on its investments.

Alternative 1: Keep the old freezer and have it repaired. If the old freezer is repaired, it will be kept for another eight years and then sold for its salvage value.

Cost of old freezer	$75,000
Cost of repair	50,000
Annual expected revenues generated	63,000
Annual cash operating costs after repair	55,000
Salvage value of old freezer in 8 years	3,000

Alternative 2: Sell the old freezer and buy a new one. The new freezer is larger than the old one and will allow the company to expand its product offerings, thereby generating more revenues. Also, it is more energy efficient and will yield substantial operating cost savings.

Cost of new freezer	$150,000
Salvage value of old freezer now	5,000
Annual expected revenues generated	68,000
Annual cash operating costs	30,000
Salvage value of new freezer in 8 years	8,000

Required

1. Determine the net present value of alternative 1.

2. Determine the net present value of alternative 2.

3. Which alternative do you recommend that management select? Explain.

Problem 11-5B
Payback period, break-
even time, and net
present value

P1 A1

Aster Company is considering an investment in technology to improve its operations. The investment will require an initial outlay of $800,000 and yield the following expected cash flows. Management requires investments to have a payback period of two years, and it requires a 10% return on its investments.

Period	Cash Flow
1	$300,000
2	350,000
3	400,000
4	450,000

Required

1. Determine the payback period for this investment.

2. Determine the break-even time for this investment.

3. Determine the net present value for this investment.

Analysis Component

4. Should management invest in this project? Explain.

Retsa Company is considering an investment in technology to improve its operations. The investment will require an initial outlay of $800,000 and will yield the following expected cash flows. Management requires investments to have a payback period of two years, and it requires a 10% return on its investments.

Period	Cash Flow
1	$450,000
2	400,000
3	350,000
4	300,000

Required

1. Determine the payback period for this investment. (Round the answer to one decimal.)

2. Determine the break-even time for this investment. (Round the answer to one decimal.)

3. Determine the net present value for this investment.

Analysis Component

4. Should management invest in this project? Explain.

5. Compare your answers for parts 1 through 4 with those for Problem 11-5B. What are the causes of the differences in results and your conclusions?

Check   (1) Payback period, 1.9 years

(This serial problem began in Chapter 1 and continues through most of the book. If previous chapter segments were not completed, the serial problem can begin at this point. It is helpful, but not necessary, to use the Working Papers that accompany the book.)

SP 11   Santana Rey is considering the purchase of equipment for Business Solutions that would allow the company to add a new product to its computer furniture line. The equipment is expected to cost $300,000 and to have a six-year life and no salvage value. It will be depreciated on a straight-line basis. Business Solutions expects to sell 100 units of the equipment's product each year. The expected annual income related to this equipment follows.

SERIAL PROBLEM
Business Solutions

P1   P2

Sales	$375,000
Costs	
Materials, labor, and overhead (except depreciation).	200,000
Depreciation on new equipment	50,000
Selling and administrative expenses	37,500
Total costs and expenses	287,500
Pretax income	87,500
Income taxes (30%)	26,250
Net income	$ 61,250

Required

Compute the (1) payback period and (2) accounting rate of return for this equipment. (Record answers as percents, rounded to one decimal.)

Beyond the Numbers

BTN 11-1   Assume Apple invested $2.12 billion to expand its manufacturing capacity. Assume that these assets have a 10-year life and that Apple requires a 10% internal rate of return on these assets.

Required

1. What is the amount of annual cash flows that Apple must earn from these projects to have a 10% internal rate of return? (*Hint:* Identify the 10-period, 10% factor from the present value of an annuity table, and then divide $2.12 billion by this factor to get the annual cash flows necessary.)

REPORTING IN ACTION

P3

APPLE

Fast Forward

2. Access Apple's financial statements for fiscal years ended after September 28, 2013, from its website (Apple.com) or the SEC's website (SEC.gov).

 a. Determine the amount that Apple invested in capital assets for the most recent year. (*Hint:* Refer to the statement of cash flows.)

 b. Assume a 10-year life and a 10% internal rate of return. What is the amount of cash flows that Apple must earn on these new projects?

COMPARATIVE ANALYSIS

P3   P4

APPLE

GOOGLE

BTN 11-2   Assume that Google invests $2.42 billion in capital expenditures, including $1.08 billion related to manufacturing capacity. Assume that these projects have a seven-year life and that management requires a 15% internal rate of return on those projects.

Required

1. What is the amount of annual cash flows that Google must earn from those expenditures to achieve a 15% internal rate of return? (*Hint:* Identify the seven-period, 15% factor from the present value of an annuity table and then divide $1.08 billion by the factor to get the annual cash flows required.)

2. BTN 11-1 must be completed to answer part 2. How does your answer to part 1 compare to Apple's required cash flows determined in BTN 11-1? What does this imply about each company's cash flow requirements for these types of projects?

ETHICS CHALLENGE

P3

BTN 11-3   A consultant commented that "too often the numbers look good but feel bad." This comment often stems from estimation error common to capital budgeting proposals that relate to future cash flows. Three reasons for this error often exist. First, reliably predicting cash flows several years into the future is very difficult. Second, the present value of cash flows many years into the future (say, beyond 10 years) is often very small. Third, it is difficult for personal biases and expectations not to unduly influence present value computations.

Required

1. Compute the present value of $100 to be received in 10 years assuming a 12% discount rate.

2. Why is understanding the three reasons mentioned for estimation errors important when evaluating investment projects? Link this response to your answer for part 1.

COMMUNICATING IN PRACTICE

P1   P2   P3   P4

BTN 11-4   Payback period, accounting rate of return, net present value, and internal rate of return are common methods to evaluate capital investment opportunities. Assume that your manager asks you to identify the type of measurement basis and unit that each method offers and to list the advantages and disadvantages of each. Present your response in memorandum format of less than one page.

TAKING IT TO THE NET

P1   P3

BTN 11-5   Capital budgeting is an important topic, and there are websites designed to help people understand the methods available. Access TeachMeFinance.com's capital budgeting web page (teachmefinance.com/capitalbudgeting.html). This web page contains an example of a capital budgeting case involving a $15,000 initial cash outflow.

Required

Compute the payback period and the net present value (assuming a 10% required rate of return) of the following investment—assume that its cash flows occur at year-end. Compared to the example case at the website, the larger cash inflows in the example below occur in the later years of the project's life. Is this investment acceptable based on the application of these two capital budgeting methods? Explain.

Year	Cash Flow
0	$(15,000)
1	1,000
2	2,000
3	3,000
4	6,000
5	7,000

BTN 11-6 Break into teams and identify four reasons that an international airline such as Southwest or Delta would invest in a project when its direct analysis using both payback period and net present value indicate it to be a poor investment. (*Hint:* Think about qualitative factors.) Provide an example of an investment project that supports your answer.

TEAMWORK IN ACTION

P1 P3

BTN 11-7 Read the chapter opener about Limor Fried and her company, Adafruit Industries. Suppose Limor's business continues to grow, and she builds a massive new manufacturing facility and warehousing center to make her business more efficient and reduce costs.

ENTREPRENEURIAL DECISION

P1 P2 P3 P4

Required

1. What are some of the management tools that Limor can use to evaluate whether the new manufacturing facility and warehousing center will be a good investment?
2. What information does Limor need to use the tools that you identified in your answer to part 1?
3. What are some of the advantages and disadvantages of each tool identified in your answer to part 1?

BTN 11-8 Visit or call a local auto dealership and inquire about leasing a car. Ask about the down payment and the required monthly payments. You will likely find the salesperson does not discuss the cost to purchase this car but focuses on the affordability of the monthly payments. This chapter gives you the tools to compute the cost of this car using the lease payment schedule in present dollars and to estimate the profit from leasing for an auto dealership.

HITTING THE ROAD

P3

Required

1. Compare the cost of leasing the car to buying it in present dollars using the information from the dealership you contact. (Assume you will make a final payment at the end of the lease and then own the car.)
2. Is it more costly to lease or buy the car? Support your answer with computations.

BTN 11-9 Samsung's annual report includes information about its debt and interest rates. Its annual report reveals that Samsung recently issued bonds with an interest rate of 4.1%.

GLOBAL DECISION

P3 P4

Samsung

Required

Explain how Samsung would use that 4.1% rate to evaluate its investments in capital projects.

ANSWERS TO MULTIPLE CHOICE QUIZ

1. a

2. e;

	Net Cash Flow	Present Value of an Annuity of 1 at 12%	Present Value of Cash Flows
Years 1–3	$3,600 + $30,000	2.4018	$ 80,700
Amount invested			(90,000)
Net present value . . .			$ (9,300)

3. a

4. c; Payback = $270,000/$61,200 per year = 4.4 years.

5. d; Accounting rate of return = $8,550/[($180,000 + $0)/2] = 9.5%.

Reporting Cash Flows

Chapter Preview

BASICS OF CASH FLOW REPORTING

C1 Purpose, measurement, and classification

Noncash activities

P1 Format and preparation

CASH FLOWS FROM OPERATING

P2 Indirect and direct methods of reporting

Illustration of indirect method

Summary of indirect method adjustments

CASH FLOWS FROM INVESTING

P3 Three-stage process of analysis

Analyzing noncurrent assets

Analyzing other assets

CASH FLOWS FROM FINANCING

P3 Three-stage process of analysis

Analyzing noncurrent liabilities

Analyzing equity

Overall summary using T-accounts

A1 Analyzing cash

Learning Objectives

CONCEPTUAL

C1 Distinguish between operating, investing, and financing activities, and describe how noncash investing and financing activities are disclosed.

ANALYTICAL

A1 Analyze the statement of cash flows and apply the cash flow on total assets ratio.

PROCEDURAL

P1 Prepare a statement of cash flows.

P2 Compute cash flows from operating activities using the indirect method.

P3 Determine cash flows from both investing and financing activities.

P4 *Appendix 12A*—Illustrate use of a spreadsheet to prepare a statement of cash flows.

P5 *Appendix 12B*—Compute cash flows from operating activities using the direct method.

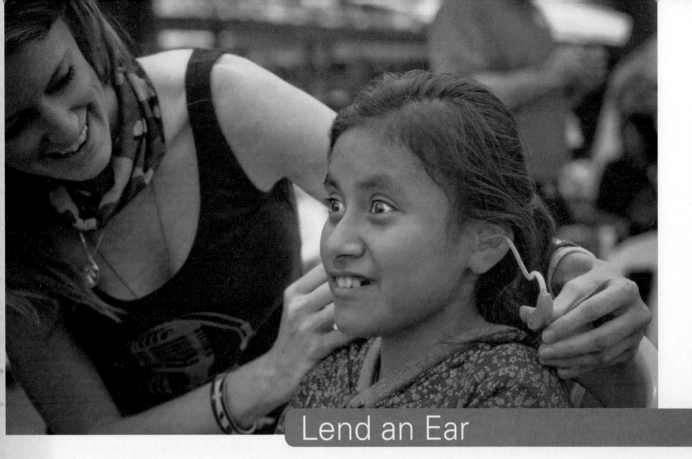

Lend an Ear

LOS ANGELES—"To have never heard music, laughter, nature—that's unimaginable for me," explains Bridget Hilton. "I'm inspired to enable people to have that joy in their lives." That inspiration led Bridget, along with Joe Huff, to launch **LSTN** (**LSTNheadphones.com**), a social enterprise "making headphones that sounded good, looked good, and were doing good!" Bridget explains that "we set forth on a mission that would set us apart—we'd produce great headphones made from reclaimed wood and, for every pair sold, LSTN would help restore hearing to a person in need."

To make her mission a reality, Bridget had to learn to run a manufacturing business with little cash. First, she set up what she says are "the two most important things—a manufacturer and a charity partner." However, cash shortage was still a problem. In response, Bridget "launched the site as a pre-order—in this day and age, you can launch a company with next to no money."

Bridget admits that as business grew and revenue flowed in, it was hard to find the cash from operations to expand. Many entrepreneurs turn to external cash financing in such cases. However, Bridget tightened her belt and focused on a lean operation. "Keep the spending down as long as possible. You don't need an office right away, or T-shirts with your logo, big events, a super fancy website, a bunch of employees,

"Consider your social values"
—Bridget Hilton

etc.," insists Bridget. "Work out of your house and coffee shops, use your network as much as possible, and put your head down and work hard. If you have a physical product, buy or make as little as possible (a minimum viable product) and test it to see if people even want it before you dump all your money into inventory."

Bridget monitors and controls cash flows for each of her operating, investing, and financing activities. "Being frugal will help you not only financially, but it will also force you to be creative," insists Bridget. Yet it is the mission that inspires her. "I love my company and what I do, so working is exciting." Even her analysis of LSTN's statement of cash flows, and its individual inflows and outflows, is embraced as it helps her stay on track.

To date, Bridget has successfully controlled cash outflows while growing cash inflows. She relies on cash flow information to make important business decisions, but never loses touch with her mission. "I recently returned from a trip to Peru," says Bridget. "When I saw the faces that lit up when children connected and communicated with their families, I lost it. It was truly life changing . . . to even change one person's life through our business proved that our plan was working."

Sources: *LSTN's website,* January 2015; *Trend Hunter,* August 2012; *Upstart,* May 2014; *SocialEarth,* August 2012; *Women 2.0,* January 2014

BASICS OF CASH FLOW REPORTING

This section describes the basics of cash flow reporting, including its purpose, measurement, classification, format, and preparation.

Purpose of the Statement of Cash Flows

The purpose of the **statement of cash flows** is to report cash receipts (inflows) and cash payments (outflows) during a period. This includes separately identifying the cash flows related to operating, investing, and financing activities. It is the detailed disclosure of individual sources and uses of cash that makes this statement useful to users. Information in this statement helps users answer questions such as these:

Point: Internal users rely on the statement of cash flows to make investing and financing decisions. External users rely on this statement to assess the amount and timing of a company's cash flows.

- What explains the change in the cash balance?
- Where does a company spend its cash?
- How does a company receive its cash?

- Why do income and cash flows differ?
- How much is paid in dividends?
- Is there a cash shortage?

Importance of Cash Flows

Information about cash flows can influence decision makers in important ways. For instance, we look more favorably at a company that is financing its expenditures with cash from operations than one that does it by selling its assets. Information about cash flows helps users decide whether a company has enough cash to pay its existing debts as they mature. It is also relied upon to evaluate a company's ability to meet unexpected obligations and pursue unexpected opportunities. External information users, especially, want to assess a company's ability to take advantage of new business opportunities. Internal users such as managers use cash flow information to plan day-to-day operating activities and make long-term investment decisions.

Macy's striking turnaround is an example of how analysis and management of cash flows can lead to improved financial stability. Several years ago Macy's obtained temporary protection from bankruptcy. It desperately needed to improve its cash flows, and did so by engaging in aggressive cost-cutting measures. As a result, Macy's annual cash flow rose to $210 million, up from a negative cash flow of $38.9 million in the prior year. Macy's eventually met its financial obligations and then successfully merged with **Federated Department Stores**.

The case of **W. T. Grant Co.** is a classic example of the importance of cash flow information in predicting a company's future performance and financial strength. Grant reported net income of more than $40 million per year for three consecutive years. At that same time, it was experiencing an alarming decrease in cash provided by operations. For instance, net cash outflow was more than $90 million by the end of that three-year period. Grant soon went bankrupt. Users who relied solely on Grant's income numbers were unpleasantly surprised. This reminds us that cash flows as well as income statement and balance sheet information are crucial in business decisions.

Bloomberg via Getty Images

▌ Decision Insight

Do You Know Your Cash Flows?   "A lender must have a complete understanding of a borrower's cash flows to assess both the borrowing needs and repayment sources. This requires information about the major types of cash inflows and outflows. I have seen many companies, whose financial statements indicate good profitability, experience severe financial problems because the owners or managers lacked a good understanding of cash flows."—Mary E. Garza, **Bank of America** ▪

Measurement of Cash Flows

Cash flows are defined to include both *cash* and *cash equivalents*. The statement of cash flows explains the difference between the beginning and ending balances of cash and cash equivalents. We continue to use the phrases *cash flows* and the *statement of cash flows,* but remember that both phrases refer to cash *and* cash equivalents.

Recall that a cash equivalent must satisfy two criteria: (1) be readily convertible to a known amount of cash and (2) be sufficiently close to its maturity so its market value is unaffected by interest rate changes. In most cases, a debt security must be within three months of its maturity

Cash Equivalents

to satisfy these criteria. Companies must disclose and follow a clear policy for determining cash and cash equivalents and apply it consistently from period to period. **American Express**, for example, defines its cash equivalents as "time deposits and other highly liquid investments with original maturities of 90 days or less."

Classification of Cash Flows

Since cash and cash equivalents are combined, the statement of cash flows does not report transactions between cash and cash equivalents, such as cash paid to purchase cash equivalents and cash received from selling cash equivalents. However, all other cash receipts and cash payments are classified and reported on the statement in one of three categories—operating, investing, or financing activities. Individual cash receipts and payments for each of these three categories are labeled to identify their originating transactions or events. A net cash inflow (source) occurs when the receipts in a category exceed the payments. A net cash outflow (use) occurs when the payments in a category exceed the receipts.

C1_____

Distinguish between operating, investing, and financing activities, and describe how noncash investing and financing activities are disclosed.

Operating Activities   **Operating activities** include those transactions and events that determine net income. Examples are the production and purchase of inventory, the sale of goods and services to customers, and the expenditures to operate the business. Not all items in income, such as unusual gains and losses, are operating activities (we discuss these exceptions later). Exhibit 12.1 lists the more common cash inflows and outflows from operating activities.

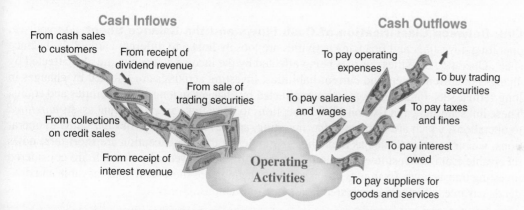

EXHIBIT 12.1

Cash Flows from Operating Activities

Investing Activities   **Investing activities** generally include those transactions and events that affect long-term assets—namely, the purchase and sale of long-term assets. They also include (1) the purchase and sale of short-term investments in the securities of other entities, *except* trading securities, and (2) lending and collecting money for notes receivable. Exhibit 12.2 lists examples of cash flows from investing activities. Cash from collecting the principal amounts of notes that result from a loan to another party are classified as investing. However, the FASB requires that the collection of interest on notes be reported as an operating activity; also, if a note results from sales to customers, it is classified as operating.

Point: The FASB requires that *cash dividends received* and *cash interest received* be reported as operating activities.

EXHIBIT 12.2

Cash Flows from Investing Activities

Financing Activities **Financing activities** include those transactions and events that affect long-term liabilities and equity. Examples are (1) obtaining cash from issuing debt and repaying the amounts borrowed and (2) receiving cash from or distributing cash to owners. These activities involve transactions with a company's owners and creditors. They also involve borrowing and repaying principal amounts relating to both short- and long-term debt. GAAP requires that payments of interest expense be classified as operating activities. Exhibit 12.3 lists examples of cash flows from financing activities.

Point: Interest payments on a loan are classified as operating activities, but payments of loan principal are financing activities.

EXHIBIT 12.3

Cash Flows from Financing Activities

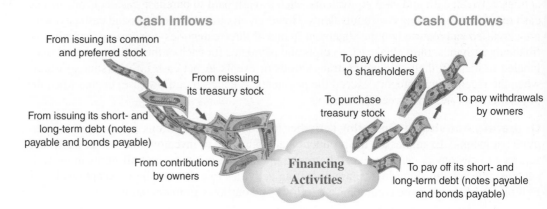

Cash Inflows   **Cash Outflows**

From issuing its common and preferred stock

From reissuing its treasury stock

From issuing its short- and long-term debt (notes payable and bonds payable)

From contributions by owners

Financing Activities

To pay dividends to shareholders

To purchase treasury stock

To pay withdrawals by owners

To pay off its short- and long-term debt (notes payable and bonds payable)

Link Between Classification of Cash Flows and the Balance Sheet As you see, operating, investing, and financing activities are loosely linked to different parts of the balance sheet. Operating activities, besides being affected by the income statement, are also affected by changes in current assets and current liabilities. Investing activities are affected by changes in long-term assets. Financing activities are affected by changes in long-term liabilities and equity. These links are shown in Exhibit 12.4. Exceptions to these links are: (1) current assets *unrelated* to operations, which are then treated as investing, and (2) current liabilities *unrelated* to operations, which are then treated as financing. Examples of the first exception are short-term notes receivable from noncustomers and marketable (not trading) securities, which are considered investing transactions. Examples of the second exception are short-term notes payable and dividends payable, which are considered financing transactions.

EXHIBIT 12.4

Linkage of Cash Flow Classifications to the Balance Sheet

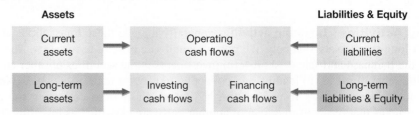

Assets		Liabilities & Equity
Current assets →	Operating cash flows	← Current liabilities
Long-term assets →	Investing cash flows Financing cash flows	← Long-term liabilities & Equity

■ **Decision** Insight ➤

Where in the Statement Are Cash Flows? Cash flows can be delayed or accelerated at the end of a period to improve or reduce current period cash flows. Also, cash flows can be misclassified. Cash outflows reported under operating activities are interpreted as expense payments. However, cash outflows reported under investing activities are interpreted as a positive sign of growth potential. Thus, managers face incentives to misclassify cash flows. For these reasons, cash flow reporting warrants our scrutiny. ■

Noncash Investing and Financing

Some important investing and financing activities do not affect cash receipts or payments. One example of such a transaction is the purchase of long-term assets using a long-term note payable (loan). This transaction involves both investing and financing activities but does not affect any cash inflow or outflow, so it is not reported in any of the three sections of the statement of cash flows. Such transactions are reported at the bottom of the statement of cash flows or in a note to the statement because of their importance and the *full-disclosure principle.* Exhibit 12.5 lists transactions commonly disclosed as noncash investing and financing activities.

- Retirement of debt by issuing equity stock.
- Conversion of preferred stock to common stock.
- Lease of assets in a capital lease transaction.
- Purchase of long-term assets by issuing a note or bond.
- Exchange of noncash assets for other noncash assets.
- Purchase of noncash assets by issuing equity or debt.

EXHIBIT 12.5

Examples of Noncash Investing and Financing Activities

Format of the Statement of Cash Flows

A statement of cash flows must report information about a company's cash receipts and cash payments during the period. Exhibit 12.6 shows the usual format. A company must report cash flows from three activities: operating, investing, and financing. The statement then shows the net increase or decrease from those activities. Finally, it explains how transactions and events impact the prior period-end cash balance to produce its current period-end balance. Any non-cash investing and financing transactions are disclosed in a note disclosure or separate schedule.

P1_____

Prepare a statement of cash flows.

COMPANY NAME		
Statement of Cash Flows		
For period Ended date		
Cash flows from operating activities		
[Compute operating cash flows using indirect or direct method]		
Net cash provided (used) by operating activities	$ #	
Cash flows from investing activities		
[List of individual inflows and outflows]		
Net cash provided (used) by investing activities	#	
Cash flows from financing activities		
[List of individual inflows and outflows]		
Net cash provided (used) by financing activities	#	
Net increase (decrease) in cash	$ #	
Cash (and equivalents) balance at prior period-end	#	
Cash (and equivalents) balance at current period-end	$ #	

Separate schedule or note disclosure of any noncash investing and financing transactions is required.

EXHIBIT 12.6

Format of the Statement of Cash Flows

Point: Positive cash flows for a section are titled net cash "provided by" or "from." Negative cash flows are labeled as net cash "used by."

■ **Decision Maker**

Entrepreneur You are considering purchasing a start-up business that recently reported a $110,000 annual net loss and a $225,000 annual net cash inflow. How are these results possible? ■ [Answers follow the chapter's Summary.]

Preparing the Statement of Cash Flows

Preparing a statement of cash flows involves five steps, as shown in Exhibit 12.7.

1. Compute the net increase or decrease in cash.
2. Compute and report the net cash provided or used by operating activities (using either the direct or indirect method; both are explained).
3. Compute and report the net cash provided or used by investing activities.
4. Compute and report the net cash provided or used by financing activities.
5. Compute the net cash flow by combining net cash provided or used by operating, investing, and financing activities, and then *prove it* by adding it to the beginning cash balance to show that it equals the ending cash balance.

Point: View the change in cash as a *target* number (or check figure) that we will fully explain and prove in the statement of cash flows.

EXHIBIT 12.7

Five Steps in Preparing the
Statement of Cash Flows

Step 1 Compute net increase or decrease in cash.

Step 2 Compute net cash from operating activities.

Step 3 Compute net cash from investing activities.

Step 4 Compute net cash from financing activities.

Step 5 Prove and report beginning and ending cash balances.

Computing the net increase or net decrease in cash is a simple but crucial computation. It equals the current period's cash balance minus the prior period's cash balance. This is the *bottom-line* figure for the statement of cash flows and is a check on accuracy.

Analyzing the Cash Account A company's cash receipts and cash payments are recorded in the Cash account in its general ledger. The Cash account is therefore a natural place to look for information about cash flows from operating, investing, and financing activities. To illustrate, see the summarized Cash T-account of Genesis, Inc., in Exhibit 12.8. The Cash account increased $5,000, from $12,000 to $17,000. Individual cash transactions are summarized in this Cash account according to the major types of cash receipts and cash payments. For instance, only the total of cash receipts from all customers is listed. Individual cash transactions underlying these totals can number in the thousands. Accounting software is available to provide summarized cash accounts.

EXHIBIT 12.8

Summarized Cash Account

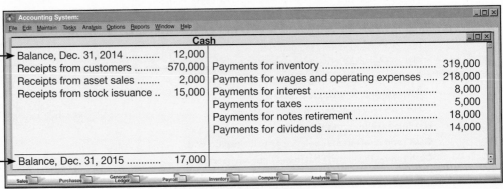

Accounting System:		
File Edit Maintain Tasks Analysis Options Reports Window Help		
Cash		
Balance, Dec. 31, 2014	12,000	
Receipts from customers	570,000	Payments for inventory 319,000
Receipts from asset sales	2,000	Payments for wages and operating expenses 218,000
Receipts from stock issuance ..	15,000	Payments for interest 8,000
		Payments for taxes 5,000
		Payments for notes retirement 18,000
		Payments for dividends 14,000
Balance, Dec. 31, 2015	17,000	
Sales Purchases General Ledger Payroll Inventory Company Analysis		

The statement of cash flows summarizes and classifies the transactions that led to the $5,000 increase in the Cash account. Preparing a statement of cash flows from Exhibit 12.8 requires determining whether an individual cash inflow or outflow is an operating, investing, or financing activity, and then listing each by activity. However, preparing the statement of cash flows from an analysis of the summarized Cash account has two limitations. First, most companies have many individual cash receipts and payments, making it difficult to review them all. Accounting software minimizes this burden, but it is still a task requiring professional judgment for many transactions. Second, the Cash account does not usually carry an adequate description of each cash transaction, making assignment of all cash transactions according to activity difficult.

Analyzing Noncash Accounts A second approach to preparing the statement of cash flows is analyzing noncash accounts. This approach uses the fact that when a company records cash inflows and outflows with debits and credits to the Cash account (see Exhibit 12.8), it also records credits and debits in noncash accounts (reflecting double-entry accounting). Many of these noncash accounts are balance sheet accounts—for instance, from the sale of land for cash. Others are revenue and expense accounts that are closed to equity. For instance, the sale of services for cash yields a credit to Services Revenue that is closed to Retained Earnings for a corporation. In sum, *all cash transactions eventually affect noncash balance sheet accounts.* Thus, we can determine cash inflows and outflows by analyzing changes in noncash balance sheet accounts.

Exhibit 12.9 uses the accounting equation to show the relation between the Cash account and the noncash balance sheet accounts. This exhibit starts with the accounting equation (at the top). It is then expanded in line (2) to separate cash from noncash asset accounts. To isolate cash on one side of the equation, line (3) shows noncash asset accounts being subtracted from both sides of the equation. Cash now equals the sum of the liability and equity accounts *minus* the noncash asset accounts. Line (4) points out that *changes* on one side of the accounting equation equal *changes* on the other side. It shows that we can explain changes in cash by analyzing changes in the noncash accounts consisting of liability accounts, equity accounts, and noncash asset accounts. By analyzing noncash balance sheet accounts and any related income statement accounts, we can prepare a statement of cash flows.

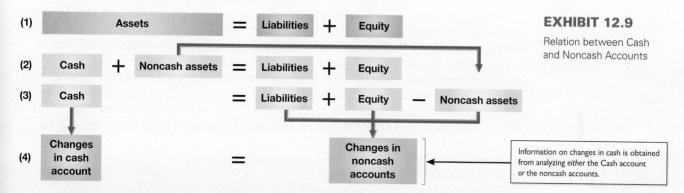

EXHIBIT 12.9

Relation between Cash and Noncash Accounts

Information to Prepare the Statement Information to prepare the statement of cash flows usually comes from three sources: (1) comparative balance sheets, (2) the current income statement, and (3) additional information. Comparative balance sheets are used to compute changes in noncash accounts from the beginning to the end of the period. The current income statement is used to help compute cash flows from operating activities. Additional information often includes details on transactions and events that help explain both the cash flows and non-cash investing and financing activities.

Classify each of the following cash flows as operating, investing, or financing activities.

___ **a.** Purchase equipment for cash

___ **b.** Cash payment of wages

___ **c.** Issuance of stock for cash

___ **d.** Receipt of cash dividends from investments

___ **e.** Cash collections from customers

___ **f.** Note payable issued for cash

___ **g.** Cash paid for utilities

___ **h.** Cash paid to acquire investments

___ **i.** Cash paid to retire debt

___ **j.** Cash received as interest on investments

___ **k.** Cash received from selling investments

___ **l.** Cash received from a bank loan

NEED-TO-KNOW 12-1

Classifying Cash Flows

C1

QC1

Solution

a. Investing	**c.** Financing	**e.** Operating	**g.** Operating	**i.** Financing	**k.** Investing
b. Operating	**d.** Operating	**f.** Financing	**h.** Investing	**j.** Operating	**l.** Financing

Do More: QS 12-1, QS 12-2, E 12-1

CASH FLOWS FROM OPERATING

Indirect and Direct Methods of Reporting

Cash flows provided (used) by operating activities are reported in one of two ways: the *direct method* or the *indirect method*. These two different methods apply only to the operating activities section.

Operating

The **direct method** separately lists each major item of operating cash receipts (such as cash received from customers) and each major item of operating cash payments (such as cash paid for inventory). The cash payments are subtracted from cash receipts to determine the net cash provided (used) by operating activities.

The **indirect method** reports net income and then adjusts it for items necessary to obtain net cash provided or used by operating activities. It does *not* report individual items of cash inflows and cash outflows from operating activities. Instead, the indirect method reports the necessary adjustments to reconcile net income to net cash provided or used by operating activities. **The net cash amount provided by operating activities is** *identical* **under both the direct and indirect methods.** This equality always exists. The difference in these methods is with the computation and presentation of this amount. The FASB recommends the direct method, but because it is not required and the indirect method is arguably easier to compute, nearly all companies report operating cash flows using the indirect method.

To illustrate, we prepare the operating activities section of the statement of cash flows for Genesis. Exhibit 12.10 shows the December 31, 2014 and 2015, balance sheets of Genesis along with its 2015 income statement. We use this information to prepare a statement of cash flows that explains the $5,000 increase in cash for 2015 as reflected in its balance sheets. This $5,000 is computed as Cash of $17,000 at the end of 2015 minus Cash of $12,000 at the end of 2014.

EXHIBIT 12.10

Financial Statements

> *The next section describes the indirect method. Appendix 12B describes the direct method. An instructor can choose to cover either one or both methods. Neither section depends on the other. If the indirect method is skipped, then read Appendix 12B and return to the section (five pages ahead) titled "Cash Flows from Investing."*

GENESIS Income Statement For Year Ended December 31, 2015		
Sales		$590,000
Cost of goods sold	$300,000	
Wages and other operating expenses	216,000	
Interest expense	7,000	
Depreciation expense...........	24,000	(547,000)
		43,000
Other gains (losses)		
Loss on sale of plant assets	(6,000)	
Gain on retirement of notes ...	16,000	10,000
Income before taxes		53,000
Income taxes expense		(15,000)
Net income		$ 38,000

Additional information for 2015

a. The accounts payable balances result from inventory purchases.

b. Purchased $60,000 in plant assets by issuing $60,000 of notes payable.

c. Sold plant assets with a book value of $8,000 (original cost of $20,000 and accumulated depreciation of $12,000) for $2,000 cash, yielding a $6,000 loss.

d. Received $15,000 cash from issuing 3,000 shares of common stock.

e. Paid $18,000 cash to retire notes with a $34,000 book value, yielding a $16,000 gain.

f. Declared and paid cash dividends of $14,000.

GENESIS Balance Sheets December 31, 2015 and 2014			
	2015	**2014**	**Change**
Assets			
Current assets			
Cash....................	$ 17,000	$ 12,000	$ 5,000 Increase
Accounts receivable	60,000	40,000	20,000 Increase
Inventory.................	84,000	70,000	14,000 Increase
Prepaid expenses...........	6,000	4,000	2,000 Increase
Total current assets........	167,000	126,000	
Long-term assets			
Plant assets	250,000	210,000	40,000 Increase
Accumulated depreciation....	(60,000)	(48,000)	12,000 Increase
Total assets	$357,000	$288,000	
Liabilities			
Current liabilities			
Accounts payable...........	$ 35,000	$ 40,000	$ 5,000 Decrease
Interest payable............	3,000	4,000	1,000 Decrease
Income taxes payable	22,000	12,000	10,000 Increase
Total current liabilities.......	60,000	56,000	
Long-term notes payable.......	90,000	64,000	26,000 Increase
Total liabilities	150,000	120,000	
Equity			
Common stock, $5 par........	95,000	80,000	15,000 Increase
Retained earnings	112,000	88,000	24,000 Increase
Total equity	207,000	168,000	
Total liabilities and equity	$357,000	$288,000	

Applying the Indirect Method of Reporting

Net income is computed using accrual accounting, which recognizes revenues when earned and expenses when incurred. Revenues and expenses do not necessarily reflect the receipt and payment of cash. The indirect method of computing and reporting net cash flows from operating activities involves adjusting the net income figure to obtain the net cash provided or used by operating activities. This includes subtracting noncash increases from net income and adding noncash charges back to net income.

To illustrate, the indirect method begins with Genesis's net income of $38,000 and adjusts it to obtain net cash provided by operating activities of $20,000. Exhibit 12.11 shows the results of the indirect method of reporting operating cash flows, which adjusts net income for two types of adjustments. There are ① adjustments to income statement items that neither provide nor use cash and ② adjustments to reflect changes in balance sheet current assets and current liabilities (linked to operating activities). This section describes each of these adjustments.

P2

Compute cash flows from operating activities using the indirect method.

EXHIBIT 12.11

Operating Activities Section—Indirect Method

GENESIS
Statement of Cash Flows—Operating Section under Indirect Method
For Year Ended December 31, 2015

Cash flows from operating activities	
Net income	$ 38,000
Adjustments to reconcile net income to net cash provided by operating activities	
Income statement items not affecting cash	
① Depreciation expense	24,000
Loss on sale of plant assets	6,000
Gain on retirement of notes	(16,000)
Changes in current assets and liabilities	
Increase in accounts receivable	(20,000)
Increase in inventory	(14,000)
② Increase in prepaid expenses	(2,000)
Decrease in accounts payable	(5,000)
Decrease in interest payable	(1,000)
Increase in income taxes payable	10,000
Net cash provided by operating activities	**$20,000**

① Adjustments for Income Statement Items Not Affecting Cash   The income statement usually includes some expenses and losses that do not reflect cash outflows. Examples are depreciation, amortization, depletion, bad debts expense, loss from an asset sale, and loss from retirement of notes payable. When there are expenses and losses that do not reflect cash outflows, the indirect method for reporting operating cash flows requires the following adjustment:

Expenses and losses with no cash outflows are added back to net income.

To see the logic of this adjustment, recall that items such as depreciation, amortization, and depletion have *no* cash effect, and adding them back cancels their deductions. To see the logic for losses, consider that items such as a plant asset sale and a notes retirement are usually recorded by recognizing the cash, removing all plant asset or notes accounts, and recording any loss or gain. The cash received or paid is part of either investing or financing cash flows. *No* operating cash flow effect occurs, and adding it back to net income cancels the deduction.

Similarly, when net income includes revenues that do not reflect cash inflows, the indirect method for reporting operating cash flows requires the following adjustment:

Revenues and gains with no cash inflows are subtracted from net income.

We apply these adjustments to the income statement items in Exhibit 12.10 that do not affect cash.

Depreciation.   Depreciation expense is Genesis's only operating item that has no effect on cash flows. We must add back the $24,000 depreciation expense to net income when computing

Point: An income statement reports revenues, gains, expenses, and losses on an accrual basis. The statement of cash flows reports cash received and cash paid for operating, financing, and investing activities.

cash provided by operating activities. Adding it back cancels the expense. (We later explain that any cash outflow to acquire a plant asset is reported as an investing activity.)

Loss on sale of plant assets. Genesis reports a $6,000 loss on sale of plant assets as part of net income. This loss is a proper deduction in computing income, but it is *not part of operating activities*. Instead, a sale of plant assets is part of investing activities. Thus, the $6,000 nonoperating loss is added back to net income (see Exhibit 12.11). Adding it back cancels the loss. We later explain how to report the cash inflow from the asset sale in investing activities.

Gain on retirement of debt. A $16,000 gain on retirement of debt is properly included in net income, but it is *not part of operating activities*. This means the $16,000 nonoperating gain must be subtracted from net income to obtain net cash provided by operating activities (see Exhibit 12.11). Subtracting it cancels the recorded gain. We later describe how to report the cash outflow to retire debt.

These three adjustments to net income for "items not affecting cash" are shown as follows in the operating section:

Net income	$ 38,000
Adjustments to reconcile net income to net cash provided by operating activities	
Income statement items not affecting cash	
Depreciation expense	24,000
Loss on sale of plant assets	6,000
Gain on retirement of notes	(16,000)

② **Adjustments for Changes in Current Assets and Current Liabilities** This section describes adjustments for changes in current assets and current liabilities.

Adjustments for changes in current assets. Decreases in current assets require the following adjustment:

Decreases in current assets are added to net income.

Increases in current assets require the following adjustment:

Increases in current assets are subtracted from net income.

Adjustments for changes in current liabilities. Increases in current liabilities require the following adjustment to net income when computing operating cash flows:

Increases in current liabilities are added to net income.

Conversely, when current liabilities decrease, the following adjustment is required:

Decreases in current liabilities are subtracted from net income.

To illustrate, we apply these adjustment rules to the three noncash current assets and three current liabilities in Exhibit 12.10, which are then reported as follows in the operating section:

Reconstructed Entry
Cash . . . . #
   Current Asset . . . . . .   #
Reconstructed Entry
Current Asset . . . . #
   Cash . . . .   #

Reconstructed Entry
Cash . . . . #
   Current Liabilities . . .   #
Reconstructed Entry
Current Liabilities . . . . . #
   Cash . . . .   #

Net income	$ 38,000
Adjustments to reconcile net income to net cash provided by operating activities	
Increase in accounts receivable	(20,000)
Increase in inventory	(14,000)
Increase in prepaid expenses	(2,000)
Decrease in accounts payable	(5,000)
Decrease in interest payable	(1,000)
Increase in income taxes payable	10,000

Following is an explanation, including T-account analysis, for how these adjustments result in cash receipts and cash payments.

Accounts receivable. Following the rule above, the $20,000 increase in the current asset of accounts receivable is subtracted from income. This increase implies that Genesis collects less cash than is reported in sales. To see this it is helpful to use *account analysis.* This involves setting up a T-account and reconstructing its major entries to compute cash receipts or payments as follows.

Point: Operating activities are typically those that determine income, which are often reflected in changes in current assets and current liabilities.

Numbers in black are taken from Exhibit 12.10. The red number is the computed (plug) figure.

Accounts Receivable			
Bal., Dec. 31, 2014	40,000		
Sales	590,000	Cash receipts =	570,000
Bal., Dec. 31, 2015	60,000		

We see that sales are $20,000 greater than cash receipts. This $20,000—reflected in the increase in Accounts Receivable—is subtracted from net income when computing cash provided by operating activities.

Inventory. The $14,000 increase in inventory is subtracted from income. This increase implies that Genesis had greater cash purchases than cost of goods sold, as reflected in the following account analysis:

Inventory			
Bal., Dec. 31, 2014	70,000		
Purchases =	314,000	Cost of goods sold	300,000
Bal., Dec. 31, 2015	84,000		

Prepaid expenses. The $2,000 increase in prepaid expense is subtracted from income, implying that Genesis's cash payments exceed its recorded prepaid expenses and is reflected in the following T-account:

Prepaid Expenses			
Bal., Dec. 31, 2014	4,000		
Cash payments =	218,000	Wages and other operating exp.	216,000
Bal., Dec. 31, 2015	6,000		

Accounts payable. The $5,000 decrease in the current liability for accounts payable is subtracted from income. This decrease implies that cash payments to suppliers exceed purchases, which is reflected in the following T-account:

Accounts Payable			
		Bal., Dec. 31, 2014	40,000
Cash payments =	319,000	Purchases	314,000
		Bal., Dec. 31, 2015	35,000

Interest payable. The $1,000 decrease in interest payable is subtracted from income. This decrease indicates that cash paid for interest exceeds interest expense, which is reflected in the following T-account:

Interest Payable			
		Bal., Dec. 31, 2014	4,000
Cash paid for interest =	8,000	Interest expense	7,000
		Bal., Dec. 31, 2015	3,000

Income taxes payable. The $10,000 increase in income taxes payable is added to income. This increase implies that reported income taxes exceed the cash paid for taxes, which is reflected in the following T-account:

Income Taxes Payable			
		Bal., Dec. 31, 2014	12,000
Cash paid for taxes =	5,000	Income taxes expense	15,000
		Bal., Dec. 31, 2015	22,000

Summary Adjustments for Operating Activities—Indirect Method

Exhibit 12.12 summarizes the adjustments to net income when computing net cash provided or used by operating activities under the indirect method.

EXHIBIT 12.12

Summary of Adjustments for Operating Activities— Indirect Method

---

Net Income (or Loss)

① Adjustments for operating items not providing or using cash

   + Noncash expenses and losses

     Examples: Expenses for depreciation, depletion, and amortization; losses from disposal of long-term assets and from retirement of debt

   − Noncash revenues and gains

     Examples: Earnings from equity-method investments; gains from disposal of long-term assets and from retirement of debt

② Adjustments for changes in current assets and current liabilities

   + Decrease in noncash current operating asset

   − Increase in noncash current operating asset

   + Increase in current operating liability

   − Decrease in current operating liability

Net cash provided (used) by operating activities

■ Decision Insight

How Much Cash Is in Income? The difference between net income and operating cash flows can be large and sometimes reflects on the quality of earnings. This bar chart shows the net income and operating cash flows of three companies. Operating cash flows can be either higher or lower than net income. ■

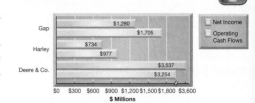

A company's current-year income statement and selected balance sheet data at December 31 of the current and prior years follow. Prepare the cash flows from operating activities section only of its statement of cash flows using the indirect method for the current year.

Reporting Operating Cash Flows (Indirect)

P2

Income Statement For Current Year Ended December 31	
Sales revenue	$120
Expenses	
Cost of goods sold	50
Depreciation expense	30
Salaries expense	17
Interest expense	3
Net income	$ 20

Selected Balance Sheet Accounts		
At December 31	**Current Yr**	**Prior Yr**
Accounts receivable	$12	$10
Inventory	6	9
Accounts payable	7	11
Salaries payable	8	3
Interest payable	1	0

Solution

Cash Flows from Operating Activities—Indirect Method For Current Year Ended December 31		
Cash flows from operating activities		
Net income		$20
Adjustments to reconcile net income to net cash provided by operating activities		
Income statement items not affecting cash		
Depreciation expense	$30	
Changes in current assets and current liabilities		
Increase in accounts receivable	(2)	
Decrease in inventory	3	
Decrease in accounts payable	(4)	
Increase in salaries payable	5	
Increase in interest payable	1	33
Net cash provided by operating activities		$53

> Do More: QS 12-3, QS 12-4,
> E 12-4, E 12-5, E 12-6

QC2

CASH FLOWS FROM INVESTING

The third major step in preparing the statement of cash flows is to compute and report cash flows from investing activities. We normally do this by identifying changes in (1) all noncurrent asset accounts and (2) the current accounts for both notes receivable and investments in securities (excluding trading securities). We then analyze changes in these accounts to determine their effect, if any, on cash and report the cash flow effects in the investing activities section of the statement of cash flows. **Reporting of investing activities is identical under the direct method and indirect method.**

Three-Stage Process of Analysis

Information to compute cash flows from investing activities is usually taken from beginning and ending balance sheets and the income statement. We use a three-stage process to determine cash provided or used by investing activities: (1) identify changes in investing-related accounts, (2) explain these changes using reconstruction analysis, and (3) report their cash flow effects.

P3_____

Determine cash flows from both investing and financing activities.

Analyzing Noncurrent Assets

Information about the Genesis transactions provided earlier reveals that the company both purchased and sold plant assets during the period. Both transactions are investing activities and are analyzed for their cash flow effects in this section.

Plant Asset Transactions   The *first stage* in analyzing the Plant Assets account and its related Accumulated Depreciation account is to identify any changes in these accounts from comparative balance sheets in Exhibit 12.10. This analysis reveals a $40,000 increase in plant assets from $210,000 to $250,000 and a $12,000 increase in accumulated depreciation from $48,000 to $60,000.

The *second stage* is to explain these changes. Items *b* and *c* of the additional information in Exhibit 12.10 affect plant assets. Recall that the Plant Assets account is affected by both asset purchases and sales; its Accumulated Depreciation account is normally increased from depreciation and decreased from the removal of accumulated depreciation in asset sales. To explain changes in these accounts and to identify their cash flow effects, we prepare *reconstructed entries* from prior transactions; *they are not the actual entries by the preparer*.

Point: Investing activities include (1) purchasing and selling long-term assets, (2) lending and collecting on notes receivable, and (3) purchasing and selling short-term investments other than cash equivalents and trading securities.

Point: Financing and investing info is available in ledger accounts to help explain changes in comparative balance sheets. Post references lead to relevant entries and explanations.

To illustrate, item *b* reports that Genesis purchased plant assets of $60,000 by issuing $60,000 in notes payable to the seller. The reconstructed entry for analysis of item *b* follows.

Reconstruction	Plant Assets	60,000	
	Notes Payable		60,000

Next, item *c* reports that Genesis sold plant assets costing $20,000 (with $12,000 of accumulated depreciation) for $2,000 cash, resulting in a $6,000 loss. The reconstructed entry for analysis of item *c* follows.

Reconstruction	Cash	2,000	
	Accumulated Depreciation	12,000	
	Loss on Sale of Plant Assets	6,000	
	Plant Assets		20,000

Point: When determining cash flows from investing, T-account analysis is key to reconstructing accounts and amounts.

We also reconstruct the entry for Depreciation Expense from the income statement. Depreciation expense results in no cash flow effect.

Reconstruction	Depreciation Expense	24,000	
	Accumulated Depreciation		24,000

These three reconstructed entries are reflected in the following plant asset and related T-accounts.

Plant Assets				
Bal., Dec. 31, 2014	210,000			
Purchase	60,000	Sale	20,000	
Bal., Dec. 31, 2015	250,000			

Accumulated Depreciation—Plant Assets				
		Bal., Dec. 31, 2014	48,000	
Sale	12,000	Depr. expense	24,000	
		Bal., Dec. 31, 2015	60,000	

Example: If a plant asset costing $40,000 with $37,000 of accumulated depreciation is sold at a $1,000 loss, what is the cash flow? What is the cash flow if this asset is sold at a gain of $3,000? *Answers:* +$2,000; +$6,000.

This reconstruction analysis is complete in that the change in plant assets from $210,000 to $250,000 is fully explained by the $60,000 purchase and the $20,000 sale. Also, the change in accumulated depreciation from $48,000 to $60,000 is fully explained by depreciation expense of $24,000 and the removal of $12,000 in accumulated depreciation from the asset sale.

The *third stage* in analyzing the Plant Assets account looks back at the reconstructed entries to identify any cash flows. The identified cash flow effect is reported in the investing section of the statement as follows:

Cash flows from investing activities	
Cash received from sale of plant assets	$2,000

The $60,000 purchase described in item *b* and financed by issuing notes is a noncash investing and financing activity. It is reported in a note or in a separate schedule to the statement as follows:

Noncash investing and financing activity	
Purchased plant assets with issuance of notes	$60,000

Analyzing Additional Assets

Genesis did not have any additional noncurrent assets (or nonoperating current assets) and, therefore, we have no additional investing transactions to analyze. If other investing assets did exist, we would identify and report the investing cash flows using the same three-stage process illustrated for plant assets.

Use the following information to determine this company's cash flows from investing activities.

a. A factory with a book value of $100 and an original cost of $800 was sold at a loss of $10.

b. Paid $70 cash for new equipment.

c. Long-term stock investments were sold for $20 cash, yielding a loss of $4.

d. Sold land costing $175 for $160 cash, yielding a loss of $15.

NEED-TO-KNOW 12-3

Reporting Investing
Cash Flows

P3

Solution

Cash flows from investing activities	
Cash received from sale of factory*	$ 90
Cash paid for new equipment	(70)
Cash received from sale of long-term investments	20
Cash received from sale of land	160
Net cash provided by investing activities	$200

Do More: QS 12-5, QS 12-6,
QS 12-9, E 12-7

QC3

*Cash received from sale of factory = Book value − Loss = $100 − $10 = $90

CASH FLOWS FROM FINANCING

The fourth major step in preparing the statement of cash flows is to compute and report cash flows from financing activities. We normally do this by identifying changes in all noncurrent liability accounts (including the current portion of any notes and bonds) and the equity accounts. These accounts include long-term debt, notes payable, bonds payable, common stock, and retained earnings. Changes in these accounts are then analyzed using available information to determine their effect, if any, on cash. Results are reported in the financing activities section of the statement. **Reporting of financing activities is identical under the direct method and indirect method.**

Three-Stage Process of Analysis

We again use a three-stage process to determine cash provided or used by financing activities: (1) identify changes in financing-related accounts, (2) explain these changes using reconstruction analysis, and (3) report their cash flow effects.

Analyzing Noncurrent Liabilities

Information about Genesis provided earlier reveals two transactions involving noncurrent liabilities. We analyzed one of those, the $60,000 issuance of notes payable to purchase plant assets. This transaction is reported as a significant noncash investing and financing activity in a footnote or a separate schedule to the statement of cash flows. The other remaining transaction involving noncurrent liabilities is the cash retirement of notes payable.

Point: Financing activities generally refer to changes in the noncurrent liability and the equity accounts. Examples are (1) receiving cash from issuing debt or repaying amounts borrowed and (2) receiving cash from or distributing cash to owners.

Notes Payable Transactions   The *first stage* in analysis of notes is to review the comparative balance sheets from Exhibit 12.10. This analysis reveals an increase in notes payable from $64,000 to $90,000.

The *second stage* explains this change. Item *e* of the additional information in Exhibit 12.10 reports that notes with a carrying value of $34,000 are retired for $18,000 cash, resulting in a $16,000 gain. The reconstructed entry for analysis of item *e* follows:

Reconstruction	Notes Payable	34,000	
	Gain on retirement of debt		16,000
	Cash		18,000

This entry reveals an $18,000 cash outflow for retirement of notes and a $16,000 gain from comparing the notes payable carrying value to the cash received. This gain does not reflect any cash inflow or outflow. Also, item *b* of the additional information reports that Genesis purchased plant assets costing $60,000 by issuing $60,000 in notes payable to the seller. We reconstructed this entry when analyzing investing activities: It showed a $60,000 increase to notes payable that is reported as a noncash investing and financing transaction. The Notes Payable account is explained by these reconstructed entries as follows:

Notes Payable			
		Bal., Dec. 31, 2014	64,000
Retired notes	34,000	Issued notes	60,000
		Bal., Dec. 31, 2015	90,000

The *third stage* is to report the cash flow effect of the notes retirement in the financing section of the statement as follows:

Cash flows from financing activities
Cash paid to retire notes . . . . $(18,000)

Analyzing Equity

The Genesis information reveals two transactions involving equity accounts. The first is the issuance of common stock for cash. The second is the declaration and payment of cash dividends. We analyze both.

Common Stock Transactions   The *first stage* in analyzing common stock is to review the comparative balance sheets from Exhibit 12.10, which reveal an increase in common stock from $80,000 to $95,000.

The *second stage* explains this change. Item *d* of the additional information in Exhibit 12.10 reports that 3,000 shares of common stock are issued at par for $5 per share. The reconstructed entry for analysis of item *d* follows:

Reconstruction   Cash   15,000
                Common Stock   15,000

This entry reveals a $15,000 cash inflow from stock issuance and is reflected in (and explains) the Common Stock account as follows:

Common Stock		
	Bal., Dec. 31, 2014	80,000
	Issued stock	15,000
	Bal., Dec. 31, 2015	95,000

The *third stage* discloses the cash flow effect from stock issuance in the financing section of the statement as follows:

Cash flows from financing activities
Cash received from issuing stock $15,000

Retained Earnings Transactions   The *first stage* in analyzing the Retained Earnings account is to review the comparative balance sheets from Exhibit 12.10. This reveals an increase in retained earnings from $88,000 to $112,000.

The *second stage* explains this change. Item *f* of the additional information in Exhibit 12.10 reports that cash dividends of $14,000 are paid. The reconstructed entry follows:

Reconstruction	Retained Earnings	14,000	
	Cash		14,000

This entry reveals a $14,000 cash outflow for cash dividends. Also see that the Retained Earnings account is impacted by net income of $38,000. (Net income was analyzed under the operating section of the statement of cash flows.) The reconstructed Retained Earnings account follows:

		Retained Earnings		
		Bal., Dec. 31, 2014	88,000	
Cash dividend	14,000	Net income	38,000	
		Bal., Dec. 31, 2015	112,000	

The *third stage* reports the cash flow effect from the cash dividend in the financing section of the statement as follows:

Cash flows from financing activities
Cash paid for dividends .... $(14,000)

Point: Financing activities not affecting cash flow include *declaration* of a cash dividend, *declaration* of a stock dividend, issuance of a stock dividend, and a stock split.

We now have identified and explained all of the Genesis cash inflows and cash outflows and one noncash investing and financing transaction.

Proving Cash Balances

The fifth and final step in preparing the statement is to report the beginning and ending cash balances and prove that the *net change in cash* is explained by operating, investing, and financing cash flows. This step is shown here for Genesis.

Net cash provided by operating activities	$20,000
Net cash provided by investing activities	2,000
Net cash used in financing activities	(17,000)
Net increase in cash	**$ 5,000**
Cash balance at 2014 year-end	12,000
Cash balance at 2015 year-end	$17,000

The preceding table shows that the $5,000 net increase in cash, from $12,000 at the beginning of the period to $17,000 at the end, is reconciled by net cash flows from operating ($20,000 inflow), investing ($2,000 inflow), and financing ($17,000 outflow) activities. This is formally reported at the bottom of the complete statement of cash flows as shown in Exhibit 12.13.

Global: There are no requirements to separate domestic and international cash flows, leading some users to ask, "Where in the world is cash flow?"

■ **Decision** Maker

Reporter Management is in labor contract negotiations and grants you an interview. It highlights a recent $600,000 net loss that involves a $930,000 extraordinary loss and a total net cash outflow of $550,000 (which includes net cash outflows of $850,000 for investing activities and $350,000 for financing activities). What is your assessment of this company? ■ [Answers follow the chapter's Summary.]

EXHIBIT 12.13

Complete Statement of
Cash Flows—Indirect
Method

GENESIS Statement of Cash Flows For Year Ended December 31, 2015		
Cash flows from operating activities		
Net income	$ 38,000	
Adjustments to reconcile net income to net cash provided by operating activities		
Income statement items not affecting cash		
Depreciation expense	24,000	
Loss on sale of plant assets	6,000	
Gain on retirement of notes	(16,000)	
Changes in current assets and liabilities		
Increase in accounts receivable	(20,000)	
Increase in inventory	(14,000)	
Increase in prepaid expenses	(2,000)	
Decrease in accounts payable	(5,000)	
Decrease in interest payable	(1,000)	
Increase in income taxes payable	10,000	
Net cash provided by operating activities		$20,000
Cash flows from investing activities		
Cash received from sale of plant assets	2,000	
Net cash provided by investing activities		2,000
Cash flows from financing activities		
Cash received from issuing stock	15,000	
Cash paid to retire notes	(18,000)	
Cash paid for dividends	(14,000)	
Net cash used in financing activities		(17,000)
Net increase in cash		$ 5,000
Cash balance at prior year-end		12,000
Cash balance at current year-end		$17,000

Point: Refer to Exhibit 12.10
and identify the $5,000 change
in cash. This change is what
the statement of cash flows
explains; it serves as a check.

Point: The statement of
cash flows is usually the last
prepared of the four required
financial statements.

NEED-TO-KNOW 12-4

**Reporting Financing
Cash Flows**

P3

Use the following information to determine this company's cash flows from financing activities.
a. Issued common stock for $40 cash.
b. Paid $70 cash to retire a note payable at its $70 maturity value.
c. Paid cash dividend of $15.
d. Paid $5 cash to acquire its treasury stock.

Solution

Cash flows from financing activities	
Cash received from issuance of common stock	$ 40
Cash paid to settle note payable	(70)
Cash paid for dividend	(15)
Cash paid to acquire treasury stock	(5)
Net cash used by financing activities	$(50)

Do More: QS 12-9, QS 12-10,
QS 12-13, E 12-8

OVERALL SUMMARY USING T-ACCOUNTS

A statement of cash flows is prepared by analyzing changes in noncash balance sheet accounts.
Exhibit 12.14 uses T-accounts to summarize how changes in Genesis's noncash balance sheet
accounts affect its cash inflows and outflows (dollar amounts in thousands). The top of the
exhibit shows the company's Cash T-account, and the lower part shows T-accounts for its

remaining balance sheet accounts. We see that the $20,000 net cash provided by operating activities and the $5,000 net increase in cash shown in the Cash T-account agree with the same figures in the statement of cash flows in Exhibit 12.13.

We explain Exhibit 12.14 in five parts (amounts in $ thousands):

a. Entry (1) records $38 net income in the credit side of the Retained Earnings account and the debit side of the Cash account. This $38 net income in the Cash T-account is adjusted until it reflects the $5 net increase in cash.

b. Entries (2) through (4) add the $24 depreciation and $6 loss on asset sale to net income, and subtract the $16 gain on retirement of notes.

c. Entries (5) through (10) adjust net income for changes in current asset and current liability accounts.

d. Entry (11) records the noncash investing and financing transaction involving a $60 purchase of assets by issuing $60 of notes.

e. Entries (12) and (13) record the $15 stock issuance and the $14 dividend.

EXHIBIT 12.14

Balance Sheet T-Accounts to Explain the Change in Cash ($ thousands)

Cash			
(1) Net income	38		
(2) Depreciation	24	(4) Gain on retirement of notes	16
(3) Loss on sale of plant assets	6		
(10) Increase in income taxes payable	10	(5) Increase in accounts receivable	20
		(6) Increase in inventory	14
		(7) Increase in prepaid expanse	2
		(8) Decrease in accounts payable	5
		(9) Decrease in interest payable	1
Net cash provided by operating activities	20		
(3) Cash received from sale of plant assets	2	(4) Cash paid to retire notes	18
(12) Cash received from issuing stock	15	(13) Cash paid for dividends	14
Net increase in cash	5		

Data to prepare statement of cash flows

Accounts Receivable		
Beg.	40	
(5)	20	
End.	60	

Inventory		
Beg.	70	
(6)	14	
End.	84	

Prepaid Expenses		
Beg.	4	
(7)	2	
End.	6	

Plant Assets		
Beg.	210	
		(3) 20
(11)	60	
End.	250	

Accumulated Depreciation		
	Beg.	48
(3) 12	(2)	24
	End.	60

Accounts Payable		
	Beg.	40
(8) 5		
	End.	35

Interest Payable		
	Beg.	4
(9) 1		
	End.	3

Income Taxes Payable		
	Beg.	12
	(10)	10
	End.	22

Long-Term Notes Payable		
	Beg.	64
(4) 34		
	(11)	60
	End.	90

Common Stock		
	Beg.	80
	(12)	15
	End.	95

Retained Earnings		
	Beg.	88
	(1)	38
(13) 14		
	End.	112

GLOBAL VIEW

The statement of cash flows, which explains changes in cash (including cash equivalents) from period to period, is required under both U.S. GAAP and IFRS. This section discusses similarities and differences between U.S. GAAP and IFRS in reporting that statement.

Samsung

Reporting Cash Flows from Operating Both U.S. GAAP and IFRS permit the reporting of cash flows from operating activities using either the direct or indirect method. Further, the basic requirements underlying the application of both methods are fairly consistent across these two accounting systems. Appendix A shows that Samsung reports its cash flows from operating activities using the indirect method, and in a manner similar to that explained in this chapter. Further, the definition of cash and cash equivalents is roughly similar for U.S. GAAP and IFRS.

There are, however, some differences between U.S. GAAP and IFRS in reporting operating cash flows. We mention two of the more notable. First, U.S. GAAP requires that cash inflows from interest revenue and dividend revenue be classified as operating, whereas IFRS permits classification under operating or investing provided that this classification is consistently applied across periods. Samsung reports its cash from interest received under operating, consistent with U.S. GAAP (no mention is made of any dividends received). Second, U.S. GAAP requires cash outflows for interest expense be classified as operating, whereas IFRS again permits classification under operating or financing provided that it is consistently applied across periods. (Some believe that interest payments, like dividend payments, are better classified as financing because they represent payments to financiers.) Samsung reports cash outflows for interest under operating, which is consistent with U.S. GAAP and acceptable under IFRS.

Reporting Cash Flows from Investing and Financing U.S. GAAP and IFRS are broadly similar in computing and classifying cash flows from investing and financing activities. A quick review of these two sections for Samsung's statement of cash flows shows a structure similar to that explained in this chapter. One notable exception is that U.S. GAAP requires that cash outflows for income tax be classified as operating, whereas IFRS permits the splitting of those cash flows among operating, investing, and financing depending on the sources of that tax. Samsung reports its cash outflows for income tax under operating, which is similar to U.S. GAAP.

Sustainability and Accounting LSTN, as introduced in this chapter's opening feature, places an emphasis on being a socially conscious and environmentally friendly alternative within the luxury headphone market. LSTN partners with The Starkey Hearing Foundation "to provide hearing for children in deaf schools," explains Bridget Hilton, its founder. "Ninety-five percent of children in deaf schools worldwide can be helped . . . [and] eighty percent of those people live in developing countries." LSTN also recognizes the need to work within the local markets so that its successes are sustainable. Our hearing products and services "will not undercut the local economies—these are basic senses that everyone on earth should be able to experience," explains Bridget. "To me, success in business is doing something you love while being financially secure." That is something we all hope is sustainable.

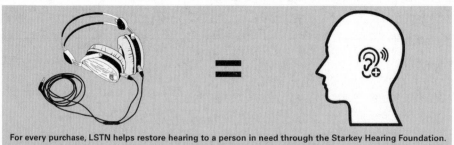

For every purchase, LSTN helps restore hearing to a person in need through the Starkey Hearing Foundation.

Courtesy of Bridget Hilton

Decision Analysis 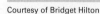 Cash Flow Analysis

A1

Analyze the statement of cash flows and apply the cash flow on total assets ratio.

Analyzing Cash Sources and Uses

Most managers stress the importance of understanding and predicting cash flows for business decisions. Creditors evaluate a company's ability to generate cash before deciding whether to lend money. Investors also assess cash inflows and outflows before buying and selling stock. Information in the statement of cash flows helps address these and other questions such as (1) How much cash is generated from or used in operations? (2) What expenditures are made with cash from operations? (3) What is the source of cash for debt payments? (4) What is the source of cash for distributions to owners? (5) How is the increase in investing activities financed? (6) What is the source of cash for new plant assets? (7) Why is cash flow from operations different from income? (8) How is cash from financing used?

To effectively answer these questions, it is important to separately analyze investing, financing, and operating activities. To illustrate, consider data from three different companies in Exhibit 12.15. These companies operate in the same industry and have been in business for several years.

($ thousands)	BMX	ATV	Trex
Cash provided (used) by operating activities	$90,000	$40,000	$(24,000)
Cash provided (used) by investing activities			
Proceeds from sale of plant assets			26,000
Purchase of plant assets	(48,000)	(25,000)	
Cash provided (used) by financing activities			
Proceeds from issuance of debt			13,000
Repayment of debt	(27,000)		
Net increase (decrease) in cash	$15,000	$15,000	$ 15,000

EXHIBIT 12.15

Cash Flows of Competing Companies

Each company generates an identical $15,000 net increase in cash, but its sources and uses of cash flows are very different. BMX's operating activities provide net cash flows of $90,000, allowing it to purchase plant assets of $48,000 and repay $27,000 of its debt. ATV's operating activities provide $40,000 of cash flows, limiting its purchase of plant assets to $25,000. Trex's $15,000 net cash increase is due to selling plant assets and incurring additional debt. Its operating activities yield a net cash outflow of $24,000. Overall, analysis of these cash flows reveals that BMX is more capable of generating future cash flows than is ATV or Trex.

Decision Insight

Free Cash Flows Many investors use cash flows to value company stock. However, cash-based valuation models often yield different stock values due to differences in measurement of cash flows. Most models require cash flows that are "free" for distribution to shareholders. These *free cash flows* are defined as cash flows available to shareholders after operating asset reinvestments and debt payments. Knowledge of the statement of cash flows is key to proper computation of free cash flows. A company's growth and financial flexibility depend on adequate free cash flows. ■

Point: CFO (Cash flow from operations)
Less: Capital Expenditures
Less: Debt Repayments
= FCF (free cash flows)

Cash Flow on Total Assets

Cash flow information has limitations, but it can help measure a company's ability to meet its obligations, pay dividends, expand operations, and obtain financing. Users often compute and analyze a cash-based ratio similar to return on total assets except that its numerator is net cash flows from operating activities. The **cash flow on total assets** ratio is shown in Exhibit 12.16.

$$\text{Cash flow on total assets} = \frac{\text{Cash flow from operations}}{\text{Average total assets}}$$

EXHIBIT 12.16

Cash Flow on Total Assets

This ratio reflects actual cash flows and is not affected by accounting income recognition and measurement. It can help business decision makers estimate the amount and timing of cash flows when planning and analyzing operating activities.

To illustrate, the 2013 cash flow on total assets ratio for Nike is 18.3%—see Exhibit 12.17. Is an 18.3% ratio good or bad? To answer this question, we compare this ratio with the ratios of prior years (we could also compare its ratio with those of its competitors and the market). Nike's cash flow on total assets ratio

EXHIBIT 12.17

Nike's Cash Flow on Total Assets

Year	Cash Flow on Total Assets	Return on Total Assets
2013.........	18.3%	15.0%
2012.........	12.5	14.6
2011.........	12.3	14.5
2010.........	22.9	13.8
2009.........	13.5	11.6

for several prior years is in the second column of Exhibit 12.17. Results show that its 18.3% return is its second highest return over the past five years. This is probably reflective of the recent recessionary period.

Point: Cash flow ratios are often used by financial analysts.

As an indicator of *earnings quality,* some analysts compare the cash flow on total assets ratio to the return on total assets ratio. Nike's return on total assets is provided in the third column of Exhibit 12.17. Nike's cash flow on total assets ratio exceeds its return on total assets in three of the five years, leading some analysts to infer that Nike's earnings quality is good for that period because much of its earnings are realized in the form of cash.

Decision Insight

Point: The following ratio helps assess whether operating cash flow is adequate to meet long-term obligations:

Cash coverage of debt = Cash flow from operations ÷ Noncurrent liabilities.

A low ratio suggests a higher risk of insolvency; a high ratio suggests a greater ability to meet long-term obligations.

Cash Flow Ratios Analysts use various other cash-based ratios, including the following two:

(1)
$$\text{Cash coverage of growth} = \frac{\text{Operating cash flow}}{\text{Cash outflow for plant assets}}$$

where a low ratio (less than 1) implies cash inadequacy to meet asset growth, whereas a high ratio implies cash adequacy for asset growth.

(2)
$$\text{Operating cash flow to sales} = \frac{\text{Operating cash flow}}{\text{Net sales}}$$

When this ratio substantially and consistently differs from the operating income to net sales ratio, the risk of accounting improprieties increases. ■

NEED-TO-KNOW

COMPREHENSIVE

Preparing Statement of Cash Flows—Indirect *and* Direct Methods

Umlauf's comparative balance sheets, income statement, and additional information follow.

UMLAUF COMPANY
Balance Sheets
December 31, 2015 and 2014

	2015	2014
Assets		
Cash	$ 43,050	$ 23,925
Accounts receivable	34,125	39,825
Inventory	156,000	146,475
Prepaid expenses	3,600	1,650
Total current assets	236,775	211,875
Equipment	135,825	146,700
Accum. depreciation—Equipment	(61,950)	(47,550)
Total assets	$310,650	$311,025
Liabilities		
Accounts payable	$ 28,800	$ 33,750
Income taxes payable	5,100	4,425
Dividends payable	0	4,500
Total current liabilities	33,900	42,675
Bonds payable	0	37,500
Total liabilities	33,900	80,175
Equity		
Common stock, $10 par	168,750	168,750
Retained earnings	108,000	62,100
Total liabilities and equity	$310,650	$311,025

UMLAUF COMPANY
Income Statement
For Year Ended December 31, 2015

Sales		$446,100
Cost of goods sold	$222,300	
Other operating expenses	120,300	
Depreciation expense	25,500	(368,100)
		78,000
Other gains (losses)		
Loss on sale of equipment	3,300	
Loss on retirement of bonds	825	(4,125)
Income before taxes		73,875
Income taxes expense		(13,725)
Net income		$ 60,150

Additional Information

a. Equipment costing $21,375 with accumulated depreciation of $11,100 is sold for cash.

b. Equipment purchases are for cash.

c. Accumulated Depreciation is affected by depreciation expense and the sale of equipment.

d. The balance of Retained Earnings is affected by dividend declarations and net income.

e. All sales are made on credit.

f. All inventory purchases are on credit.

g. Accounts Payable balances result from inventory purchases.

h. Prepaid expenses relate to "other operating expenses."

Required

1. Prepare a statement of cash flows using the indirect method for year 2015.

2.[B] Prepare a statement of cash flows using the direct method for year 2015.

PLANNING THE SOLUTION

- Prepare two blank statements of cash flows with sections for operating, investing, and financing activities using the (1) indirect method format and (2) direct method format.
- Compute the cash paid for equipment and the cash received from the sale of equipment using the additional information provided along with the amount for depreciation expense and the change in the balances of equipment and accumulated depreciation. Use T-accounts to help chart the effects of the sale and purchase of equipment on the balances of the Equipment account and the Accumulated Depreciation account.
- Compute the effect of net income on the change in the Retained Earnings account balance. Assign the difference between the change in retained earnings and the amount of net income to dividends declared. Adjust the dividends declared amount for the change in the Dividends Payable balance.
- Compute cash received from customers, cash paid for inventory, cash paid for other operating expenses, and cash paid for taxes as illustrated in the chapter.
- Enter the cash effects of reconstruction entries to the appropriate section(s) of the statement.
- Total each section of the statement, determine the total net change in cash, and add it to the beginning balance to get the ending balance of cash.

SOLUTION

Supporting computations for cash receipts and cash payments.

(1)	*Cost of equipment sold	$ 21,375
	Accumulated depreciation of equipment sold.	(11,100)
	Book value of equipment sold	10,275
	Loss on sale of equipment	(3,300)
	Cash received from sale of equipment	$ 6,975
	Cost of equipment sold	$ 21,375
	Less decrease in the Equipment account balance	(10,875)
	Cash paid for new equipment	$ 10,500
(2)	Loss on retirement of bonds	$ 825
	Carrying value of bonds retired	37,500
	Cash paid to retire bonds	$ 38,325
(3)	Net income.	$ 60,150
	Less increase in retained earnings	45,900
	Dividends declared	14,250
	Plus decrease in dividends payable	4,500
	Cash paid for dividends	$ 18,750
(4)[B]	Sales	$ 446,100
	Add decrease in accounts receivable	5,700
	Cash received from customers	$451,800
(5)[B]	Cost of goods sold.	$ 222,300
	Plus increase in inventory.	9,525
	Purchases	231,825
	Plus decrease in accounts payable	4,950
	Cash paid for inventory	$236,775
(6)[B]	Other operating expenses	$ 120,300
	Plus increase in prepaid expenses	1,950
	Cash paid for other operating expenses	$122,250
(7)[B]	Income taxes expense	$ 13,725
	Less increase in income taxes payable	(675)
	Cash paid for income taxes	$ 13,050

* Supporting T-account analysis for part 1 follows:

Equipment				Accumulated Depreciation—Equipment			
Bal., Dec. 31, 2014	146,700					Bal., Dec. 31, 2014	47,550
Cash purchase	10,500	Sale	21,375	Sale	11,100	Depr. expense	25,500
Bal., Dec. 31, 2015	135,825					Bal., Dec. 31, 2015	61,950

1. Indirect method:

UMLAUF COMPANY
Statement of Cash Flows (Indirect Method)
For Year Ended December 31, 2015

Cash flows from operating activities		
Net income		$60,150
Adjustments to reconcile net income to net cash provided by operating activities		
Income statement items not affecting cash		
Depreciation expense	25,500	
Loss on sale of plant assets	3,300	
Loss on retirement of bonds	825	
Changes in current assets and current liabilities		
Decrease in accounts receivable	5,700	
Increase in inventory	(9,525)	
Increase in prepaid expenses	(1,950)	
Decrease in accounts payable	(4,950)	
Increase in income taxes payable	675	
Net cash provided by operating activities		$79,725
Cash flows from investing activities		
Cash received from sale of equipment	6,975	
Cash paid for equipment	(10,500)	
Net cash used in investing activities		(3,525)
Cash flows from financing activities		
Cash paid to retire bonds payable	(38,325)	
Cash paid for dividends	(18,750)	
Net cash used in financing activities		(57,075)
Net increase in cash		$19,125
Cash balance at prior year-end		23,925
Cash balance at current year-end		$43,050

2.B Direct method (Appendix 12B):

UMLAUF COMPANY
Statement of Cash Flows (Direct Method)
For Year Ended December 31, 2015

Cash flows from operating activities		
Cash received from customers	$451,800	
Cash paid for inventory	(236,775)	
Cash paid for other operating expenses	(122,250)	
Cash paid for income taxes	(13,050)	
Net cash provided by operating activities		$79,725
Cash flows from investing activities		
Cash received from sale of equipment	6,975	
Cash paid for equipment	(10,500)	
Net cash used in investing activities		(3,525)
Cash flows from financing activities		
Cash paid to retire bonds payable	(38,325)	
Cash paid for dividends	(18,750)	
Net cash used in financing activities		(57,075)
Net increase in cash		$19,125
Cash balance at prior year-end		23,925
Cash balance at current year-end		$43,050

Spreadsheet Preparation of the Statement of Cash Flows

12A

This appendix explains how to use a spreadsheet (work sheet) to prepare the statement of cash flows under the indirect method.

Preparing the Indirect Method Spreadsheet   Analyzing noncash accounts can be challenging when a company has a large number of accounts and many operating, investing, and financing transactions. A *spreadsheet,* also called *work sheet* or *working paper,* can help us organize the information needed to prepare a statement of cash flows. A spreadsheet also makes it easier to check the accuracy of our work. To illustrate, we return to the comparative balance sheets and income statement shown in Exhibit 12.10. We use the following identifying letters *a* through *g* to code changes in accounts, and letters *h* through *m* for additional information, to prepare the statement of cash flows:

P4

Illustrate use of a spreadsheet to prepare a statement of cash flows.

a. Net income is $38,000.
b. Accounts receivable increase by $20,000.
c. Inventory increases by $14,000.
d. Prepaid expenses increase by $2,000.
e. Accounts payable decrease by $5,000.
f. Interest payable decreases by $1,000.
g. Income taxes payable increase by $10,000.
h. Depreciation expense is $24,000.
 i. Plant assets costing $20,000 with accumulated depreciation of $12,000 are sold for $2,000 cash. This yields a loss on sale of assets of $6,000.
 j. Notes with a book value of $34,000 are retired with a cash payment of $18,000, yielding a $16,000 gain on retirement.
k. Plant assets costing $60,000 are purchased with an issuance of notes payable for $60,000.
 l. Issued 3,000 shares of common stock for $15,000 cash.
m. Paid cash dividends of $14,000.

Exhibit 12A.1 shows the indirect method spreadsheet for Genesis. We enter both beginning and ending balance sheet amounts on the spreadsheet. We also enter information in the Analysis of Changes columns (keyed to the additional information items *a* through *m*) to explain changes in the accounts and determine the cash flows for operating, investing, and financing activities. Information about noncash investing and financing activities is reported near the bottom.

Entering the Analysis of Changes on the Spreadsheet   The following sequence of procedures is used to complete the spreadsheet after the beginning and ending balances of the balance sheet accounts are entered:

① Enter net income as the first item in the statement of cash flows section for computing operating cash inflow (debit) and as a credit to Retained Earnings.
② In the statement of cash flows section, adjustments to net income are entered as debits if they increase cash flows and as credits if they decrease cash flows. Applying this same rule, adjust net income for the change in each noncash current asset and current liability account related to operating activities. For each adjustment to net income, the offsetting debit or credit must help reconcile the beginning and ending balances of a current asset or current liability account.
③ Enter adjustments to net income for income statement items not providing or using cash in the period. For each adjustment, the offsetting debit or credit must help reconcile a noncash balance sheet account.
④ Adjust net income to eliminate any gains or losses from investing and financing activities. Because the cash from a gain must be excluded from operating activities, the gain is entered as a credit in the operating activities section. Losses are entered as debits. For each adjustment, the related debit and/or credit must help reconcile balance sheet accounts and involve reconstructed entries to show the cash flow from investing or financing activities.
⑤ After reviewing any unreconciled balance sheet accounts and related information, enter the remaining reconciling entries for investing and financing activities. Examples are purchases of plant assets,

Point: Analysis of the changes on the spreadsheet are summarized here:

1. Cash flows from operating activities generally affect net income, current assets, and current liabilities.

2. Cash flows from investing activities generally affect noncurrent asset accounts.

3. Cash flows from financing activities generally affect noncurrent liability and equity accounts.

EXHIBIT 12A.1

Spreadsheet for Preparing
Statement of Cash
Flows—Indirect Method

	A	B	C	D	E	F	G
1				GENESIS			
2				Spreadsheet for Statement of Cash Flows—Indirect Method			
3				For Year Ended December 31, 2015			
4			Dec. 31,		Analysis of Changes		Dec. 31,
5			2014		Debit	Credit	2015
6	**Balance Sheet—Debit Bal. Accounts**						
7	Cash		$ 12,000				$ 17,000
8	Accounts receivable		40,000	(b)	$ 20,000		60,000
9	Inventory		70,000	(c)	14,000		84,000
10	Prepaid expenses		4,000	(d)	2,000		6,000
11	Plant assets		210,000	(k1)	60,000	(i) $ 20,000	250,000
12			$336,000				$417,000
13	**Balance Sheet—Credit Bal. Accounts**						
14	Accumulated depreciation		$ 48,000	(i)	12,000	(h) 24,000	$ 60,000
15	Accounts payable		40,000	(e)	5,000		35,000
16	Interest payable		4,000	(f)	1,000		3,000
17	Income taxes payable		12,000			(g) 10,000	22,000
18	Notes payable		64,000	(j)	34,000	(k2) 60,000	90,000
19	Common stock, $5 par value		80,000			(l) 15,000	95,000
20	Retained earnings		88,000	(m)	14,000	(a) 38,000	112,000
21			$336,000				$417,000
22	**Statement of Cash Flows**						
23	Operating activities						
24	Net income			(a)	38,000		
25	Increase in accounts receivable					(b) 20,000	
26	Increase in inventory					(c) 14,000	
27	Increase in prepaid expenses					(d) 2,000	
28	Decrease in accounts payable					(e) 5,000	
29	Decrease in interest payable					(f) 1,000	
30	Increase in income taxes payable			(g)	10,000		
31	Depreciation expense			(h)	24,000		
32	Loss on sale of plant assets			(i)	6,000		
33	Gain on retirement of notes					(j) 16,000	
34	Investing activities						
35	Receipts from sale of plant assets			(i)	2,000		
36	Financing activities						
37	Payment to retire notes					(j) 18,000	
38	Receipts from issuing stock			(l)	15,000		
39	Payment of cash dividends					(m) 14,000	
40							
41	**Noncash Investing and Financing Activities**						
42	Purchase of plant assets with notes			(k2)	60,000	(k1) 60,000	
					$317,000	$317,000	

issuances of long-term debt, stock issuances, and dividend payments. Some of these may require entries in the noncash investing and financing section of the spreadsheet (reconciled).

⑥ Check accuracy by totaling the Analysis of Changes columns and by determining that the change in each balance sheet account has been explained (reconciled).

We illustrate these steps in Exhibit 12A.1 for Genesis:

Step	Entries
①·········	(a)
②·········	(b) through (g)
③·········	(h)
④·········	(i) through (j)
⑤·········	(k) through (m)

Since adjustments *i, j,* and *k* are more challenging, we show them in the following debit and credit format. These entries are for purposes of our understanding; they are *not* the entries actually made in the journals. Changes in the Cash account are identified as sources or uses of cash.

i.	Cash—Receipt from sale of plant assets **(source of cash)**	2,000	
	Loss from sale of plant assets	6,000	
	Accumulated depreciation	12,000	
	Plant assets		20,000
	To describe sale of plant assets.		
j.	Notes payable	34,000	
	Cash—Payments to retire notes **(use of cash)**		18,000
	Gain on retirement of notes		16,000
	To describe retirement of notes.		
kl.	Plant assets	60,000	
	Cash—Purchase of plant assets financed by notes		60,000
	To describe purchase of plant assets.		
k2.	Cash—Purchase of plant assets financed by notes	60,000	
	Notes payable		60,000
	To issue notes for purchase of assets.		

APPENDIX

Direct Method of Reporting Operating Cash Flows

12B

P5

Compute cash flows from operating activities using the direct method.

We compute cash flows from operating activities under the direct method by adjusting accrual-based income statement items to the cash basis. The usual approach is to adjust income statement accounts related to operating activities for changes in their related balance sheet accounts as follows:

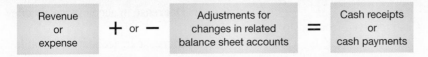

The framework for reporting cash receipts and cash payments for the operating section of the cash flow statement under the direct method is presented in Exhibit 12B.1. We consider cash receipts first and then cash payments.

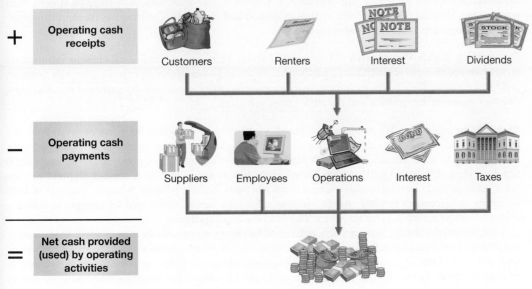

EXHIBIT 12B.1

Major Classes of Operating Cash Flows

Operating Cash Receipts A review of Exhibit 12.10 and the additional information reported by Genesis suggests only one potential cash receipt: sales to customers. This section, therefore, starts with sales to customers as reported on the income statement and then adjusts it as necessary to obtain cash received from customers to report on the statement of cash flows.

Cash Received from Customers If all sales are for cash, the amount received from customers equals the sales reported on the income statement. When some or all sales are on account, however, we must adjust the amount of sales for the change in Accounts Receivable. It is often helpful to use *account analysis* to do this. This usually involves setting up a T-account and reconstructing its major entries, with emphasis on cash receipts and payments.

Point: An accounts receivable increase implies that cash received from customers is less than sales (the converse is also true).

To illustrate, we use a T-account that includes accounts receivable balances for Genesis on December 31, 2014 and 2015. The beginning balance is $40,000 and the ending balance is $60,000. Next, the income statement shows sales of $590,000, which we enter on the debit side of this account. We now can reconstruct the Accounts Receivable account to determine the amount of cash received from customers as follows:

Reconstructed Entry

Cash 570,000	
Accts Recble. 20,000	
Sales	590,000

Accounts Receivable			
Bal., Dec. 31, 2014	40,000		
Sales	590,000	Cash receipts =	570,000
Bal., Dec. 31, 2015	60,000		

Example: If the ending balance of Accounts Receivable is $20,000 (instead of $60,000), what is cash received from customers? *Answer:* $610,000

This T-account shows that the Accounts Receivable balance begins at $40,000 and increases to $630,000 from sales of $590,000, yet its ending balance is only $60,000. This implies that cash receipts from customers are $570,000, computed as $40,000 + $590,000 − [?] = $60,000. This computation can be rearranged to express cash received as equal to sales of $590,000 minus a $20,000 increase in accounts receivable. This computation is summarized as a general rule in Exhibit 12B.2. Genesis reports the $570,000 cash received from customers as a cash inflow from operating activities.

EXHIBIT 12B.2

Formula to Compute Cash Received from Customers—Direct Method

$$\text{Cash received from customers} = \text{Sales} \quad \text{or} \quad \begin{array}{l} + \textbf{ Decrease in accounts receivable} \\ - \textbf{ Increase in accounts receivable} \end{array}$$

Other Cash Receipts While Genesis's cash receipts are limited to collections from customers, we often see other types of cash receipts, most commonly cash receipts involving rent, interest, and dividends. We compute cash received from these items by subtracting an increase in their respective receivable or adding a decrease. For instance, if rent receivable increases in the period, cash received from renters is less than rent revenue reported on the income statement. If rent receivable decreases, cash received is more than reported rent revenue. The same logic applies to interest and dividends. The formulas for these computations are summarized later in this appendix.

Point: Net income is measured using accrual accounting. Cash flows from operations are measured using cash basis accounting.

Operating Cash Payments A review of Exhibit 12.10 and the additional Genesis information shows four operating expenses: cost of goods sold; wages and other operating expenses; interest expense; and taxes expense. We analyze each expense to compute its cash amounts for the statement of cash flows. (We then examine depreciation and the other losses and gains.)

Cash Paid for Inventory We compute cash paid for inventory by analyzing both cost of goods sold and inventory. If all inventory purchases are for cash and the ending balance of Inventory is unchanged from the beginning balance, the amount of cash paid for inventory equals cost of goods sold—an uncommon situation. Instead, there normally is some change in the Inventory balance. Also, some or all purchases are often made on credit, and this yields changes in the Accounts Payable balance. When the balances of both Inventory and Accounts Payable change, we must adjust the cost of goods sold for changes in both accounts to compute cash paid for inventory. This is a two-step adjustment.

First, we use the change in the account balance of Inventory, along with the cost of goods sold amount, to compute cost of purchases for the period. An increase in inventory implies that we bought more than we sold, and we add this inventory increase to cost of goods sold to compute cost of purchases. A decrease in inventory implies that we bought less than we sold, and we subtract the inventory decrease from cost of goods sold to compute purchases. We illustrate the *first step* by reconstructing the Inventory account of Genesis:

Inventory			
Bal., Dec. 31, 2014	70,000		
Purchases =	314,000	Cost of goods sold	300,000
Bal., Dec. 31, 2015	84,000		

The beginning balance is $70,000, and the ending balance is $84,000. The income statement shows that cost of goods sold is $300,000, which we enter on the credit side of this account. With this information, we determine the amount for cost of purchases to be $314,000. This computation can be rearranged to express cost of purchases as equal to cost of goods sold of $300,000 plus the $14,000 increase in inventory.

The second step uses the change in the balance of Accounts Payable, and the amount of cost of purchases, to compute cash paid for inventory. A decrease in accounts payable implies that we paid for more goods than we acquired this period, and we would then add the accounts payable decrease to cost of purchases to compute cash paid for inventory. An increase in accounts payable implies that we paid for less than the amount of goods acquired, and we would subtract the accounts payable increase from purchases to compute cash paid for inventory. The *second step* is applied to Genesis by reconstructing its Accounts Payable account:

Accounts Payable			
		Bal., Dec. 31, 2014	40,000
Cash payments =	319,000	Purchases	314,000
		Bal., Dec. 31, 2015	35,000

Reconstructed Entry

COGS.	300,000
Inventory	14,000
Accounts Payable . .	5,000
Cash	319,000

Its beginning balance of $40,000 plus purchases of $314,000 minus an ending balance of $35,000 yields cash paid of $319,000 (or $40,000 + $314,000 − [?] = $35,000). Alternatively, we can express cash paid for inventory as equal to purchases of $314,000 plus the $5,000 decrease in accounts payable. The $319,000 cash paid for inventory is reported on the statement of cash flows as a cash outflow under operating activities.

We summarize this two-step adjustment to cost of goods sold to compute cash paid for inventory in Exhibit 12B.3.

Example: If the ending balances of Inventory and Accounts Payable are $60,000 and $50,000, respectively (instead of $84,000 and $35,000), what is cash paid for inventory? *Answer:* $280,000

EXHIBIT 12B.3

Two Steps to Compute Cash Paid for Inventory—Direct Method

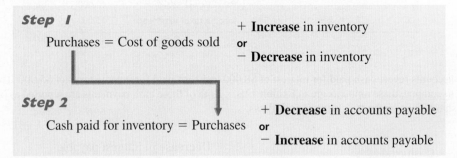

Step 1

Purchases = Cost of goods sold or
+ **Increase** in inventory
− **Decrease** in inventory

Step 2

Cash paid for inventory = Purchases or
+ **Decrease** in accounts payable
− **Increase** in accounts payable

Cash Paid for Wages and Operating Expenses (Excluding Depreciation)   The income statement of Genesis shows wages and other operating expenses of $216,000 (see Exhibit 12.10). To compute cash paid for wages and other operating expenses, we adjust this amount for any changes in their related balance sheet accounts. We begin by looking for any prepaid expenses and accrued liabilities related to wages and other operating expenses in the balance sheets of Genesis in Exhibit 12.10. The balance sheets show prepaid expenses but no accrued liabilities. Thus, the adjustment is limited to the change in prepaid expenses. The amount of adjustment is computed by assuming that all cash paid for wages and other operating expenses is initially debited to Prepaid Expenses. This assumption allows us to reconstruct the Prepaid Expenses account:

Prepaid Expenses			
Bal., Dec. 31, 2014	4,000		
Cash payments =	218,000	Wages and other operating exp.	216,000
Bal., Dec. 31, 2015	6,000		

Reconstructed Entry

Wages and Other Expenses.	216,000
Prepaid Expenses . .	2,000
Cash	218,000

Point: A decrease in prepaid expenses implies that reported expenses include an amount(s) that did not require a cash outflow in the period.

Prepaid expenses increase by $2,000 in the period, meaning that cash paid for wages and other operating expenses exceeds the reported expense by $2,000. Alternatively, we can express cash paid for wages and other operating expenses as equal to its reported expenses of $216,000 plus the $2,000 increase in prepaid expenses.[1]

Exhibit 12B.4 summarizes the adjustments to wages (including salaries) and other operating expenses. The Genesis balance sheet did not report accrued liabilities, but we include them in the formula to explain the adjustment to cash when they do exist. A decrease in accrued liabilities implies that we paid cash for more goods or services than received this period, so we add the decrease in accrued liabilities to the expense amount to obtain cash paid for these goods or services. An increase in accrued liabilities implies that we paid cash for less than what was acquired, so we subtract this increase in accrued liabilities from the expense amount to get cash paid.

EXHIBIT 12B.4

Formula to Compute Cash Paid for Wages and Operating Expenses— Direct Method

Cash paid for wages and other operating expenses	=	Wages and other operating expenses	**+ Increase** in prepaid expenses or **− Decrease** in prepaid expenses	**+ Decrease** in accrued liabilities or **− Increase** in accrued liabilities

Cash paid for interest and income taxes   Computing operating cash flows for interest and taxes is similar to that for operating expenses. Both require adjustments to their amounts reported on the income statement for changes in their related balance sheet accounts. We begin with the Genesis income statement showing interest expense of $7,000 and income taxes expense of $15,000. To compute the cash paid, we adjust interest expense for the change in interest payable and then the income taxes expense for the change in income taxes payable. These computations involve reconstructing both liability accounts:

Reconstructed Entry

Int. Expense	7,000	
Int. Payable	1,000	
Cash		8,000

Interest Payable			
		Bal., Dec. 31, 2014	4,000
Cash paid for interest =	8,000	Interest expense	7,000
		Bal., Dec. 31, 2015	3,000

Reconstructed Entry

Inc. Tax Exp.	15,000	
Inc. Tax Pay.	10,000	
Cash		5,000

Income Taxes Payable			
		Bal., Dec. 31, 2014	12,000
Cash paid for taxes =	5,000	Income taxes expense	15,000
		Bal., Dec. 31, 2015	22,000

These accounts reveal cash paid for interest of $8,000 and cash paid for income taxes of $5,000. The formulas to compute these amounts are in Exhibit 12B.5. Both of these cash payments are reported as operating cash outflows on the statement of cash flows.

EXHIBIT 12B.5

Formulas to Compute Cash Paid for Both Interest and Taxes—Direct Method

Cash paid for interest	=	Interest expense	**+ Decrease** in interest payable or **− Increase** in interest payable
Cash paid for taxes	=	Income taxes expense	**+ Decrease** in income taxes payable or **− Increase** in income taxes payable

Analyzing Additional Expenses, Gains, and Losses   Genesis has three additional items reported on its income statement: depreciation, loss on sale of assets, and gain on retirement of debt. We must consider each for its potential cash effects.

---

[1] The assumption that all cash payments for wages and operating expenses are initially debited to Prepaid Expenses is not necessary for our analysis to hold. If cash payments are debited directly to the expense account, the total amount of cash paid for wages and other operating expenses still equals the $216,000 expense plus the $2,000 increase in prepaid expenses (which arise from end-of-period adjusting entries).

Depreciation Expense   Depreciation expense is $24,000. It is often called a *noncash expense* because depreciation has no cash flows. Depreciation expense is an allocation of an asset's depreciable cost. The cash outflow with a plant asset is reported as part of investing activities when it is paid for. Thus, depreciation expense is *never* reported on a statement of cash flows using the direct method; nor is depletion or amortization expense.

Loss on Sale of Assets   Sales of assets frequently result in gains and losses reported as part of net income, but the amount of recorded gain or loss does *not* reflect any cash flows in these transactions. Asset sales result in cash inflow equal to the cash amount received, regardless of whether the asset was sold at a gain or a loss. This cash inflow is reported under investing activities. Thus, the loss or gain on a sale of assets is *never* reported on a statement of cash flows using the direct method.

Gain on Retirement of Debt   Retirement of debt usually yields a gain or loss reported as part of net income, but that gain or loss does *not* reflect cash flow in this transaction. Debt retirement results in cash outflow equal to the cash paid to settle the debt, regardless of whether the debt is retired at a gain or loss. This cash outflow is reported under financing activities; the loss or gain from retirement of debt is *never* reported on a statement of cash flows using the direct method.

Point: The direct method is usually viewed as *user friendly* because less accounting knowledge is required to understand and use it.

Summary of Adjustments for Direct Method   Exhibit 12B.6 summarizes common adjustments for net income to yield net cash provided (used) by operating activities under the direct method.

EXHIBIT 12B.6

Summary of Selected Adjustments for Direct Method

Item	From Income Statement	Adjustments to Obtain Cash Flow Numbers	
Receipts			
From sales	Sales Revenue	{ +Decrease in Accounts Receivable −Increase in Accounts Receivable	
From rent	Rent Revenue	{ +Decrease in Rent Receivable −Increase in Rent Receivable	
From interest	Interest Revenue	{ +Decrease in Interest Receivable −Increase in Interest Receivable	
From dividends	Dividend Revenue	{ +Decrease in Dividends Receivable −Increase in Dividends Receivable	
Payments			
To suppliers	Cost of Goods Sold	{ +Increase in Inventory −Decrease in Inventory	{ +Decrease in Accounts Payable −Increase in Accounts Payable
For operations	Operating Expense	{ +Increase in Prepaids −Decrease in Prepaids	{ +Decrease in Accrued Liabilities −Increase in Accrued Liabilities
To employees	Wages (Salaries) Expense	{ +Decrease in Wages (Salaries) Payable −Increase in Wages (Salaries) Payable	
For interest	Interest Expense	{ +Decrease in Interest Payable −Increase in Interest Payable	
For taxes	Income Tax Expense	{ +Decrease in Income Tax Payable −Increase in Income Tax Payable	

Direct Method Format of Operating Activities Section   Exhibit 12B.7 shows the Genesis statement of cash flows using the direct method. Major items of cash inflows and cash outflows are listed separately in the operating activities section. The format requires that operating cash outflows be subtracted from operating cash inflows to get net cash provided (used) by operating activities.

The FASB recommends that the operating activities section of the statement of cash flows be reported using the direct method, which is considered more useful to financial statement users. *However, the FASB requires a reconciliation of net income to net cash provided (used) by operating activities when the direct method is used* (which can be reported in the notes). This reconciliation follows the preparation of the operating activities section of the statement of cash flows using the indirect method.

Point: Some preparers argue that it is easier to prepare a statement of cash flows using the indirect method. This likely explains its greater frequency in financial statements.

 IFRS

Currently, U.S. GAAP and IFRS allow cash flows from operating activities to be reported using either the indirect method or the direct method. The IASB and FASB are working on joint guidance that would require the direct method for the operating section with the indirect method's operating section disclosed in the footnotes. Stay tuned . . . ∎

EXHIBIT 12B.7

Statement of Cash
Flows—Direct Method

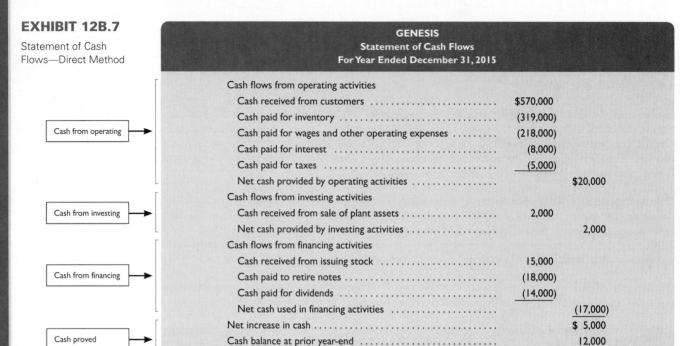

	Cash from operating
	Cash from investing
	Cash from financing
	Cash proved

GENESIS
Statement of Cash Flows
For Year Ended December 31, 2015

Cash flows from operating activities		
Cash received from customers	$570,000	
Cash paid for inventory	(319,000)	
Cash paid for wages and other operating expenses	(218,000)	
Cash paid for interest	(8,000)	
Cash paid for taxes	(5,000)	
Net cash provided by operating activities		$20,000
Cash flows from investing activities		
Cash received from sale of plant assets	2,000	
Net cash provided by investing activities		2,000
Cash flows from financing activities		
Cash received from issuing stock	15,000	
Cash paid to retire notes	(18,000)	
Cash paid for dividends	(14,000)	
Net cash used in financing activities		(17,000)
Net increase in cash		$ 5,000
Cash balance at prior year-end		12,000
Cash balance at current year-end		$17,000

NEED-TO-KNOW 12-5

**Reporting Operating
Cash Flows (Direct)**

P5

A company's current-year income statement and selected balance sheet data at December 31 of the current and prior years follow. Prepare the cash flows from operating activities section only of its statement of cash flows using the direct method for the current year.

Income Statement	
For Current Year Ended December 31	
Sales revenue	$120
Expenses	
Cost of goods sold	50
Depreciation expense	30
Salaries expense	17
Interest expense	3
Net income	$ 20

Selected Balance Sheet Accounts		
At December 31	Current Yr	Prior Yr
Accounts receivable	$12	$10
Inventory	6	9
Accounts payable	7	11
Salaries payable	8	3
Interest payable	1	0

Solution

Cash Flows from Operating Activities—Direct Method
For Current Year Ended December 31

Cash flows from operating activities*	
Cash received from customers	$118
Cash paid for inventory........................	(51)
Cash paid for salaries..........................	(12)
Cash paid for interest	(2)
Net cash provided by operating activities	$53

Do More: QS 12-12,
QS 12-13, QS 12-14, E 12-12,
E 12-14, E 12-15, E 12-16

QC4

*Supporting computations:
  Cash received from customers = Sales of $120 − Accounts Receivable increase of $2.
  Cash paid for inventory = COGS of $50 − Inventory decrease of $3 + Accounts
                              Payable decrease of $4.
  Cash paid for salaries = Salaries Expense of $17 − Salaries Payable increase of $5.
  Cash paid for interest = Interest Expense of $3 − Interest Payable increase of $1.

Summary

C1 **Distinguish between operating, investing, and financing activities, and describe how noncash investing and financing activities are disclosed.** The purpose of the statement of cash flows is to report major cash receipts and cash payments relating to operating, investing, or financing activities. Operating activities include transactions and events that determine net income. Investing activities include transactions and events that mainly affect long-term assets. Financing activities include transactions and events that mainly affect long-term liabilities and equity. Noncash investing and financing activities must be disclosed in either a note or a separate schedule to the statement of cash flows. Examples are the retirement of debt by issuing equity and the exchange of a note payable for plant assets.

A1 **Analyze the statement of cash flows and apply the cash flow on total assets ratio.** To understand and predict cash flows, users stress identification of the sources and uses of cash flows by operating, investing, and financing activities. Emphasis is on operating cash flows since they derive from continuing operations. The cash flow on total assets ratio is defined as operating cash flows divided by average total assets. Analysis of current and past values for this ratio can reflect a company's ability to yield regular and positive cash flows. It is also viewed as a measure of earnings quality.

P1 **Prepare a statement of cash flows.** Preparation of a statement of cash flows involves five steps: (1) Compute the net increase or decrease in cash; (2) compute net cash provided or used by operating activities (*using either the direct or indirect method*); (3) compute net cash provided or used by investing activities; (4) compute net cash provided or used by

financing activities; and (5) report the beginning and ending cash balances and prove that the ending cash balance is explained by net cash flows. Noncash investing and financing activities are also disclosed.

P2 **Compute cash flows from operating activities using the indirect method.** The indirect method for reporting net cash provided or used by operating activities starts with net income and then adjusts it for three items: (1) changes in noncash current assets and current liabilities related to operating activities, (2) revenues and expenses not providing or using cash, and (3) gains and losses from investing and financing activities.

P3 **Determine cash flows from both investing and financing activities.** Cash flows from both investing and financing activities are determined by identifying the cash flow effects of transactions and events affecting each balance sheet account related to these activities. All cash flows from these activities are identified when we can explain changes in these accounts from the beginning to the end of the period.

P4ᴬ **Illustrate use of a spreadsheet to prepare a statement of cash flows.** A spreadsheet is a useful tool in preparing a statement of cash flows. Six key steps (see Appendix 12A) are applied when using the spreadsheet to prepare the statement.

P5ᴮ **Compute cash flows from operating activities using the direct method.** The direct method for reporting net cash provided or used by operating activities lists major operating cash inflows less cash outflows to yield net cash inflow or outflow from operations.

Guidance Answers to Decision Maker

Entrepreneur   Several factors might explain an increase in net cash flows when a net loss is reported, including (1) early recognition of expenses relative to revenues generated (such as research and development), (2) cash advances on long-term sales contracts not yet recognized in income, (3) issuances of debt or equity for cash to finance expansion, (4) cash sale of assets, (5) delay of cash payments, and (6) cash prepayment on sales. Analysis needs to focus on the components of both the net loss and the net cash flows and their implications for future performance.

Reporter   Your initial reaction based on the company's $600,000 loss with a $550,000 decrease in net cash is not positive. However, closer scrutiny reveals a more positive picture of this company's performance. Cash flow from operating activities is $650,000, computed as [?] − $850,000 − $350,000 = $(550,000). You also note that net income *before* the extraordinary loss is $330,000, computed as [?] − $930,000 = $(600,000).

Key Terms

Cash flow on total assets	Indirect method	Operating activities
Direct method	Investing activities	Statement of cash flows
Financing activities		

Multiple Choice Quiz   Answers at end of chapter

1. A company uses the indirect method to determine its cash flows from operating activities. Use the following information to determine its net cash provided or used by operating activities.

Net income	$15,200
Depreciation expense	10,000
Cash payment on note payable	8,000
Gain on sale of land	3,000
Increase in inventory	1,500
Increase in accounts payable	2,850

   a. $23,550 used by operating activities
   b. $23,550 provided by operating activities
   c. $15,550 provided by operating activities
   d. $42,400 provided by operating activities
   e. $20,850 provided by operating activities

2. A machine with a cost of $175,000 and accumulated depreciation of $94,000 is sold for $87,000 cash. The amount reported as a source of cash under cash flows from investing activities is
   a. $81,000.
   b. $6,000.
   c. $87,000.
   d. Zero; this is a financing activity.
   e. Zero; this is an operating activity.

3. A company settles a long-term note payable plus interest by paying $68,000 cash toward the principal amount and

$5,440 cash for interest. The amount reported as a use of cash under cash flows from financing activities is
   a. Zero; this is an investing activity.
   b. Zero; this is an operating activity.
   c. $73,440.
   d. $68,000.
   e. $5,440.

4. The following information is available regarding a company's annual salaries and wages. What amount of cash is paid for salaries and wages?

Salaries and wages expense	$255,000
Salaries and wages payable, prior year-end	8,200
Salaries and wages payable, current year-end ...	10,900

   a. $252,300   c. $255,000   e. $235,900
   b. $257,700   d. $274,100

5. The following information is available for a company. What amount of cash is paid for inventory for the current year?

Cost of goods sold	$545,000
Inventory, prior year-end...................	105,000
Inventory, current year-end.................	112,000
Accounts payable, prior year-end	98,500
Accounts payable, current year-end	101,300

   a. $545,000   c. $540,800   e. $549,200
   b. $554,800   d. $535,200

A(B) *Superscript letter A (B) denotes assignments based on Appendix 12A (12B).*

▮ Icon denotes assignments that involve decision making.

Discussion Questions

1. What is the reporting purpose of the statement of cash flows? Identify at least two questions that this statement can answer.

2. What are some investing activities reported on the statement of cash flows?

3. What are some financing activities reported on the statement of cash flows?

4. Describe the direct method of reporting cash flows from operating activities.

5. When a statement of cash flows is prepared using the direct method, what are some of the operating cash flows?

6. Describe the indirect method of reporting cash flows from operating activities.

7. Where on the statement of cash flows is the payment of cash dividends reported?

8. ▮ Assume that a company purchases land for $1,000,000, paying $400,000 cash and borrowing the remainder with a long-term note payable. How should this transaction be reported on a statement of cash flows?

9. ▮ On June 3, a company borrows $200,000 cash by giving its bank a 90-day, interest-bearing note. On the statement of cash flows, where should this be reported?

10. ▮ If a company reports positive net income for the year, can it also show a net cash outflow from operating activities? Explain.

11. ▮ Is depreciation a source of cash flow?

12. Refer to Apple's statement of cash flows in Appendix A. (*a*) Which method is used to **APPLE** compute its net cash provided by operating activities? (*b*) Its balance sheet shows an increase in accounts (trade) receivable from September 29, 2012, to September 28, 2013; why is this increase in accounts (trade) receivable subtracted when computing net cash provided by operating activities for the fiscal year ended September 28, 2013?

13. Refer to Google's statement of cash flows in Appendix A. What are its **GOOGLE**

cash flows from financing activities for the year ended December 31, 2013? List the items and amounts.

14. Refer to Samsung's 2013 statement of cash flows in Appendix A. **Samsung** List its cash flows from operating activities, investing activities, and financing activities.

15. Refer to Samsung's statement of cash flows in Appendix A. What **Samsung** investing activities result in cash outflows for the year ended December 31, 2013? List items and amounts.

▪ connect

Classify the following cash flows as either operating, investing, or financing activities.

_____ **1.** Sold long-term investments for cash.
_____ **2.** Received cash payments from customers.
_____ **3.** Paid cash for wages and salaries.
_____ **4.** Purchased inventories for cash.
_____ **5.** Paid cash dividends.
_____ **6.** Issued common stock for cash.
_____ **7.** Received cash interest on a note.
_____ **8.** Paid cash interest on outstanding notes.
_____ **9.** Received cash from sale of land at a loss.
_____ **10.** Paid cash for property taxes on building.

QUICK STUDY

QS 12-1
Transaction classification by activity C1

Label the following headings, line items, and notes with the numbers *1* through *13* according to their sequential order (from top to bottom) for presentation of the statement of cash flows.

_____ **a.** "Cash flows from investing activities" title
_____ **b.** "For *period* Ended *date*" heading
_____ **c.** "Cash flows from operating activities" title
_____ **d.** Company name
_____ **e.** Schedule or note disclosure of noncash investing and financing transactions
_____ **f.** "Statement of Cash Flows" heading
_____ **g.** Net increase (decrease) in cash .... $ #
_____ **h.** Net cash provided (used) by operating activities .... $ #
_____ **i.** Cash (and equivalents) balance at prior period-end ..... $ #
_____ **j.** Net cash provided (used) by financing activities........ $ #
_____ **k.** "Cash flows from financing activities" title
_____ **l.** Net cash provided (used) by investing activities .... $ #
_____ **m.** Cash (and equivalents) balance at current period-end ... $ #

QS 12-2
Statement of cash flows
P1

For each of the following three separate cases X, Y and Z, compute cash flows from operations using the indirect method. The list includes all balance sheet accounts related to cash from operating activities.

QS 12-3
Indirect: Computing cash flows from operations
P2

	Case X	Case Y	Case Z
Net income	$ 4,000	$100,000	$72,000
Depreciation expense	30,000	8,000	24,000
Accounts receivable increase (decrease)	40,000	20,000	(4,000)
Inventory increase (decrease)	(20,000)	(10,000)	10,000
Accounts payable increase (decrease)	24,000	(22,000)	14,000
Accrued liabilities increase (decrease)	(44,000)	12,000	(8,000)

QS 12-4

Indirect: Computing cash from operations **P2**

Use the following information to determine this company's cash flows from operating activities using the indirect method.

MOSS COMPANY Selected Balance Sheet Information December 31, 2015 and 2014		
	2015	2014
Current assets		
Cash	$84,650	$26,800
Accounts receivable	25,000	32,000
Inventory	60,000	54,100
Current liabilities		
Accounts payable	30,400	25,700
Income taxes payable	2,050	2,200

MOSS COMPANY Income Statement For Year Ended December 31, 2015		
Sales		$515,000
Cost of goods sold		331,600
Gross profit		183,400
Operating expenses		
Depreciation expense	$ 36,000	
Other expenses	121,500	157,500
Income before taxes		25,900
Income taxes expense		7,700
Net income		$ 18,200

The following information is necessary to answer QS 12-5 and QS 12-6.

QS 12-5

Indirect: Computing investing cash flows

P2

The plant assets section of the comparative balance sheets of Anders Company is reported below.

Anders Company Comparative Balance Sheets		
	2015	2014
Plant assets		
Equipment	$ 180,000	$270,000
Accum. Depr.—Equipment	(100,000)	(210,000)
Equipment, net..................	$ 80,000	$ 60,000
Buildings	$ 380,000	$400,000
Accum. Depr.—Buildings..........	(100,000)	(285,000)
Buildings, net	$ 280,000	$115,000

Refer to the balance sheet data above from Anders Company. During 2015, equipment with a book value of $40,000 and an original cost of $210,000 was sold at a loss of $3,000.

1. How much cash did Anders receive from the sale of equipment?

2. How much depreciation expense was recorded on equipment during 2015?

3. What was the cost of new equipment purchased by Anders during 2015?

QS 12-6

Indirect: Computing investing cash flows

P2

Refer to the balance sheet data above from Anders Company. During 2015, a building with a book value of $70,000 and an original cost of $300,000 was sold at a gain of $60,000.

1. How much cash did Anders receive from the sale of the building?

2. How much depreciation expense was recorded on buildings during 2015?

3. What was the cost of buildings purchased by Anders during 2015?

QS 12-7

Computing cash from asset sales

P3

The following selected information is from Ellerby Company's comparative balance sheets.

At December 31	2015	2014
Furniture...........................	$132,000	$ 184,500
Accumulated depreciation—Furniture	(88,700)	(110,700)

The income statement reports depreciation expense for the year of $18,000. Also, furniture costing $52,500 was sold for its book value. Compute the cash received from the sale of furniture.

Compute cash flows from investing activities using the following company information.

Sale of short-term investments	$ 6,000
Cash collections from customers	16,000
Purchase of used equipment	5,000
Depreciation expense	2,000

QS 12-8
Computing cash flows from investing

P3

The following selected information is from Princeton Company's comparative balance sheets.

At December 31	2015	2014
Common stock, $10 par value	$105,000	$100,000
Paid-in capital in excess of par	567,000	342,000
Retained earnings	313,500	287,500

QS 12-9
Computing financing cash flows

P3

The company's net income for the year ended December 31, 2015, was $48,000.

1. Compute the cash received from the sale of its common stock during 2015.
2. Compute the cash paid for dividends during 2015.

Compute cash flows from financing activities using the following company information.

Additional short-term borrowings	$20,000
Purchase of short-term investments	5,000
Cash dividends paid	16,000
Interest paid	8,000

QS 12-10
Computing cash flows from financing

P3

Use the following balance sheets and income statement to answer QS 12-11 through QS 12-16.

QS 12-11
Indirect: Computing cash from operations

P2

CRUZ, INC. Comparative Balance Sheets December 31, 2015		
	2015	**2014**
Assets		
Cash	$ 94,800	$ 24,000
Accounts receivable, net	41,000	51,000
Inventory	85,800	95,800
Prepaid expenses	5,400	4,200
Total current assets	227,000	175,000
Furniture	109,000	119,000
Accum. depreciation—Furniture	(17,000)	(9,000)
Total assets	$319,000	$285,000
Liabilities and Equity		
Accounts payable	$ 15,000	$ 21,000
Wages payable	9,000	5,000
Income taxes payable	1,400	2,600
Total current liabilities	25,400	28,600
Notes payable (long-term)	29,000	69,000
Total liabilities	54,400	97,600
Equity		
Common stock, $5 par value	229,000	179,000
Retained earnings	35,600	8,400
Total liabilities and equity	$319,000	$285,000

CRUZ, INC. Income Statement For Year Ended December 31, 2015		
Sales		$488,000
Cost of goods sold		314,000
Gross profit		174,000
Operating expenses		
Depreciation expense	$37,600	
Other expenses	89,100	126,700
Income before taxes		47,300
Income taxes expense		17,300
Net income		$ 30,000

Required

Use the indirect method to prepare the cash provided or used from operating activities section only of the statement of cash flows for this company.

QS 12-12

Computing cash from asset sales

P3

Refer to the data in QS 12-11.
Furniture costing $55,000 is sold at its book value in 2015. Acquisitions of furniture total $45,000 cash, on which no depreciation is necessary because it is acquired at year-end. What is the cash inflow related to the sale of furniture?

QS 12-13

Computing financing cash outflows

P3

Refer to the data in QS 12-11.
1. Assume that all common stock is issued for cash. What amount of cash dividends is paid during 2015?
2. Assume that no additional notes payable are issued in 2015. What cash amount is paid to reduce the notes payable balance in 2015?

QS 12-14ᴮ

Direct: Computing cash received from customers

P5

Refer to the data in QS 12-11.
1. How much cash is received from sales to customers for year 2015?
2. What is the net increase or decrease in cash for year 2015?

QS 12-15ᴮ

Direct: Computing operating cash outflows

P5

Refer to the data in QS 12-11.
1. How much cash is paid to acquire inventory during year 2015?
2. How much cash is paid for "other expenses" during year 2015? (*Hint:* Examine prepaid expenses and wages payable.)

QS 12-16ᴮ

Direct: Computing cash from operations

P5

Refer to the data in QS 12-11.
Use the direct method to prepare the cash provided or used from operating activities section only of the statement of cash flows for this company.

QS 12-17

Analyses of sources and uses of cash

A1

Financial data from three competitors in the same industry follow.
1. Which of the three competitors is in the strongest position as shown by its statement of cash flows?
2. Analyze and compare the strength of Moore's cash flow on total assets ratio to that of Sykes.

	A	B	C	D
1	($ thousands)	Moore	Sykes	Kritch
2	Cash provided (used) by operating activities	$ 70,000	$ 60,000	$ (24,000)
3	Cash provided (used) by investing activities			
4	Proceeds from sale of operating assets			26,000
5	Purchase of operating assets	(28,000)	(34,000)	
6	Cash provided (used) by financing activities			
7	Proceeds from issuance of debt			23,000
8	Repayment of debt	(6,000)		
9	Net increase (decrease) in cash	$ 36,000	$ 26,000	$ 25,000
10				
11	Average total assets	$790,000	$625,000	$300,000

When a spreadsheet for a statement of cash flows is prepared, all changes in noncash balance sheet accounts are fully explained on the spreadsheet. Explain how these noncash balance sheet accounts are used to fully account for cash flows on a spreadsheet.

QS 12-18ᴬ
Noncash accounts on a spreadsheet

P4

Use the following financial statements and additional information to (1) prepare a statement of cash flows for the year ended December 31, 2016, using the *indirect method,* and (2) analyze and briefly discuss the statement prepared in part 1 with special attention to operating activities and to the company's cash level.

QS 12-19
Indirect: Preparation of statement of cash flows

P1 P2 P3

MONTGOMERY INC.
Comparative Balance Sheets
December 31, 2016 and 2015

	2016	2015
Assets		
Cash	$ 30,400	$ 30,550
Accounts receivable, net	10,050	12,150
Inventory	90,100	70,150
Total current assets..................	130,550	112,850
Equipment	49,900	41,500
Accum. depreciation—Equipment	(22,500)	(15,300)
Total assets	$157,950	$139,050
Liabilities and Equity		
Accounts payable	$ 23,900	$ 25,400
Salaries payable	500	600
Total current liabilities...............	24,400	26,000
Equity		
Common stock, no par value	110,000	100,000
Retained earnings	23,550	13,050
Total liabilities and equity	$157,950	$139,050

MONTGOMERY INC.
Income Statement
For Year Ended December 31, 2016

Sales		$45,575
Cost of goods sold		(18,950)
Gross profit		26,625
Operating expenses		
Depreciation expense	$7,200	
Other expenses	5,550	
Total operating expense		12,750
Income before taxes		13,875
Income tax expense		3,375
Net income		$10,500

Additional Information

a. No dividends are declared or paid in 2016.
b. Issued additional stock for $10,000 cash in 2016.
c. Purchased equipment for cash in 2016; no equipment was sold in 2016.

Answer each of the following questions related to international accounting standards.

1. Which method, indirect or direct, is acceptable for reporting operating cash flows under IFRS?
2. For each of the following four cash flows, identify whether it is reported under the operating, investing, or financing section (or some combination) within the indirect format of the statement of cash flows reported under IFRS and under U.S. GAAP.

QS 12-20
International cash flow disclosures

C1

Cash Flow Source	US GAAP Reporting	IFRS Reporting
a. Interest paid		
b. Dividends paid		
c. Interest received		
d. Dividends received		

■ connect

EXERCISES

Exercise 12-1
Indirect: Cash flow classification C1

The following transactions and events occurred during the year. Assuming that this company uses the *indirect method* to report cash provided by operating activities, indicate where each item would appear on its statement of cash flows by placing an *x* in the appropriate column.

	Statement of Cash Flows			Noncash Investing and Financing Activities	Not Reported on Statement or in Notes
	Operating Activities	Investing Activities	Financing Activities		
a. Declared and paid a cash dividend	____	____	____	____	____
b. Recorded depreciation expense	____	____	____	____	____
c. Paid cash to settle long-term note payable	____	____	____	____	____
d. Prepaid expenses increased in the year	____	____	____	____	____
e. Accounts receivable decreased in the year	____	____	____	____	____
f. Purchased land by issuing common stock	____	____	____	____	____
g. Inventory increased in the year	____	____	____	____	____
h. Sold equipment for cash, yielding a loss	____	____	____	____	____
i. Accounts payable decreased in the year	____	____	____	____	____
j. Income taxes payable increased in the year	____	____	____	____	____

Exercise 12-2
Indirect: Reporting cash flows from operations

P2

Hampton Company reports the following information for its recent calendar year. Prepare the operating activities section of the statement of cash flows for Hampton Company using the *indirect method.*

Income Statement Data		Selected Year-End Balance Sheet Data	
Sales	$160,000	Accounts receivable increase.	$10,000
Expenses		Inventory decrease	16,000
Cost of goods sold	100,000	Salaries payable increase	1,000
Salaries expense	24,000		
Depreciation expense	12,000		
Net income	$ 24,000		

Exercise 12-3
Indirect: Reporting and interpreting cash flows from operations

P2

Arundel Company disclosed the following information for its recent calendar year.

Income Statement Data		Selected Year-End Balance Sheet Data	
Revenues	$100,000	Accounts receivable decrease	$24,000
Expenses		Purchased a machine for cash	10,000
Salaries expense	84,000	Salaries payable increase	18,000
Utilities expense	14,000	Other accrued liabilities decrease	8,000
Depreciation expense	14,600		
Other expenses	3,400		
Net loss	$(16,000)		

Required

1. Prepare the operating activities section of the statement of cash flows using the *indirect method.*
2. What were the major reasons that this company was able to report a net loss but positive cash flow from operations?
3. Of the potential causes of differences between cash flow from operations and net income, which are the most important to investors?

The following income statement and information about changes in noncash current assets and current liabilities are reported.

SONAD COMPANY
Income Statement
For Year Ended December 31, 2015

Sales		$1,828,000
Cost of goods sold		991,000
Gross profit		837,000
Operating expenses		
Salaries expense	$245,535	
Depreciation expense	44,200	
Rent expense	49,600	
Amortization expenses—Patents	4,200	
Utilities expense	18,125	361,660
		475,340
Gain on sale of equipment		6,200
Net income		$ 481,540

Changes in current asset and current liability accounts for the year that relate to operations follow.

Accounts receivable	$30,500 increase	Accounts payable	$12,500 decrease
Inventory	25,000 increase	Salaries payable	3,500 decrease

Required

Prepare only the cash flows from operating activities section of the statement of cash flows using the *indirect method*.

Fitz Company reports the following information. Use the *indirect method* to prepare only the operating activities section of its statement of cash flows for the year ended December 31, 2015.

Selected 2015 Income Statement Data		Selected Year-End 2015 Balance Sheet Data	
Net income	$374,000	Accounts receivable decrease	$17,100
Depreciation expense	44,000	Inventory decrease....................	42,000
Amortization expense.............	7,200	Prepaid expenses increase.............	4,700
Gain on sale of plant assets.........	6,000	Accounts payable decrease	8,200
		Salaries payable increase.............	1,200

Salud Company reports the following information. Use the *indirect method* to prepare only the operating activities section of its statement of cash flows for the year ended December 31, 2015.

Selected 2015 Income Statement Data		Selected Year-End 2015 Balance Sheet Data	
Net income	$400,000	Accounts receivable increase.	$40,000
Depreciation expense	80,000	Prepaid expenses decrease	12,000
Gain on sale of machinery..........	20,000	Accounts payable increase.............	6,000
		Wages payable decrease................	2,000

Use the following information to determine this company's cash flows from investing activities.

a. Equipment with a book value of $65,300 and an original cost of $133,000 was sold at a loss of $14,000.
b. Paid $89,000 cash for a new truck.
c. Sold land costing $154,000 for $198,000 cash, yielding a gain of $44,000.
d. Long-term investments in stock were sold for $60,800 cash, yielding a gain of $4,150.

Exercise 12-8
Cash flows from
financing activities
P3

Use the following information to determine this company's cash flows from financing activities.
a. Net income was $35,000.
b. Issued common stock for $64,000 cash.
c. Paid cash dividend of $14,600.
d. Paid $50,000 cash to settle a note payable at its $50,000 maturity value.
e. Paid $12,000 cash to acquire its treasury stock.
f. Purchased equipment for $39,000 cash.

Exercise 12-9
Indirect: Statement of
cash flows under IFRS
P1

Peugeot S.A. reports the following financial information for the year ended December 31, 2011 (euros in millions). Prepare its statement of cash flows under the *indirect method*. (*Hint:* Each line item below is titled, and any necessary parentheses added, as it is reported in the statement of cash flows.)

Net income	€ 784	Cash paid for purchases of treasury stock	€ (199)
Depreciation and amortization	3,037	Cash paid for other financing activities............	(2,282)
Gains on disposals and other	(883)	Cash from disposal of plant assets and intangibles ...	189
Net increase in current operating assets....	(1,183)	Cash paid for plant assets and intangibles	(3,921)
Cash paid for dividends	(290)	Cash and cash equivalents, December 31, 2010......	10,442

Exercise 12-10
Analyses of cash flow on
total assets   **A1**

A company reported average total assets of $1,240,000 in 2014 and $1,510,000 in 2015. Its net operating cash flow was $102,920 in 2014 and $138,920 in 2015. Calculate its cash flow on total assets ratio for both years. Comment on the results and any change in performance.

Exercise 12-11
Indirect: Preparation of
statement of cash flows
P1 P2 P3 A1

The following financial statements and additional information are reported.

IKIBAN INC. Comparative Balance Sheets June 30, 2015 and 2014		
	2015	**2014**
Assets		
Cash	$ 87,500	$ 44,000
Accounts receivable, net	65,000	51,000
Inventory	63,800	86,500
Prepaid expenses	4,400	5,400
Total current assets....................	220,700	186,900
Equipment	124,000	115,000
Accum. depreciation—Equipment	(27,000)	(9,000)
Total assets	$317,700	$292,900
Liabilities and Equity		
Accounts payable	$ 25,000	$ 30,000
Wages payable	6,000	15,000
Income taxes payable	3,400	3,800
Total current liabilities.................	34,400	48,800
Notes payable (long term).............	30,000	60,000
Total liabilities	64,400	108,800
Equity		
Common stock, $5 par value	220,000	160,000
Retained earnings	33,300	24,100
Total liabilities and equity	$317,700	$292,900

IKIBAN INC. Income Statement For Year Ended June 30, 2015		
Sales		$678,000
Cost of goods sold		411,000
Gross profit		267,000
Operating expenses		
Depreciation expense	$58,600	
Other expenses	67,000	
Total operating expenses		125,600
		141,400
Other gains (losses)		
Gain on sale of equipment		2,000
Income before taxes		143,400
Income taxes expense		43,890
Net income		$ 99,510

Additional Information

Check   (*b*) Cash paid for
dividends, $90,310

a. A $30,000 note payable is retired at its $30,000 carrying (book) value in exchange for cash.
b. The only changes affecting retained earnings are net income and cash dividends paid.

c. New equipment is acquired for $57,600 cash.

d. Received cash for the sale of equipment that had cost $48,600, yielding a $2,000 gain.

e. Prepaid Expenses and Wages Payable relate to Other Expenses on the income statement.

f. All purchases and sales of inventory are on credit.

(*d*) Cash received
from equip. sale, $10,000

Required

1. Prepare a statement of cash flows for the year ended June 30, 2015, using the *indirect method.*

2. Compute the company's cash flow on total assets ratio for its fiscal year 2015.

Refer to the information in Exercise 12-11. Using the *direct method,* prepare the statement of cash flows for the year ended June 30, 2015.

Exercise 12-12^B

Direct: Preparation of statement of cash flows

P1   P3   P5

Complete the following spreadsheet in preparation of the statement of cash flows. (The statement of cash flows is not required.) Prepare the spreadsheet as in Exhibit 12A.1; report operating activities under the *indirect method.* Identify the debits and credits in the Analysis of Changes columns with letters that correspond to the following transactions and events *a* through *h.*

Exercise 12-13

Indirect: Cash flows spreadsheet

P4

a. Net income for the year was $100,000.

b. Dividends of $80,000 cash were declared and paid.

c. Scoreteck's only noncash expense was $70,000 of depreciation.

d. The company purchased plant assets for $70,000 cash.

e. Notes payable of $20,000 were issued for $20,000 cash.

f. Change in accounts receivable.

g. Change in inventory.

h. Change in accounts payable.

	A	B	C	D	E	F	G
1		SCORETECK CORPORATION					
2		Spreadsheet for Statement of Cash Flows—Indirect Method					
3		For Year Ended December 31, 2015					
4				Analysis of Changes			
5		Dec. 31, 2014		Debit		Credit	Dec. 31, 2015
6	**Balance Sheet—Debit Bal. Accounts**						
7	Cash	$ 80,000					$ 60,000
8	Accounts receivable	120,000					190,000
9	Inventory	250,000					230,000
10	Plant assets	600,000					670,000
11		$1,050,000					$1,150,000
12	**Balance Sheet—Credit Bal. Accounts**						
13	Accumulated depreciation	$ 100,000					$ 170,000
14	Accounts payable	150,000					140,000
15	Notes payable	370,000					390,000
16	Common stock	200,000					200,000
17	Retained earnings	230,000					250,000
18		$1,050,000					$1,150,000
19	**Statement of Cash Flows**						
20	Operating activities						
21	Net income						
22	Increase in accounts receivable						
23	Decrease in inventory						
24	Decrease in accounts payable						
25	Depreciation expense						
26	Investing activities						
27	Cash paid to purchase plant assets						
28	Financing activities						
29	Cash paid for dividends						
30	Cash from issuance of notes						
31							

Exercise 12-14ᴮ
Direct: Cash flow classification

C1   P5

The following transactions and events occurred during the year. Assuming that this company uses the *direct method* to report cash provided by operating activities, indicate where each item would appear on the statement of cash flows by placing an *x* in the appropriate column.

	Statement of Cash Flows			Noncash Investing and Financing Activities	Not Reported on Statement or in Notes
	Operating Activities	Investing Activities	Financing Activities		
a. Retired long-term notes payable by issuing common stock	___	___	___	___	___
b. Paid cash to acquire inventory	___	___	___	___	___
c. Sold inventory for cash	___	___	___	___	___
d. Paid cash dividend that was declared in a prior period	___	___	___	___	___
e. Accepted six-month note receivable in exchange for plant assets	___	___	___	___	___
f. Recorded depreciation expense	___	___	___	___	___
g. Paid cash to acquire treasury stock	___	___	___	___	___
h. Collected cash from sales	___	___	___	___	___
i. Borrowed cash from bank by signing a nine-month note payable	___	___	___	___	___
j. Paid cash to purchase a patent	___	___	___	___	___

Exercise 12-15ᴮ
Direct: Computation of cash flows

P5

For each of the following three separate cases, use the information provided about the calendar-year 2016 operations of Sahim Company to compute the required cash flow information.

Case X: Compute cash received from customers:	
Sales	$515,000
Accounts receivable, December 31, 2015	27,200
Accounts receivable, December 31, 2016	33,600
Case Y: Compute cash paid for rent:	
Rent expense	$139,800
Rent payable, December 31, 2015	7,800
Rent payable, December 31, 2016	6,200
Case Z: Compute cash paid for inventory:	
Cost of goods sold	$525,000
Inventory, December 31, 2015	158,600
Accounts payable, December 31, 2015	66,700
Inventory, December 31, 2016	130,400
Accounts payable, December 31, 2016	82,000

Exercise 12-16ᴮ
Direct: Cash flows from operating activities   P5

Refer to the information about Sonad Company in Exercise 12-4. Use the *direct method* to prepare only the cash provided or used by operating activities section of the statement of cash flows for this company.

Exercise 12-17ᴮ
Direct: Preparation of statement of cash flows and supporting note

P1   P3   P5

Use the following information about the cash flows of Ferron Company to prepare a complete statement of cash flows (*direct method*) for the year ended December 31, 2015. Use a note disclosure for any non-cash investing and financing activities.

Cash and cash equivalents balance, December 31, 2014	$ 40,000
Cash and cash equivalents balance, December 31, 2015	148,000
Cash received as interest	3,500
Cash paid for salaries	76,500

[continued on next page]

[continued from previous page]

Bonds payable retired by issuing common stock (no gain or loss on retirement)	185,500
Cash paid to retire long-term notes payable.....................................	100,000
Cash received from sale of equipment	60,250
Cash received in exchange for six-month note payable	35,000
Land purchased by issuing long-term note payable	105,250
Cash paid for store equipment	24,750
Cash dividends paid	10,000
Cash paid for other expenses	20,000
Cash received from customers	495,000
Cash paid for inventory...	254,500

The following summarized Cash T-account reflects the total debits and total credits to the Cash account of Thomas Corporation for calendar-year 2015.

1. Use this information to prepare a complete statement of cash flows for year 2015. The cash provided or used by operating activities should be reported using the *direct method*.

2. Refer to the statement of cash flows prepared for part 1 to answer the following questions *a* through *d*: (*a*) Which section—operating, investing, or financing—shows the largest cash (i) inflow and (ii) out-flow? (*b*) What is the largest individual item among the investing cash outflows? (*c*) Are the cash proceeds larger from issuing notes or issuing stock? (*d*) Does the company have a net cash inflow or outflow from borrowing activities?

Exercise 12-18B

Direct: Preparation of statement of cash flows from Cash T-account

P1   P3   P5

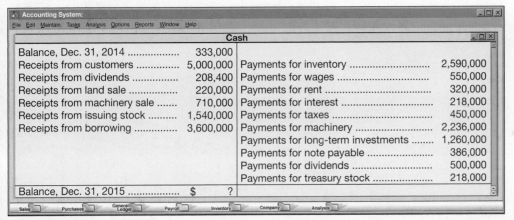

Cash

Balance, Dec. 31, 2014	333,000	Payments for inventory	2,590,000
Receipts from customers	5,000,000	Payments for wages	550,000
Receipts from dividends	208,400	Payments for rent	320,000
Receipts from land sale	220,000	Payments for interest	218,000
Receipts from machinery sale	710,000	Payments for taxes	450,000
Receipts from issuing stock	1,540,000	Payments for machinery	2,236,000
Receipts from borrowing	3,600,000	Payments for long-term investments	1,260,000
		Payments for note payable	386,000
		Payments for dividends	500,000
		Payments for treasury stock	218,000
Balance, Dec. 31, 2015	$?		

connect

Lansing Company's 2015 income statement and selected balance sheet data (for current assets and current liabilities) at December 31, 2014 and 2015, follow.

PROBLEM SET A

Problem 12-1A
Indirect: Computing cash flows from operations

P2

LANSING COMPANY
Selected Balance Sheet Accounts

At December 31	2015	2014
Accounts receivable	$5,600	$5,800
Inventory	1,980	1,540
Accounts payable........	4,400	4,600
Salaries payable	880	700
Utilities payable	220	160
Prepaid insurance	260	280
Prepaid rent............	220	180

LANSING COMPANY
Income Statement
For Year Ended December 31, 2015

Sales revenue	$97,200
Expenses	
Cost of goods sold	42,000
Depreciation expense	12,000
Salaries expense	18,000
Rent expense	9,000
Insurance expense	3,800
Interest expense	3,600
Utilities expense	2,800
Net income	$ 6,000

Required

Prepare the cash flows from operating activities section only of the company's 2015 statement of cash flows using the *indirect method*.

Check   Cash from operating activities, $17,780

Problem 12-2A[B]
Direct: Computing cash flows from operations

P5

Refer to the information in Problem 12-1A.

Required

Prepare the cash flows from operating activities section only of the company's 2015 statement of cash flows using the *direct method*.

Problem 12-3A
Indirect: Statement of cash flows

A1   P1   P2   P3

Forten Company, a merchandiser, recently completed its calendar-year 2015 operations. For the year, (1) all sales are credit sales, (2) all credits to Accounts Receivable reflect cash receipts from customers, (3) all purchases of inventory are on credit, (4) all debits to Accounts Payable reflect cash payments for inventory, and (5) Other Expenses are paid in advance and are initially debited to Prepaid Expenses. The company's income statement and balance sheets follow.

FORTEN COMPANY
Comparative Balance Sheets
December 31, 2015 and 2014

	2015	2014
Assets		
Cash	$ 49,800	$ 73,500
Accounts receivable	65,810	50,625
Inventory	275,656	251,800
Prepaid expenses	1,250	1,875
Total current assets	392,516	377,800
Equipment	157,500	108,000
Accum. depreciation—Equipment	(36,625)	(46,000)
Total assets	$513,391	$439,800
Liabilities and Equity		
Accounts payable	$ 53,141	$114,675
Short-term notes payable	10,000	6,000
Total current liabilities	63,141	120,675
Long-term notes payable	65,000	48,750
Total liabilities	128,141	169,425
Equity		
Common stock, $5 par value	162,750	150,250
Paid-in capital in excess of par, common stock	37,500	0
Retained earnings	185,000	120,125
Total liabilities and equity	$513,391	$439,800

FORTEN COMPANY
Income Statement
For Year Ended December 31, 2015

Sales		$582,500
Cost of goods sold		285,000
Gross profit		297,500
Operating expenses		
Depreciation expense	$ 20,750	
Other expenses	132,400	153,150
Other gains (losses)		
Loss on sale of equipment		(5,125)
Income before taxes		139,225
Income taxes expense		24,250
Net income		$114,975

Additional Information on Year 2015 Transactions

a. The loss on the cash sale of equipment was $5,125 (details in *b*).

b. Sold equipment costing $46,875, with accumulated depreciation of $30,125, for $11,625 cash.

c. Purchased equipment costing $96,375 by paying $30,000 cash and signing a long-term note payable for the balance.

d. Borrowed $4,000 cash by signing a short-term note payable.

e. Paid $50,125 cash to reduce the long-term notes payable.

f. Issued 2,500 shares of common stock for $20 cash per share.

g. Declared and paid cash dividends of $50,100.

Required

Check Cash from operating activities, $40,900

1. Prepare a complete statement of cash flows; report its operating activities using the *indirect method*. Disclose any noncash investing and financing activities in a note.

Analysis Component

2. Analyze and discuss the statement of cash flows prepared in part 1, giving special attention to the wisdom of the cash dividend payment.

Refer to the information reported about Forten Company in Problem 12-3A.

Problem 12-4A^A
Indirect: Cash flows
spreadsheet
P1 P2 P3 P4

Required

Prepare a complete statement of cash flows using a spreadsheet as in Exhibit 12A.1; report its operating activities using the *indirect method*. Identify the debits and credits in the Analysis of Changes columns with letters that correspond to the following list of transactions and events.

a. Net income was $114,975.

b. Accounts receivable increased.

c. Inventory increased.

d. Prepaid expenses decreased.

e. Accounts payable decreased.

f. Depreciation expense was $20,750.

g. Sold equipment costing $46,875, with accumulated depreciation of $30,125, for $11,625 cash. This yielded a loss of $5,125.

h. Purchased equipment costing $96,375 by paying $30,000 cash and **(i.)** by signing a long-term note payable for the balance.

j. Borrowed $4,000 cash by signing a short-term note payable.

k. Paid $50,125 cash to reduce the long-term notes payable.

l. Issued 2,500 shares of common stock for $20 cash per share.

m. Declared and paid cash dividends of $50,100.

Check Analysis of Changes column totals, $600,775

Refer to Forten Company's financial statements and related information in Problem 12-3A.

Problem 12-5A^B
Direct: Statement of
cash flows P1 P3 P5
Check Cash used in
financing activities, $(46,225)

Required

Prepare a complete statement of cash flows; report its operating activities according to the *direct method*. Disclose any noncash investing and financing activities in a note.

Golden Corp., a merchandiser, recently completed its 2015 operations. For the year, (1) all sales are credit sales, (2) all credits to Accounts Receivable reflect cash receipts from customers, (3) all purchases of inventory are on credit, (4) all debits to Accounts Payable reflect cash payments for inventory, (5) Other Expenses are all cash expenses, and (6) any change in Income Taxes Payable reflects the accrual and cash payment of taxes. The company's balance sheets and income statement follow.

Problem 12-6A
Indirect: Statement of
cash flows
P1 P2 P3

GOLDEN CORPORATION
Comparative Balance Sheets
December 31, 2015 and 2014

	2015	2014
Assets		
Cash	$ 164,000	$107,000
Accounts receivable	83,000	71,000
Inventory	601,000	526,000
Total current assets	848,000	704,000
Equipment	335,000	299,000
Accum. depreciation—Equipment	(158,000)	(104,000)
Total assets	$1,025,000	$899,000
Liabilities and Equity		
Accounts payable	$ 87,000	$ 71,000
Income taxes payable	28,000	25,000
Total current liabilities	115,000	96,000
Equity		
Common stock, $2 par value	592,000	568,000
Paid-in capital in excess of par value, common stock	196,000	160,000
Retained earnings	122,000	75,000
Total liabilities and equity	$1,025,000	$899,000

GOLDEN CORPORATION
Income Statement
For Year Ended December 31, 2015

Sales		$1,792,000
Cost of goods sold		1,086,000
Gross profit		706,000
Operating expenses		
Depreciation expense	$ 54,000	
Other expenses	494,000	548,000
Income before taxes		158,000
Income taxes expense		22,000
Net income		$ 136,000

Additional Information on Year 2015 Transactions

a. Purchased equipment for $36,000 cash.

b. Issued 12,000 shares of common stock for $5 cash per share.

c. Declared and paid $89,000 in cash dividends.

Required

Check Cash from operating activities, $122,000

Prepare a complete statement of cash flows; report its cash inflows and cash outflows from operating activities according to the *indirect method*.

Problem 12-7A[A]
Indirect: Cash flows spreadsheet

P1 P2 P3 P4

Refer to the information reported about Golden Corporation in Problem 12-6A.

Required

Prepare a complete statement of cash flows using a spreadsheet as in Exhibit 12A.1; report operating activities under the *indirect method*. Identify the debits and credits in the Analysis of Changes columns with letters that correspond to the following list of transactions and events.

a. Net income was $136,000.

b. Accounts receivable increased.

c. Inventory increased.

d. Accounts payable increased.

e. Income taxes payable increased.

f. Depreciation expense was $54,000.

g. Purchased equipment for $36,000 cash.

Check Analysis of Changes column totals, $481,000

h. Issued 12,000 shares at $5 cash per share.

i. Declared and paid $89,000 of cash dividends.

Problem 12-8A[B]
Direct: Statement of cash flows

P1 P3 P5

Check Cash used in financing activities, $(29,000)

Refer to Golden Corporation's financial statements and related information in Problem 12-6A.

Required

Prepare a complete statement of cash flows; report its cash flows from operating activities according to the *direct method*.

PROBLEM SET B

Problem 12-1B
Indirect: Computing cash flows from operations

P2

Salt Lake Company's 2015 income statement and selected balance sheet data (for current assets and current liabilities) at December 31, 2014 and 2015, follow.

SALT LAKE COMPANY
Income Statement
For Year Ended December 31, 2015

Sales revenue	$156,000
Expenses	
Cost of goods sold	72,000
Depreciation expense	32,000
Salaries expense	20,000
Rent expense	5,000
Insurance expense	2,600
Interest expense	2,400
Utilities expense	2,000
Net income	$ 20,000

SALT LAKE COMPANY
Selected Balance Sheet Accounts

At December 31	2015	2014
Accounts receivable	$3,600	$3,000
Inventory	860	980
Accounts payable	2,400	2,600
Salaries payable	900	600
Utilities payable	200	0
Prepaid insurance	140	180
Prepaid rent	100	200

Required

Prepare the cash flows from operating activities section only of the company's 2015 statement of cash flows using the *indirect method*.

Check Cash from operating activities, $51,960

Refer to the information in Problem 12-1B.

Required

Prepare the cash flows from operating activities section only of the company's 2015 statement of cash flows using the *direct method*.

Problem 12-2B[B]
Direct: Computing cash flows from operations
P5

Gazelle Corporation, a merchandiser, recently completed its calendar-year 2015 operations. For the year, (1) all sales are credit sales, (2) all credits to Accounts Receivable reflect cash receipts from customers, (3) all purchases of inventory are on credit, (4) all debits to Accounts Payable reflect cash payments for inventory, and (5) Other Expenses are paid in advance and are initially debited to Prepaid Expenses. The company's balance sheets and income statement follow.

Problem 12-3B
Indirect: Statement of cash flows
A1 P1 P2 P3

GAZELLE CORPORATION Comparative Balance Sheets December 31, 2015 and 2014		
	2015	**2014**
Assets		
Cash	$123,450	$ 61,550
Accounts receivable	77,100	80,750
Inventory	240,600	250,700
Prepaid expenses	15,100	17,000
Total current assets...................	456,250	410,000
Equipment	262,250	200,000
Accum. depreciation—Equipment	(110,750)	(95,000)
Total assets	$607,750	$515,000
Liabilities and Equity		
Accounts payable	$ 17,750	$102,000
Short-term notes payable	15,000	10,000
Total current liabilities................	32,750	112,000
Long-term notes payable	100,000	77,500
Total liabilities	132,750	189,500
Equity		
Common stock, $5 par	215,000	200,000
Paid-in capital in excess of par, common stock	30,000	0
Retained earnings	230,000	125,500
Total liabilities and equity	$607,750	$515,000

GAZELLE CORPORATION Income Statement For Year Ended December 31, 2015		
Sales		$1,185,000
Cost of goods sold		595,000
Gross profit		590,000
Operating expenses		
Depreciation expense	$ 38,600	
Other expenses	362,850	
Total operating expenses		401,450
		188,550
Other gains (losses)		
Loss on sale of equipment		(2,100)
Income before taxes		186,450
Income taxes expense		28,350
Net income		$ 158,100

Additional Information on Year 2015 Transactions

a. The loss on the cash sale of equipment was $2,100 (details in *b*).

b. Sold equipment costing $51,000, with accumulated depreciation of $22,850, for $26,050 cash.

c. Purchased equipment costing $113,250 by paying $43,250 cash and signing a long-term note payable for the balance.

d. Borrowed $5,000 cash by signing a short-term note payable.

e. Paid $47,500 cash to reduce the long-term notes payable.

f. Issued 3,000 shares of common stock for $15 cash per share.

g. Declared and paid cash dividends of $53,600.

Required

1. Prepare a complete statement of cash flows; report its operating activities using the *indirect method*. Disclose any noncash investing and financing activities in a note.

Analysis Component

2. Analyze and discuss the statement of cash flows prepared in part 1, giving special attention to the wisdom of the cash dividend payment.

Problem 12-4B[A]
Indirect: Cash flows spreadsheet

P1   P2   P3   P4

Refer to the information reported about Gazelle Corporation in Problem 12-3B.

Required

Prepare a complete statement of cash flows using a spreadsheet as in Exhibit 12A.1; report its operating activities using the *indirect method*. Identify the debits and credits in the Analysis of Changes columns with letters that correspond to the following list of transactions and events.

   a. Net income was $158,100.
   b. Accounts receivable decreased.
   c. Inventory decreased.
   d. Prepaid expenses decreased.
   e. Accounts payable decreased.
   f. Depreciation expense was $38,600.
   g. Sold equipment costing $51,000, with accumulated depreciation of $22,850, for $26,050 cash. This yielded a loss of $2,100.
   h. Purchased equipment costing $113,250 by paying $43,250 cash and **(i.)** by signing a long-term note payable for the balance.
   j. Borrowed $5,000 cash by signing a short-term note payable.
   k. Paid $47,500 cash to reduce the long-term notes payable.
   l. Issued 3,000 shares of common stock for $15 cash per share.
   m. Declared and paid cash dividends of $53,600.

Problem 12-5B[B]
Direct: Statement of cash flows

P1   P3   P5

Refer to Gazelle Corporation's financial statements and related information in Problem 12-3B.

Required

Prepare a complete statement of cash flows; report its operating activities according to the *direct method*. Disclose any noncash investing and financing activities in a note.

Problem 12-6B
Indirect: Statement of cash flows

P1   P2   P3

Satu Company, a merchandiser, recently completed its 2015 operations. For the year, (1) all sales are credit sales, (2) all credits to Accounts Receivable reflect cash receipts from customers, (3) all purchases of inventory are on credit, (4) all debits to Accounts Payable reflect cash payments for inventory, (5) Other Expenses are cash expenses, and (6) any change in Income Taxes Payable reflects the accrual and cash payment of taxes. The company's income statement and balance sheets follow.

SATU COMPANY
Comparative Balance Sheets
December 31, 2015 and 2014

	2015	2014
Assets		
Cash............................	$ 58,750	$ 28,400
Accounts receivable	20,222	25,860
Total current assets...................	78,972	54,260
Inventory	165,667	140,320
Equipment	107,750	77,500
Accum. depreciation—Equipment	(46,700)	(31,000)
Total assets	$305,689	$241,080
Liabilities and Equity		
Accounts payable	$ 20,372	$157,530
Income taxes payable	2,100	6,100
Total current liabilities................	22,472	163,630
Equity		
Common stock, $5 par value	40,000	25,000
Paid-in capital in excess		
of par, common stock	68,000	20,000
Retained earnings	175,217	32,450
Total liabilities and equity	$305,689	$241,080

SATU COMPANY
Income Statement
For Year Ended December 31, 2015

Sales		$750,800
Cost of goods sold		269,200
Gross profit		481,600
Operating expenses		
Depreciation expense	$ 15,700	
Other expenses..............	173,933	189,633
Income before taxes		291,967
Income taxes expense...........		89,200
Net income		$202,767

Additional Information on Year 2015 Transactions

a. Purchased equipment for $30,250 cash.

b. Issued 3,000 shares of common stock for $21 cash per share.

c. Declared and paid $60,000 of cash dividends.

Required

Prepare a complete statement of cash flows; report its cash inflows and cash outflows from operating activities according to the *indirect method*.

Check   Cash from operating activities, $57,600

Refer to the information reported about Satu Company in Problem 12-6B.

Required

Prepare a complete statement of cash flows using a spreadsheet as in Exhibit 12A.1; report operating activities under the *indirect method*. Identify the debits and credits in the Analysis of Changes columns with letters that correspond to the following list of transactions and events.

a. Net income was $202,767.

b. Accounts receivable decreased.

c. Inventory increased.

d. Accounts payable decreased.

e. Income taxes payable decreased.

f. Depreciation expense was $15,700.

g. Purchased equipment for $30,250 cash.

h. Issued 3,000 shares at $21 cash per share.

i. Declared and paid $60,000 of cash dividends.

Problem 12-7B[A]
Indirect: Cash flows spreadsheet

P1 P2 P3 P4

Check   Analysis of Changes column totals, $543,860

Refer to Satu Company's financial statements and related information in Problem 12-6B.

Required

Prepare a complete statement of cash flows; report its cash flows from operating activities according to the *direct method*.

Problem 12-8B[B]
Direct: Statement of cash flows

P1 P3 P5

Check   Cash provided by financing activities, $3,000

SERIAL PROBLEM

Business Solutions
(Indirect)

P1 P2 P3

(This serial problem began in Chapter 1 and continues through most of the book. If previous chapter segments were not completed, the serial problem can begin at this point. It is helpful, but not necessary, to use the Working Papers that accompany the book.)

SP 12   Santana Rey, owner of Business Solutions, decides to prepare a statement of cash flows for her business.

BUSINESS SOLUTIONS Income Statement For Three Months Ended March 31, 2016		
Computer services revenue.		$25,307
Net sales		18,693
Total revenue		44,000
Cost of goods sold	$14,052	
Depreciation expense— Office equipment	400	
Depreciation expense— Computer equipment	1,250	
Wages expense	3,250	
Insurance expense	555	
Rent expense	2,475	
Computer supplies expense	1,305	
Advertising expense	600	
Mileage expense	320	
Repairs expense—Computer	960	
Total expenses		25,167
Net income		$18,833

BUSINESS SOLUTIONS Comparative Balance Sheets December 31, 2015, and March 31, 2016		
	Mar. 31, 2016	**Dec. 31, 2015**
Assets		
Cash	$ 68,057	$48,372
Accounts receivable	22,867	5,668
Inventory	704	0
Computer supplies	2,005	580
Prepaid insurance	1,110	1,665
Prepaid rent	825	825
Total current assets	95,568	57,110
Office equipment	8,000	8,000
Accumulated depreciation—Office equipment	(800)	(400)
Computer equipment	20,000	20,000
Accumulated depreciation— Computer equipment	(2,500)	(1,250)
Total assets	$120,268	$83,460
Liabilities and Equity		
Accounts payable	$ 0	$ 1,100
Wages payable	875	500
Unearned computer service revenue	0	1,500
Total current liabilities	875	3,100
Equity		
Common stock	98,000	73,000
Retained earnings	21,393	7,360
Total liabilities and equity	$120,268	$83,460

Required

Check   Cash flows used by operations: $(515)

Prepare a statement of cash flows for Business Solutions using the *indirect method* for the three months ended March 31, 2016. Recall that owner Santana Rey contributed $25,000 to the business in exchange for additional stock in the first quarter of 2016 and has received $4,800 in cash dividends.

GENERAL LEDGER PROBLEM

Available in Connect

The following General Ledger assignments highlight the impact, or lack thereof, on the statement of cash flows from summary journal entries derived from consecutive trial balances. Prepare summary journal entries reflecting changes in consecutive trial balances. Then prepare the statement of cash flows (direct method) from those entries. Finally, prepare the reconciliation to the indirect method for net cash provided (used) by operating activities.

GL 12-1   General Ledger assignment based on Exercise 12-11

GL 12-2   General Ledger assignment based on Problem 12-3

GL 12-3   General Ledger assignment based on Problem 12-6

Beyond the Numbers

BTN 12-1   Refer to Apple's financial statements in Appendix A to answer the following.

1. Is Apple's statement of cash flows prepared under the direct method or the indirect method? How do you know?
2. For each fiscal year 2013, 2012, and 2011, is the amount of cash provided by operating activities more or less than the cash paid for dividends?
3. What is the largest amount in reconciling the difference between net income and cash flow from operating activities in fiscal 2013? In fiscal 2012? In fiscal 2011?
4. Identify the largest cash inflow and cash outflow for investing *and* for financing activities in fiscal 2013 and in fiscal 2012.

Fast Forward

5. Obtain Apple's financial statements for a fiscal year ending after September 28, 2013, from either its website (Apple.com) or the SEC's database (www.SEC.gov). Since September 28, 2013, what are Apple's largest cash outflows and cash inflows in the investing and in the financing sections of its statement of cash flows?

**REPORTING IN
ACTION**

A1

APPLE

BTN 12-2   Key figures for Apple and Google follow.

($ millions)	Apple			Google		
	Current Year	1 Year Prior	2 Years Prior	Current Year	1 Year Prior	2 Years Prior
Operating cash flows...........	$ 53,666	$ 50,856	$ 37,529	$ 18,659	$16,619	$14,565
Total assets.................	207,000	176,064	116,371	110,920	93,798	72,574

**COMPARATIVE
ANALYSIS**

A1

**APPLE
GOOGLE**

Required

1. Compute the recent two years' cash flow on total assets ratios for Apple and Google.
2. What does the cash flow on total assets ratio measure?
3. Which company has the highest cash flow on total assets ratio for the periods shown?
4. Does the cash flow on total assets ratio reflect on the quality of earnings? Explain.

BTN 12-3   Katie Murphy is preparing for a meeting with her banker. Her business is finishing its fourth year of operations. In the first year, it had negative cash flows from operations. In the second and third years, cash flows from operations were positive. However, inventory costs rose significantly in year 4, and cash flows from operations will probably be down 25%. Murphy wants to secure a line of credit from her banker as a financing buffer. From experience, she knows the banker will scrutinize operating cash flows for years 1 through 4 and will want a projected number for year 5. Murphy knows that a steady progression upward in operating cash flows for years 1 through 4 will help her case. She decides to use her discretion as owner and considers several business actions that will turn her operating cash flow in year 4 from a decrease to an increase.

**ETHICS
CHALLENGE**

C1   A1

Required

1. Identify two business actions Murphy might take to improve cash flows from operations.
2. Comment on the ethics and possible consequences of Murphy's decision to pursue these actions.

BTN 12-4   Your friend, Diana Wood, recently completed the second year of her business and just received annual financial statements from her accountant. Wood finds the income statement and balance sheet informative but does not understand the statement of cash flows. She says the first section is especially confusing because it contains a lot of additions and subtractions that do not make sense to her. Wood adds, "The income statement tells me the business is more profitable than last year and that's most important. If I want to know how cash changes, I can look at comparative balance sheets."

**COMMUNICATING
IN PRACTICE**

C1

Required

Write a half-page memorandum to your friend explaining the purpose of the statement of cash flows. Speculate as to why the first section is so confusing and how it might be rectified.

TAKING IT TO THE NET

A1

BTN 12-5   Access the March 31, 2014, filing of the 10-K report (for year ending December 31, 2013) of Mendocino Brewing Company, Inc. (ticker: MENB), at www.SEC.gov.

Required

1. Does Mendocino Brewing use the direct or indirect method to construct its consolidated statement of cash flows?
2. For the year ended December 31, 2013, what is the largest item in reconciling the net income to net cash provided by operating activities?
3. In the recent two years, has the company been more successful in generating operating cash flows or in generating net income? Identify the figures to support the answer.
4. In the year ended December 31, 2013, what was the largest cash outflow for investing activities *and* for financing activities?
5. What item(s) does Mendocino Brewing report as supplementary cash flow information?
6. Does Mendocino Brewing report any noncash financing activities for 2013? Identify them, if any.

TEAMWORK IN ACTION

C1   A1   P2   P5

BTN 12-6   Team members are to coordinate and independently answer one question within each of the following three sections. Team members should then report to the team and confirm or correct teammates' answers.

1. Answer *one* of the following questions about the statement of cash flows.
    a. What are this statement's reporting objectives?
    b. What two methods are used to prepare it? Identify similarities and differences between them.
    c. What steps are followed to prepare the statement?
    d. What types of analyses are often made from this statement's information?
2. Identify and explain the adjustment from net income to obtain cash flows from operating activities using the indirect method for *one* of the following items.
    a. Noncash operating revenues and expenses.
    b. Nonoperating gains and losses.
    c. Increases and decreases in noncash current assets.
    d. Increases and decreases in current liabilities.
3.[B] Identify and explain the formula for computing cash flows from operating activities using the direct method for *one* of the following items.
    a. Cash receipts from sales to customers.
    b. Cash paid for inventory.
    c. Cash paid for wages and operating expenses.
    d. Cash paid for interest and taxes.

Note: For teams of more than four, some pairing within teams is necessary. Use as an in-class activity or as an assignment. If used in class, specify a time limit on each part. Conclude with reports to the entire class, using team rotation. Each team can prepare responses on a transparency.

ENTREPRENEURIAL DECISION

C1   A1

BTN 12-7   Review the chapter's opener involving LSTN and its entrepreneurial owner, Bridget Hilton.

Required

1. In a business such as LSTN, monitoring cash flow is always a priority. Even though it is off to a successful start and is growing with a positive net income, explain how cash flow can lag behind net income.
2. LSTN is a privately owned company. What are potential sources of financing for its future expansion?

BTN 12-8   Jenna and Matt Wilder are completing their second year operating Mountain High, a down-hill ski area and resort. Mountain High reports a net loss of $(10,000) for its second year, which includes an $85,000 extraordinary loss from fire. This past year also involved major purchases of plant assets for renovation and expansion, yielding a year-end total asset amount of $800,000. Mountain High's net cash outflow for its second year is $(5,000); a summarized version of its statement of cash flows follows:

Net cash flow provided by operating activities	$295,000
Net cash flow used by investing activities	(310,000)
Net cash flow provided by financing activities	10,000

Required

Write a one-page memorandum to the Wilders evaluating Mountain High's current performance and assessing its future. Give special emphasis to cash flow data and their interpretation.

BTN 12-9   Visit The Motley Fool's website (Fool.com). Enter the *Fool's School* (at *Fool.com/School*). Identify and select the link "How to Value Stocks." (This site might ask you to register with your email address; registration had been free and did grant access to articles on the site.)

HITTING THE ROAD

C1

Required

1. Click on "Introduction to Valuation Methods," and then "Cash-Flow-Based Valuations." How does the Fool's school define cash flow? What is the school's reasoning for this definition?
2. Per the school's instruction, why do analysts focus on earnings before interest and taxes (EBIT)?
3. Visit other links at this website that interest you such as "How to Read a Balance Sheet," or find out what the "Fool's Ratio" is. Write a half-page report on what you find.

BTN 12-10   Key comparative information for Samsung (www.Samsung.com), which is a leading manufacturer of electronic consumer products, follows.

GLOBAL DECISION

C1

Samsung
APPLE
GOOGLE

(W in millions)	Current Year	1 Year Prior	2 Years Prior
Operating cash flows	W 46,707,440	W 37,972,809	W 22,917,901
Total assets	214,075,018	181,071,570	155,800,263

Required

1. Compute the recent two years' cash flow on total assets ratio for Samsung.
2. How does Samsung's ratio compare to Apple's and Google's ratios from BTN 12-2?

ANSWERS TO MULTIPLE CHOICE QUIZ

1. b;

Net income	$15,200
Depreciation expense	10,000
Gain on sale of land	(3,000)
Increase in inventory	(1,500)
Increase in accounts payable	2,850
Net cash provided by operations	$23,550

2. c; Cash received from sale of machine is reported as an investing activity.

3. d; FASB requires cash interest paid to be reported under operating.
4. a; Cash paid for salaries and wages = $255,000 + $8,200 − $10,900 = $252,300
5. e; Increase in inventory = $112,000 − $105,000 = $7,000
Increase in accounts payable = $101,300 − $98,500 = $2,800
Cash paid for inventory = $545,000 + $7,000 − $2,800 = $549,200

Analysis of Financial Statements

Chapter Preview

BASICS OF ANALYSIS

C1 Analysis: Its purpose, building blocks, and information needs

C2 Standards for comparisons, and analysis tools

HORIZONTAL ANALYSIS

P1 Application of:

Comparative balance sheets

Comparative income statements

Trend analysis

VERTICAL ANALYSIS

P2 Application of:

Common-size balance sheet

Common-size income statement

Common-size graphics

RATIO ANALYSIS AND REPORTING

P3 Liquidity and efficiency

Solvency

Profitability

Market prospects

A1 Analysis reports

Learning Objectives

CONCEPTUAL

C1 Explain the purpose and identify the building blocks of analysis.

C2 Describe standards for comparisons in analysis.

ANALYTICAL

A1 Summarize and report results of analysis.

A2 *Appendix 13A*—Explain the form and assess the content of a complete income statement.

PROCEDURAL

P1 Explain and apply methods of horizontal analysis.

P2 Describe and apply methods of vertical analysis.

P3 Define and apply ratio analysis.

In Search of Truth

ALEXANDRIA, VA—In Shakespeare's Elizabethan comedy *As You Like It,* only the fool could speak truthfully to the king without getting his head lopped off. Inspired by Shakespeare's stage character, Tom and David Gardner vowed to become modern-day fools who tell it like it is. With under $10,000 in start-up money, the brothers launched **The Motley Fool (Fool.com).** And befitting of a Shakespearean play, the two say they are "dedicated to educating, amusing, and enriching individuals in search of the truth."

The Gardners do not fear the wrath of any king, real or fictional. They are intent on exposing the truth, as they see it, "that the financial world preys on ignorance and fear." As Tom explains, "There is such a great need in the general populace for financial information." Who can argue, given their brilliant success through practically every medium, including their website, radio shows, newspaper columns, online store, investment newsletters, and global expansion.

Despite the brothers' best efforts, however, ordinary people still do not fully use information available in financial

"The Motley Fool . . . is similar to what goes on in a library"
—Tom Gardner

statements. For instance, discussions keep appearing on The Motley Fool's online bulletin board that can be easily resolved using reliable and published accounting data. So, it would seem that the Fools must continue their work of "educating and enriching" individuals and showing them the advantages of financial statement analysis.

Following The Motley Fool's objectives, this chapter introduces horizontal and vertical analyses—tools used to reveal crucial trends and insights from financial information. It also expands on ratio analysis, which gives insight into a company's financial condition and performance. By arming ourselves with the information contained in this chapter and the investment advice of The Motley Fool, *we* can be sure to not play the fool in today's financial world.

Sources: *Motley Fool website,* January 2015; *Washington Business Journal,* January 2011; *What to Do with Your Money Now,* June 2002; *USA Weekend,* July 2004; *Washington Post,* November 2007; *Money After 40,* April 2007

BASICS OF ANALYSIS

C1_____

Explain the purpose and identify the building blocks of analysis.

Financial statement analysis applies analytical tools to general-purpose financial statements and related data for making business decisions. It involves transforming accounting data into more useful information. Financial statement analysis reduces our reliance on hunches, guesses, and intuition as well as our uncertainty in decision making. It does not lessen the need for expert judgment; instead, it provides us an effective and systematic basis for making business decisions. This section describes the purpose of financial statement analysis, its information sources, the use of comparisons, and some issues in computations.

Purpose of Analysis

Internal users of accounting information are those involved in strategically managing and operating the company. They include managers, officers, internal auditors, consultants, budget directors, and market researchers. The purpose of financial statement analysis for these users is to provide strategic information to improve company efficiency and effectiveness in providing products and services.

Point: Financial statement analysis tools are also used for personal financial investment decisions.

External users of accounting information are *not* directly involved in running the company. They include shareholders, lenders, directors, customers, suppliers, regulators, lawyers, brokers, and the press. External users rely on financial statement analysis to make better and more informed decisions in pursuing their own goals.

We can identify other uses of financial statement analysis. Shareholders and creditors assess company prospects to make investing and lending decisions. A board of directors analyzes financial statements in monitoring management's decisions. Employees and unions use financial statements in labor negotiations. Suppliers use financial statement information in establishing credit terms. Customers analyze financial statements in deciding whether to establish supply relationships. Public utilities set customer rates by analyzing financial statements. Auditors use financial statements in assessing the "fair presentation" of their clients' financial results. Analyst services such as Dun & Bradstreet, Moody's, and Standard & Poor's use financial statements in making buy-sell recommendations and in setting credit ratings. The common goal of these users is to evaluate company performance and financial condition. This includes evaluating (1) past and current performance, (2) current financial position, and (3) future performance and risk.

Point: Financial statement analysis is a topic on the CPA, CMA, CIA, and CFA exams.

Building Blocks of Analysis

Financial statement analysis focuses on one or more elements of a company's financial condition or performance. Our analysis emphasizes four areas of inquiry—with varying degrees of importance. These four areas are described and illustrated in this chapter and are considered the *building blocks* of financial statement analysis:

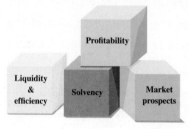

- **Liquidity** and **efficiency**—ability to meet short-term obligations and to efficiently generate revenues.
- **Solvency**—ability to generate future revenues and meet long-term obligations.
- **Profitability**—ability to provide financial rewards sufficient to attract and retain financing.
- **Market prospects**—ability to generate positive market expectations.

Applying the building blocks of financial statement analysis involves determining (1) the objectives of analysis and (2) the relative emphasis among the building blocks. We distinguish among these four building blocks to emphasize the different aspects of a company's financial condition or performance, yet we must remember that these areas of analysis are interrelated. For instance, a company's operating performance is affected by the availability of financing and short-term liquidity conditions. Similarly, a company's credit standing is not limited to satisfactory short-term liquidity but depends also on its profitability and efficiency in using assets. Early in our analysis, we need to determine the relative emphasis of each building block. Emphasis and analysis can later change as a result of evidence collected.

■ **Decision** Insight

Chips and Brokers   The phrase *blue chips* refers to stock of big, profitable companies. The phrase, comes from poker, where the most valuable chips are blue. The term *brokers* refers to those who execute orders to buy or sell stock. The term comes from wine retailers—individuals who broach (break) wine casks. ■

Information for Analysis

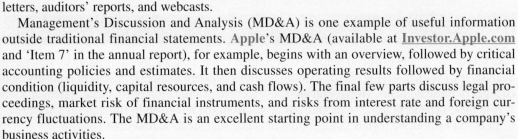

Some users, such as managers and regulatory authorities, are able to receive special financial reports prepared to meet their analysis needs. However, most users must rely on **general-purpose financial statements** that include the (1) income statement, (2) balance sheet, (3) statement of stockholders' equity (or statement of retained earnings), (4) statement of cash flows, and (5) notes to these statements.

Financial reporting refers to the communication of financial information useful for making investment, credit, and other business decisions. Financial reporting includes not only general-purpose financial statements but also information from SEC 10-K or other filings, press releases, shareholders' meetings, forecasts, management letters, auditors' reports, and webcasts.

Management's Discussion and Analysis (MD&A) is one example of useful information outside traditional financial statements. **Apple**'s MD&A (available at **Investor.Apple.com** and 'Item 7' in the annual report), for example, begins with an overview, followed by critical accounting policies and estimates. It then discusses operating results followed by financial condition (liquidity, capital resources, and cash flows). The final few parts discuss legal proceedings, market risk of financial instruments, and risks from interest rate and foreign currency fluctuations. The MD&A is an excellent starting point in understanding a company's business activities.

■ **Decision** Insight

Analysis Online   Many websites offer free access and screening of companies by key numbers such as earnings, sales, and book value. For instance, **Investor's Business Daily** has information for more than 10,000 stocks (**www.investors.com**). ■

Standards for Comparisons

When interpreting measures from financial statement analysis, we need to decide whether the measures indicate good, bad, or average performance. To make such judgments, we need standards (benchmarks) for comparisons that include the following:

C2

Describe standards for comparisons in analysis.

- *Intracompany*—The company under analysis can provide standards for comparisons based on its own prior performance and relations between its financial items. Apple's current net income, for instance, can be compared with its prior years' net income and in relation to its revenues or total assets.
- *Competitor*—One or more direct competitors of the company being analyzed can provide standards for comparisons. **Coca-Cola**'s profit margin, for instance, can be compared with **PepsiCo**'s profit margin.
- *Industry*—Industry statistics can provide standards of comparisons. Such statistics are available from services such as Dun & Bradstreet, Standard & Poor's, and Moody's.
- *Guidelines (rules of thumb)*—General standards of comparisons can develop from experience. Examples are the 2:1 level for the current ratio or 1:1 level for the acid-test ratio. Guidelines, or rules of thumb, must be carefully applied because context is crucial.

Point: Each chapter's *Reporting in Action* problems engage students in *intracompany* analysis, whereas *Comparative Analysis* problems require competitor analysis (Apple vs. Google vs. Samsung).

All of these comparison standards are useful when properly applied, yet measures taken from a selected competitor or group of competitors are often best. Intracompany and industry measures are also important. Guidelines or rules of thumb should be applied with care, and then only if they seem reasonable given past experience and industry norms.

Tools of Analysis

Three of the most common tools of financial statement analysis are

1. **Horizontal analysis**—comparison of a company's financial condition and performance across time.
2. **Vertical analysis**—comparison of a company's financial condition and performance to a base amount.
3. **Ratio analysis**—measurement of key relations between financial statement items.

The remainder of this chapter describes these analysis tools and how to apply them.

Decision Insight

Fraud Fighters.   Horizontal, vertical, and ratio analysis tools can uncover fraud by identifying amounts out of line with expectations. One can then follow up and ask questions that can either identify a logical reason for such results or confirm/raise suspicions of fraud. Many past fraud schemes could have been identified much earlier had people applied these tools and pressured management for explanations. ■

QC1

HORIZONTAL ANALYSIS

P1
Explain and apply methods of horizontal analysis.

Analysis of any single financial number is of limited value. Instead, much of financial statement analysis involves identifying and describing relations between numbers, groups of numbers, and changes in those numbers. Horizontal analysis refers to examination of financial statement data *across time*. (The term *horizontal analysis* arises from the left-to-right [or right-to-left] movement of our eyes as we review comparative financial statements across time.)

Comparative Statements

Comparing amounts for two or more successive periods often helps in analyzing financial statements. **Comparative financial statements** facilitate this comparison by showing financial amounts in side-by-side columns on a single statement, called a *comparative format*. Using figures from **Apple**'s financial statements, this section explains how to compute dollar changes and percent changes for comparative statements.

Computation of Dollar Changes and Percent Changes   Comparing financial statements over relatively short time periods—two to three years—is often done by analyzing changes in line items. A change analysis usually includes analyzing absolute dollar amount changes and percent changes. Both analyses are relevant because dollar changes can yield large percent changes inconsistent with their importance. For instance, a 50% change from a base figure of $100 is less important than the same percent change from a base amount of $100,000 in the same statement. Reference to dollar amounts is necessary to retain a proper perspective and to assess the importance of changes. We compute the *dollar change* for a financial statement item as follows:

Example: Which is a more significant change, a 70% increase on a $1,000 expense or a 30% increase on a $400,000 expense? *Answer:* The 30% increase.

$$\text{Dollar change} = \text{Analysis period amount} - \text{Base period amount}$$

Analysis period is the point or period of time for the financial statements under analysis, and *base period* is the point or period of time for the financial statements used for comparison purposes. The prior year is commonly used as a base period. We compute the *percent change* by dividing the dollar change by the base period amount and then multiplying this quantity by 100 as follows:

$$\text{Percent change } (\%) = \frac{\text{Analysis period amount} - \text{Base period amount}}{\text{Base period amount}} \times 100$$

We can always compute a dollar change, but we must be aware of a few rules in working with percent changes. To illustrate, look at four separate cases in this chart:

Case	Analysis Period	Base Period	Change Analysis Dollar	Change Analysis Percent
A	$ 1,500	$(4,500)	$ 6,000	—
B	(1,000)	2,000	(3,000)	—
C	8,000	—	8,000	—
D	0	10,000	(10,000)	(100%)

When a negative amount appears in the base period and a positive amount in the analysis period (or vice versa), we cannot compute a meaningful percent change; see cases A and B. Also, when no value is in the base period, no percent change is computable; see case C. Finally, when an item has a value in the base period and zero in the analysis period, the decrease is 100 percent; see case D.

It is common when using horizontal analysis to compare amounts to either average or median values from prior periods (average and median values smooth out erratic or unusual fluctuations).[1] We also commonly round percents and ratios to one or two decimal places, but practice on this matter is not uniform. Computations are as detailed as necessary, which is judged by whether rounding potentially affects users' decisions. Computations should not be excessively detailed so that important relations are not lost among a mountain of decimal points and digits.

Comparative Balance Sheets Comparative balance sheets consist of balance sheet amounts from two or more balance sheet dates arranged side by side. The usefulness of this method of analysis is often improved by showing each item's dollar change and percent change to highlight large changes.

Analysis of comparative financial statements begins by focusing on items that show large dollar or percent changes. We then try to identify the reasons for these changes and, if possible, determine whether they are favorable or unfavorable. We also follow up on items with small changes when we expected the changes to be large.

Exhibit 13.1 shows comparative balance sheets for Apple Inc. (Nasdaq: AAPL). A few items stand out on the asset side. Apple's inventories show a substantial 123.0% increase. While some of this increase can be explained by growth in operations as evidenced by a 9.2% increase in sales, the bulk of this increased inventory seems inefficient (with increased risks from obsolescence and consumer fads). Other notable increases occur with (1) short-term (and long-term) securities and cash, reflecting Apple's success but also a limited vision for reinvestment; (2) goodwill and property, plant and equipment, reflecting Apple's continued growth; and (3) accounts receivable, which warrants attention as it exceeds the growth in sales. Its sizable total asset growth of 17.6% must be accompanied by future income to validate Apple's asset reinvestments. Some of Apple's shareholders are concerned about its growing assets and declining return on assets.

On Apple's financing side, we see the 17.6% increase is driven by a 44.2% increase in liabilities (equity increased only 4.5%). The largest increase is due to issuance of long-term debt, followed by various increases in current liabilities. We also see a 2.9% growth ($2,967) in retained earnings, which is much less than its $37,037 in net income. This is in part due to cash dividends and stock repurchases.

Comparative Income Statements Comparative income statements are prepared similarly to comparative balance sheets. Amounts for two or more periods are placed side by side, with additional columns for dollar and percent changes. Exhibit 13.2 shows Apple's comparative income statements.

Apple reports substantial sales growth of 9.2% in 2013. This finding helps support management's 17.6% growth in assets as reflected in the comparative balance sheets. The 21.4% growth in cost of sales with only a 9.2% sales increase raises a concern with Apple's control over its

Example: When there is a value in the base period and zero in the analysis period, the decrease is 100%. Why isn't the reverse situation an increase of 100%? *Answer:* A 100% increase of zero is still zero.

Point: Spreadsheet programs can help with horizontal, vertical, and ratio analyses, including graphical depictions of financial relations.

Point: Business consultants use comparative statement analysis to provide management advice.

Point: Percent change can also be computed by dividing the current period by the prior period and subtracting 1.0. For example, the 9.2% sales increase in Exhibit 13.2 is computed as: ($170,910/$156,508) − 1.

---

[1] *Median* is the middle value in a group of numbers. For instance, if five prior years' incomes are (in 000s) $15, $19, $18, $20, and $22, the median value is $19. When there are two middle numbers, we can take their average. For instance, if four prior years' sales are (in 000s) $84, $91, $96, and $93, the median is $92 (computed as the average of $91 and $93).

EXHIBIT 13.1

Comparative Balance
Sheets

APPLE

APPLE INC.
Comparative Balance Sheets
September 28, 2013 and September 29, 2012

(in millions)	2013	2012	Dollar Change	Percent Change
Assets				
Cash and cash equivalents......................	$ 14,259	$ 10,746	$ 3,513	32.7%
Short-term marketable securities................	26,287	18,383	7,904	43.0
Accounts receivable, net......................	13,102	10,930	2,172	19.9
Inventories................................	1,764	791	973	123.0
Deferred tax assets..........................	3,453	2,583	870	33.7
Vendor non-trade receivables	7,539	7,762	(223)	(2.9)
Other current assets.........................	6,882	6,458	424	6.6
Total current assets.......................	73,286	57,653	15,633	27.1
Long-term marketable securities.................	106,215	92,122	14,093	15.3
Property, plant and equipment, net..............	16,597	15,452	1,145	7.4
Goodwill.................................	1,577	1,135	442	38.9
Acquired intangible assets, net	4,179	4,224	(45)	(1.1)
Other assets...............................	5,146	5,478	(332)	(6.1)
Total assets..............................	$207,000	$176,064	$30,936	17.6
Liabilities				
Accounts payable...........................	$22,367	$21,175	$1,192	5.6%
Accrued expenses	13,856	11,414	2,442	21.4
Deferred revenue...........................	7,435	5,953	1,482	24.9
Total current liabilities.....................	43,658	38,542	5,116	13.3
Deferred revenue—noncurrent.................	2,625	2,648	(23)	(0.9)
Long-term debt	16,960	—	16,960	—
Other noncurrent liabilities....................	20,208	16,664	3,544	21.3
Total liabilities	83,451	57,854	25,597	44.2
Stockholders' Equity				
Common stock	19,764	16,422	3,342	20.4
Retained earnings...........................	104,256	101,289	2,967	2.9
Accumulated other comprehensive income	(471)	499	(970)	—
Total stockholders' equity.....................	123,549	118,210	5,339	4.5
Total liabilities and stockholders' equity............	$207,000	$176,064	$30,936	17.6

EXHIBIT 13.2

Comparative Income
Statements

APPLE

APPLE INC.
Comparative Income Statements
For Years Ended September 28, 2013, and September 29, 2012

(in millions, except per share)	2013	2012	Dollar Change	Percent Change
Net sales	$170,910	$156,508	$14,402	9.2%
Cost of sales	106,606	87,846	18,760	21.4
Gross margin	64,304	68,662	(4,358)	(6.3)
Research and development	4,475	3,381	1,094	32.4
Selling, general and administrative................	10,830	10,040	790	7.9
Total operating expenses......................	15,305	13,421	1,884	14.0
Operating income	48,999	55,241	(6,242)	(11.3)
Other income, net...........................	1,156	522	634	121.5
Income before provision for income taxes	50,155	55,763	(5,608)	(10.1)
Provision for income taxes	13,118	14,030	(912)	(6.5)
Net income	$ 37,037	$ 41,733	(4,696)	(11.3)
Basic earnings per share......................	$ 40.03	$ 44.64	($4.61)	(10.3)
Diluted earnings per share....................	$ 39.75	$ 44.15	($4.40)	(10.0)

costs of sales. Similarly, we see a 14.0% increase in operating expenses, which exceeds the 9.2% sales growth (not good news). However, much of this is due to increased research and development costs, from which management hopes to reap future rewards. Apple reports a decline of 11.3% in net income, which is again mainly attributed to the 21.4% growth in cost of sales.

Trend Analysis

Trend analysis, also called *trend percent analysis* or *index number trend analysis,* is a form of horizontal analysis that can reveal patterns in data across successive periods. It involves computing trend percents for a series of financial numbers and is a variation on the use of percent changes. The difference is that trend analysis does not subtract the base period amount in the numerator. To compute trend percents, we do the following:

1. Select a *base period* and assign each item in the base period a weight of 100%.
2. Express financial numbers as a percent of their base period number.

Specifically, a *trend percent,* also called an *index number,* is computed as follows:

Point: *Index* refers to the comparison of the analysis period to the base period. Percents determined for each period are called *index numbers.*

$$\text{Trend percent (\%)} = \frac{\text{Analysis period amount}}{\text{Base period amount}} \times 100$$

To illustrate trend analysis, we use the Apple data shown in Exhibit 13.3.

(in millions)	2013	2012	2011	2010	2009
Net sales...............	$170,910	$156,508	$108,249	$65,225	$42,905
Cost of sales.............	106,606	87,846	64,431	39,541	25,683
Operating expenses	15,305	13,421	10,028	7,299	5,482

EXHIBIT 13.3

Sales and Expensess

These data are from Apple's current and prior financial statements. The base period is 2009 and the trend percent is computed in each subsequent year by dividing that year's amount by its 2009 amount. For instance, the revenue trend percent for 2013 is 398.3%, computed as $170,910/$42,905. The trend percents—using the data from Exhibit 13.3—are shown in Exhibit 13.4.

Point: Trend analysis expresses a percent of base, not a percent of change.

	2013	2012	2011	2010	2009
Net sales...............	398.3%	364.8%	252.3%	152.0%	100.0%
Cost of sales.............	415.1	342.0	250.9	154.0	100.0
Operating expenses	279.2	244.8	182.9	133.1	100.0

EXHIBIT 13.4

Trend Percents for Sales and Expenses

Graphical depictions often aid analysis of trend percents. Exhibit 13.5 shows the trend percents from Exhibit 13.4 in a *line graph,* which can help us identify trends and detect changes in direction or magnitude. It reveals that the trend line for revenue consistently exceeds that for both operating expenses and for cost of sales (except for 2010 and 2013). The marked increase in cost of sales in 2013 is concerning for Apple because its long-run profitability will suffer if those costs are not controlled. The trend line for operating expenses is encouraging because it lags revenue growth for each year from 2010–2013; however, the 2013 cost of sales reflects a marked rise in its trend line and exceeds that for net sales, which is worrying.

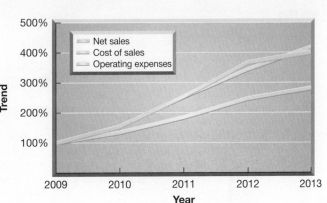

EXHIBIT 13.5

Trend Percent Lines for Sales and Expenses of Apple

EXHIBIT 13.6

Revenue Trend Percent Lines—Apple, Google and Samsung

APPLE

GOOGLE

Samsung

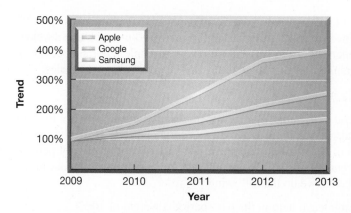

Exhibit 13.6 compares Apple's revenue trend line to that of **Google** and **Samsung** for this same period. Apple is able to grow its revenue in each year relative to its base year. In this respect Apple outperforms its competitors, although both Google and Samsung performed well over this same period of time. These data indicate that Apple's products and services have met with great consumer acceptance.

Trend analysis of financial statement items can include comparisons of relations between items on different financial statements. For instance, Exhibit 13.7 compares Apple's revenue and total assets. The rate of increase in total assets (435.8%) is more than the increase in revenues (398.3%) since 2009. Is this result favorable or not? The answer is that Apple was *less* efficient in using its assets in 2013 versus 2009. Management has not generated revenues sufficient to compensate for the asset growth.

EXHIBIT 13.7

Sales and Asset Data for Apple

(in millions)	2013	2009	Trend Percent (2013 vs. 2009)
Net sales...........	$170,910	$42,905	398.3%
Total assets.........	207,000	47,501	435.8

Overall we must remember that an important role of financial statement analysis is identifying questions and areas of interest, which often direct us to important factors bearing on a company's future. Accordingly, financial statement analysis should be seen as a continuous process of refining our understanding and expectations of company performance and financial condition.

■ **Decision** Maker

Auditor   Your tests reveal a 3% increase in sales from $200,000 to $206,000 and a 4% decrease in expenses from $190,000 to $182,400. Both changes are within your "reasonableness" criterion of ±5%, and thus you don't pursue additional tests. The audit partner in charge questions your lack of follow-up and mentions the *joint relation* between sales and expenses. To what is the partner referring? ■   [Answers follow the chapter's Summary.]

NEED-TO-KNOW 13-1

Horizontal Analysis

P1

Compute trend percents for the following accounts, using 2012 as the base year (round percents to whole numbers). State whether the situation as revealed by the trends appears to be favorable or unfavorable for each account.

($ millions)	2015	2014	2013	2012
Sales....................	$500	$350	$250	$200
Cost of goods sold........	400	175	100	50

Solution

($ millions)	2015	2014	2013	2012
Sales....................	250%	175%	125%	100%
	($500/$200)	($350/$200)	($250/$200)	($200/$200)
Cost of goods sold........	800%	350%	200%	100%
	($400/$50)	($175/$50)	($100/$50)	($50/$50)

Do More: QS 13-3, QS 13-4, E 13-3

Analysis: The trend in sales is favorable; however, we need more information about economic conditions such as inflation rates and competitors' performances to better assess it. Cost of sales is also rising (as expected with increasing sales); however, cost of sales is rising faster than the increase in sales, which is unfavorable and bad news. A quick analysis of the gross margin percentage would highlight this concern.

VERTICAL ANALYSIS

Vertical analysis is a tool to evaluate individual financial statement items or a group of items in terms of a specific base amount. We usually define a key aggregate figure as the base, which for an income statement is usually revenue and for a balance sheet is usually total assets. This section explains vertical analysis and applies it to **Apple**. (The term *vertical analysis* arises from the up-down [or down-up] movement of our eyes as we review common-size financial statements. Vertical analysis is also called *common-size analysis*.)

P2

Describe and apply methods of vertical analysis.

Common-Size Statements

The comparative statements in Exhibits 13.1 and 13.2 show the change in each item over time, but they do not emphasize the relative importance of each item. We use **common-size financial statements** to reveal changes in the relative importance of each financial statement item. All individual amounts in common-size statements are redefined in terms of common-size percents. A *common-size percent* is measured by dividing each individual financial statement amount under analysis by its base amount:

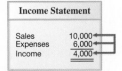

$$\text{Common-size percent (\%)} = \frac{\text{Analysis amount}}{\text{Base amount}} \times 100$$

Common-Size Balance Sheets Common-size statements express each item as a percent of a *base amount*, which for a common-size balance sheet is usually total assets. The base amount is assigned a value of 100%. (This implies that the total amount of liabilities plus equity equals 100% since this amount equals total assets.) We then compute a common-size percent for each asset, liability, and equity item using total assets as the base amount. When we present a company's successive balance sheets in this way, changes in the mixture of assets, liabilities, and equity are apparent.

Exhibit 13.8 shows common-size comparative balance sheets for Apple. Some relations that stand out on both a magnitude and percentage basis include (1) a 2.3% point increase in short-term securities, which equates to a $7,904 million increase; (2) a new issuance of $16,960 million in long-term debt; and (3) a 7.1% decrease in retained earnings, which equates to a $2,967 million decrease. The lack of substantial change in the balance sheet suggests a mature company, but with some lack of focus as evidenced by the increasing amount in short- and long-term securities. This buildup in securities is a concern as the return on securities is historically smaller than the return on operating assets from successful reinvestment. Time will tell whether Apple can continue to generate sufficient revenue and income from its growing asset base.

Point: The *base* amount in common-size analysis is an *aggregate* amount from that period's financial statement.

Point: Common-size statements often are used to compare two or more companies in the same industry.

Point: Common-size statements are also useful in comparing firms that report in different currencies.

Common-Size Income Statements Analysis also benefits from use of a common-size income statement. Revenue is usually the base amount, which is assigned a value of 100%. Each common-size income statement item appears as a percent of revenue. If we think of the 100% revenue amount as representing one sales dollar, the remaining items show how each revenue dollar is distributed among costs, expenses, and income.

Exhibit 13.9 shows common-size comparative income statements for each dollar of Apple's revenue. The past two years' common-size numbers are similar with a few exceptions. One important exception is the decrease of 5.0 cents in net income per each net sales dollar—evidenced by the decrease in income as a percent of net sales from 26.7% to 21.7%. This implies that management is *not* effectively controlling costs. Much of this is attributed to the rise in cost of sales from 56.1% to 62.4% as a percent of net sales. In sum, analysis here shows that common-size percents for successive income statements can uncover potentially important changes in a company's cost management. (Evidence of no changes, especially when changes are expected, is also informative.)

Global: International companies sometimes disclose "convenience" financial statements, which are statements translated in other languages and currencies. However, these statements rarely adjust for differences in accounting principles across countries.

Common-Size Graphics

Two of the most common tools of common-size analysis are trend analysis of common-size statements and graphical analysis. The trend analysis of common-size statements is similar to that of comparative statements discussed under vertical analysis. It is not illustrated here because the only difference is the substitution of common-size percents for trend percents. Instead, this

EXHIBIT 13.8

Common-Size Comparative
Balance Sheets

APPLE

APPLE INC. Common-Size Comparative Balance Sheets September 28, 2013, and September 29, 2012			Common-Size Percents*	
(in millions)	2013	2012	2013	2012
Assets				
Cash and cash equivalents	$ 14,259	$ 10,746	6.9%	6.1%
Short-term marketable securities	26,287	18,383	12.7	10.4
Accounts receivable, net	13,102	10,930	6.3	6.2
Inventories	1,764	791	0.9	0.4
Deferred tax assets	3,453	2,583	1.7	1.5
Vendor non-trade receivables	7,539	7,762	3.6	4.4
Other current assets	6,882	6,458	3.3	3.7
Total current assets	73,286	57,653	35.4	32.7
Long-term marketable securities.	106,215	92,122	51.3	52.3
Property, plant and equipment, net	16,597	15,452	8.0	8.8
Goodwill.	1,577	1,135	0.8	0.6
Acquired intangible assets, net.	4,179	4,224	2.0	2.4
Other assets.	5,146	5,478	2.5	3.1
Total assets.	$207,000	$176,064	100.0%	100.0%
Liabilities				
Accounts payable	$ 22,367	$ 21,175	10.8%	12.0%
Accrued expenses	13,856	11,414	6.7	6.5
Deferred revenue.	7,435	5,953	3.6	3.4
Total current liabilities	43,658	38,542	21.1	21.9
Deferred revenue—noncurrent.	2,625	2,648	1.3	1.5
Long-term debt	16,960	0	8.2	0.0
Other noncurrent liabilities	20,208	16,664	9.8	9.5
Total liabilities.	83,451	57,854	40.3	32.9
Stockholders' Equity				
Common stock.	19,764	16,422	9.5	9.3
Retained earnings	104,256	101,289	50.4	57.5
Accumulated other comprehensive income	(471)	499	(0.2)	0.3
Total stockholders' equity	123,549	118,210	59.7	67.1
Total liabilities and stockholders' equity	$207,000	$176,064	100.0%	100.0%

* Percents are rounded to tenths and thus may not exactly sum to totals and subtotals.

EXHIBIT 13.9

Common-Size Comparative
Income Statements

APPLE

APPLE INC. Common-Size Comparative Income Statements For Years Ended September 28, 2013, and September 29, 2012			Common-Size Percents*	
(in millions)	2013	2012	2013	2012
Net sales	$170,910	$156,508	100.0%	100.0%
Cost of sales	106,606	87,846	62.4	56.1
Gross margin	64,304	68,662	37.6	43.9
Research and development	4,475	3,381	2.6	2.2
Selling, general and administrative.	10,830	10,040	6.3	6.4
Total operating expenses.	15,305	13,421	9.0	8.6
Operating income	48,999	55,241	28.7	35.3
Other income, net.	1,156	522	0.7	0.3
Income before provision for income taxes	50,155	55,763	29.3	35.6
Provision for income taxes	13,118	14,030	7.7	9.0
Net income	$ 37,037	$ 41,733	21.7%	26.7%

* Percents are rounded to tenths and thus may not exactly sum to totals and subtotals.

section discusses graphical analysis of common-size statements.

An income statement readily lends itself to common-size graphical analysis. This is so because revenues affect nearly every item in an income statement. Exhibit 13.10 shows Apple's 2013 common-size income statement in graphical form. This pie chart highlights the contribution of each cost component of net sales for net income (for this graph, "other income, net" is included in selling, general, administrative, and other costs).

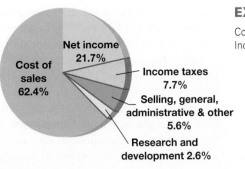

EXHIBIT 13.10

Common-Size Graphic of Income Statement

Exhibit 13.11 previews more complex graphical analyses available and the insights they provide. The data for this exhibit are taken from Apple's *Segments* footnote. Apple reports six operating segments for 2013: (1) Americas, (2) Europe, (3) China, (4) Japan, (5) Asia Pacific, and (6) Retail.

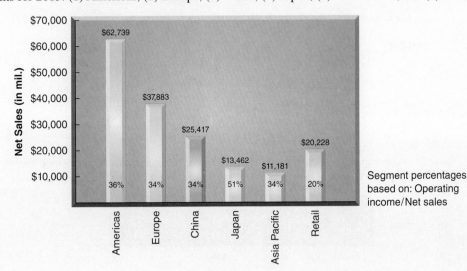

EXHIBIT 13.11

Sales and Operating Income Margin Breakdown by Segment

The bars in Exhibit 13.11 show the level of net sales for each of the six reportable segments of Apple. Its Americas segment generates $62,739 million of its total net sales, which is roughly 37% of its total sales. The five other bars show the level of sales generated from each of the other international segments, including its retail segment. At the bottom of each bar is that segment's operating income margin, defined as segment operating income divided by segment net sales. The Americas segment yields a 36% operating income margin; margins for the other five segments are shown at the bottom of each of the other segment bars. This type of graphic presentation can lead to questions about the profitability of each segment and discussion of potential expansions into the more lucrative segments. For example, the Japan segment yields an operating margin of 51%. A natural question for management is what potential is there to further expand sales into the Japan segment and maintain the similar operating margin? This type of analysis can help users in determining strategic plans and actions.

Graphical analysis is also useful in identifying (1) sources of financing including the distribution among current liabilities, noncurrent liabilities, and equity capital and (2) focuses of investing activities, including the distribution among current and noncurrent assets. To illustrate, Exhibit 13.12 shows a common-size graphical display of Apple's assets. Common-size balance sheet

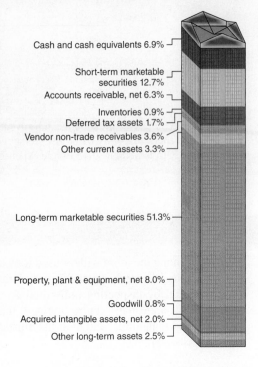

EXHIBIT 13.12

Common-Size Graphic of Asset Components

analysis can be extended to examine the composition of these subgroups. For instance, in assessing liquidity of current assets, knowing what proportion of *current* assets consists of inventories is usually important, and not simply what proportion inventories are of *total* assets.

Common-size financial statements are also useful in comparing different companies. Exhibit 13.13 shows common-size graphics of Apple, Google, and Samsung on financing sources. This graphic highlights the larger percent of equity financing for Google versus Apple and Samsung. It also highlights the somewhat larger noncurrent (debt) financing of Apple versus Google and Samsung. Comparison of a company's common-size statements with competitors' or industry common-size statistics alerts us to differences in the structure or distribution of its financial statements but not to their dollar magnitude.

EXHIBIT 13.13

Common-Size Graphic of Financing Sources—Competitor Analysis

APPLE
GOOGLE
Samsung

Current liabilities
Noncurrent liabilities
Equity

	Apple	Google	Samsung
Current liabilities	21%	14%	24%
Noncurrent liabilities	19%	7%	6%
Equity	60%	79%	70%

NEED-TO-KNOW 13-2

Vertical Analysis

P2

Express the following comparative income statements in common-size percents and assess whether or not this company's situation has improved in the most recent year (round percents to whole numbers).

Comparative Income Statements
For Years Ended December 31, 2015 and 2014

	2015	2014
Sales	$800	$500
Total expenses	560	400
Net income	$240	$100

Solution

	2015	2014
Sales	100%	100%
	($800/$800)	($500/$500)
Total expenses	70%	80%
	($560/$800)	($400/$500)
Net income	30%	20%

Do More: QS 13-5, E 13-4, E 13-6

QC2

Analysis: This company's situation has improved. This is evident from its substantial increase in net income as a percent of sales for 2015 (30%) relative to 2014 (20%). Further, the company's sales increased from $500 in 2014 to $800 in 2015 (while expenses declined as a percent of sales from 80% to 70%).

RATIO ANALYSIS

P3

Define and apply ratio analysis.

Ratios are among the more widely used tools of financial analysis because they provide clues to and symptoms of underlying conditions. A ratio can help us uncover conditions and trends difficult to detect by inspecting individual components making up the ratio. Ratios, like other analysis tools, are usually future oriented; that is, they are often adjusted for their probable future trend and magnitude, and their usefulness depends on skillful interpretation.

A ratio expresses a mathematical relation between two quantities. It can be expressed as a percent, rate, or proportion. For instance, a change in an account balance from $100 to $250 can be expressed as (1) 150% increase, (2) 2.5 times, or (3) 2.5 to 1 (or 2.5:1). Computation of a ratio is a simple arithmetic operation, but its interpretation is not. To be meaningful, a ratio must refer to an economically important relation. For example, a direct and crucial relation exists between an item's sales price and its cost. Accordingly, the ratio of cost of goods sold to sales is meaningful. In contrast, no obvious relation exists between freight costs and the balance of long-term investments.

This section describes an important set of financial ratios and their application. The selected ratios are organized into the four building blocks of financial statement analysis: (1) liquidity and efficiency, (2) solvency, (3) profitability, and (4) market prospects. The purpose here is to organize and apply them under a summary framework. We use four common standards, in varying degrees, for comparisons: intracompany, competitor, industry, and guidelines.

Point: Some sources for industry norms are *Annual Statement Studies* by Robert Morris Associates, *Industry Norms & Key Business Ratios* by Dun & Bradstreet, *Standard & Poor's Industry Surveys*, and Reuters.com/finance.

Liquidity and Efficiency

Liquidity refers to the availability of resources to meet short-term cash requirements. It is affected by the timing of cash inflows and outflows along with prospects for future performance. Analysis of liquidity is aimed at a company's funding requirements. *Efficiency* refers to how productive a company is in using its assets. Efficiency is usually measured relative to how much revenue is generated from a certain level of assets.

Both liquidity and efficiency are important and complementary. If a company fails to meet its current obligations, its continued existence is doubtful. Viewed in this light, all other measures of analysis are of secondary importance. Although accounting measurements assume the company's continued existence, our analysis must always assess the validity of this assumption using liquidity measures. Moreover, inefficient use of assets can cause liquidity problems. A lack of liquidity often precedes lower profitability and fewer opportunities. It can foretell a loss of owner control. To a company's creditors, lack of liquidity can yield delays in collecting interest and principal payments or the loss of amounts due them. A company's customers and suppliers of goods and services also are affected by short-term liquidity problems. Implications include a company's inability to execute contracts and potential damage to important customer and supplier relationships. This section describes and illustrates key ratios relevant to assessing liquidity and efficiency.

Working Capital and Current Ratio The amount of current assets less current liabilities is called **working capital,** or *net working capital.* A company needs adequate working capital to meet current debts, to carry sufficient inventories, and to take advantage of cash discounts. A company that runs low on working capital is less likely to meet current obligations or to continue operating. When evaluating a company's working capital, we must not only look at the dollar amount of current assets less current liabilities, but also at their ratio. The *current ratio* is defined as follows.

$$\text{Current ratio} = \frac{\text{Current assets}}{\text{Current liabilities}}$$

Drawing on information in Exhibit 13.1, Apple's working capital and current ratio for both 2013 and 2012 are shown in Exhibit 13.14. Also, Google (4.58), Samsung (2.16), and the industry's current ratio (2.5) are shown in the margin. Apple's 2013 ratio (1.68) is lower than competitors' ratios, but it is not in danger of defaulting on loan payments. A high current ratio suggests a strong liquidity position and an ability to meet current obligations. A company can, however, have a current ratio that is too high. An excessively high current ratio means that the company has invested too much in current assets compared to its current obligations.

EXHIBIT 13.14
Apple's Working Capital and Current Ratio

(in millions)	2013	2012
Current assets	$ 73,286	$ 57,653
Current liabilities	43,658	38,542
Working capital	$29,628	$19,111
Current ratio		
$73,286/$43,658 =	1.68 to 1	
$57,653/$38,542 =		1.50 to 1

Current ratio
Google = 4.58
Samsung = 2.16
Industry = 2.5

An excessive investment in current assets is not an efficient use of funds because current assets normally generate a low return on investment (compared with long-term assets).

Many users apply a guideline of 2:1 (or 1.5:1) for the current ratio in helping evaluate a company's debt-paying ability. A company with a 2:1 or higher current ratio is generally thought to be a good credit risk in the short run. Such a guideline or any analysis of the current ratio must recognize at least three additional factors: (1) type of business, (2) composition of current assets, and (3) turnover rate of current asset components.

Type of business.   A service company that grants little or no credit and carries few inventories can probably operate on a current ratio of less than 1:1 if its revenues generate enough cash to pay its current liabilities. On the other hand, a company selling high-priced clothing or furniture requires a higher ratio because of difficulties in judging customer demand and cash receipts. For instance, if demand falls, inventory may not generate as much cash as expected. Accordingly, analysis of the current ratio should include a comparison with ratios from successful companies in the same industry and from prior periods. We must also recognize that a company's accounting methods, especially choice of inventory method, affect the current ratio. For instance, when costs are rising, a company using LIFO tends to report a smaller amount of current assets than when using FIFO.

Point: When a firm uses LIFO in a period of rising costs, the standard for an adequate current ratio usually is lower than if it used FIFO.

Composition of current assets.   The composition of a company's current assets is important to an evaluation of short-term liquidity. For instance, cash, cash equivalents, and short-term investments are more liquid than accounts and notes receivable. Also, short-term receivables normally are more liquid than inventory. Cash, of course, can be used to immediately pay current debts. Items such as accounts receivable and inventory, however, normally must be converted into cash before payment is made. An excessive amount of receivables and inventory weakens a company's ability to pay current liabilities. The acid-test ratio (see below) can help with this assessment.

Turnover rate of assets.   Asset turnover measures a company's efficiency in using its assets. One relevant measure of asset efficiency is the revenue generated. A measure of total asset turnover is revenues divided by total assets, but evaluation of turnover for individual assets is also useful. We discuss both receivables turnover and inventory turnover next.

▋ Decision Maker ◀━━━━━━━━━━━━━━━━━━━━━

Banker   A company requests a one-year, $200,000 loan for expansion. This company's current ratio is 4:1, with current assets of $160,000. Key competitors carry a current ratio of about 1.9:1. Using this information, do you approve the loan application? Does your decision change if the application is for a 10-year loan? ■   [Answers follow the chapter's Summary.]

Acid-Test Ratio   Quick assets are cash, short-term investments, and current receivables. These are the most liquid types of current assets. The *acid-test ratio,* also called *quick ratio,* reflects on a company's short-term liquidity.

$$\text{Acid-test ratio} = \frac{\text{Cash} + \text{Short-term investments} + \text{Current receivables}}{\text{Current liabilities}}$$

Apple's acid-test ratio is computed in Exhibit 13.15. Apple's 2013 acid-test ratio (1.23) is lower than that for Google (4.25) and Samsung (1.37), but is greater than the 1:1 common guideline for

EXHIBIT 13.15
Acid-Test Ratio

(in millions)	2013	2012
Cash and equivalents	$14,259	$10,746
Short-term securities.	26,287	18,383
Current receivables	13,102	10,930
Total quick assets.	$53,648	$40,059
Current liabilities	$43,658	$38,542
Acid-test ratio		
$53,648/$43,658	1.23 to 1	
$40,059/$38,542		1.04 to 1

Acid-test ratio
Google = 4.25
Samsung = 1.37
Industry = 0.9

an acceptable acid-test ratio. The ratio for Apple is also greater than the 0.9 industry norm; thus, we are not concerned. As with analysis of the current ratio, we need to consider other factors. For instance, the frequency with which a company converts its current assets into cash affects its working capital requirements. This implies that analysis of short-term liquidity should also include an analysis of receivables and inventories, which we consider next.

Accounts Receivable Turnover   We can measure how frequently a company converts its receivables into cash by computing the *accounts receivable turnover*. This ratio is defined as follows. (see Chapter 7 for additional explanation).

$$\text{Accounts receivable turnover} = \frac{\text{Net sales}}{\text{Average accounts receivable, net}}$$

Short-term receivables from customers are often included in the denominator along with accounts receivable. Also, accounts receivable turnover is more precise if credit sales are used for the numerator, but external users generally use net sales (or net revenues) because information about credit sales is typically not reported. Apple's 2013 accounts receivable turnover is computed as follows ($ millions).

$$\frac{\$170,910}{(\$10,930 + \$13,102)/2} = 14.2 \text{ times}$$

Apple's value of 14.2 exceeds that of both Google's 7.1 and Samsung's 8.4. Accounts receivable turnover is high when accounts receivable are quickly collected. A high turnover is favorable because it means the company need not commit large amounts of funds to accounts receivable. However, an accounts receivable turnover can be too high; this can occur when credit terms are so restrictive that they negatively affect sales volume.

Point: Some users prefer using gross accounts receivable (before subtracting the allowance for doubtful accounts) to avoid the influence of a manager's bad debts estimate.

Accounts receivable turnover
Google = 7.1
Samsung = 8.4
Industry = 5.0

Point: Ending accounts receivable can be substituted for the average balance in computing accounts receivable turnover if the difference between ending and average receivables is small.

Inventory Turnover   How long a company holds inventory before selling it will affect working capital requirements. One measure of this effect is *inventory turnover,* also called *merchandise turnover* or *merchandise inventory turnover,* which is defined as follows.

$$\text{Inventory turnover} = \frac{\text{Cost of goods sold}}{\text{Average inventory}}$$

Using Apple's cost of goods sold and inventories information, we compute its inventory turnover for 2013 as follows (if the beginning and ending inventories for the year do not represent the usual inventory amount, an average of quarterly or monthly inventories can be used).

$$\frac{\$106,606}{(\$791 + \$1,764)/2} = 83.45 \text{ times}$$

Inventory turnover
Google = 55.55
Samsung = 7.47
Industry = 7.0

Apple's inventory turnover of 83.45 is more than Google's 55.55 and Samsung's 7.47, and the industry's 7.0. A company with a high turnover requires a smaller investment in inventory than one producing the same sales with a lower turnover. Inventory turnover can be too high, however, if the inventory a company keeps is so small that it restricts sales volume.

Days' Sales Uncollected   Accounts receivable turnover provides insight into how frequently a company collects its accounts. Days' sales uncollected is one measure of this activity, which is defined as follows.

$$\text{Days' sales uncollected} = \frac{\text{Accounts receivable, net}}{\text{Net sales}} \times 365$$

Any short-term notes receivable from customers are normally included in the numerator.

Rita Qian/AFP/Getty Images

Apple's 2013 days' sales uncollected follows.

Days' sales uncollected
Google = 54.2
Samsung = 44.5

$$\frac{\$13,102}{\$170,910} \times 365 = 28.0 \text{ days}$$

Both Google's days' sales uncollected of 54.2 days and Samsung's 50.7 days are more than the 28.0 days for Apple. Days' sales uncollected is more meaningful if we know company credit terms. A rough guideline states that days' sales uncollected should not exceed 1⅓ times the days in its (1) credit period, *if* discounts are not offered or (2) discount period, *if* favorable discounts are offered.

Days' Sales in Inventory *Days' sales in inventory* is a useful measure in evaluating inventory liquidity. Days' sales in inventory is linked to inventory in a way that days' sales uncollected is linked to receivables. We compute days' sales in inventory as follows.

$$\text{Days' sales in inventory} = \frac{\text{Ending inventory}}{\text{Cost of goods sold}} \times 365$$

Apple's days' sales in inventory for 2013 follows.

Days' sales in inventory
Google = 6.0
Samsung = 50.7
Industry = 35

$$\frac{\$1,764}{\$106,606} \times 365 = 6.0 \text{ days}$$

Point: *Average collection period is estimated by dividing 365 by the accounts receivable turnover ratio. For example, 365 divided by an accounts receivable turnover of 6.1 indicates a 60-day average collection period.*

If the products in Apple's inventory are in demand by customers, this formula estimates that its inventory will be converted into receivables (or cash) in 6.0 days. If all of Apple's sales were credit sales, the conversion of inventory to receivables in 6.0 days *plus* the conversion of receivables to cash in 28.0 days implies that inventory will be converted to cash in about 34.0 days (6.0 + 28.0).

Total Asset Turnover *Total asset turnover* reflects a company's ability to use its assets to generate sales and is an important indication of operating efficiency. The definition of this ratio follows.

$$\text{Total asset turnover} = \frac{\text{Net sales}}{\text{Average total assets}}$$

Apple's total asset turnover of 0.89 for 2013 follows, which is greater than that for Google (0.58) but less than that for Samsung (1.16).

Total asset turnover
Google = 0.58
Samsung = 1.16
Industry = 1.2

$$\frac{\$170,910}{(\$176,064 + \$207,000)/2} = 0.89 \text{ times}$$

Solvency

Solvency refers to a company's long-run financial viability and its ability to cover long-term obligations. All of a company's business activities—financing, investing, and operating—affect its solvency. Analysis of solvency is long term and uses less precise but more encompassing measures than liquidity. One of the most important components of solvency analysis is the composition of a company's capital structure. *Capital structure* refers to a company's financing sources. It ranges from relatively permanent equity financing to riskier or more temporary short-term financing. Assets represent security for financiers, ranging from loans secured by specific assets to the assets available as general security to unsecured creditors. This section describes the tools of solvency analysis. Our analysis focuses on a company's ability to both meet its obligations and provide security to its creditors *over the long run*. Indicators of this ability include *debt* and *equity* ratios, the relation between *pledged assets and secured liabilities,* and the company's capacity to earn sufficient income to *pay fixed interest charges.*

Debt and Equity Ratios   One element of solvency analysis is to assess the portion of a company's assets contributed by its owners and the portion contributed by creditors. This relation is reflected in the debt ratio (also described in Appendix C). The *debt ratio* expresses total liabilities as a percent of total assets. The **equity ratio** provides complementary information by expressing total equity as a percent of total assets. Apple's debt and equity ratios follow.

Point: For analysis purposes, noncontrolling interest is usually included in equity.

(in millions)	2013	Ratios	
Total liabilities	$ 83,451	40.3%	[Debt ratio]
Total equity	123,549	59.7	[Equity ratio]
Total liabilities and equity	$207,000	100.0%	

Debt ratio :: Equity ratio
Google = 21.3% :: 78.7%
Samsung = 29.9% :: 70.1%
Industry = 35% :: 65%

Apple's financial statements reveal more equity than debt. A company is considered less risky if its capital structure (equity and long-term debt) contains more equity. One risk factor is the required payment for interest and principal when debt is outstanding. Another factor is the greater the stockholder financing, the more losses a company can absorb through equity before the assets become inadequate to satisfy creditors' claims. From the stockholders' point of view, if a company earns a return on borrowed capital that is higher than the cost of borrowing, the difference represents increased income to stockholders. The inclusion of debt is described as *financial leverage* because debt can have the effect of increasing the return to stockholders. Companies are said to be highly leveraged if a large portion of their assets is financed by debt.

Point: Bank examiners from the FDIC and other regulatory agencies use debt and equity ratios to monitor compliance with regulatory capital requirements imposed on banks and S&Ls.

Debt-to-Equity Ratio   The ratio of total liabilities to equity is another measure of solvency. We compute the ratio as follows.

$$\text{Debt-to-equity ratio} = \frac{\text{Total liabilities}}{\text{Total equity}}$$

Apple's debt-to-equity ratio for 2013 is

$$\$83,451/\$123,549 = 0.68$$

Debt-to-equity
Google = 0.27
Samsung = 0.43
Industry = 0.6

Apple's 0.68 debt-to-equity ratio is higher than that of Samsung (0.43) and Google (0.27), and greater than the industry ratio of 0.6. Consistent with our inferences from the debt ratio, Apple's capital structure has less debt than equity, which helps limit risk. Recall that debt must be repaid with interest, while equity does not. These debt requirements can be burdensome when the industry and/or the economy experience a downturn. A larger debt-to-equity ratio also implies less opportunity to expand through use of debt financing.

Times Interest Earned   The amount of income before deductions for interest expense and income taxes is the amount available to pay interest expense. The following *times interest earned* ratio reflects the creditors' risk of loan repayments with interest.

Point: The times interest earned ratio and the debt and equity ratios are of special interest to bank lending officers.

$$\text{Times interest earned} = \frac{\text{Income before interest expense and income taxes}}{\text{Interest expense}}$$

The larger this ratio, the less risky is the company for creditors. One guideline says that creditors are reasonably safe if the company earns its fixed interest expense two or more times each year. Apple's times interest earned ratio follows. Apple's 369.8 result suggests that its creditors have little risk of nonrepayment.

Times interest earned
Google = 184.2
Samsung = 76.3

$$\frac{\$37{,}037 + \$136 + \$13{,}118}{\$136} = 369.8 \text{ times}$$

■ Decision Insight

Bears and Bulls A *bear market* is a declining market. The phrase comes from bear-skin jobbers who often sold the skins before the bears were caught. The term *bear* was then used to describe investors who sold shares they did not own in anticipation of a price decline. A *bull market* is a rising market. This phrase comes from the once popular sport of bear and bull baiting. The term *bull* came to mean the opposite of *bear.* ■

Profitability

We are especially interested in a company's ability to use its assets efficiently to produce profits (and positive cash flows). *Profitability* refers to a company's ability to generate an adequate return on invested capital. Return is judged by assessing earnings relative to the level and sources of financing. Profitability is also relevant to solvency. This section describes key profitability measures and their importance to financial statement analysis.

Profit Margin A company's operating efficiency and profitability can be expressed by two components. The first is *profit margin,* which reflects a company's ability to earn net income from sales. It is measured by expressing net income as a percent of sales (*sales* and *revenues* are similar terms). Apple's profit margin follows.

Profit margin
Google = 21.6%
Samsung = 13.3%
Industry = 11%

$$\text{Profit margin} = \frac{\text{Net income}}{\text{Net sales}} = \frac{\$37{,}037}{\$170{,}910} = 21.7\%$$

To evaluate profit margin, we must consider the industry. For instance, an appliance company might require a profit margin between 10% and 15%, whereas a retail supermarket might require a profit margin of 1% or 2%. Both profit margin and *total asset turnover* make up the two basic components of operating efficiency. These ratios reflect on management because managers are ultimately responsible for operating efficiency. The next section explains how we use both measures to analyze return on total assets.

Return on Total Assets *Return on total assets* is defined as follows.

$$\text{Return on total assets} = \frac{\text{Net income}}{\text{Average total assets}}$$

Apple's 2013 return on total assets is

Return on total assets
Google = 12.6%
Samsung = 15.4%
Industry = 9%

$$\frac{\$37{,}037}{(\$176{,}064 + \$207{,}000)/2} = 19.3\%$$

Point: Many analysts add back *Interest expense* × *(I − Tax rate)* to net income in computing return on total assets.

Apple's 19.3% return on total assets is higher than that for many businesses and is higher than Google's 12.6%, Samsung's 15.4%, and the industry's 9% return. We also should evaluate any trend in the rate of return.

The following equation shows the important relation between profit margin, total asset turnover, and return on total assets.

$$\textbf{Profit margin} \times \textbf{Total asset turnover} = \textbf{Return on total assets}$$

or

$$\frac{\textbf{Net income}}{\textbf{Net sales}} \times \frac{\textbf{Net sales}}{\textbf{Average total assets}} = \frac{\textbf{Net income}}{\textbf{Average total assets}}$$

Both profit margin and total asset turnover contribute to overall operating efficiency, as measured by return on total assets. If we apply this formula to Apple, we get

$$21.7\% \times 0.89 = 19.3\% \text{ (with rounding)}$$

Google: 21.6% × 0.58 = 12.6%
Samsung: 13.3% × 1.16 = 15.4%
(with rounding)

This analysis shows that Apple's superior return on assets versus that of both Google and Samsung is driven by its higher profit and, in the case of Google, also by its better asset turnover.

Return on Common Stockholders' Equity Perhaps the most important goal in operating a company is to earn net income for its owner(s). *Return on common stockholders' equity* measures a company's success in reaching this goal and is defined as follows.

$$\textbf{Return on common stockholders' equity} = \frac{\textbf{Net income} - \textbf{Preferred dividends}}{\textbf{Average common stockholders' equity}}$$

Apple's 2013 return on common stockholders' equity is computed as follows:

$$\frac{\$37,037 - \$0}{(\$118,210 + \$123,549)/2} = 30.6\%$$

Return on common equity
Google = 16.2%
Samsung = 22.5%
Industry = 15%

The denominator in this computation is the book value of common equity (noncontrolling interest is often included in common equity for this ratio). In the numerator, the dividends on cumulative preferred stock are subtracted whether they are declared or are in arrears. If preferred stock is noncumulative, its dividends are subtracted only if declared. Apple's return on common stockholders' equity (30.6%) is superior to Google's 16.2% and Samsung's 22.5%.

 Decision Insight ━━━━━━━━━━━━━━━━━━━━━━━━━━━

Wall Street   *Wall Street* is synonymous with financial markets, but its name comes from the street location of the original New York Stock Exchange. The street's name derives from stockades built by early settlers to protect New York from pirate attacks. ∎

Market Prospects

Market measures are useful for analyzing corporations with publicly traded stock. These market measures use stock price, which reflects the market's (public's) expectations for the company. This includes expectations of both company return and risk—as the market perceives it.

Price-Earnings Ratio   Computation of the *price-earnings ratio* follows.

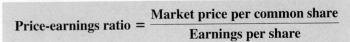

$$\textbf{Price-earnings ratio} = \frac{\textbf{Market price per common share}}{\textbf{Earnings per share}}$$

Predicted earnings per share for the next period is often used in the denominator of this computation. Reported earnings per share for the most recent period is also commonly used. In both cases, the ratio is used as an indicator of the future growth and risk of a company's earnings as perceived by the stock's buyers and sellers.

The market price of Apple's common stock at the start of fiscal year 2014 was $477.25. Using Apple's $40.03 basic earnings per share, we compute its price-earnings ratio as follows (some analysts compute this ratio using the median of the low and high stock price).

$$\frac{\$477.25}{\$40.03} = 11.9$$

Apple's price-earnings ratio is less than that for Google, but it is higher than that for Samsung and near the norm for this period.

Dividend Yield   *Dividend yield* is used to compare the dividend-paying performance of different investment alternatives. We compute dividend yield as follows.

$$\text{Dividend yield} = \frac{\textbf{Annual cash dividends per share}}{\textbf{Market price per share}}$$

Apple's dividend yield, based on its fiscal year-end market price per share of $477.25 and its $11.40 cash dividends per share, is computed as follows.

$$\frac{\$11.40}{\$477.25} = 2.4\%$$

Some companies, such as Google, do not declare and pay dividends because they wish to reinvest the cash to grow their businesses in the hope of generating greater future earnings and dividends.

Summary of Ratios

Exhibit 13.16 summarizes the major financial statement analysis ratios illustrated in this chapter. This summary includes each ratio's title, its formula, and the purpose for which it is commonly used.

 Decision Insight

Ticker Prices   *Ticker prices* refer to a band of moving data on a monitor carrying up-to-the-minute stock prices. The phrase comes from *ticker tape*, a 1-inch-wide strip of paper spewing stock prices from a printer that ticked as it ran. Most of today's investors have never seen actual ticker tape, but the phrase survives. ■

© Comstock Images/Jupiter Images

EXHIBIT 13.16

Financial Statement Analysis Ratios*

Ratio	Formula	Measure of
Liquidity and Efficiency		
Current ratio	$= \dfrac{\text{Current assets}}{\text{Current liabilities}}$	Short-term debt-paying ability
Acid-test ratio	$= \dfrac{\text{Cash + Short-term investments + Current receivables}}{\text{Current liabilities}}$	Immediate short-term debt-paying ability
Accounts receivable turnover	$= \dfrac{\text{Net sales}}{\text{Average accounts receivable, net}}$	Efficiency of collection
Inventory turnover	$= \dfrac{\text{Cost of goods sold}}{\text{Average inventory}}$	Efficiency of inventory management
Days' sales uncollected	$= \dfrac{\text{Accounts receivable, net}}{\text{Net sales}} \times 365$	Liquidity of receivables
Days' sales in inventory	$= \dfrac{\text{Ending inventory}}{\text{Cost of goods sold}} \times 365$	Liquidity of inventory
Total asset turnover	$= \dfrac{\text{Net sales}}{\text{Average total assets}}$	Efficiency of assets in producing sales
Solvency		
Debt ratio	$= \dfrac{\text{Total liabilities}}{\text{Total assets}}$	Creditor financing and leverage
Equity ratio	$= \dfrac{\text{Total equity}}{\text{Total assets}}$	Owner financing
Debt-to-equity ratio	$= \dfrac{\text{Total liabilities}}{\text{Total equity}}$	Debt versus equity financing
Times interest earned	$= \dfrac{\text{Income before interest expense and income taxes}}{\text{Interest expense}}$	Protection in meeting interest payments
Profitability		
Profit margin ratio	$= \dfrac{\text{Net income}}{\text{Net sales}}$	Net income in each sales dollar
Gross margin ratio	$= \dfrac{\text{Net sales} - \text{Cost of goods sold}}{\text{Net sales}}$	Gross margin in each sales dollar
Return on total assets	$= \dfrac{\text{Net income}}{\text{Average total assets}}$	Overall profitability of assets
Return on common stockholders' equity	$= \dfrac{\text{Net income} - \text{Preferred dividends}}{\text{Average common stockholders' equity}}$	Profitability of owner investment
Book value per common share	$= \dfrac{\text{Shareholders' equity applicable to common shares}}{\text{Number of common shares outstanding}}$	Liquidation at reported amounts
Basic earnings per share	$= \dfrac{\text{Net income} - \text{Preferred dividends}}{\text{Weighted-average common shares outstanding}}$	Net income per common share
Market Prospects		
Price-earnings ratio	$= \dfrac{\text{Market price per common share}}{\text{Earnings per share}}$	Market value relative to earnings
Dividend yield	$= \dfrac{\text{Annual cash dividends per share}}{\text{Market price per share}}$	Cash return per common share

* Additional ratios also examined in previous chapters included days' cash expense coverage; cash coverage of growth; cash coverage of debt; free cash flow; cash flow on total assets; and payout ratio.

NEED-TO-KNOW 13-3

Ratio Analysis

P3

For each ratio listed, identify whether the change in ratio value from 2014 to 2015 is regarded as favorable or unfavorable.

Ratio	2015	2014	Ratio	2015	2014
1. Profit margin	6%	8%	4. Accounts receivable turnover	8.8	9.4
2. Debt ratio	50%	70%	5. Basic earnings per share	$2.10	$2.00
3. Gross margin	40%	36%	6. Inventory turnover	3.6	4.0

Solution

Ratio	2015	2014	Change
1. Profit margin ratio...................	6%	8%	Unfavorable
2. Debt ratio.........................	50%	70%	Favorable
3. Gross margin ratio	40%	36%	Favorable
4. Accounts receivable turnover.........	8.8	9.4	Unfavorable
5. Basic earnings per share	$2.10	$2.00	Favorable
6. Inventory turnover	3.6	4.0	Unfavorable

Do More: QS 13-6, E 13-7,
E 13-8, E 13-9, E 13-10,
E 13-11, P 13-4

QC3

GLOBAL VIEW

The analysis and interpretation of financial statements is, of course, impacted by the accounting system in effect. This section discusses similarities and differences for analysis of financial statements when prepared under U.S. GAAP vis-à-vis IFRS.

Horizontal and Vertical Analyses   Horizontal and vertical analyses help eliminate many differences between U.S. GAAP and IFRS when analyzing and interpreting financial statements. Financial numbers are converted to percentages that are, in the best-case scenario, consistently applied across and within periods. This enables users to effectively compare companies across reporting regimes. However, when fundamental differences in reporting regimes impact financial statements, such as with certain recognition rule differences, the user must exercise caution when drawing conclusions. Some users will reformulate one set of numbers to be more consistent with the other system to enable comparative analysis. This reformulation process is covered in advanced courses. The important point is that horizontal and vertical analyses help strip away differences between the reporting regimes, but several key differences sometimes remain and require adjustment of the numbers.

Ratio Analysis   Ratio analysis of financial statement numbers has many of the advantages and disadvantages of horizontal and vertical analyses discussed above. Importantly, ratio analysis is useful for business decisions, with some possible changes in interpretation depending on what is and what is not included in accounting measures across U.S. GAAP and IFRS. Still, we must take care in drawing inferences from a comparison of ratios across reporting regimes because what a number measures can differ across regimes. Piaggio, which manufactures two-, three- and four-wheel vehicles and is Europe's leading manufacturer of motorcycles and scooters, offers the following example of its own ratio analysis applied to its financing objectives: "The object of capital management . . . , [and] consistent with others in the industry, the Company monitors capital on the basis of a total liabilities to equity ratio. This ratio is calculated as total liabilities divided by equity."

Getty Images

Sustainability and Accounting   The Motley Fool, as introduced in this chapter's opening feature, emphasizes the importance of a sustainable and vibrant work environment. The Gardners wrote, "Sustainable advantage will not always be easy. That's one of the reasons that we value discussion in The Motley Fool . . . When determining a subjective attribute like sustainable advantage, we should all be interested in discovery." Morgan Housel, a Fool employee, explains that. "At the Motley Fool, we observe that the best . . . culture [is] built on trust and respect" (*USA Today,* April 2014). Thus, sustainability at the Fool means a dynamic, energetic, questioning workforce to analyze and interpret the information conveyed through financial reports.

Decision Insight

Not Created Equal Financial regulation has several goals. Two of them are to ensure adequate accounting disclosure and to strengthen corporate governance. For disclosure purposes, companies must now provide details of related-party transactions and material off-balance-sheet agreements. This is motivated by several major frauds. For corporate governance, the CEO and CFO must now certify the fairness of financial statements and the effectiveness of internal controls. Yet, concerns remain. A study reports that 23% of management and administrative employees observed activities that posed a conflict of interest in the past year (KPMG 2009). Another 12% witnessed the falsifying or manipulating of accounting information. The bottom line: All financial statements are not of equal quality. ■

Analysis Reporting **Decision Analysis**

Understanding the purpose of financial statement analysis is crucial to the usefulness of any analysis. This understanding leads to efficiency of effort, effectiveness in application, and relevance in focus. The purpose of most financial statement analyses is to reduce uncertainty in business decisions through a rigorous and sound evaluation. A *financial statement analysis report* helps by directly addressing the building blocks of analysis and by identifying weaknesses in inference by requiring explanation: It forces us to organize our reasoning and to verify its flow and logic. A report also serves as a communication link with readers, and the writing process reinforces our judgments and vice versa. Finally, the report helps us (re) evaluate evidence and refine conclusions on key building blocks. A good analysis report usually consists of six sections:

A1

Summarize and report results of analysis.

1. **Executive summary**—brief focus on important analysis results and conclusions.
2. **Analysis overview**—background on the company, its industry, and its economic setting.
3. **Evidential matter**—financial statements and information used in the analysis, including ratios, trends, comparisons, statistics, and all analytical measures assembled; often organized under the building blocks of analysis.
4. **Assumptions**—identification of important assumptions regarding a company's industry and economic environment, and other important assumptions for estimates.
5. **Key factors**—list of important favorable and unfavorable factors, both quantitative and qualitative, for company performance; usually organized by areas of analysis.
6. **Inferences**—forecasts, estimates, interpretations, and conclusions drawing on all sections of the report.

We must remember that the user dictates relevance, meaning that the analysis report should include a brief table of contents to help readers focus on those areas most relevant to their decisions. All irrelevant matter must be eliminated. For example, decades-old details of obscure transactions and detailed miscues of the analysis are irrelevant. Ambiguities and qualifications to avoid responsibility or hedging inferences must be eliminated. Finally, writing is important. Mistakes in grammar and errors of fact compromise the report's credibility.

Decision Insight

Short Selling *Short selling* refers to selling stock before you buy it. Here's an example: You borrow 100 shares of Nike stock, sell them at $40 each, and receive money from their sale. You then wait. You hope that Nike's stock price falls to, say, $35 each and you can replace the borrowed stock for less than you sold it for, reaping a profit of $5 each less any transaction costs. ■

Use the following financial statements of Precision Co. to complete these requirements.
1. Prepare comparative income statements showing the percent increase or decrease for year 2015 in comparison to year 2014.
2. Prepare common-size comparative balance sheets for years 2015 and 2014.

NEED-TO-KNOW

COMPREHENSIVE

3. Compute the following ratios as of December 31, 2015, or for the year ended December 31, 2015, and identify its building block category for financial statement analysis.

    a. Current ratio

    b. Acid-test ratio

    c. Accounts receivable turnover

    d. Days' sales uncollected

    e. Inventory turnover

    f. Debt ratio

    g. Debt-to-equity ratio

    h. Times interest earned

    i. Profit margin ratio

    j. Total asset turnover

    k. Return on total assets

    l. Return on common stockholders' equity

PRECISION COMPANY
Comparative Income Statements
For Years Ended December 31, 2015 and 2014

	2015	2014
Sales	$2,486,000	$2,075,000
Cost of goods sold	1,523,000	1,222,000
Gross profit	963,000	853,000
Operating expenses		
Advertising expense	145,000	100,000
Sales salaries expense	240,000	280,000
Office salaries expense	165,000	200,000
Insurance expense	100,000	45,000
Supplies expense	26,000	35,000
Depreciation expense	85,000	75,000
Miscellaneous expenses	17,000	15,000
Total operating expenses	778,000	750,000
Operating income	185,000	103,000
Interest expense	44,000	46,000
Income before taxes	141,000	57,000
Income taxes	47,000	19,000
Net income	$ 94,000	$ 38,000
Earnings per share	$ 0.99	$ 0.40

PRECISION COMPANY
Comparative Balance Sheets
December 31, 2015 and 2014

	2015	2014
Assets		
Current assets		
Cash	$ 79,000	$ 42,000
Short-term investments	65,000	96,000
Accounts receivable, net	120,000	100,000
Merchandise inventory	250,000	265,000
Total current assets	514,000	503,000
Plant assets		
Store equipment, net	400,000	350,000
Office equipment, net	45,000	50,000
Buildings, net	625,000	675,000
Land	100,000	100,000
Total plant assets	1,170,000	1,175,000
Total assets	$1,684,000	$1,678,000
Liabilities		
Current liabilities		
Accounts payable	$ 164,000	$ 190,000
Short-term notes payable	75,000	90,000
Taxes payable	26,000	12,000
Total current liabilities	265,000	292,000
Long-term liabilities		
Notes payable (secured by		
mortgage on buildings)	400,000	420,000
Total liabilities	665,000	712,000
Stockholders' Equity		
Common stock, $5 par value	475,000	475,000
Retained earnings	544,000	491,000
Total stockholders' equity	1,019,000	966,000
Total liabilities and equity	$1,684,000	$1,678,000

PLANNING THE SOLUTION

- Set up a four-column income statement; enter the 2015 and 2014 amounts in the first two columns and then enter the dollar change in the third column and the percent change from 2014 in the fourth column.

- Set up a four-column balance sheet; enter the 2015 and 2014 year-end amounts in the first two columns and then compute and enter the amount of each item as a percent of total assets.

● Compute the required ratios using the data provided. Use the average of beginning and ending amounts when appropriate (see Exhibit 13.16 for definitions).

SOLUTION

1.

PRECISION COMPANY
Comparative Income Statements
For Years Ended December 31, 2015 and 2014

	2015	2014	Increase (Decrease) in 2015 Amount	Percent
Sales	$2,486,000	$2,075,000	$411,000	19.8%
Cost of goods sold	1,523,000	1,222,000	301,000	24.6
Gross profit	963,000	853,000	110,000	12.9
Operating expenses				
Advertising expense	145,000	100,000	45,000	45.0
Sales salaries expense	240,000	280,000	(40,000)	(14.3)
Office salaries expense	165,000	200,000	(35,000)	(17.5)
Insurance expense	100,000	45,000	55,000	122.2
Supplies expense	26,000	35,000	(9,000)	(25.7)
Depreciation expense	85,000	75,000	10,000	13.3
Miscellaneous expenses	17,000	15,000	2,000	13.3
Total operating expenses	778,000	750,000	28,000	3.7
Operating income	185,000	103,000	82,000	79.6
Interest expense	44,000	46,000	(2,000)	(4.3)
Income before taxes	141,000	57,000	84,000	147.4
Income taxes	47,000	19,000	28,000	147.4
Net income	$ 94,000	$ 38,000	$ 56,000	147.4
Earnings per share	$ 0.99	$ 0.40	$ 0.59	147.5

2.

PRECISION COMPANY
Common-Size Comparative Balance Sheets
December 31, 2015 and 2014

	December 31		Common-Size Percents	
	2015	2014	2015*	2014*
Assets				
Current assets				
Cash	$ 79,000	$ 42,000	4.7%	2.5%
Short-term investments	65,000	96,000	3.9	5.7
Accounts receivable, net	120,000	100,000	7.1	6.0
Merchandise inventory	250,000	265,000	14.8	15.8
Total current assets	514,000	503,000	30.5	30.0
Plant assets				
Store equipment, net	400,000	350,000	23.8	20.9
Office equipment, net	45,000	50,000	2.7	3.0
Buildings, net	625,000	675,000	37.1	40.2
Land	100,000	100,000	5.9	6.0
Total plant assets	1,170,000	1,175,000	69.5	70.0
Total assets	$1,684,000	$1,678,000	100.0	100.0

[continued on next page]

[continued from previous page]

Liabilities

Current liabilities

Accounts payable	$ 164,000	$ 190,000	9.7%	11.3%
Short-term notes payable	75,000	90,000	4.5	5.4
Taxes payable	26,000	12,000	1.5	0.7
Total current liabilities	265,000	292,000	15.7	17.4

Long-term liabilities

Notes payable (secured by mortgage on buildings)	400,000	420,000	23.8	25.0
Total liabilities	665,000	712,000	39.5	42.4

Stockholders' Equity

Common stock, $5 par value	475,000	475,000	28.2	28.3
Retained earnings	544,000	491,000	32.3	29.3
Total stockholders' equity	1,019,000	966,000	60.5	57.6
Total liabilities and equity	$1,684,000	$1,678,000	100.0	100.0

* Columns do not always exactly add to 100 due to rounding.

3. **Ratios for 2015:**

   a. Current ratio: $514,000/$265,000 = 1.9:1 (liquidity and efficiency)

   b. Acid-test ratio: ($79,000 + $65,000 + $120,000)/$265,000 = 1.0:1 (liquidity and efficiency)

   c. Average receivables: ($120,000 + $100,000)/2 = $110,000

   Accounts receivable turnover: $2,486,000/$110,000 = 22.6 times (liquidity and efficiency)

   d. Days' sales uncollected: ($120,000/$2,486,000) × 365 = 17.6 days (liquidity and efficiency)

   e. Average inventory: ($250,000 + $265,000)/2 = $257,500

   Inventory turnover: $1,523,000/$257,500 = 5.9 times (liquidity and efficiency)

   f. Debt ratio: $665,000/$1,684,000 = 39.5% (solvency)

   g. Debt-to-equity ratio: $665,000/$1,019,000 = 0.65 (solvency)

   h. Times interest earned: $185,000/$44,000 = 4.2 times (solvency)

   i. Profit margin ratio: $94,000/$2,486,000 = 3.8% (profitability)

   j. Average total assets: ($1,684,000 + $1,678,000)/2 = $1,681,000

   Total asset turnover: $2,486,000/$1,681,000 = 1.48 times (liquidity and efficiency)

   k. Return on total assets: $94,000/$1,681,000 = 5.6% or 3.8% × 1.48 = 5.6% (profitability)

   l. Average total common equity: ($1,019,000 + $966,000)/2 = $992,500

   Return on common stockholders' equity: $94,000/$992,500 = 9.5% (profitability)

13A

Sustainable Income

A2

Explain the form and assess the content of a complete income statement.

When a company's revenue and expense transactions are from normal, continuing operations, a simple income statement is usually adequate. When a company's activities include income-related events not part of its normal, continuing operations, it must disclose information to help users understand these events and predict future performance. To meet these objectives, companies separate the income statement into continuing operations, discontinued segments, extraordinary items, comprehensive income, and earnings per share. For illustration, Exhibit 13A.1 shows such an income statement for ComUS. These separate distinctions help us measure *sustainable income,* which is the income level most likely to continue into the future. Sustainable income is commonly used in PE ratios and other market-based measures of performance.

Continuing Operations   The first major section (①) shows the revenues, expenses, and income from continuing operations. Users especially rely on this information to predict future operations. Many users view this section as the most important.

ComUS
Income Statement
For Year Ended December 31, 2015

Net sales		$8,478,000
Operating expenses		
Cost of goods sold	$5,950,000	
Depreciation expense	35,000	
Other selling, general and administrative expenses	515,000	
Interest expense	20,000	
① { Total operating expenses		(6,520,000)
Other gains (losses)		
Loss on plant relocation		(45,000)
Gain on sale of surplus land		72,000
Income from continuing operations before taxes		1,985,000
Income taxes expense		(595,500)
Income from continuing operations		1,389,500
Discontinued segment		
② { Income from operating Division A (net of $180,000 taxes)	420,000	
Loss on disposal of Division A (net of $66,000 tax benefit)	(154,000)	266,000
Income before extraordinary items		1,655,500
Extraordinary items		
③ { Gain on land expropriated by state (net of $85,200 taxes)	198,800	
Loss from earthquake damage (net of $270,000 tax benefit)	(630,000)	(431,200)
Net income		$1,224,300
Earnings per common share (200,000 outstanding shares)		
Income from continuing operations		$ 6.95
④ { Discontinued operations		1.33
Income before extraordinary items		8.28
Extraordinary items		(2.16)
Net income (basic earnings per share)		$ 6.12

Discontinued Segments   A **business segment** is a part of a company's operations that serves a particular line of business or class of customers. A segment has assets, liabilities, and financial results of operations that can be distinguished from those of other parts of the company. A company's gain or loss from selling or closing down a segment is separately reported. Section ② of Exhibit 13A.1 reports both (1) income from operating the discontinued segment for the current period prior to its disposal and (2) the loss from disposing of the segment's net assets. The income tax effects of each are reported separately from the income taxes expense in section ①.

Extraordinary Items   Section ③ reports **extraordinary gains and losses,** which are those that are *both unusual* and *infrequent.* An **unusual gain or loss** is abnormal or otherwise unrelated to the company's regular activities and environment. An **infrequent gain or loss** is not expected to recur given the company's operating environment. Reporting extraordinary items in a separate category helps users predict future performance, absent the effects of extraordinary items. Items usually considered extraordinary include (1) expropriation (taking away) of property by a foreign government, (2) condemning of property by a domestic government body, (3) prohibition against using an asset by a newly enacted law, and (4) losses and gains from an unusual and infrequent calamity ("act of God"). Items *not* considered extraordinary include (1) write-downs of inventories and write-offs of receivables, (2) gains and losses from disposing of segments, and (3) financial effects of labor strikes.

Gains and losses that are neither unusual nor infrequent are reported as part of continuing operations. Gains and losses that are *either* unusual *or* infrequent, but *not* both, are reported as part of continuing operations *but* after the normal revenues and expenses.

■ Decision Maker

Small Business Owner You own an orange grove near Jacksonville, Florida. A bad frost destroys about one-half of your oranges. You are currently preparing an income statement for a bank loan. Can you claim the loss of oranges as extraordinary? ■ [Answers follow the chapter's Summary.]

Earnings per Share The final section ④ of the income statement in Exhibit 13A.1 reports earnings per share for each of the three subcategories of income (continuing operations, discontinued segments, and extraordinary items) when they exist.

Changes in Accounting Principles The *consistency concept* directs a company to apply the same accounting principles across periods. Yet a company can change from one acceptable accounting principle (such as FIFO, LIFO, or weighted-average) to another as long as the change improves the usefulness of information in its financial statements. A footnote would describe the accounting change and why it is an improvement.

> **Point:** Changes in principles are sometimes required when new accounting standards are issued.

Changes in accounting principles require retrospective application to prior periods' financial statements. *Retrospective application* involves applying a different accounting principle to prior periods as if that principle had always been used. Retrospective application enhances the consistency of financial information between periods, which improves the usefulness of information, especially with comparative analyses. Accounting standards also require that *a change in depreciation, amortization, or depletion method for long-term operating assets is accounted for as a change in accounting estimate*—that is, prospectively over current and future periods. This reflects the notion that an entity should change its depreciation, amortization, or depletion method only with changes in estimated asset benefits, the pattern of benefit usage, or information about those benefits.

QC4

Summary

C1 **Explain the purpose and identify the building blocks of analysis.** The purpose of financial statement analysis is to help users make better business decisions. Internal users want information to improve company efficiency and effectiveness in providing products and services. External users want information to make better and more informed decisions in pursuing their goals. The common goals of all users are to evaluate a company's (1) past and current performance, (2) current financial position, and (3) future performance and risk. Financial statement analysis focuses on four "building blocks" of analysis: (1) liquidity and efficiency—ability to meet short-term obligations and efficiently generate revenues; (2) solvency—ability to generate future revenues and meet long-term obligations; (3) profitability—ability to provide financial rewards sufficient to attract and retain financing; and (4) market prospects—ability to generate positive market expectations.

C2 **Describe standards for comparisons in analysis.** Standards for comparisons include (1) intracompany—prior performance and relations between financial items for the company under analysis; (2) competitor—one or more direct competitors of the company; (3) industry—industry statistics; and (4) guidelines (rules of thumb)—general standards developed from past experiences and personal judgments.

A1 **Summarize and report results of analysis.** A financial statement analysis report is often organized around the building blocks of analysis. A good report separates interpretations and conclusions of analysis from the information underlying them. An analysis report often consists of six sections: (1) executive summary, (2) analysis overview, (3) evidential matter, (4) assumptions, (5) key factors, and (6) inferences.

A2ᴬ **Explain the form and assess the content of a complete income statement.** An income statement has four *potential* sections: (1) continuing operations, (2) discontinued segments, (3) extraordinary items, and (4) earnings per share.

P1 **Explain and apply methods of horizontal analysis.** Horizontal analysis is a tool to evaluate changes in data across time. Two important tools of horizontal analysis are comparative statements and trend analysis. Comparative statements show amounts for two or more successive periods, often with changes disclosed in both absolute and percent terms. Trend analysis is used to reveal important changes occurring from one period to the next.

P2 **Describe and apply methods of vertical analysis.** Vertical analysis is a tool to evaluate each financial statement item or group of items in terms of a base amount. Two tools of vertical analysis are common-size statements and graphical analyses. Each item in common-size statements is expressed as a percent of a base amount. For the balance sheet, the base amount is usually total assets, and for the income statement, it is usually sales.

P3 **Define and apply ratio analysis.** Ratio analysis provides clues to and symptoms of underlying conditions. Ratios, properly interpreted, identify areas requiring further investigation. A ratio expresses a mathematical relation between two quantities such as a percent, rate, or proportion. Ratios can be organized into the building blocks of analysis: (1) liquidity and efficiency, (2) solvency, (3) profitability, and (4) market prospects.

Guidance Answers to Decision Maker

Auditor The *joint relation* referred to is the combined increase in sales and the decrease in expenses yielding more than a 5% increase in income. Both *individual* accounts (sales and expenses) yield percent changes within the ±5% acceptable range. However, a joint analysis suggests a different picture. For example, consider a joint analysis using the profit margin ratio. The client's profit margin is 11.46% ($206,000 − $182,400/$206,000) for the current year compared with 5.0% ($200,000 − $190,000/$200,000) for the prior year—yielding a 129% increase in profit margin! This is what concerns the partner, and it suggests expanding audit tests to verify or refute the client's figures.

Banker Your decision on the loan application is positive for at least two reasons. First, the current ratio suggests a strong ability to meet short-term obligations. Second, current assets of $160,000

and a current ratio of 4:1 imply current liabilities of $40,000 (one-fourth of current assets) and a working capital excess of $120,000. This working capital excess is 60% of the loan amount. However, if the application is for a 10-year loan, our decision is less optimistic. The current ratio and working capital suggest a good safety margin, but indications of inefficiency in operations exist. In particular, a 4:1 current ratio is more than double its key competitors' ratio. This is characteristic of inefficient asset use.

Small Business Owner The frost loss is probably not extraordinary. Jacksonville experiences enough recurring frost damage to make it difficult to argue this event is both unusual and infrequent. Still, you want to highlight the frost loss and hope the bank views this uncommon event separately from continuing operations.

Key Terms

Business segment	Financial statement analysis	Ratio analysis
Common-size financial statement	General-purpose financial statements	Solvency
Comparative financial statements	Horizontal analysis	Unusual gain or loss
Efficiency	Infrequent gain or loss	Vertical analysis
Equity ratio	Liquidity	Working capital
Extraordinary gains and losses	Market prospects	
Financial reporting	Profitability	

Multiple Choice Quiz   Answers at end of chapter

1. A company's sales in 2014 were $300,000 and in 2015 were $351,000. Using 2014 as the base year, the sales trend percent for 2015 is:

a. 17%   **c.** 100%   **e.** 48%
b. 85%   **d.** 117%

Use the following information for questions 2 through 5.

GALLOWAY COMPANY
Balance Sheet
December 31, 2015

Assets

Cash	$ 86,000
Accounts receivable	76,000
Merchandise inventory	122,000
Prepaid insurance	12,000
Long-term investments	98,000
Plant assets, net	436,000
Total assets	$830,000

Liabilities and Equity

Current liabilities	$124,000
Long-term liabilities	90,000
Common stock	300,000
Retained earnings	316,000
Total liabilities and equity	$830,000

2. What is Galloway Company's current ratio?
a. 0.69
b. 1.31
c. 3.88
d. 6.69
e. 2.39

3. What is Galloway Company's acid-test ratio?
a. 2.39
b. 0.69
c. 1.31
d. 6.69
e. 3.88

4. What is Galloway Company's debt ratio?
a. 25.78%
b. 100.00%
c. 74.22%
d. 137.78%
e. 34.74%

5. What is Galloway Company's equity ratio?
a. 25.78%
b. 100.00%
c. 34.74%
d. 74.22%
e. 137.78%

^A *Superscript letter A denotes assignments based on Appendix 13A.*
[i] Icon denotes assignments that involve decision making.

Discussion Questions

1. Explain the difference between financial reporting and financial statements.

2. What is the difference between comparative financial statements and common-size comparative statements?

3. Which items are usually assigned a 100% value on (*a*) a common-size balance sheet and (*b*) a common-size income statement?

4. [i] What three factors would influence your evaluation as to whether a company's current ratio is good or bad?

5. [i] Suggest several reasons why a 2:1 current ratio might not be adequate for a particular company.

6. [i] Why is working capital given special attention in the process of analyzing balance sheets?

7. [i] What does the number of days' sales uncollected indicate?

8. [i] What does a relatively high accounts receivable turnover indicate about a company's short-term liquidity?

9. [i] Why is a company's capital structure, as measured by debt and equity ratios, important to financial statement analysts?

10. [i] How does inventory turnover provide information about a company's short-term liquidity?

11. [i] What ratios would you compute to evaluate management performance?

12. [i] Why would a company's return on total assets be different from its return on common stockholders' equity?

13. Where on the income statement does a company report an unusual gain not expected to occur more often than once every two years or so?

14. Refer to **Apple**'s financial statements in Appendix A. Compute its profit margin for the years ended September 28, 2013, and September 29, 2012.   **APPLE**

15. Refer to **Google**'s financial statements in Appendix A to compute its equity ratio as of December 31, 2013, and December 31, 2012.   **GOOGLE**

16. Refer to **Samsung**'s financial statements in Appendix A. Compute its debt ratio as of December 31, 2013, and December 31, 2012.   **Samsung**

17. Use **Samsung**'s financial statements in Appendix A to compute its return on total assets for fiscal year ended December 31, 2013.   **Samsung**

[Mc Graw Hill] **connect**

QUICK STUDY

QS 13-1
Financial reporting
C1

Which of the following items *a* through *i* are part of financial reporting but are *not* included as part of general-purpose financial statements?

  ____ **a.** Income statement

  ____ **b.** Balance sheet

  ____ **c.** Prospectus

  ____ **d.** Financial statement notes

  ____ **e.** Company news releases

  ____ **f.** Statement of cash flows

  ____ **g.** Stock price information and analysis

  ____ **h.** Statement of shareholders' equity

  ____ **i.** Management discussion and analysis of financial performance

---

QS 13-2
Standard of comparison
C2

Identify which standard of comparison, (*a*) intracompany, (*b*) competitor, (*c*) industry, or (*d*) guidelines, is best described by each of the following.

  ____ **1.** Is often viewed as the best standard of comparison.

  ____ **2.** Rules of thumb developed from past experiences.

  ____ **3.** Provides analysis based on a company's prior performance.

  ____ **4.** Compares a company against industry statistics.

QS 13-3
Horizontal analysis
P1

Compute the annual dollar changes and percent changes for each of the following accounts.

	2015	2014
Short-term investments	$374,634	$234,000
Accounts receivable	97,364	101,000
Notes payable	0	88,000

Use the following information for Tide Corporation to determine the 2014 and 2015 trend percents for net sales using 2014 as the base year.

($ thousands)	2015	2014
Net sales	$801,810	$453,000
Cost of goods sold	392,887	134,088

Refer to the information in QS 13-4. Use that information for Tide Corporation to determine the 2014 and 2015 common-size percents for cost of goods sold using net sales as the base.

For each ratio listed, identify whether the change in ratio value from 2014 to 2015 is usually regarded as favorable or unfavorable.

Ratio	2015	2014	Ratio	2015	2014
____ 1. Profit margin	9%	8%	____ 5. Accounts receivable turnover. . . .	5.5	6.7
____ 2. Debt ratio	47%	42%	____ 6. Basic earnings per share	$1.25	$1.10
____ 3. Gross margin. . . .	34%	46%	____ 7. Inventory turnover	3.6	3.4
____ 4. Acid-test ratio. . .	1.00	1.15	____ 8. Dividend yield	2.0%	1.2%

The following information is available for Morgan Company and Parker Company, similar firms operating in the same industry. Write a half-page report comparing Morgan and Parker using the available information. Your discussion should include their ability to meet current obligations and to use current assets efficiently.

	A	B	C	D	E	F	G	H
1		**Morgan**				**Parker**		
2		**2015**	**2014**	**2013**		**2015**	**2014**	**2013**
3	Current ratio	1.7	1.6	2.1		3.2	2.7	1.9
4	Acid-test ratio	1.0	1.1	1.2		2.8	2.5	1.6
5	Accounts receivable turnover	30.5	25.2	29.2		16.4	15.2	16.0
6	Merchandise inventory turnover	24.2	21.9	17.1		14.5	13.0	12.6
7	Working capital	$70,000	$58,000	$52,000		$131,000	$103,000	$78,000
8								

A review of the notes payable files discovers that three years ago the company reported the entire $1,000 cash payment (consisting of $800 principal and $200 interest) toward an installment note payable as interest expense. This mistake had a material effect on the amount of income in that year. How should the correction be reported in the current-year financial statements?

Answer each of the following related to international accounting and analysis.

a. Identify a limitation to using ratio analysis when examining companies reporting under different accounting systems such as IFRS versus U.S. GAAP.

b. Identify an advantage to using horizontal and vertical analyses when examining companies reporting under different currencies.

connect
_____

Match the ratio to the building block of financial statement analysis to which it best relates.

A. Liquidity and efficiency   **B.** Solvency   **C.** Profitability   **D.** Market prospects

____ **1.** Equity ratio	____ **6.** Accounts receivable turnover
____ **2.** Return on total assets	____ **7.** Debt-to-equity
____ **3.** Dividend yield	____ **8.** Times interest earned
____ **4.** Book value per common share	____ **9.** Gross margin ratio
____ **5.** Days' sales in inventory	____ **10.** Acid-test ratio

Exercise 13-2
Identifying financial ratios

C2

Identify which of the following six metrics *a* through *f* best completes questions *1* through *3* below.

a. Days' sales uncollected

b. Accounts receivable turnover

c. Working capital

d. Return on total assets

e. Total asset turnover

f. Profit margin

1. Which two ratios are key components in measuring a company's operating efficiency? _____ _____
Which ratio summarizes these two components? _____

2. What measure reflects the difference between current assets and current liabilities? _____

3. Which two short-term liquidity ratios measure how frequently a company collects its accounts?
_____ _____

Exercise 13-3
Computation and analysis of trend percents

P1

Compute trend percents for the following accounts, using 2011 as the base year (round the percents to whole numbers). State whether the situation as revealed by the trends appears to be favorable or unfavorable for each account.

	2015	2014	2013	2012	2011
Sales	$282,880	$270,800	$252,600	$234,560	$150,000
Cost of goods sold	128,200	122,080	115,280	106,440	67,000
Accounts receivable	18,100	17,300	16,400	15,200	9,000

Exercise 13-4
Common-size percent computation and interpretation

P2

Express the following comparative income statements in common-size percents and assess whether or not this company's situation has improved in the most recent year (round the percents to one decimal).

GOMEZ CORPORATION		
Comparative Income Statements		
For Years Ended December 31, 2015 and 2014		
	2015	**2014**
Sales	$740,000	$625,000
Cost of goods sold	560,300	290,800
Gross profit	179,700	334,200
Operating expenses	128,200	218,500
Net income	$ 51,500	$115,700

Exercise 13-5
Determination of income effects from common-size and trend percents

P1   P2

Common-size and trend percents for Rustynail Company's sales, cost of goods sold, and expenses follow. Determine whether net income increased, decreased, or remained unchanged in this three-year period.

	Common-Size Percents			**Trend Percents**		
	2015	**2014**	**2013**	**2015**	**2014**	**2013**
Sales	100.0%	100.0%	100.0%	105.4%	104.2%	100.0%
Cost of goods sold	63.4	61.9	59.1	113.1	109.1	100.0
Total expenses	15.3	14.8	15.1	106.8	102.1	100.0

Simon Company's year-end balance sheets follow. Express the balance sheets in common-size percents. Round amounts to the nearest one-tenth of a percent. Analyze and comment on the results.

Exercise 13-6
Common-size percents

P2

At December 31	2015	2014	2013
Assets			
Cash	$ 31,800	$ 35,625	$ 37,800
Accounts receivable, net	89,500	62,500	50,200
Merchandise inventory	112,500	82,500	54,000
Prepaid expenses	10,700	9,375	5,000
Plant assets, net	278,500	255,000	230,500
Total assets	$523,000	$445,000	$377,500
Liabilities and Equity			
Accounts payable	$129,900	$ 75,250	$ 51,250
Long-term notes payable secured by mortgages on plant assets	98,500	101,500	83,500
Common stock, $10 par value	163,500	163,500	163,500
Retained earnings	131,100	104,750	79,250
Total liabilities and equity	$523,000	$445,000	$377,500

Refer to Simon Company's balance sheets in Exercise 13-6. Analyze its year-end short-term liquidity position at the end of 2015, 2014, and 2013 by computing (1) the current ratio and (2) the acid-test ratio. Comment on the ratio results. (Round ratio amounts to two decimals.)

Exercise 13-7
Liquidity analysis

P3

Refer to the Simon Company information in Exercise 13-6. The company's income statements for the years ended December 31, 2015 and 2014, follow. Assume that all sales are on credit and then compute: (1) days' sales uncollected, (2) accounts receivable turnover, (3) inventory turnover, and (4) days' sales in inventory. Comment on the changes in the ratios from 2014 to 2015. (Round amounts to one decimal.)

Exercise 13-8
Liquidity analysis and interpretation

P3

For Year Ended December 31	2015		2014	
Sales		$673,500		$532,000
Cost of goods sold	$411,225		$345,500	
Other operating expenses	209,550		134,980	
Interest expense	12,100		13,300	
Income taxes	9,525		8,845	
Total costs and expenses		642,400		502,625
Net income		$ 31,100		$ 29,375
Earnings per share		$ 1.90		$ 1.80

Refer to the Simon Company information in Exercises 13-6 and 13-8. Compare the company's long-term risk and capital structure positions at the end of 2015 and 2014 by computing these ratios: (1) debt and equity ratios—percent rounded to one decimal, (2) debt-to-equity ratio—rounded to two decimals, and (3) times interest earned—rounded to one decimal. Comment on these ratio results.

Exercise 13-9
Risk and capital structure analysis

P3

Refer to Simon Company's financial information in Exercises 13-6 and 13-8. Evaluate the company's efficiency and profitability by computing the following for 2015 and 2014: (1) profit margin ratio—percent rounded to one decimal, (2) total asset turnover—rounded to one decimal, and (3) return on total assets—percent rounded to one decimal. Comment on these ratio results.

Exercise 13-10
Efficiency and profitability analysis

P3

Exercise 13-11
Profitability analysis

P3

Refer to Simon Company's financial information in Exercises 13-6 and 13-8. Additional information about the company follows. To help evaluate the company's profitability, compute and interpret the following ratios for 2015 and 2014: (1) return on common stockholders' equity—percent rounded to one decimal, (2) price-earnings ratio on December 31—rounded to one decimal, and (3) dividend yield—percent rounded to one decimal.

Common stock market price, December 31, 2015	$30.00
Common stock market price, December 31, 2014	28.00
Annual cash dividends per share in 2015	0.29
Annual cash dividends per share in 2014	0.24

Exercise 13-12
Analysis of efficiency and financial leverage

A1

Roak Company and Clay Company are similar firms that operate in the same industry. Clay began operations in 2013 and Roak in 2010. In 2015, both companies pay 7% interest on their debt to creditors. The following additional information is available.

	Roak Company			Clay Company		
	2015	2014	2013	2015	2014	2013
Total asset turnover	3.1	2.8	3.0	1.7	1.5	1.1
Return on total assets	9.0%	9.6%	8.8%	5.9%	5.6%	5.3%
Profit margin ratio	2.4%	2.5%	2.3%	2.8%	3.0%	2.9%
Sales	$410,000	$380,000	$396,000	$210,000	$170,000	$110,000

Write a half-page report comparing Roak and Clay using the available information. Your analysis should include their ability to use assets efficiently to produce profits. Also comment on their success in employing financial leverage in 2015.

Exercise 13-13[A]
Income statement categories

A2

In 2015, Randa Merchandising, Inc., sold its interest in a chain of wholesale outlets, taking the company completely out of the wholesaling business. The company still operates its retail outlets. A listing of the major sections of an income statement follows:

A. Income (loss) from continuing operations

B. Income (loss) from operating, or gain (loss) from disposing, a discontinued segment

C. Extraordinary gain (loss)

Indicate where each of the following income-related items for this company appears on its 2015 income statement by writing the letter of the appropriate section in the blank beside each item.

Section	Item	Debit	Credit
_____	1. Net sales		$2,900,000
_____	2. Gain on state's condemnation of company property (net of tax)		230,000
_____	3. Cost of goods sold	$1,480,000	
_____	4. Income taxes expense	217,000	
_____	5. Depreciation expense	232,500	
_____	6. Gain on sale of wholesale business segment (net of tax)		775,000
_____	7. Loss from operating wholesale business segment (net of tax)	444,000	
_____	8. Salaries expense	640,000	

Exercise 13-14[A]
Income statement presentation   A2

Use the financial data for Randa Merchandising, Inc., in Exercise 13-13 to prepare its income statement for calendar year 2015. (Ignore the earnings per share section.)

Nintendo Company, Ltd., reports the following financial information as of, or for the year ended, March 31, 2013. Nintendo reports its financial statements in both Japanese yen and U.S. dollars as shown (amounts in millions).

Exercise 13-15
Ratio analysis under different currencies

P3

Current assets	¥1,192,250	$12,683,516
Total assets.	1,447,878	15,402,966
Current liabilities	194,475	2,068,887
Net sales	635,422	6,759,818
Net income	7,099	75,527

1. Compute Nintendo's current ratio, net profit margin, and sales-to-total-assets using the financial information reported in (a) yen and (b) dollars. Round amounts to two decimals.
2. What can we conclude from a review of the results for part 1?

connect

Selected comparative financial statements of Haroun Company follow.

PROBLEM SET A

Problem 13-1A
Calculation and analysis of trend percents

A1   P1

HAROUN COMPANY Comparative Income Statements For Years Ended December 31, 2015–2009							
($ thousands)	**2015**	**2014**	**2013**	**2012**	**2011**	**2010**	**2009**
Sales	$1,694	$1,496	$1,370	$1,264	$1,186	$1,110	$928
Cost of goods sold	1,246	1,032	902	802	752	710	586
Gross profit	448	464	468	462	434	400	342
Operating expenses	330	256	234	170	146	144	118
Net income	$ 118	$ 208	$ 234	$ 292	$ 288	$ 256	$224

HAROUN COMPANY Comparative Balance Sheets December 31, 2015–2009							
($ thousands)	**2015**	**2014**	**2013**	**2012**	**2011**	**2010**	**2009**
Assets							
Cash	$ 58	$ 78	$ 82	$ 84	$ 88	$ 86	$ 89
Accounts receivable, net	490	514	466	360	318	302	216
Merchandise inventory	1,838	1,364	1,204	1,032	936	810	615
Other current assets	36	32	14	34	28	28	9
Long-term investments	0	0	0	146	146	146	146
Plant assets, net	2,020	2,014	1,752	944	978	860	725
Total assets	$4,442	$4,002	$3,518	$2,600	$2,494	$2,232	$1,800
Liabilities and Equity							
Current liabilities	$1,220	$1,042	$ 718	$ 614	$ 546	$ 522	$ 282
Long-term liabilities	1,294	1,140	1,112	570	580	620	400
Common stock	1,000	1,000	1,000	850	850	650	650
Other paid-in capital	250	250	250	170	170	150	150
Retained earnings	678	570	438	396	348	290	318
Total liabilities and equity	$4,442	$4,002	$3,518	$2,600	$2,494	$2,232	$1,800

Required

1. Compute trend percents for all components of both statements using 2009 as the base year. (Round percents to one decimal.)

Analysis Component

2. Analyze and comment on the financial statements and trend percents from part 1.

Check   (1) 2015, Total assets trend, 246.8%

Problem 13-2A
Ratios, common-size
statements, and trend
percents

P1   P2   P3

Selected comparative financial statements of Korbin Company follow.

KORBIN COMPANY Comparative Income Statements For Years Ended December 31, 2015, 2014, and 2013			
	2015	2014	2013
Sales	$555,000	$340,000	$278,000
Cost of goods sold	283,500	212,500	153,900
Gross profit	271,500	127,500	124,100
Selling expenses	102,900	46,920	50,800
Administrative expenses	50,668	29,920	22,800
Total expenses	153,568	76,840	73,600
Income before taxes	117,932	50,660	50,500
Income taxes	40,800	10,370	15,670
Net income	$ 77,132	$ 40,290	$ 34,830

KORBIN COMPANY Comparative Balance Sheets December 31, 2015, 2014, and 2013			
	2015	2014	2013
Assets			
Current assets	$ 52,390	$ 37,924	$ 51,748
Long-term investments	0	500	3,950
Plant assets, net	100,000	96,000	60,000
Total assets	$152,390	$134,424	$115,698
Liabilities and Equity			
Current liabilities	$ 22,800	$ 19,960	$ 20,300
Common stock	72,000	72,000	60,000
Other paid-in capital	9,000	9,000	6,000
Retained earnings	48,590	33,464	29,398
Total liabilities and equity	$152,390	$134,424	$115,698

Required

1. Compute each year's current ratio. (Round ratio amounts to one decimal.)
2. Express the income statement data in common-size percents. (Round percents to two decimals.)

Check   (3) 2015, Total
assets trend, 131.71%

3. Express the balance sheet data in trend percents with 2013 as the base year. (Round percents to two decimals.)

Analysis Component

4. Comment on any significant relations revealed by the ratios and percents computed.

Problem 13-3A
Transactions, working
capital, and liquidity
ratios

P3

Plum Corporation began the month of May with $700,000 of current assets, a current ratio of 2.50:1, and an acid-test ratio of 1.10:1. During the month, it completed the following transactions (the company uses a perpetual inventory system).

May   2   Purchased $50,000 of merchandise inventory on credit.
       8   Sold merchandise inventory that cost $55,000 for $110,000 cash.
      10   Collected $20,000 cash on an account receivable.
      15   Paid $22,000 cash to settle an account payable.

Check   May 22: Current
ratio, 2.19; Acid-test ratio, 1.11

      17   Wrote off a $5,000 bad debt against the Allowance for Doubtful Accounts account.
      22   Declared a $1 per share cash dividend on its 50,000 shares of outstanding common stock.

26 Paid the dividend declared on May 22.
27 Borrowed $100,000 cash by giving the bank a 30-day, 10% note.
28 Borrowed $80,000 cash by signing a long-term secured note.
29 Used the $180,000 cash proceeds from the notes to buy new machinery.

May 29: Current
ratio, 1.80; Working capital,
$325,000

Required

Prepare a table showing Plum's (1) current ratio, (2) acid-test ratio, and (3) working capital after each transaction. Round ratios to two decimals.

Selected year-end financial statements of Cabot Corporation follow. (All sales were on credit; selected balance sheet amounts at December 31, 2014, were inventory, $48,900; total assets, $189,400; common stock, $90,000; and retained earnings, $22,748.)

Problem 13-4A
Calculation of financial
statement ratios

P3

CABOT CORPORATION Income Statement For Year Ended December 31, 2015	
Sales	$448,600
Cost of goods sold	297,250
Gross profit	151,350
Operating expenses	98,600
Interest expense	4,100
Income before taxes	48,650
Income taxes	19,598
Net income	$ 29,052

CABOT CORPORATION Balance Sheet December 31, 2015			
Assets		**Liabilities and Equity**	
Cash	$ 10,000	Accounts payable	$ 17,500
Short-term investments	8,400	Accrued wages payable	3,200
Accounts receivable, net	29,200	Income taxes payable	3,300
Notes receivable (trade)*	4,500	Long-term note payable, secured	
Merchandise inventory	32,150	by mortgage on plant assets	63,400
Prepaid expenses	2,650	Common stock	90,000
Plant assets, net	153,300	Retained earnings	62,800
Total assets	$240,200	Total liabilities and equity	$240,200

* These are short-term notes receivable arising from customer (trade) sales.

Required

Compute the following: (1) current ratio, (2) acid-test ratio, (3) days' sales uncollected, (4) inventory turnover, (5) days' sales in inventory, (6) debt-to-equity ratio, (7) times interest earned, (8) profit margin ratio, (9) total asset turnover, (10) return on total assets, and (11) return on common stockholders' equity. Round to one decimal place; for part 6, round to two decimals.

Check Acid-test ratio, 2.2
to 1; Inventory turnover, 7.3

Summary information from the financial statements of two companies competing in the same industry follows.

Problem 13-5A
Comparative ratio
analysis A1 P3

	Barco Company	Kyan Company		Barco Company	Kyan Company
Data from the current year-end balance sheets			**Data from the current year's income statement**		
Assets			Sales	$770,000	$880,200
Cash	$ 19,500	$ 34,000	Cost of goods sold	585,100	632,500
Accounts receivable, net	37,400	57,400	Interest expense	7,900	13,000
Current notes receivable (trade) ...	9,100	7,200	Income tax expense	14,800	24,300
Merchandise inventory	84,440	132,500	Net income	162,200	210,400
Prepaid expenses	5,000	6,950	Basic earnings per share	4.51	5.11
Plant assets, net	290,000	304,400	Cash dividends per share..........	3.81	3.93
Total assets	$445,440	$542,450			
			Beginning-of-year balance sheet data		
Liabilities and Equity			Accounts receivable, net	$ 29,800	$ 54,200
Current liabilities	$ 61,340	$ 93,300	Current notes receivable (trade) ...	0	0
Long-term notes payable	80,800	101,000	Merchandise inventory	55,600	107,400
Common stock, $5 par value	180,000	206,000	Total assets	398,000	382,500
Retained earnings	123,300	142,150	Common stock, $5 par value	180,000	206,000
Total liabilities and equity	$445,440	$542,450	Retained earnings	98,260	93,666

Required

Check (1) Kyan: Accounts
receivable turnover, 14.8;
Inventory turnover, 5.3

(2) Barco: Profit
margin, 21.1%; PE, 16.6

1. For both companies compute the (*a*) current ratio, (*b*) acid-test ratio, (*c*) accounts (including notes) receivable turnover, (*d*) inventory turnover, (*e*) days' sales in inventory, and (*f*) days' sales uncollected. Identify the company you consider to be the better short-term credit risk and explain why. Round to one decimal place.

2. For both companies compute the (*a*) profit margin ratio, (*b*) total asset turnover, (*c*) return on total assets, and (*d*) return on common stockholders' equity. Assuming that each company's stock can be purchased at $75 per share, compute their (*e*) price-earnings ratios and (*f*) dividend yields. Round to one decimal place. Identify which company's stock you would recommend as the better investment and explain why.

Problem 13-6A[A]
Income statement
computations and format

A2

Selected account balances from the adjusted trial balance for Olinda Corporation as of its calendar year-end December 31, 2015, follow.

	Debit	Credit
a. Interest revenue...		$ 14,000
b. Depreciation expense—Equipment...........................	$ 34,000	
c. Loss on sale of equipment..................................	25,850	
d. Accounts payable		44,000
e. Other operating expenses..................................	106,400	
f. Accumulated depreciation—Equipment		71,600
g. Gain from settlement of lawsuit............................		44,000
h. Accumulated depreciation—Buildings........................		174,500
i. Loss from operating a discontinued segment (pretax)..........	18,250	
j. Gain on insurance recovery of tornado damage (pretax and extraordinary).........		29,120
k. Net sales...		998,500
l. Depreciation expense—Buildings	52,000	
m. Correction of overstatement of prior year's sales (pretax)......................	16,000	
n. Gain on sale of discontinued segment's assets (pretax)......................		34,000
o. Loss from settlement of lawsuit	23,750	
p. Income taxes expense	?	
q. Cost of goods sold	482,500	

Required

Answer each of the following questions by providing supporting computations.

1. Assume that the company's income tax rate is 30% for all items. Identify the tax effects and after-tax amounts of the four items labeled pretax.

2. What is the amount of income from continuing operations before income taxes? What is the amount of the income taxes expense? What is the amount of income from continuing operations?

3. What is the total amount of after-tax income (loss) associated with the discontinued segment?

4. What is the amount of income (loss) before the extraordinary items?

5. What is the amount of net income for the year?

Check (3) $11,025

(4) $243,425

(5) $263,809

Selected comparative financial statements of Tripoly Company follow.

PROBLEM SET B

Problem 13-1B
Calculation and analysis
of trend percents

A1 P1

TRIPOLY COMPANY Comparative Income Statements For Years Ended December 31, 2015–2009							
($ thousands)	2015	2014	2013	2012	2011	2010	2009
Sales	$560	$610	$630	$680	$740	$770	$860
Cost of goods sold	276	290	294	314	340	350	380
Gross profit	284	320	336	366	400	420	480
Operating expenses	84	104	112	126	140	144	150
Net income	$200	$216	$224	$240	$260	$276	$330

TRIPOLY COMPANY Comparative Balance Sheets December 31, 2015–2009							
($ thousands)	2015	2014	2013	2012	2011	2010	2009
Assets							
Cash	$ 44	$ 46	$ 52	$ 54	$ 60	$ 62	$ 68
Accounts receivable, net	130	136	140	144	150	154	160
Merchandise inventory	166	172	178	180	186	190	208
Other current assets	34	34	36	38	38	40	40
Long-term investments	36	30	26	110	110	110	110
Plant assets, net	510	514	520	412	420	428	454
Total assets	$920	$932	$952	$938	$964	$984	$1,040
Liabilities and Equity							
Current liabilities	$148	$156	$186	$190	$210	$260	$280
Long-term liabilities	92	120	142	148	194	214	260
Common stock	160	160	160	160	160	160	160
Other paid-in capital	70	70	70	70	70	70	70
Retained earnings	450	426	394	370	330	280	270
Total liabilities and equity	$920	$932	$952	$938	$964	$984	$1,040

Required

1. Compute trend percents for all components of both statements using 2009 as the base year. (Round percents to one decimal.)

Check (1) 2015, Total assets trend, 88.5%

Analysis Component

2. Analyze and comment on the financial statements and trend percents from part 1.

Problem 13-2B

Ratios, common-size statements, and trend percents

P1   P2   P3

Selected comparative financial statement information of Bluegrass Corporation follows.

BLUEGRASS CORPORATION			
Comparative Income Statements			
For Years Ended December 31, 2015, 2014, and 2013			
	2015	2014	2013
Sales	$198,800	$166,000	$143,800
Cost of goods sold	108,890	86,175	66,200
Gross profit	89,910	79,825	77,600
Selling expenses	22,680	19,790	18,000
Administrative expenses	16,760	14,610	15,700
Total expenses	39,440	34,400	33,700
Income before taxes	50,470	45,425	43,900
Income taxes	6,050	5,910	5,300
Net income	$ 44,420	$ 39,515	$ 38,600

BLUEGRASS CORPORATION			
Comparative Balance Sheets			
December 31, 2015, 2014, and 2013			
	2015	2014	2013
Assets			
Current assets	$ 54,860	$ 32,660	$ 36,300
Long-term investments	0	1,700	10,600
Plant assets, net	112,810	113,660	79,000
Total assets	$167,670	$148,020	$125,900
Liabilities and Equity			
Current liabilities	$ 22,370	$ 19,180	$ 16,500
Common stock	46,500	46,500	37,000
Other paid-in capital	13,850	13,850	11,300
Retained earnings	84,950	68,490	61,100
Total liabilities and equity	$167,670	$148,020	$125,900

Required

Check   (3) 2015, Total assets trend, 133.18%

1. Compute each year's current ratio. (Round ratio amounts to one decimal.)
2. Express the income statement data in common-size percents. (Round percents to two decimals.)
3. Express the balance sheet data in trend percents with 2013 as the base year. (Round percents to two decimals.)

Analysis Component

4. Comment on any significant relations revealed by the ratios and percents computed.

Problem 13-3B

Transactions, working capital, and liquidity ratios   P3

Check   June 3:
Current ratio, 2.88;
Acid-test ratio, 2.40

Koto Corporation began the month of June with $300,000 of current assets, a current ratio of 2.5:1, and an acid-test ratio of 1.4:1. During the month, it completed the following transactions (the company uses a perpetual inventory system).

June   1   Sold merchandise inventory that cost $75,000 for $120,000 cash.
      3   Collected $88,000 cash on an account receivable.
      5   Purchased $150,000 of merchandise inventory on credit.
      7   Borrowed $100,000 cash by giving the bank a 60-day, 10% note.
    10   Borrowed $120,000 cash by signing a long-term secured note.
    12   Purchased machinery for $275,000 cash.
    15   Declared a $1 per share cash dividend on its 80,000 shares of outstanding common stock.
    19   Wrote off a $5,000 bad debt against the Allowance for Doubtful Accounts account.
    22   Paid $12,000 cash to settle an account payable.
    30   Paid the dividend declared on June 15.

June 30: Working capital, $(10,000); Current ratio, 0.97

Required

Prepare a table showing the company's (1) current ratio, (2) acid-test ratio, and (3) working capital after each transaction. Round ratios to two decimals.

Selected year-end financial statements of Overton Corporation follow. (All sales were on credit; selected balance sheet amounts at December 31, 2014, were inventory, $17,400; total assets, $94,900; common stock, $35,500; and retained earnings, $18,800.)

Problem 13-4B
Calculation of financial statement ratios

P3

OVERTON CORPORATION Income Statement For Year Ended December 31, 2015	
Sales	$315,500
Cost of goods sold	236,100
Gross profit	79,400
Operating expenses	49,200
Interest expense	2,200
Income before taxes	28,000
Income taxes	4,200
Net income	$ 23,800

OVERTON CORPORATION Balance Sheet December 31, 2015			
Assets		**Liabilities and Equity**	
Cash	$ 6,100	Accounts payable	$ 11,500
Short-term investments	6,900	Accrued wages payable	3,300
Accounts receivable, net	12,100	Income taxes payable	2,600
Notes receivable (trade)*	3,000	Long-term note payable, secured	
Merchandise inventory	13,500	by mortgage on plant assets	30,000
Prepaid expenses	2,000	Common stock, $5 par value	35,000
Plant assets, net	73,900	Retained earnings	35,100
Total assets	$117,500	Total liabilities and equity	$117,500

* These are short-term notes receivable arising from customer (trade) sales.

Required

Compute the following: (1) current ratio, (2) acid-test ratio, (3) days' sales uncollected, (4) inventory turnover, (5) days' sales in inventory, (6) debt-to-equity ratio, (7) times interest earned, (8) profit margin ratio, (9) total asset turnover, (10) return on total assets, and (11) return on common stockholders' equity. Round to one decimal place; for part 6, round to two decimals.

Check Acid-test ratio, 1.6 to 1; Inventory turnover, 15.3

Summary information from the financial statements of two companies competing in the same industry follows.

Problem 13-5B
Comparative ratio analysis A1 P3

	Fargo Company	Ball Company		Fargo Company	Ball Company
Data from the current year-end balance sheets			**Data from the current year's income statement**		
Assets			Sales	$393,600	$667,500
Cash	$ 20,000	$ 36,500	Cost of goods sold	290,600	480,000
Accounts receivable, net	77,100	70,500	Interest expense	5,900	12,300
Current notes receivable (trade) ...	11,600	9,000	Income tax expense	5,700	12,300
Merchandise inventory	86,800	82,000	Net income	33,850	61,700
Prepaid expenses	9,700	10,100	Basic earnings per share	1.27	2.19
Plant assets, net	176,900	252,300			
Total assets	$382,100	$460,400			
			Beginning-of-year balance sheet data		
			Accounts receivable, net	$ 72,200	$ 73,300
Liabilities and Equity			Current notes receivable (trade) ...	0	0
Current liabilities	$ 90,500	$ 97,000	Merchandise inventory	105,100	80,500
Long-term notes payable	93,000	93,300	Total assets	383,400	443,000
Common stock, $5 par value	133,000	141,000	Common stock, $5 par value	133,000	141,000
Retained earnings	65,600	129,100	Retained earnings	49,100	109,700
Total liabilities and equity	$382,100	$460,400			

Required

1. For both companies compute the (*a*) current ratio, (*b*) acid-test ratio, (*c*) accounts (including notes) receivable turnover, (*d*) inventory turnover, (*e*) days' sales in inventory, and (*f*) days' sales uncollected. Identify the company you consider to be the better short-term credit risk and explain why. Round to one decimal place.

2. For both companies compute the (*a*) profit margin ratio, (*b*) total asset turnover, (*c*) return on total assets, and (*d*) return on common stockholders' equity. Assuming that each company paid cash dividends of $1.50 per share and each company's stock can be purchased at $25 per share, compute their (*e*) price-earnings ratios and (*f*) dividend yields. Round to one decimal place; for part *b*, round to two decimals. Identify which company's stock you would recommend as the better investment and explain why.

Problem 13-6B[A]
Income statement
computations and format

A2

Selected account balances from the adjusted trial balance for Harbor Corp. as of its calendar year-end December 31, 2015, follow.

		Debit	Credit
a.	Accumulated depreciation—Buildings		$ 400,000
b.	Interest revenue		20,000
c.	Net sales		2,640,000
d.	Income taxes expense	$?	
e.	Loss on hurricane damage (pretax and extraordinary)	64,000	
f.	Accumulated depreciation—Equipment		220,000
g.	Other operating expenses	328,000	
h.	Depreciation expense—Equipment	100,000	
i.	Loss from settlement of lawsuit	36,000	
j.	Gain from settlement of lawsuit		68,000
k.	Loss on sale of equipment	24,000	
l.	Loss from operating a discontinued segment (pretax)	120,000	
m.	Depreciation expense—Buildings	156,000	
n.	Correction of overstatement of prior year's expense (pretax)		48,000
o.	Cost of goods sold	1,040,000	
p.	Loss on sale of discontinued segment's assets (pretax)	180,000	
q.	Accounts payable		132,000

Required

Answer each of the following questions by providing supporting computations.

1. Assume that the company's income tax rate is 25% for all items. Identify the tax effects and after-tax amounts of the four items labeled pretax.

2. What is the amount of income from continuing operations before income taxes? What is the amount of income taxes expense? What is the amount of income from continuing operations?

3. What is the total amount of after-tax income (loss) associated with the discontinued segment?

4. What is the amount of income (loss) before the extraordinary items?

5. What is the amount of net income for the year?

**SERIAL
PROBLEM**
Business Solutions

P3

(This serial problem began in Chapter 1 and continues through most of the book. If previous chapter segments were not completed, the serial problem can begin at this point. It is helpful, but not necessary, to use the Working Papers that accompany the book.)

SP 13 Use the following selected data from Business Solutions's income statement for the three months ended March 31, 2016, and from its March 31, 2016, balance sheet to complete the requirements below: computer services revenue, $25,307; net sales (of goods), $18,693; total sales and revenue, $44,000; cost of goods sold, $14,052; net income, $18,833; quick assets, $90,924; current assets, $95,568; total assets, $120,268; current liabilities, $875; total liabilities, $875; and total equity, $119,393.

Required

1. Compute the gross margin ratio (both with and without services revenue) and net profit margin ratio (round the percent to one decimal).

2. Compute the current ratio and acid-test ratio (round to one decimal).

3. Compute the debt ratio and equity ratio (round the percent to one decimal).

4. What percent of its assets are current? What percent are long term (round the percent to one decimal)?

Beyond the Numbers

BTN 13-1 Refer to Apple's financial statements in Appendix A to answer the following.

1. Using fiscal 2011 as the base year, compute trend percents for fiscal years 2011, 2012, and 2013 for net sales, cost of sales, operating income, other income (expense) net, provision for income taxes, and net income. (Round percents to one decimal.)

2. Compute common-size percents for fiscal years 2012 and 2013 for the following categories of assets: (*a*) total current assets, (*b*) property, plant and equipment, net, and (*c*) goodwill plus acquired intangible assets, net. (Round percents to one decimal.)

3. Comment on any notable changes across the years for the income statement trends computed in part 1 and the balance sheet percents computed in part 2.

Fast Forward

4. Access Apple's financial statements for fiscal years ending after September 28, 2013, from its website (Apple.com) or the SEC database (www.SEC.gov). Update your work for parts 1, 2, and 3 using the new information accessed.

REPORTING IN ACTION

A1 P1 P2

APPLE

BTN 13-2 Key figures for Apple and Google follow.

($ millions)	Apple	Google
Cash and equivalents	$ 14,259	$18,898
Accounts receivable, net	13,102	8,882
Inventories	1,764	426
Retained earnings.	104,256	61,262
Cost of sales	106,606	25,858
Revenues	170,910	59,825
Total assets.	207,000	110,920

COMPARATIVE ANALYSIS

C2 P2

APPLE

GOOGLE

Required

1. Compute common-size percents for each of the companies using the data provided. (Round percents to one decimal.)

2. Which company retains a higher portion of cumulative net income in the company?

3. Which company has a higher gross margin ratio on sales?

4. Which company holds a higher percent of its total assets as inventory?

BTN 13-3 As Beacon Company controller, you are responsible for informing the board of directors about its financial activities. At the board meeting, you present the following information.

ETHICS CHALLENGE

A1

	2015	2014	2013
Sales trend percent	147.0%	135.0%	100.0%
Selling expenses to sales	10.1%	14.0%	15.6%
Sales to plant assets ratio	3.8 to 1	3.6 to 1	3.3 to 1
Current ratio	2.9 to 1	2.7 to 1	2.4 to 1
Acid-test ratio	1.1 to 1	1.4 to 1	1.5 to 1
Inventory turnover	7.8 times	9.0 times	10.2 times
Accounts receivable turnover	7.0 times	7.7 times	8.5 times
Total asset turnover	2.9 times	2.9 times	3.3 times
Return on total assets	10.4%	11.0%	13.2%
Return on stockholders' equity.	10.7%	11.5%	14.1%
Profit margin ratio	3.6%	3.8%	4.0%

After the meeting, the company's CEO holds a press conference with analysts in which she mentions the following ratios.

	2015	2014	2013
Sales trend percent	147.0%	135.0%	100.0%
Selling expenses to sales	10.1%	14.0%	15.6%
Sales to plant assets ratio	3.8 to 1	3.6 to 1	3.3 to 1
Current ratio	2.9 to 1	2.7 to 1	2.4 to 1

Required

1. Why do you think the CEO decided to report 4 ratios instead of the 11 prepared?

2. Comment on the possible consequences of the CEO's reporting of the ratios selected.

COMMUNICATING IN PRACTICE

A1   P3

BTN 13-4   Each team is to select a different industry, and each team member is to select a different company in that industry and acquire its financial statements. Use those statements to analyze the company, including at least one ratio from each of the four building blocks of analysis. When necessary, use the financial press to determine the market price of its stock. Communicate with teammates via a meeting, e-mail, or telephone to discuss how different companies compare to each other and to industry norms. The team is to prepare a single one-page memorandum reporting on its analysis and the conclusions reached.

TAKING IT TO THE NET

P3

BTN 13-5   Access the February 21, 2014, filing of the December 31, 2013, 10-K report of The Hershey Company (ticker HSY) at www.SEC.gov and complete the following requirements.

Required

Compute or identify the following profitability ratios of Hershey for its years ending December 31, 2013, *and* December 31, 2012. Interpret its profitability using the results obtained for these two years.

1. Profit margin ratio (round the percent to one decimal).

2. Gross profit ratio (round the percent to one decimal).

3. Return on total assets (round the percent to one decimal). (Total assets at year-end 2011 were $4,407,094 in thousands.)

4. Return on common stockholders' equity (round the percent to one decimal). (Total shareholders' equity at year-end 2011 was $880,943 in thousands.)

5. Basic net income per common share (round to the nearest cent).

TEAMWORK IN ACTION

P1   P2   P3

BTN 13-6   A team approach to learning financial statement analysis is often useful.

Required

1. Each team should write a description of horizontal and vertical analysis that all team members agree with and understand. Illustrate each description with an example.

2. *Each* member of the team is to select *one* of the following categories of ratio analysis. Explain what the ratios in that category measure. Choose one ratio from the category selected, present its formula, and explain what it measures.

Hint: Pairing within teams may be necessary for part 2. Use as an in-class activity or as an assignment. Consider presentations to the entire class using team rotation with transparencies.

   a. Liquidity and efficiency   **c.** Profitability

   b. Solvency   **d.** Market prospects

3. Each team member is to present his or her notes from part 2 to teammates. Team members are to confirm or correct other teammates' presentations.

ENTREPRENEURIAL DECISION

A1   P1   P2   P3

BTN 13-7   Assume that David and Tom Gardner of The Motley Fool (Fool.com) have impressed you since you first heard of their rather improbable rise to prominence in financial circles. You learn of a staff opening at The Motley Fool and decide to apply for it. Your resume is successfully screened from the thousands received and you advance to the interview process. You learn that the interview consists of analyzing the following financial facts and answering analysis questions below. (The data are taken from a small merchandiser in outdoor recreational equipment.)

	2015	2014	2013
Sales trend percents	137.0%	125.0%	100.0%
Selling expenses to sales	9.8%	13.7%	15.3%
Sales to plant assets ratio	3.5 to 1	3.3 to 1	3.0 to 1
Current ratio	2.6 to 1	2.4 to 1	2.1 to 1
Acid-test ratio	0.8 to 1	1.1 to 1	1.2 to 1
Merchandise inventory turnover	7.5 times	8.7 times	9.9 times
Accounts receivable turnover	6.7 times	7.4 times	8.2 times
Total asset turnover	2.6 times	2.6 times	3.0 times
Return on total assets	8.8%	9.4%	11.1%
Return on equity	9.75%	11.50%	12.25%
Profit margin ratio	3.3%	3.5%	3.7%

Required

Use these data to answer each of the following questions with explanations.

1. Is it becoming easier for the company to meet its current liabilities on time and to take advantage of any available cash discounts? Explain.
2. Is the company collecting its accounts receivable more rapidly? Explain.
3. Is the company's investment in accounts receivable decreasing? Explain.
4. Is the company's investment in plant assets increasing? Explain.
5. Is the owner's investment becoming more profitable? Explain.
6. Did the dollar amount of selling expenses decrease during the three-year period? Explain.

BTN 13-8   You are to devise an investment strategy to enable you to accumulate $1,000,000 by age 65. Start by making some assumptions about your salary. Next compute the percent of your salary that you will be able to save each year. If you will receive any lump-sum monies, include those amounts in your calculations. Historically, stocks have delivered average annual returns of 10–11%. Given this history, you should probably not assume that you will earn above 10% on the money you invest. It is not necessary to specify exactly what types of assets you will buy for your investments; just assume a rate you expect to earn. Use the future value tables in Appendix B to calculate how your savings will grow. Experiment a bit with your figures to see how much less you have to save if you start at, for example, age 25 versus age 35 or 40. (For this assignment, do not include inflation in your calculations.)

HITTING THE ROAD

C1   P3

BTN 13-9   Samsung (www.Samsung.com), which is a leading manufacturer of consumer electronic products, along with Apple and Google, are competitors in the global marketplace. Key figures for Samsung follow (in KRW millions).

GLOBAL DECISION

A1

Samsung
APPLE
GOOGLE

Cash and equivalents	₩ 16,284,780	Cost of sales	₩137,696,309
Accounts receivable, net	27,875,934	Revenues	228,692,667
Inventories	19,134,868	Total assets	214,075,018
Retained earnings	148,600,282		

Required

1. Compute common-size percents for Samsung using the data provided. (Round percents to one decimal.)
2. Compare the results with Apple and Google from BTN 13-2.

ANSWERS TO MULTIPLE CHOICE QUIZ

1. d; ($351,000/$300,000) × 100 = 117%
2. e; ($86,000 + $76,000 + $122,000 + $12,000)/$124,000 = 2.39
3. c; ($86,000 + $76,000)/$124,000 = 1.31
4. a; ($124,000 + $90,000)/$830,000 = 25.78%
5. d; ($300,000 + $316,000)/$830,000 = 74.22%

appendix A

Financial Statement Information

This appendix includes financial information for (1) Apple, (2) Google, and (3) Samsung. Apple states that it designs, manufactures, and markets mobile communication and media devices, personal computers, and portable digital music players, and sells a variety of related software, services, peripherals, networking solutions, and third-party digital content and applications; it competes with both Google and Samsung in the United States and globally. The information in this appendix is taken from their annual 10-K reports (or annual report for Samsung) filed with the SEC or other regulatory agency. An **annual report** is a summary of a company's financial results for the year along with its current financial condition and future plans. This report is directed to external users of financial information, but it also affects the actions and decisions of internal users.

A company often uses an annual report to showcase itself and its products. Many annual reports include photos, diagrams, and illustrations related to the company. The primary objective of annual reports, however, is the financial section, which communicates much information about a company, with most data drawn from the accounting information system. The layout of an annual report's financial section is fairly established and typically includes the following:

- Letter to Shareholders
- Financial History and Highlights
- Management Discussion and Analysis
- Management's Report on Financial Statements and on Internal Controls
- Report of Independent Accountants (Auditor's Report) and on Internal Controls
- Financial Statements
- Notes to Financial Statements
- List of Directors and Officers

This appendix provides the financial statements for Apple (plus selected notes), Google, and Samsung. The appendix is organized as follows:

- Apple **A-2** through **A-9**
- Google **A-10** through **A-13**
- Samsung **A-14** through **A-17**

Many assignments at the end of each chapter refer to information in this appendix. We encourage readers to spend time with these assignments; they are especially useful in showing the relevance and diversity of financial accounting and reporting.

APPLE
GOOGLE
Samsung

Special note: The SEC maintains the EDGAR (**E**lectronic **D**ata **G**athering, **A**nalysis, and **R**etrieval) database at www.SEC.gov for U.S. filers. The **Form 10-K** is the annual report form for most companies. It provides electronically accessible information. The **Form 10-KSB** is the annual report form filed by small businesses. It requires slightly less information than the Form 10-K. One of these forms must be filed within 90 days after the company's fiscal year-end. (Forms 10-K405, 10-KT, 10-KT405, and 10-KSB405 are slight variations of the usual form due to certain regulations or rules.)

APPLE

Apple Inc.
CONSOLIDATED BALANCE SHEETS
(In millions, except number of shares which are reflected in thousands)

	September 28, 2013	September 29, 2012
ASSETS:		
Current assets:		
Cash and cash equivalents	$ 14,259	$ 10,746
Short-term marketable securities	26,287	18,383
Accounts receivable, less allowances of $99 and $98, respectively	13,102	10,930
Inventories	1,764	791
Deferred tax assets	3,453	2,583
Vendor non-trade receivables	7,539	7,762
Other current assets	6,882	6,458
Total current assets	73,286	57,653
Long-term marketable securities	106,215	92,122
Property, plant and equipment, net	16,597	15,452
Goodwill	1,577	1,135
Acquired intangible assets, net	4,179	4,224
Other assets	5,146	5,478
Total assets	$ 207,000	$ 176,064
LIABILITIES AND SHAREHOLDERS' EQUITY:		
Current liabilities:		
Accounts payable	$ 22,367	$ 21,175
Accrued expenses	13,856	11,414
Deferred revenue	7,435	5,953
Total current liabilities	43,658	38,542
Deferred revenue – non-current	2,625	2,648
Long-term debt	16,960	0
Other non-current liabilities	20,208	16,664
Total liabilities	83,451	57,854
Commitments and contingencies		
Shareholders' equity:		
Common stock, no par value; 1,800,000 shares authorized; 899,213 and 939,208 shares issued and outstanding, respectively	19,764	16,422
Retained earnings	104,256	101,289
Accumulated other comprehensive income/(loss)	(471)	499
Total shareholders' equity	123,549	118,210
Total liabilities and shareholders' equity	$ 207,000	$ 176,064

See accompanying Notes to Consolidated Financial Statements.

Apple Inc.
CONSOLIDATED STATEMENTS OF OPERATIONS
(In millions, except number of shares which are reflected in thousands and per share amounts)

Years ended	September 28, 2013	September 29, 2012	September 24, 2011
Net sales	$ 170,910	$ 156,508	$ 108,249
Cost of sales	106,606	87,846	64,431
Gross margin	64,304	68,662	43,818
Operating expenses:			
Research and development	4,475	3,381	2,429
Selling, general and administrative	10,830	10,040	7,599
Total operating expenses	15,305	13,421	10,028
Operating income	48,999	55,241	33,790
Other income/(expense), net	1,156	522	415
Income before provision for income taxes	50,155	55,763	34,205
Provision for income taxes	13,118	14,030	8,283
Net income	$ 37,037	$ 41,733	$ 25,922
Earnings per share:			
Basic	$ 40.03	$ 44.64	$ 28.05
Diluted	$ 39.75	$ 44.15	$ 27.68
Shares used in computing earnings per share:			
Basic	925,331	934,818	924,258
Diluted	931,662	945,355	936,645
Cash dividends declared per common share	$ 11.40	$ 2.65	$ 0.00

Apple Inc.
CONSOLIDATED STATEMENTS OF COMPREHENSIVE INCOME
(In millions)

Years ended	September 28, 2013	September 29, 2012	September 24, 2011
Net income	$ 37,037	$ 41,733	$ 25,922
Other comprehensive income/(loss):			
Change in foreign currency translation, net of tax effects of $35, $13 and $18, respectively	(112)	(15)	(12)
Change in unrecognized gains/losses on derivative instruments:			
Change in fair value of derivatives, net of tax benefit/(expense) of $(351), $73 and $(50),respectively	522	(131)	92
Adjustment for net losses/(gains) realized and included in net income, net of tax expense/(benefit) of $255, $220 and $(250), respectively	(458)	(399)	450
Total change in unrecognized gains/losses on derivative instruments, net of tax	64	(530)	542
Change in unrealized gains/losses on marketable securities:			
Change in fair value of marketable securities, net of tax benefit/(expense) of $458, $(421) and $17, respectively	(791)	715	29
Adjustment for net losses/(gains) realized and included in net income, net of tax expense/(benefit) of $82, $68 and $(40), respectively	(131)	(114)	(70)
Total change in unrealized gains/losses on marketable securities, net of tax	(922)	601	(41)
Total other comprehensive income/(loss)	(970)	56	489
Total comprehensive income	$ 36,067	$ 41,789	$ 26,411

See accompanying Notes to Consolidated Financial Statements.

Apple Inc.
CONSOLIDATED STATEMENTS OF SHAREHOLDERS' EQUITY
(In millions, except number of shares which are reflected in thousands)

	Common Stock		Retained Earnings	Accumulated Other Comprehensive Income/ (Loss)	Total Shareholders' Equity
	Shares	Amount			
Balances as of September 25, 2010	915,970	$ 10,668	$ 37,169	$ (46)	$ 47,791
Net income	0	0	25,922	0	25,922
Other comprehensive income/(loss)	0	0	0	489	489
Share-based compensation	0	1,168	0	0	1,168
Common stock issued under stock plans, net of shares withheld for employee taxes	13,307	561	(250)	0	311
Tax benefit from equity awards, including transfer pricing adjustments	0	934	0	0	934
Balances as of September 24, 2011	929,277	13,331	62,841	443	76,615
Net income	0	0	41,733	0	41,733
Other comprehensive income/(loss)	0	0	0	56	56
Dividends and dividend equivalent rights declared	0	0	(2,523)	0	(2,523)
Share-based compensation	0	1,740	0	0	1,740
Common stock issued under stock plans, net of shares withheld for employee taxes	9,931	200	(762)	0	(562)
Tax benefit from equity awards, including transfer pricing adjustments	0	1,151	0	0	1,151
Balances as of September 29, 2012	939,208	16,422	101,289	499	118,210
Net income	0	0	37,037	0	37,037
Other comprehensive income/(loss)	0	0	0	(970)	(970)
Dividends and dividend equivalent rights declared	0	0	(10,676)	0	(10,676)
Repurchase of common stock	(46,976)	0	(22,950)	0	(22,950)
Share-based compensation	0	2,253	0	0	2,253
Common stock issued under stock plans, net of shares withheld for employee taxes	6,981	(143)	(444)	0	(587)
Tax benefit from equity awards, including transfer pricing adjustments	0	1,232	0	0	1,232
Balances as of September 28, 2013	899,213	$ 19,764	$104,256	$ (471)	$ 123,549

See accompanying Notes to Consolidated Financial Statements.

Apple Inc.
CONSOLIDATED STATEMENTS OF CASH FLOWS
(In millions)

Years ended	September 28, 2013	September 29, 2012	September 24, 2011
Cash and cash equivalents, beginning of the year	$ 10,746	$ 9,815	$ 11,261
Operating activities:			
Net income	37,037	41,733	25,922
Adjustments to reconcile net income to cash generated by operating activities:			
Depreciation and amortization	6,757	3,277	1,814
Share-based compensation expense	2,253	1,740	1,168
Deferred income tax expense	1,141	4,405	2,868
Changes in operating assets and liabilities:			
Accounts receivable, net	(2,172)	(5,551)	143
Inventories	(973)	(15)	275
Vendor non-trade receivables	223	(1,414)	(1,934)
Other current and non-current assets	1,080	(3,162)	(1,391)
Accounts payable	2,340	4,467	2,515
Deferred revenue	1,459	2,824	1,654
Other current and non-current liabilities	4,521	2,552	4,495
Cash generated by operating activities	53,666	50,856	37,529
Investing activities:			
Purchases of marketable securities	(148,489)	(151,232)	(102,317)
Proceeds from maturities of marketable securities	20,317	13,035	20,437
Proceeds from sales of marketable securities	104,130	99,770	49,416
Payments made in connection with business acquisitions, net	(496)	(350)	(244)
Payments for acquisition of property, plant and equipment	(8,165)	(8,295)	(4,260)
Payments for acquisition of intangible assets	(911)	(1,107)	(3,192)
Other	(160)	(48)	(259)
Cash used in investing activities	(33,774)	(48,227)	(40,419)
Financing activities:			
Proceeds from issuance of common stock	530	665	831
Excess tax benefits from equity awards	701	1,351	1,133
Taxes paid related to net share settlement of equity awards	(1,082)	(1,226)	(520)
Dividends and dividend equivalent rights paid	(10,564)	(2,488)	0
Repurchase of common stock	(22,860)	0	0
Proceeds from issuance of long-term debt, net	16,896	0	0
Cash generated by/(used in) financing activities	(16,379)	(1,698)	1,444
Increase/(decrease) in cash and cash equivalents	3,513	931	(1,446)
Cash and cash equivalents, end of the year	$ 14,259	$ 10,746	$ 9,815
Supplemental cash flow disclosure:			
Cash paid for income taxes, net	$ 9,128	$ 7,682	$ 3,338

See accompanying Notes to Consolidated Financial Statements.

APPLE

APPLE INC.
SELECTED NOTES TO CONSOLIDATED FINANCIAL STATEMENTS

Basis of Presentation and Preparation

The Company's fiscal year is the 52- or 53-week period that ends on the last Saturday of September. The Company's fiscal years 2013, 2012 and 2011 ended on September 28, 2013, September 29, 2012 and September 24, 2011, respectively. An additional week is included in the first fiscal quarter approximately every six years to realign fiscal quarters with calendar quarters. Fiscal year 2012 spanned 53 weeks, with a 14th week included in the first quarter of 2012. Fiscal years 2013 and 2011 spanned 52 weeks each. Unless otherwise stated, references to particular years, quarters, months and periods refer to the Company's fiscal years ended in September and the associated quarters, months and periods of those fiscal years.

Revenue Recognition

Net sales consist primarily of revenue from the sale of hardware, software, digital content and applications, peripherals, and service and support contracts. The Company recognizes revenue when persuasive evidence of an arrangement exists, delivery has occurred, the sales price is fixed or determinable, and collection is probable. Product is considered delivered to the customer once it has been shipped and title and risk of loss have been transferred. For most of the Company's product sales, these criteria are met at the time the product is shipped. For online sales to individuals, for some sales to education customers in the U.S., and for certain other sales, the Company defers revenue until the customer receives the product because the Company retains a portion of the risk of loss on these sales during transit. The Company recognizes revenue from the sale of hardware products, software bundled with hardware that is essential to the functionality of the hardware, and third-party digital content sold on the iTunes Store in accordance with general revenue recognition accounting guidance. The Company recognizes revenue in accordance with industry specific software accounting guidance for the following types of sales transactions: (i) standalone sales of software products, (ii) sales of software upgrades and (iii) sales of software bundled with hardware not essential to the functionality of the hardware.

For the sale of most third-party products, the Company recognizes revenue based on the gross amount billed to customers because the Company establishes its own pricing for such products, retains related inventory risk for physical products, is the primary obligor to the customer and assumes the credit risk for amounts billed to its customers. For third-party applications sold through the App Store and Mac App Store and certain digital content sold through the iTunes Store, the Company does not determine the selling price of the products and is not the primary obligor to the customer. Therefore, the Company accounts for such sales on a net basis by recognizing in net sales only the commission it retains from each sale. The portion of the gross amount billed to customers that is remitted by the Company to third-party app developers and certain digital content owners is not reflected in the Company's Consolidated Statements of Operations.

The Company records deferred revenue when it receives payments in advance of the delivery of products or the performance of services. This includes amounts that have been deferred for unspecified and specified software upgrade rights and non-software services that are attached to hardware and software products. The Company sells gift cards redeemable at its retail and online stores, and also sells gift cards redeemable on the iTunes Store for the purchase of digital content and software. The Company records deferred revenue upon the sale of the card, which is relieved upon redemption of the card by the customer. Revenue from AppleCare service and support contracts is deferred and recognized over the service coverage periods. AppleCare service and support contracts typically include extended phone support, repair services, web-based support resources and diagnostic tools offered under the Company's standard limited warranty.

The Company records reductions to revenue for estimated commitments related to price protection and other customer incentive programs. For transactions involving price protection, the Company recognizes revenue net of the estimated amount to be refunded. For the Company's other customer incentive programs, the estimated cost of these programs is recognized at the later of the date at which the Company has sold the product or the date at which the program is offered. The Company also records reductions to revenue for expected future product returns based on the Company's historical experience. Revenue is recorded net of taxes collected from customers that are remitted to governmental authorities, with the collected taxes recorded as current liabilities until remitted to the relevant government authority.

Shipping Costs

For all periods presented, amounts billed to customers related to shipping and handling are classified as revenue, and the Company's shipping and handling costs are included in cost of sales.

Warranty Expense

The Company generally provides for the estimated cost of hardware and software warranties at the time the related revenue is recognized. The Company assesses the adequacy of its pre-existing warranty liabilities and adjusts the amounts as necessary based on actual experience and changes in future estimates.

Apple Inc. Notes—continued

Software Development Costs

Research and development costs are expensed as incurred. Development costs of computer software to be sold, leased, or otherwise marketed are subject to capitalization beginning when a product's technological feasibility has been established and ending when a product is available for general release to customers. In most instances, the Company's products are released soon after technological feasibility has been established. Costs incurred subsequent to achievement of technological feasibility were not significant, and software development costs were expensed as incurred during 2013, 2012 and 2011.

Advertising Costs

Advertising costs are expensed as incurred and included in selling, general and administrative expenses. Advertising expense was $1.1 billion, $1.0 billion and $933 million for 2013, 2012 and 2011, respectively.

Earnings Per Share

Basic earnings per share is computed by dividing income available to common shareholders by the weighted-average number of shares of common stock outstanding during the period. Diluted earnings per share is computed by dividing income available to common shareholders by the weighted-average number of shares of common stock outstanding during the period increased to include the number of additional shares of common stock that would have been outstanding if the potentially dilutive securities had been issued.

Cash Equivalents and Marketable Securities

All highly liquid investments with maturities of three months or less at the date of purchase are classified as cash equivalents. The Company's marketable debt and equity securities have been classified and accounted for as available-for-sale. Management determines the appropriate classification of its investments at the time of purchase and reevaluates the designations at each balance sheet date. The Company classifies its marketable debt securities as either short-term or long-term based on each instrument's underlying contractual maturity date. Marketable debt securities with maturities of 12 months or less are classified as short-term and marketable debt securities with maturities greater than 12 months are classified as long-term. The Company classifies its marketable equity securities, including mutual funds, as either short-term or long-term based on the nature of each security and its availability for use in current operations. The Company's marketable debt and equity securities are carried at fair value, with the unrealized gains and losses, net of taxes, reported as a component of shareholders' equity. The cost of securities sold is based upon the specific identification method.

Accounts Receivable (Trade Receivables)

The Company has considerable trade receivables outstanding with its third-party cellular network carriers, wholesalers, retailers, value-added resellers, small and mid-sized businesses, and education, enterprise and government customers. The Company's cellular network carriers accounted for 68% and 66% of trade receivables as of September 28, 2013 and September 29, 2012, respectively. The additions and write-offs to the Company's allowance for doubtful accounts during 2013, 2012 and 2011 were not significant.

Allowance for Doubtful Accounts

The Company records its allowance for doubtful accounts based upon its assessment of various factors. The Company considers historical experience, the age of the accounts receivable balances, credit quality of the Company's customers, current economic conditions, and other factors that may affect customers' ability to pay.

Inventories

Inventories are stated at the lower of cost, computed using the first-in, first-out method, or market. If the cost of the inventories exceeds their market value, provisions are made currently for the difference between the cost and the market value.

Inventories	2013	2012
Components	$ 683	$124
Finished goods	1,081	667
Total inventories	$1,764	$791

Property, Plant and Equipment

Property, plant and equipment are stated at cost. Depreciation is computed by use of the straight-line method over the estimated useful lives of the assets, which for buildings is the lesser of 30 years or the remaining life of the underlying building; between two to five years for machinery and equipment, including product tooling and manufacturing process equipment; and the shorter of lease terms or ten years for leasehold improvements. The Company capitalizes eligible costs to acquire or develop internal-use software that are incurred subsequent to the preliminary project stage. Capitalized costs related to internal-use software are amortized using the straight-line method over the estimated useful lives of the assets, which range from three to five years. Depreciation and amortization expense on property and equipment was $5.8 billion, $2.6 billion and $1.6 billion during 2013, 2012 and 2011, respectively.

Property, Plant and Equipment	2013	2012
Land and buildings	$ 3,309	$ 2,439
Machinery, equipment and internal-use software	21,242	15,984
Leasehold improvements	3,968	3,464
Gross property, plant and equipment	28,519	21,887
Accumulated depreciation and amortization	(11,922)	(6,435)
Net property, plant and equipment	$16,597	$15,452

APPLE

Apple Inc. Notes—continued

Long-Lived Assets Including Goodwill and Other Acquired Intangible Assets

The Company reviews property, plant and equipment, inventory component prepayments, and certain identifiable intangibles, excluding goodwill, for impairment. Long-lived assets are reviewed for impairment whenever events or changes in circumstances indicate the carrying amount of an asset may not be recoverable. Recoverability of these assets is measured by comparison of their carrying amounts to future undiscounted cash flows the assets are expected to generate. If property, plant and equipment, inventory component prepayments, and certain identifiable intangibles are considered to be impaired, the impairment to be recognized equals the amount by which the carrying value of the assets exceeds its fair value. The Company did not record any significant impairments during 2013, 2012 and 2011.

The Company does not amortize goodwill and intangible assets with indefinite useful lives, rather such assets are required to be tested for impairment at least annually or sooner whenever events or changes in circumstances indicate that the assets may be impaired. The Company performs its goodwill and intangible asset impairment tests in the fourth quarter of each year. The Company did not recognize any impairment charges related to goodwill or indefinite lived intangible assets during 2013, 2012 and 2011. The Company established reporting units based on its current reporting structure. For purposes of testing goodwill for impairment, goodwill has been allocated to these reporting units to the extent it relates to each reporting unit. In 2013 and 2012, the Company's goodwill was allocated to the Americas and Europe reportable operating segments.

The Company amortizes its intangible assets with definite useful lives over their estimated useful lives and reviews these assets for impairment. The Company is currently amortizing its acquired intangible assets with definite useful lives over periods typically from three to seven years.

Goodwill and Other Intangible Assets

The Company's acquired intangible assets with definite useful lives primarily consist of patents and licenses and are amortized over periods typically from three to seven years. The following table summarizes the components of gross and net intangible asset balances as of September 28, 2013 (in millions):

	Gross Carrying Amount	Accumulated Amortization	Net Carrying Amount
Definite lived and amortizable acquired intangible assets	$ 6,081	$ (2,002)	$ 4,079
Indefinite lived and non-amortizable trademarks	100	0	100
Total acquired intangible assets	$ 6,181	$ (2,002)	$ 4,179

The Company's gross carrying amount of goodwill was $1.6 billion and $1.1 billion as of September 28, 2013 and September 29, 2012, respectively. The Company did not have any goodwill impairment during 2013, 2012 or 2011. Amortization expense related to acquired intangible assets was $960 million, $605 million and $192 million in 2013, 2012 and 2011, respectively.

Fair Value Measurements

The Company applies fair value accounting for all financial assets and liabilities and non-financial assets and liabilities that are recognized or disclosed at fair value in the financial statements on a recurring basis. The Company defines fair value as the price that would be received from selling an asset or paid to transfer a liability in an orderly transaction between market participants at the measurement date. When determining the fair value measurements for assets and liabilities, which are required to be recorded at fair value, the Company considers the principal or most advantageous market in which the Company would transact and the market-based risk measurements or assumptions that market participants would use in pricing the asset or liability, such as risks inherent in valuation techniques, transfer restrictions and credit risk. Fair value is estimated by applying the following hierarchy, which prioritizes the inputs used to measure fair value into three levels and bases the categorization within the hierarchy upon the lowest level of input that is available and significant to the fair value measurement:

Level 1—Quoted prices in active markets for identical assets or liabilities.

Level 2—Observable inputs other than quoted prices in active markets for identical assets and liabilities, quoted prices for identical or similar assets or liabilities in inactive markets, or other inputs that are observable or can be corroborated by observable market data for substantially the full term of the assets or liabilities.

Level 3—Inputs that are generally unobservable and typically reflect management's estimate of assumptions that market participants would use in pricing the asset or liability.

The Company's valuation techniques used to measure the fair value of money market funds and certain marketable equity securities were derived from quoted prices in active markets for identical assets or liabilities. The valuation techniques used to measure the fair value of all other financial instruments, all of which have counterparties with high credit ratings, were valued based on quoted market prices or model driven valuations using significant inputs

Apple Inc. Notes—continued

derived from or corroborated by observable market data. In accordance with the fair value accounting requirements, companies may choose to measure eligible financial instruments and certain other items at fair value. The Company has not elected the fair value option for any eligible financial instruments.

Accrued Warranty and Indemnification

The Company offers a basic limited parts and labor warranty on its hardware products. The basic warranty period for hardware products is typically one year from the date of purchase by the end-user. The Company also offers a 90-day basic warranty for its service parts used to repair the Company's hardware products. The Company provides currently for the estimated cost that may be incurred under its basic limited product warranties at the time related revenue is recognized. Factors considered in determining appropriate accruals for product warranty obligations include the size of the installed base of products subject to warranty protection, historical and projected warranty claim rates, historical and projected cost-per-claim, and knowledge of specific product failures that are outside of the Company's typical experience. The Company assesses the adequacy of its pre-existing warranty liabilities and adjusts the amounts as necessary based on actual experience and changes in future estimates. The following table shows changes in the Company's accrued warranties and related costs for 2013, 2012 and 2011 (in millions):

	2013	2012	2011
Beginning accrued warranty and related costs	$ 1,638	$ 1,240	$ 761
Cost of warranty claims	(3,703)	(1,786)	(1,147)
Accruals for product warranty	5,032	2,184	1,626
Ending accrued warranty and related costs	$ 2,967	$ 1,638	$ 1,240

Accrued Expenses	2013	2012
Accrued warranty and related costs	$ 2,967	$ 1,638
Accrued taxes	1,200	1,535
Deferred margin on component sales	1,262	1,492
Accrued marketing and selling expenses	1,291	910
Accrued compensation and employee benefits	959	735
Other current liabilities	6,177	5,104
Total accrued expenses	$13,856	$11,414

Non-Current Liabilities	2013	2012
Deferred tax liabilities	$16,489	$13,847
Other non-current liabilities	3,719	2,817
Total other non-current liabilities	$20,208	$16,664

Long-Term Debt

In May 2013, the Company issued floating- and fixed-rate notes with varying maturities for an aggregate principal amount of $17.0 billion (collectively the "Notes"). The Notes are senior unsecured obligations, and interest is payable in arrears, quarterly for the floating-rate notes and semi-annually for the fixed-rate notes. As of September 28, 2013, the fair value of the Company's Notes, based on Level 2 inputs, was $15.9 billion.

Segment Information and Geographic Data

The following table shows information by operating segment for 2013, 2012 and 2011 (in millions):

	2013	2012	2011
Americas:			
Net sales	$62,739	$57,512	$38,315
Operating income	$22,817	$23,414	$13,111
Europe:			
Net sales	$37,883	$36,323	$27,778
Operating income	$13,025	$14,869	$11,209
Greater China:			
Net sales	$25,417	$22,533	$12,690
Operating income	$ 8,541	$ 9,843	$ 5,246
Japan:			
Net sales	$13,462	$10,571	$ 5,437
Operating income	$ 6,819	$ 5,861	$ 2,415
Rest of Asia Pacific:			
Net sales	$11,181	$10,741	$ 9,902
Operating income	$ 3,753	$ 4,253	$ 4,004
Retail:			
Net sales	$20,228	$18,828	$14,127
Operating income	$ 4,025	$ 4,613	$ 3,075

Google Inc.
CONSOLIDATED BALANCE SHEETS
(In millions, except share and par value amounts which are reflected in thousands, and par value per share amounts)

As of December 31	2012	2013
Assets		
Current assets:		
Cash and cash equivalents	$ 14,778	$ 18,898
Marketable securities	33,310	39,819
Total cash, cash equivalents, and marketable securities (including securities loaned of $3,160 and $5,059)	48,088	58,717
Accounts receivable, net of allowance of $581 and $631	7,885	8,882
Inventories	505	426
Receivable under reverse repurchase agreements	700	100
Deferred income taxes, net	1,144	1,526
Income taxes receivable, net	0	408
Prepaid revenue share, expenses and other assets	2,132	2,827
Total current assets	60,454	72,886
Prepaid revenue share, expenses and other assets, non-current	2,011	1,976
Non-marketable equity investments	1,469	1,976
Property and equipment, net	11,854	16,524
Intangible assets, net	7,473	6,066
Goodwill	10,537	11,492
Total assets	$ 93,798	$ 110,920
Liabilities and Stockholders' Equity		
Current liabilities:		
Accounts payable	$ 2,012	$ 2,453
Short-term debt	2,549	3,009
Accrued compensation and benefits	2,239	2,502
Accrued expenses and other current liabilities	3,258	3,755
Accrued revenue share	1,471	1,729
Securities lending payable	1,673	1,374
Deferred revenue	895	1,062
Income taxes payable, net	240	24
Total current liabilities	14,337	15,908
Long-term debt	2,988	2,236
Deferred revenue, non-current	100	139
Income taxes payable, non-current	2,046	2,638
Deferred income taxes, net, non-current	1,872	1,947
Other long-term liabilities	740	743
Commitments and contingencies		
Stockholders' equity:		
Convertible preferred stock, $0.001 par value per share, 100,000 shares authorized; no shares issued and outstanding	0	0
Class A and Class B common stock and additional paid-in capital, $0.001 par value per share: 12,000,000 shares authorized (Class A 9,000,000, Class B 3,000,000); 329,979 (Class A 267,448, Class B 62,531) and par value of $330 (Class A $267, Class B $63) and 335,832 (Class A 279,325, Class B 56,507) and par value of $336 (Class A $279, Class B $57) shares issued and outstanding	22,835	25,922
Class C capital stock, $0.001 par value per share: 3,000,000 shares authorized; no shares issued and outstanding	0	0
Accumulated other comprehensive income	538	125
Retained earnings	48,342	61,262
Total stockholders' equity	71,715	87,309
Total liabilities and stockholders' equity	$ 93,798	$ 110,920

See accompanying notes.

Google Inc.
CONSOLIDATED STATEMENTS OF INCOME
(In millions, except per share amounts)

Year Ended December 31	2011	2012	2013
Revenues:			
Google (advertising and other)	$37,905	$46,039	$55,519
Motorola Mobile (hardware and other)	0	4,136	4,306
Total revenues	$37,905	$50,175	$59,825
Costs and expenses:			
Cost of revenues—Google (advertising and other) [(1)]	13,188	17,176	21,993
Cost of revenues—Motorola Mobile (hardware and other)[(1)]	0	3,458	3,865
Research and development[(1)]	5,162	6,793	7,952
Sales and marketing[(1)]	4,589	6,143	7,253
General and administrative[(1)]	2,724	3,845	4,796
Charge related to the resolution of Department of Justice investigation	500	0	0
Total costs and expenses	26,163	37,415	45,859
Income from operations	11,742	12,760	13,966
Interest and other income, net	584	626	530
Income from continuing operations before income taxes	12,326	13,386	14,496
Provision for income taxes	2,589	2,598	2,282
Net income from continuing operations	$ 9,737	$10,788	$12,214
Net income (loss) from discontinued operations	0	(51)	706
Net income	$ 9,737	$10,737	$12,920
Net income (loss) per share of Class A and Class B common stock—basic:			
Continuing operations	$ 30.17	$ 32.97	$ 36.70
Discontinued operations	0.00	(0.16)	2.12
Net income (loss) per share of Class A and Class B common stock—basic	$ 30.17	$ 32.81	$ 38.82
Net income (loss) per share of Class A and Class B common stock—diluted:			
Continuing operations	$ 29.76	$ 32.46	$ 36.05
Discontinued operations	0.00	(0.15)	2.08
Net income (loss) per share of Class A and Class B common stock—diluted	$ 29.76	$ 32.31	$ 38.13
[(1)]Includes stock-based compensation expense as follows:			
Cost of revenues—Google (advertising and other)	$ 249	$ 359	$ 469
Cost of revenues—Motorola Mobile (hardware and other)	0	14	18
Research and development	1,061	1,325	1,717
Sales and marketing	361	498	578
General and administrative	303	453	486
	$ 1,974	$ 2,649	$ 3,268

See accompanying notes.

GOOGLE

Google Inc.
CONSOLIDATED STATEMENTS OF STOCKHOLDERS' EQUITY
(In millions, except for share amounts which are reflected in thousands)

	Class A and Class B Common Stock and Additional Paid-In Capital		Accumulated Other Comprehensive Income	Retained Earnings	Total Stockholders' Equity
	Shares	Amount			
Balance at January 1, 2011	321,301	$ 18,235	$ 138	$ 27,868	$ 46,241
Common stock issued	3,594	621	0	0	621
Stock-based compensation expense		1,974	0	0	1,974
Stock-based compensation tax benefits		60	0	0	60
Tax withholding related to vesting of restricted stock units		(626)	0	0	(626)
Net income		0	0	9,737	9,737
Other comprehensive income		0	138	0	138
Balance at December 31, 2011	324,895	20,264	276	37,605	58,145
Common stock issued	5,084	736	0	0	736
Stock-based compensation expense		2,692	0	0	2,692
Stock-based compensation tax benefits		166	0	0	166
Tax withholding related to vesting of restricted stock units		(1,023)	0	0	(1,023)
Net income		0	0	10,737	10,737
Other comprehensive income		0	262	0	262
Balance at December 31, 2012	329,979	22,835	538	48,342	71,715
Common stock issued	5,853	1,174	0	0	1,174
Stock-based compensation expense		3,343	0	0	3,343
Stock-based compensation tax benefits		449	0	0	449
Tax withholding related to vesting of restricted stock units		(1,879)	0	0	(1,879)
Net income		0	0	12,920	12,920
Other comprehensive income		0	(413)	0	(413)
Balance at December 31, 2013	335,832	$ 25,922	$ 125	$ 61,262	$ 87,309

Google Inc.
CONSOLIDATED STATEMENTS OF COMPREHENSIVE INCOME
(In millions)

Year Ended December 31	2011	2012	2013
Net income	$9,737	$10,737	$12,920
Other comprehensive income (loss):			
Change in foreign currency translation adjustment	(107)	75	89
Available-for-sale investments:			
Change in net unrealized gains	348	493	(392)
Less: reclassification adjustment for net gains included in net income	(115)	(216)	(162)
Net change (net of tax effect of $54, $68, $212)	233	277	(554)
Cash flow hedges:			
Change in unrealized gains	39	47	112
Less: reclassification adjustment for gains included in net income	(27)	(137)	(60)
Net change (net of tax effect of $2, $53, $30)	12	(90)	52
Other comprehensive income (loss)	138	262	(413)
Comprehensive income	$9,875	$10,999	$12,507

See accompanying notes.

Google Inc.
CONSOLIDATED STATEMENTS OF CASH FLOWS
(In millions)

Year Ended December 31	2011	2012	2013
Operating activities			
Net income	$ 9,737	$ 10,737	$ 12,920
Adjustments:			
Depreciation and amortization of property and equipment	1,396	1,988	2,781
Amortization of intangible and other assets	455	974	1,158
Stock-based compensation expense	1,974	2,692	3,343
Excess tax benefits from stock-based award activities	(86)	(188)	(481)
Deferred income taxes	343	(266)	(437)
Impairment of equity investments	110	0	0
Gain on divestiture of businesses	0	(188)	(700)
Other	6	(28)	106
Changes in assets and liabilities, net of effects of acquisitions:			
Accounts receivable	(1,156)	(787)	(1,307)
Income taxes, net	731	1,492	401
Inventories	(30)	301	(234)
Prepaid revenue share, expenses and other assets	(232)	(833)	(696)
Accounts payable	101	(499)	605
Accrued expenses and other liabilities	795	762	713
Accrued revenue share	259	299	254
Deferred revenue	162	163	233
Net cash provided by operating activities	14,565	16,619	18,659
Investing activities			
Purchases of property and equipment	(3,438)	(3,273)	(7,358)
Purchases of marketable securities	(61,672)	(33,410)	(45,444)
Maturities and sales of marketable securities	48,746	35,180	38,314
Investments in non-marketable equity investments	(428)	(696)	(569)
Cash collateral related to securities lending	(354)	(334)	(299)
Investments in reverse repurchase agreements	5	45	600
Proceeds from divestiture of businesses	0	0	2,525
Acquisitions, net of cash acquired, and purchases of intangibles and other assets	(1,900)	(10,568)	(1,448)
Net cash used in investing activities	(19,041)	(13,056)	(13,679)
Financing activities			
Net payments related to stock-based award activities	(5)	(287)	(781)
Excess tax benefits from stock-based award activities	86	188	481
Proceeds from issuance of debt, net of costs	10,905	16,109	10,768
Repayments of debt	(10,179)	(14,781)	(11,325)
Net cash provided by (used in) financing activities	807	1,229	(857)
Effect of exchange rate changes on cash and cash equivalents	22	3	(3)
Net increase (decrease) in cash and cash equivalents	(3,647)	4,795	4,120
Cash and cash equivalents at beginning of period	13,630	9,983	14,778
Cash and cash equivalents at end of period	$ 9,983	$ 14,778	$ 18,898
Supplemental disclosures of cash flow information			
Cash paid for taxes	$ 1,471	$ 2,034	$ 1,932
Cash paid for interest	$ 40	$ 74	$ 72
Non-cash investing and financing activities:			
Receipt of Arris shares in connection with divestiture of Motorola Home	$ 0	$ 0	$ 175
Fair value of stock-based awards assumed in connection with acquisition of Motorola	$ 0	$ 41	$ 0
Property under capital lease	$ 0	$ 0	$ 258

See accompanying notes.

GOOGLE

Samsung Electronics Co., Ltd. and its subsidiaries
CONSOLIDATED STATEMENTS OF FINANCIAL POSITION

(In millions of Korean won)	December 31, 2013	December 31, 2012
	KRW	KRW
Assets		
Current assets		
Cash and cash equivalents	16,284,780	18,791,460
Short-term financial instruments	36,722,702	17,397,937
Available-for-sale financial assets	1,488,527	1,258,874
Trade and other receivables	27,875,934	26,674,596
Advances	1,928,188	1,674,428
Prepaid expenses	2,472,950	2,262,234
Inventories	19,134,868	17,747,413
Other current assets	2,135,589	1,462,075
Assets held for sale	2,716,733	—
Total current assets	110,760,271	87,269,017
Non-current assets		
Available-for-sale financial assets	6,238,380	5,229,175
Associates and joint ventures	6,422,292	8,785,489
Property, plant and equipment	75,496,388	68,484,743
Intangible assets	3,980,600	3,729,705
Long-term prepaid expenses	3,465,783	3,515,479
Deferred income tax assets	4,621,780	2,516,080
Other non-current assets	3,089,524	1,541,882
Total assets	214,075,018	181,071,570
Liabilities and Equity		
Current liabilities		
Trade and other payables	17,633,705	16,889,350
Short-term borrowings	6,438,517	8,443,752
Advances received	1,706,313	1,517,672
Withholdings	1,176,046	966,374
Accrued expenses	11,344,530	9,495,156
Income tax payable	3,386,018	3,222,934
Current portion of long-term borrowings and debentures	2,425,831	999,010
Provisions	6,736,476	5,054,853
Other current liabilities	467,973	343,951
Total current liabilities	51,315,409	46,933,052
Non-current liabilities		
Long-term trade and other payables	1,053,756	1,165,881
Debentures	1,311,068	1,829,374
Long-term borrowings	985,117	3,623,028
Net defined benefit liabilities	1,854,902	1,729,939
Deferred income tax liabilities	6,012,371	3,429,467
Provisions	460,924	408,529
Other non-current liabilities	1,065,461	472,094
Total liabilities	64,059,008	59,591,364
Equity attributable to owners of the parent		
Preferred stock	119,467	119,467
Common stock	778,047	778,047
Share premium	4,403,893	4,403,893
Retained earnings	148,600,282	119,985,689
Other components of equity	(9,459,073)	(8,193,044)
Non-controlling interests	5,573,394	4,386,154
Total equity	150,016,010	121,480,206
Total liabilities and equity	214,075,018	181,071,570

The accompanying notes are an integral part of these consolidated financial statements.

Samsung Electronics Co., Ltd. and its subsidiaries
CONSOLIDATED STATEMENTS OF INCOME

(In millions of Korean won)

For the year ended December 31,	2013	2012
	KRW	KRW
Revenue	228,692,667	201,103,613
Cost of sales	137,696,309	126,651,931
Gross profit	90,996,358	74,451,682
Selling and administrative expenses	54,211,345	45,402,344
Operating profit	36,785,013	29,049,338
Other non-operating income	2,429,551	1,552,989
Other non-operating expense	1,614,048	1,576,025
Share of profit of associates and joint ventures	504,063	986,611
Finance income	8,014,672	7,836,554
Finance costs	7,754,972	7,934,450
Profit before income tax	38,364,279	29,915,017
Income tax expense	7,889,515	6,069,732
Profit for the year	**30,474,764**	**23,845,285**
Profit attributable to owners of the parent	29,821,215	23,185,375
Profit attributable to non-controlling interests	653,549	659,910
Earnings per share for profit attributable to owners of the parent (in Korean Won)		
—Basic	197,841	154,020
—Diluted	197,800	153,950

Samsung Electronics Co., Ltd. and its subsidiaries
CONSOLIDATED STATEMENTS OF COMPREHENSIVE INCOME

(In millions of Korean won)

For the year ended December 31,	2013	2012
	KRW	KRW
Profit for the year	30,474,764	23,845,285
Other comprehensive income		
Items not to be reclassified subsequently to profit or loss:		
Remeasurement of net defined benefit liabilities, net of tax	(213,113)	(504,120)
Items to be reclassified subsequently to profit or loss:		
Changes in value of available-for-sale financial assets, net of tax	186,480	962,184
Share of other comprehensive income (loss) of associates and joint ventures, net of tax	20,756	(350,491)
Foreign currency translation, net of tax	(1,000,961)	(1,824,653)
Other comprehensive loss for the year, net of tax	(1,006,838)	(1,717,080)
Total comprehensive income for the year	29,467,926	22,128,205
Comprehensive income attributable to:		
Owners of the parent	28,837,590	21,499,343
Non-controlling interests	630,336	628,862

The accompanying notes are an integral part of these consolidated financial statements.

Samsung Electronics Co., Ltd. and its subsidiaries
CONSOLIDATED STATEMENTS OF CHANGES IN EQUITY

(In millions of Korean won)	Preferred stock	Common stock	Share premium	Retained earnings	Other components of equity	Equity attributable to owners of the parent	Noncontrolling interests	Total
Balance at January 1, 2012	119,467	778,047	4,403,893	97,622,872	(5,833,896)	97,090,383	4,223,247	101,313,630
Profit for the year	—	—	—	23,185,375	—	23,185,375	659,910	23,845,285
Changes in value of available-for-sale financial assets, net of tax	—	—	—	—	960,688	960,688	1,496	962,184
Share of other comprehensive loss of associates and joint ventures, net of tax	—	—	—	—	(350,491)	(350,491)	—	(350,491)
Foreign currency translation, net of tax	—	—	—	—	(1,789,877)	(1,789,877)	(34,776)	(1,824,653)
Remeasurement of net defined benefit liabilities, net of tax	—	—	—	—	(506,351)	(506,351)	2,231	(504,120)
Total comprehensive income (loss)	—	—	—	23,185,375	(1,686,031)	21,499,344	628,861	22,128,205
Dividends	—	—	—	(827,501)	—	(827,501)	(373,632)	(1,201,133)
Capital transaction under common control	—	—	—	—	(1,089,835)	(1,089,835)	(104,395)	(1,194,230)
Changes in consolidated entities	—	—	—	—	—	—	12,844	12,844
Disposal of treasury stock	—	—	—	—	455,377	455,377	—	455,377
Stock option activities	—	—	—	—	(33,071)	(33,071)	—	(33,071)
Others	—	—	—	4,943	(5,588)	(645)	(771)	(1,416)
Total transactions with owners	—	—	—	(822,558)	(673,117)	(1,495,675)	(465,954)	(1,961,629)
Balance at December 31, 2012	119,467	778,047	4,403,893	119,985,689	(8,193,044)	117,094,052	4,386,154	121,480,206
Profit for the year	—	—	—	29,821,215	—	29,821,215	653,549	30,474,764
Changes in value of available-for-sale financial assets, net of tax	—	—	—	—	187,477	187,477	(997)	186,480
Share of other comprehensive income (loss) of associates and joint ventures, net of tax	—	—	—	—	20,949	20,949	(193)	20,756
Foreign currency translation, net of tax	—	—	—	—	(986,691)	(986,691)	(14,270)	(1,000,961)
Remeasurement of net defined benefit liabilities, net of tax	—	—	—	—	(205,360)	(205,360)	(7,753)	(213,113)
Total comprehensive income (loss)	—	—	—	29,821,215	(983,625)	28,837,590	630,336	29,467,926
Dividends	—	—	—	(1,206,622)	—	(1,206,622)	(42,155)	(1,248,777)
Capital transaction under common control	—	—	—	—	(312,959)	(312,959)	600,042	287,083
Changes in consolidated entities	—	—	—	—	—	—	(918)	(918)
Disposal of treasury stock	—	—	—	—	41,817	41,817	—	41,817
Stock option activities	—	—	—	—	(11,999)	(11,999)	—	(11,999)
Others	—	—	—	—	737	737	(65)	672
Total transactions with owners	—	—	—	(1,206,622)	(282,404)	(1,489,026)	556,904	(932,122)
Balance at December 31, 2013	119,467	778,047	4,403,893	148,600,282	(9,459,073)	144,442,616	5,573,394	150,016,010

The accompanying notes are an integral part of these consolidated financial statements.

Samsung Electronics Co., Ltd. and its subsidiaries
CONSOLIDATED STATEMENTS OF CASH FLOWS

(In millions of Korean won)

For the year ended December 31,	2013	2012
	KRW	KRW
Cash flows from operating activities		
Profit for the year	30,474,764	23,845,285
Adjustments	23,804,832	22,759,559
Changes in operating assets and liabilities	(1,313,245)	(5,777,949)
Cash flows from operating activities	52,966,351	40,826,895
Interest received	1,034,074	789,397
Interest paid	(434,857)	(576,379)
Dividend received	592,217	1,112,940
Income tax paid	(7,450,345)	(4,180,044)
Net cash generated from operating activities	46,707,440	37,972,809
Cash flows from investing activities		
Net increase in short-term financial instruments	(19,391,643)	(5,965,611)
Net decrease (increase) in short-term available-for-sale financial assets	33,663	(589,072)
Proceeds from disposal of long-term available-for-sale financial assets	1,691,463	106,208
Acquisition of long-term available for-sale financial assets	(1,531,356)	(870,249)
Proceeds from disposal of associates and joint ventures	240	41,091
Acquisition of associates and joint ventures	(181,307)	(279,022)
Disposal of property and equipment	377,445	644,062
Purchases of property and equipment	(23,157,587)	(22,965,271)
Disposal of intangible assets	4,562	61,497
Purchases of intangible assets	(934,743)	(650,884)
Cash outflows from business combination	(167,155)	(464,279)
Others	(1,490,601)	(390,024)
Net cash used in investing activities	(44,747,019)	(31,321,554)
Cash flows from financing activities		
Net repayment of short-term borrowings	(1,861,536)	(800,579)
Disposal of treasury stock	34,390	88,473
Proceeds from long-term borrowings and debentures	26,672	1,862,256
Repayment of long-term borrowings and debentures	(1,368,436)	(522,899)
Payment of dividends	(1,249,672)	(1,265,137)
Net increase (decrease) in noncontrolling interests	281,551	(1,200,134)
Others	—	(26,488)
Net cash used in financing activities	(4,137,031)	(1,864,508)
Effect of exchange rate changes on cash and cash equivalents	(330,070)	(687,048)
Net increase (decrease) in cash and cash equivalents	**(2,506,680)**	**4,099,699**
Cash and cash equivalents		
Beginning of the year	18,791,460	14,691,761
End of the year	16,284,780	18,791,460

The accompanying notes are an integral part of these consolidated financial statements.

B

appendix

Time Value of Money

Appendix Preview

PRESENT AND FUTURE VALUE CONCEPTS

C1 Time is money and the concept of interest

VALUE OF A SINGLE AMOUNT

P1 Present value of a single amount

P2 Future value of a single amount

VALUE OF AN ANNUITY

P3 Present value of an annuity

P4 Future value of an annuity

Learning Objectives

CONCEPTUAL

C1 Describe the earning of interest and the concepts of present and future values.

PROCEDURAL

P1 Apply present value concepts to a single amount by using interest tables.

P2 Apply future value concepts to a single amount by using interest tables.

P3 Apply present value concepts to an annuity by using interest tables.

P4 Apply future value concepts to an annuity by using interest tables.

PRESENT AND FUTURE VALUE CONCEPTS

The old saying "Time is money" reflects the notion that as time passes, the values of our assets and liabilities change. This change is due to *interest,* which is a borrower's payment to the owner of an asset for its use. The most common example of interest is a savings account asset. As we keep a balance of cash in the account, it earns interest that the financial institution pays us. An example of a liability is a car loan. As we carry the balance of the loan, we accumulate interest costs on it. We must ultimately repay this loan with interest.

Present and future value computations enable us to measure or estimate the interest component of holding assets or liabilities over time. The present value computation is important when we want to know the value of future-day assets *today.* The future value computation is important when we want to know the value of present-day assets *at a future date.* The first section focuses on the present value of a single amount. The second section focuses on the future value of a single amount. Then both the present and future values of a series of amounts (called an *annuity*) are defined and explained.

C1_____

Describe the earning of interest and the concepts of present and future values.

Decision Insight

What's Five Million Worth?   A maintenance worker duped out of a $5 million scratch-off ticket got his winnings seven years later. Robert Miles bought the ticket in 2006 at a convenience store where the owner and his two sons convinced Miles the ticket was worth $5,000 and paid him $4,000 for it. The brothers waited until 2012 to claim the jackpot, prompting an investigation, which uncovered the fraud. The $5 million will be paid to Miles as a $250,000 annuity over 20 years or as a lump-sum payment of $3,210,000, which results in about $2,124,378 after taxes. ■

PRESENT VALUE OF A SINGLE AMOUNT

We graphically express the present value, called p, of a single future amount, called f, that is received or paid at a future date in Exhibit B.1.

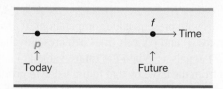

EXHIBIT B.1

Present Value of a Single Amount Diagram

P1_____

Apply present value concepts to a single amount by using interest tables.

The formula to compute the present value of a single amount is shown in Exhibit B.2, where p = present value (PV); f = future value (FV); i = rate of interest per period; and n = number of periods. (Interest is also called the *discount,* and an interest rate is also called the *discount rate.*)

$$p = \frac{f}{(1 + i)^n}$$

EXHIBIT B.2

Present Value of a Single Amount Formula

To illustrate present value concepts, assume that we need $220 one period from today. We want to know how much we must invest now, for one period, at an interest rate of 10% to provide for this $220. For this illustration, the p, or present value, is the unknown amount—the specifics are shown graphically as follows:

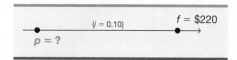

Conceptually, we know p must be less than $220. This is obvious from the answer to this question: Would we rather have $220 today or $220 at some future date? If we had $220 today, we could invest it and see it grow to something more than $220 in the future. Therefore, we would prefer the $220 today. This means that if we were promised $220 in the future, we would take less than $220 today. But how much less? To answer that question, we compute an estimate of the present value of the $220 to be received one period from now using the formula in Exhibit B.2 as follows:

$$p = \frac{f}{(1 + i)^n} = \frac{\$220}{(1 + 0.10)^1} = \$200$$

Point: The FV factor when n = 2 and i = 10%, is 1.2100. Its reciprocal, 0.8264, is the PV factor when n = 2 and i = 10%.

We interpret this result to say that given an interest rate of 10%, we are indifferent between $200 today or $220 at the end of one period.

We can also use this formula to compute the present value for *any number of periods*. To illustrate, consider a payment of $242 at the end of two periods at 10% interest. The present value of this $242 to be received two periods from now is computed as follows:

$$p = \frac{f}{(1 + i)^n} = \frac{\$242}{(1 + 0.10)^2} = \$200$$

Together, these results tell us we are indifferent between $200 today, or $220 one period from today, or $242 two periods from today given a 10% interest rate per period.

The number of periods (n) in the present value formula does not have to be expressed in years. Any period of time such as a day, a month, a quarter, or a year can be used. Whatever period is used, the interest rate (i) must be compounded for the same period. This means that if a situation expresses n in months and i equals 12% per year, then i is transformed into interest earned per month (or 1%). In this case, interest is said to be *compounded monthly*. For example, the present value of $1 when n is 12 months and i is 12% compounded monthly follows:

$$p = \frac{1}{(1 + .01)^{12}} = \$0.8874$$

A present value table helps us with present value computations. It gives us present values (factors) for a variety of both interest rates (i) and periods (n). Each present value in a present value table assumes that the future value (f) equals 1. When the future value (f) is different from 1, we simply multiply the present value (p) from the table by that future value to give us the estimate. The formula used to construct a table of present values for a single future amount of 1 is shown in Exhibit B.3.

EXHIBIT B.3

Present Value of 1 Formula

$$p = \frac{1}{(1 + i)^n}$$

This formula is identical to that in Exhibit B.2 except that f equals 1. Table B.1 at the end of this appendix is such a present value table. It is often called a **present value of 1 table**. A present value table involves three factors: p, i, and n. Knowing two of these three factors allows us to compute the third. (A fourth is f, but as already explained, we need only multiply the 1 used in the formula by f.) To illustrate the use of a present value table, consider three cases.

Case 1 (solve for p when knowing i and n). To show how we use a present value table, let's look again at how we estimate the present value of $220 (the f value) at the end of one period (n = 1) where the interest rate (i) is 10%. To solve this case, we go to the present value table (Table B.1) and look in the row for 1 period and in the column for 10% interest. Here we find a present value (p) of 0.9091 based on a future value of 1. This means, for instance, that $1 to be received one period from today at 10% interest is worth $0.9091 today. Since the future value in this case is not $1 but $220, we multiply the 0.9091 by $220 to get an answer of $200.

Case 2 (solve for n when knowing p and i). To illustrate, assume a $100,000 future value (f) that is worth $13,000 today (p) using an interest rate of 12% (i) but where n is unknown. In particular, we want to know how many periods (n) there are between the present value and the future value. To put this in context, it would fit a situation in which we want to retire with $100,000 but currently have only $13,000 that is earning a 12% return and we will be unable to save any additional money. How long will it be before we can retire? To answer this, we go to Table B.1 and look in the 12% interest column. Here we find a column of present values (p) based on a future value of 1. To use the present value table for this solution, we must divide $13,000 ($p$) by $100,000 ($f$), which equals 0.1300. This is necessary because *a present value table defines* f *equal to 1, and* p *as a fraction of 1*. We look for a value nearest to 0.1300 (p), which we find in the row for 18 periods (n). This means that the present value of $100,000 at the end of 18 periods at 12% interest is $13,000; alternatively stated, we must work 18 more years.

Case 3   (solve for i when knowing p and n). In this case, we have, say, a $120,000 future value ($f$) worth $60,000 today ($p$) when there are nine periods (n) between the present and future values, but the interest rate is unknown. As an example, suppose we want to retire with $120,000 in nine years, but we have only $60,000 and we will be unable to save any additional money. What interest rate must we earn to retire with $120,000 in nine years? To answer this, we go to the present value table (Table B.1) and look in the row for nine periods. To use the present value table, we must divide $60,000 ($p$) by $120,000 ($f$), which equals 0.5000. Recall that this step is necessary because a present value table defines f equal to 1 and p as a fraction of 1. We look for a value in the row for nine periods that is nearest to 0.5000 (p), which we find in the column for 8% interest (i). This means that the present value of $120,000 at the end of nine periods at 8% interest is $60,000 or, in our example, we must earn 8% annual interest to retire in nine years.

A company is considering an investment expected to yield $70,000 after six years. If this company demands an 8% return, how much is it willing to pay for this investment today?

NEED-TO-KNOW B-1

Present Value of Single Amount

P1

Solution

$70,000 × 0.6302 = $44,114 (using PV factor from Table B.1, i = 8%, n = 6).

FUTURE VALUE OF A SINGLE AMOUNT

We must modify the formula for the present value of a single amount to obtain the formula for the future value of a single amount. In particular, we multiply both sides of the equation in Exhibit B.2 by $(1 + i)^n$ to get the result shown in Exhibit B.4.

P2

Apply future value concepts to a single amount by using interest tables.

EXHIBIT B.4

Future Value of a Single Amount Formula

$$f = p \times (1 + i)^n$$

The future value (f) is defined in terms of p, i, and n. We can use this formula to determine that $200 ($p$) invested for 1 ($n$) period at an interest rate of 10% (i) yields a future value of $220 as follows:

$$\begin{aligned} f &= p \times (1 + i)^n \\ &= \$200 \times (1 + 0.10)^1 \\ &= \$220 \end{aligned}$$

This formula can also be used to compute the future value of an amount for *any number of periods* into the future. To illustrate, assume that $200 is invested for three periods at 10%. The future value of this $200 is $266.20, computed as follows:

$$\begin{aligned} f &= p \times (1 + i)^n \\ &= \$200 \times (1 + 0.10)^3 \\ &= \$200 \times 1.3310 \\ &= \$266.20 \end{aligned}$$

Point: The FV factor in Table B2 when n = 3 and i = 10% is 1.3310.

A future value table makes it easier for us to compute future values (f) for many different combinations of interest rates (i) and time periods (n). Each future value in a future value table assumes the present value (p) is 1. As with a present value table, if the future amount is something other than 1, we simply multiply our answer by that amount. The formula used to construct a table of future values (factors) for a single amount of 1 is in Exhibit B.5.

EXHIBIT B.5

Future Value of 1 Formula

$$f = (1 + i)^n$$

Table B.2 at the end of this appendix shows a table of future values for a current amount of 1. This type of table is called a **future value of 1 table**.

Point:
1/PV factor = FV factor.
1/FV factor = PV factor.

There are some important relations between Tables B.1 and B.2. In Table B.2, for the row where $n = 0$, the future value is 1 for each interest rate. This is so because no interest is earned when time does not pass. We also see that Tables B.1 and B.2 report the same information but in a different manner. In particular, one table is simply the *reciprocal* of the other. To illustrate this inverse relation, let's say we invest $100 for a period of five years at 12% per year. How much do we expect to have after five years? We can answer this question using Table B.2 by finding the future value (f) of 1, for five periods from now, compounded at 12%. From that table we find $f = 1.7623$. If we start with $100, the amount it accumulates to after five years is $176.23 ($100 × 1.7623). We can alternatively use Table B.1. Here we find that the present value (p) of 1, discounted five periods at 12%, is 0.5674. Recall the inverse relation between present value and future value. This means that $p = 1/f$ (or equivalently, $f = 1/p$). We can compute the future value of $100 invested for five periods at 12% as follows: f = $100 × (1/0.5674) = $176.24 (which equals the $176.23 just computed, except for a 1 cent rounding difference).

A future value table involves three factors: f, i, and n. Knowing two of these three factors allows us to compute the third. To illustrate, consider these three possible cases.

Case 1 (solve for f when knowing i and n). Our preceding example fits this case. We found that $100 invested for five periods at 12% interest accumulates to $176.24.

Case 2 (solve for n when knowing f and i). In this case, we have, say, $2,000 ($p$) and we want to know how many periods (n) it will take to accumulate to $3,000 ($f$) at 7% interest ($i$). To answer this, we go to the future value table (Table B.2) and look in the 7% interest column. Here we find a column of future values (f) based on a present value of 1. To use a future value table, we must divide $3,000 ($f$) by $2,000 ($p$), which equals 1.500. This is necessary because *a future value table defines* p *equal to 1, and* f *as a multiple of 1.* We look for a value nearest to 1.50 (f), which we find in the row for six periods (n). This means that $2,000 invested for six periods at 7% interest accumulates to $3,000.

Case 3 (solve for i when knowing f and n). In this case, we have, say, $2,001 ($p$), and in nine years ($n$) we want to have $4,000 ($f$). What rate of interest must we earn to accomplish this? To answer that, we go to Table B.2 and search in the row for nine periods. To use a future value table, we must divide $4,000 ($f$) by $2,001 ($p$), which equals 1.9990. Recall that this is necessary because a future value table defines p equal to 1 and f as a multiple of 1. We look for a value nearest to 1.9990 (f), which we find in the column for 8% interest (i). This means that $2,001 invested for nine periods at 8% interest accumulates to $4,000.

NEED-TO-KNOW B-2

Future Value of Single Amount

P2

Assume that you win a $150,000 cash sweepstakes today. You decide to deposit this cash in an account earning 8% annual interest, and you plan to quit your job when the account equals $555,000. How many years will it be before you can quit working?

Solution

$555,000/$150,000 = 3.7000 (the future value factor)

Table B.2 shows this value is not achieved until reaching 17 years at 8% interest.

PRESENT VALUE OF AN ANNUITY

An *annuity* is a series of equal payments occurring at equal intervals. One example is a series of three annual payments of $100 each. An *ordinary annuity* is defined as equal end-of-period payments at equal intervals. An ordinary annuity of $100 for three periods and its present value (*p*) are illustrated in Exhibit B.6.

P3

Apply present value concepts to an annuity by using interest tables.

EXHIBIT B.6

Present Value of an Ordinary Annuity Diagram

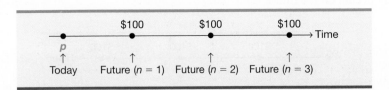

One way to compute the present value of an ordinary annuity is to find the present value of each payment using our present value formula from Exhibit B.3. We then add each of the three present values. To illustrate, let's look at three $100 payments at the end of each of the next three periods with an interest rate of 15%. Our present value computations are

$$p = \frac{\$100}{(1 + 0.15)^1} + \frac{\$100}{(1 + 0.15)^2} + \frac{\$100}{(1 + 0.15)^3} = \$228.32$$

This computation is identical to computing the present value of each payment (from Table B.1) and taking their sum or, alternatively, adding the values from Table B.1 for each of the three payments and multiplying their sum by the $100 annuity payment.

A more direct way is to use a present value of annuity table. Table B.3 at the end of this appendix is one such table. This table is called a **present value of an annuity of 1 table**. If we look at Table B.3 where $n = 3$ and $i = 15\%$, we see the present value is 2.2832. This means that the present value of an annuity of 1 for three periods, with a 15% interest rate, equals 2.2832.

A present value of an annuity formula is used to construct Table B.3. It can also be constructed by adding the amounts in a present value of 1 table. To illustrate, we use Tables B.1 and B.3 to confirm this relation for the prior example:

From Table B.1		From Table B.3	
$i = 15\%, n = 1$	0.8696		
$i = 15\%, n = 2$	0.7561		
$i = 15\%, n = 3$	0.6575		
Total	2.2832	$i = 15\%, n = 3$	2.2832

Point: Excel functions follow:

$= -\text{PV (rate, periods, payment)}$
$= -\text{PV (0.15, 3, 100)}$
$= \$228.32$

We can also use business calculators or spreadsheet programs to find the present value of an annuity.

■ **Decision** Insight ━━━━━━━━━━━━━━━━━━

Count Your Blessings   "I don't have good luck—I'm blessed," proclaimed Andrew "Jack" Whittaker, a sewage treatment contractor, after winning the largest ever undivided jackpot in a U.S. lottery. Whittaker had to choose between $315 million in 30 annual installments or $170 million in one lump sum ($112 million after-tax). ■

A company is considering an investment that would produce payments of $10,000 every six months for three years. The first payment would be received in six months. If this company requires an 8% annual return, what is the maximum amount it is willing to pay for this investment today?

NEED-TO-KNOW **B-3**

Present Value of an Annuity

P3

Solution

$10,000 × 5.2421 = $52,421 is the maximum (using PV of annuity factor from Table B.3, $i = 4\%, n = 6$).

FUTURE VALUE OF AN ANNUITY

P4
_____

Apply future value concepts to an annuity by using interest tables.

The future value of an *ordinary annuity* is the accumulated value of each annuity payment with interest as of the date of the final payment. To illustrate, let's consider the earlier annuity of three annual payments of $100. Exhibit B.7 shows the point in time for the future value (*f*). The first payment is made two periods prior to the point when future value is determined, and the final payment occurs on the future value date.

EXHIBIT B.7

Future Value of an Ordinary Annuity Diagram

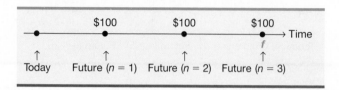

Point: An ordinary annuity is a series of equal cash flows, with the payment at the *end* of each period.

One way to compute the future value of an annuity is to use the formula to find the future value of *each* payment and add them. If we assume an interest rate of 15%, our calculation is

$$f = \$100 \times (1 + 0.15)^2 + \$100 \times (1 + 0.15)^1 + \$100 \times (1 + 0.15)^0 = \$347.25$$

This is identical to using Table B.2 and summing the future values of each payment, or adding the future values of the three payments of 1 and multiplying the sum by $100.

A more direct way is to use a table showing future values of annuities. Such a table is called a **future value of an annuity of 1 table**. Table B.4 at the end of this appendix is one such table. Note that in Table B.4 when $n = 1$, the future values equal 1 ($f = 1$) for all rates of interest. This is so because such an annuity consists of only one payment and the future value is determined on the date of that payment—no time passes between the payment and its future value. The future value of an annuity formula is used to construct Table B.4. We can also construct it by adding the amounts from a future value of 1 table. To illustrate, we use Tables B.2 and B.4 to confirm this relation for the prior example:

From Table B.2		From Table B.4	
$i = 15\%, n = 0$	1.0000		
$i = 15\%, n = 1$	1.1500		
$i = 15\%, n = 2$	1.3225		
Total	3.4725	$i = 15\%, n = 3$	3.4725

Point: Excel functions follow:

= −FV (rate, periods, payment)
= −FV (0.15, 3, 100)
= $347.25

Note that the future value in Table B.2 is 1.0000 when $n = 0$, but the future value in Table B.4 is 1.0000 when $n = 1$. Is this a contradiction? No. When $n = 0$ in Table B.2, the future value is determined on the date when a single payment occurs. This means that no interest is earned because no time has passed, and the future value equals the payment. Table B.4 describes annuities with equal payments occurring at the end of each period. When $n = 1$, the annuity has one payment, and its future value equals 1 on the date of its final and only payment. Again, no time passes between the payment and its future value date.

NEED-TO-KNOW   **B-4**

Future Value of an Annuity

P4

A company invests $45,000 per year for five years at 12% annual interest. Compute the value of this annuity investment at the end of five years.

Solution

$45,000 × 6.3528 = $285,876 (using the FV of annuity factor from Table B.4, $i = 12\%, n = 5$).

Summary

C1 **Describe the earning of interest and the concepts of present and future values.** Interest is payment by a borrower to the owner of an asset for its use. Present and future value computations are a way for us to estimate the interest component of holding assets or liabilities over a period of time.

P1 **Apply present value concepts to a single amount by using interest tables.** The present value of a single amount received at a future date is the amount that can be invested now at the specified interest rate to yield that future value.

P2 **Apply future value concepts to a single amount by using interest tables.** The future value of a single amount

invested at a specified rate of interest is the amount that would accumulate by the future date.

P3 **Apply present value concepts to an annuity by using interest tables.** The present value of an annuity is the amount that can be invested now at the specified interest rate to yield that series of equal periodic payments.

P4 **Apply future value concepts to an annuity by using interest tables.** The future value of an annuity invested at a specific rate of interest is the amount that would accumulate by the date of the final payment.

ꙥ connect

Assume that you must make two-year-ahead future value estimates using the *future value of 1 table* (Table B.2). Which interest rate column *and* number-of-periods row do you use when working with the following rates?

1. 8% annual rate, compounded quarterly
2. 12% annual rate, compounded annually
3. 6% annual rate, compounded semiannually
4. 12% annual rate, compounded monthly (the answer for number-of-periods in part 4 is not shown in Table B.2)

QUICK STUDY

QS B-1
Identifying interest rates in tables

C1

Ken Francis is offered the possibility of investing $2,745 today and in return to receive $10,000 after 15 years. What is the annual rate of interest for this investment? (Use Table B.1.)

QS B-2
Interest rate on an investment   P1

Megan Brink is offered the possibility of investing $6,651 today at 6% interest per year in a desire to accumulate $10,000. How many years must Brink wait to accumulate $10,000? (Use Table B.1.)

QS B-3
Number of periods of an investment   P1

Flaherty is considering an investment that, if paid for immediately, is expected to return $140,000 five years from now. If Flaherty demands a 9% return, how much is she willing to pay for this investment?

QS B-4
Present value of an amount   P1

CII, Inc., invests $630,000 in a project expected to earn a 12% annual rate of return. The earnings will be reinvested in the project each year until the entire investment is liquidated 10 years later. What will the cash proceeds be when the project is liquidated?

QS B-5
Future value of an amount   P2

Beene Distributing is considering a project that will return $150,000 annually at the end of each year for the next six years. If Beene demands an annual return of 7% and pays for the project immediately, how much is it willing to pay for the project?

QS B-6
Present value of an annuity   P3

Claire Fitch is planning to begin an individual retirement program in which she will invest $1,500 at the end of each year. Fitch plans to retire after making 30 annual investments in the program earning a return of 10%. What is the value of the program on the date of the last payment (30 years from the present)?

QS B-7
Future value of an annuity   P4

EXERCISES

Exercise B-1
Present value of an
amount P1

Mike Derr Company expects to earn 10% per year on an investment that will pay $606,773 six years from now. Use Table B.1 to compute the present value of this investment. (Round the amount to the nearest dollar.)

Exercise B-2
Present value of an
amount P1

On January 1, 2015, a company agrees to pay $20,000 in three years. If the annual interest rate is 10%, determine how much cash the company can borrow with this agreement.

Exercise B-3
Number of periods
of an investment P2

Tom Thompson expects to invest $10,000 at 12% and, at the end of a certain period, receive $96,463. How many years will it be before Thompson receives the payment? (Use Table B.2.)

Exercise B-4
Interest rate on
an investment P2

Bill Padley expects to invest $10,000 for 25 years, after which he wants to receive $108,347. What rate of interest must Padley earn? (Use Table B.2.)

Exercise B-5
Future value of an
amount P2

Mark Welsch deposits $7,200 in an account that earns interest at an annual rate of 8%, compounded quarterly. The $7,200 plus earned interest must remain in the account 10 years before it can be withdrawn. How much money will be in the account at the end of 10 years?

Exercise B-6
Future value of an
amount P2

Catten, Inc., invests $163,170 today earning 7% per year for nine years. Use Table B.2 to compute the future value of the investment nine years from now. (Round the amount to the nearest dollar.)

Exercise B-7
Interest rate on an
investment P3

Jones expects an immediate investment of $57,466 to return $10,000 annually for eight years, with the first payment to be received one year from now. What rate of interest must Jones earn? (Use Table B.3.)

Exercise B-8
Number of periods
of an investment P3

Keith Riggins expects an investment of $82,014 to return $10,000 annually for several years. If Riggins earns a return of 10%, how many annual payments will he receive? (Use Table B.3.)

Exercise B-9
Present value of an
annuity P3

Dave Krug finances a new automobile by paying $6,500 cash and agreeing to make 40 monthly payments of $500 each, the first payment to be made one month after the purchase. The loan bears interest at an annual rate of 12%. What is the cost of the automobile?

Exercise B-10
Present values of
annuities

P3

C&H Ski Club recently borrowed money and agrees to pay it back with a series of six annual payments of $5,000 each. C&H subsequently borrows more money and agrees to pay it back with a series of four annual payments of $7,500 each. The annual interest rate for both loans is 6%.

1. Use Table B.1 to find the present value of these two separate annuities. (Round amounts to the nearest dollar.)
2. Use Table B.3 to find the present value of these two separate annuities. (Round amounts to the nearest dollar.)

Exercise B-11
Present value with
semiannual compounding

C1   P3

Otto Co. borrows money on April 30, 2015, by promising to make four payments of $13,000 each on November 1, 2015; May 1, 2016; November 1, 2016; and May 1, 2017.

1. How much money is Otto able to borrow if the interest rate is 8%, compounded semiannually?
2. How much money is Otto able to borrow if the interest rate is 12%, compounded semiannually?
3. How much money is Otto able to borrow if the interest rate is 16%, compounded semiannually?

Exercise B-12
Present value of bonds

P1   P3

Spiller Corp. plans to issue 10%, 15-year, $500,000 par value bonds payable that pay interest semiannually on June 30 and December 31. The bonds are dated December 31, 2015, and are issued on that date. If the market rate of interest for the bonds is 8% on the date of issue, what will be the total cash proceeds from the bond issue?

Compute the amount that can be borrowed under each of the following circumstances:

1. A promise to repay $90,000 seven years from now at an interest rate of 6%.

2. An agreement made on February 1, 2015, to make three separate payments of $20,000 on February 1 of 2016, 2017, and 2018. The annual interest rate is 10%.

Exercise B-13
Present value of an amount and of an annuity
P1   P3

Algoe expects to invest $1,000 annually for 40 years to yield an accumulated value of $154,762 on the date of the last investment. For this to occur, what rate of interest must Algoe earn? (Use Table B.4.)

Exercise B-14
Interest rate on an investment   P4

Steffi Derr expects to invest $10,000 annually that will earn 8%. How many annual investments must Derr make to accumulate $303,243 on the date of the last investment? (Use Table B.4.)

Exercise B-15
Number of periods of an investment   P4

Kelly Malone plans to have $50 withheld from her monthly paycheck and deposited in a savings account that earns 12% annually, compounded monthly. If Malone continues with her plan for two and one-half years, how much will be accumulated in the account on the date of the last deposit?

Exercise B-16
Future value of an annuity   P4

Starr Company decides to establish a fund that it will use 10 years from now to replace an aging production facility. The company will make a $100,000 initial contribution to the fund and plans to make quarterly contributions of $50,000 beginning in three months. The fund earns 12%, compounded quarterly. What will be the value of the fund 10 years from now?

Exercise B-17
Future value of an amount plus an annuity
P2   P4

---

a. How much would you have to deposit today if you wanted to have $60,000 in four years? Annual interest rate is 9%.

b. Assume that you are saving up for a trip around the world when you graduate in two years. If you can earn 8% on your investments, how much would you have to deposit today to have $15,000 when you graduate?

c. Would you rather have $463 now or $1,000 ten years from now? Assume that you can earn 9% on your investments.

d. Assume that a college parking sticker today costs $90. If the cost of parking is increasing at the rate of 5% per year, how much will the college parking sticker cost in eight years?

e. Assume that the average price of a new home is $158,500. If new homes are increasing at a rate of 10% per year, how much will a new home cost in eight years?

f. An investment will pay you $10,000 in 10 years, and it will also pay you $400 at the end of *each* of the next 10 years (years 1 thru 10). If the annual interest rate is 6%, how much would you be willing to pay today for this type of investment?

g. A college student is reported in the newspaper as having won $10,000,000 in the Kansas State Lottery. However, as is often the custom with lotteries, she does *not* actually receive the entire $10 million now. Instead she will receive $500,000 at the end of the year for *each* of the next 20 years. If the annual interest rate is 6%, what is the present value (today's amount) that she won? (Ignore taxes.)

Exercise B-18
Practical applications of the time value of money
P1   P2   P3   P4

For each of the following situations, identify (1) the case as either (*a*) a present or a future value and (*b*) a single amount or an annuity, (2) the table you would use in your computations (but do not solve the problem), and (3) the interest rate and time periods you would use.

a. You need to accumulate $10,000 for a trip you wish to take in four years. You are able to earn 8% compounded semiannually on your savings. You plan to make only one deposit and let the money accumulate for four years. How would you determine the amount of the one-time deposit?

b. Assume the same facts as in part (*a*) except that you will make semiannual deposits to your savings account.

c. You want to retire after working 40 years with savings in excess of $1,000,000. You expect to save $4,000 a year for 40 years and earn an annual rate of interest of 8%. Will you be able to retire with more than $1,000,000 in 40 years? Explain.

d. A sweepstakes agency names you a grand prize winner. You can take $225,000 immediately or elect to receive annual installments of $30,000 for 20 years. You can earn 10% annually on any investments you make. Which prize do you choose to receive?

Exercise B-19
Using present and future value tables
C1   P1   P2   P3   P4

TABLE B.1*

Present Value of 1

$$p = 1/(1 + i)^n$$

| | | | | | | Rate | | | | | | |
Periods	1%	2%	3%	4%	5%	6%	7%	8%	9%	10%	12%	15%
1	0.9901	0.9804	0.9709	0.9615	0.9524	0.9434	0.9346	0.9259	0.9174	0.9091	0.8929	0.8696
2	0.9803	0.9612	0.9426	0.9246	0.9070	0.8900	0.8734	0.8573	0.8417	0.8264	0.7972	0.7561
3	0.9706	0.9423	0.9151	0.8890	0.8638	0.8396	0.8163	0.7938	0.7722	0.7513	0.7118	0.6575
4	0.9610	0.9238	0.8885	0.8548	0.8227	0.7921	0.7629	0.7350	0.7084	0.6830	0.6355	0.5718
5	0.9515	0.9057	0.8626	0.8219	0.7835	0.7473	0.7130	0.6806	0.6499	0.6209	0.5674	0.4972
6	0.9420	0.8880	0.8375	0.7903	0.7462	0.7050	0.6663	0.6302	0.5963	0.5645	0.5066	0.4323
7	0.9327	0.8706	0.8131	0.7599	0.7107	0.6651	0.6227	0.5835	0.5470	0.5132	0.4523	0.3759
8	0.9235	0.8535	0.7894	0.7307	0.6768	0.6274	0.5820	0.5403	0.5019	0.4665	0.4039	0.3269
9	0.9143	0.8368	0.7664	0.7026	0.6446	0.5919	0.5439	0.5002	0.4604	0.4241	0.3606	0.2843
10	0.9053	0.8203	0.7441	0.6756	0.6139	0.5584	0.5083	0.4632	0.4224	0.3855	0.3220	0.2472
11	0.8963	0.8043	0.7224	0.6496	0.5847	0.5268	0.4751	0.4289	0.3875	0.3505	0.2875	0.2149
12	0.8874	0.7885	0.7014	0.6246	0.5568	0.4970	0.4440	0.3971	0.3555	0.3186	0.2567	0.1869
13	0.8787	0.7730	0.6810	0.6006	0.5303	0.4688	0.4150	0.3677	0.3262	0.2897	0.2292	0.1625
14	0.8700	0.7579	0.6611	0.5775	0.5051	0.4423	0.3878	0.3405	0.2992	0.2633	0.2046	0.1413
15	0.8613	0.7430	0.6419	0.5553	0.4810	0.4173	0.3624	0.3152	0.2745	0.2394	0.1827	0.1229
16	0.8528	0.7284	0.6232	0.5339	0.4581	0.3936	0.3387	0.2919	0.2519	0.2176	0.1631	0.1069
17	0.8444	0.7142	0.6050	0.5134	0.4363	0.3714	0.3166	0.2703	0.2311	0.1978	0.1456	0.0929
18	0.8360	0.7002	0.5874	0.4936	0.4155	0.3503	0.2959	0.2502	0.2120	0.1799	0.1300	0.0808
19	0.8277	0.6864	0.5703	0.4746	0.3957	0.3305	0.2765	0.2317	0.1945	0.1635	0.1161	0.0703
20	0.8195	0.6730	0.5537	0.4564	0.3769	0.3118	0.2584	0.2145	0.1784	0.1486	0.1037	0.0611
25	0.7798	0.6095	0.4776	0.3751	0.2953	0.2330	0.1842	0.1460	0.1160	0.0923	0.0588	0.0304
30	0.7419	0.5521	0.4120	0.3083	0.2314	0.1741	0.1314	0.0994	0.0754	0.0573	0.0334	0.0151
35	0.7059	0.5000	0.3554	0.2534	0.1813	0.1301	0.0937	0.0676	0.0490	0.0356	0.0189	0.0075
40	0.6717	0.4529	0.3066	0.2083	0.1420	0.0972	0.0668	0.0460	0.0318	0.0221	0.0107	0.0037

*Used to compute the present value of a known future amount. For example: How much would you need to invest today at 10% compounded semiannually to accumulate $5,000 in 6 years from today? Using the factors of n = 12 and i = 5% (12 semiannual periods and a semiannual rate of 5%), the factor is 0.5568. You would need to invest $2,784 today ($5,000 × 0.5568).

TABLE B.2**

Future Value of 1

$$f = (1 + i)^n$$

| | | | | | | Rate | | | | | | |
Periods	1%	2%	3%	4%	5%	6%	7%	8%	9%	10%	12%	15%
0	1.0000	1.0000	1.0000	1.0000	1.0000	1.0000	1.0000	1.0000	1.0000	1.0000	1.0000	1.0000
1	1.0100	1.0200	1.0300	1.0400	1.0500	1.0600	1.0700	1.0800	1.0900	1.1000	1.1200	1.1500
2	1.0201	1.0404	1.0609	1.0816	1.1025	1.1236	1.1449	1.1664	1.1881	1.2100	1.2544	1.3225
3	1.0303	1.0612	1.0927	1.1249	1.1576	1.1910	1.2250	1.2597	1.2950	1.3310	1.4049	1.5209
4	1.0406	1.0824	1.1255	1.1699	1.2155	1.2625	1.3108	1.3605	1.4116	1.4641	1.5735	1.7490
5	1.0510	1.1041	1.1593	1.2167	1.2763	1.3382	1.4026	1.4693	1.5386	1.6105	1.7623	2.0114
6	1.0615	1.1262	1.1941	1.2653	1.3401	1.4185	1.5007	1.5869	1.6771	1.7716	1.9738	2.3131
7	1.0721	1.1487	1.2299	1.3159	1.4071	1.5036	1.6058	1.7138	1.8280	1.9487	2.2107	2.6600
8	1.0829	1.1717	1.2668	1.3686	1.4775	1.5938	1.7182	1.8509	1.9926	2.1436	2.4760	3.0590
9	1.0937	1.1951	1.3048	1.4233	1.5513	1.6895	1.8385	1.9990	2.1719	2.3579	2.7731	3.5179
10	1.1046	1.2190	1.3439	1.4802	1.6289	1.7908	1.9672	2.1589	2.3674	2.5937	3.1058	4.0456
11	1.1157	1.2434	1.3842	1.5395	1.7103	1.8983	2.1049	2.3316	2.5804	2.8531	3.4785	4.6524
12	1.1268	1.2682	1.4258	1.6010	1.7959	2.0122	2.2522	2.5182	2.8127	3.1384	3.8960	5.3503
13	1.1381	1.2936	1.4685	1.6651	1.8856	2.1329	2.4098	2.7196	3.0658	3.4523	4.3635	6.1528
14	1.1495	1.3195	1.5126	1.7317	1.9799	2.2609	2.5785	2.9372	3.3417	3.7975	4.8871	7.0757
15	1.1610	1.3459	1.5580	1.8009	2.0789	2.3966	2.7590	3.1722	3.6425	4.1772	5.4736	8.1371
16	1.1726	1.3728	1.6047	1.8730	2.1829	2.5404	2.9522	3.4259	3.9703	4.5950	6.1304	9.3576
17	1.1843	1.4002	1.6528	1.9479	2.2920	2.6928	3.1588	3.7000	4.3276	5.0545	6.8660	10.7613
18	1.1961	1.4282	1.7024	2.0258	2.4066	2.8543	3.3799	3.9960	4.7171	5.5599	7.6900	12.3755
19	1.2081	1.4568	1.7535	2.1068	2.5270	3.0256	3.6165	4.3157	5.1417	6.1159	8.6128	14.2318
20	1.2202	1.4859	1.8061	2.1911	2.6533	3.2071	3.8697	4.6610	5.6044	6.7275	9.6463	16.3665
25	1.2824	1.6406	2.0938	2.6658	3.3864	4.2919	5.4274	6.8485	8.6231	10.8347	17.0001	32.9190
30	1.3478	1.8114	2.4273	3.2434	4.3219	5.7435	7.6123	10.0627	13.2677	17.4494	29.9599	66.2118
35	1.4166	1.9999	2.8139	3.9461	5.5160	7.6861	10.6766	14.7853	20.4140	28.1024	52.7996	133.1755
40	1.4889	2.2080	3.2620	4.8010	7.0400	10.2857	14.9745	21.7245	31.4094	45.2593	93.0510	267.8635

**Used to compute the future value of a known present amount. For example: What is the accumulated value of $3,000 invested today at 8% compounded quarterly for 5 years? Using the factors of n = 20 and i = 2% (20 quarterly periods and a quarterly interest rate of 2%), the factor is 1.4859. The accumulated value is $4,457.70 ($3,000 × 1.4859).

$$p = \left[1 - \frac{1}{(1 + i)^n}\right]/i$$

TABLE B.3†

Present Value of an Annuity of 1

Periods	1%	2%	3%	4%	5%	6%	7%	8%	9%	10%	12%	15%
1	0.9901	0.9804	0.9709	0.9615	0.9524	0.9434	0.9346	0.9259	0.9174	0.9091	0.8929	0.8696
2	1.9704	1.9416	1.9135	1.8861	1.8594	1.8334	1.8080	1.7833	1.7591	1.7355	1.6901	1.6257
3	2.9410	2.8839	2.8286	2.7751	2.7232	2.6730	2.6243	2.5771	2.5313	2.4869	2.4018	2.2832
4	3.9020	3.8077	3.7171	3.6299	3.5460	3.4651	3.3872	3.3121	3.2397	3.1699	3.0373	2.8550
5	4.8534	4.7135	4.5797	4.4518	4.3295	4.2124	4.1002	3.9927	3.8897	3.7908	3.6048	3.3522
6	5.7955	5.6014	5.4172	5.2421	5.0757	4.9173	4.7665	4.6229	4.4859	4.3553	4.1114	3.7845
7	6.7282	6.4720	6.2303	6.0021	5.7864	5.5824	5.3893	5.2064	5.0330	4.8684	4.5638	4.1604
8	7.6517	7.3255	7.0197	6.7327	6.4632	6.2098	5.9713	5.7466	5.5348	5.3349	4.9676	4.4873
9	8.5660	8.1622	7.7861	7.4353	7.1078	6.8017	6.5152	6.2469	5.9952	5.7590	5.3282	4.7716
10	9.4713	8.9826	8.5302	8.1109	7.7217	7.3601	7.0236	6.7101	6.4177	6.1446	5.6502	5.0188
11	10.3676	9.7868	9.2526	8.7605	8.3064	7.8869	7.4987	7.1390	6.8052	6.4951	5.9377	5.2337
12	11.2551	10.5753	9.9540	9.3851	8.8633	8.3838	7.9427	7.5361	7.1607	6.8137	6.1944	5.4206
13	12.1337	11.3484	10.6350	9.9856	9.3936	8.8527	8.3577	7.9038	7.4869	7.1034	6.4235	5.5831
14	13.0037	12.1062	11.2961	10.5631	9.8986	9.2950	8.7455	8.2442	7.7862	7.3667	6.6282	5.7245
15	13.8651	12.8493	11.9379	11.1184	10.3797	9.7122	9.1079	8.5595	8.0607	7.6061	6.8109	5.8474
16	14.7179	13.5777	12.5611	11.6523	10.8378	10.1059	9.4466	8.8514	8.3126	7.8237	6.9740	5.9542
17	15.5623	14.2919	13.1661	12.1657	11.2741	10.4773	9.7632	9.1216	8.5436	8.0216	7.1196	6.0472
18	16.3983	14.9920	13.7535	12.6593	11.6896	10.8276	10.0591	9.3719	8.7556	8.2014	7.2497	6.1280
19	17.2260	15.6785	14.3238	13.1339	12.0853	11.1581	10.3356	9.6036	8.9501	8.3649	7.3658	6.1982
20	18.0456	16.3514	14.8775	13.5903	12.4622	11.4699	10.5940	9.8181	9.1285	8.5136	7.4694	6.2593
25	22.0232	19.5235	17.4131	15.6221	14.0939	12.7834	11.6536	10.6748	9.8226	9.0770	7.8431	6.4641
30	25.8077	22.3965	19.6004	17.2920	15.3725	13.7648	12.4090	11.2578	10.2737	9.4269	8.0552	6.5660
35	29.4086	24.9986	21.4872	18.6646	16.3742	14.4982	12.9477	11.6546	10.5668	9.6442	8.1755	6.6166
40	32.8347	27.3555	23.1148	19.7928	17.1591	15.0463	13.3317	11.9246	10.7574	9.7791	8.2438	6.6418

†Used to calculate the present value of a series of equal payments made at the end of each period. For example: What is the present value of $2,000 per year for 10 years assuming an annual interest rate of 9%. For (n = 10, i = 9%), the PV factor is 6.4177. $2,000 per year for 10 years is the equivalent of $12,835 today ($2,000 × 6.4177).

$$f = [(1 + i)^n - 1]/i$$

TABLE B.4‡

Future Value of an Annuity of 1

Periods	1%	2%	3%	4%	5%	6%	7%	8%	9%	10%	12%	15%
1	1.0000	1.0000	1.0000	1.0000	1.0000	1.0000	1.0000	1.0000	1.0000	1.0000	1.0000	1.0000
2	2.0100	2.0200	2.0300	2.0400	2.0500	2.0600	2.0700	2.0800	2.0900	2.1000	2.1200	2.1500
3	3.0301	3.0604	3.0909	3.1216	3.1525	3.1836	3.2149	3.2464	3.2781	3.3100	3.3744	3.4725
4	4.0604	4.1216	4.1836	4.2465	4.3101	4.3746	4.4399	4.5061	4.5731	4.6410	4.7793	4.9934
5	5.1010	5.2040	5.3091	5.4163	5.5256	5.6371	5.7507	5.8666	5.9847	6.1051	6.3528	6.7424
6	6.1520	6.3081	6.4684	6.6330	6.8019	6.9753	7.1533	7.3359	7.5233	7.7156	8.1152	8.7537
7	7.2135	7.4343	7.6625	7.8983	8.1420	8.3938	8.6540	8.9228	9.2004	9.4872	10.0890	11.0668
8	8.2857	8.5830	8.8923	9.2142	9.5491	9.8975	10.2598	10.6366	11.0285	11.4359	12.2997	13.7268
9	9.3685	9.7546	10.1591	10.5828	11.0266	11.4913	11.9780	12.4876	13.0210	13.5795	14.7757	16.7858
10	10.4622	10.9497	11.4639	12.0061	12.5779	13.1808	13.8164	14.4866	15.1929	15.9374	17.5487	20.3037
11	11.5668	12.1687	12.8078	13.4864	14.2068	14.9716	15.7836	16.6455	17.5603	18.5312	20.6546	24.3493
12	12.6825	13.4121	14.1920	15.0258	15.9171	16.8699	17.8885	18.9771	20.1407	21.3843	24.1331	29.0017
13	13.8093	14.6803	15.6178	16.6268	17.7130	18.8821	20.1406	21.4953	22.9534	24.5227	28.0291	34.3519
14	14.9474	15.9739	17.0863	18.2919	19.5986	21.0151	22.5505	24.2149	26.0192	27.9750	32.3926	40.5047
15	16.0969	17.2934	18.5989	20.0236	21.5786	23.2760	25.1290	27.1521	29.3609	31.7725	37.2797	47.5804
16	17.2579	18.6393	20.1569	21.8245	23.6575	25.6725	27.8881	30.3243	33.0034	35.9497	42.7533	55.7175
17	18.4304	20.0121	21.7616	23.6975	25.8404	28.2129	30.8402	33.7502	36.9737	40.5447	48.8837	65.0751
18	19.6147	21.4123	23.4144	25.6454	28.1324	30.9057	33.9990	37.4502	41.3013	45.5992	55.7497	75.8364
19	20.8109	22.8406	25.1169	27.6712	30.5390	33.7600	37.3790	41.4463	46.0185	51.1591	63.4397	88.2118
20	22.0190	24.2974	26.8704	29.7781	33.0660	36.7856	40.9955	45.7620	51.1601	57.2750	72.0524	102.4436
25	28.2432	32.0303	36.4593	41.6459	47.7271	54.8645	63.2490	73.1059	84.7009	98.3471	133.3339	212.7930
30	34.7849	40.5681	47.5754	56.0849	66.4388	79.0582	94.4608	113.2832	136.3075	164.4940	241.3327	434.7451
35	41.6603	49.9945	60.4621	73.6522	90.3203	111.4348	138.2369	172.3168	215.7108	271.0244	431.6635	881.1702
40	48.8864	60.4020	75.4013	95.0255	120.7998	154.7620	199.6351	259.0565	337.8824	442.5926	767.0914	1,779.0903

‡Used to calculate the future value of a series of equal payments made at the end of each period. For example: What is the future value of $4,000 per year for 6 years assuming an annual interest rate of 8%. For (n = 6, i = 8%), the FV factor is 7.3359. $4,000 per year for 6 years accumulates to $29,343.60 ($4,000 × 7.3359).

Chart of Accounts

Following is a typical chart of accounts, which is used in several assignments. Each company has its own unique set of accounts and numbering system. *An asterisk denotes a contra account.

Assets

Current Assets
101 Cash
102 Petty cash
103 Cash equivalents
104 Short-term investments
105 Fair value adjustment, _____ securities (S-T)
106 Accounts receivable
107 Allowance for doubtful accounts*
108 Legal fees receivable
109 Interest receivable
110 Rent receivable
111 Notes receivable
119 Merchandise inventory (or Inventory)
120 _____ inventory
121 _____ inventory
124 Office supplies
125 Store supplies
126 _____ supplies
128 Prepaid insurance
129 Prepaid interest
131 Prepaid rent
132 Raw materials inventory
133 Work in process inventory, _____
134 Work in process inventory, _____
135 Finished goods inventory

Long-Term Investments
141 Long-term investments
142 Fair value adjustment, _____ securities (L-T)
144 Investment in _____
145 Bond sinking fund

Plant Assets
151 Automobiles
152 Accumulated depreciation—Automobiles*
153 Trucks
154 Accumulated depreciation—Trucks*
155 Boats
156 Accumulated depreciation—Boats*
157 Professional library
158 Accumulated depreciation—Professional library*
159 Law library
160 Accumulated depreciation—Law library*
161 Furniture
162 Accumulated depreciation—Furniture*
163 Office equipment
164 Accumulated depreciation—Office equipment*
165 Store equipment
166 Accumulated depreciation—Store equipment*
167 _____ equipment
168 Accumulated depreciation—_____ equipment*
169 Machinery
170 Accumulated depreciation—Machinery*
173 Building _____
174 Accumulated depreciation—Building _____*
175 Building _____
176 Accumulated depreciation—Building _____*
179 Land improvements _____
180 Accumulated depreciation—Land improvements _____*
181 Land improvements _____
182 Accumulated depreciation—Land improvements _____*
183 Land

Natural Resources
185 Mineral deposit
186 Accumulated depletion—Mineral deposit*

Intangible Assets
191 Patents
192 Leasehold
193 Franchise
194 Copyrights
195 Leasehold improvements
196 Licenses
197 Accumulated amortization—_____*

Liabilities

Current Liabilities
201 Accounts payable
202 Insurance payable
203 Interest payable
204 Legal fees payable
207 Office salaries payable
208 Rent payable
209 Salaries payable
210 Wages payable
211 Accrued payroll payable
212 Factory payroll payable
214 Estimated warranty liability
215 Income taxes payable
216 Common dividend payable
217 Preferred dividend payable
218 State unemployment taxes payable
219 Employee federal income taxes payable
221 Employee medical insurance payable
222 Employee retirement program payable
223 Employee union dues payable
224 Federal unemployment taxes payable
225 FICA taxes payable
226 Estimated vacation pay liability

Unearned Revenues
230 Unearned consulting fees
231 Unearned legal fees
232 Unearned property management fees
233 Unearned _____ fees
234 Unearned _____ fees
235 Unearned janitorial revenue
236 Unearned _____ revenue
238 Unearned rent

Notes Payable
240 Short-term notes payable
241 Discount on short-term notes payable*
245 Notes payable
251 Long-term notes payable
252 Discount on long-term notes payable*

Long-Term Liabilities
253 Long-term lease liability
255 Bonds payable
256 Discount on bonds payable*
257 Premium on bonds payable
258 Deferred income tax liability

Equity

Owner's Equity
301 _____, Capital
302 _____, Withdrawals
303 _____, Capital
304 _____, Withdrawals
305 _____, Capital
306 _____, Withdrawals

Paid-In Capital
307 Common stock, $ _____ par value
308 Common stock, no-par value
309 Common stock, $ _____ stated value
310 Common stock dividend distributable
311 Paid-in capital in excess of par value, Common stock
312 Paid-in capital in excess of stated value, No-par common stock

313 Paid-in capital from retirement of common stock
314 Paid-in capital, Treasury stock
315 Preferred stock
316 Paid-in capital in excess of par value, Preferred stock

Retained Earnings

318 Retained earnings
319 Cash dividends (or Dividends)
320 Stock dividends

Other Equity Accounts

321 Treasury stock, Common*
322 Unrealized gain—Equity
323 Unrealized loss—Equity

Revenues

401 _____ fees earned
402 _____ fees earned
403 _____ revenues
404 Revenues
405 Commissions earned
406 Rent revenue (or Rent earned)
407 Dividends revenue (or Dividends earned)
408 Earnings from investment in _____
409 Interest revenue (or Interest earned)
410 Sinking fund earnings
413 Sales
414 Sales returns and allowances*
415 Sales discounts*

Cost of Sales

Cost of Goods Sold

502 Cost of goods sold
505 Purchases
506 Purchases returns and allowances*
507 Purchases discounts*
508 Transportation-in

Manufacturing

520 Raw materials purchases
521 Freight-in on raw materials
530 Direct labor
540 Factory overhead
541 Indirect materials
542 Indirect labor
543 Factory insurance expired
544 Factory supervision
545 Factory supplies used
546 Factory utilities
547 Miscellaneous production costs
548 Property taxes on factory building
549 Property taxes on factory equipment
550 Rent on factory building
551 Repairs, factory equipment
552 Small tools written off
560 Depreciation of factory equipment
561 Depreciation of factory building

Standard Cost Variances

580 Direct material quantity variance
581 Direct material price variance
582 Direct labor quantity variance
583 Direct labor price variance
584 Factory overhead volume variance
585 Factory overhead controllable variance

Expenses

Amortization, Depletion, and Depreciation

601 Amortization expense—_____
602 Amortization expense—_____
603 Depletion expense—_____
604 Depreciation expense—Boats
605 Depreciation expense—Automobiles
606 Depreciation expense—Building _____
607 Depreciation expense—Building _____
608 Depreciation expense—Land improvements _____
609 Depreciation expense—Land improvements _____
610 Depreciation expense—Law library
611 Depreciation expense—Trucks
612 Depreciation expense—_____ equipment
613 Depreciation expense—_____ equipment
614 Depreciation expense—_____
615 Depreciation expense—_____

Employee-Related Expenses

620 Office salaries expense
621 Sales salaries expense
622 Salaries expense
623 _____ wages expense
624 Employees' benefits expense
625 Payroll taxes expense

Financial Expenses

630 Cash over and short
631 Discounts lost
632 Factoring fee expense
633 Interest expense

Insurance Expenses

635 Insurance expense—Delivery equipment
636 Insurance expense—Office equipment
637 Insurance expense—_____

Rental Expenses

640 Rent expense
641 Rent expense—Office space
642 Rent expense—Selling space
643 Press rental expense
644 Truck rental expense
645 _____ rental expense

Supplies Expenses

650 Office supplies expense
651 Store supplies expense
652 _____ supplies expense
653 _____ supplies expense

Miscellaneous Expenses

655 Advertising expense
656 Bad debts expense
657 Blueprinting expense
658 Boat expense
659 Collection expense
661 Concessions expense
662 Credit card expense
663 Delivery expense
664 Dumping expense
667 Equipment expense
668 Food and drinks expense
671 Gas and oil expense
672 General and administrative expense
673 Janitorial expense
674 Legal fees expense
676 Mileage expense
677 Miscellaneous expenses
678 Mower and tools expense
679 Operating expense
680 Organization expense
681 Permits expense
682 Postage expense
683 Property taxes expense
684 Repairs expense—_____
685 Repairs expense—_____
687 Selling expense
688 Telephone expense
689 Travel and entertainment expense
690 Utilities expense
691 Warranty expense
692 _____ expense
695 Income taxes expense

Gains and Losses

701 Gain on retirement of bonds
702 Gain on sale of machinery
703 Gain on sale of investments
704 Gain on sale of trucks
705 Gain on _____
706 Foreign exchange gain or loss
801 Loss on disposal of machinery
802 Loss on exchange of equipment
803 Loss on exchange of _____
804 Loss on sale of notes
805 Loss on retirement of bonds
806 Loss on sale of investments
807 Loss on sale of machinery
808 Loss on _____
809 Unrealized gain—Income
810 Unrealized loss—Income
811 Impairment gain
812 Impairment loss

Clearing Accounts

901 Income summary
902 Manufacturing summary

MANAGERIAL ANALYSES AND REPORTS

① Cost Types
Variable costs: Total cost changes in proportion to volume of activity
Fixed costs: Total cost does not change in proportion to volume of activity
Mixed costs: Cost consists of both a variable and a fixed element

② Cost Sources
Direct materials: Raw materials costs directly linked to finished product
Direct labor: Employee costs directly linked to finished product
Overhead: Production costs indirectly linked to finished product

③ Costing Systems
Job order costing: Costs assigned to each unique unit or batch of units
Process costing: Costs assigned to similar products that are mass-produced in a continuous manner

④ Costing Ratios
Contribution margin ratio = (Net sales − Variable costs)/Net sales
Predetermined overhead rate = Estimated overhead costs/Estimated activity base
Break-even point in units = Total fixed costs/Contribution margin per unit

⑤ Planning and Control Metrics
Cost variance = Actual cost − Standard (budgeted) cost
Sales (revenue) variance = Actual sales − Standard (budgeted) sales

⑥ Capital Budgeting
Payback period = Time expected to recover investment cost
Accounting rate of return = Expected annual net income/Average annual investment
Net present value (NPV) = Present value of future cash flows − Investment cost
NPV rule: 1. Compute net present value (NPV in $)
2. If NPV ≥ 0, then accept project; If NPV < 0, then reject project
Internal rate 1. Compute internal rate of return (IRR in %)
of return rule: 2. If IRR ≥ hurdle rate, accept project; If IRR < hurdle rate, reject project

⑦ Costing Terminology
Relevant range: Organization's normal range of operating activity.
Direct cost: Cost incurred for the benefit of one cost object.
Indirect cost: Cost incurred for the benefit of more than one cost object.
Product cost: Cost that is necessary and integral to finished products.
Period cost: Cost identified more with a time period than with finished products.
Overhead cost: Cost not separately or directly traceable to a cost object.
Relevant cost: Cost that is pertinent to a decision.
Opportunity cost: Benefit lost by choosing an action from two or more alternatives.
Sunk cost: Cost already incurred that cannot be avoided or changed.
Standard cost: Cost computed using standard price and standard quantity.
Budget: Formal statement of an organization's future plans.
Break-even point: Sales level at which an organization earns zero profit.
Incremental cost: Cost incurred only if the organization undertakes a certain action.
Transfer price: Price on transactions between divisions within a company.

⑧ Standard Cost Variances

Total materials variance	=	Materials price variance + Materials quantity variance

Total labor variance	=	Labor (rate) variance + Labor efficiency (quantity) variance

Total overhead variance	=	Overhead controllable variance + Fixed overhead volume variance

Overhead controllable variance = Actual total overhead − Budgeted total overhead per flexible budget
Fixed overhead volume variance = Budgeted fixed overhead − Applied fixed overhead
Variable overhead variance = Variable overhead spending variance + Variable overhead efficiency variance
Fixed overhead variance = Fixed overhead spending variance + Fixed overhead volume variance
} = Total overhead variance

Materials price variance	= [AQ × AP] − [AQ × SP]
Materials quantity variance	= [AQ × SP] − [SQ × SP]
Labor (rate) variance	= [AH × AR] − [AH × SR]
Labor efficiency (quantity) variance	= [AH × SR] − [SH × SR]

Variable overhead spending variance = [AH × AVR] − [AH × SVR]
Variable overhead efficiency variance = [AH × SVR] − [SH × SVR]
Fixed overhead spending variance = Actual fixed overhead − Budgeted fixed overhead

where AQ is Actual Quantity of materials; AP is Actual Price of materials; AH is Actual Hours of labor; AR is Actual Rate of wages; AVR is Actual Variable Rate of overhead; SQ is Standard Quantity of materials; SP is Standard Price of materials; SH is Standard Hours of labor; SR is Standard Rate of wages; SVR is Standard Variable Rate of overhead.

⑨ Sales Variances

Sales price variance	= [AS × AP] − [AS × BP]
Sales volume variance	= [AS × BP] − [BS × BP]

where AS = Actual Sales units; AP = Actual sales Price; BP = Budgeted sales Price; BS = Budgeted Sales units (fixed budget)

Schedule of Cost of Goods Manufactured
For _period_ Ended _date_

Direct materials		
Raw materials inventory, Beginning	$	#
Raw materials purchases		#
Raw materials available for use		#
Raw materials inventory, Ending		(#)
Direct materials used		#
Direct labor		#
Overhead costs		
Total overhead costs		#
Total manufacturing costs		#
Add work in process inventory, Beginning		#
Total cost of work in process		#
Deduct work in process inventory, Ending		(#)
Cost of goods manufactured	$	#

Contribution Margin Income Statement
For _period_ Ended _date_

Net sales (revenues)............................	$	#
Total variable costs.............................		#
Contribution margin.............................		#
Total fixed costs		#
Net income (pretax)	$	#

Flexible Budget
For _period_ Ended _date_

	Flexible Budget		Flexible Budget for Unit Sales of #
	Variable Amount per Unit	Fixed Cost	
Sales (revenues)	$ #		$ #
Variable costs			
Examples: Direct materials, Direct labor,			
Other variable costs	#		#
Total variable costs	#		#
Contribution margin	$ #		#
Fixed costs			
Examples: Depreciation, Manager		$ #	#
salaries, Administrative salaries		#	#
Total fixed costs		$ #	#
Income from operations			$ #

Budget Performance Report*
For _period_ Ended _date_

	Budget	Actual Performance	Variances†
Sales: In units	#	#	
In dollars......................	$ #	$ #	$ # F or U
Cost of sales			
Direct costs	#	#	# F or U
Indirect costs	#	#	# F or U
Selling expenses			
Examples: Commissions	#	#	# F or U
Shipping expenses...........	#	#	# F or U
General and administrative expenses			
Examples: Administrative salaries	#	#	# F or U
Total expenses	$ #	$ #	$ # F or U
Income from operations	$ #	$ #	$ # F or U

† F = Favorable variance; U = Unfavorable variance. * Applies to both flexible and fixed budgets.

Master Budget Sequence

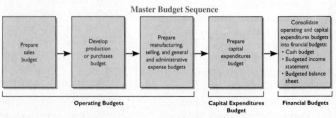

| Operating Budgets | | | Capital Expenditures Budget | Financial Budgets |